202

0038285

DATE DUE	
NOV 0 4 1992	
DEC 1 5 1992	
FEB 1 0 1993	
FEB 0 2 1996	
MAR 0 5 1996	
JUL 1 1 1996	
JUL 2 4 1996	
DEC 0 2 1996	
FEB 2 0 1997	
JAN 0 2 1998	
MAR 0 4 1998	

BRODART, INC.   Cat. No. 23-221

$28.50

© THE BAKER & TAYLOR CO.

THE
United States

Sixth Edition
Combined Edition

Winthrop D. Jordan - Leon F. Litwack

University of Mississippi

University of California, Berkeley

Richard Hofstadter - William Miller - Daniel Aaron

Prentice-Hall, Inc., Englewood Cliffs, New Jersey 07632

Library of Congress Cataloging-in-Publication Data

The United States.
    Includes bibliographies and index.
      Contents: v. 1. Conquering a continent—v. 2. Becoming a world power / Leon F. Litwack . . . [et al.].
      1. United States—History. I. Jordan, Winthrop D. II. Litwack, Leon F.
E178.1.U5532 1987b   973   86-23127
ISBN 0-13-938374-3 (v. 1)
ISBN 0-13-938432-4 (v. 2)

Editorial/production supervision: Mary Bardoni
Cover and interior design: Jayne Conte
Manufacturing buyer: Ray Keating
Acquisitions editor: Steve Dalphin
Photo research: Barbara Schultz
Photo editor: Lorinda Morris
Cover photo: Upper and Lower Bay of N.Y.: undated Lithograph by Currier & Ives.
Credit The Granger Collection.

Photo credits: p. xvi, The Granger Collection; p. 18, New York Historical Society; p. 44, Independence National Historic Park, Phil., Pa.; p. 66, New York Historical Society; p. 84, New York Historical Society; p. 106, Copyright Yale University Art Gallery; p. 126, Independence National Historic Park, Phil., Pa.; p. 148, New York Historical Society; p. 168, Alan P. Kirby Collection, Lafayette College; p. 188, The Metropolitan Museum of Art, Gift of Lyman G. Bloomingdale, 1901; p. 214, The Boatman's National Bank of St. Louis; p. 236, Cincinnati Art Museum; p. 260, San Jacinto Museum of History Association; p. 282, The Historic New Orleans Collection; p. 302, The Metropolitan Museum of Art, Purchase, 1941, Joseph Pulitzer Bequest; p. 322, Kennedy Galleries, Inc., 40 W. 57th St., New York, N.Y.; p. 346, New York Historical Society; p. 370, Collection of Jay P. Altmayer, Mobile, Ala; p. 402, The Granger Collection; p. 422, Museum of the City of New York; p. 450, Library of Congress; p. 476, New York Historical Society; p. 500, The Granger Collection; p. 518, The Granger Collection; p. 540, The Los Angeles County Museum of Art, Los Angeles County Funds; p. 572, New York Historical Society; p. 592, The Granger Collection; p. 630, Courtesy Vanity Fair. Copyright © 1933 (renewed 1961) by the Conde Nast Publications, Inc.; p. 662, The West Point Museum Collections, U.S. Military Academy, West Point, N.Y.; p. 696, Courtesy of the Norman Rockwell Museum at Stockbridge, Mass.; p. 730, Los Alamos National Laboratory; p. 760, James Pickerell, Black Star; p. 794, Dennis Brack, Black Star; p. 822, Paul Shambroom, Photo Researchers.

Printed in the United States of America

10 9 8 7 6 5 4 3 2

ISBN 0-13-938473-1 01

Prentice-Hall International (UK) Limited, *London*
Prentice-Hall of Australia Pty. Limited, *Sydney*
Prentice-Hall Canada Inc., *Toronto*
Prentice-Hall Hispanoamericana, S.A., *Mexico*
Prentice-Hall of India Private Limited, *New Delhi*
Prentice-Hall of Japan, Inc., *Tokyo*
Prentice-Hall of Southeast Asia Pte. Ltd., *Singapore*
Editora Prentice-Hall do Brasil, Ltda., *Rio de Janeiro*

CONTENTS

PART II: Becoming a World Power

Chapter 22

THE EMERGENCE OF URBAN AMERICA 477

Chapter 23

CULTURE AND THOUGHT 501

Chapter 24

THE AMERICAN EMPIRE 519

Chapter 25

PEOPLE AND POLITICS: THE PROGRESSIVE ERA 541

Chapter 26

WORLD WAR AND WORLD REVOLUTION 573

Chapter 27

THE TWENTIES: BUSINESS AND CULTURE 593

Chapter 28

THE GREAT DEPRESSION AND THE NEW DEAL 631

Chapter 33

THE POLITICS OF RIGHTEOUSNESS: NIXON AND CARTER 795

Chapter 34

THE POLITICS OF NOSTALGIA: THE REAGAN ERA 823

APPENDIX 839

INDEX 851

PHOTO ESSAYS

MAPS AND CHARTS

A NOTE OF INTRODUCTION

The word "history" actually has a double meaning. It refers to what did in fact take place in the past. It also refers to our study and understanding of what actually occurred and how we talk and write about those events.

These two meanings are often confused. We all have met such expressions as: "history tells us;" "history shows;" and "the lessons of history are. . . ." These expressions assume that the actual events of the past can themselves teach us about the present and perhaps even something about the future. Yet past events cannot themselves speak, let alone teach. But we can and in fact do learn from what has been said and written about them. We learn from and about ourselves when we interact with what other people today are saying about what went on in the past, as well as from what people in our past said about their past.

Here things get tricky simply because historians are people. No two historians look at past events in exactly the same manner. They draw differing conclusions about the meaning of what went on and sometimes about what actually did go on. They also disagree about what was important enough to bother discussing. For example, historians still disagree as to exactly when President Woodrow Wilson suffered his first stroke. At a different level of inquiry they disagree about the causes and consequences of the American Civil War. Much more than they used to, historians are learning and writing about the lives of ordinary men and women. Whether Joe and Josephine Smith went to the supermarket on July 3, 1947, is in itself obviously not of great importance, but the fact that millions of Americans were getting their food in such a manner obviously is, especially since we know that the Smiths' parents could not have fed themselves or their families that way.

Why bother with the past in any form? The most basic answer is that we cannot do without it. As individuals, we use it all the time. Each of us lives in the present, but our immediate experiences, thoughts, and perceptions are shaped by our previous ones. We are, in a very real sense, what we have been—and what we think we have been. An important part of our present is our awareness of our past. Similarly, an entire society is shaped by its past and by its consciousness of that past. As individuals and as a nation, we cannot tell where we are (much less where we are going) without knowing where we have been. And because the United States is a vast and profoundly complex entity, including over the years more than a half billion individual lives and millions of groups, the task of understanding this nation is not an easy one.

Working at such a task can be very rewarding and even fun. This book has a number of thematic chapters, such as those dealing with important intellectual and literary developments. Nonetheless we have adhered to a fundamentally chronological structure, an approach that is dictated by the unfolding of events. We are convinced that anyone who thinks that the U.S. Constitution was adopted before the American Revolution is not going to be able to understand the nature of either one of those two major developments. The same may be said of the Cold War and World War II, or of the invention of the atomic bomb and the machine gun.

A few words about this new edition of *The United States*: As authors of this extensively re-written and revised edition, we have tried to convey both the personalities and importance of such public leaders as George Whitefield, Andrew Jackson, and Dorothea Dix; of Franklin Roosevelt, Martin Luther King, Jr., and Ronald Reagan. We have also especially emphasized the history of less powerful people. The ordinary folk who have made up the great bulk of American society expressed themselves in various ways in the past, as they still do today. We have stressed their experiences and their voices—the lives of Indians, blacks, Hispanic-Americans, dozens of immigrant groups from Europe and Asia, as well as working people in the fields, boats, shops, factories, mines, and homes of the nation.

This edition has much more about women because a solid body of scholarship in women's history has emerged in very recent years. We have dealt with women in such various roles as young daughters and child laborers, mothers and grandmothers, factory and office workers, farmers and westward pioneers, reformers, intellectuals, professionals, and politicians. As we have with ethnic, racial, and religious groups, we have dealt with the record of women's achievements and with the record of the obstacles and defeats that barred their way.

This edition also includes a new and (we believe) unique feature—a series of boxes entitled *Words and Names in American History*. These are miniature essays about the specifically American background of words that are in common use today or until quite recently. Some are political: such as *lobby, logrolling, gerrymander, platform;* others geographical, such as *Mississippi, Wall Street,* and the *Mason-Dixon Line;* others defy classification, such as *Uncle Sam, cafeteria, deadline, lynch,* and *hazing.* All of them cast small shafts of light on the American past. As with the previous edition, the chapters through the Civil War have been done by Winthrop Jordan; those from Reconstruction and Restoration to the present, by Leon Litwack.

From these boxes, from the greatly expanded and carefully selected illustrative materials, from the boxes that offer some "voices" of the American people, and from the text itself, we hope that readers will gain more than a formal knowledge of American history. We hope they will also gain an appreciation of the richness and diversity of American cultural expression, and a deeper, more sub-tle sense of what it means to live in this somewhat ambiguous, ever-changing nation.

As aids to teaching and learning, a number of supplemental items are available with the text. These include a **Two-Volume Study Guide,** prepared by Helena Mast Krohn, Constance Jones, and Derris Raper of Tidewater Community College, Virginia Beach, Virginia. For students with access to an Apple or IBM-PC, an **Interactive Study Guide** draws questions from the study guides and offers self-scoring review quizzes. An **Instructor's Manual,** authored by Matthew Panczyk of Bergen Community College and a separate **Test Item File** by Paul Harvey of the University of California at Berkeley provide, respectively, teaching suggestions, chapter outlines, film lists, and over 1000 objective test and essay questions. The test item file material is also available on **Floppy Disk** for the IBM-PC and Apple computers; or the instructor may make use of Prentice-Hall's **Telephone Test Preparation Service. Full-color Transparencies** of 40 maps are available on adoption as are **Free Videos and Films** of high quality, award-winning documentaries, and docudramas.

In its development, many instructors have read the manuscript and have offered helpful suggestions for improvement. They include William C. Hine, South Carolina State College; Roger L. Nichols, University of Arizona; George H. Skau, Bergen Community College; Alwyn Barr, Texas Tech University; and Robert Haws, University of Mississippi. Also, Robert D. Cross, University of Virginia; Leonard L. Richards, University of Massachusetts; Peyton McCrary, University of South Alabama; Richard Wightman Fox, Yale University; Robert G. Pope, SUNY at Buffalo; Joseph C. Morton, Northeastern Illinois University; Thomas A. Krueger, University of Illinois at Urbana; John Mayfield, University of Kentucky; Linda Dudik Guerrero, Palomar College; Bradley R. Rice, Clayton Junior College; David C. Hammack, Princeton University; Alasdair Macphail, Connecticut College; Harvey H. Jackson, Clayton Junior College; and Jerry Rodnitzky, The University of Texas at Arlington. We would especially like to thank our editors at Prentice-Hall, Mary Bardoni and Steve Dalphin, as well as the many others whose hard work is reflected in this new edition.

WINTHROP D. JORDAN
LEON F. LITWACK

MIGRANTS TO THE NEW WORLD

Chapter 1

The first Americans were immigrants from Asia. They came, probably in search of big game, somewhere between 15,000 and 40,000 years ago. They traveled on foot in small groups at several times when lower sea levels exposed an ancient land bridge between Asia and North America at what is now the Bering Strait. As thousands of years went by, they fanned out over North, Central, and South America. This geographic dispersion resulted in the development of hundreds of different languages and a wide variety of physical characteristics, social organizations, and levels of technology. For thousands of years they remained in isolation as melting icecaps put the ancient land bridge under three hundred feet of water.

Then, five hundred years ago, came a remarkably sudden burst of immigration by sea from Western Europe and Western Africa. At first that immigration was largely Spanish, but then other Atlantic nations began to take an interest in what Europeans called a New World. People from Portugal, France, the Netherlands, and the British Isles began to arrive. They brought with them—against their will—many different peoples from Africa.

From about 1500, therefore, the history of North America was no longer isolated from developments in the Old World. At

that time Western Europe was developing a new, dynamic economic system: commercial capitalism. The Atlantic nations of Western Europe were becoming more centralized than before, usually under powerful new monarchs. They developed strong international rivalries that greatly affected events in America as well as Europe. At the same time, the great Western Christian church was split by the Reformation; for several centuries hostility between Roman Catholics and Protestants shaped rivalries among nations.

When Europeans migrated to the New World, they had a profound and usually disastrous impact on the descendants of the original settlers—the Indians as the Europeans called them. Some of this impact was cultural and technological. But the most important result was that European diseases took an appalling toll among the Indians. In its early phases, European migration to America resulted in one of the most drastic drops in population over a large area that humankind has ever experienced.

In turn, however, the Indians influenced European and African settlement in various ways. They did a great deal to reshape Old World agricultural practices, patterns of settlement, and military tactics. So did the New World environment, especially the climate and such natural resources as precious metals, timber, fish, fur, and plants.

Historians have used a good many terms to describe this sudden burst of migration from the Old World to the New. It was called a "discovery" by Europeans, despite the fact that Christoforo Columbo died in the stubborn conviction that the lands he had seen on his voyages lay just off the coasts of China and Japan, and despite the fact that other Europeans had touched American shores five hundred years earlier. Recent writers have referred to the "invention" of America, assuming that Europeans needed to find a different sort of world in order to understand their own. The coming of the Europeans has also been called an "invasion" of the Indians' lands. Finally, it should be borne in mind that Indian America was settled not just by Europeans, but by Africans as well. ■

THE FIRST AMERICANS

Little is known about the long history of the original American immigrants. Much of the available evidence is *archeological* and has literally been dug up. Some is *geological;* it is known, for example, that at a time when Indians were spearing mammoths in New Mexico, northern New England was covered with ice. There are written materials from a few Indian cultures, including the famous calendar of the Aztecs in Mexico, but most Indian peoples used oral tradition rather than writing. Much of what is known about these people comes from the early reports of European explorers and conquerors, reports that have to be treated with great caution in order to screen out the prejudices and lack of comprehension of the observers.

1500, 16.Jh.

Five hundred years ago, the peoples of the New World were as various as those of the Old. They spoke some twelve hundred different dialects and languages, and they varied enormously in appearance, dress, customs, technology, and political organization. Some went about nearly naked, clad only around the waist with animal skin, and used stones and shells as tools. Some produced stunning works of art in gold or silver, constructed highways, and built enormous pyramids of stone. Some lived on nuts and berries, others cooked food in baskets of reeds or bark, or in clay pots. Some dwelt in cities comparable in size to those of Europe; others roamed as nomadic hunters. Some were governed by "divine" kings; others knew no greater authority than their own family. Traditionally, historians have concentrated on the "high civilizations" of Mexico and Peru—the Aztec, Maya, and Inca—but for the history of the early United States, it seems more appropriate to concentrate on the peoples who lived along the North Atlantic coast.

Technology in the Eastern Woodlands

Indians arrived along the Atlantic seaboard relatively late in the long process of settling the American continents. In the region stretching from what is now Georgia to Maine, eastern woodland Indians shared many common characteristics,

Secota, an unfortified village in the Carolina Coast, as drawn by John White. (*Reproduced by courtesy of the Trustees of the British Museum*)

WORDS AND NAMES IN AMERICAN HISTORY

Succotash is a mixture of boiled corn and lima or butter beans. The dish, still commonly served in New England, is actually much older than the first arrival of English Puritans there. It was a staple of the New England Indians, and the word itself comes directly from the Algonkian word for the mixture. For the Indians there it was an obvious combination, since they planted both beans and squash in their corn-fields. It is now realized what a clever agricultural practice this was, for the leaves of the bean and squash plants shaded out the growth of weeds, and the corn stalks provided natural poles on which the bean plants could climb. The succotash mixture provided a nutritious dietary base. One can even buy frozen succotash in some markets today, though not nationwide.

though with considerable variations. Anthropologists usually divide them into three large groups, principally on the basis of language. The Algonkian tribes who lived from Canada to North Carolina and as far west as the Great Lakes became, for the early English migrants, the "typical" Indians. Farther south and west were several large groups who spoke Muskogean languages: the Choctaw, Chickasaw, Creek, and Seminole. The Cherokee in Georgia were similar in living habits but appear to have been a more recently arrived group who spoke a dialect of a third language, Iroquoian, which prevailed in the area around the eastern Great Lakes. Those Iroquoian peoples were probably also relative newcomers, having come from the Mississippi Valley into what is now upstate New York and neighboring parts of Canada.

All these people shared common cultural characteristics, but climate plus available food and housing made for important differences. Although they had several technological skills Europeans lacked, lack of other skills put them at a severe disadvantage when they were confronted by the Europeans. The Iroquois and Algonkian had developed a highly efficient means of transportation at a time when roads in most parts of the world were inferior to the highways of ancient Rome. The Indian elm and birch-bark canoes were brittle, but they had the great advantage of light weight for portages between lakes and streams. Hollowed-out logs were also used, but more often on the ocean. Many of the coastal Indians fished with great efficiency in shallow waters, using nets and weirs. They did not, however, go into deep water, for they had not developed sails.

All the eastern woodland Indians grew corn (maize) and various kinds of squash, pumpkins, and beans. And of course they hunted deer and bears, which provided clothing as well as food,

and they trapped and hunted a variety of smaller animals unknown in the Old World, such as beaver, opossum, and raccoon. Hunting was done with bows and arrows, which in skillful hands were as accurate as European muskets and much more rapid firing. They also used tomahawks in warfare. The Muskogean carried, in addition, spears and shields woven from bark and vines. Their housing usually consisted of bent poles covered with thatch or hides; the word *wigwam* is the Algonkian term for "house." Metalworking was unknown; stones and shells served as weapons and tools. And these peoples lacked three technological advantages widely used by Europeans: the wheel, the plow, and draft animals such as oxen and horses.

Nature and Society

Eastern woodland Indians lived closer to nature than Europeans did, though of course Europeans then lived much closer to nature than we do now. They still kept time by the sun or moon or walking distances, in an age when Europeans were increasingly using clocks and calendars. The Indians had a close psychological rapport with animals and even with trees and mountains; many tribes believed that animals had souls. Their religious faiths reflected their strong ties with the natural surroundings. Most—perhaps all—believed in a high god, a single deity superior to other deities. These less powerful spirits were often identified with specific animals, vegetation, or places. The same affinity with nature was reflected in the way they thought about their societies. Many tribes considered themselves to be divided into *clans*, groups of people thought to be related to one another, and these clans were often identified by such names as wolf, bear, deer, and beaver.

The Indians were strongly attached to their land, which they felt was theirs by reason of tradition and use, not because they "owned" it. The land almost seemed to own them. This way of thinking was very different from the one that prevailed in Europe, where various groups of people staked out their own turf by means of national boundaries and carved up those spaces among individuals who "owned" land as "real estate." The gap between these concepts about land was to prove an enduring source of conflict between Indians and Europeans in America.

The social and political organization of the tribes varied considerably, but it is impossible today to describe them accurately, largely because early Europeans tended to talk about Indian societies in terms based on their own experience. European observers expected to find kings, nobles, and commoners, and they became confused when they discovered that such categories did not fit. There was similar confusion about the different Indian groups, which the English variously called "nations," "tribes," or simply "sorts." It is clear, however, that there were at least a hundred Algonkian tribes; sometime groups of them were shaped into confederacies by forceful leaders.

The famous League of the Iroquois in upstate New York came about because five tribes fashioned a sophisticated, powerful, and remarkably enduring political alliance. Each tribe sent a specific number of representatives to a central council for decisions about war and diplomacy. The Iroquois fascinate historians and anthropologists because of the unusual strength of this confederation and also because of other distinguishing aspects of their society: their "longhouses," huge wigwams occupied by four to six families; their reputation as fierce warriors; their reliance on communal interpretation of individual dreams; and the powerful influence of Iroquois women, who farmed while their men hunted and warred and who chose which men would lead them in both war and peace. Among all eastern Indians, political leadership depended on maturity, wisdom, and forcefulness much more than on heredity or the accumulation of wealth.

The division of labor between these Indian men and woman was even more rigid than it was in Europe at the time. Men hunted, trapped, and fished; in short, they concentrated on getting animal resources. Women cleaned and processed animals and did almost all the farming and prep-

aration of food. Men went to war, but women did more than half the labor that provided food, clothing, and shelter.

The woodland Indians were no more peaceful than Europeans: They fought frequently against each other, more for sport and manhood than for territory. By European standards, casualties were low. Silence and surprise were the usual methods of attack. Many tribes practiced ritual torture of captives and/or formal tribal adoption. Their style of peace resembled their style of war; Europeans were struck by their quiet dignity in diplomatic negotiations. They spoke with brief eloquence, weighing their words with confident assurance that those few words would seal whatever agreement was being made.

THE OLD WORLD MEETS THE NEW

People from the western part of the Old World discovered Indian America at least twice, but the first discovery had little effect. The impact of the second was momentous, in Europe as well as America. In both instances, "America" was not discovered as a whole; rather, European navigators stumbled onto particular landfalls without the slightest notion that they had found two "new" continents.

The Norsemen

The Norse contacts with America took place about a thousand years ago. Bold Norwegians had long been settled in Iceland; from there they pushed westward along the steppingstone islands of the North Atlantic. In about 980 they established tiny settlements near the southern tip of Greenland. In the thirteenth century some four thousand were living there, but for unknown reasons they lost contact with Europe in the second half of the fifteenth century and died out for lack of food and supplies.

Yet that thrust westward had gone further. In 986 Biarni Heriulfson set sail from Iceland to join his father, Heriulf, in Greenland. By mistake his course was too far south. He missed that island and ended up cruising along a shore he was sure could not be Greenland because it was "a flat and wooded country" and had no mountains of ice. He was, in fact, running along the coasts of Baffin

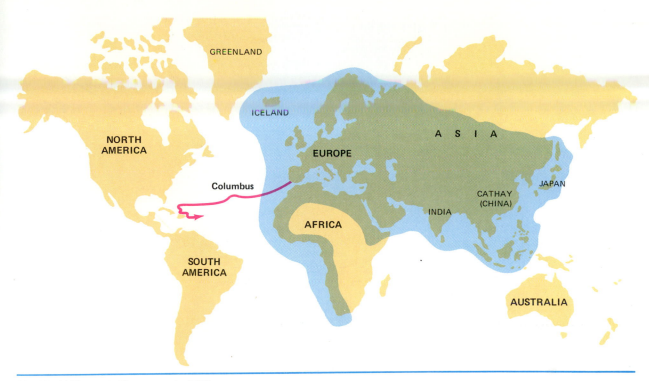

The World Known to Europeans in 1492

Island and Labrador, but he did not land because he was aiming for Greenland.

Although Biarni was the first European we know of who saw American shores, Leif Ericsson was the first to set foot on American soil. Sailing westward from Greenland in the same boat Biarni had used, he landed on Baffin Island and then made his way south down the coast of Labrador. At last the voyagers came ashore at a place they called Vinland "in accordance with all the good things they found in it."

There has been much conjecture about the location of this spot; some people have claimed that Leif got as far south as Massachusetts or even Virginia. But the site has recently been pinpointed to be L'Anse aux Meadows on the northern tip of Newfoundland. Archeological evidence there shows conclusively that Norwegians established a fishing colony which lasted for several years.

This original European discovery of America remained unknown except in some obscure old Norse sagas until the nineteenth century. Some people have made claims for earlier contact with Indian America—by ancient Phoenicians from the Mediterranean, by black Africans, and even by Pacific Islanders. None of these claims is totally improbable, but all are very far from firmly

established. Much more to the point, if such contacts did occur, they had no widespread effect. The voyages of Christopher Columbus did.

European Expansion (15 th.)

There is no easy explanation for the sudden wanderlust of Western Europeans in the fifteenth century. Various factors contributed to their thrust overseas, which we might label as economic, political, technological, and demographic.

For centuries Europeans had traded with the peoples of southeastern Asia for highly valued commodities that could not be found or grown in Europe, among them jewels, silk, and spices. (Spices improved the taste of food and, in an age without refrigeration, preserved meat and disguised its taste when rotten.) That trade was carried on over thousands of miles across the Indian Ocean, through the Middle East, over the Mediterranean Sea to the ports of southern Europe, and then overland to the north and west. At the western ports of entry, the trade was controlled by the merchants of Venice and other city-states in what is now Italy.

As time went on, merchants in the western parts of Europe grew more and more discontented with

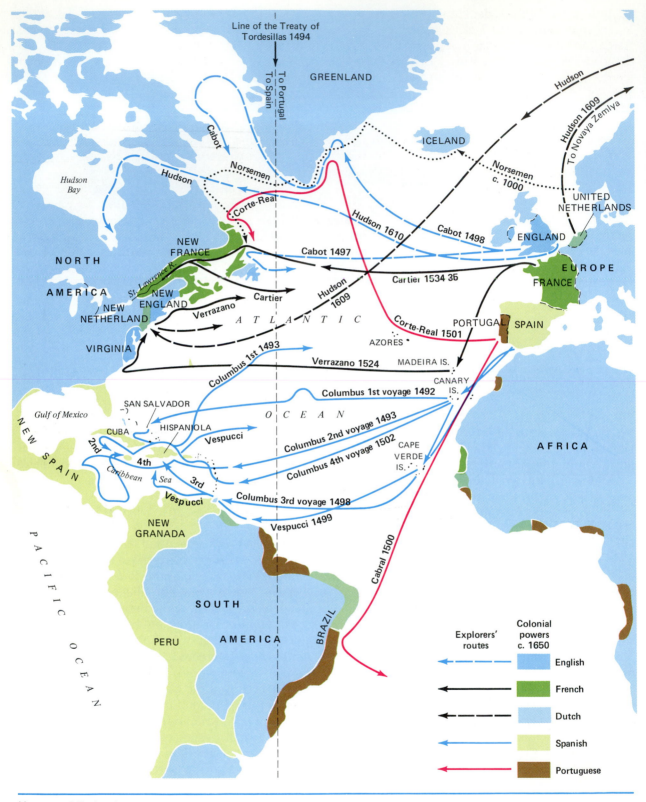

Voyages of Exploration

the problems of this trade: high prices, piracy, too many middlemen, and lack of reliability. At the same time, new financial practices developed in Italy were beginning to spread north and west: double-entry bookkeeping of financial records, pooling of capital among several individuals or families, rudimentary banks, and the use of Arabic rather than Roman numerals in account books.

Politically, the monarchs of Western Europe were becoming more successful in their struggles with powerful feudal warlords. Geographic areas that are now single countries, like France, Portugal, and Spain, were then collections of separate provinces and dukedoms. During the fifteenth century, monarchs consolidated their authority over larger territories, and it was these powerful new monarchies that became the modern countries of Western Europe. Many historians summarize these developments as *the rise of nation-states.*

A third development in European society was just as complicated but much less dramatic. Trade with the Far East had resulted in knowledge of both gunpowder and the compass. Although neither of these Chinese inventions had an immediate impact on methods of warfare and navigation, in the long run they helped give Europeans a sense of mastery over other peoples and the sea. Also important to overseas expansion were hundreds of small improvements in ship design. Taken together, these improvements enabled Europeans to build vessels that could handle ocean swells without capsizing, be steered by workable rudders, and be propelled entirely by sails, without the need for oars.

The demographic change that helped set off expansion was the result of a disaster. In the fourteenth century Europe was struck by bubonic plague, a deadly infection carried by infected lice on rats. The Black Death swept away about a third of Western Europe's population. Even though it damaged the economy, the tragedy raised the economic and social status of the agricultural laborers (serfs) who survived, because it meant that their labor was in great demand. The notion that people were bound to the land began to break down. People grew restless and no longer assumed they had to stay where they had been born.

Portugal Takes the Lead

These four factors interacted in various ways in different parts of Western Europe, but together they produced a mood of adventure. Early in the fourteenth century, Italian, Spanish, and French sailors began to explore the west coast of Africa in search of a way around that continent. They came upon and occupied the Canary Islands, then the Madeiras, and then the Azores. But it was the Portuguese, after 1420, who began the systematic collection of geographic information that enabled them to transform the Atlantic into a path of adventure and commerce. And it was they who first brought enslaved blacks back by sea from Africa to Europe in 1442.

In 1420, Prince Henry the Navigator set up his great maritime research institute at Sagres on Portugal's southernmost tip, "where the two seas, the Mediterranean and the Great Ocean, fight together." There, until his death in 1460, he conducted a laboratory in astronomy, cosmography, mapmaking, ship and sail design, and instruments of navigation. Some of his most valuable information came from returning sailors and ship captains who were making longer and longer voyages down the western coast of Africa. Prince Henry's work was crowned in 1488, many years after he died, when Bartholomeu Diaz at last rounded the Cabo Tormentoso (Cape of Storms) at Africa's southernmost tip, opening the first all-water route from Europe to the Indies. The king of Portugal was so impressed by this fact that he renamed that treacherous neck of land the Cape of Good Hope.

Nine years after Diaz's voyage, a flotilla of four Portuguese ships under Vasco da Gama sailed for India from Lisbon and returned in triumph in 1499, laden with spices and jewels. Da Gama's voyage meant the end of Levantine (Middle East) supremacy in the Oriental trade, the eclipse of the Italian merchants, and the decline of the Mediterranean. The Portuguese, moreover, soon drove Muslim merchants and pirates from the Indian Ocean itself, reduced their strongholds at the sources of supply for Oriental goods, and established a Far Eastern empire of their own that lasted, at least in fragments, almost to our day.

THE SPANISH AND FRENCH IN AMERICA

While the Portuguese were attempting to reach Asia by sailing south and east, a singleminded man decided to attempt the same goal by sailing directly west. He came upon a puzzling barrier on that route, and died dejected because he had not found Japan and China. By his own standards Columbus failed, but in doing so he laid the foundation for an enormous and extremely profitable

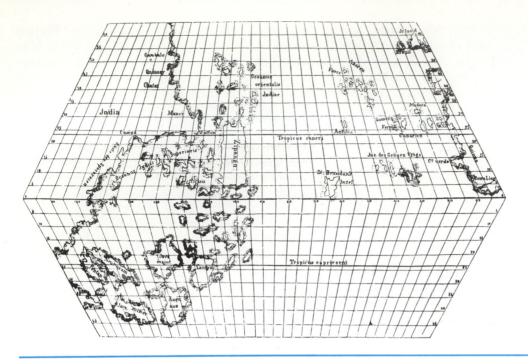

Columbus's belief that he could reach the Orient by sailing westward was backed by Paolo Toscanelli, a scholar who sent Columbus this map of the world in 1481. (*Windsor,* History of America, *vol. II, 1886*)

Spanish empire in America. Through his exploits, Spain claimed control over most of the two American continents. Other European nations refused to accept that claim, so soon European rivalries found a new field of battle in America.

Christoforo Columbo

The son of a tailor, Christoforo Columbo was born in Genoa, one of the major maritime Italian city-states. At an early age he turned to the sea and became an experienced navigator and shipmaster. His private dream was of reaching the Orient by sailing westward. Like most educated people, he believed that the world was round, but he grossly underestimated the size of the globe by discounting the quite accurate estimates of ancient Greek scholars. For five years, he pleaded for financial backing at the courts of the monarchs of Spain, England, France, and Portugal. He was turned down everywhere.

In 1492, a dramatic event changed the minds of the jointly reigning Spanish monarchs, King Ferdinand and Queen Isabella. For centuries the Spanish had struggled to expel the Muslim conquerors who had invaded their land from North Africa. They finally succeeded in 1492. Immediately they moved to expel other non-Catholics,

Christoforo Columbo. (*The Metropolitan Museum of Art, Gift of J. Pierpont Morgan, 1900*)

particularly the Jews, whose wealth had helped finance the long wars against the Moors.

The Spanish had conducted their campaigns as a religious crusade, and now Ferdinand and Isabella were willing to help spread Christianity elsewhere, as Columbus promised to do. They were also eager for profits from trade with "the lands of India," or the "Indies" as the Far East was called. So they agreed to back the eccentric sailor who insisted he could reach the Indies by sailing west. Columbus was given the title (as he carefully noted) of "Admiral-in-Chief of the Ocean Sea and Viceroy and Perpetual Governor of all the lands and mainlands that I should discover."

On August 3, 1942, Columbus's expedition set sail from the little Spanish port of Palos aboard three vessels, the *Niña*, the *Pinta*, and the *Santa Maria*. After stopping at the Canary Islands off the coast of West Africa, Columbus set a course due west. He had calculated that he was on the same latitude as Cipangu (Japan), which was regarded as the richest part of "the lands of India." The crew, mostly Spanish, did not fully trust their Italian captain. He, in turn, doctored the ship's log by underestimating the daily mileage of his little fleet.

Having doubled all records for ocean sailing beyond sight of shore, *Santa Maria's* crew mutinied. The boredom of an endless voyage strained the nerves of sailors made idle by the easy passage. Columbus managed to quiet the crew by promising to turn back if no land was sighted within three days. Then, just past 2 A.M. on October 12, *Pinta's* lookout called, "Tierra! Tierra!"

"To the first island which I found," Columbus later wrote to Ferdinand and Isabella, "I gave the name San Salvador, in remembrance of the Divine Majesty, Who had marvelously bestowed all this." The inhabitants of the island called it Guanahani. Columbus called them Indians on the assumption that he was on the outskirts of the Indies. Soon, "I found very many [other] islands," Columbus added in his letter to Ferdinand and Isabella, "filled with innumerable people, and I have taken possession of them all for their Highnesses, done by proclamation and with the royal standard unfurled, and no opposition was offered to me."

After a few months of exploring the Caribbean, Columbus left some of his men behind on the large island of Hispaniola and set out for Spain with a few gold nuggets and several "Indians" to prove the success of his venture. None of the Indians survived the voyage. Columbus made three more trips to the New World. His search on these visits was for a passageway through the barrier beyond which, he remained certain, must lie Japan. He found no such passage. Not until Ferdinand Magellan's men sailed around the world in the service of Spain (1519–1522) did the truth become known about the enormous distance of the westward passage to the Far East.

Upon learning of Columbus's great discoveries, the Pope proceeded to divide up the newly discovered world between the Spanish and the Portuguese. In 1494, in the Treaty of Tordesillas, Spain and Portugal agreed on the specific boundary separating their territories. In effect, Portugal received the Orient and Spain the New World, except for the region that became Brazil. In 1500, on a voyage around Africa to the Orient, a Portuguese captain, Cabral, was blown off course and found himself on a New World shore which he promptly claimed for his native land. Cabral's discovery became known as Brazil. But the Portuguese took little interest in the New World for another half century.

Soon after Columbus's first triumphant return, Spain encouraged other mariners to occupy this New World claim, search out its limits, convert its inhabitants, and seize its wealth. One of the first to sail under Spanish colors was Amerigo Vespucci, a native of the Italian city, Florence. In 1497 he began a series of voyages on which he explored the coastline southeast from Mexico all the way to Brazil. Ten years later, a German geographer first called the New World "America" in his honor.

The Spanish and the Indians

Long before other Atlantic nations offered a challenge, Spain had established a vast empire in the New World. Small numbers of Spaniards occupied the largest Caribbean islands: Cuba, Hispaniola, Puerto Rico, and Jamaica. Led by Hernando Cortes, the Spanish went on to conquer the Indian civilizations in Mexico. Francisco Pizarro began the occupation of Peru in 1528. In both regions the Spanish found fabulous sources of gold and silver. Other Spanish explorers wandered through Florida, the lower Mississippi Valley, and the North American Southwest, but they were discouraged by not finding precious metals in those regions.

The Indians of the Caribbean Islands—the Arawaks and Caribs—were relatively primitive in technology and political organization, although they had mastered the art of interisland boating. The first European drawings of these Indians

European imaginations conjured up visions of Indian cannibals. *The New York Public Library, Astor, Lenox, and Tilden Foundation)*

brutal, but the Aztecs in Mexico were themselves conquerors of earlier peoples and practiced ritual human sacrifice and perhaps cannibalism as well. The Spanish advantage was mainly psychological. Many more Indians were overawed by Spanish firearms than were killed by them. And the Indians also were amazed by the sight of men on horseback, who they thought were single animals.

In recent years, however, it has become clear that the Spanish had one enormous advantage of which neither they nor the Indians were aware. Over hundreds of centuries, most of the peoples of the Old World had developed partial immunity to certain diseases unknown in the New World. Within fifty years of first contact with the Spanish, the Indians of Hispaniola nearly died out. In Mexico the Indian population appears to have dropped to something like 10 percent of its previous level. Measles and especially smallpox were probably the two chief killers. Whatever the diseases, it is clear that no society can survive when it loses 90 percent of its people in one or two generations. Unwittingly the Indians had their revenge, for Columbus's sailors introduced syphilis into Europe. But that disease did not kill masses of people in a short period of time.

In the New World, the political and social consequences of disease were profound. Many Indian societies were virtually destroyed. Depopulation was largely responsible for the demand for slaves from the Old World to work the fields and mines of the New. Starting about 1522, the Spanish began importing slaves from Africa. Though they too died in large numbers, the Africans had had sufficient

showed them eating human flesh. They may or may not have been cannibals; what is certain is that the Arawaks told the Spanish that the Caribs, their enemies, were. On the mainland of Mexico and Peru, the Spanish found densely populated, advanced civilizations, genuine empires with powerful kings, highway systems, enormous temples, and stunning works of art in silver and gold.

Until recently, the success of the small numbers of Spanish explorers has been explained largely in terms of their superior boldness and technology. The Spanish conquerors were indeed

THE AZTEC VIEW OF THE SPANIARDS

One of the few Indian texts about early contact with Europeans described the reaction of the Spanish conquerors to gifts of gold sent by Montezuma, King of the Aztecs:

Then Motecuhzoma dispatched various chiefs. Tzihuacpopocatzin was at their head, and he took with him a great many of his representatives. They went out to meet the Spaniards in the vicinity of Popocatepetl and Iztactepetl, there in the Eagle Pass.

They gave the "gods" ensigns of gold, and ensigns of quetzal feathers, and golden necklaces. And when

they were given these presents, the Spaniards burst into smiles; their eyes shone with pleasure; they were delighted by them. They picked up the gold and fingered it like monkeys; they seemed to be transported by joy, as if their hearts were illumined and made new.

The truth is that they longed and lusted for gold. Their bodies swelled with greed, and their hunger was ravenous; they hungered like pigs for that gold. They snatched at the golden ensigns, waved them from side to side and examined every inch of them. They were like one who speaks a barbarous tongue: everything they said was in a barbarous tongue.

THE EUROPEAN VIEW OF THE DEMOGRAPHIC CHANGE

Some European settlers thought the heavy mortality among the Indians was a sign that God favored the cause of European settlement. Edward Johnson, an early settler and historian of Puritan New England, expressed this view in "The Wonderful Preparation the Lord Christ by His Providence Wrought for His People's Abode in this Western World." Speaking of the New England Indians before the arrival of the Puritans, he wrote: "There befell a great mortality among them; the greatest that ever the memory of father or son took notice of, desolating chiefly those places where the English afterward planted; sweeping away whole families, but chiefly young men and children, the very seeds of increase. . . . Their wigwams lie full of dead corpses. . . . By this means, Christ, whose great and glorious works throughout the earth are all for the benefit of his churches and chosen, not only made room for his people to plant, but also tamed the hearts of these barbarous Indians."

contact with Europeans across the Sahara Desert to acquire partial immunities themselves, so they did not suffer the drastic mortality rates of the Indians. But they too had a measure of revenge, for many European slave traders died from tropical diseases. The dimensions of this human tragedy, then, were enormous and bitterly ironic.

The French

Except in Brazil, the Spanish claimed a monopoly on the entire New World, one that was endorsed by the Pope. Yet other Christian nations refused to recognize Spain's exclusive jurisdiction. The French were the first to challenge it. In 1524 another Florentine, Giovanni da Verrazano, sailed westward in the service of the French king along the coast of North America. He was looking for a passageway to the Far East.

Ten years later, the French monarch sent Jacques Cartier on a similar mission in search of what had become known as the Northwest Passage—not because it was expected to run northwest, but because it was supposed to be in the north and to run directly westward to the Indies. Cartier hit upon the mouth of the St. Lawrence River, and he was able to sail so far up that stream he was convinced that he had found the route to the Orient. But then, at the site of modern Montreal, he came up against rapids that prevented further progress to the west. Despite his disappointment, he was impressed by "the immense numbers of people in Hochelga" and by "their kindness and peacefulness."

The Spanish showed little interest in the northern voyages, but they were deeply concerned by a French settlement in Florida that was uncomfortably close to the shipping lanes of their treasure ships from Peru and Mexico. They wiped it out

and confidently built Fort Augustine on the northeast coast of that region. From there they sent missionaries farther north, but established no permanent settlements. Although as early as the 1540s Vásquez de Coronado had explored as far north as present-day Kansas, it was the French and not the Spanish who gained control in North America.

In the early seventeenth century, under the leadership of Samuel de Champlain, French explorers established outposts at Quebec, Montreal, and various other points along the great gateway to the interior of the continent, the St. Lawrence River. Then they pressed on through the regions of the Great Lakes and the Ohio and Mississippi valleys. The French also established settlements at New Orleans and Biloxi on the Gulf of Mexico, and at St. Domingue, the western end of the island of Hispaniola.

Most French settlements in the Midwest were not really towns; they were forts and trading stations, aimed primarily at serving the fur trade. Many French fur traders married Indian women and adopted Indian ways. French farmers were widely scattered and remained sufficiently few in number to take very little land from the Indians. Thus the French avoided conflict with the native inhabitants, unlike the Spanish and unlike the English.

THE ENGLISH IN THE NEW WORLD

Among the Atlantic nations of Europe, England and the Netherlands lagged behind Portugal, Spain, and France in taking an interest in the New World. In the sixteenth century, the Dutch were still fighting for national unity and independence from the Spanish. They established no claims in North America until 1609, when Henry

Hudson, an Englishman in the employ of a Dutch trading company, sailed up the river which he named for himself. The first English claim was established much earlier along the northern coast by two voyages sponsored by King Henry VII in 1497 and 1498. But the expeditions led by John and Sebastian Cabot provoked little interest in England, and for more than seventy-five years the only Englishmen to see American shores were summertime fishermen.

This delay had two important consequences. During the latter half of the sixteenth century, the economies of England and the Netherlands were becoming committed to commercial capitalism, much more so than the economies of the other Atlantic nations. Thus the English and Dutch settlements in America in the early seventeenth century were financed largely by private merchants rather than by royal wealth. Fully as important, by the time they attempted to establish colonies in America, the Dutch and the English had become Protestants and were locked in bitter opposition to the supporters of the Roman Catholic Church.

The Reformation

The Protestant Reformation began in Germany in 1517 when Martin Luther publicly denounced the Catholic Church for selling pardons for sins. Luther contended that people could be saved "by faith alone," not by outward observances, charity, and good behavior—mere "good works." He went on to claim that Christians must acquire faith directly from the Bible, the Word of God. Luther's assault on Catholic hierarchy and doctrine triggered more than a century of religious war in Europe. Eventually religious divisions came to coincide roughly with national boundaries. Spain and Portugal remained Roman Catholic, as did France, except for a strong minority of Protestants called Huguenots. England, Scotland, the Netherlands, and the Scandinavian countries became Protestant.

The reformers were not a united group. Protestants in France, the Netherlands, and Scotland followed the doctrines of John Calvin, a French refugee who established a religious government in Geneva, Switzerland. Calvin stressed human helplessness in the face of an all-powerful God. He also emphasized the doctrine of *predestination,* the idea that God, from the beginning of time, had decided the eternal fate of every individual—whether he or she was to be saved or damned. Calvin also sought to eliminate from Protestant

services the forms and ceremonies of Roman Catholic ritual, and he insisted that all members of the religious community must constantly examine the condition of their souls. Although people do not earn their way into Heaven by good deeds, diligent labor in their job or "calling," Calvin taught, was often a sign of redemption. It seemed to Calvinists that God would favor communities that were committed to His ways.

Calvinist ideas began to seep into England in the middle of the sixteenth century. By then, however, the English nation had already broken away from the Roman Catholic Church. In the 1530s Henry VIII had become entangled in marital problems that involved both the Pope and Spain, whose monarch was rapidly becoming the defender of Catholicism. Henry established a national English church with himself as Supreme Governor and confiscated the vast landholdings of the monasteries. Two short reigns followed Henry's death— one Protestant, the next Catholic. Then Queen Elizabeth, monarch from 1558 to 1603, tried to achieve a compromise between the nationalized Protestant Church of England, still partly Catholic in ceremony and doctrine, and the growing number of English Calvinists who demanded further reform of the national church.

England versus Spain

Queen Elizabeth became the champion of Protestantism against the Catholic Counterreformation being mounted by Spain. She secretly financed Dutch Protestants in their wars against the Spanish and eventually sent English troops into the Netherlands to help them. She also quietly invested in voyages of English ship captains who wanted to raid the Spanish treasure ships bringing back gold and silver from Mexico and Peru.

In 1577, even though the two nations were supposedly at peace, she backed a brilliantly successful expedition led by Francis Drake, who sailed through the Strait of Magellan, raided Spanish ships and settlements along the western coast of South America, touched at California, which he claim for England as "Nova Albion," and returned to England in 1580 after having circled the world. In Plymouth harbor Elizabeth knighted Drake on the deck of his ship, the *Golden Hind.* Elizabeth rather deviously assured the Spanish ambassador that she had no hostile intentions toward his country. Drake's exploits helped establish a tradition among European nations, which lasted until the middle of the eighteenth century, that they

Queen Elizabeth. (*Cooper-Bridgeman Library, Collection Thyssen-Bornemiszo*)

Ursprung?

could war against each other in the New World while remaining at peace in the Old. As the common phrase went, "No peace beyond the Line."

For a generation England and Spain held onto a shaky peace, but in 1588 the Spanish mounted a massive attempt to invade England. The famous Spanish Armada was probably the largest naval force ever assembled up to that time. The population of England was less than half of Spain's. But the Spanish fleet was hit by gale winds and the guns of the English ships. The result, for the Spanish, was a disastrous defeat. For the English, it was a glorious victory for the cause of Protestantism and the English nation. The war with Spain dragged on until 1604, but the defeat of the Armada established England as a major power. As such, it began to think more seriously about challenging its international rivals in the New World.

Frobisher and Gilbert

English interest in America was not merely a matter of challenging Catholic Spain. In the 1550s London merchants began to organize joint stock companies for trading overseas with Russia, Africa, and the Levant (the Middle East). In the 1570s a new Cathay (China) Company financed three voyages led by Martin Frobisher to find the Northwest Passage.

Frobisher sailed directly west below the southern tip of Greenland and then northwest until he came on the enormous, forbidding island of Baffin not far below the Arctic Circle. Finding further passage blocked by ice and barren land, Frobisher brought back to England several tons of ore that glittered with specks of gold. When tested it proved to be pyrite, or "fool's gold," and for years piles of the ore lay blocking one of the interior gates of the Tower of London.

Another Englishman was dreaming about a more promising destiny for his country in America. Sir Humphrey Gilbert was the first Englishman to see the New World as a place where profit could be had by permanent settlement rather than by setting up trading posts. He organized two expeditions. Virtually nothing is known about the first one in 1578, but in the summer of 1583 he set sail with five ships and reached Newfoundland with four.

There he found a little community of European fishermen who for years had been drying fish in the summer. He took possession of the land in the name of Elizabeth, and then sailed south in search of a more favorable climate. But winter was beginning to close in, and his ships (now reduced to two) were running short of supplies. On the return voyage they ran into a storm, and one of the vessels was lost. Sir Humphrey Gilbert was last seen sitting in the stern of a ten-ton fishing boat reading a copy of Thomas More's *Utopia*.

Raleigh's Roanoke

- Gilbert's mantle fell to his half-brother, Sir Walter Raleigh, a dashing, impulsive favorite of Elizabeth.
- Raleigh had no trouble in getting a royal charter to

Sir Walter Raleigh. (*By courtesy of the National Portrait Gallery, London*)

found a colony in America. In 1584 he sent out an expedition with instructions to explore much farther south along the coast. The men came back with glowing descriptions of the land around Chesapeake Bay, which Raleigh called Virginia after the unmarried queen. The next year he equipped an expedition which included an artist, John White, who made superb paintings of the Indians, and Thomas Cavendish, who later became the third European to sail around the world.

They settled on Roanoke Island in Albemarle Sound. The men were frustrated in their search for gold and for a water passage to the Pacific, so when Sir Francis Drake stopped at the colony the next year on his way back from robbing Spanish gold in the West Indies, the Roanoke settlers returned with him to London.

Raleigh was as persistent as he was impulsive: In 1587 he sent out a large expedition of 120 people, which for the first time included women. Virginia Dare, the first English child born in America, was the grandaughter of the group's leader, John White. Leaving his family in the colony, White returned to England to help arrange for supplies. But because of the Spanish Armada and the war with Spain, every English vessel was pressed into service. When a supply ship finally reached the colony in 1590, all the settlers were gone. To this day, no one knows what happened to them.

Marked by bad luck, unrealistic expectations, lack of financial resources, and the ongoing war with Spain, English colonizing efforts seemed to be going nowhere. Yet in the closing decades of the sixteenth century there were significant changes in England that may in the long run have been more important than all these early expeditions. More and more capital was accumulating in the hands of English merchants. The transfers of land that began with Henry VIII's seizure of the monasteries helped trigger a process by which some people were gaining great wealth and others were being thrown off the land altogether to become the roving "beggars" of Elizabethan England.

The mood of the English people was becoming nationalistic. Defeating the Armada did nothing to diminish this feeling. One man captured this mood so well that he became known as the "trumpet" of English colonization. Richard Hakluyt was a friend of Gilbert and Raleigh, a clergyman, and a propagandist for overseas expansion. In 1584 he set forth a comprehensive case for English settlement in the New World. In the 1590s he capti-

A Carolina Indian dance, painted around 1585 by John White. (*Reproduced by courtesy of the Trustees of the British Museum*)

vated a wide audience with his *The Principal Navigations, Voyages, Traffiques, and Discoveries of the English Nation.*

Yet clearly it would require more than this kind of pleading to make English colonization in America a success. The necessary ingredients for successful "planting" in America did not become obvious until the English found them in the next century by a process of trial and error, greed and faith.

SUMMARY

European voyages of exploration and discovery had by the late fifteenth century reached the Americas, which until then had known only Asian immigrants. This new expansionism was motivated by desire for the trade and wealth on which the new economic system of commercial capitalism was based, as well as by political rivalry. The latter, in turn, was based on the religious conflicts that had grown out of the Protestant Reformation.

The most important immediate effect of this "invasion" by Europeans of the New World was the destruction of the native populations living there; they died by the thousands of diseases to which they had no resistance. These "Indians," as the Europeans called them, were extremely varied in language, culture, and appearance. Their societies and political organizations ranged from the sophisticated empires of the Aztecs and Incas to the simple family or tribal groupings of nomadic hunters.

The woodland Indians of the Atlantic seacoast lived primarily by hunting, fishing, trapping, and simple agriculture. Political organization was based on tribes or nations, and sometimes on confederations of alliances of a number of tribes. These societies were remarkably "classless"; there were leaders, but leadership was based on age and merit, not birth.

Although we say Christopher Columbus "discovered" America, it had actually been known to Europeans much earlier. The tenth-century Scandinavians who found and settled Iceland and Greenland also made their way to Labrador and Newfoundland. But it was not until late in the fifteenth century that economic, political, and technological development made long sea voyages and large-scale colonization both possible and desirable.

Portuguese navigators were the first to venture out in search of a sea route to India and the Far East. They sailed south and east around the southern tip of Africa to find the route to the "Indies." Then Spanish and later French and English explorers tried to reach the "east" by sailing west. When Columbus landed in the Caribbean, he thought he was near Japan.

The Pope divided the world between the Spanish and the Portuguese in the Treaty of Tordesillas. The Spanish got the New World except for Brazil; the Portuguese got the Orient. By the time the English, the French, and the Dutch realized the potential of Spain's new possessions, the Spanish had built a huge overseas empire and extracted from it enormous amounts of gold and silver. It was not until 1534 that Cartier found the St. Lawrence River and Canada for the French, and even then the French settlements were really trading outposts that did not greatly disturb the Indians. The Dutch did not arrive until 1609, when Henry Hudson discovered the river that bears his name. The English had actually come earlier, in 1497 and 1498, but it was seventy-five years before they attempted to establish a settlement.

Martin Luther's challenge of the supreme authority of the Catholic Church in 1517 started centuries of religious conflict in Europe. As a result, Spain, Portugal, and France became loyal supporters of the Pope; England, Scotland, the Netherlands, and Scandinavia were split among various Protestant denominations. The defeat of the Spanish Armada in 1588 made England a major maritime power; its merchants were by this time eager to share in the rewards of overseas trade. But the first attempts to establish English settlements in North America—in Newfoundland in 1578 and 1583, and at Roanoke, Virginia, in 1584 and 1587—all failed. It would take much trial and error before the English would find the right formula for overseas empire in North America.

Suggested Readings

The emergence of expansionist Europe and the beginnings of the thrust overseas are the subject of R. Reynolds, *Europe Emerges: Transition toward an Industrial World-Wide Society, 1660–1750* (1961); see also D. Whittlesy, *Environmental Foundations of European History* (1949). An important and stimulating recent work is I. Wallerstein, *The Modern World System: Capitalist Agriculture and the Origins of the European World-Economy in the Sixteenth Century* (1974).

J. Hobson, *Imperialism: A Study* (1902), places the European invasion of the New World in a broader context. C. Verlinden, *Beginnings of Modern Colonization* (1970), emphasizes the medieval antecedents to European expansion. There is extremely interesting material in C. Cipolla, *European Culture and Overseas Expansion* (1970); and R. Davis, *The Rise of the Atlantic Economies* (1973), covers the fifteenth through the eighteenth centuries.

The matter of the Norse voyages has long been controversial. Perhaps the best start may be made with W. Washburn (ed.), *Proceedings of the Vinland Map Conference* (1971); C. Sauer, *Northern Mists* (1968); and F. Pohl, *The Viking Settlements of North America* (1972).

Easily the best survey of the subject is C. Gibson, *Spain in America* (1966), which contains a good bibliography. See also the same author's *The Aztecs under Spanish Rule: A History of the Indians in the Valley of Mexico, 1519–1810* (1966). J. Hardoy, *Pre-Columbian Cities* (1973), has an informative text and magnificent pictures. A complex and fascinating subject is dealt with by M. Morner, *Race Mixture in the History of Latin America* (1967). J. Parry, *The Spanish Seaborne Empire* (1966) is a vivid account.

A beginning may be made on other European nations in the New World with two works by C. Boxer: *Race Relations in the Portuguese Colonial Empire, 1415–1825* (1963), and *The Dutch Seaborne Empire, 1600–1800* (1965). For the French, see W. Eccles, *France in America* (1972). The superb prose of Francis Parkman is still worth reading in this connection. There is an excellent selection in *The Parkman Reader* (1955), edited by S. Morison.

During the past twenty years there have been numerous works published on the Amerindians, most of them great improvements over older studies. Probably the best survey is H. Driver, *Indians of North America* (2nd ed., 1970). This may be supplemented with G. Willey, *An Introduction to American Archaeology*,

Vol. I, *North and Middle America* (1966), and with R. Underhill, *Red Man's America: A History of Indians in the United States* (rev. ed., 1971). A useful collaboration between anthropologists and historians is E. Leacock and N. Lurie (eds.), *North American Indians in Historical Perspective* (1971). For further citations, see the splendid bibliographical essay in W. Washburn, *The Indian in America* (1975).

The discovery of the New World by European voyagers has received loving attention from several distinguished historians. S. Morison's *Admiral of the Ocean Sea* (2 vols., 1942) remains one of the great biographies of American history. Morison, who was both a sailor and a superb stylist, capped his long historical career with *European Discovery of America: The Northern Voyages* (1971); and *European Discovery of America: The Southern Voyages* (1974). A fine survey of European maritime expansion, especially good on the significance of ship design, is J. Parry, *The Age of Reconnaissance* (1963). Several other works whose titles are largely self-explanatory are well worth looking at: See D. Quinn, *England and the Discovery of America, 1481–1620: From the Bristol Voyages of the Fifteenth Century to the Pilgrim Settlement at Plymouth; The Exploration, Exploitation, and Trial and Error Colonization of America by the English* (1974); J. Axtell (ed.), *The Indian Peoples of Eastern America, A Documentary History of the Sexes* (1981); A. Rowse, *The Expansion of Elizabethan England* (1955); and H. Baudet, *Paradise on Earth: Thoughts on European Images of Non-Europeans* (1965). A different perspective is offered in R. Brown, *Historical Geography of the United States* (1948).

There is an enormous body of works on the Reformation in England and in Western Europe as a whole. Partly because of differing religious perspectives, no single study stands out as the place to begin. A bibliography that focuses on the English Reformation is found in R. Lockyer, *Tudor and Stuart Britain, 1471–1714* (1964).

AN OVERSEAS EMPIRE

Chapter 2

Between 1600 and 1700, England acquired a permanent empire in the New World, and the New World acquired a new society. The colonies that grew up on the coast of North America became linked with one another and with England in a mercantile system of empire. It was an economy based on the exchange and sale of goods in a pattern designed to build the prosperity and power of England as the center. Founding and running an overseas empire was a new venture for England; making a new life was a new venture for the colonists. It was inevitable that there would be problems, particularly because England sent colonists rather than conquerors to North America. The colonies themselves differed from one another because they were established for different reasons.

By the end of the century, government officials in England began to realize that they had the makings of an overseas empire. In actuality, that empire consisted of nearly twenty different settlements stretching from the Caribbean to New England. They knew what they wanted the colonies to become; but enforcing their wishes was difficult at a time when it took three months to get an answer in London to the simplest question about what was going on in America. But none of this was apparent in 1603–1604, when events in England made permanent settlement on the Atlantic coast a real possibility. ■

CHANGES IN ENGLAND

Several factors combined to make many English people decide to emigrate to the forbidding wilderness in America. The war between Spain and England came to an end in 1604, and peace encouraged merchants to invest their capital in overseas enterprises. James I, who had succeeded Elizabeth, tried to support some of these efforts, but the royal treasury lacked funds. James was hostile to the growing number of Calvinists in his church. Many of these "Puritans," as they were called, decided that truly godly communities would be more easily established in America than in England. Many of them also thought James was undermining the traditional English freedoms of representative government, free speech, taxation by consent, and trial by due process. In addition, economic dislocations led to the idea that England was overpopulated; there seemed to be too many "beggars" roaming the countryside and flooding into London. Finally, a sense of exhilaration and expansive power was sweeping the nation after its victories over Catholic Spain.

A learned and well-intentioned man, James I was also tactless and opinionated. It was a bad combination for a ruler who had to deal with an unruly Parliament and a growing Puritan party within the national church. Although he willingly presided over the great English translation of the Bible, the King James version, he came into conflict with Puritans, who thought the Church of England was still too much like the Church of Rome. He also clashed with Parliament over taxation and free speech. At the bottom of these and other issues was that of parliamentary versus royal power.

James I died in 1625, but his son Charles I took a hard line on taxation and the privileges of Parliament. After a mjaor constitutional crisis in the late 1620s, Charles I tried for more than a decade to rule without Parliament. When forced by financial necessity to call Parliament together in 1639, he became involved in a civil war that resulted in his execution in 1649. It was followed by the Puritan dictatorship of Oliver Cromwell and his "saints." After Cromwell's death, the monarchy was "restored" in 1660.

The Restoration of Charles II marked a turning point in English history that had a great effect on the colonies, just as the outbreak of the civil war had in 1640. After twenty years of civil turmoil, the English government was able to encourage the establishment of more colonies and to set up a system for supervising them. Yet the religious issue in England was only partially settled. Most people still belonged to the Church of England, but a large minority still held Puritan principles in the face of some persecution. The constitutional issue remained less clear. It was not until another revolution in 1689 that the primacy of Parliament over the Crown was firmly established.

VIRGINIA: THE FIRST COLONY

When James I assumed the throne in 1603, he was quite willing to issue land grants in America. James gave his backing to the Virginia Company, which had two branches, one in London and the other in the little port city of Plymouth. He awarded Sir Ferdinando Gorges's Plymouth branch an enormous territory on the northern portion of the Altantic coast, and in the spring of 1607 Sir Ferdinando sent an expedition to Sagadohoc on the Kennebec River in Maine. The settlement lasted barely one winter. After an "extreme, unseasonable, and frosty" season, the men simply quit. It was the Jamestown settlement that finally succeeded.

This first permanent English settlement in the New World came very close to failure; only an accident of timing saved it from going the way of Roanoke. At first it was an all-male enterprise, but gradually a few women braved the hardships of the Atlantic voyage and the crude life in the struggling colony. In order to survive, an overseas colony needed a reliable source of income, and this first successful settlement found one in a new crop, tobacco. The early English settlers also had to deal with the fact that the land was already occupied. The Indian residents of the area could easily have wiped out the tiny settlement, and they came quite close to doing so.

In December 1606 the *Susan Constant*, *Godspeed*, and *Discovery*, with 160 men under the command of Captain Christopher Newport, weighed anchor in the name of the Virginia Company of London. Four months later they sighted "the Bay of Chesupiac," or Chesapeake. The three tiny ships sailed up a broad river the settlers tactfully named the James and chose an island they called Jamestown, a site well situated for defense— and also, as it turned out, for the spread of disease. Here, after the most terrible experiences, England won its first foothold in America.

During the bleak winter of 1608–1609, the "starving time," the colony was held together by the efforts of Captain John Smith, an energetic and iron-willed war veteran. Smith was aided by

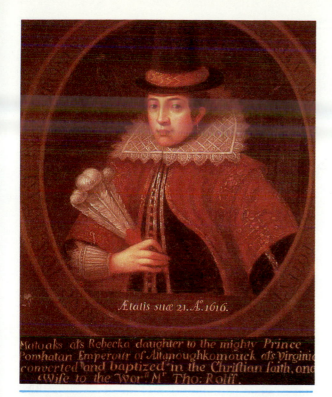

Matoaka (Pocahontas), born in Virginia, as she adapted to London in 1617. Her father's name is given in Latin on the left. (*Architect of the Capitol*)

Powhatan, a chief who had forged a powerful confederacy of Indian tribes in the area. Powhatan at first regarded the English as pawns in his power game and befriended them with food supplies, as he would any local tribe whose loyalty he wished to gain.

The English undertaking in Virginia had three principal objectives: to find a northwest water passage to the wealth of Asia, to exploit the gold and silver of America, and to find suitable lands for producing crops like silk, grapes, dyes, and oranges. All three efforts failed. The James River did not go very far west. Smith's explorations aroused the hostility of Powhatan's people, who soon realized that the English had come not merely to trade metal for corn, but to take Indian land. Powhatan's daughter Matoaka, whom the English called Pocahontas, voiced this resentment when she said: "Many do inform me that your coming is not for trade but to invade my people and possess my country."

In addition to meeting growing hostility from the Indians, the settlers failed to find the gold that the Spanish experience in Mexico told them ought to be lying about for the taking. But that did not stop the "gentlemen" the Virginia Company had sent out from spending their time looking for trea-

sure instead of providing shelter or food or establishing plantations.

By late 1608, more colonists arrived. Smith tried to force Powhatan to trade; Powhatan chose to let the English starve. When Smith was injured in 1609 and left Virginia for good, the settlement remained, as he accurately described it, "a miserie, a ruine, a death, a Hell." By 1610, although Christopher Newport on successive visits had brought almost two hundred newcomers, only sixty settlers lived in Jamestown. The Virginia Company struggled to support its overseas enterprise, but met with little success. By 1624, when James I revoked the colony's charter and made Virginia a royal province, it had only 1200 people. About 6000 had set out for Jamestown, but 4000 had perished on the ocean voyage or in the New World, and hundreds of others had given up and gone home.

The Colony Grows

By then, however, conditions had begun to improve. The first settlers had been mere servants of the promoters, men who had signed contracts called *indentures*, by which they agreed to work for a certain number of years in exchange for their passage. Once they reached Virginia, these servants became very hard to control. Many ran off to seek gold, and those who fulfilled their contracts had little incentive to work. In 1619, the promoters gave each of the "ancient planters" 100 acres of his own and instituted the *head right* system, under which any new settler received 50 acres for every servant he induced to come to America. The government of the colony was liberalized by the creation of a House of Burgesses. This first legislature of elected representatives in America held its first meeting in 1619. By that time, a few women had arrived in the colony. Their presence helped change Virginia from a military outpost to a permanent settlement.

Fully as important was the discovery in 1612 that tobacco could be grown successfully. A market for this product had been growing in Europe since the middle of the sixteenth century. In 1618, Virginia shipped 30,000 pounds to England, mostly for reexport to the Continent. By 1627, the colony was exporting more than 500,000 pounds a year. Not until sugar in the Caribbean, a generation later, or until the invention of the cotton gin nearly two centuries later, would a single staple New World crop "take off" in such spectacular fashion.

A SERVANT IN VIRGINIA

In 1623, the year after the great Indian massacre in Virginia, a young English servant owned by the Virginia Company wrote his parents in hopes that they would arrange to buy his freedom.

Loveing and kind father and mother my most humble duty remembered to you hopeing in God of your good health, as I my selfe am at the makeing hereof, this is to let you understand that I your Child am in a most heavie Case by reason of the nature of the Country is such that it Causeth much sicknes, as the scurvie and the bloody flux and divers other diseases, wch maketh the bodie very poore, and Weake, and when wee are sicke there is nothing to Comfort us: for since I came out of the ship, I never at[e] anie thing but pease, and loblollie (that is water gruell) as for deare or venison I never saw anie since I came into this land, ther is indeed some foule, but Wee are

not allowed to goe, and get it, but must Worke hard both earelie, and late for a messe of water gruell, and a mouthfull of bread, and beife, a mouthfull of bread for a pennie loafe must serve for 4 men wch is most pitifull. . . .

Living as he was on an isolated plantation, Richard Ffrethorne also referred to the continuing danger from Indians: "Wee are but 32 to fight against 3000 if they should Come, and the nighest helpe that Wee have is ten miles of us." He had been befriended by a kindly freeman, he said, who "much marvailed that you would send me a servaunt to the Companie, he saith I had beene better knockd on the head, and Indeede so I find it now to my great greife and miserie, and saith, that if you love me you will redeeme me suddenlie, for wch I doe Intreate and begg. . . ."

This explosion of tobacco production had important social and political effects. Tobacco rapidly depleted the fertility of the soil; four years on the same ground was the usual limit. In their search for more and more land, the great planters gradually pushed small farmers back from good water transportation in the Tidewater, the rich coastal plain. Some of these farmers ventured into the Piedmont, the upland area west of the Fall Line (see map).

These developments resulted in the concentration of economic and political power in the hands of a relatively small ruling class. Daughters of wealthy planters began to marry the sons of wealthy planters—even their first cousins. The planting class became a network of interrelated families. The ruling "heads" of these households translated their economic and familial positions into political power by restricting voting and representation in the House of Burgesses, both financially (with a property requirement) and geographically (by overrepresenting the Tidewater). The tobacco planters mercilessly exploited their indentured servants—but they could not always prevent them from moving on after their terms had expired. What they needed was a labor force they could control for life.

Bacon's Rebellion

The one-crop system became the source for some of the grievances that led in 1676 to Bacon's Rebellion. In 1622, several years after tobacco cul-

ture had begun to push settlers into Indian territory, Powhatan's successor led an attack on the English settlements and killed nearly a third of the settlers. The English response was bitter and violent. All Indians, whether friendly or not, were now enemies. Instructions from London directed settlers "to root out [the Indians] from being any longer a people."

There was another conflict in the 1640s. When the fighting was over, in 1646, leaders on both sides agreed to occupy separate territories. The Indians and the English lived in relative peace for the next three decades, until a new wave of settlers began spreading onto the Indian lands. In the 1670s these settlers complained of Indian raids on their hogs and demanded official permission to push the Indians out of the lands near white settlements. Virginia's Governor William Berkeley was reluctant, so the frontiersmen took matters into their own hands. They attacked a group of about 400 Susquehannocks living in an abandoned fort. Weakened by European diseases and warfare, they and several other local tribes were extremely vulnerable. In the war of extermination that followed, revenge was taken on both sides. When Governor Berkeley failed to provide a force that could remove or destroy the Indians, Nathaniel Bacon had his chance.

An aristocrat with a shady past, Bacon was in his twenties when he arrived in Virginia and set himself up on more than 1000 acres in the interior. The elderly governor was his cousin by marriage, and within a year of his arrival Bacon was given a seat on the governor's council. Bacon, however, remained an outsider. The Virginia country, he said, wanted dead Indians, not friendly ones, and he demanded that Berkeley grant him a military commission to do the job. When Berkeley refused, Bacon set himself up as the leader of an anti-Berkeley party. He gathered a force of volunteers and led them in successful raids against the Indians and then against Jamestown itself. They burned the capital.

News reached England in September 1676, and the king shipped out 1100 soldiers to restore order. But by that time Nathaniel Bacon had died of "swamp fever," and his followers had scattered into the woods. Probably less than a hundred Englishmen died in the rebellion, but Governor Berkeley—a man of vengeance—had 23 of the rebels hanged.

PURITAN NEW ENGLAND

The Puritans who migrated to New England were very different from the settlers of the tobacco colonies. They were committed to dynamic religious beliefs that had profound and lasting effects on the settlement of the region and later on much of English America as well. They were not seeking religious liberty. Rather, they intended to set up their own Puritan churches, and they expected all settlers to follow Puritan principles and leadership. In order to do this, Puritan leaders tried to control the pattern of settlement; they wanted compact village communities rather than scattered farms. And the Puritans migrated as families rather than as individuals. Thus, from the beginning there were more women and children in New England than in the other English colonies.

Puritan Ideology

Much nonsense has been written about the Puritans. They did not all wear tall black hats and drab clothing. They drank liquor, but not to excess. "Wine is from God," one of them wrote, "but drunkenness is from the devil." Far from denouncing sex, they declared that it should be enjoyed by both women and men. But they firmly believed that sex ought to take place only between a married man and woman. Not only that, they insisted that a husband and wife *ought* to love each other both physically and spiritually. On this score they had only one reservation—that married love should not distract the partners from the higher love of God.

John Calvin. (*New York Public Library*)

These English Calvinists kept God at the center of their attention. As Calvin himself had taught, they were certain that from the beginning of creation God had either saved or damned every single person for all eternity. Yet this conviction did not make Puritans give up trying to lead good and moral lives. Both God and His word, the Bible, required good behavior on the part of the individual and the community as a whole. Puritans knew that God would see fit to punish violations of His laws both in this world and in the next; surely He would punish an individual sinner. It was also entirely within His power to show His displeasure with entire communities by means of storms, disease, and other natural disasters.

What could a person do in order to be saved? Strictly speaking, the answer was "nothing," because the decision was in the hands of God. At the same time, Puritans believed they should watch for signs of God's pleasure toward them. They should prepare their hearts to receive salvation. Through Christ, people should try to gain assurance that they were saved.

The problem was that a person could never be absolutely certain about God's decision. In daily life, therefore, Puritans were constantly examining themselves for signs about their eternal life. Puritans also watched their neighbors. They believed they had excellent reasons for doing so, since God, speaking through the Bible, required good behavior of everyone. So the Puritans looked for sinful words and deeds in their communities. They expected to find them, and of course they did, for they regarded all people as sinful by nature. They kept a watchful eye out for such sins as swearing, drunkenness, unlawful sex, theft, assault, murder, and idleness.

Puritans included "idleness" in the catalog of sins because they believed God required everyone to be busy at his or her work. God "called" men and women to their jobs—minister, farmer, mother, servant, seamstress, or carpenter. Whatever the job or "calling," God required that men and women work long and hard at it. Thus the members of the wealthiest merchant's family shared the same duties as those required in the household of the humblest farmer.

As we look back now, we can easily see that these requirements produced men and women of great faith and little tolerance. In the early years of New England settlement, this world view resulted in impatience toward anyone who stood in the Puritans' way, whether it was an English king and his bishops, the Atlantic Ocean, or the Indians who already lived on land the Puritans decided ought to be their own.

Pilgrims in Plymouth

The first Puritans who migrated to New England were a small and somewhat peculiar group. Though today we know them as Pilgrims, at the time they were called Separatists because they wished to break completely from the Church of England. The Separatists regarded the English Church as hopelessly corrupt. King James and the Church authorities responded by harassing their ministers and little congregations. In 1614 one of these congregations fled to Holland, where the

authorities were more tolerant. After several years there, however, some of them grew worried about the condition of their own piety and particularly about the behavior of their children. They finally decided to attempt to go to America, where they could "live as a distinct body by themselves."

After obtaining financial backing from some London businessmen, 35 Pilgrims set out aboard the *Mayflower* in the autumn of 1620. Also in the ship's company were some 60 "strangers"—artisans, soldiers, and indentured servants. The entire group was led by William Bradford and Captain Miles Standish, the military commander. Finding themselves off Cape Cod in November 1620, they decided not to seek "Virginia," where they had been given a land grant. Rather, they would find a suitable harbor in the region where God had sent them.

A month later their search was rewarded by discovery of the place they called Plymouth, on the inner shoreline of Massachusetts Bay. Anchored offshore, 41 adult men signed a written compact of government: "solemnly and mutually in the presence of God and one of another, [we] Covenant and Combine ourselves together into a Civil Body Politic, for our better ordering and preservation." In effect, the Mayflower Compact established a government based on the consent of the governed. The governor of the settlement would be elected annually by free adult males. In a world of hereditary monarchies, this was a radical step.

The Pilgrims knew very little about fishing and hunting and not much more about farming in the extreme New England climate. The tiny settlement barely survived the "starving time" of that first winter, when half the group died. Yet even-

---

THE HARDSHIPS OF LIFE IN PLYMOUTH

William Bradford described the early trials of the Pilgrims with an eloquence that made plain the importance of the Pilgrims' religious faith. Early in his history *Of Plymouth Plantation,* Bradford conceded that the Indians

. . . showed them no small kindness in refreshing them, but these savage barbarians, when they met with them (as after will appear) were readier to fill their sides full of arrows than otherwise. And for the season it was winter, and they that know the winters of that country know them to be sharp and violent, and subject to cruel and fierce storms,

dangerous to travel to known places, much more to search an unknown coast. Besides, what could they see but a hideous and desolate wilderness, full of wild beasts and wild men—and what multitudes there might be of them they knew not. . . . For summer being done, all things stand upon them with a weather-beaten face, and the whole country, full of woods and thickets, represented a wild and savage hue. If they looked behind them, there was the mighty ocean which they had passed and was now as a main bar and gulf to separate them from all the civil parts of the world. . . .What could now sustain them but the Spirit of God and His grace?

---

24 AN OVERSEAS EMPIRE

tually it grew by means of luck, fortitude, and faith.

Only a few years before, a plague carried by European fishermen had wiped out many Indians in southeastern New England. Those the English met were wary but not unfriendly. The new settlers were greatly aided by Squanto, an Indian who had been to England. He and several other Indians showed the Pilgrims how to plant corn. Squanto also served as a translator between the Pilgrims and Massasoit, the chief sachem of the region. Characteristically, Bradford described Squanto as "a special instrument sent by God" for the good of the English settlers.

Six years after they landed, the Pilgrims were able to buy out their financial backers with shipments of lumber and furs. That purchase virtually cut their connection with England. After ten years on their own, with new towns scattering southward and onto Cape Cod, the Pilgrims adopted a system of elective, representative government, very much in the spirit of the original Mayflower Compact. Each town sent representatives to the central government at Plymouth. Still, only those orthodox in religion and wealthy enough to rank "freemen" were given the vote.

Until 1691, when their little towns were absorbed into the Massachusetts Bay Colony, the Pilgrims led an independent existence, sustained by fish, fur, lumber, and religious faith. They were, as one of their friends in England wrote, "the instruments to break the ice for others."

The Commonwealth of Massachusetts Bay

Unlike the Separatist Pilgrims, most English Puritans intended to remain within the Church of England. By the late 1620s, however, many had grown discouraged about the future of their movement. The new king, Charles I, tried to suppress their preachers. This made some Puritans toy with the idea of emigrating to America in order to establish a holy commonwealth of their own. In 1629 a wealthy Puritan lawyer, John Winthrop, led a successful effort to establish a company with rights of settlement in New England. Winthrop became the first governor of the Massachusetts Bay Company.

The company's charter from the king resembled those granted to other trading companies, except that it did not specify the company's official residence or place of administration. This was an unusual omission and may well have been deliberate on the part of Winthrop and his friends. In any event, when these Puritans migrated in 1630

John Winthrop (1588–1649). His strength and determination are clearly shown in this portrait, painted before he immigrated to America. (*Massachusetts Historical Society*)

they took their charter with them, thereby transferring the entire enterprise to New England. As the Reverend Cotton Mather later explained, "We would have our posterity settled under the pure and full dispensation of the gospel; defended by rulers who should be ourselves."

The Great Migration began in 1630. By the end of that year, a thousand selected settlers had landed in Massachusetts. Moving outward, from Boston, these Puritan families laid out other little towns. Migrants kept coming, and by the end of the decade, about 15,000 persons had crossed the Atlantic.

This large migration sustained the prosperity of the colony; there was no "starving time" in Massachusetts. Few of the Puritan settlers were very wealthy, but many of them were able to pay for their own passage, with enough savings left over to support themselves for the first few months. The earlier settlers prospered by selling food and other articles to the newcomers.

The arrangement worked very well as long as immigration lasted. But about 1640 the Great Migration came to a halt when civil war broke out in England. Massachusetts faced its first economic depression. Yet the colony escaped disaster because, as Winthrop wrote, "the Lord was pleased to open up a trade with the West Indies." After

The meetinghouse of the Third Church of Boston (1669), the largest to be built in seventeenth-century New England. (*From William Burgis, "View of Boston," 1722; New York Public Library*)

only a dozen years of settlement, Massachusetts found its economic prosperity resting not on any single staple crop, but on overseas trade with other colonies and with England.

The quest for a suitable form of government proved more difficult. The colony had control over its own charter and thus was able to act like an independent republic while acknowledging allegiance to the king. But it was not at all clear which settlers should control that government. Winthrop and other Puritan leaders, convinced that most settlers were not truly godly persons, struggled to keep control in the hands of the Puritan elite. They never thought Puritan ministers should rule the holy commonwealth, though they often turned to them for advice and support. They simply assumed that any truly godly community should be governed by thoroughly orthodox Puritan men.

This leadership was challenged from two directions. The leaders were, as a group, wealthier than the other settlers. So their control of the colony was resented for both religious and economic reasons. Other men of lesser religious and economic status began grumbling about their rights. As freeborn Englishmen, they argued, they had the right to participate in government. After all, they had done so at home in England, if only by being allowed to vote. They had no wish to allow servants or the poor to vote, and they agreed that the

wicked and irreligious should be excluded. But they balked at being governed by a handful of self-appointed gentlemen on the governor's council.

There was a quiet but very real struggle for power between these two groups. After about fifteen years, a series of compromises was hammered out. Most adult male members of the churches would be allowed to vote. A representative legislature—the General Court—would be divided into two houses. The smaller upper house would be made up of relatively wealthy men. The larger lower house would consist of humbler representatives, with each town able to send two of its own. The governorship would remain an annually elective office. This workable compromise was possible because so many of the settlers shared a common belief in English liberties and Puritan values. The firmness of that ground is apparent in the fact that John Winthrop was elected governor almost every year until his death in 1649.

The Dissidents of Rhode Island

The rule of orthodox Puritans in Massachusetts was also challenged by two outstanding but very different individuals: Roger Williams and Anne Hutchinson. Roger Williams was a Separatist minister who migrated to Massachusetts in 1631. He was greatly admired for his piety and talents, but he soon began to irritate the authorities with alarming ideas. Williams announced that the settlers had no just claim to land unless they *purchased* it from the Indians. Williams also insisted that the government had no right to interfere in religious matters, not even the right to punish violations of the Sabbath. Most Puritans thought such proposals both absurd and dangerous. And much as they liked him, Massachusetts authorities were unwilling to tolerate his preaching. So in 1636, Roger Williams was banished from the colony.

In the dead of winter, Williams tramped southward through the snow to the headwaters of Narragansett Bay. For a time he lived with the Narragansett Indians and even took the trouble to learn their language—one of the few English settlers ever to do so. Soon he was joined by sympathizers from Massachusetts. They established the town of Providence, which became the center of a new colony, Rhode Island. In 1644, during the English civil war, Williams went back to England and successfully obtained a charter for his new settlement from a sympathetic Puritan Parliament.

Rhode Island's charter provided for a government similar to that of Massachusetts, but it contained unusual provisions that reflected Williams's personal views. All Christian groups were allowed to worship as they pleased, without any interference from the government. Even men who were not members of any church were permitted to vote. In these matters, Rhode Island remained unique among the colonies for many years.

The other early challenger of the authorities in Massachusetts, Anne Hutchinson, was a quick-witted and forceful person who jolted that colony even more than Williams had. She began discussing Sunday sermons with an ever-widening circle of admirers and announcing her conclusion that most ministers in the colony were wrong about the process of salvation. She publicly claimed the ministers were wrongly preaching that proper outward behavior could be a sign of salvation. She also announced that saints who had been saved were under no obligation to obey the outward laws of God.

These unorthodox views, known to theologians as Antinomianism, attracted a considerable following in the colony. The authorities were alarmed by the threat she posed to the social order, and they brought her to trial in 1638. At first she defended herself well before a frustrated court, but she made one fatal mistake. When asked where she obtained her unorthodox ideas, she replied that she had heard from God "by an immediate voice." Most Puritans believed that God no longer spoke directly to individuals but only through His holy word, the Bible, and that the only proper interpreters of the Bible were educated ministers.

The court banished Anne Hutchinson from Massachusetts. She moved with her family and numerous supporters to Rhode Island. Several years later she migrated westward, where she was killed by Indians—a brutal end several Massachusetts leaders interpreted as a positive sign of God's providence.

Connecticut, New Hampshire, and Maine

In the meantime, orthodox Puritan settlers were venturing far from the cluster of towns around Boston. Some moved northward onto land between the Merrimack and Kennebec rivers claimed by Massachusetts and also by several wealthy individuals in England. After considerable confusion about boundaries and land titles, New Hampshire emerged as a separate Puritan colony with a governor appointed by the king. The coastal land to the northeast, known as the district of Maine, remained part of Massachusetts.

Other Puritans left Massachusetts in favor of the fertile lands of the lower Connecticut valley. The Reverend Thomas Hooker led the first sizable

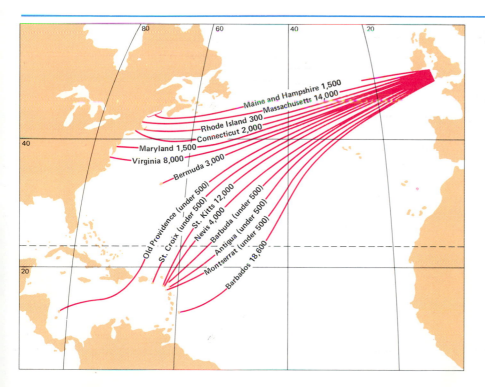

Migrations from England before 1640

migration and established the town of Hartford in 1636. More settlers from Massachusetts arrived and set up towns of their own. Puritans from England migrated to the Connecticut coast, where they founded New Haven. Eventually these towns banded together, applied for a charter much like those of Massachusetts and Rhode Island, and emerged in 1662 as the separate colony of Connecticut.

Thus five separate colonies had been established in New England. Of the five, Massachusetts was by far the most populous. All were thoroughly Puritan in their origins, and only Rhode Island was wayward and unorthodox. Yet Rhode Island was Puritan too. Religious tolerance in that colony demonstrated that orthodox Puritanism contained the seeds of disagreement and of change.

Puritans and Indians

The Puritans in Massachusetts, like the Pilgrims in Plymouth, had at first encountered small and sparsely settled Indian tribes who usually were peaceful and even generous to them. The colonists were not as generous in return. Although the Puritans talked about an obligation to convert the Indians to Christianity, they did little about it. The first missionary activity did not take place until thirteen years after the Puritans' arrival, and even then only a few ministers took any interest. Puritan governments forbade the sale of firearms to Indians and barred them from entering English settlements.

The Indians were puzzled and angered by the English encroachment on their lands. For their part, the Puritans wished the Indians would become civilized or simply go away. Intent on establishing their holy commonwealths, the English settlers regarded the Indians with a combination of hostility, contempt, and indifference. When smallpox killed several thousand Indians in eastern Massachusetts, for example, Governor John Winthrop explained the tragedy by saying: "The Lord hathe cleared our title to what we possess."

Given these attitudes, conflict was unavoidable. Usually the Puritans took advantage of old hostilities between Indian tribes. In 1637 the Pequots chose to resist the English by force. In May of that year, the English and their allies, the Narragansetts, set fire to the last Pequot stronghold, a fort on the Mystic River. They slaughtered or cap-

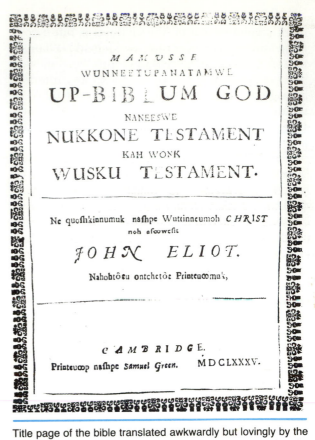

Title page of the bible translated awkwardly but lovingly by the Reverend Mr. John Eliot into an Algonkian dialect spoken by several Indian groups in eastern New England. Published in the Massachusetts Bay Colony in 1685. (*Rare Book Division, The New York Public Library, Astor, Lenox, and Tilden Foundation*)

tured nearly the entire nation. Plymouth's Governor William Bradford wrote of the massacre:

It was a fearful sight to see them thus frying in the fire and the streams of blood quenching the same, . . . but the victory seemed a sweet sacrifice, and they [the Puritans] gave the praise thereof to God, who had wrought so wonderfully for them . . . and given them a speedy victory over so proud and insulting an enemy.

The Narragansetts, shocked at this savagery, thought that the warfare of their English allies "is too furious and slays too many men."

A generation later, one tribe, the Wampanoags, organized a last-ditch offensive to oust the white invaders. The alliance was led by Metacom (or King Philip, as the Puritans called him), who won support from tribes whose lands and livelihood had been taken by the whites. These Indians had become dependent on European trade goods but could no longer supply beaver pelts in exchange, since the animals had been hunted out of their eastern territories.

Successful guerrilla raids on outlying Puritan villages attracted more and more tribes (including the Narragansetts) to the Wampanoags' cause. During the winter of 1675–1676 the Indians devastated the New England frontier. By March they were attacking towns 20 miles west of Boston. In response, the Puritans followed the usual policy of extermination, massacring both friendly and hostile tribes.

Food shortages and disease finally halted Metacom's forces. Of some 90 Puritan villages, 52 had been attacked and 12 destroyed, and the white frontier had been moved back. A higher proportion of the white New England population had died than in any American war before or since. Many of the surviving Indians were placed in "praying villages" (so-called Christianized Indian reservations) or shipped off to the West Indies as slaves. They had gone the way of the coastal tribes in Virginia in the face of European pressure for their land.

New England's Economy: Trade

The geography and climate of New England did a great deal to shape the life of the new arrivals. In Maine and New Hampshire, the colder weather restricted farming for the English as it had for the Indians. Except for the Connecticut and Merrimack valleys, New England was much more hilly and far less fertile than the Chesapeake region. Small farms were the rule. Farming families settled in villages where the houses clustered around the church and the village green instead of being scattered over the countryside.

When a group wished to establish a new town, it obtained permission from the colonial legislature to settle a block of land of approximately 6 square miles, usually adjoining an older town. All freemen were eligible to draw for the town lots and to use the woods and meadows. The richer settlers sometimes got additional lots, but even they never received more than two or three times as much land as the poorest. The system had certain disadvantages: By keeping control of the

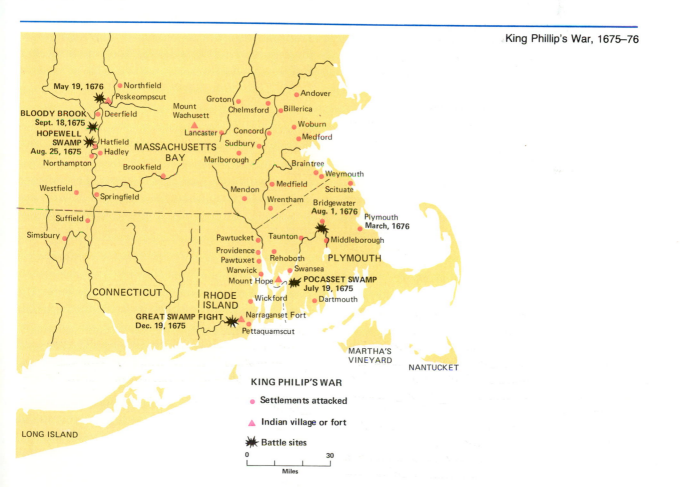

King Phillip's War, 1675–76

Northfield
May 19, 1676
Peskeompscut
BLOODY BROOK
Sept. 18, 1675
Deerfield
HOPEWELL SWAMP
Aug. 25, 1675
Hatfield
Hadley
MASSACHUSETTS BAY
Northampton
Brookfield
Westfield
Springfield
Suffield
Simsbury
Groton
Mount Wachusett
Chelmsford
Lancaster
Concord
Sudbury
Marlborough
Mendon
Medfield
Wrentham
Pawtucket
Providence
Pawtuxet
Warwick
Mount Hope
Andover
Billerica
Woburn
Medford
Braintree
Weymouth
Scituate
Bridgewater
Aug. 1, 1676
Plymouth
March, 1676
Taunton
Middleborough
Rehoboth
PLYMOUTH
Swansea
POCASSET SWAMP
July 19, 1675
CONNECTICUT
RHODE ISLAND
Wickford
Dartmouth
GREAT SWAMP FIGHT
Dec. 19, 1675
Narraganset Fort
Pettaquamscut
MARTHA'S VINEYARD
NANTUCKET
LONG ISLAND

KING PHILIP'S WAR
● Settlements attacked
▲ Indian village or fort
✳ Battle sites
0   30
Miles

undivided land, the original owners could discriminate against newcomers, who often formed a deprived majority, along with landless and voteless tenants and laborers. Disputes between old and new settlers frequently ended with the newcomers moving west or north to areas beyond the town's control. Eventually the system of planned expansion broke down. During most of the seventeenth century, however, the system worked, and Puritan culture was carried to new frontiers.

Most settlers in this period lived by farming and home industry, with relatively little hired help or indentured labor. As early as 1644, iron was being smelted commercially in Massachusetts, rum was being made from West Indian molasses, and cider pressed from local fruits had become available for sale locally and overseas. New England craftsmen also made many of the commodities needed in the colony, such as furniture, pottery, hardware, and tools. Three vital products were made primarily by women: clothing, soap, and candles. Since New Englanders did not have an export staple such as tobacco, they could not easily pay to import such articles from abroad.

Some New Englanders turned to the sea for a living. Fishing off the banks of Newfoundland became so important in Massachusetts that the cod became the symbol of the colony. Enough fish were caught for export to the West Indies and elsewhere, along with foodstuffs, horses, lumber, rum, and even captive Indians to be sold as slaves.

Puritan trading in black slaves began in 1638 when the Salem ship *Desire* brought Africans from the West Indies. Blacks were imported in small numbers; by 1700 the region's population of 90,000 included about a thousand blacks, most of them slaves. It was the traffic *to* the West Indies, not from it, that soon dominated the slave trade. Early in the 1640s, Puritan captains began visiting the West African coast. Before the end of the century, Massachusetts and Rhode Island merchants were involved in the trade, with their main customers in the Caribbean islands. Gradually they won larger markets in the mainland colonies as well.

Overseas commerce, like fishing, stimulated shipbuilding. New England ships were so seaworthy and so inexpensive that they were soon being built for foreign as well as domestic merchants and captains. Once on the sea, Puritan ships, like those of other maritime nations, sought out all kinds of cargoes and sailed to any port, legal or illegal. By the end of the seventeenth century Boston had become an international port where goods of many nations were transshipped. Boston merchants and traders were becoming as rich and powerful as the planters of the Tidewater. They also had interests that extended beyond their ties with England.

THE DUTCH BEACHHEAD

While the English were establishing themselves in the Chesapeake and New England areas, the Dutch suddenly grabbed the most valuable portion of the eastern seaboard. The Netherlands had established its credentials as a Protestant nation during Elizabeth's reign by fighting for independence against a Catholic Spanish monarch. It became a commercial and naval power strong enough to rival England during the first half of the seventeenth century.

In much the same way as the English, the Dutch organized trading companies and naval flotillas, and successfully challenged the Spanish in the Caribbean and the Portuguese in Brazil, in the East Indies, and in West Africa. Almost incidentally, a Dutch trading company sent Henry Hudson (an Englishman) in the *Half Moon* to scout the northern coast of America. He found the Hudson River, the major seaway into the interior. On a little island at its mouth, the Dutch set up a fort they called New Amsterdam.

They then established Fort Orange (later renamed Albany) at the critical junction of the Mohawk and Hudson rivers. From there they extended their influence westward to the most powerful and politically sophisticated group of Indians in northeastern America, the Iroquois Confederacy. By the 1630s, the Dutch had established enormous landed estates along the Hudson. They traded for furs with the Iroquois and probed east to the Connecticut River and south to the Delaware, where there was a tiny settlement of Swedes and Finns. The English were not yet fully aware that the three major water-level routes into the interior of the continent—the St. Lawrence, the Mississippi, and the Hudson—were in the hands of foreign powers.

During the first half of the seventeenth century, the Dutch dominated the slave trade in West Africa, the international carrying trade (what we would call the merchant marine), the East Indies and trade with India, and the sugar industry in Brazil. But almost as soon as it began, the bubble collapsed. England and the Netherlands battled at sea in a series of three wars in the mid-seventeenth century, and the English won. New Netherland, as the Dutch colony in North America was called,

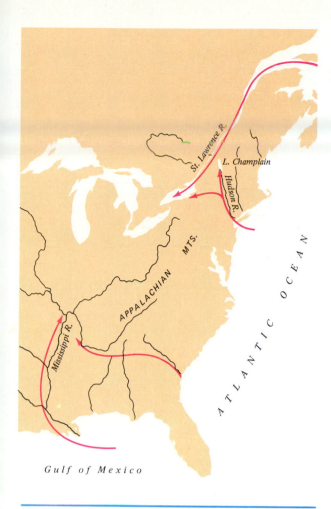

Routes to the Interior

changed hands several times, but ended up as New York. Because of its half-century of Dutch settlement and government, New York remained for many years the most culturally varied province among the English colonies.

THE PROPRIETARY COLONIES

Most of the early English colonies, except Rhode Island and Connecticut, were founded by joint stock trading companies. By the 1630s, however, the English Crown had begun to take a more direct interest in controlling land grants. King Charles I granted a portion of the American coast—Maryland—to a single individual and his heirs. Then, after the Restoration of 1660, his son Charles II gave out enormous tracts of land to various wealthy individuals. Recipients of these grants were called *proprietors* because they literally owned the land. Yet in the long run the proprietary colonies developed along much the same

lines as the earlier settlements, largely because the proprietors found that the settlers insisted on having representative legislatures of their own.

Maryland

King Charles I was married to a Roman Catholic. One of the major figures in his court, Sir George Calvert, was also a Catholic—and one who wanted to found a colony in America. Partly he hoped to profit financially from such a venture; partly too, Calvert wanted to establish a haven for English Catholics, who remained a small and unhappy minority group in England. The king was well aware that the settlements around Jamestown did not occupy all the land of "Virginia." So he was happy to respond to Calvert's request for a land grant.

Charles simply gave Calvert the area of "Virginia" that surrounded the northern part of Chesapeake Bay. The gift was personal. Calvert and his heirs were to be the proprietors of an entire colony. The royal charter provided that the Calvert family would actually own the land and collect rents from people who settled on it. The charter gave Calvert broad powers of government in the colony, but it did provide for a representative assembly. Calvert and his son gratefully named the colony Maryland in honor of Charles's Catholic queen.

George Calvert died while the charter was still being processed by royal bureaucrats. His son Lord Baltimore organized the expedition that set out for the Chesapeake in 1634 and first settled on an island in the upper part of the bay. There was no starving time in Maryland; the settlers had learned from the sad experiences at Jamestown. They brought plenty of provisions, and they were able to trade for supplies with the other colonies. They soon discovered that tobacco grew as well in Maryland as in Virginia. Economically, the two colonies became almost twins.

The Calvert-Baltimore family realized from the start that Protestant settlers might outnumber Catholics in Maryland, even though the early leaders of the settlement were Catholic. The Baltimores had no desire to persecute Protestants, and as things turned out, they had little opportunity. When Protestants settled in large numbers in Maryland, Lord Baltimore began to fear that Catholics in the colony might themselves become victims of religious persecution.

In 1649 he requested the Maryland assembly to pass his Toleration Act, and the assembly did so. This landmark act provided for freedom of worship for all Christians except for those few who did not believe in the Holy Trinity. For a time there was political friction between Protestants and Catholics in Maryland. But the important principle of religious toleration was firmly established, largely out of necessity.

Carolina

Carolina, which extended from the southern boundary of Virginia to the borders of Spanish Florida and as far westward as the continent itself, was the first colony established after the Restoration of Charles II. This enormous territory was granted by Charles II in 1663 to eight friends who had helped place him on the throne. The first permanent settlement began in 1670. Some colonists sailed directly from England; others came from the island of Barbados, where several of the Carolina proprietors had made large fortunes. The growth of large sugar plantations there had squeezed many men off the land, and they were eager to seek new opportunities. From the beginning Carolina was something of an offshoot of Barbados.

The new colony grew slowly, but without starvation. In 1680 the capital of Charles Town was moved to its present site at the junction of two rivers about 3 miles from the ocean. Charles Town (later Charleston) became a thriving commercial center. The colonists traded with the Indians for deerhides; they also established a thriving cattle industry. They experimented with a variety of crops, but the weather proved too warm for to-bacco and too cold for tropical fruit.

Finally they found a crop that could be profitably exported—rice. It came to be the staple crop of Carolina and the source of great wealth for successful planters. Some African slaves had been brought in at the very beginning, and it was they who probably introduced the cultivation of rice—a crop not grown in England but well known in parts of West Africa.

Rice came to dominate the low country lands near Charleston in the same way that tobacco dominated the Virginia and Maryland Tidewater. Since rice cultivation required much labor, planters imported more and more Africans and enslaved large numbers of Indians as well. By the early decades of the eighteenth century, the majority of settlers in southern Carolina were black.

The northern part of the Carolina land grant had already been partly settled by people from Virginia. The area was handicapped by lack of good ports, and for many years it remained a land of small farms, with fewer slaves than in Virginia or in the southern part of the colony. The proprietors placed a deputy governor over this territory and provided for separate elected assemblies for the two areas. As the years went by, settlers in both parts of Carolina grew increasingly unhappy about proprietary rule. That rule was in fact inefficient because of the large number of proprietors, and the situation grew more confused as some of them died and willed their rights to their heirs. In 1721 the king made South Carolina a royal colony; henceforth the governor was appointed. A few years later, North Carolina was also made a royal colony. Both kept their representative assemblies,

Charles Town, South Carolina, 1760. (*Colonial Williamsburg Foundation*)

AN OVERSEAS EMPIRE

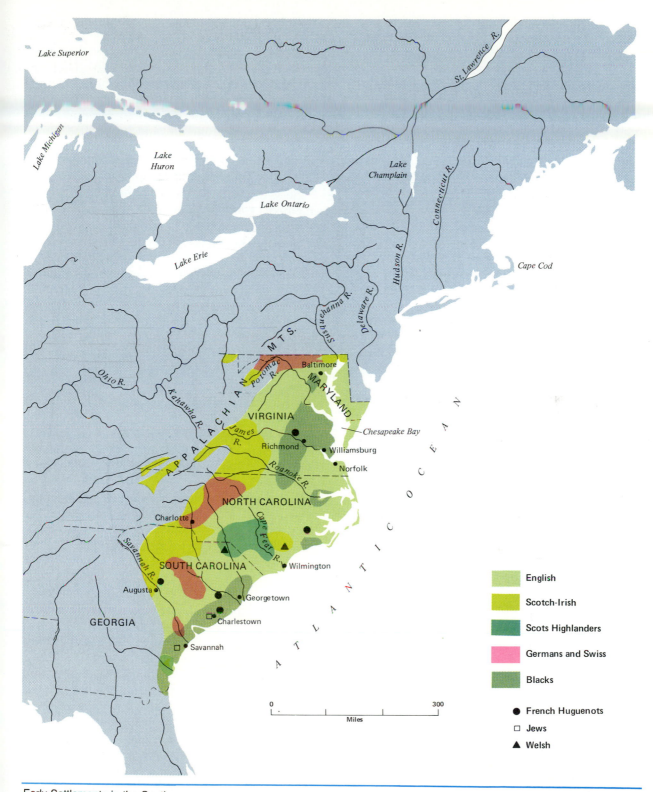

Early Settlements in the South

Legend:
- English
- Scotch-Irish
- Scots Highlanders
- Germans and Swiss
- Blacks
- ● French Huguenots
- □ Jews
- ▲ Welsh

for by this time assemblies were regarded as normal and essential parts of colonial governments.

New Jersey

King Charles II had been generous to the Carolina proprietors, and he was even more so to his younger brother James, the Duke of York. He turned over to James all the territory captured from the Dutch. Partly because the Dutch settlers were foreigners, no provision was made for a representative assembly. James simply sent over a royal governor to rule the colony, which was renamed New York. James also granted the southern portion of this vaguely defined territory to two of his friends. This area eventually became the colony of New Jersey, but only after a series of events produced great confusion.

A large group of Puritan New Englanders moved into northeastern New Jersey. They were encouraged to do so by the royal governor of New York, who expected to collect rents from them. In the meantime, the two proprietors were also encouraging settlement in the same area, also in the hope of collecting rents. The inevitable result of this situation was widespread uncertainty about who owned what land. Residents of East Jersey were still quarreling about land titles a century later.

There was further confusion about government. The two proprietors had no authority to appoint a governor or permit a legislative assembly, yet they went ahead and did so. Then the proprietors split the colony into East and West Jersey, and sold West Jersey to a group of English Quakers.

The situation was finally resolved in 1702, when the two halves were joined into the single colony of New Jersey. The Quaker proprietors retained some land rights, but none in government. From now on the governor was to be appointed by the king, and there was to be a representative assembly. Yet the confusion could not be ended at once. For more than thirty years, New Jersey's royal governor was the royal governor of New York. Yet the colony's economy rested on a solid basis of small farming, which provided food for two growing cities in neighboring colonies, New York, and Pennsylvania.

Pennsylvania and Delaware

Only one section of the Atlantic seaboard remained to be given away, and Charles II gave it to a most unlikely person. William Penn was the son of an admiral and was raised as a conventional gentleman. He learned some Latin, some law, and how to duel with a sword, and at the age of sixteen was introduced to the king at court. Years later, in 1681, King Charles II gave him a huge tract of land that ran north and west from the Delaware River and its bay. The king owed Admiral Penn both gratitude and money, and he decided to repay the son. But rather than naming his colony after a member of the royal family, William Penn chose to call it Penn's Woods, or Pennsylvania.

The younger Penn had become a Quaker. He remained a gentleman, but his Quaker ideas were regarded by many people as radical, foolish, and dangerous. The Quakers (who called themselves Friends) had emerged from the turmoil of the English civil war as a religiously and socially radical group of Protestant Christians. They pressed certain Christian beliefs to extremes. All Christians, for example, believed in good will toward men; Quakers acted upon this principle. They believed that love of God could best be shown by love for every man and woman, and they believed that everyone could be saved.

Quakers insisted that there was an Inner Light in every person that enabled him or her to learn God's will. Accordingly, Quakers had no distinct class of ministers, for they felt that every person was both a minister and a child of God. Quakers insisted on a life of simplicity, and for this reason dressed plainly. They refused to honor customary social distinctions. They called everyone "thee" or "thou" in an age when most people used the plural "you" when speaking to people of high station. They refused to swear legal oaths because they believed there should not be two standards of Truth. In addition, Quakers were firm pacifists.

To most Christians, Quakerism was Christianity gone mad. When Quakers tried to gain converts, not only in England but elsewhere, they met outraged resistance. In Massachusetts, the Puritan authorities hanged two Quakers who returned after being banished. In England, many Quakers were jailed for holding religious meetings. As time went on, however, the group became somewhat more conventional and conservative. People began to realize that Quakers were not trying to undermine all good government. It was in this changing atmosphere that William Penn received the charter for his colony in 1681.

Penn provided a liberal plan of government for his colony. He kept his own authority at a minimum, and gave the right to vote to all adult male landowners and taxpayers. All Christians of whatever sort were to have complete freedom of wor-

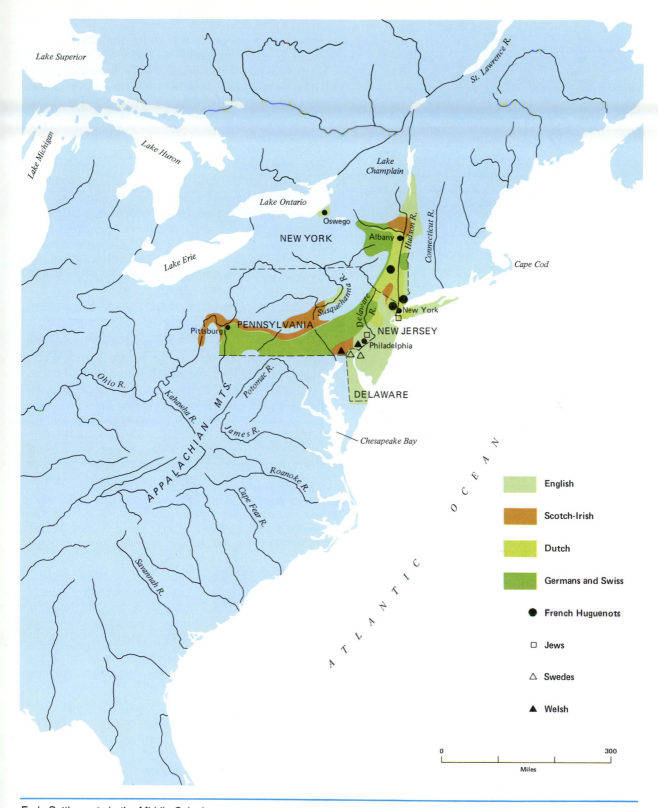

Lake Superior

Lake Michigan

Lake Huron

Lake Ontario

Lake Erie

St. Lawrence R.

Lake Champlain

Cape Cod

Oswego

NEW YORK

Albany

Hudson R.

Connecticut R.

Susquehanna R.

Delaware R.

New York

Pittsburg

PENNSYLVANIA

NEW JERSEY

Philadelphia

DELAWARE

Ohio R.

Kahawha R.

Potomac R.

James R.

APPALACHIAN MTS.

Roanoke R.

Cape Fear R.

Chesapeake Bay

Savannah R.

A T L A N T I C   O C E A N

English

Scotch-Irish

Dutch

Germans and Swiss

● French Huguenots

□ Jews

△ Swedes

▲ Welsh

0   300
Miles

Early Settlements in the Middle Colonies

William Penn. (*Historical Society of Pennsylvania*)

ship. Penn had every reason to think his plan would work, so he grew puzzled and discouraged when he met opposition. He had given the smaller upper house of the assembly the power to introduce legislation. Members of the lower house wanted that power. Characteristically, Penn told the legislators to draft a plan of their own.

The result was the Charter of Liberties of 1701, which provided for a single-house legislature. It was the only such legislature in all the English colonies, and the only one to depart from the mode of the two Houses of Parliament in England. The Charter of Liberties also provided for a separate assembly for the three southern counties along Delaware Bay. Delaware gained a somewhat separate existence, but it continued to have the same governors Penn and his heirs appointed for Pennsylvania.

The colony proved to be a great success. Its liberal government and its policy of religious freedom attracted large numbers of settlers. At first most of the colonists were English and Welsh Quakers, and they continued to dominate the government of the colony. But Penn's policies attracted many other groups. When he sent agents to western Germany to advertise the virtues of his

William Penn's Treaty with the Indians in 1681, as depicted nearly a century later (1771) by Benjamin West, 1739–1820, one of the first noted American-born artists. Historians came to question if such a conference took place, but the legend persisted and West no doubt prolonged it with his persuasive and much reproduced painting. The painting did capture the spirit in which William Penn sought to establish peaceful relations with the Delaware tribe inhabiting his colony and his recognition of the Indians as the lawful owners of the land included in his grant. (*The Thomas Gilcrease Institute, Tulsa, Oklahoma*)

colony, large numbers of German Protestants emigrated, drawn by promises of religious freedom and cheap land.

The immediate success of Pennsylvania showed how much the colonists had learned since Jamestown and Plymouth. Penn carefully selected the site for Philadelphia before the first settlers arrived, and he laid out his city with foresight. His province turned out to be highly fertile. As in New England, a flourishing trade quickly sprang up with the West Indies, where Pennsylvania pork, beef, wheat, and flour were in great demand.

A unique feature of this colony was the Quaker policy of nonviolence and peaceful coexistence with the Indians. Penn was one of the few Englishmen to learn an Indian language. He recognized Indian ownership of the land and allowed colonists to settle only on tracts he had purchased from tribal chiefs. Contact between the Delawares (the largest tribe in the area) and the settlers was limited in the early years because there was little trade in furs. That enterprise had been monopolized much earlier by the Susquehannocks and the Dutch.

The situation began to change by the end of the seventeenth century, when non-Quakers came to the colony in large numbers. They did not share Quaker convictions about Indians' rights to the land, and treaties with the Delawares were broken. Alcohol became a bargaining tool. The Indians eventually migrated westward, but the resentment they felt would be unleashed a generation later.

William Penn's colony became the most populous and the richest in North America. But he did not share in its good fortune. After turning to England in 1701 to keep the Crown from taking his charter, Penn had financial difficulties, spent a short time in debtor's prison, and died in 1718. More than any other proprietor, Penn had sought to establish a good society, what he called a "Holy Experiment." As things turned out, the experiment worked very well.

BUILDING AN EMPIRE

The permanent settlement of the mainland colonies—their economic growth, political maturity, and territorial expansion—all took place within the framework of an emerging imperial system. The English government struggled to bring the colonies under its control so that they would benefit the mother country. But England was far from stable in the second half of the seventeenth century; in fact, there was another revolution in 1689. It had important consequences in the colonies. Once that revolution was over, however, England began to consolidate its empire.

The Mercantile System: Theory and Practice

The English had a theory of empire long before they had an empire. That theory, known as *mercantilism,* was simple, and was not used only by England. It was the way in which all the Atlantic nations operated their economies and their overseas empires. In that age, people saw two main sources of national strength: wealth and military power. National leaders were well aware that the two were closely related, and they spent much time and energy trying to enlarge their own and diminish their rivals'.

Mercantilists in the home country assumed that economic activity should be regulated by the government for the sake of the nation as a whole. They thought of the "nation" as including both the mother country and its overseas settlements. They also thought the colonies should contribute to the nation's wealth and power by providing products not found or grown or made in the mother country. In particular, they assumed colonies should provide raw materials for manufacturing. The making of finished goods, or manufacturing, should take place in the mother country, which would then sell these items in the colonies or to foreign countries. National wealth could best be increased by selling more goods to other nations than were purchased from them. Today we would call this simply a favorable balance of trade.

Mercantilists were also very much concerned about military strength, which for the English meant naval power. The ships of His Majesty's navy had to be built and supplied and manned. The vessels could be built in England, but trees for masts and spars had to be imported. Before the colonies existed, pine trees were bought from Sweden and other Scandinavian countries. Such imports violated mercantilist principles in two ways. They cost the nation money, and they made England dependent on foreign powers for a vital article of defense. So English authorities turned to the colonies, where after 1729 the largest pines in northern New England were reserved for the use of His Majesty's navy.

At that time there was no clear dividing line between naval warships and the civilian merchant marine. Many merchant ships were armed with cannon, and in wartime were given licenses to prey on enemy shipping. For this reason, the English government encouraged the construction of ships of all sorts. Although authorities in London agreed that manufacturing should normally be done in England, in this case the importance of defense overrode the economic principle. The English government thus encouraged one kind of manufacturing in the colonies—shipbuilding.

Ships needed sailors. Here was another reason to encourage shipbuilding and a large merchant marine. Skilled seamen on merchant vessels could be pressed into service during wartime. The government encouraged the fishing industry for the same reason. The "fisheries," it was said, were "nurseries for seamen." The government even tried to retain the old Roman Catholic tradition of not eating meat on Fridays. By eating fish instead, the English people would help build England's maritime power.

The twin aspects of mercantilism—financial and naval—usually worked well together. In the seventeenth century and even later, these principles were in the best interests of the colonies. The colonies did not have enough people for large-scale manufacturing. The colonists produced raw materials that sold well in England, and English manufacturers could supply them with a broad range of finished goods. Yet the fit between mercantilist principles and the interests of the colonies was not a perfect one. Left to themselves, the colonists might prefer to buy cloth from French or Dutch manufacturers. They might prefer to sell masts, pitch, and tar to outfitters of Dutch ships rather than English ones. To work well, the mercantilist system required supervision by the home government.

The royal government never doubted that it had the right to undertake such supervision. Nor did the colonists—although they sometimes found it convenient to evade regulations that hurt their interests. Obviously the colonists had no desire to weaken England's naval power or to lessen its wealth. But what if the choice was filling colonists' pockets or those of London merchants? The colonists would have been less than human if they had not chosen their own.

And although the need for supervision was clear, setting up an effective system was not easy. The colonies were 3000 miles and many weeks away from London. English bureaucrats had no experience or training in administering overseas lands. They did have experience in regulating economic activity at home, and they had little doubt that they could do the same abroad. But if they knew what sort of activity *ought* to be going on in the colonies, they often found it difficult to discover what actually *was* going on. And sometimes the colonists were less than helpful in letting them know.

The mercantilist system worked best when the colonies produced agricultural staples, such as the tobacco of Virginia and Maryland, the rice of South Carolina, and the sugar of the West Indies. Planters found a protected market for their products in the mother country, and were granted credit for the manufactures they bought. British exporters, assured of payment in marketable crops each year, encouraged the colonial planters to live well—indeed, well beyond their means.

The system had fewer attractions for merchants of the Middle Colonies and fewest of all for those of New England, who had no staple crops that were marketable in England. The northern colonies developed an extensive trade with the West Indies and looked for other means of profiting from overseas trade. Meanwhile, England was still battling the Dutch for maritime supremacy.

The struggle included three naval wars and the capture of New Netherland. It also included several important acts of Parliament aimed at regulating the trade of the American colonies as well as weakening the Dutch merchant marine. These were the Navigation Acts, which were intended to encourage English shipping and trade at the expense of the Dutch.

The Navigation Acts: Regulation and Enforcement

The Navigation Acts of 1660 and 1663 set up certain basic regulations that were later enlarged and tinkered with, but never abandoned. The various Navigation Acts embodied both the naval and the economic principles of mercantalism. First, they banned all trade with the colonies except in colonial or English-built ships. These vessels had to be manned by crews at least three-quarters English or colonial. Second, the acts required that certain colonial products be exported only to England or another colony. The list included such important items as sugar and tobacco. Third, most European goods imported by the colonies had to be shipped by way of England.

The system was tightened up and extended over a period of many years with four important modifications. First, certain rules and paperwork were imposed on ship captains to prevent evasion of the acts. Second, the list of goods was enlarged to include important colonial crops such as rice and

Many people today use the expression *to keel over* without any awareness of its origins. We all know what is meant by such a sentence as, "Well, Joe looked perfectly all right when he was telling me about his trip, but then he suddenly just keeled over, and it took us quite a while to get an ambulance." Actually, the term is nautical, from the days of sailing vessels. The keel of a sailing ship was originally the main beam running fore and aft at the bottom of the hull. In order to achieve greater stability and better sailing qualities, ship designers extended wooden plates downward. Modern recreational sailboats have keels, or sometimes a "centerboard" that can be raised and lowered from inside the cockpit of the boat. For such a boat to keel over is obviously disastrous; it means that the boat has capsized, with its keel showing horizontally on the surface of the water or, in some cases, sticking straight up in the air, in which case the boat's mast(s) are underwater, pointing straight at the bottom.

the wood products known as naval stores (masts, smaller spars, pitch, tar, and turpentine). Indigo, a plant that produced a purple-blue dye, was also added to the list, partly because it was used for sailors' uniforms. Third, the English government began to pay bounties, or cash supplements, to colonial exporters of naval stores and indigo. Fourth, the government restricted certain colonial manufacturing enterprises that developed in the eighteenth century. These included woolen cloth, hats, and finished iron products. The Iron Act of 1750, for example, encouraged the colonists to make iron in bulk bars or sheets for export to England, but it prohibited them from making such finished iron products as nails and tools.

These regulations were intended to benefit English subjects everywhere. But some subjects benefited more than others. For example, the Iron Act of 1750 helped English makers of finished iron products by banning colonial competition, but English producers of bulk iron were hurt. One part of the English iron industry had won out over the other. Similar differences of economic interest existed in the various colonies, and sometimes they appeared within a single colony. In Pennsylvania, for example, producers of bulk iron were happy with the Iron Act, while manufacturers of finished iron products were not.

There were also important differences among the colonies. These differences were especially clear in the case of the Molasses Act of 1733, which placed a high tax on molasses imported from the colonies of other countries. It aimed at protecting the interests of the British sugar island colonies by making foreign molasses more expensive. But the act was a blow to New England merchants who imported molasses for making rum. If they had observed the Molasses Act, they would have had to buy high-priced molasses from the English islands. Instead, they preferred to pay lower prices in the French islands. In short, they smuggled.

Problems of Enforcement

Somehow all these laws had to be enforced. But even while the Navigation Acts were being passed, Charles II was giving away powers of government in the colonies. He gave huge territories to individual colonies, to proprietors, and to colonial assemblies. He authorized new charters for Rhode Island and Connecticut which gave those colonies almost complete control over their own affairs, including the right to elect their own governors. Except in New York, Charles's proprietary grants provided for representative assemblies. Because the men who sat in these assemblies usually took a different view of colonial interests than bureaucrats in London, there was bound to be friction between the assemblies and appointed agents of the crown.

Within the English government, a small group of bureaucrats was responsible for colonial affairs. They were commonly known as the Lords of Trade, but the group's powers were not clear. In 1664 the Lords of Trade sent a royal commission to the colonies to find out what was going on and to remind the colonists about their obligations under the new Navigation Acts. The commissioners decided to investigate New England. Both Virginia and Maryland were exporting large quantities of tobacco, on which the royal government was collecting handsome taxes, but New England did not seem to fit into the system nearly so well. These colonies were exporting masts and spars, but otherwise were not contributing to the wealth and power of the mother country.

The royal commissioners were suspicious of the New Englanders for still another reason. Most were Puritans, and both Charles II and the royal commissioners hated Puritans. After all, English Puritans had chopped off the head of Charles's father only fifteen years before. The commissioners suspected that the Puritan authorities in New

England wanted as much independence from the Crown's authority as they could manage. Their suspicions were correct.

When the commissioners arrived in Boston, the leaders of Massachusetts did their best to ignore them and then questioned their authority to make inquiries. Accustomed to having their own way for thirty-five years, leaders of the Bay Colony did not take kindly to the agents of a monarch who was persecuting Puritans in England. The frustrated commissioners reported back that Massachusetts was a nest of arrogant "independency." They recommended that the colony be compelled to observe the Navigation Acts and that its charter be recalled and canceled. But nothing was done about this first imperial inspection of an American colony; Massachusetts went on as it had before.

Eventually, however, authorities in London managed to bring the colony into line. The Board of Trade sent Edmund Randolph, an able and energetic young bureaucrat, to the colonies several times. On each visit Randolph collected more damaging information about violations of the Navigation Acts. Randolph also discovered that Massachusetts had been passing laws contrary to the laws of England, which was specifically forbidden by the original charter.

Over the years, Randolph and other royal officials repeated the same recommendation: The Massachusetts charter ought to be revoked. Charles II was finally convinced. Canceling a royal charter was not easy, but it could be done. Randolph presented his evidence to an English court, which declared the charter null and void in 1684. The most populous English colony in America no longer had any legal basis.

THE "GLORIOUS REVOLUTION"

Very shortly afterward, a great and general crisis shook the English-speaking world. At first it had nothing to do with Massachusetts. When Charles II died in 1685 he was succeeded by his brother, the Duke of York, who became James II. As king, James remained the proprietor of New York. Far more important, he had become a Roman Catholic. At the time he had no children and therefore no Roman Catholic heir, but he was still young and might yet produce one. His Protestant subjects were appalled by this possibility. In addition, James was determined to rule with an iron hand. A stubborn and tactless man, he had little idea how much his subjects valued their Protestantism and the privileges of their Parliament.

The king took sweeping and drastic action to settle the Massachusetts problem. With a stroke of his pen he created a single vast colony called the Dominion of New England, a new administrative unit that included all the New England colonies, as well as New York and East and West Jersey. This huge territory was to be administered from Boston by a royal governor and by a deputy governor in New York. A governor's council was to be appointed by the crown, and there were to be no representative assemblies in any part of the Dominion.

This sweeping reorganization sent a shudder through the colonies. Virginia was already a royal colony, but what did the future hold for Pennsylvania, Maryland, and Carolina? What would government be like without the protections provided by elected assemblies? The man James II appointed governor of the Dominion of New England did nothing to calm these fears. Edmund Andros was an able administrator, but he was arrogant and high-handed. Within a few weeks of arriving in Boston, Andros managed to make thousands of enemies.

Traditional political leaders found themselves out in the cold because the assemblies had been abolished. Andros and his counselors simply levied taxes on their own authority. Puritan leaders pointed out that such taxes violated their rights as Englishmen; Andros replied that such rights did not necessarily exist in the Dominion of New England. He went further. He announced that the town governments established under the old Massachusetts charter were illegal; therefore, the land grants these towns had made to individuals were void. Landowners would have to reconfirm their titles with Dominion authorities and pay rents to the Dominion as well. As if this were not enough, Andros questioned the lawfulness of the Puritan churches. The proper church for English colonists, he said, was the established Church of England. He also made it clear that the Navigation Acts would be enforced, and brought in customs officers to do so.

The colonists were outraged. In one way or another, Andros had stepped on the toes of just about everyone in the colony. In 1687 Massachusetts sent its most prominent minister, Increase Mather, to London. Mather's task was to get the old charter revived and Andros recalled. But just as Mather was putting his diplomatic skills to work, the entire political picture was changed by a bloodless revolution.

During his brief reign, James II managed to produce almost as much resentment in England as Andros had in Massachusetts. James knew better than to try to rule without Parliament, but he did his best to get around Parliament's laws. He openly favored English Roman Catholics and began tinkering with the organization of the army. The people began to wonder if he meant to use the army at home rather than abroad. Worst of all, James fathered a baby, and England was faced with a continued line of Roman Catholic monarchs.

A group of parliamentary leaders boldly invited William of Orange to become their new king. William was Dutch, but he was Protestant and married to James's Protestant daughter Mary. He accepted and landed in England with an army that met no opposition. James fled abroad, and William and Mary were installed as joint monarchs. Parliament proceeded to pass a series of laws that set forth the rights of Englishmen, enlarged the powers of Parliament, and restricted the power of the monarch. An Act of Toleration gave religious freedom to Dissenters—that is, to English Puritans. Roman Catholics were forever excluded from the English throne. Ever afterward, the English described all these events as their Glorious Revolution.

When Puritan leaders in Massachusetts learned that William had landed in England, they decided to attempt a revolution of their own. Without waiting to hear whether William had gained the throne, a group of armed citizens marched on Andros's house in Boston and forced him to take refuge in an island fort in Boston harbor. Later, in London, Increase Mather succeeded in gaining the official recall of Andros and the abolition of the Dominion of New England. The northern colonies were returned to their previous status. But Massachusetts still had no charter. Mather tried and failed to get the old one restored.

In 1691, however, a new charter was issued that incorporated the old Plymouth colony into Massachusetts. It combined features of royal government with features from the old colony form. A royal governor was to be appointed. But the governor did not have the power to appoint members of his council, as he did in other royal colonies. The council would serve as the upper house of the assembly, just as in all the royal colonies. But in Massachusetts the council was to be elected by the lower house. The charter of 1691 also provided for religious toleration; Puritans would no longer be able to persecute such groups as Quakers and members of the Church of England. Puritan leaders were not altogether happy with the new charter, but they could live with it. And more and more,

they were turning away from religious concerns and toward the more profitable path of trade.

In New York, Andros's deputy, Francis Nicholson, resigned. In May 1689, Jacob Leisler, a German trader in Manhattan since its Dutch days, took advantage of Nicholson's absence to call on neighboring counties and towns to set up a representative government. With the support of those alarmed by rumors of a French invasion and a Catholic conspiracy, Leisler managed civil affairs for several months.

But by disregarding a message he had intercepted from the Crown ordering Nicholson to conduct colonial affairs until new authorities took over, he gave support to the charges that he was a revolutionary. When in March 1691 Leisler resisted the deputy sent by William III, he was captured, tried, and sentenced to death along with seven of his men. Leisler and his son-in-law, his closest follower, were hanged in May. The others were pardoned by the king, who then established royal and representative government in New York. But the rebellion poisoned the atmosphere of New York politics for years afterward.

New Imperial Regulations

William III brought with him to England his rivalry with the Catholic French, which was intensified by Louis XIV's hospitality to James II. As early as 1689, this rivalry led to war. And as things turned out, the conflict was the beginning of a series of world wars in the eighteenth century.

To bolster his position in the New World, William III established a new committee for governing the colonies in 1696 and strengthened the administration of the navigation system. The old Lords of Trade were replaced by a group known as the Board of Trade, a committee made up of high royal officials, private gentlemen, and merchants who had business interests in the colonies. The Board of Trade had no power to make or enforce regulations for the colonies. It could not appoint royal governors or other officials. But the board could offer its advice on such matters, and its advice was usually taken, because the Board of Trade was the only government agency that knew much about the colonies.

New navigation acts strengthened the board's hand. Customs offices were set up in each colony, with the same powers as those in England, including access to "writs of assistance" by which officials could use police power to search private premises. Offenders against the new navigation code were to be tried in admiralty courts, which were staffed by royal judges and had no juries. Admiralty courts became one of the most detested of all English institutions in the colonies. The navigation code itself was strengthened by the "enumeration" of more commodities to be shipped exclusively to England.

Yet the colonies prospered, and the richness of America's natural resources contributed heavily to their success. Smuggling and other kinds of evasion continued to go largely unpunished. American as well as English merchants benefited from the exclusion of other nations from their trade and from protection against enemies at sea. With all these benefits, the colonists took pride in their roles as overseas subjects. They were not yet conscious that they were creating a distinctive American way of life.

SUMMARY

The pattern of English colonization and the push to establish permanent settlements in North America were the result of several conditions in England and Europe at the turn of the seventeenth century: religious and political discontent, economic changes that uprooted people, and a sense of power and opportunity after the victory over Spain.

The first permanent English settlement in North America was at Jamestown in Virginia. It survived early hardships and began to prosper with the discovery of a valuable export crop: tobacco. Another factor in the growth of Virginia and all the agricultural southern colonies was the discovery of a new system of cheap labor: black slaves imported from Africa.

The Jamestown settlement was followed by the Puritan migration to New England, which grew into the Commonwealth of Massachusetts Bay and set yet another colonial economic pattern: shipping and trade. By the middle of the seventeenth century, New England included Connecticut, Rhode Island, New Hampshire, and Maine, as well as Massachusetts.

What were to become the Middle Colonies—New York, New Jersey, Pennsylvania, and Delaware—began with the Dutch settlement of New York after the voyages of Henry Hudson. Except for New York, all the Middle Colonies, as well as Maryland and Carolina, began as proprietary colonies—huge grants of land to wealthy individuals—rather than as grants to joint stock companies.

Although the colonies were settled by different types of people and for different reasons, they soon began to develop a new way of life. One factor in this development was the colonists' attachment to representative assemblies and representative government. By the time the English king and government in London became aware of the role the colonies could play in the new mercantile system of world empire, certain patterns of independence and self-government were already set.

The close supervision by governors and agents sent from London was not always welcome in America. Nor were the Navigation Acts, a series of laws passed by Parliament to regulate the commerce and defense of the empire.

Open discontent with these ideas began when James II, in an effort to tighten control, lumped New York, New Jersey, and the New England colonies into the Dominion of New England, a new unit that was to be ruled by a royal governor without any colonial assemblies. The Glorious Revolution of 1688 in England reversed this trend, but not that of greater control from London. William III established a new committee to govern the colonies, the Board of Trade, and had new acts passed to strengthen the mercantile system; these included lists of items that could be shipped only to England, and admiralty courts staffed by royal judges to try offenders. By the beginning of the eighteenth century, the system was working and the colonies were growing and prospering.

Suggested Readings

The course of events in England is best charted by Lockyer, *Tudor and Stuart Britain*. Two works that focus more specifically on settlement in America are C. Bridenbaugh, *Vexed and Troubled Englishmen, 1590–1642* (1968), and W. Notestein, *The English People on the Eve of Colonization* (1954). For a deeper appreciation of English society at the time, try the subtle and sophisticated Marxist view in C. Hill, *Society and Puritanism in Pre-Revolutionary England* (1964).

R. Simmons, *The American Colonies: From Settlement to Independence* (1976), an excellent overview of the entire colonial period, has a good bibliography. W. F. Craven, *The Southern Colonies in the Seventeenth Century, 1607–1689* (1949), is outstanding. A. Vaughn's *American Genesis: Captain John Smith and the Founding of Virginia* (1975), discusses a man who has fascinated historians ever since he undertook to write a history of his own career. Bacon's Rebellion in

Virginia has received such partisan treatment from historians that it is safest to begin with R. Middlekauff's edited collection of documents, *Bacon's Rebellion* (1964).

The New England colonies have received much attention because settlers there kept and preserved so many more original records. The two best introductions to Puritan thought and society are E. Morgan, *The Puritan Dilemma: The Story of John Winthrop* (1958), a superb example of the way in which biography can be enlarged to become broad history; and G. Haskins, *Law and Authority in Massachusetts* (1960), much more general than the title suggests.

Puritan theology is complex. Perry Miller's brilliant studies are essential but not easy reading. Crucial are his *Errand into the Wilderness* (1964); *The New England Mind: The Seventeenth Century* (1939); *The New England Mind: From Colony to Province* (1953). Some of Miller's contentions have since been modified by first-rate studies such as E. Morgan's *Visible Saints: The History of a Puritan Idea* (1966); D. Hall, *The Faithful Shepherd: A History of the New England Ministry in the Seventeenth Century* (1972); R. Dunn, *Puritans and Yankees: The Winthrop Dynasty of New England, 1630–1717* (1962).

By far the most important modifications of Miller's studies are in R. Middlekauff, *The Mathers: Three Generations of Puritan Intellectuals, 1596–1728* (1971). A fine biography of the last of the three is K. Silverman, *The Life and Times of Cotton Mather* (1984). See also P. Gura, *A Glimpse of Sion's Glory: Puritan Radicalism in New England, 1620–1660* (1984). A powerful recent work lays bare many historical and personal aspects of Puritanism: C. Cohen, *God's Caress: The Psychology of Puritan Religious Experience* (1986).

New England's history has been greatly enriched by superb local studies. Two of the most widely read are K. Lockridge, *A New England Town, The First Hundred Years: Dedham, Massachusetts, 1636–1736* (1970); and P. Greven, Jr., *Four Generations: Population, Land, and Family in Colonial Andover, Massachusetts* (1970). S. Powell, *Puritan Village: The Formation of a New England Town* (1963), does much more with the migration of English customs and institutions.

The tiny colony of Plymouth has received fine treatment in G. Langdon, *Pilgrim Colony: A History of New Plymouth, 1620–1691* (1966). A much more controversial work is J. Demos, *A Little Commonwealth: Family Life in Plymouth Colony* (1970) which, like several of the books cited in the previous paragraph, deals with family relationships. In this connection, the best place to start is E. Morgan, *The Puritan Family* (1966). The great original account of Plymouth is William Bradford's *Of Plymouth Plantation, 1620–1647*, best read in S. Morison's 1952 edition.

A new approach to history is W. Cronon, *Changes in the Land: Indians, Colonists, and the Ecology of New England* (1983). For the various offshoots of the Massachusetts Bay colony, probably the most interesting reading bears upon Rhode Island. O. Winslow, *Master Roger Williams* (1957), is a traditional biography. S. James, *Colonial Rhode Island: A History* (1975), deals with what was called the "sinkhole" of New England.

The early years of the Restoration colonies have received less attention from historians. A. Trelease, *Indian Affairs in Colonial New York: The Seventeenth Century* (1960), and L. Leder, *Robert Livingston, 1654–1728, and the Politics of Colonial New York* (1961), deal with the turmoil that followed the transition from Dutch to English rule. For Pennsylvania, see G. Nash, *Quakers and Politics: Pennsylvania, 1681–1726* (1968), and M. Dunn, *William Penn: Politics and Conscience* (1967). Though there are several specialized studies, the best beginning on the Carolinas is W. Craven, *The Colonies in Transition, 1660–1713* (1969), which has much information on other Restoration colonies and a good bibliography.

Several of the most interesting books on the seventeenth and eighteenth centuries deal with intercultural contacts and cultures: See G. Nash, *Red, White, and Black: The Peoples of Early America* (1974); A. Wallace, *The Death and Rebirth of the Seneca* (1969), K. Kupperman, *Settling with the Indians: The Meeting of English and Indian Cultures in America, 1580–1640* (1980); and J. Axtell, *The Invasion Within: The Contest of Cultures in Colonial North America* (1985).

D. Lovejoy, *The Glorious Revolution in America* (1972), is the best place to start on that subject. See also J. Sosin, *English America and the Revolution of 1688: Royal Administration and the Structure of Provincial Government* (1982). An old account of the first colonial system still stands up very well: C. Andrews, *The Colonial Period of American History* (Vol. IV, 1938). Also see S. Webb, *The Governors General: The English Army and the Definition of the Empire, 1569–1681* (1979).

THE COLONIAL PEOPLE

Chapter 3

18 Jh. - 1700

During the first two-thirds of the eighteenth century, the Anglo-American colonies grew rapidly. This population growth meant geographical expansion, and it had important social and economic consequences. Many new settlers in the English colonies were not English at all, and outside New England ethnic diversity became the rule rather than the exception.

As the colonies grew, distinct social patterns emerged in various regions. Along the southern part of the Atlantic coast, slavery transformed the English settlements; after about 1720 it begins to make sense to speak of "southern" and "northern" colonies. To the west, in all the colonies, we can begin to talk about a "frontier" culture. In the east, with the rapid growth of towns, it is possible to detect the emergence of an "urban" way of life.

Yet it is important to bear in mind that the single most common experience of the colonists was life on a family farm. This dominance of rural over urban life was of course exactly opposite to the situation in the United States today; it did a good deal to shape the structure and practices of colonial politics. Yet political life in the colonies was shaped by other factors as well. Among them were the continuing ties with the mother country, the nature of the colonial economy, and the idea that government should remain in the hands of the rich, the well born, and the able. ■

PATTERNS OF POPULATION

In many ways the population of the English colonies in America was unique. The number of people grew faster, probably, than anywhere else in the world. This rapid growth had a deep impact on the colonial economy and the nature of colonial society. In addition, the English colonies attracted a great many non-English peoples. By the time of the American Revolution, colonists of English descent made up only slight more than half the entire population.

The Population Explosion

At the end of the Great Migration in 1640, the non-Indian population of the colonies was about 27,000. This figure includes all the English colonies along the Atlantic seaboard, as well as New Netherland, but not the English colonies in the West Indies. It does not include Indians, because no one knows how many Indians there were. Today, 27,000 people would make a very small town; modern football stadiums hold about three times that number.

By 1700 the non-Indian population in these colonies was nearly ten times as large, about 250,000. This rapid growth continued during the eighteenth century. No other European settlements in the New World grew as fast. Though this increase

David, Joanna, and Abigail Mason posed for their portrait by an unknown itinerant painter in Massachusetts about 1670. (*The Fine Arts Museums of San Francisco, Gift of Mr. and Mrs. John D. Rockefeller 3rd*)

was remarkable, we still need to bear in mind that 250,000 is about the population of a medium-sized city in the United States today. Put another way, the town that Roger Williams founded—Providence, Rhode Island—today has nearly as many people as lived in *all* the colonies in 1700.

There were several reasons for the rapid increase. One, of course, was the founding of new colonies; each new colony offered more land, and more land attracted more settlers. Another was the continued migration from England to the older colonies. Some of these people returned to England, but most stayed in America. In addition, the birth rate in the colonies was considerably higher than that in England. Probably this was largely because of the relative ease of obtaining land, which enabled couples to marry younger and therefore to have more children. Parents on farms found children useful, since they could be put to work at an early age. Most parents assumed that their children would get land of their own when they grew up, so a large family—five or six children was the average—seemed to have advantages rather than disadvantages.

Rapid population growth also reflected a relatively low death rate. After the early years of settlement, the death rate in the American colonies was far lower than in England. This difference was caused partly by large cities like London. Two and three hundred years ago, large cities killed off people much faster than they produced them. Crowding encouraged the spread of disease, especially because the drinking water in almost all cities was badly polluted by garbage and sewage. In 1700 London was the largest city in the world. By comparison, Boston, New York, and Philadelphia were tiny towns. And because they were so much smaller, they had far fewer urban problems.

Even though the death rate in the colonies was lower than in Europe, it was far higher than it is today, especially among babies and young children. There were no effective cures for disease; no one knew that germs even existed, let alone how to kill them. The American colonists had a higher death rate in the early years of settlement than later on. Virginia remained an especially unhealthy place for fifty years. Overwork, malnutrition, and bad treatment made the typical Virginia laborer's life a short one; but two diseases took the greatest toll: malaria (from mosquitoes) and typhoid fever (from polluted drinking water). After about 1650 the health of the Virginia colonists improved considerably. The reasons are not entirely clear, but the death rate dropped and population began to increase rapidly.

Charles Willson Peale (1741–1827), Family Group, 1773. (*The New York Historical Society*)

By contrast, the New England colonies were more healthy from the beginning. It was largely for this reason that early Massachusetts had a far larger population than Virginia. New England, and later the Middle Colonies of New York, New Jersey, and Pennsylvania, had one of the lowest death rates in the entire world.

Another brake on population growth in the colonies was the proportion of women and men. In early Virginia, most settlers were male. Since the number of children in any society depends upon the number of young women, not the number of men, Virginia's early growth was far slower than New England's. The English migration to all the northern colonies was usually by entire families. Single settlers were more common in the southern colonies. As the years went by, children born in America became a larger and larger part of the population. Because males and females were born in about equal numbers, the proportion of men and women in the population gradually evened out, and fewer men remained unmarried. This was an important development, for married men tend to settle down and to think more about security and less about adventure. The American colonies were becoming "settled" in more ways than one.

Specialization of Labor

The population explosion in the American colonies had several important effects. It stimulated economic growth and helped raise the standard of living, since a growing population meant more mouths to feed and a growing market for farmers. A small settlement could afford only to cultivate food and make clothes and shelters. A larger one could support a greater variety of jobs.

As an example, let us take John, a young shoemaker who arrived in Massachusetts as part of the Great Migration of the 1630s. He had little money, but was a skilled bootmaker. He settled in the little town of Hingham outside Boston. With the help of his neighbors, he built a glorified hut which he called a house. In turn he helped his neighbors at the same task, and together they constructed a meetinghouse to serve as a church and as a meeting place for the voters of the town. But John had to eat; so he had to farm. His neighbors, including the minister, did the same.

Yet John remained a shoemaker at heart, for he was better at his craft than at raising squash and corn. He used his little remaining cash to buy some leather. In his spare time, our shoemaker lovingly made some boots, which he sold to his neighbors. There were more and more of them as time went by. They paid him in food and firewood more often than in cash, but eventually he was able to stop farming, sell his land, and move to Boston.

Once in town, John bought a small house and hung out his sign—a piece of wood in the shape of a boot. One room in his two-room house was his place of work and his retail store. Boston was growing from a village into a real town, and could

A Shoemaker prospers by his trade. (*American Antiquarian Society*)

of the colonies was relatively small. The colonists did their best to meet the situation by setting the age for service in the colonial militias between sixteen and sixty. People often referred to the "men and boys" of colonial armies.

The youthfulness of the colonial population had an even more important result: the absence of a large group of people who were too old to work. Some people lived to be seventy or eighty, but not many. Elderly people assumed they should work until they died or became too feeble. The age of sixty-five had no particular meaning, and no one thought about "retirement." Most people did a full day's work from about age twelve on, unless they were disabled.

This situation contrasts sharply with today, when the United States has a very large group of old people who either do not or cannot work. They are supported partly by savings from their working years and by the social security and welfare systems. But as a group they are not self-supporting; they are supported by younger people who can and do work.

The colonists did have large numbers of dependent children. But we also have such a large group today, despite a lower birth rate. This is because people today do not do much productive work until they are eighteen or even thirty, and the law at least supposedly prevents them from working before the age of sixteen. In the colonies, a much higher proportion of the population engaged in productive work, and the group of nonworking dependents was relatively small. So many people working made for economic growth and a rising standard of living.

no longer feed itself. Nearby farmers drove their wagons into town with food and firewood for sale, and they were happy for the chance to buy John's boots. There were more and more of them every year. John died at his workbench of a heart attack, reasonably secure in the knowledge that he had labored hard at his calling. That, at least, is the way he would have looked at it. We would call it increasing specialization of labor, fueled by population growth.

The Young and the Old

The high birth rate also shaped early American society by making it very youthful. Today, fewer than half the people of the United States are under the age of thirty. In the seventeenth and eighteenth centuries, half the people were under the age of sixteen. This youthfulness had several important effects. Obviously, only a relatively small number of men could take part in politics and government. It also meant that the military power

NON-ENGLISH IMMIGRANTS

In the early years of the eighteenth century, social conditions in western Germany and northern Ireland created a large pool of discontented people who were willing to migrate overseas. The Palatines (as Americans called most Germans) and the Scotch-Irish (as those from the province of Ulster in northern Ireland were called) made up by far the largest groups of newcomers. However, by far the largest group of non-English immigrants came from West Africa, and of course they came against their will.

The Germans

Continuous German immigration began in 1683, when small groups of Mennonites and Quakers established Germantown, near Philadelphia. During the next three decades other radical German Protestants founded Pennsylvania towns such as Bethlehem, Lititz, and Nazareth. These early immigrants were mainly well-educated people who paid their own passage, brought property from the Old World, and bought land on their arrival. They built substantial communities where many original buildings still stand. All the radical sects were opposed to domination of the church by the state, a position that took its most extreme form in their refusal to bear arms. They also refused to swear oaths, a fact that annoyed and concerned British administrators of the Navigation Acts and other officials.

Along with the sects, many German Lutherans and German Reformed Calvinists also settled in Pennsylvania early in the eighteenth century. These denominations, with Lutherans predominant, were by far the most numerous of the German-speaking immigrants to America. They were usually called "church people." Most of them, too poor to pay their way to America, came as *redemptioners*, one of the many forms of white servitude.

The indentured servants who were first shipped to Virginia and Maryland early in the seventeenth century had made contracts with the joint stock companies or proprietary agents abroad. They agreed to work in the colonies in exchange for passage across the Atlantic. Redemptioners of the eighteenth century sold themselves to ship captains or "soul brokers" in European ports.

In 1750, Gottlieb Mittelberger warned Germans about the voyage to America: "There is on board these ships terrible misery . . . stench, fumes, horror, vomiting . . . fever, dysentery . . . heat, constipation, boils, scury, cancer, mouthrot . . . from old and sharply salted food and . . . foul water, so that many die miserably." On one ship arriving in Philadelphia in 1745, only 40 of 400 passengers survived. As many as a third of the redemptioners may have died at sea. Sometimes the survivors were forced into extra years of servitude to pay back the cost of the passage of their dead relatives.

Once in America, the redemptioners' contracts were sold to the highest bidders. Since the healthiest were sold first, ship captains kept the sick and old on board until their contract was sold or they died. Parents were often forced to sell their children into service. The usual term was from four to seven years, at the end of which the servant was to receive "freedom dues," usually 50 acres of land, tools, and clothing. The evidence suggests that these dues were often withheld or, when granted,

that the servant sold off the land for a small amount of cash. Not surprisingly, runaways were frequent.

German immigration reached its high point between 1749 and 1754, when over 5000 Germans arrived in American ports each year, most in Philadelphia. Although many of the church people tried to learn English ways, others held to their own language and traditions. The Pennsylvania Germans became celebrated throughout the country for their rich gardens and orchards, their sturdy barns and well-tended livestock. German artisans developed the famous long rifle, first manufactured in Lancaster and later adopted and improved by frontiersmen everywhere. Yet many English Pennsylvanians became concerned about the fact that more than one-third of the colony was German and that the colony might be becoming a New Germany.

The Scotch-Irish

The large number of German immigrants in the eighteenth century was exceeded by the so-called Scotch-Irish. Their ancestors were the lowland Scottish Calvinists who moved to Ulster early in the seventeenth century. James I deliberately encouraged this migration in order to strengthen Protestantism in Ireland. At first they prospered as farmers and artisans. After 1696, however, new Navigation Acts hurt the economy of Ireland. Then, in the early years of the eighteenth century, British absentee landlords started doubling rents. The people of Ulster began leaving in thousands.

Poverty in Ireland, as in England, helped fill the prisons with debtors. In time of war, male prisoners were often thrown into the army. But when poverty and unemployment spread during periods of peace, as it did after the Peace of Utrecht in 1713, something was needed to empty the jails. The common penalties of "burning in the hand and whipping" were inadequate. As a substitute, thousands of English and Scotch-Irish debtors were shipped to Maryland and Virginia to work in the tobacco fields. A Treasury decision in 1716 to pay merchants for transporting them overseas created a powerful special interest in the practice.

Paying passengers probably accounted for no more than one in ten of the Scotch-Irish immigrants. The rest, like most of the Germans, obtained their passage by signing indentures. Many landed in Philadelphia or in nearby Newcastle, Delaware. As they continued to arrive by the thousands each year and indentures expired, they moved beyond the Germans on Philadelphia's western frontier, across the Susquehanna to the Cumberland Valley. Here mountain passes led southwest to Maryland, western Virginia, and North Carolina. This course took them along the outer rim of a smaller number of Germans who had earlier moved in the same direction.

The West Africans

1619 →

The first Africans brought to the English colonies were sold by a Dutch shipmaster at Virginia in 1619, the same year the first legislative body met in America. Whether these early arrivals were treated as slaves for life or servants for term is uncertain, but they were never regarded as just another kind of settler. After 1640 in Virginia and Maryland, some of the Africans and their children were being enslaved for life. By 1660, a pattern had clearly emerged: "Negroes" (a term borrowed from the Portuguese-Spanish word for "black") customarily were lifetime, hereditary slaves. They were forbidden to bear arms, and—a crucial, enduring, and often overlooked distinction—Negro women were routinely put to work "in the fields." White women generally were not, nor would they ever be.

African Origins of the Slave Trade

Head of a Negro, by John Singleton Copley. By 1780, some 600,000 slaves worked the lands of the south. (*The Detroit Institute of Arts, Founders Society Purchase, Gibbs-Williams Fund*)

At the same time, about 1660, the legislatures of Virginia and Maryland began to enact laws to permit, and even require, the status of slavery for Africans, and Africans only. The irony was that the English, who prided themselves on being the freest people of all Europe, hammered out in the New World the legal framework for slavery. By the early 1770s, complex slave codes had been enacted in the southern colonies. Yet the system was not watertight. At least a few Negroes were "free," no matter how much they might otherwise be degraded. From the beginning, race and slavery never matched completely.

The general pattern, however, rapidly became clear. There were not a great many blacks in the Chesapeake colonies until about 1700. From then until the Revolution, they were imported in huge numbers into the tobacco colonies and South Carolina. A relative trickle reached the middle and northern colonies. From 1720 to the American Revolution, Africans and Americans of African descent constituted some 20 percent of the mainland colonial population, a far higher proportion than before or since.

The West African migration to the British mainland colonies was a very small part of the slave trade to the New World. Between 9 and 12 million slaves were brought to the Americas during the 350 years of the slave trade. Ninety percent went to tropical America; according to the best current assessment, only some 350,000 arrived in North America.

The cruelty of this forced migration has usually and perhaps rightly drawn attention away from its enormous significance. Brutality began with war-

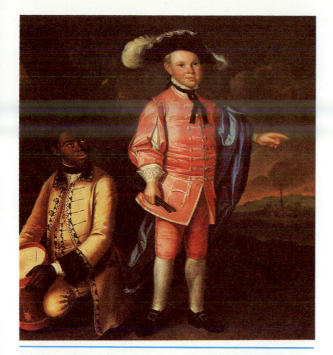

Charles Calvert with a slave boy, painted in Maryland in 1761 by John Hesselius. (*The Baltimore Museum of Art: Gift of Alfred R. and Henry G. Riggs, in Memory of Generae Lawrason Riggs*)

time capture or kidnapping or conviction for a crime. Warfare among various African tribes was the most common cause of enslavement, but sometimes European raiding parties attacked Africans directly. During the marches to the sea, often for hundreds of miles, many died or were killed. On the coast, survivors were chained, herded into open stockades, branded, and segregated by age and sex.

The greatest shock of all was perhaps the sudden, enforced separation from familiar surroundings, the awful sight of the great, pounding ocean, and the tall-masted vessels that rode offshore with such seeming grace and confidence. (It seems small compensation for anyone then or since for us to discover that mortality among European slave trade sailors was even higher than among the victims.) Despite the careful organization of the trade on the African coast, vessels frequently rode offshore for weeks before finding a full load or a favorable wind.

Slaves rebelled most often during these periods, sometimes with complete success. On the high seas some captives threw themselves into shark-infested waters. What Europeans saw as

Treatment of African slaves, as illustrated in an eighteenth-century treatise on "Methods of Procuring Slaves": (a) "Manner of yoking slaves" when marching to port; (b) mouthpiece and neck brace with hooks, to prevent escape when pursued in the woods; (c) dealer branding recently purchased slaves; (d) plan for stowing slaves below decks for the long sea voyage. (*Library of Congress*)

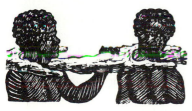

(a)

(b)

(c)

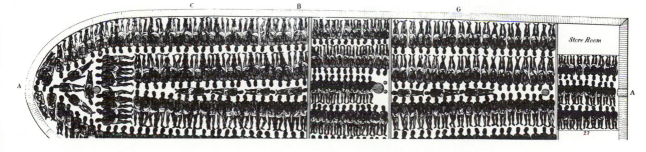

The musical instrument the *banjo*—and the word itself—came to the United States and to other parts of the New World from West Africa. A few banjoes may perhaps have been brought across the Atlantic aboard slave ships, but knowlege of the instrument and the skill to construct it most certainly did. There are many references to the *banjo* (variously spelled) as early as the mid-eighteenth century. Thomas Jefferson referred to it in 1784: "The instrument proper to them [the blacks] is the Banjor, which they brought hither from Africa." The original version had five strings (as most still do) and depended on a small drum for its reasonance, unlike the wooden box of the European guitar. Since West African music made such extensive use of drumming, the combination of strings with a drum was a natural development. After generations of homemade construction and strumming on slave plantations, the banjo was taken up by whites in their blackface minstrel shows in the 1830s. Throughout American history, and probably in Africa, the instrument has customarily been played by men rather than women.

---

suicide was actually a thoroughly rational action, since many West Africans believed that Europeans were cannibals and that only through death and spiritual remigration could they return to their homeland.

Slave traders announced their sales in newspaper advertisements and broadsides like this one, from South Carolina. Note the imbalanced sex ratio among the slaves in the cargo. (*American Antiquarian Society*)

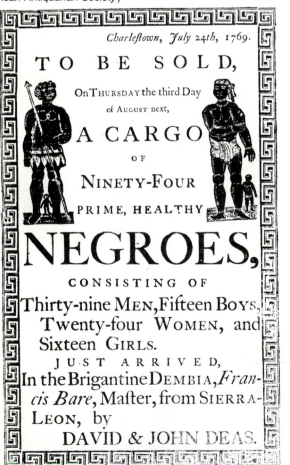

Charlestown, *July 24th*, 1769.

TO BE SOLD,

On THURSDAY the third Day of AUGUST next,

A CARGO

OF

NINETY-FOUR

PRIME, HEALTHY

NEGROES,

CONSISTING OF

Thirty-nine MEN, Fifteen BOYS, Twenty-four WOMEN, and Sixteen GIRLS.

JUST ARRIVED,

In the Brigantine DEMBIA, *Francis Bare*, Master, from SIERRA-LEON, by

DAVID & JOHN DEAS.

Britain was one of the last of the Western powers to enter the slave trade on a commercial basis, but the British came to dominate the trade in the eighteenth century. Of the relatively small number of slaves who were sold to the mainland colonies, at least 85 percent came directly from Africa. The remainder came from the Caribbean islands, usually after staying there for only a few weeks. Because males were in greater demand, they greatly out-numbered the female slaves. In addition, like servants from the British Isles, the African migrants tended to be young, many of them in their teens.

We will never know the exact nature of the cultural contact between the English colonists and their slaves. Both sides seem to have survived the shock. Africans and their immediate descendants learned English manners and language rapidly—because they had to. The English who came in day-to-day contact also became to some extent bicultural. Africans and their children learned to accommodate themselves to powerlessness. English masters and their children learned a new role of great personal power.

For obvious reasons, historians know more about the white side of this equation than the black. We know the whites saw blacks as enemies, and there is nothing to suppose that the reverse was not the case. The tyranny that resulted was self-reinforcing. As the slave system developed in the early years of the eighteenth century, it tightened the bonds on the personal and civil freedom of whites and blacks alike. But it was blacks who suffered the chains of slavery.

In Virginia and Maryland, "new Negroes" from Africa were normally put "into the ground" on a "quarter" of some sixteen people and one overseer, far from the larger home plantation of the actual owner. In the Chesapeake colonies, many men of the second and third generations were trained or permitted to practice as "tradesmen" or skilled laborers on the home plantations, which served as commercial and manufacturing centers because there were no large towns. In South Carolina and Georgia, the rice plantations contained larger numbers of Africans and fewer whites. This heavy concentration in the coastal low country of South Carolina and Georgia meant that Africans were able there, as nowhere else in America, to preserve many of the cultural patterns and languages they had known in West Africa. That style and the resultant language (known usually as Gullah) survives there to this day.

CLASSES AND LIFE STYLES

During the eighteenth century the English settlements were turning into more mature societies. They became much more diverse in terms of ethnic makeup, and differences in their economies made for differences in social organization. Although most colonists still farmed, or had servants and slaves to farm for them, an increasing number moved to urban areas. All the colonies maintained social distinctions among people, an arrangement which at the time seemed perfectly ordinary and proper.

Tidewater Gentry

Throughout the colonial period, most of the white population of tidewater Virginia and Maryland and of adjacent parts of North Carolina was of English extraction. Here, although corn and other food crops continued to be grown, the production and export of tobacco was the main focus of economic activity, along with land speculation.

Led by a small elite group, the Chesapeake planters kept close ties with Britain and copied the manners of its aristocracy. The Carters, Lees, Byrds, Randolphs, and Fitzhughs of Virginia, the Carrolls, Dulaneys, and Galloways of Maryland lived in great Georgian mansions. They filled the well-proportioned rooms with the finest imported furniture or hired astisans to carry out the designs of foreign cabinetmakers. Contemporary artists painted the Chesapeake gentry in all their imported finery.

A few planters owned large libraries with books in several languages, although learning and schools were not emphasized. In 1693 William and Mary College, endowed by the established Anglican church, opened in Williamsburg, Virginia, which was soon to become the provincial

Robert Carter of Nomini Hall, Virginia. (*Painting by Joshua Reynolds; Colonial Williamsburg Photography*)

capital. But few students spent more than a year there. Some planters sent their sons to England for their education, but those who profited from the opportunity often did not come back. The Chesapeake gentry were an outdoor people, fonder of fox hunting, horse racing, and partying than of learning.

The Chesapeake planters had to take the management of their plantations seriously. But they seemed driven to keep up the good life, or at least the appearance of it. Land, which represented their greatest wealth, was also their downfall. "Such amazing property," observed Philip Fithian, a tutor to the Carters, "no matter how deeply it is involved in debt, blows up the owners to an imagination which is visible to all." They "live up their suppositions," a Londoner remarked, "without providing against calamities and accidents."

From the 1730s to the 1750s, when the price of Virginia tobacco soared, rising profits made the planters' land more valuable. The Chesapeake gentry enjoyed a golden age. Yet few could long keep up the high life, the expenditures for clothes, carriages, body slaves, mansions, parks, and wine. Eventually, the debts for imported goods grew too high. To those who crashed, the West was a refuge or a new springboard to success. It also fed ideas of empire among such Virginians as young George Washington.

Slave quarters and the big house. (*Carolina Art Association; Gibbs Art Gallery*)

Of all the mainland settlements, tidewater South Carolina, extending inland about 60 miles and southward to the Savannah River, was closest to the West Indian sugar islands in character. Eighteenth-century South Carolina was the only mainland colony where blacks outnumbered whites, as in the islands. The whites below the 2000 leading families, moreover, were the most depressed on the continent. They had the lowest literacy rate and some of the strongest antagonisms toward the ruling group.

Carolina rice proved to be the single most profitable staple in all the mainland colonies, and the rice barons of South Carolina became the wealthiest of American planters. By midcentury, they were encouraged to grow indigo, heavily in demand as the source of a dye for the booming English textile industry. Indigo and rice were less subject than tobacco to price fluctuations and other market hazards, so the Carolina planters, unlike the Chesapeake gentry, had stable incomes and few problems with debt.

Carolina rivers were not deep enough for seagoing vessels to sail directly to the plantations, as they did in the Chesapeake region, so the colony's produce was brought to Charleston for shipment abroad. Although the Chesapeake region remained virtually without towns for generations, Charleston by the 1750s had become the fourth largest colonial city. Its mid-century population of 10,000 was almost equally divided by color, with a sizable proportion of the blacks serving as household and personal slaves to planters who maintained homes there. The masters, living much of the year far from the heat and disease of the rice fields, left overseers and blacks to the labors and hazards of producing the crops.

Back Parts of the South

Although the entire southern back country at first was a paradise for hunters and trappers, European settlers developed a mixed subsistence agriculture of cereals, potatoes, fruits, meat, flax, and hemp. In the Chesapeake, small market centers grew up along the main routes and at ferry crossings. Even before mid-century there were such tiny thriving crossroads communities as Fredericksburg and Hagerstown in Maryland (dominated by German newcomers), Martinsburg and Winchester in Virginia, and Charlotte in North Carolina (where the Scotch-Irish prevailed).

GROWING UP IN VIRGINIA

Devereaux Jarrett, an Anglican minister, was born in tidewater Virginia, where simplicity and frugality characterized his upbringing during the years before the American Revolution:

Our food was altogether the produce of the farm, or plantation, except a little sugar, which was rarely used; and our raiment was altogether my mother's manufacture, except our hats and shoes, the latter of which we never put on, but in the winter season. We made no use of tea or coffee for breakfast, or at any other time; nor did I know a single family that made any use of them. Meat, bread and milk was the ordinary food of all my acquaintance. I suppose the richer sort might make use of those and other luxuries, but to such people I had no access. We were accustomed to look upon, what were called gentle folks, as beings of a superior order. For my part, I was quite shy of them, and kept off to a humble

distance. A periwig, in those days, was a distinguishing badge of gentle folk—and when I saw a man riding the road, near our house, with a wig on, it would so alarm my fears, and give me such a disagreeable feeling, that, I dare say, I would run off, as for my life. Such ideas of the difference between gentle and simple, were, I believe, universal among all of my rank and age....

My parents neither sought nor expected any titles, honors, or great things, either for themselves or children. Their highest ambition was to teach their children to read, write, and understand the fundamental rules of arithmetic. I remember also, they taught us short prayers, and made us very perfect in repeating the Church Catechism. They wished us all to be brought up in some honest calling, that we might earn our bread, by the sweat of our brow, as they did....

Yet rough conditions continued to breed rough manners. The back parts of the Carolina country were more isolated than those of the Chesapeake region. Settlers fresh from Ulster or German villages found it hard to spend lonely years in such a wild, disease-ridden country. But the major difficulty was the unending labor of clearing the land. Many settlers soon fell into a semi-nomadic life. Some became herdsmen of wild swine and cattle often stolen from the Indians. Itinerant clergymen reported with dismay how the people in the back country dwelt together in "Concubinage, swapping their wives as Cattel, and living in a State of Nature, more irregularly and unchastely than the Indians." A few made fortunes out of meat, skins, and tallow, forming a back-country gentry living on great cattle ranges.

Gradually, tidewater institutions, both legal and political, were imposed on the Maryland and Virginia back country, although not without resistance. Antagonism to Charleston's domination in South Carolina was even stronger. Throughout the eighteenth century, farmers in the interior complained frequently about the lack of courts and the "parasites" who came from Charleston to collect taxes.

The Middle Colonies

During the eighteenth century, the Middle Colonies formed the most culturally varied part of British North America. Pennsylvania, the newest,

quickly became the largest and most diversified of these colonies. By 1755, Philadelphia was the largest city in the colonies, with about 18,000 people. Though Quakers no longer were a majority, Quaker merchants made up Philadelphia's wealthiest group and dominated the entire colony. Quaker religious beliefs, like those of the Puritans, inspired the thrift, industry, and reliability essential to business success.

Persecution in Europe and America had scattered Friends all over the Atlantic world, a situation they used to advantage by establishing business contacts with Friends in other colonies. The industrious farmers Penn brought to his colony supplied Philadelphia merchants with excellent grain and other staples for export and a thriving market for imported goods.

Travelers passing through New Jersey in the eighteenth century sometimes stopped long enough to comment on its natural beauty, its prosperity, or its wonderful oysters, but there was little more to detain the curious. Jerseyites often felt the same way about their settlement. In the 1750s many of them looked upon their colony as a "keg tapped at both ends," transporting its surplus hemp, grain, flax, hay, and Indian corn to New York or Philadelphia to feed those cities or for shipment overseas.

Nature had endowed New York with the finest harbor in the Atlantic world, yet the growth of that colony was far slower than that of New England, Pennsylvania, or the southern colonies. Huge

Philadelphia landowners kept elaborate carriages to carry them from town to their country estates, like this one belonging to Isaac Norris. (*From a 1717 drawing; the Historical Society of Pennsylvania*)

landed estates along the Hudson River Valley and Iroquois control of the interior were partly responsible. From the start of the eighteenth century, British governors of New York, copying the Dutch, had rewarded their favorites with land grants ranging from 50,000 to 1 million acres in the Hudson Valley. These *patroons,* as they were called, sometimes paid nothing but a token tax and thus had small incentive to sell or lease their property. German, Scotch-Irish, and other squatters, however, took advantage of the unused land. When later on the patroons tried to collect rents from families that had squatted there for generations, they met armed resistance.

At mid-century, New York City had 13,000 inhabitants, many of them living in houses built, as a visitor reported, "after the Dutch model." But the city had begun to lose many of its Dutch features, and the Dutch language itself was dying out. Yet Dutch influence persisted in the Hudson Valley, in towns like Albany, where the language remained predominant as late as the 1740s. Exposed to Indian raiders from French Canada until the British defeated the French in 1763, colonial Albany kept the look of a frontier outpost. Wooden walls enclosed the town, and at its center stood a square stone fortress.

Tilling the soil on a farm in Pennsylvania. (*Library of Congress*)

New England

Connecticut, like all New England, was dominated by family farms and Puritan churches; it became known as "the land of steady habits." The same could have been said of rural New Hampshire, Rhode Island, and Massachusetts, except that the latter two each boasted a large town. Newport, Rhode Island, was a favorite summer vacation spot for southern planters. The city also thrived on the slave trade and the distilling of molasses into "rumbullion"—a drink we call rum.

THE COLONIAL PEOPLE

The city of Boston was the heart of Massachusetts, as Massachusetts was the heart of New England. North of Boston such ports as Salem, Marblehead, and Gloucester, which much later were to supply many of the "proper Bostonians" of the Victorian era, were already trading centers. But the capital of the commonwealth, with over 15,000 people in 1750, a fine harbor, and the biggest inland markets, was far ahead of the other towns.

In the seventeenth century, Boston's merchants had been quick to take advantage of England's wars with the Dutch, which diverted the ships of the two greatest commercial nations from their regular trading routes. Early in the eighteenth century, peace gave a strong boost to Boston's prosperity. In the West Indies, the growing demand for necessities sent prices and profits soaring. By the terms of the Peace of Utrecht (1713), Britain took New Foundland and Nova Scotia from France, and their vast fisheries were opened to Yankees. At the same time, Nantucket whalers began to sail to the Arctic Ocean and to Brazil.

Throughout New England, the demand for more and better ships promoted such land-based businesses as rope and sailmaking. These drew artisans from nearby and foreign towns. Their growing number brought new home and business construction, and prosperity to the surrounding countryside.

As in Pennsylvania and the South, in Massachusetts wealth brought a change in social style. Calvin, it is true, had warned the Saints against "all superfluities" and luxuries. But by the eighteenth century, many of the richest Puritans, like the richest Quakers, shifted to the more tolerant Anglican Church. Boston's "codfish aristocracy" and its imitators in other Yankee ports now wore swords, satins, and English broadcloth and lived in elegant homes.

Yankee merchants, like those elsewhere, often installed their brothers, sons, and in-laws as agents in foreign lands. In Britain itself they turned to relatives. If there were no family connections, they, like the Quakers, sought out other Puritans. As a last resource in foreign ports, they employed their own countrymen to look after their interests. Family businesses were enlarged and family ties multiplied by intermarriage among the merchant group.

North, south, and west of Boston, new settlements grew up everywhere in the first part of the eighteenth century. To outsiders, rural New England villages were remarkable for two qualities that seemed contradictory: proper social order, and at the same time, a "democratic" style. One visitor commented on the relative lack of social distinctions: "They seem to be a good substantial Kind of Farmers, but there is no break in their Society; their Government, Religion, and Manners all tend to support an equality. Whoever brings in your Victuals sits down and chats to you." Here were the makings of a more democratic society than prevailed in many of the other colonies.

Family Farms

From Pennsylvania northward the typical way of life was that of the family farm. Even in the southern colonies, the majority of whites were farmers. Anyone who has ever lived on a family farm knows that such a life involves long hours and hard work for everyone. Children worked at least some of the time from the age when they could be shown how to shell peas, shuck corn, or fetch firewood. Older girls and women had an unending round of tasks. They cooked in metal pots hung over the open fireplace, and they baked in the hollow compartment in the chimney that served as an oven. Many of them spun and wove rough cloth and sewed it into clothing for the family. They washed clothes and bedding in wooden tubs, with soap they made themselves, and then hung it out to dry on a fence or anything else that was handy.

Mothers fed their babies at the breast. They used a nursing can with cow's milk only if they had to. When the baby was old enough, he or she was fed a mixture of potatoes or cornmeal or wheatmeal, mashed with vegetables or fruit. Meat was sometimes available for the family, but not every day. Stringy chicken meat was fresh when available, but pork and beef were usually salted or smoked. In winter, some foods could be kept cold in an underground compartment; the warmer months were more of a problem because there was no way to keep food from spoiling.

For the most part, a woman's work outdoors was confined to lighter tasks, such as feeding livestock and slopping the hogs, which ate most of the family's garbage. Only at harvest time did women join in the heavier jobs; even then, it was regarded as necessary rather than normal and desirable. There was an important exception: Widows worked in the fields because they had to—which is one reason widows remarried as soon as they could.

The men of farming families did most of the heavy outdoor work. They cleared the fields, steering the plow around boulders and tree stumps be-

A colonial housewife spinning wool. (*American Antiquarian Society*)

hind a horse or ox or mule. They set the seed, prayed for rain, chopped the weeds, and prayed for clear skies at harvest time. After harvest, they had time to build a shed, cut fence rails, mend the harness, trap raccoons, fix the chimney, and help the women teach the children to obey, to work, to read, and to pray.

For all the members of farming families, life was busy but not rushed. Certain things had to be done. If you did not chop firewood, you went hungry, and in the winter you froze. As always and everywhere, there were emergencies and sudden strokes of bad luck. If the new baby died, a little grave had to be dug. If lightning struck the house, another had to be built. If Indians gave trouble, they had to be talked to or shot at. If the field just planted for corn was washed out by a thunderstorm, it had to be reseeded. If the planks over the creek on the way to town washed out, they had to be replaced.

In many ways this was a simple life by modern standards. There was very little paperwork—or paper of any kind. There were practically no bills to pay, for exchanges of goods and services were usually done on the spot, often without any cash. Credit normally depended on one's reputation with a peddler or the owner of a tiny general store or with a neighbor. As time went on, however, rents became a problem for the minority of family farmers who did not own their own land.

Taxes, whether from the town, the county, or the colony's government, could also become a problem. But the purpose of such taxes was obvious. The farmer who voted on the local tax rate had a very good idea of what he was paying for. His taxes would go toward support for a couple of widows and several orphans, toward the minister's salary, and to pay the travel costs of the town's or county's representatives in the colonial assembly. Taxes also went for maintenance of the meetinghouse, and to pay minor expenses for several neighbors who were helping to clear a road to a nearby settlement.

There were dozens of such local expenses, plus taxes to the colony as well. But many farmers voted annually for representatives to the colonial assembly, and they therefore had a sense of control, or at least of participation, in the process of taxation and government.

These farmers were not well off by modern standards; they lived with more hardship and far less leisure than modern Americans. Compared to the farmers of Europe, however, they were prosperous. They had a far better chance of owning land of their own. Because land was easy to get, American farmers wasted what they had. They knew it would be easy to move on, so they often simply abandoned fields that had been worn out. Many farming families moved from one place to another, from old land to new. Family farming was a hard life, but one could always hope to start again on better soil.

Colonial Cities

All the colonies remained closely tied to the Atlantic Ocean. The sea had its dangers, but it was the great highway of trade and migration. Water transportation was crucial. As settlers moved westward, they settled the river valleys first, partly because the soil was more fertile, but also because river transportation was easier and cheaper. Even the best roads consisted of twin ruts worn down by

THE EXPLOITATION OF THE LAND

Peter Kalm, a Swedish naturalist who traveled extensively in the colonies, was one of the few commentators of that time who even glimpsed the connections between rapid population growth, the availability of land, and wasteful exploitation of natural resources. As for population, Kalm wrote:

It does not seem difficult to find out the reasons, why the people multiply more here than in Europe. As soon as a person is old enough, he may marry in these provinces, without any fear of poverty; for there is such a tract of good ground yet uncultivated, that a new-married man can, without difficulty, get a spot of ground, where he may sufficiently subsist with his wife and children. The taxes are very low, and he need not be under any concern on their account. The liberties he enjoys are so great, that he considers himself as a prince in his possessions.

Yet these "possessions" were exploited with little eye to their future value:

The Europeans coming to America found a rich and fine soil before them, lying as loose between the trees as the best bed in a garden. They had nothing to do but to cut down the wood, put it up in heaps, and to clear the dead leaves away. They could then immediately proceed to ploughing, which in such loose ground is very easy; and having sown their corn, they got a most plentiful harvest. This easy method of getting a rich crop has spoiled the English and other European inhabitants, and induced them to adopt the same method of agriculture which the Indians make use of; that is, to sow uncultivated grounds, as long as they will produce a crop without manuring, but to turn them into pastures as soon as they can bear no more, and to take in hand new spots of ground, covered since time immemorial with woods, which have been spared by the fire or the hatchet ever since the creation. This is likewise the reason why agriculture, and the knowledge of this useful branch, is so imperfect here. . . .

Pat Lyon at the forge. (*Museum of Fine Arts, Boston*)

the wheels of wagons.

All the important urban centers were Atlantic ports. In 1740 Boston was still the largest colonial city, with a population of 17,000. But the size of Boston was limited because it was built on a small neck of land, so Philadelphia and New York soon grew to be larger. Charles Town and Newport remained the fourth and fifth largest cities in the colonies. By the time of the American Revolution, Philadelphia had about 35,000 inhabitants. London was more than ten times as large, but Philadelphia was by then one of the two or three largest cities in the English-speaking world.

To the country farmers of eighteenth-century America, the city was an impressive place. Many of the streets were actually paved with stones, and later some of them were even lit by oil lamps! Many country people never saw a city in their entire lives. Those who did were astounded by the crowding and the bustle. The farmer's wagon was only one of many that creaked and rattled through the narrow streets, piled high with corn or wheat, vegetables and fruits, boards or firewood. Now and then a brightly painted gentleman's carriage made its way through the traffic. Dogs yapped and nipped at the horses and oxen, and pigs and an occasional goat jostled for the garbage in the

To His Excellency IOHN MONTGOMERIE Esq.
Cap.t Gene.l & Gov.r in Chief of his May.ties Province of New York,
New Jersey, & Territories depending thereon, & Vice Admiral of the
Same &c. This View of Fort George is Most humbly Dedicated, by his Excellen.cy Most humble & Most Obed.t Ser.t W.m Burgis

View of New Amsterdam. (*Courtesy of the New York Historical Society, New York City*)

streets. Sheep and cattle were herded along to slaughterhouses, while hundreds of screaming seagulls circled overhead, waiting to feed on the refuse. Hundreds more circled the masts of the sailing vessels tied up at the wharves or lying at anchor in the harbor, watching for more garbage from the ships.

Hundreds of doorways beckoned the curious visitor. The visitor could tell a good deal about what went on behind these doors by peering through the windows on either side, or by just watching what sort of person went in and out. Gentlemen wearing wigs and their well-dressed ladies shopped at the silversmith and the cloth merchant. Ship captains visited the chandler's shops to purchase clocks, telescopes, and ship fittings of all kinds. Weatherbeaten sailors clambered ashore from longboats on their way to the sailmakers and ropemakers who worked in buildings far larger than the meetinghouse in the farmer's own village.

There seemed to be taverns everywhere. Some obviously were for gentlemen or at least men of middling wealth. The windows of these taverns were filled with printed political and commercial notices. There were other taverns of a different sort. Sailors headed into them on their sea legs and staggered out on legs weakened by rum. Next to some of these taverns were little houses with the wooden shutters closed over the windows even in the daytime. Sailors and fishermen went in and out, and, indeed, so did an occasional farmer. A visitor knew what sort of women were behind that door.

The visitor was also tempted by all the things for sale. The grand merchants sold goods just off the ship from England. Some of these articles might find their way to crossroads stores in the country, but here in the city there was a far greater variety of things to buy. There were bells, buckles, brass buttons, and books. There were copper kettles, iron nails, and steel knives. There were heads for axes and heads for hoes. There were hinges, pulleys, hooks, and harness fittings, medicines in glass bottles, a nursing can for his baby, and a whalebone corset for his wife. A man could empty

THE COLONIAL PEOPLE

his pocket without any difficulty.

The inhabitants of the cities saw these surroundings rather differently. A small group was wealthy enough to live a comfortable life. But the majority of people, even the wealthy, worked hard. Wealthy merchants worked long hours supervising their account books. They wrote out instructions for ship captains and corresponded with their agents in other colonies, in the West Indies, and in London.

Already there were urban problems that did not exist in the countryside. All the cities had exhausted their local supplies of firewood. This early energy crisis had to be met by bringing in wood from greater and greater distances. Part-time watchmen dealt with crime, much of which was associated with the large temporary population of sailors. Sanitation remained a problem, but gradually sewers and pipes for drinking water were put into place underground. Fires were a serious menace because the wooden houses were packed so tightly together. Every colonial city experienced fires that wiped out whole sections of town. There was no city fire department; instead, citizens organized volunteer companies.

Only about 5 percent of the colonial population lived in cities. As a group, though, the city dwellers were more skilled and better educated than the population as a whole, and they also had a somewhat higher standard of living. Most important, they were better informed about politics and what was going on in other colonies and in Europe. By the 1730s printers were publishing newspapers once a week in every sizable colonial city. Boston, Philadelphia, and New York had more than one. These four-page newspapers were heavy with advertisements by local merchants and news from Europe. Colonial newspapers provided very little local news, since people knew what was happening in their own home town. If a warehouse burned down on Monday, there was not much point in putting the information in Friday's newspaper; everyone already knew about it.

COLONIAL POLITICS

When John Adams of Massachusetts attended the Continental Congress in Philadelphia in 1774, he saw for the first time haughty southerners attended by their slaves. In a state of some anxiety, he wrote to his wife Abigail how he dreaded "the consequences of this dissimilitude of character" between Yankees and planters; ". . . without the utmost caution on both sides, and the most considerate forbearance with one another, . . . they will certainly be fatal."

By then it was apparent that such a diverse collection of colonies was not a likely candidate for national unity. Style, customs, and economic interests divided them. Vague boundaries in the colonial charters caused many conflicts. Boundary disputes grew especially bitter in the middle of the eighteenth century, when ambitious land speculators staked out overlapping claims. The disputes turned colony against colony in feuds that later helped drag out the Revolutionary War and postponed the establishment of a permanent federal government after independence. Other issues, involving currency, piracy, smuggling, religion, and politics, also strained intercolonial relationships. Many people, in fact, saw British control as the only really stabilizing influence in the colonial situation.

And yet unifying influences were at work, especially among colonial leaders. Despite their differences, they shared many interests, beliefs, experiences, and hopes. Trade united the merchants. Family ties united distant kin. The colonists read one another's newspapers, sermons, pamphlets, and almanacs. Literate colonists had information on matters outside their immediate sphere of interest that linked them with all the colonies and the continent.

Most important of all, the colonists shared a common legal and political heritage. They were all committed to the ancient English common law. This legal system was peculiar to England; it did not exist in France, Spain, or other European countries. The "common law" rested on years and even centuries of decisions by courts and judges, with each decision based on previous decisions. Thus, in contrast to statutes passed by Parliament or colonial legislatures, the common law was established from previous custom and not made or enacted by lawmakers at one specific moment.

The colonists valued traditional English liberties, such as trial by jury and due process. At the very center of this common experience was the English tradition of representative government— a tradition colonial politics did a great deal to strengthen.

Governors and Assemblies

Each of the colonies was headed by a governor, sometimes an American but more often an Englishman. In Connecticut and Rhode Island, the governor was elected by the legislature. In Maryland and Pennsylvania, he continued to be appointed by the absentee proprietor in England. In all the other colonies he was appointed by the king upon recommendation by the Board of Trade.

Most governors had broad powers. They could summon and dissolve the assemblies, veto legislation, and appoint minor officials. Except in Massachusetts, the royal governors also recommended appointees to the governor's council, a body that served as the upper house of the legislature, as an advisory board to the governor, and as the colony's highest court.

Technically, it was the Board of Trade who appointed the members of the councils, but the governor's recommendations carried great weight. So wealthy and ambitious Americans were inclined to cultivate good relations with their governors. At the same time, since most council members were Americans, they easily came into conflict with the governor when he insisted on the wishes of the crown.

With all his dignity and authority, the governor often found himself caught in a crossfire. As the symbol and spokesman of the king or proprietor, he was expected to follow instructions from England that reflected policies made thousands of miles away. At the same time, he had to respect the needs of the colony and its leaders, among whom he had to live. The job called for remarkable tact, a quality some governors lacked.

Sharing the responsibility for government were the lower houses of the elected legislatures, the assemblies. These bodies had two principal functions: to enact legislation and to appropriate money for the colony's expenses. Although either the governor or the Board of Trade could veto such legislation, neither could force the assemblies to pass specific laws. As time went on, the assemblies grew more and more powerful. They used the power of the purse to gain concessions of all kinds from the governor, including approval of legislation he was not supposed to sign.

In many cases the assemblies controlled the governor's salary, and they were happy to use this weapon to gain more power for themselves. In almost every colony there were struggles between assemblies and governors as representatives of royal or proprietary power. But by the 1760s it was clear that the assemblies had won.

This was a triumph for the power of representative government, not for democracy. The assemblies were usually controlled by wealthy planters, lawyers, or merchants. The degree of this control varied from colony to colony and was far stronger in the southern colonies than in New England—but everywhere the assemblies were in the hands of the "better sort" of gentlemen.

Two conditions helped sustain their power. One was the property requirement for voting and holding public office. Here too there was considerable variation from one region to another. In the New England colonies, perhaps as many as 90 percent of white adult males had the right to vote; in the Middle Colonies, the proportion was somewhat lower; and in the southern colonies, the figure was as low as 50 percent. Even that latter proportion, however, was far higher than in England. Some colonies also had religious qualifications for voting, but with the exception of Catholics and Jews, these tended to matter less and less when property qualifications could be met.

Property qualifications for officeholding were usually considerably higher than for the vote itself. A member of the South Carolina assembly, for example, had to own at least 500 acres of land, 10 slaves, or other property worth £1000; requirements for members of the council were even higher. Propertied *women* were allowed to vote in New Jersey—and actually did so occasionally. Historians have never been able to explain why this practice, so strange at that time, was permitted or even thought of by men in control of voting procedures.

Another factor in limiting control to the wealthy was that new inland settlements had few representatives in the colonial assemblies. Except in New England, the assemblies themselves often refused to establish new counties and towns in distant regions and to reapportion seats according to changing population patterns. In addition, men on the frontier often did not bother to vote, even when they could. These settlements sometimes were happy not to have to pay for county or town governments or for representation in the assembly. They had few complaints until they were aroused by crises involving Indians, courts, or taxation.

Consensus and Conflict

There were remarkably few objections to the system of property requirements for voting. People simply assumed that servants and the poor did not have enough at stake in society to participate in government. Most people also assumed that it was right for government to be in the hands of men of wealth, refinement, and education. Most farmers, whether literate or not, could think of no worse experience than having to address public meetings or sit in legislative bodies.

City artisans, shopkeepers, and laborers shared these feelings. By and large, most voters were still proud to be represented by the great men of their neighborhood. Thus they returned to office generation after generation of gentlemen from the same distinguished families.

Even in Massachusetts, where the voting qualifications were not as strict and educational levels and literacy were higher than elsewhere, members of the same families were repeatedly returned to office. Social and political deference was still the cement that held the various colonial societies together. The word "gentleman" was not yet a sign meaning merely that "ladies" should use the other door.

This is not to suggest that colonial politics were free from conflict. In many colonies, in some periods, rival factions in the assemblies struggled for power. In New York, for example, the factions were shaped by family rivalries, religious differences, and the poisonous legacy of Leisler's Rebellion. In Pennsylvania, Quakers and non-Quakers battled for control. In Rhode Island, two factions emerged on the basis of political rivalry between Newport and Providence. In some colonies, however, politics remained remarkably free from this kind of conflict. In Virginia, especially, a stable group of elite families remained in control. They strengthened and harmonized their rule with a complicated network of intermarriages among leading families.

The most important source of political conflict was money. Farmers were often in debt; urban merchants were usually their creditors. The normal scarcity of cash in the colonies was aggravated by the mercantilist system, which drained gold and silver to the mother country. It became common for debtors to demand more and more paper money. Out of necessity, all the colonies issued paper money at one time or another. But since paper money had a tendency to be overissued and to decline in value, easy money policies usually were reversed during periods of economic downswing. At such times, taxes, interest, rent, and loans went unpaid; on occasion, creditors who tried to collect were chased from the debtor's door at gunpoint.

Conflicts over the money supply, taxation, and debt were not necessarily sectional ones, though farmers in frontier regions were more likely to fall into debt than those close to water transportation. Other political conflicts were sectional in origin. One of the most persistent arose over the complaints of new settlers on the frontier about the failure of the government to protect them from the Indians, the French, and the Spanish. Failure to provide passable roads to markets was a second source of sectional conflict. A third was the failure of the assemblies to establish courts in the back country and thus save the farmers the time and cost of several days' travel. A fourth was the collection of tithes for the established churches, which had few ministers and few members in the wilderness. It was these issues that made back-country people begin to take an interest in representation in the assemblies.

As important as these issues were, other matters seem to have concerned the colonists more. New ways of thought were sweeping the colonies. The new sciences presented a novel view of humankind's proper relationship to the natural world. Many people found a more traditional concern more important: their relationship with God. Simple farming folk worried about their children, their debts, the condition of their souls, and the proper allotment of firewood for their minister.

SUMMARY

As the colonies grew, they developed not only new forms of politics, but also new kinds of societies. The population exploded because of easy access to land, and this growth speeded up the economy and raised the standard of living. No longer was it necessary for everyone to farm; artisans, craftspeople, and merchants could support themselves in the new urban centers. And since most of the population was young, and almost everyone, young or old, worked, productivity was high. The new settlers were no longer exclusively English; immigrants began to come from western Germany and northern Ireland; there were the Dutch in New York and the West Africans in the South.

Distinctions were drawn between social classes in all the colonies. In the South, the Tidewater gentry copied the life style and manners of the English aristocracy; in the North, wealthy Quaker and Puritan merchants lived in elegant homes filled with fine furnishings. But poor whites in the South lived in misery. The Middle Colonies and New England had a more varied social structure; there were prosperous artisans and farmers among the variety of people and classes that lived in the thriving new cities—Boston, Philadelphia, New York, Newport. Most people, however, lived on family farms, where everyone worked long and hard and almost everything the family needed was made at home. Only about 5 percent of the population actually lived in the cities.

Colonial politics were marked by both unity and diversity. The colonies were certainly different from one another, but common interests, such as trade and legal and political traditions, drew them together. The American colonists shared a commitment to representative government as embodied in the colonial assemblies.

Eventually, the struggle for power between royal governors and the colonial assemblies was won by the colonists. Voting qualifications kept voting power in the hands of a small and wealthy group of men. Yet there was little objection to this arrangement, since most people thought this was the way things ought to be. While there was some conflict between sections and classes over such issues as money and debt, taxation, and government protection on the frontier, the issues remained less troublesome and more local than they would later become.

Suggested Readings

The best demographic study of the period prior to the first national census of 1790 is R. Wells, *The Population of the British Colonies in America before 1776, A Survey of Census Data* (1975). P. Curtin, *The African Slave Trade: A Census* (1969), estimates the number of people forced from Africa to the New World. A. Smith, *Colonists in Bondage* (1947), remains the best book on the servant trade from England. Also see S. Kim, *Landlord and Tenant in Colonial New York: Manorial Society, 1664–1774* (1975).

Non-English immigrants have been dealt with by R. Dickson, *Ulster Emigration to Colonial America, 1718–1775* (1966); J. Leyburn, *The Scotch-Irish: A Social History* (1962); and D. Rothermund, *The Layman's Progress: Religious and Political Experience in Colonial Pennsylvania, 1740–1770* (1961). Somewhat indirectly, one of the best studies of ethnic pluralism in colonial America is J. Lemon, *The Best Poor Man's Country: A Geographical Study of Early Southeastern Pennsylvania* (1972).

There are several books about the early years of heavy African migration to this country: G. Mullin, *Flight and Rebellion: Slave Resistance in Eighteenth-Century Virginia* (1972); P. Wood, *Black Majority: Negroes in Colonial South Carolina from 1670 through the Stono Rebellion* (1974); T. Tate, Jr., *The Negro in Eighteenth-Century Williamsburg* (1965); B. Wood, *Slavery in Colonial Georgia, 1730–1775* (1984); L. Greene, *The Negro in Colonial New England* (1942); and A. Kullikoff, *Tobacco and Slaves: The Development of Southern Cultures in the Chesapeake, 1680–1800* (1986).

Several other books on eighteenth-century American society are especially rewarding. R. Hooker's edition of *The Carolina Backcountry on the Eve of the Revolution: The Journal of Charles Woodmason* (1953) is highly readable because the Rev. Mr. Woodmason was such a crusty chap. C. Bridenbaugh's *The Colonial Craftsman* (1950) is a broader work than the title suggests, as are J. Blake, *Public Health in the Town of*

Boston, 1630–1822 (1959), and R. Bushman, *From Puritan to Yankee: Character and Social Order in Connecticut, 1690–1765* (1967). O. Winslow, *Meetinghouse Hill, 1630–1783* (1952), is a fine social history of New England. C. Bridenbaugh's *Myths and Realities* (1952) gives a useful introduction to eighteenth-century southern society.

It is sad commentary on the condition of women's history that J. Spruill, *Women's Life and Work in the Southern Colonies* (1938), remains one of the most useful books on that topic. Though heavily polemical, there is much information not found elsewhere in M. Ryan, *Womanhood in America: From Colonial Times to the Present* (1975).

Social history is also touched upon by some of the better works on eighteenth-century politics: L. Labaree, *Royal Government in America: A Study of the British Colonial System before 1783* (1930); and J. Greene, *The Quest for Power: The Lower Houses of Assembly in the Southern Royal Colonies, 1689–1763* (1963). B. Bailyn's short interpretive essay, *The Origins of American Politics* (1965) and E. Cook's comprehensive analysis of power in local governments, *The Fathers of Towns: Leadership and Community Structure in Eighteenth Century New England* (1976), bear on social as well as political themes.

Two important books on the workings of the eighteenth-century British empire are M. Kammen, *Empire and Interest: The American Colonies and the Politics of Mercantilism* (1970); and J. Henretta, "Salutary Neglect": Colonial Administration under the Duke of Newcastle* (1972).

Some of the very best studies of eighteenth-century politics focus on a particular colony or group of people. C. Sydnor, *Gentlemen Freeholders: Political Practices in Washington's Virginia* (1952), is a vivid account of the politics of deference. Different styles of giving way to one's betters are described by C. Grant, *Democracy in the Connecticut Frontier Town of Kent* (1961). F. Tolles,

James Logan and the Culture of Provincial America (1957), focuses on the well-rounded American "gentleman." P. Bonomi, *A Factious People: Politics and Society in Colonial New York* (1971), emphasizes ethnic tensions. R. Isaac looks at society in eighteenth-century Virginia almost as an anthropologist might view a foreign culture in *The Transformation of Virginia* (1982). The safest discussion of an especially tricky topic is C. Williamson, *American Suffrage: From Property to Democracy, 1760–1860* (1961).

NEW WAYS OF THOUGHT

Chapter 4

When we speak of the "mind" of an entire society, we are talking about a concept that we use as an organizing principle. There were, in fact, as many actual minds as there were colonists. But because they shared so many common ideas and assumptions, it seems both fair and useful to treat them as a unit, even though we need to remember that there was dissent. In doing this we are doing what historians always do: We generalize about the past, and select from it, because we cannot re-create it in all its infinite detail.

During the first half of the eighteenth century, religious concerns were still primary for a great many Americans. Yet concern about religion could take many different forms. Individuals might worry about their own souls—and large numbers of people did. Ministers and congregations might argue about their proper relationship. Different denominations might fret about their relative status and about proper church organization. And many people might grow concerned about the state of religion in general, and ask themselves about the general health of society as a whole. Americans still ask this question today.

These were not new questions, nor have they ever been fully answered. But they were framed in new ways largely because of the impact of other ideas. These eighteenth-century ideas, which may perhaps be better described as a mental posture, originated in Europe. They have become known as the Enlightenment. Enlightened thinkers deliberately chose science over superstition, thought over feeling, order over chaos, and the powers of the individual as opposed to the state.

The very term Enlightenment captures much of the new mood: if human beings would only cast the light of reason on nature and society, they would see the world with a new clarity. And by doing so they would be able to improve and perhaps even perfect the nature of the human condition.

All attitudes are adopted under specific circumstances. The Enlightenment in the colonies was strongly shaped by Calvinist convictions and by the seemingly boundless opportunities the new land offered. The colonists tended to see their own prosperity and political freedom as the cutting edges of human progress. If other people stood in their way, like the French, the Spanish, and the Indians, they would have to be removed—by force if necessary. ■

RELIGIOUS CONVICTIONS

The English colonists were slow to give up the assumption that there could be only one true and lawful church in a Christian society. Yet eventually they had to face the fact that competing denominations existed in the colonies. They also had to deal with a general consensus that religion was in a state of decline. Then suddenly, in 1740, a firestorm of religious enthusiasm swept their settlements. Afterwards they had to deal with its consequences, most of which they had not foreseen at all.

Established Churches

Since England had a national church, the Anglican church, it should have logically been the church of the English colonies as well. But the Church of England was established only in the southern colonies and parts of New York. Those Anglican churches were supported by taxes assessed on everyone, no matter whether they belonged or not. Yet there were no Anglican bishops in the colonies, and ministers had to go all the way to London to be ordained. So ministers were scarce and parishes enormous. Effective control of the affairs of these churches was in the hands of vestrymen, who were usually wealthy, slaveholding planters.

Elsewhere the situation was different. In Pennsylvania, New Jersey, and Rhode Island, there were no established churches. In the three remaining New England colonies, the Puritan churches, now often called Congregational, were established by law and supported by public taxes. The Massachusetts charter of 1691 prevented the Puritans from persecuting other denominations, but groups like Baptists, Quakers, and Anglicans had to support their churches by voluntary contributions rather than with money from the government. And they were still taxed for the support of the local Congregational minister.

The Great Awakening

The early decades of the eighteenth century saw a decline in church membership. Many people seemed to be doing so well in this world that they paid less attention to the next, and many preachers seemed to lack spiritual warmth and enthusiasm. There was a general feeling that religion was in a state of decline.

Certain ministers tried to promote "revivals" in their churches. Theodore Frelinghuysen led several such revivals among the Dutch Reformed churches of New Jersey in the 1720s. In the next decade William Tennent and his son Gilbert stirred up the Presbyterians of Pennsylvania. In 1735 there was a successful revival in the Congregational church of Northhampton in western Massachusetts led by the local minister, Jonathan Edwards.

Edwards was perhaps the most profound philosopher and theologian ever to live in America. His writings dealt with fundamental and very difficult questions about human existence. In his *Freedom of the Will* (1754), for example, Edwards struggled with the following problem: Is a person ever free not to do what he actually does do? Edwards reemphasized Calvin's original insistence that humankind was helpless in the hands of an all-powerful God. He declared that people must do more than recognize their own sinfulness. They must *feel* it, and they must *feel* the necessity of opening themselves to God. Unless they did so, they were doomed. Edwards saw conversion as a profoundly emotional experience of the heart rather than the head. It was this view that led him to active and successful preaching.

It took a different sort of person, however, to bring about a more widespread revival. This re-

Jonathan Edwards. (*Library of Congress*)

NEW WAYS OF THOUGHT

The charismatic George Whitefield preaching. (*National Portrait Gallery, London*)

vival began in the colonies in 1740, and it produced such excitement that it soon became known as the Great Awakening. The man who sparked it was a remarkable young Englishman named George Whitefield. When he arrived in the colonies, Whitefield had already gained fame as a popular preacher. Technically, he was a minister of the Church of England. But he had no special attachment for any particular church. When he arrived in America, he was persuaded to a Calvinist view by Gilbert Tennent. But it was not *what* Whitefield preached that drew the crowds. It was *how*.

No building in all the colonies could hold the astonishing numbers of people who flocked to hear him, so he often preached outdoors. In Philadelphia, Benjamin Franklin made a very careful estimate and concluded that 30,000 people could hear him at the same time. (This sounds like an absurdly high number for someone without a microphone, but Franklin was not a man to exaggerate.) Whitefield traveled from one colony to another, and everywhere he drew huge crowds.

His fame spread as the newspapers reported his progress. He was aided, it has recently been discovered, by a friend who planted newspaper stories on Whitefield's behalf. At the end of 1740 he returned to England, leaving the colonies in a state of general excitement and turmoil. In later years he made more trips to the colonies, but these trips failed to cause the great stir of 1740. As we look back on this famous preacher, however, we can see a significance the colonists could not: Whitefield was the first person known to almost everyone in every colony.

Effects of the Great Revival

Much controversy developed in the wake of Whitefield's passage through the colonies. Some ministers, including the Tennents and Edwards, saw his preaching as the work of God and tried to do the same themselves. People, especially young women, flocked to join the churches. But some ministers got carried away. In Connecticut, James Davenport made a specialty of torchlit evening meetings where he stripped to the waist and did imitations of the devil. More conservative ministers thought this sort of behavior was more the devil's work than God's. Jonathan Edwards was not disturbed when his preaching caused members of the congregation to fall on the floor and scream aloud for mercy. But some ministers were profoundly shocked.

They were also disturbed that uneducated, unqualified men were wandering about preaching to anyone who would listen. Charles Chauncy of Boston referred to these itinerant preachers as "Men who, though they have no Learning, and but small Capacities, yet imagine they are able, and without Study too, to speak to the spiritual Profit of such as are willing to hear them." Chauncy especially attacked the Revival's "bitter Shriekings and Screaming; Convulsionlike Tremblings and Agitations, Struggling and Tumblings." None of this turmoil, Chauncy declared, meant genuine conversion. In turn, Chauncy and other conservatives found themselves called cold, lifeless men of letters, "'dead at heart" and lacking God's saving grace.

Church members began to take sides. Individual congregations split over the proper qualifications of their minister. By 1742 the two largest Calvinist groups, the Congregationalists and the Presbyterians, were divided into two camps which became known as New Lights and Old Lights.

As the names implied, Old Lights emphasized the need for learned preaching and a thoroughly educated ministry; New Lights stressed the importance of emotional experience. There were arguments over doctrine and church organization. In New England especially, many people left the Congregational churches and founded independent Baptist churches of their own.

NEWS FROM HEAVEN

Nathan Cole, a simple Connecticut farmer, described the impact of George Whitefield's arrival:

Now it pleased God to send Mr. Whitefield into this land; and my hearing of his preaching at Philadelphia . . . and many thousands flocking to hear him . . . and great numbers . . . converted to Christ; I felt the Spirit of God drawing me . . . I longed to see and hear him, and wished he would come this way. . . . [T]hen on a Sudden, in the morning . . . there came a messenger and said Mr. Whitefield . . . is to preach at Middletown this morning . . . I was in my field at

Work, I dropt my tool that I had in my hand and ran home to my wife telling her to make ready quickly. . . . [W]hen we came within about half a mile . . . of the Road that comes down from Hartford . . . to Middletown . . . I saw before me a Cloud or fogg rising . . . [and] I heard a noise something like a low rumbling thunder and . . . found it was the noise of Horses feet . . . [A]nd as I drew nearer it seemed like a steady Stream of horses and their riders . . . all of a Lather and foam with sweat . . . every horse seemed to go with all his might to carry his rider to hear news from heaven.

The general excitement of the Great Awakening was pretty well over by the end of 1742. Yet it never really died out completely, for local revivals kept breaking out from time to time. The southern colonies had been less affected by the Awakening. But over the course of the next generation, Presbyterians, Baptists, and Methodists began organizing churches there. This process was not confined to the South; in fact, it has gone on everywhere in this country ever since. Yet the process has not always worked to multiply churches, for sometimes churches have united. Both the Presbyterians and the Congregationalists managed to reunite within fifteen years of the split. In general, New Light views prevailed; revivalism was here to stay in American culture.

The Great Awakening had two other results. First, the prestige of ministers was undermined. People were evaluating religious leaders as never before. Members of individual congregations even felt free to debate whether their minister was saved or damned. Second, the multiplication of churches gave people more choices. If they did not like one church and its minister, they could always choose another. The Great Awakening worked in the direction of spiritual democracy, planting an idea that could easily be applied to politics as well.

Another development was the revival meeting. The huge crowds that came to hear Whitefield and the other preachers yearned for social contact. At the vast outdoor meetings that were to become a common feature of revivals, women, men, and children found release for their emotions and meaning for their lives. Despite the excesses accompanying the Great Awakening and the backsliding that followed, a new social form had been created in America. It was one especially suited to a spiritually and socially lonely rural people.

Although many revivalists mistrusted an educated clergy, the Great Awakening led to the founding of a number of educational institutions. William Tennent's Log College at Neshaminy, Pennsylvania, founded in 1736, was the first of similar schools for the preparation of Presbyterian ministers. The Baptists lagged behind the Presbyterians, but they established their own schools—Hopewell Academy, and later the College of Rhode Island (Brown) in 1764. Other colleges, such as Princeton (Presbyterian), Rutgers (Dutch Reformed), and Dartmouth (Congregational), all started with the revival movement. At first their main purpose was to prepare ministers. In time, however, some of the new colleges dropped that original purpose and became leaders in science, the arts, and literature.

The Awakening, Blacks, and Slavery

The Great Awakening also quickened the humanitarian spirit of the eighteenth century. When Jonathan Edwards defined virtue as "love of Being in general," he was suggesting that there was a divine element in everyone. Orphans, paupers, Indians, and even slaves shared in this Being and were thus the objects of Christian concern. Whitefield's original purpose in coming to America was to establish an orphanage.

Revivalists did not challenge slavery as an institution. But they preached that every person, no matter what his or her color, was "conceived and born in sin." Thus the Great Awakening strongly implied the spiritual equality of blacks. Indeed, the Great Revival marked the beginning of the slow but effective Christianization of Afro-Americans. Blacks began attending revival meetings, and joining various churches, especially the Baptists. The religious egalitarianism of the Awakening permitted and even encouraged the rise of preaching by blacks themselves. Eventually this meant the growth of a leadership class within black communities. Finally, by becoming Christians in increasing numbers, blacks were becoming more like whites. They, in turn, sought other grounds for distinguishing themselves from blacks.

Although the Quakers did not participate in the Great Awakening, the Society of Friends underwent its own revival in the mid-1750s and in the process became increasingly hostile to slavery. Quakers were led to adopt this view by John Woolman, a determined humanitarian who never ceased to admonish that:

Placing on men the ignominious Title, Slave, dressing them in uncomely Garments, keeping them to servile Labour, in which they are often dirty, tends gradually to fix a notion in the Mind, that they are a sort of people below us in Nature, and leads us to consider them as such in all our Conclusions about them.

It was Woolman who first clearly realized that whites were "prejudiced" against blacks and that slavery and prejudice were intertwined. The term *prejudice* itself, as it concerned attitudes toward racial groups, was first used in America about 1760. Woolman was joined in the antislavery cause by the pamphleteer and teacher Anthony Benezet. By speaking to the world at large as well as other Quakers, Benezet helped to broaden the issue. Yet action remained largely confined to the Society of Friends, which took an increasingly hard line on slaveholding among its members. By the time of the American Revolution, the Society had nearly rid its membership of the moral taint of slaveholding and had raised the fundamental issue for everyone.

Many Protestant Religions

Despite all these developments, at the time of the Revolution a majority of Americans had no church affiliation. Yet the spirit of Protestantism, especially in its Calvinist forms, remained strong. It took on a new energy as denominations splintered and new sects sprang up, and it affected many people who were not members of a particular church. The great number of religions promoted practical tolerance and a growing acceptance of what finally came to be the American principle of the separation of church and state.

Despite the variety of sects and the ethnic and geographical divisions among the denominations, the following generalizations about colonial religion in the 1750s seem valid. First, it was overwhelmingly Protestant. Although the colonies provided a refuge for the persecuted of all religions, only about 25,000 Catholics and 2,000 Jews were living in America on the eve of the Revolution.

Protestant colonists, in a real sense children of the Reformation, differed among themselves in creed and doctrine, yet stood united in their opposition to Rome. Catholics were not physically molested in eighteenth-century America, but they were the targets of propaganda spread by ministers, educators, editors, and publishers of popular almanacs. England's wars with Catholic France partly explain this anti-Catholic feeling, but the hostility went far deeper.

Second, American Protestantism was strongly colored by the Calvinist heritage. That is, the great majority of churches shared, in varying degree, certain common emphases. They tended to favor simple ceremony that was grounded in biblical theology, and they emphasized individual piety rather than control by a strong clergy.

Third, the doctrine and organization of American churches reflected, in a very rough way, the social background of their members. The wealthiest denominations in the colonies were the New England Congregationalists, the Presbyterians, and the Anglicans. These churches numbered among their members many poorer people in addition to most of the merchant and landed families. A higher proportion of those of modest means was found in the Baptist churches, among the Methodists who emerged in the late 1760s, and in various small sects. By their frankly evangelical appeals, these two denominations reached elements in the colonial population neglected by the elite churches. Especially because of their successes in the South and on the frontier, these two groups eventually emerged as the two largest Protestant denominations.

Fourth, although the churches of the non-English-speaking settlers in the eighteenth century had little influence on the main currents of colonial religion, they served as vital social organizations. It took some time for European immigrants to adjust to American ways, and they often looked to religious leaders for guidance. The German churches survived best, though they faced a continual problem about whether English should

Many American surnames—"last" names—originally came from occupations that thrived in the colonies but are now nearly extinct. Some names came from other sources, such as names ending in son, John(son) and Jack(son) (British Isles and Scandanavia) or similarly in Ireland O'Riley (of the Riley's) or Scotland McNeil (of the Neil family). Many American names have also come from dozens of countries and several continents. But even if one confines oneself to a survey of English names in the New York City telephone book, there are numerous entries that once were the names of particular callings or occupations. We can start with the name *Smith*. Originally it meant someone who worked with metal, though there has been a tendency to drop that refinement (as in Tinsmith, Goldsmith) or to keep it in favor of dropping the "Smith," as in the name Black(smith). Some such names are obvious and common, such as Carpenter; others are equally obvious but less common, as with the jockey Willie Shoemaker. Taylors made clothes. Wheelwrights made wheels. Wagners drove wagons. Coopers made barrels. Chandlers made candles and branched out into retailing, specializing in equipping ships. Fullers processed wool and Tanners leather. Some of the these names (picked from a telephone book of a small American town) scarcely need explanation: Boatwright, Brewer, Walker, Weaver, Miller, Mason, Marshall, Shepard, Marchbanks, Fisher, and (without further comment) Lovelady.

---

be substituted for their native tongue.

Fifth, the tendency throughout the eighteenth century was toward greater religious freedom. Even in orthodox New England, the persecution of Quakers and Baptists had ceased by 1700. A minister like John Wise of Ipswich could almost singlehandedly stop an organized group of ministers from centralizing church government and destroying the independence of its congregations. In defending the congregational principle and church democracy, Wise introduced arguments that were later adopted in defense of political democracy. All men are born free, he said; "Democracy is Christ's government in Church and State."

As eighteenth-century Americans became more humanitarian, secular, and liberal, and turned their attention away from God in heaven toward people on earth, their God also grew more tractable, less demanding, more involved with the happiness of His children. By 1755, John Adams could speak of "the frigid John Calvin" and turn elsewhere for peace of mind.

THE ENLIGHTENMENT

Religious belief continued to be of great importance to many Americans of the eighteenth century; yet new ideas were in the air. These ideas were closely connected with the beginnings of modern science. Since we have inherited these ideas, they now seem normal and reasonable. At the time, however, they were revolutionary.

The End of Witchcraft

A dramatic example of this kind of change can be found in the witchcraft crisis in Salem, Massachusetts, in 1692. Several girls accused certain townspeople of bewitching them. There were official trials and more accusations. Before the crisis was over, 20 people had been executed for witchcraft and another 100 had been jailed on the same charge. The excitement began to die down when prominent people were accused. Some ministers finally convinced the court not to accept evidence from the supposed victims. But the episode has fascinated Americans ever since.

Historians have recently discovered that personal hostility between two groups of townspeople had a good deal to do with what happened. But it is impossible to understand the episode without recognizing one important fact. Everyone involved, including the ministers, believed that witches and witchcraft really existed. In Europe, thousands of people were executed for this crime. Yet the Salem trials were the last witchcraft prosecutions in the colonies, for soon after people began to doubt the reality of witches. William Penn dismissed a case against a woman charged with riding a broomstick by saying: "There is no law in Pennsylvania against riding on broomsticks."

The World of Isaac Newton

The relationship between the earth and the sun seems to be a simple matter. Everyday observation clearly suggests that the sun goes around the

The trial of George Jacobs for witchcraft. (*Courtesy, Essex Institute, Salem, Massachusetts*)

earth, since the sun rises in the morning, moves through the sky, and disappears on the other side of the earth at night. By ordinary observation, we cannot see or feel the earth rotate. The obvious conclusion is that the sun moves around a stationary earth. Western Europeans took this very sensible view of the matter until the sixteenth century.

In 1543 Copernicus proposed a completely opposite view, that the earth moves once a year around the sun and that the earth itself does one full rotation every twenty-four hours. Copernicus saw things in a new way, partly because he looked at more bits of information and because he handled data mathematically. His discovery had important implications for the way people looked at God's universe: now the earth was no longer at the center.

During the next few centuries scientists made many other advances in understanding the natural world, and one man in particular dominated the thinking of the eighteenth century. The work of Sir Isaac Newton suggested that the world was not governed by chance or miracles, but rather that the universe was a perfect machine governed by fixed mathematical laws. The universal force of gravity, for example, governed both the falling of an apple and the movement of planets around the sun. Newton showed that apparently unrelated facts and events were part of a unified plan. Many other scientists set out to follow his example in hopes of discovering all the laws of the natural world.

But there were dangers in this new way of thinking. Perhaps God was merely a great watchmaker who had wound up the universe and left it to run by itself forever. By the end of the eighteenth century, a few Americans had adopted this view, although most still saw God in a more traditional way. Some ministers took an active interest in scientific matters, proceeding with the full assurance that God wanted them to understand His works.

John Locke: Social Scientist

Human reason seemed to be the key to unlocking the secrets of the natural world. It also seemed to be the key to an understanding of human beings and society. Another great English thinker dominated eighteenth-century views on these subjects. John Locke argued that human beings were born with blank minds. They learned things, Locke said, by using their senses to accumulate experience. The mind had the ability to organize this experience into true understanding.

This view of human knowledge had important implications. It was experience that counted, not previous ideas. People could learn about the world through experiments. Reason was the process of ordering the information the senses provided, and proper order was the goal. This was what Newton had shown for the natural world.

Locke also spread new and important ideas about society and government. People, he declared, had originally existed in a "state of nature," totally without laws or government. In order to gain protection, human beings agreed to come together in an organized society. In this new condition they retained certain "natural" rights God had originally given them. There were three such natural rights: life, liberty, and property.

In order to protect them, people made a contract with a ruler. In return for the ruler's protection, they agreed to obey him. If the ruler protected their natural rights, they owed obedience, but if the ruler violated these rights, the people no longer had any obligation to obey. Indeed, the people could replace such a tyrant with a ruler who would respect their natural rights.

Locke's influence in the colonies was powerful but often indirect. Probably more widely read were certain English "Commonwealth writers" of the early eighteenth century, especially John Trenchard and Thomas Gordon. They were themselves much indebted to Locke, but they wrote as critics of the British monarchy. Their theme was that the English court and crown tended toward dissipation, extravagance, and corruption. Their writings were widely read and struck a responsive chord in the colonies.

Other beliefs strengthened the natural rights philosophy. The common law rights of free-born Englishmen, for example, were closely identified with the natural rights of all people. And these legal rights were sustained by two English authorities who were immensely influential in America: Sir William Blackstone, known through his *Commentaries on the Laws of England* (1765–1769), and Sir Edward Coke, the seventeenth-century lawyer and scholar. The colonists quoted Blackstone to the effect that a person's first allegiance was to a God whose will was the universal law of nature, and that human laws in conflict with natural law were clearly invalid.

All these ideas seemed to fit perfectly with the colonists' own experiences. Because so many people owned property in the colonies, property did seem like a natural right. And all these ideas supported political freedom. Locke himself wrote in support of religious toleration, and others called for a free press and free speech. Most Englishmen at home and in the colonies prided themselves on having the freest government in the world.

Benjamin Franklin: The Enlightened American

One American became a living example of the ideals of the Enlightenment. Benjamin Franklin was born in Boston, where his father owned a tannery, and at age twelve was apprenticed to his older brother as a printer's assistant. They did not get along together, so the younger Franklin took off for Philadelphia, where he soon set himself up as a printer. This was the beginning of the most varied and successful career in early American history. By the age of forty Franklin had made a small fortune and was able to retire from business. Then he began a half-dozen careers at once, all of them distinguished.

In Philadelphia, Franklin founded the first American public library, the first American volunteer fire company, and the first American scientific society. He made many useful inventions, including a fuel-efficient stove, bifocal eyeglasses, improved carriage wheels, a musical instrument, an improved watering trough for horses, and a fan for his chair to keep off the flies. He worked out accurate ideas about the paths of hurricanes, and he showed ship captains how to shorten the voyage to Europe by taking advantage of the Gulf Stream.

He achieved international fame as a scientist by his work with electricity. Most of that work was a

good deal more sophisticated (and less dangerous) than flying a kite in a thunderstorm. He was the first to propose the concept of positive and negative currents. His famous kite experiment was helpful, however, for it showed that lightning and electricity (which was then regarded as a toy) were in fact the same thing. Characteristically, Franklin gave his discovery a practical application—the lightning rod.

Franklin refused to take out patents on his inventions because he felt that the benefits of sci-

Benjamin Franklin, by Robert Feke, and "Poor Richard's Almanac." The portrait was painted about the time of Franklin's retirement from business. Thirty years later Franklin's image was completely transformed. (*Fogg Art Museum, Harvard University Portrait Collection*)

Benjamin Franklin, portrait by Charles Willson Peale. (*The Historical Society of Pennsylvania*)

FRANKLIN'S *POOR RICHARD'S ALMANACK*

Keep thy shop, and thy shop will keep thee.

Why does the blind man's wife paint herself?

God heals, and the doctor takes the Fees.

Neither a fortress nor a maid will hold out long after they begin to parley.

Creditors have better memories than debtors.

Keep your eyes wide open before marriage, half shut afterwards.

Wish not so much to live long as to live well.

Sin is not hurtful because it is forbidden but it is forbidden because it's hurtful.

Historians relate, not so much what is done, as what they would have believed.

ence should be available to everyone. He explained this attitude by saying: "As we enjoy great advantages from the inventions of others, we should be glad of an opportunity to serve others by any invention of ours." In the same quiet and open spirit, he kept his own newspaper open to a wide variety of opinions.

When he was an elderly man, Franklin became the American ambassador to France. By then he was internationally famous. At the extremely formal court of the French king, Franklin stood out in his simple clothes. He wore a long-haired wig, as all gentlemen did, but no one else walked the streets of Paris wearing a fur cap. At age seventy-five, he charmed the ladies and greatly impressed the gentlemen by his direct, modest, and reasonable manner. They saw him as a Pennsylvanian, as an American, and as a man who applied reason and good will to the problems of the natural and the human world.

Science in the Colonies

The brilliance of Franklin's career, including his important work on electricity, has tended to make us forget the achievements of his contemporaries. They shared his reliance on Enlightenment thought and, like him, believed that natural philosophy could be put to practical use. They were also motivated by curiosity and a desire for recognition. Indeed, they sensed very keenly their colonial status in the international realm of science. Living in a society without a distinct group of scholars, they looked to Europe for encouragement and support.

European scholars were keenly interested in the New World, and they encouraged Americans to report their findings on plant and animal life, Indians, medicine, and earthquakes. By collecting unknown plants, for example, Americans helped the great Swedish scholar Carl Linnaeus to complete his encyclopedic classifications of what he thought were all the species of living things. By the middle of the eighteenth century, European and American scientists had developed a system of communication that kept them informed about one another's findings. Through the efforts of Peter Collinson, a Quaker merchant of London and an influential member of the Royal Society, the reports of the Americans were transmitted to interested Europeans. To have an article published in the Royal Society's *Transactions* was an honor most American scientists yearned for.

In the early years, New England was the leader in scientific investigation. Many of its leaders and professional men had been trained at English universities, and Harvard teachers and graduates had been elected to the Royal Society before 1700. John Winthrop, Jr., of Connecticut, a charter member of the society, donated a telescope to Harvard in 1672. It enabled Thomas Brattle to observe the comet of 1676. Newton used Brattle's observations in his *Principia Mathematica* to illustrate how the orbits of comets are fixed by gravitational force.

No less important were the eighty-two letters Cotton Mather sent to the Royal Society's *Transactions* between 1712 and 1724. Among them were reports on inoculation against smallpox, which Mather learned from his African slave, who reported on the practice in Africa. Equally characteristic of Mather's contributions, though rather less useful and scientifically impressive, was his article on a snake supposed to be growing in a horse's eye.

By 1750, however, Philadelphia had clearly become the capital of colonial science. Commercial prosperity was partly responsible for the willingness of Philadelphians to support scientific enterprises. Equally important was the Quaker connection with intellectuals abroad. It was the English merchant Collinson who put the self-taught naturalist John Bartram in touch with

Cotton Mather. (*Library of Congress*)

Linnaeus, who was regarded at the time as the Newton of the natural world. When Peter Kalm, a pupil of Linnaeus, visited America in 1748, he came straight to Philadelphia to see Bartram. According to Kalm, their discussions ranged from silk culture, vineyards, stalactites, and truffles to Indian pottery, hummingbirds, and cures for snakebite. Bartram had a genius for collecting specimens and a knack for communicating his enthusiasm to others.

In 1743 Franklin and Bartram tried unsuccessfully to establish a scientific society. Twenty-five years later their plan took form in the American Philosophical Society, today the oldest learned society in the United States. The 1771 *Transactions* of the society carried reports by a number of colonial scientists on a transit of Venus across the sun that had occurred in 1769. In Philadelphia, where the observation took on the proportions of a community enterprise, David Rittenhouse, an ingenious clockmaker and builder of the celebrated orrery (a mechanical planetarium), was the principal contributor. European scientists hailed the Society's *Transactions* as evidence that American science had attained maturity.

A People of the Written Word

Benjamin Franklin was never a good public speaker; in fact, he admired his friend George Whitefield for that ability. In small groups or in private conversation, Franklin was enormously persuasive, partly because he was so quietly logical and partly because he was always so careful to offer his deepest convictions as merely sensible possibilities. In order to reach a large number of people, Franklin relied on the printed word. Although he had fewer years of formal education than most readers of this book, he made himself a master of words by reading. And he wrote largely for an American public that was more literate than people anywhere else in the world.

The proportion of people who knew how to read was highest in New England. Even more than most Protestants, the Puritans insisted that members of a godly community had to know how to read the Word of God. That principle applied to both sexes, though in application boys were given preference over girls. The New England pattern of orderly settlement by towns made it possible to set up arrangements for formal schooling. From the 1640s, Massachusetts law required all towns with more than fifty families to support a schoolmaster. In effect, all children were to be taught to read at public expense.

The New England ideal set very high standards. A later law in Massachusetts required that towns with over 100 families support a schoolmaster who knew both Latin and Greek. Other New England colonies passed somewhat similar laws. Often, however, these laws were not observed, especially in small towns or in those exposed to attack by Indians. None of the townspeople liked the expense, but in general they believed in the ideal. Many children were taught to read by their parents without benefit of formal schooling. Yet by the 1720s many New England towns found they could maintain schools that ran from the end of harvest until spring planting. In the eighteenth century, more than 90 percent of New Englanders could read and write, at least on a very simple level.

In the Middle Colonies, the literacy rate was lower. There were no laws requiring public support of schools, and farms were more scattered. Yet various Calvinist churches provided the same incentive the New England churches did. The situation in the southern colonies was more complicated. More than 40 percent of the people were slaves, and virtually no slaves knew how to read. Few people lived in towns, and there was little formal schooling. Yet Anglicans shared in the general Protestant insistence on reading the Bible. The literacy rate among southern whites was probably about 50 percent, which was about the same as that for adult males in England.

In all the colonies, women were not excluded from education, but they were left behind. Many girls learned to read English, a few learned French, but practically none were taught Latin and Greek. Sometimes girls were taught the piano and fancy sewing, rather than the fundamentals of arithmetic. Despite these disadvantages, however, the level of women's education in the colonies was considerably higher than in England.

No women attended college, and in comparison to today, very few men did either. The first American college was Harvard, founded in 1636, as a training ground for ministers. From the beginning, however, students there studied the subjects that were traditional at English universities. These included Latin and Greek, mathematics, some sciences, and the philosophy of morals. After about 1700, more than half the graduates of Harvard went into occupations other than the ministry. By that time two other colleges had been established: William and Mary (1693) and Yale (1703). Later, of course, at least five more colleges were founded as a result of the Great Awakening. Most of these

Pages from a 1727 textbook. (*New York Public Library*)

An early view of the campus of Harvard College. (*Massachusetts Historical Society*)

remained connected to some church group, though attendance was not restricted to church members.

The largest colleges were smaller than most high schools today. Usually the students came from well-to-do families, but there were bright farm boys at all of them. Only one of these little colleges (William and Mary) was located in a southern colony. As time went on, the liberal and rational influences of the age began to affect all the colleges. In mid-century King's College (later to become Columbia University) advertised that while the teaching of religion was its principal objective, "it is further the Design of this College to instruct and perfect the Youth in . . . The Arts of Numbering and Measuring, of Surveying and Navigation, of Geography and History, of Husbandry, Commerce and Government."

The colleges also became important centers of the new science. None of the college professors matched Benjamin Franklin or John Bartram in originality. But America's most competent astronomer, John Winthrop, taught at Harvard, and David Rittenhouse, astronomer, model maker, and mathematician, lectured at the College of Philadelphia, as did Dr. Benjamin Rush, the first professor of chemistry in America and later the new nation's most prominent physician.

A People of the Printed Word

When Benjamin Franklin became a printer—and hence an editor and author—he also became head of an important educational institution. Today we tend to contrast our various mass media, such as television, radio, newspapers, and magazines, with formal learning in school. Such a distinction made much less sense in the colonies, where transmission of knowledge and information was by face-to-face contact or through print. A wide assortment of books was imported from England and printed in the northern colonies. Until the political controversies of the 1760s, the most widely printed works were sermons. On many farms they were the only books in the house except the Bible.

Annual almanacs were popular; pocket-sized and paperbound, they served as calendars, astrological guides, recipe books, and children's school books. Sandwiched in between bits of practical information were jokes, poems, and sayings. The better almanacs offered simplified summaries of the new science, and presented selections from the best British authors. Franklin's *Poor Richard's Almanack,* first published in 1732, soon sold 10,000 copies a year.

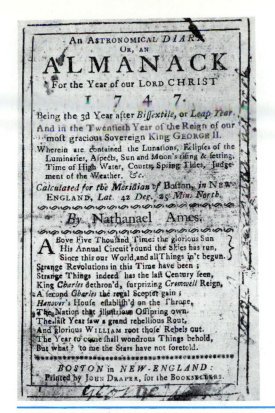

Title page of Nathaniel Ames's *Almanack,* published in Boston in 1747. (*Library of Congress*)

Newspapers were even more widely read—and read aloud. The first colonial newspaper appeared in Boston at the beginning of the eighteenth century. By 1765, twenty-five newspapers were being published in the colonies. When Franklin was postmaster of the colonies, he managed to reduce mailing rates for newspapers and speed their circulation. The papers appeared once a week, with only four pages, the last two mostly devoted to advertisements in very small print. The only illustrations were a few small woodcuts showing the outline of a ship (just arrived) or a runaway (servant or slave). There were no other drawings and of course no photographs. The news was known as "latest advices." Much of it was copied directly from English and other European newspapers. This news usually occupied the front page. On the second page one might find "advices" copied from newspapers published in other colonies.

Sometimes the newspapers carried accounts about the latest activities of the colony's governor and assembly, and from time to time there were letters from readers. Often there were brief stories and poems. But newspapers gave very little local news, since everyone knew what was going on in his or her own town.

Colonial newspapers served as the most important public tie among the colonies. Their circulations were small by modern standards. Many backwoods farmers rarely saw one, even if they knew how to read. Yet newspapers were passed from hand to hand and read aloud at crossroads stores. They served as a vital network of communication among a relatively literate people. And as time went on, that communication link became more and more vital to their interests.

STRUGGLE FOR A PROTESTANT AMERICA

The ideas of the Enlightenment were downright intoxicating. They suggested to many Americans that they had only to continue what they were already doing in order to achieve a better society. Yet Protestant Americans saw their future in rather special terms.

The Threat of New France

As time went on, the English settlements occupied more and more territory. Indians east of the Appalachians were drastically reduced in numbers and in power as they moved westward or succombed to disease. To the north and west lay the French settlements, forts along the St. Lawrence Valley, the southern Great Lakes, and the Mississippi River all the way to New Orleans. French Catholic missionaries and fur traders had established friendly relations with the Indians, for the fur traders did not take the Indian land. They often lived in Indian villages and had children by Indian wives. French royal officials tried to encourage settlement by farmers, but they were not very successful. In 1760 there were only about 60,000 French people in all of New France; the British colonists numbered nearly 1.5 million.

English numerical superiority was partly balanced by the weight of Indian power. Whenever there was war between England and France, the colonial French encouraged their Indian friends to raid English settlements. The balance of power between the French and British in North America was also affected by the fact that a large proportion of the French colonists were males of fighting age. In contrast, the British colonies had many more women and children.

New York became the crucial battleground because it included the only water-level break in the Appalachian mountain chain. Fortunately for the English, the Iroquois Confederacy controlled the Mohawk Valley. To the north and west of the Iroquois were the Hurons. The French had long ago befriended the Hurons, without knowing that they were traditional enemies of the Iroquois. Thus the English were able to make alliances with the Iroquois against their common enemies, the Hurons and the French.

When William of Orange came to the English throne, he brought with him an old feud with Louis XIV of France. From 1689 to 1713 there was almost continuous war between England and France, which by this time were the two most powerful nations in Europe. Europe remained the main scene of the conflict, and neither country sent troops to their colonies. But the English and French settlers in America sent raiding expeditions against each other, and Indians became involved in most of this fighting. By and large, the English won.

When the wars finally ended in 1713, the Peace of Utrecht gave important new American territories to the British. The French ceded the rich island of St. Christopher (St. Kitt's) in the West Indies, and recognized British claims to the territory around Hudson Bay. The British also acquired the peninsula of Nova Scotia (previously known as Acadia), which New Englanders had captured. The French acknowledged the Iroquois as British subjects and their territory as British domain.

The Founding of Georgia

For twenty-five years after the Peace of Utrecht there was no further warfare between Great Britain and France. But the southern border of the mainland colonies remained in dispute with Spain, and the British moved to strengthen their position in that region. They did so by founding a new colony, the last of the thirteen that later became the United States.

In 1732 General James Oglethorpe and several other English gentlemen obtained a royal charter for a new colony to be located south of the Savannah River. The charter gave Oglethorpe and the other "trustees" the right to govern the colony for twenty-one years. Thereafter the colony of Georgia would have a royal governor. Two reasons prompted the establishment of the new colony. The British government wanted a military outpost for defense against the Spanish in Florida. Oglethorpe was interested in setting up a place of refuge for those who had been imprisoned for debt. The Georgia trustees laid down certain rules they

Georgia and the Carolinas

Map labels: INDIAN COUNTRY, VIRGINIA, Jamestown, ROANOKE ISLAND, Albemarle Sound, NORTH CAROLINA, New Bern, SOUTH CAROLINA, Cape Fear, Charleston, GEORGIA, Savannah, ATLANTIC OCEAN, SPANISH FLORIDA, Added to Georgia 1763

colonies. Rumors about possible invasion swept some cities, but they all proved false. Then, in 1745, something truly amazing happened. For years, the famous fort of Louisburg had stood on Cape Breton Island as the sentry for the St. Lawrence River. Louisburg was the gateway to New France, and it was heavily fortified. That year, Massachusetts and other New England colonies sent milita and sailors to assault Louisburg. To almost everyone's surprise, the expedition succeeded.

The victory fired the colonists' imagination. They had proved their own strength. Colonial leaders (especially in Massachusetts) began to think in grander terms. Some began to predict that all of New France would eventually fall to Anglo-American power. Here would be a stunning triumph for British-Americans and for the cause

General Sir William Pepperell, the victor of Louisburg. (*Library of Congress*)

hoped would help realize both aims: Landholdings were limited to 500 acres; rum and brandy were banned, since farmers and militiamen ought to be sober; slavery was prohibited not because it was wrong, but because it would weaken the colony as a military outpost.

Most of these plans for the new colony fell through. The trustees did support settlement of some debtors from England, but they were soon outnumbered by land-hungry men from South Carolina and other established colonies. The trustees withdrew their ban on rum in the face of protests. Planters from South Carolina brought in slaves, bought up large tracts of land in the low country, and began planting rice. By the time Georgia became a royal colony in 1752, it was a small copy of its neighbor to the north. The Georgia assembly simply copied many of South Carolina's laws. Rice and slaves dominated the colony. Still, at the time of the American Revolution Georgia had fewer people than any of the other thirteen colonies.

Louisburg as Citadel and Symbol

Shortly after the founding of Georgia, war broke out again in Europe. From 1739 to 1748 Britain was at war, first with Spain and then with France. At first there was little action in the American of Protestantism as well. Perhaps the entire continent might become a citadel of enlightened government and true religion.

Peace came three years later, in 1748. The Treaty of Aix-la-Chapelle ended the conflict known in the colonies as King George's War. One of the provisions rather casually handed Louisburg back to the French. That concession produced resentment in the colonies, especially in Massachusetts. Yet it was widely believed that the treaty was merely a temporary truce. King George's War had been a sideshow to the main conflict in Europe.

France remained more populous and perhaps more powerful than Great Britain.

No one was sure on the latter point—but it was clear in London and Paris and the colonial capitals that a showdown was coming. It seemed possible that North America might become an important scene of the fighting. No one thought of another possibility—that such a conflict might set off a chain of events that would lead to war *within* the British empire. And no one realized that revivalism and the Enlightenment might contribute to such a development.

SUMMARY

In the eighteenth century the concern about religion that had brought so many people to America was still very important. But it was affected by a whole new set of ideas called the Enlightenment—the birth of a belief in human reason and science.

Because at the beginning of the eighteenth century many Americans thought religion was in decline, some ministers began to promote revivalism. The most widespread revival, the Great Awakening, was led and preached by a young and popular English preacher, George Whitefield. Thousands came to hear him, and the effects of his work lasted long after he returned to England. Many ministers followed Whitefield's example, and the outdoor meeting at which emotionalism could be freely expressed became an American institution. Congregations split over the new and the old types of worship, and new denominations were formed. People had more choices. As a result, the foundations were laid for the transfer of the new spiritual democracy to other areas of life.

New educational institutions were set up, among them Princeton, Rutgers, and Dartmouth. Quakers began to question the morality of slaveholding. And though Americans were overwhelmingly Protestant, the many sects and denominations promoted ideas of toleration, religious freedom, and the separation of church and state.

These trends away from rigid belief and strict doctrine were encouraged by Enlightenment ideas of rationality and the power of human reason. Trials of witches came to an end, and magic and witchcraft came to seem ridiculous. New discoveries about the workings of the natural world changed people's perspective and increased confidence in their ability to understand and therefore control nature.

The same was true for politics and philosophy. John Locke's ideas were particularly influential. Benjamin Franklin became a living example of Enlightenment ideas in America through his public service and his inventions and interest in science. With Franklin's help, a community of American scientists began to develop. Public education was the rule in New England, and literacy rates were high. Colleges began to expand their teaching to subjects other than religion and to become centers for the new science. Almanacs and newspapers were widely circulated and read. Weekly newspapers became an important link among the colonies. All these trends and events made Americans an alert people, open to and eager for new ideas.

Political events also fostered a spirit of optimism and expansionism. English colonists, moving west, began to encounter French settlements near the eastern Great Lakes. After a series of wars between England and France from 1689 to 1713, the English gained new territories in America by the Peace of Utrecht. In the south, Georgia was set up as a buffer colony against the Spanish presence in Florida. Still another war in Europe was ended by treaty in 1748. But by then it was clear a showdown was coming, which this time might well involve the overseas colonies as well as the mother countries.

Suggested Readings

Two sweeping studies deal with eighteenth-century religious thought: S. Ahlstrom, *A Religious History of the American People* (1972), which has a fine bibliography; and R. Handy, *A History of the Churches of the United States and Canada* (1977).

The best place to start is J. Bumsted and J. Van de Wetering, *What Must I Do to Be Saved? The Great Awakening in Colonial America* (1976). Three very different biographies are probably more useful than the regional studies: O. Winslow's straightforward *Jonathan*

Edwards (1940); P. Miller's subtle but difficult *Jonathan Edwards* (1949); and S. Henry's *George Whitefield: Wayfaring Witness* (1957). Especially good on the continuing reverberations of the Awakening is W. McLoughlin's short biography, *Isaac Backus and the American Pietistic Tradition* (1967). Of the various denominational histories, see particularly L. Trinterud, *The Forming of an American Tradition: Presbyterianism during the Colonial Period* (1968); C. Goen, *Revivalism and Separatism in New England, 1740–1800: Strict Congregationalism and Separate Baptists in the Great Awakening* (1962); and C. Wright, *Beginnings of Unitarianism in America* (1955). A. Heimert and P. Miller (eds.), *The Great Awakening, Documents Illustrating the Crisis and Its Consequences* (1967), provides a fascinating collection of contemporary accounts.

The best place to start on the Salem witchcraft episode is J. Demos, *Entertaining Satan* (1982). Miller, *The New England Mind,* and Middlekauff, *The Mathers,* deal with that crisis. K. Thomas, *Religion and the Decline of Magic* (1971), sets witchcraft in a much broader context.

S. James, *A People among Peoples: Quaker Benevolence in Eighteenth-Century America* (1963), deals with antislavery sentiment. The complex relationship between religion and the growth of humanitarianism is also discussed in D. Davis, *The Problem of Slavery in Western Culture* (1964), and W. Jordan, *White over Black: American Attitudes toward the Negro, 1550–1812* (1968).

Many of these books deal with the American Enlightenment (as do many cited in Chapter 3). A. Tourtellot's *Benjamin Franklin: The Shaping of Genius, The Boston Years* (1977), and R. Clark, *Benjamin Franklin: A Biography* (1983) wrestle quite successfully with an incredible man. Franklin headed off historians by writing his own *Autobiography,* available in many editions. S. Bedini, *Thinkers and Tinkers: Early American Men of Science* (1975), is encyclopedic. R. Shyrock, *Medicine and Society in America, 1600–1860* (1960), is a model of how to convey a lot with few words. John Locke's *Two Treatises* is an eighteenth-century political tract much more closely connected with "science" than would at first appear. For a subtle interpretation of Enlightenment thinkers (both European and American) and their impact on American religious thought, see H. May, *The Enlightenment in America* (1976). D. Boorstin's cultural history, *The Americans: The Colonial Experience* (1958), emphasizes the practical bent of the American mind.

L. Cremin, *American Education: The Colonial Experience, 1607–1783* (1970), discusses both formal and informal educational agencies. R. Middlekauff, *Ancients and Axioms: Secondary Education in Eighteenth-Century New England* (1963), is the best single monograph. There is a fine but dated bibliographical essay in the latter half of B. Bailyn, *Education in the Forming of American Society* (1960), which is as much about the colonial family as it is about "education."

Finally, there are books on very different subjects well worth looking at: L. Levy, *Legacy of Suppression: Freedom of Speech and Press in Early American History* (1960); and L. Ziff, *The Literature of America: Colonial Period* (1970). R. Slotkin, *Regeneration through Violence: The Mythology of the American Frontier, 1600–1860* (1973), grapples with the literature generated by the conflict between European settlers and Indians in North America.

THE MAKINGS OF REVOLT

Chapter 5

When war is expected, it usually comes. France and Great Britain slipped into war almost as if they had scheduled the conflict in advance. This time North America became a main theater in a worldwide war that also included fighting in Europe, Africa, India, and the West Indies. British victories resulted in a stunning enlargement of the British empire. In North America, all of New France came under British rule.

Officials in London quite naturally thought that an enlarged empire needed better administration and firmer control. Since Great Britain had piled up a huge debt for the war, they also felt the colonies ought to pay a fair share of the costs of running such an empire. Anglo-American colonists had been paying taxes for years. A few of these were part of the navigation laws, but most were levied by the colonial assemblies to support colonial governments. When Parliament decided to raise revenue in the colonies there were howls of protest, even though most of that revenue was earmarked for the defense of the colonists themselves.

For a dozen years the colonies and the mother country pushed and shoved each other on the matter. Other issues arose, and self-interest and high principles became so entangled that no one could tell them apart. The two sides staggered from crisis to crisis, each one never knowing exactly what to expect from the other. At some point they stepped onto the slippery slope of no return. Grievances on both sides finally exploded in armed conflict—a conflict neither wanted and both had tried to avoid.

Some of the British colonies did not revolt. Canada and Nova Scotia remained within the empire, as did Jamaica, Barbados, and the other British islands in the West Indies. Thirteen continental colonies took up arms against their lawful government. From the beginning, a major issue was whether these colonies would act separately or together, and in the long run this problem proved to be as difficult as making the break with Britain. Ideas about self-government helped support the thirteen colonies; so did the values of the Enlightenment and the emotions of the Great Awakening. Yet the colonists had little to guide them concerning the question of unity—little, that is, except the powerful force of necessity. ■

VICTORY OVER THE FRENCH

Before the ink was dry on the Treaty of Aix-la-Chapelle, both sides began to prepare for a showdown. The French refortified Louisburg and constructed a long string of forts from Lake Erie south to the "forks of the Ohio." There, where the Allegheny and Monongahela rivers join to form the Ohio, they built Fort Duquesne.

The Ohio Country

The westward pressure of Anglo-American settlement soon spilled against the line of French forts. In 1747 a group of wealthy Virginia planters formed the Ohio Company in hopes of acquiring land in the Ohio Valley. Two years later, the Virginia government gave the company 200,000 acres west of the Monongahela River in an area claimed not only by France and Virginia, but by Pennsylvania. Authorities in London approved the grant in hopes of encouraging further settlement. In 1751 Robert Dinwiddie arrived in Virginia as the new royal governor and was induced to join the Ohio Company. His appointment meant that the interests of imperial officials in London were interlocked with those of Virginia's ruling aristocrats.

Both as a British patriot and as a land speculator, Dinwiddie took a keen interest in the Ohio country. In 1753 he sent out a small group of Virginians to find out what the French were doing in the area, and they returned with news of the construction of Fort Duquesne. The next year, in 1754, he asked the leader of the previous expedition to lead a force of Virginia militiamen to get rid of the French intruders.

George Washington was then twenty-two years old, a young man with excellent connections including two brothers in the Ohio Company and an appointment as colonel in the Virginia militia. Washington led his small force toward the forks of the Ohio. When he learned that the fort was heavily fortified, he and his men built a stockade some fifty miles to the south, naming it Fort Necessity. The French attacked, and the badly outnumbered Virginians surrendered.

Because the two nations were not officially at war, the French released the Virginians so that they might return with word that the Ohio country was firmly in the hands of France. The skirmish at Fort Necessity was, in fact, the opening battle of a great war that lasted until 1763. Anglo-Americans called it the French and Indian War. But since the worldwide conflict was not officially declared until 1756, it became known in Europe as the Seven Years' War.

The Albany Congress

While Washington and his men were returning from Fort Necessity, an important meeting was taking place in Albany, New York. The London government had summoned delegates from all the colonies from Virginia northward to meet with leaders of the Iroquois Confederacy. Officials in London knew that the various colonies would have to cooperate if there was renewed conflict with the French. They also regarded the Iroquois as crucial allies in any such war.

In Albany, the Iroquois leaders listened solemnly to the customary speeches of welcome and high regard and gravely accepted the usual gifts, which on this occasion were particularly generous. But they refused to make promises of support. They were aware of growing French power in the west and had no desire to back a losing cause.

At the Albany Congress, Benjamin Franklin and other delegates proposed a general "plan of union" for the mainland colonies. The plan provided for a grand council of representatives from all the colonies. The powers of the council would cover western lands and settlement, joint defense, and relations with the Indians. The council would have the power to raise taxes on its own. The presiding officer would be appointed by the king and have a veto over actions by the council.

The Albany delegates sent the plan to the various colonies for their approval. In every colony, it

This cartoon compared the squabbles of the colonies to the separated parts of a snake, warning that they must "Join, or die." (*Library of Congress*)

was rejected or ignored. The plan aimed to please all parties and ended up pleasing none. Authorities in London were relieved, for they had no desire to see the colonies united on a permanent basis. The various assemblies had no wish to share their taxation power, and many of them wanted to press their own claims in the west.

Fruits of Victory

After the Albany Congress, the government in London decided for the first time to send regular troops to the colonies. In the spring of 1755 General Edward Braddock arrived at the head of an impressive army of 1400 redcoats. Dinwiddie and Braddock planned a major expedition to destroy Fort Duquesne and drive the French from the Ohio country. The British troops were joined by 1000 colonial militiamen, but only eight Indian guides could be found. Together they marched off through western Maryland and then north into Pennsylvania toward the forks of the Ohio. It was the same route Washington had taken a year before.

Only eight miles south of the fort, they were suddenly ambushed and badly mauled by a combined force of French and Indians. Braddock was mortally wounded, and his army suffered nearly a thousand casualties. This stunning defeat shook the reputation of the British redcoats, and it also badly weakened the prestige of the British among the western Indians.

By 1756 the war that had started in the American wilderness spread over the continent of Europe. At first it went very badly for the British, both in Europe and America. Important forts in northern and western New York fell to French and Indian attacks. In 1758, however, a new chief minister took charge in London and within a year turned the conflict completely around. William Pitt subsidized German armies on the European continent, leaving Britain free to pursue the war on the sea and in America. For Pitt, the central objective was the conquest of Canada and the American interior. He used British superiority at sea to strike hardest at two focal points of French power: Louisburg and Quebec.

In 1758 the British recaptured Louisburg. The event was celebrated with great bonfires in London, Philadelphia, Boston, and New York. In the same year, George Washington had the satisfaction of taking part in the capture of Fort Duquesne. The climax of the fighting came in 1759, when the brilliant young General James Wolfe, after bringing a large army up the St. Lawrence from

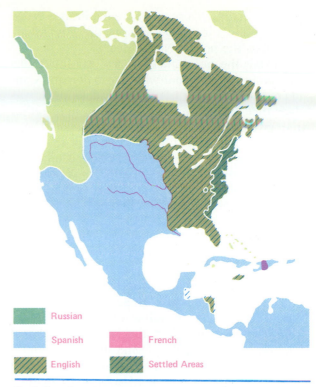

Russian

Spanish

English

French

Settled Areas

North America after the Treaty of Paris, 1763

Louisburg, stormed the Heights of Abraham outside Quebec and took the city from a smaller force under General Montcalm. Both Wolfe and Montcalm were killed in the battle, but Wolfe lived long enough to know that he had won Canada for the empire.

The next year, British troops captured Montreal. They continued a long string of victories at sea, in the West Indies, in India, and in the American West. "Some time ago," said Pitt in the middle of all these triumphs, "I would have been content to bring France to her knees, now I will not rest till I have laid her on her back." The war dragged on until 1763, but Britain's new young monarch, George III, was determined to bring it to an end. He fired Pitt and found ministers who were willing to make peace.

The Treaty of Paris (1763) was a general settlement of what had become a major world war. France ceded to Britain all of Canada and all the great interior east of the Mississippi River except the crucial port of New Orleans. Britain returned to France two captured islands in the West Indies—Martinique and Guadaloupe. France retained fishing rights and two small islands off the coast of Newfoundland. Spain surrendered East and West Florida to the British in exchange for Cuba, which the British had captured the year before. Finally, by a separate treaty, France ceded to Spain all its territories west of the Mississippi, as well as the port of New Orleans.

During the negotiations there was much discussion in Britain about whether to demand Canada or the rich sugar island of Guadaloupe. It was clear that France would continue to fight rather than give up both. That such a choice should have even been considered was evidence of the great value of the sugar plantations. The decision to ask for Canada resulted in large part from pressure by British owners of sugar plantations in colonies like Jamaica and Barbados. They had no wish for more competition. In addition, British merchants were beginning to realize that having colonies on the North American continent provided a growing market for their manufactured goods.

During the arguments over the proposed treaty, several British politicians suggested that someday Canada might revolt and win its independence from Great Britain. They also pointed out that if the French were expelled from Canada, the American colonists would no longer feel as dependent on Britain for protection. Benjamin Franklin, then in London as an agent for Pennsylvania, wrote a pamphlet on the subject in which he argued for retaining Canada as part of the British empire. Franklin brushed aside the idea of independence. If the North American colonists could not unite against the French and Indians, he asked, could they unite against "their own nation" which "they love much more than they love one another?" A union among the colonies, he went on, "is not merely improbable, it is impossible."

But Franklin went on to say: "When I say such a union is impossible, I mean without the most grievous tyranny and oppression." Few people knew it at the time, but some British officials were already considering new regulations for the American colonies. Whether these regulations would constitute "grievous tyranny and oppression" was, of course, a matter of opinion.

NEW IMPERIAL MEASURES

After the French and Indian War, Great Britain adopted certain policies toward the colonies that aroused great resentment. The colonists' major grievance was taxes—direct taxes laid upon them by Parliament. But other imperial policies angered various segments of the colonial population. Westerners and land speculators resented London's ideas about how to handle the Indians. Merchants were troubled by enforcement of the Navigation Acts and by new currency regulations. And when the British government decided to station regular troops in the colonies, many Americans grew suspicious about the intentions of the king's ministers.

Two factors added to the deepening sense of alienation many Americans felt. One was the instability of the English government. In the early years of his reign, beginning in 1760, George III could not find a chief minister who really satisfied him. The king was intensely patriotic and intelligent, but so unsure of himself that he dismissed ministers almost as fast as he named them. (The young monarch showed no signs yet of the insanity that surfaced some twenty-five years later, when he clambered down from his carriage in a London park and began an animated conversation with an oak tree.) At that time, the king had the right to choose a first minister, who then chose other members of Parliament to form a "ministry." For ten years various ministries came and went, and with them Britain's policies toward the colonies. No one could be sure whether today's policy would be reversed tomorrow.

Second, many colonists were extraordinarily suspicious about British intentions. When officials

King George III. (*National Portrait Gallery, London*)

in London proposed efficiency, officials in the colonies smelled attack. They had grown so attached to self-government that they were inclined, as a British statesman told the House of Commons, to "sniff the approach of tyranny in every tainted breeze."

Writs of Assistance

Rumblings of serious trouble in America were heard even before the end of the French and Indian War. From the start of the war, colonial merchants, with characteristic disregard for British policy, had traded with the enemy in Canada and in the West Indies. In 1760 Pitt's ministry ordered colonial governors to make greater efforts to enforce customs regulations. In Massachusetts, the center of illegal trade, royal customs collectors needed help to search the premises of merchants suspected of smuggling. They applied to the Superior Court of the colony for *writs of assistance* that would allow them to use police constables.

Writs of assistance had been in common use for a long time, both in Britain and America. Authorized by acts of Parliament, they had to be renewed each time a new sovereign came to the throne. When George II died in 1760, new writs had to be authorized in the name of George III. Some Massachusetts merchants took this opportunity to criticize the whole practice. They hired as counsel a brilliant but eccentric young Boston lawyer named James Otis.

Early in 1761, Otis appeared in court and delivered an astounding attack on these writs. John Adams, who was there, recalled years later: "Otis was a flame of fire! . . . he hurried away everything before him." Although the speech itself has been lost, we know that Otis rested his case on broad principles derived from John Locke and the Commonwealth writers. He claimed that the writs violated the people's rights of property, and that an act of Parliament contrary to natural law must be regarded as void. Parliament had no legal right, he said, to violate natural law either in Britain or in America.

Otis lost his case, and the writs were issued. But men in other colonies soon joined in the protest against their legality. And despite the pleas and threats of imperial customs officials, colonial judges often refused to grant them. Otis had established an important precedent, moreover, by basing his argument on the bedrock of natural rights.

Problems in the West

So long as France owned Canada, Americans were forced to rely on Britain for protection. The defeat of France removed one menace, but it failed to settle the colonists' relationship with the Indians.

Established fur traders in the thirteen colonies and in Canada wanted the West permanently reserved for Indian hunters and trappers. Newly influential land speculators, on the other hand, were urging settlers to go west; they wanted the Indians cleared out or "pacified." Both sides had powerful friends in Britain.

Colonial land speculators were particularly active in Pennsylvania and Virginia, and their claims often conflicted with one another, as well as with those of rivals abroad. Benjamin Franklin represented a group of wealthy Pennsylvanians interested in lands along the Ohio. One of the Virginia enterprises was promoted by George Washington, whose Mississippi Company, formed as a successor to the old Ohio Company, had its eye on thousands of acres at the junction of the Ohio and Mississippi rivers.

During the war, fearful of British expansionism, most of the northwestern Indian tribes had

The Proclamation of 1763

—— Proclamation line of 1763

chosen to ally themselves with the French. The victory of the British renewed their anxiety. Goaded by French traders who talked of the return of French power to North America, Indians in New York and Pennsylvania launched an attack on British forts. They were led by the Ottawa chief Pontiac. With the objective of sweeping the entire white population into the sea, Pontiac's followers destroyed seven of the nine British garrisons west of Niagara.

Soon after news of these attacks reached London, the government issued the royal Proclamation of 1763. It set boundaries for three new royal colonies: Quebec, East Florida, and West Florida. Most other western territory—from the Alleghenies to the Mississippi and from Florida to 50° north latitude—was reserved for the Indians. The Proclamation excluded all white fur traders, land speculators, and settlers. It was intended as a temporary measure to give Britain time to work out a permanent western policy, but it aroused the anger of the colonists.

No proclamation issued thousands of miles away could keep speculators and frontiersmen out. Many colonists agreed with George Washington when he urged that the Proclamation of 1763 be disobeyed: "I can never look upon that proclamation in any other light . . . than as a temporary expedient to quiet the minds of Indians. . . . Any person, therefore, who neglects the present opportunity of hunting out good lands, and in some measure marking and distinguishing them for his own (in order to keep others from settling them), will never regain it." Washington practiced what he preached. He and other land speculators sent agents into the Ohio Valley to stake out claims.

Opposition to the Proclamation of 1763 grew so strong that within a few years the British revised their western policy. They made a series of treaties with the Indians to give the speculators room. In each case the treaties pushed the map of English control farther westward, and before long the paper fence was in shreds. Every extension of the boundary line touched off new bursts of speculation. In 1768 the first settlers to penetrate the Blue Ridge barrier occupied the Watauga Valley of

Daniel Boone escorting settlers through the Cumberland Gap, 1851–52. (*Washington University Gallery of Art, Steinberg Hall*)

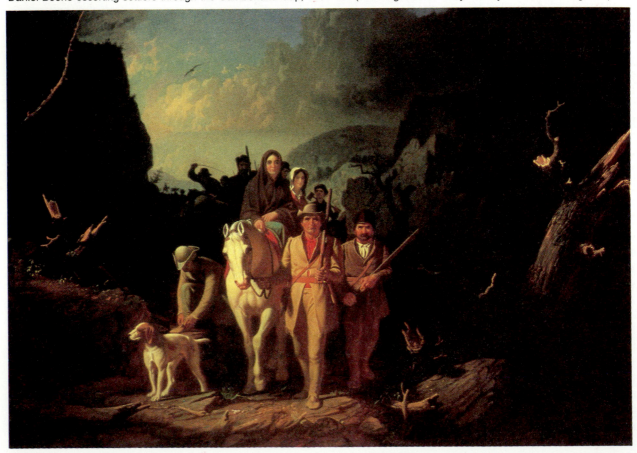

North Carolina. In 1769, having made his first trip west two years before, Daniel Boone crossed the future Wilderness Road through the Cumberland Gap into Kentucky. In 1775, he guided the first group of permanent settlers to the bluegrass region. As Americans moved deeper into the West, away from older centers of power, they became more and more determined to control their own destinies.

Discontent in Virginia

Britain's new policies caused strong resentment in Virginia, one of the most populous of all the colonies. By concentrating on one money-making crop, tobacco planters had depleted their best soil; cheap lands in the west seemed their only salvation. But land policy was only one source of planter discontent. British merchants served as middlemen for everything the planters bought or sold abroad, and British shipowners charged high rates for carrying the planters' produce and purchases across the ocean.

As the return from their lands dwindled, the planters' debts mounted. Thomas Jefferson once estimated that Virginia planters owed at least £2 million to British merchants and observed that these debts "had become hereditary from father to son, for many generations." Many planters grew concerned about their inability to finance their own agricultural expansion.

Troops and Taxation

The worst problem raised by the French and Indian War was taxation. Britain's long, costly struggles for empire had boosted tax rates so much that by 1763 British landowners were turning over about a third of their income to the government. Now the British had to face the cost of protecting their expanded possessions. Several bureaucrats estimated that 10,000 troops were needed for the colonies, and Parliament felt that the colonists should share the cost of their own protection.

There was also a more sinister motive behind the British plan to station regular troops in America. War veterans could be taken care of and a large army maintained without the distrust that would come if it were on home soil. As things turned out, colonial Americans had strong suspicions about what was then known as "a standing army at home."

The colonists had long since learned to manage their finances without British interference. They began to demand that the British solve their own financial crisis. For one thing, the colonies had piled up a war debt of £2.5 million. In addition, by Pitt's estimate, British merchants made profits of at least £2 million a year on colonial commerce. Such profits seemed to Americans, and to Pitt himself, to be "tax" enough. The very prosperity that made the colonists fair game to the British had given them the self-assurance to stand against Parliament.

The Sugar, Currency, and Quartering Acts

The task of handling postwar problems of imperial government and finance fell upon the ministry of George Grenville, who got his appointment chiefly because of his reputation as a fiscal expert. Grenville discovered that the American customs service cost four times as much as it was collecting. The Molasses Act of 1733 had imposed a duty of 6 pence per gallon on foreign-made molasses. Everyone knew that New England merchants were importing vast quantities of relatively cheap molasses from the French sugar islands without paying any duties. Grenville thought he saw a way of stopping the smuggling and increasing revenue. His instrument was the Sugar Act, which he pushed through Parliament in 1764.

The Sugar Act actually reduced the duty on foreign molasses, from 6 pence to 3. Previously merchants had been bribing customs officials at about 1 pence per gallon. Now bribery would be less profitable. In addition, the Sugar Act placed duties on many other essential imports. Finally, it provided new mechanisms of enforcement. Violations of the Sugar Act would be tried in admiralty courts.

Previously the colonists had successfully steered most smuggling cases into colonial courts with juries. The local people on those juries had been understanding, and acquittals were easy to obtain. Now violators would have to deal with courts presided over by unfriendly judges sent from England.

The Sugar Act provisions alarmed colonial merchants, and they and other colonists found the title and preamble downright ominous. Its official title was the Revenue Act, and the preamble stated that its purpose was to raise money in the colonies. Previously all taxes laid by Parliament had been passed for the purpose of regulating trade.

The Revenue Act would serve that aim, but it introduced the new and important principle that Parliament had the right to tax the colonies directly for the benefit of the British treasury.

George Grenville was a determined, precise, and energetic man, and he regarded the Sugar Act merely as one of several steps necessary to set colonial financial affairs in order. The next year he came up with still another means of getting the colonists to help pay for the cost of supporting British troops in America. The Quartering Act required any colony where troops were stationed to provide living quarters, certain supplies, and traditional rations of cider, beer, or rum. English law had many precedents for such requirements, but the colonists had never before been asked to support a standing army in their midst.

As part of his American revenue package, George Grenville persuaded Parliament to pass the Currency Act of 1764. Although the Currency Act did not get much attention at the time, it was actually a serious blow to merchants outside New England. In 1750 the New England colonies had been told not to issue paper money not backed by gold or silver; then in 1764 all the colonies were prohibited from printing money that could not be exchanged for either gold or silver. Because these two metals were scarce in the colonies, merchants everywhere found it difficult to pay their debts to English businessmen.

Grenville's measures had different effects in different colonies. The Quartering Act affected only those places where British troops were actually stationed. As things turned out, most British troops were stationed in New York. The Currency Act probably had the greatest impact on the colonial economy, but its effects were slow and not easy to detect. The Sugar Act received the most attention, since it seemed the most radical departure from previous practices and struck directly at the influential merchants' pocketbooks. It affected Boston more than any other colonial city, and the Boston town meeting reacted accordingly.

In written instructions to its representatives in the General Court, the town asked an ominous question: "If taxes are laid upon us in any shape without ever having a legal representation where they are laid, are we not reduced from the character of free subjects to the miserable state of tributary slaves?" James Otis wrote a pamphlet that declared flatly, "No parts of his Majesty's dominions can be taxed without their consent." The Massachusetts General Court appointed a "Committee of correspondence" to write to other provinces about the Sugar Act.

The Stamp Act Crisis

When Grenville announced the Sugar Act, he also announced that his ministry was preparing still another revenue measure. This was the Stamp Act, passed by Parliament in March 1765. The act required that a tax stamp (ranging in value from a halfpenny to £10) be purchased and placed on all legal documents, licenses, newspapers, pamphlets, almanacs, playing cards, and dice. The Stamp Act also provided that violators be tried in admiralty courts. To provide time for printing the stamps and shipping them to special distributors in the colonies, the new duties were scheduled to take effect on November 1. A few members of Parliament warned that the colonists would resist such a tax, but similar duties had been levied before in England, and the Stamp Act passed overwhelmingly. Grenville settled back to wait for the money to come in.

He never got any: No stamps were ever bought or used in the colonies. The moment word of the Stamp Act arrived, there was an outburst of protest and defiance. The colonial assemblies took the first steps. In Virginia, a fiery young lawyer named Patrick Henry took the floor of the assembly to offer a set of resolutions. The house adopted several which took the position that Virginians could be taxed only by the Virginia assembly, but it rejected others that called for outright disobedience. Newspapers picked up both sets of resolu-

Patrick Henry (1736–99). (*National Portrait Gallery, Smithsonian Institution, Washington, D.C. 20560*)

THE IMPORTANCE OF INFORMATION

One astute observer of the prerevolutionary crisis was profoundly impressed by the impact and importance of the printed word. As he described it, he saw

. . . a spectacle never before displayed among man, and even yet without a parallel on earth. It is the spectacle, not of the learned and the wealthy only, but of the great body of the people; even a large portion of that class of the community which is destined to daily labor, having free and constant access to public prints, receiving regular information of every occurrence, attending to the course of political affairs, discussing public measures, and having thus presented to them constant excitement to the acquisition of knowledge, and continual means of obtaining it. Never, it may be safely asserted, was the number of political journals so great in proportion to the population of a country as at present in ours. Never were they, all things considered, so cheap, so universally diffused, so easy of access.

---

tions and printed them as if they had all been passed. Other colonial assemblies rejected the more radical position and modeled their own resolutions on Virginia's more moderate ones. They simply denied the right of Parliament to tax the colonists.

The assemblies took a truly crucial step by deciding on joint protest. In June, the Massachusetts General Court called upon the other assemblies to name delegates to a congress to meet in New York City for the purpose of asserting the rights of British-Americans. Delegates from nine colonies met there in October. (Several colonies had been prevented by their royal governors from selecting delegates.) The Stamp Act Congress quickly agreed on a Declaration of Rights and Grievances.

It began by acknowledging "all due subordination" to the crown and Parliament, but went on to claim that the people of the colonies could be taxed only by their elected representatives. Only people chosen by themselves could represent the colonists, and "the people of these colonies are not, and from their local circumstances cannot be, represented in the House of Commons in Great Britain." No taxes could ever be rightly imposed on the colonies by Parliament. Nor could Parliament expand the jurisdiction of admiralty courts beyond their traditional limits. The declaration closed by demanding repeal of both the Sugar Act and the Stamp Act. It seemed to the colonists that Grenville was trying to deny them their rights as freeborn Englishmen.

The colonists' position was clear and consistent. For them, the matter was one of rights, principles, and common sense. To tax a man was to take away his property, to which he had a natural right. It could be rightly taken from him only if he consented, and the only way he could give his consent was to elect his own representatives. The colonial assemblies were the only bodies which represented the people of the colonies, and therefore they were the only bodies which could rightfully tax them. All this was simple and obvious. The phrase "no taxation without representation" was therefore more than a slogan. So far as the colonists were concerned, it described the heart of the relationship between government and the people.

The British rejected the American position by advancing the old idea of "virtual representation." The colonists, they argued, were represented in Parliament because members of Parliament were elected to represent all English people everywhere. The people of such large English cities as Birmingham and Manchester, they pointed out, sent no representatives to Parliament but were represented by members elected by other localities. So too with the colonists, who elected no one to Parliament but were "virtually" represented there by its current membership.

As far as most Americans were concerned, virtual representation was no representation at all. If some English cities were not permitted to elect anyone to Parliament, they should be. A representative, the colonists claimed, had to be *elected by the people he represented*. He should live among his constituents and be responsive to their interests.

The colonial argument had one flaw. Even before the Stamp Act crisis, it had been suggested that the colonists elect representatives to Parliament, but the idea got nowhere. Both sides recognized that the Atlantic was a real barrier to effective representation. The British were not anxious to press the matter because they sensed that any discussion might well open the whole question of the lack of representation *within* England. The Americans were even less anxious to open the question. They knew that any fair representation of the colonies in Parliament would be very small in comparison to the total of English

The Bostonians paying the excise man or Tarring and Feathering. (*Library of Congress*)

members. The colonists would probably always be outvoted. They sensed that their own interests were much better served by the local assemblies.

By the time of the Stamp Act Congress in October, some colonists were willing to go far beyond passing resolutions. That summer, secret organizations began forming in the port cities. Calling themselves Sons of Liberty, these self-appointed groups were composed largely of shopkeepers, artisans, and laborers, but they were often led by gentlemen of property and social standing. They aimed at defending American liberties by making sure that no stamps were distributed.

In August a shouting mob of Bostonians burned the records of the admiralty court, ransacked the house of stamp distributor Andrew Oliver, and called for his resignation or his head. The next day Oliver was forced to read his resignation aloud before a jeering, cheering crowd. Similar mobs assembled in other cities, and they proved remarkably effective without actually killing anyone. By the fateful day of November 1, every stamp agent in the colonies had been forced to resign or prom-

ise not to issue any stamps.

Rioting in colonial cities was not altogether new; there had been riots against British navy press gangs during the wars against the French. But the Stamp Act riots were a new kind of demonstration: they were well-organized, frequently led by citizens of wealth and standing, and aimed at a clear political objective. Here was a new form of politics. Like the crowds of the Great Awakening, the crowds of the 1760s worked outside traditional institutions. In doing so, they established a new mode of public expression that was to surface again and again at times of crisis in American history.

This development coincided with and was connected to a similar development in England. There, mob action swirled about the person and name of John Wilkes, a clever, unstable agitator. In 1763 Wilkes came crashing onto the public stage by criticizing Lord Bute, an intimate friend of George III who pressed through the Treaty of Paris. Wilkes's remarks were published in number 45 of a magazine called *North Briton,* and he

John Wilkes. (*British Crown copyright; reproduced by the kind permission of the Rt. Hon. Mr. Speaker of the House of Commons*)

was arrested for libel. His career turned into a dizzying round of trials, jailings, flight abroad, election to Parliament, and later lord mayor of London. Wilkes successfully equated himself with the cause of liberty at home and in the colonies, and the colonists made him a popular hero. "Wilkes and Liberty" became a common rallying cry in America, and the number 45 an almost sacred symbol.

After the Stamp Act Congress, hundreds of merchants signed agreements not to buy British goods until the act was repealed. When the Stamp Act went into force on November 1, 1765, merchants suspended business in protest. They resumed trading at the end of the year, but without using stamps. By then, Grenville had been fired after a quarrel with George III about the king's mother. The new ministry under the Marquis of Rockingham faced opposition not only in America, but from merchants at home who were feeling the pinch of the American boycott.

Parliament reluctantly repealed the Stamp Act on March 17, 1766. Rockingham realized it was both unwise and unenforceable. William Pitt was one of the few members of Parliament to think that it was, as he put it, "founded on an erroneous principle." Most members regarded taxation of the colonists as entirely fair. On the day of repeal they voted overwhelmingly for a Declaratory Act which asserted that Parliament had the full right to make laws "to bind the colonies and people of America . . . in all cases whatsoever." In the colonies, news of repeal was greeted with the tolling of bells and joyous celebrations. The colonists were so happy about their victory that they scarcely noticed the Declaratory Act.

The Townshend Acts

Several months after repeal of the Stamp Act, Rockingham's ministry went the way of Grenville's. The king recalled William Pitt, now the Earl of Chatham, to form a new ministry. But Pitt, by far the ablest of British statesmen, soon became so ill with gout that he was forced to retire temporarily. Control of the government fell into the hands of the Chancellor of the Exchequer, Charles Townshend, a dashing man of great energy and little sense.

During the Stamp Act crisis Townshend had been led by American arguments to believe the colonists would accept revenue-raising acts if they were presented as traditional "external" trade regulation, rather than as "internal" taxes. In 1767, on his recommendation, Parliament passed the Townshend Acts, imposing new import duties on glass, lead, paints, paper, and tea. These duties were labeled regulations of trade, but in fact they made little sense according to traditional mercantilist principles because they taxed manufactured goods sent to the colonies from the mother country.

In addition, the Townshend Acts reasserted the legitimacy of writs of assistance and placed enforcement in the hands of admiralty courts. They also provided for a new means of enforcement, a Board of Customs Commissioners to be located in Boston, a city which by this time had the reputation of being the principal nest of smuggling and tax resistance in the colonies. The Townshend Acts also provided that customs officials would be paid out of fines levied by the admiralty courts—a sure recipe for official corruption.

And as part of his entire program, Townshend included an act to settle the disputes over the Quartering Act. Because New York's assembly had refused to vote supplies for British troops, the act voided all the assembly's new laws until it provided suitable quarters and rations.

The American response to the Townshend Acts followed a somewhat different pattern than during the Stamp Act crisis in 1765. The new duties lacked the symbolic impact of the hated tax stamps. And this time merchants were more directly affected than anyone else. They revived the technique of boycotting imports from England. The nonimportation movement gathered strength month after month. As with all boycotts, there was great difficulty in gaining everyone's cooperation. If merchants in one port agreed on nonimportation, other merchants in neighboring ports were tempted to continue business as usual.

The Sons of Liberty made a three-pronged attack on this problem. They visited offending merchants and talked persuasively about the rights of the colonies. They also pointed out the dangers of not going along. In addition, the Sons of Liberty mounted a campaign in the newspapers to persuade the public to give up British-made luxuries. They sang the virtues of homespun cloth and the life of domestic simplicity. In doing so they touched the feelings of the populace as a whole. Simplicity and hard work had long been regarded as virtues by a people with a Calvinist outlook on life; now these traditional virtues could serve the cause of liberty.

As nonimportation grew more and more effective, some colonists grew busy with their pens. Pennsylvania's John Dickinson published a series of *Letters from a Farmer in Pennsylvania* which gained a wide audience through the newspapers. Dickinson denounced the Townshend duties as a violation of the unwritten constitution of the British empire. He admitted that Parliament had the right to regulate trade with taxes. These taxes might even result in some revenue. But taxes imposed for the purpose of raising money for the English treasury were another matter. They were no more acceptable in the form of import duties than in the form of stamps. Dickinson also pointed out that if Parliament could shut down the New York assembly, it could shut down others.

DEEPENING CRISIS

In Boston a clever agitator took advantage of the Townshend Acts. Samuel Adams was a Bostonian who had failed in the brewery business but then turned with great success to local politics. Adams saw every new British measure as evidence of tyranny. For several years he was successful at sustaining a high level of public indignation and even at establishing a network of cooperation among the thirteen colonies. In the early 1770s, however, British policies seemed to most Americans much less oppressive than during the previous decade.

Trouble in Massachusetts

Not long after publication of Dickinson's *Letters*, the Massachusetts General Court sent a circular letter to the other colonial assemblies. The actual author was Sam Adams. Using the Boston town meeting as his power base, Adams was rapidly building a career as a professional patriot and popular agitator. With the Massachusetts circular letter, Adams played his cards beautifully. Its tone angered the British, who ordered all colonial governors to dissolve their assemblies if they attempted to endorse it. This was exactly what Adams hoped would happen.

By the time these orders were received, three other colonies had endorsed the Massachusetts letter, and Virginia's assembly had produced one of its own. The ministry had specifically instructed Governor Francis Bernard of Massachusetts to dissolve the General Court if it failed to repeal the letter. On June 30, 1768, the General Court voted 92 to 17 not to rescind. The next day Bernard dissolved the house, and the numbers 92 and 17 promptly joined 45 in the colonists' vocabulary of liberty.

The atmosphere in Boston was further heated by the activities of the new customs commissioners. They would have been resented whatever they did, for neither smugglers nor legitimate merchants liked to pay taxes, and few people welcomed the arrival of a swarm of bureaucrats. Here were men who came with power to line their own pockets by prosecutions in admiralty courts.

And the customs officials proved to be far from saintly. The provisions of the Sugar Act and the Townshend duties furnished them with perfect tools for trapping the most innocent merchants in a snare of red tape. Shippers had to post bonds and fill out long forms concerning their cargoes and destinations. It was easy to file the wrong form or the right form in the wrong way; many "violations" were possible. Some were punishable by seizure of the entire cargo and the ship as well.

Abuses by customs officials were numerous, but one incident became notorious. The sloop *Liberty* belonging to a wealthy merchant named John Hancock was tied up at one of the Boston wharves, when word got out that Madeira wine was aboard. Hancock thought he owed no duty, but some customs officials decided he did. They ordered the *Liberty* seized and towed out to anchor beside a British warship in the harbor. Crowds assembled on the wharf and outside the commissioners' homes. As things turned out there was no real violence, but the incident had important results.

For his part, John Hancock's feeling for American liberty deepened considerably; he became something of a popular hero in Massachusetts. The commissioners were badly shaken and went to Castle William on an island in Boston harbor. From there they wrote London (not actually for the first time) requesting that troops be sent for their protection.

The Boston Massacre

Rumors about the possible arrival of British troops ran through Boston during that summer of 1768, and Sam Adams and other Sons of Liberty talked up the idea of active resistance. Two well-equipped regiments did finally arrive in late September, headed by General Thomas Gage. As the redcoats marched in, the townspeople watched with apprehension and resentment. But there was no violence. A Boston silversmith and engraver sat down to sketch the arrival of British soldiers in a peaceful Anglo-American town. His name was Paul Revere.

In looking back, it is easy to see that the arrival of British soldiers in Boston was an important turning point in relations between the American colonies and Great Britain. For more than a cen-

John Singleton Copley's portrait of Paul Revere remembers him as a silversmith and craftsman. He also cast cannon for the army and designed the state seal still used by Massachusetts. (*Courtesy, Museum of Fine Arts, Boston*)

Paul Revere's drawing of "The Bloody Massacre" in Boston. (*Library of Congress*)

tury, Englishmen in England and elsewhere had regarded a standing army at home in peacetime as a threat to their liberties. They almost automatically thought of the dictatorship of Oliver Cromwell after the English civil wars and the threat of oppression by James II before the Glorious Revolution. All the history they knew gave evidence that troops were the spearheads of tyranny.

It seems remarkable that British redcoats lived in Boston for eighteen months before a serious incident occurred. The British found the town both dull and hostile. A major cause of friction was competition for jobs between local laborers and redcoats looking for work in off-duty hours. On the afternoon of March 5, 1770, a fistfight broke out over this issue. That evening a mob gathered in front of the customshouse, where ten armed British soldiers stood guard outside. Someone threw something at the soldiers, and soon the air was filled with snowballs, garbage, and pieces of manure. For a while, the frustrated soldiers simply stood their ground, but finally they sent a volley of musketfire into the crowd. Five of the rioters were killed and six others wounded. To head off further clashes, Lieutenant Governor Thomas

Hutchinson ordered the troops to islands in the harbor. They remained there for the next four years.

Samuel Adams immediately labeled this incident a "massacre" and made certain that it received wide publicity throughout the colonies. John Adams defended the soldiers in court. The civilian dead, he said later, were among "the most obscure and inconsiderable [men] . . . upon this continent." Adams contended they were not even genuine Bostonians, but outsiders looking for trouble. In fact, the five victims had all been artisans or seamen, and one of them, Crispus Attucks, was a mulatto.

Adam's plea won acquittal on the murder charge. Two soldiers, found guilty of manslaughter, were released after minor punishment. But the "massacre" itself became a favorite theme for oratory, pamphleteering, and another famous engraving by Paul Revere. At the same time, the nonimportation movement proved increasingly effective as colonial trade with Britain fell off by a third.

Samuel Adams by J. S. Copley. (*Courtesy, Museum of Fine Arts, Boston*)

Relative Quiet

In the meantime, events in England were moving in a more peaceful direction. When Charles Townshend died, George III finally found a chief minister he could get along with. The ministry of Lord North began in January 1770, and lasted for twelve years. King George and Lord North understood each other largely because they were rather alike. Both were hardworking English patriots but lacking in imagination.

North realized that the Townshend Acts were costing much more to enforce than they would ever bring in. English merchants were complaining loudly about the colonial boycott of their goods. So Lord North called upon Parliament to repeal all the duties except the one on tea. He saw two obvious reasons for retaining this one tax. Americans drank a lot of tea and seemed willing to pay a good price for it. More important, continuation of this tax would maintain the principle of Parliament's power to tax the colonists. Parliament did as North asked in April 1770.

When word reached the colonies, the nonimportation movement collapsed. Sam Adams and the Sons of Liberty in other cities tried to keep the boycott alive, but they had no success. In the early days of the boycott, many merchants had found that nonimportation permitted them to sell off goods from already well-stocked warehouses. At

first, profit and patriotism had dovetailed very nicely. As time went on, however, and stocks ran low, merchants found it increasingly costly to support their political principles. They therefore happily abandoned nonimportation when they learned of Lord North's concessions. Business boomed. The political atmosphere became more relaxed than at any time since word of the Sugar Act had arrived in 1764.

This relative quiet lasted for three years, even though there were incidents which Sam Adams and other agitators tried to take advantage of. In 1772, for example, word arrived that the salaries of Massachusetts judges would now be paid by the crown rather than by the colony. Adams decided that Lord North's ministry was trying to place the judges under its thumb, and he publicly announced that Americans would soon become "as complete slaves as the inhabitants of Turkey or Japan." At that time, all Englishmen regarded those countries as having no freedoms at all.

Adams also made the most of a more serious incident that year in Rhode Island. For months the British customs schooner *Gaspee* had been harassing colonial vessels on Narragansett Bay, boarding them to see if they were smuggling goods. Sailors from the *Gaspee* went ashore and cut down fruit trees for firewood and stole pigs and chickens. On June 9 the *Gaspee* ran aground while pursuing a local vessel. That night eight boatloads of men rowed out from Providence to the stranded schooner, boarded the vessel, wounded its captain, removed its crew, and burned it.

Several of the attackers were prominent merchants, but their identities were not known to British authorities. When word reached London, Lord North's ministers quite correctly concluded that no convictions could be obtained from local juries in Rhode Island courts. The king named a special commission to seek out the guilty and bring them back to England for trial.

The plan to drag colonial Americans to England for trial aroused widespread suspicion and hostility in the colonies. Rather than call a congress, as the assemblies had done at the time of the Stamp Act, they set up more permanent machinery for cooperation. The assemblies of Massachusetts and Virginia were the first to appoint "committees of correspondence" to communicate with other colonies about threats to American liberties. By February 1774 most colonies had established such committees. They were unofficial in the sense that the governors had nothing to do with their formation; the various assemblies simply appointed several members to serve as a committee. By doing so the assemblies established a network among the colonies entirely outside the framework of imperial government.

TOWARD CONCORD AND LEXINGTON

In the early months of 1773, very few American colonists realized they were on the verge of war with Great Britain. Only a handful had the faintest idea about the possibility of American independence. But as often happens, a single and apparently trivial decision in one place started a chain of events that led to outright conflict in another. People in the thirteen colonies rapidly came to realize that they had to establish a united front against Great Britain. In doing so they fell back upon their previous experience at the time of the Stamp Act, on their representative assemblies, and on their commitment to ideas about English liberties and natural rights.

Tea and the Intolerable Acts

In those same months, Lord North found himself dealing with a problem that arose halfway around the world from the American colonies. The East India Company was teetering on the brink of bankruptcy. The company was a gigantic private business to which the British government had given a monopoly on trade with India and the responsibility for governing English territories there. Largely because the company had become riddled with corruption and mismanagement, its warehouses were bulging with 17 million pounds of unsold tea. North had to save the East India Company or watch Britain's imperial ambitions in India go down the drain.

He chose to push the Tea Act through Parliament in an attempt to save the company by helping it to get rid of its surplus in the American colonies. He had no idea that the act would arouse a storm of protest. Previously tea had been purchased at auction in London and then sold through a series of middlemen in the colonies. North's new act gave the East India Company a monopoly on the colonial tea market and thus would provide the colonists with cheaper tea by eliminating the middlemen's profits. So far so good. But North forgot about the possible reaction of established tea merchants in the colonies and the fact that the

WORDS AND NAMES IN AMERICAN HISTORY

The word *boss*, which is of course both a noun and a verb, comes originally from the Dutch *baas*, which was the rough equivalent of the English word *master*. Over the years in the American colonies and states the word underwent some interesting transformations, aside from the change in spelling. The term took on stronger suggestions of social and political and even physical power than the English *master*. Thus one could master the skill of carpentry but not boss it; on the other hand, factory managers could boss their workers but not necessarily master them. The term *master* is closely associated with *mastery*, with a skill, while the word *boss* suggests personal power. Thus we have political bosses, and even prison bosses,—the term carries a faint whiff of illegitimacy. In the army, we have master sergeants, not boss sergeants, although master sergeants boss privates around. And the American system of higher education commonly offers two degrees, one of which, the M.A., stands for Master of Arts, and the other, the B.A., does *not* stand for Boss of Arts, no matter how well deserved.

colonists might not like a quasi-government monopoly controlling a highly valued import.

When news of the Tea Act arrived in the colonies, mass protest meetings were held in most colonial ports. Tea agents of the East India Company were persuaded to resign, much like the Stamp Act commissioners nearly eight years before. Tea ships were turned back or the tea unloaded and placed in warehouses unsold. In Boston, however, Governor Thomas Hutchinson decided the act would have to be obeyed. He refused to let the tea ships clear the harbor without first discharging their cargoes. (Hutchinson, a high-minded, aristocratic native of Massachusetts, was devoted to the cause of established authority. This commitment had made him enormously unpopular; in this case his position was weakened by the fact that two of his sons and a nephew were newly appointed tea agents.) On the evening of December 16, 1773, a well-organized group of Bostonians disguised themselves as Indians, boarded the tea ships, broke open the tea boxes with hatchets, and tossed them overboard into the waters of Boston harbor.

Many colonists thought the Boston men had gone too far. After all, those "Indians" had destroyed private property, and Americans had been busy defending property rights for ten years. Their minds changed very rapidly, however, when they learned of Lord North's reaction to the "Boston Tea Party."

Lord North and the king took aim at Boston and Massachusetts. North easily got Parliament to pass a series of measures that came to be known in the colonies as the Intolerable (or Coercive) Acts. The Port of Boston was closed until the East India Company and the customs service were paid for their losses. Royal officials charged with a capital crime would be tried in England rather than in the colonies. The Massachusetts council was to be appointed by the crown rather than elected by the General Court. Judges and sheriffs who had previously been elected by the people were now to be appointed by the royal governor. Town meetings were to be held only when called by the governor.

Finally, a new Quartering Act authorized military commanders to house their men in private homes as well as in barracks. The Quartering Act applied to all the colonies, but British authorities made clear where it was aimed. The troops stationed on islands in Boston harbor were reinforced and brought into the city itself. General Thomas Gage, commander of all British troops in the colonies, was appointed the new governor of Massachusetts.

While pressing through this legislation, Parliament also passed the Quebec Act, a law that had nothing to do with the situation in Boston. But the timing and the provisions of the Quebec Act seemed as "intolerable" and "coercive" to the colonists as any of the others. The Quebec Act provided the first civilian government for the conquered French province of Canada. As a concession to the traditions of the French inhabitants, the new government was to have no representative assembly, and court cases were to be tried by judges rather than juries. The Roman Catholic Church was given a privileged position.

In London, all these provisions seemed like a generous way of treating a conquered people. In the thirteen colonies, however, they appeared as an ominous new form of colonial government and a cowardly concession to followers of the Pope. Worse still, the Quebec Act enlarged that province to include all the territory north of the Ohio River, ignoring the land claims of Virginia, Pennsylvania, and other colonies.

The First Continental Congress

The reaction of the colonists to the Intolerable Acts was very different from what Lord North and the king expected. They had hoped to isolate Massachusetts by singling it out for special punishment. Instead, their actions drove the colonies together. People in other cities collected supplies to send to the suffering residents of Boston. Illegal conventions met in one colony after another. For the most part these conventions were composed of men who a few weeks before had been sitting as members of the colony's legislative assembly. They debated whether to try the strategy of nonimportation again, but most of them felt that events had moved beyond such measures.

The various committees of correspondence worked at keeping each other informed and at coordinating some kind of joint effort. At the urging of the Massachusetts General Court, they agreed at last that each colonial convention should name delegates to a "continental" congress in Philadelphia in September 1774. The congress that assembled on September 5 in Philadelphia represented only twelve colonies, for the royal governor of Georgia, James Wright, had outmaneuvered all attempts to send delegates.

THE FARMINGTON RESOLVES

At the outset, the delegates made a crucial decision: They decided that they represented individual colonies rather than the colonists in general. As a result, they agreed to count their votes by colony rather than by individuals. The delegates from Rhode Island and North Carolina would have equal voting power with those from far more populous colonies like Massachusetts, Pennsylvania, and Virginia.

The First Continental Congress then agreed to endorse several resolutions which had been adopted by a meeting of town delegates in Suffolk County in eastern Massachusetts. The Suffolk Resolves denounced the Intolerable Acts and asked the colonies to raise troops and suspend trade with the rest of the empire. After this show of support for Massachusetts, the delegates considered a plan of union proposed by one of their most cautious and conservative members, Joseph Galloway of Pennsylvania.

The Galloway Plan was for a grand council of all the colonies to share power with Parliament. Each body would be able to veto the actions of the other concerning colonial matters. Galloway's plan ran into heavy opposition, especially from New England delegates, who objected to any arrangement that might curtail the powers of the colonial assemblies, and it was voted down.

Defeat of the Galloway Plan showed how far the thinking of many colonists had shifted since the Stamp Act crisis of 1765. The colonists began by denying Parliament's right to tax them. Now a majority of those at the First Continental Congress denied that Parliament had the right to pass any sort of laws for the colonies. The Congress did admit, however, that Parliament could regulate trade by means of moderate customs duties. In effect, its members asked that the clock be turned back eleven years to the situation that had prevailed until 1763.

Yet the delegates were well aware that they were dealing with a new kind of political crisis. They were determined to establish mechanisms for combatting the Intolerable Acts. They set up a Continental Association to enforce a real boycott of British imported goods; the association would enforce not only nonimportation, but nonexportation as well. With that aim in mind, the Congress called upon every colonial assembly to appoint local committees which would publish the names of all violators of the boycott as "enemies of American liberty." Within months, local "committees of safety" were in operation in most of the colonies.

Before adjourning on October 26, the Continental Congress agreed to meet again in May 1775 unless American grievances were fully met. As they cast their ballots, the delegates were well aware that the countryside around Boston was becoming a powder keg that could explode at any moment.

Painting by Amos Doolittle of the outbreak of war on Lexington green on April 19, 1775. (*Museum of Art, Carnegie Institute, Pittsburgh*)

War

Many people in the towns of eastern New England felt encouraged by the Continental Congress to proceed with military preparations. Special units of their militias prepared to assemble at a minute's notice, and these "minutemen" began stockpiling firearms and gunpowder. In Boston, General Gage found out about these activities and began writing London for more men. On April 14 he received a letter (dated January 27) ordering him to attack the rebellious minutemen with the soldiers he had. He immediately prepared to strike at Concord, 21 miles northwest of Boston, where informants told him there was a large collection of arms.

General Gage realized he could not conceal his preparations, since he had to bring in longboats from anchored warships in order to ferry his men across the Charles River. On the night of April 18, 700 British soldiers set out for Concord. Paul Revere and two other American riders rode off to spread word of the intended destination. The countryside rang with churchbells and gunshots— prearranged signals sent from one town to the next.

The first British troops reached Lexington, five

miles short of Concord, at dawn. There they found about 70 minutemen drawn up on the village green. The commanding British officer ordered them to lay down their guns and disperse. The Americans began to do so but without putting down their arms. Someone fired a shot—no one knows who—and the redcoats sent a volley into the dispersing militiamen. Eight were killed.

The British troops then pressed on to Concord, which they reached at about 8 A.M. There they drove off a small group of minutemen and searched for the supposed store of arms, but all that remained were a few gun carriages, digging tools, some flour, and a stripped tree—a "liberty pole" the Americans had erected to celebrate their cause. After burning this disappointing collection of objects, the redcoats regrouped in a thin column for the march back to Boston. They knew they had still another 20 miles to go with their heavy packs and muskets, but they did not know they were about to become involved in a kind of battle none of them had ever experienced.

The entire day's march was a disaster. The road to Boston seemed to be lined with riflemen who fired from behind trees and stone walls. In fact, some three to four thousand armed New England farmers had assembled in about twelve hours. The redcoats fell by the dozens, and only the arrival of reinforcements from Boston saved them from complete defeat. As it was, they suffered nearly four times as many casualties as the farmers they had always held in such contempt. Exhausted, humiliated, and bewildered, the British soldiers struggled back into Boston that night. They were probably too tired to notice that the surrounding hills were dotted with the campfires of colonial Englishmen who had somehow become their enemies.

SUMMARY

The American Revolution had its seeds in the long war between France and England from 1756 to 1763. This conflict began in America and then spread to Europe, unlike those that had preceded it. American militia fought in this war, alongside regular British troops sent to the colonies for the first time. The Treaty of Paris, which settled what had been a major world war, gave Britain all of Canada and the interior lands east of the Mississippi River except for New Orleans, plus Florida. Spain got from France all its lands west of the Mississippi, plus the port of New Orleans.

The Seven Years' War changed the balance of power in America. The British were now in command—but they were also in debt; the war had been expensive. Royal officials thought the colonists should help pay at least some of the expenses of empire—in particular, those of their own defense. London's vehicle was new taxes, which Americans very much resented. They also resented the western land policy of the Proclamation of 1763, the use of writs of assistance to enforce the Navigation Acts, the new currency regulations, and the stationing of British troops in the colonies at the colonists' expense.

Colonial leaders began to talk to one another about these developments, and a new network of communication—the committees of correspondence—came into being. The colonists focused on the question of taxation without representation. The first real crisis came with the Stamp Act of 1765, which the colonists refused outright to obey. No stamps were ever bought or used in the colonies. At a Stamp Act Congress in October 1765, delegates from nine colonies met and drew up a Declaration of Rights and Grievances demanding repeal of two tax acts: the Sugar Act and the Stamp Act. Groups called Sons of Liberty began to enforce the protest by mob action and riots.

Repeal of the Stamp Act in March 1766 brought the colonists joy, but within a few months the king's new chief minister, Charles Townshend, managed to enrage them once again. The Townshend Acts, passed by Parliament in 1767, imposed new import duties on manufactured goods sent to the colonies from the mother country, reaffirmed the use of writs of assistance, and put enforcement in the hands of admiralty courts. A Board of Customs Commissioners was to be sent to Boston, the center of resistance. Assemblies that refused to pay for British troops stationed in their colonies had the laws they passed declared null and void. The American response to Townshend's program was nonimportation—a boycott of British goods—plus a widespread and effective propaganda campaign.

For three years after the so-called Boston Massacre

of March 1770, there was relative quiet. The Townshend Acts were repealed, except for the tax on tea, and the colonists relaxed their suspicions about what the British really meant to do. But then in 1773 a new crisis arose concerning—of all things—tea. Passage of the Tea Act, followed by the Boston Tea Party, brought retaliation in the form of the Intolerable Acts. But to the surprise of the British—and perhaps of the colonists themselves—instead of isolating the troublemakers in Massachusetts, the new laws united the colonists.

The First Continental Congress met in September 1774 to find effective ways to combat British policies. Other colonists, especially in New England, began to stockpile firearms and train militia. In the spring of 1775, British troops quartered in Boston had their first skirmishes with colonial minutemen. Without anyone quite realizing it, and with the colonists never intending it, the American Revolution had begun.

Suggested Readings

The great international conflict Americans have called the French and Indian War has not received the treatment it deserves. One of the best beginnings is a biography: J. Schutz, *William Shirley: King's Governor of Massachusetts* (1961). H. Peckam, *The Colonial Wars, 1689–1762* (1964), is succinct; the thirteen volumes of L. Gibson, *The British Empire before the American Revolution* (1936–67), contain a great deal of interesting information. The perspective of the Indians during that war is examined by G. Nash in *Red, White, and Black* (1974). A truly fresh approach is taken by F. Anderson in *A People's Army: Massachusetts Soldiers and Society in the Seven Years' War* (1984).

A number of works deal with the Revolution as a whole. E. Morgan, *The Birth of the Republic, 1763–1789* (1956), gives a pro-patriot view. D. Lacy, *Meaning of the American Revolution* (1964), a well-balanced short survey, carries the story through to the adoption of the Constitution. An English author, E. Wright, has written another good survey, *Fabric of Freedom, 1763–1800* (1961). H. Aptheker, *The American Revolution, 1763–1783* (1960), gives a Marxist interpretation. The best place to gain a sense of the wide variety of historical interpretations on the subject is J. P. Greene, *The Reinterpretation of the American Revolution, 1763–1776* (1968). The most recent synthesis is grounded in a wide variety of sources: R. Middlekauff, *The Glorious Cause: The American Revolution* (1982), which is especially useful also for the next two chapters. There are other good studies with differing points of view, such as M. Jensen, *The Founding of a Nation: A History of the American Revolution, 1763–1776* (1968); E. Robson, *The American Revolution, 1763–1783* (1955); and M. Smelser, *The Winning of Independence* (1972). R. Palmer, *The Age of Democratic Revolution: A Political History of Europe and America, 1760–1800* (1959), places the American revolt in the context of the upheavals then occurring in Europe.

Some of the very best books about the Revolution have been concerned with ideology. B. Bailyn, *The Ideological Origins of the American Revolution* (1967), stresses the colonists' near paranoia over what they regarded as Britain's conspiratorial intentions. R. Merritt, *Symbols of American Community, 1735–1775* (1966), an intriguing analysis of the press during this period, attempts to discover when Americans began to think of themselves as such. A superb original study is R. Bloch, *Visionary Republic: Millennial Themes in American Thought, 1756–1800* (1986).

Many other books focus on political events. A. Schlesinger, *Colonial Merchants and the American Revolution, 1763–1776* (1918), emphasizes the conflict between wealthy conservatives and the more radical common folk. C. Bridenbaugh, *Cities in Revolt: Urban Life in America, 1743–1776* (1955), catalogues many aspects of American material and cultural life in those little towns. E. and H. Morgan, *The Stamp Act Crisis: Prologue to Revolution* (1953), and B. Labaree, *The Boston Tea Party* (1964), focus on two key crises. For the maneuvering on the British side of the Stamp Act, see P. Thomas, *British Politics and the Stamp Act Crisis: The First Phase of the American Revolution, 1763–1767* (1975). The course of political events in the various colonies is charted by J. Main in *The Upper House in Revolutionary America, 1763–1788* (1967). A. Jones, *American Colonial Wealth: Documents and Methods* (3 vols., 1977), is a statistical study of wealth and its distribution in all parts of the colonies. P. Maier, *From Resistance to Revolution: Colonial Radicals and the Development of American Opposition to Britain, 1756–1776* (1972), probes the organization of "mob" action in the cities.

J. Hutson and S. Kurtz, *Essays on the American Revolution* (1973), is a good collection, especially on social history. R. Brown, *The South Carolina Regulators: The Story of the First American Vigilante Movement* (1963), makes clear why there was so much guerrilla warfare in the lower South. For the West, see J. Sosin, *The Revolutionary Frontier, 1763–1783* (1967), and F. Philbrick, *The Rise of the West,*

1754–1830 (1965). T. Breen, *Tobacco Culture, The Mentality of the Great Tidewater Planters on the Eve of Revolution* (1986), offers a refreshing approach. The context of the Revolution is clarified in D. Robson, *Educating Republicans: The College in the Era of the American Revolution, 1750–1800* (1985).

For a concise but comprehensive account of the Revolution as a whole that is solidly grounded in economics, see E. Ferguson, *The American Revolution: A General History, 1763–1790* (1974). Another general history, which is both balanced and imaginative, is N. J. Risjord, *Forging an American Republic, 1760–1815* (1973).

THE AMERICAN REVOLUTION

Chapter 6

The American Revolution was one of the major events in the history of the modern world. It was the first major rebellion by overseas European emigrants against a mother country. It set an example that was widely followed, especially in Latin America. The American Revolution was the first in modern times to be based on ideas about equal rights for "all men." American revolutionaries claimed that their principles applied to people everywhere, not just to themselves. They saw themselves, self-consciously, as leaders in a universal struggle for liberty, and they hoped others would follow their lead. A similar way of thinking has been true of the other great revolutions of modern times, including those in France, Russia, and China.

Yet the American Revolution was full of contradictions and inconsistencies. It was many things at once, and historians have never agreed as to exactly what it was. In two respects it was a civil war: It was a struggle between the English in England and the British-Americans in the colonies, and it was also a conflict between colonists who supported independence and those who did not. The American Revolution has been called a simple war for independence. Yet the fighting went on for a year before many colonists accepted independence as a goal. The struggle was carried on in the name of liberty by men who owned slaves. The armies in this major revolution rarely numbered more than a few thousand men. The Americans could not have won the war without the aid of the French, whom they had been fighting for years. The revolution was made by fourteen separate governments, one of which was a shaky union of the others. Finally, one of its major leaders claimed it was over before it began.

Looking back many years afterward, John Adams asked: "What do we mean by the Revolution? The War? That was no part of the Revolution. It was only an effect and consequence of it. The Revolution was in the minds of the people, and this was effected, from 1760 to 1775, in the course of fifteen years before a drop of blood was drawn at Lexington." It is very possible that John Adams was right, that the "real" revolution was one of human consciousness. ■

TOWARD INDEPENDENCE

There were many people on both sides who refused to realize that a real war had begun. Actual revolt began before the actual revolution; that is why twentieth-century Americans celebrate 1776 rather than 1775. As news of the fighting spread, colonists looked anxiously to a Philadelphia meeting for leadership. Very few Americans thought about the possibility of independence; for more than a year they insisted on their loyalty to the king. Finally, when they broke that tie and declared their independence, they met considerable opposition from other colonists.

The Second Continental Congress

The Second Continental Congress met in Philadelphia in May 1775. An atmosphere of crisis hovered over the meeting; everyone knew that blood had already been shed. The delegates from the thirteen colonies made up a distinguished if divided group; and three of them were later to become presidents of the United States. None of these men imagined that they would remain in session almost continuously for fourteen years.

It was clear at the outset that the Congress would support the action Massachusetts had taken. Yet there was no formal resolution that the Continental Congress create an army. The existence of an intercolonial fighting force was recognized only in an offhand announcement that the Congress would "adopt" the army then gathering around Boston, for "the general defense of the rights of America." At the urging of John Adams, the delegates selected George Washington, a Virginian, as commander-in-chief of the army. Adams was well aware that his home colony of Massachusetts needed outside support.

On July 6, 1775, the Congress voted a Declaration of the Causes and Necessity of Taking up Arms: "Our cause is just," they confidently declared: "Our union is perfect." Then came an open threat: "Our internal resources are great, and, if necessary, foreign assistance is undoubtedly attainable. . . . The arms we have been compelled by our enemies to assume, we will . . . employ for the preservation of our liberties, being with one mind resolved to die free men rather than live slaves." But there was also a note of hope: "We have not raised armies with ambitious designs of separating from Great Britain, and establishing independent States."

Nearly at the same time, the Congress adopted the Olive Branch Petition, the work of its most

Abigail Adams. (*New York State Historical Association, Cooperstown*)

John Adams. (*Boston Athenaeum*)

ABIGAIL AND JOHN ADAMS ON THE STATUS OF WOMEN

In March 1776, when John Adams was away from home at the Second Continental Congress in Philadelphia, his wife Abigail sent him some unusual thoughts which have since become famous:

I long to hear that you have declared an independancy—and by the way in the new Code of Laws which I suppose it will be necessary for you to make I desire you would Remember the Ladies, and be more generous and favourable to them than your ancestors. Do not put such unlimited power into the hands of the Husbands. Remember all Men would be tyrants if they could. If perticuliar care and attention is not paid to the Laidies we are determined to foment a Rebelion, and will not hold ourselves bound by any Laws in which we have no voice, or Representation.

That your Sex are Naturally Tyrannical is a Truth so thoroughly established as to admit of no dispute, but such of you as wish to be happy willingly give up the harsh title of Master for the more tender and endearing one of Friend. Why then, not put it out of the power of the vicious and the Lawless to use us with cruelty and indignity with impunity. Men of Sense in all Ages abhor those customs which treat us only as the vassals of your Sex. Regard us then as Beings placed by providence under your protection and in immitation of the Supreem Being make use of that power only for our happiness.

John Adams was somewhat taken aback; he protested to his beloved wife that men "have only the Name of Masters," and that "in Practice you know We are the subjects."

cautious members. This document begged King George to keep Parliament from passing further measures so that a plan of reconciliation could be worked out. On receiving it in August, however, the king brushed it aside. In a royal proclamation, he called the Americans rebels and warned all loyal persons not to help them. Still, there were peacemakers in Britain. Edmund Burke, in one of his great speeches, urged Parliament to meet American demands and surrender the right to tax. "An Englishman," he exclaimed, "is the unfittest person on earth to argue another Englishman into slavery." Lord North himself persuaded Parliament to offer concessions that might have helped in 1765 but in 1775 were too late.

Early Fighting

By the time North's concessions reached Philadelphia, the two sides had met at the Battle of Bunker Hill, the bloodiest engagement of the entire war. The main battle actually took place on nearby Breed's Hill, overlooking Boston, where American militiamen had gathered soon after the British had returned from Concord. On June 17, 1775, General Gage, with fresh troops, decided to drive the Americans off. His troops finally managed to dislodge them, but at great cost. The Americans lost almost 400 men; Gage lost more than 1000—over 40 percent of those he had ordered into battle. Two weeks later, Washington arrived at Cambridge, outside Boston, to take command.

By this time too, fighting had begun farther north. In May, in an effort to gain control of Canada, Ethan Allen captured the British posts at Crown Point and Ticonderoga in New York. Congress approved an address to "fellow-sufferers" in Canada, inviting them to join the rebellion. But the Canadians' "sufferings" had been taken care of by the Quebec Act of 1774, and they remained loyal to the British crown. Washington decided upon an invasion of Canada. He ordered Benedict Arnold to set out for Quebec from Cambridge with about 1000 men. Arnold was joined below the city by a smaller group of Americans under Richard Montgomery. On New Year's Eve, 1775, Arnold and Montgomery made their assault. It ended in Montgomery's death and Arnold's defeat.

Elsewhere American arms proved more successful. A British fleet was beaten from the harbor

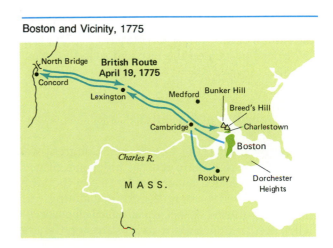

Boston and Vicinity, 1775

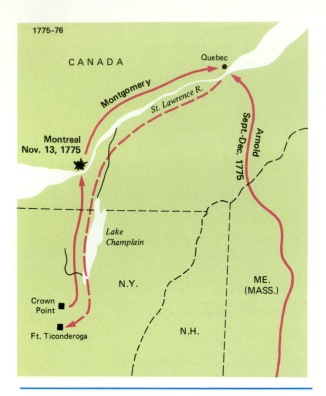

1775–76

CANADA

Quebec

Montgomery

St. Lawrence R.

Montreal
Nov. 13, 1775

Arnold
Sept.–Dec. 1775

Lake
Champlain

N.Y.

ME.
(MASS.)

Crown
Point

Ft. Ticonderoga

N.H.

Canadian Campaigns, 1775–76

and authorized the creation of a navy.

All these actions were undertaken while the Congress was still expressing its loyalty to the king. Most Americans felt such loyalty very deeply. Rather than blaming George III, they insisted that their difficulties were the fault of his corrupt and misguided ministers. As commander-in-chief, Washington was always careful to refer to the enemy as the "ministerial army." Americans remained loyal to the king in the face of royal proclamations declaring them to be in a state of rebellion. They protested that they were merely defending their rights and that they would stop fighting as soon as those rights were restored.

It was an English writer newly arrived in America who broke the logjam of public sentiment. In *Common Sense*, published anonymously in January 1776, Thomas Paine attacked the monarchy, not merely the king's ministers, and called for establishment of an independent republic. Having assailed "the Royal brute of Britain," he went on to declare: "There is something very absurd in supposing a Continent to be perpetually governed by an island." Paine's *Common Sense* was widely read

of Charles Town, South Carolina. In Virginia the royal governor, Lord Dunmore, took refuge on a British warship. When he publicly invited Virginia slaves to join the British cause several hundred answered his call, but there was no general slave uprising. Dunmore's action horrified white Virginians and united them in their conviction that blacks should have no part in a white man's war.

In Massachusetts, the siege of Boston finally came to an end. The Americans obtained heavy cannons by hauling them on sleds hundreds of miles overland from Fort Ticonderoga in New York. Once set in place on Dorchester Heights just south of Boston, they commanded the city and much of the harbor. On March 17, 1776, British troops evacuated the city and sailed for Nova Scotia.

The Question of Loyalty

In the meantime, the Continental Congress was acting more and more like an independent government. It issued paper money to pay the army and established a committee for negotiating with foreign countries. It set up a postal department with Benjamin Franklin as Postmaster General

Thomas Paine. (*Independence National Historic Park*)

THE AMERICAN REVOLUTION

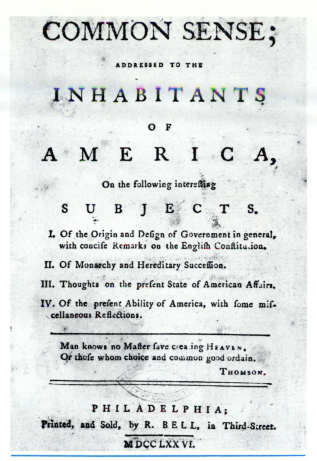

Title page of first edition of Thomas Paine's *Common Sense,* 1776. (*Library of Congress*)

with a formal declaration of principles. They decided to issue a statement with the broadest possible appeal: to British-Americans in the colonies, to Englishmen at home, and to the people of the "world," meaning especially those in Western Europe, with an eye particularly on allies in France.

The Declaration of Independence

The Congress appointed a committee to draft this public declaration. The committee in turn asked Thomas Jefferson of Virginia to draw up a draft. Jefferson's draft, somewhat modified by John Adams and Benjamin Franklin, was then debated by Congress. One major change was made: Jefferson's attack on King George for promoting the slave trade was deleted. The charge was unfair, but it was removed for a different reason. South Carolina and Georgia, the two colonies most dependent on slaves, objected to Jefferson's description of the slave trade as "war upon humanity itself." In order to gain the votes of those two colonies, the offending passage was deleted. The amended declaration was "authenticated and printed" on July 4, though it was not signed by all members until November.

The Declaration of Independence was a masterpiece of political writing. The famous words of the preamble remain far better known than the long list of accusations aimed at George III. For people at the time, however, that list summarized the "long train of abuses" of the preceding dozen years. The accusations were not entirely fair, since George III did not bear personal responsibility for many of the actions the Declaration condemned. But Americans were finally breaking their one remaining tie with Britain, the king, so Jefferson aimed his propaganda at that final link.

Many years later, John Adams belittled Jefferson's achievement in the preamble by claiming that it merely repeated what everyone had been saying all along. But Jefferson replied that this was exactly what he had intended: The Declaration, he said, was "to be an expression of the American mind." In framing it, he had "turned to neither book nor pamphlet." He had simply given expression to common ideas about natural rights and the right of the people to rebel.

In fact, these ideas no longer belonged just to John Locke or the Commonwealth writers, or even to the Scottish philosophers who had influenced him. They were simply the way most Americans thought about government. It was "self-evident" that the powers of government derived from the

and widely acclaimed; it was, in fact, one of the most immediately influential political pamphlets ever written.

Public opinion shifted rapidly. On April 6, 1776, the Congress opened American ports to the commerce of all nations except Britain. This measure in itself made America independent, as many delegates realized. A month later, the Congress advised all colonies to form new state governments if they had not already done so. Nine hours of debate on July 1 helped to bring some reluctant delegates around; on July 2, 1776, Congress adopted Richard Henry Lee's Resolution of Independence:

RESOLVED, That these United Colonies are, and of right ought to be, free and independent States, that they are absolved from allegiance to the British Crown, and that all political connection between them and the State of Great Britain is, and ought to be, totally dissolved.

Adoption of this resolution was crucial; but the delegates also wanted to set forth their position

The drafting committee presents their proposed version of the Declaration of Independence for adoption and signing by members of the Continental Congress. This picture is a nineteenth-century lithograph based on a much earlier oil painting. The drum and flags on the wall are fanciful, placed there by the original artist for visual balance. But each face is a real portrait of a real person. The president of the Congress, John Hancock (seated) accepts the draft from the hands of its principal author, Thomas Jefferson. The artist knew what went on in the drafting committee, for he places the other two members who had some impact (John Adams, left, and Benjamin Franklin, right) almost on a line with Jefferson. Roger Sherman and Robert R. Livingston (both of whom merely approved the draft) are also standing, but somewhat behind the others. (*Architect of the Capitol*)

people, who could rightly take them back if they were abused; and in any such revolution, the people should then establish governments that would protect their natural rights.

When Jefferson came to naming those rights, he changed the traditional trinity of "life, liberty, and property" to "life, liberty, and the pursuit of happiness." His rewording has prompted the joke that the Declaration gives everyone the right to pursue happiness, but not the right to catch up with it. But the point of this remark rests on a thorough misunderstanding of Jefferson's use of the word "pursuit." He used it not in the sense of a chase, but in the older meaning of "practice" or "cultivation." To "pursue" something was to cultivate it, to learn and perfect it by practicing it repeatedly, by improving it with attention and care.

Jefferson regarded property as a means to happiness, as a way of leading the good life, rather than as a goal in itself. He had in mind the typical American farmer, who led a life of "happiness" precisely because he was so much more likely to own property than the typical farmer in Europe.

The Declaration of Independence stated flatly that "all men are created equal." This idea has proved in the long run to be the most enduring of all. At the time, it merely expressed the common assumption that free citizens were politically equal. It was not intended to include women or blacks, or to exclude them. It was not meant to suggest that all people were the same in ability or ought to be the same in wealth. It obviously did not apply to slaves. Later, however, the Declaration's principle of equality took on a life of its own.

THE AMERICAN REVOLUTION

The phrase "all men" could very easily be interpreted as meaning all human beings, not just the white men of America in 1776. It might even be extended—and eventually was—to include blacks and women.

The Loyalists

Some Americans opposed independence and the war. These *Loyalists*—or *Tories*, as the patriots called them—varied in number from place to place and also from time to time. The best modern estimates suggest that they never numbered more than a fifth of the white population. But numbers alone do not tell why some people chose to remain loyal to the British Crown. For many, the decision was a crisis of conscience; for others, it was a matter of self-interest. Men who had held positions as royal officials, for example, found it easy to remain loyal. Some Loyalists had a distaste for popular rule. Certain ethnic groups in certain places tended to become Loyalist because other ethnic groups in the same area were becoming patriots. Quakers and German pacifists could not become active patriots because their principles prevented them from supporting war.

Probably the most important factor in pushing people toward a decision was the presence of armed men in the immediate neighborhood. The presence of British troops in an area could work in two ways: It could make Loyalists out of those who wished to pick the winning side; or it could make patriots out of outraged farmers who watched helplessly as redcoats made off with their corn and livestock. As the major fighting moved from one part of the colonies to another, more and more Americans had to make a choice. This pattern placed the Loyalists at a tremendous disadvantage; British troops came and went, while their armed American opponents remained. The patriot majority remained a majority mostly through its long-term control of the countryside.

Committees of patriots, backed with bayonets, drove many Loyalists from their homes and communities. The new states provided legal machinery for taking Loyalist property. There were brutalities on both sides, but few Loyalists lost their lives except in open battle. Throughout the war, the British constantly overestimated the number of Loyalists. Yet at the same time they failed to take full advantage of Loyalist support. Professional British army officers often treated potential allies with the same contempt they had for all colonials.

One basic fact about the domestic opposition to the American Revolution has often been overlooked. Many of the Loyalists could simply leave without going permanently into exile. They could return "home" to England or move to another part of the British empire. Many did so. When British troops evacuated Boston, some one thousand Loyalists left with them for Nova Scotia. The same pattern was repeated whenever the British evacuated an American port. For many Loyalists, these journeys were heart-wrenching departures from their homes. But they were moving to places where people spoke English and had similar loyalties to the British crown. Many even received financial compensation from the British government for their losses. Few exiled refugees from a major revolution have had the same opportunity.

The departure of so many Loyalists had an important impact on the future of the new country. It meant that the most determined opponents of the revolution were no longer on the scene when vic-

---

WORDS AND NAMES IN AMERICAN HISTORY

The growth of *bureaucracy* is one of the most important and characteristic developments of modern industrial societies. Almost every American today has to deal with various bureaucracies at one time or another, whether they be government, business, health, military, educational, and so on. A great many Americans work for bureaucracies and are therefore bureaucrats themselves. The word itself is not of American origin. It derives from a synthetic combination of two words, one French and the other Greek. The original French word *bureau* was the name of a cloth used for covering writing desks. Gradually it became the name of the desk itself and eventually a term for a large office (especially a government one) equipped with many such desks. From there it was a small step to using the term for large offices themselves. The term *cracy* derives from the ancient Greek root word meaning "rule," as in *democracy,* or rule by the *demos* or "people." The terms *bureaucracy* and *bureaucrat* came into common use in England and the United States in the middle of the nineteenth century, at a time of marked growth in the size of governments. When John Marshall was secretary of state in 1800 (before moving to the Supreme Court), he had working for him one chief clerk, seven regular clerks (no Xerox machines), and one messenger. Today, the State Department has about 24,000 employees.

---

tory was won. After the war, Americans were able to deal with the problems of nation-building without having to worry about a large group of people who opposed the entire enterprise.

WAR—AND PEACE

The war had begun in Massachusetts, but then the arena of conflict shifted to the Middle Colonies when the British decided to isolate New England by capturing New York. For several years, most of the fighting took place in New York, New Jersey, and Pennsylvania. During the final years, the theater of war shifted to the southern colonies. All in all, the Americans lost more battles than they won, but eventually they achieved a final victory. That triumph would have been impossible without the aid of their old enemies, the French.

Strengths and Weaknesses

The colonists faced enormous military disadvantages. They had a population of about 2.5 million, of whom nearly 20 percent became Loyalists and another 20 percent were slaves. The population of Great Britain was four times as large, and the British could put far many more troops on the field. And these were veteran troops who had been trained and seasoned during the Seven Years' War. The British navy was the largest and probably the most efficient in the world. In addition, Great Britain could afford to buy manpower. Early in the war it did so by hiring 30,000 Germans. The largest number came from the state of Hesse-Cassel in western Germany, which was why all German mercenaries came to be called Hessians by resentful Americans.

Yet the British also faced disadvantages. Chief among them was the Atlantic Ocean. In addition, they had to fight on unfamiliar, badly mapped stretches of territory that seemed to be crawling with hostile farmers. British troops and generals were accustomed to the better roads and more open country of Europe. Any army requires good transportation for cannon, troops, and supplies. One British officer complained after the war that transportation difficulties "absolutely prevented us this whole war from going fifteen miles from a navigable river."

The Americans were fighting on their own ground. But they lacked a sizable navy, for Congress was able to find funds for only a few vessels. Even the successful efforts of John Paul Jones, who with one ship raided British shipping in the English Channel, did nothing to change the fact that for most of the war the British controlled the sea lanes and the American coastline. The Americans also had great difficulty keeping an army together. In any given place, the colonists would turn out in large numbers to fight. But staying in the army and marching off to other colonies was not an attractive prospect; long service in the army meant low pay, rigid discipline, cold, hunger, and disease. There were no pensions for soldiers disabled by wounds, no insurance payments for their widows if they died. So it is scarcely any wonder that many American farmers enlisted for three months and then went back home to their crops.

An advertisement for a runaway slave suspected of joining Lord Dunmore—a common sight in Virginia and Maryland newspapers during the fall and winter of 1775 to 1776. (*The Virginia State Library*)

RUN away from *Hampton*, on *Sunday* last, a lusty Mulatto Fellow named ARGYLE, well known about the Country, has a Scar on one of his Wrists, and has lost one or more of his fore Teeth; he is a very handy Fellow by Water, or about the House, &c. loves Drink, and is very bold in his Cups, but dastardly when sober. Whether he will go for a Man of War's Man, or not, I cannot say; but I will give 40s. to have him brought to me. He can read and write.

NOVEMBER 2, 1775.   JACOB WRAY.

George Washington's great achievement was that he managed to keep something resembling an army in the field for eight years. He commanded two varieties of soldiers: militiamen from the various states, and the men of the Continental Army, so called because they were drawn from all the states and because they were paid (or supposed to be paid) by the Continental Congress. The Continental soldiers served longer periods and therefore became better trained and much more reliable in battle. As the war went on, the Continentals began to take pride in themselves both as professional soldiers and as the truest of patriots. They grew intensely loyal to their tall, somewhat aloof, but always devoted commander.

For his part, Washington was a firm yet fair administrator of military discipline. He was deeply committed to his new country, and he spent much of his time dealing with military problems that arose from the weaknesses of the civilian government. He constantly had to plead with the Congress for men, money, and supplies. The Congress, in turn, could and did print paper money, which quickly depreciated, but it had to beg the states to furnish men and supplies. It had no authority to raise taxes.

Fighting in the Middle Colonies

The British pulled out of Boston in March 1776. During the next fifteen months, American forces suffered one defeat after another and lost control of their two largest cities, New York and Philadelphia. The British, having won all these victories, then proceeded to lose an entire army in a confrontation that proved to be the major turning point of the war.

In the spring of 1776, the British decided to seize New York as their headquarters. Two brothers, General Sir William Howe and Admiral Richard Howe, were sent in command of an awe-

Central Campaigns, 1776–78

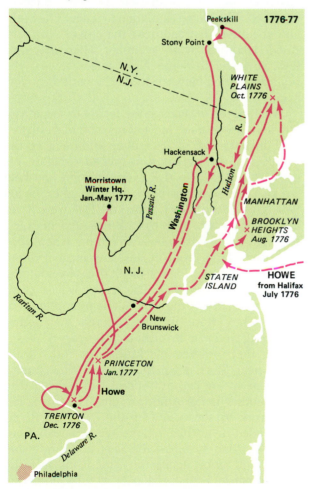

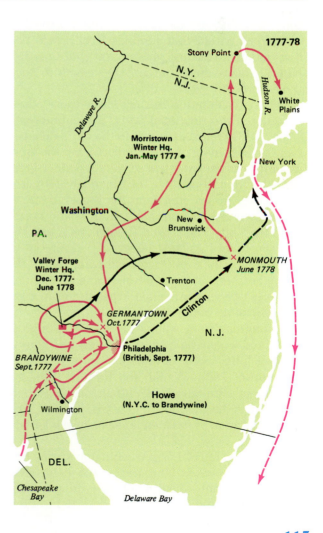

LIFE, LIBERTY, AND THE PURSUIT OF HAPPINESS: EIGHT MASSACHUSETTS SOLDIERS

Early in the war, eight Massachusetts soldiers petitioned the Provincial Congress for redress of their grievances. Their spelling was somewhat shaky, but they had a firm grip on certain ideological aspects of the Revolution. Addressing their words to the "Jentlemen Representitives of this province," they wrote:

Know dout it is a truth acknowlidged among men that god [has] placd men in greater and Lower Stations in life, and that Inferiours are moraly Bound to obay their Superiors in all their lawful Commands, But altho our king is our Superiour, yet his Commands are unlawful. Therefore we are not bound to obay, but are in providence Cald to rise up against Such tiranical usurpations, and our province at this difficult Day is Necessiated to Chuse Representitives and officers to Rule as king over us. To which we Cheerfully Submit in all things lawful or just and Count it our hapiness, but if their laws are greavious to bare, then the agreaved is by the Same Rule au-

thorized to Rise up in oppisition to Said laws. . . .

Having made their point, they went on to complain about scarcities in camp, even though many men had already gone back to their farms:

[by those men] that Remain Here are much Deuty Required, to which we, animated from a Spirit of Liberty, would Chearfully Submit, provided we had a Sufficient Support from day to day. we many times have drawn Such Roten Stinkin meat that the Smell is Sufficient to make us lothe the Same. . . . their is a large Number of men in verious Ragements that Rsents Their treatment with Regard to provision So fare that they have Sworn by the god that made them that, if the[y] Cannot have a Sufficient Support, they will Either Raise a mob and go to the general and Demand provision and obtain it that way, or they will Swing their packs Emediately and go home boldly throu all the Guards.

---

some military and naval force, which arrived at New York harbor that summer. The Howes had instructions to discuss peace terms, but they also had 32,000 soldiers and 10,000 seamen to back their words.

When Washington learned about these plans, he ordered the American army, then numbering some 23,000 men, to march to the city's defense. Not only was his army outnumbered, but the great majority were inexperienced militia. Under great pressure from the British, the Americans retreated with heavy losses, first from the Brooklyn end of Long Island, then from Manhattan Island northward to White Plains, and from there across the Hudson River into New Jersey.

Following their first victory on Long Island, the Howe brothers invited the Americans to send delegates to a peace conference. Washington doubted that anything would come of it, but both he and the Congress were willing to try. The Congress appointed a geographically balanced negotiating team of John Adams of Massachusetts, Benjamin Franklin of Pennsylvania, and Edward Rutledge of Virginia. The talks broke off almost as soon as they began because the Howes demanded that the Declaration of Independence be rescinded immediately.

By the late fall of 1776, Washington's army had been pushed across New Jersey into Pennsylvania. By then, only about 8000 men remained under his command; the rest had deserted to their farms or had died of disease, or been killed or captured. The Howes had men to spare. They sent an expedition that captured the city of Newport, Rhode Island, early in December. Then, leaving a few garrisons in some New Jersey towns, the brothers settled back to sit out the winter in New York.

Washington was desperate for some sort of victory to revive morale. Most of his men had enlisted only until the end of December, and he faced the prospect of seeing his army dissolve before his eyes. He decided to risk everything on one bold stroke. On Christmas night, in icy weather, he led 2400 men in boats back across the Delaware River into New Jersey. By 8 o'clock the next morning they had marched 9 miles to Trenton, where they surprised a large group of Hessians, most of whom were still asleep. They took 900 captives at the cost of only 5 casualties. The victory was so stunning that many of the Americans promptly reenlisted. They were further cheered by another smashing victory at Princeton on January 5. Washington then ordered his little army into winter camp near Morristown in northern New Jersey.

When spring came, General Howe decided to take another major American city. His troops left New York by sea, sailed up the Delaware River, and landed near Philadelphia. Washington's Continentals tried to block the way at Brandywine Creek, but once again the Americans lost the pitched battle. British redcoats occupied Philadel-

Watercolor of colonial troops. (*Anne S. K. Brown Military Collection, Brown University Library*)

phia in September, and the pleasure-loving General Howe settled back by his fireside to enjoy the hospitality of the city's Loyalists. A week later, Washington's little army mounted an attack on the major British encampment outside the city at Germantown. At first things went well for the Americans, but patches of dense fog created so much confusion that at one point they were firing on each other. Once again, the British won.

Saratoga and the French Alliance

In the meantime, one of Howe's fellow generals was marching straight into the jaws of disaster. General John Burgoyne had persuaded the high command in London to let him lead a major army down the route of lakes from Canada to Albany, where he intended to link up with Howe's troops coming north from New York City. This strategy aimed at cutting off the New England colonies, which British authorities regarded as the hotbed of rebellion. But when Burgoyne set out from Canada he did not know that Howe had gone off to Philadelphia.

"Gentleman Johnny" Burgoyne also had little idea how to mount an expedition through trackless forest with 4000 British regulars, 3000 Hessians, and some 1400 Indians. He had 138 pieces of artillery, a good supply of wine and fine clothes, camp-following women for his men, his own mistress, and a four-poster bed. The farther he pene-

trated south of Lake Champlain, the more resistance he met. Local farmers cut trees to slow his progress. His food supplies ran low.

Though he did not know it, American militiamen and Continentals were gathering from all over New York and New England. One skirmish fol-

Northern Campaigns, 1777

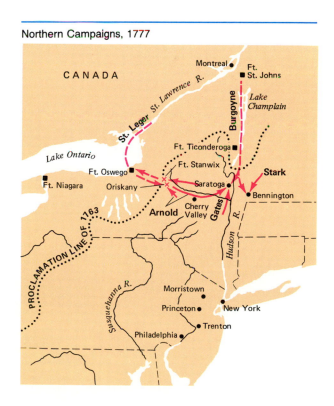

lowed another, and every time the two sides clashed, Burgoyne lost several hundred men. The massed Americans finally brought Burgoyne's army to a standstill at Saratoga, New York, and the dashing British general surrendered his battered army on October 17, 1777. The importance of Saratoga was more psychological than military. Americans now had proof that they could defeat British regulars. The real impact of the battle came in London and Paris.

From the start, European governments had watched the conflict in America with mixed feelings. The French and Spanish governments had hoped to see the British humbled. Yet the monarchs of Spain and France were not at all anxious to encourage revolutions, for they had no desire to have ideas about popular government and natural rights spread among their subjects. Within the French government, however, hopes for humiliation of Great Britain eventually won out over fears of revolution.

Even before the French knew the Americans had declared independence, they decided to send aid to them secretly. Early in 1776, the Congress sent Silas Deane as its agent to Paris. When he arrived, Deane received a favorable response, and soon the Americans were importing about 80 percent of their gunpowder from France. A few months later, the Congress sent Benjamin Franklin to help Deane push the French into a formal alliance. But even Franklin's charm failed to move the French government into risking open aid to the Americans. When New York City fell to British forces the French decided not to back a hopeless cause, since to do so would surely bring another war with Great Britain.

For the Americans, victory at Saratoga brought concessions from London and a triumph at the negotiating table in Paris. Lord North's ministry was so shaken that it offered to suspend all laws concerning America passed since 1763. Two years earlier, the Americans probably would have ceased fire on such terms. Now they refused. American agents in Paris used the news of North's offer to prod the French into making an open alliance with the Congress of the United States. The French were now more than willing, for they smelled revenge in the news from Saratoga.

A formal treaty of alliance between France and the United States was concluded in March 1778.

Starving American prisoners on board the prison ship *Jersey*. (*Frick Art Reference Library*)

THE AMERICAN REVOLUTION

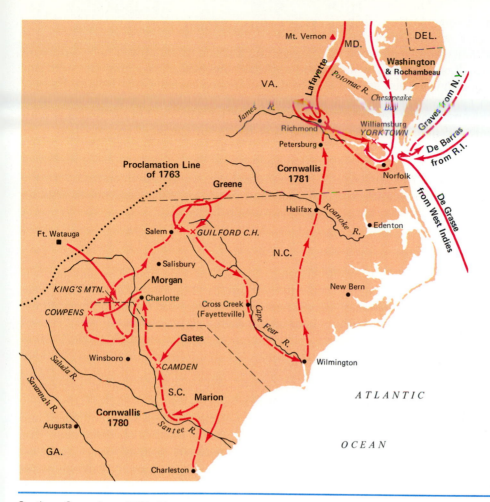

Southern Campaigns, 1780–81

War in the South

The stated aim of the treaty was the independence of the United States. The new nation would be permitted to keep all North American territories conquered from the British. The French and Americans also agreed that if war came between France and England, neither ally was to make peace without the consent of the other. When the British government learned about the treaty, it immediately declared war on France. The American war for independence was now transformed into still another European struggle for dominance in North America. In 1779 Spain joined the war as France's ally.

War in the South

The French alliance of 1778 was followed by three years of deep discouragement for the Americans. While the three American negotiators were at work in Paris, Washington's Continentals were in win-

ter camp at Valley Forge. There they suffered from cold, hunger, and desertions while General Howe reclined comfortably on his couch in Philadelphia only 20 miles away. In the spring of 1778, Lord North and the king decided to replace Howe with Sir Henry Clinton.

General Clinton turned out to be more imaginative but even less capable of making up his mind about when and where to attack. Rumors about a French assault on New York City caused Clinton to order British troops to leave Philadelphia, cross New Jersey, and return to New York. Washington's forces pursued them but were unable to prevent their reaching their destination. The Americans then camped outside the British-occupied city, and there the two armies sat facing each other for three long years.

That same summer of 1778, the British high command in London decided to shift major military efforts to the southern colonies. They did this because they thought most people in the South remained loyal. They were wrong, but a British expedition captured Savannah at the end of that year. After months of hesitation, Clinton combined all his forces for a major assault on Charles Town, South Carolina. There the British won their greatest victory of the war. They captured not only the city, but the entire force of American defenders, some 5500 men. Thoroughly satisfied, Clinton retired to New York, leaving General Lord Cornwallis in charge of mopping up the Carolinas.

At first Cornwallis was successful. At Camden, South Carolina, he smashed the American forces. As his army advanced into North Carolina, however, he was hit by a series of reverses. Several times his troops were outfought by southern militiamen and by Continentals commanded by Washington's ablest general, Nathaniel Greene of Rhode Island. Cornwallis concluded that he might do better by moving north into Virginia. Greene elected not to pursue him, but to mop up the remaining British units farther south.

Cornwallis then made the fateful mistake of leading his army out onto the peninsula between the James and the York rivers. His troops camped at Yorktown, not many miles from the original English settlement at Jamestown.

Very suddenly, in 1781, a combination of good luck and well-timed decisions favored the American cause. A major French army had assembled at Newport, Rhode Island. Two French fleets, one from Newport and the other from the West Indies, appeared within sight of the Yorktown peninsula. Upon learning of Cornwallis's exposed position, Washington ordered his army to march for Virginia from outside New York City. On the peninsula the combined French and American armies laid siege to Cornwallis's 7000 British regulars.

In New York, Clinton decided to save the situation by sending a fleet of warships to the York River. Usually the British navy ruled the seas, but for just a moment the British fleet was outnumbered and outgunned. The jaws of the trap closed rapidly. For the first time, the British could not escape by sea. On land, they were badly outnumbered. Cut off from reinforcements, Cornwallis agreed to have his men lay down their arms, but to French officers rather than to the despised Americans. As the redcoats marched forward to stack their arms, the British army band played a popular song. "The World Turned Upside Down."

The world was. When Lord North heard of the surrender at Yorktown he cried out again and again, "Oh God! It is all over." He resigned to make way for a ministry that could make peace with an independent American republic.

The Treaty of Paris

Negotiating a peace treaty proved to be a delicate and difficult business. Four nations were involved—the United States, Great Britain, France, and Spain—and each had different interests. Spain had no formal ties with the United States and indeed was hostile to the new nation's hopes for independence and a western boundary on the Mississippi River. The French-American treaty of 1778 required the Americans to consult with the French and obtain their consent before signing any treaty with England.

One of the American negotiators, John Jay of New York, described France's position very accurately: "We can depend upon the French only to see that we are separated from England, but it is not in their interest that we should become a great and formidable people, and therefore they will not help us to become so."

The Congress sent an extremely able team of negotiators to Paris. John Jay, Benjamin Franklin, and John Adams soon found out that the French were secretly encouraging the English to insist on a boundary well to the east of the Mississippi. They decided to ignore the French for the moment and to deal directly with the British delegation. The British and Americans worked out a tentative agreement that included a western boundary at the Mississippi and the giving up of American claims to Canada.

By agreeing to this western boundary, the British hoped to drive a wedge between the Americans and the French. The Americans laid this agreement before the French as an accomplished fact. Vergennes, the French foreign minister, was annoyed by these deals. But Franklin managed to soothe him and even to extract another fat loan for the United States.

The Treaty of Paris between the United States and Great Britain was signed in September 1783 and ratified in Philadelphia in January 1784. Britain formally acknowledged American independence. The boundaries of the new nation were established at Florida in the south, the Mississippi in the west, and a border with Canada much like the present one. The British recognized American fishing rights off Newfoundland. The Americans agreed that private British creditors would be free to collect any debts owed by citizens of the United States. Finally, the Congress was to "earnestly recommend" to the various states that they return property taken from Loyalists. By a separate treaty, the British granted Florida back to Spain.

The treaty was highly favorable to the United

North America in 1783

duced considerably less social change than almost any major modern revolution. The main reason for this is obvious: A great deal of change had already taken place during the century before the Revolution. The great majority of white people already had some property and good hopes of getting more. So there were few demands for taking property from the wealthy. There was no widespread cry for freedom of religious worship, because that freedom already existed. There were no calls for changing the economic system, because that system seemed to be working rather well. By and large, Americans were well off, and prosperous people do not like to rock the foundations of their prosperity.

Slavery

One group of Americans had no share in this freedom and prosperity. Black slaves and slavery itself stood out as the one great exception to the principles of the American Revolution. What happened with slavery was easily the most important social result of that Revolution. The war itself changed the lives of some slaves, for several thousand served in the armed forces of both sides, and often gained their freedom by doing so. Rhode Island recruited a battalion of black soldiers. Black seamen served in the tiny American navy, and most privateering vessels had black sailors aboard. In the South, however, most whites opposed even the idea of placing firearms in the hands of potentially dangerous black slaves or the few free blacks.

Thousands of slaves were carried off by the British when they left Georgia and South Carolina. Some of them were carried to freedom in Nova Scotia and eventually to Sierre Leone in Africa. Others, however, continued in slavery in the West Indies. For the great majority of American blacks, though, the war meant continued toil in the fields.

Yet the ideas of the Revolution brought into question the entire institution of slavey, for it was obvious to many white Americans that their claims about "liberty" and the rights of "all men" meant that holding slaves was wrong. There were major barriers to freeing the slaves. First, slaves were property, and for years white Americans had argued that no government could deprive people of their property without their consent. In this case, one principle of the Revolution, the owner's natural right of property, collided directly with another, the slave's natural right of liberty.

Second, many white Americans thought that

States. George Washington watched the last British troops board their transports in New York harbor, bade farewell to his assembled officers, and then rode off to present his resignation as commander-in-chief to the Congress. He told the assembly he was leaving "all the employments of public life."

SOCIAL CHANGES

Historians have often asked an obvious question about the American Revolution. How much change did it produce in American society? We usually think of revolutions as being periods of great and rapid social change. Certainly the French Revolution of 1789 and the more recent Russian and Chinese revolutions produced profound changes in those societies. Was the American Revolution, in this sense, really revolutionary? The answer to this apparently simple question is, in fact, a complicated one.

It is clear that the American Revolution pro-

Elizabeth Freeman was a black Massachusetts woman who successfully sued for her freedom in 1783. (*Massachusetts Historical Society, Boston*)

there was much discussion about getting rid of it. The major difficulty was that most whites wanted to get rid of blacks if they were freed, and there was no realistic way of doing this. A number of masters went ahead and privately freed some or all of their slaves. In doing so they often cited the principles of the revolution. But just as frequently they referred to principles of Christian brotherhood; and in many cases, they referred to both. In those states there had always been free blacks, but now their numbers increased considerably.

Farther south there was little discussion and no action. In South Carolina and Georgia, slavery was highly profitable and slaves far more numerous in proportion to the white population. Thus white Americans succeeded in living up to their principles where it was easy to do so, but failed where it was difficult. The author of the Declaration of Independence continued to own slaves.

The revolution had still another important impact on the pattern of American slavery. The coming of the war brought the importation of slaves from Africa to a halt. Several factors worked to make this change nearly permanent. A majority of white Americans had begun to recognize the outrageous cruelty and injustice of the Atlantic slave trade. Slaves were in great demand only in South Carolina and Georgia; elsewhere in the South, planters had more slaves than they could use. And most whites also thought there was a surplus of black people. They feared and disliked the ones they already had, whether slave or free, and they wanted no more. The great majority of white Americans wanted the new nation to be a white man's country.

Churches, Property, and Women

The revolution gave Americans a chance to make certain changes in the relationship between church and state. In New York and the southern states, the established Anglican church lost its privileged position. Yet most states still continued to tax their citizens for the support of the churches. Usually the taxpayer could name the church he wanted to support. The Congregational churches in Massachusetts and Connecticut kept certain special privileges until the nineteenth century. Only Virginia provided for the complete separation of church and state. Virginia's advanced position was largely due to Thomas Jefferson, James Madison, and Baptists who refused to pay taxes for a state-supported church.

Although the principles of the American Revo-

freed slaves would become a drain on society, a hostile group of people who would either rob and kill or starve. And many whites simply did not want to live with free blacks; they would have been happy to see them free if they would somehow go away. Many slaveowners opposed emancipation simply because they were profiting from slave labor.

The net result of these feelings was that some states took steps toward abolishing slavery and others did not. From Pennsylvania northward, where there were few slaves, it was relatively easy to bring the practice to an end. In Massachusetts, court decisions found that slavery violated the state constitution's assertion that "all men are born free and equal."

Elsewhere in the North, the states passed gradual emancipation laws. These acts did not abolish slavery outright; they provided that slaves born after passage of the act would become free at a certain age such as 21 or 28. In many cases, the laws named July 4 as the date when they would go into effect. That date itself pointed to the force of revolutionary principles. By 1802 all northern states had provided for the gradual end of slavery.

In the southern states, the principles were the same but the number of slaves was much greater. In Virginia and Maryland, slavery was less profitable than farther south, and in those two states

Lemuel Haynes, 1753–1833, the first black minister of the Congregational Church in America. (*Museum of Art, Rhode Island School of Design; Gift of Mrs. Lucy T. Aldrich*)

lution strongly supported the idea of private property, the war itself resulted in a slightly more equal distribution of property among white Americans. We do not know exactly how great this change actually was. Widespread printing of paper money resulted in its depreciation, a process which favored poorer people who borrowed money because they were able to repay their debts with inflated currency. Many wealthy merchants suffered great losses during the war. Some farmers profited by selling food supplies to one army or the other and sometimes to both. Others lost most of what they had. The seizure of Loyalist lands by the states resulted in somewhat broader landholding, since the states usually sold these lands at public auction. However, many of these estates were purchased by large speculators who then made money from resales to small farmers. The Revolution resulted in somewhat wider possession of land—an unexpected outcome that supported a growing conviction among Americans that ownership of land gave them special virtues.

One important group of Americans may have benefitted from the Revolution, but it is very hard to say how widely and how much. Many white women were left completely in charge of the family farm for the first time in their lives. With their husbands in the army they had to tackle heavy jobs that they had never done before, such as plowing. Perhaps more important, they had to take responsibility for crucial farming decisions, such as when to plant and when to begin harvesting. Thus the Revolution thrust on many women a degree of independence that they had never before experienced. Though their legal and political rights remained untouched by the Revolution, these experiences on the part of tens of thousands of American women may have had subtle but important effects not only on the wives themselves but on their daughters.

In addition, a much smaller number of women actually accompanied their husbands and boyfriends as part of the Continental Army. They were usually poor, but these "camp followers" were not all prostitutes. Many of them received army rations. In return they cooked, washed and mended, cared for the sick and wounded, and even helped bury the dead. Though Washington never really liked these arrangements, he put up with them for fear that if he threw the women out of his army, many of the men would follow them. All told, it is estimated that about one-sixteenth of the patriot army was female. Many of them suffered greatly, like the soldiers, but few of them could have been unaffected by the travel and widening of horizons that such an experience involved.

The winning of independence and the establishment of new governments caused Americans to examine their society more closely than ever before. By and large, they liked what they saw. Yet there were obvious flaws. Especially in the northern states, efforts were made to make punishments for crime more humane. Many states ended the practice of putting debtors in jail until they had paid their debts. New private schools and colleges were established because Americans thought they needed better educated citizens for the new republic. These and other reforms were stimulated by the Revolution. Yet they probably would have been undertaken even without it. Most of the constructive energies of the nation's leaders were going into problems of government. Independence raised pressing political problems which had somehow to be solved. It was in the realm of politics that the American Revolution turned out to be truly revolutionary.

SUMMARY

The American Revolution, the war for independence, was a long process. It was also a first: the first major and successful rebellion by overseas Europeans against a mother country. Other events also made this revolution different. One was that armed rebellion began before formal independence was declared. When the Second Continental Congess met in May 1775, there were still hopes for settling the dispute, both in the colonies and in England. Most Americans, including those at the Congress, were still loyal to King George, if not to his ministers. Some continued that loyalty and never agreed to the idea of independence. Many of these Loyalists left the colonies at some point during the long struggle, so that the rebels, or patriots as they called themselves, had the advantage of controlling the American countryside.

It was Thomas Paine's widely read pamphlet, *Common Sense*, that pushed the colonists past the point of no return. About a year after the fighting began, the Congress began opening American ports to commerce with all nations except Britain, telling colonies to form state governments, and declaring independence. The Declaration of Independence, a masterpiece of political writing that has stood to this day, embodied the principles on which the colonists based their revolt. But masterful as the Declaration was, it did not solve the rebels' military and financial problems. The British had trained men, money, and supplies; the colonists did not. The British navy controlled the seas; the Americans had just a few small ships. And American militiamen were ordinary citizens who left their farms to fight.

Despite all these problems—and military defeats—Washington managed to keep something resembling an army in the field for eight years. The American victory over the British at Saratoga in New York in the autumn of 1777 brought a major advantage: a formal alliance with the French, who up to then had kept their support secret.

As the war went on, the scene of the fighting shifted from New England to the Middle Colonies and then to the South. The British shifted their forces in hopes of winning a decisive victory. In 1781 Cornwallis, in command of the British forces in the South, made the mistake of going to Yorktown, Virginia, located on a peninsula. The Americans, with the help of the French, took advantage of the momentary British vulnerability to force a surrender that ended the war by cutting Cornwallis off on land and on sea.

Four nations were involved in the Treaty of Paris, which ended the war—the United States, Britain, France, and Spain. Signed in 1783, that treaty was highly favorable to the United States. Its two most important provisions were that Great Britain recognized American independence, and that the new nation's western boundary was to be the Mississippi River.

In military and political terms, the American Revolution was indeed revolutionary. But in social and economic terms, change was more limited. More than half the newly independent states began the gradual abolition of slavery. Yet slavery continued in the southern areas where it was most profitable, although the Atlantic slave trade nearly ended. The lives of a great many American women were drastically changed by the war, though the long-term effects of their experiences are hard to gauge. Tens of thousands of women had to supervise farms for the first time in their lives. Thousands of others served with the patriot armies. The idea of established churches began to fade, although in a few states citizens still paid taxes for church support. Land ownership was somewhat broadened, as lands taken from the Loyalists were redistributed. But the economic system remained the same. Americans were mainly well off and conscious of their country as the land of opportunity.

Suggested Readings

C. Becker, *The Declaration of Independence* (1922), offers conclusions about its intellectual origins which are now outmoded; but his discussion of the style of the document and his own style remain unsurpassed. G. Wood, *The Creation of the American Republic, 1776–1787* (1969), is central to an understanding of the political philosophies of the founders of the new nation. The extraordinarily influential pamphlet *Common Sense* by Tom Paine (1776) is available in many editions.

For the continuing development of political events, the J. Main book cited in Chapter 5 is pertinent, along with his *The Sovereign States, 1775–1783* (1973). In fact, a good many of the works cited in Chapter 5 are relevant to the material discussed in Chapter 6. B. Graymont, *The Iroquois in the American Revolution* (1972), tells how British and Americans both abandoned the Iroquois. The standard account on blacks is B. Quarles, *The Negro in the American Revolution* (1967).

Historians have shown considerable interest in slavery in this period. D. MacLeod, *Slavery, Race and the American Revolution* (1972), criticizes W. Jordan, *White Over Black*. See also D. Davis, *The Problem of Slavery in the Age of Revolution, 1770–1823* (1975); D. Robinson, *Slavery in the Structure of American Politics, 1765–1820* (1971); and R. McColley, *Slavery and Jeffersonian Virginia* (1964).

There has been a flurry of scholarly activity recently on the subject of American opponents of the Revolution. There are three general studies: W. Nelson, *The American Tory* (1961); W. Brown, *The Good Americans: The Loyalists in the American Revolution* (1969); and R. Calhoun, *The Loyalists in Revolutionary America* (1973). In addition, there are more specialized works. J. Ferling, *The Loyalist Mind: Joseph Galloway and the American Revolution* (1977), analyzes the thinking of one of the American Revolution's most notable loyalists.

There is a superb biography of another prominent loyalist: B. Bailyn, *The Ordeal of Thomas Hutchinson* (1974).

M. Norton, *The British-Americans: The Loyalist Exiles in England, 1774–1789* (1975), is a fine study. Finally, the four essays in E. Wright (ed.), *A Tug of Loyalties: Anglo-American Relations, 1765–1785* (1975), are very useful in comparing the mind sets of rebels and loyalists.

In recent years, the military history of the Revolution has received increasingly sophisticated treatment by historians interested in the relationship between armies and the larger societies from which they are drawn. See D. Higgenbotham, *The War of American Independence: Military Attitudes, Policies, and Practices, 1763–1789* (1971); J. Martin and M. Lender, *A Respectable Army: The Military Origins of the Republic, 1763–1789* (1982); L. Cress, *Citizens in Arms: The Army and Militia in American Society to the War of 1812* (1982); R. Wright, *The Continental Army* (1983); C. Royster, *A Revolutionary People at War: The Continental Army and American Character, 1775–1783* (1979); E. Carp, *To Starve the Army at Pleasure: Continental Army Administration and American Political Culture, 1775–1783* (1984).

Naval action during the Revolution is explained in S. Morison, *John Paul Jones: A Sailor's Biography* (1959). G. Sheer (ed.), *Private Yankee Doodle* (1962), is an interesting memoir by a common soldier. The best account of the central American figure who lost so many battles but won the war is J. Flexnor, *George Washington in the American Revolution, 1775–1783* (1968). An important aspect of the conflict is dealt with by J. Dull in *A Diplomatic History of the American Revolution* (1985).

For women's status and roles in revolutionary America, see M. Norton, *Liberty's Daughters* (1980), and L. Kerber, *Women of the Republic* (1980).

PROBLEMS OF GOVERNMENT

Chapter 7

In many ways the American revolutionaries were lucky when it came to dealing with problems of government. The idea of natural rights gave them a very clear idea of how governments ought to work. They already shared strong ideas about such matters as representation, taxation, the dangers of standing armies, courts without juries, and public officials over whom they had no control. And the American rebels had one thing most other revolutionaries lacked. They already possessed certain institutions that embodied their ideas about government. These institutions—notably the courts and representative assemblies—provided a foundation for carrying on the work of change. No other single fact does more to explain the character of the American Revolution.

Yet old institutions and practices can create problems as well. Americans were used to having their forms of government set down in writing. The governments of the colonies had been based on royal charters issued to a joint stock company, to proprietors, or to an individual colony. Once the king had been rejected, the question arose as to who should write and issue new written frames of government. Theory suggested that "the people" should draw up the fundamental framework, but here there were obvious difficulties. Exactly how did "the people" go about drafting and

approving a charter of government, a constitution? Given their experience with Great Britain, Americans were anxious to write down not only what their governments could do, but what they could not.

A related problem was the relationship of the various states. At first the Continental Congress called them the United Colonies and then the United States, but it was not at all clear what the "United States" actually was—or were. If the "United States" was to be anything more than a temporary alliance, there had to be some agreement about what it could and could not do.

As the war ended, the touchiest question remained the same one that had dominated politics in the 1760s: taxation. Other problems also came to the surface. A major one was how to deal with the vast territory won in the West. Another was the relationships of the new country (or thirteen countries) with foreign powers, Spain and Britain remained hostile, and France not overly friendly to American interests. Could Americans solve these problems and still remain faithful to the principles of the Revolution? In the modern world, most ex-colonies have ended up as dictatorships. Thanks to their own historical experience, however, Americans were able to find another way. ■

THE STATE CONSTITUTIONS

In 1776 the states were governed by provincial congresses composed mostly of men who had served in the colonial assemblies. Indeed, at first the old assemblies simply transformed themselves into the governing bodies of the new states. Everyone assumed that more permanent arrangements needed to be made and written down in a state constitution. Despite wartime difficulties, every state adopted a written document of fundamental law long before the war ended.

Power to the Legislatures

For the most part, the new constitutions continued old forms and practices. Rhode Island and Connecticut simply kept their old charters after eliminating references to Great Britain and the king. All the states retained their assemblies. Only Pennsylvania had lacked a governor's council to serve as the upper house of the legislature, and Pennsylvania was the only state to adopt a unicameral legislature; all the other states provided for two houses.

But they made important changes in the upper one. Rather than being appointed by the governor, the upper houses were now elected by the people or by the lower house. In addition, the upper houses lost their roles of advising the governors and serving as high courts. As things turned out, the members tended to be the same sort of people who sat in the lower house.

Most of the new constitutions also broadened the suffrage somewhat by lowering property requirements for voting. Yet Americans did not abandon the old idea that a man ought to possess at least some property in order to vote, and they continued the practice of having higher qualifications for those seeking public office. In contrast to Europe, however, the suffrage was so broad that the United States seemed really to be ruled by the people.

Fundamental Power of the People

In most states, the revolutionary provincial congresses drew up and adopted new constitutions without consulting the voters. Massachusetts, however, set a different example that was later followed by the others in rewriting their basic law, and by the Republic itself when the Great Convention of 1787 wrote the fundamental law of the land. This new procedure emphasized one of the American Revolution's most important contributions to modern democratic government—the idea that constitutions are derived directly from the will of the people.

In Massachusetts, when the provincial congress asked the towns for power to draw up the new state constitution the majority agreed, but Concord objected. The Concord town meeting asked: If the provincial legislature makes the constitution, what is to prevent it from unmaking it? If the fundamental law has no standing above ordinary legislation, what will protect our liberties? Concord demanded that a special "Convention . . . be immediately Chosen, to form & establish a Constitution."

The Massachusetts provincial government ignored Concord's proposal and drafted a new constitution. But the Concord notion spread; and when the provincial congress presented its work to the people in 1778, they rejected it by a 5 to 1 majority. Recognizing that the principal objection to the constitution was its authorship, the provincial congress voted in June 1779 to follow the Concord idea. By March 1780, under the leadership of John Adams, a specially elected convention completed a new framework of government, which the voters approved in June.

Bills of Rights

Most state constitutions set forth at the outset a "bill" or "declaration" of "unalienable" or "natural" or "inherent" rights. These rights included "acquiring, possessing, and protecting property"; freedom of worship, speech, and assembly; moderate bail, prompt hearings, trial by jury, and punishments to fit the crime; protection from general search warrants and from liability to serve in, or support, standing armies.

Above all, "when any government shall be found inadequate or contrary to [the people's wishes] . . . a majority of the community hath an indubitable, unalienable and indefeasible right to reform, alter or abolish it." To reduce the likelihood of revolutions, elections must be "free, . . . frequent, certain, and regular." And in such elections, all "men having sufficient evidence to permanent common interest with, and attachment to the community, have the right of suffrage."

For some time conservatives found it easy enough to live with these generalizations. Yet the "bills of rights" gave the people, in the language of the times, "a standing law to live by." Without promises of such a bill of rights they almost certainly would have rejected the new federal Constitution of 1787. Eventually, reformers used the liberal language of these bills to abolish imprisonment for debt, provide free schools, prohibit the use of public funds for favored religious sects, promote free expression in the press, reform the courts, improve the jails, liberalize qualifications for officeholding, and broaden the franchise.

THE ARTICLES OF CONFEDERATION

It took the Second Continental Congress more than two years to draft an instrument that its members would agree to submit to the states. John Dickinson of Pennsylvania, the principal author of the new document, tried to establish a national government without weakening the individual commonwealths. Dickinson's name for his government, "a firm league of friendship," strongly suggested that where conflict of authority arose, the states, not the new central government, would triumph. The Congress was aware of defects in its proposal. In its request to the states for formal approval, it apologized for the "uncommon embarrassment and delay" in framing the Articles.

Strengths and Weaknesses

Under the proposed Articles of Confederation, each state elected and paid the salaries of its delegates and reserved the right to recall them. In the single-chamber legislature voting was to be by state. Each state had only one vote, no matter what its population and wealth or how many delegates it sent. Important legislation required a two-thirds majority, or nine of the thirteen states, a margin made more difficult to reach by the provision nullifying a state's vote if its delegates were evenly split. The administration of laws was made difficult by the provision making the executive a "committee of the states" consisting of one delegate from each state. The weakest link of all was that the Articles could be amended only with the *unanimous* consent of the states.

Yet the Articles gave the new central government considerable powers. It could make war and treaties of alliance and of peace. It could establish the amounts of men and money the states should provide for national purposes. It could settle dis-

ADAMS ON GOVERNMENT

Even before the Declaration of Independence, John Adams was thinking about long-range plans for a new government. His sense of optimism is clear in this letter of January 1776.

As politics is the art of securing human happiness, and the prosperity of societies depends upon the constitution of government under which they live, there cannot be a more agreeable employment to a benevolent mind than the study of the best kinds of government.

It has been the will of Heaven that we should be thrown into existence at a period when the greatest philosophers and lawgivers of antiquity would have wished to live. A period when a coincidence of circumstances without example, has afforded to thirteen Colonies, at once, an opportunity of beginning government anew from the foundation, and building as they choose. How few of the human race have ever had any opportunity of choosing a system of government for themselves and their children! How few have ever had any thing more of choice in government than in climate! These Colonies have now their election; and it is much to be wished that it may not prove to be like a prize in the hands of a man who has no heart to improve it.

John Adams. (*Boston Athenaeum*)

putes between states, admit new ones, borrow money, set standards for coins and weights and measures, establish a postal service, deal with Indians, appoint naval and military officers, and otherwise support national armed forces. But the new government was denied the power of levying taxes, raising troops, and regulating commerce, all of which were basic to sovereignty.

In retrospect it is clear that the Articles proposed a very new kind of government. They divided the fundamental powers of government between two levels of government. Many people had long thought such an arrangement impossible. Most people had previously assumed that the supreme or sovereign power of any government could not be shared. Out of wartime necessity, the Congress was proposing that sovereignty be divided between the states and the national government. For this reason, they naturally described their union as a "confederation," a term that literally means "with trust."

The Problem of Land Claims

The framers of the Articles, having made every concession they could to the states' freedom of action, expected quick approval by state governments. One last concession to Virginia, however, aroused the suspicions of Maryland and other "landless" states and delayed ratification for almost four years. This concession was that "no state should be deprived of territory for the benefit of the United States."

Seven "landed" states, on the basis of their original charters or on other grounds, laid claim to territory extending either to the Ohio or Mississippi rivers or all the way to the Pacific. By the Quebec Act of 1774, Britain had overridden these claims. Maryland, a state without claims to western lands, now argued that since the Revolutionary War was a common effort, the territories claimed by the landed states should be "considered as common property." New Jersey and Delaware agreed with Maryland.

As the costs of the war mounted, the landless states became alarmed at the high taxes they would be forced to levy. The landed states would be able to pay their costs out of land sales. The landless states were also troubled by the probable growth in population and power of the landed ones. Their own people, they said, would be lured by low taxes to the western territories of the landed states, making such states dominant in any central government. Speculators added their voices to those

of their representatives. Before the revolution, these speculators had purchased millions of acres from Indians in areas claimed especially by Virginia. If Virginia's claims were allowed, their own would not be.

The deadlock over ratification of the Articles lasted until February 1780, when New York, a "landed" state, proposed to offer its lands to Congress to cement "the federal alliance." Connecticut followed suit. When Virginia at last yielded in January 1781, Maryland withdrew its objections. In February, Congress named March 1 as the day to proclaim the start of the new government. The Second Continental Congress then became the formal ruling body of "The United States of America."

Foreign Affairs

At the close of the revolution, an Englishman predicted that the Americans would be "a disunited people till the end of time, suspicious and distrustful of each other . . . divided and subdivided into little commonwealths or principalities . . . with no centre of union and no common interest." In 1783 there was real justification for such a view. For several months, Congress lacked enough members to form a quorum. It proved impossible to gather enough delegates to ratify the peace treaty before the specified six-month time limit ran out, though the British permitted the treaty to go into effect two months late. Charles Thomson, the "secretary" of Congress, admitted that "a government without a visible head must appear a strange phenomenon to European politicians."

According to the peace treaty, the British were to surrender their military and fur-trading posts in the Northwest "with all convenient speed." But the British held onto the posts in order to protect the rich Canadian fur trade until, as they hoped, the new nation collapsed. They stirred up Indians against American settlers, and they used force to deny Americans the use of the Great Lakes.

Spain, an ally of France in the Revolutionary War, proved to be as much an enemy to the Americans as Britain. In 1783 the Spanish had received East and West Florida from the British. They established forts there and proceeded to make treaties with the Indians of the region. The treaties obligated the Indians to join in the harassment of American settlers. Congress was unable to force Spain to stop, and this weakness cost it support in the South and Southwest, just as weakness against the British angered Americans in the Northwest.

Western Lands Ceded by the States, 1782–1802

On the map:

BRITISH CANADA

Claimed by Great Britain

Lake Superior

Lake Huron

St. Lawrence R.

VT. (1791)

MAINE (To Mass.)

Lake Michigan

Lake Ontario

Lake Erie

Ceded by Mass. 1785

Ceded by Conn. 1786

Ceded by Conn. 1800

Ceded by New York 1782

N.H.

NEW YORK

MASS.

CONN. R.I.

PENNSYLVANIA

NEW JERSEY

MD.

DEL.

LOUISIANA (Spanish)

Ohio R.

Mississippi R.

VIRGINIA

Ceded by Virginia 1792

Ceded by North Carolina 1790

NORTH CAROLINA

Ceded by South Carolina 1787

SOUTH CAROLINA

Ceded by Georgia 1802

GEORGIA

Ceded by South Carolina 1787
Claimed by Spain until 1795

SPANISH FLORIDA

ATLANTIC OCEAN

Gulf of Mexico

Legend:
Western lands ceded by states
Ceded by Virginia 1784 ("Northwest Territory")
Disputed territories

0   300
Miles

British and Spanish stubbornness over the West was hardened by American failures on other international issues. The peace treaty, for example, declared that no legal barriers should prevent creditors on either side from collecting old debts. Actually the great bulk of the debts were owed by the ex-colonists. Although Congress urged the new states to honor the treaty provision, it had no power to prevent their passing laws to frustrate collection. Not until 1802 did the United States settle private debts incurred by Americans before the revolution by agreeing to pay the sum of £600,000 to British creditors.

In accordance with the terms of the peace treaty, Congress also made "earnest recommendation" to the states to restore confiscated property to former Loyalist owners. Most states chose to ignore this recommendation; even after the war, patriots continued to confiscate Loyalist lands without being punished by the courts.

Financial Problems

With no power to levy taxes, Congress had to face its problems without a sound financial base. With no money to pay the troops, Congress was physically menaced by its own army. Sharing the almost universal lack of confidence in the government, several units of the army refused to disband without being paid. In June 1783, told that the Philadelphia militia would not raise a single musket against mutinous Pennsylvania regiments and having no force of their own to use, the few delegates in attendance removed themselves to the hamlet of Princeton, New Jersey. One Pennsylvania officer called Congress "a jest."

Many other claims arising from the war poured in. There was the back interest, not to speak of the principal, to be paid on the public debt. Robert Morris, named secretary of finance in 1781, urged Congress to establish a national tariff so that it would no longer have to beg states for funds. He also proposed a land tax, a poll tax, and an excise tax on distilled liquors. But the delegates refused all these proposals. When Congress in 1782 requested $10 million from the states for the next year, it received less than $1.5 million.

When Morris finally left his post in 1784, the treasury was empty as usual. Yet his efforts had not been wholly in vain. In 1781, at his suggestion, Congress chartered the Bank of North America, the first commercial bank in the nation. It was to be located in Philadelphia. The bank eventually lent millions to the government and saw it through some critical situations. But most of the bank's business was with private businessmen. Like other American institutions under the Confederation, this bank—and others modeled after it in New York and Massachusetts in 1784—performed more effectively than the central government.

Congress and the Private Economy

There were other postwar economic problems. American shipowners were especially hard hit by the loss of their favored trading position with Britain and the British West Indies. When the Americans tried to get Britain to reopen the West Indian trade to American ships, they were laughed out of court. The loss of British trade was only partially offset by the new trade opened up with China in 1784 and by increased trade with France and other European countries.

American importers grew as discontented as American shipowners. Just after the war, importers had a taste of prosperity when the ex-colonists

---

WORDS AND NAMES IN AMERICAN HISTORY

The word *logrolling* is an almost perfect example of the way the meaning of words can reflect the workings of American history. Originally, *logrolling* meant something rather simple. It came into use when the earliest settlers, both European and African, had to cut down trees in the heavily forested lands along the Atlantic coast. These settlers cut wood for several purposes: for fuel, for housing, for export, for shipbuilding, and (in many cases) to get it out of the way so they could grow crops. Moving trees that had been cut down required a great deal of power, and no elephants or bulldozers were available. So the logs had to be "rolled" by people in groups. Since logrolling always took place on one person's property, with the cooperation of others who did not own that land, the job and the term always suggested that services were being exchanged: "if you'll roll my log, I'll roll yours." The same feeling spilled over eventually into American politics. In the national Congress and in the state legislatures, *logrolling* came to describe exactly the same ethic as the original effort: In short: you help me with mine, I'll help you with yours. I'll vote for your favorite bill if you'll vote for mine.

went on a buying splurge. But the market for luxuries was small, and the splurge was quickly over. American manufacturers and artisans, who had had the American market for coarse goods largely to themselves during the war, also suffered from the foreign competition. They demanded protective tariffs to keep foreign goods out and subsidies to support their own industrial expansion—neither of which Congress could provide.

There was a brighter side. Most Americans were subsistence farmers who did not depend on Congress for their well-being. Even the loudest critics of Congress often found ways to help themselves. Philadelphia, New York, and Baltimore merchants profited from illegal West Indian trade. Public creditors, though unpaid by Congress, apparently still had enough money to sponsor new business ventures. Immediately following the war there was unprecedented activity in river and road improvements, house building, land transactions, and banking. The resumption of immigration from the British Isles and from Europe also helped the basic soundness of the economy.

Congress and the Frontier

In writings about American history, "frontier" usually describes the West in an early phase of its development. But this use of the word ignores the opening of the "northern frontier" of Vermont, New Hampshire, and Maine.

Vermont was the last part of the northern frontier to be entered by white settlers. Both New York and New Hampshire claimed the territory. After Ethan Allen's victory for the rebel states at Fort Ticonderoga in 1775, he and his brother Levi tried to get the governor of Canada to guarantee Vermont's independence in exchange for neutrality in the war. Failing here, in 1777, when about 30,000 persons had settled in Vermont, the Allens set up an independent government. Not until 1791 did Vermont become the fourteenth state.

Far to the southwest, other adventurers were staking out land for independent settlements. During the 1770s, James Robertson and John Sevier, two Virginia speculators, led settlers into the region of the Watauga and Holston rivers. In 1784, when North Carolina ceded its claims in this region to Congress, the Wataugans, now 10,000 strong and aware that Congress could do nothing for them that they could not do better themselves, set up the independent state of Franklin. Eventually, however, Franklin was ab-

sorbed into the sixteenth state, Tennessee.

Much the same pattern occurred beyond the Virginia mountains in the regions that became Kentucky in 1792. It was a pattern repeated in many frontier areas where settlement outran the reach of eastern governments. In the long run, what was most striking was the ease with which these little, supposedly independent, "republics" were absorbed into the larger one. The key to the matter was, of course, that the federal union was itself, from the beginning, a union of little republics.

The Northwest Ordinance

Settlement of the vast area northwest of the Ohio River was somewhat more orderly, partly because of the New England tradition of controlled settlement and partly because of Thomas Jefferson's liking for planning. Jefferson wrote much of the Northwest Ordinance of 1785, which set the basic pattern. It established the crucial principle that the settled portions of the West would be admitted to the Union on an equal basis with the original provinces. Jefferson's original ordinance was modified two years later by the addition of provisions for the transition from organized territories to full-fledged states.

This Northwest Ordinance of 1787 was probably the Confederation Congress's most important piece of legislation. Under it, the Northwest Territory became a single unit with a governor appointed by Congress. When 5000 free male inhabitants had settled in the territory, those who owned at least 50 acres were to elect a territorial legislature whose acts would be subject only to the governor's veto. The voters would also send a nonvoting delegate to Congress. No less than three and no more than five states were to be carved out of the territory. The boundaries of three future states were laid out. When a potential state had 60,000 free inhabitants, it was to be admitted to the Union on an equal footing with the original states. The ordinance also prohibited slavery in the territory and in all the states to be carved from it.

Following adoption of the ordinance, there was a rush of settlement. The Ohio Company sent out a small group of pioneers and established the village of Marietta at the junction of the Ohio and Muskingam rivers. A second group, sent out by a New Jersey speculator, laid the foundations of Cincinnati in 1788. Eight years later, Moses Cleaveland led a band of pioneers to build a town on the shores of Lake Erie.

Detroit in 1794. (*Courtesy of the Burton Historical Collection, Detroit Public Library*)

Shays' Rebellion

Apart from the Northwest Ordinance, Congress had few successes during the postwar years. Even in the Northwest, pioneers were left almost entirely to their own resources in fighting the Indians and the British. Frontier violence and threats of violence weakened the demand for land and left speculators a great deal less than happy.

Other postwar developments aroused the anger of the largest single economic class in the new nation, the farmers. The war had piled up what appeared to be monstrous debts for the states. As a result, the men who were owed money by state governments stood in conflict with the general mass of taxpayers, many of whom were debtors. In addition, as in any inflationary situation, private debtors were happy to pay off their debts in currency of reduced value, to the dismay of their creditors. Debtors demanded abundant paper money, lower taxes and "stay laws" that would delay mortgage foreclosures. Creditors wanted heavy taxes in gold or silver and swift and rigid enforcement of legal contracts.

Seven states issued some form of paper money, often with good effect. But in New England in particular, creditors and merchants in the coastal

commercial towns usually managed to avoid paper money and also to shift much of the tax burden onto inland farmers. By 1786, conditions had grown so bad in New Hampshire that the militia had to be called out to disperse a mob of farmers who surrounded the legislative meeting house in an effort to force the members to issue paper money. It was in Massachusetts, however, where farmers appear to have been taxed as much as one-third of their income, that conservatives received their greatest shock. In 1785, Massachusetts farmers in the western part of the state decided to take the same sort of action Boston merchants had thought legitimate ten years earlier: domestic rebellion.

Daniel Shays was not very different from the thousand men who became his followers. He had seen action at Bunker Hill. "A brave and good soldier," as a subordinate described him, he waited four years for a promised commission to captain. In 1780 he returned home to await payment for his long service to his country. His farming went badly, his army compensation was delayed, his obligations accumulated, and he faced being jailed for debt.

His neighbors shared his bitterness. Many western towns were too poor to send delegates to the

Daniel Shays and Joe Shattuck. (*National Portrait Gallery, Smithsonian Institution, Washington, D.C.*)

legislature in Boston. Without any voice in the state government, the debtor leaders resorted to the now-familiar device of county conventions. Men from neighboring towns gathered at county seats to voice their political sentiments by means of resolutions and petitions to the legislature.

After the Massachusetts General Court adjourned in July 1786, having ignored these petitions, more and more county conventions met. Shays and other leaders warned the members to "abstain from all mobs and unlawful assemblies until a constitutional method of redress can be obtained." But popular discontent overrode such advice, and mobs began to threaten civil courts where foreclosure proceedings were scheduled. After forcing the suspension of many civil court sessions, the mobs attacked the criminal courts to prevent trials of the rioters. Finally, when armed mobs of farmers threatened federal arsenals, the government took action.

By October 1786, Shays had somehow become the focus of the whole movement, and the rebels who followed him soon became the targets of state forces gathered by General Benjamin Lincoln at the request of Governor James Bowdoin. Fighting between the Shays forces and Lincoln's continued from mid-January to the end of February 1787, when the rebellion finally was crushed.

Shays fled to Vermont. A number of his followers, captured during the fighting, were freed by the legislature in June. The bitterness that followed this uprising emerged in the subsequent elections, when Governor Bowdoin was voted down at the polls. No real punishment was imposed on Shays or his followers. The Massachusetts legislature eased off on taxes and passed laws exempting household goods and workmen's tools from confiscation for debt.

News of Shays' Rebellion shocked many propertied Americans. They were already alarmed by the weakness of Congress, the discontent of the army, and the vulnerability of government to mob action. Washington himself described Congress as "a half-starved, limping" body "always moving upon crutches and tottering at every step."

THE CONSTITUTION

The movement for a stronger central government was sparked by a small group of energetic and dedicated nationalists. We know now that they

JOHN JAY ON GOVERNMENT

Late in October 1786, John Jay wrote from New York the following gloomy assessment to ambassador Thomas Jefferson in Paris. His sentiments echoed those of most nationalists throughout the states.

The inefficacy of our Government becomes daily more and more apparent. Our Credit and our Treasury are in a sad Situation, and it is probable that either the Wisdom or the Passions of the People will produce Changes.

A Spirit of Licentiousness has infected Massachusetts, which appears more formidable than some at first apprehended; whether similar Symptoms will soon mark a like Disease in several other States, is very problematical.

The public Papers herewith sent contain everything generally known about these Matters. A Reluctance to Taxes, an Impatience of Government, a Rage for Property, and little Regard to the Means of acquiring it, together with a Desire of Equality in all Things, seem to actuate the Mass of those who are uneasy in their Circumstances; to these may be added the influence of ambitious Adventurers, and the Speculations of the many Characters who prefer private to public good, and of others who expect to gain more from Wrecks made by Tempests, than from the Produce of patient and honest Industry. . . .

In short, my Dr. Sir; we are in a very unpleasant Situation. Changes are Necessary, but what they ought to be, what they will be, and how and when to be produced, are arduous Questions. I feel for the Cause of Liberty and for the Honor of my Countrymen who have so nobly asserted it, and who at present so abuse its Blessings. If it should not take Root in this Soil little Pains will be taken to cultivate it in any other.

succeeded with the Constitution of the United States. At the time, however, they faced enormous obstacles and came extremely close to failure. In the early 1780s many of the new nation's leaders thought it was going through a "critical period." Some had grown so discouraged about the whole experiment that they thought it should be given up. "Some of our more enlightened men," wrote Benjamin Rush in 1786, "have secretly proposed an Eastern, Middle, and Southern Confederacy, to be united by an alliance." Others spoke of the possibility of preserving the Union by means of a monarchy. "What a triumph for our enemies," exclaimed Washington, "to verify their predictions! What a triumph for the advocates of despotism to find we are incapable of governing ourselves."

Washington, steadfast in his nationalism and republicanism, would tolerate neither disunion nor despotism. Even before the Articles of Confederation had been ratified, he and other nationalists were advocating their improvement to strengthen the union. They carried the day, but only by taking revolutionary steps of their own.

George Washington. (*The Cleveland Museum of Art, Hinman B. Hurlbut Collection*)

The Constitutional Convention

A strong movement for a new form of government emerged from the efforts of practical men to achieve what the Articles could not—a more satisfactory regulation of interstate commerce. Early in 1785, delegates from Maryland and Virginia met at Alexandria in an attempt to settle their differences over navigation of the Potomac River and Chesapeake Bay. The delegates decided to move to Washington's home at Mount Vernon, where they extended their sessions so that delegates from neighboring Delaware and Pennsylvania could attend. These discussions finally resulted in a recommendation to the Virginia legislature that it call a general meeting of all the states at Annapolis in September 1786.

Only five states responded, but one was New York. Among its delegates was Alexander Hamilton, whose ideas about government went far beyond commercial matters. To attempt much more in the way of change with only five states, however, seemed impractical. At Hamilton's and James Madison's suggestion, the Annapolis convention adjourned with a call for a new convention to meet in Philadelphia the following May to amend the Articles. Meanwhile, since Shays' Rebellion had aroused so much concern, the state legislatures responded far more positively than they had to Virginia's call a few months earlier. All

except Rhode Island eventually sent representatives to Philadelphia.

The men the states chose were a remarkably able group. Some prominent political leaders were not available: John Adams and Thomas Jefferson were abroad on diplomatic missions; Sam Adams was not named a delegate; Patrick Henry, appointed by Virginia, refused to attend. Otherwise the famous names of the country were there: Benjamin Franklin and James Wilson from Pennsylvania; James Madison, Edmund Randolph, and George Washington from Virginia; and Alexander Hamilton from New York.

Of the seventy-four men named to the convention, only fifty-five actually attended. Their average age was forty-two. Many had been army officers in the war, and twenty-seven belonged to the Society of the Cincinnati, a group formed to look after army officer interests. Only eight were signers of the Declaration of Independence. In an age when few Americans went to college, a majority of the delegates were college graduates. For the most part they were lawyers, merchants, and planters.

The convention was supposed to assemble on May 14, but delegates from the required minimum of seven states did not assemble in Philadelphia until May 25. On that day twenty-nine delegates unanimously elected Washington presiding officer. Next, uneasy about local rumors and the press, they voted unanimously to keep their discussions secret. Debate then took place on their purpose in coming together. Some maintained that they must follow their instructions to "amend" the Articles. But others, led by Hamilton, argued that they must not "let slip the golden opportunity." The convention decided to replace, not amend, the Articles. It adopted Edmund Randolph's resolution,

That a national government ought to be established consisting of a supreme legislative, executive, and judiciary.

Fundamental Assumptions

Although the delegates had many disagreements, most of them shared certain basic assumptions about the nature of people and of government. They agreed that people were basically driven by self-interest and that the structure of any government had to deal with this fact. If people were, as Hamilton said, "ambitious, vindictive, and rapacious," how did one go about controlling them without establishing a tyranny? Most delegates agreed with Madison that vice could not be stopped by virtue; vice must be stopped with vice: "Ambition must be made to counteract ambition."

The delegates wholeheartedly agreed that the people ought to have a voice in government. But they felt they knew from both history and recent experience that the people could be stampeded

James Madison. (*Library of Congress*)

into following demagogues and dictators. So the people's role must be limited. Although most of the delegates were men of property who distrusted excessive democracy, they had no illusions about the benevolence of the rich. Even a wealthy aristocrat like Gouverneur Morris of Pennsylvania acknowledged that "wealth tends to corrupt the mind," and that rich men as well as poor would use power to their own advantage if given the opportunity. Thus the greed and pride of the rich, like the gullibility and passions of the poor, must also be held in check.

The delegates were as reluctant to entrust power to special interests as to individuals or social classes. They believed that a landed interest, a slaveholding interest, a creditor interest, a debtor interest, a commercial interest, or a religious interest would tyrannize the rest of society if given the opportunity. And the danger would be even greater if several interests were to join forces. To meet this problem, the advocates of a strong constitution turned to a variety of arrangements, including the division of sovereignty in a federal republic. But they also had in mind balancing powers within the fundamental units of government. Political selfishness among the parts would offset attempts to monopolize power by various interests working together.

The concept of offsetting competing interests was as old as Aristotle. It had been elaborately set forth by Montesquieu, one of the *philosophes* of the French Enlightenment. He had argued that the various parts of the government should check and balance one another. It was John Adams, though, who gave the best statement of the idea of "checks and balances":

A legislative, an executive, and a judicial power comprehend the whole of what is meant and understood by government. It is by balancing each of these powers against the other two, that the efforts of human nature toward tyranny can alone be checked and restrained, and any degree of freedom preserved in the constitution.

Traditional American political practices gave the delegates an opportunity to introduce such balancing into the new national government. In the provincial and state legislatures, the lower house usually served as the "democratical branch," elected by a broad suffrage. In the new national legislature, most delegates agreed, there must also be two houses, the democratic one to check and in turn be checked by a second, which would represent the wealthier elements.

John Adams declared that there could be "no

free government without a democratical branch in the constitution." A few delegates thought that a two-house legislature, by pulling in opposite directions, would be incapable of effective action. But advocates of bicameralism pointed out that a strong and independent executive could prevent this.

Naturally the convention could not agree unanimously even on these general principles. Some delegates were concerned about state power. Others, certain that the establishment of a national sovereignty would swallow up traditional personal liberties, earned reputations as obstructionists. Hamilton himself stood on the extreme conservative side and believed that concessions to the people made the Constitution "a frail and worthless fabric," though he later urged ratification of the document. John Adams expressed the spirit of the Founding Fathers and the spirit of the age when he observed that "the blessings of society depend entirely on the constitutions of government." Helped by that faith, the delegates at the convention managed to balance out contending claims and complete the instrument that has proved so durable.

Two Compromises

The first of the two most divisive controversies was that of the relative power to be granted large and small states. Once the delegates had agreed to go beyond the idea of amending the Articles, they took up Edmund Randolph's so-called Virginia Plan for a new government structure. Randolph proposed a two-house National Legislature with membership in both houses allotted among the states in proportion to their free population. Members of the upper house were to be elected by the members of the lower, who were themselves to be elected by the people. The whole National Legislature was then to elect the National Judiciary.

This proposal obviously violated the principle of balancing separate powers within the government, and it aroused considerable opposition. It particularly alarmed the small-state delegates, who feared that their commonwealths would be overwhelmed in the popularly elected house and that some states might have no representatives at all in the upper chamber.

As a counterproposal, the small states offered a plan of their own, presented to the convention by William Paterson of New Jersey and known since as the New Jersey Plan. It proposed to have Congress remain a single house, as under the Articles,

with each state having one vote. The delegates quickly rejected this suggestion because it continued the current situation and because it based representation on states rather than people. The convention returned to the Virginia Plan as the preliminary model from which to construct the final document.

Rejection of Randolph's proposals for the makeup of the new national legislature brought the issue of large and small state representation to a head. At one point the small-state delegations threatened, as a Delaware member put it, to "find some foreign ally, of more honor and good faith" than his large-state colleagues. They were on the verge of going home.

Disaster was avoided by the appointment of a special committee to restudy the whole issue of representation. Early in July this committee brought in a compromise devised largely by Benjamin Franklin: There would be a two-house legislature, with membership in the lower house according to population, thus satisfying the large states, and membership in the upper house equal for all states, thus satisfying the small ones. This arrangement, adopted after a great deal of debate, provided the basis for the Great Compromise of the Constitution. It determined the general character of the two bodies that were named the House of Representatives and the Senate.

The two-house plan enabled the delegates to establish the lower house as the people's branch. Members of this house were to be elected by all voters in each state who were eligible to vote for "the most numerous branch of the State Legislature." The matter of suffrage requirements was left to the states. The upper house, whose members were to be chosen by state legislatures, was expected to be more friendly to propertied classes and generally more conservative.

The Great Compromise raised several issues that divided the delegates along completely different lines—sectional ones that concerned slavery. None of the delegates seemed to have expected this line of division.

The first such issue concerned the "direct taxes" the new government could levy. The convention agreed that such taxes should be apportioned among the states according to population, just as representation was to be apportioned in the lower house. But the slave states wanted their blacks, if they were counted at all in apportioning taxes, to be given less weight than free men. The North wanted blacks to be given less weight only for congressional representation. In the debate, the proportion of three-fifths was proposed many times. But Wilson of Pennsylvania "did not well see on what principle the admission of blacks in the proportion of three-fifths could be explained. Are they admitted as Citizens? Are they admitted as property? Then why is not other property admitted into the computation?" Wilson nevertheless admitted "the necessity of compromise," and the others yielded on the three-fifths rule. For both direct taxes and representation, five blacks were to be counted as equivalent to three whites.

Another issue that split the states along sectional lines was foreign commerce. Delegates from the commerical North urged that the new government be granted full power to regulate interstate and foreign commerce and to make treaties the states must obey. The convention easily agreed on these points. But delegates from the southern states, fearful of being outvoted in the new Congress, demanded that commercial regulations and all treaties require the consent of two-thirds of the Senate rather than a simple majority. Southerners, whose constituents depended so heavily on agricultural exports, were concerned about export taxes and possible treaties requiring them. They were dependent on selling tobacco and rice in competitive world markets.

The Lower South was even more concerned about the slave trade. If Congress had control over commerce, it could ban the slave trade or tax it out of existence. Delegates from South Carolina and Georgia warned that their states would never approve the proposed constitution if their supply of slaves was threatened. From North Carolina and Virginia northward there was no demand for slave imports, and a great many people had decided that the slave trade was unjust and inhumane. To placate South Carolina and Georgia, the majority of delegates reluctantly agreed on a compromise: Congress would be prohibited from interfering with the slave trade for a period of twenty years. The convention also compromised by prohibiting all taxes on exports. Finally, the South won the provision requiring a two-thirds vote in the Senate for the ratification of treaties. In exchange for these concessions, the northerners won their point on a simple congressional majority for acts regulating commerce, both among the states and with foreign nations.

The Executive

The convention next turned to the problem of the executive branch. The delegates discussed the questions of whether it should be composed of one or several men, how long he or they should serve, whether its holder(s) could serve for another term, and what name to give the executive office holder(s). Discussion of these matters took far longer than others that now seem more important. Yet at the time it was not at all obvious, for example, how long the new "president" should hold office. Seven years was the term most commonly suggested. Eventually the delegates settled on an arrangement that prevails to this day (with one exception concerning reelection): a single executive, elected for four renewable years, called a president.

The method of the president's election presented one last test. Strong nationalists wanted the president elected directly by the people; state-sovereignty men wanted him chosen by state legislatures. After many arguments, the convention devised the elaborate electoral college plan (Article II, Section 1). Each state was to have as many electors as it had representatives and senators, and the method of choosing these electors was left up to the state legislatures.

Almost all the delegates assumed that the presidential electors in each state would usually vote for men from their own state. They expected that no candidate would receive the majority required for election. In that case, or in case two candidates, each with a majority, were tied, the election would be decided in the House of Representatives. Each state, regardless of population, would cast one vote. This arrangement appeared to give the small states equal standing with the large ones in the ultimate choice of the president. The members of the convention assumed that, in effect, the president would be nominated by the large states in the electoral college, but actually elected by all the states in the House of Representatives.

This complex scheme was based on the assumption that each state would constitute its own party. Only a few years later, the emergence of national political parties made this elaborate machinery useless. The two-party system eventually made it possible for voters throughout the country to choose electors pledged to one of a few leading candidates. But electors retained the privilege of exercising personal choice in the electoral college.

Toward Sovereign Power

Among the flaws of government under the Confederation, two were fatal: Congress had neither the power of the purse nor the power of the sword. Although distracted at the outset by problems of apportioning power to the states and the people, most delegates had come to Philadelphia mainly to solve these problems by giving a new national government such sovereign strength.

Every delegate but Elbridge Gerry of Massachusetts voted to give the new national government power to levy and collect taxes and tariffs. The clause permitting Congress to pay the debts of the United States passed unanimously. No one opposed giving Congress the power to coin money and "regulate the value thereof," or the power to borrow money on the credit of the United States, or the power to regulate commerce among the states and foreign nations, or to deal with Indian tribes.

When Madison complained about state laws, he had in mind those that made credit more risky, investment more hazardous, and long-term business planning more uncertain. The big problem was paper money. The delegates agreed with Madison's position, and they almost unanimously forbade the states to issue "bills of credit" (paper money); to make anything but gold and silver legal tender for the payment of private or public debts; to interfere with the obligations of contracts; or to tax imports or exports in commercial wars with one another.

The Constitution's provisions for a military establishment also shifted power from the states to the national government. The new government alone was enabled to "provide for the common defence"; "to declare war"; "to raise and support armies"; "to provide and maintain a navy"; "to provide for calling forth the militia to execute the laws of the Union, suppress insurrections and repel invasions"; and more broadly, to provide for the "general welfare of the United States." To ensure that national sovereignty would not be impaired by technicalities, the framers added what later became known as the "elastic clause," enabling Congress "to make all laws which shall be necessary and proper for carrying into execution the foregoing powers."

A third flaw in the Confederation had been the absence of an independent executive. In remedying this defect, the Constitution made the president commander-in-chief of the army and navy and of the state militias when called into federal service. His power of appointing federal officers was extensive, and he was required to obtain the consent of the Senate only for his highest aides. The president could make treaties with foreign nations with the consent of two-thirds of the Senate. He could call Congress into extraordinary session and could veto acts of Congress, although his veto could be overridden by a two-thirds vote in both houses.

For protection against possible wrongdoing, the convention provided that the president could be impeached by majority vote in the House and then convicted by a two-thirds vote after a trial in the Senate, with the chief justice presiding.

A fourth flaw of the Confederation was its lack of a judiciary independent of state courts. The Constitution provided for a national judicial system. At the head of the system stood the Supreme Court of the United States: It could decide cases on appeal from lower federal courts, which Congress was empowered to establish, and from state courts in cases involving the Constitution, the laws of the United States, or treaties with other nations. The Constitution made no specific provision for "judicial review" of federal legislation, the power of federal courts to declare acts of Congress unconstitutional and void. But the Supreme Court later clarified this issue. Article II, Section 2, of the Constitution made possible the conclusion that any state actions or laws that encroached on the supreme powers of the federal government must be found unconstitutional by the federal courts. It was a short step for the Supreme Court to decide that it also had the power to declare acts of the federal Congress and president to be unconstitutional.

A Government for the Ages

The Philadelphia convention proposed a government that could act with speed, strength, and dignity. The Constitution radically shifted sovereign power away from the states toward a truly national government. No one knew at the time whether the arrangement would work. It took Americans about forty years before they began to regard the federal government as truly permanent. They were helped by the flexibility of the Constitution, and by the fact that its framers built into it their convictions about the fallibility—and the long-range bedrock importance—of "the people."

While the framers wanted mainly to substitute a strong central government for the weak Articles of Confederation, they also hoped to create a government, as Madison put it, "for the ages." Their success rested in part on features they introduced and on others unforeseen, but that proved at least as important.

From the framers' point of view, the Constitution's built-in checks and balances were the best safeguards of the Republic. No chief executive could become a dictator. And no temporary surge

Scene at the signing of the Constitution of the United States. (*Architect of the Capitol*)

of popular feeling, reflected in the "democratical branch" of the legislature, could unseat the president or overturn the courts.

A second source of the Constitution's lasting strength was its amending process. Trying to amend the Articles by unanimous consent of the states had proved impossible. The easier amending process in the Constitution was at first used sparingly—but only after the first ten amendments, the much-desired federal Bill of Rights, had been adopted.

A third source of the Constitution's long life lay in the brevity of its wording. The framers avoided going into great detail because they assumed that the principles of good government were universal. They left important powers to the states, but they spelled out the powers of the national government so broadly that these powers could later be expanded.

Several later developments unexpectedly added to the strength of the Constitution. They included the two-party system and the cabinet, both of which developed within ten years of the Constitution's adoption. Two other innovations came much later: the committee system in the House and Senate, and the civil service.

The constitutional convention, for all its conservatism, set up what was by world standards a radical government. Under the Constitution, said John Marshall, who rose as a new leader during the ratification controversy in Virginia, "It is the people that give power, and can take it back. What shall restrain them? They are the masters who give it, and of whom their servants hold it."

For all its stress on private property, which in the eighteenth century was thought to be the best foundation for public responsibility, the Constitution required no property qualification for office, not even that of president. It also required "a compensation—to be ascertained by law, and paid out of the Treasury of the United States" for all elective posts, so that the poor as well as the rich might hold them. In the Constitution itself, before the Bill of Rights was added, the provisions forbade religious tests for any federal position. It provided that "for any speech or debate in either House," senators and representatives "shall not be questioned in any other place," thereby assuring their fullest freedom of expression. It also guaranteed trial by jury for all crimes, "except in cases of impeachment," and forbade suspension of "the privilege of the writ of habeas corpus" except in times of invasion or rebellion. These provisions, which were similar to freedoms won in England in the seventeenth century, were important protections for legislative debate and individual liberty.

RATIFICATION

The constitutional convention was in session from May 25 to September 16, 1787. Of the fifty-five delegates who took part, forty-two stayed to the end, and thirty-nine signed the document. The other three—Gerry of Massachusetts, and Randolph and Mason of Virginia, refused to go along. Their refusals gave warning of the storm ahead when the Constitution would be brought to the people for approval.

Antifederalist Arguments

The day after the convention adopted the Constitution a copy was sent to Congress, largely out of courtesy, with a letter that did not mince words. "In all our deliberations on this subject," said the signers, "we kept steadily in our view that which appeared to us the greatest interest of every true American—the consolidation of the Union—in which is involved our prosperity, felicity, safety, perhaps our national existence." They did not ask Congress for a vote. Nor would they ask the state legislatures for confirmation; in the Constitution itself they asked for the consent of nine special state conventions like their own.

While the election of delegates to these conventions was in progress, the Constitution was discussed and debated throughout the country. Rufus King, a member of the Massachusetts ratifying convention, summed up the feelings of the opposition, though he did not share them, when he wrote to Madison in January 1788: "An apprehension that the liberties of the people are in danger, and a distrust of men of property and education have a more powerful effect upon the minds of our opponents than any specific objections against the Constitution."

But the Constitution's critics, named Antifederalists by the Constitution's friends, did offer many specific objections. There was no Bill of Rights; state sovereignty would be destroyed; the president might become king; the standing national army would be everywhere; only the rich could afford to hold office; tax collectors would swarm over the countryside; the people could not bear to be taxed by both state and national governments; commercial treaties would sell out the West and the South; debtors would no longer be able to defend themselves through recourse to state paper money and state stay laws. Many state politicians feared that a stronger national government would mean that they would lose their influence. More important, many ordinary citizens worried about so drastic an innovation and about centralized political power.

The First Ratifications

At first, ratification went smoothly. In December and January 1787–1788, five states approved the Constitution. The conventions of Delaware, New Jersey, and Georgia did so without a single opposing vote. Connecticut ratified by 123 to 40. Only in Pennsylvania, among the first five, was there controversy. By staying away, opponents of the Constitution tried to prevent the legislature from forming the quorum necessary before it could vote to call a ratifying convention. Federalists seized enough of their opponents and pushed them into the chamber to make a quorum. Pennsylvania voted to ratify, 46 to 23.

In the key state of Massachusetts, the next to ratify, the contest was close. Its convention debated for a month, but Federalist leaders maneuvered to win over opponents such as John Hancock and Sam Adams. They won over others by promising to support amendments guaranteeing popular liberties. Finally, Massachusetts voted for the Constitution, 187 to 168.

In the less crucial states of Maryland and South Carolina, ratification won easily. In New Hampshire, opposition was powerful. After a first convention failed to reach a vote, a second convention narrowly ratified on June 21, 1788. Technically speaking, the new government could now go into effect, for nine states had accepted it. But no one believed it could function without Virginia and New York, and in these two states the outcome remained doubtful.

Virginia and New York

In Virginia, an extraordinarily thorough and brilliant review of the issues took place, with the opposition led by George Mason and Patrick Henry. Washington's influence and the certain knowledge that he would consent to serve as first pres-

REDEUNT SATURNIA REGNA.

On the erection of the Eleventh PILLAR of the great *Na-*
tional DOME, *we beg leave most sincerely to felicitate* " OUR DEAR COUNT;

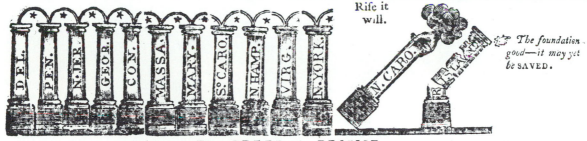

Rise it will.

The foundation good—it may yet be SAVED.

The FEDERAL EDIFICE.

ELEVEN STARS, in quick succession rise—
ELEVEN COLUMNS strike our wond'ring eyes,
Soon o'er the *whole*, shall swell the beauteous DOME,
COLUMBIA's boast—and FREEDOM's hallow'd home.
   Here shall the ARTS in glorious splendour shine !
And AGRICULTURE give her stores divine !
COMMERCE refin'd, dispense us more than gold,
And this new world, teach WISDOM to the old—
RELIGION here shall fix her blest abode,
Array'd in *mildness*, like its parent GOD !
JUSTICE and LAW, shall endless PEACE maintain,
And *the* " SATURNIAN AGE," *return again.*

North Carolina and Rhode Island were needed to help the other "pillars" support the new nation. (*Library of Congress*)

John Hancock. (*Museum of Fine Arts, Boston*)

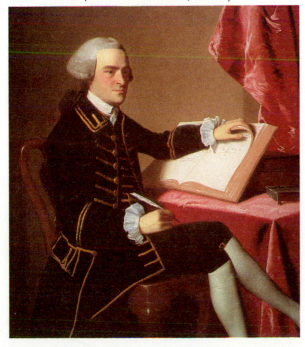

ident were responsible for the unexpected conversion of Edmund Randolph, who had refused to sign the Constitution. The promised addition of a Bill of Rights further softened the opposition. Four days after New Hampshire had ratified, Virginia fell in line, 89 to 79. By arrangement between Madison and Hamilton, couriers were quickly dispatched with the news to New York, where an extremely close struggle was in process.

In New York, Hamilton led the Federalist fight in support of ratification; Governor Clinton led the opposition. Well aware of Clinton's strength, Hamilton, John Jay, and James Madison had undertaken a series of anonymous newspaper articles supporting the Constitution. Later published as *The Federalist*, these articles provide the best commentary on the Constitution by contemporary advocates. But there was no landslide in New York. More important in the voting here was the news of Federalist success in New Hampshire and Virginia. Once again, the promise of a Bill of Rights overcame opposition. Having agreed to support

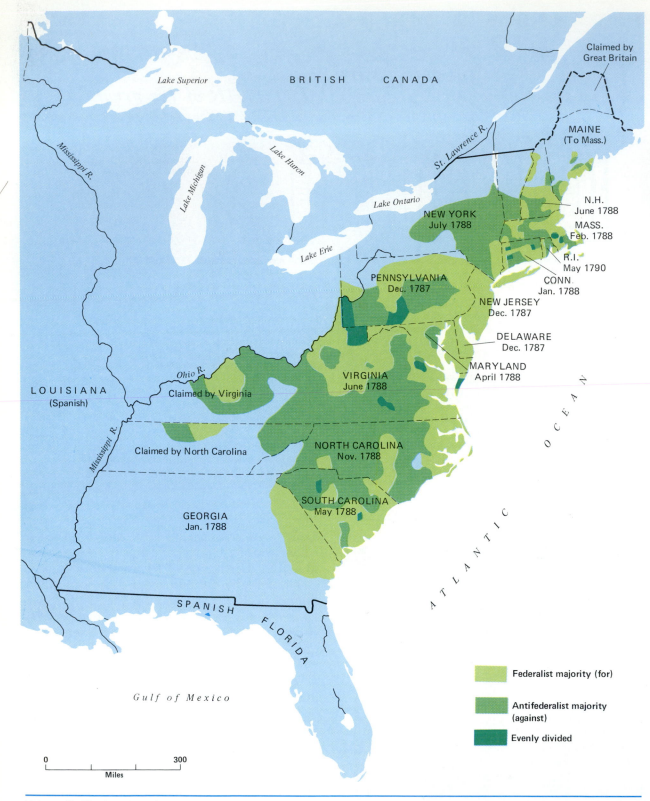

Vote on Ratification of the Constitution

Legend:
- Federalist majority (for)
- Antifederalist majority (against)
- Evenly divided

Map labels:
- BRITISH CANADA
- Lake Superior
- Lake Michigan
- Lake Huron
- Lake Ontario
- Lake Erie
- St. Lawrence R.
- Claimed by Great Britain
- MAINE (To Mass.)
- N.H. June 1788
- MASS. Feb. 1788
- R.I. May 1790
- CONN. Jan. 1788
- NEW YORK July 1788
- PENNSYLVANIA Dec. 1787
- NEW JERSEY Dec. 1787
- DELAWARE Dec. 1787
- MARYLAND April 1788
- VIRGINIA June 1788
- Claimed by Virginia
- Ohio R.
- Mississippi R.
- LOUISIANA (Spanish)
- Claimed by North Carolina
- NORTH CAROLINA Nov. 1788
- SOUTH CAROLINA May 1788
- GEORGIA Jan. 1788
- SPANISH FLORIDA
- Gulf of Mexico
- ATLANTIC OCEAN

Scale: 0 — 300 Miles

such amendments, Federalists in New York finally won by a narrow margin.

Rhode Island and North Carolina rejected the Constitution. But when the new national government got underway, they had little choice but to join. North Carolina, by a wide margin, decided to join in November 1789. Rhode Island held out for a few months. Congress was considering a bill placing it on the footing of a foreign nation. Even then, Rhode Island decided to enter by the narrowest of margins.

Ratification: An Appraisal

Among historians there has long been controversy about all these events, and even today there is no complete agreement. Interpretations have varied all the way from a coup d'état by conservative counterrevolutionaries to the divinely inspired work of intellectual giants bent upon fulfilling the aims of the revolution. The truth lies not exactly in between, but somewhere off center between these two poles.

At the national level it is clear that leaders who favored the new Constitution had the edge in talent. Men who had previously participated in politics outside their own state tended to favor adoption. Wealthy persons were inclined toward adoption, and some who favored the Constitution knew they would gain financially from a stronger central government. Within each state politics were important, especially the influence of popular local leaders like John Hancock (who wanted ratification) and Patrick Henry (who did not). Cities and towns and regions of commercial activity tended to be Federalist; small farmers in more isolated areas tended to be Antifederalist. Representation in the ratifying conventions favored the commercial regions, and it is quite clear that a majority of actual voters opposed the Constitution.

Finally, had George Washington not favored it, the Federalist cause would have been doomed. It was almost universally assumed that he would be the first president under the new government. He was widely admired and trusted—but it remained to be seen whether a victorious general would make a good president, and whether the new system would work.

SUMMARY

By winning independence the United States had become a nation so far as the world was concerned. But Americans had yet to set up the most important institution of all, a national government. New state governments, with written constitutions, had been established during the war. These documents gave governing power to legislatures elected by the people. Fundamental power was reserved to the people themselves, who were protected by bills of rights guaranteeing individual liberties.

The great problem was the national government. The Articles of Confederation, drawn up by the Second Continental Congress, provided for a loose association of states to be governed by a one-house legislature in which voting was by state. Each state had one vote, no matter how many delegates it sent. A two-thirds majority was required for important legislation, and a unanimous vote for amendments. The government could declare war and make treaties; could settle disputes between states and admit new ones; could borrow money, establish a postal

service, and appoint military officers. But it could not levy taxes, raise troops, or regulate commerce.

More difficulties came with the disputes between the "landed" states (those with claims to western lands) and those without such resources. The question of how to keep the landless states from paying a greater share of the cost of the war, in fact, delayed ratification and the start of the new government until March 1781. It then immediately ran into problems with foreign relations and with money. Neither the British nor the Spanish wanted the new nation to succeed, so they did their best to get the Indians of Florida and the Northwest to harass the Americans. In the meantime, Congress could not depend on its own army, which it did not have the money to pay. Nor did it have the authority to force the states to supply funds to pay back the national debt and to run the government.

The most significant accomplishment of the government under the Articles was the Northwest Ordinance of

1787, which established the terms for the settlement of the Northwest Territory, that vast area northwest of the Ohio River. The ordinance unified the whole territory under a governor, laid out tentative boundaries for new states, and set the terms for their admission. It also prohibited slavery in the territory and in the states to be carved from it.

The worst problem for the government was money and credit. Farmers, who were taxpayers and often also debtors, wanted paper money to ease the pressure of their money payments. Creditors wanted payment in specie—gold or silver coin—so they would not be paid back with devalued currency. The agitation and discontent over this issue reached a peak in western Massachusetts in the autumn of 1786 in Shays' Rebellion, which the government finally managed to put down by early 1787.

By that year it was clear something had to be done. The Articles had constructed a government that was simply too weak. Work on a new and stronger central government actually began in 1785, when delegates from Maryland, Virginia, Delaware, and Pennsylvania met to discuss problems of interstate commerce. The result was a call for a general meeting of all the states at Annapolis in September 1786. Only five sent delegates, but the convention did recommend a new gathering to meet in Philadelphia in May 1787.

It was this convention that eventually replaced the Articles with a new federal government. The Constitution set up not only a strong government, but a new kind of national structure. By means of checks and balances, power was divided among three branches of government—executive, legislative, and judicial—so that no one class, interest group, or faction could dominate for any length of time. The balance of power between large and small states was solved by the two-house legislature. The sectional division caused by slavery was handled by several compromises. And the new federal government had two powers the Confederation Congress had lacked: the power to tax and the power to raise an army. It also had an independent executive (a president), and an independent judiciary.

The new Constitution of the United States was ratified only after a long and difficult campaign in the states, and only after immediate amendment by a Bill of Rights was promised. By June 1788 nine states had ratified. But Virginia and New York had strong opposition groups. Ratification, especially in New York, came late and by a narrow margin. But by the end of 1788, all except Rhode Island and North Carolina had ratified. The new government, with George Washington as first president, was ready to go to work.

Suggested Readings

M. Jensen, *The New Nation: A History of the United States during the Confederation, 1781–1789* (1950) argues that postwar economic and political conditions were not chaotic. Several studies of states illuminate the various issues involved. See especially V. Hall, *Politics Without Parties: Massachusetts, 1780–1791* (1972); I. Polishook, *Rhode Island and the Union, 1774–1795* (1969); and S. Lynd, *Anti-Federalism in Duchess County, New York* (1962). R. Beeman, *The Old Dominion and the New Nation, 1788–1801* (1972), has a fine discussion of Antifederalist sentiment in Virginia.

A fine account of the "father of the Constitution" is I. Brant, *James Madison* (6 vols., 1941–1961). Hamilton's political views and his role in the adoption process is covered by C. Rossiter, *Alexander Hamilton and the Constitution* (1950). The correspondence between Madison and Jefferson, who was in Paris during this time, provides fascinating insights. It is available in volumes 13 and 14 of J. Boyd (ed.), *The Papers of Thomas Jefferson* (1950—).

E. Ferguson, *The Power of the Purse, A History of American Public Finance, 1776–1790* (1961), is complex but crucial to a full understanding of the adoption of the Constitution. Much of the recent writing on that subject has revolved around claims made by Charles Beard in *An Economic Interpretation of the Constitution of the United States* (1913) that the Constitution was written by, and in the interest of wealthy public security holders and landowners. Beard's views have been challenged by F. McDonald, *We the People: The Economic Origins of the Constitution* (1958). An alternative picture is presented by J. Main, *The Antifederalists, Critics of the Constitution, 1781–1788* (1961), who stresses that the commercial areas of the new nation were most favorable to the Constitution. See also R. Rutland and J. Main, *Political Parties before the Constitution* (1973).

For economic developments during the period, in addition to Ferguson, See R. East, *Business Enterprise in the American Revolutionary Era* (1938); and C. Nettels, *The Emergence of a National Economy, 1775–1815* (1962). On the issue of slavery, see the works cited in Chapter 6. In addition, S. Lynd, *Class, Conflict, Slavery and the United States Constitution* (1967), offers an economic interpretation. M. Starkey, *A Little Rebellion* (1955), describes Shays' Rebellion, the event that so frightened the upper classes and ensured a conservative footing for the new federal government. See also D. Szatmary, *Shays' Rebellion: The Making of an Agrarian Insurrection* (1980).

Easily the best discussion of the political thought of the Founding Fathers is by Wood (cited in Chapter 6).

But see also A. O. Lovejoy, *Reflections on Human Nature* (1961). More directly focused on the instrument itself are L. Levy (ed.), *Essays on the Making of the Constitution* (1969), and M. Jensen, *Making of the American Constitution* (1964). The best text of the Constitution, with an analysis of each clause and summaries of Supreme Court interpretations, is E. S. Corwin, *The Constitution of the United States of Amer-* ica (1953). The classic commentary on the Constitution is *The Federalist*, written 1787–1788 by Hamilton, Madison, and Jay. The definitive modern edition is J. E. Cooke (1961). Richard Henry Lee, *Letters from the Federal Farmer*, orginally published in 1787 and 1788 and available in F. McDonald (ed.), *Empire and Nation* (1962), became the Antifederalist equivalent of the Federalist papers. C. Kenyon (ed.), *The Antifederalists* (1966), is an outstanding anthology. There is no substitute for reading the original records of the fascinating debates. See M. Farrand (ed.), *Records of the Federal Convention* (4 vols., 1911–1937).

THE FEDERALIST ERA

Chapter 8

The new national government faced grave problems. For one thing, it had to create parts of itself. At first there were only two members of the executive branch—the president and vice-president—and no judicial system at all. The government was badly in debt. In the West, Spain claimed a huge portion of United States territory, and the British still occupied forts on American soil. Various Indian tribes regarded most of the western lands as their own. The monarchs of Europe hoped to see the new nation fall apart. Before long a major war broke out in Europe in the wake of the French Revolution, and the United States found itself involved in bitter battles on the high seas.

President Washington hoped for a spirit of unity in the national government. He disliked political factionalism, which he regarded as poisonous. But he soon discovered that the American people and their leaders disagreed on such critical matters as the powers of the new federal government, its fiscal policies, and the best way to deal with the war in Europe. Despite Washington's intentions, by the time he left office in 1797 two political parties had come into existence: the Federalists and the Republicans. (Though the name was the same, the Republican party of that time was completely different from the modern one of the same name.)

The president was not alone in his dislike for political parties; no one expected or welcomed the development of a system which has proved to be a basic feature of American political life. At the time, members of each party regarded the other as a troublemaking and even dangerous faction made up of the enemies of the nation. And John Adams, who succeeded Washington as president, discovered that deep divisions could take place *within* a party. A long time passed before Americans came to believe that political parties were a legitimate and useful means of working out differences about public policy. ■

THE NEW GOVERNMENT AT WORK

The president and the new Congress were acutely aware of the pitfalls and importance of their first actions. At the start of his administration, Washington wrote: "My station is new, and, if I may use the expression, I walk on untrodden ground. . . . There is scarcely any part of my conduct which may not hereafter be drawn into precedent." As the emerging leader of Congress, James Madison used much the same metaphor: "We are in a wilderness," he wrote, "without a single footstep to guide us." The president and Congress had to establish executive offices and a judicial system. They also had to find ways of raising money for operating expenses and for paying off the debts inherited from the Confederation government. But they dealt first with amendments to the constitution, amendments widely demanded (and promised) during the campaign for ratification.

The Bill of Rights

Almost everyone agreed that Congress's first business should be adoption of a set of amendments which would constitute a Bill of Rights. Members of the Philadelphia convention had considered including such a list in the constitution. They had rejected the idea because the powers of the new federal government were carefully enumerated, and they assumed such enumeration would prevent the national government from doing anything it was not specifically authorized to do. Yet many Americans wanted to set specific restrictions on the powers of the new government. As things turned out during the ratification process, the nationalists in Philadelphia may have been lucky in their omission. Promises of a Bill of Rights won over many votes in the state ratifying conventions. Nearly half the states proposed such amendments during ratification.

Even a quick reading of the Bill of Rights gives a good glimpse into the distrust of government that prevailed at the time. The first group of ten amendments protects freedom of religion, freedom of speech and of the press, the right to assemble peacefully with other persons, and the right to petition the federal government to correct wrongs. It requires federal officials to obtain search warrants from a court before searching a person's home. The Bill of Rights also provides for trial by jury in criminal cases and prohibits excessive bail and "cruel and unusual punishments." The Fifth Amendment gives individuals the right not to testify against themselves in court. The Ninth and Tenth Amendments limit the powers of the federal government to those not specifically named in the Constitution. All other powers were, in a phrase that was both clear and ambiguous, "reserved to the States respectively, or to the people."

These first ten amendments to the Constitution, the Bill of Rights, were ratified by the states in December 1791. Like many provisions of the Constitution, the various provisions of the Bill of Rights have undergone considerable interpretation and reinterpretation by the courts. Though the Founding Fathers thought they were writing for the ages, changing circumstances have raised (and will continue to raise) such questions as whether a person is free to advocate overthrow of the government; whether police may search a person's automobile without a warrant; whether the death penalty is a "cruel and unusual punishment"; whether "the right of the people to keep and bear arms" makes gun control laws unconstitutional. Yet the Constitution wisely provided for a mechanism for dealing with changes in its interpretation by means of amendments or the federal courts.

The Judiciary

The Judiciary Act of 1789 did a great deal to cement the federal system. The first Congress spelled out the procedure by which federal courts could review—and if necessary declare void—state laws and state court decisions involving powers

Plan of the new center of the federal government, 1792. The government remained in Philadelphia until 1800. (*New York Public Library*)

and duties the Constitution delegated to the federal government. It also specified that the Supreme Court be staffed by a chief justice and five associate justices. (Congress retains the power of numbering the members of the Supreme Court; it could change the present number of nine today without violating the Constitution.)

In 1789 the system of federal courts was completed by three circuit courts and thirteen district courts. Attached to each district court were United States prosecuting attorneys, as well as marshals and deputies to serve as federal police. It was the duty of these marshals to supervise the taking of the first federal census in 1790, as required by the Constitution.

The Executive

The executive had been one of the weakest elements in the old Confederation. Nonetheless, Congress was slow in creating executive departments. In the summer of 1789 Congress created a Department of State to manage foreign relations, a War Department, and a Department of the Treasury. In 1792, Congress stipulated that there should be "one Postmaster General," but this official remained within the Treasury Department until 1829. The Judiciary Act of 1789 created the office of attorney general, but a separate Department of Justice was not established until 1870.

While Congress busied itself with these measures, the president gave his attention to appointments. Washington wanted to surround himself with the best men available, but he had other things in mind as well. He was acutely aware of the thinness of the thread that held the states together and of the need not to offend local people in filling even minor posts. "A single disgust excited in a particular state," he wrote, "might perhaps raise the flame of opposition that could not easily, if ever, be extinguished."

At the same time, Washington was reluctant to appoint any opponent of the Constitution to office. He also had in mind sectional considerations, and when he could he chose men he had known personally during the war. He appointed General Henry Knox of Massachusetts, his old chief of artillery and one of the army's most outspoken opponents of the old Congress, as the first secretary of war. He named Edmund Randolph of Virginia, one of his wartime aides-de-camp, as attorney general. The Treasury went to Hamilton, another of his military aides. John Jay, also of New York, had been in charge of foreign affairs for the old

The first cabinet: Knox, Jefferson, Hamilton, and Washington. (*Library of Congress*)

Congress and had continued to direct them until 1790. Then Thomas Jefferson of Virginia took over as secretary of state, and Jay became the first chief justice of the Supreme Court.

The Constitution made no provision for a presidential cabinet, but early in his administration Washington established the practice of taking action only on matters that had been referred to him by the secretaries of his three departments and the attorney general. Gradually he began to consult these men on questions outside their departments. In the spring of 1791, before a journey to the South that would keep him away for an extended period, Washington instructed the three secretaries that they should consult together if "any serious and important cases arise during my absence." While holding himself ready to return to the capital in an emergency, he told them to take whatever "measures . . . may be legally and properly pursued without the immediate agency of the President," and "I will approve and ratify" them. Thereafter, the secretaries began to meet periodically. Afer a crisis in foreign affairs in 1793 arising from the wars of the French Revolution, these meetings became regular. The cabinet thus became a permanent feature of the federal machinery.

PROBLEMS OF FINANCE

Hamilton was the driving force behind the solution of the new nation's financial difficulties. His goals were political as well as fiscal. He was determined to win the support of wealthy financiers for the new government by giving them a personal stake in its success. In doing so, however, he aroused great opposition, especially from southerners who were not in a position to benefit from his measures. Yet he was largely successful in solving the financial problems that had so badly weakened the old Confederation government.

Hamilton's Funding Plan

At thirty-four years of age, Alexander Hamilton was a vigorous, ambitious, and extraordinarily able young man, and he proposed a bold financial program. Not content merely to propose, he worked

Alexander Hamilton. (*National Portrait Gallery, Smithsonian Institution, Washington, D.C., gift of Henry Cabot Lodge*)

closely with members of Congress; one senator declared that "nothing is done without him."

The government of the old Confederation had piled up a huge debt. Hamilton argued that the new United States government was obligated to take responsibility for it. No one really disagreed with his claim that "the debt of the United States . . . was the price of liberty. The faith of America has been repeatedly pledged for it." About one-fifth of the money was owed to foreigners. The remainder was in the form of various public securities or government bonds, which the Confederation government had sold to patriots during and after the war and had used to pay soldiers. Hamilton proposed to "fund" this foreign and domestic debt by exchanging new government securities for the old ones. He wanted to issue new bonds at the same face value as the old ones, plus any unpaid interest.

Hamilton's plan ran into opposition in Congress because the old bonds had dropped in value and because many of these securities had been bought up by wealthy speculators. During and shortly after the war, United States securities had fallen in value to a point where they were worth only 25 percent of their face value. This lower value reflected widespread doubts about the government's ability to pay interest or buy back the bonds. Many war veterans sold their bonds for less to speculators. Adoption of the new, stronger form of government increased confidence in the government's ability to pay, and the value of the bonds began rising.

In the early months of the new government there was an orgy of speculation. Wealthy speculators sent agents into the back country to buy up as many bonds as they could find, at the lowest possible price. In such a situation, there was great profit in knowing about Hamilton's proposals ahead of time. His subordinates in the Treasury Department leaked advance word of his plan to their friends. By the time the proposal became public, the old securities had risen to 80 percent of their face value; if it passed, their value would rise to 100 percent.

Most of the speculators were northern capitalists. Few landholders in the South could compete with the northerners, since southern money was tied up in land and slaves. What really made the situation politically explosive, however, was that many northern speculators sat in Congress. They were in a superb position to vote in favor of their own pocketbooks.

Far from being horrified by the situation, Hamilton had planned it. He was deeply committed to the success of the new government. In his view, the way to strengthen the new nation was to involve the personal interests of powerful men in its continued success. Thus he deliberately set out to gain backing for the government from those who had a personal interest in maintaining its ability to pay its debts. Hamilton had neither the time nor inclination to profit personally from the situation; he had little interest in making money for himself. But he was interested in power—both for himself and for the new government.

Madison's Discrimination

James Madison had opposite inclinations. Not a particularly wealthy man, he was in no position to profit personally in public securities, nor would he have done so even if able. He saw the situation as basically unfair to the war veterans and other original owners of the securities. He was shocked by the scramble for personal profit by those who would gain at the expense of ordinary soldiers and citizens. He and his friend and neighbor Thomas Jefferson (who was just taking over as secretary of state) grew increasingly opposed to Hamilton's policies.

Madison introduced a counterproposal in the House of Representatives. He conceded the need to pay off the foreign debt at face value in order to establish the new government's credit with other nations. There was no argument on that matter. But Madison proposed to "discriminate" between original holders of public securities and those who had bought them later for speculative purposes. He suggested that possessors of bonds which had not been resold should be offered new ones at face value. Those holding securities they had bought from someone other than the government—that is, speculators—should fall into a separate group which would receive half the original face value. He, and Jefferson even more, began to see the matter as one of justice to ordinary soldiers and farmers as against the interests of the northern merchants.

Madison's proposal lost for two reasons: One was the voting weight of those in Congress who were actively engaged in speculation; the other was that "discrimination" among holders of public securities was impractical, since some securities had changed hands five or six times. It was therefore virtually impossible to work out a plan that would be fair to everyone. The proposal failed in the House of Representatives by a wide margin.

Assumption

Hamilton also proposed that the federal government assume responsibility for paying the debts of the individual states, an amount that added up to nearly half the national debt. This "assumption" plan ran into greater opposition than the "funding" one. Speculators were involved in state securities, so there was bound to be opposition. More important, some states had almost paid off their debts, while others had not. A majority of the states that had done so were in the South. Virginians, for example, were unhappy with the prospect of being taxed to help pay for the unpaid debts of Massachusetts. Madison was able to gather enough opposition to defeat the proposal on a test vote.

Yet assumption eventually passed. The speculators in Congress threatened to vote against funding unless they could have assumption as well. Madison and his followers were unwilling to oppose the principle of funding because they knew it was essential for establishing the government's credit. Furthermore, Hamilton held out a suggestion that was particularly attractive to southern representatives. Rather than locate the capital in New York or Philadelphia, why not build a new city on the banks of the Potomac? So Congress passed both parts of Hamilton's program, plus a bill to establish a new "federal city" that would become the capital in 1800. It was soon named Washington, after the first president.

The National Bank

Hamilton made another financial proposal that again stirred up sectional strife. He called for a Bank of the United States, modeled on the Bank of England. One-fifth of the capital was to be subscribed by the government, the rest by private investors. The Federalists, opposed on principle to government paper money, planned to have the Treasury issue only minted gold and silver. Hamilton argued that a commercial bank was needed to supply notes which would serve as currency in business transactions. This bank would also assist the government by lending it money to meet its short-term obligations and by serving as a depository for government funds. Finally, by providing personal loans, the bank would make it easier for individuals to pay taxes.

"This plan for a national bank," objected Representative James Jackson of Georgia, "is calculated to benefit a small part of the United States, the mercantilist interests only; the farmers, the yeomanry, will derive no advantage from it." But Hamilton's bill passed the House because the commercial North was able to outvote the agrarian South. In 1791 the Bank of the United States was chartered for twenty years, with headquarters in Philadelphia. Ultimately eight branches were established in port cities from Boston to New Orleans.

In the House debate, Madison had argued that a national bank would be unconstitutional. The 1787 convention, he insisted, had rejected the proposition that the federal government be given power to charter companies. When the bank bill was sent to Washington, the president asked Jefferson, Hamilton, and Attorney General Randolph for their opinions. Jefferson supported Madison. Hamilton argued that since the government had been given the power to regulate currency, it had the "implied power" to establish a bank to issue currency.

Randolph could not decide on the constitutional problem, and Washington himself never resolved it. He rejected Jefferson's and Madison's "strict interpretation" of the Constitution in favor of Hamilton's "broad interpretation." But his decision was based more on instinct than on constitutional reasoning. Washington ordinarily gave his support, when in doubt on an issue, to the cabinet member whose office was most closely involved. On these grounds Hamilton won his bank. Yet he did not win the broader constitutional issue, and it remained unresolved for years.

Early Crises

Hamilton's second proposal for raising money was an excise tax on various commodities, including distilled liquor. It was enacted quietly in 1791, but it soon raised a storm that tested the inexperienced government. Opposition was especially strong in the West, because whiskey was the most easily transported grain product. The most violent resistance to Hamilton's measure occurred in western Pennsylvania, where resistance to tax collection gained such strong support that it became known as the Whiskey Rebellion. Here, as on other frontiers not close to water transportation, whiskey was regarded as an important means of raising cash. It was also thought of as a personal right and necessity. In addition, the new tax added to a general resentment of government meddling. Opponents of the excise, meeting in Pittsburgh, resolved that "it is insulting to the feelings of the

people to have their vessels marked, houses . . . ransacked, to be subject to informers."

In 1794, the federal court in Philadelphia issued writs against seventy-five western Pennsylvania distillers, who would have to travel across the state to answer them in Philadelphia. When federal marshals came west with the writs, a mob attacked them. Hamilton interpreted the uprising against federal collectors as a rebellion against the United States. He prevailed upon Washington to order the mobilization of 13,000 militiamen to crush the farmers. Characteristically, Hamilton rode west with the troops. Although they found no organized opposition, the militia rounded up about a hundred men. Two were later convicted of treason and sentenced to death, but Washington eventually pardoned them.

While the Federalist administration aroused opposition with its financial measures, it managed to appear ridiculous in its dealings with the Indians and with foreign powers. Spain continued to claim much of the Southwest and to keep the Mississippi River closed at New Orleans to American shipping. In the Northwest Territory, Britain persisted in using military power to help Canadian fur trappers. British forts on American soil were deeply resented by settlers who looked to a strong central government for protection against Indian raids.

Yet the new government failed them. In 1791 most of Governor St. Clair's 2000 ill-equipped and untrained men deserted before they even met the Indians against whom they had been mobilized. The rest were trapped and forced to flee for their lives. Washington stormed: "Here in this very room, I warned General St. Clair against being surprised." Not until 1794, in the Battle of Fallen Timbers, did General "Mad Anthony" Wayne subdue the northwestern tribes. And not until 1795, by the Treaty of Fort Greenville, did these tribes yield most of their Ohio land to the United States. But the Treaty of Fort Greenville came too late for the Federalists to retrieve the political support that earlier failures on the northwestern frontier had cost them.

The awareness that a substantial opposition party was beginning to form only served to intensify a sense of crisis in Federalist ranks. In 1792 Daniel Carroll, one of the commissioners for the development of the federal city, explained that Congress's delay in making appropriations for the new capital arose from suspicions that the government was about to be dissolved. In 1793, Oliver Wolcott of Connecticut, who was to succeed Hamilton at the Treasury two years later, observed

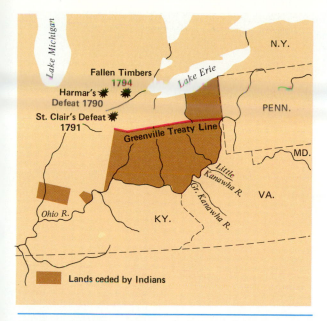

Treaty of Greenville, 1795

that if the funding and assumption policies did break up the Union, "the separation ought to be eternal." In 1795 another commentator, observing the new state capitol at Hartford, Connecticut, wrote that it "excites the suspicion . . . that it is contemplated by some to make this a Capitol [of New England], should there be a division of the Northern from the Southern States."

PARTY POLITICS

No specific dates can be given for the beginnings of political parties in the United States. During the colonial period, factions came and went with little continuity. In the new government Washington regarded factions as unpatriotic. He was appalled as he watched opponents of his administration develop into a well-organized, permanent political party. He was unaware of his own contribution to this process, even as he became increasingly influenced by Hamilton. As Jefferson and Madison organized their political forces, he grew more and more upset. He could not know it, but a strange four-handed game was shaping the course of the nation's politics.

Four Politicians

It was their differing visions of the proper future for the new country that separated Hamilton from Madison and Jefferson. Hamilton envisioned a powerful nation resting on a balanced economy of agriculture, trade, finance, and manufacturing. Agriculture, he thought, needed no special encouragement. After all, the country was predominantly agricultural, and other branches of the economy were more in need of help from the government. Hamilton saw finance as the major weakness of the old government. An elitist by temperament, Hamilton distrusted "the people." This view reflected his own personal background. Born illegitimate in the West Indies, he had made his way by marriage into the highest financial circles in New York. An outsider, he liked men of wealth and power.

Jefferson, on the other hand, thought farmers would always be the chief supporters of the republic and the eternal guardians of public virtue. More than Madison, he distrusted the world of cities, commerce, and finance. He thought of them as breeding grounds for moral and political corruption, and he described urban workers as "debased by ignorance, indigence, and oppression." Born to the life of a Virginia slaveholding country gentleman, Jefferson felt deep attachment to the land and had an unquestioning trust in the common people who tilled it. He was neither the first nor last public person to hate privilege because he had it himself.

Madison also owned a plantation (very near Jefferson's), but his interest was concentrated on the art and practice of politics. Deeply committed to balance and moderation, he thrived on the give and take of political horsetrading. But now he saw his own goal of strengthening the national government being pushed too far by Hamilton's program. It was natural that he should join with his Virginian friend in the executive branch.

For his part, Washington remained deeply attached to country and to duty. Convinced that his proper role was to stand at the head of the new nation, he felt he should take no part in quarreling over details of public policy. Although he was one of the wealthiest planters in the South, he never shared Jefferson's distrust of commercial interests. Unfamiliar with the complications of fiscal matters, he was happy to leave them to Hamilton. He tried evenhandedly to soothe the mounting hostility between Hamilton and Jefferson in the cabinet. He intervened more in foreign than in domestic affairs because he thought himself obligated and more competent to do so. When Hamilton assured him that no members of Congress were speculating in government securities, Washington believed him. The patriotic old gen-

The Washington family by Edward Savage. (*National Gallery of Art, Washington; Andrew W. Mellon Collection*)

eral found it hard to recognize that some men might place their own intersts above the government's.

Organizing

As tension mounted over Hamilton's financial program in 1791–1792, Madison and Jefferson set out to gain support for their position in the country at large as well as in Congress. They toured several New England states and especially New York to express their views to political leaders there. In New York they won over Governor George Clinton. Clinton had long been a rival of Hamilton's wealthy father-in-law, and he still had personal reasons for supporting state power.

Jefferson and Madison also backed a new newspaper, the *National Gazette*, as a vehicle for criticizing Hamilton's policies. Madison wrote several articles for this newspaper supporting his position, and he referred to those who backed his views as "the Republican party, as it may be termed." Many readers responded enthusiastically.

Hamilton was not a man to sit by while his opponents organized. He and his allies, taking the name Federalists, backed a newspaper of their own. Like the Republicans, the Federalists began organizing local clubs. The Federalists had several important advantages. They had a well-thought-out, positive program. The great majority of newspaper editors and clergy supported Federalist ideas, and so did a majority of wealthy men. In addition, Federalists in government were able to reward party workers with jobs.

By the time of the 1792 national election, the Republicans were not well enough organized to run a candidate for president. Furthermore, Washington had reluctantly agreed to serve again, and it would have been futile and perhaps damaging to oppose him. John Adams, who had been elected vice-president in the first election, was again the vice-presidential candidate. The Republicans organized behind George Clinton for vice-president. Washington and Adams were both reelected. But the election returns showed that the Republicans were a new force in American politics. During the

THE FEDERALIST ERA

WORDS AND NAMES IN AMERICAN HISTORY

The name *Mississippi* was originally an Algonkian Indian term meaning "big river." Algonkian-speaking Indians ranged all the way from the northern Atlantic coast westward through the Great Lakes region. Western Algonkian tribes gave that name to the northern part of a large river without knowing anything about the southern region through which it flowed to the Gulf of Mexico. French explorers first heard the name "Messipi" in 1666 as they pressed westward from the St. Lawrence river valley through and beyond the Great Lakes. Farther south, different Indian groups, speaking different languages, each had their own name for the great river. Hernando de Soto, the Spanish explorer who was buried in the southern part of the river, piously named it *Espiritu Santo,* or Holy Spirit. But as French adventurers pressed southward they used the northern Algonkian name for the entire waterway. In 1798 Congress created a U.S. territory in what was then the southwestern frontier and named it after the river. Later, in 1817, part of that territory was admitted to the Union as the state of Mississippi.

---

next few years, voting in Congress did not take place according to firm party lines. Yet by 1795 certain developments in foreign affairs further clarified and deepened the division into two national political parties.

FOREIGN AFFAIRS UNDER WASHINGTON

During Washington's first administration, party lines had been drawn over financial issues. In his second administration, problems of foreign policy, as a contemporary said, "not merely divided parties, but moulded them," and "gave them . . . their bitterness." Some of these problems were carry-overs from the war with Britain. But the French Revolution, which began just a few weeks after Washington first took office in 1789, was the source of most of the trouble.

Citizen Genêt and the Neutrality Proclamation

At first, most Americans welcomed the French Revolution. They felt their own revolutionary principles were spreading to Europe. In 1790, when Lafayette sent the key to the fortress-prison—the Bastille—to Washington, the president acknowledged it as a "token of victory gained by liberty over despotism." Within a year, however, the Hamiltonians had aligned themselves against the French Revolution, while the Jeffersonians still praised it.

The execution of Louis XVI in January 1793 alarmed American conservatives, and the Jacobin "reign of terror" that followed confirmed their misgivings about excessive democracy. In the meantime, the French wars against the continen-

tal monarchs, who had combined to end the threat of republicanism, had begun in 1792.

For weeks, westerly gales kept news of the executions and the wars from reaching America. When all the news flooded in at once, in April 1793, it strengthened the Hamiltonians in their stand against France. The Jeffersonians, on the other hand, remained distrustful of monarchy and confident about the people of France.

It was not long before the conflict of opinion was deepened by specific issues of foreign policy. The French treaty of 1778 obligated the United States to defend the French West Indies in case of an attack on France itself. It also provided that French privateers and men-of-war could bring captured ships to American ports. In 1792 the group of revolutionaries ruling France assumed that this treaty remained in force—as indeed it did under international law. They sent "Citizen" Edmond Genêt as envoy to America to see that it was carried out.

Genêt had other instructions. He was to organize expeditions from the United States to seize Louisiana and Florida from Spain, and outfit American ships to prey on British shipping. These enterprises were to be financed with American funds made available by a speedup in American payments on the old French loan. Genêt had one more project: to organize Jacobin clubs in America, to advance the cause of "Liberty, Equality, and Fraternity." This happened just when Jefferson himself had begun to sponsor Republican political clubs of his own.

Genêt, an attractive and enterprising young man, landed in Charleston, South Carolina, in 1793. After a warm welcome, he went to work without even bothering to present his credentials to the government in Philadelphia. By the time he finally arrived at the capital, the president, after consulting Jefferson and Hamilton, had issued a

Neutrality Proclamation making it clear that the United States would not participate in the French wars.

Jefferson defended the Girondist position that the treaty of 1778 was with the French nation, no matter what its government might be. He also argued that since only Congress could declare war, only Congress could proclaim neutrality. Jefferson also felt that if such a proclamation were issued, Britain should be forced to make certain concessions in return. Hamilton held that the French treaty had died with the French king, and that neutrality in any case was the only possible American policy. Jefferson, having made these arguments, did not persist in opposing the practical step: Washington's proclamation followed.

By this time, Genêt had already commissioned enthusiastic Charleston ship captains as French privateers to prey on British shipping. He had also organized a South Carolina military adventure against Spain in Florida and had persuaded a group of Kentuckians to float down the Mississippi and dislodge the Spanish from New Orleans. The warmth of Genêt's reception had convinced him that the American people were with him, whatever the government might do. When Washington received Genêt with forbidding coldness and gave him to understand that the government would no longer tolerate his operations, let alone support them, Genêt decided to ignore the president.

Even Jefferson was put out by this persistence; and when Genêt, contrary to Washington's express warnings, permitted *Little Democrat,* a prize ship converted into an armed vessel, to sail as a privateer, Jefferson voted with the president and the rest of the cabinet to ask for Genêt's recall. By then, Genêt's group had fallen out of favor at home. Fearing for his life, the young envoy remained in America, married Governor Clinton's daughter, and retired to a country estate on the Hudson.

The repercussions of this affair were less romantic. Washington's Neutrality Proclamation had reflected the president's determination to keep the nation at peace. Jefferson shared this hope, but his apparent sympathy with Genêt's early activities led the president to read the most sinister meaning into the conduct of his secretary of state and of those "self-constituted societies," as Washington called the new Republican clubs Jefferson sponsored. "It is not the cause of France, nor I believe of liberty, which they regard," he wrote in 1793, but only the "disgrace" of the new nation under Federalist rule. By the end of the year, Washington accepted Jefferson's resignation from the cabinet. As for Jefferson himself, his nerves were frayed by political battling; he longed only to retire to his beloved Monticello.

Neutrality: Profits and Problems

The war in Europe opened the way for a shipping boom in the neutral nations. As a leading maritime nation, the United States was among the greatest gainers. Since the French had a relatively small merchant fleet that was vulnerable to British attack, they desperately needed neutral assistance. Early in the war, France at last surrendered its monopoly of the French West Indian trade and opened the island ports to American ships and produce. American ships began a brisk trade with the French sugar islands, supplying them with foodstuffs and barrels and returning with sugar and molasses.

The British retaliated. They resurrected their "rule of the War of 1756," which held that trade barred to a nation in peacetime could not be opened

---

WASHINGTON ON THE ROLE OF THE ARMY, 1795

As an ex-military man and leader of a war for national liberation, President Washington took a view of the army which few such leaders have adopted; in 1795 he wrote Major General Daniel Morgan:

Still it may be proper constantly and strongly to impress upon the Army that they are mere agents of Civil power; that out of Camp, they have no other authority, than other citizens[,] that offences against the laws are to be examined, not by a military officer, but by a Magistrate; that they are not exempt from arrests and indictments for violations of the law; that officers ought to be careful, not to give orders, which may lead the agents into infractions of the law; that no compulsion be used towards the inhabitants in the traffic, carried on between them and the army; that disputes be avoided, as much as possible, and be adjusted as quickly as may be, without urging them to an extreme; and that the whole country is not to be considered as within the limits of the camp.

THE FEDERALIST ERA

JAY'S TREATY

By the time of Jay's Treaty, even the great wartime leader was being denounced in the opposition press. The following "Political CREED of a Western American" was copied in several newspapers.

I believe that the treaty formed by Jay and the British king is the offspring of a vile aristocratic few who have too long governed in America, and who are enemies to the equality of men, friends to no government but that whose funds they can convert to their private employment.

I do not believe that Hamilton, Jay or King and their minions, are devils incarnate: but I do believe them so filled with pride, and so fattened on the spoils of America, that they abhor every thing which

partakes of Democracy, and that they most ardently desire the swinish multitude humbled in dust and ashes.

I believe the period is at hand when the inhabitants of America will cease to admire or approve the conduct of the Federal executive, because they esteem the man who fills the chair of state. . . .

I believe that the political dotage of our good old American chief, has arrived, and that while we record his virtues in letters of gold, we should consign his person to the tender offices due to virtuous age, and transfer him from the chair of state to the chair of domestic ease. . . .

to it during hostilities. This applied with special force to the French West Indian trade. In 1793 they announced that all shipping to or from the French colonies would be subject to British seizure. American ships by then had swarmed into the Caribbean to serve the French islands. The British seized about 300 United States vessels, abused their passengers, and forced many of their sailors into the British navy.

Even so, American trade thrived. Many ships were captured, but many more slipped through. These losses served as an additional stimulus to the shipbuilding industry. By 1794, however, the British had become so brazen that even Federalists expected war. The United States insisted that "neutral ships made neutral goods," but the British enforced their self-proclaimed right to search for enemy supplies anywhere on any ship. The United States insisted that a blockade must be enforced by actual patrols of the closed ports. But the British simply announced "paper blockades" and undertook to enforce them wherever they found a vessel presumably bound for a forbidden harbor. The United States insisted that foodstuffs could not be classified as contraband, but the British did not hesitate to capture ships carrying food for France and its allies.

In addition, British authorities in Canada continued to encourage Indians to resist American settlers moving west. The British government made clear that it still had no intention of giving up its armed posts in northwestern American territory. It based this refusal to evacuate on the fact that the United States had not lived up to the provisions of the peace treaty of 1783, especially concerning Loyalist property and American debts.

Jay's Treaty

President Washington decided to try diplomatic negotiation in order to meet these problems. He named John Jay his special envoy, with instructions to get the British to surrender their military posts in the Northwest, to pay for American ships that had been captured illegally, and to respect the American position on the rights and privileges of neutrals. Jay was also to negotiate the best commercial treaty he could. If he could not get the British to agree on all these points, Jay was to try to get the northern countries of Europe to agree jointly with the United States to enforce neutral rights.

Jay had a good case, and the British needed American friendship. But Hamilton undercut these advantages. As early as 1789, he had told Major Beckwith, his secret British contact reporting on American affairs: "I have always preferred a connexion with you, to that of any other country. We think in English, and have a similarity of prejudices and predilections."

In 1794, while Jay was still on his way to England, Washington received a proposal from Sweden and Denmark, two of the northern neutrals Jay was to consult if he failed to gain British concessions. They suggested just what Jay was instructed to suggest to them—that all three nations unite to combat British assaults on neutral shipping. Washington was favorably inclined. But Hamilton managed to stop him, arguing that far from strengthening Jay's hand, such action would only make the British more difficult to deal with. Hamilton, moreover, promptly told George Hammond, the British minister in New York, of

Washington's decision. Hammond lost little time in sending this information to the British negotiators. The result was an uphill fight for Jay and a very unsatisfactory agreement.

By the Treaty of London (completed in November 1794 and known in America as Jay's Treaty), the British agreed again to evacuate their Northwest posts. By 1796 they had done so, but Jay had to barter away a great deal in return. The British could still carry on the fur trade on the American side of the Canadian border with Indians hostile to advancing American settlement. This concession almost canceled out the surrender of the posts and deeply angered westerners.

As for the British paying for captured ships, settlement of this issue was left to a future joint commission that would determine what, if anything, was owed. On the rights of neutrals, Jay failed altogether. His efforts to gain commercial concessions also fell completely flat.

Jay's whole agreement was so unsatisfactory that Washington hesitated a long time before sending it to the Senate. The Senate, in turn, made every effort to hide the terms from the people. But there were leaks. When the Senate on June 25, 1795, by the slenderest possible two-thirds majority ratified the treaty, the public outcry was as violent as expected. In the months following, "Sir John Jay" was hanged in effigy throughout the country. One person chalked up in large letters on a Boston street wall: "DAMN JOHN JAY! DAMN EVERY ONE WHO WON'T DAMN JOHN JAY!! DAMN EVERY ONE WHO WON'T SIT UP ALL NIGHT DAMNING JOHN JAY!!!"

In the Congress that met in December 1795, the question was asked whether the House of Representatives, by failing to vote appropriations required under the agreement, could in effect reject the treaty, even though the Senate had accepted it. The House voted 57 to 35 that it had the constitutional right to reject treaties by withholding funds, but it went on to approve the appropriations by a vote of 51 to 48.

Pinckney's Treaty

In June 1795, while the Senate was considering Jay's Treaty with Britain, Spain withdrew from the British coalition against France and made peace with the revolutionary government there. This step made Spain fearful of British reprisals, which might take the form of attacks on its empire

"Stop the Wheels of Government".

A Federalist cartoon of Congressman Albert Gallatin, 1796. Gallatin argued that by withholding appropriations, the House of Representatives could, in effect, veto the Jay Treaty and thus "stop the wheels of government." The guillotine is a Federalist reminder of the dangerous implications of Gallatin's French-speaking ancestry. (*New York Public Library*)

in America. It also feared attacks from American frontiersmen. When Britain and America concluded Jay's Treaty, Spain's fears for its empire grew.

The Spanish decided to try to win American friendship. After several proposals failed to lure Thomas Pinckney, the American minister who had gone to Madrid on Spain's invitation in 1794, Pinckney wrote home that the King of Spain was now prepared "to sacrifice something of what he considered as his right, to testify to his good will to us."

Pinckney proceeded to negotiate the Treaty of San Lorenzo, usually called Pinckney's Treaty, which the Spanish signed in 1795 and the United States Senate unanimously approved in 1796. This agreement settled the northern boundary of Florida at the latitude of 31°. Much more important, Spain opened the Mississippi "in its whole length from its source to the ocean" to American river traffic and allowed Americans use of the port of New Orleans for three years, after which time the arrangement could be renewed.

Line claimed by Spain after 1783
Line of Pickney's Treaty, 1795
● Spanish settlements

Pinckney's Treaty, 1795

The Election of 1796

Washington had felt so strongly about not running for president again in 1792 that he had asked Madison and others to draw up ideas for his "valedictory" to the nation. Early in 1796 he turned these old papers over to Hamilton for a new draft. This time he was utterly determined not to serve again. He looked with deepest dismay, he said, on the "baneful effects of the spirit of party." But at the same time he took keen satisfaction in many of his accomplishments.

Washington did not deliver his Farewell Address in person; he simply published it in the newspapers on September 17, 1796. That date was so close to the presidential elections that it stirred resentment among opposition leaders, who felt that his delay in announcing his decision handicapped them in mounting an effective campaign. They also felt his warnings on party spirit were attacks on them and not on the Federalist party.

The party strife Washington hated was nearing its peak when he retired. Debate in the House over Jay's Treaty had continued well into 1796, and Washington's own decision intensified the conflict by opening up the highest office to the rising political machines. The Federalists brought out a ticket of John Adams of New England and Thomas Pinckney of South Carolina. The Republicans named Jefferson and Aaron Burr of New York.

Hamilton and Adams had long since grown cool toward each other, and Hamilton went to great pains to maneuver Pinckney into the presidency. His elaborate scheme backfired. Adams won with 71 votes. Jefferson, with 68 votes, was second in the balloting and defeated Pinckney for the vice-presidency. Thus the president and the vice-president represented two different political parties.

THE ADAMS ADMINISTRATION

Americans now take the transition from one presidential administration to another as a matter of course. In 1796 the public was experiencing the

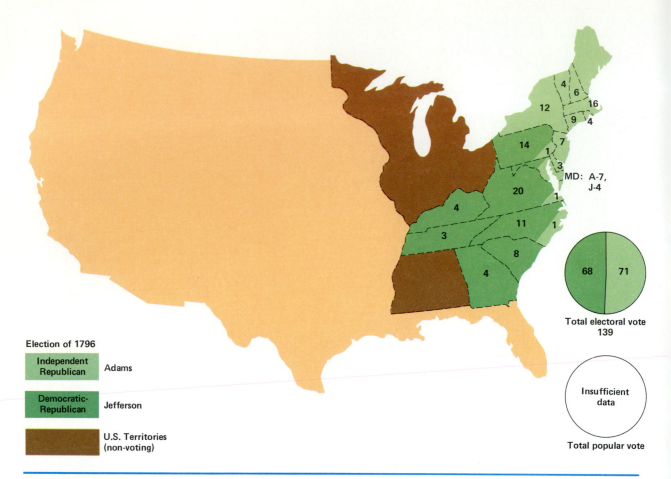

Election of 1796

■ Independent Republican — Adams

■ Democratic-Republican — Jefferson

■ U.S. Territories (non-voting)

MD: A-7, J-4

Total electoral vote 139 (68 | 71)

Insufficient data

Total popular vote

Election of 1796

first transfer of presidential power from one man to another. Anxiety was deepened by the fact that a leader of Washington's stature was about to retire. The president, writes one historian, "had already determined to demonstrate to the world the supreme achievement of democratic government—the peaceful and orderly change of the head of the state in accordance with the voice of the people." John Adams himself was moved by the historic event to write to his wife on his inauguration: "All agree that . . . it was the sublimest thing ever exhibited in America."

Foreign Policy

During John Adams's presidency, the new government nearly lost control over its own foreign policy. No statesman in the United States had written more than John Adams about human nature. But Jefferson shrewdly observed that in practice Adams was "a bad calculator" of the "mo-

tives of men." He made the mistake of retaining in his cabinet second-rate Hamiltonians, such as Secretary of State Timothy Pickering and Secretary of the Treasury Oliver Wolcott, who had surrounded Washington toward the end. Worse, Adams spent a great deal of time at home in Massachusetts. In later years, after his retirement, Adams counted as one of his major accomplishments that he, like Washington, had kept the United States at peace with France. Yet Hamilton's anti-French friends in Adams's virtually independent cabinet carried the administration to the brink of all-out hostilities.

The French government interpreted Jay's Treaty as a British diplomatic victory. They intensified their attacks on American ships bound for British ports. By the time of Adams's inauguration in March 1797, the French had captured about 300 American vessels and had manhandled their crews.

In the meantime, Washington had recalled James Monroe and sent Charles C. Pinckney to

162

THE FEDERALIST ERA

replace him as minister to France. After he had been in France the two months allowed to foreigners, the French police notified Pinckney that unless he got a permit to remain, they would arrest him. Pinckney fled to Amsterdam in a rage. When news of Pinckney's treatment reached Philadelphia, Adams (now president) had to deal with Federalist demands for war with the French.

Adams refused to give in. Without asking the French government, he decided to send a three-man mission to Paris to persuade the French to end their raids on American shipping. When Talleyrand, then Foreign Minister of France, refused to negotiate until the Americans had given a bribe of $250,000 to three subordinates, the mission collapsed. In their reports home, the American envoys referred to Talleyrand's three subordinates as X, Y, and Z. When the reports became public, an uproar broke out among both parties over the so-called XYZ dispatches, during which someone is said to have cried, "Millions for defense, but not one cent for tribute." Congress did vote millions for the expansion of the army and navy in 1798 and 1799; it also created a separate Navy Department and repealed all treaties with France.

To the disappointment of Hamilton, who wanted to lead it into battle, the new army grew very slowly. Adams himself saw little use for land forces in fighting for the freedom of the seas. He was also reluctant to burden the country with needless expense. The new Navy Department, on the other hand, promptly pushed to completion three well-armed frigates then under construction, produced twenty other ships of war, and sent hundreds of American privateers to prey on the French. In 1798 and 1799, an "undeclared naval war" raged with France. American ships, operating mainly in the Caribbean, took almost a hundred French vessels and suffered serious losses themselves.

Hamilton's friends in the cabinet and Congress, meanwhile, were pushing the expansion of the army so hard that many people suspected a plan to use it against domestic as well as foreign enemies. Their suspicions were confirmed in February 1799, when troops were sent once more to western Pennsylvania to put down a rebellion led by John Fries against the collection of the new taxes to pay for the army.

The Hamiltonians even persuaded Washington, only a few months before his death, to take nominal command of the army once again. This step helped push Adams, much against his inclination,
to name Hamilton as next in command and effectively in charge. But Adams would go no further; he refused to ask Congress to make an official declaration of war against France.

The Alien and Sedition Acts

At the time of Adams's election, Madison had written to Jefferson: "You know the temper of Mr. A. better than I do, but I have always conceived it to be rather a ticklish one." One thing Adams quickly became "ticklish" about was the Republican taunt that he was "President by three votes." Other attacks on him and his administration aroused him, early in the summer of 1798, to lash back at his opponents.

Many of the most vocal were recent immigrants, including Albert Gallatin, the Swiss banker who became Republican leader of the House when Madison retired. The English radical Thomas Cooper, who had come to America in 1794 and soon proved himself a vigorous Republican pamphleteer, was another. Adams suspected a number of recently arrived French intellectuals of engaging in espionage. Most offensive of all, perhaps, were the defeated fighters for Irish freedom who brought to the United States their hatred of Britain. Nor did Adams forget American-born Republican journalists.

Adams might easily have gotten over his anger if extremists in his party, in 1798, had not pushed through Congress four laws known as the Alien and Sedition Acts. The first was a Naturalization Act that raised the residence requirement for American citizenship from five to fourteen years. The second, the Alien Act, empowered the president, even in peacetime, to order any alien from the country and to imprison any who refused to go. The third, the Alien Enemies Act, permitted the president to jail enemy aliens in wartime. No arrests were made under either alien act, but they did frighten hundreds of foreigners from the country.

The fourth measure was the Sedition act. Its key clause provided severe fines and jail penalties for anyone speaking, writing, or publishing "with intent to defame . . . or bring into contempt or disrepute" the president or other members of the government. That its purpose was to gag the Republican opposition until after the next presidential election was evident in the provision continuing the act "in force until March 3, 1801, and no longer."

A number of Republican editors were actually jailed, and some Republican papers were forced to shut down. The trials were travesties of justice dominated by judges who saw treason everywhere. Juries were hand-picked by Federalist United States marshals in defiance of statutes prescribing orderly procedures. The presiding judges often ridiculed the defendants' lawyers and interrupted their presentations so much that many walked out and left their clients to the mercy of the courts.

The Virginia and Kentucky Resolutions

The entire collection of acts aroused indignant opposition. Madison called the Sedition Act "a monster that must forever disgrace its parents." He and Jefferson both recognized it as the beginning of the Federalist campaign for the election of 1800. They moved quickly to a broad attack on the whole Federalist philosophy. Their offensive took the form of a series of resolutions for which their allies won the approval of the legislatures of Kentucky and Virginia in 1798. The resolutions were then circulated among the other states.

Jefferson wrote the Kentucky Resolutions; Madison wrote those adopted in Virginia. Both sets attacked the "broad interpretation" of the Constitution and developed the state rights position later used to justify nullification and secession. In Jefferson's words, "the several states composing the United States of America, are not united on the principle of unlimited submission to their general government." That government, in Madison's terms, is but a "compact to which the states are parties." The Kentucky Resolutions held that, as parties to the "compact," the states had the right to declare what measures went beyond their agreement and were "unauthoritative, void, and of no force," and to decide what remedies were appropriate. Madison, in the Virginia Resolutions, said that the states together might "interpose" to check the exercise of unauthorized federal powers. Jefferson went further; he held that the legislature of each individual state had this right.

No interpretation of the intent or action of the Great Convention of 1787 could have been more far-fetched than that expressed in these resolutions. But in pressing their argument this far, Madison and Jefferson at least had a liberalizing goal that was not part of later state rights movements. In the Kentucky Resolutions, Jefferson said that the Alien and Sedition Acts, by employing the loosest construction of the Constitution to impose the tightest tyranny, soured "the mild spirit of our country and its laws."

In both states the resolutions asked other state legislatures to adopt the same position. None did so. Federalists in several northern states passed resolutions denouncing Virginia and Kentucky for misinterpreting the nature of the Constitution. They argued that the Constitution was much more than an agreement among independent states and that only the federal courts could decide whether actions of the other two branches violated it. So the Virginia and Kentucky Resolutions had little effect at the time, except to remind Americans that the relationship of the states to the national government was not a settled one. No one at the time realized how often the question would arise again.

The Election of 1800

While the XYZ affair and other actions by France had cost the Republicans some strength in the country, their prospects for the presidential campaign of 1800 were brightened by the sharp split in Federalist ranks between the Adams men and the Hamiltonians.

For the campaign of 1800, the Republican caucus named Jefferson and Aaron Burr of New York. The Federalists were badly divided, but they finally brought out a ticket of Adams and C. C. Pinckney. After the election, the electoral college voted 65 for Adams and 64 for Pinckney; Jefferson and Burr each received 73 votes.

The Republicans had won, but they faced an unexpected difficulty because of the tie between the Republican candidates for president and vice-president. Burr had no ambitions to be president at this time; but many Federalists, especially those from commercial New England and New York, saw his tie vote with Jefferson as an opportunity to keep Jefferson out.

The *Washington Federalist* described Burr as "a friend of the Constitution . . . a friend of the commercial interests . . . the firm and decided friend of the navy." The newspaper went on to argue for geographical balance: "The Eastern States [New England] have had a President and Vice President; So have the Southern. It is proper that the middle states should also be respected."

According to the Constitution, the House would have to decide between the two Republicans. There the voting was to be by states, and nine states (out of the sixteen) were needed to win. The

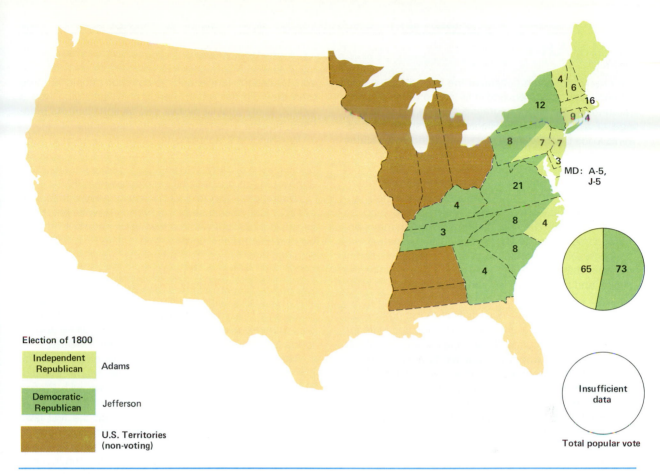

Election of 1800

Election of 1800

Independent Republican — Adams

Democratic-Republican — Jefferson

U.S. Territories (non-voting)

MD: A-5, J-5

65 | 73

Insufficient data

Total popular vote

first ballot was taken on February 11, with the results that Jefferson had foreseen: He carried eight states, Burr six, and two were undecided. And so it went for a feverish week, during which thirty-five ballots were taken. The deadlock was broken on the thirty-sixth ballot. Certain Federalist congressmen took their states out of Burr's camp by voting blanks.

The next Congress put an end to this kind of problem by writing the Twelfth Amendment, ratified by the states in 1804. This amendment provided that henceforth, "The electors . . . shall name in their ballots the person voted for as President, and in distinct ballots the person voted for as Vice-President."

Despite the viciousness of the election campaign, the transfer of power from the Federalists to the Republicans had been accomplished peaceably. Americans were beginning to realize that an organized political opposition had to be permitted its own free voice and hopes for power.

Although the Republicans captured the presidency and control of both the House and the Senate, the country's first great shift in political power was not quite complete. Just before adjourning in March 1801, the retiring Federalist Congress gave Adams a new judiciary act. It relieved Supreme Court justices, as well as district court justices, from the burden of riding to the circuit courts, created a whole new group of circuit court judges, and increased the number of district court judges. Adams put Federalist sympathizers in these lifetime jobs and other new judicial posts. Most important, he named his interim Secretary of State, John Marshall, as chief justice of the Supreme Court. Adams was the last Federalist president. After him, as the country became more Republican and expansive, his party became more sectional and narrow. Yet for more than thirty years of Republican political rule, the new chief justice continued to hand down Federalist, nationalist interpretations of the law despite continuous crises generated by wars in Europe and an expanding economy.

SUMMARY

The new Constitution described the United States government; now its leaders had to fill in the framework. The first item on the new Congress's agenda was the passage of a federal Bill of Rights—the first ten amendments to the Constitution. They were ratified by the states late in 1791. The Judiciary Act of 1789 set up the federal court system and spelled out its powers. The building of the executive branch was begun with three departments—State, War, and Treasury. Washington appointed secretaries for each, a chief justice, and an attorney general. The secretaries and the attorney general became the basis for a presidential cabinet.

Congress, meanwhile, turned to the urgent money problems that had caused so much trouble under the Articles and passed the first money-raising law, a tariff. Hamilton was the driving force behind longer-range solutions to the nation's financial difficulties. He proposed a variety of plans to deal with the public debt and to tie the fate of the new nation to the fortunes of the merchants and the wealthy, whom he saw as its most important citizens. He succeeded in establishing a national bank modeled on the Bank of England. But he had less success with an excise tax on commodities. Opposition to the tax resulted in the so-called Whiskey Rebellion in western Pennsylvania in 1794. The fact that the new government was not immediately able to deal firmly with the Indians, the British, and the Spanish on the frontiers also added to its troubles.

All these controversies helped to build factions, and eventually political parties. Four men—Hamilton, Madison, Jefferson, and Washington—were the country's leading figures. But they were not in agreement, and from their opposing views of how government should work and where power should reside—whether with the national government or with the states—came political parties. The Federalists, led by Hamilton, favored a strong, wealthy nation led by commercial and financial interests. The Republicans, led by Jefferson and Madison, trusted the farmer and the common people far more than they did the urban merchant. Washington was a patriot, firmly against parties and factionalism. As president, he saw it as his duty not to take sides.

Washington's agreeing to serve for a second term meant there was no presidential contest in 1792. But the parties were already active in the vice-presidential race and would run presidential candidates in 1796.

Washington's second term was occupied with foreign affairs, mostly because of the French Revolution. It had begun in 1789, but within a few years its effects spread beyond the French borders and caused war between England and France. The subversive activities of Citizen Genêt, the problems of neutrality on the seas, and the unpopularity of the treaty John Jay negotiated with the British in 1794 all caused discontent in the United States. Pinckney's treaty with Spain in 1795 had a better reception, primarily because the United States gained access to the Mississippi and to the port of New Orleans.

The election of 1796, the first peaceful transfer of power, was won by the Federalist John Adams. Much of his attention was devoted to avoiding war with France and to battling political enemies at home. It was also in his administration that Congress passed the first laws abridging individual freedoms—the Alien and Sedition Acts. The Republican reaction to these measures was sharp. Madison and Jefferson, through the Virginia and Kentucky Resolutions, began a debate over state rights and federal power that would become part of American politics for many years.

With the Republican capture of the presidency in 1800, the Federalist party faded. But before Adams left office, he appointed a new Chief Justice of the Surpeme Court, John Marshall. The decisions of this Federalist in favor of a broad, nationalist interpretation of the Constitution were to have a permanent influence on the new nation and to turn it in a direction opposite to that which the Republicans intended.

Suggested Readings

J. Miller, *The Federalist Era, 1789–1801* (1960), a well-balanced survey, contains an extensive bibliography. An interesting, sweeping approach is taken by J. Fliegelman, *Prodigals and Pilgrims: The American Revolution against Patriarchal Authority, 1750–1800* (1982).

Hamilton was, of course, a central figure in this period, and he remains almost as controversial now as he was then. The best approach to his thinking lies through his *Papers,* currently being edited by H. Syrett and J. Cooke. J. Miller, *Alexander Hamilton* (1959), is probably the most balanced biography, though there is much more information in B. Mitchell, *Alexander Hamilton* (2 vols., 1957, 1962). J.Boyd, the Sherlock Holmes of modern historians, has unraveled Hamilton's machinations in *Number 7, Alexander Hamilton's Secret Attempts to Control American Foreign Policy* (1964). Hamilton's economic program has received impressive analysis by Mitchell (above) and Ferguson (cited in Chapter 7).

Washington is brought to life in the third and fourth volumes of the biography by J. Flexner, *George Washington and the New Nation, 1783–1793* (1969), and *George Washington: Anguish and Farewell, 1793–1799* (1972). D. Freeman, *George Washington* (7 vols., 1948–1957), provides more detail and is itself a monument to monumental biography. For Madison, see Brant's biography (cited in Chapter 7); for Jefferson, see the citations in Chapter 9.

Partly because the Founding Fathers disliked the very notion of political parties, historians have been fascinated by the parties' rapid emergence: J. Chambers, *Political Parties in a New Nation, The American Experience, 1776–1809* (1963); N. Cunningham, Jr., *The Jeffersonian Republicans: The Formation of Party Organization, 1789–1801* (1957); and M. Borden, *Parties and Politics in the Early Republic, 1789–1815* (1967). J. Banner, *To the Hartford Convention: The Federalists and the Origins of Party Politics in Massachusetts* (1970), gives a sensible discussion at the state level.

Foreign affairs in the Federalist period and their impact on party development are dealt with in A. De Conde, *Entangling Alliance: Politics and Diplomacy under George Washington* (1958); and his *The Quasi-War: The Politics and Diplomacy of the Undeclared War with France, 1797–1801* (1966); P. Varg, *Foreign Policies of the Founding Fathers* (1963); and J. Combs, *The Jay Treaty: Political Battleground of the Founding Fathers* (1970). Perhaps the best writer on foreign policy for this and later periods is B. Perkins, *The First Rapprochement: England and the United States, 1795–1805* (1955).

The new nation's foreign policy in this period was intertwined with westward expansion. On this matter, see F. Philbrick, *The Rise of the West, 1754–1830* (1965); R. Horseman, *The Frontier in the Formative Years, 1783–1815* (1970); and M. Rohrbough, *Land Office Business: Public Lands, 1789–1837* (1968). West-

ern policy and several of the key characters involved receive attention in J. Daniels, *Ordeal of Ambition: Jefferson, Hamilton, Burr* (1970). Gore Vidal's *Burr: A Novel* (1973), is fun, but it is what it purports to be—fiction.

There is no fully adequate biography of John Adams. G. Chinard, *Honest John Adams* (1933), is brief but out of date. Z. Haraszti, *John Adams and the Prophets of Progress* (1952), takes advantage of the fact that Adams filled the margins of the books he read with biting criticisms. No study has yet caught the fundamentally Puritan nature of Adams's thought and feeling. The best way of getting at this puzzling man is through his *Diary and Autobiography*, edited by L. Butterfield et al. (4 vols., 1961); and Butterfield et al., *The Book of Abigail and John: Selected Letters of the Adams Family, 1762–1784* (1975). There are, however, two good political studies: M. Dauer, *The Adams Federalists* (1953), and S. Kurtz, *The Presidency of John Adams: The Collapse of Federalism, 1795–1800* (1958).

A free press was not so taken for granted in this period as is often thought. On early repression, see J. Miller, *Crisis in Freedom: The Alien and Sedition Acts* (1951); J. Smith, *Freedom's Fetters* (1956); and D. Stewart, *The Opposition Press of the Federal Period, 1789–1800* (1969). R. Buel, *Securing the Revolution: Ideology in American Politics, 1789–1815* (1972), affords a brand of psychohistory while examining certain political leaders during the period of the Alien and Sedition Acts.

THE JEFFERSONIAN ERA

Chapter 9

Of all the great figures among the Founding Fathers, Thomas Jefferson was both the most approachable and the most aloof. He dressed casually and informally, even on solemn public occasions. A Pennsylvania senator described him when he took up his duties as secretary of state in 1790: "His clothes seem too small for him. He sits in a lounging manner, on one hip commonly, and with one of his shoulders elevated much above the other. . . . His whole figure has a loose, shackling air." The senator went on to describe Jefferson's "rambling vacant look," which had "nothing of that firm collected deportment which I expected." The senator "looked for gravity," but found "rather the air of stiffness in his manner." "The people," writes one of Jefferson's biographers, "could have quite taken him to their hearts if they had not felt, as every one felt in his presence, that he was always graciously but firmly holding them off."

Thomas Jefferson called the Republican victory that brought him to office "the revolution of 1800." Never a man to see much shading between good and evil, he wrote: "The Federalists wished for everything which would approach our new government to a monarchy; the Republicans to preserve it essentially republican."

Few historians today would agree with Jefferson. His election was followed by change, but not as much as he thought or would have liked. Jefferson himself felt that the great majority of Federalists had been led astray by a few wealthy, power-hungry persons, and he wanted to bring them to his own party. He was somewhat successful, for Federalists never again controlled the presidency. Yet they continued for at least fifteen years to be an active political party. And they continued to control the courts. Today, what seems most impressive about Jefferson's "revolution" was the peaceful transfer of political power from one political group to another.

Jefferson and his two hand-picked successors, James Madison and James Monroe, wanted to avoid further entanglement with European conflicts. Jefferson's eyes were on what he called America's "continental destiny." He used that phrase despite the fact that the rest of the continent was still claimed by European powers and occupied by Indians. As things turned out, Jefferson doubled the size of the United States. But then James Madison allowed the country to drift into involvement in European wars. Only after those wars were over was the United States free to concentrate on internal expansion. ■

JEFFERSON IN POWER

The new president immediately set out to correct what he regarded as the injustices of the previous administration. He also cut the federal budget. He struggled against Federalists in the judiciary, but with very little success. His greatest interest, however, was more positive. Most of the North American continent, he was convinced, was destined to fall into the hands of the young republic. He gave destiny a helping hand by sending out explorers and by approving the purchase of a territory so large that it doubled the size of the United States.

Cleaning House

Jefferson's inaugural address extended the hand of peace to his opponents. "We are all Republicans; we are all Federalists," he declared in a statement that was more hopeful than accurate. Jefferson also announced his faith that enemies of the republic should be allowed to "stand undisturbed as monuments of the safety with which error of opinion may be tolerated where reason is left free to combat it." When he spoke these words, John Adams was already rattling along in a coach headed back to Massachusetts.

The new administration did indeed seem very different from the old Federalist ones. Jefferson's inauguration was the first to take place in the new federal city on the Potomac. Grand plans had been made for the city. A French architect, Pierre L'Enfant, had been hired to draw up an imposing plan of streets.

In 1801, however, the city was anything but imposing. The streets were ruts of dust and mud,

except when they were frozen. Pennsylvania Avenue ran from the Capitol through a swamp. The few public buildings were still under construction. The rest of the city consisted of one stationery shop, one grocer, one shoemaker, one printer, one washerwoman's, one tailor shop, one dry goods shop, and one oyster house. Elected and appointed officials lived in seven or eight crammed boarding houses, seeing too much of each other in quarters far too close for privacy or comfort. Members of Congress spent as little time as possible in Washington. Philadelphia had been far more attractive, a real city with paved and lighted streets, established taverns, social life with ladies, and even a theater.

Upon taking office, Jefferson and the Republicans immediately set about to nullify the Alien and Sedition Acts. Since these laws were due to expire within a few months, the only positive action needed was changing the period of naturalization back from fourteen to five years. As a matter of personal and symbolic justice, the men convicted under the Sedition Act were pardoned and their fines returned with interest.

Jefferson's first appointments to his cabinet indirectly showed how important Washington's example had been. He appointed Republicans, men who basically agreed with him, but kept a careful eye on geographical balance. His most influential appointees were trusted comrades from the days when the Republicans had been a minority in Congress. James Madison was named secretary of state and Albert Gallatin secretary of the treasury. Gallatin agreed with Jefferson's instructions to cut the cost of government. He supervised one of the few reductions of the federal bureaucracy which has ever taken place. The new administration reduced the size of the army, stopped the scheduled

BELKNAP ON THE GOOD SOCIETY

At the end of the eighteenth century a New England intellectual, Jeremy Belknap, described his ideal community in Jeffersonian terms:

Were I to form a picture of happy society, it would be a town consisting of a due mixture of hills, valleys and streams of water: The land well fenced and cultivated; the roads and bridges in good repair; a decent inn for the refreshment of travellers, and for public entertainments: The inhabitants mostly husbandmen; their wives and daughters domestic manufacturers; a suitable proportion of handicraft workmen and two or three traders; a physician and lawyer, each of whom should have a farm for his

support. A clergyman of any denomination, which should be agreeable to the majority, a man of good understanding, of a candid disposition and exemplary morals; not a metaphysical, nor a polemic, but a serious and practical preacher. A school master who should understand his business and teach his pupils to govern themselves. A social library, annually increasing, and under good regulation. A club of sensible men, seeking mutual improvement. A decent musical society. No intriguing politician, horse jockey, gambler or sot; but all such characters treated with contempt. Such a situation may be considered as the most favourable to social happiness of any which this world can afford.

expansion of the navy, shrank the diplomatic corps, and cut expenses on government social functions.

Such reductions were easier then than they would be today, for the federal bureaucracy was tiny. When Jefferson took office, the State Department had nine employees. He urged Gallatin to undertake the nearly impossible job of making the government's financial affairs so simple "that every member of Congress and every man of any mind in the Union should be able to comprehend them." Jefferson wanted to achieve a simple style appropriate for a republic. He graciously greeted foreign envoys while wearing bedroom slippers. Rather than give his first annual State of the Union address in person, he sent it to Congress by messenger.

Jefferson hoped that financial economies and a simple style of government would have several happy results. Taxes could be reduced. The national debt could be paid off and speculators kept out of government. Government could be made simple, inexpensive, and responsive to the needs of the people.

When he was forced to deal with challenges from foreign countries, Jefferson proved to be a strong nationalist. To the surprise and delight of Federalist leaders, he quickly decided to face down the pirates who for years had been raiding American ships off the coast of North Africa. The rulers of several small Muslim states on the southwest shores of the Mediterranean (known as the Barbary Coast) had been running an extortion game on the ships of other countries. Britain, the United States, and other European nations had been paying "tribute" to these rulers. Sometimes Muslim rulers seized American ships and enslaved their crews.

In 1801, when one of the North African states demanded more money, Jefferson responded by sending a naval squadron to bottle up the pirates in their own ports. The undeclared "Barbary war"

Artist Michel F. Corne's painting of United States naval vessels shelling the port of Tripoli in North Africa, August, 1804. (*U.S. Naval Academy Museum*)

dragged on until 1805. The United States "won" only the right to make lower payments than other nations, a practice which did not end for another ten years.

Struggles with the Judiciary

Jefferson also set out to correct certain injustices at home. He felt particularly strongly about the "midnight" judicial appointments the Federalists and Adams had slipped through at the last moment. The president presuaded Congress to pass another Judiciary Act (1802) which reduced the number of federal judgeships. This was the opening gun of Jefferson's "war" on the Federalist judiciary.

A minor incident in this struggle was transformed into a major constitutional case by Chief Justice John Marshall. Known as *Marbury v. Madison* (1803), the case arose out of Adams's last-minute appointment of William Marbury as a federal justice of the peace. Marbury's commission was signed so late that it was not delivered to him before Jefferson took office. Madison refused to deliver Marbury's commission. (The secretary of state in those days was charged with certain domestic duties as well as the conduct of foreign affairs.)

Marbury asked the Supreme Court to issue a writ ordering Madison to hand it over. The Court, by the Judiciary Act of 1789, had the power to do

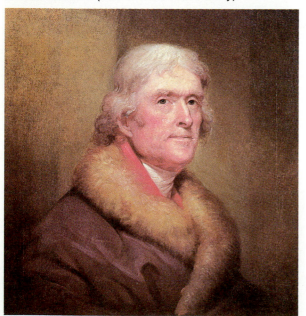

Thomas Jefferson. (*New York Historical Society*)

as Marbury asked. But John Marshall, in his decision in *Marbury v. Madison* (1803), refused to use it. He held that Marbury, despite the Judiciary Act, had no case at all.

The Constitution, Marshall argued, stated explicitly in what actions the Supreme Court had original jurisdiction, and Marbury's complaint was not among them. Only an amendment to the Constitution could extend the Court's jurisdiction to it. That being so, Marshall continued, the provision in the Judiciary Act of 1789 that granted the Supreme Court the authority to issue such writs as Marbury sought was unconstitutional.

Marshall's decision did not set a precedent. In 1792, a United States circuit court in Pennsylvania had declared a federal law unconstitutional. But *Marbury v. Madison* was memorable because Marshall firmly and effectively confronted Jefferson's state rights theory of the Kentucky Resolutions. It was also the first time, and the only one for more than fifty years, that the Supreme Court declared an act of Congress unconstitutional.

Marshall's own proclamations have stood the test of time. The Constitution, he said, was law, to be enforced by courts. It was, moreover, the supreme law, to which even federal legislation must conform. In conflicts over the meaning of the Constitution as law or over the validity of legislation under it, "it is emphatically the province and duty of the judicial department—and not of the states or the legislature— "to say what the law is."

That the power of judicial review should be assigned to the Surpeme Court by a Federalist so early in the first Republican administration made Jefferson furious. If Federalist judges could check legislation simply by declaring it unconstitutional, the legislature must have some means to counteract them. Congress, some Republican legislators claimed, had these means in the power of impeachment. The most important victim of the impeachment policy was Supreme Court Justice Samuel Chase, who had a habit of entertaining juries with anit-Republican speeches before sentencing Republican victims. Chase had become especially outrageous in cases involving the Sedition Act. The House impeached him for misconduct in 1805, though he escaped conviction in the Senate. The Republicans were unable to convict Chase because they were not united.

The so-called Old Republicans, led by John Randolph of Virginia, were the "democratic" wing of the party. They distrusted executive and judicial power and independence in particular, and the federal government in general. The moderate wing of the Republican party, led by the more national-minded Madison, was less willing to let government be led by the "whims" of the people. On the issue of Chase's impeachment—and on many other issues, as things turned out—the moderates were usually able to defeat the more radical members of their own party, both at the national and state levels. Sometimes they had the help of moderate Federalists and, generally, Jefferson's backing.

Jefferson and the West

In 1801, though other Europeans were not challenging the Americans' right to settle the region east of the Mississippi, the land was not vacant. Indians had lived there for centuries and continued to do so. Yet over the next forty years these original Americans were systematically driven from their homelands by means of one-sided "treaties" and naked force.

To encourage white settlement of the "public" lands, Congress in 1796 and 1800 had lowered both the minimum acreage pioneers had to buy and the actual cash they had to put down. In 1804 Jefferson got Congress to reduce requirements to the point where, for a down payment of only $80, white settlers could gain title to a "quarter section" of 160 acres. These measures speeded the pace of westward migration by farmers into the Northwest Territory. In 1803 the new state of Ohio was admitted to the Union.

Jefferson also promoted settlement in the Southwest. After much confusion and quarreling about Georgia's western land claims, two new states were eventually carved out of the lands along the Gulf Coast between Georgia and the Mississippi River. By that time Jefferson had retired from office, but he had been instrumental in the establishment and eventual admission of Mississippi (1817) and Alabama (1819).

As president, Jefferson had even larger plans for the West. Early in 1803, he persuaded Con-

American Explorations of the Far West

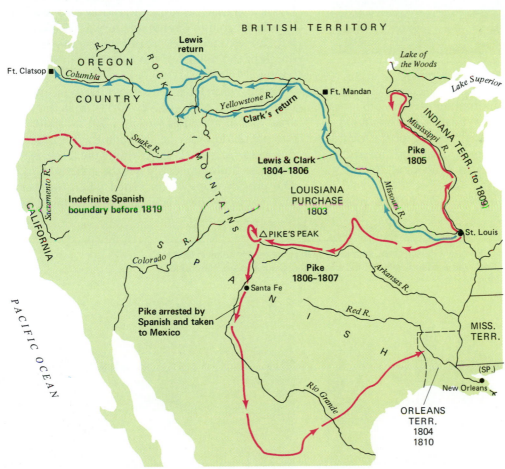

Meriwether Lewis. (*New York Public Library*)

opportunities, and possible routes for overland migration. Jefferson's scientific interest was genuine, but his explanation to Spain's ambassador was less than honest. He told the Spanish minister that the expedition "would have no other view than the advancement of geography."

The Lewis and Clark expedition took two years, but it was a great success. In 1804 a party of nearly fifty men followed the Missouri River northwestward, crossed the Rockies, and descended along the Columbia River to the Pacific. The expedition added greatly to knowlege of the West and showed that overland travel was possible in that enormous region. It also strengthened American claims to the vaguely defined "Oregon country" on the Pacific northwest coast. Jefferson sent two other expeditions, both led by Zebulon Pike, to find the source of the Mississippi River and to explore the Southwest. Pike's second expedition went through territory that clearly belonged to Spain.

The Louisiana Purchase

Lewis and Clark assumed that they also would be traveling through foreign territory. But before they left, an extraordinary series of events had put much of the middle of the continent in American hands.

Spain, with Jefferson's blessing, held the vast Louisiana territory—or New Orleans, as the whole area was often called—from 1762 to 1800. "Till our population can be sufficiently advanced [in numbers] to gain it from them piece by piece," Jefferson thought it could not "be in better hands." The president grew concerned when he learned that Napoleon, by a secret treaty in October 1800,

gress to secretly appropriate money to send Meriwether Lewis and William Clark on an expedition to the Pacific Coast. As one of the United States' leading scientists, Jefferson instructed them to keep careful journals about all the plants and animals they found. They were also told to record all information about Indian tribes, trading

Sketches from the journal of Sergeant Patrick Gass, who accompanied Lewis and Clark in their travels; (left) Lewis and Clark hold a council with the Indians; (right) Clark and his men hunt bears. (*New York Public Library*)

had retrieved Louisiana for France. Napoleon intended to develop Louisiana into a breadbasket for the French West Indies, thereby ending the islands' dependence on the United States for food. But he could not go on with this plan until his position in Europe was secure.

In western Santo Domingo (Haiti), moreover, a spectacular slave insurrection led by the black General Toussaint L'Ouverture threatened to ruin Napoleon's vision of a new American empire. Once Napoleon had quieted Europe with the Peace of Amiens in 1802, he sent some 20,000 men to crush Toussaint and then to occupy the port of New Orleans. His campaign in Haiti failed when his troops lost to the rebellious blacks and to tropical diseases.

That same year Jefferson learned about Napoleon's previously secret deal with Spain. He warned the French that their action might "completely reverse all . . . political relations" and drive the United States into the arms of England. In May 1802, Jefferson instructed Robert Livingston in Paris to try to get France to put a price on the city of New Orleans. Before Livingston could make much progress, Jefferson learned that the Spanish official still in charge at New Orleans had suspended the American right, under Pinckney's Treaty, to deposit cargoes there. Nothing could have more strongly confirmed American suspicions of the French.

Yet Jefferson was determined to avoid war. He won from Congress an appropriation of $2 million to be used by James Monroe, who sailed to Paris in March 1803, to assist Livingston. Monroe's instructions were to buy the city of New Orleans. If France refused to sell and kept New Orleans shut to American commerce, Monroe and Livingston were to suggest to Britain that it join the United States in case of a new war with Napoleon. By the time Monroe arrived in Paris, he found his instructions obsolete. Napoleon needed money. To get it, he offered the entire Louisiana Territory to the United States. Livingston and Monroe almost immediately closed the deal for $15 million.

To negotiate such a "bargain" was one thing; to get the money for it, quite another. One difficulty was that the Constitution did not give the federal government power to purchase territory. Jefferson was so worried that he at first suggested a constitutional amendment to make the treaty legitimate. But delay might cause Napoleon to change his mind, so Jefferson pushed the treaty through.

The Senate ratified it, 26 to 5, and the House appropriated the money, 90 to 25. On December 20, the United States formally took possession of the heartland of the North American continent. By long-range financial, per-acre comparison, the original $24 Dutch purchase of Manhattan Island was downright expensive.

The next year, two territories were made of the purchase, to be administered under the terms of the Northwest Ordinance of 1787. Under these terms, Louisiana, with its present boundaries, became a state in 1812. Florida had not been included in the arrangement, since Spain had never actually given it to France. But Jefferson was not discouraged. "If we push them strongly with one hand, holding out a price in the other," he said, "we shall certainly obtain the Floridas, and all in good time."

WORLD POLITICS: THE NAPOLEONIC WARS

John Randolph, reflecting in his old age on the first three years of Jefferson's presidency, declared: "Never was there an administration more brilliant than that of Mr. Jefferson up to this period. We were indeed in the 'full tide of successful experiment.' Taxes repealed; the public debt amply provided for . . . ; sinecures abolished; Louisi-

---

JEFFERSON ON NEW ORLEANS

Though he was a friend of France, Jefferson opposed French acquisition of New Orleans. Such a move, he thought, would force the United States to ally with France's traditional enemy.

The cession of Louisiana and the Floridas by Spain to France works most sorely on the U.S. . . . There is on the globe one single spot, the possessor of which is our natural and habitual enemy. It is New Orleans, through which the produce of three-eighths of our territory must pass to market, and from its fertility it will ere long yield more than half of our whole produce and contain more than half our inhabitants. France placing herself in that door assumes to us the attitude of defiance. . . . The day that France takes possession of N. Orleans . . . seals the union of two nations who in conjunction can maintain exclusive possession of the ocean. From that moment we must marry ourselves to the British fleet and nation.

ana acquired; public confidence unbounded." Even in New England the congressional elections of 1802–1803 showed the Republican strength. And the next year Jefferson carried every state except Connecticut and Delaware. The new vice-president was George Clinton, to whom Jefferson had entrusted the distribution of Republican patronage in New York.

Jefferson's first administration coincided roughly with the first years of peace in Europe since the French Revolution, and he had made the best of it. His second administration had hardly begun when the country was buffeted once more by renewed war in Europe. In 1805 Napoleon's victory at Austerlitz gave France control of much of the European continent. Nelson's naval victory at Trafalgar had given Britain control of the seas. This stalemate has been aptly called "a war between the lion and the whale." The conflict had disastrous results for neutral carriers, especially the United States.

Freedom of the Seas

Between 1804 and 1807, hundreds of American ships were confiscated by the British. Even worse was the *impressment* of American seamen. The British navy was chronically short of men, and British policy was that anyone who had ever been a subject of His Majesty could be forced to serve aboard any of His Majesty's naval vessels. There were many British subjects sailing aboard American vessels. Given these circumstances, British officers were not fussy about citizenship papers when boarding an American ship in search of "British deserters."

There was bound to be an incident. In June 1807, the new U.S. frigate *Chesapeake* was cruising just outside the three-mile limit off Virginia. When *H.M.S. Leopard* ordered her to heave to and permit search for a named deserter, *Chesapeake's* captain refused. *Leopard* opened fire. *Chesapeake*, her new guns poorly mounted and her decks still cluttered with gear, suffered twenty-one casualties before being boarded by *Leopard's* officers. They found their deserter and also took three Americans who had served in the British navy.

To most Americans, this attack meant war. But Jefferson insisted on a policy of "peaceful coercion." To save ships and men from capture and thereby save the country from provocation, he decided to keep American ships off the high seas. He thought withholding American goods and carriers would force the European nations to respect neu-

tral rights. Congress went along. The famous Embargo Act passed easily on December 27, 1807.

The Embargo Act resulted in ruin for American commerce and American ports. Despite ship losses, commerce had doubled between 1803 and 1807. Under the embargo it came to a standstill, and the northern industries associated with it, such as shipbuilding and sailmaking, simply shut down. There were immediate protests from those directly affected. Merchants, seamen, ropemakers—everyone whose livelihood came from international trade—saw Jefferson's policy as weak-kneed, unworthy of the republic, and subservient to agrarian interests.

James Madison: The War of 1812

Though in the long run agricultural exporters would have been drastically affected, the immediate effect of the embargo was to worsen sectional feelings. It appeared to many people that the cities and New England would suffer most, while the agricultural interests—Virginia, in particular—would suffer hardly at all. The embargo did, in fact, throw thousands of laborers out of work. It also temporarily resurrected the Federalist party for the national election of 1808. James Madison, Jefferson's handpicked successor, seemed for a time to face an uphill fight for election.

By the summer of 1808, every Republican New England governor had been turned out in favor of a Federalist. Federalist representation in the house doubled between 1807 and 1809. For the presidential campaign of 1808, the Federalists renamed the ticket of 1804—Charles C. Pinckney of South Carolina and Rufus King of New York as his running mate. They carried Maryland, North Carolina, and Delaware, as well as all of New England except Vermont. Yet the results of the election made clear how far the Jeffersonian Republicans had carried the new nation since the election of 1800. Despite diplomatic reverses, Madison won by a considerable margin.

Jefferson was happy to retire. He believed deeply that "the earth belongs to the living not to the dead," that each generation must make its own laws. One of his last acts as president was to sign an act repealing the embargo.

James Madison proved to be temperamentally unsuited for the crisis he inherited. Some men have clearly grown in the presidency; Madison, more than any president in American history, seemed to shrink. "Our President," a young Congressman observed during Madison's first term,

WORDS AND NAMES IN AMERICAN HISTORY

The verb to *gerrymander* is peculiarly American and is scarcely known outside this country. It refers to the forming of an electoral district for some political office by drawing boundaries which will virtually ensure that one political party (the one in control of the legislature doing the mapping) will have its own candidate elected from that district. When the voting districts of a state or even county are drawn with this aim in mind, the result can be weirdly shaped districts. The name of this practice, which has been common in American politics, comes from Elbridge Gerry, who was not really personally responsible for starting it. Gerry was an enthusiastic supporter of the American cause during the revolution. He was one of the few delegates to the Constitutional Convention in Philadelphia to end up opposing its ratification. Later he became a Jeffersonian Republican. When he was governor of Massachusetts in 1812, the legislature redrew all the electoral districts in the hope of maintaining Republican control. One result was a district in eastern Massachusetts so oddly shaped that some people thought it looked on a map like the small reptile called the salamander. It rapidly became known as a *Gerrymander,* and the practice became so common in most states that the word is no longer capitalized. Most historians have concluded that Mr. Gerry would have preferred to have his name immortalized in some other way

---

"tho a man of amiable manners and great talents, has not I fear those commanding talents which are necessary to control those about him." In congresses, conferences, and conversations, Madison's mind had been telling. He was much less effective at political infighting and cloakroom bargaining. At the very beginning, he lost control of his cabinet and appointments. Lack of unity in the administration was aggravated by sectional conflicts carried over from Jefferson's time. Madison also had to deal with a new generation of politicians in Congress: men like Henry Clay, the idol of the West; John C. Calhoun, the idol of the South; and Daniel Webster, the idol of New England. All these men were young enough never to have been British subjects.

Driven from the sea by Jefferson's embargo, northern businessmen after 1807 began to take greater interest in manufacturing, especially in cotton and in wool. In the South, meanwhile, cotton was booming. These changes in the American economy, which were to have such great effect at home in later decades (see Chapter 10), were not lost on British industrialists.

At the same time, many people in Britain still had not forgiven their American cousins. They were happy to see the American flag wiped from the seas. Their policy was to keep up the impressments and captures that had forced Jefferson to use the embargo. Napoleon and his minister Talleyrand played their own game with Madison and Congress. In 1811 they tricked them into cutting off commerce with Great Britain.

Popular disgust with administration fumbling in foreign affairs showed itself in the elections of 1810 and 1811, in which the voters unseated most of the Eleventh Congress. The replacements arriving in Washington in November 1811 included young men from the frontiers. Little concerned with Europe's attacks on American ships, these newcomers hoped to extend American territory at Europe's expense.

On the southern frontier, Spain still held the Floridas, long a haven for runaway slaves, marauding pirates, and hostile Indians. By 1810, many permanent settlers in West Florida were Americans. They asked to be annexed by the United States. Madison, as eager as Jefferson to acquire new territory, agreed. Early in 1812 an armed American expedition set out to take East Florida as well. But when Spain threatened war and New England threatened secession if war came, Madison had to recall the troops.

On the frontier in the Ohio and Mississippi valleys, the trend was even more ominous. Here, between 1801 and 1810, a dozen crushed Indian tribes were forced to make treaties by which they ended up granting more than 100 million acres of prime land to the United States. They were soon being driven off their old preserves.

In 1811, Tecumseh, the great Shawnee chief, decided on a stand. He attempted to organize an alliance of all the Indian nations from Florida to the upper Missouri, with the goal of establishing the Ohio River as a permanent Indian border. The plan was ruined by a premature military attack ordered by Tecumseh's brother, known as the Prophet. Governor William Henry Harrison, one of the hardest negotiators of Indian treaties, attacked Tecumseh's headquarters at Tippecanoe while the Shawnee chief was away mobilizing other tribes. The Prophet ordered a defense of the village, which resulted in a terrible defeat for the Indians. Tecumseh vowed revenge.

Tecumseh. (*Field Museum of Natural History*)

1811 between the American frigate *President* and the British corvette *Little Belt*. The *President's* captain mistook the *Little Belt* for the much more formidable British *Guerrière,* known to be active in impressment raids off New York harbor. Believing she had spotted *Guerrière* off Sandy Hook, *President* gave chase. When the other ship refused to identify herself, *President's* captain gave the order to fire. Nine British seamen were killed and twenty-three wounded. *President* suffered no casualties.

At home, the pounding of *Little Belt* was hailed as a great triumph. A few months after the *Little Belt* affair, public disclosure of the "Henry Letters" further inflamed Americans. John Henry was a Canadian secret agent. Among his letters were reports on the extent of disunion feeling in New England. British interest in this subject enraged many Americans and brought the pressure on Madison to a peak.

On June 1, 1812, the president reluctantly sent a message to Congress asking for war on Britain. The House and Senate complied. "I verily believe that the militia of Kentucky are alone competent to place Montreal and Upper Canada at your feet," boasted Henry Clay during the House debate. Congress must have believed him, for when it adjourned it had voted no new taxes and only a few additional men to carry on the war it had declared.

The maritime sections of the Middle States as well as of New England voted against the war, mainly because they knew their ships would bear the brunt of the fighting and their commerce the brunt of the cost. The South supported the war. It had lost its European tobacco market because of Napoleon's decrees, and it was losing cotton sales because the British could not sell manufactured cotton textiles across the Channel. Except in upper New York State and part of upper Vermont, where relations with Canada were close and trade across the border profitable, the war had the strong support of the frontier.

In his war message, Madison had named impressment as the most important cause. He said nothing of Canada and Florida and little of the Indians. Yet all these issues were tied together, as was made clear in a letter written the previous March by Andrew Jackson, a rising figure in Tennessee:

We are going to fight for the reestablishment of our national character, . . . for the protection of our maritime citizens impressed on board British ships of war, . . . to vindicate our right to a free trade, and open markets for the productions of our soil, . . . to seek some indemnity for past injuries, some security against fu-

But the Battle of Tippecanoe spelled the beginning of the end; from then on, Tecumseh's power steadily declined. Frontier settlers had long believed that the British had been arming Tecumseh and egging him on. They saw Tippecanoe as a victory over the British as well as the Indians. They also saw Tecumseh's revenge as part of a British plot. They began calling for the conquest of all Canada to drive the British from "Our Continent," and for the conquest of all Florida.

Among those who brought this idea to Congress in November 1811 were John Calhoun of South Carolina, whose grandmother had been scalped by Cherokees; Felix Grundy of Tennessee, who had lost three brothers in Indian raids; and their leader, Harry of the West, Henry Clay of Kentucky. The easterners promptly labeled them the War Hawks.

Taking advantage of political quarrels among older members of the Republican party, Clay's friends elected him Speaker of the House. He used this power to name them chairmen of major committees. Soon Clay and his backers presented the House with bills for an enlarged army and navy. Madison found it difficult to withstand the pressure, coming as it did on top of the failure of diplomacy and more incidents at sea.

Two events in particular played into the hands of the war party. One was the encounter in May *ture aggression, by the conquest of all the British dominions upon the continent of North America.*

The War on Land and Sea

Confusion in American minds over the nature and objectives of the war muddied preparations and strategy. Money, men, ships, and supplies had to be provided. Yet early in 1811, Congress had allowed the Bank of the United States to die at the expiration of its twenty-year charter, just when it was to be needed most. Despite the urging of Secretary of the Treasury Gallatin, Congress put off new taxes until 1813. Throughout the war, taxes were voted reluctantly and evaded expertly. Loans were authorized but hard to float.

Congress did not appropriate money to enlarge the navy until six months after war had been declared. The army faced a different problem. Early in 1812 Madison was authorized to accept 50,000 volunteers for one year's service. But in six months only 5000 signed up. Later the president was au- thorized to call out 100,000 state militia, but few would follow their officers across the borders of their own states. The army probably was no worse than its generals deserved. "The old officers," observed Winfield Scott at the beginning of hostili- ties, "had very generally sunk into either sloth, ignorance, or habits of intemperate drinking."

Canada, it was agreed, was the only place to engage the British. But New England, the logical base for an invasion of Canada, opposed the war. The South was no more enthusiastic. It feared that the acquisition of Canada would put the slave states in the minority. Popular opinion in the West was much more favorable, but would not tolerate withdrawal of troops from the garrisons guarding the frontier against the Indians.

At the opening of the war, the United States tried three timid forays against Canada, scattered over almost a thousand miles of border. In the first of these, in July 1812, General William Hull not only failed to enter Canada, but was forced to yield Detroit to the brilliant Canadian General Isaac

The U.S.S. *Constitution* demolishes the British ship *Guerrière*. (*U.S. Naval Academy Museum*)

Brock. American forces attempted a second attack early in October. Captain John Wool led an American detachment across the Niagara River and took Queenstown Heights, where New York militia were to join him and push on. But New York's militiamen refused to cross their state line and stood by while Canadian reinforcements mowed down Wool's men.

The third foray in November was directed against Montreal from Plattsburgh on Lake Champlain in New York. Here, militia under General Henry Dearborn marched north twenty miles, decided that was far enough from home, and marched back again. Before 1812 was over, a new American force under General William Henry Harrison was frustrated in its efforts to regain Detroit. Capturing Canada thus proved somewhat less easy than anyone had supposed. Far from occupying it, the Americans after six months of fighting found their own frontier pushed back to Ohio.

Things went better at sea. The United States navy was no match for the enemy in numbers. In the opening months of hostilities American ships won several stunning victories over British men-of-war in single-ship engagements. Yet the winter of 1812–1813 found most of the American navy back in harbor, where the British succeeded in bottling it up for the rest of the war. But even the British navy failed to control American privateers.

All told, they captured more than 800 British merchantmen.

In the November election of 1812, De Witt Clinton of New York, named by the "peace party" among the Republicans and supported by the Federalists, carried every northern state except Pennsylvania and Vermont. Madison, however, with the support of the South and West, won.

Perhaps the war party's political victory inspired more successful efforts in the field. The first step seemed to be to regain Detroit. General Harrison and others agreed that control of Lake Erie was essential to success here. The task of clearing the Canadians from the lake was given to young Captain Oliver Hazard Perry. By August 1813, Perry's lake fleet was ready, and on September 10, he found the British squadron in Put-in-Bay at the western end of the lake. At the end of the engagement, Perry reported to Harrison, "We have met the enemy and they are ours."

Harrison followed up immediately by defeating the British at the Thames River in Canada. Tecumseh, who had earlier gone over to the British, was killed in this engagement, and his Indian forces ceased to be a factor in the war. To the east, on Lake Ontario, United States troops raided York (now Toronto), burned the Parliament houses, and fled.

In April 1814, Napoleon abdicated. Britain was eager for a general peace, but not before putting

Northern Campaigns, 1812–14

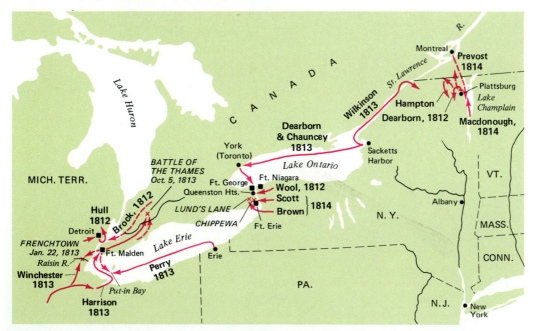

In August, 1814, the British captured and burned the city of Washington, including the president's house, the Capitol, the Treasury, and the War Office. (*The Granger Collection*)

the Americans in their place. In May the British extended their blockade of Atlantic ports to northern New England and strengthened it elsewhere, steps that permitted the harassment of American seaboard cities all the way to Maine.

On one such adventure, a force of British regulars supported by a British fleet began a march from Chesapeake Bay toward Washington. The hastily mobilized defenders, led by the incompetent General William H. Winder, were defeated at Bladensburg, Maryland, leaving Washington open. On August 24, in revenge for the burning of York, the British set fire to the Capitol and the White House. But the next month, an unsuccessful assault against Baltimore and Fort McHenry led them to withdraw from the area.

More important than the burning of Washington was a three-pronged attack the British directed against Niagara, Lake Champlain, and New Orleans, starting in the summer of 1814. All phases of this attack failed. At Niagara, new American commanders—General Jacob Brown and his subordinate, Winfield Scott—fought the British to a standstill. A month later, 10,000 veterans of Wellington's Napoleonic campaigns arrived at Montreal ready to march south toward Lake Champlain. Their objective may have been to detach northern New York and New England and restore them to the British empire. Whatever their purpose, they were foiled at the battle of Plattsburgh Bay, the last armed clash of the war

before the Treaty of Ghent officially ended hostilities.

But it was not the last battle, for the Americans won a stunning victory at New Orleans without either side knowing that a treaty of peace had just been signed in Europe. In the Southwest, Andrew Jackson had been leading his own more or less private campaign against the Indians. After defeating Creek warriors at the battle of Horseshoe Bend in Alabama in March 1814, he forced them to sign a treaty giving up huge tracts of land. Jackson's actions brought him full command in the southwestern theater and the responsibility for checking the British attack in that sector—the third prong of the comprehensive assault. Aware that the British might use Pensacola in Spanish Florida as a base, Jackson highhandedly invaded the area and burned the town. Then he marched to New Orleans and was ready for the British when they arrived.

The battle between General Sir Edward Pakenham's 8000 veterans of the Napoleonic wars and the collection of militiamen, blacks, sailors, and pirates under Jackson took place two weeks after the Treaty of Ghent had been signed, but more than a month before news of the signing had reached Washington. The British lost more than 2000 men in this encounter. American casualties numbered twenty-one. Jackson became the hero of New Orleans, the country's most popular man since George Washington.

Gulf of Mexico

Southwest Campaigns, 1813–15

The Hartford Convention

If the British were trying to detach New England from the United States, many New Englanders would have wished them luck. As early as January 1811, during the opening stages of the debate over the admission of Louisiana as a state, Josiah Quincy of Massachusetts told the House of Representatives that favorable action would make it "the duty of some to prepare definitely for a separation—amicably if they can, violently if they must." Once "Mr. Madison's War" began, New England decided to have as little to do with it as possible, except to make a profit. Yankee farmers and manufacturers grew rich selling supplies to the army their sons refused to serve in.

The Hartford Convention of December 1814 marked the climax of this refusal to cooperate. Many of the convention's organizers hoped that New England would secede from the Union. The Hartford meeting was originally called by the Massachusetts legislature, but when the participants assembled they found that only Massachusetts, Rhode Island, and Connecticut had sent formal delegations. And there were enough moderates among them to outvote the hotheads. Secession was postponed.

Yet even the demands of the moderates exposed the workings of sectionalism. One amendment proposed by the convention's report eliminated the "three-fifths" clause of the Constitution, depriving the South of that part of its representation based on slaves. Another limited the presidency to one term and prohibited the election of successive presidents from the same state—a proposal clearly aimed at Virginia. Others required a two-thirds majority in each house for the admission of new states, for stopping commerce with foreign nations, and declarations of war. The members of the Hartford Convention threatened to meet again if Congress rejected these proposals. They were saved from themselves by the ending of the war.

The battle of New Orleans, with the victorious American troops entrenched on the left. (*New York Historical Society*)

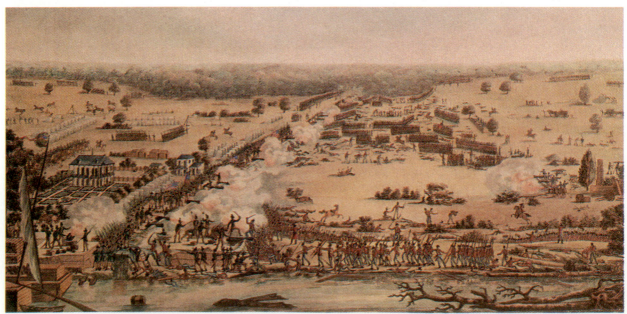

The Treaty of Ghent

Britain had launched its military offensive in the summer of 1814 partly to gain a better position from which to dictate terms at the war's end. When peace commissioners from both sides met in the Belgian town of Ghent in August 1814, the British stalled because they expected reports of new victories. They also presented Madison's negotiators with sweeping demands. Their terms created much conflict among the American negotiators, especially between Henry Clay of Kentucky and John Quincy Adams of Massachusetts, whose temperamental differences sharpened their sectional ones.

The British opened by demanding western territory to provide for an Indian buffer state between the United States and Canada and to give Canada access to the Mississippi. They seemed determined to concede nothing on maritime matters, including New England's privilege (granted in 1783 but withdrawn in 1812) to fish in Newfoundland and Labrador waters.

Britain's claims to the American West angered Clay, but not nearly so much as Adams's willingness to acknowledge them if necessary in order to recover the fishing privileges. Clay was ready to trade away these privileges for territorial demands of his own. Another member of the American mission, Albert Gallatin, kept the negotiations from breaking down by keeping peace among the American delegates.

At the same time, however, Britain's expected victories in America did not take place. Gradually, the British negotiators backed down. On Christmas Eve, both sides at last agreed. The Treaty of Ghent, ratified by the Senate in February 1815, left most issues just as they were at the war's start. It provided for commissions to settle questions of boundaries, fisheries, and the terms of commerce. Few people were optimistic about the future. Adams called the treaty an "armistice." Clay declared that "we are destined to have war after war with Great Britain, until, if one of the two nations be not crushed, all grounds of collision shall have ceased between us."

Although without funds, Congress voted in March 1815 to set up a standing army of 10,000 men, to enlarge appropriations for West Point, and to spend $8 million for warships. New wars, as it turned out, were avoided, but many "grounds of collision" kept the threat of new fighting alive.

POSTWAR ANGLO-AMERICAN RELATIONS: THE MONROE DOCTRINE

The coming of peace did not end all conflict between the United States and Great Britain. British businessmen adopted a policy of dumping manufactured goods in the United States at bargain prices. They did so, as one member of Parliament declared, "to stifle in the cradle those rising manufactures in the United States which the war has forced into being." Henry Clay had this rivalry in mind when he spoke of Britain's determination to crush America.

When petitions poured into Congress demanding that these British moves be stopped, he led the fight for the first protective tariff in the nation's history, the tariff of 1816.

Trade and Territory

The tariff of 1816 had solid support in all parts of the country. When it failed to stop the flood of imports, Clay said it was because of Britain's "mean, barefaced, cheating, by fraudulent invoices and false denominations." While the British forced themselves into United States markets, they still insisted on excluding Americans from the British West Indies.

Despite friction over economic matters and widespread expectations of more armed conflict, the original "mother country" and the new independent and united former colonies never again went to war against each other. No one at the time thought the "armistice" of Ghent would last. Yet diplomatic negotiations, with concessions freely offered by both sides, preserved peace, until in the twentieth century the two nations became the firmest of allies. The first success of negotiation came in 1817 shortly after the War of 1812. The Rush-Bagot Treaty (named after the two negotiators) amounted to a disarmament agreement on the Great Lakes. At the time, that string of enormous lakes made up nearly half the border between the United States and Canada. Both sides agreed to maintain no more than four small armed vessels on the Lakes. Except for technical changes, the Rush-Bagot agreement is still in force. With westward expansion, the U.S.–Canadian border has become what has rightly been called "the longest undefended international border in the world."

This demilitarization of the Great Lakes was a

good omen for the settlement of the boundary issues left to commissions by the treaty. By 1818 four separate commissions had worked out the permanent boundary between the United States and Canada as far west as the "Great Stony (Rocky) Mountains." Knowledge of geography beyond the mountains was still vague, and Britain and the United States agreed to occupy the Oregon Country jointly. When settlement was extended to this region in the 1840s, America's "continental destiny" had become an obsession, and joint occupation became intolerable enough to inspire new talk of war (see Chapter 15).

The Spanish and Indians

The apparent improvement in Anglo-American relations that resulted from peaceful negotiations over the Canadian boundary was endangered by events on the Spanish and Indian frontiers even before those negotiations were over. The first trouble occurred in the area between American West Florida and Spanish East Florida. When Indian-white violence in this region seemed to endanger settlers moving into western Georgia after the war, the state asked the federal government for help. Early in 1817, General Andrew Jackson got the nod, or so he believed, to perform this service. In his usual manner he performed it ruthlessly, burning Indian villages and hanging Indian chiefs.

Jackson also arrested, court-martialed, and executed two British citizens—an old Scottish trader, Alexander Arbuthnot, and a young adventurer, Robert Ambrister—who, he believed, had stirred up the Indians. He then marched on the Spanish in Pensacola, where the Seminoles had found refuge, ejected the governor, installed his own garrisons, and claimed the territory for the United States, as he had promised he would do "in sixty days."

New Boundaries Established by Treaties

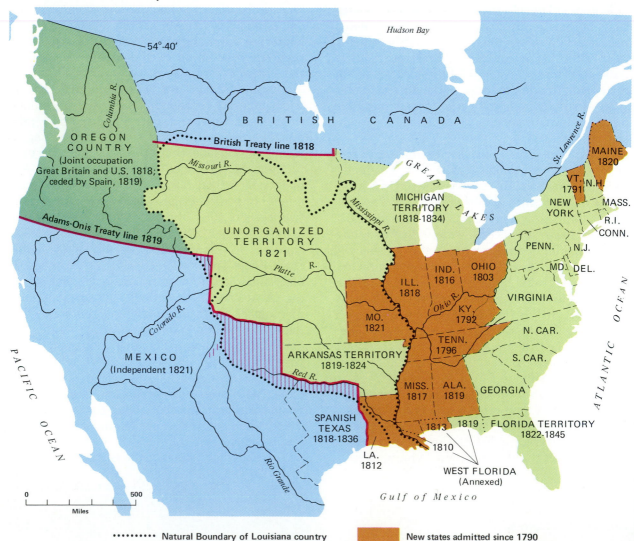

Many people in Britain demanded war over the execution of Ambrister and Arbuthnot. The Spanish, outraged over the invasion of their territory, also made angry gestures. Peace was kept, but Jackson's adventure gave Spain just the push Jefferson believed the Spanish needed to make them sell Florida to the United States before the Americans simply took it.

In the Adams-Onís Treaty of 1819, Spain surrendered its remaining claims to West Florida and ceded East Florida. In exchange, the United States agreed to assume, up to $5 million, the claims of American merchants who had lost ships and cargoes to Spain during the Napoleonic wars. The Adams-Onís Treaty also established the boundary between the United States and Mexico all the way to the Pacific.

Secretary of State John Quincy Adams was disappointed in not gaining Texas as well. The absorption of all North America by the United States, he said in 1819, was "as much a law of nature . . . as that the Mississippi should flow to the sea." But American interest in Texas was only just awakening. Adams, finding little support, did not press the issue.

The boundary agreements with Britain and Spain sharpened the definition of the United States's vast inland empire. But this "empire" was the homeland of hundreds of thousands of Indians. Land-hungry whites could not settle there without, they thought, dealing with those original settlers. Tecumseh's death had taken away the leader of the northern tribes and Britain's retirement from the Great Lakes area had removed their only remaining friend. The situation encouraged the United States to embark on an ambitious fort-building program.

To discourage Indians from seeking any new allegiance to Canada, the government added a string of trading centers where they could buy goods below cost. This stick-and-carrot policy gradually pressured the Indians in the Northwest Territory to agree, in a series of new treaties, to move beyond the Mississippi.

In the Southwest, the Indians had been overawed by Jackson's wartime victories. Now the government offered them (in what was regarded by most whites as a humane move) the choice of taking up agriculture on the lands where they lived or moving west. To the disappointment of the whites, most of the Indians preferred farming to abandoning their homes. Not until Jackson became president in 1829 were they forcibly removed from their lands.

Latin America and the Monroe Doctrine

In 1800, Spain had yielded its claim to the Oregon Country to Britain and Russia, and its vast territory of Louisiana to France. But it still owned an immense New World empire ranging from Upper California to Cape Horn. Portugal owned Brazil, a land soon to cover half of South America. Twenty-five years later, Spain's New World empire had been reduced to Cuba and Puerto Rico; Portugal's, to nothing.

The immediate cause of this shattering collapse was Napoleon's successful invasion of Portugal (1807) and Spain (1808). The Spanish empire was the personal possession of the monarchs. When they fell, the colonies refused allegiance to their successors. Revolts began in Spanish America about 1810, and the independence of the last of the new separate states was completed in 1824.

After Napoleon's downfall in 1814 and the restoration of the Bourbons, the Spanish made a serious effort to regain their New World lands. But they were successfully defied by such Latin American patriots as José de San Martin, founder of Argentina; Simon Bolivar, founder of Venezuela; and Bernardo O'Higgins, dictator of Chile.

The restoration of the Bourbons in Spain in 1814, besides heightening the revolutionary spirit in Spanish America, led to repression and revolution at home. By 1822 the Holy Alliance of the European countries that had defeated Napoleon was ready to suppress the Spanish revolt. When in 1823 France invaded Spain, Britain and the United States both believed the invasion might easily reach across the Atlantic to suppress the colonial revolutions. Britain had already developed a profitable trade with the new republics. That spring, Britain's Foreign Secretary Canning "unofficially and confidentially" suggested to Richard Rush, the American minister in London, that their countries declare to the world, for the benefit of France, that "we conceive the recovery of the [American] colonies by Spain to be hopeless." Canning also suggested further that they state "we could not see any portion of them transferred to any other Power with indifference."

Canning's proposal was forwarded to Washington, where it immediately became the subject of debate in the cabinet and of consideration by two elder statesmen, Jefferson and Madison. Jefferson, acknowledging that "Great Britain is the nation which can do us the most harm of any one," advised that "with her on our side we need not fear the whole world." He recommended accepting

Canning's proposal. Madison agreed.

Secretary of State John Quincy Adams feared that Canning's proposal for joint protection of the rebel countries was an attempt to head off future American acquisition of any territory still held by Spain, particularly Cuba. He urged that the United States should act alone in the Western Hemisphere. President Monroe yielded to Adams's arguments, and in his annual address to Congress in December 1823 used the words later called the Monroe Doctrine:

The political system of the allied powers [of Europe] is essentially different . . . from that of America. . . . We owe it, therefore, to candor and to the amicable relations existing between the United States and those powers to declare that we should consider any attempt on their part to extend their system to any portion of this hemisphere as dangerous to our peace and safety. . . . With the governments who have declared their independence and maintained it, and whose independence we have . . . acknowledged, we could not view any interposition . . . by any European power in any other light than as the manifestation of an unfriendly disposition towards the United States.

Latin America was not the only area of the Western Hemisphere in which European aggression worried Monroe's government. The Russians had been in Alaska for decades. They had built a fort as far south as the coast of northern California. In 1821, the ambitious Czar Alexander I decreed that "the pursuits of commerce, whaling, and fishery, and of all other industry on all islands, posts, and gulfs, including the whole of the northwest coast of America, beginning from Behring Straits to the 51° of northern latitude . . . is exclusively granted to Russian subjects."

Nothing could have aroused Secretary Adams more. He immediately advised the American minister in Russia that "the United States can admit no part of these claims." Monroe, in turn, added, "as a principle," in his message to Congress that the American continents "are henceforth not to be considered as subjects for future colonization by any European powers." The following April the president learned that the czar had agreed on 54° 40' as Russia's southern boundary in North America. With this development, the United States entered a period of thirty years of freedom from serious involvement with foreign powers.

SUMMARY

Thomas Jefferson came to the presidency determined to move the country in a Republican rather than a Federalist direction. He nullified the Alien and Sedition Acts, cut the federal bureaucracy, reduced the size of the army, and stopped the expansion of the navy. His aim was financial economy and a simple style of government.

One way toward this aim was to try to stop the Federalist Supreme Court, where Chief Justice Marshall continued to hand down decisions based on a broad interpretation of the Constitution. But in the landmark *Marbury v. Madison,* Marshall and the Court won.

Although a Republican, Jefferson was a strong nationalist. He sent the navy to the coast of North Africa to battle the Barbary pirates who harassed American shipping. And he believed it was America's destiny to expand over the North American continent. In 1803, he got Congress to sponsor the Lewis and Clark expedition to the Pacific Coast and the two Pike expeditions to find the source of the Mississippi and explore the Spanish/French Southwest. His most ambitious undertaking was the Louisiana Purchase of 1803. For $15 million, Napoleon sold the Louisiana Territory to the United States, the whole middle of the continent.

Jefferson's second administration saw the beginnings of international problems caused by the Napoleonic wars in Europe. American hostility was directed against the British over the issues of the rights of neutrals, freedom of the seas, and the impressment of American seamen into the British navy. An Embargo Act keeping American ships off the seas passed Congress at the end of 1807. It resulted not in keeping the United States out of war, but in the ruin of American commerce and American ports.

It also brought the revival of the Federalist party, James Madison as president, sectional conflict, and then war with England. The War of 1812 ended in 1814 with the Treaty of Ghent, which left most issues to be settled by commissions: boundaries, fishing rights, and the terms of commerce. The war also made a national figure of Andrew Jackson, the hero of New Orleans.

American-British hostilities continued in the form of trade wars. But relations eventually improved, and a Canadian boundary dispute was settled peacefully. In the South, the issue of Spanish Florida was settled in 1819 after another military adventure by General Andrew Jackson. The Adams-Onís Treaty also established the boundary between the United States and Mexico all the way to the Pacific. In 1823, the Monroe Doctrine set forth the principle that in the Western Hemisphere the United States would act alone. The settlement of Russia's southern limit in 1822 ended American boundary problems for the time being and gave the Untied States thirty years of freedom from trouble with foreign powers. The troubles now were to be growing pains at home.

Suggested Readings

Much the best approach to Jefferson is to read his own writings. The great modern edition, J. Boyd (ed.), *The Papers of Thomas Jefferson,* is not yet complete. For the period of his administration, one must rely on the far less satisfactory edition by P. Ford (10 vols., 1892–1899). L. Cappon (ed.), *The Adams–Jefferson Letters* (2 vols., 1959), furnishes one of the great correspondences of American history, especially after 1812, when the two political foes were reconciled.

The standard multivolume biography is D. Malone, *Jefferson and His Time* (5 vols., 1948–1974). M. Peterson, *Thomas Jefferson and the New Nation: A Biography* (1970), is also first rate. F. Brodie, *Thomas Jefferson: An Intimate History* (1974), provides details on his personal life but makes him rather too much a twentieth-century man. For insights into his personality, A. Nock, *Thomas Jefferson* (1926), remains unsupplanted. The focus is much more political in A. Koch, *Jefferson and Madison, The Great Collaboration* (1950), which is highly favorable to Jefferson, and in L. Levy, *Jefferson and Civil Liberties, The Darker Side* (1963), which is decidedly hostile. D. Boorstin, *The Lost World of Thomas Jefferson* (1948), is a brilliant re-creation of the Jeffersonian world view. W. Jordan, *White Over Black: American Attitudes toward the Negro 1550–1812* (1968), analyzes his views on race.

M. Cunliffe, *The Nation Takes Shape, 1789–1837* (1959), offers a very good summary and analysis of the period. For the rise of the Republican party, see N. Cunningham, Jr., *The Jeffersonian Republicans in Power, 1801–1809* (1963); and W. Chambers, *Political Parties in a New Nation, The American Experience, 1776–1809* (1963). These should be read in light of R. Ellis, *The Jeffersonian Crisis: Courts and Politics in the Young Republic* (1971), which emphasizes divisions in the Jeffersonian ranks between "radicals" and "moderates," especially on judiciary issues. See also N. Cunningham, Jr., *The Process of Government under Jefferson* (1978).

On the Federalists in this era, see J. Banner (cited in Chapter 8); D. Fischer, *The Revolution of American Conservatism* (1965); S. Livermore, Jr., *The Twilight of Federalism . . . 1815–1830* (1962); and L. Kerber, *Federalists in Dissent: Imagery and Ideology in Jeffersonian America* (1970).

Physical and social conditions in the new federal city get lively treatment in J. Young, *The Washington Community, 1800–1829* (1966). Another good account is C. Green, *Washington: Village and Capital, 1800–1878* (1962). Two other aspects of the social history of the new capital are discussed in L. Brown, *Free Negroes in the District of Columbia, 1790–1846* (1972); and M. Smith (ed.), *The First Forty Years of Washington Society* (1906), a woman's account of the political and social scene.

On the war with the judiciary see C. Miller, *The Supreme Court and the Uses of History* (1969). For American expansionism in general, A. Weinberg, *Manifest Destiny: A Study of National Expansionism in American History* (1935), is still useful. For the Louisiana Purchase in particular, see G. Dangerfield's superb biography, *Chancellor Robert Livingston of New York, 1746–1813* (1960); and I. Brant, *James Madison and American Nationalism* (1968). On the people, animals, and geography this new territory contained, B. De Voto (ed.), *The Journals of Lewis and Clark* (1953), makes fascinating reading. Another important episode during Jefferson's administration is covered in T. Abernethy, *The Burr Conspiracy* (1954).

Major issues of Anglo-American diplomatic relations are best handled in a fine series by B. Perkins: *The First Rapprochement: England and the United States, 1795–1805* (1955); *Prologue to War . . . 1805–1812* (1961); and *Castlereagh and Adams . . . 1812–1823* (1964). National prestige as a factor in bringing on the war is examined in R. Brown, *The Republic in Peril: 1812* (1964). H. Coles, *The War of 1812* (1965), surveys the war itself. On the diplomacy of the war and the peace, see S. Bemis, *John Quincy Adams and the Foundations of American Foreign Policy* (1949). F. Engleman, *The Peace of Christmas Eve* (1962), focuses on the Treaty of Ghent. J. Stagg, *Mr. Madison's War: Politics, Diplomacy, and Warfare in the Early American Republic, 1783–1830* (1983), places the War of 1812 in a much broader context.

The Hartford Convention is discussed in Banner, mentioned above; see also S. Morison, *Harrison Gray Otis* (1969). The latter and G. Dangerfield's *The Awakening of American Nationalism, 1815–1828* (1965) are perceptive treatments of the postwar period.

Various aspects of the postwar years are examined in the following: H. Ammon, *James Monroe* (1971); D. Perkins, *A History of the Monroe Doctrine* (1955). The rise of West Point and militaristic ambitions among Americans especially after 1815 are discussed in M. Cunliffe, *Soldiers and Civilians: The Martial Spirit in America, 1775–1865* (1973). R. A. Humphreys and J. Lynch, *The Origins of the Latin American Revolutions, 1808–1826* (1965), is a good introduction to the subject.

INTERNAL DEVELOPMENT

Chapter 10

The War of 1812 is often called America's "second war of independence," and there is much truth in that label. The coming of peace in 1815 set the stage for important developments in the American political system and the American economy. The two–party system fell apart, largely because the Federalists had opposed the war and Republicans had adopted so much of the Federalist program. The nation's economy boomed—and then went bust. John Marshall produced an impressive series of court decisions, many of which had as much to do with economic matters as with federal supremacy. And the issue the Founding Fathers had swept under the rug came spilling out: Slavery suddenly emerged and exposed deep sectional hostilities. An aging Thomas Jefferson, alarmed, called it "a firebell in the night."

Slavery was the main issue in this sectional division, but economic differences also contributed to the split. Alexis de Tocqueville, in his famous *Democracy in America* (1935) and in his letters home during his visit to the United States, made the usual observations about the free North ("everything is activity, industry; labor is honored") and the slave South ("you think yourself on the other side of the world; the enterprising spirit is gone"). Yet the South too enjoyed a strong westward and economic surge. And like that of the North, it added to the strength of the union. ■

THE ERA OF GOOD FEELINGS

With Madison's support, James Monroe became the Republican candidate for the 1816 election. His Federalist opponent was Rufus King of New York, chosen by the New Englanders who still dominated the Federalist party to make it appear less sectional than it actually was. In the election, King carried only Massachusetts, Connecticut, and Delaware. He was the last Federalist candidate.

Monroe had been an admirer of Jefferson. Later on, he thought himself a competitor to Madison. But he lacked their imagination and intellect and was slow to shed his narrow localism. Monroe had served twice as governor of Virginia. On the national scene, American military activity in the last phases of the War of 1812 reflected credit on his performance in the War Department and helped him win the nomination and the election in 1816. Sixty-one years old at the time of his election, he seemed a solid link with the old revolutionary generation. He was the last president to wear a powdered wig.

James Monroe. (*National Portrait Gallery, Smithsonian Institution*)

Unlike many men jealous of power, Monroe felt strong enough to surround himself with able associates. His cabinet was probably the strongest since Washington's first administration. Shortly before his inauguration in March 1817, he made a triumphal journey through the northeastern states. His visit was topped by a cordial reception in Boston. There, soon after, the *Columbia Sentinel* published an article called "Era of Good Feelings," in which it hailed a new era of political peace. By then, the Republicans had shown so much concern for manufacturing and a protective tariff, for an army and a navy, even for chartering a national bank, that the old issues seemed no longer to stand in the way of national unity. Virginia and Massachusetts appeared to have made peace at last. Monroe was reelected in 1820 with only one electoral vote cast against him.

Boom, Bank, and Bust

The War of 1812 had apparently converted Republicans to the support of American commercial, industrial, and financial growth. Jefferson himself acknowledged that "manufactures are as necessary to our independence as to our comforts." But once the war ended, most of the "war babies" among American factories lost out to British competition, despite efforts at tariff protection.

Britain's own postwar boom soon promoted another kind of boom in the United States. The spurt in British textile manufacturing brought an enormous demand for southern cotton. The end of the war also reopened European markets for southern tobacco. Poor European harvests in 1816 and 1817 added to the demand for American grain. Agricultural exports helped provide the hard money Americans needed to pay for postwar imports.

The boom in agriculture quickly inspired a boom in land speculation, especially in the West, where population soared. By 1820, Ohio had more people than Massachusetts, and the entire West had more people than New England. Land, naturally, was in great demand. Settlers and speculators bought and sold it with the aid of several hundred state and private banks that had been established after the first Bank of the United States went out of existence in 1811. Such banks had issued $100 million in paper money by 1817, much of it nonnegotiable even in neighboring communities.

Congress established a Second Bank of the United States in 1816. Like the first national bank, the Second Bank was chartered for twenty years as the sole depository for government funds. Its capital was set at three and a half times that of the earlier bank. Of this amount, the government was to subscribe one-fifth and private capitalists the rest. Five of the bank's twenty-five directors were to be appointed by the president of the United States; the rest by American stockholders. Foreign stockholders were to have no say in the bank's affairs.

The Second Bank had the right to establish branches in different parts of the country. But influential local bankers had persuaded some states to write into their constitutions provisions against "foreign banks"—that is, branches of the national bank doing business within their borders. The Second Bank proceeded to justify local fears by outdoing even the state banks with enormous loans. These loans, made in the form of national bank notes, were more acceptable as currency than the notes of most local banks. Injured local bankers soon got their states to try to tax out of existence both its branches and its notes.

In the summer of 1818, when the postwar boom was at its height, the Second Bank decided to try deflationary measures to control speculation. But the sudden contraction of credit prevented many people from keeping up payments on their debts. Before 1819 was over, for this and other reasons, the whole boom collapsed. The Second Bank became as unpopular with the public as it had always been with local financiers. The country was gripped by its first major economic depression.

Actually, the economic collapse was worldwide.

The revival of European agriculture after the Napoleonic wars and the weakening of the post-war textile boom created a glut both of wheat and cotton in world markets. But the depression was most severe in the United States and most devastating in the West. The crisis prompted a number of states to abolish the practice of punishing debtors with imprisonment and to pass liberal bankruptcy laws. Congress also came to the aid of the West with a new land act in 1820, which permitted a settler to buy an 80-acre homestead for $100 in cash. The next year it added a relief act to assist land purchasers who had run into trouble with the credit provisions in earlier land acts.

The Marshall Court

Against this background of local self-assertion, economic crisis, and conflict between debtors and creditors, John Marshall issued a series of historic Supreme Court decisions. He had sustained the Court's power to declare acts of Congress unconstitutional (*Marbury v. Madison*, 1803), and he had upheld the obligation of contracts against state interference (*Fletcher v. Peck*, 1810).

The question of contracts gave Marshall the chance for two decisions in 1819 that alarmed states righters. The first issue was raised in *Dartmouth College v. Woodward*. Could the royal charter granted to the college in 1769 and later acknowledged by the New Hampshire legislature be altered by the legislature without the college's

MARSHALL ON FEDERAL POWER

In his vigorous decision in *McCulloch v. Maryland* (1819), John Marshall set forth a powerful case for the broad exercise of national powers under the Constitution:

We admit, as all must admit, that the powers of the government are limited, and that its limits are not to be transcended. But we think the sound construction of the Constitution must allow to the national legislature that discretion, with respect to the means by which the powers it confers are to be carried into execution, which will enable that body to perform the high duties assigned to it, in the manner most beneficial to the people. Let the end be legitimate, let it be within the scope of the Constitution, and all means which are appropriate, which are plainly adapted to that end, which are not prohibited, but consist with the letter and spirit of the Constitution, are constitutional.

John Marshall. (*Library of Congress*)

consent? In a decision that interested business corporations chartered by state legislatures more than colleges, Marshall decided that a charter was a contract between two parties, neither one of whom alone could change it. In a second decision in 1819, *Sturges v. Crowninshield*, Marshall declared a New York bankruptcy law unconstitutional for seeking to relieve a debtor of his contractual debts. He held that the legislature could not constitutionally interfere with private contracts.

In several important cases not involving contracts, Marshall's court set aside state laws as contrary to the federal Constitution. One of the most far-reaching was *McCulloch v. Maryland*, also decided in 1819. The state of Maryland had attempted to tax the Baltimore branch of the Second Bank of the United States out of existence. But, said Marshall in finding the Maryland tax law unconstitutional, "the power to tax involves the power to destroy." If the states were permitted to nullify acts of Congress by attacking its agencies, they could "defeat and render useless the power to create." In broad language, Marshall asserted the constitutionality of the act creating the bank. His decision laid the foundation for a broad interpretation of the implied powers of Congress.

Finally, in the case of *Gibbons v. Ogden* (1824), Marshall spoke out on the power of Congress to regulate commerce. New York had granted Robert Fulton and Robert R. Livingston a monopoly of steam navigation in state waters, and Aaron Ogden had bought from them the right to operate a ferry between New York and New Jersey. When Thomas Gibbons set up a competing ferry under a federal coasting license, Ogden tried to use the state-sanctioned monopoly to stop him from running it. The original grant by New York interfered with the exclusive right of Congress to regulate interstate commerce. But Marshall was not content with throwing out the New York monopoly. He went on to interpret the term *commerce* to include commerce "among the several states" that extended into the interior of any state. No state could act on such commerce when its acts intruded on the powers of Congress.

It is often said that Marshall handed down Federalist law from the fortress he held for thirty-four years in the Supreme Court. But it is closer to the truth to say that, once his battle with Jefferson had ended, Marshall gave all his energies to extending national power, just as Jefferson gave his to extending the national domain. Both were expansionists; the work of one complemented that of the other. Together they gave Americans physical and legal room for an expanding economy.

The Missouri Compromise

One notable feature of the constitutional and economic growth of the country was the orderly admission of new states to the Union. After Ohio in 1803 and Louisiana in 1812, in the three years after the war came the admissions of Indiana, Mississippi, and Illinois. This easy procession was suddenly interrupted by a controversy over the admission of Missouri, which reopened the issue of the extension of slavery.

Slavery had been forbidden in the Northwest Territory in 1787. The first real conflict over it occurred just beyond, in the so-called Upper Louisiana Territory, whose settlers first applied for admission to the Union under the name of Missouri in 1818. There was no problem until Representative James Tallmadge of New York shocked the South by offering an amendment to the Missouri enabling act to prohibit the introduction of additional slaves into the new state. He also proposed that all children born of slaves in that region be freed when they reached the age of twenty-five.

The Tallmadge Amendment passed the House by a narrow margin, reflecting the populous North's strength there. The story in the Senate was different. Even though the free states outnumbered the slave states eleven to ten at the time, a number of northern senators who had been born and brought up in the South voted with southern senators and helped defeat the Tallmadge Amendment.

The deadlock carried over to the next session of Congress, which opened in December 1819. Now, along with Missouri's petition for admission as a slave state, came Alabama's as well. There was no issue about admitting Alabama as a slave state. It became the twenty-second state and established a balance between slave and free states at eleven each. Admission of Missouri would give the South a virtual veto in the Senate of all legislation enacted by the House. The northern majority in the House insisted on keeping Missouri closed to slavery. When the northeastern part of Massachusetts applied for admission to the Union as the independent state of Maine, some members of Congress, led by Henry Clay, took the chance to break the deadlock.

The series of measures known as the Missouri Compromise arranged for the temporary preserva-

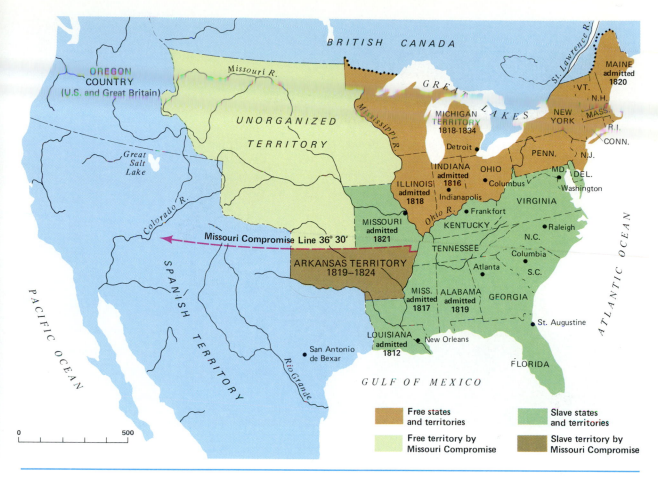

The Missouri Compromise, 1820

tion of the balance of power in the Senate by admitting Missouri as a slave state and Maine as a free one. The most significant part of the compromise permitted slavery in Missouri, but prohibited it "forever . . . in all territory ceded by France to the United States . . . which lies north of 36° 30' . . . not included within the limits of [that] state." President Monroe signed the compromise measures on March 6, 1820.

There the slavery issue rested for a generation. But the Missouri controversy intensified sectionalism and threatened the spirit of nationalism. At the same time, a booming economy was making fundamental changes in the lives of many Americans.

AN EXPANDING ECONOMY

In 1815, and for several decades thereafter, the majority of white Americans in the South as well as in the North still lived on family farms. These people or their ancestors had come to America in search of personal freedom based on economic independence. Isolated on their farms, they were not fully aware that new technology and expanding business enterprise were fundamentally altering American life.

Fishing and Lumbering

Some Americans continued to make their living from fishing long after the revolution. In 1821, Timothy Dwight, reporting on his travels through New England, said of the fishing ports south of Boston: "The whole region wears remarkably the appearance of stillness and retirement; and the inhabitants seem to be separated in a great measure, from all active intercourse with their country."

Fisherman in these ports went out, like farmers, only for the day. Each had his own boat and brought back his catch for his family and for buy-

Celebrating the Fourth of July in "the good old days," a watercolor by J. L. Krimmel. (*Historical Society of Pennsylvania*)

ing grain, clothing, and equipment. At more active fishing centers like Newburyport and Beverly and on Cape Cod, voyages were longer and better organized. But here too, the rule was that each man supplied his own gear and provisions in return for a share of the catch. The fisherman always preferred going out "on his own hook," a phrase that originated with these Yankees.

One specialized occupation—whaling—ranked very high until kerosene supplanted whale oil for lighting after the Civil War. Until the War of 1812, just about every New England port had its whaling fleet. Afterward, Nantucket and New Bedford, Massachusetts, nearly monopolized the industry, with New Bedford having perhaps a third of the international fleet.

The concentration of whaling activities in New Bedford added to the efficiency of operations. Yet whaling remained a conservative industry. The only significant changes since colonial times were that voyages grew longer and that crews—paid, like fishermen, with a share of the catch—were more ruthlessly exploited. Rebellious hands, when they did not mutiny or desert, often were aban-

doned on some foreign shore by a captain who thus avoided paying them their shares. On return voyages, crews were often made up of men from a dozen different lands. Even Fiji islanders and Polynesians, like the harpooner Queequeg in Melville's *Moby Dick,* could be seen walking the streets of New Bedford after a whaler had put in.

In lumbering, as in farming, fishing, and whaling, few changes were made in the first third of the nineteenth century. The industry grew, of course, but until the railroads brought a huge demand for wood for fuel, ties; and rolling stock, lumbering remained the occupation of individual loggers, who supplied timber to widely scattered and independently owned sawmills.

The Indians had taught the first settlers how to grow corn, harpoon whales, and bring down trees. For more than two centuries, these basic techniques of farming, fishing, and lumbering spread unchanged as the country gradually expanded. The making of commodities such as flour, leather goods, and ironware was done according to the old methods, generation after generation in the same family. It was a living and a way of life. Until vast

INTERNAL DEVELOPMENT

new markets were opened up by improved transportation, this traditional system continued to characterize the American economy.

Expansion: The Fur and China Trades

No one in early nineteenth-century America was more isolated than the fur trapper and trader. But unlike the other primary occupations, the fur trade soon gave a new direction to American life, a new method to American business and a new spirit to the American economy. Fur—mink, otter, lynx, fox, and beaver, as well as bear, wolf, deer, rabbit, muskrat, "coon," and "possum"—had been one of the first staples exported by the colonies. The finer pelts were used in hats, cloaks, and robes; the coarser ones, in blankets. The Indians, who did most of the actual trapping, traded furs for guns, ironware, and liquor.

From the start, profits had been large and competition keen. As early as 1700, overtrapping had depleted the fur-bearing animals on lands along the Atlantic seaboard. In the next fifty years, French traders from Canada and Spanish traders from Mexico, as well as the English colonists, forced their way a thousand miles inland, far in advance of European settlement.

Two thousand miles beyond even the farthest inland fur trading post in the Mississippi Valley were the sea otter waters off the Oregon coast. Sea captains from New England and New York in the China trade discovered a market for the beautiful otter skins (as well as for other domestic furs) among the wealthy of North China. New Englanders were attracted to the sea otter because it gave them a commodity to export in exchange for the tea, silk, spices, willowware china, and cheap cottons of the Orient.

By the early 1800s, the sea otter was nearly extinct. Profits from Chinese imports, however, had proved even greater than those from the sale of furs in China. When the sea otter supply failed, around the outbreak of the War of 1812, ship captains began to carry Hawaiian sandalwood to the Orient, where it was used for incense. Upright

Foreign trading stations in Canton harbor about 1840. (*Peabody Museum of Salem*)

Yankee traders also began to smuggle opium from the Dutch East Indies and neighboring islands into China. But the American opium traffic always remained a small fraction of that carried on by the British East India Company, which used cannon and bayonets to force immense quantities of Indian opium into China.

The fur market in China had attracted land trappers and traders as well as sea captains. After Lewis and Clark returned from their expedition across the continent in 1806, trappers began to exploit the upper Missouri, the Yellowstone, the Green and other northwestern rivers, and the Colorado and the Gila in the southwestern desert. The farther trappers and traders went from their Mississippi base at St. Louis, however, the harder it was to carry on business. One reason was the hostility of the Plains Indians. Of greater importance was the fact that time and distance cost money; only well-financed organizations could send trappers and traders into far-off regions for a year or more.

It was the New Yorker John Jacob Astor, by 1800 the city's leading fur merchant and one of its most creative businessmen, who most successfully met the new conditions. His instrument was the American Fur Company. In 1810 Astor sent out two expeditions, one by sea and another by land, to set up a trading post (named Astoria) at the mouth of the Columbia River in Oregon. With the outbreak of the War of 1812, Astor's men were forced to sell out to the Canadian fur traders of the Oregon country. But this setback did not stop him. In 1816 he persuaded Congress to prohibit foreigners from the fur trade on United States soil except as licensed employees of American traders. He then persuaded the governor of the Michigan Territory to issue licenses almost exclusively to employees of the American Fur Company.

Until the 1830s, when European hat styles changed from fur to silk, Astor's company averaged an annual profit of $5 million. Astor became the first American millionaire. But he was not the last to make a fortune out of a dwindling natural resource, or the last to obtain the assistance of the government in doing so.

The Sante Fe Trail

Less dramatic than the fur trade, and involving far fewer men and far less capital, was the trade along the Santa Fe Trail. Spain had established the iso-lated outpost of Sante Fe in the desert of New Mexico early in the seventeenth century and had supplied it from Vera Cruz, 1500 miles away. Early American efforts to trade at Santa Fe were frustrated by Spain's rigid colonial policy, which excluded foreigners. Soon after Mexico won its independence from Spain in 1821, however, it opened Santa Fe to its northern neighbor, a step it later regretted and reversed.

In 1825, the United States Army surveyed the Santa Fe Trail westward from Independence, Missouri. Thereafter, for twenty years, caravans of American farm wagons trekked across it, hauling all sorts of goods from the East and from Europe and exchanging them for Spanish gold and silver.

The arrival of the caravan each year was a great event in the Spanish town. Gradually, some Americans settled in Santa Fe. Others, attracted by the land bordering the eastern part of the trail, staked out farms along the way. When Santa Anna, the Mexican leader, closed the trail in 1844, Americans viewed his act as interference with their rights and "destiny."

The Santa Fe trade never involved more than a few hundred persons a year. But like the fur trade, it opened a new path across the continent, lured American business into new country, and led to a political and territorial claim that eventually would be enforced by war (see Chapter 15).

The Rise of the Middle West

Well to the east of fur trappers and traders, traveling over trails they had marked through the wilderness, thousands of settlers moved on to the lands of the Middle West. Some were new immigrants from Europe. Many more were second-, third-, and fourth-generation Americans who moved westward in successive steps of a few dozen or a few hundred miles. The wealthier ones had wagons, usually pulled by oxen. Other women and men walked, often pushing all their possessions in handcarts. Many of these families suffered from periodic bouts of "ague," as malaria was then called.

In 1810 only one-seventh of the American population of 7.2 million lived west of the Alleghenies; by 1840 more than a third of 17.2 million Americans lived there. Production of corn and wheat rose, but not dramatically. The new lands were more fertile than those in the East, which had been worn out by years of repeated crops. The

LIFE ON THE FRONTIER

The lives of these westward-moving pioneers consisted mostly of hard work and sickness. When they moved, they traveled on foot, carrying their possessions in a wheelbarrow or pushcart or strapped to the backs of a few scrawny cows. When they settled, they had to clear land and build shelter. Many of them suffered from the "ague" (malaria).

Thomas Lincoln's experience was typical of these pioneers of the early nineteenth century. Part backwoodsman, part farmer, part handyman-carpenter, Thomas was a native of the western Virginia hills but grew up in Kentucky. "A wandering laboring boy,"

without schooling, he married the illiterate Nancy Hanks, who bore their son Abe in 1809. The Lincolns and the Hankses rarely stayed put for long. By 1816 the whole tribe had reached Indiana, where they "squatted" the first year.

"We lived the same as the Indians," one of the Hankses said years later, "ceptin' we took an interest in politics and religion." They managed to build a log cabin, without floor, door, or windows. A roof stuffed with mud and dry grass was the only protection from the rain. This cabin remained their home for a decade before they pushed on to Illinois.

Population Density, 1820

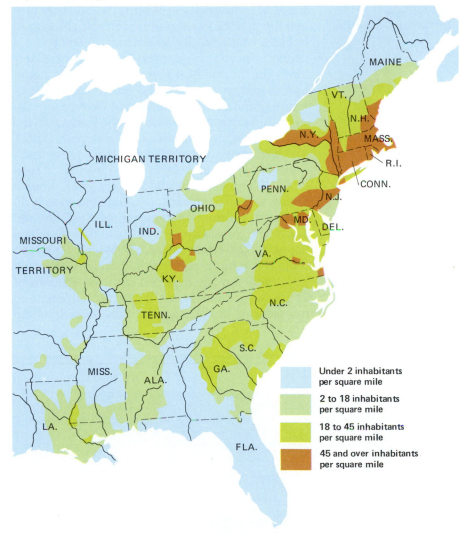

Under 2 inhabitants per square mile

2 to 18 inhabitants per square mile

18 to 45 inhabitants per square mile

45 and over inhabitants per square mile

result was that many unproductive farms in New England were simply abandoned.

Until settlers reached the more open prairie country in Indiana and Illinois, the supply of trees seemed unlimited. Farmers wanted wood for fuel, fences, tool handles, and house construction. But they also regarded standing trees as a barrier to farming. Piles of fallen dead trees were burned outdoors simply to get them out of the way.

One symbol of this wastefulness was the log-cabin method of constructing houses. First introduced in the seventeenth century by Swedes and Finns along the Delaware River, this technique was adopted by westward-moving pioneers. It was probably the most labor-efficient way of turning trees into housing; it wasted a lot of wood, but it saved a lot of work. Since wood was far more plentiful than labor, Americans did not think twice about wasting it; when it ran out, settlers could always move on to where there was more. This attitude was part of a general assumption that the abundant natural supplies of the continent would exist forever.

The New Cotton Empire

In the Southwest, westward settlement was encouraged by the expansion of upland cotton. Commercial cotton growing had made great strides in the South after 1790, when British East Indian indigo destroyed the market for that product. For two generations, it had been a staple of the South Carolina and Georgia planters. Between 1790 and 1793, the indigo planters turned their land to cotton. Most of this cotton was of the fragile long-staple variety, the finest kind, and the only kind that could be cleansed of its oily black seed at reasonable cost.

In America, however, the climate and soil requirements of long-staple cotton limited it to the South Carolina and Georgia sea islands and the coastal plain extending into Spanish Florida. The other type of cotton, the coarser, short-staple, green-seed boll, could be grown on almost any soil, provided the warm season was long enough. Its single drawback was the difficulty of removing the seed: One worker could clean only a single pound in a day.

One technological invention solved this problem and brought about a major economic revolution in the American South. In 1793 Eli Whitney, a young man from Massachusetts, invented an engine for cleaning the green-seed plant. Whitney was in Georgia as a tutor to a planter's family. His solution, the cotton gin, was so simple that he soon was involved in patent suits.

By 1794, however, short-staple cotton production was spreading rapidly. One worker operating a single gin by hand could clean 50 pounds a day. Rapid improvements in Whitney's and other gins and the application of power to the machine multiplied its capacity. By 1800 about 75,000 bales of cotton went to market, most of it the short-staple kind. On the eve of the War of 1812, this figure had soared to over 175,000 bales, nearly three-fourths from South Carolina and Georgia.

Within a few years, however, the Piedmont land was used up, as tidewater land had been earlier. The piedmont, a traveler said in 1820, presented a scene of "dreary and uncultivated wastes . . . half-clothed negroes, lean and hungry stock, houses falling to decay, and fences wind-shaken and dilapidated." Cotton planters pushed west into Alabama and Mississippi. By 1830, the combined population of these states exceeded 400,000, even though the large planters had bought up many small farms in the best cotton areas. Sections of Tennessee, Arkansas, and Florida suitable for cotton planting also became heavily settled, as did

HOW AMERICA GREW

The last French governor of Louisiana offered this description of the thousands of Americans pouring into the Old Southwest:

They set up their huts, cut and burn the timber, kill the savages or are killed by them, and disappear from the country either by dying or ceding to some steadfast cultivator the land they have already begun to clear. When a score of new colonists are thus gathered in a certain spot, they are followed by two printers, one a federalist and the other an anti- *federalist, then by doctors, lawyers and adventurers; they propose toasts and nominate a speaker; they erect a city; they beget children without end; they vainly advertise vast territories for sale; they attract and deceive as many buyers as possible; they increase the figures of the population till they reach a total of 60,000 souls, at which time they are able to form an independent state and send a representative to Congress . . . and there is one more star in the United States flag.*

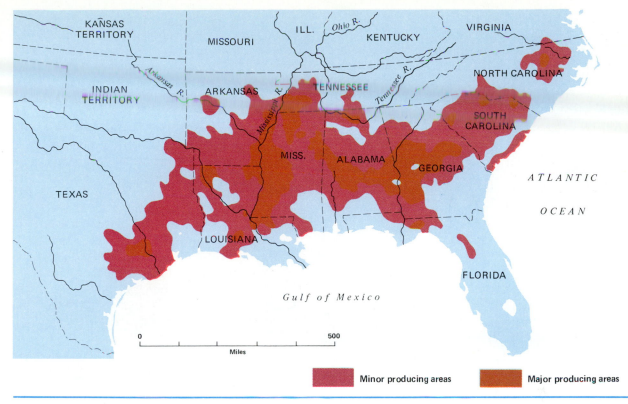

Cotton-Growing Areas

Minor producing areas   Major producing areas

the Louisiana sugar country.

The traffic at New Orleans reflected the rapid growth of the new regions. In 1816, only 37,000 bales of cotton were shipped from this port; by 1822, the figure was 161,000 bales; by 1830, it was 428,000. Most of this cotton went to English textile factories, though some fed the mills of New England.

The Cotton Kingdom's growing need for food and work animals gave westerners an opportunity. As markets and prices improved, western farmers went into debt to acquire more land. They were thus forced to concentrate on cash crops to meet their financial obligations. Southern specialization in cotton brought western specialization in grain and meat and mules. The marvelous Mississippi River system tied the two sections together, and the steamboat tightened the knot.

TRANSPORTATION AND TRADE

In colonial America, the ocean was the easiest means of communication and trade. As farms and plantations spread inland among the eastern rivers, they too began to carry their share of people and goods. Settlement in the West brought the Mississippi River system into the transportation network, and the steamboat made it the foremost inland carrier of all.

The Steamboat

The first steamboat on the western waters was the *New Orleans*, built in 1811 by Robert Fulton, four years after his success with *Clermont* on the Hudson. As he had in New York, Fulton won a monopoly of the carrying trade of the West. It lasted until 1824. Then John Marshall, in *Gibbons v. Ogden*, dealt a death blow to monoplies on interstate waters. By 1830, there were nearly 200 steamboats on the western rivers.

Keelboat rates between Louisville and New Orleans had been about $5 per 100 pounds of freight. By 1820, steamboat rates for this trip had fallen to $2 per 100 pounds. By 1842, competition had driven them down to 25 cents. Western staples now moved down to New Orleans for shipment overseas or for distribution to the rest of the South and Southwest and even to the Northeast. Commodities from aborad or from the Northeast also were funneled into New Orleans for trans-

The Cincinnati waterfront as viewed from the Kentucky side of the river. (*Public Library of Cincinnati and Hamilton County*)

shipment inland.

The Mississippi system, however, was less ideal than it seemed. The river itself and most of its tributaries were filled with snags, shifting sandbars, floating trees, and unpredictable eddies. Pirates infested the entire system. Summer droughts pinched the river channels into narrow ribbons, stranding many vessels in shallow water.

New Roads

The difficulties of road transportation presented even greater challenges. From the earliest times, many Americans chose to settle far from neighbors on land several miles from water routes. And yet somehow they had to travel to grist mills, tobacco warehouses, cotton gins, forges, country stores, county courts, and to the rivers themselves. As time went on, a crude network of roads spread across the countryside, often following old Indian trails and the paths of trappers and traders. Only a few such roads had been made wide enough for wagons or carts. Rains transformed them into muddy pools, while winter cold froze them into ruts.

As early as 1806, Congress chartered a National

Highway to be built with federal funds. Not until 1811, however, did the first crews begin to cut the road westward from Cumberland, Maryland. By 1818 it had been pushed to Wheeling, Virginia, on the Ohio River. The failure of Congress to provide additional money stopped construction there. But work was resumed in 1825, and by mid-century the road reached Vandalia, Illinois, its western point. The National Highway, paved with stone over much of its length, became an efficient carrier, "the path of empire" for hundreds of thousands of Americans on the move westward.

Other useful roads included the privately financed Lancaster Turnpike, built in 1794 across the 62-mile stretch from Philadelphia to Lancaster, Pennsylvania. At first only a dirt road, the Lancaster pike was reconstructed, after many accidents, on the principles worked out by the Scottish engineer John L. McAdam. These principles ruled roadbuilding in America and England until asphalt began to be used in the automobile age.

"It is the native soil," McAdam wrote, "which really supports the weight of traffic." But the soil had to be kept dry by a covering impenetrable to rain. This covering was made of small stones carefully broken into the right sizes. Tolls collected along the Lancaster pike more than paid for its

INTERNAL DEVELOPMENT

WORDS AND NAMES IN AMERICAN HISTORY

cost, and the idea proved profitable enough to encourage the construction of similar roads elsewhere.

By 1825, private companies, mostly in New England and the middle states, built more than 10,000 miles of turnpike. State and local governments often helped with the cost by buying their stock and granting them proceeds from the sale of government bonds. Most turnpikes, however, remained modest enterprises, and the short stretches of road did little to improve the network of country paths. High tolls for the transportation of heavy agricultural goods discouraged shippers. By the 1830s, management and maintenance of privately operated turnpikes had become so costly, and returns so little that thousand of miles of such roads were abandoned or turned over to the states.

The Canal Boom

New York, Philadelphia, Boston, and the other eastern seaports turned to canals to link the great waterways of the American continent. But canals were far more expensive than turnpikes, and they took not a year or two, but seven to ten years to build. They presented new problems in finance and management as well as in engineering.

In 1816, the country had only 100 miles of canals. As early as 1810, however, the New York State legislature had appointed a committee to investigate the possibility of digging a canal to the West, and in 1816 De Witt Clinton again raised the issue. His arguments were so convincing that even his political opponents voted for his project—a canal to connect the Hudson River with Lake Erie, a breathtaking 363 miles.

Construction of the Erie Canal began in 1817. By 1823, a 280-mile stretch was in operation from Albany to Rochester. The tolls that came pouring in from traffic helped finance the final leg to Buffalo, completed in 1825. In 1823, New York had also opened the Champlain Canal, connecting the Hudson River and Lake Champlain to the north. Two figures tell the story of the Erie's success: It reduced freight rates between Albany and Buffalo from $100 to $15 a ton, and travel time from twenty to eight days.

In 1825 Boston persuaded the Massachusetts legislature to consider building a canal into the interior, but the hilly Massachusetts terrain discouraged people. When Boston did finally gain entry to the West in 1842, it was by way of three railroads across Massachusetts to the eastern terminal of the Erie Canal at Albany. In 1826, Philadelphia won state approval for still another scheme to tap the West, a project even bigger than the one Boston had abandoned. This system included both a main canal and railroad track. It was completed to Pittsburgh in 1834 at a cost of more than $10 million, all of it supplied by the state.

In 1827, Baltimore joined the race for western business by announcing plans for the Chesapeake and Ohio Canal. Maryland's legislature refused to finance the project, but work began with private and federal funds. The state legislators turned out to be right, for construction of the Canal stopped at the mountains. In 1828, a private corporation began to lay track for the Baltimore and Ohio Railroad, the first successful line in America. But many years passed before the B&O reached the Ohio River in the 1850s.

Internal Improvements

Westerners became as energetic as easterners in seeking ways to promote trade. They soon discovered that their rich soil could produce more wheat and corn, and their corn could fatten more hogs,

Principal Canals and Roads

than southern markets could absorb. In the 1820s westerners turned a sympathetic ear to Henry Clay's program for high tariffs and "internal improvements." The first was to promote the growth of eastern factory towns; the second was to provide the means for opening towns to western produce. "Internal improvements" would also mean that manufactured goods could be shipped more cheaply from the East than through New Orleans.

Congress never adopted Clay's program. But even without federal assistance, Ohio and other western states started ambitious canal and railroad projects. By 1840, some 3,326 miles of canals, most of them in the North and West, had been built in the United States. Private investors supplied only a small part of this money. Federal and state subscriptions to the securities of private canal companies accounted for some of the balance, but more than half the total was provided directly by the states out of revenues or through the sale of state bonds abroad, mainly in England.

The impact of the canals, the first enterprises to receive large-scale public financial backing, proved as beneficial as expected. The South remained a valuable, growing customer of the West, and the Ohio and Mississippi river systems continued to be heavily used. But the West's connection with the North and East became stronger as the canal system developed. Without that connection, the history of American sectional conflict would have been very different.

Travel over canals was much cheaper than over turnpikes, but for about four months of the year the northern canals were frozen solid. Railroads soon freed shippers from the weather and from the medieval pace of oxen and tow horses. By 1840, the United States had 3,328 miles of railroad, almost exactly equal to the canal mileage. But only 200 of these railroad miles were in the West. For some time after 1840, rivers, canals, and turnpikes remained the principal channels of inland commerce.

Artist's view of the wonders of transportation that contributed to the prosperity of the time, including the stage coach, the barge, the steamboat, and—most spectacular of all—the suspension bridge. (*Library of Congress*)

Exciting trial of speed between Mr. Peter Cooper's locomotive, "Tom Thumb," and one of Stocton & Stoke's Horse-Cars. (*Library of Congress*)

New York City's Spectacular Rise

From this discussion and a glance at a map of the physical geography of the northeastern United States, it is clear why New York City suddenly became so prominent. Until the revolution, New York had remained the third largest of the Atlantic cities of North America (behind Philadelphia and Boston). Situated as it was at the gateway to the only gap through the Appalachian Mountains, it was bound to grow. As people and commerce moved westward, and as technological innovations began to transform this route, the settlement that had once been New Amsterdam rapidly became one of the world's largest metropolitan centers. Its population of about 150,000 in 1830 dwarfed other American cities.

New York won its eventual supremacy through the enterprise of its businessmen. The promotion and construction of the Erie Canal, of course, was the most rewarding accomplishment. But even before canal digging began, New Yorkers had thought of attractive innovations. One was a modified auction system for disposing of imports. Most American ports held auctions at which common practice was for traders to offer imports for sale and then withdraw them if bids were too low. In New York City, after 1817, merchants decided to

guarantee that the highest bid would be accepted and that purchases would be delivered promptly at the price named.

This change drew merchants to New York from all over the country. And where merchants gathered, shippers were bound to bring their goods. Another New York innovation was a transatlantic packet service with vessels running on regular schedules, "full or not full." Before this, ocean commerce had depended on the weather and the convenience of ship captains. New York's Black Ball Line, first in the world to operate on the new basis, sent the ship *James Monroe* from New York on January 5, 1818, in a snowstorm that would have been regarded as a valid excuse for delay by any ordinary vessel.

Even after the Black Ball Line began operations, irregular sailings continued to characterize most ocean shipping. The American merchant marine carried cargo around the world to the Middle East, the Baltic states, Africa, and the East Indies, as well as to the West Indies, South America, Western Europe, China, and India. In an age without wireless communication, shipowners could not tell when a vessel might return to its home port, what it might be carrying, or where it might have been.

The shipowners of Boston thrived on this old-

Broadway and Canal Street, 1835. (*New York Public Library*)

fashioned worldwide carrying trade. Nevertheless, the so-called Atlantic shuttle grew in importance as cotton exports soared and the United States offered expanding markets for manufactured goods. And New York became most important among shuttle ports. By 1828, New York's share of the American merchant marine almost equaled that of Philadelphia, Boston, and Baltimore combined.

Since dependable auctions and scheduled sailings brought business and goods into New York, the city needed an export staple to balance its trade. Western produce pouring in over the Erie Canal helped. But in the 1820s New York's shippers began to sail directly to New Orleans, Mobile, and other southern ports to pick up cotton to carry to Britain and the Continent. There they exchanged the cotton for other goods, which they brought back to New York for distribution in the city and the interior.

So successful were the New York merchants that by 1830 it was estimated that 40 cents of every dollar paid for raw cotton went north—al-most exclusively to New York—to cover freight charges, insurance, commissions, and interest. In 1837, a convention in the South, called to promote the revival of direct trade with Europe, reminded southern merchants: "You hold the element from which [the New York merchant] draws his strength. You have but to speak the word, and his empire is transferred to your own soil." But the word was not spoken. Two years later, a similar convention declared that "the importing merchants of the South [had become] an almost extinct race, and her direct trade, once so great, flourishing, and rich, [had] dwindled down to insignificance." The South had become an economic colony of the North.

THE INDUSTRIAL REVOLUTION

The expansion of commercial agriculture in the West, the rapid growth of population, and access to western markets all gave a strong push to the development of eastern industry. Concentration on cotton in the South also made it a market for the coarse textiles worn by slaves and for other manufactures. Until western and southern markets were opened, however, factory industry had difficulty getting started in America.

First Factories

Back in 1791, in his *Report on Manufactures* to Congress, Alexander Hamilton had written, "The expediency of encouraging manufactures in the United States . . . appears at this time to be pretty generally admitted." He was too optimistic. In its first decades, America had neither surplus capital to invest in factories nor surplus labor to work in them. In 1791, Hamilton himself had helped organize the Society for Establishing Useful Manufactures. In the next few years, this corporation founded the city of Paterson, New Jersey, where there was a large waterfall. It built numerous buildings to house its works, smuggled in skilled British mechanics, and began manufacturing yarn, cloth, hats, and other commodities. By 1796, however, both the works and the town were dead.

Other undertakings suffered the same fate. Cautious financiers at that time chose to keep their money in trade, shipping, and land. Federalist businessmen in northern cities and Republican planters in the South, both with English commercial connections, had no interest in manufacturing at home. They wanted imported English woolens, linens, china, cutlery, furniture, and tools.

The first successful full-time factory in America was the cotton-spinning plant of Almy & Brown, Providence merchants. Under the direction of an experienced Englishman, Samuel Slater, this factory began operations at Pawtucket in 1791. As Hamilton had suggested, this early factory employed only children at 12 to 25 cents a day—wages unacceptable to adult males. After the outbreak of the Napoleonic wars in Europe, Americans found it more and more difficult to get British products. To supply their needs, Slater's mill expanded operations, and many hopeful imitators started up.

The Entry of Big Capital

The first textile mills were small operations rarely capitalized at more than $10,000—perhaps $120,000 in terms of today's dollar. Since their managers had little experience in keeping accounts, handling money and workers, and supplying markets, conservative banks would have nothing to do with them. But in 1813 a group of wealthy Boston investors headed by Francis Cabot Lowell organized the Boston Manufacturing Company, which built the first cotton manufacturing plant in the world in which *all* operations were under one roof, from the unbaling of the raw cotton to the dyeing and printing of the finished cloth. They even established their own selling agencies instead of depending on local jobbers.

After the depression of 1819, the opening of the West and the expansion of cotton in the South brought a general business upturn. The revolutions against Spain in Latin America opened new foreign markets for American manufactured goods. More and more such goods found their way to China to help pay for the tea Americans were drinking in ever larger quantities.

All these changes were reflected in the expansion of firms that had survived the depression and in the great numbers of new textile corporations that set up business during the 1820s and 1830s. Some of these new companies were organized and chartered by the same group that had started the

Samuel Slater. (*Library of Congress*)

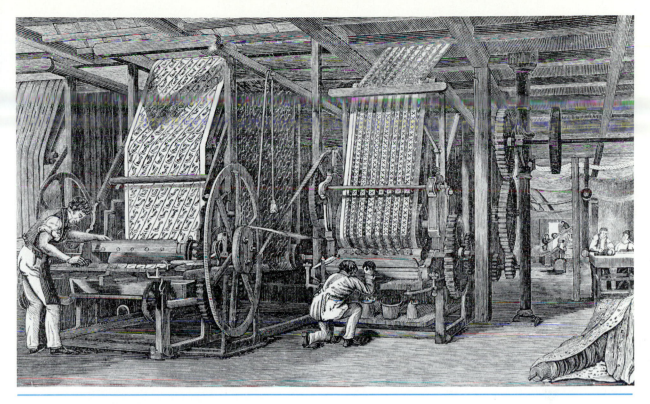

Power-driven spinning machine. (*Library of Congress*)

Boston Manufacturing Company. Between 1821 and 1835, these men, often called the Boston Associates, opened nine new companies in Massachusetts and southern New Hampshire. Each specialized in a particular textile or product on a large scale.

More important, during and after the depression, these men founded insurance companies and banks to maintain and concentrate their supply of capital. They established real estate companies to take over the best factory sites. They formed water power companies to control dams and dam sites for harnessing the power of the rivers. The fifteen families of the Boston Associates directed much of Massachusett's economic, political, and cultural life. They controlled 20 percent of the cotton manufacturing in the state, 30 percent of the railroad mileage, 39 percent of the insurance capital, and 40 percent of Boston's banking resources.

These financial enterprises were aided by the development of the *corporation,* a legal device used by capitalists to accumulate large amounts of money through the sale of shares to subscribers. By the time the canal and railroad companies were being formed in the 1810s and 1820s, the idea of

limited liability had also become well established in law and finance. It meant that owners of corporation stock were liable for the obligations of the company only to the extent of their own investment, regardless of how large their personal fortunes might be. This protection helped to attract the capital required for costly, long-term projects. Since corporate securities could be more easily disposed of than investments in partnerships or single-owner businesses, corporate enterprises also could look forward to a long life. They would not be affected by the death or withdrawal of investors.

Women and Industrial Labor

Many of the new textile mills found a cheap and eager source of labor in young women from surrounding rural areas. A major reason was that rural New England had a shortage of men. Many young males had headed west—to upper New York State and beyond—for better and more plentiful farmland. Like most human migrations, the westward movement from the New England states was

"Lowell Girls," as they were called, operate looms in one of the town's mills. The girls, most of whom came from local farm families, were very closely chaperoned. (*Museum of American Textile History*)

Lowell, Massachusetts, 1850. (*Library of Congress*)

THE WOMEN IN THE MILLS

Early in the 1840s one radical American reformer, Orestes Brownson, offered a dissenting view of the frequently praised Lowell mills, whose female operatives were said to be so well and carefully treated. This picture of "well dressed" and "healthy and happy" workers, he wrote, was

the fair side of the picture; the side exhibited to distinguished visitors. There is a dark side, moral as well as physical. Of the common operatives, few, if any, by their wages, acquire a competence.... The great mass wear out their health, spirits, and morals, without becoming one whit better off than when they commenced labor. The bills of mortality in these factory villages are not striking, we admit, for the girls when they can toil no longer go home to die. The average life—working life, we mean—of the girls that come to Lowell ... is only about three years. What becomes of them then? Few of them ever marry, fewer still ever return to their native places with reputations unimpaired."

heavily male. The first census of 1790 showed that New England was the only major section of the new nation to have significantly more women than men. Young women in Massachusetts and the other New England States found husbands in short supply.

Thus in the early nineteenth century, unmarried farm girls flocked to such new mill towns as Lowell, Waltham, Lawrence, and Dover (Boston Associate factories). There they endured long and difficult hours on the job and a completely controlled environment in boarding houses off the job. All their visitors were screened and their hours carefully restricted by matrons. They were required to attend church and forbidden to discuss grievances even among themselves. At the mills, their wages were kept low and they were subject to fines for the slightest infringement. Many of the women were forced to sign contracts agreeing not to form any sort of alliance, at the risk of losing their wages. Since most factories paid workers only two to four times a year, this threat carried considerable weight.

At first the "dormitory" factories drew considerable admiration from foreign visitors. Here were young ladies industriously earning their own dowries in hopes of eventual marriage. As time went by, however, factory work became more onerous and less respectable. Increasingly, "nice" young ladies shunned it. The poorest of New England women and children were joined by women just off the boat from Ireland and other European countries. In 1840 the reformer Orestes Brownson described the situation of Lowell women who had gone to work just long enough to accumulate a dowry, add to the family income, or send a brother to school: "The great mass wear out their health, spirits, and morals without becoming one whit better off than when they commenced labor. The bills of mortality in these factory villages are not striking, we admit, for the poor girls when they can toil no longer go home to die."

Conditions for these women textile workers as well as other industrial workers worsened during the frequent and severe economic crises in the United States. When demand lagged behind expanding production, shops and factories closed. Workers were laid off, and many small businesses were swallowed up by bigger ones that were able to absorb the losses.

In the seventy years before the Civil War, American workers slowly came to learn that their interests were best served by joining together. Skilled male artisans first broke away from their employers in the 1790s by joining mutual aid societies. By the beginning of the nineteenth century, improvements in transportation had opened larger markets to master artisans, some of whom gave up their handwork to become merchant capitalists—that is, businessmen who gathered up larger orders than one artisan and a few helpers could fill and who employed others to work for them. Those who had never been artisans also entered various crafts as merchant capitalists. By the 1820s, as competition became keen, wages were cut. Artisans were further embittered by the loss of their independent status. Worse still, the integrity of their work and their product was being destroyed as skills were being broken down into simpler tasks to be performed by lower-paid apprentices.

The first unions in America were formed in protest against these conditions. From the start, big business, with the aid of the government, made it hazardous for workers to join these alliances. Until 1842 labor unions were frequently declared by the courts to be "conspiratorial combinations." In a trial of Pittsburgh cordwainers in 1815, the artisans were found guilty of "combining to raise wages" and the Court Recorder wrote of the verdict: ". . . it is most important to the manufacturing interests of the community for it puts an end to these associations which have been so prejudicial to the successful enterprize of the capitalist in the western country."

Neither court decisions nor coercion could prevent laborers from organizing. Economic depressions, however, slowed the labor movement considerably during the first half of the nineteenth century. In the 1819–1822 depression, 40,000 laborers were thrown out of work in Philadelphia and New York alone. Budding labor unions were crushed, and no relief for the unemployed was offered by the government. It was not until the late 1820s that labor revived, with the movement for a ten-hour day.

In Philadelphia the first citywide federation of labor, the Mechanics' Union, emerged out of this struggle for shorter hours. Carpenters, masons, stonecutters, hatters, tailors, riggers, stevedores, cabinetmakers, cordwainers, and other workers joined to secure their "right, derived from their creator, to have sufficient time in each day for the cultivation of their minds and for self-improvement." Through strikes and labor solidarity among the different trades, the ten-hour day was eventually won by workers in most eastern cities.

The first recorded strike of factory workers was conducted by children in 1828. The mill owners in Paterson, New Jersey, tried to change the dinner hour from twelve to one. The children went out on strike, "for fear," said one observer, "if they assented to this, the next thing would be to deprive them of eating at all." The militia was called in to break the strike. Soon after, the other large group in the textile mills, working women, went on strike, and 400 of them paraded through the streets of Dover, New Hampshire. For Yankee "young ladies" to take to the streets required courage in a period when any kind of public activity was thought to disgrace a woman.

From 1833 to 1837, labor organizations, particularly those of artisans, grew at a rate not to be matched again in the century. Trade unions grew from 26,000 members to 300,000 during that period. In New York City nearly two-thirds of the workers were organized, and unions were beginning to move west to Buffalo, St. Louis, and Pittsburgh. During these four years there were over 170 strikes. Wage earners who had never before been organized—including seamstresses, tailors, bookbinders, and shoemakers—formed unions and went on strike.

Women textile workers were again in the forefront of the labor struggle. In 1834 a thousand or more Lowell girls walked out in protest against a 15 percent wage cut. "One of the leaders," reported the *Boston Transcript,* "mounted a stump, and made a flaming . . . speech on the rights of women and the iniquities of the 'monied aristoc-

CHILD LABOR

Small textile factories employed women and children drawn from the poorest farm families in an area. They could be paid less, and they were thought to be more obedient than men. Children were especially cheap to hire, and their small, thin hands could fit easily into the narrow slots of the machines. But the mill children had to be swift and careful, or the machines would grab their fingers or their hair and a bit of scalp. The children worked twelve and thirteen hours a day, rarely seeing their families, much less the sun. The older ones had to watch over the younger ones to make sure they did not fall asleep on the job.

Such miserable conditions were pointed to with pride by the mill owners. They were keeping the children out of trouble, teaching them the value of money and the virtue of hard work. This "educational" program actually provided high profits for the new entrepreneurs and abject poverty for many New England families, whose sole support became the scanty wages of their children. Cheap child labor in many cases put the father out of a job. In 1820, half the factory workers in America were children, earning 33 to 67 cents a week.

racy' which produced a powerful effect on her auditors, and they determined to 'have their way, if they died for it.' " The strike was broken, and many of the women went home.

Those who stayed, however, continued to fight back, forming a Factory Girls' Association in 1836, with a membership of 2500. They declared: "As our fathers resisted unto blood the lordly avarice of the British ministry, so we, their daughters, never will wear the yoke which has been prepared for us." When they went out on strike they were evicted from the company-owned boarding houses and starved into defeat. But the struggle inspired other women textile workers, whose strikes were later successful.

The business collapse of 1837 crushed the early labor movement when unemployment threatened all workers. Layoffs were becoming harsher for industrial workers. Women, children, and men had moved off their farms and had become dependent on the factory for a living. In many cases European immigrants were also tied to the factories. Having arrived penniless, they had to remain in the cities. Industrialization did provide jobs for these new Americans, as well as for many poor farming families. But the cost in the quality of life was great. Farm work did not disrupt families and subject individuals to lonely, alienating, and dangerous jobs.

These changes in the lives of Americans were not so obvious then as they are now. Many people were conscious that something was going on, but they were not sure what. They welcomed what they called the "age of improvement." But they grew vaguely anxious about the direction of social change. There was an inherent tension between these reactions, a tension that easily spilled over into politics.

SUMMARY

America experienced a boom after the War of 1812, and then a bust in 1819. The Second Bank of the United States was chartered for twenty years. Federal power and the national economy was strengthened by a series of Supreme Court decisions by Chief Justice John Marshall.

The problem of admitting new states that allowed slavery and those that forbade it was settled for a time by the Missouri Compromise of 1820. Slavery was permitted in Missouri; Maine was admitted as a free state; and slavery was prohibited "forever" in the entire Louisiana Territory north of a line drawn westward from Missouri's southern border—36′ 30°.

The economy began to grow and change. Farming, fishing, and lumbering remained traditional ways of earning a living. But now the fur trade in the West and the China trade in the Pacific began to expand American horizons. So did the trade on the Santa Fe Trail in the Mexican Southwest. Meanwhile, thousands of settlers poured onto the lands of the Middle West and mid-South. The lives of these western settlers were hard, but it was clear the land was fertile and could be a source of agricultural wealth. The demand for cotton in world markets, especially Britain, led the Southern plantation system to expand westward into Alabama and Mississippi. Eli Whitney's cotton gin, invented late in the eighteenth century, greatly expanded production. This new Cotton Kingdom provided a market for the agricultural products of the West. Southern specialization in cotton brought western specialization in grain and meat and mules.

Trade and regional specialization fostered the growth of a national transportation system. The steamboat revolutionized inland water transport. So did the many miles of canals built to link the inland waterways. The longest and biggest was the Erie Canal in New York, completed in 1825. On land, a national highway was built from Cumberland, Maryland, to Vandalia, Illinois. Private turnpikes were built in other areas, mostly in New England and the middle states. But by the 1830s most of these roads had been turned over to the states. They now formed the basis for a national system of public roads.

Henry Clay in the 1820s lured westerners with a program for high tariffs and "internal improvements." The tariff was to promote eastern factory towns; the internal improvements were to open towns to western products. By 1840, the United States had about 3000 miles of canals and an equal number of railroad track.

In the East, New York suddenly rose to dominance as

a port and a trading center. Its merchants pioneered a modified auction system and the idea of running ships on a regular schedule, full or not full, in all kinds of weather. These merchants helped make the South an economic colony of the North.

The North was also helped by the fact that the Industrial Revolution in America took root in New England. The first successful full-time factory in America was a textile plant in Rhode Island. Most of the early factories were small, but in 1813 a group of wealthy Boston investors organized the Boston Manufacturing Company. It grew to include not only textile plants, but insurance companies and banks to maintain and concentrate capital, real estate companies to buy factory sites, and water power companies to control the sources of power.

Women and children of both sexes began to work in the new textile factories. Especially in New England, a surplus of women contributed to this development. Children and women could be paid much less than men. Many of these new industrial workers suffered on their jobs from long hours, harsh discipline, and dangerous machinery. All kinds of working people, including skilled male artisans as well as women and children in the factories, took the first steps toward organizing in "unions" and even striking for better working conditions. These efforts at first had some success, but were thoroughly crushed by the economic depression that struck in 1837.

Americans generally began to realize that economic progress could have disastrous costs, but for the most part they welcomed the "improvements" that were bringing prosperity to the nation. This twin sense of improvement and suffering spilled over into the realm of politics.

Suggested Readings

R. Burlingame, *Rise of the Iron Men* (1938), is a readable social history of American technology before the Civil War. More conventional is the survey by G. Taylor, *The Transportation Revolution, 1815–1860* (1951). Two books by D. North, *Economic Growth of the United States, 1790–1860* (1961), and *Growth and Welfare in the American Past: A New Economic History* (2nd ed. 1974), should be compared with the appraisal of causation by S. Bruchey, *The Roots of American Economic Growth, 1607–1861* (1965).

For the history of agriculture in this period, see P. Gates, *The Farmers' Age: Agriculture, 1815–1860* (1960). The stunning development of events in the North is traced in C. Danhof, *Change in Agriculture, the Northern United States, 1820–1870* (1969). An older work that still contains information on production and slave populations not found elsewhere is L. Gray, *History of Agriculture in the Southern United States to 1860* (2 vols., 1933). S. Bruchey (ed.), *Cotton and the Growth of the American Economy, 1790–1860* (1967), deals with that extraordinary expansion. J. Mirsky and A. Nevins, *The World of Eli Whitney* (1952), describes not only the invention of the cotton gin, but also the development of interchangeable parts in the manufacture of guns.

One of the most authoritative descriptions of whaling is contained in Herman Melville's great novel, *Moby Dick* (1851). Also very readable is the scholarly work by S. Morison, *The Maritime History of Massachusetts, 1783–1860* (1921). T. Karamanski, *Fur Trade and Exploration: Opening the Far Northwest, 1821–1852* (1983), emphasizes exploration. Race relations are stressed in L. Saum, *The Fur Trader and the Indian* (1965).

River transportation before the age of steam is discussed in L. Baldwin, *The Keelboat Age on Western Waters* (1941); the later period is covered by L. Hunter, *Steamboats on the Western Rivers* (1939). A popular work by W. Langdon, *Everyday Things in American Life, 1776–1876* (1941), includes material on road construction and use. See also O. Holmes and P. Rohrbach, *Stagecoach East: Stagecoach Days in the East from the Colonial Period to the Civil War* (1983).

A lifetime of study is reflected in C. Goodrich, *Government Promotion of American Canals and Railroads, 1800–1890* (1960). Two more recent works bear on important canals: R. Shaw, *Erie Water West: A History of the Erie Canal, 1792–1854* (1966), and H. Scheiber, *The Ohio Canal Era: A Case Study of Government and the Economy, 1820–1861* (1968). M. Reed, *New Orleans and the Railroads: The Struggle for Commercial Empire, 1830–1860* (1966), is an interesting study of the South's greatest city, which was a river and an ocean port, as well as a railroad terminal. For more on railroads, see the citations in Chapter 13, and Vol. II of J. Dorfman, *The Economic Mind in American Civilization* (5 vols., 1946–1959).

R. Albion, *The Rise of New York Port, 1815–1860* (1939), is a stunning work. S. Warner, *The Urban Wilderness: A History of the American City* (1972), contains a section covering 1820 to 1870 that discusses transportation, technology, land use, and social problems. A fine study of one of the new manufacturing centers is D. Cole, *Immigrant City: Lawrence, Massachusetts, 1845–1921* (1963).

All phases of America's first modern industry are presented in C. Ware, *The Early New England Cotton Manufacture* (1931); and H. Josephson, *The Golden*

Threads: New England's Mill Girls and Magnates (1949). On business more generally, see E. Dodd, *American Business Corporations until 1860* (1954), and T. Cochran, *Business in American Life: A History* (1972), a magnificent and broadly interpretive work. There is much information but virtually no interpretation in V. Clark, *History of Manufactures in the United States* (3 vols., 1928). M. Smith, *Harpers Ferry Armory and the New Technology: The Challenge of Change* (1977), is a marvelously comprehensive account of the development of the machine-tool industry and its social impact. On technology and the enterprising spirit, see the widely ranging J. Ellul, *The Technological Society* (1967).

The history of labor in the early years of the United States has not received the recent treatment it deserves. A beginning may be made with N. Ware, *The Industrial Worker, 1840–1860* (1924); L. Ulman, *The Rise of the National Trade Union* (1955); and Vol I of P. Foner, *History of the Labor Movement in the United States* (3 vols., 1947–1964). B. Wertheimer, *We Were There: The Story of Working Women In America* (1977), treats early women's unionization particularly well.

NEW POLITICS FOR A NEW AGE

Chapter 11

When James Monroe left the White House in 1825, the age of the Founding Fathers had clearly ended. The nation was free from foreign entanglements. Monroe himself was the last president of the Virginia dynasty and the last one of the revolutionary generation. His successor was in many ways a transitional figure. John Quincy Adams inherited his position in diplomacy and politics from his distinguished father. He himself was the last president who could possibly be called an intellectual until the twentieth century. His famous father was still alive in Quincy, busily corresponding with Thomas Jefferson about statecraft, religion, and the nature of man. The two elder statesmen died on the same day during the presidency of the younger Adams. The symbolism of their passing was not lost on Americans, for the date was July 4, 1826, the fiftieth anniversary of the Declaration of Independence. Surely God's providence was guiding the American nation.

The resulting outburst of oratory and self-congratulation was very brief. Americans returned to political bickering in an extremely nasty campaign for the presidency in 1828. The outlines of two new political parties were beginning to emerge, and the next few years saw the development of what has been called the "second political party system." In 1828 the voters rejected the incumbent president, who was the last ever to look upon political parties with distaste. They elected an old war hero who loved having political opposition so he could fight against it.

President Jackson so dominated the political scene that the 1830s are often called the Age of Jackson. He greatly enlarged the power of the presidency and in doing so aroused controversy that cast a shadow over American politics long after his death. Both he and his opponents adapted their styles to a changed society. Neither would have put the matter that way; rather, they talked about "democracy" and "the common man." Exactly what these phrases meant was not clear, though some historians have continued to use them.

It is clear, however, that the American people were in a changed mood. They no longer turned for leadership to aristocratic gentlemen of wealth and breeding. Many of them praised the virtues of the common people, even while they admired those who forged ahead in the world of business. They welcomed the new age, yet at the same time grew nostalgic for the simpler days of the early republic. They hailed the achievements of the nation, while at the same time, as we will see in the next chapter, they denounced its failings. We can sense in these self-assessments a response to profound changes they knew were taking place but did not fully understand.

Yet there was more to Jacksonian politics than a change in mood and style. A changed economy presented Americans with very real issues. Westward expansion raised problems of how to treat Indians and whether to construct "internal improvements." The complexity of the economy raised questions about the National Bank and the tariff. These matters often raised important questions about the proper interpretation of the Constitution. At the center of these controversies stood the figure of Andrew Jackson, who stamped the era with his iron will and vigorous style. ■

THE BEGINNINGS OF THE NEW POLITICS

The Age of Jackson may be said to have begun in 1824, when he won the popular vote, lost the election, and had friends pushing him for the presidency all during the administration of John Quincy Adams. One important development often associated with Jackson actually took place before he was a political candidate and owed nothing to his ideas or actions. And oddly enough, the extension of the franchise through elimination of property requirements was one of the few important political developments that did *not* arouse debate about constitutional issues.

Expanding the Electorate

During the first quarter of the nineteenth century most states quietly eliminated property qualifications for voting, thus opening up the franchise to almost all adult white males. In Europe, particularly in Great Britain, broadening the suffrage was a major public issue throughout much of the nineteenth century. The United States escaped major quarrels on this matter largely because the Founding Fathers had left suffrage requirements to the states: Americans did not have to deal with the matter as a national issue. Nonetheless, it is clear that public feeling was in favor of giving the vote to "all men."

The Vermont constitution of 1777 put some restrictions on voting, but it was the first to remove propertyholding or taxpaying qualifications. This constitution was intact when Vermont entered the Union in 1791. Kentucky, New Jersey, Maryland, and Connecticut then widened the franchise. Connecticut became a model for northern states such as Maine, Massachusetts, and New York. Between 1816 and 1821, six new states entered the Union with constitutions that required no property qualifications for voting.

The South generally lagged behind. Virginia, despite the Jeffersonian tradition, was the last state to surrender the property test. Only a few years earlier, Louisiana broadened the franchise by reducing its heavy taxpaying qualification. Elsewhere in the slave states, the more liberal example of Maryland had been followed. "We ought," said a Virginia Senator in 1829, "to spread wide the foundation of our government, that all white men have a direct interest in its protection." What he meant was protection against slave revolts.

Restricting Blacks

The democratic spirit failed to carry over to one significant class of the population—free blacks. As late as 1820, they were permitted by law to vote equally with whites in northern New England, New York, Pennsylvania, and even in Tennessee and North Carolina. This right, however, usually came from omissions in the law and was denied in practice until the law itself was tightened. As a delegate to the Pennsylvania constitutional convention of 1837 said on his way to the meeting that would disenfranchise free blacks: "The people of this state are for continuing this commonwealth, what it always has been, a political community of white persons."

By 1837, the free blacks' right to vote survived only in the New England states north of Connecticut. In Connecticut, after 1818 previous black voters could continue to vote, but newly freed slaves were disenfranchised. In the other states where they once voted, free blacks were now deprived of the vote, usually by the very same article that for the first time provided full manhood suffrage for whites. No state entering the Union between 1819 and the Civil War permitted free blacks to vote.

Loss of the right to vote was only one of the

lengthening list of restrictions on blacks in the free states. They were cooped up in miserable slums, confined by curfews, placed outside the judicial and educational systems, barred from all but the most menial occupations and from the land as well. An Oregonian said that the free black was "cast upon the world," even in his own distant commonwealth in the 1850s, "with no defense; his life, liberty, his property, his all, are dependent on the caprice, the passion, and the inveterate prejudices of not only the community at large but of every felon who may happen to cover an inhuman heart with a white face." By then, many western states would not allow free blacks even to enter.

National Elections

For the "political community of white persons," on the other hand, even more important than the suffrage was the greater interest of men in exercising that right on the national level. While proportions running up to 70 percent of the electorate had voted earlier in hot local contests, presidential elections until 1828 seem to have left most voters cold. Even in 1824, when Jackson first was a candidate, only 27 percent of those eligible voted, compared with 56 percent in 1828. Popular enthusiasm for presidential elections reached its peak in 1840, after Jackson had retired, when 78 percent of the eligible votes went to the polls.

That proportion was new in American politics and has never been equaled or surpassed in any presidential election since. One reason for the new interest was the gradual emergence of a new two-party system after 1824 and sharper party differences on issues. Another was voter participation in actually naming the candidates.

Presidential candidates had been nominated by a *caucus*, or meeting, of congressmen in Washington, a system that kept cliques in power. Its success was prolonged by the availability of strong candidates from populous Virginia, who won over opponents put forward by scattered factions in other states. Rising politicians hated the caucus and even opposed Jefferson's nomination of Madison in 1808. The first genuine break in the system came in 1824.

Sectionalism at last made it impossible for the Republicans to smooth over their differences, and four major candidates ran. The modern method of

A political orator of the Jackson period holds his audience spellbound. (*Boatman's National Bank of St. Louis*)

nominating candidates in a national convention was begun by a short-lived minor party, the Anti-Masons, when they held the first such convention in 1831. The new major parties, the Democrats and Whigs, adopted this innovation in time for the election of 1832.

Still another institution gave way before the rising demand to bring government closer to the people. In most states, presidential electors had been chosen by the legislatures. By 1828, every state except Delaware and South Carolina had provided for popular election of members of the electoral college. The change forced presidential candidates to appeal to the people rather than a small group of politicians. Jackson, as he often reminded his opponents, was the first president who could claim to have been elected directly by the voters. The claim was not altogether justified, since members of the electoral college kept personal discretion in casting ballots. Governors also began to be popularly elected, and property qualifications for that office and others were swept away. Finally, by the 1840s state judges were being elected rather than appointed.

This trend toward popular participation did not, of course, bring many backwoodsmen in coonskin caps, lumberjacks, fishermen, artisans, or even farmers to high political office. A man still needed standing in the community, achievement, or at least a certain eloquence to win office. But popular participation in politics remained more broadly based in the United States than in any other country in the world. It would not be long before it would occur to some reformers that women too should be included in the process.

The Election of 1824

Everyone assumed that Monroe would not run for a third term, chiefly because of the precedent established by Washington. The Republicans had lost their unity and were unable to present a single candidate. Four contenders for the presidency emerged in 1824, all of them rather vaguely claiming to be "Republicans."

One was Andrew Jackson, who had little government experience but a great reputation as an Indian fighter and especially as the Hero of New Orleans. In 1822 his supporters in Tennessee had pushed him into the United States Senate because they wanted to nominate the somewhat reluctant general as a presidential candidate two years later. Another candidate was John Quincy Adams of Massachusetts, the heir apparent because by this

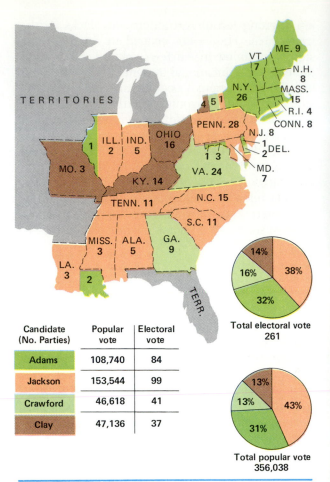

Candidate (No. Parties)	Popular vote	Electoral vote
Adams	108,740	84
Jackson	153,544	99
Crawford	46,618	41
Clay	47,136	37

Total electoral vote 261
14% 38% 32% 16%

Total popular vote 356,038
13% 43% 31% 13%

Election of 1824

time it was assumed that the secretary of state would succeed to the presidency. Adams could legitimately present himself as a skillful, hard-working diplomat, a committed American nationalist, and an uncorruptible man of honor. William Crawford of Georgia was a personally attractive man who presented himself as the true heir of Thomas Jefferson. He would have polled more votes if he had not suffered a stroke during the campaign. Finally, Kentucky's Henry Clay had built a strong power base as Speaker of the House, as well as a broad popular following for his American System.

Clay's American System was one of the most thoroughly worked out platforms ever devised by a presidential candidate. Clay pictured an industrial East providing a growing home market for southern cotton and western grain and meat. An agricultural West and South would provide an expanding market for eastern factory goods. For the East he would supply protective tariffs; for the

NEW POLITICS FOR A NEW AGE

West and South, "internal improvements" such as canals and turnpikes to reduce transportation costs. Trade between the sections was to be aided by a stable credit system underwritten by a national bank. This plan, said Clay, would "place the confederacy upon the most solid of all foundations, [that] of common interest."

The results of the election showed that Jackson had won a heavy plurality of the popular vote. In the electoral college, however, his 99 votes fell short of the required majority, so the contest was thrown into the House of Representatives. Here Clay, having polled the lowest electoral total, was eliminated under the terms of the Twelfth Amendment. Of the top three, Crawford was ill. The contest was left to Jackson and Adams.

Clay, a power in the House, had no love for Jackson. "I cannot believe," he said, "that killing 2500 Englishmen at New Orleans qualifies [him] for the various difficult and complicated duties of the Chief Magistracy." After a private talk with Adams, Clay swung his supporters to him. Clay's influence was largely responsible for Adams's election. One of Adams's first presidential acts was to name Clay as secretary of state.

In popular opinion, this was like naming him as his successor. The Jackson men lost little time in charging that a "corrupt bargain" had been made.

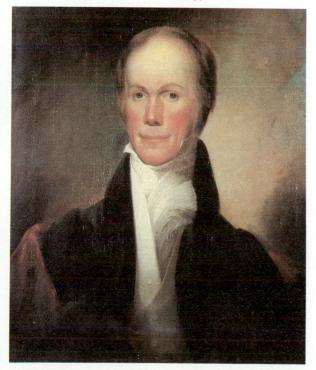

Henry Clay. (*Chicago Historical Society*)

The charge was not really fair, since Clay and Adams agreed on most matters. But "bargain and corruption" became the Jacksonian slogan for the 1828 campaign, which opened as soon as they learned of their defeat in 1824.

John Quincy Adams in Office

The alleged "deal" was not the only issue that haunted Adams in the White House. A sensitive and high-minded man, he regretted having to accept the presidency with, as he said, "perhaps two-thirds of the whole people adverse to the actual result." Popular opinion, however, did not stop Adams from launching a program he considered right for the country. With stubborn courage and political ineptitude, he argued for an active national government and for internal improvements.

He was warned by Clay and most of his cabinet that, at a time when states' rights feelings were rising and sectional jealousies were strong, it was all but suicidal for a president—and a minority president at that—to urge such a policy. Adams himself agreed that his program was a "perilous experiment."

Congress under the Constitution, Adams argued in his message, had the power to "provide for the common defense and general welfare." The "common defense" seemed a clear enough obligation; the "general welfare," not nearly so. Adams proposed to stretch the latter to justify establishing a national university, financing scientific expeditions, building astronomical observatories, reforming the patent system, and developing a national transportation system. A dozen years later, Adams explained that "the great effort of my administration" was to put "all the superfluous revenue of the Union into internal improvement."

Adams continued with an analysis of the defeat of his program: "When I came to the Presidency this principle of internal improvement was swelling the tide of public prosperity." However, he went on, "the South saw the signs of its own inevitable downfall in the unparalleled progress of the general welfare in the North, and fell to cursing the tariff and internal improvements, and raised the standard of free trade, nullification, and state rights." In fact, many in the middle states and the Midwest, with their own "mass of local jealousies," joined the South in rejecting the Adams program. At the same time, many "self-made" men (Clay first coined this term to describe the rising manufacturers of Kentucky) were on Adams's side.

John Quincy Adams, taken long after he left the White House and was serving in the House of Representatives. This picture is one of the first *photographs* of a United States president. (*Metropolitan Museum of Art*)

der Jacksonian leadership, the new Congress made its single purpose the advancement of the general's presidential prospects in 1828.

The Jacksonian strategy was to win support in all key or questionable states by means of legislative handouts. Beyond that, the Jacksonian press blackened Adams's name. The attacks continued during the 1828 campaign, when Jackson's supporters also introduced a carnival spirit into the presidential contest. They paraded with hickory sticks to symbolize the toughness of Old Hickory and waved hickory brooms to suggest the need for sweeping the rascals out. Adams's supporters replied with similar tactics, but Adams himself characteristically tried to remain above such a campaign. Said he: "If my country wants my services, she must ask for them."

Apart from personalities, the major issue in 1828 was the protective tariff on manufactured goods, adopted in 1824. The act had gained the support of the industrial middle states and the Old Northwest, which continued to look to eastern cit-

Adams's comprehensive program for centralized economic and cultural development, and his failure to push it through, encouraged states rights opponents everywhere to mobilize their own machines behind Jackson. An especially humiliating outcome resulted from the president's efforts to preserve the lands of the Creek and Cherokee Indians in Georgia against outraged opposition from the state, its speculators, and potential frontier settlers.

Jackson's Election

By the time of the congressional elections of 1826, Adams's program had gained for his followers the name of National Republicans. His opponents became known as the Democratic Republicans. In these elections, for the first time in the history of the country, a president lost his majority in Congress after two years in office. On convening un-

Election of 1828

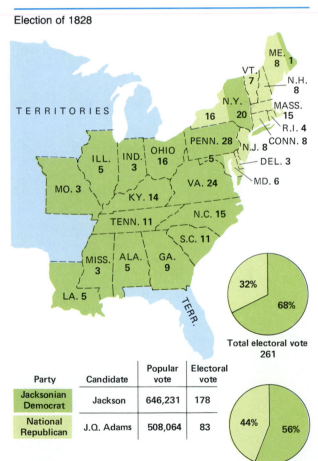

Party	Candidate	Popular vote	Electoral vote
Jacksonian Democrat	Jackson	646,231	178
National Republican	J.Q. Adams	508,064	83

Total electoral vote 261

32% / 68%

Total popular vote 1,154,295

44% / 56%

ies for markets for its agricultural surplus. New England, with large manufacturers of its own, was still heavily committed to commerce, and had split on the measure. The South, which had given up its hopes for manufacturing, overwhelmingly opposed it.

From this alignment, Jackson's lieutenants hoped to make more political hay. Their means was the Tariff of 1828. Its object, said one political observer, was to encourage "manufactures of no sort but the manufacture of a President of the United States." But the scheme backfired. Because it raised the general level of duties, southerners called it "the tariff of abominations." And because it failed to protect woolen manufactures while it raised duties on raw wool and other raw materials, the tariff also angered certain northern industrialists.

Yet Jackson's candidacy survived—with the help of his supporters in Congress, who made large grants of federal lands to politically doubtful states. In 1828, the Hero of New Orleans, the victim of the Adams-Clay "corrupt bargain," the most visible old soldier in the country for four solid years, polled 647,000 votes. The surprise, if any, was that Adams received 508,000 votes. Several other U.S. presidents have won election by a wider margin.

Andrew Jackson. (*Library of Congress*)

OLD HICKORY IN THE WHITE HOUSE

Jackson's inauguration attracted an immense crowd to Washington. People surged through the unpaved streets, pressed into the White House, stood on sofas, smashed glasses, and generally impressed observers with the fact that the presidency had somehow been brought to the masses. Jackson himself did nothing to discourage this mood. He thought of himself as a man of humble background, a man of the common people. He had been born in poverty in the Carolina back country, the son of Scotch-Irish immigrants, and both he and his supporters made a great deal of this fact. He was the first American president since Washington to have no college training.

At the time of his election at the age of sixty-one, however, he was scarcely one of the common people. He had built a highly successful career in Tennessee in law, politics, land speculation, cotton planting, and soldiering. His home, the Hermitage, was a mansion, not a log cabin. Anyone who owned more than a hundred slaves, as Jackson did, was a very wealthy man.

He was also a man of strong convictions but few ideas. As president, he saw himself as the one government official who had been elected by all the people, and he therefore regarded himself as representing the national interest. Always suspicious, Jackson disliked special interest groups and men whose power came from special privilege. Lurking just beneath the surface of his iron will was a deep streak of anger. When crossed, he lashed back, whether it was at the British army, Indians, Spanish officials, judges, bank officers, or political opponents. He was the least forgiving of men. He was the only president ever to have killed a man in a duel.

In sheer physical presence, he was more commanding than any public figure since George Washington. Yet while Washington had commanded widespread respect, Jackson commanded widespread popularity. He seemed to symbolize the virtues of the new America—a common man successfully on the make, ready to tackle and destroy aristocratic privilege wherever he found it. His opponents sensed that he had all the qualities of a democratic emperor. The National Republicans soon began calling themselves Whigs to symbolize their resistance to "King Andrew I." As president, Jackson moved quickly to defend the political spoils system, to veto internal improvements, and to challenge the Supreme Court.

The Spoils System

When the new chief executive set about to name his major department heads, his most important appointment went to Martin Van Buren of New York as secretary of state. But Jackson liked to rely on the advice of personal friends. His administration was marked by the rise to power of a category of men who became known as the Kitchen Cabinet—a small group of what we would call White House advisors. Three were trusted western newspaper editors. Whatever these men or Jackson may have thought about the new issues in national politics—the tariff, internal improvements, the bank, land, and Indian policy—they all shared his feeling about the need for a strong presidency.

Jackson's policy toward the executive civil service was consistent with his independent view of his high office. He shocked the Adams men by firing about 900 jobholders from among the 10,000 he found on the payroll. Actually, his party chiefs, having made many commitments in two campaigns, wanted even more heads to roll, but Jackson restrained them. The Adams press protested against this new "reign of terror" and the grim "purge" that was bloodying Washington's streets. But in the long run it was the president's defense of the *spoils system*, rather than the particular replacements, that so firmly associated his name with it. Earlier presidents had removed opposition people from office without raising many eyebrows.

Jackson was the first to make the spoils system seem a social and moral as well as a political "reform." In his first annual message to Congress in December 1829, he defended "that rotation [in office] which constitutes a leading principle in the republican creed." Such rotation, he continued, would nullify the prevailing idea that "office is . . . a species of property, and government . . . a means of promoting individual interests, . . . an engine for the support of the few at the expense of the many." Jackson was ready to exclude judges, cabinet officers, and high-ranking diplomats from this rule. Otherwise, "the duties of public offices" are "plain and simple," and plain and simple men could best perform them in the people's interest.

The Rights of the States

In his relations with Congress and the courts, the new chief executive proved equally aggressive. Earlier presidents had been content to administer the laws passed by Congress. But Jackson took the constitutional power given the executive to participate in making (or unmaking) the law as well as executing it. In his two terms, Jackson vetoed more legislation than all former presidents combined.

Such actions appear remarkable in a man so openly attached to popular government. But Jackson, especially after losing the election of 1824 in the House, had come to regard Congress as the home of "aristocratical establishments" like the national bank. He saw his own office as the only popular defense against such "interests" as the new industrialists.

One of his most famous vetoes killed the Maysville Road Bill of 1830, which would have required the federal government to buy stock in a private corporation. The company was to build an internal improvement, a road in Clay's home state, Kentucky. Because the road would lie within a single state, Jackson's stand was easy to justify. He was well aware that he would be strongly supported in such states as New York and Pennsylvania, for they had helped his election and had developed transportation systems at their own expense. He knew he would also find support from the South Atlantic states, committed to slavery and state rights. These states were also becoming opposed to protective tariffs, which supplied most of the federal money for internal improvements.

But throughout his presidency, Jackson approved large appropriations for river and harbor improvement bills and similar pork barrel legislation sponsored by worthy Democrats, in return for local election support. Yet he told Congress: "The great mass of legislation relating to our internal affairs was intended to be left where the Federal Convention found it—in the State governments. . . . I can not . . . too strongly or too earnestly . . . warn you against all encroachments upon the legitimate sphere of State sovereignties." Jackson viewed the presidency as the only direct reflection of the people's will. Almost inevitably this view resulted in a clash with the Supreme Court as well as Congress. Once again, he based his stand on the rights of the states.

The Cherokee Indians

In 1803, after Georgia had ceded its western lands to the United States, the federal government agreed to settle Creek and Cherokee claims to the region (see Chapter 10). Federal action, however, was slow; and as cotton growing spread in the state, the planters' patience ran out. Georgia's militant governor, George M. Troup, ordered a state survey of Creek lands in 1826. When President

JACKSON AND INDIANS

President Jackson stated his views about removing the southern Indians in a formal message to Congress:

The consequences of a speedy removal will be important to the United States, to individual States, and to the Indians themselves. The pecuniary advantages which it promises to the Government are the least of its recommendations. It puts an end to all possible danger of collision between the authorities of the General and State Governments on account of the Indians. It will place a dense and civilized population in large tracts of country now occupied by a few savage hunters. By opening the whole territory between Tennessee on the north and Louisiana on the south to the settlement of the whites it will incalcu- *lably strengthen the southwestern frontier and render the adjacent States strong enough to repel future invasions without remote aid. It will relieve the whole State of Mississippi and the western part of Alabama of Indian occupancy, and enable those States to advance rapidly in population, wealth, and power. It will separate the Indians from immediate contact with settlements of whites; free them from the power of the States; enable them to pursue happiness in their own way and under their own rude institutions; will retard the progress of decay, which is lessening their numbers, and perhaps cause them gradually, under the protection of the Government and through the influence of good counsels, to cast off their savage habits and become an interesting, civilized, and Christian community.*

Adams threatened to stop the survey with federal forces, Governor Troup said he would resist force with force. Conflict was avoided only by the Creek surrender and their removal beyond the Mississippi.

Far more than most Indian ethnic groups, the Cherokee, like the Creek, had embraced the white man's ways. They had established farms and factories, built schools, and begun a newspaper. They also adopted a constitution. In 1827 they decided to form an independent state on the American model. Georgia responded by nullifying all federal Indian laws and ordering seizure of Cherokee lands.

When Georgia courts convicted a Cherokee of murder, the Supreme Court of the United States ordered that conviction set aside. Governor Troup and the state legislature ignored the federal government's "interference" and executed the prisoner. By then, Jackson had become president. It was well known that his feeling for Indians was as cold as his sympathy for the planters was warm. The Cherokee sought an injunction in the Supreme Court prohibiting the extension of Georgia law to Indian residents and Georgia's seizure of Indian lands.

In 1831 John Marshall denied the rule that Indian tribes were like "foreign nations" with whom the United States made treaties. The Indians, he said, were "domestic dependent nations" who could not sue in United States courts. He denied the injunction, but he asserted that the United States alone, and no single state, had sovereignty over Indians and over their lands.

In 1832 Marshall took the opportunity to strengthen this opinion in *Worcester v. Georgia* by saying that the Cherokee nation was a legitimate political community, with clearly defined territories, where "the laws of Georgia can have no force, and which the citizens of Georgia have no right to enter" without Cherokee consent. In effect, Marshall was saying that the Cherokee nation would exist or not at the pleasure of the federal government, not that of any single state. The state ignored the Court's decision.

The Jackson-dominated House of Representatives tabled the enforcement order to restrain Georgia from evicting the Cherokee. This meant that no federal troops would be made available to support Marshall's decision, and the takeover of the Indian lands continued. By 1835, only a few southwestern Indians retained their lands. After the subjugation of the Florida Seminoles (1835–1842), millions of acres were thrown open to whites.

The Indians, meanwhile, were forced onto a westward trek that became known as the Trail of Tears. Many of these people died on the journey. Officals overseeing them robbed them of their money. Of the Cherokee removal, one critic cried that "such a dereliction of all faith and virtue, such a denial of justice, and such deafness to screams for mercy were never heard of in time of peace . . . since the earth was made."

The Webster-Hayne Debate

While the head of the federal government was asserting his leadership, the heads of the geographical regions in Congress were arguing about

"Trail of Tears" by Robert Lindneux. (*Woolarac Museum, Bartlesville, Oklahoma*)

sectional differences. Many issues divided slave from free states, and the free West from the free East. While the Missouri Compromise of 1820 seemed to have settled the question of slavery in the West, new developments in the rapidly expanding country once again aroused sectional quarrels. Two of the most persistently disruptive issues were public land policies and protective tariffs. The Webster-Hayne debate in 1830 revealed the extent of both.

For a generation, pioneers had been calling for cheap government land and for protection of squatters who staked out such land before it was surveyed and put on the market. Squatters who had improved their land during their illegal tenures demanded the right to buy it at the minimum rate of $1.25 an acre when it came up for sale. This right became known as *preemption*. It was permitted for short periods in the 1830s, but not until 1841 was it enacted for an unlimited period for male citizens (meaning whites only) and for aliens having declared their intention of becoming citizens.

Many westerners, for whom Senator Thomas Hart Benton of Missouri became the spokesman, went further. As early as 1824 Benton had proposed that the price of unsold government land be gradually reduced to 75 cents an acre and then to 50 cents. If no buyers appeared at that price, the land should be given away. This proposal came to be known as *graduation*. For the first time, a senator formally proposed that the work of pioneers opening the country was more valuable to the nation than money from the sale of land would be to the Treasury.

Easterners saw Benton's plan as a scheme to tap their labor supply and raise their wage costs. They also saw development of the West as a threat to their political strength. On the other hand, it was obvious that land sales at the established prices would flood the Treasury with money. And a wealthy Treasury would destroy the most respectable argument for high tariffs—the need for revenue to pay off the national debt and support government services.

In an effort to eat their cake and have it too, some easterners offered the policy of *distribution*: keep up the price of land and the tariff, and distribute the surplus revenue among the states to help them improve public education and business

NEW POLITICS FOR A NEW AGE

morality. When nothing came of this, they turned to the rather desperate proposal that the West be closed to settlement altogether.

In December 1829, Senator Samuel A. Foot of Connecticut offered a resolution that public land surveys be stopped for a time and that future sales be limited to lands already on the market. Senator Benton, speaking for the West, called Foot's resolution a manufacturers' plot. Spokesmen for the slave South supported Benton in hopes that they could aggravate the growing differences between the free East and the free West. The South's purpose was to lure the West away from the protective tariff part of the American system.

Senator Robert Y. Hayne of South Carolina presented the South's case. His most divisive remarks were derived from an antitariff essay published anonymously by Vice-President John Calhoun in 1828. According to Calhoun, the Tariff of 1828 made southerners serfs to northern industrialists. "The tariff is unconstitutional and must be repealed," Calhoun wrote. "The rights of the South have been destroyed, and must be restored, . . . the Union is in danger, and must be saved." No free government, Calhoun argued, would permit the transfer of "power and property from one class or section to another." The tyranny of the majority could be met by the constitutional right of each state to nullify an unconstitutional act of Congress.

In an address for many years regarded as a model of eloquence (and therefore parts of it memorized by several generations of northern schoolchildren), Daniel Webster of New Hampshire replied that the Union was no mere compact among state legislatures; it was "the creature of the people." They had erected it, and therefore they alone were sovereign. It was for the Supreme Court, not the states, to decide whether laws passed by Congress followed the Constitution. If a single state had that right, the Union would be dissolved. Webster closed his four-hour speech with what Senator Benton called "a fine piece of rhetoric misplaced," a vision of two Americas. One was a land "rent with civil feuds, or drenched . . . in fratricidal blood"; the other, a republic "now known and honored throughout the earth, still full high advanced, its arms and trophies streaming in their original lustre." He ended with the famous words: "Liberty and Union, now and forever, one and inseparable."

Once the debate ended, the first question everyone asked was, where does Jackson stand? There was a long delay before he responded. When he finally decided to talk he confronted not Hayne, the spokesman, but John C. Calhoun, the philosopher behind Hayne.

Nullification

The doctrine of nullification was a strange way for the South to choose to capture the heart of the West. Beyond the coastal tier of the thirteen original states, all the new ones had been created by the national government of the United States. None had ever known independence. Where they stood on nullification finally became clear to Jackson himself. And since the Union was involved, he was with them. He was for states rights; about that there was to be no mistake. But he was for state rights within the Union. There was to be no mistake about that either.

A few months after the Webster-Hayne debate, when leading Democrats gathered at a Jefferson birthday dinner, Old Hickory raised his pain-wracked body to its feet and, looking Calhoun straight in the eye, proposed this toast: "Our Union—it must be preserved!" (Before news of Jackson's toast was released, Hayne got the president to soften it by inserting the word "federal"

John C. Calhoun by Charles Bird King. (*National Portrait Gallery, Smithsonian Institution*)

before Union.) But federal or not, Calhoun refused to back down. To Jackson's words, he rose to reply: "The Union—next to our liberty, the most dear."

In the months following the famous dinner toasts in Washington, Jackson and Calhoun came to a complete break. The grounds for the split were personal and political. A social scandal involving the reputation of a cabinet member's wife found Jackson on one side of the controversy and Calhoun on the other. Martin Van Buren maneuvered behind the scenes to strengthen his own position as a future presidential candidate. Calhoun's enemies let Jackson know that Calhoun, as secretary of war in 1818, had severely criticized Jackson's actions in Florida.

The vice-president tried to explain away these reports, but Jackson remained unforgiving. The break was nearly out in the open when, on Jackson's urging, in 1832 Congress began to consider a tariff act to reduce the rates. Calhoun found this an insult to his constituency. The president had thought a reduction in duties would please the South, but the most immediate result of his proposal was to send Calhoun into a huff. He resigned the vice-presidency and went home to South Carolina to rally support.

The Tariff of 1832 passed, and Calhoun immediately resurrected the doctrine of nullification. This time, South Carolina moved to put Calhoun's theories into action. Despite strong opposition within the state, the legislature ordered the election of delegates to a special state convention in November 1832. There, an ordinance of nullification was adopted which pronounced the tariffs of 1828 and 1832 "unauthorized by the Constitution" and therefore "null, void, and no law, nor binding upon this state."

The convention also demanded that the legislature prohibit collection of duties in state ports after February 1, 1833. If federal troops were used to collect the duties, the convention declared, South Carolina would secede from the federal union.

Jackson was furious. He replied with his ringing Nullification Proclamation:

I consider . . . the power to annul a law of the United States, assumed by one State, incompatible with the existence of the Union, contradicted expressly by the letter of the Constitution, unauthorized by its spirit, inconsistent with every principle on which it was founded, and destructive of the great object for which it was formed.

Jackson warned that the laws of the United States compelled him to meet treason with force.

In February 1833 the Senate passed a Force Bill empowering the president to use the army and navy if South Carolina resisted federal customs officials. While the Force Bill was being debated in the House, Henry Clay introduced a compromise by sponsoring a new tariff bill calling for gradual reduction of the 1832 duties. South Carolina leaders, having learned that other southern states would not go along with nullification and that a strong Unionist faction inside their own borders would continue to fight it, anxiously awaited the decision on these two measures. Jackson signed both Clay's tariff bill and the Force Bill on the same day in March 1833—a carrot and a stick.

Faced with these twin measures, South Carolina withdrew its nullification ordinance. But to save face, the state adopted a new ordinance nullifying the Force Act. Jackson was wise enough to disregard this last challenge. Both sides claimed victory, but most Americans knew that the national government had weathered a major constitutional crisis. Outright conflict had been avoided, and John Calhoun's career as a national states-

THE NATION'S FIRST "NEWSPAPERWOMAN" VIEWS THE WASHINGTON SCENE

Amid the political excitement of the election year of 1832, public attention in the nation's capital focused on a cholera epidemic and public health. Anne Royall, an eccentric but talented writer and editor, described the situation:

That the location of Washington is unhealthy cannot be denied. The principal part of the city [Pennsylvania Avenue], being built in a marsh, which a common shower [rain] overflows, and from want of sewers and proper attention, it is overspread with standing puddles which are choked with filth. The whole flat land between the settled part of the city and the Potomac, much of which is marsh, is also overspread with stagnant pools. There are besides great, oblong, deep holes, from which the earth has been scooped out years past, intended for a canal, but has been the receptacle for dead cats, dogs, puppies, and we grieve to add, infants. Scientific men ought to be engaged to put in sewers and drain the marsh.

man had been brought to an end. Most important, the idea of nullification appeared to be dead.

THE BANK WAR

Not long before his reelection in 1832, Jackson settled into brooding hostility toward the Bank of the United States. Rechartering was not due for another four years, but the question of the bank's continuation came up during the election campaign. Although real and serious financial issues were involved, the fact that Jackson carried on a war against "the monster" bank, even after he had won the election, suggests that his opposition came as much from what the bank symbolized as from what it actually did. Many of the political developments of the 1830s had this same symbolic quality.

The Anti-Masonic Party

It was this atmosphere of symbolic politics that partly explains the rapid rise of an unexpected third party during the 1832 campaign. It was at this time that the Jacksonians formally adopted the name Democrats. The National Republicans would soon adopt the label Whig. The Anti-Masonic party also seized upon something it was against, rather than for.

The Masons were a national fraternal order with local lodges. Little was known about the organization, except that its members were sworn to secrecy, practiced mysterious rituals, and on occasion dressed in odd costumes. In fact, Masonry was an international fraternity, much more interested in its own internal affairs than anything else. Yet Masonry's secrecy became the source of suspicion and hostility.

The rise of the Anti-Masonic party was triggered by a mysterious murder in upper New York state. It became strong enough in a number of states to hold a national political convention in 1832, at which Anti-Masons talked about the "horrid, oath binding system" which threatened American Christianity and the openness of a democratic society. Jackson himself had once been a Mason, and for that reason alone the Anti-Masons opposed him.

The new party had no permanent impact on American politics, though at the time its existence and ideas worried many politicians. Anti-Masonic candidates carried only one state in the 1832 election and then disappeared as a factor on the polit-

ical scene. Most supporters went over to the Whigs because they opposed the president. But this brief comet across the political skies strongly suggested how badly Americans wanted to find a villain responsible for a changing world they did not fully understand.

President Jackson versus President Biddle

For ten years prior to the 1832 election, the Second Bank of the United States had been managed by Nicholas Biddle of Philadelphia. A former Federalist, Biddle was appointed a director of the bank by President Monroe. In 1824 and 1828 he voted for Jackson. On becoming president of the bank, Biddle intensified the deflationary policies his predecessor had introduced during the Panic of 1819.

Biddle was cautious about issuing notes of his own bank. By refusing to accept at face value the notes of state and local banks that had issued more paper than their reserves warranted, he forced them into more cautious policies. They resented it, and so did their clients.

In addition, the Second Bank was an enormous institution with far-reaching powers. It had considerable control over the private economy as well as custody of government funds. Its enemies were apparently justified in denouncing it as a monopoly. Whether it really was a "monster" was a matter of opinion.

Nobody attacked the bank more vigorously than the Democratic senator from Missouri, Thomas Hart Benton. In February 1831 Benton introduced a resolution against rechartering the bank and spoke for several hours on its threat to democracy. He exploited feelings against the bank: "It tends to aggravate the inequality of fortunes; to make the rich richer and the poor poorer; to multiply nabobs and paupers."

The Senate rejected Benton's resolution, but he had helped antibank sentiment. His fear that the bank was "too great and powerful" reflected a widespread conviction that the bank was corrupting the nation's virtue. It granted financial favors to senators, congressmen, and newspapermen. Many of the old Republican school, moreover, had never accepted the bank's constitutionality.

Jackson grew increasingly upset about the bank. It began to take on personal importance. When urged by one of his advisors to say nothing, he said, "My friend, I am pledged against the bank." When the time came to submit his message in December, Jackson remained silent almost to the end. Then he said it was not too soon for the

Nicholas Biddle. (*New York Public Library*)

issue of rechartering the bank in 1836 to be submitted "to the deliberate consideration of the Legislature and the people." With words that made his own position clear, he added: "Both the constitutionality and the expedience of the law creating this bank are well questioned by a large portion of our fellow-citizens."

Jackson would have preferred to keep the Second Bank out of the 1832 campaign. His secretary of state and secretary of the treasury were busy talking to Biddle's friends about renewal after the election. But Webster and Clay, grossly overestimating public support for the bank, urged Biddle to take the offensive. Biddle, increasingly confused, gave in to their advice. On July 3, 1832, as forecast, the recharter bill passed both houses.

Jackson, bedridden for the moment, grimly observed to his heir apparent: "The Bank, Mr. Van Buren, is trying to kill me, but I will kill it." In his veto message of July 10, Jackson noted at the start that the recharter bill had come to him on the Fourth of July and that he had considered it "with that solemn regard to the principles of the Constitution which the day was calculated to inspire." His closing remarks were well suited to the coming election:

Distinctions in society will always exist under every just government. Equality of talents, of education, or of wealth cannot be produced by human institutions: ... but when the laws undertake to add to these natural and just advantages artificial distinctions ... to make the rich richer, and the potent more powerful, the humble members of the society—the farmers, mechanics, and laborers—who have neither the time nor the means of

securing like favors to themselves, have a right to complain of the injustice of their government.

To the Panic of 1837

Jackson's victory over Clay in the election caused him to interpret his triumph as a mandate for his war against Biddle's "hydra of corruption." The president's opening shot was to order the removal of government deposits from the Second Bank's branches. His reason: Biddle's policies no longer insured the safety of public funds. He then ordered that these deposits and all new government revenue be placed in selected state institutions, which became known as Jackson's "pet banks."

His orders were more easily issued than carried out, however, for the secretary of the treasury alone had legal power to withdraw government deposits, and Jackson's secretary was a friend of the bank. Such obstacles did not stop Old Hickory. He fired two secretaries of the treasury until he found in Roger B. Taney of Maryland someone who would do as he wished. Late in 1833, Taney began the removal of the deposits. By the end of the year, twenty-three state banks had been named to receive federal funds.

Even though his bid for a new charter had been defeated, Biddle refused to accept this assault on his bank. If the bank was to be forced to close, it must begin to call in loans and limit new business. After the federal deposits had been removed, Biddle embarked on this policy. His object was to create a business panic so widespread that public opinion would force Jackson to reverse his stand. For some months in 1833 and 1834, a panic indeed seemed imminent. But once again Biddle miscalculated the political effects. To those who began to press Jackson for help, the president replied, "Go to Nicholas Biddle."

In time, segments of the conservative business community, alienated by Jackson's high-handed political maneuvers in the Treasury, did appeal to Biddle to relent. And finally he gave in. Relief turned the near panic into a boom, especially in the South and West. Speculation was further stimulated by the inflationary practices of the pet banks, which used the federal deposits as reserves for many bad loans. By throwing millions of acres of public land on the market, the administration itself encouraged wholesale borrowing.

The land boom quickly heightened the demand for internal improvements, leading to reckless investments in turnpikes, canals, and railroads. Many projects were financed in part by foreign

WORDS AND NAMES IN AMERICAN HISTORY

In this country, few such simple words as *stump* have such eloquent histories. The phrase *to be up a stump* goes back to the eighteenth century and indicated a state of helplessness and frustration. It came from the fact that wagons and coaches traveling on the incredibly crude roads of the time sometimes caught their axles or even their floorboards on the stumps of trees left between the two ruts that formed the road. In the antebellum era, in the days of popular electioneering and political oratory, candidates often stood on tree stumps to address the crowd. Hence we have the phrase *stump speeches*. Even today, without ever actually standing on one, political candidates *stump* their district or state or even the entire nation in search of votes. And the meaning of the phrase *to stump* someone with a question to which the person does not know the answer comes from that same political tradition, where candidates often debated one another by asking for answers to difficult questions.

---

capitalists who would not risk their money in private American corporations. They were willing to purchase state bonds, backed by state revenues, which many states issued to support internal improvement schemes.

The optimistic state programs got a boost in the summer of 1836 when it became clear that the federal government was about to distribute to the states most of the $35 million surplus that had accumulated in the Treasury from tariff revenues and public land sales. Distribution began in time to sustain the boom.

Before payments could be completed, however, the surplus evaporated. Responsibility for this rested largely on another administration measure, Jackson's Specie Circular. Issued on July 11, 1836, this circular required that all land purchased from the federal government after August 15 be paid for in silver or gold. Settlers were allowed to use bank notes for an additional four months, provided their purchases were under 320 acres.

This drastic reversal of policy slowed land sales and sent prices plunging. In the spring of 1837, after Jackson had left office, stock and commodity prices also broke. Soon the Panic of 1837 was on in earnest. Like other panics, that of 1837 was worldwide and had international as well as American causes and effects. British banks engaged in financing American trade, mainly in cotton and the new railroads, called in their loans and forced many American merchants to the wall. The failure of Biddle's bank, which had been operating since 1836 under a Pennsylvania charter, helped deepen the depression that followed the panic. After suspending activities twice, the bank was finally turned over to trustees for liquidation in 1841. Biddle was charged with fraud, but subsequently acquitted. In 1844, at age fifty-eight, he died a broken man.

After a brief economic recovery in 1839, the country sank into a severe depression that lasted until the mid-1840s. Banks and businesses folded. Farms and plantations were lost by those who had borrowed more than they could repay. Men, women, and children were thrown out of work. The streets of the cities became crowded with hungry, frightened people—a new class in the United States, people who wanted work but could find none. Many state governments had to stop paying interest on their bonds. A few states defaulted completely and announced they could not even pay back the face amount they had borrowed. British leaders, who themselves were under strain, were outraged as they saw their loans go down the drain.

They blamed the Americans. Americans, in turn, blamed everyone. They blamed British capitalists, American bankers, their state governments, the federal government, President Van Buren, ex-President Jackson, Nicholas Biddle, the Whig party, the Democratic party, alcohol, their food, and the moral fiber of the American people. When a man worked hard and then lost his farm, his business, his job, his plantation, who else was there to blame? When people could no longer support their children or even themselves, who could explain it?

No American fully realized that large, impersonal, international market forces were at work. Van Buren himself could only offer the suggestion that the depression was caused by "overbanking" and "overtrading." He was not altogether wrong, but the dimensions and nature of the problem were not well understood.

The national and international market economy was far more complex and interwoven than it had been a generation before, but it was not easy to see the relationships. It was not yet obvious that a bank failure in New Orleans might be connected with failure of a New York cotton merchant, a bank in Boston, and a cotton factory in Manchester, England. It was even more difficult to see the relevance of a rise in silver exports from Mexico or a temporary interruption of the opium trade in China. Such developments, in fact, could affect a farmer in Illinois or Alabama. It was easier to find the cause of one's own difficulties closer to home. It is no wonder that many Americans in this era turned inward to reform their own society, without realizing that it was rapidly becoming part of a much larger and more impersonal world.

JACKSONIAN POLITICS WITHOUT JACKSON

President Jackson barely escaped the economic storm and its political consequences. The election of 1836 took place before financial panic set in, and Van Buren's nomination was assured by Jackson's support. Having failed four years earlier with Henry Clay, the Whigs were unable to decide on a candidate. At their national convention, they resolved matters by running four regional candidates in the hope of depriving Van Buren of a majority and throwing the election into the House of Representatives.

With national prosperity at its height, Van Buren won. But his popular and electoral majorities were far smaller than his predecessor's. In the election of 1840, he paid the political price of presiding over a depression. The Whigs out-ballyhooed the Democrats and finally won control of the presidency—only to lose it a month later because their candidate caught a chill at his inauguration.

Critics of the Jackson Presidency

President Jackson's enlargement of presidential power cast a long shadow over American politics. Not for another generation would an American president use the office with such vigor. In part this was because no successor until Lincoln had Jackson's force of personality. But it was also because Jackson himself had aroused fears about a strong president.

The principal complaint against Jackson was that of "executive usurpation." After Jackson had fired two Treasury secretaries who would not do what he wanted, Henry Clay bitterly attacked the "revolution, hitherto bloodless, but rapidly tend-

ing toward . . . the concentration of all power in the hands of one man." In 1834, the Senate gave Jackson a taste of his own medicine by adopting, 26 to 20, the following unprecedented resolution:

Resolved, That the President, in the late Executive proceedings in relation to the public revenue, has assumed upon himself authority and power not conferred by the Constitution and laws, but in derogation of both.

Jackson responded with an eloquent "Protest," which the Senate refused to enter in the journal of its proceedings. Jackson's supporters in the Senate fought for almost three years to have the censure resolution removed from the record, and at last they had their way. During the debate, Clay again expressed the resentment of many senators over what they regarded as Jackson's enlargement of the executive's rights:

The Senate has no army, no navy, no patronage, no lucrative offices, nor glittering honors to bestow . . . How is it with the President? . . . By means of principles which he has introduced, and innovations which he has made in our institutions, alas! but too much countenanced by Congress and a confiding people, he exercises uncontrolled the power of the state. In one hand he holds the purse and in the other brandishes the sword of the country! . . . He has swept over the government like a tropical tornado.

Others voiced similar judgments. "I look upon Jackson," wrote Chancellor Kent of New York, "as a detestable, ignorant, reckless, vain and malignant tyrant. . . . This American elective monarchy frightens me. The experiment, with its foundations laid on universal suffrage and our unfettered press, is of too violent a nature for our excitable people." In the Senate, Webster roared out this protest: "The President carries on the government; all the rest are subcontractors."

Van Buren Carries On

Martin Van Buren stepped into the much criticized shoes of his predecessor and almost immediately stumbled into an economic depression. He was a capable politician. He made his career in politics, first in New York state and then at the national level, and his cleverness at always landing on his feet earned him the nickname of The Little Magician. A man of honesty and instinctive sympathy with the common people, he lacked the forcefulness of Jackson, the charm of Clay, the

Martin Van Buren. (*Library of Congress*)

eloquence of Webster, the subtle and complicated mind of Calhoun.

The new president spent much of his administration trying to deal with the vacuum left by the disappearance of the "monster" bank. Van Buren was convinced that banks in general were a threat to the working man. He pressed for what he called an Independent Treasury, a "divorce of bank and state." The government would deposit its temporary surplus funds in vaults in various cities. They would not be tied in any way to state banks or a central federal financial institution.

Whig leaders were not happy with the proposed system, but they had no better alternative. In 1840, in the darkest year of the depression, Congress finally went along with Van Buren's plan.

The Election of 1840

The Independent Treasury did little for economic recovery, and as the election of 1840 drew near, Whig leaders scented victory. Clay, defeated in

Election of 1840

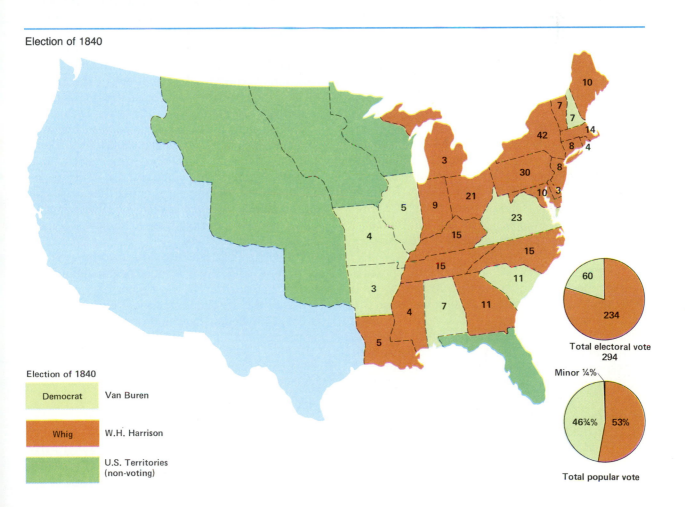

Election of 1840

Democrat	Van Buren
Whig	W.H. Harrison
U.S. Territories (non-voting)	

Total electoral vote 294

60
234

Minor ¼%

46¾% 53%

Total popular vote

the election on the bank issue in 1832 and by-passed in 1836 for strategic reasons, now hoped to win. This time, however, he received no support from Webster, who looked upon him as a rival. With little hope of winning the nomination himself, Webster backed General William Henry Harrison.

At the Whig convention "Old Tippecanoe" was nominated. John Tyler of Virginia was named the general's running mate to strengthen Whig chances in the South. The Democrats renominated Van Buren. But since Jackson's retirement, they had become so divided that they were not able to agree on a candidate for vice-president and were forced to leave that choice to the states.

The presidential campaign of 1840 was one of the most dramatic in American history. The Whig campaigners lashed out at the hard times under the Democrats. They focused on the president's supposedly luxurious tastes. A campaign document, "Royal Splendor of the President's Palace," pictured Van Buren in the White House as an Oriental potentate eating French cookery from golden plates and resting on a "Turkish divan." By contrast, the Whigs stressed the stern simplicity of Old Tippecanoe. When a Baltimore newspaper taunted the Whigs by saying that Harrison would be perfectly satisfied with a log cabin and a good supply of cider, his managers picked up the log cabin as a party symbol. "It tells of virtues," New York's Thurlow Weed declared, "that dwell in obscurity, of the privations of the poor, of toil and danger." The log cabin, this "emblem of simplicity," was as foreign to Harrison's gentlemanly origins and living habits as Van Buren's Turkish divan, but the symbol helped elect him. Seventy-eight percent of eligible voters went to the polls, by far the highest percentage ever in the history of the nation.

Having given over the nomination to a popular hero for the sake of winning the presidency, such Whig leaders as Clay and Webster planned to run the administration once he took office. In fact, during his single month as president, Harrison yielded to them. Of Clay, a New York newspaper correspondent reported: "He predominates over the Whig Party with despotic sway. Old Hickory himself never lorded it over his followers with authority more undisputed, or more supreme." But Harrison died on April 4, 1841, having established two presidential records: the shortest presidency (one month) and the longest inaugural address (a mere one and three-quarter hours). Tyler became

president, and the situation changed drastically.

Tyler was a Whig only because he had followed Calhoun out of the Democratic party after the break with Jackson. A veteran of the Virginia legislature and of both houses of Congress, he had had many opportunities to disclose his strong antitariff views, his antagonism to Biddle's bank, his dislike for federal aid to internal improvements. Beyond these issues, he sided with Calhoun on nullification. The Whigs had named him for the vice-presidency in order to attract southern anti-Jackson support, despite his enthusiasm for states rights. They soon wished they had made another choice.

Tyler's presidency was less than successful. Henry Clay thought the time had come for putting his American System into full effect. As a states rights man, Tyler thought otherwise. He vetoed bills for internal improvements and only reluctantly agreed to a higher tariff in 1842. He also agreed to repeal of Van Buren's Independent Treasury. But when the Whigs tried to reestablish another national bank, Tyler vetoed one proposal after another. The government continued to use state banks.

Gradual economic recovery made the issue of a national bank seem less and less important. As politicians turned to other matters in the 1840s, the banking issue disappeared as a major factor in American politics for more than twenty years.

Tyler's vetoes outraged Whig leaders, but they lacked enough votes in Congress to override them. National domestic legislation came almost to a standstill. Angry Whig congressmen issued a formal statement reading Tyler out of the party. The entire cabinet resigned except for Webster, who stayed on as secretary of state to complete certain diplomatic negotiations.

The victory of 1840 turned out to be a nearly empty one, and Whig leaders began falling out among themselves. They lost their majority in the House in the 1842 congressional elections. Clay resigned his Senate seat to try once again for the presidency.

The Jacksonian Legacy

The sheer force of Andrew Jackson's personality did a great deal to bring about the second party system. During the 1830s, two distinct parties emerged, each with considerable strength in ev-

Figurehead of Andrew Jackson carved for the frigate *Constitution*. An angry anti-Jacksonian sawed off the upper part of the head, but it was later restored. (*Museum of the City of New York*)

ery section of the nation and each with a large core of loyal followers who identified themselves as lifetime Whigs or Democrats. The Anti-Masonic party disappeared as quickly as it arose. By this time almost all Americans accepted parties as a fact of political life. Once regarded as an evil, political parties—especially *two* political parties— were now seen as beneficial and even necessary to the functioning of national government.

The style of politics had changed drastically. Politicians appealed more to passions than to reason. They courted popularity in a way that John Quincy Adams and his predecessors could never have brought themselves to do. Far more Americans than ever before were involved, often quite emotionally, in the political process. In an age lacking visual mass media, long political speeches became a form of popular entertainment.

Jackson himself set a precedent for a strong, activist presidency—the kind we are accustomed to now. Few men could fill that role as well as he, though some would attempt to do so. Jackson was not the last president to remind other politicians that he alone was elected by all the people and represented them in all their majestic power. He thought (incorrectly as things turned out) that he had settled the question of the relationship of the states and the federal government. But he had considerable justification at the time for thinking he had helped strengthen the permanence of the national union.

Both Jackson and his opponents had to wrestle with problems created by the new economy. They did their best in a new world which in many ways was confusing and mysterious. For ten years, the major issue in American politics was banking, or rather The Bank. The rapid disappearance of this issue suggests that it was in large measure symbolic. Yet there was another issue both Jackson and the Whigs managed to keep off center stage, and it was both symbolic and very real. Already in the 1830s a small but noisy band of men and women were trying to bring it to the nation's attention. They insisted that American democracy contained a serious flaw. If Americans were a free and democratic people, why were some Americans slaves?

That issue came to dominate American politics in the years after John Tyler's presidency. But in order to understand why, it is necessary to turn away from politics to examine important changes in the minds of Americans as they stepped onto the slippery slope that led to civil war.

SUMMARY

The political tone of the Age of Jackson began even before Andrew Jackson became president in 1828. During the first quarter of the nineteenth century, most states opened up the vote to almost all adult white males. And interest in national politics grew as government seemed to become more accessible to the people. A new two-party system gradually emerged after 1824, and voters began to participate in naming the candidates in national conventions. By 1828, most states allowed voters rather than legislators to choose members of the electoral college, and governors were being popularly elected.

The election of 1824 brought John Quincy Adams to the presidency, with Henry Clay as secretary of state. But Adams's program for national economic and cultural development failed, and he lost his congressional majority in the midterm elections. In 1828 Andrew Jackson— Old Hickory and the Hero of New Orleans in the War of 1812—became president.

Jackson greatly enlarged the power of the presidency. His administration was marked by the rise to power of the Kitchen Cabinet—a small group of advisors who were also personal friends. Jackson's name also became linked with the "spoils system," the right of a president to put his own people in the executive branch upon election. He clashed with Congress and with the Supreme Court, and warred on the Second Bank of the United States. During his administration, the heads of the various geographical sections in Congress solidified their positions. They lashed out at one another on various issues: The Webster-Hayne debate of 1829 was one instance; South Carolina's nullification was another.

The campaign of 1832 brought a third party to national prominence for the first time. The Anti-Masonic party had no permanent effect on American politics, but it showed that a single issue could generate political force. Almost immediately after his reelection, Jackson continued his war with the Second Bank of the United States.

He had vetoed the bill for rechartering before the election, and saw his victory as a sign that the public approved. Jackson succeeded in removing the government's money from the bank and placing it in selected state banks, known as "pet banks." President Biddle of the bank responded by calling in loans and limiting new business. He relented finally, but the shaky economic boom became a panic in 1837. After a brief recovery in 1839, the country went into a severe depression that lasted until the mid-1840s.

Andrew Jackson cast a long shadow over American politics. His enlargement of presidential power aroused fears of a strong executive. His successor, Martin Van Buren, had to cope with an economic depression and with the vacuum left by the disappearance of the Bank of the United States. As a result, though renominated he lost the election of 1840 to a Whig, William Henry Harrison. Harrison died within a month of his inauguration, and John Tyler of Virginia became president. Tyler, nominated only in order to attract southern support, was a supporter of nullification and of states rights. He vetoed the legislation of his own party, and Congress came almost to a standstill; his entire cabinet resigned except for the secretary of state.

Jackson's presidency did a great deal to create a second two-party system. During the 1830s the Whigs and the Democrats emerged as two distinct groups, and the idea of a two-party system came to be seen as beneficial to the functioning of national government. Both parties had to deal with economic problems they did not fully understand, and with social changes that seemed to come from nowhere.

Suggested Readings

R. McCormick, *The Second American Party System: Party Formation in the Jacksonian Era* (1966), is an impressive state-by-state electoral analysis. More oriented toward prevailing thought than simple voting behavior is R. Hofstadter, *The Idea of a Party System: The Rise of Legitimate Opposition in the United States, 1780–1840* (1969).

C. Williamson, *American Suffrage, from Property to Democracy, 1760–1860* (1960), is the standard account of the suffrage. A comprehensive anthology of contemporary accounts on the subject is gathered in M. Peterson (ed.), *Democracy, Liberty, and Property: The State Constitutional Conventions of the 1820s* (1966). The developing exclusion of blacks from the franchise is dealt with by L. Litwack, *North of Slavery: The Negro in the Free States, 1790–1860* (1961). L. Benson, *The Concept of Jacksonian Democracy: New York as a Test Case* (1961), is a controversial work that stresses the correlation between ethnic affiliation and party alignments. C. Sellers, *James K. Polk, Jacksonian, 1795–1843* (2 vols., 1957–1966), is a first-rate biography and reveals much about political practices in the Jacksonian era.

Several other studies bear more directly on the machinery of the Jacksonian party: J. Curtis, *The Fox at Bay: Martin Van Buren and the Presidency, 1837–1841* (1970); R. Remini, *The Election of Andrew Jackson* (1963); and L. White, *The Jacksonians: A Study in Administrative History, 1829–1861* (1954), which is especially informative on the spoils system and its effects. The types of men appointed to high office in the early republic are discussed in S. Aronson, *Status and*

Kinship in the Higher Civil Service . . . in the Administrations of John Adams, Thomas Jefferson, and Andrew Jackson (1964).

G. Dangerfield, *The Era of Good Feelings* (1952), and his *The Awakening of American Nationalism, 1815–1828* (1965), give smoothly written analyses of American life and politics leading to the election of Jackson. S. Bemis, *John Quincy Adams and the Union* (1956), is the second volume of a compelling biography; this one covers not only his presidency but his later career in Congress where he battled against the refusal to receive antislavery petitions.

For clashing views, see the piece on Jackson in R. Hofstadter, *The American Political Tradition* (1948), which contains essays on various political figures throughout American history; J. Dorfman, *The Economic Mind in American Civilization, 1606–1865* (5 vols., 1946–1959); M. Meyers, *The Jacksonian Persuasion: Politics and Belief* (1957), a brilliant study stressing the nostalgic yearning Jacksonians felt about the supposedly golden years of the founding of the republic; and J. Ward, *Andrew Jackson, Symbol for an Age* (1962), which relates key events in Jackson's life to the historical period and discusses his reputation as a popular leader. For a rich portrait of the habits and attitudes of ordinary Americans in this period, see the well-known work by the French traveler Alexis de Tocqueville, *Democracy in America* (1835).

Other key figures in that era of senatorial giants are given attention in the following works: C. Eaton, *Henry Clay and the Art of American Politics* (1957); S. Nathans, *Daniel Webster and Jacksonian Democracy* (1973), dealing with the period 1828–1844; and C. Wiltse, *John C. Calhoun, Nullifier, 1829–1839* (1949). The latter should be balanced against the brilliant essay on Calhoun, "The Marx of the Master Class," in Hofstadter, above. W. Freehling, *Prelude to Civil War: The Nullification Controversy in South Carolina, 1816–1836* (1966), presents a masterly analysis that stresses the profound impact of slavery on South Carolina politics. For President Tyler, there is R. Seager II, *And Tyler Too* (1963).

It has only fairly recently become clear that Indian policy is crucial to an understanding of the Jacksonian age. Prevailing ideas about the Indian are discussed with a literary emphasis in R. Pearce, *The Savages of America: A Study of the Indian and the Idea of Civilization* (rev. ed., 1965). See also T. Wilkins, *Cherokee Tragedy: The Story of the Ridge Family and the Decimation of a People* (1970). The political rationale for these national travesties is covered in F. Prucha, *American Indian Policy in the Formative Years: The Indian Trade and Intercourse Acts, 1790–1834* (1962). M. Rogin, *Fathers and Children: Andrew Jackson and the Subjugation of the American Indian* (1975) is an important and fascinating study, though many readers may find it overly psychoanalytic in orientation.

A short introduction to the bank war (also treated in many of the works cited above) is found in G. Taylor (ed.), *Jackson versus Biddle* (1949). More recent studies are B. Hammond's sweeping *Banks and Politics in America: From the Revolution to the Civil War* (1957); T. Govan, *Nicholas Biddle, Nationalist and Public Banker, 1786–1844* (1959), pro-Biddle and J. McFaul, *The Politics of Jacksonian Finance* (1972), which disagrees with Hammond's claim that Jacksonians were opposed to banks and business as such. J. Sharp, *The Jacksonians versus the Banks; Politics in the States after the Panic of 1837* (1970), covers the years following the great financial crash.

THE SPIRIT OF ANTEBELLUM AMERICA

Chapter 12

America was a far more complex society in the antebellum period (1815–1860) than it had been in the eighteenth century. The variety of occupations and life styles, and the pace of life, had increased greatly. Families of all kinds—farming, industrial, professional, commercial, planting, and slave—were less isolated than ever before from the wider world of neighborhood, town, city, state, and nation. The mood of Americans was also changed; a new spirit was abroad in the land. Perhaps we ought to say spirits, for Americans exhibited many qualities, some of which seemed downright inconsistent with others.

Historians have a remarkably full picture of Americans in this period, thanks in large part to the hundreds of curious Europeans who came to the United States to observe and report on this astounding and often disturbing new phenomenon among nations. And Americans themselves were acutely conscious of living in a new and changing society; they too commented on their characteristics and examined themselves and their lives.

It is therefore possible for historians to generalize about the mood and mind of antebellum America. One central difficulty, however, arises from the need to disentangle two interwoven facts. Granted that the United States was different from other Western countries; yet while the United States was changing in many ways, becoming more "modern," so were other Western nations. It is often easy to call such attributes as optimism and egalitarianism peculiarly American, when in fact those attributes were part of the modernization of Western culture.

It was during this period that a truly American literature was born, that the fine arts began to be more than an aristocratic pastime, that a movement for free public education gained strength, and that reformers began to try to achieve social justice. These activities reflected contradictions and inconsistencies that touched many Americans. The drive for material success brought increasingly unequal wealth, a fact that ran squarely into widespread insistence on social equality. Religious principles that tolerated slavery also led many Americans to denounce slavery as an institution. ■

AMERICAN QUALITIES

Restlessness, Money, and Violence

All observers agreed that Americans worked harder, ate faster, spat tobacco juice further, moved around more, and relaxed less than Europeans. People seemed to be perpetually on the move, always in transit, going from here to somewhere better. Much of this restlessness came from a sense of unlimited possibilities on what seemed an "empty" continent.

In 1832 an anonymous writer listed some of the reasons for America's glorious prospects: "an extensive seacoast, abundantly provided with capacious ports and harbors"; "magnificent rivers" providing the means for a "lucrative internal trade"; a tremendous waterpower potential; "every variety of soil and climate"; "a capacity for raising cotton to supply the demand of the whole world"; a population "active, energetic, enterprising, and ingenious"; the most liberal, and most cheaply administered government in the world; the absence of a nobility; and an "abundant room for all the superfluous population of Europe." What more could anyone want? Faith in the American future had been strong before the revolution. But after 1820 all signs seemed to confirm the prospects of "indefinite perfectibility."

What seemed to drive the country was the dynamic "engine" of business enterprise. Even while Jacksonian Americans lashed out at the national bank, they praised their business-oriented society. They praised the fact that "the resources of this country are controlled chiefly by the class which, in our own peculiar phraseology, we term 'business community'—embracing all those who are engaged in the great occupation of buying, selling, exchanging, importing and exporting merchandise." As Americans saw it, one principle motivated the commercial class: "it is . . . money-making which constitutes the great business of our people—it is the use of money which controls and regulates everything."

Even America's severest critics usually agreed there was something great and even heroic in this pursuit of wealth. People regarded making money as a source of virtue as well as a good in itself. Merchants and financiers who shared this view supported humanitarian and cultural enterprises. Wealthy men had always had influence in America, but now wealth itself was worshipped. In the 1840s, in several cities people could buy privately published directories of their wealthiest citizens, complete with names, addresses, and the estimated size of their fortunes.

More hostile foreign critics pointed to the American liking for the gun and the Bowie knife. Stories from the frontier and the cities told of stabbings and shootings, of ambushes, river piracy, deadly feuds, and ordinary fights that included eye-gouging. By the 1830s, violence in the cities had become a public issue. Prostitutes, thieves, and murderers could be explained, if not approved, as the inevitable consequences of social injustices or of human wickedness.

Yet many people refused to condemn the law of "Judge Lynch." The motives behind lynchings and mobbings in northern cities and in the South and West were much the same. Mobs were sometimes composed of solid middle-class citizens who demanded conformity in public behavior. It was during the Age of Jackson that so many American men banded into crowds that whipped, burned, hanged, exiled, or shot people they thought dangerous or subversive—gamblers, Mormons, abolitionists, Roman Catholics, and especially blacks. Whoever seemed different to them also seemed evil.

Equality, Individualism, and Cooperation

Despite their admiration for wealth, Americans also championed social and political equality. Many new immigrants were particularly impressed by American egalitarianism. A new citizen wrote old friends in Germany in the late 1830s: "Our President walks across the street the same as I do—no Royal Highness or Majesty would ever do that. They do not even call him "Mister." . . . When talking to the President you say simply: "How are you, President?" and he answers: "Thank you, how are you?"

There is a special irony in the growth of the ideal that in the United States every person is as good as every other. That ideology began to flourish

238

at a time when economic forces were actually causing wider differences in wealth. The distribution of wealth among Americans was becoming *less* equal rather than more.

There are probably several reasons for this lack of fit between belief and fact. For one thing, the egalitarian ideal was an extremely attractive one. Observers of American society tended to talk with people who were relatively well off and expecting to do better. Further, the economic distinctions among Americans were still much less obvious—and much less real—than in the older societies of Europe. Finally, the economic and social environment in the United States was open and fluid enough to allow some people to rise from rags to riches, and so give the ideal convincing support.

It was partly the opportunities afforded by an expanding economy that gave Americans a strong sense of the power of the individual. Many foreign observers commented on this quality of individualism, on the common American belief that what a person did was what counted, rather than what he or she was. Without realizing it, they too came from societies that gave individual concerns priority over group interests. If the observers had come from, for example, traditional societies of Africa or the Orient, they would have been appalled by the way in which the interests of individual Americans were allowed to override the claims of the general welfare.

Paradoxically once again, these same outside commentators found Americans engaged in an orgy of "association." They found businessmen joining in clubs, which should not have been a surprise, but they also found "clubbiness" everywhere. Immigrants formed mutual aid associations. Citizens set up libraries, art associations, and "societies for mutual improvement." The charitable, reform, fraternal, and benefit organizations that were being established flowered in an atmosphere where there seemed to be no ruling class with a tradition of social responsibility.

Revivalism, Sectarianism, and Anti-Catholicism

If Americans poured their energies into organizations pulling in many directions at once, what was it that held their society together? Many observers

Camp meeting, around 1835. (*New York Historical Society*)

during the 1830s and 1840s were disturbed by the diffuseness of American activity, by the "lack of a common skeleton." Ralph Waldo Emerson, one of the nation's most distinguished writers, pointed to his country's odd combination of "immense resources" and "village littleness."

One major unifying bond was religious revivalism. There was no burst of revivalism such as had swept the colonies during the Great Awakening, though a massive outdoor camp meeting at Cane Ridge, Kentucky, in 1800 led some people to speak hopefully of a "second great awakening." Yet revivals occurred at various times and various places. Outdoor camp meetings, often lasting for days at a time, attracted people from hundreds of miles. At these gatherings audiences could listen to a dozen different preachers of nearly as many denominations.

Revivals could take place in unexpected places: letters from students at the University of North Carolina, for example, indicate that outbreaks of religious enthusiasm sometimes swept that college. It is less surprising that upper New York state, settled largely by New Englanders, was so frequently swept by the fires of religious passion that it became known as the "burned-over district." Revivals were not confined to rural areas; in 1857, there was an outbreak in several eastern cities.

Perhaps the most astute comment on revivalism was made by Alexis de Tocqueville, the famous French analyst of American society in the early 1830s. Tocqueville found a "fanatical and almost wild spiritualism" in America and decided that religious enthusiasm was probably natural in a society "exclusively bent upon the pursuit of material objects."

Americans seemed to be the most religious of peoples, and yet the most torn by denominational conflict. The United States had always provided a fertile soil for new sects. But in the 1830s and 1840s the splintering of dissenting churches, with

The Beecher family, the nation's most famous family of preachers. Lyman Beecher, the father, is seated center, with Harriet Beecher Stowe on his left and Catherine Beecher on his right; Henry Ward Beecher is standing at the far right. (*Library of Congress*)

each group claiming to have the true faith, reached a new peak. Baptists and Methodists, the fastest-growing denominations, were most susceptible to schisms. New cults sprang up everywhere, and the competition for the souls of immigrants pouring into the Mississippi Valley was often uncharitable. Doctrinal differences created a good deal of friction, and different denominations catered to different social classes. Presbyterians, Congregationalists, Episcopalians, and Unitarians differed in theology and in church organization, but drew their membership especially from the well-to-do. Baptists, Methodists, Campbellites, and Universalists were held to be socially a cut lower. Immigrant Catholic and Free Negro churches stood, so people thought, at the bottom.

Most Protestants shared a common hatred of the Roman Catholic Church. Even to sophisticated ministers like Lyman Beecher, the father of Harriet Beecher Stowe and president of Lane Seminary in Cincinnati, Catholicism still meant the torturing of Protestants and dictatorship by the Pope. Gullible Americans swallowed stories about Catholic atrocities and sensational "exposés" of Catholic depravity.

Anti-Catholic prejudice deepened after 1830, when immigration began to rise. In the following twenty years, 2.5 million newcomers arrived, many of them Catholics from Ireland and Germany. In 1830, there were 500 priests in the United States and about 500,000 Catholics. Twenty years later, 1,500 priests served 1,750,000 of their faith. In addition, the Roman Catholic Church had established seminaries, schools, colleges, monasteries, convents, hospitals, and other institutions. A Catholic press, starting with the *United States Catholic Miscellany* in 1822, had come into being, along with a Catholic Tract Society, founded in Philadelphia in 1827 to combat Protestantism and to propagate the religion of Rome.

Yet the general acceptance of democracy, private property, and Christian faith seemed somehow to give a national character to American society. Even in religion, powerful clergymen like the great revivalist Charles Grandison Finney had begun in the 1820s to preach a "social gospel." The idea was to redeem entire communities, not just individuals. Many clergy equated sin with social selfishness. Indifference toward enterprises like Sunday schools, home missions, and temperance crusades was a sign of a "backslidden heart." Not all religious leaders went along with Finney's ideas, but his social Christianity gave religion a relevance that helped rescue it from self-destruction in sectarian battles.

WRITERS AND POETS: A NATIONAL LITERATURE

In the four decades before the Civil War, the United States experienced a literary flowering. In 1802, when Washington Irving began to write, America had no literature and hardly a reading public. When Irving died, a year before the Civil War began, Emerson, Thoreau, Hawthorne, Poe, Melville, and Whitman had already written masterpieces.

The achievements of these writers seem all the more remarkable when we consider the environment from which they came. Besides the prevailing hostility to intellectual activity in general, there was specific hostility to literature, and particularly to American literature. After the revolution, some people had called for a national literature that would reflect the greatness of the new nation. But American poets such as Timothy Dwight and Joel Barlow, who planned mighty epics, turned out only pale and unreadable imitations of English literary forms. Among the writers of this period, only the poet Philip Freneau and the Philadelphia novelist Charles Brockden Brown had more than minor talent. Most American readers found the works of British authors such as Sir Walter Scott and Charles Dickens much more interesting. There was to be no new patriotic literature.

American writers in turn also looked toward Europe. Washington Irving was only one of a long line of Americans who felt the need to go to Europe to find the necessary romantic background for writing. Besides being conscious of living in a materialistic, unromantic society, American writers had to contend with religiously inspired distrust of literature; some Protestant sects regarded fiction as softening to the mind and dangerous to morals.

New York and New England Writers

Washington Irving, an urbane New Yorker, was the first professional man of letters to win wide popularity at home and applause abroad. Irving spent a good deal of time in Europe and wrote his best books about it. When still in his twenties, however, he wrote and published in America his *History of New York* (1809), a burlesque of the early Dutch and later backwoods democrats. It had the whole country laughing. Even more popular was *The Sketch Book* (1819–1820), which had immediate success in Britain and in the United

States. It made Rip Van Winkle and Ichabod Crane unforgettable American characters in the rural and village setting of his native state.

An even more illustrious New Yorker was the novelist and moralist James Fenimore Cooper. In Europe, where he lived and wrote for a number of years, Cooper defended the government and institutions of his native land. In America, he scolded Americans for bad manners, chauvinism, contempt for privacy, and slavish submission to public opinion. Cooper's upbringing among the landed gentry of rural New York did not prevent him from having sympathy with Jacksonian America. His thoughtful depiction of republican government, *The American Democrat* (1838), remains one of the best political essays ever written by an American.

A prolific writer, Cooper remains best known for his celebrated Leatherstocking series, the romance of the white hunter Natty Bumppo among the Indians of the woods, lakes, and open country: *The Pioneers* (1823), *The Last of the Mohicans* (1826), *The Prairie* (1827), *The Pathfinder* (1840), and *The Deerslayer* (1841). Natty, in his first incarnation, was only a composite of some of the types Cooper had known during his boyhood in New York. He grew into a mythic figure, a kind of forest philosopher-king mediating between white men and red, and immune to the viciousness of civilization and the barbarism of the frontier.

A surer sign of American taste in this early period was the phenomenal success of the New England poet Henry Wadsworth Longfellow. Like Irving and Cooper, Longfellow spent some years in Europe. There he prepared himself to become a professor of modern languages, first at Bowdoin and later at Harvard. Sitting in his Cambridge study, Longfellow composed volume after volume of flowing verse that made him famous throughout the world. *Hyperion* (1839), *Evangeline* (1847), *Hiawatha* (1855), and *The Courtship of Miles Standish* (1858) delighted the largest audience, perhaps, that any American poet ever commanded. His sentimentality, his moralistic tone, his optimism, and his sense of the past satisfied popular taste. If his Hiawatha smacked more of Cambridge, Massachusetts, than of the shores of Gitchie Gumee, and if the brawny "Village Blacksmith" was a dream of the docile and respectful worker, poems like "A Psalm of Life" expressed without irony the aspirations of middle-class America:

> Let us, then, be up and doing
>   With a heart for any fate;
> Still achieving, still pursuing,
>   Learn to labor and to wait.

Longfellow and his Boston and Cambridge associates belonged to the group of writers who contributed to what one critic has called "the flowering of New England." The emphasis placed by historians on this regional renaissance has partially hidden the intellectual and artistic activity of other sections, notably New York. Yet New England's "golden day" was real enough. The output of New England between 1830 and 1850 remains impressive, and the great names live on: Francis Parkman and William H. Prescott, historians; James Russell Lowell, Oliver Wendell Holmes, John Greenleaf Whittier, Ralph Waldo Emerson, and Henry David Thoreau, essayists and poets; Nathaniel Hawthorne, writer of romances and tales.

Poe

One Bostonian who did not agree with Boston's appreciation of itself was Edgar Allan Poe. Although born in the "hub of the universe," a city he sarcastically referred to in later life as "Frogpond," Poe regarded himself as a Virginian. He spent much of his short life writing and editing brilliantly for inferior men, publishing poems, stories, and critical essays that brought him little money

Edgar Allan Poe. (*John Miller Documents*)

or recognition. In his most productive year, 1843, Poe earned $300.

In 1836 he had married his thirteen-year-old cousin, Virginia Clemm. "I became insane," he wrote after her death ten years later, "with long intervals of horrible sanity." In 1849, Poe was found lying unconscious in a Baltimore street and died in delirium at the age of forty.

Poe was no apostle of progress. He disliked middle-class democracy. As a literary critic, he wrote cruel reviews of bad books and performed a tremendous service by attacking American provincialism. His own poetry and fiction contained most of the weaknesses he detected in his inferiors: theatricality, bombast, and sentimentality. But stories like "The Fall of the House of Usher," "The Imp of the Perverse," "The Black Cat," "The Man in the Crowd," and "The Premature Burial"—tales of murderers, neurotics, the near-insane—were redeemed by an extraordinary intelligence and intensity. The owner who sorrowfully cuts out the eyes of his pet, the brother who entombs his sister alive, the lover who pulls out the teeth of his mistress while she sleeps in a cataleptic trance—all live in a tormented world far removed from Emerson's optimistic America. Yet Poe's works profoundly influenced later poets and critics in Europe and America. In "The Gold Bug" Poe helped lay the foundation for modern detective fiction.

Ralph Waldo Emerson. (*International Museum of Photography at George Eastman House*)

Emerson and Transcendentalism

The most compelling literary figure of his generation was Ralph Waldo Emerson. Boston-born and Harvard-educated, he entered the ministry, as his father and grandfather had. But he resigned his pastorate in 1832 because he found church formality meaningless and devoted himself to writing and lecturing. *Nature* (1836), which presented in condensed form most of the themes of his later books, was followed by two volumes of essays and then by *Poems* (1847), *Representative Men* (1850), and several other works.

Emerson contained within himself the warring tendencies of his age. Part of him belonged to the practical American world of banks and railroads. No one more enthusiastically celebrated the deeds of powerful individuals (in his essays "Wealth," "Power," and "Napoleon"). At the same time, Emerson was a mystic and idealist who looked upon the external world as a passing show and detected an unchanging reality behind it. He wanted to revive old-time Puritan fervor without the rigidity of Puritan theology.

Quakerism, with its doctrine of the inner light, its gentleness, and its humanitarianism, moved him deeply. He was drawn to any philosophy that broke down the barriers between mind and matter, and he found support for his idealism in the works of certain European and Scottish philosophers, Oriental poets and sages, and in English romantic poetry.

Transcendentalism, the philosophy associated with Emerson and his sympathizers, was not a systematic faith. It had no creed and could not easily be defined. To Emerson, "transcendentalist" meant "all those who contend for perfect freedom, who look for progress in philosophy and theology, and who sympathize with each other in the hope that the future will not always be as the past."

Although vague in its outlines, transcendental doctrine was clearly formulated in Emerson's essays and lectures, in which he announced to Americans that they too could speak to God directly without churches and creeds. He urged them to be self-reliant, to get their experience at first hand. Every object in the physical world had a spiritual meaning, and those capable of seeing that material things were the symbols of spiritual truths would best understand nature's purpose. The ability to communicate with God, or the "Over Soul," was everyone's gift. But only a few poets, scholars, and philosophers develop this capacity. From them, others might learn that only the idea is real, that evil is negative (the mere absence of good), and that a kindly destiny awaited them.

Emerson expressed these thoughts in bold and fresh language. Even in his most abstract utterances, he used simple, concrete words and homely illustrations. In urging every person to maintain his or her own views, he wrote: "Let him not quit his belief that a popgun is a popgun, though the ancient and honorable of the earth affirm it to be the crack of doom." Each person, Emerson insisted, should stand up against the tyranny of public opinion, must be, in short, an individual: "What I must do is all that concerns me, not what the people think. . . . It is easy in the world to live after the world's opinion, it is easy in solitude to live after our own; but the great man is he who in the midst of the crowd keeps with perfect sweetness the independence of solitude."

Thoreau

Like Emerson, Henry David Thoreau was a graduate of Harvard and a resident of Concord, Massachusetts. "He declined," Emerson later wrote of him, "to give up his large ambition of knowledge and action for any narrow craft or profession, aiming at a much more comprehensive calling, the art of living well." Thoreau gave all his time to self-cultivation and self-exploration. He entered the results in his literary medium, the diarylike record of his experiences. As he once wrote, "I have traveled much in Concord."

In *Civil Disobedience* (1849) and especially *Walden or Life in the Woods* (1854), Thoreau expressed his unconventional conclusions about literature, religion, government, and social relations.

Like most transcendentalists, Thoreau was a forthright egoist. He wrote about himself, he said, because he knew no one else so well. His accounts of how he discovered the miraculous in the commonplace contained suggestions for those who led "lives of quiet desperation." The wealth of the world, he said, is a lesser reward than one true vision: "The ways by which you may get money almost without exception lead downward. . . .

There is no more fatal blunderer than he who consumes the great part of his life getting his living . . . you must get your living by loving."

Thoreau advised Americans to simplify their private lives and their government. He regarded the state as a threat to independence. Abolitionist, naturalist, poet, rebel, and a down to earth but subtle writer, he attracted little notice while he lived. Yet in our day, *Walden* is considered a literary masterpiece, and its author—who discovered a universe in Concord—is regarded as one of the most original minds of New England's "flowering."

Whitman

In 1842 Emerson had written: "We have yet had no genius in America. . . . Our log-rolling, our stumps and their politics, our fisheries, our Negroes and Indians . . . the northern trade, the southern planting, the western clearing, Oregon and Texas, are yet unsung. Yet America is a poem in our eyes; its ample geography dazzles the imagination, and it will not wait long for metres."

Walt Whitman of New York proved to be that

Walt Whitman. (*National Portrait Gallery, Smithsonian Institution, Washington, D.C.*)

poet. Whitman worked as a schoolteacher, printer, carpenter, journalist, publisher, and editor. When *Leaves of Grass,* his first volume of poems, appeared in 1855, its open references to the body and sex caused people to attack him as the "dirtiest beast of his age." The most friendly review, except for three he wrote himself, described his verse as "a sort of excited compound of New England transcendentalism and New York rowdy." Emerson was the only eminent writer who instantly recognized Whitman's freshness and found (as he wrote to the poet) "incomparable things, said incomparably well."

Whitman's poems, like Emerson's essays, embody the idea of progress, celebrate the innate goodness of humankind, and idealize nature. They insist on the spiritual reality underlying the material world. But Whitman looked more to the people than to his own soul for inspiration. Both poets and scholars, he said, have tried to "form classes by themselves, above the people, and more refined than the people." But he was not ashamed to embrace "what is vulgar." He wrote poems about blacks and Indians, carpenters, coach drivers, sailors and trappers, felons and prostitutes, and above all, himself:

> *I celebrate myself, and sing myself*
> *And what I assume, you shall assume,*
> *For every atom belonging to me as good belongs*
>   *to you.*

In his poems, Whitman imagined ranks, races, and civilizations mingling together. It was to be America's mission, he thought, to promote this joining of peoples. His optimism was severely tested by the Civil War, and his faith in America's destiny was shaken by the events after 1865. But he did not despair:

> *Do I contradict myself?*
> *Very well then I contradict myself,*
> *(I am large, I contain multitudes.)*

Whitman died believing that his people still possessed "a miraculous wealth of latent power and capacity."

Hawthorne and Melville

Emerson and Whitman made many criticisms of American society, but their optimism never flagged. Some other writers, however, were less sure.

Nathaniel Hawthorne was one who could not shake off the pessimistic doctrines of his Puritan

Nathanial Hawthorne. (*National Portrait Gallery, Smithsonian Institution, Washington, D.C.*)

ancestors. The son of a Massachusetts shipmaster, Hawthorne held government jobs and enjoyed human contacts. But his ideas went against the grain of his age. In his tales, sketches, and novels—notably *The Scarlet Letter* (1850)—Hawthorne painted a somber moral landscape where men and women were devoured by vices they were forced to keep secret. These terrible facts of life mocked the claims of progress. In Hawthorne's hands, schemes for human reform came to nothing, and reformers changed into monstrous villains thwarted in their search for perfection.

Hawthorne's New York friend Herman Melville was also haunted by the idea of original sin. After his father's bankruptcy, Melville endured the humiliations of genteel poverty. In 1841 he quit city life and sailed to the South Pacific on a whaling ship. Three years of adventure there provided materials for his two best-selling books, *Typee* (1846) and *Omoo* (1847).

His reputation declined after he stopped writing sketches of Polynesian life and turned to public as well as to private conflicts. An ardent nationalist and celebrator of "the great democratic God," Melville pronounced slavery "a blot, foul as the craterpool of hell" and predicted that the southern states "may yet prove battlefields." A saddened observer of the war he predicted, he wrote in *Battle-Pieces* (1866) some of the noblest poetry on the Civil War.

In rejecting transcendental optimism, Melville reacted even more strongly than Hawthorne against Emerson's bland optimism. Evil, for Melville, resided not merely in the tainted heart; it hung over the world like a curtain. In *Moby Dick* (1851), perhaps this country's finest novel, Melville struck through the "pasteboard mask" of life to confront this eternal menace. Ahab, a Yankee whaling captain, the doomed hero of this great book, exhausts himself in pursuit of Moby Dick, a gigantic white whale that symbolized the beauty, evil, and mystery of nature and of life. The pursuit fails; Ahab dies. If humans were half-divine, as the transcendentalists insisted, they still faced a tragic destiny. God remained unknowable, progress an illusion.

FORMAL CULTURE AND EDUCATION

To many Americans of the Jacksonian Age, the fine arts, even more than literature, seemed particularly aristocratic; painting and sculpture were associated with the "corrupt and despotic courts" of Europe. In an environment in which few people found much usefulness in the arts, it is not surprising that someone like Samuel F. B. Morse turned to mechanical inventions after spending half his life struggling as an artist.

Fine Arts in the Jacksonian Age

Many American artists began their careers as artisans and mechanics. The sculptor Hiram Powers worked in a Cincinnati organ factory and made wax statues before turning to art as a career. Powers's work pleased the critics of the 1830s, who praised only art that was "uplifting." Artists were invited to contemplate native forests, rivers, and sunsets, which "inspired the soul of man with visions of the ideal, the beautiful, the immortal." American contemporaries of the Hudson River School painted scenic wonders on a grand scale. By 1860, a realistic school of landscape painters had emerged. They caught the character of the horses, buffalo, Indians, and white settlers on the Great Plains, the real flavor of the frontier. Among the best were George Catlin and Alfred Jacob Miller.

A change in the national attitude toward the fine arts could be observed after 1840, when wealthy patrons in the larger cities began to support talented painters, sculptors, and architects. In the two decades before the Civil War, New York City, Philadelphia, and Boston competed in establishing "academies" and "athenaeums." Artists began to exhibit their work in private and public galleries. New schools of design appeared, along with magazines devoted to the fine arts. The Gothic style of architecture was the most popular.

The ordinary citizen, meanwhile, continued to derive more enjoyment from "a carnival of wild beasts" and from huge painted panoramas, unwound from rollers, that presented the Mississippi River or historical scenes like George Washington crossing the Delaware. The depiction of native scenes sometimes attained lasting artistic merit, as in the work of John James Audubon and the famous team of Currier and Ives. By fusing science and art, Audubon produced meticulous studies of American bird and animal life. Currier and Ives flooded the country with carefree lithographs of forest and farm, railroads, sleigh rides, and skating and boating scenes.

Some moralists had stern reservations about literature and the plastic arts, and they felt even more strongly about the theater. Dramatic productions, as one of them declared, "lead the minds of youth from serious reflection." Lay preachers

Park Theatre. (*New York Historical Society*)

attacked the "vagabond profession" and the indecency of "displays of half-clad females." Despite these objections, the theater flourished. Audiences applauded everything from Shakespeare to the broadest farces. New York was the center, but cities in every section supported theaters, and stars like Edwin Forrest, Effie Ellsler, and Fanny Kemble won national popularity.

In the 1820s a peculiarly American form of entertainment, the blackface minstrel show, began to draw enthusiastic crowds in northern cities. The performers were white men, masquerading as blacks by means of burnt-cork makeup. They caricatured the songs and dances of the Afro-American slave quarters in the South. They mixed old English tunes with imitations of what they supposed was the peculiar pronunciation of blacks. They popularized the banjo—an instrument which had in fact originally come from Africa. The supposedly happy "dancing darky" was portrayed in a way that suggested blacks had scarcely a care in the world. Both the performers and the characters they played were always male. Because these minstrel shows appealed to popular prejudices about blacks, they gained wide popularity. As one of the new small group of entertainment promoters said, "I've got only one method, and that is to find out what the people want and then give them that thing. . . . There's no use trying to force the public into a theater."

The Age of Oratory

For Americans of the 1980s it is especially difficult to appreciate the importance of public speaking, of formal oratory, in pre-Civil War America. As we look back now, it seems astonishing that huge audiences should have sat and stood in rapt attention to listen to speeches that lasted for two, three,

and even four hours. Politicians like Daniel Webster spoke that long without notes, though only after hours of hard preparation. When Webster or another prominent senator spoke, the Senate gallery was crowded with attentive listeners. Abraham Lincoln's two-minute Gettysburg address was preceded by Edward Everett's two-hour oration, and many people at the time thought Everett's effort the centerpiece of that occasion. Many years earlier, after he left the presidency, John Quincy Adams had acquired the nickname Old Man Eloquent by speaking to the House of Representatives on a topic that is now nearly forgotten. The popularity of public speaking was most evident on the Fourth of July, where in cities and towns all across the country speakers carried on for an hour or more about the magnificent past and future of the nation.

These public performances reflected several aspects of the growing society. For one thing, people were accustomed to and expected long sermons in church and at camp meetings. For another, there was little other popular entertainment: no sports on TV (let alone professional games to attend) or "news" on the radio. Speechmaking provided an open door for talented men and even a few women—a door to fame as masters of the spoken word. Most Americans could name more popular orators than musicians, actors and actresses, or even authors. Speeches drew people together in enormous crowds, without electronic help, and provided opportunities for sociability and communal sharing in "uplifting" experiences.

The Popular Press

"The influence and circulation of newspapers," wrote an astonished visitor to the United States about 1830, "is great beyond anything known in

Webster on the Union

The following is an example of the kind of flowery oratory that made Daniel Webster's speeches so famous.

When my eyes shall be turned to behold, for the last time, the sun in heaven, may I not see him shining on the broken and dishonored fragments of a once glorious Union; on States dissevered, discordant, belligerent; on a land rent with civil feuds, or drenched, it may be, in fraternal blood! Let their last feeble and lingering glance, rather, behold the gorgeous ensign of the republic, now known and honored throughout the earth, still full high advanced,

its arms and trophies streaming in their original lustre, not a stripe erased or polluted, nor a single star obscured, bearing for its motto no such miserable interrogatory as, What is all this worth? Nor those other words of delusion and folly, Liberty first, and Union afterwards: but every where, spread all over in characters of living light, blazing on all its ample folds, as they float over the sea and over the land, and in every wind under the whole heavens, that other sentiment, dear to every true American heart—Liberty and Union, now and for ever, one and inseparable!

Europe. . . . Every village, nay, almost every hamlet, has its press." Even today, despite the recent tendency toward consolidation of American newspapers, the American press remains much more diversified than that of European countries.

During the first third of the nineteenth century, the number of newspapers rose from 200 to 1200. Most were weeklies. The larger cities had many daily papers, and competition was ferocious. New York City in 1830 had 47 papers, and only one daily among them claimed as many as 4000 subscribers. Enterprising editors reduced the price of their papers to a penny. They were able to produce them faster and cheaper by means of a new invention, the steam-driven rotary press. Newspapers successfully lured more readers by featuring "robberies, thefts, murders, awful catastrophes and wonderful escapes."

Benjamin Day's *New York Sun* pioneered in the new sensationalism. Day's rival, James Gordon Bennett of the *Herald*, rapidly surpassed him. Bennett played up New York "society" (he headlined his own marriage) and developed circulation techniques that were quickly copied throughout the country.

Some newspapers were sponsored by business groups and by religious organizations, but many more were devoted to the interests of a political party. Most people expected that any given newspaper was either "Democratic" or "Whig" or the organ of some other political party. No one expected neutrality in news about national politics. The ideal of "objective" reporting was entirely foreign to nineteenth-century editors and their readers.

Magazines also sprang up by the dozen, but few survived for long. With no generally accepted literary standards, always in danger of offending the prudish, yet aware of the "vulgar" preferences of their public, harassed magazine editors scarcely knew which way to turn. Many subscribers failed to pay their bills. The penny newspapers and cheap editions of pirated English books also reduced their audience. A few metropolitan monthlies or quarterlies gained national audiences—*The North American Review* (Boston), *The Knickerbocker Magazine* (New York), *Graham's Magazine* (Philadelphia), and *The Southern Literary Messenger* (Richmond). They printed pieces by such authors as Cooper, Poe, Bryant, Hawthorne, and Longfellow. Monthly agricultural journals like the *Southern Cultivator* probably had wider circulations.

Perhaps the most significant change in popular writing—in novels as well as magazines—was its increasing orientation toward women. After about 1820, more than half the novels published in the United States were written by women, often prefaced with apologies for "imposing upon the reading public a product of the weaker sex." Not only were more women writing for the general public, women as a group were becoming an identifiable and separate group of reading consumers. New magazines were published for a specifically female audience. The two that circulated most widely were *The Ladies Magazine* and *Godey's Lady's Book*, which merged under the editorship of Sarah Josepha Hale in 1836.

Sarah Hale's career was one of the most remarkable in the history of American magazine publishing. She was born in 1788, the year the Constitution was adopted. Widowed just before the birth of her fifth child, she ran a millinery shop and wrote a competent novel (*Northwood*, 1827) "literally with my baby in my arms." The next year she began editing the *Ladies' Magazine*. In her first issue she pledged that it would "mark the progress of female improvement, and cherish the effusions of female intellect." She firmly believed that women had no proper role in politics or public affairs, yet she strenuously backed the struggling new movement for higher education for women. Intensely patriotic, she urged construction of the Bunker Hill Monument and the renovation of

WORDS AND NAMES IN AMERICAN HISTORY

Sometimes a person's name becomes attached to an invention or new product, or to a new way of producing it. Unlike, say, the Ford motor car, some of these names have become extinct. When Robert Fulton designed the first commercially successful steamboats in the early 1800s, one of the first was called Fulton's Folly, because many people thought the strange thing would never work. Because of DeWitt Clinton's years of advocating and sponsoring the canal that came to be known as the Erie, skeptics called it Clinton's Ditch. And Amelia Bloomer, a temperance and women's rights advocate who became active in the 1840s, was immortalized by her call for reforms in women's dress, especially for the long, loose trousers worn under a short dress that became known and ridiculed as "bloomers."

Bloomers. (*The Granger Collection, 1841 Broadway, New York, New York*)

tion "to civil broils, or resistance to lawful authority, but commands all men to follow peace, and to obey magistrates that are set over them, whatever the form of government may be."

Despite the lip service paid to Christian, democratic, and practical education, crusaders for free schools faced an apathetic and often hostile public. Parents who could afford to educate their children in private academies saw no reason why they should be taxed to educate the children of the poor. They saw education as a benefit to their own children rather than to society in general. Administrators of private and parochial schools, farmers, and non-English-speaking groups joined in fighting the free school movement.

But the advocates of free public schools had strong arguments. Everyone would benefit, said one publicist in 1832: "The man who is poor must see that this is the only way he can secure education for his children. The man in moderate circumstances . . . will have his children taught for a less sum that he pays at present. The rich man, who will be heavily taxed, must see that his course secures to the rising generation the only means of perpetuating our institutions."

The leaders of the free school movement—Horace Mann in Massachusetts, Henry Barnard in Connecticut, and Calvin Stowe in Ohio—hammered away in widely circulated reports and articles based on thorough investigations. They began to win their battle. By 1860, most northern states had a tax-supported school program. One motive behind this movement was the itch on the part of many working-class Americans for education as a means of personal advancement. Another was the hope that free public schools would help assimilate the large number of immigrants coming to America. These European immigrants often joined the ranks of the urban poor, whose children could not afford to stop working to attend school.

Even after the establishment of free public schools, it was chiefly the middle class and not the poorer workers or farmers whose children benefited. Education on all levels continued to suffer from low salaries, rigid teaching methods, large classes, and a short school year. The one-room schoolhouse really did exist, but whether youngsters suffered or benefited from being taught in the same room with students ten years younger or older is not at all clear. Reformers suggested a variety of schemes to raise the educational level, but these usually met opposition. Yet the quality of education remained high enough to allow foreign visitors to comment on the exceptional liter-

Washington's old home at Mount Vernon. She also campaigned successfully for recognition of Thanksgiving Day as a national holiday. In addition, she wrote poems for children, including the now classic "Mary Had a Little Lamb." Though *Godey's Lady's Book* declined in quality and influence after the Civil War, in its heyday it had a circulation of 150,000, a figure that dwarfed most other American magazines. Sarah Hale finally retired at the age of seventy-nine and then, as so often happens with energetic people, died within the year.

Public Schools

During this same period there were important accomplishments in the field of education. Most Americans favored Bible teaching in the schools because, as the famous evangelical minister Lyman Beecher expressed it, the Bible gave no sanc-

Punishment for a student. (*Addison Gallery of American Art*)

acy of the American public—which was in fact the most literate in the world.

Schools began to be "graded" by age and accomplishment, and the curriculum was pushed more and more away from the classical languages toward the three Rs: reading, writing, and 'rithmetic. Formal teacher training came about largely through the work of Horace Mann, who established the first "normal schools" for the preparation of teachers, and Henry Barnard, one of the founders of the American Association for the Advancement of Education (1855) and editor of the *American Journal of Education*. Public high schools were rare until 1840, but during the next two decades the number increased, especially in Massachusetts, New York, and Ohio. Such schools offered a more practical kind of education than private schools and were open to girls and boys.

Education for Girls and Women

As opportunities for formal education broadened, young women were included—gradually and reluctantly. This was a new and radical development. Before the revolution, formal education of girls and young women had been regarded as an entirely subsidiary matter, a kind of decorative parsley on the steak of providing young men with the essentials of the ancient languages, moral philosophy, and even arithmetic. Yet many young women had always been taught how to read, since ability to read the Bible had been thought vital, especially in New England and Pennsylvania.

The successful American Revolution provided a new reason for educating women. The new republic would require an educated and virtuous citizenry. Young men would, of course, be nurtured by their mothers. How could ignorant women raise up the rising generation of young men to support the new experiment if they themselves were ignorant? So education of future mothers was crucial. Dr. Benjamin Rush, among others, insisted that the educators themselves be educated according to true republican principles.

More than a generation after the revolution, such ideas began to have an effect on formal education for young ladies. Most secondary academies did not admit girls, largely because they assumed that sufficient education would be provided at home. Emma Willard was raised on a small Connecticut farm, but her father adopted the unusual view that she was qualified to read John Locke and philosophical essays. When she was only twenty-two, she published *An Address to the Public . . . Proposing a Plan for Improving Female Education*, a pamphlet that was vigorously argued and received considerable favorable attention. In 1821 she opened the Troy (New York) Female Seminary, which proved a great and longlasting success. Young ladies there learned some polite accomplishments, but they also studied many subjects that were normally restricted to

Emma Hart Willard. (*New York Public Library*)

the better men's colleges. One of her pupils reported in the 1830s: "We had reading, writing, spelling, arithmetic, grammar, geometry, trigonometry, astronomy, natural philosophy, chemistry, botany, physiology, mineralogy, geology, and zoology in the morning; and dancing, drawing, painting, French, Italian, Spanish, and German in the afternoon. Greek and the higher branches of mathematics were only studied by the *tall* girls [i.e., the oldest ones]." Altogether, Mrs. Willard aimed at producing polished young ladies who at the same time could hold their own in the supposedly masculine intellectual world of men. Many of her pupils came from families with domestic servants, but at the school the girls made their own beds.

Mary Lyon, who came from a background similar to Emma Willard's, also founded an academy for girls. She had had the quite unusual experience of attending one of the new academies that admitted girls as well as boys. Her Mt. Holyoke Female Seminary later became a college and has good claim to being the oldest women's college in the country.

Coeducational colleges seemed, to some people, to be a logical next step. The new Oberlin College in Ohio admitted women as well as men from its start in 1837, though its women students were given an essentially second-class status, since most of them could not take Latin and none could be valedictorians. Several of the new state colleges in the West began to admit women: Michigan was the first to do so on paper in 1837, but Iowa was the first to do so in fact in 1858.

These developments in formal schooling for girls and women took place largely in the North, especially in New England and in parts of the upper West that were settled by New Englanders. Clearly the old Puritan emphasis on literacy and education was having long-term effects. Yet even in the South the winds of change were blowing. One of the country's most challenging female seminaries was in Huntsville, Alabama; and the first women's college to require both classical languages and a full four years of study was Mary Sharp College, founded in 1851 in Winchester, Tennessee.

Colleges and Lyceums

The number of so-called colleges grew from 16 in 1799 to 182 in 1860. In those same years, 412 others started and died. Colleges, said a prominent educator in 1848, "rise up like mushrooms on our luxuriant soil. They are duly lauded and puffed for a day; and then they sink to be heard of no more." The multiplication of colleges resulted in part from the difficulties and expenses of travel. But sectarian rivalry and local pride were probably the major causes.

Each important denomination and many minor ones supported one or more colleges. Most of them were hardly more than dressed-up academies which students might enter at fourteen or fifteen; so-called universities were hardly more than large colleges. Most professional schools in this period, law and medical schools in particular, were separate institutions.

College and university curriculums varied little throughout the country. Latin, Greek, mathematics, science, political economy, and moral philosophy offered a solid enough program. Teaching by rote memory was as popular at upper levels as in lower schools. Before the Civil War, a few professors found time to write and experiment, but in general the college atmosphere offered little stimulation.

Franklin, Jefferson, and other philosophers of democracy had insisted that only an educated electorate could maintain a republican government. Many, too busy or too old to go to school, continued to believe them. The most popular informal educational institution was the *lyceum*, which grew out of the proposals of an Englishman, Lord Henry Brougham. Admirers in America, spurred on by a New Englander, Joseph Holbrook, put his ideas into practice.

By 1835, lyceums could be found in fifteen states, their activities coordinated by a national lyceum organization. By 1860 more than 3000 lyceums had been set up, mainly in New England, New York, and the upper Mississippi Valley, where public school sentiment was strong. The lyceums sponsored public lectures on every conceivable topic, with scientific and practical subjects arousing greatest interest. Eminent personages like Emerson addressed lyceum audiences (women as well as men) on such themes as "Wealth" and "Power." The education that the lyceums offered was often superficial and remote from the interests of those for whom it was theoretically designed. Yet lyceums helped bridge the gulf between the learned minority and the community, and they fostered some intellectual ideals in a predominantly commercial society.

AMBIGUITY

The inclusion of young women in formal education and the beginnings of "free," tax-supported schools were in fact revolutionary. Yet historians often treat these educational developments as reflections of the new spirit of reform that swept the northern states especially, beginning about 1820 and blossoming in the 1830s and 1840s. The very term "reform" suggests going back to better days, the remedying of evils that have crept into an essentially sound system. Yet the label "the age of reform" has fastened itself on this period for good reason. Even changes in education sought to broaden participation in institutions that were regarded as crucial to the young republic, institutions and practices that needed improvement—perhaps even a little repair—but not overthrowing. The same may be said of many other reforming movements of this era, movements that sought to eliminate flaws in American society. These flaws seemed more and more in need of reformation as Americans congratulated themselves on the progress of democratic government and the ex-

AMERICAN HUMANITARIANISM

The typical American fusion of humanitarian benevolence and missionary zeal is evident in the following appeal by Samuel Gridley Howe, a leader in education for the blind.

The advantage, nay the necessity, of printing the Gospel in raised letters for the use of the blind will be apparent to every thinking Christian. Here is a large number of our fellow creatures within our reach, who might be supplied with the New Testament at small expense, compared with that laid out in sending it among distant heathens. It may be said in-

deed, that the blind can hear the Bible read by their friends, while the heathen cannot; but, on the other hand, let one consider what a precious treasure a copy of the Testament in raised letters would be to a blind man; he would pore over it, read and re-read it, until every word became familiar; and how much greater probability there would be of its producing a good effect than in the hands of those who have a thousand other things to occupy their thoughts. . . . In fine, let any pious Christian put the case to himself and say, whether he could be content with having the Scriptures read by another.

panding prosperity of their young nation.

But at the same time that Americans very generally were congratulating themselves on the increasing successes of their society, some of them began to denounce its remaining defects. The more the country seemed to improve, the more its remaining faults stood out and cried for elimination. The spirit of optimism and mastery could also cry out for innovations (such as we have just seen in education) that would even further improve an already improving society. Thus the impulses of this age of reform had a dual quality: the elimination of evil and the advancement of good. Obviously both aims pointed in the same direction.

Temperance

The first specific reform movement—and the one that enlisted by far the largest number of people—was "temperance" with alcohol, and then its prohibition. This movement was partly a response to a very real need, since the consumption of alcohol was on the rise. It has recently been shown that these reformers were dealing with a very real fact, that the American people (mostly men) were on a binge. During the period 1790–1830, they drank more alcohol than ever before or since—not in the form of "cocktails," but as hard cider, corn whiskey, wheat whiskey, rum, beer, and (for the wealthy) wine. They gulped it down in all sorts of places and on all sorts of occasions, the hard stuff often without the benefit of dilution with "branch water."

It is hard to say why this national binge took place. The causes most frequently pointed to are the increasing mobility of the American population, the breakup of families and disruption of community life, the loneliness and fatigue of the farmer, and the long hours of the industrial worker. The 1810 census claimed that there were 14,000 distilleries in the United States. In 1820, census takers would not list distilling as a separate industry, since almost everyone in rural areas engaged in it. In some cities, saloons numbered in the thousands.

The agitation against drinking was first given strong support by the publication in 1805 of Dr. Benjamin Rush's *Inquiry into the Effect of Ardent Spirits upon the Human Mind and Body*. As a physician, Rush attacked drinking for its bad effects on health. Increasingly, however, religious revivalists dominated the campaign against "demon rum." The younger temperance reformers

Five Points, New York City, 1827, a place known for drinking and other vices. (*New York Historical Society*)

The Drunkard's Progress. (*Library of Congress*)

A One-Woman Crusade

Most reform movements involved organizations. One cause, however, the treatment of the insane and feebleminded, was dominated by a single person. Dorothea Dix taught school for a time in her native Massachusetts, but a chance experience led her to challenge the widespread abuses of such "unfortunate" people. For the most part, she operated alone, though she had backing from a number of prominent New England reformers.

When she was about forty years old, Dorothea Dix undertook a personal survey of nearly every jail and almshouse in Massachusetts. It took her eighteen months. Her notebook recorded the awful conditions in which she found "lunitics" and "idiots": "confined . . . in *cages, closets, cellars, stalls, pens! Chained, naked, beaten with rods,* and *lashed* into obedience." She gathered her data into a published *Memorial to the Legislature of Massachusetts* (1843). It was a powerful and eloquent document that began with the simple statement: "I come to place before the Legislature . . . the condition of the miserable, the desolute, the outcast." It was also effective, for after much debate the Massachusetts General Court voted substantial funds for improved facilities and treatment for mentally ill and retarded people.

Heartened by this success, Dorothea Dix used the same strategy in other states. In three years

stressed its moral viciousness. Lyman Beecher and other evangelical preachers—with the support of Bible and Tract Societies and missionary boards—persuaded millions to take the pledge as "teetotalers." Beecher claimed: "Intemperance is a sin upon our land and with boundless prosperity is coming in upon us like a flood."

In 1826 the American Temperance Society was organized in Boston to coordinate the activities of hundreds of local groups. The crusaders went beyond persuasion to legislation, and from advocating moderation to insisting on abstinence. The first prohibition law was enacted in Maine in 1846, and within five years twelve other states, all in the North, had adopted some kind of liquor control law. Many people who supported such legislation were opposed to total prohibition, and their quarrels with the teetotalers weakened the movement. Yet the campaign against "ardent spirits" actually helped reduce the consumption of alcohol. The movement had enlisted "cold water armies" of children, women, and men, who marched and sang in support of abstinence. For the first time in America the crusade against alcohol led to private organization of large groups who battled in the cause of righteousness for the entire society.

Dorothea Dix. (*Library of Congress*)

she traveled 30,000 miles, as far west and south as Illinois and Mississippi. She investigated conditions, then sent one of her increasingly famous "memorials" to one state legislature after another. Her only major defeat was at the hands of the U.S. Congress itself, which thought care of the insane a matter for the states. All together she was principally responsible for the founding of thirty-two state mental institutions, and her work inspired many more in the United States and abroad in Europe.

Unlike so many reformers, Dorothea Dix remained largely devoted to a single cause. It may have been this very singlemindedness that made her one of the most directly effective humanitarian reformers of all time.

Communitarians

In the early stages of the Industrial Revolution in America, as in Britain and France, the condition of the workers often seemed so terrible that even some leading industrialists thought there ought to be an alternative. Cooperatives—even entire new cooperative communities—were one idea. Before the militant abolitionism of William Lloyd Garrison heightened feelings and hopes on the slave issue in the 1830s, the idea of black communities as an alternative to slavery also attracted followers. Of the scores of different communitarian experiments in this period, we may take three of the most controversial sorts as examples. While many of these communities were started by Americans, two Scots and a Frenchman provided considerable inspiration. One was Robert Owen, a successful manufacturer and industrial reformer from New Lanark, Scotland. He helped inspire a young Scotswoman, Frances Wright, who wrote an enthusiastic account of her travels in America (1821) which was widely read and (for the most part) well received in Great Britain as well as in America. Charles Fourier was much more a library person, a theorist who developed a somewhat eccentric proposal for a socialist society.

Robert Owen came to America in 1825 to found a community at New Harmony, Indiana, on a site he had purchased from a group of German communitarians. A number of gifted European scholars came to Owen's utopia, and for a time the community offered the best education in the country. But the rank and file had more than their share of human frailties. According to one observer, New Harmony attracted "the indolent, the unprincipled, men of desperate fortunes, moon-worshippers, romantic young men . . . those who had dreamed about earthly Elysiums, a great many honest aspirants after a better order of things, poor men simply desiring an education for their children."

Owen's experiment did fail after two years, hastened to its end more by its founder's intolerance of established social norms than by his main purpose: the establishment of a rational system of society. Owen's attack on "marriage, . . . private or individual property, . . . [and] absurd and irrational systems of religion" as a "trinity of the most monstrous evils that could be combined to inflict mental and physical evil" got him into the most trouble. Owen was classed by his critics with "whores and whoremongers," and his community was called "one great brothel."

The collapse of New Harmony in 1827 speeded the end of Nashoba, the black community set up by the Owenite Frances Wright in 1826 in Shelby County, Tennessee. Ironically, Nashoba was situated on 300 acres once forcibly taken from the Chickasaw Indians. From 50 to 100 slaves were to be taken there to earn enough money to purchase their freedom while learning the attitudes and skills needed to sustain it.

Wright, however, soon imposed on Nashoba a full-scale communitarian scheme open to whites

Frances Wright. (*National Portrait Gallery, Smithsonian Institution, Washington, D.C.*)

as well as blacks. She also went further than Owen in attacking marriage and religion. One of her lieutenants proceeded to publish in a popular magazine accounts of the free sexual relationships there. Frances Wright defended these. If "the possession of the right of free action," she said, "inspire not the courage to exercise the right, liberty has done but little for us." Nashoba did not survive long. Yet its end was happier than that of many other communities. Frances Wright sailed with Nashoba's slaves to Haiti, where they were emancipated.

Owenism had threatened middle-class Americans with free thought and free love. The doctrines of Charles Fourier seemed less dangerous, and during the 1840s were advocated by a number of talented and respectable people. The Fourierists regarded private capitalism as wasteful and degrading. If people would only abandon the ethic of competition and gather in "phalanxes," or associated groups, they could transform the world into a paradise. What particularly appealed to the Fourierists, many of whom were New England transcendentalists, was the emphasis Fourier placed on practical idealism and the dignity of the worker.

Between 1840 and 1850, Fourier's followers organized more than forty phalanxes in the United States. All had been abandoned by 1860, but one at least became a lasting legend, the subject of Hawthorne's *The Blithedale Romance*. This was Brook Farm in Massachusetts, organized by a group of transcendentalist intellectuals in 1841 and converted to Fourierism a few years later. The Brook Farmers decided to demonstrate the possibility of combining the life of the mind with manual labor.

"After breakfast," Nathaniel Hawthorne noted in his diary, "Mr. Ripley put a four-pronged instrument into my hands, which he gave me to understand was called a pitch-fork; and he and Mr. Farley being armed with similar weapons, we all commenced a gallant attack upon a heap of manure." The community, never more than 100 people, attracted about 4000 visitors a year. But its practical side proved less successful. In 1847 a fire ruined the already failing enterprise, and it was abandoned. Secular communities like Owen's, and Wright's, and Fourier's, may have failed partly because of the personalities of their promoters. Yet Americans as a rule proved too individualistic to trust their glowing private prospects to group projects.

Abolition

From the early 1830s on, the issue of slavery attracted more and more attention until it overshadowed all others. The origins of antislavery commitment lay in the mid-eighteenth century, when Quakers denounced the buying and selling of slaves. Many political leaders in revolutionary and post-revolutionary America deplored slavery. They also deplored the presence of blacks. This conviction inspired the American Colonization Society, founded in 1817 with private, state, and federal support, to establish Liberia in 1822 as an African colony for ex-slaves.

Despite the hopes of many whites, the idea of ridding the United States of black people by sending them to Africa never worked. By 1860 no more than 15,000 American blacks had been settled in Liberia, most of them ex-slaves who had been freed on condition that they go there. This number was far less than the natural increase of the American black population. The failure of the colonization plan and the ineffectiveness of those who backed gradual liberation encouraged radical abolitionists to start their campaign for immediate emancipation.

In 1831, William Lloyd Garrison began publishing *The Liberator*, an abolitionist periodical that described slavery as a hideous evil and a terrible sin. Its appearance marked the beginning of a great antislavery offensive. Garrison was a Massachusetts journalist, a gentle but somewhat neurotic man with a hatred of injustice. As with many of his followers, abolition was only one of Garrison's causes. He was an ardent worker for women's rights and international peace, an opponent of capital punishment and imprisonment for debt. But after 1830 he focused primarily on slavery.

He attacked slavery not because it was inefficient or undemocratic or unjust, but because it was sinful. Garrison shouted that slaveholders must give up their slaves immediately, since slaveholding was a sin and no one could give up sin by gradual methods. He called the Constitution, which "guaranteed" slavery by not interfering with it, "the most bloody and heaven-daring arrangement ever made by men for the continuance and protection of a system of the most atrocious villainy ever exhibited on earth." Garrison's attacks on the "Southern oppressors" did much to intensify antiabolition sentiment in the South. His fanaticism frightened moderate antislavery people everywhere. A majority of subscribers to *The Lib-*

William Lloyd Garrison. (*New York Public Library*)

erator were northern free blacks. Garrison's refusal to resort to political action also reduced his effectiveness.

A different approach was taken by Theodore Dwight Weld of Ohio, who preferred patient organization to dramatic pronouncements. His followers, well versed in the techniques of revival meetings, converted thousands to the abolitionist cause. Throughout the North, thousands of women organized "female" antislavery societies and raised money by holding "antislavery fairs," where they sold such articles as handkerchiefs embroidered with a picture of a chained, kneeling slave and the motto, "Am I Not a Man and Brother." By 1850, almost 2000 societies had been formed with a membership close to 200,000.

Though it was always a minority movement in the North, abolition had the backing of many prominent intellectuals and reformers. John Greenleaf Whittier of Massachusetts became the poet of abolition; Emerson, Thoreau, Whitman, Longfellow, and Melville all condemned slavery. Boston's Wendell Phillips thundered against it, as did ministers like Theodore Parker, William Ellery Channing, and the Quaker Lucretia Mott. Southerners like James G. Birney and the Grimké sisters renounced their slave property, and joined the antislavery forces. Many blacks who moved north—Frederick Douglass and Sojourner Truth were the most famous—worked as speakers for the cause.

Abolitionist strength lay in the movement's unselfish dedication to Christian principles. Its weakness lay in not realizing the social barriers blacks had to overcome once they were free. Practically all abolitionists opposed the idea of violent revolution by the slaves. They did not want a civil war over slavery. But in the mid-1830s, even in the North, public opinion saw the abolitionists as a band of misguided bigots whose activities on behalf of a hopelessly inferior people would destroy the nation. Many northern cities were swept by antiabolitionist riots in defiance, or with the approval, of local authorities. Garrison was dragged through the streets of Boston by an angry mob. George Thompson, an English abolitionist, was howled down and threatened with bodily harm. Elijah Lovejoy, an antislavery editor in Alton, Illinois, was murdered by a mob in 1837.

The issue of abolition was thrust onto the floor of Congress. By the mid-1830s petitions against the slave trade in the nation's capital were pouring into that body, often signed by thousands of northern men and women. The petitions raised constitutional issues. Clearly Congress had jurisdiction over the District of Columbia. Yet some petitions called for abolition of slavery in the states, even though few people thought Congress had any such power. Southern congressmen, with considerable northern support, passed a resolution in 1836 ordering that petitions relating "in any way" to slavery be immediately tabled and thus ignored.

This was the famous Gag Rule which became the target of eight years of attack by the only former President who has ever sat in the House of Representatives. John Quincy Adams, representing his home district in Massachusetts, carried on an eloquent and for a time nearly solitary war against the Gag Rule. His case had great force, since it was based on the First Amendment provision that Congress could not deny "the right of the people . . . to petition the government for a redress of grievances." Adams was not an abolitionist, though he detested slavery. As an old son of the American Revolution, however, he thought the Gag Rule itself smelled of tyranny. Finally, in 1844, Adams's campaign succeeded. The resolution was repealed.

All these petitions, in addition to more flagrant abolitionist activities, made southerners more and more uneasy. They demanded laws against antislavery activists. Southern postmasters confiscated suspected abolitionist literature. Fears of slave insurrections and resentment against atrocity stories in abolitionist propaganda caused the South to overestimate the strength of the antislavery movement in the North. This southern response only increased northern feeling. As the sectional conflict deepened, the dream of peace and justice that had stirred the hearts of the reformers in the 1830s and 1840s faded.

Yet the issue would not go away. It continued to reverberate, especially in two important arenas.

Slavery as a practice and antislavery as an ideal continued to affect all Americans, both black and white and North and South. As we will see, the question of slaveholding eventually came to dominate American politics. Even sooner, though, it became intertwined with other issues in American culture, especially the role of another subordinate group—women. Yet the position of women, and the roles of their fathers, mothers, daughters, and sons, was undergoing change that had more to do with the nation's demographic patterns, its economy and its social values than its formal politics.

SUMMARY

Antebellum America was a changing society, one in which ideals, tradition, and material progress battled for the attention and loyalty of the public. It was also a time when Americans became conscious of themselves as different—as a restless people forever chasing the dollar or a new style of life, as a people more tolerant of violence than others. Americans were also an idealistic people: equality, individualism, and opportunity remained strong ideas, despite the fact that economic forces were causing the distribution of wealth to become less equal rather than more.

Religion was still an active force in American life, but religion also had its contradictions; along with tolerance there was intolerance, and along with the unifying bond of revivalism there was sectarianism. Yet the general acceptance of democracy, private property, and Christian faith seemed somehow to give American society a national character.

In the four decades before the Civil War, the United States experienced an intellectual flowering. In New England and New York, writers such as Washington Irving, James Fenimore Cooper, and the poet Henry Wadsworth Longfellow became world figures. Edgar Allan Poe's short stories influenced later generations of poets, critics, and writers. Two compelling figures of this period were Ralph Waldo Emerson and Henry David Thoreau. Walt Whitman's poetry celebrated the new America in language that shocked his generation but foretold and influenced the work of those to come. And in the work of Nathaniel Hawthorne and Herman Melville, Americans had treasures of world literature.

The fine arts began to grow in America as well. After 1840 there was a change in the traditional distrust of the arts. Wealthy patrons in the larger cities began to support talented painters, sculptors, and architects. The theater flourished, from Shakespeare to black face minstrel shows. Newspapers boomed, and magazines sprang up by the dozen, including ones edited by and for women. In addition hundreds of public speakers—political, patriotic, and religious—held thousands of Americans spellbound in this "age of oratory."

Free public education began to spread, though its advocates had a difficult time persuading the taxpayers that it was a worthwhile investment. Horace Mann established the first normal schools to train teachers. Schools began to be graded, and the curriculum to focus not on classical languages, but on the three Rs. Colleges and lyceums grew in number as well. For the first time, some institutions sought to meet the growing demand for better educational opportunities for women.

The free school and lyceum movements were reflections of another new spirit in society, that of reform. During the 1830s and 1840s, many men and women devoted their lives to stamping out social evils or supporting social innovations: temperance with alcohol; education for the deaf, dumb, and blind; world peace, and the abolition of slavery. Dorothea Dix waged a successful one-woman campaign for better treatment of the insane and feeble-minded.

The activities of abolitionists made the South uneasy and deepened sectional conflict. When hundreds of antislavery petitions poured into Congress, the House of Representatives refused to receive them. Ex-president John Quincy Adams fought a long and lonely battle against this Gag Rule. Finally he succeeded, but soon afterwards the issue of whether slavery should be allowed to expand westward into newly acquired territories came to dominate American politics and national life.

Suggested Readings

Alexis de Tocqueville remains one of the most acute commentators on antebellum American society. R. Nye, *Society and Culture in America, 1830–1860* (1974), is an excellent introduction to the social history of the period. E. Branch, *The Sentimental Years, 1836–1860* (1934), a neglected classic, contains fascinating information on a society that was in many ways fundamentally Victorian.

D. Davis, *Homicide in American Fiction, 1798–1860* (1967), and F. Somkin, *Unquiet Eagle: Memory and Desire in the Idea of American Freedom, 1815–1860* (1967), are analytical studies of social violence and literary reflection. Some of the important individual writers are covered by the following: K. House, *Cooper's Americans* (1965); A. Quinn, *Edgar Allan Poe* (1941); M. Van Doren, *Nathaniel Hawthorne* (1949); C. Olson, *Call Me Ishmael: Herman Melville, Moby Dick and America* (1968); J. Porte, *Emerson and Thoreau: Transcendentalists in Conflict* (1966); and G. Allen, *The Solitary Singer: A Critical Biography of Walt Whitman* (1955). D. Lawrence, *Studies in Classic American Literature* (1923), is available, along with other penetrating literary studies, in a superb anthology by E. Wilson (ed.), *The Shock of Recognition* (2nd ed., 1955). F. Matthiessen, *American Renaissance: Art and Expression in the Age of Emerson and Whitman* (1941), is a brilliant interpretation of America's literary flowering; L. Marx, *The Machine in the Garden* (1964), of innocence under pressure.

O. Larkin, *Art and Life in America* (1949), covers the history of painting and sculpture. See also R. McLanathan, *The American Tradition in the Arts* (1968), an illuminating study with emphasis on the period before the Civil War. N. Harris, *The Artist in American Society: The Formative Years 1790–1860* (1968), presents a searching analysis. J. McCoubray's illustrated essay, *American Tradition in Painting* (1963), suggests the American ambivalence toward the vast and uncultivated landscape as reflected in American painting. R. Toll, *Blacking Up: The Minstrel Show in Nineteenth-Century America* (1974), is a revealing study of one of the most popular American "art" forms in this period. For the relationship between newspapers and the government, see C. Smith, *The Press, Politics, and Patronage: The American Government's Use of Newspapers, 1789–1875* (1977). For oratory, see B. Baskerville, *The People's Voice: The Orator in American Society* (1979).

P. Cohen, *A Calculating People: The Spread of Numeracy in Early America* (1983), is a sweeping study of great value. C. Kaestle, *The Evolution of an Urban School System: New York City, 1750–1850* (1973), describes the shift away from reliance on the family, the church, and apprenticeship for socializing the child, and toward formal schooling. M. Katz, *The Irony of Early School Reform: Educational Innovations in Mid-Nineteenth-Century Massachusetts* (1968), contends that early reforms served the interests of the middle class while programming working-class youngsters to acceptance of industrial work routines. S. Schultz, *Boston Public Schools, 1789–1860* (1973), includes discussion of the experience of blacks in the educational system. B. Wishy, *The Child and the Republic: The Dawn of Modern American Nurture* (1968), deals with tensions arising from the training of children to fit an increasingly competitive society. Higher education is treated in F. Rudolph, *The American College and University* (1962),

and with more specific focus in R. Hofstadter and W. Metzger, *The Development of Academic Freedom in the United States* (1955).

For a sense of the variety of antebellum reform movements; see L. Ratnor, *Pre-Civil War Reforms: The Variety of Principle and Programs* (1967). Two of the most suggestive books are much broader in scope than their titles suggest: D. Rothman, *The Discovery of the Asylum: Social Order and Disorder in the New Republic* (1971), and G. Grob, *Mental Institutions in America: Social Policy to 1875* (1973). R. Walters, *American Reformers, 1815–1860* (1978), gives a fine overview. The casualties of urbanization are evident in J. Hawes, *Children in Urban Society: Juvenile Delinquency in Nineteenth-Century America* (1971). The best place to start for the various utopian experiments is a collection of original documents: R. Fogarty (ed.), *American Utopianism* (1972). See also W. and J. Pease, *Black Utopia: Negro Communal Experiments in America* (1963).

For revivalism itself, the best introduction is W. McLoughlin, *Revivals, Awakenings, and Reform: An Essay on Religion and Social Change in America, 1607–1977* (1980). The first section of P. Miller, *The Life of the Mind in America, from the Revolution to the Civil War* (1966), is a brilliant study of the broader aspects of the evangelical impulse. T. Smith, *Revivalism and Social Reform in Mid-Nineteenth-Century America* (1957), emphasizes the importance of the cities. C. Griffin, *Their Brother's Keepers, Moral Stewardship in the United States, 1800–1865* (1960), deals with the rise of a benefactor class.

Two good studies on the temperance movement are W. Rorabaugh, *The Alcoholic Republic: An American Tradition* (1981), and I. Tyrrell, *Sobering Up: From Temperance to Prohibition in Antebellum America, 1800–1860* (1979).

The best introduction to abolitionism is R. Walters, *The Antislavery Appeal: American Abolitionism after 1830* (1976). Studies providing important information include an older collection of essays, M. Duberman (ed.), *The Antislavery Vanguard: New Essays on the Abolitionists* (1965); J. Stewart, *Holy Warriors: The Abolitionists and American Slavery* (1976); L. Perry and M. Fellman (eds.), *Antislavery Reconsidered: New Perspectives on the Abolitionists* (1979). D. Davis, *The Problem of Slavery in the Age of Revolution, 1770–1823* (1975), emphasizes international attitudes toward slavery.

Important biographies are J. Thomas, *The Liberator, William Lloyd Garrison* (1963); G. Lewis, *The Grimké Sisters from South Carolina: Pioneers for Women's Rights and Abolition* (1971); B. Wyatt-Brown, *Lewis Tappan and the Evangelical War Against Slavery* (1969). Some of the best perspectives on abolitionism have been furnished by a study of its opponents: L. Richards, *"Gentlemen of Property and Standing": Anti-Abolition Mobs in Jacksonian America* (1970); and by two works focusing on the efforts of northern blacks: B. Quarles, *Black Abolitionists* (1969), and J. and W. Pease, *They Who Would Be Free: Blacks' Search for Freedom, 1830–1861* (1974).

SOCIETY IN THE NORTH

Chapter 13

Most of the developments described in the previous chapter took place in the northern states that had gradually done away with slavery. From about 1820 to the outbreak of the Civil War in 1861, the slave states south of the Mason-Dixon Line began to take a separate road. There, the notion of reform and change was smothered by devotion to the status quo. James Madison and several others among the Founding Fathers had suggested that the slave/agricultural southern states had different interests from those of the free/commercial states of the North, and Madison predicted that the two regions might have difficulty in maintaining a stable union. His fears about an eventual rift proved well founded. But neither he nor any of his contemporaries foresaw how different the two regions would become.

The northern states became increasingly prosperous, expansive, and committed to manufacturing, efficient transportation, new technology, and even the mechanization of agriculture. The southern states became increasingly defensive about slavery, while people in the North became convinced that free wage labor and the family farm were the proper foundations for the young republic. Yet the tendencies that prevailed in the North also existed in the South. No one in either section fully understood that fundamental demographic changes were taking place in American society. ■

DEMOGRAPHIC CHANGE

The Growth of Cities

There were several such demographic changes. They were all important, but they affected American society in different ways. One was the rapid growth of cities. Before the revolution, the largest urban areas were, by modern standards, nothing more than small towns. The growth of those settlements was astounding. This explosion may be seen in the table below. If we take the U.S. Census Bureau's traditional definition of "urban" as population centers of 2,500 or more, in the year 1790, 5 percent of the U.S. population was urban. By 1860, that figure had risen to 25 percent.

While tables and percentages give some information about the actual and relative growth of cities, they say nothing about what it was like to live in them. Because cities like New York grew so rapidly, they were unable to keep up with needs for adequate supplies of unspoiled food; the disposal of garbage and of human and animal waste; drinkable water; public transportation; adequate housing; and protection against crime. While these services (which many of us today take for granted) lagged, the pattern of settlement in cities began to reflect differences in wealth. Poor people began to crowd into certain areas. The wealthier enjoyed far more space in their neighborhoods.

While this pattern of settlement had prevailed in urban areas for centuries, the sheer size of the new cities emphasized the distinctions between wealthy and poor neighborhoods. Wealthy families got the new urban services first—their garbage and trash was carried away and fresh water brought in by pipes from the new pumping stations. The poor—who were often recent immigrants from Europe—got garbage and refuse in the street, outdoor privies, and fresh water from a single public pump a block or more away from their tiny tenement apartments. Public transportation, which consisted of horse-drawn trolleys and steam railways, became a necessity because of the huge distances in these sprouting cities. Police protection, such as it was, was expanded and regularized, but the streets of New York and other large cities were probably no safer at night than they are in the 1980s.

The Dynamics of Population Growth

The growth of American cities was startling, but no more so than the growth of the American population as a whole. Nothing is more important to an understanding of American culture in this period than an appreciation of this astonishing expansion. Nothing like it had ever occurred in historic times in Europe and probably in Africa. On the eve of the American Revolution the population of the thirteen colonies was less than 2.5 million, a figure considerably smaller than the total number of people today sitting in college stadiums across the country on any given Saturday afternoon during the football season. By 1790, the first year of the national census required by the Constitution, the U.S. population had risen to 4 million. By 1830, during Jackson's first administration, it had more than tripled to 13 million. On the eve of the Civil War it was 32 million, making the United States roughly as populous as Great Britain and even France.

Sheer numbers do not tell us very much, but a little common sense will suggest certain powerful effects that this growth had on all Americans. An exploding population contributed to westward expansion. It fueled economic growth by providing an expanding workforce which provided a growing number of consumers. It created mounting demands for transportation, housing, food, education, consumer goods, banking and other financial services, and means of communication.

POPULATION OF LARGEST U.S. CITIES, 1820 AND 1860

1820		1860	
New York and Brooklyn	130,000	New York and Brooklyn	1,079,000
Philadelphia	112,000	Philadelphia	565,000
Baltimore	62,000	Baltimore	212,000
Boston	43,000	Boston	177,000
New Orleans	27,000	New Orleans	168,000
Charleston	24,000	Cincinnati	161,000
		St. Louis	160,000

(If this table were to be expanded to include somewhat smaller cities, the concentration of urbanization in the free North would be even more apparent.)

Of course, today we are well aware that an exploding population can result in economic stagnation, poverty, and famine. Such situations are tragically common in many parts of the world. But the United States was then blessed with an enormous abundance of natural resources that made for a rising rather than falling standard of living. The principal resource was land, staggering amounts of it. Americans were able to extract enormous wealth from the land partly by means of technological innovation (as we shall see), but partly because there were so many people, year after year, to do the work and consume its bounty.

An expanding population had other effects, more subtle but no less important. It lay at the base of the kind of "mass politics" that emerged in the Jacksonian era, most conspicuously in the Log Cabin campaign of 1840. It did a great deal to make local individual misfortunes and injustices seem like societal problems that cried out for "reform." It complicated people's lives by creating the loneliness and anonymity that characterizes so much of modern life. At the same time it generated a general mood of exhilaration: America was growing in wealth, power, and maturity. And by analogy with budding crops, suckling calves, and squalling babies, who could doubt that growth was anything but improvement?

Another effect of this expansion has often gone unnoticed: The American population was beginning to age, though not nearly so fast as it has recently. In 1790 half of the American people were younger than sixteen. On the eve of the Civil War, the median age (the age at which half the people were younger and half older) was between nineteen and twenty. This was the beginning of a trend that has accelerated dramatically in recent years: Today the median age of Americans is about thirty-two.

What generated this rapid growth of the American population? Two obvious possible causes may be ruled out. While the birth rate remained high, it was (as we will see shortly) actually dropping steadily during this period and continued to do so long after the Civil War. The death rate remained roughly constant, and infant mortality still hovered at a level that was ten times today's. There were no notable advances in medical practices and care, and sanitation problems and overcrowding made the cities less healthy than rural areas—as had been true throughout human history. The driving engine behind the nation's population was the arrival of massive numbers of people from northwestern and central Europe.

Immigration

The rate of European immigration had picked up after the wars in Europe and America that ended in 1815. Immigration from Africa had been slowed to an illegal trickle by the federal ban on the Atlantic slave trade in 1808. After 1830 immigrants arrived at an increasing rate until the depression that began with the Panic of 1837. Then, in the mid-1840s, Europeans poured into northern ports and New Orleans in unprecedented numbers. The return of prosperity in the United States combined with an agricultural disaster and political persecution in parts of Europe to provide the classic pull-and-push that so often accounts for major human migrations.

In 1845 Catholic Irish peasants were devastated by a blight that struck the potato crops, the main-

WORDS AND NAMES IN AMERICAN HISTORY

There are numerous American folktales about frontier boatmen and woodsmen who called themselves *half-horse, half-alligator*. These were men who bragged about their toughness and bragged about bragging about it in exaggerated terms. The phrase *half-horse, half-alligator* came to be a kind of shorthand for referring to frontiersmen in general, but particularly those of Kentucky and Tennessee. Davy Crockett was one. He was born in Tennessee and died at the Battle of the Alamo in 1836. The standard reference work, the *Dictionary of American Biography*, begins all its entries with the occupations of the person whose biography is being sketched: Crockett's entry gives his sole occupation as "frontiersman," even though he served in the U.S. Congress. One of his contemporaries claimed that Crockett said the following: "I'm that same David Crockett, fresh from the backwoods, half horse, half alligator,—a little touched with the snapping turtle; can wade the Mississippi, leap the Ohio, ride upon a streak of lightening, and . . . whip my weight in wildcats, and if any gentleman pleases, for a ten dollar bill, he may throw in a panther,—hug a bear too close for comfort, and eat any man opposed to Jackson." Historians have difficulty with such legendary quotations, because Crockett ran for office on a specifically anti-Jackson program.

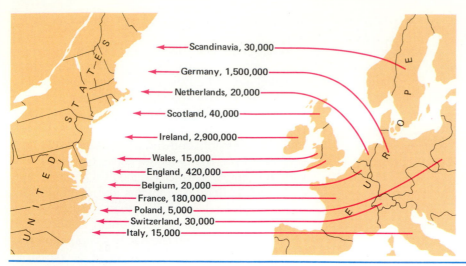

Immigration, 1840–60

stay of their miserable diets. The blight brought famine that was only partly relieved by massive emigration to America. In the following decade, about 1.3 million Irish fled to the United States. Though bred to the land rather than urban life, they were usually too poor to move inland from the coastal cities where they landed, though some traveled west as laborers with canal and railroad-building crews. An only slightly smaller wave of immigrants came from Germany, driven by religious and political persecution and by poverty. Some 940,000 Germans arrived, many of whom settled in midwestern cities such as Cincinnati, St. Louis, and Milwaukee. During that same decade, immigrants from Britain numbered about 375,000. Thousands of Scandinavians also came, along with smaller groups of Dutch, Swiss, Belgians, French, and Czechs.

All told, between 1844 and 1854 almost 3 million immigrants braved the Atlantic crossing. That figure amounted to three-fifths of the total immigration into the United States between 1815 and the beginning of the Civil War in 1861. The great majority of the newcomers avoided the South. Many were young, unmarried adults, which helps account for the rising age of the American population. Others came in family groups, among them independent, outspoken middle-class businessmen, lawyers, doctors, scientists, and journalists. They brought new skills, new learning, and new styles of leadership. The majority, however, were peasant families. Irish Roman Catholics usually remained in northeastern cities, especially Boston and New York. In 1855, more than half the population of New York City was foreign-born. The Germans, often led by their old-country pastors,

tended to settle in the Midwest, though some established communities in the western parts of the South, especially in Texas. By 1860, 30 percent of the population of Wisconsin and Minnesota was foreign-born.

Because so many people participated in this migration, it is hard to generalize about their experiences. Most of them endured a voyage across the Atlantic that normally lasted more than a month. They slept and ate below decks in foul weather, though when the wind and seas were fair they could stand on lurching decks, bracing themselves on the rails, and watch the unmarked white tassels of the endless waves that accompanied their passage from a familiar way of life toward one of unknown promise.

That promise usually differed from their expectations. On the wharves, as they got their shorelegs back, these newcomers were often victimized by hucksters of all kinds who gave false promises of immediate food, housing, jobs, and hundreds of acres of farming land somewhere in the West—all for a price. It is scarcely any wonder that the newcomers were confused and found it hard to make their way. It is no wonder that these European peasants huddled into city tenements, trying to reestablish their old communal ties, or did the same, with better luck and better leadership, in the rural West.

In the cities especially, they were greeted with outright hostility. They found it hard to get jobs. Often they saw the notice: "No Irish Need Apply." In turn, the Irish came to look down on free blacks. The new immigrants actually squeezed out many blacks, even from the dirtiest and lowest-paying jobs. And the Irish were not segregated or refused transportation on public streetcars.

In large part the Irish met hostility because they were Roman Catholic. The United States was becoming a nation of even greater religious and ethnic diversity than ever before. Despite their traditional tolerance of such diversity, native-born Americans had long prided themselves on being a Protestant Christian people. Hostility to Roman Catholicism was so widespread that it eventually formed, as we will see later, the basis of a major political movement.

AMERICAN WOMEN

The Declining Birth Rate

In the early 1800s, American women began to bear fewer and fewer children. The birth rate began to drop slowly but steadily until well into the twentieth century. Without immigration, the rate of population growth would have slowed appreciably. This dropping birth rate partially accounts for the rising median age of the population, though the immigration of so many people in their late teens and early twenties also contributed to the phenomenon.

The birth rate dropped fastest in the cities, but it dropped in rural areas as well, in the South as well as the North. It declined faster among native-born than immigrant Americans. There seems to have been no marked increase in completely childless families, though there was a slight rise in the proportion of spinsters or "old maids"—women who never married at all. But that statistical creature, the average mother, was having fewer children; six in 1800, five in 1860, and four in 1900.

But these facts do not do much to explain the causes of this new and obviously important social development. Those causes appear to have been linked with changes in the economy and especially with changing roles, expectations, and values among American mothers. These changes seem to have affected middle- and upper-class women more than the ranks of the poor. Though historians have only recently taken an interest in the matter and are not in complete agreement about it, the evidence suggests that American women felt pressure to limit the number of their children and, with or without cooperation from their husbands, were taking deliberate steps to do so.

One important pressure came from the changing economic role of the family. In the more crowded eastern rural areas, large numbers of children were more a burden than a benefit if there was not enough land to divide among them as they grew to maturity. This was especially the case in New England, though the use of children in the cotton mills helped offset rural overcrowding. In the larger cities, children could not contribute to the productive chores that normally went with farming. Indeed they could easily become an economic burden, especially as the school year lengthened for those who could go to school. In the society as a whole, westward migration played a part in making young children seem a drag on a family's fortunes. Pulling up stakes for months of hard traveling did not make two- and four-year-olds seem much of a welcome asset.

Prevailing new ideas and values about motherhood also played a part in this development. During the revolution there was a perceptible shift toward a popular view that motherhood was a domestic, hearthside role, that "the Mother" of a family carried the heavy burden of shaping the early educational, religious, and moral development of the children in order to prepare them for their roles as citizens of a virtuous republic. Here, as they so often do, economic changes dovetailed with changing values. With an increasingly complex and commercial economy, the father's work was more often separated from the home. If father was more often away, whether marketing the products of his farm or at the shop, then mother's role at home took on added importance.

A growing body of popular literature emphasized what has been called a "cult of domesticity" for women. Writers like Lydia Maria Child churned out books of advice for homemakers. Male physicians published advice manuals warning of the dangers of repeated childbirth. In fact, the dangers were not new and indeed they were very real, but the suggestion that wives avoid having too many children was new.

The term *birth control* had not yet come into use. The phrase would have shocked most Americans of this era, but in fact various folk methods toward that end were being practiced. What is especially striking is that deliberate "birth control" came before—and not as the result of—either public advocacy of the practice or any technological or medical innovations. The first little books that suggested and talked around, more than about, the practice were published in the early 1830's. Dr. Charles Knowlton, an English physician, published *Fruits of Philosophy* in 1831. Its appearance in the United States is often cited as the first American birth control manual. It is clear that some couples were starting to fear the consequences of sexual intercourse and also to engage in it less frequently. Yet at the same time that women were being placed on a pedestal, there was a rise in the use of prostitutes by middle-class men.

The practice of abortion seems to have been becoming more common, both by crude home methods and by actual "operations" by physicians. Several states for the first time passed laws against abortion, though the matter received nothing like the national attention it has had in very recent years.

The cult of motherhood and domesticity was a powerful one. Many women accepted the prevail-

ing value that "woman" was endowed with weaker intellect than "man," even though blessed with special talents for religious piety and moral purity. Yet just when this valuation of women was being advanced most fulsomely in press and pulpit, there were signs of dissent and even outright revolt.

At the same time that woman's place was being so widely defined as "in the home," many women, especially in the North, were in fact getting out of the home. This fact suggests that the prevailing ethic reflected anxiety about what was actually going on. During the first three decades of the nineteenth century, middle-class women in the North began to form church auxiliary groups. They met together in pious causes. The temperance movement also attracted women who formed

Margaret Fuller astonished many people during the reform era, especially men. She achieved her great reputation, not as a reformer, but as an intellectual adventurer. As a transcendentalist, editor, critic, author, and brilliant conversationalist, she awed famous intellectuals like Emerson. Having been pushed to master Latin by the age of 7, she later recalled: "Very early I knew that the only object in life was to grow." (*Library of Congress*)

their own organizations to advance that good work. In the larger cities, women started Magdalene Societies with the purpose of rescuing their unfortunate sisters who had fallen into lives of prostitution. In addition, more and more women were becoming schoolteachers. All these activities reflected the prevailing view that woman's sphere was essentially moral and nurturing, but the fact was that influential women were taking jobs and forming organizations on their own, away from the family hearth.

This quiet process went almost unnoticed until abolition burst on the scene in the 1830s. Some women enthusiastically joined that cause and then quite rapidly began to see similarities between the conditions of the slave and their own. Virtually all the women who became famous in the crusade for women's rights began their careers in the abolitionist movement. As Abby Kelley Foster said: "We have good cause to be grateful to the slave for the benefit we have received ourselves, in working for him. In striving to strike his irons off, we found most surely, that we were manacled ourselves."

At first, in the 1830s, the women's movement took aim against laws that reflected prevailing ideas about male dominance and superiority. At law, women were placed at the severe disadvantages accurately described by an eminent judge as late as 1860.

A married woman cannot sue for her services, as all she earns legally belongs to the husband, whereas his earnings belong to himself, and the wife legally has no interest in them. Where children have property and both parents are living, the father is the guardian. In case of the wife's death without a will, the husband is entitled to all her personal property and to a life interest in the whole of her real estate to the entire exclusion of her children, even though this property may have come to her through a former husband and the children of that marriage still be living. If a husband die without a will, the widow is entitled to one-third of the personal property and to a life interest in one-third only of the real estate. In case a wife be personally injured, either in reputation by slander, or in body by accident, compensation must be recovered in the joint name of herself and her husband, and when recovered it belongs to him. . . . The father may by deed or will appoint a guardian for the minor children, who may thus be taken entirely away from the jurisdiction of the mother at his death. . . .

The women's rights movement at first focused on these disadvantages much more than on the radical notion of women's right to vote. The cause of abolition triggered their awareness that they suffered from social and legal discriminations that had nothing to do with electoral politics. Thus the abolition movement raised the issue of whether women could properly participate in what were called "promiscuous assemblies"—public meetings attended by both sexes.

Angelina and Sarah Grimké were probably the best-known public speakers. Both sisters moved north from South Carolina because of their unpopular antislavery views. Their outspokenness in the cause of abolition drew fire from northern clergymen who thought women ought to remain silent on matters of public interest and policy. A large group of New England ministers mounted a direct attack on their efforts in 1838:

"We appreciate the unostentatious prayers of women advancing the cause of religion at home and abroad; in Sabbath-schools . . . in all such associated efforts as become the modesty of her sex. . . . But when she assumes the place and tone of a man as a public reformer . . . she yields the power which God has given her for her protection, and her character becomes unnatural."

Such opposition was widespread; the number of men willing to back the cause of women's rights was very small. Those who did, such as Garrison and James Mott, risked ridicule. It was left to a small but growing number of women to speak out

Elizabeth Cady Stanton. (*National Portrait Gallery, Smithsonian Institution, Washington, D.C.*)

on their own behalf. They did so with vigor and eloquence. Sarah Grimké declared in 1838:

[Man] has done all he could to debase and enslave her mind; now he looks triumphantly on the ruin he has wrought and says, the being he has thus deeply injured is his inferior . . . I ask no favors for my sex. I surrender not our claim to equality. All I ask of our brethren is that they will take their feet from off our necks, and permit us to stand upright on the ground which God has designed us to occupy.

As time went on, women's rights became a campaign in its own right, independent from, yet still connected with, the abolition movement. In 1848 Lucretia Mott and Elizabeth Cady Stanton organized a Woman's Rights Convention at Seneca Falls, New York. The resulting Declaration of Sentiments was deliberately modeled on an earlier Declaration: "We hold these truths to be self-evident: that all men and women are created equal. . . ." The convention was attended by 68 women and 32 men. It was characteristic of the movement as a whole that the only resolution not passed unanimously was a demand for women's suffrage.

These middle-class women were bucking not only active opposition, but common cultural assumptions about their proper place in society. During no other period of American history was so much written about woman's proper character and sphere of influence. Her place was in the home, where she was supreme. In this prevailing view, her naturally refined nature made her first duty the moral nurture of her children and the gentle encouragement of her husband, who was said to be overly busy at the countinghouse or even, alas, at the tavern. Most women accepted this role. But the demands of a vocal minority suggested that there was growing discontent on the pedestal.

For working-class women, the issues were very different. A grueling 14-hour day in a factory was an issue in itself. In 1844 five women workers organized the Lowell Female Labor Reform Association, which joined with male workers in the growing movement for the 10-hour day. Within a year, 600 women in Lowell alone had joined the association. It was in the 1840s too that Sarah Bagley became the editor of *The Voice of Industry*, the most widely read labor newspaper of the time.

Perhaps the most remarkable perspective on the problems faced by women was provided by Sojourner Truth, the ex-slave who became a popular speaker for abolition and women's rights. She told a women's rights convention in 1851:

WHAT DO WOMEN WANT?

In 1849 Lucretia Mott delivered a speech in Philadelphia which was published as "Discourse on Women." In answer to a man who had ridiculed the idea of female equality, she declared:

The question is often asked, "What does woman want more than she enjoys? What is she seeking to obtain? Of what rights is she deprived? What privileges are withheld from her?" I answer, she asks nothing as favor, but as right; she wants to be acknowledged a moral, responsible being. She is seeking not to be governed by laws, in the making of which she has no voice. She is deprived of almost every right in civil society, and is a cipher in the nation, except in the right of presenting a petition. In religious society her disabilities, as already pointed out, have greatly retarded her progress. Her exclusion from the pulpit or ministry—her duties marked out for her by her equal brother man, subject to creeds, rules, and disciplines made for her by him— this is unworthy of her true dignity. In marriage there is assumed superiority, on the part of the husband, and admitted inferiority, with a promise of obedience, on the part of the wife. This subject calls loudly for examination, in order that the wrong may be redressed.

James and Lucretia Mott. (*Friends Historical Library of Swathmore College*)

Sojourner Truth. (*National Portrait Gallery, Smithsonian Institution, Washington, D.C.*)

western portions of the free states. Mechanized agriculture first became widespread in the United States on the free family farms of the northern prairies and the eastern edges of the Great Plains. This enormously fertile country stretched from upper Indiana and Illinois north to central Wisconsin and Minnesota, then westward through Iowa and upper Missouri to the townships of eastern Kansas and Nebraska. Even more than the southern coastal plains, this flat, nearly treeless, and lush terrain invited the large-scale farming that characterizes the twentieth century.

Most settlers in this region were independent small farmers from the British Isles and Continental Europe or from neighboring states to the east. In the mid-1840s, new settlements blossomed. Germans especially moved directly into the Middle West. Technical innovations helped the development of large-scale farming. Soon farmers found themselves dealing with the profits and problems of producing for distant markets. In the East, the continued rapid growth of the urban population affected agricultural practices.

Tens of thousands of farm families in the Ohio Valley and on the borders of Lake Erie and Lake Michigan had been struck by the worldwide depression of the early 1840s. Debts forced them to

That man over there says that women need to be helped into carriages, and lifted over ditches, and to have the best place everywhere. Nobody ever helps me into carriages, or over mud-puddles, or gives me any best place! And ain't I a woman? . . . I have borne thirteen children, and seen them most all sold off to slavery, and when I cried out with my mother's grief, none but Jesus heard me! And ain't I a woman?

THE AGRICULTURAL REVOLUTION

As a former slave who had escaped the South, Sojourner Truth reflected a growing sectional division in the nation. Her words indirectly revealed how far apart the two sections were drifting. Economic forces especially were creating a bedrock of difference that was generating two kinds of value systems.

Westward Expansion

These forces were changing the pattern of work in both sections. In the North, agriculture was becoming hitched to the machine, especially in the

Settlement of the Middle West

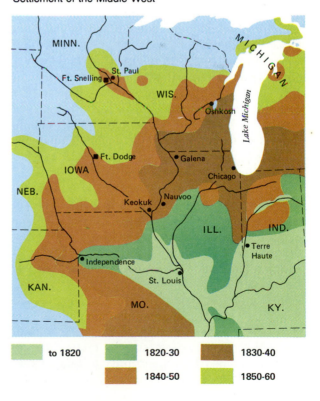

| | to 1820 | | 1820-30 | | 1830-40 |
| | 1840-50 | | 1850-60 |

sell their cleared and cultivated homesteads to newcomers.

The government's liberal land policy encouraged them to try again farther west. They migrated in such numbers that Iowa became a state in 1846, Wisconsin in 1848, and Minnesota in 1858. Admission of Kansas was delayed until 1861 for political reasons.

Groups of families sometimes settled a particular region. But even here, the whole territory being so vast, farms often were a day's travel or more apart. One reason for choosing isolated sites was the settlers' suspicion of intruders. Yet the diaries of women in this migration reveal a profound sense of loneliness. Many settlers plunked themselves down far apart partly because they hoped to add more land to the quarter section with which they usually started.

For most of the fifteen years before the Civil War, these pioneer families traveled on foot, hauling or pushing handcarts piled with their few possessions. Those who could afford the expense made the journey in wagons pulled by oxen, and crowded onto barges on the Erie Canal or the boats of the western rivers and Great Lakes. Many of them suffered from the "ague," as the intermittent attacks of malaria were called.

Having picked the land and registered it at the nearest land office, farming families built a one-room log cabin or, in treeless country, a hut made of slabs of sod and a barn of the same material. They turned out a few sheep, cows, and oxen to graze on the wild buffalo grass, and fenced them off as best they could from the vegetable garden. Once he had fenced in his main fields, at a cash outlay of $1 or $1.25 an acre, a farmer could begin cultivation. His first discovery was that his plow could hardly scratch the heavily matted virgin soil. So at a further cost of $1.75 to $2.50 per acre, he hired professional "breakers," teams of men with huge iron plows drawn by oxen, to cut the first shallow furrows on the prairie.

In following seasons, the farmer and his family would be able to plow and plant the land broken by the professionals. But the pioneers could hope to cultivate no more than an acre and a half a day; there was no possibility of one family fully cultivating an entire 160-acre section. But men who had moved their families with the idea of reestablishing an independent way of life based on self-help and Christian zeal were nonetheless quite satisfied. The sheer fertility of the soil soon inundated the pioneers with surplus crops. Many of them welcomed the opportunity to market their produce for cash and to buy more land. Every farming family seemed to want to move on from the crude log cabin or musty sod hut to a neat frame house with proper furniture and a touch of color in a table covering, a window curtain, or a picture on the wall.

Growing Markets and Production

These pioneer farmers were in fact the vanguard and support of a worldwide business surge. The increasingly industrial nations of Europe, no longer able to feed their growing urban populations, were beginning to lower tariffs on agricultural produce and to simplify procedures of international monetary exchange. It began to dawn upon observers on both sides of the Atlantic that the United States could serve as Europe's granary, with profit for everyone.

Nor was the business ferment restricted to Europe. After 1844, American ships and the vessels of other nations enjoyed new concessions in the treaty ports of China. In 1854, Commodore Matthew Perry, with a show of American naval power, opened up Japan to American trade. In 1856, Siam (modern Thailand) broadened the privileges given twenty years before to United States exporters. And all this stirring in the Pacific warmed American interest in Hawaii.

The Orient never became a market for American farms or for more than a fraction of the products of American factories. Yet Oriental trade contributed to American aspirations toward world power. It helped transform the American merchant marine into the world's largest fleet and its home ports into booming metropolises where, as in the great cities of Europe, millions clamored to be fed.

In the West itself, farmers were finding markets at frontier forts. They sold to loggers who had recently opened up the north woods of Wisconsin and Minnesota and to lead miners who, after the 1830s, extended their operations from Illinois into Wisconsin and Iowa. Gold-mining camps farther west had also begun to look to nearby farmers for flour and meal.

From the beginning of the westward movement, corn was always the frontier farmer's first marketable crop. Easily converted into fattened hogs (which were commonly turned loose in the cornfields to "hog down" the ripened ears), corn could be made to walk to market. Corn also served as winter feed for beef cattle. For human consumption, corn was distilled into "likker," eaten off the cob, baked into bread, and prepared in many other ways.

Wheat was far more selective than corn in soil and climate. Even in suitable latitudes, it grew best on land that had already produced a corn crop. In 1849, Pennsylvania, Ohio, and New York were the leading wheat states. Ten years later, the country's total wheat production had soared 75 percent, and Illinois, Indiana, and Wisconsin had moved to the head of the wheat states. In succeeding decades, reflecting the momentum of the westward surge of wheat growing, first Iowa, then Minnesota, then Kansas, and then the Dakotas became the leaders.

Acre for acre, wheat paid better than corn, over which it had advantages both in marketing and production. Unlike corn, wheat was eaten all over the world. Less bulky than corn in relation to value, it could bear high transportation costs more easily. It also withstood shipment more successfully. Finally, on the open prairies and plains, where land was plentiful but labor scarce, wheat production responded to improved tools and labor-saving machinery.

The Business of Mechanized Farming

In 1837, John Deere, an Illinois blacksmith, produced the first American steel plow. By 1858, after making many improvements on his original design, he was manufacturing 13,000 a year. Light enough for a strong man to sling over his shoulder, the Deere plow could cut deep, clean furrows in the prairie sod. Nor did it take oxen to draw it. The weaker but faster-moving horse began to replace the ox on western farms.

So great was interest in plow improvement that by the time of the Civil War 150 varieties of plows were on the market. Experimenters were working on steam-powered "plowing engines" that could cut as many as six furrows at once.

Even more striking improvements were being made in machines designed for wheat growing. Cyrus McCormick of Virginia and Obed Hussey of Ohio patented practical steel-tooth reapers in the early 1830s. With McCormick's horse-drawn machine a single man could do the work of five men equipped with scythes. Sales lagged until McCormick moved his plant to Chicago in 1848. Ten years later, by means of interchangeable parts, McCormick was producing 500 reapers a month and still not meeting the demand.

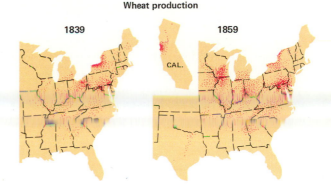

Wheat production

1839   1859

Each dot equals 100,000 bushels

Wheat Production, 1839 and 1859

The standardized parts were packed and shipped directly to the farmer, along with printed instructions on how to assemble them. At first, entire neighborhoods had to be mobilized to harvest the vast quantities of wheat the new reapers could cut down. But in the 1850s progress was being made in the design of mechanical wheat binders, and mechanical threshers were already in use. In 1800, the average American farmer spent about $15 to $20 for tools. By 1857, *Scientific American* was recommending that every farmer with 100 acres of land should have machinery worth about $600.

Once the western farmer had committed himself to machinery, his life was greatly changed. The most disturbing change came from the discovery that he was suddenly in the grip of forces over which he had little control. His principal machines, for example, such as reapers and threshers, could speed the production of wheat. But they could be used for little else when the wheat market fell off. The fact that he usually purchased these machines on credit further narrowed the farmer's range of choice.

Debts eventually had to be paid in cash; and wheat, the specialty of the new machines, was also the best cash crop. Falling wheat prices forced him to grow more wheat than ever, to get as great a cash return as at higher prices. But increasing wheat production often meant breaking or buying new land, which plunged farmers still more deeply into debt.

The continuous round of specialization, mechanization, and expansion in the free West gave a momentum to wheat production that was a priceless boon to the world. Other aspects of wheat growing, however, were hardly good for the farmer. In some years, frost, hail, and windstorms far more severe than in the East destroyed the crop before it could be harvested. Even in the best growing seasons, the servicing of distant new markets seemed to involve an endless spiral of new charges. The steps between the wheat grower and the ultimate urban consumer, for example, seemed to multiply with distance.

All along the line, weighers, graders, storage-elevator operators, rail and water carriers, warehouses, local haulers, insurers, moneylenders, and speculators—the whole apparatus of finance and distribution—mysteriously placed a hand on the farmer's fate and in his pocket. The worldwide collapse of prices in 1857 staggered the wheat farmer. In 1858, western farmers began attending protest meetings. The farmer's special place in God's plan received publicity, and farmers were urged to "assert not only their independence but their supremacy" in society. Vague proposals also began to be made for farm cooperatives and for state and federal control of railroads and other big businesses.

Out of it all, before the Civil War, came a stronger demand for two specific programs. One, a favorite among reformers, was for agricultural colleges to educate farm youth in the science of agriculture and to give them broader educational opportunities as well. These colleges were to be set up by the federal government and financed by federal land grants. The second demand, with far broader backing among farmers, was for free homesteads—free of payment and free of slaves—on the remainder of the public domain.

Over southern opposition, Congress enacted a land-grant college bill in 1859, only to have President Buchanan veto it. In June 1860 he vetoed a homestead bill that would have made western lands available at 25 cents an acre. In the elections later that year, the farmers of the West, with the slogan "Vote Yourself a Farm," helped carry the country for Lincoln.

Agricultural Revolution in the East

Right up to the outbreak of the Civil War, southern planters remained active customers of the western farmers. But the great bulk of western grain and meat flowed to the swelling population of the Northeast. So great did this volume become that the agricultural revolution in the West forced upon the East an agricultural revolution of its own.

Let the West "supply our cities with grain," said a Massachusetts man in 1838: "We will manufacture their cloth and their shoes." But he went on to point out that eastern farms could supply "what cannot so well be transported from a distance," products like meat, butter, and vegetables. What he had foreseen developed with a rush in the following twenty years not only in New England, but also on the more friendly soil of other northeastern states. Two foodstuffs he did not list became the most profitable of all—milk and fruits.

Dairying, once a routine chore in most households, had become big business by 1850. In that year, the Harlem Railroad brought about 25 million quarts of milk into New York City. Every other sizable city in the East had developed its own "milk shed," a nearby expanse of pasture land where carefully bred and carefully tended herds of cows were reared for milk production.

Fruit orchards in the East were as common as pastures. Strawberries, blackberries, and many varieties of melons added interest to the urban American's diet. The tin can, an English invention for packaging perishables, became widely used by American fruit and vegetable merchants in the late 1840s, greatly enlarging their markets.

A revival of scientific farming in the East furthered the agricultural revolution in that section. With success depending more and more on special knowledge and the latest processes, eastern farmers took a keen interest in information about climate, soils, fertilizers, methods of cultivation, and the differences among crops. Agricultural associations, fairs, magazines, books, courses, and schools multiplied. Thus the Northeast joined the Northwest in a spurt of agricultural innovation that placed the United States in a position of world leadership in the production of food.

TRANSPORTATION AND TRADE

The agricultural revolution helped the nation's position in the international marketplace; it also contributed to the growth of domestic trade. The huge territory of the United States was turning into a giant common market, its development free of the customs duties the various nations of Europe used to protect their own markets and products.

Foreign Trade

One of the most important commercial developments of the 1840s and 1850s was the revitalization of America's overseas trade. During the

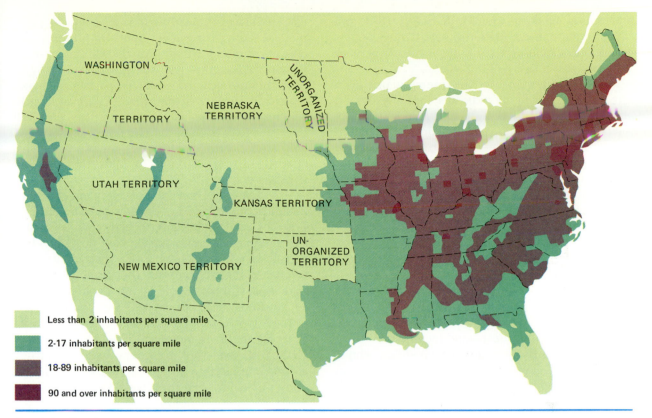

Population Density, 1860

▢	Less than 2 inhabitants per square mile
▢	2–17 inhabitants per square mile
▢	18–89 inhabitants per square mile
▢	90 and over inhabitants per square mile

depression that followed the crash of 1837, foreign trade had fallen to a point well below the level of the early years of the republic. In 1843, combined imports and exports were only $125 million. Then began an almost continuous rise to a record $687 million in 1860.

In almost every year during this period, imports exceeded exports. Eighty percent of the half-billion dollars in gold taken from the California mines before 1857 was sent abroad to make up the difference. The increasing export of western wheat and flour helped keep the imbalance within reasonable limits.

The revival of foreign trade greatly affected the pace of immigration. Without the vast fleets that sailed the Atlantic between Europe and America, millions of newcomers to the United States in those years could never have found passage to the New World. Seventy-five percent of American commerce and an even greater proportion of the immigrant traffic was carried in American sailing ships.

The average westward crossing by sail from Liverpool, England to New York took about thirty-five days. Steamships, which had been used since

1838, could make this crossing in the 1850s in ten to fifteen days. But they remained undependable and excessively costly to operate. As late as 1899, ocean steamships carried sails for auxiliary or emergency power.

Domestic Commerce

In the fifteen years before the Civil War, American domestic commerce outdid even the record foreign trade in volume and rate of growth. The vitality of foreign trading contributed to this development. The mere collection at American ports of commodities for export generated business for home carriers. Similarly, the need to distribute imports added to the demand for domestic transportation.

But domestic commerce was far more than a part of foreign trade. As the American population grew, the home market expanded. As different regions began to specialize in particular commodities, the need for exchange increased. Exchange was made easier by the gold being mined in California and by the improved credit facilities of the expanding banking system. Between 1851 and 1860, money in circulation in the United States, including specie and banknotes, rose 9 percent per capita.

But the importance of this increase was even greater than this figure indicates, for the telegraph and the railroads were now speeding up transactions and the collection of bills. Money in circulation could be used many more times in a single year than before. And since the amount of money itself was rising, the whole pace of domestic commerce quickened. Between 1843 and 1860, while American foreign trade grew 5.5 times, domestic trade grew 10 times.

The Clipper Ship Era

Before the railroad boom of the 1850s, domestic commerce was almost monopolized by water carriers. Of these, the oldest—and for a long time the most successful—were the coastal sailing ships. In 1852, the value of goods carried by American coastal vessels was three times the combined value of goods hauled by the railroads and on canals.

The most glamorous period of ocean commerce was the era of the clipper ship, the boldest commercial sailing vessel ever built. Designers of the clippers, among whom Donald McKay in East Boston, Massachusetts, was the master, lengthened the ordinary three-masted packet ships and drastically narrowed the ratio of beam to length. The result was the fastest and most graceful hull that ever took to the sea. The tallest masts available, spread with an enormous amount of canvas, challenged the courage of both seamen and shipmasters.

The first clippers were built early in the 1840s, in an attempt to shorten the voyage to the Orient. But they really came into their own with California gold mining. Since the clippers' designers had sacrificed cargo space for speed, their owners had to charge higher rates for their limited cargoes than most shippers could afford. To the California adventurers, however, speed was all-important. Conventional sailing ships arriving at San Francisco in the summer of 1850 from Boston and New York averaged 159 days for the journey around the Horn. The next summer, the clipper *Flying Cloud* arrived from New York after a voyage of 89 days, 21 hours.

The clippers were beaten at their own game,

Clipper ship *Dreadnought.* (*Museum of the City of New York*)

SOCIETY IN THE NORTH

however, just when they seemed to have perfected it. Even before the gold rush, New York steamship operators had organized an alternate route to the West Coast that took five weeks or less. This route involved an Atlantic run to Panama, land portage of the cargo across the isthmus, and then a Pacific run north again in another steamship.

The Great Lakes versus the Great Rivers

When the canals between east and west first were built, river men hoped that the artificial waterways would serve as feeders to river craft, just as the rivers fed the coastal carriers. In many eastern states, the canals did perform this function. None, of course, performed it better than the Erie Canal in New York. Yet in the long run, the Erie, along with the Ohio Canal and others completed in the West before 1837, took trade away from the western rivers.

By 1838, Buffalo, at the Erie's western end, was receiving more grain and flour annually than New Orleans. And once western canal construction began in the 1840s, almost every project was aimed at swinging more and more of the western trade away from the Mississippi River system toward the North and the East. Perhaps the most dramatic shift was brought by the completion in 1848 of the Illinois and Michigan Canal, linking Chicago on Lake Michigan with La Salle on the Illinois River. The Illinois, which joined the Mississippi north of St. Louis, quickly siphoned off so much traffic that by 1850 Chicago had become a great port even though the city was still without a single railroad connection.

In the fifteen years before the Civil War, there was a struggle for control of western commerce between the Mississippi River system and the Great Lakes. The struggle paralleled the rivalry between the free and slave states for control of the West itself. By reversing the direction of southbound traffic on the Ohio, Illinois, and northern part of the Mississippi rivers, the canals transformed these arteries into mere feeder streams. By midcentury, the canals had swung the victory to the Great Lakes.

Triumph of the Railroad

The extension of the canal system should remind us that the railroad was not so obvious an improvement over other means of inland transportation as

The train! The train! (*Kenneth M. Newman, Old Print Shop, New York City*)

we might suppose. Practical steam locomotives had been invented in England and the United States long before 1829, when their commercial feasibility was first established. But problems of roadbed construction, track scheduling, and safety continued to harass railroad operators. Nevertheless, Americans built a railroad network of 30,000 miles, one of the marvels of the world in 1860.

Passenger trains sped along at more than 20 miles per hour. Freight trains averaged about 11 miles an hour. Almost all the 3,328 miles of railroad track in the United States in 1840 lay in the Northeast and the Old South. No railroad linked the two sections, and none extended across the Appalachians to the Ohio or Mississippi Valley.

Pennsylvania, with about one-third of all the northern mileage at this time, was the nation's leader. The state government was so determined to protect its canal system that when it chartered the privately financed Pennsylvania Rail Road in 1846 for a line from Harrisburg to Pittsburgh, it required the new company to pay the state's canal administration 3 cents for each ton-mile of freight hauled. Second to Pennsylvania in 1840 was New York, where most of the lines lay in the region at the eastern end of the Erie Canal and westward roughly parallel to the canal itself.

Until 1851, New York, as eager as Pennsylva-

nia to protect its canals, forbade railroads to carry freight except when the Erie Canal was frozen over or otherwise closed to navigation. In 1840, New York City had only one tiny railroad, the New York and Harlem, which connected the metropolis with the independent town of Harlem, 7 miles to the north.

Boston's thriving entrepreneurs, always on the lookout for new investment opportunities, tried not to allow Massachusetts to lag in railroad construction. By 1850 almost every town in the state with 2000 persons or more was served by trains. Boston became the hub of the New England railroad network. More important, rail connections with the Erie Canal now made the city a competitor for western trade. Bostonians, under the leadership of John Murray Forbes, began investing in railroads in the West, successfully transferring much of their capital from seagoing ventures to what they foresaw as a new boom on land.

Like Boston, Baltimore was unhampered by a canal system's prior claims to western traffic, and railroad promoters were free to build. The Baltimore & Ohio Railroad completed a route from Baltimore to Wheeling, Virginia, in 1853. Enterprising Massachusetts and Maryland jolted Pennsylvania and New York out of confidence in canals. In 1857 the Pennsylvania Rail Road bought the

The Railroad Network, 1850–60

1850

1860

state canal system and the short railroad lines the state had built to feed the canals. From that time, the Pennsylvania Rail Road dominated the transportation structure of the commonwealth and much of its economic and political life. In similar fashion, the New York Central and the Erie Railroad rose to dominance in New York.

During the 1850s, the national rail network was expanded dramatically, especially within a 500-mile radius of Chicago. These roads faced more difficult conditions than those in the East, for private investment capital was scarce, distances were great, and population was sparse. By 1860 Congress had granted 18 million acres in ten states for the benefit of 45 different railroads. With these lands as collateral, the roads were able to market bonds through Wall Street investment bankers to American and foreign investors.

During the 1850s, issues of such bonds grew so much that many New York business firms, especially those with connections abroad, gave up handling goods and became investment bankers specializing in the distribution of railroad securities. The invention of the first-mortgage bond and the growth of investment banking were as important as iron and steel in the development of the western railroads.

All over the West, railroad construction knocked out canal systems and decimated river traffic. Railroad trains were faster than barges or steamboats, and railroad spurs could be laid to factory doors and warehouses. The competitive practices of railroad managers also helped. Where they encountered water rivals, the railroads cut rates to capture the available traffic. They got back their losses by charging all the traffic would bear at noncompetitive terminals.

Two waterways survived railroad competition. One was the Great Lakes route, over which heavy freight like wheat and iron ore could still be carried more efficiently by barge. The second was the Erie Canal. The continued use of these two waterways reflected the massive volume of the east-west trade, which needed every carrier available to meet the demands of the rising population of the western farms and the eastern cities.

As for the east-west railroads, the census of 1860 reported: "So great are their benefits that, if the entire cost of railroads between the Atlantic and the western States had been levied on the farmers of the central west, their proprietors could have paid it and been immensely the gainers." As things turned out, farmers thought otherwise.

NORTHERN INDUSTRY

In the 1850s, southern businessmen—merchants, land speculators, manufacturers, and railroad promoters—sometimes saw that their section's future lay in joining the "truly national" development of the country. Wealthy planters sometimes invested in northern lands, mines, and railroads. But these men, some of whom were among the last to yield to secessionist agitators, remained a tiny minority. Northern businessmen, on their part, valued their southern connections. Almost without exception they deplored the abolitionists in their own section. Yet few of them wished to restore to New Orleans or St. Louis the commerce New York and Chicago had captured. Fewer still were willing to grant the "slavocracy" the first transcontinental railroad or the western lands it would cross.

The New Economy

As late as 1860, the richest northerners were merchants rather than industrialists. Among them was H. B. Claflin, who had built up an enormous wholesale dry goods business on the modern principle of mass sales at low unit profits; A. T. Stewart, one of the creators of the American department store; and Charles L. Tiffany, who made a fortune selling jewelry and silverware to other merchants. Ex-China traders like John Murray Forbes supplied much of the early enterprise and capital for railroad building and for eastern manufacturing.

The first reasonably accurate census of American manufactures was taken in 1850. Its results were dramatic, for they showed that the annual output of American industry had just surpassed the value of all agricultural products, including cotton. The growth of manufacturing and of agriculture reinforced each other. As the industrial cities grew, their landless people needed to be fed. And as the number of farms increased, farm families provided an expanding market for domestic manufactures. Urban and rural communities remained intertwined: neither could do without the other, whether for wood, flour, beef, leather, or beer.

What characterized the new economy was its organization. Lumber mills, for example, began to specialize in the production of barrel staves or shingles or railroad ties, and to use single-purpose machines for the work. Specialization and mechanization appeared in other industries as well. In meatpacking, for example, the hams and shoulders of hogs were packed for eating and the rest of the flesh was rendered into oil for lubricants and shortening. The hog's bristles went into brushes, the blood into chemicals, the hooves into glue. What remained was ground into fertilizer. It is no wonder that Americans thought of themselves as being on the edge of a "newly efficient" age.

Another modern feature of meatpacking was the use of inclined tables, down which each carcass would slide past a stationary worker responsible for removing a particular part. This "continuous-flow" method was the beginning of modern assembly-line techniques.

A Spirit of Invention

At the 1851 fair at the Crystal Palace in London, few exhibits drew greater admiration than the display of American farm devices. Everything from road scrapers and sausage stuffers to currycombs and hayrakes won acclaim for ingenuity, utility, and cheapness. Few of these inventions were ever patented, and we know hardly any of the inventors' names. Nonagricultural inventions remained far fewer than agricultural ones. But they helped swell the number of patents issued by the United States Patent Office, which had opened in 1790. In 1835, a record number of patents (752) were issued. More than six times that number were issued fifteen years later.

One of the great inventions of the nineteenth century was the electric telegraph, for which the talented painter Samuel F. B. Morse received the first American patent in 1840. In fact, Morse borrowed heavily from previous inventors, and he did not construct the "code" which has since been given his name. He did, however, convince Congress to contribute money to the telegraph's development. With federal money, Morse staged the famous scene in the Supreme Court chambers in Washington in which he asked "What hath God wrought?" of a correspondent in Baltimore and got an answer.

In England, the telegraph was first used to control railroad traffic. Americans first used the telegraph for transmission of business messages and public information. Its effect on the newspaper business was immediate. The "penny press" already dominated American journalism, and printing machinery could produce 1000 newspapers an hour. With telegraphy, the demand for newspapers rose so sharply that presses needed to turn out at least 10,000 papers an hour. This volume was achieved in 1847 by a cylindrical press developed by Richard March Hoe. Other improvements in printing equipment enabled publishers to keep pace with the public's appetite for "hot news," advertising, and entertainment.

To most Americans, and to Europeans also, there seemed no end to Yankee inventiveness. "Vulcanization" of rubber was one of the most widely utilized processes. "India" rubber (most of which came from South America) had always seemed to have a unique imperviousness to rain, snow, and mud. But when exposed to heat, it

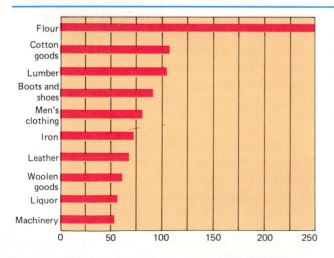

The ten leading American industries as listed in the 1860 census of manufactures are ranked here by value of product. (*John A. Garraty,* The American Nation, *fourth edition, p. 291. Copyright © 1966, 1971, 1979 by Harper & Row, Publishers, Inc. Reprinted by permission of the publisher.*)

melted, grew sticky, and collapsed. After years of effort, Charles Goodyear, a stubborn, impoverished New Englander, hit upon just the right mixture of raw rubber, chemicals, and heat that would yield a stable product at all ordinary temperatures. Before the automobile, Goodyear's rubber was used mainly in the boot and shoe industry.

A less dramatic but equally important invention was Elias Howe's sewing machine. I. M. Singer's long-term success lay in his innovative marketing. He thought of installment selling, backed by advertising. Having worked up an impressive demand for his sewing machines, Singer proceeded to mass-produce them by assembly-line methods. In doing so, he made possible mass manufacture of shoes and clothing.

The perfection of new machines often led to development of entirely new industries. In older industries, such as the manufacture of cotton and woolen goods, spectacular new inventions were no longer looked for. Yet a continuous round of inventions greatly speeded production and turnover. New dyes and new machines (like the Crompton loom, which could weave patterns) added to the variety of factory-made cloth.

An Age of Iron

The whole cycle of invention—from the simple steel plow to the sewing machine—gave the American iron industry a great boost. Most of the new agricultural machinery was made from iron and steel. When the Civil War started, about 3500 steamboats had been built for the western rivers. All required iron for their boilers—and for replacement boilers after the first ones blew up. The hulls of clipper ships were reinforced with iron forms. The telegraph was strung entirely with iron wire until copper began to replace it in the 1860s. In 1850 the world's first completely cast-iron building was built in New York City. It was shortly after that, with discovery of the far greater tensile strength of wrought iron, that the possibility of scraping the sky with a building became a reality.

By far the biggest single user of iron in the 1850s was the railroad—for rails, locomotives, wheels, axles, and hundreds of other parts. Railroads ran the most extensive machine shops in the country, making parts and repairs and their own iron and steel tools and machinery.

One of the fundamental changes in iron manufacture after 1840 was the rapid shift in fuel from wood and charcoal (half-burned wood) to anthracite (hard coal) and coke (half-burned soft coal). Much higher temperatures could be attained with these new fuels, and the rate of production was boosted to ever higher levels. Another great change was the widespread use of rolling mills in place of the hand forge for shaping iron forms. Improvements in ironmaking were reflected in a fourfold increase in the production of pig iron between 1842 and 1860.

Dramatic as all these steps were, the American iron industry in the 1850s developed very slowly in comparison with progress abroad. In 1860, the United States mined less iron ore and manufactured less pig iron than Britain had twenty years earlier. Britain's coal production in 1860 was five times that of the United States.

It is difficult for us today to recapture the sense of exhilaration that this new metal provided. To the industrial peoples of the world, iron was the staff of life. America's leading iron manufacturer observed: "The consumption of iron is a social barometer by which to estimate the relative height of civilization among nations." Certain scattered incidents, as we see them now, underline the immaturity of that industrial spirit. In 1829, drillers had brought in an oil gusher in Kentucky. It only terrified and angered the workmen, who had been looking for salt. Two years later, Joseph Henry worked out the essentials of the electric dynamo. But many decades were to pass before his "philosophical toy," as he called his electromagnetic machine, found practical use. It was not until after the Civil War that an Englishman, Henry Bessemer, successfully worked out both the process and machinery for mass steel production.

By 1860, invention and industry had just begun to transform the face of America and the character of its people. Nobody knew exactly what was taking place, but everyone was aware that the world was being rapidly transformed. By and large, people were delighted by opening horizons. It seemed to many Americans in midcentury that the generous promise of their continent was becoming real. Others were able to see only the seamy underside of the process. Even when fully employed and receiving regular wages, the members of the new industrial working class had the worst working and living conditions yet found in white America.

Thus Americans in the northern states began to realize they had important problems on their hands, problems that stemmed from a new kind of agriculture and new ways of making things. They did not fully see their difficulties, partly because new developments of this sort are hard to understand and partly because their attention became riveted on sectional tensions between the North and the South. The driving, dynamic power of economic development in the North made the South seem like another world. The South's own prosperity and its commitment to slavery caused most whites in that region to think the northern states were the enemy. Many northerners thought the aggression was on the other side.

SUMMARY

During the pre-Civil War, or antebellum, years the United States underwent fundamental changes in its population. After 1800, and especially after 1815, the size of American cities swelled dramatically. The growth of cities created numerous urban problems that were only partially solved. The nation's total population continued to expand at a much more rapid rate than Europe's. This expansion was caused chiefly by an enormous flood of immigrants from Ireland, Germany, and Great Britain, an influx of people that reached its height in the decade after 1845.

At the same time, the American birth rate was actually dropping. This new development reflected important changes that were taking place in the role of women in American culture—in the way women were regarded by men, in the functions of women in the economy, and especially in the values and ideas women held about themselves. Women seem to have begun deliberately reducing the number of children they bore by various methods of what we would now call "birth control." At the same time, middle-class women began getting out of their homes to form women's organizations. As they worked for various pious causes and social reforms, their growing commitment to the abolition of southern slavery resulted directly in the movement for women's rights in northern states and throughout the nation. Their poorer sisters had little time for such activities, but women in factories also began to show discontent with their lives.

Even as these changes took place, another revolution was underway on traditional family farms. Expansion of settlement onto the treeless lands of the western free states resulted in a new kind of farming. Growing markets for grain in the East and in Europe created an enormous demand for corn and wheat. Production of wheat, especially, helped encourage the use of newly invented farm machinery. The mechanization of farming and the longer distance from markets stimulated demand for cheap transportation, but placed farmers increasingly at the mercy of middlemen between producers and consumers. In rival areas of the northeastern states, farmers turned to fruits, vegetables, and dairy products to help feed the cities.

The new stretches of sheer distance in the expanding economy generated a pressing need for efficient transportation. Rivers, canals, and eventually railroads helped meet this demand. Coastal shipping grew in importance, and swift clipper ships added to the nation's effectiveness in international trade. For a time, there was a sectional tug in transportation developments, but eventually the new states around and west of the Great Lakes grew more tightly tied to the northeastern part of the country than to the South.

Especially during the thirty years before the Civil War, the northeastern states sprouted with new and old manufacturing enterprises. Textiles continued to be central to this development, but so did new industries that were helped by such inventions as the sewing machine and the vulcanization of rubber. Above all, iron production lay at the base of a new industrial economy and the values that accompanied it. By 1860, industrialization had proceeded so much further in the North than the South that the free and slave states seem almost to have become two different societies.

Suggested Readings

Demographic statistics are available in *Historical Statistics of the United States: Colonial Times to 1970* (1975); P. McClelland and R. Zeckhauser, *Demographic Dimensions of the New Republic: American Interregional Migration, Vital Statistics, and Manumissions, 1800–1860* (1982).

Different and extremely interesting perspectives are offered in N. Cott, *The Bonds of Womanhood: "Woman's Sphere" in New England, 1780–1835* (1977); C. Degler, *At Odds: Women and the Family from the Revolution to the Present* (1980); F. Dudden, *Serving Women: Household Service in Nineteenth-Century America* (1983); C. Smith-Rosenberg, *Disorderly Conduct: Visions of Gender in Victorian America* (1986); and J. Jensen, *Loosening the Bonds: Mid-Atlantic Farm Women, 1750–1850* (1986). Questions about family limitation are considered by L. Gordon, *Women's Body, Women's Rights: A Social History of Birth Control in America* (1976); J. Mohr, *Abortion in America: The Origins and Evolution of National Policy, 1800–1900* (1978); J. Reed, *From Private Vice to Public Virtue: The Birth Control Movement and American Society* (1978); and

K. Sklar, *Catherine Beecher: A Study in American Domesticity* (1973).

Historians have shown the close relationship between abolition and women's rights. O. Cromwell, *Lucretia Mott* (1958), and K. Lumpkin, *The Emancipation of Angelina Grimké,* (1974), present the lives of women who were strong bridges between the two movements.

Most of the books on economic history suggested for Chapter 10 are important for this later period as well. One of the best books about agricultural expansion into the northern prairies is Hamlin Garland, *A Son of the Middle Border* (1917). M. Curti and others present a painstaking examination of a frontier Wisconsin community between 1840 and 1880 in *The Making of an American Community* (1959). More recent studies are C. Danhof, *Change in Agriculture, The Northern United States, 1820–1870* (1969); and the early chapters of A. Bouge, *From Prairie to Corn Belt: Farming on the Illinois and Iowa Prairies in the Nineteenth Century* (1963).

Immigration (in this and later periods mostly to the northern states) is discussed by M. Jones, *American Immigration* (1960); and C. Wittke, *We Who Built America* (1967). One background is presented in M. Walker, *Germany and the Emigration, 1816–1885* (1964). For the more numerous Irish, see G. Potter, *To the Golden Door* (1960), and C. Woodham-Smith, *The Great Hunger* (1962). For a numerically important group sometimes not thought of as "immigrant," see R. Berthoff, *British Immigrants in Industrial America* (1953). O. Handlin, *Boston's Immigrants: A Study of Acculturation* (rev. ed., 1959), is an evocative recreation of the experience of the migrants. See also R. Ernst, *Immigrant Life in New York City, 1825–1863* (1949).

Specialized aspects of American commerce in this period are covered in R. Pineau (ed.), *The Japan Expedition, 1852–1854: The Personal Journal of Commodore Matthew C. Perry* (1969); and J. Fairbank, *Trade and Diplomacy on the China Coast* (1953), a fine account of the subtle mixture of force and diplomacy. The still stirring saga of the clipper ships receives affectionate coverage by C. Cutler in *Greyhounds of the Sea* (1930). The experience of sailing on a vessel built for the California trade was vividly recounted by Richard Henry Dana, *Two Years Before the Mast* (1840). The persistent importance of inland water transportation is detailed by L. Hunter in *Steamboats on the Western Rivers* (1949).

In this period, railroads were beginning to take over the task of linking goods and people. See A. Fishlow, *American Railroads and the Transformation of the Ante-Bellum Economy* (1965). One of the best regional studies of railroading focused on New England: E. Kirkland, *Men, Cities, and Transportation, 1820–1900* (2 vols., 1948). The crucial importance for railroad construction of capital formation and transfer is made clear in such works as I. Neu, *Erastus Corning, Merchant and Financier, 1794–1872* (1960); A. Johnston and B. Supple, *Boston Capitalists and Western Railroads* (1967); and S. Salisbury, *The State, the Investor and the Railroad: Boston and Albany, 1825–1867* (1967).

For an interesting coincidence of contrasting approaches to what appears to be the same subject, see H. Pierce, *The Railroads of New York: A Study of Government Aid, 1826–1875* (1955), and L. Benson, *Merchants, Farmers and Railroads: Railroad Regulation and New York Politics, 1850–1887* (1955). Some of the flamboyant personalities of this early age of railroading emerge in J. McCague, *Moguls and Iron Men: First Transcontinental Railroad* (1964), and H. Comstock, *The Iron Horse* (1971).

American society remains so locked into technological change that there is still no satisfactory overall assessment of our technological history. A great deal of suggestive information is offered in W. Kaempffert (ed.), *A Popular History of American Invention* (2 vols., 1924). The illustrations in M. Wilson, *American Science and Invention: A Pictoral History* (1954), add to an understanding of the newly technological world. R. Thompson, *Wiring a Continent: The History of the Telegraph Industry in the United States, 1832–1866* (1947), focuses on the shrinking of the continent.

On labor and banking, see the studies cited in Chapters 10 and 11. In addition, M. Walsh, *The Manufacturing Frontier: Pioneer Industry in Ante-Bellum Wisconsin, 1830–1860* (1972), presents a specialized regional study with implications for early manufacturing practices in all outlying areas.

A SOUTHERN NATION

Chapter 14

After 1830, white southerners began increasingly to feel that they were a separate people with their own peculiar destiny. It is of course impossible to place the beginnings of southern nationalism at any exact date, but certainly by the 1850s it was apparent to many southerners, including some slaves, that their society was on a collision course with the North.

All southerners knew, however vaguely, that their region was different from the rest of the nation: different by reason of slavery, a large number of Afro-Americans, fewer immigrants from Europe, fewer Roman Catholics, and a less rapidly expanding population. Some were also conscious that their economy was tied to cotton and other agricultural staples and that they lagged behind the North and Great Britain.

Many southern Americans, of both races, developed a deep attachment to their localities in the countryside—a commitment to home ground and to the way the sky looked and the land smelled. Sometimes knowing it and sometimes not, they grew defensive about their accomplishments. For purposes of analysis, it is useful and necessary to consider various separate aspects of southern culture in the antebellum period. But when we speak of "southernness"—of slavery, race, monoculture, economic dependency and intellectual stagnation, intolerance and violence, hospitality—we risk taking apart a culture and not being able to get it back together again. In fact, it had great coherence, even though racial antagonisms were a fatal flaw. That coherence became evident in the 1850s and the war that followed. ■

WHITE PEOPLE OF THE SOUTH

Richard Hildreth, a New England historian, visited the South in the 1830s and then published a book, *Despotism in America; or An Inquiry into the Nature and Results of the Slave-Holding System in the United States.* Within the "great social experiment of Democracy" in America, he found the South to be "another experiment, less talked about, less celebrated, but not the less real or important. It was "the experiment of Despotism." The southern states, he wrote, "are Aristocracies; and aristocracies of the sternest and most odious kind."

Hildreth saw only two classes in the South: the privileged planters and all lesser whites, on the one hand, and their "hereditary subjects, servants and bondsmen," on the other. "Extremes meet," he added. "Ferocity of temper, idleness, improvidence, drunkenness, gambling—these are vices for which the masters are distinguished, and these same vices are conspicuous traits in the character and conduct of slaves."

This was the image of Dixie in many of the abolitionist tracts of the day. Some southerners tried to expose the excessive simplicity of the image and thereby discredit it. The section's aggressive defenders, following the lead of Calhoun, preferred an equal simplicity and meeting of extremes, the better to convey an alternative image of their own. Calhoun told Congress:

This agitation [against the slave system] has produced one happy effect at least; it has compelled us in the South to look into the nature and character of this great institution, and to correct many false impressions that even we had entertained in relation to it. Many in the South once believed that it was a moral and political evil; that folly and delusion are gone; we see it now in its true light, and regard it as the most safe and stable basis for free institutions in the world.

Southern Farmers

Southern society was actually far more complex than the simple pictures sketched by Hildreth and Calhoun. There were wealthy and aristocratic planters, but not many. Easily the largest group were simple farmers who labored with their families on their own land to produce their own food, clothing, and the small amount of extra produce necessary for a little cash. A smaller but important group of whites owned one or several slaves. On their somewhat larger farms, blacks and whites labored and lived together. The "poor white trash,"

disease-ridden folk reduced to scratching subsistence from marginal lands or no land at all, were a minority of southern whites.

The farms of the plain people of the South were sometimes tucked away among the large plantations in the cotton and tobacco country, but they predominated in the upland South—in eastern Tennessee, western North Carolina, northern Georgia, Alabama, and Mississippi. There, while some produced the southern staples, most grew subsistence crops—corn, squash, greens, beans, sweet potatoes—and raised livestock. The plain people also included the storekeepers, the mechanics, and other artisans in southern villages and towns.

Seen through the perceptive eyes of Frederick Law Olmsted, a Connecticut Yankee who traveled through the South in the early 1850s, living standards seemed distinctly below those of northern farmers. And yet, though Olmsted complained of wretched cooking, vermin-filled beds, and rough manners, he also noted that these people were hospitable. "If you want to fare well in this country," he was told in northern Alabama, "you stop to poor folks' houses; they try to enjoy what they've got while they ken, but these yer big planters they don' care for nothing but to save."

Riding through an area of thin sandy soil, Olmsted reported:

The majority of dwellings are small log cabins of one room, with another separate cabin for a kitchen; each house has a well, and a garden enclosed with palings. Cows, goats, mules and swine, fowls and doves are abundant. The people are more social than those of the lower country, falling readily into friendly conversation. . . . They are very ignorant; the agriculture is wretched and the work hard. I have seen white women hoeing field crops today. A spinning-wheel is heard in every house . . . every one wears home-spun. The negroes have much more individual freedom than in the rich cotton country, and are not infrequently heard singing or whistling at their work.

Among such farmers, as one who grew up in Mississippi reported, "people who lived miles apart, counted themselves as neighbors, . . . and in case of sorrow or sickness, or need of any kind, there was no limit to the ready service" they rendered one another.

Among the white population there was also considerable cultural diversity. There were the French Creoles in Louisiana, fiercely independent mountaineers in the Ozarks and Appalachia, and Irish and German wage laborers. Though it was overwhelmingly rural, the South also had busi-

Unlike the wealthy aristocrats, the majority of southern white farmers lived in humble homes, like this one drawn in 1838 by the French naturalist Francis Comte de Castelnau in his travels through the back country. (*Library of Congress*)

ness and professional men—doctors, lawyers, editors, ministers, and industrial and commercial entrepreneurs—as well as artisans and industrial laborers.

In many parts of the South the growing season was too short for cotton, too cold for rice and sugar. It snowed every winter, and even animals needed sheltering barns. Yet the characteristic and distinguishing feature of the southern climate was the prevailing heat. If the weather drew the southerner outdoors, the terrain and what it held helped keep him there. All across the Cotton Kingdom stood dense forests that rewarded the hunter with game. As late as 1860, a large part of the slave's labor was clearing new land for cultivation. The region was also well endowed with navigable streams to carry cotton and other staples to export centers. Thousands of smaller creeks and ponds provided a choice of fish.

Despite the popularity of hunting, trapping, and fishing in the South, the region also had men who strove just as hard as any Jacksonian businessman to make their way up in the world. The Cotton Kingdom was not extended in a single generation from South Carolina to Texas by men content to loaf and dream at home. A typical Red River planter, asked to buy a "Bible Defence of Slavery," shouted: "Now you go to hell! I've told you three times I didn't want your book. . . . I own niggers; and I calculate to own more of 'em, if I can get 'em, but I don't want any damn'd preachin' about it."

The violence of white southern life has perhaps been exaggerated, but the "Arkansas toothpick" (as the Bowie knife was sometimes called) became one of the principal instruments for settling differences in the rougher sections. Even in the older and more settled regions, the dueling code prevailed.

The Planter Class

In 1860, three-fourths of southern whites owned no slaves at all. Almost half the slaveholding families owned fewer than six slaves, and only 12 percent of all slaveowners possessed twenty or more. The real "planting class" was actually a very small minority. A mere 8000 planters owned fifty or more slaves.

There were, in addition, important regional differences in slaveholdings. In the six states of the lower South (except Texas), between one-third and one-half of the white families owned slaves. Elsewhere the proportions ranged from only one-thirteenth to one-fourth. Within each state, large plantations were concentrated in areas with the most fertile soil and access to water transportation.

Some large planters lived the high life of saber-rattling, fire-breathing "cavaliers." In their youth, sons of the well-to-do were often sent West with the hope that they might settle down on plantations of their own. Many did. But many more found room for recklessness and violence. Those who were determined to develop their lands spent many years in crude surroundings. The sawmill came late to Alabama, Mississippi, and Louisiana. Even in the 1840s and 1850s, some planters continued to live in "two pen" log houses with crevices between the unhewn logs that let in the light, rain, and wind.

In the older South many of the gentry lived well—some extravagantly. Most were devoted to the simple pleasures of rustic society: hunting, horse racing, card playing, visiting, and perhaps an annual summer pilgrimage to the mountains or the sea to escape the heat. Many men found time for politics, and the planting class dominated southern political life, just as it dominated the southern economy.

Susan Dabney Smedes's account of her father conveys the beau ideal of the highest caste. Humane, upright, generous, and courteous, Mr. Dabney was most deeply concerned with sick slaves, the price of cotton, and unreliable overseers. "Managing a plantation," Mrs. Smedes observed, "was something like managing a kingdom. The ruler had need of great store, not only of wisdom, but of tact and patience as well." Nor did the planter's wife escape the domestic duties of supervising and sometimes nursing slaves.

BLACK PEOPLE OF THE SOUTH

Slavery had taken root in the South because Africans provided a cheap and readily available labor force to cultivate staple crops. Prior to the cotton gin (1794), slaves were concentrated in eastern Virginia and in lowland South Carolina and Georgia. With the westward expansion of upland cotton and with the federal prohibition of the Atlantic slave trade in 1808, there began a massive forced movement of slaves into Alabama, Mississippi, Louisiana, and beyond.

This domestic slave trade meant that hundreds of thousands of blacks were uprooted from their homes in Virginia and in the East and forced into the role of land-clearing western pioneers. Some were carried on ships to ports like Mobile, Alabama, and to New Orleans and river towns farther up the Mississippi and its tributaries. Probably more were forced by slave traders to walk the entire distance on the dusty trails of southern forests and meadows.

Most of these uprooted people were thrown onto large cotton and sugar plantations. Indeed, the slaves (unlike whites) typically lived on the factory-like plantation unit. On the eve of the Civil War, more than half the slave population lived in units with more than twenty slaves; about one-quarter in units of more than fifty. Slaves were concentrated in the richest agricultural regions. In some counties of the lower South, they greatly outnumbered whites. Only about 10 percent lived in cities and towns. Slaves were also employed in factories and in river commerce. In fact, just before the Civil War, about 6 percent of the blacks in the South were technically not chattel slaves at all; they were "free" but lived in a world of legal, social, and economic marginality.

These facts profoundly affected the lives of both blacks and whites. The predominence of large plantations meant that the principal social contacts of many blacks were with other blacks. And it meant that the families of the wealthy planting class, more than other whites, had direct contact with masses of slaves. Many blacks grew up somewhat isolated in their own Afro-American subculture. And the South's ruling class was raised in intimate contact with the actual workings of the slave system, with all its ambiguities of friendship, distrust, hostility, and fear.

WORDS AND NAMES IN AMERICAN HISTORY

Hoe cake was a common dish in the eighteenth and nineteenth centuries. It was commonly associated with blacks, because hoe cake was sometimes all that slaves had to eat at a hasty meal. Hoe cakes were flat "cakes" of ground corn, which the Algonkian Indians and later many other Americans called *hominy*. Rather than being cooked on a pan, or grill, like our pancakes, it was spread on the business end of a hoe and held over a fire of hot coals. White people in the South also ate hoe cakes. Sometimes, more commonly in the North, this food was called *Johnny cake*. Some scholars think this term was a corruption of "journey cake," since in fact there are literary references to the use of this dish by travelers. A modern book on the diet of slaves is aptly entitled *Hog Meat and Hoe Cake*.

Another characteristic of the black population immediately preceding the Civil War also had important implications for both peoples. By 1860, despite some smuggling of slaves from Africa, the overwhelming majority of American slaves were native-born, as had not been the case a century earlier. The black population was Afro-American, not African. From birth, for example, slaves spoke English, though in their own dialect. All this meant that the cultural distance between blacks and whites had narrowed.

The Slave's Outer World

Frederick Douglass was born and bred a slave in Maryland. He had various masters and mistresses, both kind and brutal. Of one especially harsh master Douglass recalled in his autobiography:

If at any one time of my life more than another, I was made to drink the bitterest dregs of slavery, that time was during the first six months of my stay with Mr. Covey. We were worked in all weathers. It was never too hot or too cold: it could never rain, blow, hail, or snow, too hard for us to work in the field. Work, work, work, was scarcely more the order of the day than of the night. The longest days were too short for him and the shortest nights too long for him. I was somewhat unmanageable when I first went there, but a few months of this discipline tamed me. Mr. Covey succeeded in breaking me.

Douglass was never completely broken, however. His early life was unusual in its variety of owners and experiences, and with some help from whites he learned to read and write. He was also an enormously talented man. Eventually he escaped from slavery and went on to become the most famous black abolitionist and champion of racial equality.

Frederick Douglass, c. 1844. (*National Portrait Gallery, Smithsonian Institution*)

Though his life as a slave was far from typical, he and millions of others would have appreciated the later words of Paul Lawrence Dunbar, son of another fugitive slave:

A crust of bread and a corner to sleep in,
A minute to smile and an hour to weep in,
A pint of joy to a peck of trouble,
And never a laugh but the moans come double:
*   And that is life!*

DOUGLASS ON SLAVERY

As a young slave in Maryland, Frederick Douglass had several different masters. One of them, a man named Covey, had the reputation of being a "slavebreaker." In his autobiography, Douglass admitted that Covey had temporarily broken his spirit. But then he went on to generalize about the effects of his being owned by a less brutal master.

Not withstanding all the improvement in my . . . home and my new master, I was still restless and discontented. . . . When entombed at Covey's and shrouded in darkness and physical wretchedness, temporal well-being was the grand desideratum, but, temporal wants supplied, the spirit put in its claims. Beat and cuff the slave, keep him hungry and spiritless, and he will follow the chain of his master like a dog, but feed and clothe him well, work him moderately and surround him with physical comfort, and dreams of freedom will intrude. Give him a bad master and he aspires to a good master; give him a good master, and he wishes to become his own master. Such is human nature. You may hurl a man so low beneath the level of his kind, that he loses all just ideas of his natural position, but elevate him a little, and the clear conception of rights rises to life and power, and leads him onward.

Douglass's own recollection caught the essence of life for slaves on most plantations: unremitting toil. On the characteristic Black Belt plantation, as elsewhere, the field hand's routine varied little from day to day, year to year. The day's work lasted, as the saying went, from "can see, 'til can't," with short breaks for breakfast and lunch, which were brought to the men and women in the fields. Physically, the heaviest work was clearing the land or "rolling logs"; anyone who has ever chopped down a tree knows that the real work has just begun.

But plowing behind a stubborn mule, weeding or "chopping" the endless rows, and finally picking the bolls of their white fiber without including in one's bag much in the way of brown leaves and stalks—this routine, 12 to 16 hours a day, was the slave's life. And no matter whether the master or overseer was brutal or kindly, this labor was forced. One of the commonest causes for a whipping was picking underweight or "trashy" cotton.

The treatment of slaves ranged all the way from hideous sadism to gentle paternalism. On some plantations, slaves found themselves continuously beaten; on others, never. Some slaves were always hungry; others ate nearly as well as the white folks. Some slaves were so poorly clad and housed that they drew sympathy from neighboring whites and blacks. Others lived so well that they were envied by poor whites and exhibited as model specimens to visiting foreigners. The major cause of this variation in treatment was not so much the region or plantation size, as the personalities involved.

On large plantations, the slave's principal contact with authority was usually with the overseer, whose personality made a great difference. But at least in the long run, the owner and the slaves decided what kind of overseer they would tolerate. The size of the crop depended on a subtle and complicated human equation, balanced among slave drivers, field hands, artisans, house servants, hired white laborers, overseers, slave masters and their wives and children. Any person involved in the equation had at least some power to alter its dynamics. The weight of power, of course, lay with whites. But they were rarely in full control.

Generalizations about "the slave experience" keep breaking down along these lines. But it is possible to make certain summary statements. Slaves in the frontier Southwest were treated with greater severity than in the older South. Slaves on large plantations were confronted with more impersonal, though not necessarily more severe, discipline than slaves on small plantations. There were greater class and occupational distinctions on large plantations than on small ones.

The distinction between house servants and field hands was never absolute. But as time went on, there was a tendency for slave children to inherit the skills and status of their parents. Slaves in the old upper South and on small farms were more likely than others to have their lives disrupted by sale away from homes and families.

The family life of slaves has been a matter of debate among historians. In the eyes of the law there was no such thing as a binding marriage between slaves, and slave children might be sold away from their parents. In practice, however, although a great many families were broken up, a far larger number managed to survive as much intact as other nineteenth-century families. Slaves wanted, and many masters actively encouraged, a stable family life with children raised by their parents, all under the same roof. On large plantations, this was the usual pattern. On smaller units, the husband was likely to live on a neighboring plantation, able to see his family once or twice a

Caesar, a slave. (*New York Historical Society, New York City*)

Slave family, photographed in Beaufort, South Carolina, 1862. (*Library of Congress*)

week, under protection of a written pass from his owner. So despite the absence of legal protection and the informality of marriage ceremonies—often "jumping over the broomstick," as it was called—many slaves were able to maintain loving and nurturing family relationships.

Many of these families lived under the threat of disruption because of sexual advances by white men. Sometimes it was a matter of outright rape. Sometimes there developed longstanding, affectionate relationships between white men and black women. Undoubtedly the most common situation was simply some variety of the sexual exploitation that takes place when men are powerful and women are helpless.

Black men could do little, of course, to defend their sexual interests, and they knew better than to approach white women. The restrictions on white women were equally clear: They had all the advantages and disadvantages of being confined to the top of a pedestal.

The Slaves' Inner World

Hemmed in as they were on so many sides, slaves struggled to create a measure of independence. Some took fierce pride in productivity; others took an equal satisfaction in malingering. Some boasted of their capacity for bearing punishment; others claimed skill at avoiding it. A great many sought the comforts of religion. It was an ambiguous refuge. Christianity could be used as an escape from the toils of this world, or it could be used as a handbook for revolutionary action. For the most part, though, slaves adapted Christianity to make their own communities a little independent of the white world.

Here again they were under pressure. After 1830, whites began to push upon slaves a brand of Christianity that supposedly would keep them docile. White preachers told slaves to serve their masters obediently, and that it was their Christian duty to do so. Left to themselves, however, slaves

AN EX-SLAVE ON RELIGION

In the 1930s an elderly ex-slave recalled religious practices on his old plantation:

Dey did allow us to go to church on Sunday about two miles down de public road, and dey hired a white preacher to preach to us. He never did tell us nothing but "Be good servants, pick up old marse and old misses' things about de place, don't steal no chickens or pigs, and don't lie about nothing." Den dey baptize you and call dat you got religion. Never did say nothing about a slave dying and going to Heaven. When we die, dey bury us next day and you is just like any of the other cattle dying on de place. . . .

We used to slip off in de woods in de old days on Sunday evening way down in de swamps to sing and pray to our liking. We prayed for dis day of freedom. We come from four and five miles to pray together to God dat if we don't live to see it, to please let our chillen live to see a better day and be free. . . . And we'd sing "our little meetin's about to break, chillen, and we must part. We got to part in body, but hope not in mind. Our little meetin's bound to break." Den we used to sing "We walk about and shake hands, fare you well my sisters, I am going home."

---

heard a very different message, one that fused eternal salvation with earthly freedom.

Music was frequently used by slaves to heighten shared feelings within the community. In no other arena of activity was their common African background more obvious. Sometimes the occasion was religious, as at a wake described by an elderly ex-slave:

When a nigger died, we had a wake an' dat was diffrunt too from what 'tis today. At de wake we clapped our han's an' kep' time wid our feet—Walking Egypt, day call hit—an' we chant an' hum all night til de nigger wus funeralized.

Singing and dancing were part of a wide variety of activities: prayer meetings, quilting bees, corn shuckings. There were ax songs, boat songs, and children's ring dancing games. What is perhaps most remarkable about the words of these songs is that there was no clear dividing line between sacred and secular concerns. One common theme runs through a great many of the songs: a resigned desire for a better life.

I know moon-rise, I know star-rise,
  Lay dis body down
I walk in de moonlight, I walk in de starlight,
  To lay dis body down.
I'll walk in de graveyeard, I'll walk through de graveyeard,
  To lay dis body down.
I'll lie in de grave and stretch out my arms;
  Lay dis body down.

"Never," said a northern officer when he first heard those words in an army camp during the Civil War, "since men first lived and suffered, was his infinite longing for peace uttered more plaintively than in that line."

Slave Resistance and White Response

Slaves also dealt with the circumstances of their lives by actively resisting the system. Throughout two centuries of slavery, slaves malingered, broke tools, abused farm animals, feigned illness, and otherwise struck out at the principal requirements of the system: hard work and productivity. There were instances of slave women remaining "pregnant" for eleven months without producing a child.

Slave driver. (*Peabody Museum, Harvard University*)

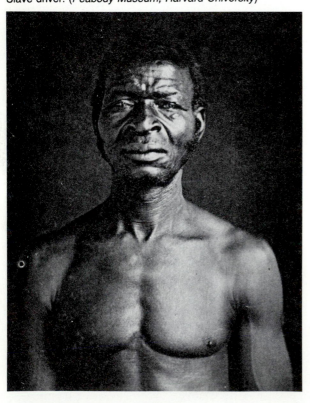

Slaveholders responded with a combination of punishments and rewards, although planters disagreed about which was more effective.

From the planters' point of view, the worst problem was running away. After about 1800, slaves in the upper South sometimes headed for freedom in the northern states. A far more common pattern involved slaves running off for a few days or weeks in the woods and then returning to face a whipping. Many runaways did not run "away" at all; they left their owners' plantation in an attempt to rejoin a spouse or other relative.

Slavery rested on a base of violence, and slaves sometimes responded in kind. There were just enough instances to keep the white population thoroughly on edge. Two of the most effective and drastic means at the slaves' disposal were arson and poisoning. Probably more common were the many instances when a slave suddenly and simply decided that he would rather fight and die than be whipped.

Some paid with their lives for their courage, but a surprising number fought their overseers to a physical and psychological standoff. Sometimes a slave might be pressed beyond the brink of rational judgment and turn upon an oppressor with a hoe or an ax and split his head open. The penalty for such "murder" was, of course, death.

Despite the overwhelming odds against them, slaves also conspired in armed rebellions. Most of these uprisings involved half a dozen to twenty-five slaves, and most were stopped when whites were told ahead of time by a slave unwilling to go along with the rebels. The most important rebellions (as opposed to panics and rumors among whites) occurred during a forty-year period following the successful slave uprising in Haiti. A flurry of conspiracies in the 1790s led up to the Gabriel plot outside Richmond in 1800.

Slaves armed themselves and gathered to march on the city, but the plot was ruined by informers and a violent rainstorm. Gabriel, "the mainspring and chief mover," and about thirty others were hanged as examples. White Virginians were badly shaken. In 1822, a Charleston freedman, Denmark Vesey, organized another large rebellion. It was also betrayed and followed by some forty public hangings.

Nat Turner, a Virginia slave preacher, led the most drastic slave revolt. He took his followers on a route of killings through Southhampton County in 1831 and left some 60 white persons dead. Terrified whites, who came to regard Turner as a fanatic, lashed back by tracking down the rebels and killing many on the spot. In the process, one or two hundred blacks who had no connection with the rebellion were slaughtered. Turner himself remained at large for a month but was finally caught, tried, and hanged.

The impact of Turner's revolt was immediate and long-lasting. The reports of suppression and bloody reprisals carried a disheartening message across the black South. The white South sharpened its defenses as abolitionist propaganda spread. Even planters rode night patrols, whiskey often giving them courage against the terrors of darkness. In the towns and cities, police costs "for the purpose of 'keeping down the niggers'," as one traveler reported, made up the largest item in municipal budgets.

Olmstead wrote that in nearly every southern city he visited, "you come to police machinery such as you never find in towns under free governments: citadels, sentries, passports, grapeshotted cannon, and daily public whippings . . . for accidental infractions of police ceremonies."

"Free people of color," along with abolitionists, came increasingly under suspicion in the South. Many black preachers among the slaves were silenced. Indeed, the religious language in which slave rebels exhorted their followers convinced many planters that Bible reading—in fact any reading—was downright dangerous. Many states outlawed teaching slaves to read and write. Yet many slaves persisted in study and in individual strikes for freedom, despite the hostility of their environment.

THE PLANTATION ECONOMY

Everyone in the South, of whatever color, sex, or status, was affected by the workings of the plantation economy. Cotton, of course, was by far the most important crop, but in certain regions other staples predominated. In the South Carolina-Georgia low country, long-staple cotton surpassed rice as the most important crop. Upland cotton held sway in the lower tier of southern states, except in southern Louisiana, where sugar cane prevailed. In the upper South the growing season was usually too short for cotton. Very little was grown, and states like Virginia and Kentucky relied on tobacco and hemp.

Secondary Staples

The first southern agricultural staple had been tobacco in the Maryland and Virginia Tidewater region. After 1800, tobacco culture spread westward across the upper South. By midcentury, more tobacco was being grown there than on the older plantations. Yet after 1850 Virginia, North Carolina, and Maryland made a spectacular comeback in tobacco production. A slave who was an overseer and blacksmith on a North Carolina plantation discovered a method of curing a type of "bright yellow" tobacco that grew better on the poor sandy soil of the Roanoke Valley and inland Maryland than on the wornout soil of the Tidewater. Large plantations once again flourished in the Old Dominion and in neighboring states. Yet compared to cotton, tobacco remained a relatively minor southern crop.

The boom in tobacco benefited both large and small farmers. The latter were most successful with hemp, another source of profit, especially in Kentucky and Missouri. Only the wealthier planters, however, could successfully produce rice or sugar, the South's two other lesser staples. Both crops required gang labor, easily drawn from the dense black populations of South Carolina and

Georgia. These plantations were unmatched in scale by those of even the Gulf states of the Cotton Kingdom. In 1860, the only estate with more than a thousand slaves was in the South Carolina rice country.

Cane-sugar planting gained after 1822, when steam engines were introduced to crush the cane. Only large plantations could support the cost of the machinery, and the cane required an exceptionally long growing season. Both conditions were fulfilled in the warm, rich lands of southern Louisiana. It was in this area that French influence was still strong. An unusual ethnic intermixture combined with climate to create a special cultural subregion for blacks and whites.

Harvesting and grinding the cane demanded intensive periods of the hardest labor by slave gangs and white and black craftsmen. During the late autumn and early winter "grinding season," the vats were kept fired twenty-four hours a day, and slaves worked nearly around the clock. At the same time, the complicated process of sugar re-

Slavery and Agricultural Production

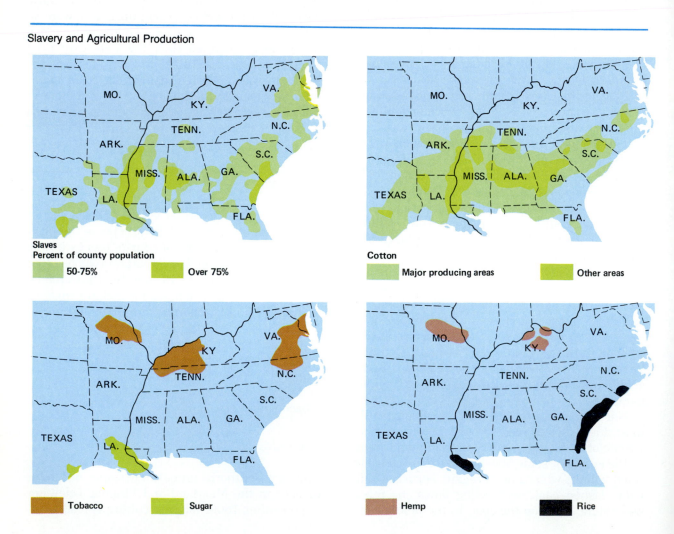

Slaves
Percent of county population
□ 50-75%   □ Over 75%

Cotton
□ Major producing areas   □ Other areas

□ Tobacco   □ Sugar

□ Hemp   ■ Rice

A SOUTHERN NATION

Slaves preparing cotton for gin on Beaufort, South Carolina plantation, 1862. (*Library of Congress*)

fining provided exceptional opportunities for slaves to acquire mechanical skills and the self-respect that went with them.

King Cotton

As early as 1820, the South's cotton crop had become more valuable than all its other crops combined. By 1835 the Cotton Kingdom had spread more than a thousand miles from South Carolina and Georgia into Texas and some 700 miles up the Mississippi Valley. Just before the Civil War, cotton accounted for two-thirds of the nation's exports.

With a little capital, small acreage, and a few slaves, a cotton farmer could still make a profit. Cotton could survive rough handling during shipping, and it did not spoil when stored. These were important considerations where poor transportation and warehousing caused marketing delays. Some of the American cotton crop, even on the frontier, was grown by small farmers. Yet cotton, with its huge market and great adaptability to gang labor, was the ideal staple for the big planters who spread over the virgin lands of the Southwest.

By 1860, slave gangs grew more than 93 percent of the Mississippi crop. Where land was plentiful and cheap, but not labor, the essence of good plantation management was high production per slave. Under effective overseers and slavedrivers, the more slaves a planter had, the greater his margin of success with cotton.

Large-scale operations gave big planters other advantages as well. Necessities they could not grow or make on the plantation, they could purchase in large quantities at wholesale rates. They could also market their crops more efficiently.

After the sale: Slaves going South from Richmond. (*Chicago Historical Society*)

Wealthier planters, moreover, were more likely to be interested in conserving the soil, more willing to experiment with new agricultural techniques.

White southerners were familiar with the contrasts drawn even by their own spokesmen between the busy North—enterprising, public-spirited, prosperous—and the indolent, poverty-stricken South. But many of them still feared the impact of factories on an agrarian slave society. Some felt that slaves working in a factory were already half-free. Others believed that blacks were incapable of mastering machinery. Many still harbored the distrust of cities that Jefferson had expressed so vividly a half-century earlier.

But in spite of such doubts and apprehensions, a favorable attitude toward manufacturing developed during the 1820s and early 1830s, when tariff debates made the South conscious of its dependence on the North. Factories, it was said, would furnish employment for unproductive poor whites and help keep southern wealth at home.

Despite some attempts at establishing cotton mills, the South remained overwhelmingly agricultural. Between 1850 and 1860, the number of industrial workers in the South rose only from 165,000 to 190,000. On the eve of the Civil War, the South was producing less than 10 percent of the nation's manufactured goods. In 1860, the Lowell mills alone operated more spindles than all the cotton-spinning factories of the South combined. The South showed even greater aversion to commerce.

At the numerous commercial conventions held in the South between 1830 and 1860, the southern imagination was fired with visions of teeming cities, happy artisans, and bustling markets, all the reward of recapturing the cotton-carrying trade from the North. But financial control of cotton marketing remained in the hands of outsiders. It was not southerners who held the reins of insurance, shipping, brokerage, and banking; the capital of the Cotton Kingdom was actually New York.

THE VALUES OF SOUTHERN WHITES

Slavery discouraged diversity in agriculture. It also speeded up the flow of southern farmers from the upper South into the free states and a false prosperity based on long-term credit, declining fertility, and expensive slaves. Yet after 1830 the allegiance of the vast majority of white southerners to the slave plantation system deepened. Their attachment varied according to class, region, and occupation, but a general consensus emerged. It depended heavily on economic self-interest, racial hostility, and the realization that slavery was under attack.

Commitment to White Domination

The consensus that supported slavery was in turn supported by certain important beliefs. The extremely heavy concentration of slaves in parts of the South generated deep-seated fears among whites that they were becoming a minority. In response to northern abolitionists, southern spokesmen replied that people living in the North, where blacks made up only a small fraction of the population, could not possibly know what things were like in South Carolina or Mississippi communities.

Many whites in the South really thought that blacks would be harmed by abolition. This belief was strengthened by reports about the condition of free blacks in the North. Everywhere in the free states, blacks were abused and discriminated against politically, economically, and socially, and then blamed for their situation. This argument had such good basis in fact that abolitionists found it very difficult to disprove.

White workers in southern cities and factories, like most northern workingmen, did not want to work alongside blacks, slave or free. They shared the common human tendency to exclude identifiable groups of people from the labor market to reserve it for themselves. At the same time, small planters, linked to the planting class by kinship or common interest, felt that their chances of rising in the world would be hurt by abolition. They, and many farmers too poor to own slaves, shared the common assumptions of the Jacksonian era. They hoped they might rise in the world and one day become masters of larger plantations.

Impoverished southern whites supported slavery as a way of preserving what little status they had. As Olmsted commented on this class of whites: "They are said to 'corrupt' the negroes and to encourage them to steal, or to work for them at night and on Sundays, and to pay them with liquor, and to constantly associate licentiously with them. They seem, nevertheless, more than any other portion of the community, to hate and de-

spise the negroes." When the crisis came in 1861, these men fought for slave property and a slaveowning class, although the planters held them in contempt.

Limitations of the Reform Spirit

Many southern writers claimed that the South had built a superior civilization on a solid base of slavery. But the claim itself was on shaky ground. New ideas were not welcome in the antebellum South. Education, literacy, and the arts lagged behind the North. In the southern mind, all "isms"—feminism, transcendentalism, Fourierism—quickly became tinged with abolitionism. Actually, there was good reason for this attitude, since northern abolitionists like Garrison, Theodore Parker, Theodore Weld, Lucretia Mott, Sarah and Angelina Grimké, and Lydia Maria Child were drawn to the whole range of reform programs.

Like many people under attack, southern writers developed code words to describe the opposition—"misguided philanthropy" and "northern fanaticism." Feminism in particular outraged the southern ideal of womanhood. Southern mavericks—notably the aristocratic Angelina and Sarah Grimké of Charleston—turned abolitionist or gave in to other "enthusiasms." But they were made to suffer for their independence and driven North.

Yet the spirit of humanitarianism and reform that flooded the North in the 1830s and 1840s did not leave the South untouched. A number of southern states changed their harsh criminal codes, improved their prisons, and humanized the treatment of the insane. Dorothea Dix was welcomed in the South for her work on behalf of the mentally ill. During the same period, schools for the deaf were patterned after northern models. Temperance was the most enthusiastically supported reform movement in the prewar South. Backed by religious and political leaders, temperance societies sprang up everywhere.

The Proslavery Argument

In the revolutionary period, many leaders in the upper South had seen the contradiction of slavery in a republic dedicated to the principles of the Declaration of Independence. They did little about it, except for scattered individuals who privately freed their own slaves. A later generation of southerners dominated the American Colonization Society, founded in 1817 with the unrealistic hope of getting rid of slavery by freeing blacks on condition that they emigrate to Africa.

In that age, the personal penalties that slavery imposed on the consciences of slaveowners could be considerable. The following extract from the will of a North Carolinian who emancipated his slaves makes this clear. He gave four reasons for his actions:

Reason the first. Agreeably to the rights of man, every human being, be his or her colour what it may, is entitled to freedom. . . . Reason the second. My conscience, the great criterion, condemns me for keeping them in slavery. Reason the third. The golden rule directs us to do unto every human creature, as we would wish to be done unto. . . . Reason the fourth and last. I wish to die with a clear conscience, that I may not be ashamed to appear before my master in a future World.

In this man's case, which was not unusual in the revolutionary era, two independent traditions merged: a devotion to natural rights and a commitment to Christian principles.

This way of thinking never completely died out in the South. But at the beginning of the 1830s a number of events caused a crisis in southern thinking about slavery. In 1829 David Walker, a free black man in Boston, published a fiery *Appeal* to southern slaves for a full-scale revolt. A shudder of horror and outrage went through the white South. Walker was later found mysteriously murdered. In January 1831, also in Boston, William Lloyd Garrison brought out the first issue of *The Liberator*, in which he began his attack on southern slavery. Abolitionism seemed to shift into high gear, and soon a price had been placed upon Garrison's head.

Late that summer, Nat Turner's rebellion horrified the nation. The following winter the Virginia legislature not only debated gradual emancipation bills, but came close to passing one. At the same time the nation was in the middle of

A cotton plantation on the Mississippi. (*Library of Congress*)

the nullification controversy with South Carolina, which itself ultimately revolved around the issue of slavery.

The response to these events was immediate and drastic. Whereas southerners had previously claimed that slavery was a "necessary evil," they now eagerly took up the proposition that slavery was a "positive good." The first full-blown defense of slavery on this basis was written in 1832 by Thomas R. Dew, a professor of legal philosophy at the College of William and Mary. As the case was elaborated over the next generation, southern writers used many authorities in support of their cause: the Bible, the Constitution, the history of Greece and Rome, the science of political economy, and the "facts" of biology. Slavery, southern writers claimed, fostered the classical form of democracy with all the Greek virtues, as distinct from the tyranny of "wage slavery" in the North.

George Fitzhugh's *Sociology for the South; Or the Failure of Free Society* (1854) and *Cannibals All! Or Slaves Without Masters* (1857) brought together many of the familiar arguments in favor of slavery. Following Calhoun's lead, Fitzhugh claimed that in the South capital and labor were not divorced. The fierce exploitation of one class by another, as in the laissez-faire economy of the North, was absent here. Northern capitalism, Fitzhugh declared, led to the impoverishment of the masses and to social revolution, not to liberty and democracy.

His arguments were a telling and sophisticated critique of the northern industrial economy. But they failed to deal with weaknesses in southern society. These weaknesses were causing many southerners to declare their society perfect in the face of the general assessment of Western civilization that it was backward and sinful.

Education and Literature

Southern society showed many characteristics of Jacksonian America, but it lacked certain dynamic elements which proved to be the cutting edges of a more modern world. Public education remained almost nonexistent in the South. In thinly populated rural areas, rich planters resisted taxation for public schools. Those who would have benefited from schools felt they bore the stigma of charity. Some 2700 private academies could be found in the South by 1850, more than in New England and middle states combined. But students were

few and the quality of education was lower than in the North. The 1850 census showed 20 percent of southern whites illiterate, 2 percent in the middle states, and 1 percent in New England.

Southern higher education compared more favorably. Some wealthy southern families continued to send their sons to Yale, Princeton, Harvard, and the University of Pennsylvania, rather than to their own new state universities and denominational colleges. At the same time, the percentage of southerners attending college was higher than that of northerners. In 1860, for example, when the northern population was 2.5 times that of the white population of the South, each section counted about 26,000 college students.

Most southern colleges were less richly endowed than those in the North. Such schools as the University of Virginia, South Carolina College, and the University of North Carolina struggled to keep up with the institutions above the Mason-Dixon line. In addition, southern colleges were dependent on the North for much of their reading material, because virtually all textbooks were published in the North. Most were also written by northern authors. One text, for example, described slavery as a "stain on the human race, which corrupts the master as much as it debases the slave"— a statement white southerners could scarcely accept.

The political and religious liberalism of the Jeffersonian South began to disappear in the early years of the nineteenth century. Enlightenment ideas began to give way before the sweep of religious fundamentalism and the necessity of defending slavery. The religious revivals of the antebellum period converted thousands of people to the Methodist and Baptist churches, and ministers of these and smaller denominations gained great influence.

These ministers tended to endorse the status quo. They thundered against the evils of infidelity, alcohol, and the ideas of the North. They denounced atheists, Deists, Unitarians, and "nothingarians" as enemies of God and social order. In 1835, a North Carolina constitutional convention voted to exclude Jews and atheists from public office.

A spirit of intellectual repressiveness was by no means confined to the South. Heresy hunts and anti-infidel crusades also flickered through the North and West. But in the South the skeptical minority was much more thoroughly pressured into silence by those who felt called to denounce what they saw as "profane sinners, downright skeptics, and God-defying wretches."

Even though a number of talented southern writers published fiction, poetry, and essays during the antebellum period, there was no literary flowering comparable to New England's. John Pendleton Kennedy's novels, such as *Swallow Barn* (1832) for example, were marred by defensiveness about slavery. No southern author treated slavery or slaves meaningfully. William Gilmore Simms, the section's most prolific novelist, offered heroes whose lips curled and eyes flashed, along with doll-like heroines who spoke in stilted phrases. His low-life characters, his traders, tavernkeepers, and poor whites, were much more real. He was the only southern novelist before the Civil War who wrote convincingly about ordinary farmers and poor whites.

But too much energy was going into defense of the South's special culture to permit either writers or readers a broader outlook. The most popular writer in the South was Sir Walter Scott, a Scottish author who filled his novels with gallant cavaliers of an earlier age. His gallant knights seemed an appropriate model for southern chivalry. It was only later, in the twentieth century, when America's southland was partially released from the pain of slavery, that southern authors like William Faulkner could fully portray their own world. In doing so, they would produce some of the nation's best literature.

Southern Women, White and Black

In many ways the burden of this thinking fell especially on southern women. Both the practice and defense of slavery led to habits of mind that affected women in different ways than men. And of course black women were affected differently.

While black women were sometimes the sexual victims of white men, they were less likely to become the victims of destructive racial stereotyping than black males. White southern literature and folklore turned adult black males into "boys" and tried to shape them into fawning, irresponsible buffoons. This dehumanizing, infantilizing stereotype was applied much less to slave women, who were often thought of in terms of the loving "Mammy" role.

"Field hands"—"Force"—"Hands"—"People" and "Niggers" are terms applied to the purchased laborers of a plantation: but "Slaves"—never. "Boys" is the general term for the men, and "women," for females. It is common to address a Negroe forty years of age as "boy." If much older he is called "daddy," or "uncle;" but "mister," or "man"—never. The females, in old age, become "aunty," "granny," or "old lady."

Then, too, black women were rarely seen as physically threatening, while black men (despite being thought of as childlike) were at times described as potential murderers and lustful rapists.

White women who lived as wives and daughters of nonslaveholders lived lives much like those of their northern counterparts, though they were more likely to be truly poor and to have fewer opportunities to visit with one another in little towns. For white women of the planting class, slavery and its defense imposed a rigid orthodoxy. Unlike many of their northern sisters, they were confined to their homes and to rounds of parties, entertaining, and social visits. Many of them found the supervision of the household slaves more a burden than a privilege. They were expected by their husbands and other male relatives to be decorative, charming, but most certainly not learned. The diaries kept by some of these women reveal that they felt injured and confined by the system of chattel slavery. They resented especially the miscegenation their men were involved in. One woman lashed out at the destructiveness of illicit interracial sex in a famous passage:

God forgive us, but ours is a monstrous system, a wrong and an iniquity! Like the patriarchs of old, our men live all in one house with their wives and concubines; and the mulattoes one sees in every family partly resemble the white children. Any lady is ready to tell you who is the father of all the mulatto children in everybody's household but her own. Those, she seems to think, drop from the clouds. My disgust sometimes is boiling over. Thank God for my country women, but alas for the men!

It is no wonder that few southern women became involved in reform causes. They had a major grievance at home, but it was one that the growing orthodoxy concerning slavery prevented their even discussing in public. That orthodoxy was increasingly making the South something of a closed society. It tightened its grip as national expansion in the West made slavery more and more the dominant issue between the sections.

The Gideon sisters with their servants. (*Western Reserve Historical Society*)

SUMMARY

The South was different from the North, and in the decades before the Civil War became more and more conscious that it was.

Among the white people of the South, the largest group were not planters or poor whites, but simple farmers who owned no slaves. The real planting class was a very small minority; only 8000 planters owned fifty or more slaves, and almost half of all slaveowning families had fewer than six slaves. Yet most of the blacks of the South were on the large plantations. More than half lived on plantations with more than twenty slaves; only about 10 percent lived in cities and towns. The principal social contact of many blacks was with other blacks; they lived somewhat isolated in an Afro-American subculture that was no longer an African culture, because by 1860 most slaves were American-born.

The treatment of slaves varied from sadism and cruelty to gentle paternalism. In general, slaves in the frontier Southwest were treated more severely than in the older South. But everywhere the white man was dominant. So the slaves created an inner world of their own, especially through religion and music. There was also resistance, mostly passive but sometimes active in the form of arson or rebellion.

The southern economy was largely a plantation economy. Cotton was the most important crop, but tobacco, rice, and sugar were also grown. As early as 1820, cotton had become more valuable than all the other crops combined. Despite some interest in the 1820s and 1830s in establishing the factory system in the South and in making the South a commercial center, the region remained overwhelmingly agricultural.

As northern pressure over slavery mounted, the allegiance of the vast majority of southern whites to the slave plantation system deepened. So did the southern belief in the rightness of white domination and the superiority of southern civilization. After 1830 there were proslavery arguments, not just the defensive attitude that slavery was a "necessary evil." White southerners contended that slavery was a "positive good" for both whites and blacks. Yet the South continued to lag behind in education. Intellectual repression became another characteristic of a society that felt itself under siege.

The women of the South, both black and white, felt the impact of the slave system in special ways. After the mid-1840s that impact grew stronger and stronger, as national expansion in the West sharpened political issues between the country's two sections, slave and free.

Suggested Readings

Two different overviews are C. Sydnor, *The Development of Southern Sectionalism, 1819–1848* (1948), and A. Craven, *The Growth of Southern Nationalism, 1848–1861* (1953). E. Genovese, *The Political Economy of Slavery* (1965), is a provocative analysis of the southern economy and its social dimensions; see also his *The World the Slaveholders Made* (1970). L. Gray, *History of Agriculture in the Southern United States to 1860* (2 vols., 1933) is one of few such works still valuable a half-century after publication. A newer approach is H. Woodman, *Slavery and the Southern Economy* (1966), and A. Cowdrey, *This Land, This South: An Environmental History* (1983).

Frederick Olmsted was by far the most astute and reliable northern observer. Some of his travel accounts are available in A. Schlesinger (ed.), *The Cotton Kingdom* (1953). Four works focus on important aspects of southern white society: J. Franklin, *The Militant South, 1800–1861* (1956), a description of the strain of violence and militarism; E. Dick, *The Dixie Frontier* (1938); F. Owsley, *Plain Folk of the Old South* (1949); and J. Oakes, *The Ruling Race: A History of American Slaveholders* (1982). White southern women are discussed in A. Scott, *The Southern Lady: From Pedestal to Politics* (1970) and C. Clinton, *The Plantation Mistress: Woman's World in the Old South* (1982). Free black women in one community are closely studied in S. Lebsock, *The Free Women of Petersburg: Status and Culture in a Southern Town, 1784–1860* (1984).

The most balanced histories of Afro-Americans are J. Franklin, *From Slavery to Freedom: A History of Negro Americans* (4th ed., 1974), and P. Foner, *History of Black Americans: From the Emergence of the Cotton Kingdom to the Eve of the Compromise of 1950* (1983). A. Weinstein and F. Gatell (eds.), *American Negro Slavery: A Modern Reader* (3rd ed., 1979), is an excellent collection of various modern views on the subject. U. Phillips, *American Negro Slavery* (1918), will repel many readers because of the author's views on blacks, but it contains useful information. K. Stampp, *The Peculiar Institution: Slavery in the Ante-Bellum South* (1956), is a modern classic, but it should be read in light of a different view of the slave's culture presented in J. Blassingame, *The Slave Community: Plantation Life in the Antebellum South* (1972). W. L. Rose, *Slavery and Freedom*, W. Freihling, ed. (1982), convincingly stresses how different slavery was in the antebellum years than earlier.

E. Genovese, *Roll, Jordan, Roll: The World the Slaves Made* (1974), is a long, richly detailed discussion of the strength of black culture. In this connection, there are two recent books of splendid quality: D. Epstein, *Sinful Tunes and Spirituals: Black Folk Music to the Civil War* (1977); and L. Levine, *Black Culture and Black Consciousness: Afro-American Folk Thought from Slavery to Freedom* (1977). An account of slavery by the victims is R. Starobin (ed.), *Blacks in Bondage: Letters of Americans Slaves* (1974). One book that is not about slavery sheds much light on it: E. Ayers, *Vengeance and Justice: Crime and Punishment in the Nineteenth Century American South* (1984).

These general studies may be supplemented by important monographs such as Starobin's *Industrial Slavery in the Old South* (1970); R. Wade, *Slavery in the Cities: The South, 1820–1860* (1972); W. Scarborough, *The Overseer: Plantation Management in the Old South* (1966); and C. Joyner, *Down by the Riverside: A South Carolina Slave Community* (1984). There are many works comparing slavery regionally in the New World. S. Elkins, *Slavery: A Problem in American Institutional and Intellectual Life* (2nd ed., 1968), a controversial study, should be read along with A. Lane (ed.), *The Debate over Slavery: Stanley Elkins and His Critics* (1971). A more balanced view is presented in C. Degler, *Neither Black nor White: Slavery and Race Relations in Brazil and the United States* (1971).

The matter of slave resistance has also been controversial. H. Aptheker, *American Negro Slave Revolts* (1943), first made an extended case for the inherent rebelliousness of American slaves. N. Yetman (ed.), *Voices from Slavery* (1970), is a fascinating collection of interviews with elderly ex-slaves in 1937; and G. Rawick has written a fine account based on those interviews, *The American Slave: A Composite Autobiography* (1972).

W. Cash, *The Mind of the South* (1941), is a penetrating study of illusion and reality. W. Taylor, *Cavalier and Yankee: The Old South and American National Character* (1961), probes different attitudes and assumptions that eventually helped break one nation apart. E. McKitrick (ed.), *Slavery Defended: The Views of the Old South* (1963), is an anthology of proslavery writings. C. Degler, *The Other South: Southern Dissenters in the Nineteenth Century* (1974), offers an analysis of southerners who opposed slavery. A recent study illuminates conflicting values in the South: D. Bailey, *Shadow on the Church: Southwestern Evangelical Religion and the Issue of Slavery, 1783–1860* (1985). An important turning point is covered in A. Freehling, *Drift Toward Dissolution: The Virginia Slavery Debate of 1831–1832* (1982).

Racial attitudes are explored in G. Frederickson, *The Black Image in the White Mind: The Debate on Afro-American Character and Destiny, 1817–1914* (1971); J. Kovel, *White Racism: A Psychohistory* (1970); and W. Stanton, *The Leopard's Spots: Scientific Attitudes toward Race in America, 1815–1859* (1960).

MANIFEST DESTINY AND SLAVERY

Chapter 15

Throughout the 1820s and 1830s, Americans were very much on the move—not only into new states in the Louisiana Purchase, but all the way to the Pacific Coast and even beyond to Pacific islands. Within little more than a quarter of a century, the unbroken expanse of the United States had been extended to its present limits, the annexation of Hawaii had been proposed, and the purchase of Alaska completed. Both Canada and Cuba still looked tempting to those who thought the United States was destined to rule the North American continent.

The phrase "manifest destiny" became identified with American expansionism about 1845, but the idea of a divine mission was much older. This notion, which had begun to tempt colonial Americans when they had captured Louisburg a century before, suggested that God had set aside the American continent and nearby islands as reservations "for the free development of our yearly multiplying millions." No physical barrier, no foreign force, could stop the American people from extending their system.

Practical politicians in charge of the country's day-to-day policies in the 1840s promoted more tangible objectives. They hoped to dominate northern Pacific waters and trade to the Orient, which they saw as a legitimate extension of the American West. They also turned their eyes to Canada, where for a time they kept running into serious border conflicts. They had to deal with the question of the Oregon Country, an area claimed by both Great Britain and the United States. In the Southwest, a new republic emerged as the result of American westward settlement. For a time Texas remained independent, but there was strong sentiment for annexing it to the United States.

In the mid-1840s an aggressive American president provoked a war with Mexico. That conflict brought great territorial gains for Americans. But it also raised the question of whether those territories should be open to slavery. That issue came close to tearing the nation apart, but it was patched over by a complex compromise in 1850. As the compromise went into effect, it produced both relief and anger. Many people began to doubt whether it would last. ■

THE CANADIAN BORDER

The westward surge of the American people and the star-spangled predictions that their flag would wave from Cape Horn to the North Pole strengthened suspicions in Europe. The British (along with the rest of Europe) saw the Yankees as a people to be watched. These opinions were based partly on the reports of British travelers who made quick tours of America. Many people in Britain were greatly angered by the American states' repudiating their debts to British creditors after the Panic of 1837.

They also disliked the boastful spirit of American democracy, which the popular author, Charles Dickens, mimicked: "We are a model of wisdom, and an example to the world, and the perfection of human reason." Britain had led the world by emancipating blacks in its colonies in 1833, and thereafter the British scoffed at the peculiar American brand of liberty which defended slavery and assaulted abolitionists. Underlying each nineteenth-century conflict between Britain and the United States was the growing commercial and industrial rivalry of the two nations.

There were more practical reasons to be watchful of the Americans. The British had very low expectations of Canada as a paying colony. But Canada had its uses—"above all," wrote a future colonial secretary, "in case of war with the United States." In such an event, he added, Canada "furnishes ample assistance in men, timber and harbours for carrying on the war, and that on the enemy's frontier." How seriously Britain took the American menace was made clear by its spending millions of pounds to build the inland Rideau Canal as an alternative to the St. Lawrence River in case control of the latter ever fell to American invaders. The British spent millions more rebuilding the strategic citadel of Quebec. In the late 1830s and early 1840s, three confrontations gave the British and Americans excuses for war: the *Caroline* affair, the Maine border, and the *Creole* incident.

The *Caroline* Affair

In 1837, inspired in part by the "great experiment" below the border, insurrections flared up in Canada. Loyal forces quickly suppressed these upris-

View of the capitol, 1824. (*Metropolitan Museum of Art, Purchase, 1942, Joseph Pulitzer Bequest*)

There are a good many theories about the parentage of *Uncle Sam*, who has come to represent the U.S. government and the United States as a nation on the international scene. Most scholars agree that no single person invented the term or the artist's view of the strong but kindly, tall and rather thin, mature but not old gentleman attired in top hat and striped trousers, all in the star-spangled colors of red, white, and blue. The name Uncle Sam first came into use during the War of 1812, and his appearance at that time suggests that he was the product of nationalistic anti-British feelings. When British-American international tensions began to subside after the American Civil War, Uncle Sam began to replace the more predominant previous American character, Brother Jonathan, who was a similarly thin man when drawn by political cartoonists as an opponent of John Bull, a solid and portly gentleman who stood for the British nation. Some scholars connect the name of Uncle Sam with the initials U.S., the United States, but this connection is uncertain. In the twentieth century, however, the character has been used by hostile foreign journalists to represent the evils of American imperialism.

ings, but not before some Americans had come to the rebels' aid. One night the *Caroline*, a small American steamer ferrying supplies to the insurgents, lay moored off the New York shore of the Niagara River. A party of loyal Canadian volunteers rowed across, threw out the *Caroline's* crew, set her afire, and watched her sink. During the scuffle one American was killed.

The United States promptly demanded an apology. But the British replied that the *Caroline*, by aiding the criminal conspiracy in Canada, had become fair game. New York authorities arrested Alexander McLeod, one of the Canadian participants in the raid on the vessel, and charged him with murder and arson. The British foreign secretary Lord Palmerston admitted that the raid had been officially planned to prevent American aid to the insurrectionists. He went on to demand McLeod's release on grounds that any actions he may have taken were done under orders. McLeod's execution, Palmerston warned, would mean war. New York's Governor William H. Seward insisted that McLeod face trial in the state courts. He promised Secretary of State Webster that if convicted, McLeod would be pardoned. Fortunately for both countries, he was acquitted.

The "Aroostook War"

The winter freeze on the St. Lawrence had hampered the movement of the troops putting down the Canadian revolts of 1837. The next year the British decided to build a road from St. John on the Bay of Fundy in New Brunswick to Quebec and Montreal. In February 1839 work began in the rich Aroostook River Valley, where conflicting claims of the state of Maine and the province of New Brunswick had grown sharper as the value of the timber in the valley rose. When "foreign" lumberjacks entered the area and began clearing trees for the road, the Maine militia chased them out.

The Aroostook war was a bloodless affair, but an angry Congress appropriated $10 million and authorized President Van Buren to enlist 50,000 volunteers. As it turned out, neither money nor men were needed. General Winfield Scott, the president's negotiator, succeeded in smoothing things over at the scene. Scott was not able to eliminate the source of the trouble, however, which lay in the vagueness of the frontier line. Not until the Webster-Ashburton Treaty of 1842 was Maine's northern boundary firmly established.

The *Creole* Incident

The *Creole* case of 1841 strained Anglo-American relations on another touchy subject, and made Canadian border issues more difficult to settle. In its attempts to stop the Atlantic slave traffic on the high seas, Britain had made treaties with many nations giving its navy the right even in peacetime to stop and search suspected ships under all flags. Palmerston boasted that Britain had enlisted in the fight against the slave trade "every state in Christendom which has a flag that sails on the ocean, with the single exception of the United States of North America." This was not entirely true. France, like the United States, had resisted Britain's assumption of their authority. But it suited Palmerston to point his finger at the United States—with some justice, for slave ships of various nations often escaped search and seizure simply by running up the Stars and Stripes.

The American brig *Creole* was carrying about

130 slaves from Virginia to New Orleans in 1841 when the blacks revolted and took over the vessel. It was the most successful slave insurrection in American history, led by a man named Madison Washington. They sailed her to the British port of Nassau in the Bahamas and went ashore, knowing that British territory would mean freedom. Only one white passenger had been killed in the revolt. The *Creole's* owners and American officials tried to reclaim the slaves. The British insisted the slaves were freed by their own action in successfully reaching a British port. The blacks remained in Nassau as free people, while white Americans fumed in indignation.

The Webster–Ashburton Treaty

Palmerston's attitude made him sufficiently unpopular to evoke sighs of relief on both sides of the Atlantic when a change of ministers threw him out of office in 1841. The new foreign secretary was far more agreeable, and he appointed as special envoy to the United States Lord Ashburton, the husband of an American heiress.

The principal point of the talks between Ashburton and Secretary of State Daniel Webster was the Canadian-American border. The talks took place in an atmosphere dominated by assumptions on both sides of the Atlantic that at some point or another, a third war between Great Britian and the United States was nearly inevitable. Ultimately, the two diplomats compromised on the Maine boundary; they also agreed on the inaccurately surveyed boundary along northern Vermont and New York and westward to Minnesota and Ontario. They smoothed over the *Caroline* and the *Creole* affairs with such skillful language that both sides were made to seem in the right.

The results did much for their historical reputations, though not their popularity at the time. Extremists in both countries protested that their country had suffered a diplomatic defeat. But the Webster-Ashburton Treaty, signed in 1842, was a model of compromise that paved the way for other peaceful settlements during the next two decades.

TEXAS

In the North, after forcible removal of the Sauk and Fox tribes in 1833, white emigrants from Illinois, Indiana, Ohio, and Kentucky began to spill into the newly opened Iowa and Wisconsin coun-

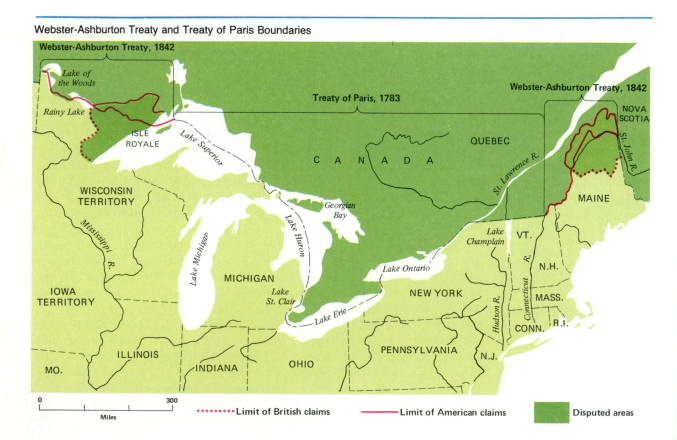

Webster-Ashburton Treaty and Treaty of Paris Boundaries

········· Limit of British claims   —— Limit of American claims   Disputed areas

MANIFEST DESTINY AND SLAVERY

try. By 1840, some 75,000 settlers had established themselves on the rich farmlands there. Smaller numbers, including lumbermen and trappers, pushed into Minnesota. Southern farmers as well as planters had no land like this at their disposal. By 1840, much of the best land on the southern Gulf plains was occupied by large planters and slaves. After the admission of Arkansas in 1836, the only remaining prospective slave state under the provisions of the Missouri Compromise was the territory of Florida.

Immediately to the west of the last southern settlements lay the "permanent Indian frontier," established in the 1820s in much of present-day Oklahoma and Kansas. That land was set aside forever, it was said, for the displaced woodland Indians of the East as well as the tribes native to the region. South and west of this "Indian territory" stretched Texas, only recently independent of Mexico. Beyond Texas lay Mexico's vaguely defined California empire, whose charms had been so lavishly publicized by American mountain men and sailors.

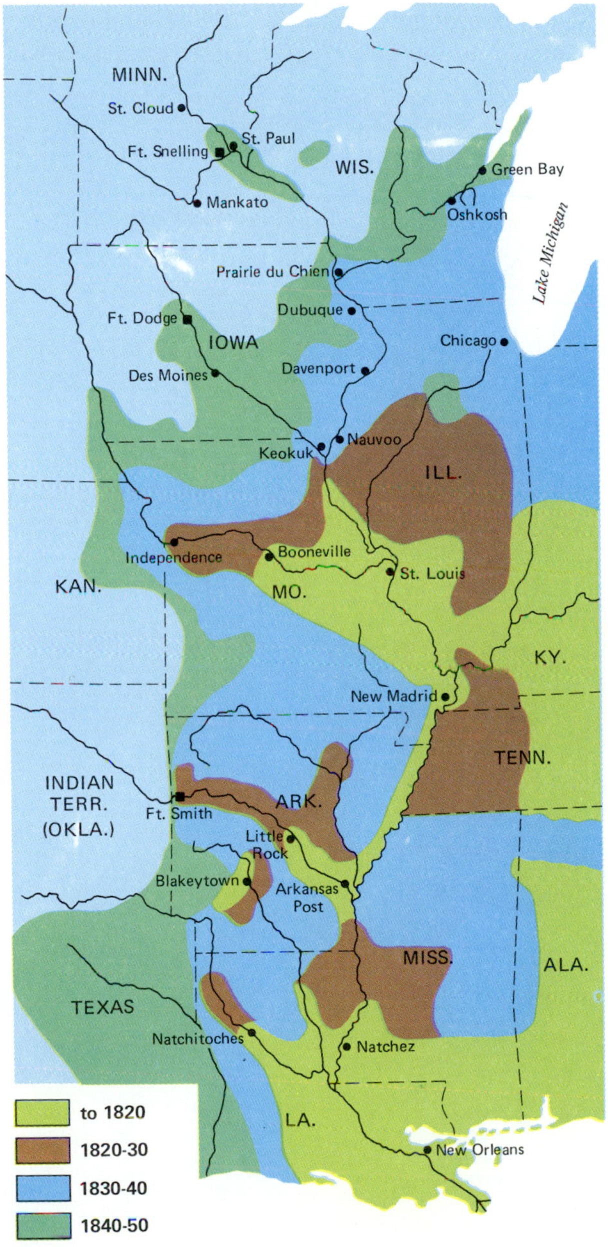

The Lone Star Republic

American claims to the Mexican province of Texas were based on the carefree geography of the Louisiana Purchase treaty. When the United States obtained Florida from Spain in 1819, it surrendered those claims. American traders and military adventurers continued the illegal commercial relations they had already established with the Mexicans, despite Spain's many warnings. When Mexico, with the assistance of these traders and fighters, won its independence from Spain in 1821, the Mexican government promptly put American commerce on a legitimate footing and invited Americans to settle in Texas. Connecticut-born Moses Austin, who obtained a land grant from the Mexican government in 1820, pioneered the American colonization of Texas. He died before developing his tract, but Mexico validated the grant for his son Stephen, who carried through the first colonization program.

Mexican officials had hoped that the settlement of Texas by Anglo-Americans would protect their sparsely settled borderland outposts from Indian raids. They soon realized they had miscalculated about the results of immigration from the United States. Between 1820 and 1830, about 20,000 Americans with approximately 2000 slaves had crossed into Texas, largely from the lower Mississippi frontier. Most were law-abiding people. But rougher elements made the Mexicans agree with John Jay's old complaint that white frontiersmen were more dangerous than Indians. Texas-Americans, on their part, soon began to complain about lack of self-government.

Offers by the United States to purchase Texas only served to deepen Mexico's anxiety. Furthermore, American settlers in Mexico had failed to become Catholics, as they were required to do by the terms of their invitation. They ignored a Mexican prohibition on bringing in slaves by substituting a thinly disguised indenture system. Some

Settlement of the Mississippi Valley

Legend:
- to 1820
- 1820-30
- 1830-40
- 1840-50

Map labels: MINN., St. Cloud, St. Paul, Ft. Snelling, Mankato, WIS., Green Bay, Oshkosh, Lake Michigan, Prairie du Chien, Dubuque, Ft. Dodge, IOWA, Chicago, Des Moines, Davenport, Nauvoo, Keokuk, ILL., Independence, Booneville, St. Louis, KAN., MO., KY., New Madrid, TENN., INDIAN TERR. (OKLA.), Ft. Smith, ARK., Little Rock, Blakeytown, Arkansas Post, MISS., ALA., TEXAS, Natchitoches, Natchez, LA., New Orleans

Americans, moreover, slipped into territory reserved by law for Mexicans.

In 1830 the Mexican government sent troops to occupy Texas, stopped further American immigration, and passed other restrictive measures, including the abolition of slavery. Shortly thereafter, General A. L. de Santa Anna, Mexico's strongman, instituted a centralist program and abolished all local rights of self-government in his distant province. Early in 1836 he led an army of 6000 into Texas. Confronted with this threat, Americans there declared their independence on March 2, 1836. They set up a provisional government under a constitution that allowed slavery, and appointed Sam Houston commander-in-chief of a Texas army.

Santa Anna already had the Alamo mission in San Antonio under seige. For ten days, 187 Americans held off a much larger number of Mexican troops, taking a heavy toll. Finally, on March 6, Mexican cannons opened holes in the walls. Their troops poured through: They killed the Americans, including the wounded and such legendary figures as Davy Crockett and James Bowie, threw oil on the bodies, and burned them. It proved to be a costly victory, for it aroused the anger of Texas-Americans. They went into later battles crying "Remember the Alamo." Three weeks later, more than 300 Americans died at Goliad after surrendering to troops led by General José Urrea.

These defeats forced Houston to retreat east until he reached the vicinity of San Jacinto creek. There, on April 21, 1836, his troops suddenly turned on the unprepared pursuers, defeated Santa Anna's army, and took the general captive. Santa Anna signed a treaty giving Texas indepen-

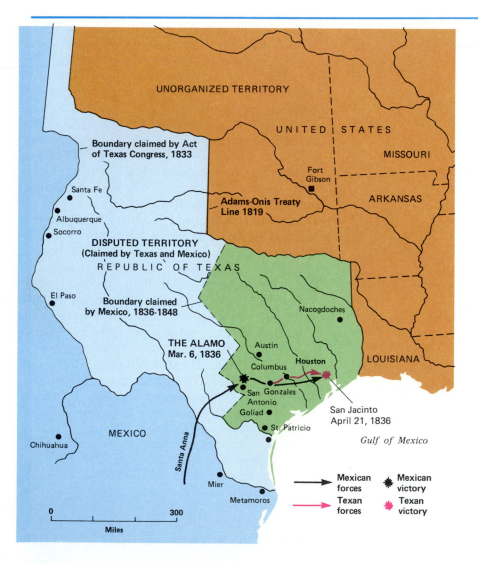

The Texas Revolution

UNORGANIZED TERRITORY

UNITED STATES

MISSOURI

Boundary claimed by Act of Texas Congress, 1833

Santa Fe

Fort Gibson

Adams-Onis Treaty Line 1819

ARKANSAS

Albuquerque
Socorro

DISPUTED TERRITORY
(Claimed by Texas and Mexico)
REPUBLIC OF TEXAS

El Paso

Boundary claimed by Mexico, 1836-1848

Nacogdoches

THE ALAMO
Mar. 6, 1836

Austin
Columbus
Houston

LOUISIANA

San
Antonio
Gonzales
Goliad

San Jacinto
April 21, 1836

MEXICO

Chihuahua

Santa Anna

St. Patricio

Gulf of Mexico

Mier

Metamoros

0   300
Miles

Mexican forces
Texan forces
Mexican victory
Texan victory

MANIFEST DESTINY AND SLAVERY

dence and fixing a vague boundary between Mexico and Texas. Although the Mexican Congress promptly disallowed the treaty, it seemed powerless to reverse it.

Annexation

Sympathy for the Texas rebels had been strong in the South and also in the Northwest, where their cause was identified with the struggles of all pioneers. There was far less support in the Northeast. Whig leaders viewed the Texans' request to enter the Union as a slaveowners' plot. Anywhere from five to seven states, they pointed out, might be carved from the huge Texas domain, thus ensuring southern control of Congress. Opponents of annexation protested so much that President Jackson waited to give diplomatic recognition to the Lone Star Republic until just before he left office in 1837. Van Buren also withstood growing annexationist pressure. The policy was to cost him his political future during Tyler's administration.

Denied admission to the United States and menaced by an unforgiving Mexico, the Lone Star Republic sought protection elsewhere. Britain welcomed an independent Texas that would export cotton and import British manufactured goods. Britain also opposed slavery, and Foreign Secretary Aberdeen declared that "with regard to Texas, we avow that we wish to see slavery abolished, as elsewhere." But the presence of slavery did not keep Britain from wanting to recognize and support Texas as an independent republic that would serve as an obstacle to continued United States expansion.

President Tyler himself worked tirelessly to gain credit for annexation before his successor took office. In April 1844 he submitted to the Senate a Texas statehood treaty drawn up by Calhoun, his newly appointed secretary of state. But with characteristic tactlessness, Calhoun attached a little essay on the virtues of slavery in response to Aberdeen's vow to abolish it. These remarks ensured the Senate's rejection of the arrangement, 36 to 16. But Tyler was not finished.

In February 1845, after President Polk's election on an expansionist platform, he persuaded Congress to annex Texas by passing a joint resolution that required only a majority vote, not the two-thirds needed for treaties. In October Texas accepted its terms, which explicitly permitted slavery under the Missouri Compromise. On December 29, 1845, Texas became the twenty-eighth state. Mexico recalled its minister from Washington.

THE FAR WEST

The grand but forbidding Pacific coastline of North America had only three first-rate natural harbors: Puget Sound, the gateway to the Oregon Country; San Francisco Bay, inside Mexico's California; and the Bay of San Diego, farther south. American spokesmen from all sections of the country were in agreement on taking these fine anchorages and keeping out rival powers, especially Britain. Americans also learned about the beauty and fertility of the Willamette Valley in the Oregon country and the stunning expanses of California.

The Oregon Country

The future of Oregon as well as the future of Texas had reached a critical point when the presidential campaign of 1844 began. Distant though it was from the mainstream of European and American politics and business, the Oregon country had long been the scene of competition among France, Spain, Russia, Britain, and the United States.

Trapper Long Jake. (*Yale University Art Gallery, Mabel Brady Gavin Collection*)

Mountain man Jim Baker. (*Colorado Historical Society*)

Early in the nineteenth century, France and Spain had surrendered their claims. The Russians had agreed to fix their own southern boundary at 54° 40′. This left Britain and the United States free to contest ownership of the remainder of "Oregon."

After John Jacob Astor's Pacific Fur Company was forced out in 1812, American interest in the region was quiet until the 1830s. Then Nathaniel J. Wyeth, an enterprising Massachusetts merchant, sent out several expeditions. Though financially unsuccessful, they called attention to the overland route that had first been explored by Lewis and Clark. Accompanying Wyeth to Oregon was a band of Methodist missionaries. The fertility and beauty of Oregon's Willamette Valley captivated this group, and they quickly became more interested in farming than in converting the Indians.

The home church in the East soon washed its hands of the enterprise, but settlement flourished. Letters from missionaries continued to praise Oregon's agricultural possibilities. By 1843, "Oregon fever" swept across the Mississippi Valley frontier. In May of that year, more than a thousand settlers started out on the nearly two-thousand-mile Ore-

"America's Progress" by artist John Gast (1872). As the Indians flee westward, the advance of civilization is headed by the trapper and the miner, followed by the settler, the farmer, and the railroad. (*Library of Congress*)

PIONEER WOMEN

Many pioneer women found that the way west was difficult emotionally as well as physically. Lavinia Porter recalled the inner pain of her move to California:

I never recall that sad parting from my dear sister on the plains of Kansas without the tears flowing fast and free. . . . We were the eldest of a large family, and the bond of affection and love that existed between us was strong indeed . . . as she with the other friends turned to leave me for the ferry which was to take them back to home and civilization, I stood alone on that wild prairie. Looking westward I saw my husband driving slowly over the plain; turning my face once more to the east, my dear sister's footsteps were fast widening the distance between us. For the time I knew not which way to go, nor whom to follow. But in a few moments I rallied

my forces . . . and soon overtook the slowly moving oxen who were bearing my husband and child over the green prairie . . . the unbidden tears would flow in spite of my brave resolve to be the courageous and valiant frontierswoman.

On the trail, Mrs. Porter began to have serious doubts about the entire enterprise:

I would make a brave effort to be cheerful and patient until the camp work was done. Then starting out ahead of the team and my men folks, when I thought I had gone beyond hearing distance, I would throw myself down on the unfriendly desert and give way like a child to sobs and tears, wishing myself back home with my friends and chiding myself for consenting to take this wild goose chase.

---

gon Trail from Independence, Missouri. As anyone who has traveled the Great Plains knows, a wagon train journey over those endless miles was a harrowing experience.

While American leaders in Oregon struggled to organize a provisional government, expansionists back east began to thunder about America's right to the territory. They rejected the old boundary at the 49th parallel, the limit of American claims in earlier discussions with Britain. The Democrats' campaign slogan for 1844 was "54° 40′ or fight." No other presidential election was so clearly fought over the issue of national expansion.

By opposing the annexation of Texas, Van Buren had forfeited his chance of renomination by the Democrats, and Calhoun seemed too closely tied to regional interests. The Democratic convention finally settled on a single-minded Jacksonian planter from Tennessee—an expansionist named James K. Polk—who promptly endorsed "the reoccupation of Oregon and the reannexation of Texas."

Having in previous years passed him over, the Whigs were almost forced to choose Henry Clay. But Clay had openly opposed the annexation of Texas, on which the Whig platform remained silent. The more he hedged during the campaign, the worse off he became. Polk won by an electoral margin of 170 to 105.

Yet the popular vote was extremely close, and Clay would have won the election if he had carried New York. There, despite its failure nationwide, the new Liberty party—which was pledged to oppose the expansion of slavery—drained enough

votes away from Clay to throw that state into the Democratic column. Its record here showed for the first time that a small third party could have an important impact on American politics. But antislavery enthusiasts could take no delight in the outcome. Polk was a slaveholder, and his fellow Democrats enlarged their House majority and gained a majority in the Senate. In fact, the election results were widely interpreted as a mandate for expansion, especially by Polk himself.

A Peaceful Solution

Polk was not so obscure as his Whig opponents tried to suggest. A veteran of state politics in Tennessee before his elevation to the White House, Polk had served fourteen years in the House of Representatives in Washington, the last four as Speaker. As president, Polk remained the solid Democrat he had always been.

He opposed protection, and in 1846 signed the Walker Tariff, which put the country back on low duties for revenue only. He opposed a national debt and meant to keep it low enough to be serviced (and reduced when possible) by current taxes. He opposed banks and restored Van Buren's Independent Treasury system for handling federal funds. He gave nullifiers no comfort. Above all, he was as expansionist and isolationist as Jefferson.

In his inaugural address, Polk asserted "the right of the United States to that portion of our territory which lies beyond the Rocky Mountains.

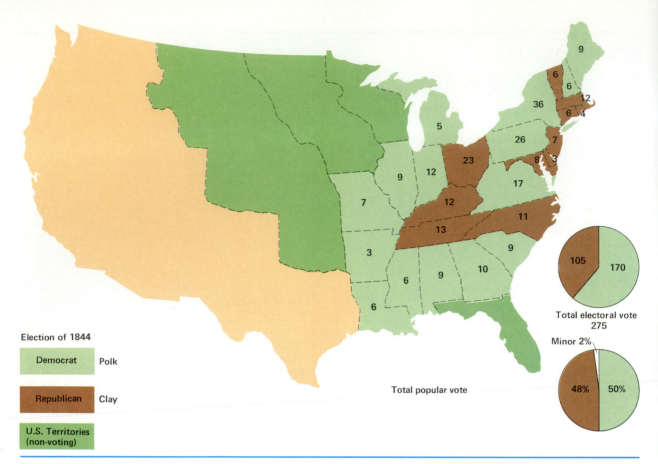

Election of 1844

Democrat — Polk

Republican — Clay

U.S. Territories (non-voting)

Total electoral vote 275

105   170

Total popular vote

Minor 2%

48%   50%

The Election of 1844

James Polk. (*White House Historical Association*)

American title to the country of the Oregon," he said, "is 'clear and unquestionable,' and already are our people preparing to perfect that title by occupying it with their wives and children." In his first annual message to Congress in 1845, Polk stretched the Monroe Doctrine by making two statements that are sometimes called the Polk Doctrine: First, that "The people of this continent alone have the right to decide their own destiny." Second, that the United States cannot allow European states to prevent an independent state from entering the Union.

While war with Mexico over Texas still threatened, a war with Britain over Oregon seemed foolish. After the election was over and the 54° 40' slogan had served its purpose, Polk found a way to back down. He had been advised that Oregon above the 49th parallel was not suited to agriculture. Below that latitude, he said, lay "the entrance of the Straits of Fuca, Admiralty Inlet, and Puget's Sound, with their fine harbors and rich surrounding soils." Britain was also beginning to think of compromise. British-Canadian authorities were

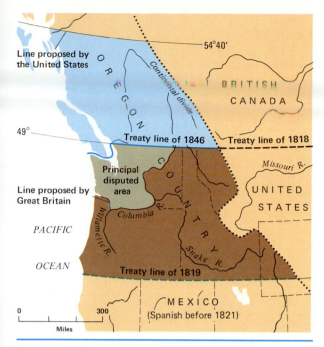

The Oregon Controversy

ecy which recalled an ancient legend that the Indians were descendants of the lost tribes of Israel and which directed Smith's followers to convert them. Given this revelation, Smith founded the Church of Jesus Christ of Latterday Saints.

Scorned as heretics, the Mormons were harried to Nauvoo, Illinois. There they found peace until Joseph Smith's practice of plural marriages began to gather notoriety. To most Victorian Americans, one wife was enough. The Nauvoo settlement was mobbed, and Smith was killed in jail by men who saw him a threat to domestic order and their own domestic tranquility. Smith's murder almost killed the Mormon movement. But it provided the Mormon church with a martyr in whose name a new leader might rally its forces.

Such a leader appeared in the person of Brigham Young, who became the new "Lion of the Lord." Forced out of Illinois after the Prophet's assassination, in the winter of 1846 Young led the Mormons westward. Eventually they found in the Salt Lake Valley a Zion isolated on a barren Mexican plateau remote from the lands of the Gentiles. There, encircled by dusty mountains and a smoking desert, the Mormon leaders created a theocracy superbly organized for survival.

Because of geography and theology, the Salt Lake community was cooperative rather than

finding it difficult to keep Americans out of Oregon. At the same time, depletion of fur-bearing animals along the Columbia River gave them a reason for getting out.

After long negotiations, both sides were able to agree by treaty in 1846 to extend the old line along the 49th parallel westward to Puget Sound and from there to the Pacific through the Straits of Juan de Fuca. Some territory north of the Columbia River, though clearly British by right of settlement, fell into American hands. Britain retained Vancouver Island and navigation rights on the Columbia. Running the original line westward had finally been accomplished without war.

The Mormons in Utah

While thousands of Americans from the North and the South were moving west to "perfect," as Polk said, American title to North America, one group moved west to escape the American government. In 1823, Joseph Smith, a visionary from Vermont, claimed to have been led by angels to a hill near Manchester, New York, where "there was a book deposited, written upon gold plates" and "two stones in silver bows." As God's helper, Smith used these stones to translate the book from its mysterious language. What was revealed was the Book of Mormon, a composite of mythology and proph-

Brigham Young. (*Library of Congress*)

competitive. Its very existence depended on control of a limited water supply. Young and his advisors laid out numerous tightly regulated communities. The Mormon desert state (eventually named Utah) was probably the most successful communitarian project ever established in America. Despite its original reputation as a gigantic brothel, the rigid sobriety and fruitful labor of its inhabitants gradually won the Mormon community respect from other Americans. One of the few religious denominations with exclusively American roots, the Mormons thought themselves

to be the chosen people—a familiar claim in American history.

On to California

The present state of California had first been opened to European expansion by Spanish Franciscan missions protected by small garrisons. The purpose had been to convert Indians and to prevent British and Russian penetration on the California coast. In theory, these missions were temporary; they were set up to teach the Indians

Trails of the Old West

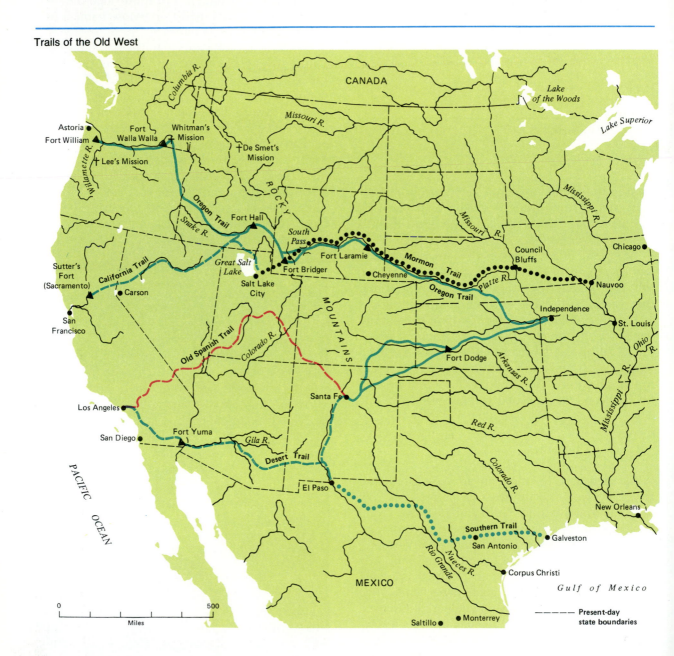

MANIFEST DESTINY AND SLAVERY

agriculture and household arts and to Christianize them. But gradually mission lands fell into private hands, and ranching became the way of life. The California Indians died rapidly from European diseases. By the time of the Mexican-American War in 1846, the various tribes were tragically dependent remnants. Few active missions remained.

During the preceding twenty-five years, Yankee whalers from Nantucket and New Bedford had begun stopping at Monterey and San Francisco, leaving behind them deserters and adventurers. They were soon joined by people from the Oregon and Mississippi frontiers. Anglo-American expansion completely disrupted the lives of the Mexican and Indian residents. Bitter conflicts arose over land, religion, and living habits. A comment from the letter of an American soldier reflected one view of this clash of cultures: "The Mexican, like the poor Indian, is doomed to retire before the more enterprising Anglo-Americans."

Although California had not been an issue in the 1844 campaign, it soon became identified with Oregon. San Francisco was the great prize—twenty times more valuable, thought Daniel Webster, than the whole of Texas. San Diego harbor, according to many observers, would outweigh Oregon. The United States had no claim to California except desire. During Jackson's and Tyler's administrations, government efforts to buy California merely deepened Mexican hostility. Anglo-Californians waited cautiously until they learned of the outbreak of war with Mexico in 1846. Then they raised a standard for a Bear Flag Republic which they hoped would be annexed to the United States.

WAR AGAINST MEXICO

In one of the most obviously aggressive wars in American history, in 1846 President Polk ordered General Zachary Taylor to occupy disputed territory on the southern boundary of Texas. Taylor had carried out his orders by the end of March. That show of force, thought Polk, might push the Mexicans into reconsidering their refusal to negotiate. Or it might cause an incident to serve as an excuse for war. Almost inevitably there was a clash of troops at the disputed border. Polk had already prepared a war message for Congress, which did as he asked. The shedding of American blood on what the United States claimed to be its own soil put the legislators in a mood to act without much debate.

Lieutenant B. W. Armstrong, American soldier. (*National Archives*)

A Divided People

The size of his congressional majorities may have raised Polk's hopes for bipartisan support of the war, but these hopes were soon dashed. His refusal to declare his war aims openly (the seizure of New Mexico and California) encouraged southern as well as northern Whigs to attack his Mexican policy.

By forcing an unwilling people into war, said northern Whigs, Polk was simply "attempting to consummate a scheme for the extension and strengthening of slavery and the Slave Power." Some southern Whigs feared that the acquisition of new territories would intensify sectional rivalries and destroy their party. But if the Whigs publicly attacked Polk, most of them quickly made all the political capital they could out of the triumphs of two Whig generals, Zachary Taylor and Winfield Scott.

Moral and political dissatisfaction with the war was greatest in the Northeast, where New England Whigs and antislavery spokesmen such as Emerson, Parker, James Russell Lowell, and Robert C. Winthrop denounced Polk's adventurism. The populous Northeast supplied only 7900 recruits for the army; some 20,000 southerners and 40,000 westerners enlisted.

The Fruits of Victory

General Taylor captured Monterrey, Mexico, on September 24, 1846, and defeated a Mexican force of 15,000 men at Buena Vista early in 1847. General Scott, appointed next to lead an expedition against Mexico City, overcame tough resistance on the coast at Vera Cruz and took Mexico City on September 14, 1847. Troops commanded by Colonel Stephen W. Kearny, starting from Fort Leavenworth, Kansas, captured Santa Fe and pushed through to California. Commodore Robert F. Stockton and a battalion under General John C. Frémont had already proclaimed the annexation of California in August 1846.

When news of the victories at Buena Vista and Vera Cruz reached Washington, Polk thought he would be able to arrange an immediate peace. When the negotiations were taken out of his hands by envoys operating on their own, Polk was outraged. He considered several angry and probably impossible alternatives: that northern Mexico and all California be annexed; that Mexico be forced to pay all costs of war; that all of Mexico be annexed. At last better sense prevailed; on February 2, 1848, he signed the Treaty of Guadalupe Hidalgo.

Polk secured the Rio Grande boundary, Upper California, including the ports of San Diego and San Francisco, as well as "New Mexico," all the territory north and westward from the Rio Grande River. In return for this vast territory, Polk agreed on payment of some $13 million to Mexico. Several years later, when southern Americans became interested in a railroad to the Pacific coast, the United States negotiated the purchase of 54,000

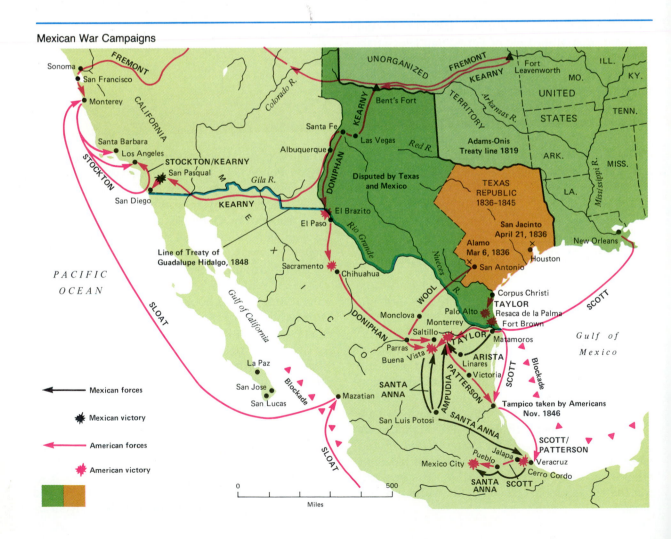

Mexican War Campaigns

MANIFEST DESTINY AND SLAVERY

War news from Mexico. (*National Academy of Design, 1083 Fifth Avenue, New York City*)

square miles along the southern New Mexico border for $10 million—the Gadsden Purchase of 1853.

THE QUESTION OF SLAVERY

As American soldiers stormed into Mexico, Ralph Waldo Emerson wrote in his journal: "The United States will conquer Mexico, but it will be as the man who swallows the arsenic, which brings him down in turn. Mexico will poison us."

Slavery in the Territories

The symptoms of poisoning appeared almost immediately. As early as August 1846, David Wilmot, a Free Soil Democrat from Pennsylvania, offered an amendment to an appropriation bill in the House. "Neither slavery nor involuntary servitude shall ever exist in any part" of the territory that might be acquired from Mexico. The more heavily northern House adopted the amendment; the Senate defeated it. But that was not the end of the matter. The Wilmot Proviso was added to bill after bill in Congress and was hotly debated there and in the country generally.

At the same time, admission of Iowa and Wisconsin to the Union was pending; Minnesota was soon to apply for statehood; and even the Oregon Territory was getting ready. For all these free states to enter the Union while the South was to be deprived of slave states in the new southern territory was intolerable for many southerners. And growing numbers of northerners saw slavery as an evil that must be contained.

Did Congress have authority to determine whether or not slavery could exist in territory obtained by the United States? Southerners who first raised this question replied that since the Constitution recognized and protected property in slaves, owners of such property could not lawfully be prohibited from carrying that property wherever they went, even across the Missouri Compromise line.

Antislavery northerners pointed out that the Constitution plainly gave Congress jurisdiction over the territories and that the Confederation Congress had exercised those rights by confirming the exclusion of slavery from the Northwest Territory in 1785. Then—and especially—the federal Congress had adopted the Missouri Compromise, in 1820.

A third position on slavery in the territories was possible. Usually called *squatter sovereignty* or *popular sovereignty,* this interpretation was set forth by Lewis Cass of Michigan and Stephen A. Douglas of Illinois. They argued that there was a long-established precedent in America for communities to act as the best judges of their own interests. Let the new territories be set up with the question of slavery left open, and then permit the people to decide for themselves.

It sounded sensible, but this doctrine was disastrously vague on the crucial matter of timing. Just when should a territory decide the question— after slaves had been brought in or before? What if free settlers had arrived before slaveowners? By leaving resolution of the question open to zealots of both camps, popular sovereignty also left it open to violence.

The Election of 1848

By 1848 the issue of the extension of slavery to new territories had become so poisonous that both major parties tried to avoid it while preparing for the presidential campaign. On taking office, Polk had pledged himself to a single term. "Regular" Democrats, at their convention in Baltimore, nom-

inated Michigan's Lewis Cass on a platform that ignored slavery. The "regular" Whigs, at their convention in Philadelphia, hoped to silence talk on all issues by nominating the "hero of Buena Vista," General Taylor.

The watchword of the regulars in both parties was "party harmony." But they reckoned without antislavery northern Democrats. In New York and New England they became known as Barnburners, because they were said to be willing to burn down the Democratic "barn" in order to get rid of the proslavery "rats." The regulars also reckoned without the "conscience" Whigs. In August 1848 antislavery Democrats and Whigs, who had left their regular party conventions, met in Buffalo with other antislavery leaders and formed the Free Soil party. Its slogan was "Free soil, Free speech, Free labor, and Free men." They named Martin Van Buren, who had won their sympathy by his stand against the annexation of Texas.

The 1848 election itself aroused little popular enthusiasm. Neither Taylor nor Cass had much popular appeal, and Van Buren—despite his antislavery position—could not live down his reputation as a slippery fox. Moreover, he had no nationwide machine behind him. In the balloting, Taylor won with 1,360,000 popular votes to Cass's 1,220,000. The Free Soilers polled only 291,000 votes. But they absorbed enough Democratic support in New York to give that state's electoral vote to Taylor, and enough Whig votes in Ohio and Indiana to throw those states to Cass.

The Free Soil party also elected nine congressmen to a closely divided House, where they might hold the balance of power. Most important, the Free Soilers had demonstrated the potential strength and disruptive power of a purely sectional party. Now there could be no glossing over the slavery issue. Southern extremists had fresh reasons with which to convince moderates in their states that the South must unite to protect slavery.

The Compromise of 1850

Sectional tensions relaxed for a moment in 1848 when news of gold in California spread across the nation. Americans of every class and occupation headed for the Pacific Coast. Men from all over the world rushed to join them. By 1849, California had an unruly population of over 100,000—and an inadequate military government. Polk had retired before a deeply divided Congress could decide California's future. President Taylor recommended that California (and New Mexico and

California gold miners. (*California State Library*)

Abandoned ships in the San Francisco harbor were abandoned by their crews, who took off to dig in the gold fields. (*Smithsonian Institution*)

Utah as well) draw up constitutions and decide without congressional direction whether or not slavery should be excluded. Congress, however, was in no mood to let the new president decide such an important matter on his own.

The fears of proslavery spokesmen were soon confirmed. The constitutions of all three territories banned slavery. Many southern congressmen then took an uncompromising stand on all sectional issues. Should the sale of slaves be banned in the District of Columbia? Should the 1793 law on fugitive slaves be tightened? Must Texas, a slave state, give part of its western lands to the proposed free territory of New Mexico? Southern unity in defense of slavery had never been so strong. Some politicians in the South began talking about the slave states seceding—withdrawing from the Union.

Everyone knew a crisis was coming except President Taylor; his reaction was to ask Congress to avoid "exciting topics of sectional character." At a time when senators and representatives carried Bowie knives and Colt revolvers, Taylor's request seemed rather less forceful than it might have been. Clearly the South had no intention of allowing California to enter the Union as a free state unless it received important concessions. And it was becoming clear that the South might secede rather than accept the Wilmot Proviso.

Henry Clay. (*The National Archives, Brady Collection*)

Yet Congress was still controlled by older men who loved the Union more than their section. They were shocked by the possibility that the Union might fail. Henry Clay, at seventy-three, remained a powerful and persuasive orator who understood the desperate mood of the South. He consulted his old rival, Daniel Webster of Massachusetts, and got his backing. In his last and finest hour, Clay rose to present the Senate with eight resolutions that carefully balanced the interests of the free and slave states. No more momentous package of compromises had ever been presented in the federal legislature—and none have equaled it since for comprehensiveness, goodwill, and ultimate failure.

The Compromise of 1850 was adopted in what amounted to the following eight propositions: (1) California admitted as a free state; (2) two separate territorial governments in Utah and New Mexico decide for themselves whether to permit or abolish slavery; (3) the disputed land between Texas and New Mexico be assigned to New Mexico; (4) the United States pay debts Texas had contracted before annexation; (5) slavery in the District of Columbia not be abolished without the consent of its residents and Maryland's and not without compensation to owners; (6) the slave trade be prohibited in the District of Columbia; (7) a stricter fugitive slave law be adopted; (8) Congress declare its own lack of jurisdiction over the domestic, interstate slave trade.

The Compromise of 1850 was one of the most hotly contested battles in congressional history. Against Clay were an angry, suspicious president, secessionists, antislavery men, and Free Soilers. President Taylor was firm in his conviction that California must be admitted to the Union without any reservations. He was prepared to treat even moderate and Union-loving southerners as traitors if they protested. Secessionists like Jefferson Davis (Mississippi), Barnwell Rhett (South Carolina), and Louis T. Wigfall (Texas) were contemptuous of compromise. Antislavery extremists and radical Free Soilers like William H. Seward (New York), Salmon P. Chase and Joshua Giddings (Ohio), and Charles Sumner (Massachusetts) stood firm for the Wilmot Proviso and spoke of a "higher law" than the Constitution—the law of God—under which slavery could never be justified.

But Clay's resolutions were sufficiently broad and conciliatory to win over the many moderates in both sections. Among the staunchest was Webster, whose moving speech in the Senate supported the entire compromise, even Clay's strict

Free states and territories

Slave states and territories

Open to slavery by principle of popular sovereignty

The United States in 1850

Daniel Webster. (*Metropolitan Museum of Art*)

new fugitive slave law. There was an immediate, angry outcry against Webster. He had underestimated northern revulsion against returning fugitive slaves, as well as the hatred of the whole plantation system. For the moment at least, his efforts strengthened the Unionist position, to which others rallied.

Outstanding among them was Stephen A. Douglas, who brought many in Congress around to the view that the Southwest was geographically unsuitable for slave labor. After the exhausted Clay retired from the battle, Douglas whipped through the measures that made up the Compromise of 1850. He was helped by the sudden death of President Taylor early in July and the succession of Vice-President Millard Fillmore, a Free Soiler who supported the compromise.

Several northern states soon virtually nullified the fugitive slave law through "personal liberty laws" that allowed alleged fugitives to have legal counsel, jury trials, and other means of defending their freedom. Northern blacks also took up the defense of fugitives. Blacks, they said, had too long been characterized as meek and yielding. "This reproach must be wiped out," declared the escaped slave Frederick Douglass, "and nothing short of resistance on the part of the colored man can wipe it out. Every slavehunter who meets a bloody death in his infernal business is an argument in favor of the manhood of our race."

The Election of 1852

The nation as a whole rejoiced when news of the compromise became known. In the presidential election of 1852, the national desire for tranquility and moderation seemed to persist. Franklin Pierce, the Democratic candidate, easily defeated General Winfield Scott, the Whig candidate, by a margin of 254 to 42 in the electoral college. The Free Soil party was mauled in the election: Its candidate, John P. Hale of New Hampshire, won only half the number of votes Van Buren had received just four years earlier in 1848.

In the long run, the issue of slavery and its extension could not be so easily settled. An ominous sign of trouble ahead was the breakup of the Whig party following the deaths of Webster and Clay in 1852. The party, said one commentator, "seems almost annihilated by the recent elections." Southern Whigs felt this was precisely what any party that accepted the guidance of antislavery men like Seward deserved. The Democrats still stood as a great national party, to which many southern Whigs were now drawn.

Northern Whigs found nowhere to go. Having lost the presidential election, with their foremost traditional leaders dead, with many of their southern followers defecting to the Democrats, and with their own adherents divided by the issues of slavery and Catholic immigration, northern Whigs seemed to have no political home. One of the two great national political parties simply fell apart almost overnight, and its disintegration left a vacuum in the nation's traditional system of politics.

SUMMARY

Along with slavery, the issue that dominated American politics during the 1840s was manifest destiny—the idea that America was destined to rule the entire continent. By the end of the decade, the United States had gone a long way toward reaching this goal.

The Canadian border conflict with Britain, aggravated during this period by incidents such as the *Caroline* affair, the Aroostook War, and the *Creole* incident, was settled peacefully by the Webster-Ashburton Treaty of 1842, which fixed the boundary as far west as Minnesota and Ontario.

In the Southwest, Texas became an independent republic in 1836, and a new state in 1845. In the Far West, Americans looked to the Oregon country and to California, which was then part of Mexico.

The election of James Polk in 1844 was a victory for expansionists. Polk promptly settled the Oregon boundary with Britain, since war with Mexico over Texas was still a possibility. By treaty in 1846, the Canadian-United States border was finally fixed to the Pacific.

In the same year, Americans who had settled in California declared themselves independent of Mexico as the Bear Flag Republic. Polk provoked war against Mexico, with the aim of winning New Mexico and California. Though the United States handily defeated Mexican armies, the war aroused great opposition, especially among northern Whigs. The Treaty of Guadalupe Hidalgo in 1848 established the Rio Grande boundary and obtained Upper California and the Utah and New Mexico

territories for a payment of $13 million to Mexico.

The joy over these new territories was marred by the urgency of the slavery issue. The question now was whether the new states that would be carved out of the territories would be slave or free and who would decide—Congress or the people who settled the new states. The issue of the extension of slavery became poisonous. In the election of 1848, it led to the formation of a new third party, with Van Buren as its candidate. The Whig candidate, General Taylor, won; but the Free Soilers elected enough representatives to a closely divided House of Representatives to threaten the balance of political and sectional power.

Open conflict was postponed another ten years with the Compromise of 1850, by which California entered the Union as a free state, and the western boundary of Texas was fixed. In two new territories—New Mexico and Utah—the question of slavery was left to the people to decide. Slave trading, but not slavery, was prohibited in the District of Columbia. A strong fugitive slave law was passed to satisfy the South.

The fugitive slave law deeply angered many northerners. Yet for a few years politics went on as usual, and in 1852 the Democratic candidate, Franklin Pierce, was elected president. Almost immediately the Whig party began to disintegrate. Its collapse resulted in the end of the nation's "second party system" (of Whigs and Democrats) and left a political vacuum.

Suggested Readings

H. N. Smith, *The Virgin Land* (1950), an imaginative literary study, analyzes nineteenth-century thoughts and feelings about the West. R. Slotkin, *Regeneration through Violence*, focuses on Indian-white relations. R. Berkhoffer, *Salvation and the Savage: An Analysis of Protestant Missions and American Indian Response, 1787–1862* (1965), should be balanced by R. Pearce, *Savages of America*. The intimate link between western expansion and militarism may be approached through F. Prucha, *The Sword of the Republic: The United States Army on the Frontier, 1783–1846* (1969). A. Moore, *The Frontier Mind* (1957), portrays the pioneer experience as a brutalizing one that turned sensitive people into unthinking toilers.

The impact of westward expansion on American society as a whole is discussed in R. Billington, *America's Frontier Heritage* (1966); it also contains a fine bibliography. D. Boorstin, *The Americans: The National Experience* (1965), is full of fascinating trivia as well as provocative analysis on material aspects of mid-nineteenth-century America. See also W. Goetzmann, *Exploration and Empire: The Explorer and the Scientist in the Winning of the American West, 1805–1900* (1973). The ecological havoc wreaked on Indian lands first by the fur trade and later by land speculation, and the governmental policies that encouraged this destruction in the early nineteenth-century are described in V. Vogel, *This Country Was Ours: A Documentary History of the American Indian* (1972).

A new and different perspective on an important region is D. Weber, *The Mexican Frontier, 1821–1846: The American Southwest Under Mexico* (1982). For the war against Mexico, the biographical works by C. Sellers, *James K. Polk: Jacksonian, 1795–1843* (1957), and *James K. Polk: Continentalist 1843–1846* (1966), are especially good. In addition, see W. Binkley, *The Texas Revolution* (1952); S. Siegel, *A Political History of the Texas Republic, 1836–1845* (1956); and A. Bill, *Rehearsal for Conflict: The War with Mexico, 1846–1848* (1947). In addition, there is a study by G. Price, *Origins of the War with Mexico: The Polk-Stockton Intrigue* (1967). See also D. Pletcher, *The Diplomacy of the Annexation of Texas, Oregon, and the Mexican War* (1973).

United States expansion into the Far West in this period is treated in C. Gates, *Empire of the Pacific: A History of the Pacific Northwest* (1957), and the relevant portion of J. Caughey, *California* (1970). In addition to Berkhoffer, above, C. Drury, *Marcus Whitman, Pioneer and Martyr* (1937), supplies information on the importance of the missionary impulse. See D. Morgan, *Jedidiah Smith and the Opening of the West* (1964), for an exciting discussion of the fur trade in the Rockies and farther west. Francis Parkman's personal and evocative account, *The California and Oregon Trail* (1849), better known as *The Oregon Trail*, is available in several modern editions.

There is interesting material on the saga of the Mormons in L. Arrington, *Great Basin Kingdom: An Economic History of the Latterday Saints, 1830–1900* (1958). F. McKiernan et al. (eds)., *The Restoration Movement: Essays on Mormon History* (1973), is a comprehensive account of church history with particular strength in analyzing the relationship between the two major branches, the Brighamites and the "Reorganization." One of the great Mormon leaders has received first-rate biographical treatment in F. Brodie, *No Man Knows My History: The Life of Joseph Smith* (1945).

An excellent account of domestic politics in this period contains considerable detail but is nonetheless highly readable: A. Nevins, *Ordeal of the Union* (2 vols., 1947). J. Silbey (ed.), *The Transformation of American Politics, 1840–1860* (1967), is a well-chosen anthology, especially revealing on the forces behind the restructuring of party alignments. A. Craven, *The Growth of Southern Nationalism, 1848–1861* (1953), presents the situation in which the South found itself. H. Hamilton, *The Compromise of 1850* (1964), offers a fine analysis of events that seemed to contemporaries to be a turning point in the course of the nation. The very strong reaction of blacks to the compromise and to the events preceding it can be found in H. Aptheker (ed.), *A Documentary History of the Negro People in the United States* (1951).

This was an age dominated by struggles among towering personalities in the political arena; hence the studies of Calhoun, Clay, and Webster cited in Chapter 11 are of particular importance. For a fascinating look at the personal writings of ordinary women who crossed the country in the mid-nineteenth century, see J. Jeffrey, *Frontier Women: The Trans Mississippi West, 1840–1880* (1979).

THE UNION COMES APART

Chapter 16

From December 1859 through February 1860, the House of Representatives was locked in struggle over the election of its own Speaker. Southern Democrats and northern Republicans attacked each other in fiery language. At one point a pistol fell onto the floor from the pocket of a New York congressman. Some members thought he had drawn to shoot, and hands were seen quickly reaching for pockets. The tension remained at a fever pitch for months. One senator commented: "The only persons who do not have a revolver and a knife are those who have two revolvers." Another wrote: "The members on both sides are mostly armed with deadly weapons, and it is said that the friends of each are armed in the galleries." The atmosphere even affected the much quieter world of women. In 1857, the wife of a new cabinet member wrote to a friend: "I avoid making myself acquainted with politics lest in an unguarded moment something slip from my lips that evil minded listeners can seize upon . . . for the newspapers."

The cause of this tension was slavery, especially slavery in the territories. In the early 1850s, slavery was brought home to northerners who had previously regarded it as a distant problem. The new fugitive slave law created widespread anger in the North. The second factor was, of all things,

publication of a novel. *Uncle Tom's Cabin* had an enormous impact on northern public opinion.

Yet it was slavery in the territories that became the central and most divisive issue. The Democrats in Congress pushed through the Kansas-Nebraska Act, which repealed the Missouri Compromise and put the future of the "free" territories in doubt. The question became cancerous. A small-scale civil war broke out between Free Soilers and proslavery elements in Kansas. When the Supreme Court was asked to settle the question in the Dred Scott case, its decision was in favor of the South. Many northerners concluded that there really was a "slave power conspiracy" to extend slavery throughout the West and perhaps eventually to the free states as well.

That decision flew directly in the face of the principal plank of the new Republican party. The collapse of the Whig party after 1852 left a political vacuum which at first was filled by the rise of the Know Nothings, a party dedicated to countering the great wave of Roman Catholic immigration. But dedication to free soil proved even stronger, and the Republicans emerged as the major counterweight to the Democrats almost overnight.

The principles of the two parties were given a thorough airing in 1858, when the

Democrat Stephen A. Douglas debated a rising lawyer, Abraham Lincoln, in a contest for a Senate seat from Illinois. By insisting on the principle that slavery must expand no farther, the Republicans made themselves a purely sectional party. Not only did the South see itself under attack from Republican victories in the North, but an antislavery zealot, John Brown, mounted a raid on a federal arsenal in Virginia in hope of stirring up a slave rebellion. John Brown confirmed the South's worst suspicions. A year later, in 1860, many southern spokesmen made clear that election of a Republican president would mean secession.

Upon Lincoln's election as a minority president in a four-way contest, the states of the lower South began to secede and organize a government of their own. The upper South remained on the fence until Lincoln maneuvered South Carolina authorities into firing the first shot, at the federal Fort Sumter in Charleston harbor. That action forced them to a decision. They split evenly, four joining the Confederacy and four remaining with the Union. Lincoln moved to suppress the "rebellion." Southerners rallied to the cause of their newly independent nation. The United States had finally come apart on the one issue the Founding Fathers had tried so hard to avoid. ■

THE FAILURE OF COMPROMISE

The Democrat Franklin Pierce of New Hampshire took office as president on March 4, 1853. A contemporary described him as a "vain, showy, and pliant man." Unfortunately, the description was close to being correct. Most Americans, including the president, still hoped that the Compromise of 1850 would stop the agitation over slavery once and for all. In the Senate, Stephen A. Douglas grandly announced: "I have determined never to make another speech on the slavery question." He urged senators to "drop the subject." But the subject would not "drop."

The weakness of the president did not help matters, but even a much stronger man would probably have been overwhelmed. Enforcement of the fugitive slave law and Harriet Beecher Stowe's vivid fictional account of slavery gave northerners a view of slavery they had never had before. Douglas's Kansas-Nebraska Act unraveled the agreements of the Missouri Compromise. And the disintegration of the Whig party, so badly rotted by sectional division and the loss of its leaders, resulted in a new political alignment.

Slavery Comes Home to the North

The fugitive slave law of 1850 provided southern slaveholders with considerable powers for recovering runaways. Its provisions were so broad that it made some free northern blacks move to Canada in fear of being legally kidnapped into slavery. Any slaveholder or his or her hired agent was empowered to seize a "runaway" slave, to ask for assistance from any federal marshal in the process, and then to go before a federal judge. Judges received $10 if they ruled that a Negro was a slave or $5 if they ruled that the person was free. The law also provided for a fine of $1000 and six months in jail for anyone convicted of aiding or assisting a fugitive slave.

These provisions outraged abolitionists. They also angered a good many people in the North who had been hostile to abolition. Black leaders like Frederick Douglass called upon the black community to resist with force. Many northern states passed "personal liberty" laws that attempted to nullify the effects of the new federal statute. Then a series of incidents brought state and federal officials into conflict.

In Ohio, for example, a crowd of students from Oberlin College—long a hotbed of abolition sentiment—forcibly rescued a fugitive from a slavecatcher. Several members of that crowd were convicted by a federal jury under terms of the Fugitive Slave Act. Then a state court ordered the arrest of the slavecatcher and all federal officials who had cooperated with him. Eventually a compromise was worked out. But it had become clear that enforcement of the act would create problems.

Other dramatic incidents inflamed public opinion. A black man named Frederick Wilkins was working quietly as a waiter in a Boston coffeehouse when he was suddenly seized by a Virginia

CAUTION!!
COLORED PEOPLE
OF BOSTON, ONE & ALL,

You are hereby respectfully CAUTIONED and advised, to avoid conversing with the

Watchmen and Police Officers of Boston,

For since the recent ORDER OF THE MAYOR & ALDERMEN, they are empowered to act as

KIDNAPPERS
AND
Slave Catchers,

And they have already been actually employed in KIDNAPPING, CATCHING, AND KEEPING SLAVES. Therefore, if you value your LIBERTY, and the *Welfare of the Fugitives* among you, *Shun* them in every possible manner, as so many *HOUNDS* on the track of the most unfortunate of your race.

Keep a Sharp Look Out for KIDNAPPERS, and have TOP EYE open.

APRIL 24, 1851.

Having failed to save a runaway slave from being returned to his master after his capture in Boston in 1851, the Reverend Theodore Parker distributed this poster. (*Library of Congress*)

slavecatcher who knew him as "Shadrach," a runaway slave. While Wilkins was being held for return to Virginia, a crowd of blacks burst in and took him away. In New York City, James Hamlet was grabbed and packed off to Maryland so fast his wife and children had no chance to say goodbye to him. As things turned out in that incident, Hamlet was lucky. His black friends and a few sympathetic whites raised $800 to purchase his freedom.

A more publicized incident occurred at Christiana, Pennsylvania. A Maryland slaveowner tried to recapture his runaway slave, the slave escaped, and the owner and his son were badly wounded in the gun battle. Several blacks and whites were indicted for murder and treason, but all were acquitted by a local jury. Only a few years later, the streets of Boston were lined with federal troops and marshals when the fugitive Anthony Burns was marched from the courthouse down to

the ship waiting to carry him back to slavery in Virginia. That federal force held back a crowd estimated at 50,000, hissing and shouting in protest. The crowd was three times larger than the entire population of Boston at the time of the Stamp Act crisis.

It cost the federal government the enormous sum of $100,000 to return Anthony Burns to slavery. The expense, as well as the injustice, was widely publicized throughout the North. About 300 blacks were returned to slavery under terms of the Fugitive Slave Act. For every slave returned, however, thousands of northerners changed their minds about slavery. It had often seemed remote, but a glimpse of Anthony Burns in chains was far more vivid than the most awful tales in abolitionist literature.

There was one exception—*Uncle Tom's Cabin*, probably the most influential novel ever published in the United States. Harriet Beecher Stowe grew up in New England. As daughter of the famous preacher Lyman Beecher, she lived for some time in Cincinnati, just across the river from slavery in Kentucky. She wrote *Uncle Tom's Cabin* as a series of magazine articles. Then, in the spring of 1852, the publisher brought out her story in book

Harriet Beecher Stowe. (*National Portrait Gallery, Smithsonian Institution*)

form. He printed only 5000 copies because he had no great expectations for heavy sales.

The first printing sold out in two days. Within another week, 10,000 copies were swept up in the North. Within a year, the novel sold 300,000 copies. In order to meet demand, the publisher kept eight of the new rotary steam presses going around the clock and bought the entire stock of three paper mills. Throughout the North, Mrs. Stowe was hailed for lifting the veil of the peculiar institution. In the South, she was denounced for having painted it in false colors.

Such widespread readership clearly indicated that *Uncle Tom's Cabin* told many people what they wanted to hear. The story focused on Uncle Tom, a loyal and deeply Christian slave who grew to manhood in Kentucky. Tom's benevolent master got into financial trouble and was forced to sell him. The forgiving slave had to leave his wife and his "Old Kentucky Home" for the long trip "down the river" to New Orleans.

While Tom is carried off by a vicious slave trader, his daughter, her baby, and her husband flee to Ohio. (The book's description of that flight provided stage producers with a fine challenge to meet the public's taste for melodrama: Liza was represented as darting across ice in the Ohio River, babe in arms, bloodhounds baying at her heels. Finally, to everyone's relief, she found herself nearly safe in the warm home of kindly Quakers.)

In New Orleans, Tom is purchased by a kindly, genteel family. But once again fate intervenes just when his new owner is about to free him. He is sold again, this time to an unfeeling slavemaster who takes him to a desolate plantation in Arkansas. His new owner, Simon Legree, grew up in New England but is heartless. In the end, Tom is beaten to death at Legree's orders. As he dies, Tom forgives the two black overseers who had been ordered to beat him.

Mrs. Stowe's story was more complicated than this. For modern tastes it is almost unbearably sentimental, and its characters and situations downright unbelievable. It has been criticized as a third- or even tenth-rate novel. But at the time it deeply touched many Americans. It had a good story. It made a strong case that slavery was evil even when good people were involved. And it

"Flight of Elisa" scene from Stowe's *Uncle Tom's Cabin.* (*New York Historical Society*)

showed that the institution itself damaged families and homes among whites and blacks. This demonstration, as much as anything, gave the novel its powerful appeal.

The Kansas-Nebraska Act

Northern incitement and protection of runaways led the planters to seek countermeasures. A minority demanded nothing less than the reopening of the African slave trade. A more influential group, supported by Pierce himself, urged the acquisition of Spain's Cuba, where slavery was flourishing. Quite possibly enough public support could have been gotten for annexation except that Congress, in 1854, passed a law which, in the words of a New York paper, "has forever rendered annexation impossible." This was the Kansas-Nebraska Act. By reopening the question of slavery in the western territories, it strengthened northern determination to stop the spread of slavery anywhere.

The Nebraska country was a vast empire ranging west of the 95th meridian all the way to Oregon Territory and north to the Canadian border. Its southern part bordered the slave state of Missouri. But slaveholders were forbidden to extend slavery there by the Missouri Compromise of 1820. This same portion and the area north of it to the Great Bend of the Missouri River, which now forms the eastern boundary of the state of Nebraska, also lay just beyond the permanent Indian frontier. Here, in the words of Stephen A. Douglas (the italics are his), the Indians, by treaty, had been guaranteed "perpetual occupancy, *with an express condition that* [the land] *should never be incorporated within the limits of a territory or state of the Union.*"

As early as the congressional session of 1843–44, Douglas, then a freshman member of the House of Representatives from Illinois, had introduced the first bill to break the Indian treaties and organize the Territory of Nebraska. Others, meanwhile, led by Senator David R. Atchison of

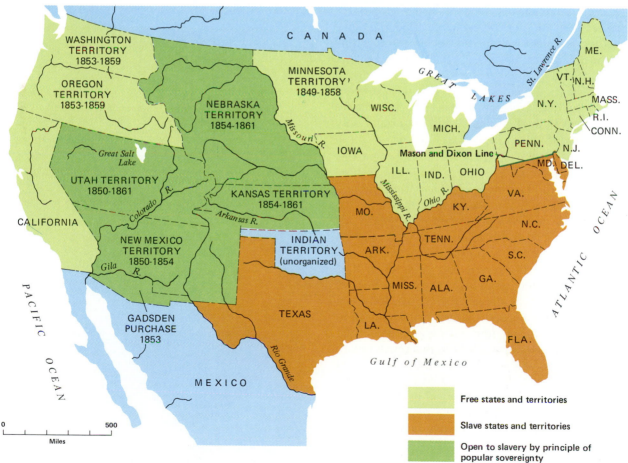

The United States in 1854

Free states and territories

Slave states and territories

Open to slavery by principle of popular sovereignty

Missouri, vowed that they would see Nebraska "sink in hell" before allowing it to be organized as a free territory. The sectional conflict was intensified by the rivalry between North and South for the first transcontinental railroad. Douglas became the leading spokesman for its construction over a northern route that would link the Pacific coast with Chicago, where he owned much real estate. He had a grand vision:

No man can keep up with the spirit of this age who travels on anything slower than the locomotive, and fails to receive intelligence by lightning. We must therefore have Rail Roads and Telegraphs from the Atlantic to the Pacific, through our own territory. Not one line only, but many lines. . . . The removal of the Indian barrier and the extension of the laws of the United States in the form of Territorial governments are the first steps toward the accomplishment of each and all of those objects.

Douglas reported his fateful Nebraska bill in the Senate on January 4, 1854. His initial report was deliberately vague. He specifically undertook to apply in Nebraska—part of the Louisiana Purchase north of 36° 30′—the "popular sovereignty" provisions of the Compromise of 1850, which allowed Utah and New Mexico to make their own decisions about slavery. Once he had enlarged the area of application of the principle of popular sovereignty, Douglas was forced to concede that the Missouri Compromise was henceforth to be "inoperative and void."

Still another concession by Douglas revolved around the railroad issue. It was clear to everyone that Congress at this time would help build only one transcontinental line. That line, according to a government-sponsored survey, would meet the fewest physical obstacles along the Mexican border. In fact, the Gadsden Purchase from Mexico had been made for the use of the railroad.

Atchison's pro-southern group in Missouri advocated a central route originating in St. Louis. They would not even consider supporting any transcontinental line, including their own, if it passed through territory closed to slavery. Fearful of their strength, and fearful that the southern part of Nebraska bordering Missouri would fall to slavery, a group of Iowa congressmen urged Douglas to divide Nebraska into two territories to ensure the passage of the transcontinental through the free valley of the Platte in the more northerly part. Although skeptical of the Iowans' fears concerning slavery in this region, Douglas felt he had to agree to their request as well. His bill

was altered to divide Nebraska into two territories: Nebraska and Kansas. Kansas was immediately marked for slavery by the South.

It took southerners outside Congress a little time to realize what they had won. One newspaper declared that the Kansas-Nebraska Act was "barren of practical benefit." But once northerners began to attack the measure, southern opinion began to rally in its favor. For their part, northerners were particularly angered by repeal of the Missouri Compromise. Lincoln wrote in his third-person autobiographical sketch that "the repeal of the Missouri Compromise aroused him as he had never been before."

While Douglas's draft was being revised, Senators Salmon P. Chase of Ohio and Charles Sumner of Massachusetts were writing an "Appeal of the Independent Democrats in Congress to the People of the United States." Their work stimulated formation of the Republican party and became the most influential attack on the Kansas-Nebraska Act.

They were determined to block passage of a "criminal betrayal of precious rights; . . . part and

Stephen A. Douglas. (*National Portrait Gallery, Smithsonian Institution*)

parcel of an atrocious plot to exclude from a vast unoccupied region immigrants from the Old World and free laborers from our own States, and convert it into a dreary region of despotism, inhabited by masters and slaves." Douglas tried to defend his legislation. Members of his own party, on home base in Chicago, hooted him off the platform, and crowds menaced him in the streets.

"Bleeding Kansas"

The Kansas-Nebraska Act failed its first test in the new Territory of Kansas. Did a new territory under "popular sovereignty" have the power to prohibit or legalize slavery before framing its constitution and before seeking statehood? Douglas said yes; southern spokesmen said no. Only a state could decide this question, southerners maintained; a territory could not keep slaves out. As settlers moved into Kansas, the issue quickly went beyond debate.

Most of the settlers were slaveless farmers from nearby states. But as in all frontier settlements, there were hustlers out to bleed the newcomers. To draw attention away from their activities, the schemers kept the slavery controversy boiling. Others also helped turn Kansas into a battle-ground. The New England Emigrant Aid Company and other northern associations financed the migration of more than a thousand "right-thinking" Yankees to Kansas to vote against slavery and to see that everyone else did. When they got there, they found packages from home—rifles!

Henry Ward Beecher, Mrs. Stowe's brother and an antislavery clergyman, preached that guns, not Bibles, would be more persuasive against slavery. So "Beecher's Bibles" went off to Kansas. Missourians came to Kansas to forestall the Yankees. Other southerners moved in, determined to pack the first Kansas territorial legislature with proslavery men.

On election day in March 1855, slightly more than 2000 Kansans were registered to vote. Over 6000 ballots were cast, most of them by Missourians who had come into Kansas for the day. The governor of the Kansas Territory tried to disqualify eight of the thirty-one members who had been elected irregularly. President Pierce refused to back the governor and eventually recalled him. The new legislature adopted a series of repressive laws that, among other punishments, prescribed the death penalty for aiding a fugitive slave. But

Free Soilers in Kansas were not intimidated. In the fall of 1855 they met in Topeka and drew up their own constitution. In January 1856, they elected their own legislature and governor. Kansas now had two rival administrations and was ripe for war.

While Pierce delayed, war came. A force of hard-drinking proslavery men raided Lawrence in search of some Free Soil leaders the proslavery legislature had indicted for treason. The raiders burned the hotel, destroyed homes, and smashed Free Soil printing presses. The "sack of Lawrence," exaggerated by northern newspapers, brought a bloodier sequel. John Brown of Osawatomie, Kansas, a fanatical abolitionist who was soon to become better known, gathered six followers, rode into the proslavery settlement at Pottawatomie Creek, and hacked five men to death. He acted, so he said, under God's authority. But his sacred vendetta started a guerrilla war in which over 200 were killed.

Violence over Kansas spread to Congress. Sumner of Massachusetts, speaking in the Senate, flailed away for two days at the "harlot slavery," but aimed his choicest remarks at Senator Andrew P. Butler of South Carolina. Two days later, Butler's nephew, a congressman, entered the floor of the Senate and beat Sumner over the head with a cane, making him an invalid for several years. The assault on Sumner by "Bully" Brooks, together with the news from Kansas, came as preparations were being made for the presidential campaign of 1856.

A New Party Alignment

The breakup of the Whig party, obvious before the election of 1852, was hastened by defeat in that campaign. The sectional strife of Pierce's administration, in turn, undermined the other great national party, the Democrats, and sent politicians looking for new homes. The first of the new parties, the American party, raised its standard in 1852. It took its name from its opposition to Catholic immigrants. Politicians in both sections were drawn to it because they thought the issue of immigration might deflect attention from slavery. They were soon proved wrong.

The American party was so concerned over its "Americanist" purity that it had secret regulations requiring members to pretend they "knew nothing" when asked for information. They soon be-

SOUTHERN REACTION TO THE BEATING OF SUMNER

A southern newspaper, the *Richmond Enquirer*, offered the following commentary on Brooks's beating of Sumner in the Senate:

In the main, the press of the South applaud the conduct of Mr. Brooks, without condition or limitation. Our approbation, at least, is entire and unreserved. We consider the act good in conception, better in execution, and best of all in consequence. The vulgar Abolitionists in the Senate are getting above themselves. They have been humored until they forget their position. They have grown saucy, and dare to be impudent to gentlemen! Now, they are a low, mean, scurvy set, with some little book-learning, but as

utterly devoid of spirit or honor as a pack of curs. Intrenched behind 'privilege,' they fancy they can slander the South and insult its representatives with impunity. The truth is, they have been suffered to run too long without collars. They must be lashed into submission. Sumner, in particular, ought to have nine-and-thirty early every morning. He is a great strapping fellow, and could stand the cowhide beautifully. Brooks frightened him, and at the first blow of the cane he bellowed like a bullcalf.... Mr. Brooks has initiated this salutary discipline, and he deserves applause for the bold, judicious manner in which he chastised the scamp Sumner. It was a proper act, done at the proper time, and in the proper place.

Brooks caning Sumner. (*New York Public Library*)

came the Know-Nothings. Secret handclasps and passwords attracted many people to the party, but enemies also emerged. One of them was Abraham Lincoln. Slower than most to disown his Whig allegiance, Lincoln wrote in 1855:

I am not a Know-Nothing. That is certain. How could I be? . . . Our progress in degeneracy appears to me to be pretty rapid. As a nation, we began by declaring that

"all men are created equal." We now practically read it "all men are created equal except Negroes." When the Know-Nothings get control, it will read "all men are created equal except Negroes and foreigners and Catholics." When it comes to this I should prefer emigrating to some country where they make no pretense of loving liberty. . . .

When in 1854 the American party's national convention voted to support the Kansas-Nebraska Act, most of its southern following joined the Democrats. Many northeastern Know-Nothings moved to the new Republican party.

That party came into being almost spontaneously in 1854. No single leader or group can claim credit for its organization. One firm principle brought its members together: the determination to keep slavery out of the territories and the conviction that Congress had the right to do so. Besides northern Know-Nothings, Free Soilers flocked to the Republicans. So did "conscience Whigs"—those whose dislike of slavery was so strong they had refused to join their party's condemnation of the Wilmot Proviso. Northern Democrats who rejected all further compromise with the South also joined, as did abolitionists and a considerable number of German immigrants. Although the Republicans opposed the extension of slavery, no more than a small minority had any interest in the well-being of blacks. North or South, blacks remained outside the land of opportunity. Most Republicans wanted free soil—not freed slaves—and the advancement of the common white man, rather than the welfare of the black.

AN ANTI-IRISH RIOT

Nativist sentiment resulted in a short-lived political party in the 1850s, but hostility toward foreign Catholics was considerably older. In Boston in 1837 a group of firemen pushed some mourners in an Irish funeral procession. The results were described by a man whose sympathies were with the Yankee firemen.

The ranks of the Irish were gradually thinned by the arrest of some of their more prominent members, who were carried off to jail amid loud shouts. . . . Finally the Irish gave up the contest just in time to save themselves from the bayonets of the [militia], several companies of which were ordered to the scene. . . .

During the conflict the firemen demolished several tenements, throwing furniture, provisions and children into the street. Featherbeds were ripped open. . . . The east wind wafted the feathers all over the city, causing such a shower as might have been taken, at a little distance, for a snow-storm. A large number of persons were badly injured on both sides, but the Irish suffered most severely. . . . There is not the least doubt that the riot originated in the assault upon the firemen. . . .

Much prejudice and ill blood had, for several years, existed between the fire department and the Irish. . . . It cannot be expected that the members of the fire department will look passively on and see their brethren assaulted, or their "machines" overturned.

(*New York Public Library Picture Collection*)

BUCHANAN'S ORDEAL

Franklin Pierce's support of southern interests in Kansas cost him renomination in 1856. The Democrats won that election, but the most important political development was the surprisingly strong showing of the Republican party in the North. The new president, James Buchanan, hoped that the Supreme Court would settle the question of slavery in the territories once and for all. The Court tackled the matter and decided that the Missouri Compromise was unconstitutional, that Congress could not keep slavery out of the territories.

Northerners were infuriated. The entire question was publicly aired in the extraordinary debates between Stephen A. Douglas and Abraham Lincoln, which first brought Lincoln to national attention. Not long afterward, the country was thrown into an uproar by one old man who decided to attack slavery directly where it already existed.

The Election of 1856

National Democratic leaders did not dare back Douglas for the presidency. His successes, as in the adoption of the Kansas-Nebraska Act, proved even more damaging to the party than Pierce's failures. Instead, they turned to a veteran of forty years in politics, the conservative Pennsylvanian James Buchanan. As minister to Britain, Buchanan had the advantage of having been out of the country during Pierce's administration. For their first presidential campaign, Republicans placed their hopes on a military hero—General John C. Frémont, the glamorous Georgia-born son-in-law of the Jacksonian Democrat Thomas Hart Benton. The American party named ex-President Millard Fillmore.

Although "Old Buck" Buchanan soon came to be despised as a "northern man with southern principles," this combination of characteristics helped the efficient Democratic machine put him

The Election of 1856

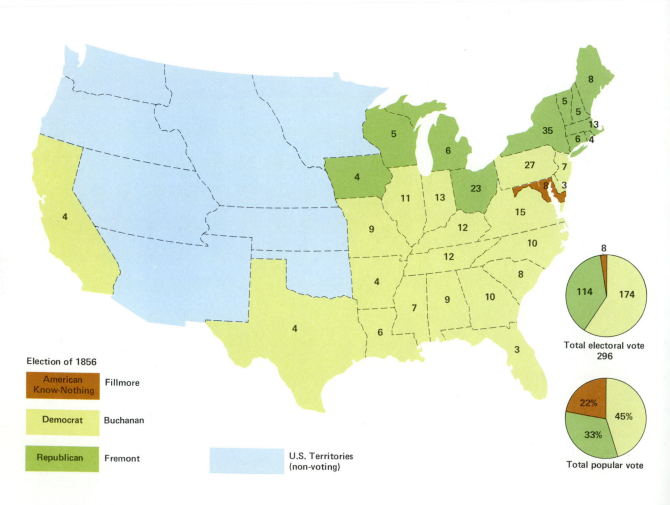

Election of 1856

American Know-Nothing — Fillmore

Democrat — Buchanan

Republican — Fremont

U.S. Territories (non-voting)

Total electoral vote 296

114   174   8

Total popular vote

22%   45%   33%

across with 174 votes in the electoral college to Frémont's 114 and Fillmore's 8. Buchanan's popular vote came to only 45 percent of the ballots cast. Nor was the sectional character of the vote a good omen. New England voted overwhelmingly for Frémont, who also won New York. Had he taken Pennsylvania and Illinois, the Republicans would have won the election. What comfort the South found in the victory hardly made up for the Republican show of strength.

Dred Scott

Buchanan was in office only a few days before the first great crisis of his administration. The trouble came over the Supreme Court decision in *Dred Scott* v. *Sandford* (1857). Dred Scott, a slave, had been taken by his master in 1834 from Missouri to the free state of Illinois, and from there to the Wisconsin Territory, where he stayed until his return to Missouri several years later. The antislavery group who backed his suit for freedom hoped to prove that Dred Scott's time in a free state and in a territory where slavery was illegal under the Missouri Compromise had made him a free man.

The Supreme Court might simply have dismissed this case on the grounds that Scott was not a citizen of Missouri or of the United States and so

Chief Justice Roger B. Taney. (*Library of Congress*)

not entitled to sue in a federal court. Or, falling back on an earlier Supreme Court decision, it might have ruled that Scott's residence in a free state suspended his slave status only temporarily. But the Court knew that Buchanan was expecting the judiciary to resolve the issue of slavery in the territories, especially in Kansas.

No fewer than eight of the nine justices on the Supreme Court wrote separate opinions on different aspects of the Dred Scott case. In speaking for the Court for more than two hours, Chief Justice Roger B. Taney spent half his time arguing that since blacks had been viewed as inferior beings at the time the Constitution was adopted, its framers did not intend to include them within the meaning of the term *citizen*. Therefore, the right of citizens of different states to sue in the federal courts could never apply to a former slave or descendant of a slave.

Only two justices agreed with Taney's racial concepts and his history. But these two and four others joined Taney in a majority finding that Scott, even had he become free, had reverted to slavery on his return to the slave state of Missouri and had no right to sue in a federal court. Five justices, conforming to the president's wishes, joined the Chief Justice in plunging further. The slave, they explained, is property, pure and simple. According to the Fifth Amendment to the Constitution, "No person shall be . . . deprived of life, liberty, or property without due process of law." It was a violation of this clause, they said, to prohibit anyone from taking slavery into the territories.

"No word can be found in the Constitution," Taney observed, "which gives Congress a greater power over slave property, or which entitles property of that kind to less protection than property of any other description." Thus Congress had no right under the Constitution to exclude slavery from the territories, and the Missouri Compromise was, and always had been, unconstitutional.

The Kansas-Nebraska Act had already declared the Missouri Compromise "inoperative and void." If, as the Court now held, the attempt of the compromise to legislate slavery out of the territories was also unconstitutional, the objective for which the Republican party had been formed was unconstitutional. Even the Douglas Democrats were troubled by the decision. For if slaves were property untouchable by law under the federal Constitution, Douglas's program for popular sovereignty on the slavery question in the territories was dead.

In June 1857, as part of his continuing cam-

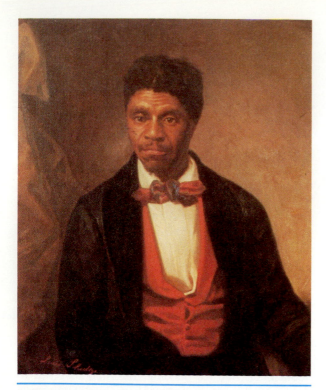

Dred Scott. (*Missouri Historical Society*)

paign against Douglas's popular sovereignty position, Lincoln said of the Dred Scott decision:

If this important decision had been made by the unanimous concurrence of the judges, and without any partisan bias, and ... had been in no part, based on assumed historical facts which are not really true; or, if ... it had been before the court more than once, and had there been affirmed and re-affirmed through a course of years, it then might be, perhaps would be, factious, nay, even revolutionary, to not acquiesce in it as a precedent.

But when, as it is true, we find it wanting in all these claims to the public confidence, it is not resistance, it is not factious, it is not even disrespectful, to treat it as not having yet quite established a settled doctrine for the country.

The Lincoln-Douglas Debates

The troublesome issue of slavery in the territories was most thoroughly examined during the contest for the Illinois senatorial seat in 1858. The rising Republican candidate, Abraham Lincoln, challenged his Democratic opponent, "the little giant" Stephen A. Douglas, to a series of debates. Before the debates began, however, two events soured the hopes of the South as much as the Dred Scott decision had sweetened them.

The first was the business panic of August 1857. The depression that followed gave antislavery Republicans strong allies in two groups of the free economy. Businessmen and their employees favored the Republican plank for high tariffs to stimulate free industry and industrial employment. Farmers liked the Republican plank for free homesteads. The sudden collapse of the economy did allow southern spokesmen to point with pride to the comparative stability and success of the slave system. But southerners were as fearful of high tariffs and free land as of the Republican party itself. They grew more determined to preserve for their section, if only for political advantage, all the western territories not yet lost to slavery.

The second event was the state constitutional convention at Lecompton, Kansas, in October 1857. Proslavery delegates named in a rigged election not only wrote a constitution guaranteeing slavery, but refused to permit the whole body of voters to ballot on it. Under severe pressure they did offer a proposition restricting the entry of new slaves, but protecting slave property already in the state. The dominant antislavery voters abstained, and the proslavery party carried the vote. After considerable maneuvering, Congress offered Kansas statehood immediately, with a federal land grant, if its voters accepted the Lecompton Constitution. The alternative was continuing territorial status if they rejected it. Given the chance, Kansas overwhelmingly turned down the Lecompton Constitution. Here the matter rested until 1861, when Kansas entered the Union as a free state.

The Illinois Republican convention that was to nominate Lincoln for the Senate, to run against Douglas, met in Springfield in June 1858. Lincoln was not so well known as he soon would be. But in Illinois he was a popular figure, a prosperous lawyer, and a Whig leader who had served a term in the United States House of Representatives. In his speech accepting the nomination, he observed that the slavery issue had grown worse each year. "In my opinion," he said, "it will not cease until a crisis shall have been reached and passed. 'A house divided against itself cannot stand.'"

This "house divided" speech was studied carefully by Douglas and furnished the basis for his attacks on Lincoln in the seven debates that followed. Douglas, who admired Lincoln personally, attacked him during the debates as a sectionalist whose philosophy would end in "a war of extermination." Why, Douglas asked, did the Republicans say that slavery and freedom could not coexist? Lincoln replied that his party did not pro-

The *Mason-Dixon Line* is named after two English surveyors, Charles Mason and Jeremiah Dixon, who surveyed part of the border between the two colonies of Maryland and Pennsylvania in 1763–67. The original proprietary grants to the Calvert family and to William Penn overlapped, resulting in a boundary dispute that was finally settled by this survey on behalf of the descendants of the original proprietors. At the time, shortly before the American Revolution, slavery existed in both Maryland and Pennsylvania (as well as Delaware). During that war, Pennsylvania became the first state to adopt a gradual emancipation law. As time went on, the *Mason-Dixon Line* came to mean the dividing line between the slave and the free states. It became a kind of shorthand way of describing the line of division between the North and the South.

pose to interfere with slavery where it existed, nor did he wish to enforce social equality between blacks and whites, as Douglas charged. In keeping with the Republican program, he opposed any extension of slavery.

In the debate at Freeport, Illinois, Lincoln asked Douglas a momentous question: "Can the people of a United States territory, in any lawful way, against the wish of any citizen of the United States, exclude slavery from its limits prior to the formation of a State constitution?" In order to answer, Douglas had to abandon popular sovereignty or defy the Dred Scott decision. If the people could not exclude slavery, popular sovereignty meant little. If they could exclude it, popular sovereignty was as much in conflict with the Dred Scott decision as the Republican principle of congressional exclusion.

Douglas answered that the people of a territory could take this step, in spite of the Dred Scott decision. Slavery could not exist for a day, he explained, if the local legislature did not pass the necessary laws to protect and police slave property. Therefore, merely by failing to arrange for slavery, a territorial legislature, without formally barring it, could make its existence impossible. Douglas's realistic answer—his "Freeport doctrine"—broadened the opposition to him in the South and widened the split in the Democratic party, as Lincoln anticipated. Douglas won the senatorial election in the Illinois state legislature, but the Democratic party and the Union were more divided than ever.

John Brown's Raid

The most emotional event in the sectional struggle was John Brown's raid on the federal arsenal at Harpers Ferry, Virginia, in 1859. Brown and his seventeen black and white men captured the arsenal and its millions of dollars worth of arms.

That night he sent a detachment to take nearby planters and some of their slaves as hostages. This mission accomplished, he awaited news of the slave uprisings he hoped would follow. "When I strike, the bees will swarm," Brown had told Frederick Douglass and other prominent abolitionists.

By dawn the next day, news of his exploit had spread across the countryside, and a hastily gathered militia counterattacked. Dangerfield Newby, a free black—his wife and seven children still slaves in Virginia—was the first of Brown's raiders to die. Brown's two sons were also mortally wounded that day, along with others. Before the

John Brown. (*National Portrait Gallery, Smithsonian Institution*)

day ended, Brown and his survivors had been trapped in the arsenal. Exaggerated stories of the adventure had by now reached Washington.

Buchanan quickly ordered the nearest federal troops to the scene. He also sent Colonel Robert E. Lee and Lieutenant J. E. B. Stuart from the capital to take charge. Having rejected Brown's truce terms, Stuart led the attack on the arsenal and soon regained it. He captured Brown and five others, leaving the rest of Brown's men dead.

Eminent abolitionists, although they did not support violence, had known of Brown's project and provided him with money and weapons, supposedly for antislavery partisans in Kansas. This only aggravated the reaction in the South, where vigilante groups assaulted anyone suspected of antislavery sympathies, and dangerous books were publicly burned. In New York, Boston, and elsewhere, huge meetings organized by northern conservatives attacked Brown and his methods. Lincoln, Douglas, and men of all parties joined in the condemnation. But when Virginia's governor rejected the plea of Brown's relatives and friends that the raider was insane and ordered him hanged, he ensured Brown's martyrdom.

Brown's bravery and dignity on the scaffold touched millions who condemned his deeds.

Lithograph of John Brown by Charles W. White, 1949. (*Library of Congress*)

"One's faith in anything is terribly shaken," a conservative New Yorker confided in his journal, "by anybody who is ready to go the gallows condemning and denouncing it." The deification of John Brown that followed was partly the work of writers like Emerson and Thoreau, who converted a brave monomaniac into an "angel of light." "A fervid Union man" of North Carolina, as he described himself, reflected the southern response in these words: "I confess the endorsement of the Harpers Ferry outrage . . . has shaken by fidelity and . . . I am willing to take the chances of every probable evil that may arise from disunion, sooner than submit any longer to Northern insolence and Northern outrage."

TOWARD SEPARATION

Four major candidates ran in the election of 1860. The Republican party nominated Lincoln. The Democrats were so divided along sectional lines that they ran two separate candidates, ensuring Lincoln's election. The states of the lower South took his victory as a signal that they must leave the Union and establish their own government. In Washington, some politicians tried to patch up another compromise during the long months between the November election and the inauguration in March.

Lincoln's Election

In April 1860 the Democratic national convention assembled at Charleston, South Carolina, the heartland of secession sentiment. Southern extremists insisted on a plank in the party platform declaring that neither Congress nor a territorial government could outlaw slavery or impair the right to own slaves. Northern Democrats, hoping to nominate Douglas without alienating the southerners, expressed willingness to accept the Dred Scott ruling. Yet they stood equally firm for popular sovereignty. "We cannot recede from this doctrine," a Douglas spokesman insisted, "without personal dishonor."

When it became clear that the extremists' plank would fail, most delegates from eight southern states withdrew. Their departure made it impossible for Douglas to get the necessary two-thirds of the ballots, and the convention adjourned. In June, Democrats reconvened in Baltimore. When the southern delegates bolted once again, the convention nominated Douglas on a popular sovereignty platform. Ten days later, the southerners met in-

Abraham Lincoln. (*National Portrait Gallery, Smithsonian Institution*)

dependently in Baltimore and chose John C. Breckinridge of Kentucky, a moderate, to represent their position on slavery in the territories. With two Democrats in the field, the last unionist bond—a great political party with support in the North and the South—had broken.

The Republicans met in Chicago. Their frontrunner was William H. Seward of New York. But Seward had a reputation as an irreconcilable because he once had spoken of the "irrepressible conflict" between North and South. The character of his backer, political boss Thurlow Weed, and the pushy behavior of Weed's henchmen at the convention also handicapped him. The way was open for Lincoln, who was strongly supported by the Illinois and Indiana delegations and acceptable to both East and West.

Six weeks before the convention Lincoln had reviewed his chances in a letter to a friend: "My name is now in the field; and I suppose I am not the first choice of a very great many. Our policy, then, is to give no offense to others—leave them in a mood to come to us, if they shall be impelled to give up their first love." This strategy paid off when Pennsylvania and Ohio switched from Seward, and Lincoln was nominated.

The Republican platform, while making a shrewd appeal to powerful economic interests, also sounded a high moral tone. It included planks for a protective tariff, free homesteads, a Pacific railroad, and the rights of immigrants. "The normal condition of all the territory of the United States," it said, "is that of freedom, . . . and we deny the authority of Congress, of a territorial legislature, or of any individuals, to give legal existence to slavery in any territory of the United States."

The campaign was further complicated by the nomination of John Bell of Tennessee, a fourth candidate, by the new Constitutional Union party, composed largely of Whigs in the border states. His platform tactfully called upon the people "to recognize no political principle other than the Constitution of the country, the Union of the states, and the enforcement of the laws."

The 1860 election presented the remarkable picture of a divided nation simultaneously carrying out two separate contests for the presidency: one between Breckinridge and Bell in the South, the second between Lincoln and Douglas in the North. Ten slave states did not even put Lincoln on the ballot. Only 1.4 percent of his popular votes came from the South. Douglas, although acknowledged as a candidate, also ran poorly there. In the North, at the same time, neither Breckinridge nor Bell found support.

Although sectional loyalties were decisive in the election, the considerable unionist vote in the South must not be overlooked. Bell won Kentucky, Tennessee, and Virginia, and only barely lost Maryland and Missouri. Although Lincoln had a decisive majority in the electoral college, he carried less than 40 percent of the popular vote. A sectional candidate had become president of the United States.

The Deep South Moves Out

After Lincoln's nomination, southern leaders had repeatedly warned that a Republican victory would mean secession. The governor of South Carolina forecast that the election of a sectional northern candidate would "ultimately reduce the southern states to mere provinces of a consolidated despotism." Such expectations perhaps best answer the question: Why did the South move out?

To understand secession, it must also be realized that few people in the South anticipated the results. It was by no means certain that the North would go to war to keep the South in the Union. And if war came, why should not the South win, and quickly? Many southerners imagined that the will to fight was weak in the North. They also looked to the sympathy of foreign aristocrats, the

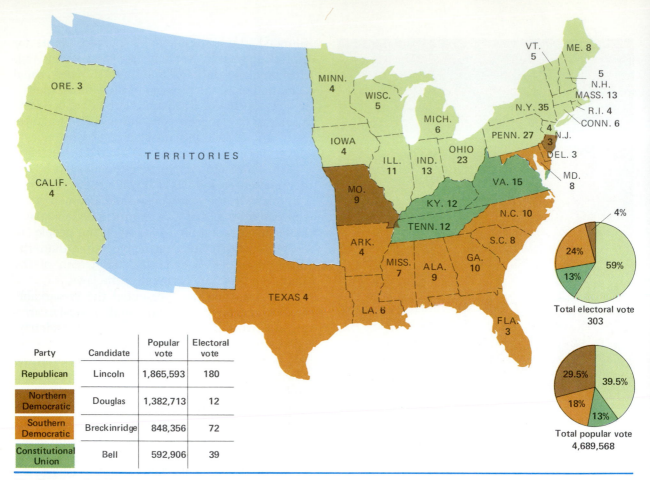

Party	Candidate	Popular vote	Electoral vote
Republican	Lincoln	1,865,593	180
Northern Democratic	Douglas	1,382,713	12
Southern Democratic	Breckinridge	848,356	72
Constitutional Union	Bell	592,906	39

Total electoral vote 303

Total popular vote 4,689,568

The Election of 1860

commercial power of King Cotton, and the help of the many pro-southerners in the North.

Secession also had a positive side. No longer would the South be drained of its resources by northern banking and shipping interests and by taxes and tariffs that chiefly benefited the North. Perhaps the slave trade would be reopened. Cuba, Santo Domingo, Mexico, and even territories in Central America might become available to enterprising planters.

On December 20, 1860, South Carolina took the initiative. A special convention formally repealed the state's ratification of the Constitution and withdrew from the Union. By February 1, 1861, six other commonwealths—Mississippi, Florida, Alabama, Georgia, Louisiana, and Texas—had followed its example. But the urge to secede proved far from from universal even in the Deep South. In almost every case, the step was taken over opposition. There were people ready to give Lincoln a chance to show whether he would really enforce the Fugitive Slave Act and meet other southern demands. But the tactics of the extremists overwhelmed the "cooperationists," as south-

ern moderates were called. Pockets of unionism persisted in the lower South. Texas Germans, Alabama and Georgia mountaineers, and small farmers in Louisiana parishes clung to their federal loyalties.

Yet the majority of southerners of all classes were ready to leave. On February 4, 1861, with seven states having seceded, but with Texas absent, delegates from six states met at Montgomery, Alabama, to form a new government. They called it the Confederate States of America, adopted a new flag, the "Stars and Bars," and wrote a new constitution.

A Federal Vacuum

Secession, having begun with Lincoln's victory, took place while Buchanan still occupied the White House. At such a moment the country had a "lame-duck" president, one without the will or the power to make commitments. Although Buchanan declared that secession was unconstitutional, he also argued that Congress had no power under the Constitution to prevent it.

While Buchanan delayed, border state leaders in particular, aware that if secession meant war their land would become a battleground, tried to avert disaster. The most seriously considered proposals were those put forward by Senator John J. Crittenden of Kentucky, two days before South Carolina's formal withdrawal from the Union. Crittenden offered these constitutional amendments: (1) Slavery was to be barred in the territories north of the Missouri Compromise line, 36° 30′. (2) It was to be permitted and protected south of that line. (3) Future states were to enter as they wished, slave or free. (4) The fugitive slave law was to be enforced and compensation paid by the federal government when enforcement failed because of the action of northerners. (5) The Constitution was never to be amended to authorize Congress to interfere with slavery in any state or the District of Columbia.

Crittenden's compromise failed to win support from either side. Southern leaders would not accept it unless it was endorsed by the Republican party. Lincoln favored enforcement of the fugitive slave law and would accept an amendment protecting slavery where it then existed. But he opposed any compromise on excluding slavery from the territories. To a friend in Congress he wrote: "Entertain no proposition for a compromise in regard to the extension of slavery. The instant you do they have us under again: all our labor is lost, and sooner or later must be done over."

FINAL FAILURE

When Abraham Lincoln stood up to take the oath of office on March 4, 1861, secession was a fact. A southern Confederacy had been formed, and important federal properties had fallen into rebel hands. Yet a far greater territory than the existing Confederacy remained very much at issue. The upper South—Virginia, Maryland, North Carolina, even Delaware—was torn by conflict as individuals, families, and neighborhoods wrestled with their alternatives. Farther west, in Tennessee, Kentucky, Arkansas, and Missouri, actual battles were fought before allegiance to North or South could be established.

Lincoln's Inaugural

In all these states, the president's inaugural address had been long awaited. Early in his speech, Lincoln stressed the perpetuity of "the more perfect Union" established by the Constitution. Then followed his sharpest words to the rebels: "No State upon its mere motion can lawfully get out of the Union; . . . acts of violence . . . against the authority of the United States, are insurrectionary or revolutionary, according to circumstance. . . . The mails, unless repelled," Lincoln added, "will continue to be furnished in all parts of the Union."

The president was as conciliatory as his office and his nature allowed. As chief executive, he said, he was bound to enforce federal regulations, including those requiring the return of fugitive slaves, in all the states. He even went so far as to say he had no objections to a proposed constitutional amendment guaranteeing that "the Federal Government shall never interfere with the domestic institutions of the States"—including slavery. Other constitutional obligations, on the other hand, required that he "hold, occupy, and possess the property and places belonging to the Government, and to collect the duties and imposts" in every American port. But in performing these acts, "there needs be no bloodshed or violence; and there shall be none, unless it be forced upon the national authority."

Near the end of his address, Lincoln reminded the South: "In your hands, my dissatisfied fellow-countrymen, and not in mine is the momentous issue of civil war." Characteristically, Lincoln did not close on a hard note; he added this eloquent paragraph:

I am loath to close. We are not enemies, but friends. We must not be enemies. Though passion may have strained, it must not break, our bonds of affection. The mystic chords of memory, stretching from every battlefield and patriot grave to every living heart and hearthstone all over this broad land, will yet swell the chorus of the Union when again touched, as surely they will be, by the better angels of our nature.

Few inaugural orations in United States history bore the burden of Lincoln's first. Few if any played so deliberately for time. In the terrible economic crisis of 1933, Franklin D. Roosevelt caught the public mood when he declared in his inaugural address: "In their need [the people of the United States] have registered a mandate that they want direct, vigorous action." But Lincoln, though pressed by those of every political creed, electrified the nation by putting action off: "My countrymen, one and all, think calmly and well upon this whole subject. Nothing valuable can be lost by taking time."

Fort Sumter Falls

And yet action was required of the president himself. In defiance of Buchanan's threat to meet force with force, the Confederacy in the early months of 1861 had seized federal forts, post offices, and custom houses throughout the South. Only Fort Sumter in Charleston harbor and three forts off the coast of Florida remained in federal hands. On the day after his inauguration, Lincoln was handed a letter from Major Robert Anderson, the commander at Sumter, reporting that he could hold the fort only with the immediate aid of 20,000 men, a large naval force, and supplies.

Anderson, in effect, recommended evacuation. If Lincoln retreated, as his advisors urged, he would have taken the first step toward recognizing the power of the Confederacy. If, on the other hand, he attempted to strengthen Sumter, he would be made to appear the aggressor. Lincoln cautiously steered a middle course. He notified South Carolina authorities that he would attempt to supply Sumter peacefully. "If such attempt be not resisted," he wrote the governor, "no effort to throw in men, arms, or ammunition will be made."

Lincoln's decision shifted the burden to Confederate authorities. If they permitted the supplying of Sumter, the fort would remain indefinitely in the mouth of their best harbor, a reproach to their prestige throughout the world. If they at-tacked a peaceful expedition bringing food, they would have fired the first shot.

When requested by Confederate authorities to surrender Sumter before the supply ships arrived, Major Anderson promised to evacuate by April 15, unless relieved or ordered to remain. But the Confederacy could not risk such a delay. On April 12 the batteries on the Charleston shore began their thirty-four-hour bombardment. When Anderson at last ran down the flag, Sumter was burning, its ammunition gone. Remarkably, not a man had been hit on either side during the engagement. But a war that was to take more casualties than even Napoleon's campaigns had in fact begun.

Before Sumter, northern opinion had divided sharply on the proper response to secession. Abolitionists like Garrison thought it pointless to enforce union "where one section is pinned to the residue by bayonets." For once, the business community, still suffering the effects of the Panic of 1857 and concerned over collecting southern debts and holding southern markets, agreed with abolitionist policy to let the "erring sisters go in peace." But warlike voices also spoke out. "If South Carolina is determined upon secession," warned *The New York Times*, "she should take the plunge with

George Hayward's watercolor caught the spirit of the flag-waving crowds cheering New York's Seventh Regiment as it marched down Broadway on April 19, 1861. (*Museum of Fine Arts, Boston*)

her eyes open. She must face the consequences—
and among them all, the most unquestionable is
war."

Disunion was especially opposed by the Northwest, where freedom for white men on the land
was the very watchword of the Lord. No section
uttered "Amen" more appreciatively to Lincoln's
March 4 statement, "Physically speaking, we cannot separate." After Sumter, peace partisans still
were heard here and there in the North. But with
the Confederacy branded as the aggressor, it became easier to portray hostilities as a defense of
the Union. Lincoln's call on April 15 for 75,000
three-month volunteers met with overwhelming
response everywhere. Walt Whitman in Manhattan, whose *Drum Taps* established him as the
Union poet of the war, caught the new surge of
spirit:

From the houses then and the workshops,
and through all the doorways

Leapt they tumultous, and lo! Manhattan
arming.

The Upper South and the Border Decide

It is sometimes said that South Carolinians, aware
that a Confederacy without Virginia would be
nothing, bombarded Fort Sumter to force that state
to join the Confederacy. Yet three months after
Virginia's "secession convention" was called, it still
refused to vote. Then, on April 15, Lincoln issued
the fateful proclamation declaring that "combinations too powerful to be suppressed" by ordinary
means existed in the seven Confederate states and
calling forth "the militia of the several States of
the Union, to the aggregate number of seventy-
five thousand, in order to suppress such combinations."

His proclamation was received with approval
throughout the North. Throughout the upper

The United States on the Eve of the Civil War

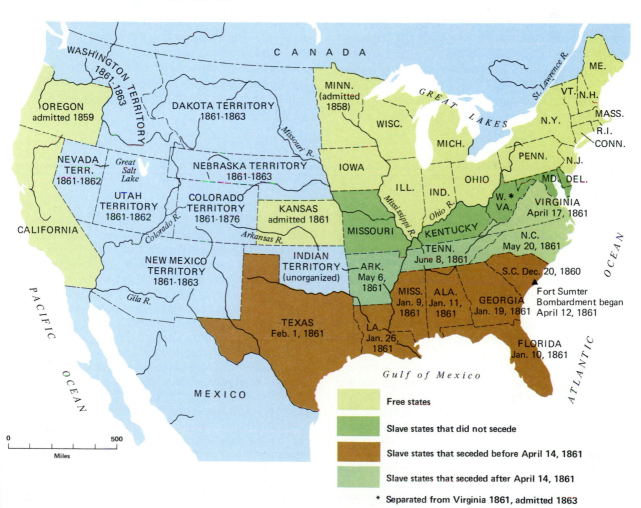

THE UNION COMES APART

South and the border states, it came like a death knell. Should Virginia and the rest answer the president's call and give their men to the Union cause? Should they stand by while the South was invaded by northern men and arms?

More than his election, more than his inaugural, more even than the attempt to provision Sumter, Lincoln's proclamation of April 15 sealed the issue of war and peace. Two days later, the Virginia convention passed its ordinance of secession, 88 to 55. The provisional Confederate government named Richmond its permanent capital and prepared to move from Montgomery. At the end of May a referendum in Virginia approved secession, though people in the western portion of the state disagreed so strongly that they began to organize to secede from the new Confederate state. Only then did the president acknowledge that all hope was gone: "The people of Virginia have thus allowed this giant insurrection to make its nest within her borders; and this government has no choice left but to deal with it where it finds it."

Lincoln had supplemented his proclamation calling out the militia with an order to the navy to blockade the ports of the first seven Confederate commonwealths. Later he extended the blockade to Virginia and North Carolina. The Supreme Court was eventually to rule that the war legally began with these blockade orders, which officially recognized that a state of "belligerency" existed between two powers. Lincoln himself never accepted this idea. He never recognized the Confederacy as a nation, nor secession as anything but "insurrection."

Other states soon followed Virginia's example. In March an Arkansas convention had rejected secession, but in May it approved. In North Carolina a convention called by the legislature voted unanimously to secede. In Tennessee, the governor and legislature took the state into the Confederacy even before the people ratified their decision. Unionist regions, nevertheless, could still be found in the upper South and on the border. Like the western Virginians, the people of eastern Tennessee would probably have rejoined the Union had Confederate troops not prevented them. Four indecisive slave states—Kentucky, Missouri, Maryland, and Delaware—remained in the Union.

Maryland's strategic position forced Lincoln to take strong unconstitutional measures against agitators there. With a show of federal force, the secessionist spirit in Maryland subsided. Rich and populous Kentucky maintained neutrality until September 1861, when the legislature voted to remain loyal to the Union. Kentucky volunteers for the Confederates numbered only half as many as those who fought with the Federals. In Missouri, the division between southern and northern supporters flared into a small civil war, though only one-fifth of Missouri's fighting men were with the South. And no one on either side thought the war would last long.

SUMMARY

By the late 1850s, tension over slavery had led to violence and threats of violence in Congress itself. The crisis came over the extension of slavery to the new territories as earlier compromises fell apart. Enforcement of the fugitive slave law of 1850, part of the compromise, and Harriet Beecher Stowe's fictional account of slavery, *Uncle Tom's Cabin,* gave northerners a view of slavery they had never had before. Dramatic incidents when "runaways" were seized led thousands to change their attitude toward slavery.

Northern incitement and protection of runaways led the planters to react. In 1854, Congress passed the Kansas-Nebraska Act, which reopened the question of slavery in the western territories and nullified the Missouri Compromise. To get a northern route for the proposed transcontinental railroad, the concession was made to divide Nebraska into two territories, Nebraska and Kansas. Kansas was marked for slavery by the South, but not by the North. The territory was turned into a battleground, and for a period there was civil war there.

After 1852, the Whig party fell apart. The election of 1856 brought new political parties: the Know-Nothings, opposed to Catholic immigrants, and the Republicans, who opposed extension of slavery to the western territories. The Democrats were now largely the party of the South and slavery. Their candidate, James Buchanan, won, but the Republican party ran strongly in the North.

Buchanan hoped the Supreme Court would settle the question of slavery in the territories. The Court, in the Dred Scott decision, decided the Missouri Compromise was unconstitutional. The issue then became the focus of the Lincoln-Douglas debates of 1858, which made Abraham Lincoln a national figure. Lincoln lost the Illinois senatorial election, but Douglas's treatment of the issue widened the split in the Democratic party. The next year John Brown's raid on the federal arsenal at Harpers Ferry, Virginia, shocked the entire country. Brown, a fervent abolitionist, was hanged—but then became a legend in the North.

Four candidates ran in the election of 1860. The winner was Abraham Lincoln, of the sectional Republican party. The South took his election as a signal. By February 1, 1861, even before Lincoln's inauguration, seven states—South Carolina, Mississippi, Florida, Alabama, Georgia, Louisiana, and Texas—had seceded from the Union. On February 4, delegates from six states met at Montgomery, Alabama, to form a new government, the Confederate States of America. Buchanan, the outgoing president, hesitated; in the Senate, senators from the border states tried a last attempt at compromise. It failed. When Lincoln took the oath of office on March 4, secession was a fact.

The taking of Fort Sumter in Charleston harbor on April 12 began the war. On April 15, by proclamation, Lincoln issued a call for 75,000 three-month volunteers to "suppress" the Confederacy. At that point the upper South and the border states were forced to make a decision: Virginia, Arkansas, North Carolina, and Tennessee seceded. Kentucky, Missouri, Maryland, and Delaware remained in the Union. And both sides prepared for what neither thought would be a long war.

Suggested Readings

With very few exceptions, general historical treatments of the 1850s have focused on the approach of the Civil War. Historians have been divided not only by sectional sympathies, but also by the factors they feel actually led to conflict. The ambitious account by A. Nevins, *Ordeal of the Union* (2 vols., 1947), and *The Emergence of Lincoln* (2 vols., 1950), is widely admired. The humane perceptions in D. Potter, *The South and the Sectional Conflict* (1968), have also commanded great respect. See also Potter's *The Impending Crisis, 1848–1861* (1976), a powerful and skillful account of the road to war.

Several books deal with important specific issues: S. Campbell, *The Slave Catchers: Enforcement of the Fugitive Slave Law, 1850–1860* (1970); G. Wolff, *Kansas-Nebraska Bill: Party, Section, and the Origin of the Civil War* (1980); R. May, *The Southern Dream of a Caribbean Empire, 1854–1861* (1973); and D. Fehrenbacher, *The Dred Scott Case: Its Significance in American Law and Politics* (1978). R. Takaki, *A Pro-Slavery Crusade: The Agitation to Reopen the African Slave Trade* (1971), focuses on the interest of certain southern leaders in protecting slavery. D. Davis, *The Slave Power Conspiracy and the Paranoid Style* (1969), discusses the mounting fear of the South's intentions.

The first outbreak of violence is dealt with in P. Gates, *Fifty Million Acres: Conflicts over Kansas Land Policy, 1854–1890* (1954); J. Rawley, *Race and Politics* (1969); a biography of John Brown by S. Oates, *To Purge This Land with Blood* (1970); and a brief, perceptive essay by C. Vann Woodward found in D. Aaron (ed.), *America in Crisis* (1952). E. Stone (ed.), *Incident at Harpers Ferry* (1956), has contemporary material on the Brown raid.

The rise and the role of the Republican party are described in many of the books cited above. Increasingly, the tendency among historians has been to concentrate on the issue of race. E. Foner, *Free Soil, Free Labor, Free Men: The Ideology of the Republican Party before the Civil War* (1970), and E. Berwanger, *The Frontier against Slavery: Western Anti-Negro Prejudice and the Slavery Extension Controversy* (1967), both stress that issue. So does H. Trefousse, *The Radical Republicans: Lincoln's Vanguard for Racial Justice* (1969). Two other studies, a biography and a study of

voting behavior, are among the most illuminating about the coming conflict: R. Durden, *James Shepherd Pike: Republicanism and the American Negro, 1850–1882* (1957), and M. Holt, *Forging a Majority: The Formation of the Republican Party in Pittsburgh, 1848–1860* (1969).

This period of rapid political realignment is dealt with by T. Alexander, *Sectional Stress and Party Strength* (1967), an examination of congressional roll calls, and more broadly in M. Holt, *The Political Crisis of the 1850s* (1978). J. Silbey's introduction to a little collection of documents, *The Transformation of American Politics, 1840–1860* (1967), offers a dazzling entrance to the political arena in this period. Several biographies also stand out: G. Van Deusen, *William Henry Seward* (1967), dealing with a puzzling and neglected figure; D. Donald, *Charles Sumner and the Coming of the Civil War* (1950), a psychological study of great value; and the long but first-rate R. Johannsen, *Stephen A. Douglas* (1973). Two unfortunate presidents have been treated in R. Nichols, *Franklin Pierce: Young Hickory of the Granite Hills* (2nd ed., 1958); and P. Klein, *President James Buchanan: A Biography* (1962).

The early career of Abraham Lincoln may be studied in C. Sandburg, *Abraham Lincoln, The Prairie Years* (one vol. ed., 1929), a classic study; D. Fehrenbacher, *Prelude to Greatness, Lincoln in the 1850s* (1962); and J. Randall, *Lincoln the President, Springfield to Gettysburg* (2 vols., 1945), part of a full-scale biography. The Lincoln-Douglas debates are printed in full in P. Angle (ed.), *Created Equal* (1958).

Of the many books on secession, state studies stand out—for example, W. Barney, *The Secessionist Impulse: Alabama and Mississippi in 1860* (1974). P. Rainwater, *Mississippi: Storm Center of Secession, 1856–1861* (1938), is an old but still impressive study. S. Channing, *Crisis of Fear: Secession in South Carolina* (1970), is a dramatic account of the background as well as the final act. An extremely interesting triangular view of the secession crisis may be had by reading the following three works: D. Potter, *Lincoln and His Party in the Secession Crisis, 1860–1861* (1942); K. Stampp, *And the War Came: The North and the Secession Crisis, 1860–1861* (1950); and R. Current, *Lincoln and the First Shot* (1963).

CIVIL WAR

Chapter 17

Secession led directly to war: it was not so easy to break the Union as southern leaders supposed. At the start, both sides seemed paralyzed. Both fervently wished that the fighting would soon be over. The Civil War became the deadliest ever fought on this continent, yet it was very slow in gathering momentum. And when it was finally over, little seemed to have been accomplished by the slaughter. Not that it was in vain. Lincoln made that clear in the Gettysburg Address: "From these honored dead we take increased devotion to that cause for which they gave the last full measure of devotion—that . . . this nation, under God, shall have a new birth of freedom—and that government of the people, by the people, for the people, shall not perish from the earth." The war pointed the way "for us the living," as Lincoln said, to dedicate themselves to "the unfinished work which they who fought here have thus far so nobly advanced."

For Lincoln, the unfinished task was restoration of the Union. But in the back of his mind he knew very well that the condition of black people was fundamental to the entire conflict. Their future was altered but scarcely settled by the war in which roughly one white man died for every six slaves "freed." ■

ENEMIES FACE TO FACE

On paper the North was far stronger than the South. It had two and a half times as many people, and it possessed far more ships, miles of railroad, and manufacturing enterprises. Southerners, however, had the advantage of fighting on home ground with better military leadership. Civilian authority was another matter. The new Confederate government ran into trouble because of one of the principles it was fighting for—states rights. In the North, moreover, Abraham Lincoln was self-confident enough to assemble a cabinet of exceptionally strong and able men. He himself assumed powers that made him as close to a dictator as the United States had ever had.

Soldiers and Supplies

At the beginning of the conflict, about 22 million persons lived in loyal states and territories, as well as an unknown number of Indians in the West. Nine million (5.5 million whites and 3.5 million blacks) lived in the South. But Union superiority in manpower was not so great as the gross figures suggest. Half a million people, scattered from Dakota to California, could make no substantial contribution to Union strength. And every year during the Civil War, Union regiments were sent to the West to fight Indians. Hundreds of thousands of Americans in loyal border states and in southern Ohio, Indiana, and Illinois worked or fought for southern independence. Many southerners, of course, remained loyal to the Union. Indeed, every state furnished men for the other side. But there is little doubt that more Federals than Confederates "crossed over."

Certain other considerations favored the Confederacy. One was the South's superior officer personnel. For twenty years before Lincoln's inauguration, southern officers had dominated the U.S. Army. Many northern West Pointers, including William T. Sherman and Ulysses S. Grant, found little opportunity for advancement and resigned their commissions early in life in favor of civilian careers. Another source of southern confidence was cotton. Secession leaders expected to exchange that staple for the foreign manufactured goods they needed, without sacrificing fighting men to factory work.

Probably the South's most important advantage was that it had only to defend relatively short interior lines against invaders who had to deal with long lines of communication and to attack on a broad front. The Confederacy also had no need to divert fighting men to tasks such as garrisoning captured cities and holding conquered territory.

The South's armies contained a considerably larger proportion of the region's white men than the North's. Taking the two white populations as separate wholes, it is clear that the war was more widely supported in the South. In addition, thousands of slaves were made to perform fatigue duty and construct fortifications. Wealthy planters and their sons took favorite slaves into the field as personal servants. On the other side, blacks were not welcomed as soldiers at first. After 1862, however, abolitionists succeeded in gaining approval for black regiments, staffed by white officers. Some of these units were recruited from the free black population in the North; others came directly from slavery in border states or in areas captured by Union forces. They suffered discrimination in pay and quarters, but their performance in battle encouraged those—black and white—who hoped to disprove the assumption that blacks could not become good fighting men.

In a short war, northern numerical superiority would not have made much of a difference. As the war continued, however, numerical strength became a psychological as well as a physical weapon. During the closing years of the conflict, Union armies, massed at last against critical strongholds, suffered terrible casualties but seemed to grow stronger with every defeat. And staggering Confederate losses sapped the southern will to fight.

The fact that the Civil War stretched over years instead of months magnified every material advantage of the North—money and credit, factories, food production, transport. It took time to redirect the economy to the requirements of war, especially because these requirements were underestimated because of wishful thinking about the length of the war. But the South found it even more difficult to convert to a war footing.

As the war lengthened, southern troops suffered from short rations, ragged clothing, and no boots. Until the end, though, the Confederacy had the basic materials of war—small arms, artillery, ammunition, and horses. Every rural home in the South had weapons. Large quantities of munitions were also taken from captured federal forts and imported by running the blockade. Under the brilliant administration of its chief of ordinance, the Confederacy also developed its own munitions plants to supplement the output of the giant Tredegar Iron Works in Richmond.

Union and Confederate soldiers took time to pose for the camera before going off to glory—and to slaughter. (*Library of Congress*)

The Confederate Government

Delegates from the first seceding states met at Montgomery, Alabama, in February 1861 to draft a frame of government. By not departing too greatly from the familiar federal document, they hoped to attract their neighbors in the upper South. Because they were so committed to states rights, however, they wrote in certain weaknesses that had been kept out of the Constitution in 1787. Its preamble declared that the Confederacy was established, not by "We, the people," but by "the people of the Confederate states, each state acting in its sovereign and independent character." Of course the new constitution "recognized and protected . . . the right of property in negro slaves."

While the Confederate Congress was granted power "to . . . provide for the common defense," no mention was made of promoting the "general welfare." "The judicial power of the Confederate States" was placed in a Supreme Court and certain lower tribunals. But no Supreme Court was ever established. The old federal district courts continued to sit, often under their old judges who applied the old rules and precedents inherited from English common law. The president's term was extended to six years. Whatever advantage in stability this brought was lost by the provision barring his reelection.

The Montgomery Constitutional Convention named Jefferson Davis of Mississippi and Alexander H. Stephens of Georgia as provisional president and vice-president, respectively. Neither man wanted his job, but in the first elections in November 1861, voters confirmed the convention's choices.

A West Pointer of the class of 1828, Jeff Davis longed to be a soldier. At the time of the war against Mexico he resigned his seat as a Democratic congressman to lead his regiment of Mississippi Rifles in a grand stand at the battle of Buena Vista. Devoted to the South, he never became an extremist. But when the question came in 1861, he backed secession. Convinced that he had been born to be a general, he proved to be a mediocre military strategist. Always well meaning, but proud, aloof, and not in good health, he often quarreled with his subordinates.

Vice-President Stephens, who stayed home in Georgia most of the time, was a scholar devoted to his studies and wracked by ill health. A stickler for states rights, he complained constantly that Davis was becoming a despot. His pessimism about the Confederate cause became contagious. And Davis's cabinet was not much more help. Four-

Jefferson Davis. (*National Portrait Gallery, Smithsonian Institution*)

teen different men filled six cabinet posts during the life of the Confederacy.

Judah P. Benjamin, a brilliant New Orleans lawyer who served through the whole administration, first as attorney-general, then as secretary of war, and finally as secretary of state, was by far the ablest. His determination to make the Confederacy face up to the grim realities of its financial, economic, and diplomatic problems led people to call him "the hated Jew," and he was frequently slandered by newspapers and legislators.

Davis was especially hard-pressed by states rights enthusiasts who saw almost no justification for central government. His military strategy came under harsh and constant criticism. Reverses on the battlefield made his life increasingly miserable. More and more the Confederacy looked to its military leaders, particularly to Robert E. Lee of Virginia.

Lincoln and the Divided Nation

Lincoln was temperamentally far better suited for a long struggle than Davis. Patient, tolerant, flexible, and crafty to the point of deviousness, Lincoln had a genius for giving men enough rope to hang themselves. Throughout the war, he was savagely abused in the press. Many people thought him not dignified enough for high office, a bungler as commander-in-chief, devious and spineless, yet out for himself. As wartime president, Lincoln absorbed the abuse quietly, often with wry self-satisfaction. Regarded by many people at the time as petty and oafish, he now seems much more an embodiment of both the narrowness and greatness of the Puritan ethic.

His reputation rests largely on his talent at statecraft, his decent magnanimity, and his stunning mastery of English prose. Even to men who knew him longest he remained something of a mystery. He enlivened cabinet meetings with his stories, yet was melancholy and aloof. His law partner, William H. Herndon, considered him a "sphinx . . . incommunicative—silent—reticent—secretive—having profound policies—and well laid—deeply studied plans."

Lincoln seldom acted until he felt public opinion would sustain him. His delay in getting on with the fighting encouraged the ambitious egotists around him—Secretary of State Seward, for example, and Secretary of the Treasury Chase—to strive for "a sort of dictatorship for the national defense." They all learned sooner or later, as Seward acknowledged after a brush with Lincoln, that "the President is the best of us. There is only one vote in the Cabinet and it belongs to him.

Abraham Lincoln. (*National Portrait Gallery, Smithsonian Institution*)

Executive ability and vigor are rare qualities, but he has them both."

He was tested early from all sides. In 1861 the federal government was filled with secessionists. Lincoln fired a great many federal employees, but he chose replacements with care. Outside his administration he faced two principal groups of opponents. Some abolitionists were pacifists, and in the early years of the war, they argued that the Union would be better off without the slave South. As the conflict continued, however, many abolitionists became Lincoln's most enthusiastic supporters.

"Peace" was also the goal of many northern Democrats, often called Copperheads, who thought the war was needless. To them, the Union seemed nothing in comparison to the thriving North. In their debating arsenal they carried a heavy weapon: "Why fight?" They underestimated popular devotion to that almost mystical entity, "the Union."

As the war continued, many abolitionists began to sense an end to slavery. At the same time, Copperheads in the North pressed their demands for compromise and became more active in obstructing enlistments. As abolitionists gradually came around to conceding the rightness of the fighting, they threw their support to those within the Republican party most in sympathy with emancipation as a war objective. This faction became known as the Radicals. The Regulars, or Conservatives, wanted only to suppress the "insurrection" and to restore the Union.

The Radicals had a formidable array of talent in both houses of Congress, led in the Senate by Sumner of Massachusetts, Benjamin Wade of Ohio, and in the House by Thaddeus Stevens of Pennsylvania, chairman of the Ways and Means Committee. Stevens regarded slavery as "a curse, a shame, and a crime." As a lawyer and businessman, he had defended fugitive slaves without fee.

Lincoln allowed nearly a whole year to pass after the first act of secession before he would even acknowledge that the gulf between the two sections could be closed only by mutual slaughter. He hated bloodshed. But he lost no time in getting the Union ready for survival. In doing so, he earned the labels "despot," "tyrant," "dictator" more deservingly than any other president. On May 3, without precedent or legislative authority, Lincoln issued a call for forty regiments of three-year United States volunteers to supplement the state militia he had called out in April. On no firmer constitutional grounds, he ordered a rapid expansion of the fleet for blockade service. The Consti-

LINCOLN ON SELF-GOVERNMENT

Probably Abraham Lincoln's major political theme was his insistence on the importance of the American experiment in self-government. He regarded the United States as a crucial example for the entire world. In his first message to Congress after the fall of Ft. Sumter, Lincoln argued that the contest between the North and the South

presents to the whole family of man, the question of whether a constitutional republic, or a democracy— a government of the people, by the same people—can, or cannot, maintain its territorial integrity, against its own domestic foes.

He brought this theme to a great climax in his address at Gettysburg, concluding with the famous words:

That from these honored dead we take increased devotion to that cause for which they gave the last full measure of devotion—that we here highly resolve that these dead shall not have died in vain—that this nation, under God, shall have a new birth of freedom—and that government of the people, by the people, for the people, shall not perish from the earth.

---

tution had stated: "No money shall be drawn from the Treasury, but in Consequence of Appropriations made by Law." Without any law, Lincoln ordered Chase to get funds to pay for the new army and navy. Chase obliged.

More widely opposed than these military and monetary moves was Lincoln's trampling of traditional safeguards of personal rights. Neither private letters nor telegrams were safe from prying federal eyes. Military commanders were empowered to make arrests without warrants and "in the extremest necessity," in Lincoln's words, to suspend the writ of habeas corpus. Eventually, at least 15,000 Americans were jailed. Despite his gestures of clemency, many remained in prison until the war's end without trial or even accusation.

Lincoln's high-handed tactics fell most heavily on citizens of the border states, which had immense strategic importance. Maryland virtually surrounded Washington and could make the national capital captive. Baltimore, Maryland's leading port and railroad center, was also Washington's main link with the outside world. Kentucky controlled the use of the Ohio River. Missouri, with Kentucky, controlled the use of the Mississippi River.

THE STRUGGLE FOR RICHMOND

The North's strategy was to strangle the South with a naval blockade, gain control of the Mississippi River, and take the Confederate capital. Few people anticipated that it would take four years of bloody war before all these aims were realized. The North lost many of the important battles, but finally, at Antietam, Union forces produced a victory that had important nonmilitary consequences.

Early Battles

Lincoln's principal military adviser during the early months was a holdover from the Mexican War, General-in-Chief of the U.S. Army Winfield Scott. Born in 1786, Scott was a year older than the Constitution. But he was one of the few men who realized the Union most prepare for a long struggle. His strategy was that the North should

"The Spirit of 1861" by Currier & Ives. (*American Heritage, Collection of Mrs. Katharine McCook Knox*)

clamp a vise of steel on the border states, take the entire length of the Mississippi, and tighten the blockade on every rebel port. This would gain time for raising and equipping armies for the final blows. Lincoln's early success in the border states provided a favorable start. The early success of Navy Secretary Gideon Welles in making Lincoln's "paper blockade" effective further improved prospects. In a few months, most rebel seaports were almost closed. The South's foreign trade had been cut at least 80 percent.

Jefferson Davis, also reluctant to abandon the fantasy that the South would be permitted to leave peacefully, had a war plan of his own that played right into Scott's hands. The South, Davis said, had seceded to get away from, not to conquer, the North. He saw a "natural frontier" stretching from the line between Maryland and Pennsylvania to the Dakota Territory. Along this border he proposed to plant a line of forts, and then to look for help from cotton-hungry Britain and France.

Almost a month before bombardment of Fort Sumter, Davis sent three commissioners to Europe to carry out his "cotton diplomacy." Their initial goal was to arrange for massive amounts of munitions and supplies. But his assumption that King Cotton would win the war was badly misplaced. Britain had filled its warehouses in anticipation of the war and in 1861 needed wheat. The Union's ability to trade massive wheat exports for munitions and supplies made it difficult for Davis's agents to do business.

While Davis opted for a defensive strategy, many other Confederate leaders urged an offensive, and without delay. They presumed that southern troops would be superior on the battlefield, and they sensed that if the South did not win quickly, it was not likely to win at all. In June 1861 the main rebel army under General P. G. T. de Beauregard was stationed at Manassas Junction in Virginia, a critical railroad crossing between Washington and Richmond. On the other side, Radical Republican congressmen and newspapers were demanding "crushing . . . overwhelming" action.

A touch of hysteria was in the air. The Confederacy, everyone said, was gathering for an assault on Washington. "Why don't they come?" was the anxious question. At last, in mid-July, with the "three-months men" nearing the end of their service, Lincoln ordered General Irvin McDowell to move.

With little training and no experience in battle, McDowell's 30,000 men were green as saplings. But so was Beauregard's force, estimated at

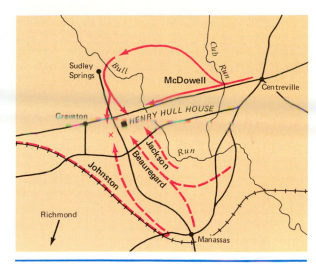

First Battle of Bull Run, 1861

24,000. As McDowell's men marched south, Beauregard's moved north to meet him. His troops dug in on the southern side of the little stream of Bull Run; and there, the next morning, the Federals found him. By noon a Union triumph seemed certain. Then General Thomas J. Jackson's "stonewall" stand in one sector, followed by a succession of counterattacks, halted the Union offensive. The southern army received reinforcements that afternoon.

McDowell, disappointed by not receiving reinforcements of his own, soon thought it better to retire. Some of his men, their three-months' service over, kept going all the way to New York, New Hampshire, and Maine, where they first had volunteered. "Give me 10,000 fresh troops, and I will be in Washington tomorrow," Stonewall Jackson is reported to have said after Bull Run. But President Davis remained devoted to his defensive plan.

"All Quiet on the Potomac"

The defeat of its forces made Congress jump. Radicals pushed through a measure which Lincoln, afraid of driving the South to revenge, said he "had some difficulty in consenting to approve." This was the so-called First Confiscation Act, making it the duty of the president to seize all property used in aiding the insurrection. Though the Radicals had hesitated to identify blacks as property, this act made slaves subject to forfeit if they were used in building fortifications and in other military and naval work. Also in the wake of the Bull Run disaster, Lincoln relieved McDowell, created a new Division of the Potomac, and placed

General George McClellan, then thirty-four years old, at its head.

"All tell me that I am held responsible for the fate of the nation," the new commander wrote to his wife. A few days later, with characteristic flourish, he told her of his plan: "I shall . . . crush the rebels in one campaign." McClellan was, in fact, a masterly organizer. His failings were his pride in smart execution of the drill and his reluctance to risk his well-drilled troops in battle. By the time Congress reconvened for its regular session in December 1861, McClellan was still grandly housed in Washington, still marching his men on parade, and beginning to try even Lincoln's patience. "Forward to Richmond!" was forgotten by the press and the people; "All Quiet on the Potomac" became the sarcastic slogan of the day.

Little more than two weeks after Congress reconvened, the Radicals succeeded in establishing a Joint Committee on the Conduct of the War, with wide powers of investigation. It was the "bounden duty" of Congress, they said, to watch "executive agents," including generals who made a practice of returning fugitive slaves and were otherwise soft on "the Negro question." McClellan, known for his "softness" on slavery, soon became the committee's pet target. Radicals began to suspect that McClellan was unwilling to fight the rebels.

The President, though still dreading a war to the finish, shared this view but he kept his own counsel. Then, his patience gone, Lincoln issued General Order No. 1, naming Washington's Birthday, February 22, as "the day for a general movement of the land and naval forces of the United States against the insurgent forces." But even this sharp command went unheeded by McClellan. "In ten days I shall be in Richmond," he boasted on February 13, 1862. Union soldiers in fact reached Richmond in 1865.

War in the West

While the federal city remained preoccupied with the long silence on the Potomac, the war was far from quiet in the West. There subordinate Union officers took things more or less into their own hands. Early in 1862, Commodore Andrew H. Foote, commanding a small fleet of gunboats under U. S. Grant's supervision, captured Fort Henry on the Tennessee River, and then took nearby Fort Donelson on the Cumberland. During the following month, Confederate General Albert Sidney Johnston was left to lead his men across the whole

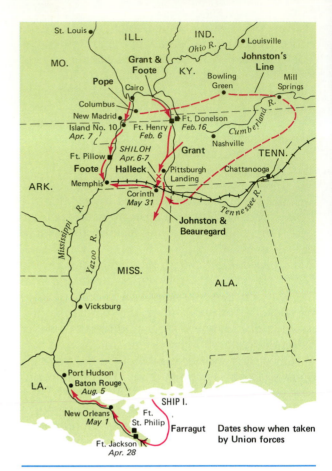

War in the West, 1862

of Tennessee to the strategic railroad center of Corinth, Mississippi. On April 6, Johnston led an attack on Grant's exposed encampment across a river at the little crossroads of Shiloh.

With the advantage of surprise, his forces pushed the Federals back the first day. On the next, the Union armies drove off the rebels, now led by Beauregard. General Henry W. (Old Brains) Halleck, recently put in command of the Department of the West, took personal charge of pressing the Union counteroffensive into Corinth. But he delayed for weeks, and the rebels got away with their army intact.

Shiloh was the first battle of the Civil War to make people on both sides realize how many men could be killed and maimed in this new kind of massive warfare. A total of 23,000 men were dead or wounded. When Grant saw that the rebels here "not only attempted to hold a line farther south, . . . but assumed the offensive and made such a gallant effort to regain what had been lost, then, indeed," he wrote in his *Memoirs,* "I gave up all idea of saving the Union except by complete conquest." Robert E. Lee, still sitting in Richmond as a pres-

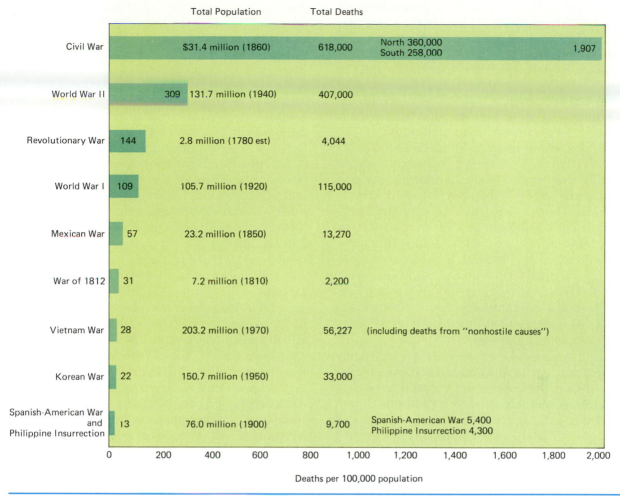

	Total Population	Total Deaths	
Civil War	$31.4 million (1860)	618,000	North 360,000 South 258,000 — 1,907
World War II	309 — 131.7 million (1940)	407,000	
Revolutionary War	144 — 2.8 million (1780 est)	4,044	
World War I	109 — 105.7 million (1920)	115,000	
Mexican War	57 — 23.2 million (1850)	13,270	
War of 1812	31 — 7.2 million (1810)	2,200	
Vietnam War	28 — 203.2 million (1970)	56,227	(including deaths from "nonhostile causes")
Korean War	22 — 150.7 million (1950)	33,000	
Spanish-American War and Philippine Insurrection	13 — 76.0 million (1900)	9,700	Spanish-American War 5,400 Philippine Insurrection 4,300

0   200   400   600   800   1,000   1,200   1,400   1,600   1,800   2,000

Deaths per 100,000 population

Deaths in the Civil War as compared to other wars. The death total for American soldiers was considerably higher in the Civil War than in any other war in which the United States has taken part. The proportion of war deaths to contemporary population, as shown in the chart, gives a truer conception of the seriousness of the losses in each war than do the absolute figures. (*Richard Current, T. Harry Williams, and Frank Freidel*, American History: A Survey, *third edition, Volume II, p. 393. Copyright © 1979 by Richard Current, T. Harry Williams, and Frank Freidel. Reprinted by permission of Alfred A. Knopf, Inc.*)

idential advisor, warned Davis that unless he held the lower Mississippi and kept the Confederacy from being split, Grant's "complete conquest" would not be far off.

Lee's warning was underscored soon after Shiloh by more decisive Union operations farther west. At the end of April, a Union fleet led by Captain David G. Farragut smashed through Confederate fortifications below New Orleans and forced the great Mississippi port to surrender. Baton Rouge fell soon after to a force under General Benjamin F. Butler. In the meantime, Foote's gunboats had pressed down the Mississippi to Memphis, where it destroyed a Confederate fleet. Between Memphis and New Orleans only Vicksburg, Mississippi, and Port Hudson, Louisiana, now blocked Union control of the entire river.

The Peninsular Campaign

Union operations in the West early in 1862 received only the barest notice in Washington, where protection of the capital and preparation of the grand assault on Richmond were the main concerns. Lincoln, who had taken to studying books on military strategy—to compensate for the inadequacy of his advisers—had formed definite opinions about how Richmond might be taken. He was for a new frontal attack, which would have the advantage of keeping the Army of the Potomoc between the Confederates and Washington itself.

Largely because he had not been consulted about it, McClellan opposed the plan. The Confederate capital, the general argued, should be approached by way of the peninsula formed by the

York River on the north and the James River on the south. The peninsular plan involved a dangerous amphibious operation. The Confederates controlled the Norfolk navy yard at the mouth of the James. At Norfolk, moreover, was the Confederate ironclad ship *Virginia,* the renamed former United States frigate *Merrimac,* which only a month before McClellan began his campaign had fought to a standstill the Union's ironclad *Monitor.*

The first contingents of McClellan's force—all told, 110,000 strong—landed successfully on the peninsula on April 4, 1862. Yorktown, the first Confederate stronghold on the way to Richmond, might have been overrun in a day. But McClellan, afraid of a new Bull Run, took a month to enter the town. Almost another month was lost while the general, awaiting expected reinforcements, advanced at a snail's pace up the peninsula. What kept McClellan's reinforcements away was Stonewall Jackson's brilliant foray up the Shenandoah Valley. As Lincoln had anticipated, he menaced Washington from the rear.

Having unnerved the Union capital sufficiently to force Lincoln to keep an even stronger army there than he had planned, Jackson dashed back to confront McClellan. Before Jackson arrived, McClellan had been drawn to within 5 miles of Richmond. There, on May 31, he narrowly averted

Peninsular Campaign, 1862

disaster at Seven Pines. McClellan might have taken advantage of the Confederates' loss of General Johnston there. Instead, he left 25,000 men under General Fitz-John Porter in the vicinity of Richmond and returned with the rest to his base at the town of White House, some 20 miles to the east. Here he waited once again for additional men to oppose the vast horde he imagined stood before the Confederate capital. While McClellan waited, Robert E. Lee at last returned to the field.

Lee possessed the abilities as well as the appearance of a hero. His many admirers regarded him as the greatest military genius of the war. His soldiers came to look upon him as a man who "communed with the angels of Heaven." Some military historians have argued that Lee was so concerned with defending his native state that he never developed a coordinated overall strategy. But for most of the war the Virginia front was his only command. He used it, with forays into the North itself, as the most effective means of relieving Union pressure elsewhere.

Other writers point to Lee's failure to provide adequate supplies for his armies, his habit of giving too much independence to his generals in the field, and his practice of taking on staff work he should have delegated to subordinates. As long as he could draw on brilliant corps commanders, however, Lee's confidence was rarely misplaced; and it was only in the later stages of the war that the caliber of his junior officers declined.

On learning how McClellan had split his army, Lee immediately formed a plan to send a small force "looking numerous and aggressive" to intimidate the general, while he himself moved in to crush Porter. McClellan and Porter, however, were prepared. Lee's "eye" in spying out McClellan's position was his cavalry chief, Jeb Stuart. It was Stuart's nature to use any opportunity for showmanship. In a marvelous display of contempt for the enemy—and of foolish disregard of risk for his own cause—for three days his cavalry circled around the Federals and brought Lee the wanted information. His exploit also alerted the Union invaders.

McClellan regrouped his forces and surprised the Confederates with his mobilized strength. Having done this much, however, he turned again to the strategy of retreat. In the Seven Days Battle, between June 26 and July 2, McClellan inflicted heavy losses on Lee's advancing troops. But his own objective was merely Harrison's Landing on the James River, where the Union navy, if necessary, could evacuate his men.

Robert E. Lee. (*National Portrait Gallery, Smithsonian Institution*)

Second Bull Run and Antietam

Lincoln visited McClellan at Harrison's Landing on July 9 and called off the whole peninsular campaign. He also named "Harry" Halleck commander of all the Union armies. In McClellan's place as commander of the Army of the Potomac, Halleck placed the rash and boastful John Pope. These men were ordered to try to take Richmond at last. But Lee routed Pope in the momentous Second Battle of Bull Run, August 29–30, 1862. This fresh setback left Union soldiers bitter and discouraged. "So long as the interests of our country are entrusted to a lying braggart like Pope," one of them wrote home, "we have little reason to hope successfully to compete with an army led by Lee, Johnston, and old 'Stonewall' Jackson."

In June 1862 McClellan had been close to Richmond. Three strong Union armies appeared to have control of the Shenandoah Valley, and western Virginia was in Union hands. Now, at the end of August, one historian has written, "the only Federals closer than 100 miles to Richmond were prisoners . . . and men . . . preparing to retreat." In desperation, Lincoln again entrusted McClellan with temporary command of the disorganized army in the East. "If he can't fight," Lincoln said, "he excels in making others ready to fight."

A Group of contrabands. Note that these men were not soldiers. They were former slaves behind the Union lines who were under the protection of the Union army and often worked as teamsters, laborers, military cooks, scouts, guides, spies, hospital workers, and blacksmiths. The name "contraband" refers to a remark made by three slaves to a confederate officer by declaring them "contraband of war." (*Library of Congress*)

Meanwhile, Lee pressed the attack, hoping to penetrate the North. Across his path lay the refurbished federal arsenal at Harpers Ferry, Virginia, with 10,000 men and munitions and supplies much needed by his own men. If he could take the arsenal and move from there into Maryland, he might win new recruits in the border states. Strengthened, he could move on to Pennsylvania. France and Britain then might recognize the Confederacy and intervene actively on its behalf. And McClellan would be driven to the defensive with a demoralized force backed by a disheartened citizenry. But his plans did not work.

On September 15, 1862, Stonewall Jackson with 25,000 men did take Harpers Ferry and all they wanted there. The Confederates also learned that McClellan had found out about this adventure in time to have smashed Lee's divided army. For two days, McClellan did nothing. When he did attack Lee on September 17 at Antietam Creek, he almost overwhelmed the rebels. By then, Jackson had returned to help stop the Federal momentum, and Lee's battered army was permitted to slip away.

Antietam has been called a defeat for both armies. But the North, at least, had repulsed an invasion on which the South had spent too much. "Our maximum strength has been mobilized," Jefferson Davis told his secretary of war after the battle, "while the enemy is just beginning to put forth his might."

WAR ON THE HOME FRONTS

The brutal, inconclusive engagement at Antietam was an appropriate symbol of the entire war. The seemingly aimless slaughter badly damaged civilian morale on both sides. As the war dragged on, its effects were felt far behind the battle lines. The South tried desperately to win aid and recognition from Great Britain; the North made every effort to keep that country neutral. And Lincoln had an important card to play in the war of nerves between the two sections—the Emancipation Proclamation.

The Confederacy in Wartime

To check criticism, Davis got his Congress to enact the first Confederate law granting the executive power to suspend the writ of habeas corpus and impose martial law. But so intense had states rights feeling become in the South that no sooner were Davis's critics locked up under Confederate authority than state authorities released them.

The military stalemate was even more acutely felt by those who had to maintain the resources and manpower of the fighting forces. As early as April 1862, the Confederate Congress had to enact the first conscription act in American history, calling up for three years' service all white men eighteen to thirty-five. Later acts raised the age limit to fifty. But anyone could escape the draft by paying for a substitute, and there were occupational exemptions. Evasion also had the support of some states rights governors.

Statistics show that the draft in the South brought in few soldiers. But the figures veil the real effects of conscription. "Conscript" became such a dirty word that many young men volunteered before their age group was called. They, more than the conscripts themselves, maintained Confederate military manpower. On the other hand, the purchasing of substitutes seemed to confirm the slogan, "a rich man's war and a poor man's fight." Desertions soared to well over 100,000—only a third, perhaps, of Union desertions, but much more keenly felt.

Symptoms of economic difficulties could be detected in the South even during the first year. Loans in money were virtually impossible to make in a country where wealth was tied up in land and slaves. By 1862 the Confederacy was trying "produce loans," by which planters were expected to buy Confederate bonds with cotton and other commodities. These loans had two drawbacks. Many planters would not surrender their commodities for government paper; and when they did, it was as difficult for the government as for citizens to transform commodities into cash.

The Confederacy had little better luck with taxes. Like other frustrated governments, it began to print paper money in 1861. By 1864 a Confederate paper dollar was worth, on average, 1.5 cents in specie. Prices soared; speculation and hoarding spread. An angry clerk in the War Department in Richmond described the situation in his diary:

In these times of privation and destitution, I see many men, who were never prominent secessionists, enjoying comfortable positions, and seeking investments for their surplus funds. . . . The true patriots . . . have sacrificed everything, and still labor in subordinate positions, with faith and patient suffering. These men and their families go in rags, and upon half rations, while the others fare most sumptuously.

The suffering was also caused by geographic maldistribution. The same clerk explained:

These evils might be remedied by the government, for there is no great scarcity of any of the substantials and necessities of life in the country, if they were only equally distributed. The difficulty is in procuring transportation, and the government monopolizes the railroads and canals. . . .

The gaunt form of wretched famine still approaches with rapid strides. Meal is now selling at $12 per bushel, and potatoes at $10. Meats have almost disappeared from the market, and none but the opulent can afford to pay $3.50 per pound for butter. . . . I am spading up my little garden, and hope to raise a few vegetables to eke out a miserable subsistence for my family.

Difficulties at home were aggravated by the collapse of diplomacy abroad. There had been some early successes. The ruling classes in Europe had no liking for slavery, but as aristocrats they would have been pleased with the failure of the "American experiment" in democratic government. Their attitude was reflected in the decision of Britain and France early in 1861 to recognize the Confederacy as a belligerent power though not as a sovereign government. Britain, moreover, threatened Lincoln's administration with war in November 1861, after a Union cruiser stopped the British mail steamer *Trent* on the high seas and removed Mason and Slidell, two Confederate diplomats, on their way to London and Paris. War was averted when Secretary of State Seward released the two rebels.

Confederate hopes for foreign military assistance, high after the *Trent* affair, died a year later with military failure at Antietam. When Lincoln took this occasion to announce his Emancipation Proclamation, the surge of Union sentiment among foreign middle- and working-class groups made it even more unlikely that foreign nations would risk discontent at home by backing the wrong horse in America.

Britain's willingness to build sea raiders for the Confederacy, however, seemed contrary to its official policy of nonintervention. International law permitted neutrals to build nonnaval craft for belligerents. But it forbade such craft to be "equipped, fitted out, or armed" for fighting. British shipbuilders evaded this restriction by allowing apparently inoffensive hulls to "escape" to obscure ports, there to take on guns and munitions. All told, eighteen such "brigands of the sea" preyed on northern shipping. Union threats in 1863 to loose a "flood of privateers" against Britain's neutral trade had the desired effect; no more Confederate raiders were launched.

By 1863 an air of caution had taken hold in France as well, where Napoleon III had dreams of reinstating a monarchy in Mexico, to which the Confederates might look for help. Maximilian of Austria, a puppet of Napoleon, actually was placed at the head of Mexico's government soon after French army units had taken over Mexico City in 1863. Thereafter he received little French support. When Maximilian was captured and executed by Mexican rebels in 1867, the French agreed quietly to the end of their hopes.

The North in Wartime

Some of the important measures enacted by the Republican Congress had little to do with the war and a great deal to do with economic goals of the Republican party. In 1861 the Morrill Tariff raised duties to their 1846 levels, from which they soared during and after the war. The next year Congress voted to build the transcontinental railroad over a central route and to help finance it with huge grants of public lands and generous cash loans. In 1863 Congress created a national banking system agreeable to northern capitalists.

Nor did Republican leaders neglect their Free Soil supporters. The Homestead Act of 1862 made available to adult "citizens of the United States" (meaning whites), and to those who declared their intention of becoming citizens, 160 acres of the public domain. The land itself was free, but only if it received "settlement and cultivation." Only men who had borne arms against the United States were excluded. Farmers also benefited from the Morrill Land Grant Act of 1862. This act donated public lands to the states and territories to support colleges where agriculture, mechanical arts, and military science became the core of the curriculum.

After a short depression in 1861–62, caused by the loss of $300 million in uncollectible southern debts and uncertainty about the war, the northern economy enjoyed a substantial boom. The splurge of government war buying helped the expansion and mechanization of agriculture, the production of shoes and other apparel, and the manufacture of munitions. Some profiteers made fortunes by selling the government huge amounts of cheap and nearly useless material, such as uniforms that fell apart in the rain. Other millionaires of the future—Rockefeller, Carnegie, Mellon, Morgan— laid the foundations of their huge fortunes in wartime activity.

But wartime prosperity hurt some people very badly. Industrial wages, for example, rose far more slowly than living costs, causing great hardship in cities where food speculators flourished. Families on fixed incomes were especially hard hit. Yet few northerners suffered the deprivation that became almost universal in the Confederacy.

Despite the boom, Lincoln's government had a

difficult time financing the war, partly because it failed to realize how long the war would last. Secretary of the Treasury Chase's monetary policies did not help. Chase distrusted debt and paper money. He got Congress to approve excise taxes and even a new experiment, an income tax, but they failed to provide the needed revenue. Before long he had to use deficit financing. After a shaky start, he sold bonds to a million persons. In 1862 he was forced to begin printing paper money. That year and the next, the Treasury issued certificates, soon known as "greenbacks," to the amount of $450 million. Unsupported by gold, greenbacks were legal tender for domestic debts. By the summer of 1864, they had fallen to their low of 39 cents on the gold dollar.

Despite its much greater population, shortages of manpower hurt the Union military effort at certain points. Large numbers of European immigrants arrived during the war, and many of them served in the northern army. So did a growing number of blacks. Yet eventually, in 1863, Congress was forced to vote the first Union draft, almost a full year after the Confederacy did so.

Far from helping the situation, the wording of the act added to social discontent. One of its provisions permitted a man to escape service simply by paying $300 to the authorities, leaving them with the responsibility of finding substitutes. Clearly the poor were to be saddled with the rich man's duty in a struggle that seemed to benefit black workers.

Riots protesting this law occurred in many towns. In Boston several would-be rioters were shot dead after stoning troops. Democratic Governor Horatio Seymour of New York helped turn the protest in New York City into a violent disturbance of major proportions. On the eve of the first drawing of names, he publicly questioned the wisdom and constitutionality of the draft. For three days, huge mobs terrorized the city. Federal troops had to be withdrawn from the battlefield to stop the violence.

The outburst of anger was aimed as much against blacks as against the draft. The leaders of the mobs were poor Irish-American workingmen, themselves discriminated against. Some were striking longshoremen whose jobs the city's free blacks had filled. Black homes and churches became the principal targets of the rioters. Fires roared out of control. At least a dozen people were killed, and hundreds wounded.

Women in a Semi-Modern War

Even more than during the American Revolution, the Civil War left grown women alone at home to manage farming, finances, and children as best they could. On both sides they suffered the wrenches that go with sending loved ones to distant battlefields. Everyone assumed that the shooting part of war was men's work. Yet the Civil War saw more women closer to the actual fighting fronts than ever before. But while a handful of women became involved in combat situations as spies and even as double agents, most American women remained at home.

In the South, many white women did most of the work on southern farms, including tasks that had usually been done by men. Wives of slaveholders were left with the new and difficult role of supervising overseers and slaves. Many of them found the job taxing and discouraging; yet many women of the planting class were exercising independent authority for the first time in their lives.

In the North, wives (and widows) of farmers in the army found their work similarly broadened, except that wealthier ones supervised other women, boys, and old men as hired hands rather than slaves. Many women entered factories for the first time. The proportion of women in the manufacturing labor force rose from one-quarter to one-third. Women had always dominated numerically in textiles and garment making, but these fields were themselves expanding to meet the mounting demand for uniforms.

In both South and North, women became nurses in far greater numbers than ever before. At first, most of the female nurses in the South were slaves, since it was felt that gentile ladies were unsuited and unsuitable for the raw, physical, and masculine atmosphere of army hospitals. As time went on and the numbers of wounded mounted, however, ladies were used as nurses in increasing numbers. In the North, nursing was better organized. In June 1861 Dorothea Dix was appointed superintendent of nurses. Dix angered some nursing applicants because she insisted that her nurses be over thirty years old and "plain in appearance"; she thought young, pretty, unmarried nurses would prove distracting and perhaps be distracted in hospitals filled with young men. Even Dix's nurses had to overcome male prejudice against women in army hospitals. One male army surgeon complained that every northern preacher "would recommend the most troublesome old maid in his congregation as an experienced nurse."

For the most part, women nurses worked in hospitals away from the fighting front; but some served in the crude and sometimes dangerous field hospitals. Clara Barton, who later founded the American Red Cross, worked in several battlefield units. Another woman, Mary Ann Bickerdyke, served with Grant's army in Tennessee, where she won the affection and gratitude of many soldiers and the lifelong respect of that crusty general.

Women also dominated numerically in the United States Sanitary Commission, a private aid and relief organization that received recognition from the government. The commission helped provide food and medical supplies, even ambulance service, for Union soldiers. As its name implied, it inspected army camps with an eye for clean food and water and safe latrines. Not only were many of the commission's nurses women, but women on the home front did much of the fundraising by holding "Sanitary Fairs."

Altogether, both North and South, the Civil War gave or forced upon women new roles outside the home, roles that gave many of them unaccustomed measures of independence and a sense of accomplishment on their own.

The Emancipation Proclamation

While Lee tried to end the slaughter by breaking the North's morale through invasion, Lincoln attempted to end the stalemate through political action.

From the day he took office, Lincoln had "struggled," as he said, against every kind of pressure—religious, journalistic, political, personal—to declare the slaves free without compensating their owners and without undertaking to "colonize" freed blacks outside the country. Even if he had sympathized with such demands, the sensitivity of slaveholding border states within the Union, and northern sentiment in general, would have made him hold back. "On the news of General Frémont having actually issued deeds of manumission" in Missouri in 1861, Lincoln declared, "a whole company of our volunteers threw down their arms and disbanded."

At first, as the fighting spread and slaves sought security behind Union lines, generals in the field were left to their own discretion in dealing with them. Then in March 1862 Congress adopted "an additional article of war" forbidding the army to return fugitive slaves to their owners. Shortly thereafter, the War Department issued specific authorization for recruitment of fugitive slaves as soldiers. The authorization was accompanied by an admonition that it "must never see daylight because it is so much in advance of public opinion."

Congress added more rungs to the ladder of freedom. In April 1862 it passed and Lincoln signed a measure abolishing slavery in the District of Columbia. Former owners were to be paid, on average, $300 per slave, not much below the going price on the eve of the war. Two months later, another act abolished slavery in United States territories, with no financial compensation. Congress then adopted the so-called Second Confiscation Act, providing for the conviction for treason of all persons engaged in rebellion, "or who shall in any way give aid . . . thereto," and including among its penalties the stipulation that "all slaves" of such persons "shall be forever free of their servitude."

In the meantime, Lincoln mounted his own effort to use emancipation to end the war and restore the Union. He cautiously awaited good news from the battlefield before taking public action. On September 22, after indecisive Antietam, he

Company "E" 4th U.S. Colored Infantry, Ft. Lincoln, Virginia. (*Chicago Historical Society*)

read to the cabinet a draft of a proclamation which the papers published the next day.

Lincoln declared that at the next meeting of Congress in December he would recommend enactment "of a practical measure" offering "pecuniary aid" to all slave states not then in rebellion against the United States and having "voluntarily adopt[ed] immediate, or gradual abolishment of slavery within their limits." He also promised to continue his efforts to "colonize persons of African descent, with their consent."

On January 1, 1863, the September proclamation went on, he would designate which states still were in rebellion, and in them, "all persons held as slaves . . . shall be then, thenceforward, and forever free," with no compensation whatever. Moreover, "the military and naval authority" of the United States would make no effort to suppress any attempts slaves might make to gain freedom; on the contrary, these authorities would do whatever necessary to shelter them.

Conservatives in the North, sick of the military stalemate and afraid that any tampering with slavery would only prolong the South's resistance, registered their disapproval in the fall elections of 1862. The Democrats cut deeply into the Republican majority in the House. The Radicals, on the other hand, attacked Lincoln's maneuverings and demanded that he get on with the "revolutionary struggle." Lincoln held to his plan. After the November elections, in accordance with his announcements, he urged Congress in his second annual message to adopt an amendment to the Constitution providing that each slave state which abolished slavery "any time before the 1st day of January, 1900, shall receive compensation from the United States." But only those not in rebellion against the United States on January 1, 1863, might participate in this offer.

On January 1, the "full period of one hundred days" of grace since his September announcement having expired with no takers among the rebellious commonwealths, Lincoln issued his final Emancipation Proclamation:

I, Abraham Lincoln, . . . in time of actual armed rebellion against the . . . United States, and as a fit and necessary war measure for suppressing said rebellion, do . . . order and declare that all persons held as slaves within . . . states and parts of states wherein the people . . . are . . . in rebellion . . . are and henceforward shall be free. . . . And I hereby enjoin upon the people so declared to be free to abstain from all violence, unless in necessary self-defense. . . . And I further declare . . . that such persons . . . will be received into the armed service of the United States.

The proclamation neither freed any slaves nor shortened the war. But it ensured the death of slavery when the war was won.

TO APPOMATTOX

No matter how great the difficulties on the home fronts, the two armies staggered from battle to battle in the field. Men died in horrifying numbers, more than in any war of the nineteenth century except the Taiping Rebellion in China. As was true of all major wars until the twentieth century, more men died of disease than in battle. For the first time, women worked near the front lines in army hospitals, nursing wounded and dying men amid the screaming and the stench of body filth, blood, and gangrene.

The Long Road to Gettysburg

After Antietam, observing that McClellan had the "slows," Lincoln replaced him with General Ambrose E. Burnside. The new commander soon showed at the battle of Fredericksburg in December 1862 that he was far worse than his predecessor. Lincoln replaced Burnside with General Joseph Hooker. "My plans are perfect," announced "Fighting Joe" in the spring of 1863, "and when I start to carry them out, may God have mercy on General Lee, for I will have none." Hooker decided to fake a movement of troops that would draw Lee's from their dug-in positions outside Fredericksburg. His tactic nearly worked, but early in May, when Hooker caught up with Lee at Chancellorsville, he, like so many of his predecessors, lost his nerve and almost lost his army.

Victory at Chancellorsville cost Lee 12,000 men and the life of Stonewall Jackson, who was shot by mistake in the dark by a Confederate soldier. But Lee now thought he saw the path open to an invasion of the North and to final victory. When Davis refused to pull men from the western theater in support of a grand assault, Lee decided to go ahead with the nearly 75,000 men in his Virginia command. "General Lee," one of his lieutenants said at this time, "believed that the Army of Northern Virginia, as it then existed, could accomplish anything." He was wrong.

Lee's army headed toward Harrisburg, Pennsylvania, on the strategic Susquehanna River. Hooker thought he saw in Lee's departure yet one more chance to move on Richmond. But Lincoln, grown wiser with the years, undertook to set him straight: "Lee's army, not Richmond, is your true objective point. If he comes toward the upper Potomac, follow on his flank and on his inside

Sargeant Baldwin. (*Chicago Historical Society*)

mand of General George Pickett to mount a frontal assault on the center of the Union line. Raked by artillery and rifle fire, they charged up the hill and for a moment broke through. But superior numbers forced them to fall back, leaving behind three-quarters of the men who on that day had sought to win independence for the Confederacy.

Lincoln telegraphed Meade, "Call no council of war. . . . Do not let the enemy escape." But Meade hesitated. He called his general officers together, and the guns were silent throughout the Fourth of July. The next morning Lee's battered army limped off toward Virginia. Lincoln was stunned. As he said later, "Our army held the war in the hollow of its hand and would not close it."

As for the battle itself, a seasoned Union officer described the awful slaughter, which characterized so many battles of the war:

track, shortening your lines while he lengthens his." By June 29 Lee's advance corps had reached a point 10 miles from Harrisburg—their deepest penetration of the war. Concerned now about the lengthening of his communications, Lee began to look for favorable terrain onto which to lure and confront the "Yanks." By then, Hooker had been replaced by "the old snapping turtle," General George Gordon Meade, who was making his own plans to invite attack on favorable ground. Both generals were to be disappointed.

On June 30, some of Lee's cavalry, searching for shoes, accidentally bumped into a Union patrol at the crossroads town of Gettysburg, Pennsylvania. They exchanged shots and attracted more troops from both sides. General Meade ordered Union troops to occupy a long north-south ridge outside the little town, with each end anchored on a hilltop. Lee instructed his forces to take up positions on a parallel ridge about a mile to the west. In between the two armies lay an open field, and the scene was set for a fight to the finish.

On July 2 the air thundered with the heaviest artillery exchange of the entire war. Wave after wave of Confederate soldiers charged across that field and up the slope of what is now known as Cemetery Ridge. Neither side gave way, but the Confederates suffered more casualties. The next day, July 3, Lee ordered the men under the com-

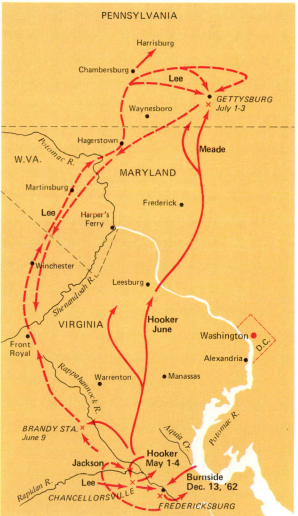

Fredericksburg to Gettysburg, 1862–63

Pursuit of Lee's army on the road near Emmitsburg, July 7, 1863. (*Library of Congress*)

We see the poor fellows hobbling back from the crest or unable to do so, pale and weak, lying on the ground with the mangled stump of an arm or leg, dripping their life-blood away; or with a cheek torn open, or a shoulder mashed. And many, alas! hear not the roar as they stretch upon the ground with upturned faces and open eyes, though a shell should burst at their very ears. Their ears and their bodies this instant are only mud.

Many months afterward the bodies of thousands who there "gave their lives" still lay unburied. The degrading spectacle led to a call for a national cemetery in their honor. It was at the dedication of this cemetery that Lincoln delivered the Gettysburg Address, promising "that these dead shall not have died in vain."

Ulysses S. Grant. (*National Portrait Gallery, Smithsonian Institution*)

Grant Takes Command

On July 4, 1863, on the heels of the victory of Gettysburg, came the report of a great Union triumph in the West. After a year of struggle, Grant had taken Vicksburg, "the Gibraltar of the Mississippi." Four days later, Port Hudson, the last Confederate stronghold on the river, surrendered. Grant's victory in the western theater focused the attention of the entire nation on this West Point graduate, a veteran of the Mexican War who had resigned his captaincy in 1854 so that he could better support his family. Grant was not glamorous, but he eventually proved to be the Union's best general. His "art of war" best sums up his military theory: "The art of war is simple enough. Find out where your enemy is. Get him as soon as you can. Strike at him as hard as you can and keep moving on."

After Vicksburg, one Confederate army and part of the Confederacy itself were isolated west of the Mississippi. But another Confederate army commanded by General Braxton Bragg was still operating in central Tennessee. In September 1863, under Grant's orders, General William Rosencrans began to pursue Bragg in earnest. But after being outmaneuvered at Chickamauga, Rosencrans's army found itself bottled up in nearby Chattanooga.

To raise the siege, Grant called on armies from the east and west. He received them because of northern railroad efficiency. On November 25 these combined forces won a spectacular victory at Chattanooga, splitting the Confederacy north and south as well as east and west.

In the spring of 1864 Lincoln rewarded Grant

CIVIL WAR FIGHTING

The first of these two views of the fighting came from a perceptive novelist, Stephen Crane, in *The Red Badge of Courage:*

There was a consciousness always of the presence of his comrades about him. He felt a subtle battle brotherhood more potent even than the cause for which they were fighting. It was the mysterious fraternity born of the smoke and danger of death. The rifles, once loaded, were jerked to the shoulder and fired without aim into the smoke, or at one of the blurred and shifting forms which, upon the field before the regiment, had been growing larger and larger like puppets under a magician's hand. . . .

The second is from a report by a Union General after the battle of Fredericksburg:

The dead were swollen to twice their natural size, black as Negroes in most cases. They sprawled in every conceivable position, some on their backs with gaping jaws, some with eyes as large as walnuts, protruding from glassy stares; some doubled up like a contortionist . . . here lay one without a head, there's one without legs, yonder a head and legs, without a trunk; everywhere horrible expressions, fear, rage, agony, madness, torture; lying in pools of blood, lying with heads half-buried in mud, with fragments of shell sticking in oozing brain, with bullet holes all over puffed limbs.

by appointing him supreme commander of all Union armies. Grant quickly set to work on his victory program. His plan was for the Army of the Potomac to keep Lee's army so busy that it could not link up with any other rebel force—and to bleed it daily in the bargain. At the same time, Sherman's army was to push eastward from Tennessee into Georgia and take Atlanta, thereby striking into the heart of rebel territory.

The first reports were disheartening. Throughout May 1864, the Army of the Potomac, under Meade and Grant himself, engaged Lee's forces in murderous but indecisive battles north of Richmond. Enormous federal casualties in the Wilderness and at Cold Harbor—Grant is said to have lost 55,000 men in this first month—aroused strong resentment in the North. Newspapers began to call him "the butcher." But Lincoln stood by him. "I have just read your dispatch," he wrote to Grant after Cold Harbor. "I begin to see it. You will succeed. God bless you all."

Grant himself, however, began to have second thoughts. He decided to swing down to the peninsula to get at Richmond once more from the south and to send General Philip Sheridan to stop Confederate thrusts northward in the Shenandoah Valley. For nearly a year there was continuous slaughter and devastation in the valley and in the Tidewater of Virginia. Sheridan executed Grant's order to leave the Shenandoah Valley "a barren waste." He reported: "A crow would have had to carry its rations if it had flown across the valley." Sheridan then joined Grant for a final thrust at Richmond.

The tide of war in the Deep South was much clearer. Starting in Tennessee, Sherman's army pushed through Georgia against weakening Confederate resistance. Sherman himself, announcing that "War is Hell," pursued a policy of devastating the countryside, of deliberately aiming at the civilian as well as the military morale of his opponents. His famous "march to the sea" was in fact a major turning point in the modern history of warfare. It was a new strategy to aim not only at

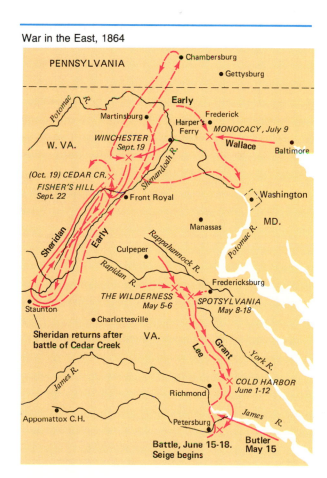

War in the East, 1864

an opposing army, but at the society supporting it.

The chaos was complicated by the enormous number of slaves suddenly set free from ruined plantations. On September 3, Sherman wired Washington: "So Atlanta is ours, and fairly won." Having left Atlanta "smouldering and in ruins," Sherman's "bummers" thrust toward Savannah. "To realize what war is," Sherman said, "one should follow in our tracks."

The End in Sight

Sherman's capture of Atlanta in September 1864 had more than military significance. Early in the year, politicians had begun to prepare for the presidential elections in November. Lincoln, for the good of the Republican party, had been urged not to seek renomination. By the time of the party convention at Baltimore in June, however, his Radical opponents had failed to agree on a candidate, and his loyal backers put him across. To bolster the ticket, they named the War Democrat Andrew Johnson of Tennessee for vice-president. Lincoln and Johnson ran under a Union party label.

The Democrats chose General McClellan. The "war failure" plank in the Democratic platform declared that hostilities should cease and that the "Federal Union of the States" should be reestablished on the old basis. This was nothing less than an armistice offer. McClellan, after serious soul-searching, decided to reject the plank and to commit himself to continuing the war. At the same time, some of Lincoln's advisers had begun to press him to make overtures to Richmond. Then came the news of Atlanta's fall.

There was a revival of confidence not only in Lincoln's generals, but in the president himself.

A defender of the Confederacy. (*Library of Congress*)

In November, Lincoln won a smashing victory. With 55 percent of the popular vote, he outdistanced McClellan in the electoral college 212 to 21. Victory, not negotiated peace, became the military theme as well.

From Savannah, in February 1865, Sherman headed north toward the "hellhole of secession," South Carolina, where, as he said, "the devil himself could not restrain his men." The "pitiless march" brought him to Columbia, South Carolina's capital. Soon, whether by accident or design, one of the most beautiful cities in the country was consumed in flames. Charleston, outflanked, was occupied the next day by Union forces blockading the harbor after the defending rebels had fled.

Sherman, meanwhile, pounded on into North Carolina. Gettysburg, Vicksburg, Atlanta, the humiliating failure of cotton diplomacy, the bruising wall of the blockade—none of these had quite managed to kill the Confederacy's capacity for war. But after Sherman's march, southern spirits drooped.

WORDS AND NAMES IN AMERICAN HISTORY

Platform, in its original and literal meaning, meant an object formed like a plate (the same root as *plateau*). That is, a platform was something flat. It came to mean something a person could stand on above the ground. Platforms were useful for outdoor public performances, since an indoor platform set before an audience is usually called a "stage." Revivalist speakers used them out-of-doors. So did politicians, especially in the early years of the nineteenth century, when outdoor platforms came to be the usual and expected place where people gathered to hear speeches. Ever since the middle of the nineteenth century, when so many politicians were speechifying from these raised platforms, the very term came to denote their political beliefs. This was an almost inevitable development, because political candidates announced their programs and then thundered forth at the end: "I stand upon this platform." Political parties started to adopt specific programs, or "platforms," after they began in the 1830s to hold national conventions. Almost inevitably, individual proposals in a party's "platform" began to be known as a "plank." Thus some candidates could claim to endorse the whole platform except for the plank on such-and-such an issue. Never before has ordinary carpentry contributed so much to political discourse.

CIVIL WAR

As early as September 1864, Davis acknowledged that "two thirds of our men are absent . . . most of them absent without leave."

In March 1865, the Confederacy took the fateful step of recruiting men "irrespective of color," slaves "who might volunteer to fight for their freedom." It was a signal of desperation. By then, Grant's 115,000 "blues" outnumbered Lee's 54,000 "grays" in Virginia. The time had come for Lee to pull out of his trenches while he still had troops and to try to join up with Johnston in North Carolina. Under cover of darkness and while Davis and his government fled, contingents of Grant's army poured into Richmond.

On April 7, his path to North Carolina sealed off, Lee asked for terms. On April 9, standing straight in a new uniform, he met the mud-spattered Grant at the McClean farmhouse at Appomattox Court House, a village some 95 miles west of Richmond. "Give them the most liberal terms," Lincoln had ordered Grant. "Let them have their horses to plow with, and, if you like, their guns to shoot crows with. I want no one punished." Grant obeyed.

As defeat loomed that terrifying spring, a patriotic and sensitive matron confided in her diary: "Such a hue and cry, everybody blamed by somebody else. Only the dead heroes left stiff and stark on the battle field escape. I cry: 'Blame every man who stayed at home and did not fight, but not one word against those who stood out until the bitter end, and stacked muskets at Appomattox.' " On April 26, Johnston surrendered his army to Sherman at Durham Station, North Carolina. On May 10, Davis was caught in Georgia and imprisoned for two years.

Lincoln's Death

When news of Richmond's fall reached Washington on April 3, the city exploded with joy. Then, on April 14, a fanatic actor, John Wilkes Booth, shot Lincoln as the president sat in his box at Ford's Theatre in Washington, watching a performance of *Our American Cousin*. At 7:20 the next morning Lincoln died. It was the first assassination of a United States president.

The victorious president had charged the nation to act "with malice towards none, with charity for all." He had acknowledged the guilt of the North as well as the South for slavery. At first Robert E. Lee would not believe the news of Lincoln's death. Then, on that Sunday, he told a visitor that he had "surrendered as much to [Lincoln's] goodness as to Grant's artillery." Now

Final campaigns of the Civil War, 1864–65

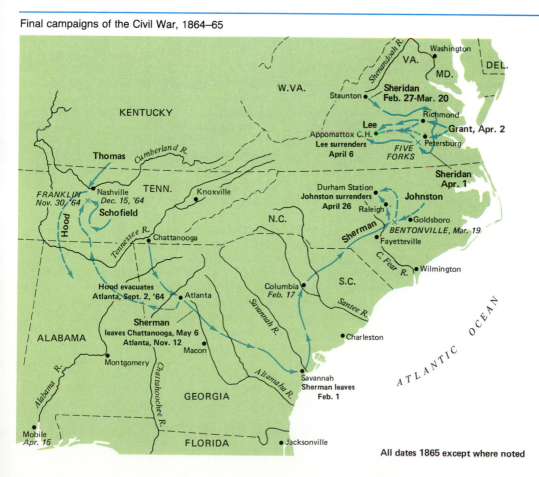

All dates 1865 except where noted

Lincoln and "goodness" were removed, with consequences Herman Melville foretold when he wrote in "The Martyr":

He lieth in his blood—
The father in his face;
They have killed him, the Forgiver—
The Avenger takes his place. . . .

SUMMARY

The Civil War became the deadliest war Americans have ever fought. It lasted four years, killed a generation of young men, and left the South devastated.

It began slowly. At first it was thought that the war would be quick, that the South, fighting on its home ground and led by talented officers, would win. In a long war, the North's advantages in terms of numerical strength and industrial resources were overwhelming. The North had other advantages in its government, which was strong and centralized, and in its political leader, Abraham Lincoln. The South, dedicated to states rights, had difficulty with even the idea of strong central government.

Lincoln immediately prepared for war, but let nearly a year go by before he acknowledged that it would be a fight to the finish. The North's strategy was to strangle the South with a naval blockade, gain control of the Mississippi, and take Richmond, the Confederate capital. The first two steps went well; the third did not. In July 1861, Union forces were beaten at Bull Run in Virginia. But Confederate military commanders anxious to push on to Washington were overruled, and the Union armies were commanded by generals whose main talent seemed to be inaction and delay.

Even with direct orders from Lincoln, the army did not move in the East and the campaign for Richmond went nowhere. Under more vigorous commanders, Union forces in the West gained control of the Mississippi except for Vicksburg in Mississippi and Port Hudson in Louisiana. The grand assault on Richmond in the spring and summer of 1862 failed utterly because of the generals' incompetence. The North was again defeated in the second battle of Bull Run in August. But at Antietam in September, the Confederate attempt to penetrate the North failed.

This was to be the turning point, for now the South's resources were being used up, and victory was still nowhere in sight. In its brutality and inconclusiveness, Antietam was also symbolic of a war that seemed to produce only aimless mutual slaughter.

By this time, there were clear signs of economic difficulties in the South. The frustrated Confederate government had begun to print paper money in 1861; by 1864 a Confederate paper dollar was worth 1.5 cents. Prices soared. Cotton diplomacy failed because the British during those years needed wheat more than cotton. In the North, there was economic boom and wartime prosperity as mechanized agriculture and expanding factories poured out huge amounts of food and supplies. The federal government also printed paper money—greenbacks—which fell in value to 39 cents on the gold dollar by the summer of 1864. While the war brought hardship to many women, especially in the South, it also brought some of them opportunities for self-assertion and independent activities. North and South, many women had no choice when their husbands and sons went off to war: They had to undertake farming chores and supervision of free and slave laborers to an extent they had never before experienced. Yet many women on both sides seized the opportunity to help in the war effort by taking jobs in factories, raising funds for the relief of soldiers in difficulty, and becoming nurses in army hospitals.

By 1862, Lincoln was ready to put in motion a plan to end the military stalemate by a bold political action—freeing the slaves. In September he issued a proclamation whose terms were to take effect on January 1, 1863. On that day, he issued the final Emancipation Proclamation. It did not shorten the war or free any slaves, but it ensured the death of slavery when the war was over.

After Antietam, the military pace of the war picked up. The North lost at Chancellorsville in May of 1863, but then came Gettysburg, July 1–July 4, and the end of Confederate hopes. On the same day the battle at Gettysburg ended, news came of Grant's victory at Vicksburg. In September, Union forces won a spectacular victory at Chattanooga in Tennessee that split the Confederacy north and south as well as east and west. Grant was made supreme commander of the Union armies in the spring of 1864, but another year of terrible fighting followed, as Union armies advanced toward Richmond in a great pincer movement. Sherman's army, starting in Tennessee, moved relentlessly toward the sea, laying waste the area over which it traveled and burning Atlanta in September 1864.

In November Lincoln was reelected on the strength of the military victories and the clear signs that the end was in sight. By the end of March 1865, Grant's army was ready to enter Richmond. On April 9, General Robert E. Lee surrendered for the Confederacy at the village of Appomattox Court House. But then on April 14, Lincoln was shot in Washington and died the next day. The war was over. It had cost the life of an American president, in addition to more American lives lost than any other war before or since.

Suggested Readings

Allan Nevins has written a magnificent survey of the Civil War era: *The War for the Union: The Improvised War, 1861–1862* (1959), *War Becomes Revolution, 1862–1863* (1960), and *The Organized War, 1863–1864* (1971). A shorter study is J. Randall and D. Donald, *The Civil War and Reconstruction* (rev. ed., 1961). See also

D. Donald and others, *Divided We Fought* (1956), a pictorial history with excellent text on military events. A good overall military history is H. Hattaway and A. Jones, *How the North Won* (1983).

The strong national feeling in the North is emphasized in G. Frederickson, *The Inner Civil War: Northern Intellectuals and the Crisis of the Union* (1965). There are many insights into the importance of the conflict in D. Aaron, *The Unwritten War: American Writers and the Civil War* (1973).

The relationship of the war to economic developments has long been debated by historians. The crucial role played by the railroads is dealt with in T. Weber, *The Northern Railroads in the Civil War, 1861–1865* (1952), and R. Black, *The Railroads of the Confederacy* (1952). Stimulating essays on the war and industrial growth may be found in D. Gilchrist and W. Lewis (eds.), *Economic Change in the Civil War Era* (1965). R. Sharkey, *Money, Class and Party, An Economic Study of the Civil War and Reconstruction* (1959), offers a more general financial analysis. Key developments in military technology are discussed in R. Bruce, *Lincoln and the Tools of War* (1956).

C. Eaton, *A History of the Southern Confederacy* (1952), is the best general survey. For the Confederacy's president and his administration, see the uncritically enthusiastic study by H. Strode, *Jefferson Davis* (2 vols., 1955, 1959). R. Durden, *The Gray and the Black: The Confederate Debate on Emancipation* (1973), reproduces portions of the 1860s debate along with a running narrative commentary.

Of the enormous number of biographical studies of Lincoln, a relatively brief one stands out: B. Thomas, *Abraham Lincoln* (1952). D. Donald, *Lincoln Reconsidered* (1956), offers insights on the man not found elsewhere; see also R. Current, *The Lincoln Nobody Knows* (1958). Also good is S. Oates, *Abraham Lincoln: The Man Behind the Myth* (1984). For Lincoln's fascinating relationships with his cabinet, see B. Thomas and J. Hyman, *Stanton: The Life and Times of Lincoln's Secretary of War* (1962), and H. Beale and A. Brownsword (eds.), *Diary of Gideon Welles, Secretary of the Navy under Lincoln and Johnson* (1960).

The strong feeling behind the Democratic opposition in the North becomes evident in F. Klement, *The Copperheads in the Middle West* (1960). For antiblack sentiment in the Midwest, see V. Voegeli, *Free But Not Equal: The Midwest and the Negro during the Civil War* (1967). The role of the abolitionists during the war is presented in J. McPherson, *The Struggle for Equality: Abolitionists and the Negro in the Civil War and Reconstruction* (1964). There are two outstanding biographies of important Radical Republicans: F. Brodie, *Thaddeus Stevens* (1959); D. Donald, *Charles Sumner and the Coming of the Civil War* (2nd ed., 1981), and his *Charles Sumner and the Rights of Man* (1976). A famous and frequently misunderstood document is placed in context in J. Franklin, *The Emancipation Proclamation* (1963).

The diplomatic aspects of the war are given in all general histories. The best single source for additional insight is M. Duberman, *Charles Francis Adams* (1961), who was the Union minister in London. There is a much larger literature on military aspects of the great conflict, enough to fill several hundred feet of shelf space. One of the best overall surveys is B. Catton, *Centennial History of the War* (3 vols., 1961–1965). Moving accounts of the Union army in the East are offered in Catton's *Mr. Lincoln's Army* (1951), *Glory Road* (1952), *A Stillness at Appomattox* (1954), and *This Hallowed Ground* (1956). There are superb photographs in W. Frassanito, *Grant and Lee: The Virginia Campaigns, 1864–1865* (1983). The Union president's agonized search for the right man is chronicled in T. Williams, *Lincoln and His Generals* (1952). Another important aspect of the struggle is treated in R. West, Jr., *Mr. Lincoln's Navy* (1957). Greatness of leadership in the South lay with a general whose spirit and skill were universally acknowledged; see D. Freeman, *R. E. Lee: A Biography* (4 vols., 1934–1935). An outstanding one-volume life is C. Dowdey, *Lee* (1965).

Many other biographies celebrate generals on both sides. For the ordinary man's role in the war, consult H. Commager (ed.), *The Blue and the Gray: The Story of the Civil War as Told by Participants* (2 vols., 1950); and B. Wiley, *The Life of Johnny Reb* (1943), and *The Life of Billy Yank* (1952). The role of blacks is discussed generally by B. Quarles, *The Negro in the Civil War* (1953); the importance of black Union troops by D. Cornish, *The Sable Arm: Negro Troops in the Union Army, 1861–1865* (1958). B. Wiley, *Southern Negroes, 1861–1865* (1938), is an old but useful account of the impact of the war behind Confederate lines; J. McPherson, *The Negro's Civil War* (1965), is a superb combination of original documents and commentary; and A. Cook, *The Armies of the Streets: The New York City Draft Riots of 1863* (1974), provides a complete analysis of that subject. The dramatic confrontation between northern troops, accompanying abolitionists, and liberated slaves in the South Carolina–Georgia Sea Islands is vividly re-created in W. Rose, *Rehearsal for Reconstruction* (1964). L. Litwack, *Been in the Storm So Long: The Aftermath of Slavery* (1979), is a sweeping account about the coming of freedom both during and after the war.

The war's impact on one slaveholding family is revealed by their letters: R. Myers (ed.), *The Children of Pride: A True Story of Georgia and the Civil War* (1972). For southern civilian life, see also B. Wiley, *The Plain People of the Confederacy* (1943). For women, see Wiley's *Confederate Women* (1975), and M. E. Massey, *Bonnet Brigades* (1966).

There are powerful literary treatments of the war: W. Whitman's *Taps* (1865), and *Speciman Days* (1875), a wrenching account of the horrors of the Union "hospitals." H. Melville, *Battle Pieces and Other Aspects of the War* (1964 ed.), is also fine. S. Crane's *The Red Badge of Courage* (1895) is one of the few novels in the English language to catch the real feelings of the ordinary soldier under fire.

AFTER THE WAR: RECONSTRUCTION AND RESTORATION

Chapter 18

After four years of warfare, the Union had withstood its most serious challenge. Measured in physical devastation and human lives, the Civil War remains the costliest war in the experience of the American people. When it ended, in April 1865, 620,000 men (in a nation of 35 million) had been killed, at least that many more had been wounded, and portions of the Confederacy lay in ruins. Two questions were firmly settled: the right of a state to secede and the right to own slaves. But new problems soon surfaced that would plunge the nation into still another period of turmoil and uncertainty.

Having won the war, the victors had no rules to guide them in how to reconstruct the South and ensure its future loyalty. Under what conditions should the ex-Confederate states be permitted to return? What if any punishment should be meted out to those southerners who had led their states out of the Union? Were the nearly 4 million freed slaves entitled to the same rights as white citizens? Finally, where did the responsibility lie for resolving these difficult questions—with the president or with Congress?

Lincoln's view of reconstruction was consistent with his theory of secession and rebellion. He held from the outset that states could not break away from the Union. The Civil War, then, had been an illegal rebellion waged by disloyal men. Now that the rebellion was over, the task of reconstruction consisted simply of restoring loyal governments to the ex-Confederate states. The rebels themselves could be quickly reinstated as citizens by presidential pardon, and they could then take part in the establishment of the new governments. Although this became known as the "moderate" approach to Reconstruction, stressing the president's generous spirit and statesmanship, the meaning of Lincoln's "moderation" should be clearly understood: After agreeing to repudiate secession and to recognize the abolition of slavery, the newly restored southern states would retain the same powers of decision enjoyed by all states, including the right to determine the status of their black residents.

The Radical Republicans, a faction within the party, believed Lincoln's program would hamper their objective; they wanted to rebuild southern society around the equality of newly freed slaves and whites. The rebel states, they argued, were reduced to the status of territories because of their "rebellion." In seeking statehood once again, they came under the jurisdiction not of the president but of Congress, which governed territorial affairs. This was not simply an argument over the respective powers of the legislative and executive branches of government; it was a battle over the very objectives and content of southern Reconstruction.

By his policy, President Lincoln hoped to build a Republican party in the South based on the votes of white men and on the leadership of those who had initially opposed secession. His successor, Andrew Johnson, also advocated a "moderate" approach, based on his strict reading of the Constitution and on his belief in white supremacy. The Radicals, on the other hand, viewed the southern black vote as the only means of winning that section of the country for the Republicans and ensuring the party's national strength. Lincoln and Johnson were willing to entrust the fate of the newly freed slaves to the defeated whites. The Radicals tried to develop a program of civil rights and education that would protect the freed blacks from the defeated whites.

Despite the war and emancipation, the white South's attitude toward blacks remained the same. The "corner-stone" of the Confederacy, Vice-President Alexander Stephens had declared in 1861, "rests upon the great truth, that the negro is not equal to the white man; that slavery— subordination to the superior race—is his natural and normal condition." Even as they acknowledged emancipation, few whites surrendered the convictions with which they had held black men and women as slaves. A planter in South Carolina gave voice to that sentiment in the questions he asked after the war: "Can not freedmen be organized and disciplined as well as slaves? Is not the dollar as potent as the lash? The belly as tender as the back?"

Neither military defeat nor the collapse of slavery suggested to whites the need to reexamine their racial relationships or assumptions. If anything, the need to maintain white supremacy took on an even greater urgency now that the slaves had been freed. The postemancipation repression of the ex-slaves made a shambles of "moderate" reconstruction. By refusing to grant blacks minimal civil rights and educational opportunities, the white South succeeded only in alienating northern public opinion, strengthening the Radical position, and helping to make possible Radical or congressional Reconstruction.

Radical rule in the South ended in 1877 (much sooner in most states), having failed to achieve the objective of a democratic, biracial society. That failure does not mean Lincoln's or Johnson's programs would have worked any better. Whatever its shortcomings, Radical Reconstruction enabled blacks to gain political experience as voters and officeholders, and it laid the legal foundations for a "second reconstruction" in the 1950s and 1960s, when black leaders and movements would seek to complete the work of emancipation. ■

THE DEFEATED SOUTH

The Civil War took a heavy toll of families in the North as well as the South, among both whites and blacks. But the physical devastation was largely limited to the South, where almost all the fighting took place. Large sections of Richmond, Charleston, Atlanta, Mobile, and Vicksburg had burned to the ground. The countryside through which the armies had passed was littered with gutted plantation houses and barns, burned bridges, and uprooted railroad lines. Many crops had been destroyed or confiscated, and much of the livestock had been slain. To rebuild the devastated areas and to restore agricultural production required outlays of capital and labor that were not readily available.

Unlike the North, where the $4 billion in direct wartime expenditures had provided huge profits, only a few southerners managed to accumulate capital during the war—some by running cotton through the northern blockade; others by demanding gold or goods instead of Confederate paper money in payment for food, clothing, and farm supplies. But most southerners were now poor.

The planters' land, worth $1.5 billion in 1860, was evaluated at half that amount ten years later. The South's $1 billion in banking capital had been wiped out, and the credit system was paralyzed. The money invested in Confederate bonds and currency was lost. Finally, and most critically, the planters' $2.5 billion investment in slaves had vanished, along with many of the slaves.

Aftermath of Slavery

After Appomattox, most planters assembled what blacks were left, acknowledged their freedom, and asked them to work for wages or shares of the crop. Having lived for years in close, day-to-day contact with the "white folks," and facing an uncertain future with a vaguely defined freedom, the emancipated slaves had to make some difficult decisions. If they remained on the old places, what relations would they now have with those who had once owned them? How adequately would they be paid for their labor? If they left, where would they go, and how would they support themselves?

For some, the first need was to test their freedom, to take some kind of action to prove to themselves that they were really free. The most direct and the quickest test was to leave the plantation. As one newly freed slave explained to his former master, "I must go, for if I stay here I'll never know I am free." By leaving, many expected to improve their economic prospects; others hoped to locate family members from whom they had been separated during slavery; and some expected greater freedom by settling in the nearest town.

To throw off a lifetime of bondage, black men and women adopted different priorities, ranging from dramatic breaks with the past to subtle though no less significant changes in demeanor and behavior. Many did not move at all, at least not in the first postwar year, choosing to remain in familiar surroundings and to find ways of exercising their freedom even as they worked in the same fields and kitchens. "Henney is still with me," a South Carolina white woman said of her former slave, "but she is not the same person that she was."

Family members who had been sold away during slavery sought each other out after emancipation—an effort that spanned several decades for some and ended for many in failure, tragedy, and disappointment. New emotional ties had sometimes replaced the old; husbands and wives who had given up any hope of seeing each other again had remarried, and children sold away from their parents had been raised by other black women or by the white mistress, creating complications. The question facing some freedmen and freedwomen was not whether to formalize their slave marriages, as so many did in the postwar years, but which marriage should take precedence. And that often proved to be a difficult and agonizing decision to make.

After emancipation, many black women opted to stop working in fields and kitchens in order to spend more time tending to their own households and children. If the women themselves did not initiate such moves, the men sometimes insisted, as a way of reinforcing their position as head of the family. "When I married my wife," a Tennessee freedman told his employer, in rejecting his request for her services, "I married her to wait on me and she has got all she can do right here for me and the children." But not all black women agreed to such a narrow definition of their roles; and even if they wanted to leave the labor force, they could seldom afford to do so. Many continued to work in the fields alongside their men, in the white family's kichen, and at other tasks to supplement the family income.

That many freedmen and freedwomen changed their lives, displayed feelings of independence, deserted their former owners, seized the land of absentee owners, engaged in work stoppages, sat where they pleased in public places and vehicles, and no longer felt the need to humble themselves

WORDS AND NAMES IN AMERICAN HISTORY

The word *miscegenation* refers to interracial sexual contact, with or without resulting children. It was an artificially coined word, made by combining the Latin *miscere*—to mix—and *genus*—race, people, or even species. The word was minted in 1863, during the Civil War, by two New York newspapermen, David Croly and George Wakeman, who were both anti-black and anti-abolitionist. They raised the matter of interracial sex in order to appeal to widely held prejudices against it. Their purposes were primarily political, yet the term has proved to be an enduring one; it pretty much replaced the more common word then in use, *amalgamation*. Perhaps because the word is long and so many Americans feel so awkward about the matter, *miscegenation* is commonly mispronounced: the accents are on the first and fourth syllables.

THE LEGACY OF SLAVERY

Several years after their forced separation during slavery, the husband of Laura Spicer had remarried in the belief that his wife had died. When he learned after the war that she was still alive, the news stung him. He dictated a letter to her:

I want to see you and I don't want to see you. I love you just as well as I did the last day I saw you, and it will not do for you and I to meet. I am married, and my wife have two children. . . . You know it never was our wishes to be separated from each other, and it never was our fault. Oh, I can see you so plain, at any-time. I had rather anything to had happened to

me most than ever have been parted from you and the children. As I am, I do not know which I love best, you or Anna. If I was to die, today or tomorrow, I do not think I would die satisfied till you tell me you will try and marry some good, smart man that will take good care of you and the children; and do it because you love me; and not because I think more of the wife I have got than I do of you. The woman is not born that feels as near to me as you do. Tell them [the children] they must remember they have a good father and one that cares for them and one that thinks about them every day.

Source: Henry L. Swint (ed.), *Dear Ones at Home: Letters from Contraband Camps* (Nashville: Vanderbilt University Press, 1966), pp. 242–43. Photograph from the Cook Collection, Valentine Museum.

in the presence of whites should not obscure the extent to which life went on very much as it had before the war. As long as whites had political and economic dominance, they were in a position to control the very content of black freedom. "The Master he say we are all free," a former South Carolina slave recalled, "but it don't mean we is white. And it don't mean we is equal. Just equal for to work and earn our living and not depend on him for no more meats and clothes."

During the war, various plans were advanced to help blacks who sought shelter and freedom behind Union lines. With federal approval, blacks in portions of the occupied South—as on the Sea Islands along the South Carolina coast and on the land in Mississippi that had belonged to Jefferson Davis and his brother—were permitted to work on the plantations with the expectation of dividing the crops and carving out plots of land for them-

selves. Some abandoned lands were offered on easy terms to ex-slaves, and many of them did well as independent farmers. But most of the land was ultimately returned to its original owners, and the freedmen's goal of becoming landowning farmers remained unrealized.

To ease the transition from slavery to freedom, Congress in March 1865 created the Freedmen's Bureau. It was authorized to furnish food, clothing, and transportation to refugees and freed blacks, to oversee labor contracts, and to settle freedmen on abandoned or confiscated lands. Although the bureau provided relief, tried to ensure the fairness of labor contracts, and helped to maintain schools for black children, it never fulfilled its promise or potential.

Oliver Otis Howard, the bureau's commissioner and a founder of Howard University, was well meaning and sympathetic, as were a number of the field agents. But many of the regional and local officers were more concerned with gaining the approval of the white communities in which they worked. Too often, bureau officers thought their main responsibility was to get the ex-slaves to accept contracts with their former masters and to prevent them from drifting into the towns. Some of the more dedicated officers who identified with the freed blacks' cause found themselves quickly removed under President Johnson.

With capital and even food in short supply, white farmers and planters often did little better than the blacks. Famine struck many parts of the South in the middle of the war. Afterward, wartime systems of relief collapsed in the general ruin of the Confederacy. In the first four years after the war, the Freedmen's Bureau fed thousands of starving whites as well as blacks. In several instances, the ex-slaves themselves came to the assistance of their former masters and mistresses, some by making small contributions for their welfare, others by agreeing to stay with those who seemed incapable of running the plantations without them.

Perhaps the heaviest blow to the white South was the moral and psychic cost of war and defeat. Purpose, morale, and aspiration declined. The losses in youth and talent hurt beyond measure. And it had all been in vain—the suffering, the self-sacrifice, the devastation. That was the most difficult fact to accept. "Now we belong to Negroes and Yankees," a South Carolina woman cried in despair. Emancipation, moreover, forcibly reminded former slaveholding families of how dependent they remained on their black laborers, of how helpless they were. "They need us all the time," a black domestic recalled.

They don't want no food unless a nigger cooks it. They want niggers to do all their washing and ironing. They want niggers to do their sweeping and cleaning and everything around their houses. The niggers handle everything they wears and hands them everything they eat and drink. Ain't nobody can get closer to a white person than a colored person. If we'd a wanted to kill 'em, they'd all done been dead.

With equal frankness, a Virginia planter conceded his dependence on black labor: "I must have niggers to work for me. I can't do nothin' on my place without 'em. If they send all the niggers to Africa, I'll have to go thar, too."

The former slaveholding class seemed less equipped, mentally and physically, to make the transition from slave to free labor than their former slaves. No matter how hard a few of them tried, they seemed incapable of learning new ways and shaking off old attitudes. That failure was demonstrated during presidential Reconstruction, when the white South was given the opportunity to reconstruct itself with a minimum of federal interference.

Lincoln's Plan

The Civil War began as a war with limited objectives. The Crittenden Resolution adopted by the House of Representatives on July 22, 1861, with only two dissenting votes, made those objectives abundantly clear:

This war is not waged . . . for any purpose . . . but to defend and maintain the supremacy of the Constitution and to preserve the Union, with all the dignity, equality, and rights of the several States unimpaired; and . . . as soon as these objects are accomplished the war ought to cease.

Three days later, the Senate adopted an almost identical resolution. Although the Emancipation Proclamation broadened the objectives of the war, President Lincoln remained faithful to the spirit of the resolution.

When in 1862 much of Tennessee, Louisiana, and North Carolina had fallen, Lincoln appointed military governors to bring these states into conformity with the Constitution. On December 8, 1863, with still other rebel states on the verge of surrender, the president issued his Proclamation of Amnesty and Reconstruction, which became known as the "10 percent plan" and set forth the terms by which the southern states would be restored to the Union.

Except for high military and civil officers of the Confederacy, any southern citizen would be granted an amnesty by the president after taking an oath of loyalty to the Constitution and the laws of the Union. Confiscated property other than slaves would be restored. As soon as 10 percent of those who had voted in the presidential election of 1860 had taken the oath and sworn allegiance to the Union, that state could proceed to write a new constitution, elect new state officers, and send members to the United States Congress. The House and Senate, of course, retained their constitutional privilege of seating or rejecting such members.

The president failed to confront the social realities of emancipation. Lincoln assured the states to which his proclamation applied that he would not object to "any provision" they might wish to make regarding the freed slaves "which may yet be consistent with their present condition as a laboring, landless, and homeless class." This was nothing short of an invitation to the ex-Confederate states to adopt the inflammatory Black Codes they enacted in 1865 and 1866.

Until late in the war, Lincoln still held that the best way to deal with "the Negro problem" was to persuade blacks to leave the country. "There is an unwillingness on the part of our people, harsh as it may be, for you free colored people to remain with us," he told a black delegation in August 1862. "It is better for us both, therefore, to be separated." But black leaders rejected Lincoln's colonization scheme, even as Radical Republicans would reject his "moderate" reconstruction program. In his last public address on April 11, 1865, Lincoln made no mention of colonizing freed blacks. In defending his reconstruction plan, he suggested that the states might wish to extend the suffrage to "the very intelligent" blacks and to "those who serve our cause as soldiers." That was for the states to decide, however, and it soon became apparent that none of them thought the president's suggestion worthy of serious consideration.

The Radical Plan

In treating the ex-Confederate states, Lincoln had urged a minimum of federal interference. The Radical Republican proposals called for a more thorough reconstruction of southern society. Under their program, the power of the old planter class would be destroyed, and the freedom of the emancipated blacks fully protected. Thaddeus Stevens of Pennsylvania, a Radical leader in the House, stated this position most forcefully. To make the Confederacy "a safe republic," he insisted, "the whole fabric of southern society must be changed."

To Stevens, this meant the confiscation of the estates of the southern ruling class and their distribution to the very people who had made the land productive—the freed slaves. In the Senate, Charles Sumner added his voice to that of Stevens; to preserve the gains of the war, giving the vote to blacks was essential, he insisted.

Practical political considerations also encouraged Republicans to favor a tougher program. With the abolition of slavery, all freedmen (rather than three-fifths of them) would be counted for purposes of representation. The South would gain additional seats in Congress, even if it denied the vote to blacks. That fact won over many conservative Republicans, who feared that northern and southern Democrats would again close ranks and overturn Republican economic legislation.

The Wade-Davis bill, adopted by Congress a few days before it adjourned in July 1864, set forth the first Radical response to Lincoln's program. It required a majority of the citizens of a state, not just 10 percent, to swear loyalty to the Union before a provisional governor could call an election for a state constitutional convention. Only those southerners able to swear that they had *always* been loyal to the Union and had not "voluntarily borne arms against the United States" were entitled to vote for delegates to the constitutional conventions. The bill also prescribed that new state constitutions in the South must abolish slavery, repudiate state debts, and deprive ex-Confederate leaders of the right to vote.

Radical strategists hoped to commit the Republican party to their program in the 1864 presidential campaign. Lincoln attempted to stop them by permitting the Wade-Davis bill to die by a pocket veto. Defending his action, Lincoln said rebel states might follow the Wade-Davis provisions if they wished, but he refused to make them mandatory. Most Radical leaders supported Lincoln in the 1864 campaign because they did not want to disrupt the party and endanger the war effort. Once the election was over, they pressed again for their program.

In January 1865 they adopted the Thirteenth Amendment, which abolished slavery throughout the United States. (It was ratified in December 1865 by the required twenty-seven states, including eight formerly of the Confederacy, which Congress for other purposes did not even recognize as states.) In February, Congress refused to admit members from Louisiana, which Lincoln had declared "reconstructed" under the 10 percent plan. In March, Congress created the Freedmen's Bureau. With these measures, Congress adjourned. When it reconvened, in December, it would have to deal with a new president and with a South that had been "reconstructed" under the president's plan.

Johnsonian Restoration

When Lincoln died on April 15, 1865, the victim of an assassin's bullet, Andrew Johnson of Tennessee became president. Like Lincoln, he was born in poverty. Uneducated, he was ultimately

While Thaddeus Stevens (left) House leader of the Radical Republicans, sought to alter "the whole fabric of southern society" and provide a legal and economic underpinning for black freedom, President Johnson (right) proceeded with a restoration of the ex-Confederate states to the Union that would have permitted southern whites to determine the status of blacks. (*Library of Congress*)

taught to read by his wife. Unlike Lincoln, he was tactless and inflexible, possessing neither humility nor the capacity for compromise. He rose to political power in nonslaveholding eastern Tennessee. When he told poor farmers of his dislike for rich cotton planters, they rallied to his support. But even though Johnson delighted his constituents with attacks on special privilege and the planter aristocracy, he never became a vocal opponent of slavery, and he held traditional southern views on race relations. "I wish to God," he said on one occasion, "every head of a family in the United States had one slave to take the drudgery and menial service off his family."

He refused, however, to give up his seat in the Senate after Tennessee left the Union. In 1864, as a demonstration of wartime unity, the Republican party nominated Johnson for the vice-presidency even though he had been a Democrat all his life. During the campaign, Johnson made himself attractive to Radicals by his fierce denunciations of rebel leaders as "traitors." But the enthusiasm with which Johnson appeared to have embraced the Radical cause proved to be short-lived.

With Congress still in recess, the new president set out to complete Lincoln's restoration of the South to the Union. Early in May 1865, he recognized Lincoln's "10 percent" governments in Lou-

isiana, Tennessee, Arkansas, and Virginia. He next appointed military governors in the seven states that had not yet complied. On May 29 he offered executive amnesty to all citizens of these states except high Confederate military and civil officers and others owning more than $20,000 worth of property. These people had to apply for amnesty to the president.

The "whitewashed" electorate—that is, those who benefited by the amnesty offer—was then to elect members to a constitutional convention in each state. They were to abolish slavery, rescind the state's secession ordinance, adopt the Thirteenth Amendment, repudiate the war debt, and call an election for a new state government. The suffrage for this election was to be determined by each state rather than by Congress, and that clearly meant blacks would be denied participation in southern political life.

By the winter of 1865, all the seceding states but Texas had complied with Johnson's terms. Given the opportunity to reconstruct themselves, the ex-Confederate states moved quickly to restore the old planter class to political power. The president cooperated in this move. For all his dislike of the southern Old Guard, Johnson's personal grants of amnesty exceeded all bounds. He pardoned the heroes of the "Lost Cause," whom the whitewashed voters proceeded to elect to national, state, and local offices. None other than Alexander Stephens, for example, the former vice-president of the Confederacy, became Georgia's duly elected United States senator.

The spirit that dominated the ex-Confederate states was apparent not only in the individuals elected to office, but in the decisions made by the new governments. Widespread reluctance to renounce the war debt was accompanied in some states by determination to resist taxation for redemption of the Union debt. That was bound to provoke northern public opinion, as was the legislation adopted to deal with the emancipated slaves.

While ratifying the Thirteenth Amendment as required, the reconstructed states, almost as a unit, warned Congress to leave the status of the freedmen to those who knew them best—the white southerners. And when the new governments confronted the question of what to do with the ex-slaves, they used the old slave codes and their previous experience with free blacks.

In the Black Codes adopted in 1865 and 1866, the new southern governments recognized the fact of emancipation in some of the rights accorded to blacks for the first time. Although still universally forbidden to serve on juries, even in cases involving blacks, freedmen could now swear out affidavits in criminal cases, sue and be sued in civil actions, appear as witnesses, and otherwise give testimony. Marriages among blacks were to be sanctified under law, but interracial marriages carried sentences up to life imprisonment for both parties. Blacks could make wills and pass on personal property. Their children could go to school and were to be protected from abuse if they were apprenticed.

But nowhere could blacks bear arms, vote, hold public office, or assemble freely. In some states they could work at any jobs and quit jobs freely. Most states, however, forbade them to leave their jobs except under stated conditions. Nor in some states could they work as artisans, mechanics, or in other capacities in which they competed with white labor. The Mississippi code forbade freedmen to rent or lease land or houses.

The idea behind these codes was that blacks would not work except under compulsion and proper supervision, and with the vigorous enforcement of contracts and vagrancy laws. The vagrancy provisions were the worst. In Georgia, for example, the law said that "all persons wandering or strolling about in idleness, who are able to work and who have no property to support them," could be picked up and tried. If convicted, they could be set to work on state chain gangs or contracted out to planters and other employers who would pay their fines and their upkeep for a stated period.

The Johnson governments confirmed the worst fears and predictions of the Radicals and shocked many moderates. The rapid return to power of the Confederate leadership suggested an unwillingness by the South to accept defeat. By defining the freedman's role in a way that was bound to keep him propertyless and voteless, the Black Codes attempted to deny the fact of black freedom. In the North, the conviction grew that the white South was preparing to regain what it had lost on the battlefield. By their actions, the South and President Johnson had set the stage for Congress to act.

THE RADICAL CONGRESS

When Congress met in December 1865, it was faced with Johnson's actions and the South's responses. As their first countermove, Radicals set up the Joint Committee of Fifteen—six senators and nine representatives—to review the work of presidential reconstruction and the qualifications of those elected in the southern states to serve in Congress. Exercising its constitutional power, Congress refused to seat them. Early in 1866, it enacted a bill continuing the Freedmen's Bureau; Johnson vetoed the bill because he believed that care and protection of the freedmen should be left to the states.

In March 1866 Johnson also vetoed a civil rights bill that forbade states to discriminate among citizens on the basis of color or race, as they had in the Black Codes. By now a sufficient number of conservative senators were ready to join the Radicals in defense of congressional power, if not of Radical principles, and both houses overrode the president. A few months later, in July 1866, Radicals pushed through a second Freedmen's Bureau bill over Johnson's veto.

Even if many Republicans, like their constituents, remained divided over the proper place of blacks in American society, they could agree that the newly freed slaves should be protected in their basic rights and given the opportunity to advance themselves economically. The actions of the southern governments and the president's vetoes undermined those possibilities. With growing unanimity, Republicans now moved to provide a constitutional basis for black freedom.

The Fourteenth Amendment

When Radicals introduced the Fourteenth Amendment in June 1866, they were concerned about the constitutionality of the Civil Rights Act and the danger that another Congress might repeal it. A civil rights amendment would end the constitutional issue and make repeal more difficult. Perhaps the most far-reaching amendment ever added to the Constitution, its importance rested largely on how it was later interpreted.

The Fourteenth Amendment, for the first time, defined citizenship in the United States as distinct from citizenship in a state. By identifying as citizens "all persons born or naturalized in the United States," it automatically extended citizenship to American-born blacks. It also forbade any state to abridge "the privileges and immunities" of United States citizens, to "deprive any person of life, liberty, or property, without due process of law," and to "deny to any person within its jurisdiction the equal protection of the laws."

The second section of the amendment did not give blacks the vote, as many Radicals hoped it would, but penalized any state for withholding it. (The penalty was never imposed and was replaced by the Fifteenth Amendment.) The third section disqualified from federal or state office all Confederates who before the war had taken a federal oath of office unless Congress specifically lifted the disqualification by a two-thirds vote. Finally, the amendment guaranteed the Union debt but outlawed the Confederate debt and any claims for compensation for loss of slaves.

The Fourteenth Amendment had a stormy history before it was finally ratified in July 1868. Many years later, the use of the word "person" in the first section of the amendment was interpreted by the federal courts as applying to "legal persons" such as business corporations as well as to blacks, who were the only persons its framers had in mind. It thus supplied legal grounds for the courts to declare unconstitutional state regulation of railroads and trusts. Still later, the phrase in Section 1 prohibiting the denial of "equal protection of the laws" supplied legal grounds for the Supreme Court's school desegregation decision in 1954.

Although far-reaching as it would later be interpreted to be, the Fourteenth Amendment failed to satisfy the Radicals as a final condition for the reconstruction of the southern states. They thought it too full of compromises, and hoped in time to stiffen its provisions. Dissatisfaction with the amendment was also voiced by Susan B. Anthony and other agitators for women's suffrage, who had hoped to win the franchise because of their contributions to victory in the Civil War. They fought valiantly to delete the word "male" from the voting provisions of the Fourteenth Amendment (and soon to add the word "sex" to "race, color, or previous condition of servitude" in the Fifteenth Amendment). But Radical leaders believed that merging women's rights with blacks' rights would weaken the chances of both.

Radicals demanded that southern states ratify the Fourteenth Amendment to regain representation in Congress. Johnson advised them not to. By mid-February 1867, all but Tennessee—that is, ten of eleven ex-Confederate states—had followed his advice. Without the required three-fourths majority of the states, the amendment was dead. But the rejection of the amendment, along with the president's defiance, only reinforced in the minds of Republicans, Radicals and moderates alike, the need to take over the process of southern reconstruction.

The Reconstruction Acts and Impeachment

The Fourteenth Amendment had drawn the issue clearly between president and Congress. In the congressional campaign of 1866, Johnson visited key cities on behalf of candidates who favored his policy. The more the president talked, however, the more he antagonized northern voters. At the same time, racial clashes in New Orleans and Memphis appeared to confirm Radical warnings about the consequences of Johnson's southern policy. The Radicals sought and won a sweeping electoral victory. With a two-thirds majority in Congress, they would be able to impose even sterner measures and carry them over presidential vetoes.

The Radicals began with the First Reconstruction Act, passed over Johnson's veto on March 2, 1867. Tennessee had been accepted back into the Union in 1866, but all other southern state governments were declared illegal. The South was organized into five military districts, each under a general to be named by the president. The general's main task was to call a new constitutional convention in each state, its delegates to be elected by universal adult male suffrage, black and white, excluding those deprived of the vote under the proposed Fourteenth Amendment. The new conventions would establish state governments in which blacks could vote and hold office. These governments were to ratify the Fourteenth Amendment as a condition for their return to the

Union and the acceptance of their representatives by Congress.

By June 1868 all but three states—Mississippi, Texas, and Virginia—had complied with these requirements, and in July the ratification of the Fourteenth Amendment was completed. The three reluctant states were readmitted in 1870. In that year Georgia, whose reconstruction had been suspended because of the expulsion of black members from the legislature, was also readmitted for the second time.

The Radicals' next step was to protect their program from the Supreme Court. In the case of *ex parte Milligan* (1866), which arose over Lincoln's suspension of habeas corpus in Indiana during the war, the Supreme Court had held that if military rule persists after the regular courts are reinstated, it is "a gross usurpation of power." That is exactly what happened when the First Reconstruction Act was passed. Southern courts were open; but by establishing military rule, the act usurped their power.

When the constitutionality of the act was challenged in *ex parte McCardle*, the Radicals attached a rider to a minor bill making it impossible to appeal a habeas corpus case to the Supreme Court. Johnson vetoed the whole bill, but the habeas corpus provision was passed over his veto in March 1868. The Supreme Court had put *ex parte McCardle* on its schedule, but it yielded to the Radicals and allowed the case to be quashed. The First Reconstruction Act survived.

Having checked the Supreme Court, the Radicals next set about defending their program from presidential sabotage. The Tenure of Office Act, passed along with the First Reconstruction Act, declared that the president could not remove federal officers who had been appointed with the consent of the Senate unless the Senate agreed. The second, the Command of the Army Act, forbade the president to issue orders to the army except through the General of the Army (Ulysses S. Grant). These measures were designed to prevent the president from using patronage or control of the army to undermine the Radical program.

The conflict between Congress and Johnson ended in a move to impeach the president. Radicals held that as long as he remained in office, their reconstruction program could never be fully or fairly implemented. Although Johnson had no real choice but to enforce the acts of Congress, he had used his executive powers to weaken them. As commander-in-chief, for example, he had removed district commanders who were overly sympathetic to Radical policies and to the cause of the freedmen. He had also helped to restore the vote to southerners of doubtful loyalty. But there was no evidence directly implicating the president in any "high crimes and misdemeanors"—the only constitutional grounds for impeachment.

After almost a year of investigation, the House Judiciary Committee in 1867 voted by a narrow majority to recommend that the president be impeached. It charged him with attempting to reconstruct the ex-Confederate states "in accordance with his own will, in the interests of the great criminals who carried them into rebellion." This charge proved too vague for the whole House to accept, and it rejected the recommendation. But by attempting to remove Secretary of War Stanton, the remaining Radical in his cabinet, in apparent violation of the Tenure of Office Act, Johnson provided new grounds for impeachment. On February 21, 1868, Stanton was formally removed. Three days later, a new impeachment resolution came before the House. This time the House voted for impeachment 126 to 47. All but one of the charges ("particular articles") referred to the Tenure of Office Act. (Johnson's lawyers would contend that the Tenure of Office Act was unconstitutional and that it could not be applied to Stanton in any case, since he was a Lincoln appointee.) The tenth article charged that Johnson had been"unmindful of the high duties of his office" and had attempted to bring Congress into "disgrace, ridicule, hatred, contempt and reproach." This proved to be the major thrust of the impeachment move.

To convict Johnson, two-thirds of the Senate would have to be convinced that the charges against him amounted to "high crimes and misdemeanors" or that impeachment could be broadened to include political conduct that rendered a president unfit to hold office. But seven Republicans could not be persuaded, and that was enough. By the barest possible margin, only one vote, the Senate refused to remove the president.

The Election of 1868: Grant

Although they had done everything possible to block the president before the election of 1868, the Radicals were determined to secure the office for themselves that year. Their choice was General Grant, who had no known political allegiances—or, for that matter, any known political ambitions. He had served the Radicals in the controversy over Stanton's removal, and his war record appeared to make him a certain winner. At the Republican convention, Grant was nominated on the first ballot. Johnson sought the Democratic nomination. But after twenty-two ballots, the Democratic convention chose former New York Governor Horatio Seymour.

In the campaign, Democrats sought to divert attention from their reconstruction record by making an issue of cheap money. In 1866 Congress had passed a measure providing for the gradual retirement of the wartime greenbacks, whose dollar value always remained below that of gold. In the next two years, almost $100 million worth were withdrawn from circulation, much to the disappointment of businessmen as well as farmers.

Western farmers, although emotionally attached to the Republican party for its liberal land policy, wanted cheap money to meet mortgage obligations and other debts. The Democrats' platform made a bid for their support by advocating the reissue of greenbacks to retire war bonds that did not specifically require repayment in gold. The leading proponent of this "soft money" plank was an early aspirant for the 1868 Democratic nomination, George H. Pendleton of Ohio. It became the Ohio Idea.

The Republicans had another idea. War bonds, they said, should be redeemed in gold; anything else would be a repudiation of a sacred debt. At the same time, they promised businessmen they would extend redemption "over a fair period," so as not to disturb the credit structure. When the time came, all bondholders would be paid in gold.

The Radicals kept the main political issue before the voters—Radical Reconstruction versus Democratic dishonor. The "bloody shirt," which had done such service in the 1866 campaign, was waved again. The Democratic party, cried Republicans, was the standard-bearer of rebellion, black repression, and financial repudiation. "In short," cried Oliver P. Morton, the Radical governor of Indiana, "the Democratic party may be described as a common sewer and loathsome receptacle, into which is emptied every element of inhumanity and barbarism which had dishonored the age."

But the campaign did not overwhelm the opposition. In 1868, against a weak opponent, Grant was elected with a popular plurality of only 310,000 (about 52.7 percent of the popular vote). If not for the seven reconstructed southern states and the black vote, he might have lost.

The part blacks played in winning the election— or rather the fact that blacks in states such as Louisiana and Georgia had been prevented from casting what might have been much-needed Republican votes—led Radicals to attempt to strengthen the Fourteenth Amendment's protec-

tion of black suffrage. When Congress convened early in 1869, it promptly passed the Fifteenth Amendment: "The right of citizens of the United States to vote shall not be denied or abridged by the United States or by any State on account of race, color, or previous condition of servitude." This amendment was ratified in March 1870. By then, blacks had already made their presence and influence known in the newly established southern governments.

RADICAL RECONSTRUCTION: LEGEND AND REALITY

With the passage of the Reconstruction Act in 1867, Congress began a new era in southern political history. The new state governments were the first to be organized on the basis of universal male suffrage and to operate on the premise that all men, white and black, were entitled to equal legal protection. For whites, as well as for the blacks themselves, this proved to be an extraordinary experience—black voters, black officeholders, black jurors, black sheriffs, black militias. Here was a society, remarked one observer, "suddenly turned bottom-side up." That statement captured the spirit of Radical rule in several of the states, even though it exaggerated black strength and influence in most of them.

Contrary to legend, blacks did not dominate any of the new governments; federal military occupation was never extensive; and only in South Carolina, Florida, and Louisiana did Radical rule last as long as eight years. The impressions that survived Reconstruction, however, and which generations of Americans would believe, added up to a "tragic era" in which corrupt carpetbaggers, poor white scalawags, and illiterate blacks ran wild in an unprecedented and outrageous orgy of misrule. The historians later supplied the footnotes, the novelists embroidered the plots, and finally the motion picture industry (in films such as *The Birth of a Nation* and *Gone with the Wind*) depicted this version of Reconstruction for millions of believing spectators.

Few periods of American history have produced a worse collection of villains—white and black. The very names by which the white South came to know them suggested deceit, treachery, and alien rule. The carpetbaggers were "those Yankees who came South like buzzards after the surrender with all their worldly possessions in one carpetbag." The scalawags were "southerners who had turned Republican very profitably" and in do-

HOW FREE IS FREE?

"Yes, yes, we are ignorant. We know it. I am ignorant for one, and they say all niggers is. They say we don't know what the word constitution means. But if we don't know enough to know what the Constitution is, we know enough to know what Justice is. I can see for myself down at my own court-house. If they makes a white man pay five dollars for doing something today, and makes a nigger pay ten dollars for doing that thing tomorrow, don't I know that ain't justice? They've got a figure of a woman with a sword hung up thar, sir; Mr. President, I don't know what you call it—["Justice," "Justice," several delegates shouted]—well, she's got a handkercher over her eyes, and the sword is in one hand and a pair o' scales in the other. When a white man and a nigger gets into the scales, don't I know the nigger is always mighty light? Don't we all see it? Ain't it so at your court-house, Mr. President?" (Delegate to a freedmen's convention, Raleigh, North Carolina, 1865)

Source: John R. Dennett, *The South As It Is, 1865–1866*, ed. Henry M. Christman (New York: Viking, 1965), pp. 150–51. Illustration from the Library of Congress.

ing so betrayed their own people. And the misled ex-slaves, as Woodrow Wilson would later write of them, had been nothing more than "a host of dusky children untimely put out of school."

Like most stereotypes, this picture is simplified, distorted, and falsified. The carpetbagger was a northerner who moved to the South after the Civil War and supported or participated in the Radical state governments. His reasons for settling in the South were as varied as his personal character. For some, legitimate business opportunities and the availability of land and natural resources provided the incentive. Others were Union veterans who had found the South an attractive place in which to live. Still others were teachers, clergy, and agents of charitable societies who had com-

AFTER THE WAR: RECONSTRUCTION AND RESTORATION

mitted themselves to the task of educating and converting the ex-slaves. Finally, there were political adventurers, but their actual numbers were small. To the white South, however, the fact that some carpetbaggers aided black voting and officeholding was enough to make them all guilty by association.

Like the carpetbaggers, the scalawags—native white Republicans who supported Radical rule—were a varied lot. In no state were they a majority of southern whites. They were not necessarily poor whites, nor did they all welcome or support black participation in political life. To those who had been Whigs before the war, the Republican party appeared to offer the best hope for promoting the industrial and economic interests of a new South. To those who had been against secession, the Radical program was a way to neutralize the dominant planters and a chance at political power. And some felt it important to participate in order to retain some control.

But whatever their individual motives, the scalawags faced ostracism in their communities. Some found it impossible to withstand the pressure, and few had any enthusiasm for racial equality. When blacks demanded a more substantial share of political power, many whites deserted the party.

Although carpetbaggers and scalawags aroused white hatred, black voters and officeholders symbolized the changes in postwar southern society far more dramatically. To find black men, many of them only recently slaves, now voting and holding public office was a change so drastic and so fearful in its implications that few white southerners could accept it.

Even a northern newspaperman, a Republican who had opposed slavery, expressed his shock at the sight of the South Carolina legislature:

The Speaker is black, the Clerk is black, the doorkeepers are black, the little pages are black, the chairman of the Ways and Means is black, and the chaplain is coal-black. At some of the desks sit colored men whose types it would be hard to find outside of Congo. . . . It is the dregs of the population habilitated in the robes of their intelligent predecessors. . . . It is barbarism overwhelming civilization by physical force. It is the slave rioting in the halls of his master.

No matter how competently carpetbaggers, scalawags, and blacks might have carried out their political responsibilities, they would have been denounced by a majority of white southerners. Their very presence in the government and their commitment to black voting and officeholding was enough to condemn them, and their successes were in many ways more threatening to whites than their failures.

Radical Rule in the South

Although blacks voted in large numbers, they did not in fact dominate any of the southern states. At the beginning of Radical Reconstruction, of the 1,350,000 citizens qualified to vote in the ex-

THE FIRST VOTE

"Mr. Judge [a northern visitor], we always knows who's our friends and who isn't. We knows the difference between the Union ticket and the Rebel ticket. We may not know all about all the men that's on it; but we knows the difference between the Union and the Rebel parties. Yes sir; we knows that much better than you do! Because, sir, some of our people stand behind these men at the table, and hear 'em talk; we see 'em in the house and by the wayside; and we know 'em from skin to core, better than you do or can do, till you live among 'em as long, and see as much of 'em as we have." (A black preacher in Georgia)

Source: Whitelaw Reid, *After the War: A Southern Tour, May 1, 1865, to May 1, 1866* (Cincinnati, 1866), p. 144. Illustration from The Granger Collection.

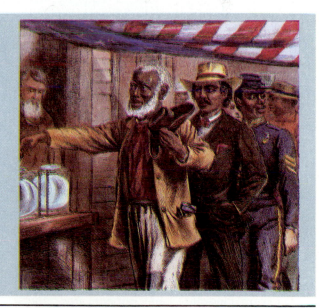

H. R. Revels of Mississippi, the first black senator in the United States, was elected to Jefferson Davis's seat in 1870 (seated at far left). The first black representatives in the Forty-first and Forty-second Congresses were: (seated) Benjamin S. Turner, Alabama; Josiah T. Walls, Florida; Joseph H. Rainey and Robert Brown Elliott, South Carolina; (standing) Robert C. Delarge, South Carolina; and Jefferson H. Long, Georgia. (*The Granger Collection*)

Confederate states, about half were black. In Alabama, Florida, Louisiana, Mississippi, and South Carolina, black voters were a majority. Only in South Carolina, however, did black legislators outnumber whites, 88 to 67. In other state legislatures, blacks made up sizable minorities. But in no state did blacks control the executive mansion.

There were black lieutenant governors, secretaries of state, state treasurers, speakers of the house, and superintendents of education. Fourteen blacks were elected to the United States House of Representatives between 1869 and 1877, and two (Hiram Revels and Blanche K. Bruce of Mississippi) to the United States Senate. The majority of black officeholders had local positions, like justice of the peace, sheriff, and county supervisor, which were important at a time of much local decision-making.

Most were young men, generally in their twenties and thirties at the outset of Reconstruction. Some were illiterate, some self-educated, and a few were graduates of northern colleges. Many were ministers, teachers, artisans, and farmers who had managed to accumulate small landholdings. Before the war, a number of them had been members of the free black class in the South. Still others had resided in the North, either northern-born or self-imposed "exiles" from their homeland. Most impressive, however, were those who had only recently been slaves. The skills they had gained from learning how to survive as slaves may explain why many of them proved to be successful politicians.

Under Radical rule, both races made political and social advances in the South. Many of the gains grew out of the new state constitutions, written by conventions in which blacks and whites participated. These constitutions eliminated property qualifications for voting and holding office among whites as well as blacks. They apportioned representation in state legislatures and in Congress more fairly. Judicial systems were revised, and juries were opened to blacks. Imprisonment

Robert Smalls (left), South Carolina legislator and U.S. Congressman and John R. Lynch (right), Speaker of the Mississippi House of Representatives and U.S. Congressman. (*Library of Congress*)

for debt was abolished, along with other archaic social legislation. Above all, for the first time in many southern states, the constitutions provided for public schools for whites and blacks.

Next to giving blacks the vote, nothing offended the white South more than Radical efforts to give blacks schooling at public expense. Even the segregation of black and white pupils did not satisfy critics. It had long been an article of faith among white southerners that education spoiled blacks as laborers, developing in them wants that could never be satisfied and expectations that could

P.B.S. Pinchback (left), president *pro tempore* of the Louisiana State Senate and an acting governor and Blanche K. Bruce (right), assessor and sheriff of Bolivar County, Mississippi, elected in 1874 to the U.S. Senate. (*Library of Congress*)

never be realized. Invariably, then, an educated black person could be expected to be discontented, frustrated, and troublesome. That was reason enough for whites to burn black schools and to threaten and harass teachers and students. Yet blacks persisted in their quest for education, and by 1877 southern schools enrolled 600,000 blacks.

Several colleges and universities, including Fisk, Howard, Atlanta, and the Hampton Institute in Virginia, had been established by the Freedmen's Bureau and northern philanthropic agencies. Night schools for adults flourished. But despite the commitment of the Radical governments to education, the financial resources of the states were often not sufficient to support a dual school system. Only the private efforts of various northern groups, such as the American Missionary Association, enabled many blacks to obtain an education.

The Radical governments displayed restraint and caution when dealing with economic matters. Even black legislators refused to interfere with the rights of private property, though land ownership remained the principal goal of their black constituents. Rather than experiment with land redistribution, most black leaders urged the familiar mid-nineteenth-century self-help creed: be thrifty and industrious and buy property. What black people needed, they argued, was simply legal equality. "Let the laws of the country be just," a South Carolina black leader declared, "that is all we ask. Place all citizens upon one broad platform; and if the Negro is not qualified to hoe his row in this contest of life, then let him go down."

Black sharecroppers and tenants knew only too well, however, that legal equality and the vote could not feed hungry mouths or end economic hardship. They needed land of their own and the means to farm that land. But neither the Radical legislatures nor Congress, although liberally giving funds and grants to railroads, were willing to make that kind of commitment to ex-slaves—even as a token payment for years of unpaid labor.

The black officeholder gained experience in governing during an era in which corruption marked much of American political life. Although corruption in the Radical governments was not as bad as painted, there was enough to tarnish them and to confirm the skepticism in the North about the entire experiment. Between 1868 and 1874, the bonded debt of the eleven ex-Confederate states grew by over $100 million. This enormous sum was not itself evidence of corruption. To raise money, the southern states had to sell bonds in the North, where southern credit was so poor that

investors often demanded a 75 percent discount from a bond's face value. Thus, for every $100 worth of bonds sold, a southern state might actually realize only $25.

Many of the social and humanitarian reforms of the reconstruction legislatures were costly, as was the relief extended to the starving and homeless of both races. Taxes to pay for such expenditures, including new "luxuries" like public schools, fell heavily on the planters, who before the war had been able to pass taxes on to other groups.

Still, much of the debt was incurred corruptly, though carpetbaggers, scalawags, and blacks were not necessarily the principal beneficiaries. Like the rest of the nation, the South suffered at the hands of railroad interests, business speculators, and contractors who sought legislative favors and were willing to pay for them. Corruption in the South, as elsewhere, tended to be bipartisan, involving men of both races and all classes, including some of the most distinguished names of the South. It had been underway before Radical rule, and it lasted long after the overthrow of Reconstruction.

A black legislator might quickly learn from white colleagues of both parties that payoffs were a natural part of the political process and often a necessary supplement to an otherwise meager income. After accepting a bribe, one black legislator, an ex-slave, offered this moral perspective: "I've been sold in my life eleven times. And this is the first time I ever got the money." For most black leaders, however, political participation entailed personal sacrifice rather than financial gain. Henry Johnson of South Carolina, for example, was a former slave, a bricklayer and plasterer by trade, and active in Republican politics. "I always had plenty of work before I went into politics," he noted, "but I have never got a job since. I suppose they do it merely because they think they will break me down and keep me from interfering with politics." Jefferson Long, a Macon tailor elected to Congress, found that his political position "ruined his business with the whites who had been his patrons chiefly." But black leaders faced more serious dangers than the loss of business—and that was the loss of their lives.

The ability of black officeholders varied considerably; most important, blacks were learning the uses of political power and gaining confidence in their ability to rule. As they did, and as they began to demand political power on a par with their electoral strength, the shaky alliance on which Radical rule rested began to fall apart. When blacks made startling gains in Mississippi and South

Carolina in the early 1870s, for example, they vividly demonstrated their new independence and self-confidence. At the same time, they may have sealed their own doom.

The idea of black success, independence, and power drove numerous whites out of the party, accelerated internal divisions, and gave the Democrats the opportunity for which they had carefully prepared. If anything about "black reconstruction" truly alarmed the white South, it was not so much the evidence of corruption, but the very real possibility that this unique experiment in biracial government might succeed! As W. E. B. DuBois wrote: "There was one thing that the white South feared more than negro dishonesty, ignorance, and incompetency, and that was negro honesty, knowledge, and efficiency."

The End of Reconstruction: The Shotgun Policy

From the beginning of Radical rule, before any evidence of corruption had come to light, the white South was determined to use every method at its disposal to restore the rightful heirs of political power—the "natural leaders"—to the positions they deserved. Nothing less was at stake than the survival of Anglo-Saxon civilization: "If the negro is fit to make laws for the control of our conduct and property," a southern educator warned, "he is certainly fit to eat with us at our tables, to sleep in our beds, to be invited into our parlors, and to do all acts and things which a white man may do."

To overthrow Radical rule and the black vote on which it rested, thousands of even the most respectable people in the South banded together in the Ku Klux Klan, the Knights of the White Camellia, and other secret groups. Between 1867 and 1879, hooded or otherwise disguised, they roamed the land, shot, flogged, and terrorized blacks and their supporters, burned homes and public buildings, and assaulted Reconstruction officials. To suppress this violence, Congress responded with the Force Act of 1870 and the Ku Klux Klan Act of 1871. These laws imposed heavy fines and jail sentences for offenses under the Fourteenth and Fifteenth amendments and gave Republican-controlled federal courts, rather than southern state courts, jurisdiction in all cases arising under the amendments or out of conspiracies or terrorism against freedmen. The president was empowered to suspend habeas corpus in any terrorized community, to declare martial law, and to send troops to maintain order. In October 1871, President Grant invoked that authority in nine South Carolina counties where the Klan was especially active.

Reconstruction

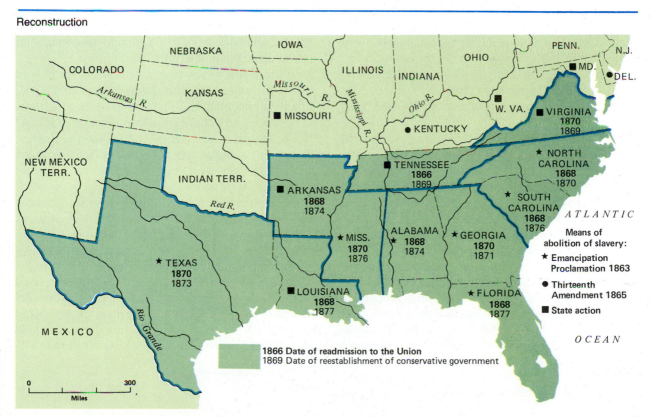

Means of abolition of slavery:
★ Emancipation Proclamation 1863
● Thirteenth Amendment 1865
■ State action

1866 Date of readmission to the Union
1869 Date of reestablishment of conservative government

Federal intervention in South Carolina marked the peak of forceful repression of southern violence. Except for the passage of the Civil Rights Act of 1875—a seldom-enforced law that guaranteed blacks equal access to public accommodations—the Republican party began to retreat from its commitment to civil rights and black voting. In May 1872 Congress passed an Amnesty Act that restored voting and officeholding privileges to all white southerners except a few hundred of the highest Confederate dignitaries. In that same year, the Freedmen's Bureau was permitted to expire. By 1877 white terrorism, economic coercion, federal indifference, and factionalism in the Radical governments brought Radical Reconstruction to an end.

The Mississippi Plan (sometimes called the "shotgun policy"), by which Democrats regained power in that state in 1875, proved to be a model of repression. It consisted of organized violence and threats, the systematic breakup of Republican gatherings, and the incitement of riots. Its aim was to force all whites into the Democratic party, and at the same time to eliminate black leadership and political participation. "Carry the election peaceably if we can, forcibly if we must," was the way one newspaper described the objective.

In communities where blacks were a majority or nearly so, the plan was carried out with full white support. Where persuasion failed, violence and terrorism were used by well-armed paramilitary units called Rifle Clubs, White Leagues, or Red Shirts. White Republicans who resisted were driven from their homes and their communities. Defiant black sharecroppers were denied credit by southern merchants; they were evicted from the land, denied other employment, assaulted, and murdered.

Even when the governor of Mississippi appealed to President Grant for assistance, claiming he had exhausted all local resources, the president refused to call upon the army to support troubled Republican regimes. Encouraged by Grant's turnabout, southern leaders in states still under Radical rule became more determined than ever to "redeem" their states through their own efforts.

The federal government's refusal to act reflected the North's growing disillusion with the reconstruction experiment. Northern whites were busy with their own economic problems. Traditional racist views persisted, and neither northern whites nor the Republicans were prepared to undertake the massive intervention and federal force necessary to sustain this unique experiment in biracial government. Northern businessmen concluded that only southern Democrats could establish the kind of stability necessary for economic advancement and investment. Alarmed over the persistent turmoil and unwilling to use federal power to sustain the reconstruction governments, northerners chose to permit the white South to work out its own solution to "the race problem."

The white southern response to Reconstruction is hardly surprising. Even honest and capable carpetbaggers came to symbolize alien rule, and even if corruption was fashionable, Radical corruption was not. Most important, if the black man were to succeed, he would no longer be content with a lower place in southern society. That was a difficult proposition for whites to accept.

While maintaining that blacks were incapable of becoming their political, social, or economic equals, many whites simultaneously betrayed the fear that they might. The black person as a buffoon, as a menial, as a servant was perfectly acceptable; indeed, many whites assumed that irresponsibility, ignorance, and submissiveness were characteristic black traits. Consequently, those blacks who failed to fit the stereotype seemed somehow abnormal, even dangerous. "The Negro as a poor ignorant creature," Frederick Douglass observed, "does not contradict the race pride of the white race. He is more a source of amusement to that race than an object of resentment. . . . It is only when he acquires education, property, and influence, only when he attempts to rise and be a man among men that he invites repression." For blacks who aspired to improve themselves, this posed an obvious dilemma.

Within ten years, then, Reconstruction was over. Although the Fourteenth and Fifteenth amendments eventually helped to make a "second reconstruction" possible in the 1950s and 1960s, that may not be enough to judge Radical Reconstruction a success. But what blacks demonstrated in that brief period of time, even if imperfectly, has too often been ignored. Despite their shortcomings, inexperience, and failure to resolve the most pressing problems of their people, black leaders exercised political responsibility with reasonable competence and gave every indication of learning from their errors. This achievement and the potential it suggested prompted W.E.B. DuBois to write in *Black Reconstruction* (1935): "The attempt to make black men American citizens was in a certain sense all a failure, but a splendid failure. It did not fail where it was expected to fail."*

---

* W. E. B. DuBois, *Black Reconstruction in America, 1860–1880* (New York: Russell & Russell, 1956). Copyright 1962, 1935 by W. E. B. DuBois.

The tragedy of Radical Reconstruction is that it failed to reconstruct southern white racial attitudes. From the very outset, this unique experiment in biracial government rested on a weak base. The commitment of the federal government was limited, and even Republicans did not seek any long-term federal intervention in southern affairs. The commitment of blacks was limited by their economic weakness and dependence. If many of them chose to withdraw from political activism altogether, it reflected not only white intimidation, but the recognition that politics had not significantly altered the quality of their day-to-day lives.

The end of Reconstruction solidified the triumph of white supremacy in the South. For blacks, the expectations raised by emancipation remained unfulfilled, and the range of choices open to them had been narrowed considerably. There was no way to assimilate, nor was there any way to separate.

THE GRANT PRESIDENCY

When Ulysses S. Grant became president in 1869, the American people expected him to exercise the same qualities of leadership he had shown in the Civil War. He would, many believed, organize a strong government, staffed by able aides, much as he had mobilized a victorious army. But the prob-

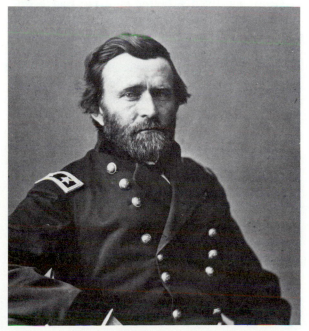

Ulysses S. Grant: the military hero as President. (*Library of Congress*)

lems Grant faced as president—turmoil in the South, the tariff, falling farm prices, and business speculation—were of a far different kind from those he had confronted on the battlefield.

He entered the White House with no political experience and few political convictions; he expected Congress to represent the will of the people and to act on that basis. A failure in business, Grant admired those who had succeeded, accepted their gracious hospitality, and tried to satisfy their needs. Moving in circles far different from those he had known, he turned for advice to people with whom he felt most comfortable. The White House staff—his "kitchen cabinet"—consisted largely of wartime friends. The regular cabinet, with few exceptions, was made up of obscure men.

The First Term: The Great Barbecue

Although personally honest, Grant permitted himself and his office to be used by self-seeking politicians and businessmen. He found it difficult to believe that many of those who befriended him were interested only in personal profit. During his administration, his secretary of war, his private secretary, and officials in the treasury and navy departments used their positions and influence to enhance their incomes. Even as a disbelieving Grant learned of the scandals, he seemed more disturbed by those who made the charges than by the revelations themselves.

Grant, no doubt, was victimized by men whose honesty and loyalty he had never thought to question. If he appointed some of his wealthy friends to cabinet posts, he did so in the conviction that these men had operated in the national interest. Many had made fortunes on war contracts, but in Grant's eyes they had also contributed to winning the war. Some of them were now sustaining the postwar boom. Positions in government were simply a recognition of their achievement and patriotism. To those who expressed alarm over the scandals, moreover, Grant could reply that he had inherited a government already far gone in corruption. The competition for war contracts and the battles for other wartime legislation covering protective tariffs, land grants, and the money system had made lobbying a full-time occupation. After the war, lobbyists often prowled the floor of House and Senate to keep their legislators in line.

Few political plums were more valuable than the tariff, which by 1870 had added to the profits of eastern manufacturing and industrial interests. But railroads also shared handsomely in congressional handouts. The last federal land grant for railroad building was made in 1871. By that time, the total distributed to the roads directly or through the states came to 160 million acres, valued conservatively at $335 million. The railroads also received lavish government loans. Each year after the Union Pacific and Central Pacific Railroads obtained their loans, Congress debated legislation that would have provided for repayment. But the railroad owners fought these measures stubbornly and successfully, often distributing company shares among the legislators "where they will do us the most good."

The Union Pacific, for example, was built by the Crédit Mobilier of America, a construction company owned largely by Union Pacific promoters. By awarding themselves large contracts on the most favorable terms, these men were able to realize huge profits. Faced with a congressional inquiry in 1868, the company directors, through Massachusetts Congressman Oakes Ames, himself a stockholder in both companies, distributed stock among key members of Congress and government officials. The scandal destroyed some political reputations, including that of Vice-President Schuyler Colfax, but only Representative Ames was censured.

Northern financiers also joined in the Great Barbecue, as Grant's regime has been called. In March 1869, fulfilling campaign promises made the year before, both houses of Congress adopted a resolution pledging the government to redeem the entire war debt in gold or in new gold bonds. This pledge, and the laws soon passed to carry it out, sent the value of war bonds soaring and brought substantial profits to speculators. These laws were also good for the government's credit. Forced during the war to offer interest as high as 6 percent, the victorious national government was soon able to borrow for as little as 2.5 percent.

Grant's Second Term: Disenchantment

In the 1872 presidential campaign, Carl Schurz of Missouri, alienated by Grant's appointments and policies, led the Liberal Republican movement. With a platform stressing civil service reform, the Liberals tried to attract candidates of "superior intelligence and superior virtue." Unfortunately, they were joined by victims of the Radical grafters, political hacks who had lost patronage, and others who were out for revenge. Many northern Democrats also joined the movement, hoping to get rid of the treasonous label of their party and win back power.

At the Liberal convention, the differences among them forced the delegates to name a less than inspiring compromise candidate, Horace Greeley, editor for more than thirty years of the *New York Tribune*. The Democrats, seeking to regain national power, gave their support to Greeley. But Grant easily won reelection, carrying all but six states.

The Democrats' hopes were by no means shattered. The scandals of the Grant administration increased public disillusion with the Republican party and those who profited by its corrupt dealings and control of patronage. The first major Grant scandal, the Crédit Mobilier affair, broke while the 1872 campaign was in progress. After the business crash of 1873, each new revelation struck with added force; and once the Democrats captured the House in 1874, the revelations and prosecutions snowballed.

Two scandals hit Grant personally. One was the uncovering of the Whiskey Ring in St. Louis, which had defrauded the government of millions of dollars in internal revenue charges. Deeply involved in this, as in other frauds, was Grant's secretary, Orville Babcock, whom the president saved from imprisonment only by interfering in his trial. The second affair led to the impeachment of Grant's third secretary of war, W. W. Belknap, who since his appointment in 1870 had been "kept" by traders in the Indian Territory under his jurisdiction. When his impeachment appeared imminent, Belknap offered his resignation to the president. Grant, with characteristic loyalty, accepted "with great regret."

Grant deserved a better fate. He had been a great military leader. But he showed little aptitude for the complex machinery of government, politics, and party. His personal honesty, trust, and naiveté made him an easy victim of interests that even the wisest politician found difficult to control. "It was the age of the audacious confidence man," Edmund Wilson has written, "and Grant was the incurable sucker. He easily fell victim to their trickery and allowed them to betray him into compromising his office because he could not believe that such people existed."

The Election of 1876: Hayes

As convention time approached in 1876, Democrats were making an issue of corruption, and Republicans were deeply divided on the best way to answer them. The Grand Old Party, as Republicans were calling themselves, separated into Stal-

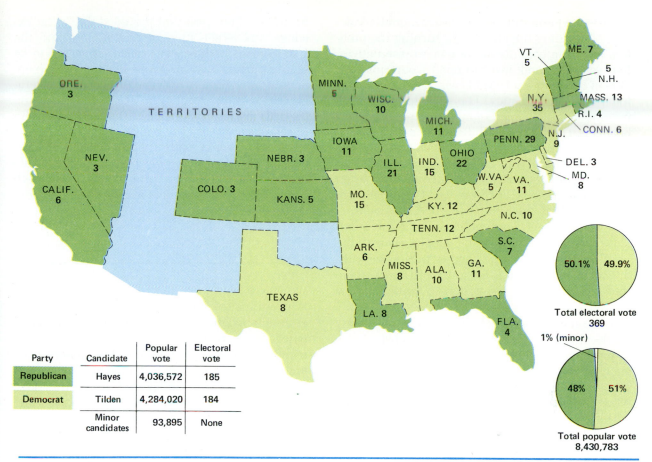

Party	Candidate	Popular vote	Electoral vote
Republican	Hayes	4,036,572	185
Democrat	Tilden	4,284,020	184
	Minor candidates	93,895	None

Total electoral vote
369
50.1% 49.9%

1% (minor)
Total popular vote
8,430,783
48% 51%

The Election of 1876

warts and Halfbreeds. Stalwarts were the hard-core political professionals who put politics first; if business wanted favors, let them pay up. Halfbreeds were Republican reformers who had not deserted to the Liberal Republicans in 1872.

Stalwarts, closest to Grant, wanted him to run for a third term. Halfbreeds lined up behind Congressman James G. Blaine of Maine, despite the dramatic disclosure of his shady relations with the Union Pacific Railroad while serving as Speaker of the House. When the movement to renominate Grant failed to materialize, the nomination went to Rutherford B. Hayes, the reform governor of Ohio.

The Democratic surge in the South, meanwhile, and the vicious repression on which it was based, accented sectional differences in that party on every issue. Hunger for the presidency, long denied them, led the Democrats to close ranks behind Samuel J. Tilden, a rich corporation lawyer and hard money man who had won a national reputation as a reform governor of New York.

The presidential scandals, the severity of the economic depression of the mid-1870s, and the ris-

ing demand for reform all seemed to work to the Democrats' advantage. The campaign they waged stressed the need to end misrule in the South and to weed out corruption in the federal government. On economic issues, little differentiated Tilden from Hayes; both were conservatives who proclaimed their belief in "sound money" and limited government.

First reports of the election results suggested a Democratic victory. Tilden had a plurality of 250,000 votes, and the press proclaimed him the new president. But Republican strategists suddenly awoke to the fact that returns from Louisiana, Florida, and South Carolina, three states still under Radical control, had not yet come in because of election irregularities. Tilden needed only one electoral vote from these states to win; Hayes needed every one. Any accurate count in the disputed states was complicated by the threats and fraud used by Democrats to keep blacks from voting. Both parties claimed to have won. Congress would have to determine which of the double sets of returns from the three states should be accepted, the Democratic count or the Republican.

The two parties agreed to the extraordinary device of deciding the election by turning the problem over to a commission of five representatives, five senators, and five Supreme Court justices. One of the justices, David Davis, presumably was independent in politics. The remaining fourteen members of the commission were equally divided between Democrats and Republicans. Unfortunately for Tilden, Davis quit the commission before it met and was replaced by a Republican justice. The Republican majority of eight then voted unanimously for Hayes. The Compromise of 1877, by which the South conceded Hayes's election, rested largely on Republican assurances that Hayes "would deal justly and generously with the South." That was understood to mean the withdrawal of the remaining federal troops and no more interference in the restoration of white political supremacy.

In his inaugural speech, Hayes spoke out clearly on the need for a permanent federal civil service beyond the reach of politics and patronage. To show that he meant business, he succeeded in getting rid of some of the party faithful from the New York Customs House, although not for long. In his southern strategy, Hayes chose David M. Key of Tennessee, a high-ranking former Confederate officer and a Democrat, as Postmaster General. By the end of April 1877 he had withdrawn the last federal troops from the South; with their departure, the last Radical state governments collapsed.

That autumn he set forth on a goodwill tour of the South. He was joined by former Confederate General Wade Hampton, just elected governor of South Carolina by the "straight-out" Democrats, chiefly by suppressing the black vote. At an enthusiastic meeting in Atlanta, Hayes assured the blacks in the audience that their "rights and interests would be safer if this great mass of intelligent white men were let alone by the general government." On his return to Washington, the president observed of his journey: "Received everywhere heartily. The country is again one and united."

The real losers in the election of 1876 were not the Democrats, but black southerners. With the withdrawal of federal troops and the continuing threats and acts of violence, the remaining Radical governments quickly collapsed. Between 1879 and 1881, however, nearly 50,000 blacks, mostly from rural Texas, Louisiana, Mississippi, and Tennessee, left for Kansas, another 5,000 for Iowa and

Nebraska. The spirit that pervaded the "great exodus" was largely that of desperation, and the Exodusters, as they were called, appeared to be more refugees than migrants, fleeing from an oppression and violence that had become intolerable. A newspaper reporter in Mississippi, observing the daily departures, described families "who seem to think anywhere is better than here." The Exodusters voted with their feet, but another quarter of a century would pass before that vote became overwhelming. Until the early twentieth century, some 90 percent of black Americans spent their whole lives in the South.

THE NEW SOUTH

With the collapse of the remaining Radical governments, politics in the South came to be dominated by a new class of men—industrialists, merchants, bankers, and railroad promoters. Calling themselves Redeemers, for having "redeemed" their states from "carpetbag rule," they envisioned a New South devoted to material progress and based on the profitable use of the region's natural resources and abundant labor supply. The old planter class found its prewar power diminished; the heavy voting strength it commanded in the rural sections, however, particularly the Black Belt, enabled it to exert considerable influence. These two classes were generally able to resolve their differences, ruling by coalition if necessary, and thus maintaining the supremacy of their values.

The new state governments set out to cut spending. The principal victims were the public schools and other state-supported services left over from the Radical years. But the same governments that cut taxes and made a virtue of economy proved to be most generous in their encouragement of economic enterprises, bestowing on them liberal charters and tax exemptions. Corruption was no less widespread under the Redeemer governments than under the previous Radical regimes, but somehow it seemed less offensive when committed by whites.

Although blacks continued to vote, they were able to exert little if any political influence. The race relations of the New South were based on the suppression of black hopes—political, economic, and social. Not even the occasional challenges to Redeemer rule altered that fact of southern life.

LABOR RELATIONS IN THE NEW SOUTH

In my condition, and the way I see it for everybody, if you don't make enough to have some left you ain't done nothin, except given the other fellow your labor. . . . Now it's right for me to pay you for usin' what's yours—your land, stock, plow tools, fertilizer. But how much should I pay? The answer ought to be closely seeked. How much is a man due to pay out? Half his crop? A third part of his crop? And how much is he due to keep for hisself? You got a right to your part—rent; and I got a right to mine. But who's the man ought to decide how much? The one that owns the property or the one that works it? (Ned Cobb, black cotton farmer, born in Alabama in 1885).

Source: Theodore Rosengarten, *All God's Dangers: The Life of Nate Shaw* (New York: Knopf, 1974), p. 108. Photograph courtesy of the Cook Collection, Valentine Museum, Richmond.

For most blacks, politics became less important in their daily lives. The need to survive—to grow a crop and to pay their debts—took precedence over a politics that offered them no real choices.

The Economics of Dependency: Agriculture

Even before the overthrow of Radical rule in the South, blacks were economically dependent on whites. Radicals had tried to reconstruct the Union by giving the ex-slaves the vote, but political priv-ileges were not backed by economic gains. During their brief hours of joy over freedom, many ex-slaves had talked about owning land and living like "white folks." With few exceptions, however, it never worked out that way. As one former slave recalled:

We thought we was going to be richer than the white folks, 'cause we was stronger and knowed how to work, and the whites didn't, and they didn't have us to work for them any more. But it didn't turn out that way. We soon found out that freedom could make folks proud, but it didn't make 'em rich.

If there was any consolation for the blacks, it would have to be the knowledge that many whites were far from being as independent as they seemed. Before the war, most large southern plantations had been heavily mortgaged. Afterward, hard-pressed creditors began demanding payment of interest and principal. Some southern planters sold off part of their land in order to finance cultivation of the rest. Others leased acreage for money rents. But obviously there was not money enough available to keep this up very long. The result was a repeat of the familiar routine of the prewar South: Planters paid no wages for labor, and their workers paid no rent for land. Instead, each was to share in the forthcoming crop.

In order to get this crop into the ground, both parties had to borrow. Since they had no other security, they had to borrow against the crop they hoped to produce. Only then would the merchants advance the required seed, fertilizer, and equipment, as well as food and clothing. For his own stock, the local merchant had to seek credit from northern suppliers. Risks in the South were so great that these suppliers demanded high prices for the goods and high interest for credit. In addition, oppressive fees were charged for transportation, insurance, and other commercial services. The merchant passed all these charges on to the landlords and sharecroppers. The merchant also added his own profit, and perhaps took a little more to reward himself for his literacy, at the expense of borrowers who could not read his account books. The South became more firmly chained to northern creditors, while the sharecropper was enslaved to the merchant.

The South drifted more and more deeply into sharecropping and crop debts because they offered a solution to the problems of labor and capital. Immediately after the war, many planters had tried to hold on to their newly freed workers by offering them cash wages. A typical contract stipulated that the planter pay wages of $10 to $12 a month, less the cost, determined by the planter, of "quarters, fuel, healthy and substantial rations." In exchange, the freedman agreed to labor faithfully "in the usual way before the War." The wage system failed because there was too little money. Few laborers received the pay they had been promised, and the freedman found little reason to trust his former master.

Sharecropping gradually stabilized labor relations in the cash-poor South. It also helped preserve the plantation system. The plantation was divided into small plots, which the landowner rented to blacks. In the typical arrangement, the freedman agreed to pay a share of the forthcoming crop, usually one-third, for use of the land, and still another share, again about one-third, for the necessary tools, seed, and work animals. To the ex-slave, once he realized the government was not about to grant him any land, sharecropping seemed better than working in gangs under an overseer or foreman.

But if sharecropping seemed to give blacks some kind of economic independence and the hope of eventually buying the land on which they worked, the financial realities of the postwar South soon turned the arrangement into a form of economic bondage. The sharecropper had to borrow continually on future crops to pay his debts to the planter and supply merchant. He was caught in a web of debt from which there was seldom any escape. Under the sharecropping system, moreover, with its emphasis on the single cash crop, overproduction soon caused cotton prices to fall.

If black southerners sensed an unfairness in their economic lives, it rested in the perception that they worked largely to enrich others—an all too familiar pattern.

The old bee makes de honey-comb
The young bee makes de honey.
Colored folks plant de cotton and corn
And de white folks gits de money.

The devastation of the war also caught up with the small white farmer. He too needed credit from the local merchants to get his land back into production and his home and barns repaired. And as in the case of the sharecroppers, the merchants dictated that the whites grow little but cotton. At first, the white farmer might give the merchant a lien on forthcoming crops. As debts mounted, the merchant demanded a mortgage on the land as well. And as the cotton market deteriorated, the merchant foreclosed. Some white farmers managed to beat the trend and became substantial landowners, even merchants. But by the 1880s, most of them had gone under and become sharecroppers or were left with the poorest land.

The Economics of Dependency: Industry

After the white South had been "redeemed," many people expected it to share in the type of industrialization that was booming in the North. To

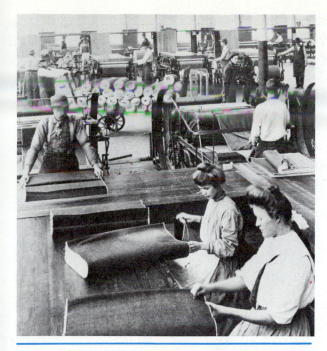
Workers in a North Carolina cotton mill, 1895. (*Brown Brothers*)

achieve self-respect as a region, some argued, the South would need to demonstrate material and financial strength. The idea of a New South was based on industrial development like that of the North, with comparable business institutions and captains of industry, and an end to the dependency that had until now characterized North-South relationships.

The movement to create a New South through industry became a crusade. After 1880, white professionals and retired generals and colonels gave their names and reputations, their energy and their capital, to the mission. The textile industry, already restored, continued to grow rapidly. During the depression of the mid-1880s, southern iron began to compete successfully with Pittsburgh's. The North Carolina tobacco industry responded to the new fad of cigarette smoking, and a bit later the cottonseed-oil industry spurted upward.

Another and more important goal of the crusade was to draw northern capital southward. It was to this goal that Henry Grady, publisher of the powerful *Atlanta Constitution,* gave most attention. Invading the North to recruit capital, Grady told a New York audience: "We have sowed towns and cities in the place of theories, and put busi-

ness in place of politics. We have challenged your spinners in Massachusetts and your ironmakers in Pennsylvania. . . . We have fallen in love with work."

In the 1880s, northern capital had good reason to look hopefully to the South. The availability of natural resources and abundant water power should have been enough. But there was more: the promise of low taxes, legislative favors, and a cheap labor force said to be immune to trade unions and strikes. As late as 1900, however, the so-called industrialized New South actually produced a smaller proportion of American manufactures than did the Old South in 1860. Fewer than 4 percent of the people in the important textile state of South Carolina were engaged in manufacturing, while 70 pecent remained in agriculture. The ratios in the rest of the South were the same. Where new industries had established themselves, they had done so largely as branches of northern-owned enterprises.

The social price exacted from the southern people proved to be considerable. In the vision of the New South, black laborers would "keep their place," growing staples in the hot sun, while whites found employment in the mills and factories. Industry would redeem the South, and the cotton mills would be the salvation of the poor whites. But when the white farmer gave up his struggle with the land to accept work in the mills, he still found that little had changed. He lived in villages that resembled the old slave quarters. He now owed his allegiance to the company store, the company landlord, and the company church. He labored long hours, rarely saw sunlight or breathed fresh air, and fell victim to a variety of diseases. "The harvest was soon at hand," Wilbur Cash writes in *The Mind of the South.*

By 1900 the cotton-mill worker was a pretty distinct type in the South. . . . A dead-white skin, a sunken chest, and stooping shoulders were the earmarks of the breed. Chinless faces, microcephalic foreheads, rabbit teeth, goggling dead-fish eyes, rickety limbs, and stunted bodies abounded—over and beyond the limit of their prevalence in the countryside. The women were characteristically stringy-haired and limp of breast at twenty, and shrunken hags at thirty or forty.

The wages paid to adult male workers varied from 40 to 50 cents a day; women and children worked for still lower pay to supplement a meager family income. But there was one compensation: The mill villages were the exclusive domain of

THE LEGACY OF THE NEW SOUTH

Unidentified black man around 1890s. (*Library of Congress*)

whites. And that, said the industrial promoters, lent dignity to their labor. For whites, moreover, the consciousness of race superiority assumed even greater importance and intensity in the late nineteenth century as the South moved systematically to repress the last vestiges of civil rights.

A Closed Society: Disfranchisement, Jim Crow, and Repression

Although Radical Reconstruction ended in 1877 and white violence at the polls persisted, black voting had not been altogether eliminated. Most blacks remained loyal to the Republicans. Redeemers or Conservatives—as southern Democrats often called themselves—became adept in some regions at making political arrangements with local black leaders whenever black votes were needed to win local elections.

Any time the black vote posed a threat, reviving the specter of "Negro domination," whites returned to the tactics of repression, ranging from crude election frauds to threats of loss of land, credit, or jobs. These same tactics might also be employed by the ruling Conservative regimes to thwart the challenge of white independents.

Forced to make political choices that had little or nothing to do with their immediate needs and problems, growing numbers of blacks withdrew from politics altogether or permitted their votes to be bought. What difference did it make who carried the election? "This is a white man's country and government," said one disillusioned black, "and he is proving it North, South, East, and West, democrats and republicans. For my part, I am tired of both parties; the Negro's back is sleek where they have rode him so much."

Despite their traditional allegiance to the Republicans as "the party of emancipation," some blacks were critical of the minimal role they were permitted to play in party affairs and the party's failure to represent the needs of common people. "The colored people are consumers," the chairman of a black meeting in Richmond declared. "The Republicans have deserted them and undertaken to protect the capitalist and manufacturer of the North."

In the late 1880s and early 1890s, agricultural hard times prompted discontented staple farmers to organize in the Populist movement. In some states, it even seemed possible that depressed white and black farmers might be able to challenge the entrenched Conservative regimes. Populist leaders like Thomas E. Watson of Georgia preached cooperation among small farmers and sharecroppers, on the grounds that their economic grievances crossed racial lines. He asked them to recognize their common plight and to subordinate race consciousness to class consciousness. At the same time, Watson made it clear that he did not believe in race mixing, nor would he tolerate "Negro domination." But why should white supremacy be jeopardized by simply telling the black sharecropper that he was "in the same boat as the white tenant; the colored laborer with the white laborer. . . . Why cannot the cause of one be made the cause of both?"

In several states, the Populists openly courted the black vote, entered into political coalitions with blacks, and named some blacks to party posts. But the degree of Populist commitment varied considerably. Many Populists refused to compromise on white supremacy, and the blacks themselves remained skeptical about the motives of white farmers who had been their traditional enemies. Only in North Carolina were the Populists able, by joining with the Republicans, to defeat the Conservative Democrats. The triumph proved to be short-lived, however. The Democratic return to power was followed by the Wilmington race riot of 1898, and by 1900 the Populists were ready to accept a constitutional amendment eliminating black participation in politics. When Populists succumbed to the rampant racism of this period, they often did so with frightening enthusiasm. Few would be more virulent than Tom Watson himself, who would write of the "hideous, ominous, national menace" of black domination, advocate depriving blacks of the vote, and condone lynching.

Between 1890 and 1915, the white South moved to disfranchise blacks. The issue was not black political power, which no longer posed a serious threat, but how to reconcile racial coexistence with white supremacy. This took on additional urgency as a new generation of blacks who had never known the discipline of slavery reached maturity. In the white southern mind, black political participation remained linked with social equality. If blacks gave up their political aspirations, they would abandon any hope of achieving social equality. And the new generation would learn that there were substantial restraints on their freedom and clear limits to their ambitions.

Mississippi had set the pattern in 1890. Some twenty years later, through such devices as the poll tax, residence requirements, and literacy tests, black voting in the South virtually ceased. In Louisiana, for example, as late as 1896, some 130,000 blacks registered to vote; eight years later, only 1,342 did so. Because the new laws "did not on their face discriminate between the races," as they were forbidden to do by the Fifteenth Amendment, the Supreme Court, in the case of *Williams* v. *Mississippi* in 1898, upheld the Mississippi scheme.

WORDS AND NAMES IN AMERICAN HISTORY

Originally, *Jim Crow* was the name of a song and dance done on the stage. During the 1820s, a growing number of white performers began blackening their faces and hands with burnt cork and offering to their audiences, mostly in northern cities, versions of what they fancied to be Negro songs and dances. These were the first blackface minstrel shows. One of these popular entertainers, T. D. Rice, copied a routine he had seen done by a crippled old black man. The song went, along with a deliberately awkward dance: "Weel about and turn about and do jus so; Ebery time I weel about, I jump Jim Crow." The word "crow" probably came from the supposed similarity of the bird's and the black man's color. Soon, however, *Jim Crow* took on a broader and more ominous meaning. It became a shorthand phrase for discrimination against and especially segregation of black people. This latter meaning was first applied to railroad cars in Massachusetts in 1841, where blacks were prohibited from sitting in the same sections with whites. Gradually *Jim Crow* came to include all the ways and places that blacks were excluded from public facilities and confined to separate, inferior accommodations throughout the country. It became, for blacks and even for whites, a code word for the entire system of humiliating racial segregation, in public transportation, in schools, in offices of the federal government, in the armed forces, in private industry, and at restaurants, movie theaters, public toilets, and water fountains. By the 1890s Jim Crow was becoming central to the way of life in the southern states, where it was rapidly becoming more rigidly and universally applied to all public situations where the two races might come in contact.

Various loopholes were provided for prospective white voters, and Democratic registration boards and "discreet" election officials could make certain that the right people qualified. The effect of the new suffrage laws, however, was to reduce white voting, too. Property qualifications were uniformly high. Poll taxes could be a financial barrier, and literacy clauses could be enforced strictly enough to discourage white illiterates from exposing their limitations.

Throughout the South, small Democratic oligarchies or machines maintained control of politics. The occasional challengers who won office by inflating the racial and class hatreds of the poor whites, "rednecks," and "wool hat boys" more often than not ended up constructing their own political machines and serving the same business interests they had challenged.

Where southern custom and etiquette had previously set the races apart, in the 1890s and early 1900s the Jim Crow laws made segregation even more systematic and extensive. Few places where the two races might come into social contact were unaffected. When the Supreme Court in 1883 declared the Civil Rights Act of 1875 unconstitutional, it ruled that the federal government had no jurisdiction over discrimination practiced by private persons or organizations. Later on, the Court sanctioned state segregation laws requiring separate public facilities for whites and blacks. In *Plessy* v. *Ferguson* in 1896, the Court decided that the blacks' equal rights under the Fourteenth Amendment were not violated if the separate facilities on railroads (and by implication, in schools and other public places) were equal. In *Cumming* v. *County Board of Education* in 1899, the Court formally extended the philosophy of "separate but equal" to schools.

Against this background of growing repression, what remained of black leadership in the 1890s found little comfort in any political party—or in politics. Disillusioned with the failure of black expectations, and fearing still more repressive measures, Bishop Henry M. Turner of the African Methodist Episcopal Church, a former black reconstruction leader in Georgia, came to advocate emigration to Africa. Like Marcus Garvey, who would launch his movement in the 1920s, Turner urged his people to think differently about themselves, to cease to despise themselves. Rather than "doing nothing day and night but cry: Glory, honor, dominion and greatness to White," the black man must look to himself, for "a man must believe he is somebody before he is acknowledged to be somebody. . . . Neither [the] Republican nor Democratic party can do for the colored race what [it] can do for [itself]. Respect Black!"

Unlike Garvey, Turner never had a substantial following; nor did he have any illusions about the realization of his African dream. Some day, though, he felt that his people would realize the true nature of their plight in white America. "They are now sullen, despondent and discontented and sooner or later these feelings will lead to trouble. The Southern whites rely upon the strong arm of power to produce submission, but they are resting upon a slumbering volcano, which sooner or later will cause a fearful eruption."

In 1900 that "fearful eruption" was still more than half a century away. The pattern of race relations established in the aftermath of Reconstruction, reinforced by the triumph of Jim Crow and disfranchisement, persisted until the 1950s and 1960s. The concept of a New South proclaimed by industrialists, promoters, and editors had little meaning for the great mass of southerners—white or black. Sunk in poverty, debt, and ignorance, ravaged by diseases of various kinds, many resigned themselves to a dreary and hopeless way of life. The southern white's fear of black domination effectively stifled dissent, class consciousness was subordinated to race consciousness, the Democrats established virtual one-party rule, and race baiting remained a necessary vehicle for every aspiring southern politician. Such was the legacy of the New South.

SUMMARY

The Civil War settled two important questions—secession and slavery—but it raised a great many new ones. What was to happen to the South? How were freed blacks to be treated? And who would decide: the president or Congress?

Lincoln's policy of presidential reconstruction, based

on the idea that the southern states had rebelled and now should be restored to the Union, free again to govern themselves like all other states, was one solution. In Congress, Radical Republicans proposed quite another. They considered the South a conquered territory under the jurisdiction of Congress and wanted to create a new southern society based on the equality of blacks and whites.

The South over which the advocates of these policies contended was a ruined land. Its people, both black and white, lacked food and clothing. Buildings, farms, factories were gone. Blacks had the additional problem of learning to deal with their new freedom. Some left to find a new life, but most stayed where they were. And life was much the same, for defeat had in no way changed the beliefs or attitudes of white southerners.

Presidential reconstruction failed, and not only because of Lincoln's assassination. The new president, Andrew Johnson, believed in white supremacy and followed policies designed to restore the old planter class to power. His liberal pardon policy, plus the sanctioning of black codes to keep the freed slaves from participating in economic and political life, brought northern public opinion and the Radicals in Congress to a boil. The war seemed to have been fought for nothing.

By December 1865, the Radicals began a legislative counterattack. A bill continuing the Freedmen's Bureau was pushed through Congress over Johnson's veto, and the Fourteenth Amendment was introduced in June 1866. When it was finally ratified in July 1868, the question of civil rights was legally settled, even though it would be another century before its provisions would be enforced. The Radical program was written into a series of laws. The First Reconstruction Act was passed over the president's veto in March 1867. It divided the South into five military districts, put each under a general to be named by the president, and directed the generals to call a constitutional convention in each former state. Delegates were to be elected by universal adult male suffrage, black and white, and the conventions were to set up new state governments in which blacks could vote and hold office. Ratification of the Fourteenth Amendment was necessary for readmittance to the Union and acceptance of representatives by Congress.

By 1870, reconstruction under this plan was complete. It was protected by other laws designed to neutralize the Supreme Court and the president. Johnson had survived an attempt to impeach him, but had lost his bid for renomination. In 1868 Ulysses Grant, military hero of the war, had become the new Republican president, thanks in large part to the black vote.

In the South, Radical Reconstruction, with its carpetbaggers and scalawags, brought blacks into government for the first time and gave them valuable experience. But it also brought corruption, white backlash, and repression—fueled by fear that blacks, given education and opportunity, might actually become equal to whites. The "shotgun policy"—terror and violence—brought Radical Reconstruction to an end. By 1877, the federal government had retreated from its commitment to civil rights, and the Republican party in the South was almost destroyed.

The scandals of Grant's presidency had not helped the Republicans. Though a successful general, Grant was a naive and trusting politician and a failure as a businessman. He was reelected in 1872, but the great Crédit Mobilier scandal that broke during the campaign, followed by the crash of 1873 and more revelations of wrongdoing in high places, diminished Republican strength and led to the disputed election of 1876. In return for southern support, the new Republican president, Rutherford B. Hayes, promised to leave the South alone.

The New South that emerged after 1877 was marked by characteristics that have only recently begun to change: white supremacy and repression of blacks; one-party rule; a small and wealthy ruling class holding both blacks and poor whites in economic bondage; and a weak industrial base very much dependent on northern capital.

Suggested Readings

The best introduction to the Reconstruction period is K. M. Stampp, *The Era of Reconstruction 1865–1877* (1965). W. E. B. DuBois, *Black Reconstruction in America 1860–1880* (1935), although ignored by historians when it first appeared, remains a classic by a leading black intellectual. K. M. Stampp and L. F. Litwack (eds.), *Reconstruction* (1969), is a collection of revisionist historical interpretations. D. Sterling (ed.), *The Trouble They Seen* (1976), is a collection of black testimony on Reconstruction. For insights into postwar southern white life and attitudes, see R. M. Myers (ed.), *The Children of Pride* (1971).

W. J. Cash, *The Mind of the South* (1941), and B. Wyatt-Brown, *Southern Honor* (1982), are stimulating studies of ethics and behavior in the Old and New South. H. M. Hyman, *A More Perfect Union* (1973), examines legal and constitutional issues during the Civil War and Reconstruction. For a broad and thoughtful examination of white racial attitudes, North and South, see G. M. Fredrickson, *The Black Image in the White Mind* (1971).

The reaction of the ex-slaves to freedom, in their own words, is exhaustively documented in G. P. Rawick (ed.), *The American Slave: A Composite Autobiography*

(41 vols., 1972–79) and in an ongoing documentary history of emancipation edited by I. Berlin and others, *Freedom* (1982–). The transition from slavery to freedom is described in E. Foner, *Nothing But Freedom* (1983), and in L. F. Litwack, *Been in the Storm So Long* (1979). For regional studies, see B. J. Fields on Maryland, *Slavery and Freedom on the Middle Ground* (1985), and C. L. Mohr on Georgia, *On the Threshold of Freedom* (1986). W. S. McFeely, *Yankee Stepfather: General O. O. Howard and the Freedmen* (1968), is a critical study of the Freedmen's Bureau. J. W. DeForest, *A Union Officer in the Reconstruction* (1948) is the personal account of a Freedmen's Bureau agent.

The evolution of Lincoln's commitment to a planter-dominated Reconstruction is examined in P. McCrary, *Abraham Lincoln and Reconstruction: The Louisiana Experiment* (1978). E. L. McKitrick, *Andrew Johnson and Reconstruction* (1960), is highly critical of Johnson. L. and J. H. Cox, *Politics, Principle and Prejudice 1865–1866* (1963), emphasizes Johnson's racial attitudes and his efforts to restore the Democratic party in the North. D. Carter, *When the War Was Over* (1985), assesses the failure of presidential reconstruction. M. Perman, in *Reunion without Compromise* (1973) and *The Road to Redemption* (1984), examines in depth southern politics after the war.

The Radical Republicans have usually fared badly at the hands of historians. The traditional view is presented in T. H. Williams, *Lincoln and the Radicals* (1941). A sympathetic treatment may be found in H. L. Trefousse, *The Radical Republicans: Lincoln's Vanguard for Racial Justice* (1969). On the economics of Republican rule, see M. W. Summers, *Railroads, Reconstruction, and the Gospel of Prosperity* (1984). J. M. McPherson, in *The Struggle for Equality* (1964) and *The Abolitionist Legacy* (1976), explores the ongoing abolitionist commitment to equal rights. Among the important biographical studies of the Radicals are F. M. Brodie, *Thaddeus Stevens* (1959); D. Donald, *Charles Sumner and the Rights of Man* (1970); and B. P. Thomas and H. M. Hyman, *Stanton* (1962). R. N. Current, *Three Carpetbag Governors* (1967), and O. H. Olsen, *Carpetbaggers' Crusade: The Life of Albion Winegar Tourgee* (1965), examine an equally maligned group.

The best study of Ulysses S. Grant and his presidency is W. S. McFeely, *Grant* (1981). On the abandonment of Radical goals, focusing on the presidents and their southern strategies, see R. W. Logan, *The Negro in American Life and Thought: The Nadir 1877–1901* (1954).

Two pioneers in exploring the neglected black role in Reconstruction were W. E. B. DuBois and A. A. Taylor. More recent state studies with the same focus are V. L. Wharton, *The Negro in Mississippi 1865–1890* (1947); J. Williamson, *After Slavery: The Negro in South Carolina during Reconstruction, 1861–1877* (1965); J. M.

Richardson, *The Negro in the Reconstruction of Florida, 1865–1877* (1965); E. L. Drago, *Black Politicians and Reconstruction in Georgia: A Splendid Failure* (1982); and T. Tunnell, *Crucible of Reconstruction: War, Radicalism and Race in Louisiana 1862–1877* (1984). Two important local studies are W. M. Evans, *Ballots and Fence Rails: Reconstruction on the Lower Cape Fear* (1966), and O. B. Burton, *In My Father's House Are Many Mansions; Family and Community in Edgefield, South Carolina* (1985). Studies of black leadership include T. Holt, *Black over White: Negro Political Leadership in South Carolina during Reconstruction* (1978); J. H. Franklin (ed.), *Reminiscences of an Active Life: The Autobiography of John Roy Lynch* (1970); H. N. Rabinowitz (ed.), *Southern Black Leaders of the Reconstruction Era* (1982); and W. E. Martin, Jr., *The Mind of Frederick Douglass* (1984).

The violent overthrow of Radical rule is described in A. W. Trelease, *White Terror: The Ku Klux Klan Conspiracy and Southern Reconstruction* (1971). The classic study of the post-Reconstruction South remains C. V. Woodward, *Origins of the New South 1877–1913* (1951). The spirit of the New South is examined in P. Gaston, *The New South Creed: A Study in Southern Mythmaking* (1970). On black labor in the New South, see G. D. Jaynes, *Branches Without Roots: Genesis of the Black Working Class in the American South, 1862–1882* (1986). On southern agrarian protest, see C. V. Woodward, *Tom Watson: Agrarian Rebel* (1938); L. Goodwyn, *Democratic Promise: The Populist Movement in America* (1976); S. Hahn, *The Roots of Southern Populism: Yeoman Farmers and the Transformation of the Georgia Upcountry, 1850–1890* (1983); W. I. Hair, *Bourbonism and Agrarian Protest: Louisiana Politics 1877–1900* (1969); and B. C. Shaw, *Wool-Hat Boys: Georgia's Populist Party* (1984).

The most ambitious and far-reaching reinterpretation of race relations in the South since emancipation, with particular focus on the post-Reconstruction period, is J. Williamson, *The Crucible of Race* (1984). A. Meier, *Negro Thought in America 1880–1915* (1963), and G. B. Tindall, *South Carolina Negroes 1877–1900* (1952), are able examinations of black organization and ideology in the post-Reconstruction South. On the disfranchisement of blacks and poor whites, see J. M. Kousser, *The Shaping of Southern Politics* (1974). On crime and punishment in the New South, see E. L. Ayers, *Vengeance and Justice* (1984). On race relations and the more rigid forms of segregation imposed after 1890, see C. V. Woodward, *The Strange Career of Jim Crow* (1974 ed.); H. N. Rabinowitz, *Race Relations in the Urban South, 1865–1890* (1978); G. M. Fredrickson, *White Supremacy* (1981); and J. W. Cell, *The Highest Stage of White Supremacy* (1982).

How blacks responded to the deterioration of race relations is examined in two works on migration movements, N. I. Painter, *Exodusters: Black Migration to Kansas after Reconstruction* (1977) and E. S. Redkey, *Black Exodus: Black Nationalist and Back-to-Africa Movements, 1890–1910* (1969). See also J. Dittmer, *Black Georgia in the Progressive Era, 1900–1920* (1977), and W. I. Hair, *Carnival of Fury: Robert Charles and the New Orleans Race Riot of 1900* (1976). In a pathbreaking study employing the folklore, music, and humor of Afro-Americans, L. W. Levine, in *Black Culture and Black Consciousness* (1977), illuminates how black southerners perceived themselves, their place in American society, and their relations with whites. Among the most compelling accounts of black life in the South is Theodore Rosengarten, *All God's Dangers: The Life of Nate Shaw* (1974), in which an 85-year-old Alabama cotton farmer recounts his life.

THE LAST AMERICAN WEST

Chapter 19

Since the first settlements on the Atlantic coast, Americans had learned to conquer new frontiers. They had moved westward, carving out of forest and plain new towns, plantations, and farm sites. By the 1840s, this movement had reached the Missouri River. From there, until they reached the West Coast, pioneers had to cross plains, mountains, and deserts. Many found other ways to reach California and Oregon; some went by clipper ship around the Horn; others sailed to Panama, made the portage across the Isthmus, and sailed up the Pacific Coast. The plains themselves were strewn with the wrecks of wagons, the bones of cows and oxen, and the graves of the unlucky.

After 1820, the western plains, which extended well into Mexico and Canada, appeared on most maps as the Great American Desert. There were few trees for fuel, houses, fences, or shade. Nor was there much rain, although the weather was violent. Hailstorms and heavy snows, gale winds and tornados were common, as were extremes of heat and cold. There was little to attract those used to the forests, rivers, and rolling hills of Europe and the East. As late as 1860, except for Texas, not a single state had been set up between the Missouri River and the Rocky Mountains. Farther west, in the mountain country of the Rockies and the Sierras and in the Great Basin between the ranges, settlement was still sparse.

On the eve of the Civil War, about 175,000 whites and a sprinkling of blacks were in the future Dakota country: Montana, Idaho, Wyoming, Colorado, New Mexico, Arizona, Utah, and Nevada. Except for the 25,000 Mormons who settled in Utah, almost all of them kept on the move, like most of the Indian inhabitants. They prospected for precious metals, hunted buffalo, trapped marten and beaver, drove cattle and sheep, guided trains bound for California and Oregon, scouted for the army, hauled overland freight and mail, and traded and fought with the Indians.

The real invasion came after the war. Miners, cattlemen, farmers, land speculators, railroad men, businessmen were drawn by newly perceived opportunities in the region. By 1890, all of the Wild West except Utah, Arizona, New Mexico, and Oklahoma had been cut up into states. Railroads spanned the continent and opened connecting lines to the mines, ranches, and farms that great corporations now controlled. The

Indian wars were over. The army had been withdrawn from the western forts, and the Indian nations had been reduced, dispersed, and humbled. The frontier was officially closed. The Wild West had become part of the American myth; and Sitting Bull and William F. (Buffalo Bill) Cody now played starring roles in a Wild West Show. ■

THE INDIANS: CONCENTRATION AND REPRESSION

Just before the Civil War, about 225,000 Indians shared the plains and mountains with the buffalo, the wild horse, the jack rabbit, and the coyote. But they would soon be overwhelmed as white Americans moved in at a breathtaking pace. The speed with which prospectors, ranchers, and farmers conquered the last frontier was made possible by the transcontinental railroads. They crisscrossed the region, transporting people and supplies and providing access to outside markets. Eager to attract settlers, the railroads made land available at low prices. The federal government also played a critical role. It proved to be as liberal in giving away land to corporations and prospective farmers as it was thorough and ruthless in moving the Indians to the less desirable places. At the same time its policies undermined Indian culture and made them the wards of government bureaucrats.

The Plains Indians

When Columbus discovered America, far more than a million people lived on the continent north of Mexico. They were grouped in more than 600 distinct tribes, few of which numbered more than 2,000 persons. By the Civil War, only about 300,000 "Indians" remained in the United States, more than two-thirds of them on the Great Plains. To the north—in southwestern Canada, the Dakotas, Montana, Minnesota, and Wyoming—the major tribes included the Blackfoot, Sioux, Crow, Cheyenne, and Arapaho. A little to the south—in Nebraska, Kansas, and Oklahoma—were the Osage, Kiowa, Iowa, Omaha, Pawnee, and Comanche. In the Southwest, on the desert of Arizona and New Mexico, rode the Navajo and Apache. Although differing in languages and customs, the Plains Indians tended to share a common culture. Most were nomadic and nonagricultural, and all depended for survival on hunting the bison, or buffalo.

Great buffalo herds, estimated at 12 to 15 million in the 1850s and 1860s, provided food, clothing, and shelter. Daily life revolved around the buffalo hunt, as did much ritual and worship. For centuries, the Plains Indians had hunted the buffalo on foot. In the sixteenth century Spaniards brought the horse to the American continent. The mounted Indian, now a more efficient hunter, steadily reduced the herds. As time went on, wars over the buffalo became more frequent and bloody. To survive, the Indians grew more nomadic and violent and more hostile to trespassers. For 250 years their pride and their skill as horsemen and warriors had been enough to hold their lands. Armed with a short bow superbly adapted to shooting from horseback, the Plains Indians were a match for cavalrymen armed with carbines and revolvers.

Not all Indians of the West were as fierce as the fighting tribes of the plains and the desert. In the naturally protected areas of the Colorado Plateau and the Southern Great Basin, agricultural tribes such as the Hopi and Zuni built their homes, called *pueblos,* into cliffs. They cultivated fields sometimes as far as 20 miles from their homes. To the north and west, in the upper regions of the Great Basin and on the Columbia Plateau, lived the Utes, Bannocks, and Snakes, whose diet consisted of bear and elk, reptiles, rodents, vermin, and grasshoppers. Still farther west lived the California Indians, whose diet was acorns, tubers, and seeds dug out of the earth. Though numerous, they were too scattered to offer resistance to the gold prospectors and other whites, who waged a brutal campaign of extermination. Completing the Indian population were the sad remnants of the Five Civilized Tribes of the East (Cherokees, Chickasaws, Choctaws, Creeks, and Seminoles), now in the Oklahoma country. There were also other "woods Indians" who had been driven west.

These groups found no welcome among the Plains tribes and got little help from the government. When Americans had deemed the Great American Desert uninhabitable and economically useless, the Plains Indians had been left relatively free to roam in the vast area west of the Missouri River. And then whites came. The migration to Oregon in the 1840s, the surveys for transcontinental railroads starting in 1853, the organization

A Sioux encampment near Pine Ridge, South Dakota, in 1891. (*Library of Congress*)

and settlement of the Kansas-Nebraska region in 1854, and the Colorado Gold Rush of 1859 all convinced the western Indians that their world was ending. If further evidence was needed, the attitudes and actions of the United States government furnished it.

The Indian Wars

In the 1840s and 1850s, when traders, travelers, and explorers demanded protection against Indians, the army established a line of forts on the plains. But even before the Civil War, the advance of the mining and agricultural frontier forced the federal government to reconsider the policy of maintaining "one big reservation." Determined to restrict if not destroy the Indians altogether, the government adopted a policy of "concentration." Individual tribes would be confined to smaller reserves, and the government would deal with each tribe separately.

The Indians also had to deal with officials of the Indian Bureau of the Department of Interior, many of whom made fortunes by supplying reservation Indians with inferior goods, by cheating them of their lands, and by selling them forbidden liquor. Between dishonest and incompetent administrators, greedy prospectors and hunters, and touchy soldiers, the Indians were either starved on the reservations or killed in the open country. In the 1850s, one western soldier wrote:

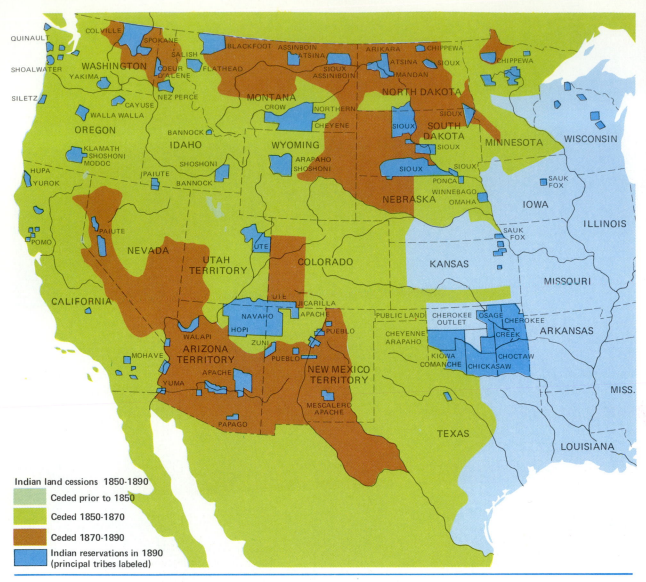

Indian Relations beyond the Mississippi, 1850–90

Indian land cessions 1850-1890
- Ceded prior to 1850
- Ceded 1850-1870
- Ceded 1870-1890
- Indian reservations in 1890 (principal tribes labeled)

It was customary to speak of the Indian man as a Buck; of the woman as a squaw.... By a very natural and easy transition, from being spoken of as brutes, they came to be thought of as game to be shot, or a vermin to be destroyed.

With that kind of attitude, the conflict between advancing white settlers and Indians determined to hold their lands was bound to be long and brutal.

The treaties of 1851 and after, which permitted the government to build roads and railroads across Indian lands, were often made only with "leaders" and small groups; most Indians were never con-sulted. But it was one thing to set aside reservations, and another to force the Indians onto them and keep them there. In 1862, when regular army units were recalled for Civil War service and replaced by new recruits, the first of the Indian wars broke out.

After a small band of Sioux murdered five whites near a reservation in the vicinity of New Ulm, Minnesota, the Sioux, under Little Crow, took to the warpath. They killed hundreds of settlers and burned their farmhouses. The militia finally caught them, and 38 Indians were hanged in a public ceremony. Fights between the eastern Sioux and the army continued until later in 1863, the year of Little Crow's death. Then Sioux lands in Minnesota were confiscated, and what was left of the tribe moved elsewhere.

Two years later, in an attempt to satisfy the miners' demands for access to supplies and civilization, the government tried to build a good wagon road along Bozeman Trail from Fort Laramie, Wyoming, north to isolated Bozeman and Helena, Montana. The road would have cut across the best hunting grounds of the western Sioux. Red Cloud, chief of the western tribes, led his warriors in a campaign to stop the work. They raided the wagon trains bringing in supplies and attacked every woodcutting party. To protect the workers, a small force under Captain W. J. Fetterman was ordered to the scene. Red Cloud's braves ambushed and massacred all 82 men, including Fetterman. Encouraged by their success, the Sioux increased the frequency and violence of their attacks. The project was abandoned.

To the south, warfare with the Cheyenne and Arapaho had been raging since 1861, when miners claimed Colorado lands that only ten years earlier the government had guaranteed to the Indians.

This phase of the Indian wars came to a climax in 1864, when a force under Colonel John M. Chivington butchered about 450 unsuspecting men, women, and children in a Cheyenne encampment at Sand Creek. The Indians, under their chief, Black Kettle, had tried to surrender peacefully, first by raising an American flag and then the traditional white flag. But Chivington was "following orders" in committing these atrocities.

General S. R. Curtis, United States army commander in the West, had said: "I want no peace till the Indians suffer more." Such savagery fed upon itself, and Indian-Army warfare in the Southwest grew more and more brutal. In 1868, at Washita in Oklahoma, an army group under Colonel George A. Custer defeated a band of Cheyenne and Arapaho warriors. Black Kettle was killed here, and his braves were forced to give up their land claims and move into a restricted area.

Many other battles took place between the army and the Indians and between the Indians and white civilians. But the Sioux and Cheyenne wars convinced Congress that the cost of controlling the Indians was too great and progress too slow.

CUSTER'S LAST STAND

More than half-a-century after the Battle of Little Big Horn (June 25, 1876), historian Stanley Vestal visited the Cheyenne River Sioux Reservation and spoke with Chief White Bull, who as a 26-year-old warrior killed a white man he later learned was General George Armstrong Custer.

I charged in. A tall, well-built soldier with yellow hair and mustache saw me coming and tried to bluff me. . . . But when I rushed him, he threw his rifle at me without shooting. I dodged it. We grabbed each other and wrestled there in the dust and smoke. . . . This soldier was very strong and brave. He tried to wrench my rifle from me. I lashed him across the face with my quirt, striking the coup. He let go, then grabbed my gun with both hands until I struck him again.

But the tall soldier fought hard. He was desperate. He hit me with his fists on the jaw and shoulders, then grabbed my long braids with both hands, pulled my face close and tried to bite my nose off. . . . I thought that soldier would kill me. . . .

Finally I broke free. He drew his pistol. I wrenched it out of his hand and struck him with it three or four times on the head, knocked him over, shot him in the head, and fired at his heart. . . .

Source: Stanley Vestal, *The Man Who Killed Custer* (University of Oklahoma Press, 1957).

General George A. Custer. (*National Archives*)

To carry the "concentration" policy one step further, peace commissioners were sent in 1867 to convince the tribes to move to selected reservations. One was in the Black Hills of Dakota; the other was in present-day Oklahoma. By 1868, treaties to this effect were forced on the Indians. Not only were they given inferior land, but they were told to submit to white rule and to give up many of their traditions.

The government had made a mistake. The Indians had no intention of keeping pledges they had no reason to believe the whites themselves would honor. They refused to give up their way of life, and the conflict became constant. Between 1869 and 1875, over 200 pitched battles were fought between the army and the Indians. On the reservations, a new civilian Board of Indian Commissioners, created in 1869, tried to break down the tribal structure and convert the Indians to agriculture. But the land was poor, and the Indians were put on welfare; unable to support themselves, they were made to depend on the government.

In the 1870s, the Indians were kept on the new reservations with great difficulty; the whites, with equal difficulty, were kept off them. Moldy flour, spoiled beef, and moth-eaten blankets were typical of the supplies the Indians received. The Sioux in Dakota were further enraged by Northern Pacific railroad crews intruding on their reservation and by the gold prospectors in the Black Hills in 1874.

Warfare broke out again in 1876. During this conflict, Custer made his famous last stand against Crazy Horse and Sitting Bull at the Battle of Little Big Horn on June 25, 1876. The Sioux killed Custer and 264 men of his Seventh Cavalry. But shortages of ammunition and food forced the Sioux to scatter, and eventually they were captured.

In Oregon, the Nez Percé, whose religious leaders urged them to drive out the whites, took to the warpath in 1877 rather than be placed on a smaller reservation. Until they gave up because of starvation and disease, the Nez Percé under Chief Joseph led 5000 government troops on a wild chase through Idaho and Montana. For almost three decades, the Apache resisted. In the 1880s they made a desperate stand in Arizona and New Mexico until their chief, Geronimo, was captured in 1886.

The end of the buffalo herds finally finished the Plains Indians. In the late 1860s the building of the Union Pacific left the animals at the mercy of every railroad worker, miner, adventurer, and traveler. Since a stampeding herd could overturn a train, buffalo hunting became a part of railroad building. Buffalo Bill Cody made his reputation by killing some 4000 buffalo in eighteen months as a hunter for the Kansas Pacific Railroad. In 1871, a

I WILL FIGHT NO MORE FOREVER

I am tired of fighting. Looking Glass is dead. Too-hul-hul-sote is dead. The old men are all dead. It is the young men who say yes or no. He who led on the young men is dead. It is cold and we have no blankets. The little children are freezing to death. My people, some of them, have run away to the hills, and have no blankets, no food; no one knows where they are—perhaps freezing to death. I want to have time to look for my children and see how many of them I can find. Maybe I shall find them among the dead. Hear me, my chiefs. I am tired; my heart is sick and sad. From where the sun now stands I will fight no more forever. (Chief Joseph of the Nez Percé)

Chief Joseph of the Nez Perce. (*Smithsonian Institution, National Anthropological Archives*)

Source: Mark H. Brown, *The Flight of the Nez Percé* (New York: Putnam, 1967), p. 407.

Pennsylvania tannery discovered it could process buffalo skins into commercial leather. Between 1872 and 1874, 3 million head a year were killed; by 1878, the southern herd had been wiped out.

"I saw buffalos lying dead on the prairie so thick that one could hardly see the ground," a hunter declared in the winter of 1881–1882. "A man could have walked for twenty miles upon their carcasses." In 1886, when the National Museum wanted to mount some buffalo, it found only about 600 of the northern herd left, deep in the Canadian woods.

Fearful that the Indians' religion contributed to the constant warfare, the government in 1884 prohibited many practices, among them the Sun Dance. The government hoped to prevent the surviving Indian bands from joining together even for ceremonies. But in 1890, a Paiute religious prophet named Wovoka attracted many Plains Indians to a faith that featured a ceremonial rite known to whites as the Ghost Dance. Although Wovoka preached love and nonviolence, the new faith promised a time in which the dead would be revived and the earth would be returned to the Indians. When the Sioux adopted this faith, alarmed officials urged military intervention.

Confronted with heavily armed cavalry, the Indians fled. The troops followed and, in December 1890, in the "battle" of Wounded Knee, they massacred the half-starved remnants of the tribe, leaving behind a two-mile trail strewn with the butchered bodies of women and children who had tried to run. "My father ran and fell down and the blood came out of his mouth," the son of Yellow Bird, the medicine man, recalled, "and then a soldier put his gun up to my pony's nose and shot him, and then I ran and a policeman got me."

The Wounded Knee massacre was a final and tragic chapter in the military conquest of the American Indians. Whatever the pride, the military prowess and the horsemanship of the Plains Indians, whatever their willingness to defend their land, families, and traditions, in the end the army's superior firepower and technology ensured the triumph of the white man on the Great Plains.

The Dawes Act and After

In 1887, three years before Wounded Knee, Congress had passed the Dawes Act, which defined the federal government's Indian policy until 1934. The act broke up the tribe as a basic unit of Indian society: Reservation land was divided, and each family head was given 160 acres to cultivate. After a probation period of twenty-five years, he was to be granted full rights of ownership and citizenship in the United States. In 1924, the United States granted citizenship to all the Indians.

The Dawes Act was the result of growing opposition to the policy of the army and the Interior Department. The alternative was forcing the Indians to become settled farmers and to adapt themselves to white ways. But the Dawes Act did the Indians little good. In dividing the land, the government usually gave them the poorest; the best was sold to white settlers. Even when an Indian obtained good land, inexperience in legal matters left him open to the same kind of cheating that had marked the making of the tribal treaties.

Again and again, Indians were tricked into selling their best holdings to white speculators. Worse still, they had neither the cultural tradition, the necessary training, nor the competitive incentive to cultivate the land they kept. Deprived of the kind of support the tribe had once provided, most became paupers. Some found outlets in alcohol or petty crime. The year the Dawes Act passed, the Indian tribes still had title to about 138 million acres of land. By 1932, some 90 million acres had found their way into white ownership.

Geronimo, Apache Chief. (*Library of Congress*)

By the 1890s the "Wild West" existed largely in the national imagination, made vivid in pulp literature and in Buffalo Bill's Wild West Exhibition featuring Sitting Bull, a Sioux medicine man, and William F. (Buffalo Bill) Cody, a scout and buffalo hunter. (*Library of Congress*)

THE GREAT AMERICAN WEST: MINERS, RANCHERS, FARMERS

With a thoroughness equaled only by their extermination of the buffalo and the Indians, Americans after the Civil War exploited the natural wealth of the West. The plains and mountains, it was discovered, were rich in agricultural and mineral wealth. The most productive of the earth's wheat lands stretched across the Dakotas and eastern Montana. In large areas of Wyoming, Colorado, and Texas, and even in sections of Nevada, Utah, and Arizona, there were grazing lands for cattle and sheep that would supply much of the world's beef, mutton, hides, and wool. Other parts of the plains and mountains held some of the world's largest and purest veins of copper and iron ore, some of the world's greatest deposits of lead and zinc, valuable seams of coal, and gold and silver. Beneath the earth in Texas (and elsewhere in the West) lay incredible reserves of crude petroleum and natural gas.

For generations Americans had had even less use for these resources than the Indians who roamed the western lands. But the demands of the booming cities and expanding industry in the postwar years changed the western landscape. Within a generation, this vast area was providing essential raw materials, meat, and grain for eastern and midwestern markets. By 1890, many individual enterprises had been replaced by corporations, frontier boom camps had been converted into company towns, and prospectors and small businessmen reduced to wage laborers.

The Mining Frontier

Although gold had brought miners to the West in the 1840s, the era of the prospector was actually short, from the mid-1850s to the mid-1870s. But during those twenty years, speculation was wild. The mining frontier changed with every new rumor of a strike; as soon as one boom ended, another developed. Towns sprang up overnight, and many of them disappeared soon after the prospectors rushed off to still another find.

THE LAST STAND

Black Elk, a holy man of the Ogalala Sioux, was present at the "battle" of Wounded Knee. Forty years later, he would recall its impact:

And so it was all over.

I did not know then how much was ended. When I look back now from this high hill of my old age, I can still see the butchered women and children lying heaped and scattered all along the crooked gulch as plain as when I saw them with eyes still young. And I can see that something else died there in the bloody mud, and was buried in the blizzard. A people's dream died there. It was a beautiful dream.

And I, to whom so great a vision was given in my youth—you see me now a pitiful old man who has done nothing, for the nation's hoop is broken and scattered. There is no center any longer, and the sacred tree is dead.

Source: John G. Neihardt, *Black Elk Speaks* (Lincoln: University of Nebraska Press, 1961), p. 276.

By the late 1850s, the fabulous discoveries in California—at Sutter's Fort and elsewhere in the San Joaquin and Sacramento valleys—were staked out and some of the best locations had begun to run thin. In a single decade, miners had extracted hundreds of millions in gold from the hills and streams, much of it by the crudest methods. Plenty of gold remained, but it was buried in hills that had to be blasted away and worked with costly equipment by teams of miners. The operations required more capital and business ability than most of the prospectors had. When surface gold ran out, a few took up more stable occupations. Some became miners for corporations, others even became farmers. But tens of thousands made "prospectin' " a way of life and quickly headed for the next strike.

On their way to California in 1848, Captain John Beck of Oklahoma country and W. Green Russell of Georgia had seen signs of gold around the South Platte River in northeastern Colorado. In 1858,

having sold out in California, they decided to go back and check into Colorado's possibilities. That July they staked out the first claim in the Pike's Peak region, near present-day Denver. Soon eastern newspapers were full of news of other Colorado strikes. By the end of 1858, "Pike's Peak or Bust" had become a national slogan. By June 1859, over 100,000 had made the trek to Colorado, some from California, but many from the East and the Mississippi Valley.

Tall stories kept them coming, but the truth soon became known: there was gold around Pike's Peak, but very little. When the trek home began, the wagons carried the complaint, "Pike's Peak and Busted." Some prospectors stayed on to try their hand at farming and grazing and to lay the foundations for Colorado's economy. In the early 1870s, rich beds of silver were worked near Leadville, and gold was found later in the region of Cripple Creek. Such discoveries, together with the

Main Street, Helena, Montana, which was originally a mining town known as Last Chance Gulch. (*Denver Public Library, Western History Collection*)

growth of Denver as a commercial center, made statehood certain. In 1876 Colorado was admitted to the Union as the Centennial State.

Before the Colorado boom had ended, news out of western Nevada in the spring of 1859 sent prospectors swarming into that area. By summer 20,000 men were seeking their fortunes, this time in silver, at the fabulous Comstock Lode on Mount Davidson. By 1877, Comstock miners had taken $306 million worth of silver. It helped to make the remarkable career of Virginia City, which overnight became a camp town and a legend. The discovery of the Comstock Lode set others looking for deposits nearby.

By 1861 Nevada had a population larger perhaps than it has ever had since. Organized as a territory in that year, Nevada became a state in 1864. This was done to secure its vote to ratify the Thirteenth Amendment and to help reelect Lincoln. Mining booms also helped the organization of Idaho (1863), Arizona (1863), and Montana (1864) as territories.

The era of the prospectors was drawing to a close when, in 1874, rumors of gold on the Sioux reservation in the Black Hills of southwestern Dakota Territory were confirmed. The area had been made unapproachable by the Sioux, who were anxious to retain their lands. The United States Army was as determined to keep the Sioux on the reservation as it was to keep out white intruders. But stories kept the lure of the Hills alive: Indians with bags of nuggets, army officers concealing their knowledge of outcroppings so troops would not desert, and a few desperate men who worked a stake and ran.

By October 1876 the army could no longer keep the prospectors out, and the reservation was opened to anyone who wanted to come. Fifteen thousand prospectors poured in almost at once, and the army did what it could to protect them. In the winter of 1876, the richest veins were discovered around Deadwood Gulch. Established as the nearby supply center, Deadwood, South Dakota, an overnight migrant city of some 25,000, soon outdid Tombstone, Arizona, as the toughest of the "badman" towns. All told, the Black Hills mines yielded ore worth $287 million. But the life of the strike was short, and the town of Deadwood quickly passed into legend too.

The first copper seam was discovered in 1881 in Butte, Montana. By the end of the decade, Montana was the leading mining state, with an annual output worth $41 million. Annual copper production had passed that of gold in value; by 1900, it neared that of gold and silver combined. Most of

The James Gang. Jesse James is seated left, with Frank James seated right; standing are Cole Younger (left) and Bob Younger (right). The Youngers were captured in 1876 and sentenced to life imprisonment. "We were drove to it, sir," Cole Younger told the judge. "Circumstances sometimes makes men what they are." Six years later Jesse James was shot in the head by a fellow gang member for the $10,000 reward money. (*Library of Congress*)

the copper went into the miles and miles of electric wiring that were lighting cities and powering factories. Lead production also increased with the growing use of electric storage batteries. Missouri remained the main source of lead. After 1880, sizable quantities from the Leadville district of Colorado and the Coeur d'Alene district of Idaho became available. In 1901, in time for the coming of the automobile, Black Gold roared onto the western scene from the gushers of the Spindletop fields in Texas, establishing the oil industry of that state.

By 1880, big business had moved in to dominate the development of the West. Exploitation of the new metals and minerals required heavy investment in plants, machinery, and hired workers. It was not long before financiers like Henry H. Rogers and the Rockefellers of New York, the Guggenheims of Philadelphia, and the Mellons of Pittsburgh dominated the economy of the West. And with their arrival, the mining frontier of the prospector came to a close.

Before that frontier closed, however, it had had

an extraordinary life of its own. The wide-open mining towns exemplified the boisterous and optimistic spirit of the last American West. The inhabitants were mostly recent arrivals, and all of them, it seemed, were on the make, sustained by the stories of instant success. The people who filled these towns gave them their unique character: desperados, deserters, prostitutes, confidence men, and gamblers preyed on the prospectors and on one another. A place like Virginia City, with its own opera house, elaborate homes, and newspaper (on which Samuel Clemens worked as "Mark Twain"), aspired to better status, but it was still largely a town of saloons, gambling houses, brothels, and dance halls.

Although the mining country was wide open and attracted an assortment of refugees from society, it soon developed a legal code. This code applied not only to personal crimes, but also to such matters as claims, assays, and water rights. Enforcement, however, was usually an individual matter. In 1866, Congress simply declared that the mining country was free to all, "subject to local customs or rules of miners in the several mining districts." But when lawbreaking grew intolerable, "law and order" citizens imposed vigilante justice, at least until the settlement of the West brought formal government agencies and stable local authorities.

The Cattle Frontier

Even as prospectors were seeking their fortunes in precious metals, cattlemen were moving into the Great Plains, turning the vast open ranges of unclaimed grassland into grazing lands for increasingly valuable herds. Before the Civil War, the number of Texas cattle alone was estimated at nearly 5 million. The incentives for reaching northern markets with these cattle multiplied along with the rapid growth of the population and the fantastic prices offered for steers. The fortunes that could be made equaled those of many of the more successful prospectors.

The Cattle Kingdom

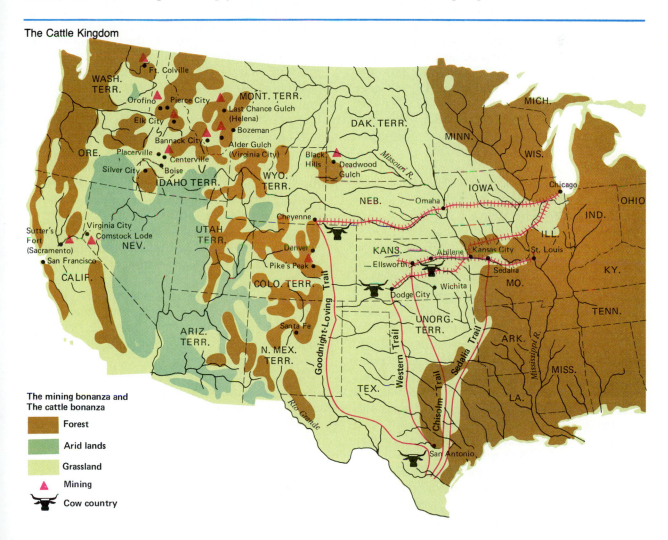

The mining bonanza and
The cattle bonanza

- Forest
- Arid lands
- Grassland
- ▲ Mining
- Cow country

Western-style ranching and cowpunching came into American life with the annexation of Texas in 1845. Long before, Mexicans had designed the bit, bridle, saddle, and spurs, the lariat, chaps, and five-gallon hat of the traditional cowboy. For centuries they had broken broncos, grazed calves, and roped steers. But they did not use the branding iron.

When Americans from Missouri, Mississippi, Alabama, and Tennessee began to trickle into Texas in the 1820s, many of them simply put their brands on what they called wild herds and set themselves up as cattle kings. Other Americans grabbed horses and cattle that had broken away from Mexican herds. In this way, the range cattle industry of Kansas and Nebraska began. The northern ranchers supplied beef and fresh horses to people going west and to mining camps and railroad crews. Compared with those of Texas, however, the northern herds were tiny.

In the 1850s, some Texas ranchers tried to drive their cattle west to the Colorado and California markets or north to Illinois. But herds and herders fell easy prey to the Indians, while the surviving steers reached their destination too thin and tough to bring a good price. The ranchers waited out the Civil War, and then began looking again for markets. When they learned that $3 or $4 Texas steers would bring as much as $40 a head in the North, they decided to try the cross-country drive once more. The risk seemed less because of the westward extension of the railroads.

In 1866, the first of the "long drives" to a railroad town—Sedalia, Missouri, on the Missouri Pacific—began. Sedalia had just been connected with Kansas City, and Kansas City with St. Louis; these thriving Missouri cities would serve as markets and distribution points for other metropolitan markets.

By the fall of that year, some 260,000 Texas steers were on the move. But the trail went through forests, which made the longhorns of the open range stampede. It also crossed over new Missouri farmland, where settlers came rushing out with guns to protect their crops. Cattle rustlers raided the herds. And the Indians, though supposedly confined to the reservations, still roamed the plains. In the end, only a few steers ever reached Sedalia. Those that did, however, brought $35 a head, a price that led many ranchers to try again the next year or to find some other route.

By then a smart Illinois meat dealer, Joseph G. McCoy, realized he could make a fortune if he could set up a convenient meeting point for northern buyers and western breeders. McCoy chose Abilene, Kansas, on the Kansas Pacific, which (with the Hannibal and St. Jo Railroad and other lines) connected Abilene with Chicago. At Abilene, McCoy built a hotel, barns, stables, pens, and loading chutes. In 1868, Abilene received 75,000 head of cattle. Within three years this number had grown nearly ten times, and Abilene became the capital of the cattle frontier. It was the legendary cow town where Wild Bill Hickok made his reputation as a straight shooter and federal marshal.

As the railroads extended westward and southward, new trails and new railroad towns nearer the cattle range were developed. Ellsworth, Kansas, received over a million head between 1872 and 1879. On the Union Pacific route, first Cheyenne and then Laramie became important cattle railheads. And Dodge City, Kansas, the "Cowboy's Capital," rivaled Tombstone, Deadwood, and Abilene. But since the drive to even the nearest railhead was not good for steers ready for market, in the 1870s ranchers began to drive Texas yearlings to the northern range—western Kansas, Nebraska, Colorado, Wyoming, Montana, the Dakotas.

Northern "feeders" bought the young cattle and fattened them free on public lands until they were ready for market. The best cows and bulls were taken from the herds, and breeds were constantly improved. The open-range cattle industry came into its own after 1878, when the business depression of the mid-1870s had ended and beef prices had revived.

Although a romantic chapter in the history of the West, the "long drive" held little glamour for the participants, the much-celebrated cowboys. Equipped with only cow ponies, lassos, and six-shooters, for two months they tried to keep safe and under control a thousand head of hungry, thirsty, touchy steers. P. A. Rollins, a veteran of the drive, wrote: "It was tiresome, grimy business for the attendant punchers, who travelled ever in a cloud of dust, and heard little but the constant chorus from the crackling of hoofs and of ankle joints, from the bellows, lows, and bleats of the trudging animals."[*]

With his picturesque outfits and reputation for daring, the cowboy captured the eastern imagination. But in actuality he was little more than a hired hand who led a lonely existence and worked long hours for low wages.

---

[*]From Philip Ashton Rollins, *The Cowboys*, (New York: Charles Scribner's Sons, 1936). Copyright 1922, 1936; copyrights renewed. Reprinted with the permission of Charles Scribner's Sons.

Like the isolated mining centers, the range too developed its own laws. Here the vital need was for water, and "range rights" along a stream became the most precious part of any ranch. Local regulations had the force of law in determining the extent of each individual's or company's "range rights," but claims often had to be backed up with a gun. Even when the ranchers respected one another's territory, the cattle did not. Here again, rules had to be established for recording brands and for disposing of unbranded cattle.

Ranches that covered as many as 30 or 40 square miles could not be policed efficiently, and rustling became common. With so much invested in their herds, ranchers needed to find ways to protect themselves. The enforcement of rude justice was one of the main objectives of the numerous stockgrowers' associations organized in the 1870s. Eventually, these groups developed hidden governments in their territories. One of their more important business objectives was to prevent competition by making it difficult for newcomers to become members and dangerous for them to operate without joining up. The ranchers were aware of the speed with which the range, endless though it seemed, could be overstocked.

But in spite of all their efforts, news soon leaked out about how $5 steers could be transformed into property worth $45 to $60 a head, with only the investment of four years of free grazing. New ranchers flocked to the range like prospectors to the mines. When great profits materialized, large investors set up corporations. By 1885, the range finally grew overcrowded, and the disastrous winter of 1885–86, followed by a blistering summer, destroyed most of the feed and cattle. The steers that found their way to market were of such poor quality that beef prices crashed despite the shortage.

It was at this time too that sheepherders began to cross the range in large numbers. Their flocks, which spoiled the water, ate not only the grass but the roots as well, leaving in their wake barren range. To add to the stockgrowers' misery, farmers began homesteading in larger numbers and fencing in the open range. Many farmers kept herds of their own on fenced fields where they could control breeding more carefully and regulate the feed. The beef they produced was superior to that grown on the open range. In 1882, range beef sold for $9.35 per hundred pounds in Chicago; by 1887, the price had fallen to $1.90. The end of the open range hastened the end of the last frontier.

The Agricultural Frontier

Although the farmers' frontier had been steadily moving westward, the expansion of agriculture in the post-Civil War decades was extraordinary. The revolution in farm machinery, transportation, and marketing and immigration from abroad were all contributing factors. Between 1870 and 1900, American farmers more than doubled their landholdings—from 407 to 841 million acres—and placed more new land under cultivation than had been farmed in the entire country since 1607.

Much of the new acreage lay in the Great Plains, which tens of thousands of homesteaders were helping to convert to an agricultural economy. But all farmers were not wealthy and comfortable. This was particularly true in the plains country. Because they had to adapt themselves to semi-arid land, harsh weather, grasshopper plagues, and isolation, the plains settlers lived hard lives.

The Homestead Act of 1862 opened public lands in the West to free settlement by American citizens or those who declared their intention of becoming citizens. Much of the best land found its way into the hands of large landholders and speculators. And although adequate for the Mississippi Valley and lavish compared to New England (the two regions from which most of the supporters of the law came), the quarter section (160 acres) offered by the Homestead Act was either too large or too small for the dry, treeless plains. It was too small for cattle or grain production and too large for irrigated farming. Prospective settlers faced high costs in transporting their families and possessions to the land and in preparing enough of the 160 acres to get a paying crop. In addition, there was the expense of irrigation, buildings, equipment, taxes, and hired help. For the large farmer or farming corporation willing to use the costly new machinery, a quarter section was hardly worth the investment.

Recognition of these problems prompted new congressional legislation to stimulate settlement and to deal with the shortage of water and timber. The Timber Culture Act of 1873 offered an additional quarter section to the settler who would put at least 40 acres of it into forest. But the act encouraged fraudulent claims, and before its repeal in 1891 fewer than 25 percent of those who took advantage of its provisions obtained final title to the land. Two other laws passed to stimulate settlement by farmers actually worked to keep them out. The Desert Land Act of 1877 allowed a settler to occupy 640 acres by paying $1.25 an acre. The

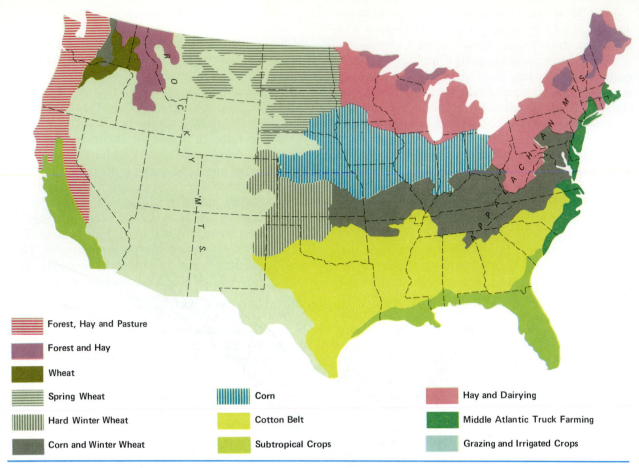

▤	Forest, Hay and Pasture				
▤	Forest and Hay				
▤	Wheat				
▤	Spring Wheat	▥ Corn		▤ Hay and Dairying
▥	Hard Winter Wheat	▥ Cotton Belt		▤ Middle Atlantic Truck Farming
▤	Corn and Winter Wheat	▤ Subtropical Crops		▤ Grazing and Irrigated Crops

Agricultural Regions of the United States

Homesteaders rest by covered wagon in Colorado in the 1870s. (*Denver Public Library, Western History Collection*)

settler could win clear title to the land in three years for an additional payment of $1 an acre, provided he could prove he had irrigated the plot. Thousands of farmers agreed to try to irrigate the land, but the job proved too difficult, and most of them quickly abandoned the effort. Cattle ranchers, however, used the act to get title to grazing range; they registered thousands of acres in the names of cowboys who then signed over the land to them. Some 2.6 million acres were taken up under the act, and an estimated 95 percent of the claims were fraudulent. Nor did settlers gain anything from the Timber and Stone Act of 1878, which operated to benefit lumber companies seeking a share of public lands. This act offered a maximum of 160 acres of rich timberland—land "unfit

WRIGHT MORRIS ON "SOD HOUSE HOME"

In the 1890's, on the plains of Nebraska, a man who had failed at the jobs he had previously attempted— salesman, farmer and medical student—became obsessed with what he saw going on around him, in particular the pioneers, some of them from the Old World, who had adapted to living in sod houses. Some of these structures were less like dwellings than caves. The camera made it possible for Solomon Butcher to document their history.

In the foreground, a settler and his wife, a dog at their feet, stand side by side. In his right hand, the man grips a pitchfork as if it were a lance or a rifle; his wife's left hand grips the back of the chair that she has just brought from the house. She wears an apron, her dark hair is parted and drawn back to a bun at the nape of her neck. He is bearded, but his

hat is tilted back to reveal the whiteness of his forehead. Behind them a small sod house, the open door framing the caged bird that hangs from the edge of the roof. A few boards and a large bleached fragment of antler hold some of the roof sod in place. Just to the right, facing the camera, a team of horses is hitched to a hay wagon.

Assembled at the front of the soddy, all the objects of value are lined up to be photographed. They include a large Christmas wreath, houseplants in pails and cans, a shiny galvanized pail, a rocking chair with a cushion. Solomon Butcher has persuaded this man and his wife to reveal themselves and their holdings, as on the day of judgment, when all would be accountable.

Source: Reprinted from The New York Times Magazine, November 7, 1982. Solomon D. Butcher Collection, Nebraska State Historical Society.

for cultivation"—in California, Nevada, Oregon, and Washington, at $2.50 an acre. With the lumber companies paying handsome bonuses to those who registered claims and then signed over the land, the act amounted to a giant giveaway of natural resources.

Between 1862 and 1900, under the Homestead Act, 80 million acres were registered, a figure that includes many dummy registrations used by speculators to accumulate large holdings. During the same period, railroads, land companies, and states receiving grants of federal land for educational purposes under the Morrill Act of 1862 sold at least five or six times as much land. These sellers charged from $2 to $10 an acre, a fair enough price for the best sites near transportation and markets. Railroads and land companies often gave mortgages on the land and extended credit for equipment to develop it.

By 1868, when the Union Pacific Railroad was nearly ready for passengers, it advertised its land in Kansas and other states on the edge of the frontier. Every land grant railroad opened a land department and a bureau of immigration. In the 1870s, the Union Pacific and the Burlington railroads each spent over $1 million for advertising abroad. Other railroads and land companies opened London offices with agents who searched Europe for settlers. Western states with land to sell and steamship companies carrying immigrants to the New World also looked for settlers abroad.

These campaigns were remarkably successful. According to the 1880 census, 73 percent of Wisconsin's population was of foreign parentage, 71 percent of Minnesota's, 66 percent of the Dakotas', and 44 percent of Nebraska's. In the following two years, "American fever" swept western and central Europe. In 1882 alone, the record year for immigration to the United States in the nine-teenth century, almost 650,000 foreigners arrived in American ports.

Large numbers remained in the coastal cities, and many others got no farther west than Pittsburgh and Cleveland. But hundreds of thousands went to the farmlands of the plains. After the war, thousands of "cotton belt" blacks from northern Louisiana and neighboring southern states joined the move to the plains areas. At first the Exodusters were welcome (they would be Republican voters). But as more and more came, Kansas officials began to send agents south to stop the flow. Most of those who did complete the journey failed to get land. Lacking the money to set up farms, some eventually found jobs as laborers, building railroads or mining coal; women took in washing or became domestics. Others joined the westward drift.

The obstacles confronting those who came to the plains were immense. To make a living was a family enterprise in which men and women worked equally hard. For the women, in addition to helping with the crops and feeding the livestock, there were household tasks made even more difficult on the prairie: keeping a dirt house clean, washing clothes with water that defied attempts to soften it, making soap and candles, undergoing childbirth with no help, and raising the children. For most women, as for most men, the loneliness of prairie life was the worst problem. On the Texas panhandle, this sign was found on an empty cabin in 1886: "250 miles to the nearest post office; 100 miles to wood; 20 miles to water; 6 inches to hell. God bless our home! Gone to live with wife's folks."

Before the new settlers could transform the country into farmland, they had to deal with the problems of shelter and water. Not even log cabins could be built on the treeless plains; the first shelters were sod huts. Lack of wood made them difficult to heat in a region that covered some of the

WORDS AND NAMES IN AMERICAN HISTORY

When Americans began living in an increasingly technological world, their everyday language was affected by technological developments. Some words have become so common that most people today are unaware of their original connection with a specific kind of technology. Take the perfectly ordinary word *sidetrack*. *To be sidetracked* is to be taken away from one's main line of activity. A bill in Congress can be *sidetracked* by a vote to send it back for further consideration by a committee. When the word is used most people do not associate it with railroads, but the term originated in the 1880s, nearly fifty years after the first railroads were built in the United States. As more and more trains began running on the single lines, it became necessary to build "sidetracks" so two trains moving in the opposite direction could pass each other, by having one train switched to wait on a short track by the side of the main line.

coldest parts of the United States. The first settlers burned dried buffalo dung. They next turned to hay, burned in special stoves designed to consume it slowly. But nothing really worked until the railroads brought in coal.

The lack of water, which increased as one moved west, made for even greater difficulties. By 1880, mechanical well-digging equipment was in use, but even when wells could be dug to the necessary depth of 200 or 300 feet, there remained the problem of getting the water to the surface.

Windmills that harnessed the power of the strong prevailing winds promised to provide an answer. But before windmills became cheap enough for the average farmer, the water problem had been solved in other ways. One was *dry farming*. With this system, a field was plowed after each rainfall in order to slow down evaporation. The turned-over mud formed a mulch to store water on which roots continued to feed long after the rain ended.

The tough sod of the plains, like the tough sod of the prairie, resisted the eastern plow. In a re-

RURAL LIFE IN THE 1880S

Born on a farm in Wisconsin in 1860, Hamlin Garland accompanied his family as they migrated to Iowa and the Dakota Territory. In 1884 he left for the East, seeking the life of a writer and teacher. Three years later, he returned for a visit to Osage, Iowa, where he had spent much of his youth.

Every house I visited had its individual message of sordid struggle and half-hidden despair. Agnes had married and moved away to Dakota, and Bess had taken upon her girlish shoulders the burdens of wifehood and motherhood almost before her girlhood had reached its first period of bloom. In addition to the work of being cook and scrubwoman, she was now a mother and nurse. As I looked around upon her worn chairs, faded rag carpets and sagging sofas—the bare walls of her pitiful little house seemed a prison. I

thought of her as she was in the days of her radiant girlhood and my throat filled with rebellious pain.

All the gilding of farm life melted away. The hard and bitter realities came back upon me in a flood. Nature was as beautiful as ever . . . but no splendor of cloud, no grace of sunset could conceal the poverty of these people; on the contrary they brought out, with a more intolerable poignancy, the gracelessness of these homes, and the sordid quality of the mechanical daily routine of these lives.

I perceived beautiful youth becoming bowed and bent. I saw lovely girlhood wasting away into thin and hopeless age. Some of the women I had known had withered into querulous and complaining spinsterhood, and I heard ambitious youth cursing the bondage of the farm. . . .

Source: Hamlin Garland, "A Visit to the West," *A Son of the Middle Border* (New York: Macmillan Co., 1962), p. 309. © The Macmillan Company 1962; Copyright by Hamlin Garland 1917; Copyright renewed 1945 by Mary I. Lord and Constance G. Williams. Photograph from the State Historical Society of Wisconsin, photo by G. J. Van Schaick.

gion blasted by hailstorms, windstorms, and sudden frosts, production was limited not by how much farmers could plant, but by how much they could harvest. With the mechanization of farming and the inventions of the 1870s and 1880s, two men and a team of horses could harvest 20 acres of wheat a day. Eastern farmers dared not plant more than 8 acres of wheat a *season*. At the end of the century, one plains farmer with a cord binder could count on harvesting 135 acres. In 1879, Illinois, the leading wheat state for twenty years, still held first place; by 1899 it had fallen out of the first ten, which were now led by Minnesota, the Dakotas, Kansas, California, and Nebraska.

During the 1870s, plains farmers began to insist that ranchers fence in their cattle. The ranchers, in turn, urged the "nesters" to move away or else pay for the fences to keep the range cattle out. Hostility between the two groups led to gunfights, but cheap fencing, not guns, eventually won the plains for the farmers. Materials for the wood and stone fences used by farmers were lacking on the plains, and neither would have been an effective barrier to cattle. In 1874, barbed wire was patented. Available in large quantities at low cost, barbed-wire fencing provided farmers with the means by which to enclose and protect their lands. By 1890, much of the farmland had been fenced.

When a disastrous series of grasshopper invasions ended early in the 1870s, everything worked in favor of the new wheat country. After 1875, Europe suffered one crop failure after another. The Russo-Turkish War of 1877–78 closed Russia's ports and cut off Europe's main source of grain. All the improvements in American farm technology coincided with the new needs of the European market. This market continued to expand as Western Europe turned from farming to industry.

The future of wheat growing on the plains appeared brighter because for eight consecutive years after 1877 the region enjoyed such good rainfall that many people believed the climate had changed.

While production soared, demand kept prices high. Good prices encouraged expansion, mainly by farmers mortgaging their land to the limit in order to raise money to acquire more land before the next person claimed it. The banks encouraged this practice. "Most of us," said a Kansas official, "crossed the Mississippi or Missouri with no money but with a vast wealth of hope and courage. Haste to get rich has made us borrowers, and the borrower has made booms, and booms made men wild, and Kansas became a vast insane asylum covering 80,000 square miles."

Just as buffalo had drawn the Indian to the West, gold the prospector, and grass the rancher, so wheat had drawn the farmer. But the agricultural West was riding for a fall. Overproduction in the United States by the mid-1880s, the entry of India and Australia into the world wheat market, the revival of Russian wheat exports—all were bad signs. By the 1870s, the commercial farmers of the plains country, like farmers elsewhere, found their freedom declining, almost in proportion to their increasing dependence on impersonal forces (markets, railroads, and middlemen) over which they had no control. For the plains farmers, that made even sharper the isolation and grim environment that drained much of the pleasure from their lives. For many of their sons and daughters, the rewards would be too meager, economically and psychologically, to sustain that kind of existence. They would seek their fortunes elsewhere—in the industrial and urban East.

SUMMARY

After the Civil War, Americans began to move in earnest into the Great Plains and to settle the land between the Mississippi and the Rockies. As they did so, they displaced and overwhelmed the Indian tribes whose home it was. But this time the Indians did not go peacefully— perhaps because there was nowhere to go. The Plains Indians were hunters and fighters, and for twenty years they battled settlers, prospectors, miners, and the United States Cavalry to keep their home.

The reservation system was no solution, for the lands given to the Indians were the poorest and most barren, and could not support a population. Eventually, by the late 1880s, the Indians were crushed; those that remained became wards of the federal government and a forgotten part of American society. What the army had

not been able to do by force, government bureaucrats did by regulations and policies that systematically stripped the Indians of their culture, their self-respect, and their independence. These were policies so cruel and so brutal that it was another half-century before most Americans even knew of the suffering expansionism had caused.

As the Indians were killed or driven onto barren reservations, white settlers poured in to exploit the resources of the West. Mines yielded great quantities of copper, iron, lead, zinc, gold, and silver. The rush of prospectors to areas where ore had been found created boomtowns overnight—and the raw, rough culture of legend.

The building of a cattle empire on the plains did the same for other areas. Growing markets for meat in the

THE LAST AMERICAN WEST

booming cities of the East made ranching profitable, and the railroad made a western cattle industry possible. Towns like Abilene, Dodge City, Tombstone, and Deadwood, where cattle were driven to be shipped to market, roared to life and contributed to the legend that was the Wild West.

Law and order was a problem in the mining and cattle areas, as was the regulation of competition. Much of the policing was done by private groups who provided their own rough justice. All this changed when the secret of farming the plains successfully was discovered. The open range was fenced in, and the Great Plains became one of the greatest grain-producing areas in the world. Farming brought stability, government, and eventually statehood, despite the great obstacles settlers had to overcome. The climate was awful, there was not even enough wood to build houses, manufactured goods were scarce, and success demanded great sacrifices in long hours of labor and great isolation and loneliness.

But new farming techniques and technology, the availability of land through such government programs as the Homestead Act, and the growing flood of European immigrants willing to work hard for a better life signaled the end of the last frontier. By the 1880s the settlement boom and the Wild West were over. Mining, cattle ranching, and farming were now businesses that entailed risk of failure when prices dropped during swings of the business cycle. For the newer immigrants and for the children of the Plains settlers, the cities and the industrialized East seemed to offer new and easier opportunities for a good life.

Suggested Readings

R. A. Billington, *Westward Expansion* (1967), and R. Bartlett, *The New Country: A Social History of the American Frontier* (1974), are informative surveys. Bernard DeVoto, *Across the Wide Missouri* (1947) provides illuminating background material and is engrossing reading. W. P. Webb, *The Great Plains* (1931), and J. C. Malin, *The Grassland of North America* (1948), are classic studies of the relationship between the natural environment and social life. H. N. Smith, *Virgin Land: The American West as Symbol and Myth* (1950), is a good study of the impact of the West on American literature and thought. Regional studies include O. O. Winther, *The Great Northwest* (1950); H. R. Lamar, *The Far Southwest 1846–1912* (1966); J. C. Caughey, *History of the Pacific Coast* (1933); and H. E. Briggs, *Frontiers of the Northwest: A History of the Upper Missouri Valley* (1940). The lure of California is imaginatively told in Kevin Starr, *Americans and the California Dream 1850–1915* (1973). Sexual imbalance on the frontier was less than many popular accounts have suggested, argues J. R. Jeffrey in her study of a much neglected subject, *Frontier Women: The Trans-Mississippi West 1840–1880* (1979).

W. E. Washburn, *The Indian in America* (1975), is an authoritative history. The plight of individual tribes is chronicled in M. H. Brown, *The Flight of the Nez Percé* (1967); Robert Utley, *Last Days of the Sioux Nation* (1963); and S. L. Marshall, *Crimsoned Prairie: The War between the United States and the Plains Indians* (1972). F. G. Roe, *The Indian and the Horse* (1955), is an important study. Wayne Gard, *The Great Buffalo Hunt* (1959), and Mari Sandoz, *The Buffalo Hunters* (1954), describe the destruction of the herds. C. C. Rister, *Border Command: General Phil Sheridan in the West* (1944), and R. G. Athearn, *William Tecumseh Sherman and the Settlement of the West* (1956), examine the army's role in the Indian wars. H. H. Jackson, *A Century of Dishonor* (1881) is a classic indictment of federal Indian policy. On the relations between the federal government and the Indians, see F. P. Prucha, *The Great Father* (2 vols., 1984); L. C. Priest, *Uncle Sam's Stepchildren: The Reformation of United States Indian Policy 1865–1887* (1942); and H. E. Fritz, *The Movement for Indian Assimilation 1860–1890* (1963).

Modern studies of the mining country include R. W. Paul, *Mining Frontiers of the Far West 1848–1880* (1963), and W. S. Greever, *The Bonanza West: The Story of the Western Mining Rushes 1848–1900* (1963). R. H. Peterson, *The Bonanza Kings,* is an informative examination of the social origins and business behavior of the western mining entrepreneurs. C. H. Shinn, *Mining Camps: A Study in American Frontier Government* (1885), is a solid study based on personal experience. Mark Twain, *Roughing It* (1872), is a stirring account of the writer's Nevada days.

On the cattle kingdom, see Lewis Atherton, *The Cattle Kings* (1961); R. R. Dykstra, *The Cattle Towns* (1970); E. S. Osgood, *The Day of the Cattleman* (1929); E. E. Dale, *The Range Cattle Industry* (1930); and Louis Pelzer, *The Cattleman's Frontier* (1936). On the cowboy, see Andy Adams, *The Log of a Cowboy* (1927); J. F. Dobie (ed.), *A Texas Cowboy* (1950); Philip Durham and E. L. Jones, *The Negro Cowboys* (1965); and J. B. Frantz and J. E. Choate, *The American Cowboy: The Myth and the Reality* (1955). On the badmen and the coming of law and order to the West, a standard study is Wayne Gard, *Frontier Justice* (1949).

F. A. Shannon, *The Farmer's Last Frontier: Agriculture 1860–1897* (1945), G. C. Fite, *The Farmer's Frontier 1865–1900* (1966), and A. G. Bogue, *From Prairie to Cornbelt: Farming on the Illinois and Iowa Prairies in the Nineteenth Century* (1963), are important scholarly studies. R. M. Robbins, *Our Landed Heritage* (1942), and P. W. Gates, *History of Public Land Development* (1968), examine the distribution and sale of the western domain. Land policy in the twentieth century is examined in E. L. Peffer, *Closing of the Public Domain* (1951). H. R. Lamar, *Dakota Territory 1861–1889* (1956), is a model study of statehood politics. On pioneer farm life, Everett Dick, *The Sod-House Frontier 1854–1890* (1937), and Mari Sandoz, *Old Jules* (1935), present detailed and dramatic stories. Equally revealing are the novels of Ole Rolvaag, especially *Giants in the Earth* (1929), Willa Cather's *O Pioneers!* (1913) and *My Antonia* (1918), and Hamlin Garland's autobiographical accounts.

THE NEW INDUSTRIAL SOCIETY

Chapter 20

With the closing of the land frontier, Americans crossed new frontiers in science, technology, and business management. The American people were to make their abundant resources—iron, coal, oil, lumber, and water power—yield wealth and riches far beyond the dreams of even the most optimistic prospectors and promoters of the past. By the turn of the century, the nation had undergone a massive economic transformation.

The population had increased 132 percent between 1870 and 1910. The proportion of Americans living in rural and urban areas, like the proportion engaged in agriculture and industry, had shifted. Tens of thousands of farm youths joined equal numbers of European immigrants in urban and industrial centers. And with rapidly expanding markets, improved transportation, new technological breakthroughs, a large and willing labor force, and a responsive federal government, the productivity of American industry seemed limitless—as did its profits.

But even as the conquests on the new frontiers pushed the United States to world industrial supremacy, Americans began to assess the price they had paid for success. The low wages paid workers, the long hours and unsafe conditions they were forced to endure, the poor structures that housed them, and the employment of women and children attested to glaring inequalities in wealth. The American labor force did not share equally in the benefits of technological advances and increased productivity. Nor could workers easily improve their lot when they had to face industries that were rapidly being dominated by monopolies, trusts, and financial mergers. The history of industrialization in the last decades of the nineteenth century yields impressive statistics of manufacturing growth. But the personal ordeals and dislocations that made that growth possible defy any easy measurement. For scores of American workers, the dream of economic success gave way to a concern for day-to-day survival. ■

THE GOSPEL OF SUCCESS

After the Civil War, succeeding by making money became more important than ever. The dominant economic, political, and educational institutions embraced a Gospel of Success that justified the accumulation of wealth, equated economic success with virtue, and excused the human costs of industrialization. To succeed was to develop those qualities of character suited to increasing profits and acquiring material goods. "Abhor one hour of idleness as you would be ashamed of one hour of drunkenness," a father instructed his son at Harvard. No less infused with the new morality, Andrew Carnegie, the millionaire steel magnate, advised aspiring young men: "Aim High. Do not rest content as head clerk, or foreman, or general manager in any concern, no matter how extensive. Say to yourself, 'My place is at the top.' Be King in your dreams."

If businessmen needed to defend their careers and operations, they could turn to a sociological interpretation in Charles Darwin's law of evolution. Herbert Spencer, an English philosopher, attracted attention in the United States by arguing that Darwin's biological theories, particularly the concept of natural selection, were relevant for human society. This interpretation found favor in intellectual circles, and its popularization by writers and lecturers soon made it an article of faith for many Americans.

Applying Darwin's "struggle for life" to the system of unregulated business competition, the Social Darwinists, as Spencer's followers became known, contended that human society too evolved by the survival of the fittest. If industrialists like John D. Rockefeller and Andrew Carnegie overcame their competitors, if their companies swallowed up smaller and weaker businesses, they had simply proved themselves the fittest to enjoy wealth and power. The progress of society demanded that business be left free to operate, just as nature was in selecting and "rejecting" species. Government intervention in economic affairs, such as the regulation of business or social legislation to assist the weak and less fortunate, only interfered with this natural process.

When Andrew Carnegie, the millionaire steel magnate, first read Spencer, he recalled in his *Autobiography,* "Light came as in a flood and all was clear." Once he discovered "the truth of evolution," he had no more doubts about the pursuit of wealth. He could now comfort himself with the thought that what he did in his business operations ultimately benefited society: "'All is well since all grows better,' became my motto, my source of comfort." But few American capitalists experienced such inspirational moments of truth, and still fewer read Spencer. Like most Americans, they had been raised in the spirit of the Protestant ethic to think of worldly success as a sign of God's favor, as outward evidence of inward moral and religious character.

And they had been taught at school and at home, as were at least three generations of Americans, the simple moral code set forth in *McGuffey's Reader.* The qualities of character and moral virtues stressed in these widely read textbooks were

AN OLD MAN AT THIRTY-FOUR

Whatever the moral virtues imparted by school readers and success manuals, many Americans came to learn that hard work, sacrifice, frugality, and punctuality did not necessarily ensure success in a rapidly industrializing society. Florence Kelley, as State Inspector of Factories and Workshops for Illinois, found that in the garment trades, for example, long hours at low wages and under unhealthy conditions took their inevitable toll among the "sweaters" who worked there.

A typical example is the experience of a cloakmaker who began work at his machine in this ward at the age of fourteen years, and was found, after twenty years of temperate life and faithful work, living in a rear basement, with four of his children apparently dying of pneumonia, at the close of a winter during which they had had, for weeks together, no food but bread and water, and had been four days without bread. The visiting nurse had two of the children removed to a hospital, and nursed the other two safely through their illness, feeding the entire family nearly four months. Place after place was found for the father; but he was too feeble to be of value to any sweater, and was constantly told that he was not worth the room he took up. A place being found for him in charge of an elevator, he could not stand; and two competent physicians, after a careful examination, agreed that he was suffering from old age. Twenty years at a machine had made him an old man at thirty-four.

Source: Florence Kelley, "The Sweating-System," *Hull-House Maps and Papers* (New York: Thomas Y. Crowell & Co., 1895), pp. 31, 37.

THE LADDER OF FORTUNE

precisely those to which the average businessman attributed his success—frugality, sobriety, industry, and piety. Applied to an industrializing society, both the Protestant ethic and *McGuffey's Reader* taught that to accumulate wealth was natural, Christian, and progressive. Those who succeeded proved that they deserved a high place in this life and salvation in the next.

The Gospel of Success taught still another important lesson: the individual was ultimately responsible for his or her economic condition. Those who succeeded had taken full advantage of the opportunities available to them. Those who fell by the wayside, whatever the circumstances, had failed to make the most of their opportunities. The failure lay in themselves, in their own weaknesses, not in any defects in the economic system. The poor were poor because they had proved themselves less fit. That they must live in slums and in poverty was unfortunate but unavoidable. In seeking to help them, social legislation and labor unions interfered with the workings of the laws of nature.

The philosophy of success hid the realities of a stratified economic society. Enough examples of rags-to-riches success stories helped to sustain the idea of upward mobility and an essentially good social system. The experiences of tens of thousands of Americans, however, contradicted this theory. No matter how hard some people worked, no matter how hard they practiced all the necessary moral virtues, their success was by no means assured. What their experiences dramatized was a basic conflict between the value of economic growth and the human cost of such growth. In nearly every phase of American industrial life, that conflict would become strikingly clear.

THE RAILROAD: MASS TRANSPORTATION AND BIG MONEY

Few enterprises were more important to American industrial development and expansion than the railroad. The United States would be joined together as never before: distant markets would be tapped, vast new regions would be opened for settlement and exploitation, mass production and mass consumption would be stimulated, and efficient distribution of goods would affect every sector of the economy. For many industries, the railroad was the key to development. For many towns and cities, the railroad was the critical factor in growth or decline.

Because of the power they had, railroad executives enjoyed an authority and influence seldom possessed by political leaders. "When the master of one of the great Western lines travels towards the Pacific on his palace car," an English writer observed in the 1880s, "his journey is like a royal progress. Governors of States and Territories bow before him; legislatures receive him in solemn session; cities and towns seek to propitiate him, for has he not the means of making or marring a city's fortune?"

In 1865 approximately 35,000 miles of railroad track served the country. By the time of the Panic of 1873, this figure had been doubled. About 5,000 miles of new track had been laid in the South. Most of the remainder was in the East and the old Northwest, where trunk lines were being extended to the Mississippi Valley and a network of feeder lines was opened up. Almost all the new construction was privately financed through security issues sold to individuals and banks. None of it enjoyed land grant benefits, and little of it received any other kind of governmental assistance.

Whatever the ultimate benefits of the growth of the railroad lines, most of them were constructed for profit rather than for society's needs. The financial stakes were high. By clever financing and by using their control of strategic routes, individuals could make fortunes. Competition among the railroad promoters was fierce and ruthless. The reputations of the railroad barons (Jay Gould, Jim Fisk, and Daniel Drew were the best-known examples) were well deserved; they made fortunes largely through speculation and stock manipulation. Like feudal chieftains, they fought for control of territories, leaving behind them a trail of ruined competitors, bribed public officials, mortgaged cities and towns, and heavily indebted and poorly constructed railroads.

The Battle for the East

As important as the opening of new roads and routes, the consolidation of independent lines enabled several large companies to control vast areas. Cornelius Vanderbilt, the shipping magnate who began investing in railroads in 1862, became one of the principal operators of the postwar period. By 1869, through a series of stock manipulations, he had secured control of the New York Central and connecting lines that gave him a direct route from New York City to Buffalo. Through a series of acquisitions and agreements with other roads, Vanderbilt subsequently extended the railroad into Chicago and beyond, all the way to Omaha, Nebraska. In 1871 Vanderbilt opened the first Grand Central Terminal in New York City, from which passenger trains made the 965-mile run to Chicago in the then incredible time of twenty-four hours.

In the 1870s the Pennsylvania Railroad, guided by its vice-president, Thomas A. Scott, also built and bought up lines to gain wholly owned routes from Philadelphia to Chicago and St. Louis. In 1871 the Pennsylvania at last gained access to New York City, and it soon would reach Baltimore and Washington. In the cutthroat competition of the postwar decades, Chicago, Cleveland, New York, and other cities that were served by rival railroads enjoyed low rates and fine service. To attract freight, competing lines often made special concessions to large shippers in the form of *rebates* (secret discounts off the published rates). But where one railroad had a monopoly of the traffic, as in Pittsburgh, cities were treated with contempt. The lines felt free to charge what the traffic would bear, and shippers had little choice but to pay.

After northern railroad building passed its peak in the 1880s, capital from that section and abroad

Railroad Network, 1890

turned to the South; between 1880 and 1890 nearly 25,000 miles of track were laid, a rate of growth almost twice that of the country as a whole. At the same time, the southern lines adopted the standard gauge, making it possible for railroad cars to move freely from one system to another throughout the country. In the South, too, consolidation accompanied expansion, and it was not long before a few northern capitalists controlled most of the lines.

The Transcontinental Railroads

Much more spectacular than railroad building in the older sections was the construction of the first transcontinental roads, which Congress chartered during the Civil War. The Union Pacific was to build westward from Omaha, and the Central Pacific eastward from Sacramento. Both companies received huge land grants and generous loans from Congress.

The Union Pacific and the Central Pacific were not built by the railroad corporations, but by separate construction companies. These companies were handsomely paid by the railroads. And since they were largely owned by the directors of the railroads they served, it was through construction rather than rail service that the promoters made their fortunes. Part of these fortunes also found their way into the pockets of congressmen and senators who looked after the railroads' legislative business.

The engineering problems of this construction had been at least as difficult as the financial ones. Although both roads had to be almost completely rebuilt some years later, the feat of crossing the broad plains and the forbidding mountain ranges remains one of the great engineering accomplishments in history.

All told, the Union Pacific construction company laid 1,086 miles of track, most of it the work of Civil War veterans and Irish immigrants. The Central Pacific, its construction crews made up largely of Chinese, laid 689 miles. With both companies competing for government subsidies

The Union Pacific Railroad joins with the Central Pacific, May 10, 1869, at Promontory Point, Utah. (*Library of Congress*)

(granted according to each mile of track laid), speed outweighed all other considerations. In the spring of 1869 the two lines approached each other, and on May 10 they were joined by golden spikes at Promontory Point, near Ogden, Utah. In the fanfare that greeted the linking by rail of the Atlantic and Pacific coasts, few people looked at the quality of the construction or the debt that resulted.

Before the Panic of 1873, three other transcontinentals were chartered by the federal government—the Northern Pacific in 1864, the Atlantic and Pacific in 1866, and the Texas and Pacific in 1871. Of the three, only the Northern Pacific eventually reached the coast. The other two, along with their land grants, were controlled by the Central Pacific's Big Four—Charles Crocker, Leland Stanford, Collis P. Huntington, and Mark Hopkins. In an effort to dominate all California railroading, this group also acquired the Southern Pacific Railroad, a company that had been chartered in California in 1865 to connect the ports of San Francisco and San Diego. After 1876, they began pushing the Southern Pacific eastward.

The Battle for the West

The Big Four were not alone. Enriched by his dealings in the stock market and in railroad financing, Jay Gould plunged into the struggle for control of the West. By 1881 Gould had pieced together a series of lines in the Southwest which so menaced the Southern Pacific that Collis Huntington, the leader of the California group, felt obliged to make a traffic-sharing and rate-fixing agreement with him. By 1890 Gould controlled nearly half the railroad mileage of the Southwest. The shippers of the area were at his mercy.

Huntington and Gould came to consider the entire West Coast, if not the entire West, as their private empire. In the North, however, they were confronted with vast transcontinental enterprises they could not quite control. One of these was the Northern Pacific, which in 1864 received the biggest of all federal land grants, some 40 million acres. German-born Henry Villard, an ex-journalist, took it over in 1881 and extended its operations to Portland, Oregon, and Tacoma, Washington. Meanwhile, James J. Hill had his own ideas about the Pacific Northwest and how to build and run railroads. With the support of Canadian financiers, he acquired the St. Paul and Pacific. In 1889 it took the name Great Northern. By then, with very little government assistance, Hill and his backers had pushed construction 2,775 miles west through Minnesota, North Dakota, and Montana, up to Winnipeg, Canada. In 1893 the Great Northern, on a route north of Villard's line, reached Puget Sound.

From the start, Hill insisted on constructing Great Northern track and roadbed with the best materials. He also chose to build around mountains rather than over them. Not only did this approach greatly reduce construction costs, but it also reduced operating costs once the road was built. The Great Northern's long trains and heavy loads, which the track for the mountainous routes of the other western roads could not carry, became the wonder of the railroad world. The proof of Hill's policies came in 1893, when only the Great Northern among the transcontinentals survived the business crash that year.

During the next decade, Hill acquired the Northern Pacific, which had been financially reorganized with the aid of J. P. Morgan and Company in 1898. In 1901, with Morgan's help, Hill also won control of the Chicago, Burlington & Quincy, the best entry to Chicago from the west, and began a bitter fight with Edward H. Harriman. The year before, Collis Huntington had died and Harriman had acquired 45 percent of Southern Pacific's stock. (Gould was already dead.) Harriman's backer, Jacob H. Schiff, was head of Kuhn, Loeb and Company, Morgan's main banking rival. Harriman also enjoyed the financial confidence of the Rockefeller Standard Oil group, always on the lookout for a place to put their millions.

Thus the stage was set and the parts assigned for one of the great financial contests of the twentieth century: Harriman, Rockefeller, the National City Bank, and Kuhn, Loeb versus Hill, the First National Bank, and Morgan. Control of the western—and the national—railroad network was the prize.

After a titanic Wall Street battle that ruined many investors but settled nothing, the antagonists, in November 1901, finally decided to merge their interests. For this purpose they formed the Northern Securities Company. In 1904 this company was broken up by a Supreme Court decision that was one of the highlights of Theodore Roosevelt's administration. The contestants quickly made new financial arrangements to keep from killing one another off.

By the turn of the century, the American railroad network of about 200,000 miles had been virtually completed. There was nothing like it anywhere else in the world. Technological advances—steel rails, heavier and faster locomotives, larger freight and passenger cars, and the double-tracking and quadruple-tracking of thousands of miles of routes in the West and in the East—also assured safer and more efficient rail service. Even so, Americans were angry with railroad management. In the 1870s and 1880s the abuses, such as discriminatory carrying charges, rebates to powerful shippers, and the corruption of public officials, had brought a strong movement for reform and regulation (see Chapter 21). Many of these abuses lasted into the new century, as did the reform efforts. But even as Americans continued to argue over them, few questioned the influence the railroads had had on industrial development.

THE AGE OF ENTERPRISE: HEAVY INDUSTRY

Railroad expansion and improvement had a great deal to do with the growth of northern industry after the war. New construction had expanded the market for all kinds of goods, from iron and steel for rails to meat and blankets for construction crews. Railroad financing attracted large amounts of foreign capital to America and helped make the public familiar with investment procedures that corporations could use to sell securities in the growing money markets of the country. Industrialists like Carnegie, Armour, and Rockefeller could use their profits to expand their own businesses and to exploit profitable by-products; others would supply the carriers to haul raw materials to their factories and manufactured products to market.

Railroad development added to the spirit of optimism that dominated the northern economy after the war. With the opening of the industrial frontier, new men emerged to vie for economic leadership. Most were possessed by ambition; they were aggressive, self-confident, and ruthless, willing to manipulate anyone who stood in their way. But they were at the same time imaginative and talented. They crushed their competitors, used the government, and ignored the human cost of their operations. But they were conscious of themselves as industrial pioneers conquering new frontiers.

Few showed these qualities more vividly than John D. Rockefeller and Andrew Carnegie. And the enterprises they directed—Standard Oil and Carnegie Steel—became models for the new wave of economic organization and consolidation.

Petroleum: Rockefeller and Standard Oil

In the 1850s, whale oil, then the world's chief commercial light source, had become so scarce that its price was almost $2 a gallon. Seepages of surface petroleum had been detected in many parts of the world for centuries. As "rock oil" it had gradually gained a reputation as a medical cure-all. Some chemical pioneers had also begun to refine petroleum into kerosene, to design lamps for burning it conveniently, and to promote it as a cheap source of lighting.

What no one knew was how to find enough petroleum to meet the rising demand. Then, in 1857, a young New York lawyer, George H. Bissell, and his associates sent Edwin L. Drake to Titusville, Pennsylvania, to make the first real attempt to drill for oil. Two years later "Drake's Folly" gushed in. By 1872, oilfields covered 2000 square miles in Pennsylvania, West Virginia, and Ohio, and annual production had soared to 40 million barrels. Of this total, John D. Rockefeller's Standard Oil Company was already refining no less than one-fifth.

Born in 1839 in Richford, New York, Rockefeller, aged twenty-six in 1865, had already made a wartime fortune in a grain and meat partnership in Cleveland. Two years earlier he had invested in a small Cleveland oil refinery, to which he was ready now to devote all his time. In 1870, Rockefeller organized the Standard Oil Company, using its capital of $1 million for an all-out attack on the competition, which was located mainly in the oil region and in Cleveland, Pittsburgh, and New York.

John D. Rockefeller. (*Brown Brothers*)

First, Rockefeller spent heavily to make his plants the most efficient in the country, so that he could undersell competitors and still make a profit. He would often sell his products well below cost in selected markets to ruin a competitor—a practice known as *cutthroat competition*. To make up his losses, he would charge more than ever once he had the market to himself.

With his volume of business soaring, Rockefeller then demanded that the railroads grant him lower freight rates than his competitors. Railroad rates were required by law to be public and equal; so Rockefeller devised a system of *rebates*. Standard Oil would pay the regular charges "on the books" and then get money back secretly. Since Cleveland was a city where competition was intense, the railroads had to agree in order to keep his business.

Having eliminated almost all his competition in Cleveland, Rockefeller applied similar techniques—rebates and discriminatory freight rates on oil shipments—to railroads in other areas and enlarged his industrial empire. By 1879, Rockefeller held about 95 percent of the refining capacity of the country and had captured almost the entire world market for his products. But by then the oil pipeline was well on the way to replacing the railroad tank car as the major oil carrier. Before long, Standard Oil used its power to gain a monopoly of pipeline transportation. Consolidating his control of the industry, Rockefeller divided the country into sales districts and sent out executives and agents to sell the products of Standard Oil.

In establishing centralized management and monopoly control, Rockefeller stabilized an industry that had once been marked by many small producers and changing prices and profits. He got rid of wasteful practices, established sound financing, and provided an efficient system of distribution. In Rockefeller's mind, that was reason enough for the methods he employed. "The day of combination is here to stay. Individualism has gone, never to return," Rockefeller observed—no doubt convinced that it was all in the national interest, as well as his own.

Steel: Andrew Carnegie

Before the Civil War, steel had been a rare and costly metal that could be made only in quantities of 25 to 50 pounds by processes that took weeks. In 1847, William Kelly of Kentucky discovered a simple method by which tons of steel could be produced in a matter of minutes. Nothing much

Andrew Carnegie. (*Culver Pictures, Inc.*)

was heard of his discovery until ten years later, when Kelly contested the application of an Englishman, Henry Bessemer, for an American patent on a process similar to his own and on an efficient "converter." The patent dispute was soon straightened out, but it was not until the early 1870s that what has since become known as Bessemer steel began to be produced in quantity in the United States.

In 1872, with long experience in railroading and the building of steel railroad bridges, Andrew Carnegie entered the steelmaking industry. He put off adopting the Bessemer process, but a trip to England the next year convinced him to use the new method. He came back and built the biggest steel mill in the world near Pittsburgh.

By 1879 American steel production had risen to 930,000 tons, three-fourths of it in the form of steel rails, almost all manufactured by the Carnegie company. By 1890 American steel production had taken another spectacular leap to an annual figure of over 4 million tons. Carnegie's success came in part from his ability as a salesman. But he also had a far better grasp of management than his competitors. Other steel men often used their profits to live in the grand style; Carnegie, like Rockefeller, plowed back his own and the company's earnings, to expand, integrate, and modernize.

Before he retired in 1901, Carnegie had acquired immense holdings in the fabulous Mesabi ore lands in Minnesota, from which as much as 85 percent of America's iron ore in the first half of the twentieth century was to come. He also bought up Pennsylvania coal fields, some limestone quarries, and the coke business of Henry Clay Frick, who became his partner. Ore, coal, limestone, and coke are the basic raw materials for the manufacture of steel; to ensure their regular delivery to his plants, Carnegie also invested heavily in ships and railroad cars.

From the mines to the market, Carnegie controlled every phase in the processing of steel. That was the meaning of integration and modernization. By 1890, although three other giant steel enterprises had grown up in the South and West, the Pittsburgh district continued to lead the industry. Carnegie maintained control until he sold out in 1901 to the newly formed United States Steel Corporation; with the Carnegie empire as its base, it became the world's leading steel producer. It controlled 70 percent of the steel business and was capitalized at nearly $1.5 billion dollars.

What made the Rockefeller and Carnegie enterprises unique was not just the scale of their operations and the monopoly they had, but the enormous profits they made. Rockefeller and Carnegie competed in giving funds to foundations, churches, and colleges. The idea was that by sharing their wealth, they helped to justify the means they had used to acquire it. A New York newspaper that kept track of their philanthropic gifts estimated Carnegie's at $332 million, Rockefeller's at $175 million. But while they competed freely in philanthropy, the techniques of monopoly control they had pioneered came to dominate American industry.

The New Technology: Telephone, Telegraph, Electric Light

Among the many new management problems in the giant enterprises emerging after the Civil War were mechanical ones, such as communication and recordkeeping. Simple mechanical devices—the typewriter, first used in business in 1867, and the adding machine, made practical by 1888—set in motion the mechanization of the office. Now recordkeeping could keep up with the flow of products and the volume of sales.

Two other advances were the electric telegraph and the telephone. In 1876, Alexander Graham Bell patented the telephone he had invented the year before. The next year, Western Union, which already controlled most of the telegraph business, entered the telephone field. But Bell sued for patent infringement and won, and during the 1880s the Bell Company bought out its remaining rivals. Thereafter, patented improvements kept the company protected from competition.

To expand long-distance telephone service, which was developed in 1884, the Bell directors set up a new corporation, the American Telephone and Telegraph Company. In 1900, AT&T became the overall holding company of the entire Bell system, with a capitalization of $250 million. In that year, 1,350,000 Bell telephones were in use in the United States. It cost New Yorkers $240 a year for a private phone, and AT&T's profits became the envy of the industry.

While Bell and others were improving the telephone, Thomas A. Edison was experimenting with electric lighting. In 1879 he perfected a reasonably priced incandescent bulb. Three years later, in New York City, he built the first central power station, from which he distributed *direct current* to eighty-five buildings. But direct current could be transmitted great distances only at great cost. With the use of transformers, *alternating current* could take direct current from a power plant, increase the voltage for distant transmission, and then lower it again for ordinary purposes. George Westinghouse and William Stanley developed the first generators and transformers for alternating current, and in 1893 Westinghouse made alternating current famous by using it to light Chicago's World Fair. The great era of electricity, however, was yet to come. Until then, the United States, as well as the rest of the world, looked to water and steam for power.

With the move toward consolidation in public utilities as well as in steel and petroleum, the

WORDS AND NAMES IN AMERICAN HISTORY

The first *iceboxes* were sometimes called *refrigerators*. The original Latin roots of the latter term meant simply "to make cold." The earliest versions were large chests with a drain hole to let the icewater run out. The ice came from frozen ponds during northern winters; it was packed in sawdust in icehouses, and occasionally shipped as a luxury item to the West Indies and the South after about 1800. After about 1900, electric models came into use, though as late as the 1930s commercial ice companies were still delivering 50-pound blocks of ice for nonelectric models throughout many American cities.

American economy changed. Now fewer and fewer industrial and financial organizations had greater and greater influence and power. In one industry after another, small enterprises disappeared. By the turn of the century, in a number of industries only one enterprise controlled more than 50 percent of the total product. The concentration of so much economic power in the hands of so few was bound to have an effect on a society that believed in free competition and the idea that anyone who was willing to work hard could succeed.

PANICS, TRUSTS, AND THE BANKS: CONGLOMERATION

By 1860, $1 billion had been invested in American industry, and the factories and shops that made up the industrial community produced goods valued at about $1.8 billion. By 1890, the investment had soared to $6.5 billion, and the annual output approached $10 billion in value. These are crude indicators of the transformation of the United States in only thirty years from a nation of farmers to one of the leading industrial powers of the world. In refining crude oil, making steel and lumber, packing meat, and extracting gold, silver, coal, and iron, the United States had passed all its rivals. In specialties like hardware, machine tools, and small arms and ammunition, it retained the leadership assumed before the Civil War. American pianos as well as locomotives ranked with the world's best.

In any age, this would have been a towering performance. In an age that worshipped bigness, it meant the achievement of the ideal. Despite frequent complaints of hard times, very few Americans blamed business or questioned the "system." Boom and depression were assumed to be natural. In the nineteenth century, and even up to the crash of 1929, depressions continued to be seen simply as the results of errors in judgment, to be followed soon by recovery.

Instead of destroying hope, depressions paid dividends for faith. They presented opportunities to expand and modernize plants at low cost, to corner raw materials at bottom prices, to capture customers by offering attractive schedules, rates, and deliveries. It was during the depression of the 1870s that Rockefeller organized his oil monopoly, Carnegie built his first great steel plant, Armour and Morris built their meatpacking empires, the Comstock Lode was exploited, and Boston capitalists began to finance Bell's telephone.

The Panic of 1873

Signs of trouble during the postwar boom had become apparent as early as 1871, when the number of business failures reached 3,000. By 1872, more than 4,000 more firms had collapsed. A clue to the problem may be found in the fact that during the boom period from 1868 to 1873, the volume of bank loans had grown seven times as fast as deposits. The Panic of 1873 began on September 8, when the New York Warehouse and Securities Company went into bankruptcy, carrying many of its creditors down with it. The greatest shock came ten days later with the failure of Jay Cooke and Company, the most famous banking house in the country.

On September 20, the New York Stock Exchange, "to save Wall Street from utter ruin," suspended all trading for ten days. Shock then gave way to depression: Railroads halted construction, mills closed down, and trade suffered. As late as 1877, over 18,000 business firms failed.

What this meant for ordinary people was unemployment, poverty, and labor violence. With large numbers of Americans dependent on factory payrolls, unemployment could quickly use up the savings of even the most frugal families. But the industrial giants did well; they had the resources to ride out any storm. "So many of my friends needed money," Carnegie explained later, "that they begged me to repay them. I did so and bought out 5 or 6 of them. That was what gave me my leading interest in this steel business."

Trusts and Pools

Once the depression of the 1870s had run its course, production boomed again, and prices fell rapidly. These changes called for greater industrial efficiency. To keep production costs down, manufacturers were forced to use the most efficient machinery in the most efficient way. Engineers branched into a new field, the factory assembly line. Even before the Civil War, firearms and farm machinery companies had speeded up production by using interchangeable parts. Meatpackers had also begun to use continuous-flow methods. In the 1870s and after, the use of interchangeable parts and their assembly along a continuous line became common in many new industries.

By mechanizing factories and simplifying workers' tasks, the new techniques made it possible for business to reduce production costs. Yet there was a catch. The machinery cost so much that the reduction in the cost of individual items was possible only when plants operated at or near full capacity. If plants produced fewer items than they were geared for, the cost of each item rose remarkably; if plants ran at capacity, so much was produced that markets were flooded and prices sank.

Each new avenue of hope for bigger markets in the postwar era—the opening of a new railroad line, a boom in immigration, a burst of exports, a rise in the tariff—promoted expansion and mechanization. But each new development soon ran its course and left behind idle plants and equipment—usually purchased with borrowed money on which interest still had to be paid. One outcome of this competitive struggle was that many family firms and independent companies were forced to shut down. A second was the move toward industrial pools and trusts. This was an effort to bring order out of the chaos of competition and ensure profits.

Pools or *pooling agreements* administered by trade associations were essentially secret agreements among competitors to restrict output, maintain prices, and divide up markets. Pools were usually created in emergencies, and they quickly collapsed when they were over. They were a temporary device. Far more permanent—and also far more secure—was the *trust*. The first trust, which became a model for all the others, was organized by Rockefeller in 1879 and reorganized in 1882.

In forming a trust, the stock of the companies involved is turned over to a group of trustees chosen by the combining firms. Trustee certificates are issued in exchange for stock, which remains in the original hands. Management of the enterprises is concentrated in the hands of a single board of trustees. After the Standard Oil Trust came the Cottonseed Oil Trust, the Salt Trust, the Whiskey Trust, the Sugar Trust, and others. Not all were actually "trust" arrangements, but the label was given to any large combination whose purpose was to restrain competition.

The power of a trust was enormous; it could shut down every one of its plants at will, or close some and keep others open. It could cut purchases of raw material, artificially limit production, raise prices to enrich itself at the public expense, and lower prices to get rid of a competitor. For business, the trust was an attractive solution. For the economy, however, it could be a problem.

The Panic of 1893: Banker Control

Pools and trusts seemed to be the answer abroad as well as in the United States. In Germany in

John Pierpont Morgan. (*Edward Steichen, The Museum of Modern Art, New York. Gift of A. Conger Goodyear.*)

particular, the *cartel*, a large pooling arrangement with powerful control, became the accepted means of regulating production, marketing, and prices. In Europe, these arrangements usually had the open approval of the government. In the United States, free competition was the ideal and the only politically acceptable position. For a long time, the government did nothing about the consolidations and the tendency toward monopoly.

The Sherman Anti-Trust Act of 1890, the first attempt at federal control, was the result of growing public anger at the artificially raised prices and artificially closed opportunities the trusts brought about. Competition, however, grew more intense than ever after the passage of the Sherman Act and especially after the Panic of 1893, when once again thousands of industrial firms failed, banks closed, and one railroad out of every six went into receivership.

This panic began in February 1893, when the Philadelphia & Reading Railroad—with negotiable assets of $100,000 and short-term debts of $18 million—was forced into bankruptcy. As the business collapse snowballed and unemployment soared, the federal government was bombarded with demands for relief. Pressure on the government intensified because even the nation's most conservative leaders now feared revolution. "It is probably safe to say," a leading industrial journal observed, "that in no civilized country in this century, not actually in the throes of war or open insurrection, has society been so disorganized as it was in the United States during the first half of 1894; never was human life held so cheap; never did the constituted authorities appear so incompetent to enforce respect for the law."

At the same time, just as the Panic of 1873 had given Carnegie and Rockefeller opportunities for expansion at bargain rates, the Panic of 1893 gave Morgan and a few other investment bankers their opportunity. Their first objective was to bring order out of chaos in railroad finance. By 1904, they had consolidated 1,040 railroad lines into six huge combinations with an aggregate capital of $10 billion. Each in turn was allied to either the Morgan or the Kuhn, Loeb interests. After this success, they moved into manufacturing and public utilities.

The return of prosperity in 1898 made it even easier to market the securities of new combines. Many of them were formed, in fact, just to make banking profits from new stocks and bonds. The strong movement toward consolidation following the Panic of 1873 had produced in twenty years only twelve great industrial trusts, with an aggregate capital under $1 billion. By contrast, Morgan's United States Steel Corporation alone had a capitalization of almost $1.5 billion.

In 1904, John Moody, in his classic study *The Truth about the Trusts,* listed no less than 318 new industrial combinations with an aggregate capital of $7.25 billion. They controlled 5,288 separate plants. Moody also listed 111 public utility combinations, all but 14 of them organized after 1893. They controlled 1,336 plants, with an aggregate capital of $3.7 billion.

The power of the investment bankers came from their ability to supply the capital for growing companies. Having gotten the money from investors who gave it largely because of confidence in the bankers themselves, the bankers felt it necessary to place their own men on the companies' boards of directors and take a hand in management. In this way, the bankers' economic power, and Morgan's especially, spread from the financial community to the heart of the big business system. By 1913 the Morgan-Rockefeller interests alone held 341 directorships in 112 corporations whose worth was estimated at more than $22 billion.

A second feature of the Morgan method was the bankers' control of, or close alliance with, other sources of capital, such as commercial banks, trust companies that administered large estates and other properties, and huge life insurance companies that collected payments from millions of small policyholders. The bankers' influence thus eventually extended over almost the entire population.

With the control it exercised over railroad lines, banks, and life insurance, steel, electrical, and shipping companies, the Morgan empire was an awesome concentration of economic power—in many ways the supreme monopoly, or *conglomerate.* Although the public might appreciate the order and efficiency Morgan and others introduced into the companies they controlled or influenced, it still had reason to feel uneasy. The sheer size and impersonality of the economic structure invited suspicion. It was as though Americans were losing control over their lives and destiny. For hundreds of thousands of workers, that realization had already become a reality. It was reflected in the changing nature of their work, hopes, and organizations.

THE WORKERS

The impact of industrialization on American life in the decades after the Civil War is clearly shown in a 300 percent rise in nonagricultural employment, as compared with a rise of only 50 percent in the number of persons working on the farms. By 1890, more than 4.6 million Americans worked in factories, and another 3 million were divided equally between construction industries and transportation. The 10 million immigrants who poured into the United States between 1870 and 1900 added to the rapidly growing labor force. But these statistics only begin to suggest what industrialization meant. Even though many workers still aspired to middle-class status and managerial positions, the facts of industrial capitalism resulted in a loss of personal autonomy, new work patterns, and a new life style to fit the new surroundings and conditions of labor.

The tension between the demands of industrial capitalism and traditional work habits and rhythms grew rapidly and sometimes erupted into open warfare. Few modern industrial nations experienced such intensive labor conflict. The battlefields on which these skirmishes were fought—Homestead, Pullman, Cripple Creek, Lawrence, Paterson, McKees Rock, and "Bloody" Ludlow—came to occupy an important place in the history of the American working class. Out of these conflicts emerged an acute awareness among workers of the meaning of industrialization for their own lives, based on their perception of class rela-

(Text continues on page 439)

THE WORK PLACE

Only a Miner

Sung in various versions from 1888 to 1961 in coal, gold, silver, copper, and lead mining regions, "Only a Miner" became known as the American miner's national anthem.

The hard-working miners, their dangers are great,
Many while mining have met their sad fate,
While doing their duties as miners all do,
Shut out from the daylight and their darling ones, too.

He's only a miner been killed in the ground,
Only a miner and one more is found,
Killed by an accident, no one can tell,
His mining's all over, poor miner farewell.

He leaves his dear wife and little ones, too,
To earn them a living as miners all do,
While he was working for those whom he loved,
He met a sad fate from a boulder above.

Chorus:

With a heart full of sorrow we bid him farewell,
How soon we may follow there's no one can tell,
Got pity the miners, protect them as well,
And shield them from danger while down in the ground.

Chorus: (twice)

Pittsburgh coal miner, 1910. (*Photograph by Lewis Hine, Library of Congress*)

In a garment sweatshop, a 12-year-old boy pulls threads. (*Photograph by Jacob Riis, The Jacob Riis Collection, Museum of the City of New York*)

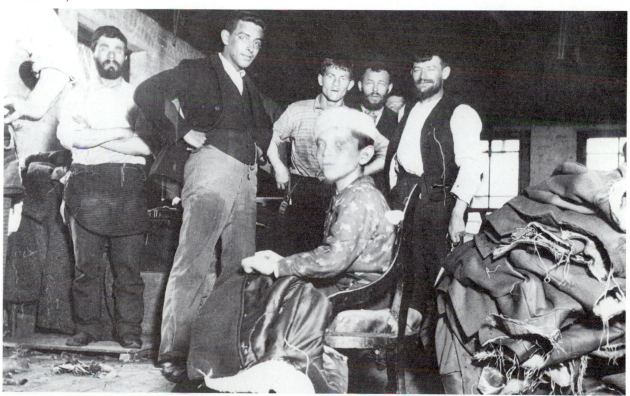

The New Feudalism

We work in *his* mill. We live in *his* houses. Our children go to *his* schools. We go to *his* YMCA. We spend our leisure in *his* reading room. Our children play in *his* streets. We go to *his* hospital. We are arrested by *his* constable and tried by *his* magistrate. And when we die we are buried in *his* cemetery.

Southern cotton mill worker, 1913

Source: A. J. McKelway, "Child Wages in the Cotton Mill: Our Modern Feudalism," *Child Labor Bulletin,* II (1913), 7.

Girl in cotton mill. (*Photograph by Lewis Hine, Library of Congress*)

Steel workers. (*Photograph by Lewis Hine, Library of Congress*)

Mighty Few Men Have Stood What I Have

Fifteen years after the Homestead Strike, John Griswold, a Scotch-Irish worker at a Pittsburgh blast furnace, assessed the conditions in his plant and his future prospects:

"Mighty few men have stood what I have, I can tell you. I've been twenty years at the furnaces and been workin' a twelve-hour day all that time, seven days in the week. We go to work at seven in the mornin' and we get through at night at six. We work that way for two weeks and then we work the long turn and change to the night shift of thirteen hours. The long turn is when we go on at seven Sunday mornin' and work through the whole twenty-four hours up to Monday mornin'. That puts us onto the night turn for the next two weeks, and the other crew onto the day. The next time they get the long turn and we get twenty-four hours off, but it don't do us much good. I get home at about half past seven Sunday mornin' and go to bed as soon as I've had breakfast. I get up about noon so as to get a bit o' Sunday to enjoy, but I'm tired and sleepy all the afternoon. . . ."

"Everybody says I'm a fool to stay here. I dunno, mebbe I am. It don't make so much difference though. I'm gettin' along, but I don't want the kids ever to work this way. I'm goin' to educate them so they won't have to work twelve hours."

(*John A. Fitch,* The Steel Workers. *New York: Russell Sage Foundation, 1911, pp. 11–12.*)

A domestic worker. (*Cook Collection, Valentine Museum*)

The Autobiography of a Black Domestic

I am a negro woman, and I was born and reared in the South. I am now past forty years of age and am the mother of three children. My husband died nearly fifteen years ago. . . . For more than thirty years—or since I was ten years old—I have been a servant in one capacity or another in white families . . .

I frequently work from fourteen to sixteen hours a day. I am compelled . . . to sleep in the house. I am allowed to go home to my own children, the oldest of whom is a girl of 18 years, only once in two weeks, every other Sunday afternoon—even then I'm not permitted to stay all night. . . . I don't know what it is to go to church; I don't know what it is to go to a lecture or entertainment or anything of the kind; I live a treadmill life . . . You might as well say that I'm on duty all the time—from sunrise to sunrise, every day in the week. I am the slave, body and soul, of this family.

Another thing—it's a small indignity, it may be, but an indignity just the same. No white person, not even the little children just learning to talk . . . ever thinks of addressing any negro man or woman as *Mr.* or *Mrs.*, or *Miss.* The women are called, "Cook," or "Nurse," or "Mammy," or "Mary Jane," or "Lou," or "Dilcey," as the case might be. . . . In many cases our white employers refer to us, and in our presence, too, as their "niggers." No matter what they call us—no matter what they teach their children to call us—we must tamely submit, and answer when we are called; we must enter no protest; if we did object, we should be driven out . . . and, in applying for work at other places, we should find it very hard to procure another situation.

(*From "More Slavery at the South," by a Negro Nurse,* The Independent, *72 (January 25, 1912), pp. 196–200.*)

Women at Work

From where I sat I could see the whole floor from end to end. I saw hundreds and hundreds of girls bending over sewing machines. The floor vibrated, beat steadily like a pulse, with the steam power. The air was filled with the whirr. I had to keep my head low to distinguish the noise of my own machine and we girls shouted and watched each other's lips when we talked. But we did not talk much! Right in front of me at a big table stood . . . the head forewoman. . . . There were also assistant forewomen and assistant foremen, and superintendents and assistant superintendents. They were all watching us.

(*Rose Cohen,* Out of the Shadow. *New York: George H. Doran, 1918.*)

A garment worker. (*Brown Brothers*)

Factory workers. (*National Archives*)

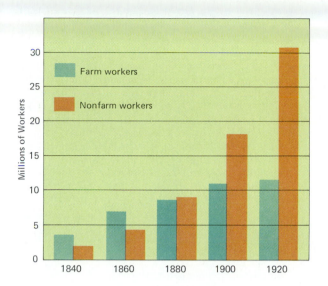

tions in the factory world. Trade unions emerged from a need to deal with these conditions. But in the last decades of the nineteenth century, workers were not sure what form their response should take.

In some industries, periodic unemployment was certain because factories worked long hours when demand was high. Work weeks ranging from 60 to over 80 hours were common; the seven-day week was the rule in steel and paper mills, oil refineries, and other mechanized plants. Advances in technology speeded up the pace of production, and the worker was expected to keep up. Fast machines greatly increased the physical danger of factory work; long hours and fatigue increased accidents, injuries, and deaths.

Another result of technology was that the machines did more and more of the skilled work, draining much of the personal satisfaction from labor. Proud craftsmen were reduced to the status and pay of menials. "When I first went to learn the trade," a twenty-three-year-old worker testified in 1883, "a machinist considered himself more than the average workingman; in fact he did not like to be called a workingman. He liked to be called a mechanic. . . . and felt he belonged in the middle class; but today he recognizes the fact that he is simply the same as any other ordinary laborer, no more and no less."

This steady lowering of the skilled craftsman's position not only made it difficult for him to sup-

port his family, but forced him to change many work habits. The informality of the old work establishments was replaced by rigid discipline. "During working hours," a Massachusetts leatherworker declared, "the men are not allowed to speak to each other, though working close together, on pain of instant discharge. Men are hired to watch and patrol the shop." To this worker, the new conditions of labor demanded a response. But like many others, he was not sure what they could or should do. "The workers of Massachusetts have always been law and order men," he concluded. "We loved the country, and respected the laws. For the last five years [1874–1879] the times have been growing worse every year, until we have been brought down so far that we have not much farther to go. What do the mechanics of Massachusetts say to each other? I will tell you: 'We must have a change. Any thing is better than this. We cannot be worse off, no matter what the change is.'"

The working class was by no means an exclusively male domain. By 1900, nearly one out of every five workers was female. In such industries as textiles, shoes, and clothing, women might make up as much as 40 to 60 percent of the work force. Most of them were young and childless, or widows. Clerical work and retail sales were becoming increasingly available to them. Nearly half of employed women, however, still worked in domestic service. Among first- and second-generation immigrant women, participation in the work force was particularly high; in New York City, for example, in 1910 nearly 60 percent of immigrant women between the ages of eighteen and twenty-four worked for wages.

For the working class women who remained at home, the daily tasks they confronted were as demanding as many industrial jobs. To maintain a household required a continual struggle with filth and disease. With sewer systems, indoor plumbing, lighting, and a decent water supply rarely available in working-class neighborhoods, that struggle proved impossible to win. To make ends meet, moreover, many families took in boarders, and housewives cooked and washed for them. When in 1909 women applying for work at a Minnesota employment bureau were asked what kind of job they preferred, many simply responded, "Anything but housework."

The Great Strike of 1877

Work in railroad transportation was freer of constant supervision than work in factories, but it took

MAN AND MACHINE

Encouraged by the increased demand for shoes, mill owners during the Civil War had introduced automatic machinery. With about 100 subdivisions in the making of shoes, the workers became specialized in one simple operation. Horace M. Eaton, general secretary-treasurer of the Boot and Shoe Workers' Union, testified in 1899 before a congressional commission on the results.

Q. *The workman only knows how to perform the labor of one department?*

A. *That is all, and he becomes a mere machine. . . . Now, take the proposition of a man operating a machine to nail on forty to sixty pairs cases of heels in a day. That is 2,400 pairs, 4,800 shoes, in a day. One not accustomed to it would wonder how a man could pick up and lay down 4,800 shoes in a day, to say nothing of putting them on a jack into a machine and having them nailed on. That is the driving method of the manufacture of shoes under these minute subdivisions. . . .*

Q. *Are there many workmen in the factory who can make a whole shoe?*

A. *No, the art of shoemaking, so far as the individual is concerned, has got to be a thing of the past. About all the actual shoemakers you can find today are located in small cobbling and custom shops—old-time* *workmen; and almost invariably you will find that they are old men. . . .*

Q. *What effect, if any, has it had on the social habits of the workman?*

A. *I think it has had quite an effect. . . . In these old shops, years ago, one man owned the shop; he took in work and three, four, five, or six others, neighbors, came in there and sat down and made shoes right in their laps, and there was no machinery. Everybody was at liberty to talk; they were all politicians. . . . Of course, under these conditions, there was absolute freedom and exchange of ideas, they naturally would become more intelligent than shoe workers can at the present time, when they are driving each man to see how many shoes he can handle, and where he is surrounded by noisy machinery. And another thing, this nervous strain on a man doing just one thing over and over and over again must necessarily have a wearing effect on him; and his ideals, I believe, must be lowered.*

Q. *What are the hours of labor?*

A. *Ten hours a day almost uniformly.*

Source: U.S. Congress, House, *Report of the Industrial Commission on the Relations and Conditions of Capital and Labor Employed in Manufactures and General Business*, 56th Cong., 2d Sess., House Doc. 495 (Washington: U.S. Government Printing Office, 1901), VII, 359, 361, 363.

---

such a heavy toll in accidents that life insurance companies rejected railroad workers as bad risks. Soon after the Civil War, and principally to establish some means of protection for their families, railroad workers began to set up labor organizations. These were called "brotherhoods" and "orders," not unions. Their members paid "premiums," not dues. Their constitutions did not mention collective bargaining or working conditions. Their main goal, as the Brotherhood of Locomotive Engineers put it, was "postmortem" security.

Working conditions on the railroads grew so bad during the depression of the 1870s that spontaneous strikes in 1877 spread across the country. The stage had been set by local railroad strikes earlier in the depression and by strikes in other industries. The Long Strike of 1875 by coal workers in Pennsylvania had been marked by the exceptional brutality of Pinkerton detectives hired by the coal operators. The six-month strike ended only when hunger forced the miners to give in and accept a 20 percent wage cut.

One of the railroad workers' major complaints by mid-1877 was the practice of blacklisting all who even dared join the brotherhoods and orders. Another sore point was the high prices charged at the railroad hotels when the men worked away from home. Discontent deepened when the roads ordered greater numbers of "doubleheaders"— that is, trains of approximately twice the normal number of cars—without added workers. The last straw was the announcement of further wage cuts, late in the spring of 1877.

The leaderless revolt began on July 16, when firemen on the B & O quit work. The *Baltimore Sun* commented:

There is no disguising the fact that the strikers in all their lawful acts have the fullest sympathy of the community. The 10 percent reduction after two previous reductions was ill advised. . . . The singular part of the disturbance is in the very active part taken by the women, who are the wives and mothers of the firemen. They look famished and wild, and declare for starvation rather than have their people work for reduced wages.

The strike soon spread to Pittsburgh. Although ordered out to break the strike, the local militia chose to side with the workers of the hated Pennsylvania Railroad. Philadelphia militiamen were then called in. They opened fire on the demonstrators, and an enraged crowd of 20,000 men and women attacked the soldiers and forced them to seek shelter. President Hayes finally had to send federal troops to restore order.

What they could not restore were 2 miles of Pennsylvania track strewn with the ruins of 104 locomotives and more than 2,000 railroad cars. Meanwhile, the strike had spread from the Pennsylvania, along the Erie and New York Central, all the way to St. Louis. Coal miners, stevedores, farmers, small businessmen, and thousands of the unemployed joined in demonstrations to support the railroad workers' cause.

The president had to order out federal troops when local militia units proved to be unreliable. "Many of us," an officer with the New York militia explained, "have reason to know what long hours and low pay mean, and any movement that aims at one or the other will have our sympathy and support. We may be militiamen, but we are workingmen first."

Within a year after its centennial celebration, the United States experienced its first national strike—not a strike at all, a St. Louis newspaper observed, but "a labor revolution." What made it so ominous was the speed with which it spread and its unplanned character. The workers lacked any real leadership or organization, and yet nothing like this had happened before: street fighting in Baltimore, Pittsburgh, and Chicago; widespread destruction of railroad equipment; the president of the United States meeting regularly with his cabinet over the crisis, sending federal troops, threatening to impose martial law, and taking precautions to safeguard public buildings in Washington, D.C. To many Americans, including those who shared the workers' grievances against the railroads, the very scale of the strike and the bitterness of the struggle raised serious concerns about the survival of society. Newspaper editors, clergymen, intellectuals, and politicians alike talked about impending disaster. Some of them attributed the unrest to newly arrived immigrants and to "the devilish spirit of communism."

By August 2, after hundreds of strikers and others had been killed and thousands injured, railroad service was forcibly restored on all lines. *The New York Times* called the outcome "a drawn battle," and there was considerable truth in this assessment. The workers had made their point. They had succeeded, with virtually no organization, in shutting down two-thirds of the nation's 75,000 miles of track. Some railroad managers wisely moved to halt further wage cuts or to take back

those made earlier: "We have seen," said one railroad president, "that a reduction of pay to employees may be as expensive to the company as an increase of the pay." Another director suggested a profit-sharing plan for employees. But at the same time, the employer class moved to firm up their defenses.

Railroad leaders now demanded that National Guardsmen in the states be trained specifically to combat "labor violence." Many states did, in fact, appropriate large sums for the expansion of their Guards and for building and equipping new armories. The railroads and many other corporations also set up private armies of their own. Detectives were used to discover union members, who were promptly fired. New employees now had to sign *yellow dog contracts* that forced them not to engage in any union activity. But the workers also learned some valuable lessons. There was talk about an organization that would include all branches of railroad labor. Some railroad men left the brotherhoods to join the new national union, the Knights of Labor.

National Unions

After the Civil War, efforts were made to organize labor nationally. The National Labor Union, formed in Baltimore in 1866, drew delegates from many local organizations and from reform groups interested in labor's welfare. In 1872, it was ambitious enough to form a Labor Reform party and to run a candidate in the presidential election. Most of its other efforts were as impractical as this one, however; and although at one time it claimed a membership of nearly 650,000, it failed to survive the Panic of 1873.

The Noble Order of the Knights of Labor was organized in Philadelphia in 1869. It achieved little until Terence V. Powderly, a Scranton machinist, became Grand Master in 1878. The Knights' principal aim was to unite all those who worked (except for liquor dealers, lawyers, gamblers, and bankers) into one huge union that would produce and distribute goods on a cooperative basis. Powderly traveled all over the country recruiting people and establishing more than thirty cooperative enterprises. Although Powderly opposed strikes and violence, his organization benefited from a successful strike against the Missouri Pacific Railroad in 1885. Certain unions affiliated with the Knights forced Jay Gould to restore a wage cut and rehire hundreds of union men he had fired. This victory so raised the Knights'

Samuel Gompers. (*AFL–CIO News*)

standing that within a year membership had grown from about 100,000 to more than 700,000.

The American Federation of Labor, given its modern form in 1886 by the "business unionists," was a very different kind of organization. Led by Samuel Gompers, its members were not individual workers, but affiliated national craft unions. The AFL imposed certain standards on its members. It insisted on regular dues to provide members and the federation (which took a share) with strike funds. It hired full-time organizers. It settled all issues of jurisdiction that arose when two or more member unions tried to organize workers in similar fields, and it sought to protect its members from raids by nonaffiliated rivals.

Avoiding politics and radical ideology, the AFL under Gompers appealed to the elite of the working class, the skilled workers, and focused on immediate economic gains. It accepted modern capitalism and the reality of a fixed working class. It proposed to protect workers from the worst abuses of the economic system, to sell their labor at the most favorable price, and to improve the standard of living of those who most likely would remain in the working class for the remainder of

their lives. The primary aim of the AFL, then, was to force employers to engage in collective bargaining with member unions on everyday issues such as wages, hours, and working conditions. An essential goal was the establishment of the *closed shop*—that is, a shop that would agree to employ only AFL members. Between 1886 and 1892, the AFL gained the affiliation of unions with some 250,000 members. By 1910, 1.5 million workers belonged to the organization. But this impressive increase in membership needs to be measured against the far more rapid increase of the industrial work force. At Gompers' death in 1924, the AFL was the dominant workers' organization in the United States, but fewer than 10 percent of the nation's wage earners were organized into trade unions. Most wage earners, many of them women, worked in the new mass production industries without protection of any kind. Long hours, low wages, and poor living conditions continued to take their toll.

The Black Worker

Although relatively few blacks had entered the industrial labor force during the early postwar decades, the race issue troubled the new unions and industrial workers generally. Should black workers be organized, or should they be left to become an industrial labor pool that would work for minimum wages and serve as strikebreakers? If organized, should black workers be invited to join with white workers, or should they be in segregated unions? The National Labor Union endorsed solidarity with black workers. "There is no concealing the fact," said one spokesman, "that the time will come when the Negro will take possession of the shops if we have not taken possession of the Negro." The leaders, however, had trouble with their followers, and no specific action was taken.

Meanwhile, under the leadership of Isaac Myers, a Baltimore ship caulker, blacks organized a National Colored Labor Union in 1869. But workers figured less prominently in the organization than black Republican party politicians, ministers, and government clerks. Reflecting a middle-class orientation, the NCLU discouraged strikes and advised blacks to try to improve themselves by self-reliance, perseverance, and economy. When politicians like Frederick Douglass replaced the union-oriented Myers, the organization became a part of the Republican party machinery and then disappeared.

At its peak of strength, the Knights of Labor included some 70,000 blacks and organized black as well as mixed locals, both in the South and the North. Organizers in the South, however, were assaulted by vigilantes and lynch mobs, often with the assistance of law enforcement officers. The mobs usually had the law on their side, since most southern state governments had passed laws declaring it a conspiracy for persons to join together to alter contracts, even oral contracts, between workers and employers.

Few blacks were admitted to the craft unions that made up the AFL; they were found mainly among the miners. Gompers' position was made clear in his annual report of 1890, when he repeated the "necessity of avoiding as far as possible all controversial questions." Certain questions did arise from time to time about AFL unions whose constitutions excluded blacks. These were handled by directives from the national leadership that were ignored. The AFL simply went along with the practices of its members—practices that reflected the racial attitudes shared by most Americans.

Racism in the trade unions, as well as the willingness of employers to exploit racial and ethnic divisions in the working class, would doom the possibility of labor solidarity. Not until World War I and the Great Migration (see Chapter 27) did black workers become a major part of the industrial labor force. But even then, except among miners and longshoremen, the advantages of union organization were denied them for a generation more.

Strikes and Confrontation: Haymarket, Homestead, Pullman

On May Day, 1886, Knights of Labor unions and other groups sponsored a massive demonstration to promote the eight-hour day. In Chicago, where an independent strike against the McCormick Harvester Company was in progress, the Knights' demonstration was followed by outdoor meetings addressed by anarchists. At a meeting in Haymarket Square on May 4, a bomb thrown at the police killed an officer. Seven more officers and four civilians died in a riot that followed.

The bomb thrower never was found, but seven of the eight anarchists arrested and accused of murder were sentenced to death. Four of the seven were executed and one committed suicide. The sentence of the other two was changed to life imprisonment. Six years later, accusing the sentenc-ing judge of "malicious ferocity," Governor John P. Altgeld courageously and unconditionally pardoned them.

The Haymarket riot outraged the general public, intensified fears of radicalism, and broke the back of the eight-hour-day movement. Although the Knights of Labor had nothing to do with the incident, newspapers and employers exploited Haymarket to ruin the entire labor movement. Within a few years, because of Haymarket and growing internal dissension, the Knights had just about disappeared.

Two massive confrontations between capital and labor in the 1890s—Homestead and Pullman—revived fears of revolution. Only two years after Gompers had negotiated a contract with the Carnegie Steel Company, the Homestead strike dealt a severe blow to the iron and steel workers. The strike was incited by the company itself when, while Carnegie was in Europe, Henry Clay Frick tried to cut wages. The powerful Amalgamated Association of Iron and Steel Workers, an AFL affiliate, refused to accept.

On July 1, 1892, Frick closed down the huge Homestead plant and hired 300 Pinkertons to protect it. When the Pinkertons arrived by barge several days later, they were met by an army of angry workers. Frick then requested the governor of Pennsylvania to call out the state militia. Only after five months did the workers begin to go back to their jobs on company terms. But by then they had lost more than the strike.

Public sympathy had been with them at first, but when Alexander Berkman, an anarchist who had nothing to do with the strike, tried to assassinate Frick, feelings changed. Fifteen years later, an investigation of conditions at Homestead revealed that wages remained low. Most of the men worked a twelve-hour day, with a twenty-four-hour stretch every two weeks when they changed day and night shifts.

The second great strike of the 1890s broke out at a Pullman "company town" near Chicago but soon spread to most of the western railroads. The control George Pullman had over the lives of the workers in his "model" town had been virtually complete. With the coming of the depression in 1893, the Pullman Company began laying off workers and cutting the pay of those who were kept on. When in May 1894 the workers asked for some reductions in rent and store prices, they were refused and their negotiators were fired. The workers then walked out and appealed for help from the American Railway Union, which many of them had joined. This was the union of all lev-

Eugene Debs of the American Railway Union recalled of his days of organizing activity: "My grip was always packed, to tramp through a railroad yard in the rain, snow, or sleet half the night. To be ordered out of the roundhouse for being an agitator or to be put off a train were all in the program." (*Brown Brothers*)

els of railroad workers Eugene V. Debs had begun to organize in 1893, when he found the individual railroad craft unions could not fight the companies.

Late in June 1894, when Pullman refused to arbitrate with Debs, 120,000 railroad workers joined the Pullman strikers. The western roads were paralyzed. By July 1, Debs thought he had won. The railroads "immediate resources were exhausted," he wrote, "and they were unable to operate their trains." All this was accomplished with "no sign of violence or disorder."

But that hopeful outlook soon changed. The General Managers Association, an employer organization representing all the railroads terminating in Chicago, had appealed to Attorney General Richard Olney for federal troops to get the trains rolling. Olney, a former railroad lawyer, was more than willing. Using the Sherman Antitrust Act, which forbade "combinations in restraint of trade,"

he obtained a series of orders in federal courts enjoining the union and "all other persons" to stop virtually every kind of activity impeding railroad operation, even "persuasion" of workers to quit their jobs. By July 3, Olney had gathered the first of thousands of federal marshals in the Chicago area to see that the injunctions were obeyed.

It is not certain how it began, but violence broke out. Using as his excuse the need to move the mail (railroad owners made a point of attaching Pullman cars to the mail trains), President Cleveland ordered in federal troops, making a bad situation worse. Workers resisted military efforts to move the trains and had to be forcibly driven from the tracks. Angered by having federal troops in his state without his invitation, as the Constitution required, Governor Altgeld poured in his own militia. By July 10 there were 14,000 soldiers in Chicago and on the railroads' right of way. In twenty states the National Guard had been mobilized, and many American Railway Union members were arrested.

To obey the federal injunctions was to break the strike. Rather than do so, Debs and three other union officers were arrested on charges of contempt of court. Harassment of union leaders soon disorganized the strikers. The American Railway Union itself disintegrated. Pullman workers who had not played an active role in the strike straggled back to work under the old conditions. In December, the United States Circuit Court convicted Debs of the contempt charge and sentenced him to six months in jail. The Supreme Court subsequently upheld the sentence.

The decision had enormous consequences for organized labor. Employers now had a powerful weapon with which to fight strikes and boycotts, and they used it widely and effectively until such injunctions were outlawed by the Norris-LaGuardia Act of 1932.

Despite the publicity given to labor warfare and organization, the vast majority of the work force remained unorganized. By 1898, there were more than 17 million factory workers, but only 500,000 were in unions. Even as the United States became the leading industrial power in the world, millions of workers did not share in its prosperity. After spending ten months in the Pittsburgh district not long after the Homestead strike, an investigator concluded that the men in the steel plants existed to work and worked to exist: "The years have done their work, and these men, with spirit dead, face a future in which they expect nothing and ask for nothing. They look dull-eyed on a world from which the brightness is gone."

The Industrial Workers of the World

In the entire history of the American labor movement, no organization provoked as much hostility, controversy, and commitment as the Industrial Workers of the World—the Wobblies—between 1905 and 1924. The kind of people it attracted suggested much about its appeal: disgruntled trade unionists like Charles Moyer, president of the battle-scarred Western Federation of Miners, and radical intellectuals like Daniel DeLeon of the Socialist Labor party. A Marxist priest, Father Thomas J. Hagerty, wrote the IWW Preamble, which began: "The working class and the employing class have nothing in common." Among IWW revolutionaries were the almost legendary Mother Jones, seventy-five years old in 1905 and an organizer for the United Mine Workers, and the young Elizabeth Gurley Flynn, "The Rebel Girl." Another of its workers, Joel Ammanuel Haagland (alias Joe Hill), supplied the IWW with songs that survived both his execution by a Utah firing squad and the end of the IWW itself.

Elizabeth Gurley Flynn of the IWW. (*Brown Brothers*)

There are women of many descriptions
In this queer world, as everyone knows.
Some are living in beautiful mansions,
And are wearing the finest of clothes.
There are blue-blooded queens and princesses,
Who have charms made of diamond and pearl;
But the only and thoroughbred lady
Is the Rebel Girl.

"The Rebel Girl" by Joe Hill

William (Big Bill) Haywood of the IWW. "I do not care a snap of my fingers whether or not the skilled workers join. We are going down in the gutter to get at the mass of workers and bring them up to a decent plane of living." (*Culver Pictures, Inc.*)

But the dominant personality, whose massive physical presence itself was impressive, proved to be William "Big Bill" Haywood, a former hardrock miner. His experiences in the Colorado mining wars had made him bitter toward both the employer class and the conservative AFL. "This is not a rival of the American Federation of Labor," he told the IWW founding convention, "for the very simple reason that this is a labor organization, in contrast with the American Separation of Labor, which was neither American, nor a federation, nor of labor."

Unlike the AFL, the Wobblies appealed to the forgotten, unskilled, casual, and marginal laborers, including the most degraded segments of the working class: lumberjacks; western gold, lead, silver, and copper miners; construction, cannery, and dock workers; migratory field hands; and the "blanket stiffs" and "bindle bums" who rode the "rattlers" and lived in railroad embankment hobo "jungles." The IWW organized black lumber workers in Louisiana and Texas as well as black dockworkers in Baltimore and Philadelphia.

Like the AFL, the Wobblies believed in direct economic action to improve workers' lives. But by direct action, the IWW meant not simply strikes, but massive work slowdowns ending in a general strike that would force the capitalist class to surrender its power and replace the state with an industrial syndicate directed by the workers. In the meantime, the IWW concentrated on improving the lives of workers. "The final aim is revolution," a Wobbly organizer explained. "But for the present let's see if we can get a bed to sleep in, water enough to take a bath and decent food to eat."

Although the IWW never attracted more than 5 percent of all trade unionists, and probably never exceeded 150,000 members at the peak of its strength, its impact was enormous. "A movement is judged," said one Wobbly, "not only by what it does itself, but also by what it compels the opposition to do." When the IWW moved east, especially into the textile industry, it won its most notable strike victory at Lawrence, Massachusetts, in 1912. Like so many IWW-led strikes, this one captured the nation's attention with its combina- tion of giant rallies, massive picket lines, flaming oratory, and revolutionary songs. This success marked the peak of IWW influence. In 1913 it participated in the strikes of textile workers in Paterson, New Jersey, and of rubber workers in Akron, Ohio; but both ended in failure.

From the beginning, sectarianism, loose orga- nization, and the withdrawal of key member unions (like the Western Federation of Miners) weakened the IWW. It failed to consolidate strike victories and to build stable local organizations. Under the growing pressure of patriotism and conformity after the entry of the United States into World War I in 1917, the IWW came under vigilante attack, federal prosecution, and harass- ment.

The Wobblies had promised to form the new society within the shell of the old. With the con- viction of its principal leaders in 1918 for under- mining the war effort, however, the IWW, as Dan Wakefield later wrote, had "to form the new soci- ety within the jails of the old." What survived were the songs, the legends, and the memory that the IWW had managed to give a new sense of power and dignity to some depressed and alienated work- ers, even if only for a short time.

THE PREACHER AND THE SLAVE

Joe Hill, songwriter for the IWW, explained that he wanted to reach the great mass of workers "who are too unintelligent and too indifferent to read a pam- phlet or an editorial on economic science." In "The Preacher and the Slave," Hill parodied the popular Salvation Army gospel hymn, "In the Sweet Bye and Bye." The Salvation Army, according to this version, advised the oppressed to be humble and content while awaiting their reward in heaven. The Wobblies, on the other hand, preached a little less hell on earth.

Long-haired preachers come out every night,
Try to tell you what's wrong and what's right;
But when asked how 'bout something to eat
They will answer with voices so sweet:

Chorus
You will eat, bye and bye,
In that glorious land above the sky;
Work and pray, live on hay,
You'll get pie in the sky when you die.

And the starvation army they play,
And they sing and they clap and they pray.
Till they get all your coin on the drum,
Then they'll tell you when you're on the bum:

Holy Rollers and jumpers come out,
And they holler, they jump and they shout.
"Give your money to Jesus," they say,
"He will cure all diseases today."

If you fight hard for children and wife—
Try to get something good in this life—
You're a sinner and bad man, they tell,
When you die you will sure go to hell.

Workingmen of all countries, unite,
Side by side we for freedom will fight:
When the world and its wealth we have gained
To the grafters we'll sing this refrain:

Last Chorus
You will eat, bye and bye,
When you've learned how to cook and to fry.
Chop some wood, 'twill do you good,
And you'll eat in the sweet bye and bye.

It is we who plowed the prairies;built the cities where
  they trade;
Dug the mines and built the workshops;endless miles
  of railroad laid.
Now we stand outcasts and starving,'mid the won-
  ders we have made;
But the Union makes us strong.

In our hands is placed a power greater than their
  hoarded gold;
Greater than the might of armies,magnified a thou-
  sand-fold.
We can bring to birth the new world from the ashes
  of the old.
For the Union makes us strong.

For the immediate future, at least, the AFL clearly dominated the portion of labor that was organized. The workers it ignored would have to wait for the emergence of the CIO in the 1930s.

Aspirations and Accommodations

In the decades after the Civil War, with new industrial giants like Rockefeller and Carnegie as their models, American farm boys swarmed into the cities with the expectation of working their way to the top. In Europe a similar movement from rural to urban life was under way. Each new influx of immigrants—first the Irish, then the Germans, then the Italians, Poles, Hungarians, and others from central and southeastern Europe—tended to start at the bottom of the economic ladder, only to be pushed upward as less experienced newcomers arrived.

The belief in individual opportunity, shared by both native American workers and newly arrived immigrants, no doubt accounted for much of their indifference to unionization. Organized or not, workers refused to surrender that dream of upward mobility. If they could not accomplish that leap themselves, they would seek it for their children. The trade union journals themselves reprinted selections from popular success novels. But despite the fact that many did manage to move into the middle class (some studies suggest as much as a quarter of the manual workers), most were not likely to make it.

"They have lost all desire to become bosses now," a machinist said of his fellow workers. "First they earn so small wages; and, next, it takes so much capital to become a boss now that they cannot think of it, because it takes all they can earn to live." With most major industries dominated by a few large companies, the success idea lost some of its credibility. Most workers learned to accommodate themselves to a position of dependency as well as to new uncertainties of livelihood.

WORDS AND NAMES IN AMERICAN HISTORY

Pork is of course meat from a pig, whether it be in the form of ham, bacon, chops, or chitterlings. It was and is a common item in the diet of many Americans. But *pork* is also a kind of legislation passed by the U.S. Congress and all the fifty states of this nation. In the days before electric refrigeration, pork was preserved by smoking it or by storing it in brine (salt water) in barrels. So sometimes this variety of legislation is called *pork barrel*. The term refers to appropriation bills that furnish money for such public projects as bridges, dams, harbor improvements, military installations, and so on that are sponsored by a particular Congressman or Senator with one eye on benefiting the constituents in his or her district and the other on his or her chances of re-election. In order to get an act passed that will benefit the folks at home, legislators support each other's bills, and the general level of governmental expenditure rises on a tide of mutual back scratching in the halls of Congress and other legislative bodies. Scholars are uncertain why this practice came to be called *pork-barreling* or why the term seems to have first come into common use in the 1880s. The authors of this book would welcome suggestions on this puzzling matter.

SUMMARY

By the turn of the twentieth century, America had undergone a massive economic transformation and become an urban, industrial giant. Settlement of the whole continent had been followed by an industrial boom in the North that turned the United States into a world power. And although economic success had great costs in terms of the dreary, miserable lives of those who labored in the factories, that cost was at first ignored.

What fueled and supported growth was the Gospel of Success, the idea that anyone could become rich if he or she was willing and able to work hard enough. Darwin's theory of the survival of the fittest was translated into social terms: those who succeeded and won out over competitors, no matter what methods they used, were those who were fit to survive and therefore deserved rewards. Those who failed did so through their own fault. These ideas justified the careers and the methods of such industrialists as Andrew Carnegie and John D. Rockefeller; they also supported the monopolies and trusts and the strangling of competition.

The first step in this economic revolution was the development of a nationwide mass transportation system—the railroads. Railroads offered a way to move vast quantities of goods easily and quickly to markets. They also offered opportunities for enormous profits, especially where there was only one line which producers of goods had to use. Great fortunes were made—but the cloud of suspicion raised by shady business practices and titanic paper battles among financiers led eventually to calls for reform and for government regulation. But despite the corruption and the "deals," by 1900 the American railroad network of 200,000 miles was the best, the most efficient, and the safest transportation system in the world.

The great expansion of northern industry after the Civil War was built on the railroads, which drew European capital to America and made Americans familiar with money markets and the idea of great corporations. Outstanding examples of the new industrial giants were Andrew Carnegie and John D. Rockefeller, whose steel and petroleum empires swallowed competitors like flies and who pioneered new kinds of vertical as well as horizontal expansion. Not only did Carnegie and Rockefeller buy up competitors, but they also bought out processors, distributors, and users of by-products, so that the Standard Oil Company and the Carnegie Corporation were, in fact, self-sufficient systems controlling every aspect of the making, distribution, and sale of their products.

The organization and management problems of these new giant corporations were solved by new technology: the telephone, the telegraph, the electric light, the typewriter, the adding machine. Public utilities in large cities also profited from economies of scale and became big enterprises. Together with the financiers and the bankers, the heads of these large businesses came to control the American economy. They soon found new ways to make even bigger combinations in the form of trusts, pools, and cartels. These monopolies were good for those who controlled them, but not always good for the economy. Americans began to experience the booms and busts of the business cycle, such as the Panics of 1873 and 1893.

Workers in particular began to realize their position in this new economic structure. They could be made to work long hours under unsafe conditions; they could be hired and fired at will; their wages could be lowered when business was bad—and there was nothing they could do about it. Furthermore, they were completely dependent upon their salaries for survival; almost no one in a city owned a house or a piece of land, and there was no such thing as welfare or unemployment insurance.

After 1870, labor conflict in the United States was intense and massive. It led eventually to the formation of trade unions, but at first there seemed little hope of workers ever acquiring any power. The Great Strike of 1877 on the railroads, a spontaneous, unorganized, and unplanned work stoppage, set the tone for much of the labor strife that followed—the Homestead and Pullman strikes, and the great Haymarket riot. Workers striking for better conditions or just against a wage cut found themselves at war not only with their employers, but with society as a whole. Governments called out troops to fire upon them, employers hired goon squads to beat them up, and sometimes after months of struggle, they would have to give in and go back to work under conditions worse than those before the strike.

Efforts to organize national unions met with mixed success. The National Labor Union founded in 1866 did not survive the Panic of 1873, and the Knights of Labor, organized in 1869, was ruined by the Haymarket riot in Chicago in 1886. The only union that grew and survived, the American Federation of Labor under Samuel Gompers, did so in part because it confined itself to economic issues such as hours and wages, and in part because it went along with other common practices, such as the exclusion of black workers. By avoiding the radical social and political activities of such movements as the IWW, the AFL survived and grew. But it did so at the expense of real labor solidarity, and the kind of influence European labor, with its political activism, was to have on major issues confronting industrial society.

Suggested Readings

E. C. Kirkland, *Industry Comes of Age* (1961), is a comprehensive examination of business, labor, and public policy between 1860 and 1897. See also D. North, *Growth and Welfare in the American Past* (1974). T. C. Cochran and W. Miller, *The Age of Enterprise* (1942), is readable and perceptive. In *Business in American Life* (1972) and *200 Years of American Business* (1977), T. C. Cochran treats business as a social institution and examines how the ideology of business reshaped American life and culture. Matthew Josephson, *The Robber Barons* (1934), is a classic indictment of business ethics. See also W. Miller (ed.), *Men in Business* (1952), and T. C. Cochran, *Railroad Leaders 1845–1890: The Business Mind in Action* (1953). A. D. Chandler, *Visible Hand: The Managerial Revolution in Business* (1977), is a masterful study of the evolution of modern management. D. F. Noble, *America by Design* (1977), examines the impact of science and technology on labor and the rise of corporate capitalism. For this and subsequent chapters, important studies are S. P. Hays, *The Response to Industrialism 1895–1914* (1957); R. H. Wiebe, *The Search for Order 1877–1920* (1967); and Alan Trachtenberg. *The Incorporation of America: Culture and Society, 1865–1893* (1980).

R. Hofstadter, *Social Darwinism in American Thought* (1955 ed.), is a thoughtful analysis. For the pervasiveness of the success myth, see M. Rischin (ed.), *The American Gospel of Success* (1965); I. G. Wyllie, *The Self-Made Man in America: The Myth of Rags to Riches* (1954); J. G. Cawelti, *Apostles of the Self-Made Man: Changing Concepts of Success in America* (1965); and D. Meyer, *The Positive Thinkers: A Study of the American Quest for Health, Wealth and Power from Mary Baker Eddy to Norman Vincent Peale* (1965).

G. R. Taylor and I. D. Neu, *The American Railroad Network 1861–1890* (1956), is a standard study of railroad development. On the transcontinentals, see R. R. Riegel, *The Story of the Western Railroads* (1926); O. Lewis, *The Big Four* (1951); and R. W. Fogel, *The Union Pacific Railroad: A Case in Premature Enterprise* (1960). A. Nevins, *John D. Rockefeller* (2 vols., 1954), is a sympathetic study. M. Klein, *The Life and Times of Jay Gould* (1986), is a reinterpretation of the legendary "robber baron." I. M. Tarbell, *The History of the Standard Oil Company* (1950 ed.), is a classic. J. F. Wall, *Andrew Carnegie* (1970), supersedes earlier biographies. See also Matthew Josephson, *Edison* (1959); R. V. Bruce, *Bell: Alexander Graham Bell and the Conquest of Solitude* (1973); and F. L. Allen, *The Great Pierpont Morgan* (1949).

The best introductions to the "new" labor history, which focuses on the social habits, expectations, and adaptations to industrialism of the working class, are H. G. Gutman, *Work, Culture, and Society in Industrializing America* (1976); David Montgomery, *Workers' Control in America: Studies in the History of Work, Technology, and Labor Struggles* (1979); J. R. Green, *The World of the Worker* (1980); and P. N. Stearns and D. Walkowitz (eds.), *Workers in the Industrial Revolution* (1974). An excellent brief analysis may be found in M. Dubofsky, *Industrialism and the American Worker 1865–1920* (1975). For critical essays on labor in the twentieth century, see D. Brody, *Workers in Industrial America* (1980). For the reactions of workers to industrialization, see L. F. Litwack (ed.), *The American Labor Movement* (1962), and Rosalyn Baxandall and others (eds.), *America's Working Women: A Documentary History* (1976). On the Knights of Labor, see two autobiographical accounts by T. V. Powderly, *Thirty Years of Labor* (1889) and *The Path I Trod* (1940). On the AFL, see Samuel Gompers, *Seventy Years of Life and Labor* (2 vols., 1925) and H. C. Livesay, *Samuel Gompers and Organized Labor in America* (1978). On Debs, see N. Salvatore, *Eugene V. Debs: Citizen and Socialist* (1982).

In *The Work Ethic in Industrial America 1850–1920* (1978), D. T. Rodgers examines the tension between the moral ideal of the work ethic and the reality. That reality is underscored in S. Yellen, *American Labor Struggles* (1936); R. V. Bruce, *1877: Year of Violence* (1959); A. Lindsey, *The Pullman Strike* (1942); M. F. Byington, *Homestead: The Households of a Mill Town* (1910); J. A. Fitch, *The Steel Workers* (1911); and D. Brody, *Steelworkers in America: The Nonunion Era* (1960). On the neglected subject of women and domestic service in industrializing America, see D. M. Katzman, *Seven Days a Week* (1978) and F. E. Dudden, *Serving Women: Household Service in Nineteenth-Century America* (1983). On American anarchism and the Haymarket riot, see P. Avrich, *The Haymarket Tragedy* (1984). The most important works on the IWW are J. L. Kornbluh (ed.), *Rebel Voices: An IWW Anthology* (1964); *The Autobiography of Big Bill Haywood* (1929); and M. Dubofsky, *We Shall Be All: A History of the IWW* (1969). For a more critical assessment of the IWW and American socialism, see A. S. Kraditor, *The Radical Persuasion, 1890–1917* (1981). The best recorded collections of labor songs are *Songs of Joe Hill* (Folkways 2039); *American Industrial Ballads* (Folkways 5251); and *Songs for a Better Tomorrow* (UAW Education Dept., 800 East Jefferson Avenue, Detroit, Michigan 48214). An important oral history is T. K. Hareven and R. Langenbach, *Amoskeag: Life and Work in an American Factory City* (1978).

PARTIES, POLITICS, AND REFORM

Chapter 21

When Mark Twain and Charles Dudley Warner coined the expression "The Gilded Age" for their novel of 1873, they wanted to suggest that the corruption of American life had made politics a sordid and shabby affair. Nor were they optimistic about the future. Neither politics nor parties could offer any solution. "The present era of incredible rottenness is not Democratic, it is not Republican, it is national. Politics are not going to cure moral ulcers like these, nor the decaying body they fester upon."

This dismal verdict would be extended by other critics to include the years from 1870 to 1900. The occupants of the White House—Grant to McKinley—were said to have been mediocre and uninspiring, the Senate was a "millionaire's club" dominated by special interests, the House was too chaotic to conduct the nation's business, the political parties differed on no vital issues. Elections offered no real choice, bosses ruled the cities, lobbyists and political machines ruled the legislatures, and the most important decisions affecting the American people were made outside the political arena. Worst of all, the promises of investigation and reform only deceived the public into thinking abuses would be cor-

rected. "All being corrupt together," E. L. Godkin, editor of *The Nation* wrote in 1873, "what is the use of investigating each other?"

But the politics of the Gilded Age, like that of any period in the nation's history, was many-sided. It was critical and creative as well as callous and corrupt, and the interplay of political, economic, and cultural interests was often complex. If the political candidates were mediocre, the turnout on election day was impressive. If the parties seemed hardly distinguishable on national issues, clear differences emerged on the state and local level and over cultural, religious, and ethnic issues.

If bosses, lobbyists, and the spoils system dominated politics, these abuses also stimulated reform movements. Narrow though these movements were in concept, and limited though they proved to be in action, they still reflected a public willingness to stop corruption. They helped to establish a merit system in the civil service, and public regulation of big business. The emergence of the Populist movement in the 1890s began a debate about the distribution of power and the role of government that would persist well into the next century. ■

THE PARTIES

Even today, with public relations and the media, political parties do not arouse the electorate as the Democrats and Republicans did in the last three decades of the nineteenth century. Speeches, torchlight parades, rallies, and picnics, along with considerable personal abuse, enlivened campaigns and gave the impression of voters making significant choices. Both parties were loose coalitions, alliances of different and often conflicting class, ethnic, and cultural interests. The Republicans were the party of high tariffs and sound money; but they included some who were sympathetic to free trade and monetary reform. The Democrats favored lower tariffs and an expanded currency, but attracted some who favored the protection of domestic industry and sound money.

Each party demonstrated strength among urban and rural, wealthy and poor, working-class and middle-class voters. Both included spokesmen for the dominant economic interests, but they sometimes differed among themselves, depending on the kind of business enterprise they represented. Agricultural regions, for example, had different needs and problems, and politicians who represented these regions might disagree on government policies, depending on whether they spoke for small or large farmers, for a single-crop economy or diversified agriculture, or for sections of the country (like the Ohio Valley) where industry and agriculture were both essential to the local economy.

Republicans: Stalwarts, Halfbreeds, and Mugwumps

For a long time, the Republicans lived off the issues of the past. They waved the "bloody shirt" of the Civil War with success for another quarter of a century. They reinforced party loyalty by attacking the Democrats as "traitors" and by providing liberal pensions for former Union soldiers and their dependents. By identifying Democrats with secession and the Confederate cause, the Republicans were able to avoid the problem of "hard times"—

Joseph Keppler's cartoon of "The Bosses of the Senate" (1889). In the same year William Allan White observed, "A United States senator . . . represented more than a state, more than a region. He represented principalities and powers in business. One senator, for instance, represented the New York Central, still another the insurance interests . . . Cotton had half a dozen senators. And so it went." (*Library of Congress*)

PARTIES, POLITICS, AND REFORM

the economic and social issues of industrialization and the growth of the cities.

As the party of high tariffs for industry, liberal aid to railroads, and conservative monetary policies, the Republicans had the support of much of the business community—especially manufacturers, bankers, and the holders of government bonds. There were internal clashes over economic issues, but before the party confronted the voters in national elections, these had usually been resolved.

Factionalism, however, continued to work against party unity throughout this period. The Stalwarts, led by Roscoe Conkling of New York, remained the hard-core machine politicians who put party success and the distribution of offices above any issue or principle. The Halfbreeds, led by James G. Blaine of Maine, gave the appearance of trying to balance party needs against the cries for reform. Essentially, however, the Stalwarts and Halfbreeds differed not over principles and policies, but rather over which group would inherit the spoils. Neither cared to be associated with the Independents (later called the Mugwumps), who had deserted the party in 1872 and were prepared to do so again to advance the crusade for good government. On economic questions like the tariff and sound money, there was little disagreement among the factions. They divided sharply, however, over commitment to civil service reform and occasionally over the quality of the presidential candidate.

Democrats: Southern Conservatives and City Bosses

The Democrats, despite the treason label, were strong contenders in national elections. After the overthrow of Radical Reconstruction and the defeat of black political aspirations, the South became solidly Democratic. White politicians waved their own kind of "bloody shirt," reminding constituents of the "horrors" of "black rule" during Reconstruction and of the need to maintain party unity in the name of "white supremacy." In northern industrial cities, where Irish bosses organized the immigrant population, the Democrats developed powerful political machines. They had less support from northern industry than the Republicans, but did have some business backers, mostly northern merchants in the import trade and commercial bankers who had southern business ties.

Conservative southern Democrats sometimes joined with western Republicans to support laws favorable to farm constituents. But they sided with the representatives of eastern commercial and financial interests against the more independent Democrats of the West and movements of economic radicalism. For a share of the spoils, they also voted in Congress with northern Republicans. It was a political alliance of convenience and conservatism that lasted well into the twentieth century.

Party Unity

On election day, Democrats came to expect a "solid South." Republicans usually counted on most of New England and the upper Middle West. To obtain votes elsewhere—especially in the key states of New York, New Jersey, Connecticut, Ohio, Indiana, and Illinois—both parties needed to attract as wide a segment of the electorate as possible. That need placed a premium on vagueness. Given a choice between the two parties, voters responded with a certain shrewdness. They refused to trust either one to dominate the federal government for a long period of time.

The Democrats lost the presidency when Lincoln was elected in 1860 and regained it only temporarily with Cleveland's two victories in 1884 and 1892. Yet the two parties showed almost equal postwar strength in numbers. In no election from 1876 to 1896 was the winning side's share of the popular vote greater than 50.8 percent. In two elections, 1876 and 1888, the Republican candidate won with fewer popular votes than his Democratic rival. In the thirteen Congresses elected between 1870 and 1894, the Democrats controlled the House nine times. Such balanced voting made party unity important.

Determined to hold their loose coalitions together, neither Democrats nor Republicans encouraged the kind of debate on issues that might sharpen internal differences. On such questions as the tariff, monetary policy, and regulation of railroads and corporations, both worded their positions to attract the widest number of voters. Neither suggested any fundamental dissatisfaction with the pace or cost of industrialization. Nor could they conceive of a need for the federal government to play a major role in the economy. No matter which party won, the industrial sector could feel reasonably secure. Perhaps that was why industrialists contributed handsomely to both parties.

But if business could feel comfortable, the politicians could not: Each election rewarded the victors with control of the patronage. With the federal payroll increasing from 53,000 to 166,000 between 1865 and 1891, the number of appointments available made the outcome of an election important. That this often resulted in inefficient public service was less important than the need to reward party faithfuls. The parties depended on the machines to deliver the votes, and the machines depended on their ability to deliver government jobs.

The efforts of the two parties to blur their differences on national economic issues in no way discouraged voter participation. Both Republicans and Democrats looked to their political machines to get out the voters on election day, and their efforts were marked with unusual success. The rate of voter turnout in the Gilded Age exceeded the earlier period and the succeeding Progressive Era. Between 1876 and 1896, 78.5 percent of the eligible voters turned out for presidential elections, 62.8 percent for off-year elections, far exceeding turnout in the twentieth century.

What voters responded to was not necessarily the ballyhoo or the machine. The outcome of elections was often determined by issues and tensions important on the state and precinct level. In many sections of the country, ethnocultural issues cut across class lines, and party identification and voting both reflected and reinforced cultural values and ethnic and religious loyalties. The Democrats drew large numbers of urban Catholics and immigrants. Republicans drew support from native-born, Anglo-Saxon Protestants. The differences and conflicts between these two blocs of voters were often expressed politically and took on added dimensions in a political campaign.

The Democrats, in representing their immigrant constituents, were more likely to oppose prohibition, Sunday closing laws, and any interference with the right of parents to send their children to parochial schools. The Republicans, reflecting the strong evangelical Protestantism that had helped to start the party during the antislavery conflict, were more sympathetic to using government to regulate morals and personal conduct: that is, they favored *blue laws* (statutes regulating work, commerce, amusements, and recreation on Sunday), restrictions on the sale and consumption of alcoholic beverages, and prohibiting the use of public funds for

The issue of state aid to private catholic schools divided the electorate and turned many state and local elections into fiercely fought contests. In this cartoon by Thomas Nast, crocodiles in the regalia of bishops are viewed as menacing the traditional public school system. (*Library of Congress*)

PARTIES, POLITICS, AND REFORM

parochial schools. At the same time, a revival of nativist agitation in the 1880s and 1890s found a warmer welcome in Republican ranks.

When any of these issues—public schools, prohibition, Sunday observance laws, or nativism—surfaced at election time, the campaigns on the local and state levels would be bitterly fought. And they determined not only the fate of the issues themselves, but the outcome of presidential and congressional races. If the voter found it difficult to understand how the tariff and currency reform affected his daily life, he could easily see affronts to his cultural values and threats to his personal and religious freedom. And he could be expected to vote accordingly.

The Reformers

Conservatives could more easily dominate parties and politics because their opponents were more divided than they were. Henry George's "single tax" (see Chapter 23), for example, aroused some interest in the cities, but had little political impact. Reformers who wanted inflation to cure rural problems won political followings only in isolated sections of the country. The Grangers, who proposed varied solutions to farmers' problems, gained only some regional, short-lived political victories in a few midwestern states. Reformers intent on changing the spoils system usually found themselves a minority in their own parties. The thrust of these various movements was the need to check abuses of economic and political power. But political and class differences set them apart, and the civil service reformers, for one, thought most other reformers were dangerous radicals.

All reformers were confronted by the spectacular development of the nation's resources and the prevailing doctrines of Social Darwinism and laissez faire, which supported absolute freedom for economic forces. The rapid pace of social and economic change, and the size of the problems they created, made it difficult to find easy solutions. If reformers could agree that unequal distribution of power lay at the root of the trouble, they could not agree on which abuses were the worst and how to correct them.

Politicians who served the needs of business resented any suggestion that they were abusing their positions. In helping to fulfill the nation's economic destiny, they viewed themselves as meeting their responsibilities to their constituents. The legislator, however, might need at times to weigh the national interest and that of his own region and political machine. If there was a growing consensus on the need to eliminate tariff abuses, for example, some who wanted reduction were ready to lower tariffs on all goods except those produced in their own districts. Candidates elected on a promise to reform the civil service found that once in office they needed to reward those who had helped elect them.

The reform politics of the period were dominated for a time by a group of men variously called Independents, Liberal Republicans, or Mugwumps. To them, the primary source of the nation's moral decline was the corruption of political power and the poor quality of government. The democratic ideals and heritage of this country were threatened because people who had once been given power on the basis of intellect, culture, and experience were no longer in command. They resented the political and economic power of the newly rich industrialists, who flaunted their wealth and influence. They expressed equal resentment for the masses of immigrants in the urban centers, the political bosses who used them, and the patronage system that kept those bosses in power.

Independent spokesmen included Carl Schurz, a German immigrant and former Union officer who had headed the Liberal Republican movement in Missouri in 1872; E. L. Godkin, editor of *The Nation;* George W. Curtis, editor of *Harper's Weekly;* and Charles Francis Adams, Jr., and his younger brother, Henry, descendants of two former presidents. What these liberal reformers worked for was civil service reform and the end of the spoils system. They wanted honest and efficient public service, and that meant a government run by men who were sufficiently disinterested and dedicated to act in the public interest—in other words, men like themselves. "We want government," said Carl Schurz, "which the best people of this country will be proud of."

Elitist, of high social standing, and university trained, the liberal reformers prided themselves on being "independents" in politics. They were prepared to cross party lines to advance their cause and return government to the hands of the virtuous. But they were committed to orthodox, laissez-faire economics and disliked those who operated outside the mainstream of American politics, particularly socialists and trade unionists. The railroad strikes of 1877, E. L. Godkin thought, must have been conceived "by a tramp by his evening fire, when full of stolen chicken and whiskey."

In the end, disillusion with the results of reform

and the refusal of the public to listen to them left reformers like Godkin bitter and frustrated men. "We all expected far too much of the human race," he conceded in 1898. "What stuff we used to talk." By that time, despite the newly established merit system, the quality of those who governed had not improved: the cities remained in the hands of the bosses; immigrants were arriving in even larger numbers; and more radical movements threatened to undermine the foundations of society.

THE REPUBLICAN YEARS: HARD TIMES AND CIVIL SERVICE REFORM

Despite the lack of results, the cry for reform was never altogether stopped. No matter how hard political leaders worked for party unity, the issues simply refused to disappear. In a period of economic fluctuations, rapid industrialization, and growing labor strife, it was difficult to keep issues like "hard times" and currency inflation out of the political arena. The alliance of business and politicians also kept alive the agitation to eliminate the spoils system. If that movement required a further push, it was soon supplied by a disappointed office seeker when he assassinated a newly elected president.

Hayes and Monetary Policy

When Rutherford B. Hayes won the Republican nomination for president in June 1876, the depression of the seventies was nearing its lowest point. Unrest was widespread. Although the federal government would not assume direct responsibility for individuals, there were traditional political steps to be taken to reverse the downward course of the economy. Most popular with debtors, especially long-term debtors like western farmers with mortgages, was an inflation of the money supply to cheapen the currency and raise prices. Creditors took the opposite view; they wanted to be paid back in currency at least equal in value in gold to that available at the time debts were incurred. The changing status of the paper money or "greenbacks" issued during the Civil War intensified the conflict.

Of the $450 million in greenbacks issued when the government required funds it could not obtain through taxes and borrowing, almost $100 million had been retired by 1868. The rest had risen in value from the wartime low of 38 cents in terms of the gold dollar. That low had resulted from concern over whether the greenbacks would be redeemed in gold or silver. In 1869, in *Hepburn* v. *Griswold*, the Supreme Court decided that Congress could not simply declare paper money legal tender without gold behind it, as Congress had done in 1862 and 1863 when it created the new currency. This decision sent the value of the greenbacks down. Then, in 1871, the Court reversed itself. In the Legal Tender cases, it said Congress could declare paper money legal tender.

With the end of the Civil War, advocates of "hard" or "sound" money wanted the government to withdraw the greenbacks from circulation and return to a standard in which money was redeemable in and backed by gold. But the supporters of "soft" money argued that an expanding economy required an expanding currency; contraction of the currency made no sense to them. And there was a particular urgency about this question. The nation was experiencing deflation, and the prices of agricultural products were declining. Farmers who had gone into debt during the war to increase production found themselves with obligations that had been incurred when prices were high and money was cheap.

Responding to these conflicting needs, Congress in the Resumption Act of 1875 sought a compromise between debtors and creditors. It freed national banks (created under the laws of 1863 and 1864) from limitations on the amounts of banknotes they could issue. It required the Treasury to retire greenbacks equal in face value to 80 percent of the new bank currency, until the amount of greenbacks in circulation was reduced to $300 million. The Resumption Act also postponed until January 1, 1879, the actual resumption of specie payments. But after that date, all government legal tender notes like greenbacks must be redeemable in gold on demand at banks and at the Treasury.

The question of whether more greenbacks must then be retired or whether the Treasury could reissue them within the $300 million limitation was left unclear. The distant date for resumption and the question of the greenbacks' future actually forced their value down in 1875 and 1876. Debtors were pleased; creditors were not.

It was just the kind of issue the parties feared the most. The Republican party was known as the party of "sound money," but western Republicans openly supported an expanded currency. Democrats were more sympathetic to "soft money" policies, but the powerful conservative wing of the party shared with their Republican counterparts an aversion to any policy that undermined public confidence in the economic system.

After Hayes took office in 1877, the issue surfaced. Hayes had backed the Resumption Act of 1875 when he was governor of Ohio. In 1877 his Secretary of the Treasury, John Sherman, began to build up government gold reserves for the retirement of greenbacks beginning in 1879, as the act required. Sherman's first step was to sell government bonds for coin. Since the public had little coin, this forced him to negotiate with banking syndicates and money brokers. Despite unfavorable public opinion, Sherman persisted and soon disposed of about $95 million in bonds. The accumulation of additional gold supplies was made easier by a favorable balance of trade when bumper wheat crops were exported to Europe.

As news of Sherman's success spread, greenbacks rose in value until they reached par with gold two weeks before January 1, 1879, the resumption deadline. Knowing there was $200 million in gold in the Treasury, few people bothered to redeem their greenbacks. They then remained at par, the creditors' goal. When debtor farmers began to agitate for more greenbacks, their campaign was supported by the newly organized Greenback Labor party, which reached its high point in 1878 by polling over a million votes and electing fourteen congressmen. But with the end of the long depression of the seventies, the drive for currency inflation had been lessened. Both the Greenback party and greenback agitation declined. The United States returned to the gold standard, and all federal issues were redeemable in gold on demand.

But the demand to increase the volume of money in circulation would soon gather new strength and take a different form. The drive for unlimited coinage of silver grew in political importance during the Hayes administration and finally ended in the depression of the nineties and the election of 1896. It had the support of silver mining interests as well as farmers. Its promoters could be found in both political parties, along with its critics.

Some argued that if the government coined large amounts of silver, the economy would be stimulated, interest rates would drop, and the prices farmers received would rise. But to "hard money" people, it was an invitation to fiscal irresponsibility that would undermine credit and wreck the economic system. The battle lines were drawn early, and each new "crisis" made the conflict worse.

In 1834, Congress had fixed the ratio of silver to gold in the dollar at 16 to 1. That is, silver could be legally exchanged for gold at a ratio of 16 ounces of silver to 1 of gold. Until 1849, this ratio reflected the market value of the two metals. Then gold came pouring in from the mines of California and other parts of the West, and its value in terms of silver declined. Owners of silver found it more profitable to sell on the open market than to present silver to the mint for coinage. So no one protested when in 1873 Congress adopted a new law ending both the minting of silver dollars and the legal tender status of the existing supply. In the depression seventies, however, western silver mines began to yield their own enormous wealth. Silver quickly fell in value in terms of gold, and it became worthwhile again to offer it to the mint. With silver overvalued at the ratio of 16 to 1, it was the cheaper metal with which to meet financial obligations. And there was an abundant supply.

On discovering the law against silver coinage, inflationists charged that a sinister group of bankers had engineered the Crime of '73. They demanded its repeal so that silver could once again be redeemed at the old 16 to 1 ratio. The first test came in November 1877, when Richard (Silver Dick) Bland of Missouri introduced a bill in the House for the unlimited coinage of silver at 16 to 1. The silver dollar at this time was worth about 89 cents and was falling. Bankers advised Hayes that the passage of the Bland bill would amount to debt repudiation. If silver became legal tender, capitalists would never again buy government bonds for gold; their confidence in the government's credit would be badly shaken. The president believed them, but he knew that Congress would override his veto.

Hayes was rescued when the Bland bill was quietly fixed in the Senate by Iowa's smooth-talking William Allison. The amended Bland-Allison bill (passed in 1878 over Hayes's veto) substituted limited for unlimited coinage of silver. It required the Treasury to buy not less than $2 million and not more than $4 million of silver every month and coin it into silver dollars at the old ratio of 16 to 1. Until 1890, silver purchases did not drive gold out of circulation or produce the kind of expanded currency "soft money" people wanted. The agitation persisted.

Garfield and Arthur: Civil Service Reform

When Hayes refused to run for a second term, the Stalwarts—with Roscoe Conkling of New York in the lead—turned to Grant. But bad management at the Republican national convention ruined their chances. At the same time, James A. Garfield, a veteran Ohio congressman, brilliantly managed the campaign of another Ohioan, Senator John Sherman. Faced with a deadlock between Sherman and Blaine, the Grant men turned to Garfield as a "dark horse." To appease the Stalwarts, the convention backed Conkling's patronage chief in New York, Chester A. Arthur, as Garfield's running mate. The delegates then proceeded to write a platform in favor of veterans' pensions and Chinese exclusion, but little else. It expressed pride in the party's accomplishments, and carefully hedged its position on civil service reform, the protective tariff, and other important issues.

Obviously desperate for a candidate, the Democrats chose Winfield Scott Hancock of Pennsylvania, whose major accomplishment was that he had been a hero of the Battle of Gettysburg. Hancock was described as "a good man weighing 250 pounds"—but he still came close to winning. Garfield squeaked into office with a plurality of 39,000 votes out of more than 9 million cast. His large electoral majority—214 to 155—was the result of narrow victories in two states, Indiana and New York. They had been carried by Republican discipline and plenty of hard cash.

After the election, Garfield rewarded Blaine with the post of secretary of state. Conkling and his Stalwart friends also expected recognition. But the new president, who had reached the top after a brilliant Civil War career and a long apprenticeship in the House, had other ideas. He broke with Conkling right after his inauguration by giving the best patronage post in the United States, Chester Arthur's old job as the collector of the Port of New York, to an anti-Conkling Republican. That infuriated Conkling, and set Republican against Republican in New York.

Before the trouble had subsided, the nation suffered the second assassination of a president in less than twenty years. On July 2, 1881, Garfield entered the Washington railroad depot and was murdered by a deranged job seeker, Charles Guiteau. As Guiteau fired, he exclaimed, "I am a Stalwart and Arthur is President now." Garfield died two months later, and though Arthur filled his cabinet with Stalwarts, his administration saw the beginning of civil service reform.

The assassination dramatized in the minds of many Americans the evils of a patronage and spoils system which had become entrenched in American government and politics. Even veteran machine politicians had grown sick of patronage. Civil service reform, its advocates insisted, was not just one issue among many. The aim, as one reformer expressed it, was to correct the "chief evil" of the day, "the alliance between industrialists and a political class which thinks like industrialists."

The first real step toward the merit system was taken with the Pendleton Act of 1883. This act gave three civil service commissioners, to be named by the president, authority to draw up practical, competitive examinations. The act forbade assessing federal employees for campaign funds or firing them for political reasons. It required that within sixty days Treasury and postal employees be classified in civil service categories,

THE CURSE OF CIVIL SERVICE REFORM

George Washington Plunkitt, a ward boss of the Fifteenth Assembly District in New York City and a powerful figure in the Tammany Hall political machine in the late nineteenth century, prided himself on his "plain talks on very practical politics."

This civil service law is the biggest fraud of the age. It is the curse of the nation. There can't be no real patriotism while it lasts. How are you goin' to interest our young men in their country if you have no offices to give them when they work for their party? Just look at things in this city today. There are ten thousand good offices, but we can't get at more than a few hundred of them. How are we goin' to provide for the thousands of men who worked for the Tammany ticket? It can't be done. These men were full of patriotism a short time ago. They expected to be servin' their city, but when we tell them that we *can't place them, do you think their patriotism is goin' to last? Not much. They say: "What's the use of workin' for your country anyhow? There's nothin' in the game." And what can they do? I don't know, but I'll tell you what I do know. I know more than one young man in past years who worked for the ticket and was just overflowin' with patriotism, but when he was knocked out by the civil service humbug he got to hate his country and became an Anarchist. . . . Isn't it enough to make a man sour on his country when he wants to serve it and won't be allowed unless he answers a lot of fool questions about the number of cubic inches of water in the Atlantic and the quality of sand in the Sahara desert?*

Source: William L. Riordon, *Plunkitt of Tammany Hall* (New York: Knopf, 1948), pp. 15–16.

and it permitted the president to extend the coverage. During Arthur's administration, about 12 percent of federal employees (compared to 85 percent in the mid-twentieth century) were classified.

The Pendleton Act, by depriving the parties of funds from public employees, forced leaders to turn more and more to big business for money for campaigns. Shrewd party managers like Matt Quay of Pennsylvania, Tom Platt of New York, and Mark Hanna of Ohio were soon representing big business clients—and so were the candidates they chose.

THE DEMOCRATIC YEARS: REGULATION AND PROTECTION

Both Democrats and Republicans claimed credit for civil service reform. But more divisive issues now demanded attention. No longer could the federal government afford to ignore corporate abuses, whether these took the form of unreasonably high tariff rates, unfair methods of competition, or industrial combinations that prevented competition. Farmers organized in Granges pushed for laws against railroad malpractices. The Great Strike of 1877 had dramatized not only the plight of railroad workers, but the degree to which the public shared their grievances against the railroad companies. If nothing else, public concern about the growth and use of corporate power had to be satisfied.

At the same time, the government did not want to tamper with "natural" economic forces by imposing restraints on industrialization. The inhabitants of the White House—Democrat or Republican—believed that the least amount of government was best. And they would cling to that belief even as the nation headed into another depression.

The Campaign of 1884: Cleveland

As president, Chester A. Arthur pleased neither the reformers nor the old guard. The Republican convention in 1884 passed him by in favor of the perennial candidate, James G. Blaine. Although Blaine had most of the qualities that make a successful presidential candidate, his many years in the House had marked him; he had grown rich without any visible means of outside income and had not allowed anyone to uncover the sources of his wealth. With his nomination, the Independents, or Mugwumps, left the party and supported the Democratic nominee, Grover Cleveland.

Cleveland had attracted notice as a reform mayor of Buffalo and as governor of New York. His defense of sound money and property rights earned him industrial and banking support. Although he was called a reformer, Cleveland carefully pointed out that "a transfer of executive control from one party to another does not mean any serious disturbance of existing conditions."

In the campaign, the parties treated the public to sensational disclosures about the private lives and personal morals of the two candidates. If Blaine's ties to railroad scandals made him unfit to hold public office, the fact that Cleveland, a bachelor, happened to be the father of a seven-year-old

---

A DISILLUSIONED INTELLECTUAL

Henry Adams, grandson of John Quincy Adams and great-grandson of John Adams, thought of himself as a displaced person in post-Civil War America and could find few virtues in the presidential electoral contests. In this letter to a friend, dated September 21, 1884, he comments on the Cleveland-Blaine race:

We are here plunged in politics funnier than words can express. Very great issues are involved. . . . The public is angry and abusive. Every one takes part. We are all doing our best, and swearing at each other like demons. But the amusing thing is that no one talks about real interests. By common consent they agree to let these alone. We are afraid to discuss them. Instead of this, the press is engaged in a most amusing dispute whether Mr. Cleveland had an ille-gitimate child, and did or did not live with more than one mistress; whether Mr. Blaine got paid in railway bonds for services as Speaker; and whether Mrs. Blaine had a baby three months after her marriage. Nothing funnier than some of these subjects has been treated in my time. I have laughed myself red with amusement over the letters, affidavits, leading articles and speeches which are flying through the air. Society is torn to pieces. Parties are wrecked from top to bottom. A great political revolution seems impending. Yet, when I am not angry, I can do nothing but laugh.

Source: Worthington Chauncey Ford (ed.), *Letters of Henry Adams* (Boston and New York: Houghton Mifflin, 1930), p. 360.

---

child was enough to define him as a moral leper. To the Republican taunt, "Ma, ma, where's my pa?" the Democrats replied: "Gone to the White House, Ha, Ha, Ha!" It was that kind of campaign. Neither party claimed to be opposed to tariff revision, as long as it did not endanger any domestic industry. Both parties also agreed that something had to be done about corporate abuses.

Blaine lost New York by 1149 votes. New York turned out to be decisive in the electoral college, where Cleveland squeaked through, 219 to 182. His popular plurality was only 23,000 out of 10 million votes. But it was enough to bring the Democrats back to the White House after a quarter of a century.

Cleveland's idea of government was almost entirely negative. He especially disliked what he called "paternalism." Early in 1887, in vetoing an act to distribute seeds in drought-stricken Texas counties, he used a phrase that returned to haunt him during the depression of the nineties: "The lesson should be constantly enforced that though the people support the Government, the Government should not support the people." In destroying "paternalism," he foiled pension grabs by veterans and tariff grabs by industry, and even retrieved 81 million acres of the public domain from the railroads. He extended the scope of civil service, but he resisted attempts to regulate business. With public pressure mounting, however, Cleveland could no longer afford to ignore the clamor for reform. By the end of his term, the railroads, tariffs, and big business were heatedly debated subjects of legislation.

Railroad Regulation

After the Panics of 1873 and 1884 had forced many speculators to the wall, the movement for railroad regulation and reform increased. Rate and dividend policies came under bitter attack from shippers and investors. When the railroads fought back by spending money to make political friends and hire the best legal talent, they made more enemies. Such open corruption raised protests against the railroads, even by impartial citizens. Reform and regulation eventually won the backing of railroad men who had come to look upon the national government as the only power that could save them from their own competitive and financial practices.

In the late 1870s and throughout the 1880s, *average* railroad freight rates went down steadily because of the competition for traffic. The trouble was that *average* rates included suicidally low ones for railroads at junctions where two or more lines crossed, and murderously high ones for shippers at monopoly points. This situation satisfied no one, least of all the railroads, which were under pressure for special consideration from all sides. Shippers at monopoly points along railroads that ended at competitive points were the worst off. They were often required to pay more for short hauls along a small portion of the road than shippers at the terminals paid for long hauls over the road's entire length.

Discriminatory carrying charges were reflected in the decline of land values where shipping costs were highest. In one rich farming area in New York State, served only by the New York Central, the railroad's high short-haul charges contributed to a decline of 20 to 25 percent in land values in 1879 alone. Rebates and other special favors to powerful shippers like Standard Oil were also a source of anger. The secrecy with which rebating had to be carried on burdened even those who profited from it.

The first regulatory commission was a state effort in Massachusetts in 1869, and it could only investigate railroad abuses and make its findings

Thomas Nast's cartoon "The Senatorial Roundhouse" in *Harper's Weekly* (1886) illustrated the power railroad corporations had. The bill on which the filibustering senator is stepping would "prevent members of Congress from accepting fees from subsidized railroads." (*Library of Congress*)

public. By 1880, fourteen states had set up railroad commissions, and some had taken more severe measures. Urban manufacturers and distributors and their banker allies sometimes began the fight, but the most persistent organization was the Patrons of Husbandry, which began organizing farmers into local granges in 1867. A year after the Panic of 1873, the Grangers had 1.5 million members, mostly in Iowa, Wisconsin, Minnesota, and Illinois. Here they won legislation setting statewide maximum rates for railroad traffic and maximum charges for the use of grain elevators, where farmers had to store their crops while awaiting shipment.

Railroad management fought Granger legislation in the courts: they attacked rate fixing by public bodies as legalized confiscation. In 1877, in *Munn* v. *Illinois,* the most important of the Granger cases to reach the Supreme Court, a majority of the justices found against the railroads and grain elevator operators. Owners of property "in which the public has an interest," said the Court, must "submit to be controlled by the public for the common good."

But single states could not regulate corporations chartered by other states and carrying on most of their business across state borders. Pressure for federal regulation mounted in the early 1880s as railroad securities slumped on the stock exchanges. By 1886, nearly 10 percent of the entire railroad system had fallen into the hands of court-appointed receivers, who would try to keep the bankrupt roads from going out of business altogether.

After the Supreme Court decision in the Wabash case (1886), which reflected conservative attitudes, the federal government could not postpone action any longer. The Wabash decision took much of the strength from *Munn* v. *Illinois* by forbidding any state to set rates even within its borders on railroad traffic entering from, or bound for, another state. With the states thus removed from the regulatory process, any effective control of the railroads now rested with the federal government.

The Interstate Commerce Act, signed by President Cleveland on February 4, 1887, provided that all charges made by railroads should be "reasonable and just." It forbade higher rates on noncompetitive short hauls than on competitive long ones and outlawed rebates to favored shippers. It also prohibited self-regulating practices, such as agreements to pool traffic and maintain high rates. Of particular importance was the establishment of the Interstate Commerce Commission, the first federal regulatory board. But its powers proved inadequate to the tasks it faced: The "cease and desist" orders the ICC was empowered to issue could be made to stick only by court action, which the railroads found easy to delay. And in the end the railroads almost always won. In the first ten years of its existence, 90 percent of the Commission's orders on rate charges were overruled by the courts. Of the sixteen cases heard by the Supreme Court between 1887 and 1905, it upheld the carrier in fifteen.

When the commission tried more vigorous prosecutions, the railroads responded with an attack on the commission itself. Some people advised them, even as early as 1892, that this was not wise. In that year, the corporation lawyer Richard S. Olney, soon to become Cleveland's attorney general, wrote to a railroad friend:

My impression would be that, looking at the matter from a railroad point of view exclusively, it would not be a wise thing to undertake to abolish the Commission. . . . The Commission, as its functions have now been limited by the Courts, is, or can be made of great use to the railroads. It satisfies the popular clamor for a government supervision of railroads, at the same time that such supervision is almost entirely nominal. Further, the older such a commission gets to be, the more inclined it will be found to take the business and railroad view of things. It thus becomes a sort of protection against hasty and crude legislation hostile to railroad interests. . . . The part of wisdom is not to destroy the Commission, but to utilize it.

Time proved Olney right. The Interstate Commerce Commission Act did not reduce rates significantly. Nor did it end cutthroat competition. Like many regulatory commissions, the ICC would frequently be staffed by individuals representing the very interests it had been created to control. What mattered was that the public's anxieties about the railroads had been satisfied, at least for a time. Yet the Interstate Commerce Commission Act was not a complete failure. It clearly affirmed the right of the federal government to regulate private interstate business, and it provided the foundation on which a system of effective regulation could be built in the twentieth century.

Protection: The Tariff

Although Democratic politicians advised him to soft-pedal the tariff issue, Cleveland was determined to achieve some reforms in this sensitive area. Beginning with the wartime duties of 1864, protection of domestic industries had increased until it covered at least 4000 items in 1887. Cleveland did not oppose those who sought to nurse "infant industries." But he saw some of the tariff rates as excessive, and he felt that such "unnecessary taxation" only encouraged Congress to spend the annual surplus that accumulated in the Treasury.

Responding to Cleveland's call for tariff reform, the House early in 1888 adopted the Mills bill. It reflected deep study of industry's real needs and recommended the moderate reductions that mild revisionists like the president wanted. The Senate responded with the "Allison substitute," which called, as usual, for a general rise in the tariff. "We all know," Joseph Wharton, the Pennsylvania iron and steel king, wrote to Senator Allison, "that the legitimate expenses of a general election are heavy, and that failure to provide for them sometimes entails defeat. I am in a position to know that the success of appeals for funds among the steel rail men will be jeopardized if the party they are asked to support proposes a measure that looks to them nearly as fatal as that proposed by the other party." The "Allison substitute" resulted in a congressional deadlock, as intended, and postponed the issue until after the presidential election of 1888.

Republican Interlude

The Democrats renominated Cleveland by acclamation. After Blaine's decision not to run again, the Republicans finally selected Benjamin Harrison, a dreary corporation lawyer from Indiana, and the grandson of President William Henry Harrison. Under the management of national party chairman Matt Quay, the Republicans charged that Cleveland's "free trade" policy (as they insisted on labeling the mild reforms of the Mills bill) would ruin American manufacturing and betray the American worker to the "pauper labor of Europe." Even the Knights of Labor believed this argument and endorsed Harrison.

Although Cleveland's popular vote topped Harrison's by more than 100,000, Harrison won an electoral majority of 65. A switch of only 6500 votes in New York would have given Cleveland that state and the election. Since Cleveland did surprisingly well in protariff regions, the effect of that issue on the election is questionable.

Like so many elections in this period, the national campaign depended largely on the ability of party organizers to mobilize supporters. When Harrison solemnly proclaimed, "Providence has given us the victory," Matt Quay exploded: "Think of the man! He ought to know that Providence hadn't a damn thing to do with it." Quay added that Harrison "would never know how close a number of men were compelled to approach the gates of the penitentiary to make him president."

After the election, Congress took care of the industrial contributors to the campaign with the McKinley tariff (1890), the highest and broadest in the nation's history. By raising already high duties even higher, the new tariff not only protected domestic industries, but made it virtually impossible for foreigners to compete. At the same time, the McKinley tariff offered protection to certain industries that had not been established, in an apparent effort to encourage their development. Secretary of State Blaine feared that exporting nations hit by the new duties would refuse to buy American farm surpluses. He got Congress to hold a club over resisting nations by inserting a "reciprocity" clause in the new tariff act. The president had authority to remove remaining items from the free list in retaliation against any discriminatory duties on American produce.

In return for western votes on the McKinley tariff, Congress in 1890 passed the Sherman Silver Purchase Act. This act authorized the Treasury to issue notes redeemable in gold or silver

WORDS AND NAMES IN AMERICAN HISTORY

The phrase *favorite son* usually refers to politics rather than to families. It is normally used to describe a candidate for the U.S. presidency whose main support comes from his home state and who has little strong support elsewhere. Occasionally, a favorite son has gone on to win the nomination. Historians look back at such a popular president as Andrew Jackson, often without realizing that his political career began as a favorite son of the state of Tennessee. Yet many historians have failed to note that the Father of His Country was its first favorite son. We have this word from the *New York Daily Gazette* of May 1, 1789: "Yesterday the Great and Illustrious Washington, the favourite son of liberty, and deliverer of his country, entered upon the execution of the office of First Magistrate of the United States of America."

FLEECING THE FARMER

A Texas farmer in 1890 describes the conditions that would give rise to the Populist movement (J. C. Peoples to A. W. Buchanan, December 12, 1890):

Every agent, pedler and Every profession of men is Fleecing the Farmer, and by the time the World Gets their Liveing out of the Farmer as we have to Feed the World We the Farmer has nothing Left, but a Bear Hard Liveing. I live in the midst of a thick Heavey populated county of Farmers 6 miles from any Town and talk Freely with them as to how much

they make. And all tell me the same Hard Tale money all gone. . . .

We have a working Energetic people that would improve if they could and Farmers in these two countys is successfull in Farming. we all make it but some way we cant Keepe it. I want you to write to me and tell me what is the matter Can our Legislator do any thing That will give us any Reliefe. I am Greately discouraged in Farming.

Source: Norman Pollack (ed.), *The Populist Mind* (Indianapolis: Bobbs-Merrill, 1967), pp. 22–23.

---

coin in exchange for greater amounts of silver than had been permitted under the Bland-Allison Act of 1878. Virtually a gift to the silver mining companies, the Silver Purchase Act was defended as an agrarian cheap money measure. But the issue was not settled; inflationists wanted unlimited silver coinage.

One more sop offered to the public was the Sherman Antitrust Act, which passed Congress in July 1890. Many states had passed antitrust statutes, but they were no more effective against trusts chartered in other states than state regulation of interstate railroads had been. After the Wabash decision of 1886 cut the ground away from stronger state measures against private corporations, the demand for federal trust regulation grew stronger.

The Sherman Antitrust Act sounded severe: It made combinations in restraint of trade illegal, subjected offenders to heavy fines and jail sentences, and ordered that triple damages be paid to persons who could prove injury by such combinations. Few courts, however, upheld any of the actions brought under the measure. Finley Peter Dunne, the political humorist, said of the act: "What looks like a stone wall to a layman is a triumphal arch to a corporation lawyer."

The Sherman Act did push certain groups of companies to change specific trust arrangements and to merge into huge corporations. Without having to act together, these companies succeeded in dominating industries at least as thoroughly as the trusts had. In other industries, the holding company device was employed. The *holding company* was an independent corporation that owned enough stock in other companies to control their policies. Dodges such as these neutralized the Sherman Act for a while, but in the twentieth century, political administrations and the courts grad-

ually began to enforce it. Although business consolidation and centralization continued, antitrust legislation did serve as a brake on many combinations considered harmful to the public interest.

The Election of 1892: Cleveland Again

Running against Cleveland in 1892, Harrison this time got 5,176,000 votes. But Cleveland got 5,556,000. Narrow though this margin was, it was the most decisive victory since 1872. The electoral college count was Cleveland 277, Harrison 145. "I am very sorry for President Harrison," Henry Frick of the Carnegie Steel Company wrote to Carnegie on learning of Cleveland's election, "but I cannot see that our interests are going to be affected one way or another by the change in administration." Carnegie replied: "Cleveland! Landslide! Well we have nothing to fear. . . . People will now think the Protected [Manufacturers] are attended to and quit agitating. . . . Off for Venice tomorrow."

Conservative industrialists may have felt safe, but conservative politicians of both parties had something new to think about: the showing of the People's party, known as the Populists, especially in the new wheat states. Organized in 1890, the party ran General James B. Weaver in 1892 in its first bid for the presidency. The general got over a million votes, more than 8 percent of the total. His party succeeded in capturing four states and brought the silver issue and the needs of the farmers to national attention.

THE POPULISTS AND THE SILVER CRUSADE

The economic crisis of the 1890s and the emergence of a strong third political party made the avoidance of critical economic issues increasingly difficult for the two major parties. Much of the unrest of the decade focused on the farmers, who, like so many industrial workers, sensed that they were no longer in control of their own lives and destiny. Farmers protested declining prices for their products and the growing percentage of their incomes falling into the hands of middlemen—marketing agents, mortgage lenders, grain elevator operators, and railroads. Farmers were joined by other groups experiencing economic hardship and concerned over corporate power and government unresponsiveness. These concerns found expression at all levels of society and soon took on political significance.

For some Americans, the 1890s raised serious questions about the survival of the economic and social order. The depression that followed the Panic of 1893 produced tens of thousands of unemployed. Labor strife peaked, with massive showdowns at Carnegie's Homestead steel works in 1892 and in the national railroad strike of 1894. Out of the Midwest emerged an "army" of unemployed who marched on Washington, D.C., to press their case for public relief. Oliver Wendell Holmes identified 1893 as the year when "a vague terror went over the earth and the word socialism began to be heard." In the nation's capital, neither the White House nor Congress seemed responsive to the growing unrest. Against this background, the Populist party made its political appeal. Whatever the ultimate fate of Populism as a third party and an economic and cultural movement, it managed to raise critical questions that would outlast both the party and the movement.

The Farmers

In 1887 Leonidas L. Polk, a North Carolina editor, expressed the views of farmers in all parts of the country when he wrote:

There is something radically wrong in our Industrial system. There is a screw loose. . . . The railroads have never been so prosperous, and yet agriculture languishes. The banks have never done a better . . . business, and yet agriculture languishes. Manufacturing enterprises never made more money, . . . and yet agriculture languishes. Towns and cities flourish and "boom," . . . and yet agriculture languishes.

What is more, farmers suffered only slightly less in good times than in bad. Broadly speaking, they blamed their plight on the high transportation rates charged by railroads, the high prices charged by producers of farm machinery, the high interest rates charged by mortgage lenders, and the high storage rates charged by monopolistic grain elevator companies. These items consumed a disproportionate share of an income already reduced by falling prices. It was said, for example, that Nebraska annually produced three principal crops: corn, freight rates, and interest, and that the last two were harvested by those who farmed the farmer.

Few enterprises had received more civic support than the railroads of the West. In return, farmers felt that the railroads owed the community moderate rates. But the farther west one moved, the worse conditions grew. In 1887, for instance, the ton-mile charge on the Pennsylvania Railroad east of Chicago was 95 cents. On the Burlington from Chicago to the Missouri River it was $1.32; on the Burlington west of the Missouri it jumped to $4.80. According to railroad officials, they had to charge high rates in sparsely populated regions. The farmers, dependent on the railroads for getting their crops to market, could hardly agree.

Heavy taxes made the high railroad rates harder to bear. Personal property then consisted chiefly of land and livestock, on which it was relatively simple to assess a personal property tax. Railroads and other corporations created new kinds of personal property—stocks and bonds—that were far easier to conceal. Since the railroads also pushed the politicians for tax exemptions or low rates on their own huge landholdings and other real property, taxes fell more and more heavily on the middle-class farmer. In a free market, he could not pass them along to the consumer, as could many large industrial corporations.

The protective tariff was still another kind of discriminatory tax that angered farmers. In their opinion, it protected the trusts, which had the power to force down the prices for raw materials produced on the farms and to force up the prices of farm machinery and other manufactures.

Falling farm prices, of course, made heavy taxes seem even worse. The price of staples began to fall in the 1880s and hit bottom in the depression years of the nineties. Wheat brought $1.20 a bushel in 1881 and 50 cents in 1895; cotton, 10.5 cents a pound in 1881 and 4.5 cents in 1894. Of course, prices of nonfarm products fell too. But the fall in farm prices hit the growers particularly hard because they were debtors with fixed *money* obligations. Their constant concern with the currency came from their need to keep these obligations stable in terms of the amount of *commodities*

THE FARMER IS THE MAN

When farmers gave voice to their grievances, they did so through songs as well as through letters, oratory, and organization. "The Farmer Is the Man" was among the best known of the Populist ballads.

Oh, the farmer comes to town
With his wagon broken down,
But the farmer is the man who feeds them all.
If you'll only look and see,
I think you will agree
That the farmer is the man who feeds them all.

The farmer is the man,
The farmer is the man,
Lives on credit till the fall;
Then they take him by the hand,
And they lead him from the land,
And the merchant is the one who gets it all.

When the banker says he's broke
And the merchant's up in smoke,
They forget that it's the farmer feeds them all.
It would put them to the test
If the farmer took a rest;

Then they'd know that it's the farmer feeds them all
The farmer is the man,
The farmer is the man,
Lives on credit till the fall;
With the interest rate so high
It's a wonder he don't die,
For the mortgage man's the one who gets it all.

Source: Edith Fowke and Joe Glazer, *Songs of Work and Freedom* (New York: Doubleday, 1960), pp. 96–97. Recorded on *American Industrial Ballads*, Folkways Records 5251.

---

needed to pay them. Farmers who had gone into debt in the 1860s to purchase new lands and machinery when farm prices were high and money cheap found themselves in the 1880s and 1890s in a period of declining prices and deflation.

Critics told the farmers they received low prices because they produced too much. But the only way the individual farmer could think of to make more money when prices were falling was to raise even larger crops. To the farmers' way of thinking, the price decline reflected a coldblooded Wall Street conspiracy to squeeze the settlers of the West. The high cost of credit seemed to confirm this view. The credit system helped force the landless southern farmer, and eventually the small southern landholder as well, into the vicious circle of sharecropping and crop lien. Tenancy came later in the West, where land was more easily obtained and more easily mortgaged. But when mortgage money cost 15 percent or more a year, as it did in Kansas and states farther west in the 1880s, the foreclosures began. Farmers faced the prospect of being evicted from the lands on which they lived and worked.

The Origins of Populism

The roots of the People's party of the 1890s lay in the farmers' alliances and in the idea of cooperatives that would free farmers from private credit merchants and bankers. The alliances had sprung up in the 1880s to replace the Grange. By 1880, many of these had consolidated into two regional

groups, the Southern Alliance, which claimed over a million members, and the somewhat smaller National Farmers' Alliance in the Northwest, mainly on the Great Plains. The Colored Farmers' Alliance, begun in 1886 by a white Baptist preacher, reportedly recruited over a million

Populist leader Mary E. Lease is said to have advised Kansas farmers to "raise less corn and more hell." (*Library of Congress*)

blacks. But it had neither the power nor the influence of the two white organizations.

The Southern and National Farmers' Alliances gave a strong stimulus to the social life and the thinking of their members. Like the Granges, they held picnics, conventions, and rallies to help overcome the isolation and bleakness of farm life. They gave out agricultural information and tried to teach their members better business methods. They sponsored economic and political discussions and established circulating libraries, which enabled members to read books of social criticism. At one time perhaps as many as a thousand local newspapers were connected with the movement.

What emerged was both a political and a cultural movement, in which farmers came together to share their experiences and to propose and act upon measures to improve their working lives and free them of the credit system. The talk ranged from the single tax to free silver, from farmers' cooperatives to government ownership of the railroads. "People commenced to think who had never thought before," one Alliance sympathizer wrote, "and people talked who had seldom spoken."

In December 1889 all the major farm organizations met in St. Louis at separate sessions. Besides the Northern and Southern Alliances, there were the Knights of Labor, the Farmers' Mutual Benefit Association, and the Colored Alliance. But a number of issues kept these groups apart. For one thing, the Southern Alliance regarded secrecy as a distinct advantage because many of its members were tenants, not landowners, and thus more vulnerable. Most northern representatives objected to it. Northern representatives resented southern insistence that black farmers be excluded, although southern spokesmen were willing to leave to each state organization the right to decide, so long as only whites were eligible for the National Council.

Another divisive issue arose over the question of creating a third political party. Certain northerners already were thinking of resorting to this tactic; southerners found it difficult to accept, since they lived in a one-party region. An independent party would have far less of a chance where politics was controlled by a single party than where two major parties were in competition and a third might tip the balance of power. Southern Alliance members also feared that a third party, by dividing voters, would endanger white supremacy.

Although little is known about the Colored Alliance, it did assert its independence of the Southern Alliance on issues like federal aid to education and enforcement of the Fifteenth Amendment,

both of which the blacks supported. More spectacularly, the Colored Alliance called a strike of black cotton pickers that the Southern Alliance (which included employers of cotton pickers) helped to defeat.

Despite organizational differences, the reform programs of the Northern and Southern Alliances proved to be very much alike. Northerners gave greater emphasis to the railroad issue, southerners to farm finances and farm credit. The most important proposal for solving the credit problem came from Dr. C. W. Macune, organizer of the Texas Alliance. Macune suggested that the federal government set up a subtreasury office and warehouse in every county that would offer for sale more than $500,000 worth of farm products annually. Farmers who placed nonperishable crops in these warehouses would receive as a loan Treasury notes in amounts up to 80 percent of the local market value of their stored crops. This loan was to be repaid when the crop was sold. Macune's plan, later incorporated into the agricultural programs of the 1930s, had the double advantage of allowing the farmer to hold a crop for the best price and of increasing the money supply.

Eastern conservatives laughed at the Alliance proposals as "hayseed socialism." But they could not laugh off the political force behind them. Between 1887 and 1890, Southern Alliance men, working at first through the Democratic party, elected three governors and won control of the legislatures of eight states. Northern Alliance candidates, in the major parties or in local "third parties" in the grain states of the Northwest, made impressive gains. It was in Kansas that the "third party" was first called the People's party. Its members there became known as Populists.

The People's Party

Although Southern Alliance members held back, by 1890 radical farmers of the Northwest went ahead with the third party idea. The first step was a convention in Cincinnati in May 1891, which attracted relics of dead organizations like the Greenback party and visionaries and utopians, as well as Northern Alliance leaders. By 1892, the Southern Alliance was ready to break with the Democratic party and to cast its lot with the new party. In February 1892, in St. Louis, the national People's party, including the Southern Alliance, was formally organized. The delegates called for a presidential nominating convention to meet in Omaha on July 4—an appropriate date on which to return the country to the creed of its founding fathers.

The key to the Populist movement lay in its rhetoric and in its cultural expression. The revivalist zeal that pervaded the Omaha convention very much influenced how the delegates chose to articulate their grievances. In their view, the dominant institutions of society—the presidency, Congress, the legislatures, the courts, and the press—had become so corrupted by industrial interests that they no longer reflected the needs of the great mass of Americans, particularly those who worked with their hands, tilled the soil, and produced the crops. The producing classes were being victimized by mortgage lenders, grain elevator interests, marketing agents, railroads, and the Wall Street bankers who manipulated the currency on behalf of creditors and industrialists. The distribution of power, like the distribution of income, had become so unbalanced that only federal action could correct it.

What the Populist platform made clear—and this marked an important break with laissez-faire ideas—was that the federal government would henceforth need to play a far more significant role in the economic life of the nation. To operate the railroads, telegraph, and telephone in the interest of the people, the Populists urged that they be owned and operated by the government. To ease the financial burden on farmers and workers, they demanded a graduated income tax. To replace the rigidly limited money supply created by the gold standard, they wanted a flexible currency based on free and unlimited coinage of silver that would increase the money supply and enable farmers to pay their debts more easily. To facilitate credit, they proposed the subtreasury plan, whereby farmers could borrow government funds at low interest rates against crops stored in public warehouses. To provide a safe deposit for their earnings, they called for postal savings banks. To return the land to the people, they demanded that all land held by the railroads and other corporations in excess of actual needs be reclaimed by the government and held for settlers only.

To restore the government to the people, they advocated the direct election of senators (who were still elected by state legislatures), the secret ballot, and the initiative and referendum. And in the hope of expanding their appeal to urban workers, the

The Legislative War of 1893. When election results in Kansas were disputed, both Populists and Republicans claimed control of the state legislature. The Republican-dominated Supreme Court decided for the Republicans, and they drove the Populists (pictured) out of the State House and assumed control. (*Kansas State Historical Society, Topeka*)

Populists promised to support the restriction of "undesirable" immigration, the eight-hour day, and abolition of the Pinkerton "standing army of mercenaries." Having adopted a platform, the Omaha convention resounded with the rhetoric of agrarian protest. "The government is the people and we are the people," announced a Populist leader. "Old man Peepul is on top. Aunt Sarah Jane is on top. We country folk are on top, and everybody is going to be happy."

The party chose James B. Weaver of Iowa as its presidential candidate. The more than one million votes he received (8 percent of the total) had to be a promising political debut. With the exception of the Republicans in 1856, no third party had done nearly as well in its first national effort. After the election, an exultant Weaver confidently predicted the demise of the Republican party. But a sober look at the distribution of the vote might have put a brake on Weaver's optimism. True, he had run well in a few Plains and Mountain states and some southern states. But in such older agricultural states as Iowa, Wisconsin, and Illinois, and in the East, he received less than 5 percent of the vote.

The Populist party hoped to unite various segments of dissent in America, but it proved to be a fragile alliance. The election returns suggested that midwestern and western farmers did not necessarily agree on the causes of their economic plight. Midwestern farmers were noticeably less enthusiastic about currency inflation, and they more readily faced up to the consequences of overproduction. In the South it proved difficult to unite farmers with different kinds of problems: landowning planters and small farmers, employing farmers and employed farmers, black croppers and tenants. And despite platform pledges to urban workers, Populists failed to understand the new realities of the urban, industrial society they wanted to change.

The Populists had shown enough strength in 1892 to worry the major parties, but no more than that. The next year, one of the worst depressions in American history began. As it spread, it set the stage for another campaign. This time the Populists would alarm conservatives, many of them unable to distinguish between Populism, free silver, and socialism.

The Crash of 1893

Many Democrats placed the blame for the Panic of 1893 on the Silver Purchase Act, which, they said, destroyed business confidence. Even the withdrawal of foreign capital, they argued, had been prompted by fears that America was going off the gold standard. This move seemed immi-

Populist Strength, 1892

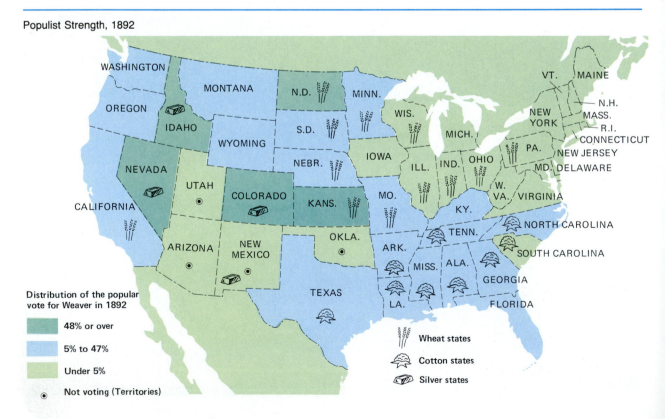

Distribution of the popular vote for Weaver in 1892

- 48% or over
- 5% to 47%
- Under 5%
- ⊙ Not voting (Territories)

🌾 Wheat states
🌿 Cotton states
⬛ Silver states

nent by April 1893, when the Treasury's gold reserve dropped below $100 million.

Cleveland's first thought was to repeal the Silver Purchase Act, which permitted holders of silver certificates to exchange them for gold. He called a special session of Congress in the summer of 1893, and Gold Democrats and Republicans closed ranks and enacted the repeal in October. By then, however, a run on the Treasury was gaining momentum.

After the failure of other measures to stop it, Cleveland, in February 1895, was forced to borrow $62 million in gold from the Morgan and Belmont banking syndicate on terms decidedly unfavorable to the government. The inflationists denounced the president as a tool of Wall Street. But the bankers, by bringing gold from Europe, succeeded in reversing the drain on the Treasury. With confidence restored, in January 1896 the government floated another loan that ended this crisis.

Cleveland's defense of the gold standard aggravated discontent in the West and South as much as it encouraged eastern financiers. It probably destroyed any hope of getting mass support for the tariff reform he had promised once again. Cleveland regarded the tariff act Congress finally passed in August 1894 (the Wilson-Gorman Tariff) as a disgrace to the party, and it became law without his signature. This act did contain one provision that the Populists wanted, a 2 percent tax on incomes over $4000. But in 1895, by a 5 to 4 decision, the Supreme Court declared the income tax unconstitutional on the ground that "direct taxes" could be apportioned among the states only on the basis of population, not personal wealth. (In 1913, the Sixteenth Amendment made the federal income tax constitutional.)

The Coxey Army, "a petition with boots," makes its way toward Washington in April 1894, to demand legislation for the unemployed. (*Library of Congress*)

As the depression deepened, the public mood grew worse. Thousands of unemployed roamed the country, sometimes in large gangs. Since the government offered them nothing, agitators proposed schemes of their own. In 1894, General Jacob S. Coxey of Massillon, Ohio, a rich man himself, convinced frightened propertyholders that a revolution had actually begun. Coxey proposed that Congress authorize a half-billion-dollar public works program. To dramatize his plan, he organized a march on Washington. "We will send a petition to Washington with boots on," he announced.

Soon "armies" all over the country were heading for the capital. Not all the marchers made it: Of the thousands who had started out, only Coxey's army of about 300 men managed to reach Washington. Police speedily dispersed them after arresting Coxey and a few of his aides for illegally carrying banners on the Capitol grounds and for trampling the grass. But Coxey's march helped make unemployment news, and an issue the Populists hoped to use in the election of 1896. The silver issue, however, soon crowded out all others: It became the focus of the campaign and of public attention.

Silver versus Gold

Propaganda from western mining interests after the repeal of the Silver Purchase Act in 1893 quickly influenced farmers who had been demanding inflation for years. They began to see the "conspiracy" against silver as another example of Wall Street treachery. In 1894, William H. Harvey, author of *Coin's Financial School,* gave the silverites a handbook that reduced the complex subject of money to terms farmers could grasp: By coining silver "you increase the value of all property by adding to the number of money units in the land. You make it possible for the debtor to pay his debts; business to start anew, and revivify all the industries of the country, which must remain paralyzed so long as silver as well as all other property is measured by a gold standard." The book was also a model of Populist rhetoric. Harvey described the country as "distracted" by the hard times, with "the jails, penitentiaries, workhouses, and insane asylums . . . full" and "hungered and half-starved men marching toward Washington."

Well illustrated and distributed in cheap editions, *Coin's Financial School* sold 300,000 copies the first year. No doubt its propaganda hurt the Gold Democrats most and contributed to a 42 per-

cent rise, in two years, in the Populist vote. In the election of 1894, when the Republicans won overwhelming control in the House, the Populists elected six senators and seven congressmen. Even more ominous for Democratic prospects, anti-administration rural Democrats in the South, men like "Pitchfork Ben" Tillman of South Carolina, viciously attacked Cleveland. "When Judas betrayed Christ," Tillman charged, "his heart was not blacker than this scoundrel, Cleveland, in deceiving the Democracy." He promised to take his pitchfork to Washington and prod the "old bag of beef in his old fat ribs."

The Election of 1896: The Cross of Gold

Trouble among the Democrats naturally encouraged the Republicans. At their national convention they showed their own solidarity by nominating on the first ballot William McKinley of Ohio, sponsor of the high tariff of 1890. McKinley was hand-picked by his fellow Ohioan Mark Hanna, the shipping and traction magnate who was emerging as the Republican national boss.

The platform, however, was a different story. Hanna wanted McKinley to straddle the money issue, to keep silverite Republicans from leaving the party. But he yielded to a sound money plank, endorsing the gold standard, in return for eastern financial support in the campaign. Silverite Republicans, led by Senator Henry M. Teller of Colorado, walked out.

The Democratic platform was written largely by Governor John P. Altgeld of Illinois, whose pardon of the Haymarket rioters in 1893 and handling of the Pullman strike the next year had made him hated by conservatives everywhere. The platform repudiated Cleveland's policies and came out flatly for *unlimited* coinage of silver at the ratio of 16 ounces of silver to 1 ounce of gold. A sharp debate over the adoption of the silver plank was resolved once a thirty-six-year-old Nebraskan, William Jennings Bryan, had spoken in its favor. The Democratic nomination was also resolved by his speech, for Bryan was voted the candidate on the fifth ballot.

Young as he was, Bryan by 1896 had already served in Congress from 1890 to 1894 as a member of the growing silver bloc. Defeated for the Senate in 1894, he became editor-in-chief of the influential *Omaha World-Herald,* and soon increased the reputation he had made in the House as a speaker by traveling throughout the country, particularly in the West and South, and giving lectures on a variety of subjects. When he made his convention speech, his friends were already working for his nomination.

Bryan's speech was calculated to appeal to the emotions of the delegates: "We are fighting in the defense of our homes, our families, and posterity," he said. He declared firmly that money was by far the most important of the issues. "You come to us and tell us that the great cities are in favor of the gold standard; we reply that the great cities rest upon our broad and fertile prairies. Burn down your cities and leave our farms, and your cities will spring up again as if by magic; but destroy our farms and the grass will grow in the streets of every city in the country." Bryan closed with the striking image by which his speech has ever since been known:

Having behind us the producing masses of this nation and the world, supported by the commercial interests, the laboring interests, and the toilers everywhere, we will answer their demand for a gold standard by saying to them: You shall not press down upon the brow of labor this crown of thorns, you shall not crucify mankind upon a cross of gold.

Despite the fiery images, Bryan's speech was really a plea that farmers too be recognized as businessmen and have equal opportunity to amass property and wealth.

The real tragedy was that the speech doomed the campaign to a debate over the silver issue. If this solution appealed to depressed southern and western farmers, it won little support among labor leaders like Samuel Gompers, who understood that "the cause of our ills lies far deeper than the question of gold or silver." Nor did this issue generate the necessary enthusiasm among many midwestern farmers, who found more reasons to blame overproduction for agricultural problems.

Even before the election of 1896, many Populists were tired of the emphasis on silver and the neglect of the more radical reforms in the party platform. Thomas E. Watson of Georgia, for example, an early Populist, thought the silver obsession had become "a trap, a pitfall, a snare, a menace, a fraud, a crime against common sense and common honesty."

When the Populists met at their convention they confronted this sad dilemma: to wage a Populist campaign would be to split the silver vote and hand the election to the Republicans; to join the Democrats in support of Bryan would mean the end of their party. Most of the delegates approved of Bryan. But the southern Populists who had

William Jennings Bryan (left) and William McKinley (right), opponents in the fiercely fought election of 1896. (*Library of Congress*)

joined the third party crusade now opposed fusion with the Democrats in their section, whom they had been fighting for years. The fusionists pointed out that the Democratic platform, besides demanding the unlimited coinage of silver, did attack Cleveland's deals with the bankers, did recommend stricter railroad regulation, and did support a constitutional amendment to make an income tax possible.

The Populists finally nominated Bryan for president, but they could not stand the Democratic vice-presidential candidate, Arthur Sewall, a rich Maine banker. In his place, they nominated Thomas E. Watson, once the staunchest third party man in the South, who actively sought white and black political unity—but on terms that in no way endangered white supremacy. Theodore Roosevelt, an active McKinley supporter and no friend of the Populists, thought Watson was superior to Bryan: "He represents the real thing while Bryan after all is more or less a sham and a compromise."

The campaign of 1896 was one of the most dramatic in American history. Bryan, handicapped by two running mates who detested and contradicted each other, concentrated on free silver. Hanna, in the meantime, was extracting millions for McKinley from those eager to sink the silver ship. Bryan traveled more than 18,000 miles and delivered over 600 speeches. McKinley stayed on the front porch of his family home in Canton, reading carefully drafted statements to delegations brought there by party leaders:

This year is going to be a year of patriotism and devotion to country. I am glad to know that people in every part of the country mean to be devoted to one flag, and that the glorious Stars and Stripes; that the people mean to maintain the financial honor of the country as sacredly as they maintain the honor of the flag. What we want, no matter to what political organization we may have belonged in the past, is a return to the good times of years ago. We have good prices and good wages, and when we have them we want them to be paid in good money.

Although Bryan won more popular votes than any previous loser, McKinley's plurality of over 600,000 was the largest of any candidate since Grant defeated Greeley in 1872. McKinley won 271 electoral votes to Bryan's 176. Even such farm strongholds as Iowa, Minnesota, and North Dakota went Republican.

No doubt the flood of propaganda, the pressure employers put on industrial workers, and the identification of Bryanism with anarchy and revolution had something to do with McKinley's success. But there were more obvious causes. The Republican prescription for "hard times" made more sense to the urban and industrial North than Democratic solutions. Republicans argued, with justice, that an inflationary price movement would leave wages far behind and that workers would be the losers. Urban workers failed to provide the mass support Bryan hoped for. Nor did he do well with the traditional Democratic Catholic vote.

In the midwestern farm states, where the agricultural depression had been less severe than in the Prairie states and the South, distrust of free silver and the Democratic analysis of agrarian problems lessened Bryan's appeal. And every middle-class American with savings invested in stocks, bonds, or insurance was, in a small way, a creditor. Recognizing that fact, Republicans pressed the point that inflation would reduce the value of personal holdings. Finally, the Republican party, learning from past mistakes, succeeded in selling itself to the voters, particularly the growing middle class, as the party of stability, political flexibility, and ethnic and cultural diversity. For a

BRYAN, BRYAN, BRYAN, BRYAN

Hundreds of thousands of agrarians must have felt the disappointment that poet Vachel Lindsay conveyed in the aftermath of the election of 1896.

Election night at midnight:
Boy Bryan's defeat.
Defeat of western silver.
Defeat of the wheat.
Victory of letterfiles
And plutocrats in miles

With dollar signs upon their coats,
Diamond watchchains on their vests
And spats on their feet.
Victory of custodians,
Plymouth Rock,
And all that in-bred landlord stock.
Victory of the neat.

Source: *The Oxford Book of American Verse* (New York: Oxford University Press, 1950), p. 622.

PARTIES, POLITICS, AND REFORM

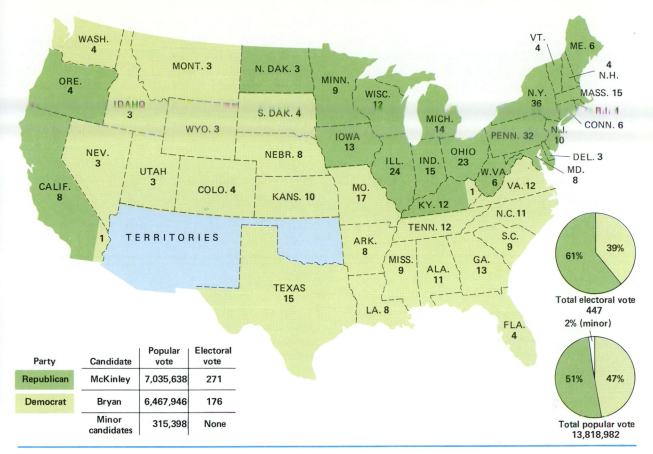

Party	Candidate	Popular vote	Electoral vote
Republican	McKinley	7,035,638	271
Democrat	Bryan	6,467,946	176
Minor candidates		315,398	None

61% 39%
Total electoral vote
447
2% (minor)

51% 47%
Total popular vote
13,818,982

The Election of 1896

people grown weary of social conflict and alleged conspiracies, that was an attractive appeal.

The election of 1896 did bring about a significant realignment of the party system. Some twenty years of virtual political stalemate gave way to an era of Republican supremacy. The Democrats lost much of their support in the Northeast and the Midwest, maintained Irish Catholic strongholds in the urban North, and commanded some following in the West. But the Republicans made claim to being the national party, the party of Anglo-Saxon Protestant America, the party best attuned to the needs and character of the new society, and (except for Woodrow Wilson's two terms) the majority party until the election of Franklin Delano Roosevelt in 1932.

Republican "Good Times"

"God's in his Heaven, all's right with the world!" Hanna telegraphed McKinley when the returns were in.

McKinley's election in 1896 did not restore prosperity, as the Republicans claimed. But

Bryan's defeat did raise the confidence of those who stood to gain most from sound currency and protective tariffs. The Republican administration quickly adopted the Dingley Tariff of 1897, which raised schedules even above those of the McKinley Tariff of 1890. Three years later, McKinley signed the Currency Act of 1900, which made the gold dollar the single unit of value and required all paper money to be redeemable in gold.

To the losers, the results were disheartening. The silver issue had brought the Democrats their worst defeat in many years, leaving the party more divided than ever. The Populist party was finished. Some Populists joined the Socialist party; in Louisiana, for example, Eugene Debs, the party's perennial candidate, would score heavily in the hill counties where Populism had been strong. Some withdrew from politics and voting altogether. Most returned to their old political home—the Democratic party.

History takes strange turns: Not long after the election, the money supply was enlarged by new flows of gold from the Klondike, South Africa, and Australia, and by greater United States production due to a new process for extracting gold from lower grade ores. Ironically, the inflation the agrarian reformers failed to win through silver came through gold. Good harvests and good prices also brought relief. In the election of 1900, boasting of "Republican prosperity," McKinley again defeated Bryan, this time even more decisively than in 1896. The Republican slogan, "The Full Dinner Pail," seemed appropriate for a prosperous country.

Several of the radical planks in the Populist program Bryan and the Democrats had neglected for silver in 1896 soon became law: direct election of senators, the income tax, an improved national currency and credit structure, and postal savings banks. Ultimately, farmers achieved political success by adopting the strategy of Samuel Gompers and concentrating their efforts on organizing the most successful farmers in the system. What the farm movement had hoped to accomplish with the subtreasury in the 1890s it did gain in the 1930s with government price supports.

The doctrine of Populism outlived the party, and McKinley's victory did not stop the forces of protest and reform. Those forces came to focus on the cities of the nation, which had grown without direction or goals in the age of industrial power.

SUMMARY

The Gilded Age in America was a time of corrupt politics, but it was also a time of reform. Some Americans were beginning to realize that government intervention in the economy and in social policy were not necessarily bad. The ideas of the public interest and the public's right to better conditions were gaining strength, though they would not really become effective until the twentieth century.

Despite the corruption and the deals, voters came out in record numbers during the decades between 1870 and 1900; campaigns were lively events in which most people were interested. Their interest, however, was generated primarily by local issues. At the national level, both parties used rhetoric and personal attacks to avoid dealing with the hard issues that faced the country. This was the heyday of the machine and the political boss. It was also a time of considerable internal party division. Republicans were split among Stalwarts and Halfbreeds; Democrats, between southern conservatives and city bosses. But all disagreements were papered over for elections. The Democrats had the Solid South, and the Republicans New England and part of the Middle West. The rest of the country was a battleground for votes, and party unity was necessary to win.

Opposed to the parties, which were mostly dominated by conservatives, were the liberal reformers. Their goal was to check abuses of economic and political power. But class and political differences kept them apart. The liberal Republican reformers (the Mugwumps) worked for civil service reform. But they had no patience with economic or social reform and thought labor agitation dangerous to society. So the reformers mostly failed, although the problems they raised did not go away, and although the government had taken some steps toward enlarging its role in the economic and social spheres.

During the Republican years, from 1876 to 1884, under Presidents Rutherford B. Hayes, James Garfield, and Chester A. Arthur, the issue of monetary policy again became central. The old argument over paper money surfaced again because "greenbacks" had been issued during the Civil War to expand the money supply and keep the government going. Afterward, debtors once again wanted cheap money, and creditors did not. The Resumption Act of 1875 had been a compromise that postponed a return to redemption in gold until January 1879. When the government began to prepare for this by building up gold supplies in 1877 and 1878, this activity raised the value of the paper money. It also led to the formation of the Greenback party, which for a time polled a substantial number of votes among farmers.

Although the United States went back to the gold standard in 1879, the issue of expanding the money supply did not die. It reappeared next in the drive for unlimited coinage of silver. This particular issue finally died in the depression of the 1890s and the campaign of 1896. Until that time, however, it was a focus of attention for Americans.

The election of 1880 brought James Garfield to the presidency, and after his assassination in 1881, Chester A. Arthur. It also brought the first step in civil service reform and the end of the patronage system—the Pendleton Act of 1883. The Democrats who took power with Grover Cleveland in 1884 faced another explosive issue: corporate abuses, especially by the railroads. Farmers organized into granges to push for laws against discriminatory practices and high rates. Railroad workers went out on strike to protest salary cuts and unsafe working conditions. Cleveland fought the trend for federal regulation. But he was not successful: by the end of his term, the first steps had been taken to regulate railroads. The Interstate Commerce Act of 1887 created not only federal rules, but an Interstate Commerce Commission to oversee them.

Other segments of society were satisfied by the protectionist McKinley Tariff of 1890, the highest and broadest in the nation's history. Western silver interests and the farmers were somewhat pacified by the Sherman Silver Purchase Act of 1890. And critics of big business got the Sherman Antitrust Act, which passed Congress in July of 1890.

The decade of the 1890s brought new agitation over the currency and a new third party, the Populists. Formed by farmers, who were again in trouble because of high transportation costs, heavy taxes, falling prices, and expensive credit, the party was joined by other groups experiencing hardship and angry about the government's unresponsiveness. The Panic of 1893 had brought depression and widespread unemployment. Workers fought Carnegie Steel at Homestead in 1892, and railroad workers went on another nationwide strike in 1894.

A march on Washington by an "army" of the unemployed was organized the same year. Only about 300 ever reached Washington, but the march did make unemployment and the Populist cause news. The Populists ran their first presidential candidate in 1892. Then came the crash of 1893; the Populists grew strong enough to elect a number of congressmen and senators in the elections of 1894 and to worry conservatives. The tariff of that year, though not a reform, did contain one Populist provision—a 2 percent tax on incomes over $4000. But the next year, the Supreme Court declared a federal income tax unconstitutional.

All these forces gathered momentum as the 1896 election approached. But then they were all sidetracked in favor of silver, which became the focus of the campaign and of public attention. The Republicans, favoring the gold standard, nominated William McKinley of Ohio. The Democrats, taking advantage of the support for silver, chose William Jennings Bryan, whose "cross of gold" speech had swayed the convention. Despite Bryan's skill as a speaker and as a campaigner, the Democrats lost. The Populists, who had backed Bryan, lost as well: their party was finished. But some of the Populist program did eventually become law—direct election of senators, the income tax, and a better currency and credit structure.

Suggested Readings

In addition to the books by Hayes and Wiebe cited in Chapter 20, see J. A. Garraty, *The New Commonwealth 1877–1890* (1968). For a conservative interpretation of the American response to industrialism, see Morton Keller, *Affairs of State: Public Life in Late Nineteenth Century America* (1977). E. F. Goldman, *Rendezvous with Destiny* (1952) and Matthew Josephson, *The Politicos* (1938), are lively studies of politics and reform. A revealing personal account is Henry Adams' classic work, *The Education of Henry Adams* (1918).

The best study of liberal reform in the Gilded Age is J. G. Sproat, *The Best Men* (1968). G. T. Blodgett, *The Gentle Reformers: Massachusetts Democrats in the Cleveland Era* (1966), is a solid introduction to the Mugwumps. The "new" political history, utilizing quantitative techniques and stressing the critical role of cultural and social forces, is best exemplified by P. Kleppner, *The Cross of Culture: A Social Analysis of Midwestern Politics* (1970) and *The Third Electoral System, 1853–1892: Parties, Voters, and Political Cultures* (1979); R. J. Jensen, *The Winning of the Midwest* (1971); S. T. McSeveney, *The Politics of Depression: Political Behavior in the Northeast 1893–1896* (1972); and F. C. Luebke, *Immigrants and Politics: The Germans of Nebraska 1880–1900* (1969). M. Keller, *The Art and Politics of Thomas Nast* (1968), features reproductions of the cartoonist's work.

On the presidents, see H. Barnard, *Rutherford B. Hayes and His America* (1954); A. Nevins, *Grover Cleveland* (1932); and H. W. Morgan, *William McKinley and His America* (1963). On other significant politicians, see C. M. Fuess, *Carl Schurz* (1932); H. Barnard, *Eagle Forgotten: The Life of John Peter Altgeld* (1938); P. W. Glad, *The Trumpet Soundeth: William Jennings Bryan and His Democracy* (1960); and P. E. Coletta, *William Jennings Bryan* (3 vols., 1964–69). On Populist leaders, see C. V. Woodward, *Tom Watson* (1938), and Martin Ridge, *Ignatius Donnelly* (1962).

I. Unger, *The Greenback Era 1865–1879* (1964), is a solid analysis of the money issue before the rise of Populism. On patronage and the civil service reform movement, see A. Hoogenboom, *Outlawing the Spoils* (1968). C. E. Rosenberg, *The Trial of the Assassin Guiteau* (1968), is an imaginative study that goes beyond the patronage issue. D. J. Rothman, *Politics and Power: The United States Senate 1869–1901* (1966), is a sympathetic study. A pressure group that failed is described in D. L. McMurry, *Coxey's Army* (1929). L. Benson, *Merchants-Farmers-and Railroads* (1955), stresses the urban origins of the call for regulation. G. Kolko, *Railroads and Regulation 1887–1916* (1965), emphasizes the frustrations of regulation.

F. A. Shannon, *The Farmer's Last Frontier 1860–1897* (1945), is a good introduction to agricultural problems after the Civil War. S. J. Buck, *The Granger Movement* (1913), and J. D. Hicks, *The Populist Revolt* (1931), are still useful older accounts of farmer unrest and political action. Richard Hofstadter, *The Age of Reform* (1955), remains an important critical assessment of Populism and the agrarian mind. L. Goodwyn, *Democratic Promise* (1976), is a sympathetic study that stresses how farmers created a new political consciousness and movement culture. N. Pollack (ed.), *The Populist Mind* (1967), is a useful documentary collection. For analyses of Populism, see also W. T. K. Nugent, *The Tolerant Populists: Kansas Populism and Nativism* (1963); O. G. Clanton, *Kansas Populism* (1969); and R. F. Durden, *The Climax of Populism* (1966). Songs of agrarian protest may be found in P. S. Foner, *American Labor Songs of the Nineteenth Century* (1975). On the aftermath of Populism, see J. R. Green, *Grass-Roots Socialism: Radical Movements in the Southwest 1895–1943* (1978).

THE EMERGENCE OF URBAN AMERICA

Chapter 22

In moving from the country to the city, Americans in the nineteenth century were sharing in a European movement. The mechanization of agriculture and the competition of new lands in other parts of the world encouraged a continuing exodus to urban centers. But the city in Europe and the United States evoked different images. In Europe the idea of the city was always as a center of power and learning, of religion and art. The great city—Athens, Rome, Paris, London, Constantinople, Moscow—traditionally was a place of palaces, emperors, and aristocrats, of universities and cathedrals, of architects, sculptors, painters, poets, philosophers, scholars, doctors. In America, the city was viewed with suspicion, and by some as a problem. "When we get piled upon one another in large cities," Thomas Jefferson observed in 1787, "we shall become as corrupt as in Europe, and go to eating one another as they do there."

Despite Jefferson's warning, the cities carved out of the American wilderness were recognized for the role they played in shaping and reflecting the economic and cultural development of the nation. But Americans never abandoned their mixed feelings toward the city; the more urbanized they became, the more they exaggerated the virtues of their rural origins. It was a rare politician who did not, if he could, boast of his rural past and praise the superior virtues of farm life. Novelists, politicians, pamphleteers, Protestant clerics, and reformers used the same themes in discussing urban life. The city came to symbolize the loss of innocence, the corruption of virtue, and the ultimate triumph of materialism. It was the place that housed the industrialists and bankers, the Catholic Church, and the immigrants who refused to conform to American ways.

But love of country life in no way stopped the steady movement toward the city. For every urban worker who chose to migrate to the country and take up farming, twenty farm youths headed for the city. The city may have been the home of corruption, crime, squalor, and stench, but it offered incredible economic opportunities and a sense of freedom.

When thousands of freed slaves moved to towns and cities in the South, they did so, one explained, because in the city freedom was supposed to be "freer." When millions of immigrants came to the United States in the late nineteenth century, they settled in the cities because opportunities were said to be better there. And when growing numbers of Americans left the countryside for the city, they did so not only to make their fortunes, but to escape the dreariness, loneliness, and drudgery of farm life. Virtuous living and fresh country air were simply not enough for families confronted with mortgage payments, declining prices, depleted soil, crop failures, and natural disasters.

The number of new city dwellers grew so rapidly that the expansion of the city often was sudden and unplanned. Cities grappled with the problem of supplying water, dis-

posing of sewage, cleaning the streets, and constructing new housing. By the turn of the century, the results were plainly visible: crowded neighborhoods, congested tenements, uncontrolled epidemics, and unworkable governments. The reformers who tried to solve these problems had different degrees of commitment and different political ideas. But their efforts were part of the movement and ideology that came to be called Progressivism. ■

URBAN GROWTH

Although urban growth had proceeded rapidly before the Civil War, in 1840 only one-twelfth of the American people lived in cities of 8000 or more. By 1860 the proportion had grown to one-sixth, and by 1900 to one-third. By 1910, nearly one person in every two lived in the city. The number of cities with more than 100,000 people had increased since 1860 from 9 to 50, and the number of cities holding between 10,000 and 25,000 people had increased from 58 to 369. America was well on its way toward becoming one of the most urbanized nations in the world.

In 1900 more than 25 million Americans were living in cities, most of which had grown in the preceding fifty years. In 1850 New York City and independent Brooklyn together boasted a population of 1.2 million. By 1900 (after the five boroughs had been consolidated in 1898), it was over 3 million; by 1910 it approached 5 million. In the same period, again partly by annexation of neighboring communities, Philadelphia grew from 560,000 to over 1.5 million.

No other city quite matched Chicago's rise from a muddy trading post with 12 families in 1831, to 100,000 people in 1860, to nearly 2 million people in the early 1900s, making it the second largest city in the United States. The sudden growth of places that hardly existed in 1860 was equally striking. By the turn of the century, Denver, Minneapolis, Los Angeles, and Birmingham were not towns, they were cities.

Why the Cities Grew

Even before 1860, the steam railroad and the steam engine had begun to transform the urban landscape. The railroad quickly made its presence

felt. It took the best sites for rights of way, freight yards, and depots; demolished old landmarks; and established the path and pace of urban expansion. For local promoters and real estate speculators who had competed to bring the railroad to town, this seemed like a small price to pay. The rapid expansion of the railroad network reduced the cost of shipping raw materials and manufactured goods, tapped larger and more distant rural and urban markets, and stimulated large-scale manufacturing. At the same time, the steam railroad and steam power in factories transformed mill towns into soot-laden cities with hundreds of new industries and tens of thousands of new workers.

Rural and Urban Population Trends, 1860–1920. (*John A. Garraty,* The American Nation: A History of the United States, *fourth edition, p. 476. Copyright © 1966, 1971, 1975, 1976 by Harper & Row, Publishers, Inc. Reprinted by permission of the publisher*)

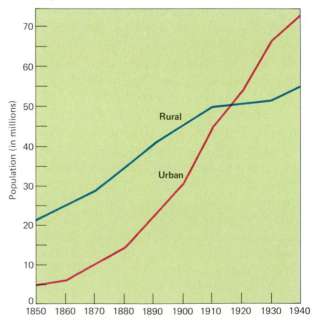

The rapid growth of American cities after the Civil War was just one sign of the enormous increase in the scale and the pace of American business. The expansion of Pittsburgh and the development of Birmingham were directly related to the modernization and growth of the iron and steel industry. Minneapolis attained city status because of its importance in the grain trade and flour milling. Denver capitalized on the mining boom.

Chicago was first a wheat port, next a railroad hub, then the meatpacking center of the world; its industry and trade boosted business activity so that it became the financial capital of the West as well. Chicago's credit facilities, in turn, attracted a great variety of new industries and business, such as the Marshall Field store and the Sears Roebuck mail order house. Philadelphia and New York, still building the commercial life that had been established earlier in their histories, also grew with new industries. One was the manufacture of ready-to-wear clothing, given a great push by the demand for uniforms during the Civil War.

Although tens of thousands of urban residents found employment as industrial workers and laborers, new opportunities were also opening up in white-collar and service occupations. Between 1870 and 1910, the number of wholesalers and retailers tripled. Salespeople and clerks in stores increased their numbers eleven times. Almost equally spectacular was the growth in number of domestics and persons employed in laundries, restaurants, boarding houses and hotels, barbershops, real estate offices, and banks. In 1910, more than 7 million persons (not all of them white-collar workers) were employed in trade and service occupations, a figure more than four times greater than that for 1870. But most newcomers were drawn into the factories and workshops. And many of these were not only new to the city, but to America as well.

The Lure of the City: Immigration

Of the 42 million city residents in 1910, some 11 million had migrated after 1880 from rural homes in the United States. The popular hero of the time was the enterprising youth described in the novels of Horatio Alger, Jr., who typically begins his life in humble circumstances in rural America, seeks fame and fortune in the city, and ultimately realizes the American Dream and becomes a respectable member of the middle class.

Although the Alger heroes were always white, the same dream attracted growing numbers of blacks from the rural South. Of the nearly 5 million black people in the United States in 1870, fewer than 500,000 lived outside the South. By 1890, 12 percent of the black population lived in cities. Like the whites from rural America, black migrants headed first for nearby towns and regional cities, and from there proceeded to the large cities in the North. Between 1870 and 1890, an average of only 41,000 blacks migrated during each decade; 200,000 blacks left the South between 1890 and 1910. But the crest of what came (text continues on page 484)

Sources of Immigrants, 1900–1920

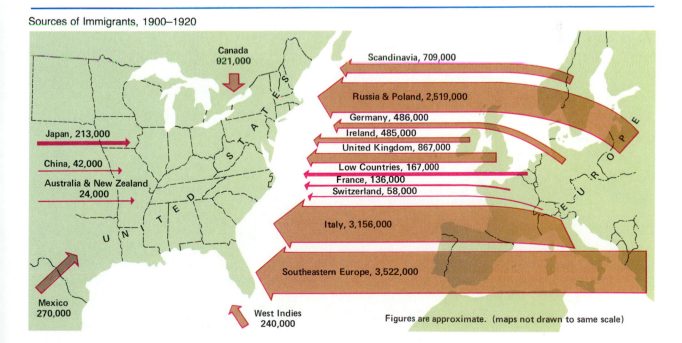

Canada 921,000
Scandinavia, 709,000
Russia & Poland, 2,519,000
Germany, 486,000
Ireland, 485,000
United Kingdom, 867,000
Low Countries, 167,000
France, 136,000
Switzerland, 58,000
Italy, 3,156,000
Southeastern Europe, 3,522,000
Japan, 213,000
China, 42,000
Australia & New Zealand 24,000
Mexico 270,000
West Indies 240,000

Figures are approximate. (maps not drawn to same scale)

Hold fast, this is most necessary in America. Forget your past, your customs, and your ideals. Select a goal and pursue it with all your might. No matter what happens to you, hold on. You will experience a bad time, but sooner or later you will achieve your goal. If you are neglectful, beware for the wheel of fortune turns quickly. You will lose your grip and be lost. A bit of advice for you: Do not take a moment's rest. Run, do, work and keep your own good in mind. . . . A final virtue is needed in America—called cheek . . . Do not say, "I cannot; I do not know." (*From a popular immigrant guidebook on how to survive in the United States, 1891.*)

Immigrants crossing the Atlantic, December 1906. (*Library of Congress*)

An Italian family on board the Immigration Service boat that carried new arrivals to Ellis Island. Sometimes the number of those waiting to be transferred was so large that they would wait for several days and nights before the little boat could bring them to the island. (*Photograph by Lewis W. Hine, Library of Congress*)

Newly arrived Russian Jewish immigrants in New York City, 1908.

(Left) An Italian grandmother and (right) a Russian Jewish girl at Ellis Island. (*Photographs by Lewis W. Hine, Library of Congress*)

(Left) A Finnish stowaway at Ellis Island, 1926, and (right) a Jewish garment worker, New York City, 1920. (*Photographs by Lewis W. Hine, Library of Congress*)

THE EMERGENCE OF URBAN AMERICA

Mulberry Street, New York City, in the heart of the immigrant area of the Lower East Side, in the early 1900s. (*Library of Congress*)

DISCOVERING URBAN AMERICA

In 1884, at the age of twenty-four, Hamlin Garland left the midwestern farm on which he had been raised and headed for the city.

With all my pay in my pocket and my trunk checked I took the train for Chicago. I shall never forget the feeling of dismay with which, an hour later, I perceived from the car window a huge smoke cloud which embraced the whole eastern horizon, for this, I was told, was the soaring banner of the great and gloomy inland metropolis, whose dens of vice and houses of greed had been so often reported to me by wandering hired men. It was in truth only a huge flimsy country town in those days, but to me it was august as well as terrible.

Up to this moment Rockford was the largest town I had ever seen, and the mere thought of a million people stunned my imagination. "How can so many people find a living in one place?" Naturally I believed most of them to be robbers. "If the city is miles across, how am I to get from the railway station to my hotel without being assaulted?" Had it not been for the fear of ridicule, I think I should have turned back at the next stop. The shining lands beyond seemed hardly worth a struggle against the dragon's brood with which the dreadful city was a-swarm. Nevertheless I kept my seat and was carried swiftly on.

Source: Hamlin Garland, *A Son of the Middle Border* (New York: Macmillan Paperbacks edition, 1962). © The Macmillan Company, 1962; copyright by Hamlin Garland 1917; copyright renewed 1945 by Mary I. Lord and Constance G. Williams.

---

to be called the Great Migration would not be reached until World War I (see Chapter 27).

A similar movement from rural to urban life was under way in Europe. Millions would cross the Atlantic in the belief that they could realize a better life for themselves and their children in the cities of the United States. The migration was in such numbers that it overwhelmed the native-born families. By 1900, more than one-third of Chicago's population was foreign-born, and New York City had more foreign-born residents than any city in the world. New York's Italian population in the 1890s equaled that of Naples; its German population, that of Hamburg. Twice as many Irish lived in New York as in Dublin. And yet the real surge of the "new" immigration had hardly begun.

Between 1866 and 1915, some 25 million immigrants came to the United States. "We are the Romans of the modern world," Oliver Wendell Holmes had said back in 1858, "the great assimilating people." Toward the end of the century, however, many people no longer shared this faith. Part of the problem was that the new immigrants—Italians, Slavs, Magyars, Croats, Serbs, Slovaks, Greeks, and Jews—came from cultures strikingly different from those of the "natives" who had preceded them.

Of the 15 million newcomers to the United States between 1890 and 1920, 80 percent were

AN IMMIGRANT WRITES HOME

Whatever the optimism with which many immigrants came to the United States, the need to adapt to the realities of day-to-day urban living could produce both cynicism and a reevaluation of expectations, as shown in this letter from Helena Brylska-Dabrowska, in the United States, to her sister Teofila Wolska, in Poland:

January 10 [1909, 1910, or 1911]
Dear Sister: I received the letter with the wafer and I thank you for thinking of me, dear sister. Now, dear sister and brother-in-law, don't be angry if I don't write to you very often, but I don't know how to write myself and before I ask somebody to write time passes away, but I try to answer you sometimes at least. You ask me how much my boys and my man earn. My man works in an iron-foundry, he earns 9, 10, 12 roubles [dollars] sometimes, and the boys earn 4 or 5 roubles. My dear, in America it is no better than in our country: whoever does well, he does, and whoever does poorly, suffers misery everywhere. I do not suffer misery, thanks to God, but I do not have much pleasure either. Many people in our country think that in America everybody has much pleasure. No, it is just as in our country, and the churches are like ours, and in general everything is alike. I wish to know with which son grandmother is. Write me. And who is farming on that land after Rykaczewski? Perhaps we shall yet meet some day or other, dear sister. . . .

Source: William I. Thomas and Florian Znaniecki, *The Polish Peasant in Europe and America*, vol. II (Boston: Richard G. Badger, The Gorham Press, 1918–20), p. 220.

from eastern and southern Europe. Between 1900 and 1914, for example, more than 3.1 million Austro-Hungarians entered the United States, more than 3 million Italians, more than 2.5 million from Russia, and nearly 900,000 from the Balkan countries of Europe and the Middle East. At the start of the twentieth century, approximately 9.5 million immigrants engulfed the North Atlantic ports of the United States; four out of five chose to settle in the industrial cities of the Northeast and Midwest, where economic opportunities were the best.

Northern and western Europeans had been the main source of immigration until 1896. Very soon the great numbers of different immigrant groups aroused "native" anxiety about Protestant and Anglo-Saxon supremacy, the survival of republican institutions, and competition over jobs. Actually, "native American stock," whatever was understood by that phrase, was in no danger of disappearing. Studies of the nation's population in the 1920s revealed that, despite the entry of more

than 35 million immigrants since the Revolution (a figure approximately ten times larger than the American population in 1783), 51 percent of the American people were descended from colonial families, and only 49 percent were foreign-born or descended from all the post-Revolutionary newcomers, including those from Great Britain. In 1880, about 12 percent of the American population was foreign-born. Between 1890 and 1910, this figure rose to 15 percent. But by 1930 it was back to 12 percent, and it declined thereafter.

Nevertheless, at the turn of the century the spectacle of cities congested with newcomers whose languages, religions, and cultures differed from their own caused considerable debate among "natives" about unrestricted immigration. Race prejudice in the West had already resulted in agitation directed at Chinese immigrants, who first came in large numbers in the 1860s to help build the Central Pacific Railroad. The earliest federal law to restrict immigration was passed in May 1882. It forbade Chinese to enter the United States

This view of Dearborn Avenue in Chicago taken in 1910 illustrates the remarkable traffic congestion characteristic of urban America around the turn of the century. (*Chicago Historical Society*)

for a decade; in 1902 another act made this exclusion permanent.

In 1885 the Knights of Labor, reflecting concern over job competition, persuaded Congress to forbid the importation of contract laborers (the previous year Hungarians and Italians had been brought in under contract to be used as strikebreakers). How to respond to the growing tide of "new" immigrants remained a source of agitation until the Immigration Restriction Act of 1921 (see Chapter 27) finally resolved the issue.

CITY LIFE: GROWTH AND DECAY

The full impact of urban growth was not felt in America until early in the twentieth century. Yet even in the nineteenth century, American cities accumulated ills and evils. Hardships were made worse by ignorance and inexperience. But a major part of the blame goes to the indifference to others that the idea of "success" encouraged.

Most city dwellers took only a halfhearted interest in civic projects that did not immediately affect their own pocketbooks or pleasure. Leaders of older nineteenth-century cities looked with satisfaction on the rising value of the urban land they owned or managed, and left those who were less well off to look after themselves. The industrialists who dominated the newer cities viewed them as sites for factories and tenements for the factory workers. Certain areas might be reserved for the industrialists, general managers, superintendents, and other ranking officials. The rest of the populace got miserable housing and almost no public facilities.

To accommodate the surge in population, real estate operators cut up city land into blocks of rectangular lots divided by a grid of roads. The lots themselves were divided simply by lines on a layout. With few restrictions on their operations, builders and landlords made maximum use of the available lots, wiping out all open space. Urban congestion fed upon itself. As sections of a city became thickly populated, more and more transportation was directed there. Water, gas, and electrical utilities might be brought in. Factories, most of them noisy and dirty, then moved in. Eventually, neighboring residential areas were overrun, land values soared, and more and more construction was undertaken to pay for higher taxes.

Under such pressures, private dwellings that had housed single families were remodeled into tenements that housed eight or twelve families or else were torn down to make room for business structures. As living conditions deteriorated, families that could afford to do so moved away. The richer ones went to nearby suburban towns. But as strong as the movement of population to the suburbs was, the flood of newcomers into the cities greatly exceeded it.

Nineteenth-century growth had a decentralizing tendency, but congestion continued to increase. The result was that land values grew every year. To offset its rising cost, land utilization became more intensive and hostile to human life. The cities also had to respond to demands for expanded services: water, gas, sewage disposal, transportation, and electrical power were now the responsibility of municipal departments that had access to large sums of tax money. Municipal debt, in fact, rose from $200 million in 1860 to $1.4 billion in 1902.

The problems created by the fast pace of urban growth were enormous. The existing and often antiquated city governments, some of them still controlled by state legislatures, were simply not equipped to undertake such imposing tasks. Without any developed science of public administration, political "machines" run by "bosses" accepted the challenge and reaped the financial benefits.

Political Corruption

When a prominent educator called America's cities in 1890 "the worst governed in Christendom—the most expensive, the most inefficient, and the most corrupt," he was underscoring the degree to which the metropolises had fallen under "boss" or "machine" rule. Designed to keep themselves and their party in office, the political machine had at its command an impressive army of county, ward, and precinct captains and workers. Few were more impressive in this era than the bosses who headed up the machines, men like William Marcy Tweed and Richard Croker of New York City, "Czar" Martin Lomasney of Boston, "King" James McManes of Philadelphia, Christopher Magee of Pittsburgh, Ed Butler of St. Louis, and "Blind Boss" Buckley of San Francisco. Of course, they charged a price for their presence—and for the essential services they rendered.

Somehow, despite the absence of professional managers, the machines made the cities work,

THE BUSINESS OF URBAN POLITICS

George Washington Plunkitt, a ward boss for Tammany Hall in New York City, discussed the problem of graft in city government in 1905.

Everybody is talkin' these days about Tammany men growin' rich on graft, but nobody thinks of drawin' the distinction between honest graft and dishonest graft. There's all the difference in the world between the two. Yes, many of our men have grown rich in politics. I have myself. I've made a big fortune out of the game, and I'm gettin' richer every day, but I've not gone in for dishonest graft—blackmailin' gamblers, saloon-keepers, disorderly people,—and neither has any of the men who have made big fortunes in politics. There's an honest graft, and I'm an example of how it works. I might sum up the whole thing by sayin': "I seen my opportunities and I took 'em." Just let me explain by examples. My party's in power in the city, and it's goin' to undertake a lot of public improvements. Well, I'm tipped off, say, that they're going to lay out a new park at a certain place. . . . I go to that place and I buy up all the land I can in the neighborhood. Then the board of this or that makes its plan public, and there is a rush to get my land, which nobody cared particular for before. Ain't it perfectly honest to charge a good price and make a profit on my investment and foresight? Of course, it is. Well, that's honest graft.

While a police reporter, Lincoln Steffens interviewed Richard Croker, who in 1886 became the Tammany Hall "boss" of New York City—a position he retained for sixteen years.

CROKER: *"Now, then, what do you want to ask me?"*

STEFFENS: *"Well, about this boss-ship. Why must there be a boss, when we've got a mayor and—a council and—"*

CROKER: *"That's why. It's because there's a mayor and a council and judges and—a hundred other men to deal with. A government is nothing but a business, and you can't do business with a lot of officials, who check and cross one another and who come and go, there this year, out the next. A business man wants to do business with one man, and one who is always there to remember and carry out the—business."*

STEFFENS: *"Business? Business? I thought government was all politics."*

CROKER: *"Ever heard that business is business? Well, so is politics business, and reporting—journalism, doctoring—all professions, arts, sports—everything is business."*

Sources: William L. Riordon, *Plunkitt of Tammany Hall* (New York: Knopf, 1948), pp. 3–4, and *The Autobiography of Lincoln Steffens* (New York: Harcourt Brace, 1931), pp. 236–37.

Members of the Tweed ring (Tweed is front left) reply to the question "Who stole the people's money?" by pointing out the next man. This and other Thomas Nast cartoons in *Harper's Weekly* annoyed Tweed, who once offered Nast $500,000 to stop his attacks. His own followers, Tweed remarked, could not read, but they could "look at the damn pictures!" (*New York Public Library*)

perhaps not efficiently or inexpensively, but with some semblance of order and service. The corruption sometimes became so obvious as to arouse upper- and middle-class residents. But their usual indifference to the needs of city dwellers had given the bosses their electoral base.

In most American cities, power resided in the mayor, in the single- or double-chambered city council, and in independent boards. These agencies determined how municipal funds should be raised and spent. They granted the franchises for street railways, awarded contracts for sewers and paving streets, constructed public buildings, bought firefighting equipment, and contracted for other services and supplies. Since most of these activities were entrusted to committees drawn from elected aldermen or council members with no training in city management, political bosses found it easy to place their people in positions where they could dip into city treasuries and enter into profitable alliances with local businessmen.

Boss Tweed's career in New York City between 1869 and 1871 became the model for all later political swindlers. As head of Tammany Hall, the New York Democratic machine, Tweed exercised control over patronage. His technique was simple. Everyone who worked for the city was required to pad his bill—at first only by 10 percent, later by 66 percent, and finally by 85 percent. The padding went to Tweed's gang. When Tweed built his famous courthouse, whose final cost ran to many times the original estimate of $3 million, an item charged to the "repair" of fixtures ran over $1,149,000 before the building was even completed. The criticism mounted, particularly in editorials in the *Times* and in Thomas Nast's cartoons in that paper and in *Harper's Weekly*. When the corruption and bonded debt reached such proportions that bankers feared the city's credit might be in jeopardy, Tweed was thrown out. Five years later, in 1876, he died in jail.

If older Americans put the blame for corruption on ignorant immigrant hordes, the immigrants themselves were wise enough to back the bosses who helped them survive in harsh new surroundings. While civic reformers talked about honest government, staged periodic "cleanup" crusades, and showed their contempt for the immigrants and lower classes, the boss provided services and earned the loyalty of constituents.

His lieutenants welcomed new arrivals at the docks, hastened their naturalization proceedings (to speed them to the polls), gave them gifts at Christmas, found city jobs for them and their sons, encouraged their ethnic customs, and mediated with the police and the courts when immigrants or their children got into trouble. The precinct captain (like the illustrious George Washington Plunkitt of Tammany Hall) worked a full day and often into the night. Everyone in the neighborhood knew him, and many were indebted to him for some favor. On election day, the voters recalled these services, not the empty promises of do-gooding reformers.

Reform programs to reduce taxes hardly touched the average immigrant's life, for he had no property to tax. Reforms to improve the efficiency of city administration aroused only suspicion, for "efficiency" in government might well mean he and his relatives would be dropped from the city payroll. Fearful of change, the immigrant disliked the very sound of "reform." And why not, since the typical upper-class reformer seemed to be attacking the very men to whom the immigrant felt most loyal—the bosses who provided the jobs and services. Reformers also had trouble with the well-educated American voter whose party loyalties were exploited by politicians. Many honest people, feeling that local reform movements would only harm their party nationally, tolerated corrupt city and state machines that delivered the vote in national elections. The ties between politics and business strengthened the tolerance of corruption arising from party loyalties. Only when the activities of the political rings became too outrageous did respectable citizens organize for "good government," and then only temporarily.

That the machines survived the challenges and demonstrated considerable staying power is a tribute to the organizational skills they employed and to their relative success in balancing the needs of the city against those of the party. It required a fine sense of priorities to survive. Few expressed it more graphically than the elected official who observed: "There comes a time in politics when a man must rise above principle."

Technical Advances

One great obstacle to good government in the nineteenth century was widespread ignorance of how to make it work. The practice of municipal borrowing, for example, so rewarding to bankers and so much more gentle on taxpayers than paying cash for "improvements," led to huge debts which, even with the best intentions, sucked up great sums for interest and periodic funding. There was no science of sewage disposal, of garbage collection, of budget procedures and effective management.

One of the worst problems was traffic congestion, especially at peak hours when millions of workers had to be carried to and from their jobs. The horsecar, with a maximum speed of 6 miles an hour, was no longer enough. The steam-driven elevated railroad was tried out in New York City in 1867 and came into everyday use there during the seventies.

Horsecar companies fought the new lines, with the support of citizens who complained of the soot and smoke and hot ashes that dropped on pedestrians' heads. As time passed, elevated steam railroads were abandoned, but not because of discomfort. It simply became too expensive to construct elevated structures strong enough to support heavy locomotives drawing long trains at fast speeds. Some other method had to be found to transport people forced by urban overcrowding to live farther and farther from their work.

The cable car, propelled by a moving underground chain, was used in San Francisco in 1873 and in Chicago ten years later. The most successful innovation, however, was the trolley car, developed by Frank Julian Sprague. Since each of Sprague's trolleys carried its own electric motor and ran on the ground, there was no need for stinking, noisy steam locomotives or the dense network of elevated track that cut off light and air. The elevated steam railroad operators fought the trolleys, but soon were forced to electrify their own lines. Electric subways, operating in London since 1886, were introduced in Boston in 1897 and New York City in 1904.

Besides providing energy for urban transportation, electricity helped improve the lighting of city streets and structures. The development of the electric arc lamp for outdoor lighting in 1897 meant the gradual disappearance of flickering gas lamps. Soon after, electric signs on buildings lit up a few streets. Interior lighting by electricity also became commercially feasible in 1897, when Edison perfected the incandescent bulb.

In dealing with such matters as water supply, waste disposal, and street cleaning, which had been handled relatively well in the past, American cities grew less and less conscientious. By 1870, the disposal of waste had reached a critical stage in the larger cities, where sanitation methods were

those used in the villages of a century before. Not one American city filtered its water, even though dumping of sewage and garbage into streams often polluted the supply. The typhoid fever epidemics common in Chicago and Philadelphia in the last decades of the century could be traced to the drinking of contaminated water.

Between 1880 and 1900, cleaner streets, purer water, and more efficient methods of fire fighting made the American metropolis more livable. Yet it retained such ugly and brutal features that Europeans who visited the United States at the end of the century often wondered why people from their country hadn't remained at home. But Europeans who could afford to travel seldom visited Europe's own urban slums, where the most desperate were trying to escape an even grimmer rural poverty.

Housing

Many American cities, especially in New England and along the eastern seaboard, retained something of their small-town character until the Civil War. For many decades, pleasant wooden houses on well-cared-for grounds stood at comfortable distances from elm-lined streets. After 1865, the general appearance of the city changed. New architectural styles came in, and machine-made pressed brick displaced wood as the standard building material.

Not all the houses in the nineties were the architectural absurdities some critics have declared them to be; many streets and districts in the major American cities were attractive and pleasant. Yet the urban landscape, as a whole, became dingier. Even the very rich, with their armies of servants, often lived in mansions near gasworks and slaughterhouses and breathed the same sooty air as the slum dwellers. In middle-class dwellings throughout the country, interiors were dark and crammed with overstuffed furniture peculiarly susceptible to dust.

The bulk and clutter of Victorian living suited a generation that overate, whose women attached bustles to their dresses, and who lived what might be described as upholstered lives. The very poor, comprising half and more of the metropolitan population, and nearly the whole of many factory towns, lived under conditions that were scarcely endurable. The names residents gave to their neighborhoods were appropriate: Hell's Kitchen,

A one-room tenement apartment in New York. (*The Jacob Riis Collection, Museum of the City of New York*)

Bandit's Roost, Poverty Gap, Kerosene Row, Bone Alley.

Even before 1840 in New York City, rows of abandoned middle-class houses in new industrial districts were being leased for conversion into tenements. After 1865, the practice spread like a disease over metropolitan America. Whole families, sometimes more than one, lived in airless closets, usually without sanitary facilities, lighting, or heat—and were victimized then as now by flourishing populations of rats and vermin.

The first tenements designed to provide cheap lodging for working-class families were erected in New York in 1850. Driven by rising land costs, their owners built on every available square inch and up to six stories, leaving no space for trees, grass, air, or light. Soon entire districts were occupied by such barracks, into which swarmed the poor, black and white, all paying extortionate rents. Substantial profits, ranging from 15 to 30 percent, were extracted from such buildings and from basements, garrets, outhouses, and stables con-

verted into dwellings. Landlords refused to repair or maintain their property and evicted those who could not or would not pay in advance.

In 1879 the "dumbbell tenement," so called because of the shape of its floor plan, was introduced as the model housing unit in New York City. It had fireproof stairways, a toilet at first for every two families, and an outside window for each room, until doubling up cut off this opening. The solid rows of these five- or six-story buildings on 25-foot lots, 90 feet deep, discouraged any real tenement reform, and they soon became as overcrowded as the old tenements. By 1894, about 39,000 dumbbell tenement houses had been erected in New York City, and nearly half of the city's population lived in them. Most lacked bathtubs, toilets, running water, and backyards.

Although New York's slums were the worst in the nation, the same conditions prevailed elsewhere. Philadelphia constructed small two-story houses instead of tenements for its working-class population, but overcrowding produced the same hideous results. Other cities used the wooden "three-decker" apartment building, first introduced in Boston during the 1840s. From there it spread west to Chicago, gaining in numbers per acre and numbers per room in the process.

The Black Ghetto

When southern blacks came to the North, they settled largely in the cities. Between 1870 and 1890, the small black population of Chicago more than tripled (from 4000 to nearly 15,000). But that was only a suggestion of what lay ahead. (The 30,000 blacks who lived in Chicago in 1900 made up less than 2 percent of the city's people, compared with nearly 25 percent sixty years later.) The black populations of New York and Philadelphia grew to about 50,000 each in 1900.

But the numbers were larger in Washington, Baltimore, and New Orleans; and the proportion of blacks to whites was far greater in Memphis, Atlanta, Savannah, and Shreveport. Only about 20 percent of whites and blacks in the South were urbanized in 1900, but almost 70 percent of northeastern blacks lived and worked in cities.

In the early postwar decades, the black populations of the older cities of the North, as of the South, often shared neighborhoods with whites. With the spread of racism in the South after 1890, however, the urban black's position declined. Jim Crow laws and attitudes brought segregation in housing and all other aspects of life. In the North at about the same time, customs and practices subjected blacks to discrimination, police harassment, and a two-faced judicial system.

"To the American white man," a northern black lawyer remarked in 1888, "a 'nigger' is a 'nigger' whether he be a Sixth Avenue dude or a Georgia mule-driver." Although the ghetto—the district marked off for black housing and thus for black life—had not yet taken on the rigidity of later decades, the outlines were already clear in the North.

Tightly knit ethnic neighborhoods were typical of large cities at the turn of the century. But when white immigrants accumulated some money, they could move. That option was closed to blacks; white hostility, often violent, shaped the pattern and quality of black settlement and housing. As the black migration northward gained momentum, the sections of the cities into which blacks could move did not expand. The congestion in the black enclaves increased.

Such housing bred its own misfortunes, which more prosperous white citizens blamed on the blacks themselves. As early as 1885, a black newspaper in New York claimed that house rent consumed at least one-third, and sometimes one-half, the earnings of most black residents, and for dwellings that hardly justified such an expenditure. To meet rent payments, which were higher than for comparable white dwellings, blacks were forced to take in lodgers and convert brownstones into roominghouses.

With the rising tide of foreign immigrants, blacks found that the few jobs to which they could aspire were now threatened. The Irish had already moved them off the docks. Hotels now replaced black employees with immigrants. Even the barbershops, which blacks had once dominated, fell to the Italians in the 1880s and 1890s. Except as members of the "marginal labor reserve," black men—prepared only for menial tasks and kept from apprenticeship training—were bypassed as factory workers.

It was once a mark of standing among the city's rich to have black servants. But as time passed, the glamour of such attendants wore off, and male black employment declined. Black nursemaids, housemaids, and other female domestic workers remained in demand, at least until the new immigrants learned enough English to compete. Many black women became the major, if not the only, breadwinners of their families, which futher undermined male morale and multiplied broken homes. Urban conditions ultimately disoriented the black family in ways that even slavery had not succeeded in doing.

Deepening urban segregation did encourage blacks to develop or expand their own social institutions. Black business enterprises, churches, political clubs, charitable organizations, fraternal and athletic clubs, insurance companies, and similar units grew in number. To serve the expanding ghettos, a black business class emerged, made up largely of self-made men who depended on black patronage and helped to promote community and racial consciousness.

But segregation also heightened the likelihood of racial strife with other segregated groups, especially the white population, which deliberately segregated itself. Race riots in New York in 1900 and in Springfield, Illinois, in 1908 caused much property damage and loss of life. Although the number of victims in no way compared to those killed by lynching in the South, the outbreaks of violence reflected growing urban tensions that would erupt again after World War I.

The Elite

The spread of urban decay depressed many observers, as did sometimes the astonishing growth in numbers and wealth of the urban middle and upper classes. Prosperous merchants and planters of earlier generations had set modest standards of elegance and public virtue on incomes of $10,000 to $20,000 a year. Now industrial magnates and railroad barons boasted incomes in the millions.

So rapid was their rise to power and privilege that few received any training in the social responsibilities of great wealth. Some millionaires, like Rockefeller and Carnegie, eventually followed the paternalistic pattern by building libraries, universities, and research foundations. But the great majority of the new rich kept their money for business and for personal luxuries.

"Conspicuous consumption" reached absurd heights in the cities during the 1890s, while the business system was sunk in a deep depression. The extravagances of the rich made newspaper copy, as did their debaucheries. At one party the guests, all on horseback, rode their mounts into a luxurious hotel. At another great dinner, cigarettes rolled in hundred-dollar bills were passed out to the guests and smoked after coffee. Harry Lehr staged a dog dinner at which his friends' dogs were invited to sup on rare dainties. Perhaps the most irritating single event was the notorious Bradley Martin ball, given at a cost of $369,000 during the severe depression winter of 1896–97. The hostess appeared as Mary Queen of Scots, displaying among her ornaments a massive ruby necklace once worn by Marie Antoinette. One of the guests, August Belmont, wore a $10,000 suit of steel armor inlaid with gold. The reaction to the ball persuaded the Bradley Martins to leave New York and take up permanent residence in England.

Yet the extravagances went on. On upper Fifth Avenue in New York City, the palaces of the rich rivaled those of the titled families of Europe. High-priced architects reproduced ancient forms in limestone and marble, while their clients decorated the interiors with genuine treasures of Europe's artistic past, as well as fraudulent reproductions.

VIEWS OF THE CITY: EDITORS AND ARCHITECTS

When writers, politicians, and clerics focused on the merits of agrarian and urban life, the city almost always suffered by comparison. Its very appearance suggested to many the alienation and depersonalization that typified urban living. In a world dominated by iron, steel, and stone, the people had come to resemble the structures they were erecting. For some, the city newspaper emphasized the differences between the rural and urban ways of life; it fed its readers on murders, scandals, and violence.

There were those who clung to a different vision of the city and what it could become. They talked of ways of altering the physical appearance of the city in order to make it a more decent place to live. That vision was captured in some of the new urban landscapes and architecture and in the Great White City that formed the nucleus of the World's Columbian Exposition in Chicago in 1893. What distinguished that "dream city" from so much of urban America was the fact that it had been planned.

Urban Journalism

The daily press, like the new popular magazines, kept up with the growing complexity of urban life and tried to satisfy the varied tastes of a growing readership. Even before the Civil War, writers and editors had discovered that crusades against corruption or vice paid off in sales. Civic vice gave such a boost to circulation that newspaper editors began to invent causes and to feature crime. Recent arrivals from the farm particularly liked stories that confirmed their ideas of life in the wicked city. Reporters who were able to "crash" the entertainments of the rich and to describe them from the inside or who could draw a tear by writing authentic reports of the experiences of the poor brought a new individuality and a new glamour to newspaper careers.

The new methods helped to enlarge daily newspaper circulation from 2.8 million in 1870 to 24 million in 1899. Increased revenue from subscriptions and sales, and above all from advertising, helped free editors from political pressure and enabled them to become powerful molders of public opinion.

Joseph Pulitzer, owner of the *St. Louis Post-*

Dispatch and later of the *World* in New York, was the model of the new type of publisher. Combining the crudest sensationalism with effective exposés, the *World* lived up to Pulitzer's promise to publish a "journal that is not only cheap, but bright, not only bright, but large, not only large but truly democratic that will expose all fraud and sham, fight all public evils and abuses."

The *World* exploited all the inventions that were revolutionizing publishing in this period: improved newsprint made from wood pulp, the Linotype machine (1886), typewriters, telephones, and the telegraph. These improvements produced startling rises in circulation—from 20,000 to 40,000 within two months after Pulitzer took over in 1883; 100,000 by 1884; and 250,000 by 1886.

Pulitzer's methods were copied by publishers in other large cities and by competitors in New York. William Randolph Hearst, fresh from Harvard and backed by his father's gold-mining millions, even outdid Pulitzer in sensationalism in his *New York Journal.* One result of the fierce newspaper rivalry was *yellow journalism,* a name derived from the yellow ink first used by Pulitzer in comics but soon made to stand for the kind of publishing he promoted.

Conservative editors were quick to criticize yellow journalism, but the only effective answer was to produce a good newspaper that sold widely without it. Adolph S. Ochs proved this could be done when he took over the moribund *New York Times* in 1896, cut its price to a penny, and revived its circulation by full and trustworthy coverage of foreign and domestic news.

When Congress in 1879 granted low postal rates to magazines, their circulation grew even more spectacularly than that of newspapers. *McCall's* (1870), *Popular Science* (1872), *Woman's Home Companion* (1873), *Cosmopolitan* (1886), *Collier's* (1888), and *Vogue* (1892) were only a few that benefited from the new postal act. By and large, these publications, as well as established monthlies like *Harper's, The Atlantic, Scribner's,* and *The Century,* appealed to the middle-class urban reader.

In the last decade of the nineteenth century, magazines became more sensational in their methods and gave more attention to current issues. New techniques in printing and heavier subsidies from advertisers helped publishers lower magazine prices. By 1900, with the additional benefit of low mailing costs, hundreds of thousands of families could subscribe.

Cyrus H. K. Curtis's *Ladies' Home Journal,* founded in 1883, became the most spectacular magazine success; it reached a million in circulation by 1900. His brilliant editor, Edward Bok, filled the *Journal* with features for women: advice on how to bring up children, decorate their homes, and preserve their health. Bok bought the fiction of the most popular American and English writers and paid them well. Soon this "monthly Bible of the American home" had become a national force which, among other accomplishments, influenced American domestic architecture and led a campaign to force municipal authorities to clean up their cities.

The New Urban Landscape

To recapture some of the rural virtues lost in an urban environment, a few far-sighted planners tried to bring the country to the city. The vision of a garden city had been caught in 1858 when Calvert Vaux and the landscape architect Frederick Law Olmsted planned Central Park in New York. Not only was the idea of a planned public park itself almost unprecedented, but their ingenious and tasteful efforts to accommodate roads, lawns, and buildings to the topography ushered in a new era in landscape design. At first, many people complained that parks were aristocratic, un-American, and unbusinesslike. But this prejudice soon disappeared, and the resistance of real estate interests was overcome. Between 1872 and 1895, Olmsted and his disciples undertook similar experiments in Boston, Washington, Buffalo, and other cities.

Architects also tried to counteract the ugliness and imitativeness that characterized so much of urban building. It took a different kind of imagination to discover originality and beauty in bridges, railroad stations, grain elevators, viaducts, warehouses, and office buildings. The Brooklyn Bridge, conceived by John Roebling in 1869 and built by his son Washington between 1869 and 1883, performed a practical function. It connected Manhattan Island with Long Island, carried tremendous loads, and eased ferryboat congestion. At the same time, its unadorned steel was breathtakingly beautiful.

Many of the skyscrapers of the period revealed a similar functional beauty, fulfilling what a pioneer Chicago architect called the "ideals of modern business life, simplicity, stability, breadth, dignity." High ground rents made the maximum use of space in business districts necessary, and the vertical, soaring office buildings seemed to escape from the city's limited dimensions. Such buildings were made possible by the electric elevator, perfected in the 1880s, and by cheap steel, which could be constructed as a light, strong cage, instead of bulky masonry walls or stone columns. But city planning or its lack also permitted the skyscraper to turn streets into canyons, to shut out light and air, and to increase congestion.

The 21 million Americans who visited the World's Columbian Exposition in Chicago in 1893 were able to see a "dream city," constructed especially for this occasion, rising miraculously from the shores of Lake Michigan. It had its own transportation facilities, water supply, sewage, and police and fire protection. Frederick Law Olmsted and his assistant, Henry Codman, scored a brilliant success in laying out the grounds. Even their skill, however, could not transform "the White City," as it came to be called, into an artistic triumph; only Louis Sullivan's Transportation Building broke with the past. The classic buildings of the Court of Honor produced a dismal succession of pillared banks, town halls, and railroad stations.

But the White City did stimulate thinking about and experiments in urban planning and beautification. Whatever the artistic merits of the exposition, critics agreed that it was an object lesson in how a well-managed city ought to be administered for the pleasure and convenience of its inhabitants. An electrified railway and electrically powered boats on the lagoons transported hundreds of thousands of visitors. Sanitation squads cleaned up the day's garbage every night. Polite and considerate guards suggested how a model police force should conduct itself. It was a striking contrast to Chicago proper, which was a jungle of disorder.

The exposition began at the outset of a severe depression and ended as the depression deepened. Even before it closed, the temporary buildings had cracked. For some Americans, it was a reflection on the society it had celebrated. But for most it had been an impressive display of American ingenuity. Rather than view the White City as an extravagance in a time of depression, those Americans concerned with the quality of urban life preferred to apply the lessons of planning and efficiency to the social problems that plagued their cities. While landscape architects tried to beautify the city, social reformers tried to help the casualties of city life.

URBAN REFORMERS

Although J. P. Morgan found New York at the turn of the century a "neighborly city," it must have appeared excessively neighborly and less enjoyable to the 30,000 persons crowded into a single East Side district of five or six blocks. This area boasted a greater density of population than any similar area anywhere in the world, even India or China. From his mansion on "Millionaires' Row," Morgan could isolate himself from this sore spot. Municipal reformers could confine themselves to developing a science of public administration that would staff city departments with university-trained experts. At the same time, social workers, philanthropists, and clergy began to deal more directly with the social ills of urbanization. Moved by moral considerations and sometimes by fear of revolution, they concerned themselves not so much with altering the structure of city government as with making life more bearable for slumdwellers.

The Humanitarian Response

Traditional explanations of poverty and misfortune had blamed the victims. The virtuous succeeded; the immoral did not. But by the 1870s urban reformers realized that the causes of poverty were far more complex. Illness, death of the breadwinner, low wages, and unemployment clearly produced more paupers and criminals than laziness and alcoholism. The advice to be frugal came to be meaningless when unemployment and miserable wages did not permit even the most thrifty families to accumulate any savings. Urban reformers placed more emphasis on the weaknesses of the economy and on the need to do something concrete to assist the victims.

The first step in relief often was simply to keep people alive. During the depression of the 1870s, the problem had grown so vast that private charities could not cope with it. In 1877, Buffalo became the first city to coordinate its relief organizations. A decade later, twenty-five affiliated charities across the country had eliminated much of the inefficiency of earlier social agencies.

By increasing the number of those most susceptible to political agitation and discontent, the slums, many believed, intensified the danger of social upheaval. Hoping to narrow the gulf between the privileged and the underprivileged, middle-class reformers and social workers, most of them women, moved into the immigrant ghettos. They learned through direct experience of the lives of the poor; they opened settlement houses in the poorest neighborhoods to offer guidance, recreation, and companionship.

The idea of the settlement house originated in London in the 1870s, and the opening of Toynbee Hall in the East London slums in 1884 provided a model. Jane Addams (1860–1935) became the leader of the settlement house movement in America. With her friend, Helen Gates Starr, in 1889 she converted the old Hull mansion in Chicago into a settlement house called Hull House. In Boston, Cleveland, Pittsburgh, and elsewhere, college men and women formed clubs for boys and girls, established playgrounds and libraries, conducted classes, transformed settlement houses into a combination nursery, gymnasium, and employment bureau, and campaigned for sanitary regulations, better housing, and penal reform.

The scientific approach to social welfare did not slow down the crusade against alcohol and the saloon. The Prohibition party, which ran its first national ticket in 1872, proved ineffective. But a powerful new organization took shape in 1874 with the founding of the Women's Christian Temperance Union. Led by Frances E. Willard, a former educator whose creed was: "No sectarianism in religion, no sectionalism in politics, no sex in citizenship," the WCTU propagandized against liquor and the people who made and sold it. Its stated policy was "mental suasion for the man who thinks and moral suasion for the man who drinks, but legal suasion for the drunkard-maker." Nothing seemed to work, however, for by 1898 only five states were legally dry. The women who led the temperance campaign were also at the head of the campaign for women's suffrage (see Chapter 25). But this campaign also had to wait until after World War I.

The Role of the Churches

The response of the churches to slums and poverty was at first slow and indecisive, for few ministers had any knowledge of the lives of working-class families. When demands for shorter hours and government regulation of working conditions grew loud, one church leader reminded them: "Whatever you suffer here from injustice of others will turn to your account hereafter. Be quiet." But such advice meant nothing in the face of urban and industrial conditions, and during the 1870s the churches began to change their stand.

The Social Gospel movement emerged during the last quarter of the nineteenth century. Organized by socially conscious ministers of various Protestant denominations, and concerned over the church's failure to reach large numbers of urban dwellers, the movement attacked the social consequences of urbanization and industrialization. The clergy who made up the movement concluded from examining conditions in their own neighborhoods that environmental forces, not immorality, lay at the root of the problem.

Some went no further than to advocate moderate reforms in wages, housing, and working conditions. The more radical insisted that the nation's business system be reformed from the bottom up. Ministers like Washington Gladden and Walter Rauschenbusch defended labor unions, wrote and preached against laissez faire, and expressed the Social Gospel ideal that Christian solutions existed for all social problems. By the 1880s, theological seminaries were offering courses in social Christianity and social ethics.

But despite the need, the Social Gospel movement was confined to a minority. Baptist, Methodist, and other churches whose membership consisted largely of artisans, shopkeepers, and farmers preferred to keep the old emphasis on individual responsibility for sin and the church's need to deal only with religious salvation. The fact that many of the newly rich were Baptists and Methodists (John D. Rockefeller was a prominent Baptist elder, Daniel Drew a fervent Methodist) may also help to explain why their churches did not quarrel with society as they found it. "People charge Mr. Rockefeller with stealing the money he gave to the church," a Baptist pastor declared. "But he has laid it on the altar and thus sanctified it."

Some Protestant ministers, concerned about the "unchurched masses," sought ways to reclaim them. One device was the revival meeting, where evangelists ignored economic and political issues and preached the "old-time" religion. Among the most effective was Dwight L. Moody. In 1870 this former shoe salesman from Boston teamed up with the singer Ira D. Sankey to launch a campaign for saving souls. Moody preached a simple but powerful message: abandon "the cold formalism that has crept into the Church of God" and persevere for Christ.

From Chicago, where Moody had evangelized successfully in Little Hell on the North Side, Moody and Sankey went to England. When they had silenced scoffers there, they returned to take by storm every large city in the United States. The Chicago Bible Institute for Home and Foreign Missions, founded in 1899, was only one of many monuments erected to them.

The evangelist spirit was also expressed in the Young Men's Christian Association, founded as the American offshoot of an English society in 1851, and the Young Women's Christian Association, founded in 1858. Both organizations dedicated themselves to "the physical, mental, social, and spiritual benefit" of men and women everywhere. By 1897, the YMCA had 263,298 members in the United States and the YWCA about 35,000. Another import from England was the Salvation Army, organized by a Wesleyan Methodist, "General" William Booth. This army of Christians helped feed and shelter urban unfortunates. After the first American branch was opened in 1880, the Salvation Army's "slum brigades" marched out into the tenement areas and skid rows and brought comfort and relief to the neglected poor.

Better-off city dwellers sought another sort of spiritual balm, provided by a remarkable woman, Mrs. Mary Baker Eddy. Her book *Science and Health* (1875) set forth the basic doctrines of the Church of Christ, Scientist, a sect that numbered 35,000 by 1900. Mrs. Eddy taught that "disease is caused by the mind alone" and that "Christian Science," the wisdom of God revealed to man by His son Jesus Christ, alone could overcome it. "Mind," she boldly wrote, "constructs the body, and with its own materials instead of matter; hence no broken bones or dislocations can occur." Her message appealed with particular force to Americans for whom science had come to have magical qualities.

The social activities of the dominant Protestant churches hardly touched the millions of Catholics in the United States—12 million by 1900—largely concentrated in the cities and especially among the city poor. The Catholic clergy, unlike the Protestants, traditionally looked to the needs of the poor. Their organized efforts in America began in 1858 when Isaac T. Hecker, a Catholic convert, organized the Paulist Fathers to serve the New York poor. After the Civil War, the Roman Catholic Church enlarged its philanthropic activities and in its schools carried on an effective program to Americanize Catholic immigrants.

Roman Catholic success with the urban masses led certain Protestant leaders to suspect that the priests were plotting to capture the country. It was not long before anti-Catholic fears surfaced once more. The American Protective Association, a secret society formed in 1887, exploited the bigotry of the rural Middle West against the influence of Roman Catholicism in labor and politics. The irony of APA activities was that they appealed to farmers. The Catholics were in the cities, where the APA leaders had no success.

Many Protestant clerics had to look only to their own congregations to note the disproportionate number of middle- and upper-class members. That perception, along with fears of growing Catholic influence among the urban masses, gradually stirred the Protestant clergy to imitate Catholic methods in the cities. During the post-Civil War decades, nondenominational mission societies were formed. The "institutional church" made its appearance, with clubrooms, reading rooms, gymnasiums, adult education classes, youth organizations, and women's societies. The "institutional church," like the social settlement house, represented a commitment to urban social reform.

But even as clerics and social workers assisted the victims of urbanization and industrialization, the conditions that bred poverty, unemployment, and urban congestion persisted. Optimism about improving the quality of urban life also persisted— the conviction that the inequalities of society could be corrected by legislation and by arousing the social conscience of the nation. For those who took up the reform standard in the Progressive Era, urban government and urban living remained a formidable challenge.

SUMMARY

After the Civil War, America became an urban nation as well as an industrial one. By 1910, almost one person in two lived in a city. New York had nearly 5 million people; Chicago, nearly 2 million. The cities grew because industry and trade grew; there were thousands of new jobs as factory workers and laborers, as salespeople, officeworkers, and clerks. The people who filled these jobs were migrants from rural America seeking success; they were also immigrants from Europe seeking a better life.

Between 1866 and 1915, about 25 million immigrants came to the United States. This great flood caused some reaction and fear of competition from those already here, and open immigration remained a source of political trouble until the Immigration Restriction Act of 1921.

The exploding nineteenth-century American city had all the problems of rapid, unplanned growth—poor sewage, bad water, inadequate housing, tangled transportation. The difficulties were compounded because no one really knew how to run a large city, and because the prevailing idea about the cause of poverty and misery was that it was the victim's fault. These attitudes led to many opportunities for political corruption, and to the growth of the political "machine" and the "boss."

In return for delivering the votes on election day, political bosses were given control of patronage—city jobs—and access to and control over how tax monies were spent. The boss gave out jobs and favors, and commanded an army of county, ward, and precinct workers. Constituents were taken care of and the city was run in a more or less orderly fashion. In return, bosses such as Tweed of New York pocketed huge amounts of the public's money.

Although the basic problems were not solved, between 1880 and 1900 the American city became a slightly more livable place. Technical advances in transportation, streetcleaning and lighting, and sanitation and water supply helped. So did the activities of editors, architects, and reformers, who planted the idea of a planned city governed in a humane way. Housing, however, remained a mess. The poor were soon crammed into a new kind of building, the dumbbell tenement, introduced in New York in 1879 as model city housing. It and several variants were soon used in cities all over the country.

The black ghetto also began to take shape during this period, as blacks were pushed out of jobs and out of certain areas of the city. Immigrants took over jobs once held by black men, black women became the breadwinners, and the stage was set for the urban black ghetto of the twentieth century.

This was the era of "conspicuous consumption" by the urban rich. Great mansions were built, and unbelievably lavish and extravagant parties were given. The spending continued through the depression of the 1890s, despite public ciriticism and resentment. The Gospel of Success said that the rich, after all, were also the righteous and the blessed.

But there were those with a new vision of the city, and those with the attitude that the city was for all people, not just the rich. New York's Central Park became the model for a new idea—the planned public park, maintained by the city for everyone's use. Architects began to design and build public structures that were beautiful as well as functional.

Newspapers and magazines, capitalizing on a growing number of readers and the increase in sales that campaigns against vice and corruption brought, became powerful molders of public opinion. This was the time of yellow journalism, of Pulitzer's *World* and Hearst's *New York Journal*. Special low postal rates helped magazines that appealed to middle-class urban readers. *The Ladies Home Journal,* founded in 1883, had a circulation of 1 million by 1900.

The problems and evils of city life were also attacked by social reformers, who tried to help those who lived in the slums and worked in the sweatshops. The challenge was great, and they could do little about the underlying conditions that caused the poverty and ignorance. But they did succeed in beginning to change the attitude of "blaming the victim" and in involving the churches, especially the Protestant churches, in social work.

A number of the reformers were women: Jane Addams, for example, began the settlement house movement in America. Frances Willard led the crusade against alcohol through the Women's Christian Temperance Union, founded in 1874. The evangelist spirit was expressed in institutions based on English models, such as the YMCA and YWCA and the Salvation Army, all well established in the United States by 1900.

All these organizations and individuals did achieve something to help the poor and to set the climate for change. But nothing substantial would happen until the twentieth century, when government would come to see social legislation and the solving of urban problems as part of its duties.

Suggested Readings

C. N. Glaab and A. T. Brown, *A History of Urban America* (1967), and Z. L. Miller, *The Urbanization of Modern America* (1973), are solid introductions to urbanization. Blake McKelvey, *The Urbanization of America 1860–1915,* (1963) is a more comprehensive survey. A. M. Schlesinger, *The Rise of the City 1878–1898* (1933), is a pioneering work that touches on many social aspects of city living. Some of the same concerns appear in H. P. Chudacoff, *The Evolution of American Urban Society* (1975), and in Gunther Barth, *City People: The Rise of Modern City Culture in Nineteenth-Century America* (1980). Dixon Wecter, *The Saga of American Society: A Record of Social Aspiration 1607–1937* (1937), examines the urban life of the elite. Paul Boyer, *Urban Masses and Moral Order in America 1820–1920* (1978), is a study of how the urban middle class sought to combat the social disintegration and moral chaos they saw around them.

Among the important studies of individual cities are C. M. Green, *Holyoke, Massachusetts: A Case History of the Industrial Revolution in America* (1939), and her two volumes on Washington, D.C.: *Village and Capital 1800–1878* (1962), and *Capital City 1879–1950* (1963); B. L. Pierce, *A History of Chicago* (3 vols., 1937–57); S. B. Warner, *The Private City: Philadelphia in Three Periods of its Growth* (1968); and W. D. Miller, *Memphis during the Progressive Era* (1957).

The process of urban growth and expansion is examined in S. B. Warner, *Streetcar Suburbs: The Process of Growth in Boston 1870–1900* (1962). Important examples of the "new" urban history, using quantitative methods and focusing on social and residential mobility, are S. Thernstrom and R. Sennett (eds.), *Nineteenth-Century Cities: Essays in the New Urban History* (1969); Thernstrom, *Poverty and Progress: Social Mobility in a Nineteenth Century City* (1964), and *The Other Bostonians: Poverty and Progress in the American Metropolis, 1880–1970* (1973); Thomas Kessner, *The Golden Door: Italian and Jewish Immigrant Mobility in New York City 1880–1915* (1977); and H. P. Chudacoff, *Mobile Americans: Residential and Social Mobility in Omaha 1880–1920* (1972).

M. A. Jones, *American Immigration* (1960), and Philip Taylor, *The Distant Magnet* (1971), provide an introduction to the immigrant. These should be supplemented by the vivid account of the "new" immigrant in Oscar Handlin, *The Uprooted* (1951). On individual immigrant groups, see R. T. Berthoff, *British Immigrants in Industrial America 1790–1950* (1953); C. Erickson, *American Industry and the European Immigrant 1860–1885* (1957); K. A. Miller, *Emigrants and Exiles: Ireland and the Irish Exodus to North America* (1985); W. I. Thomas and F. Znaniecki, *The Polish Peasant in Europe and America* (5 vols., 1918–20); and M. Rischin, *The Promised City: New York's Jews 1870–1914* (1962).

A gripping photographic study is A. Schoener (ed.), *Portal to America: The Lower East Side 1870–1925* (1967), a companion to Irving Howe's sensitive portrayal of East European Jews in New York City, *World of Our Fathers* (1976). The "new" immigration history has shown how newcomers maintained their cultures and family structure in an alien environment. See, for example, V. Yans-McLaughlin, *Family and Community: Italian Immigrants in Buffalo, 1880–1930* (1977); H. S. Nelli, *The Italians in Chicago* (1970); and J. Barton, *Peasants and Strangers: Italians, Roumanians, and Slovaks in an American City, 1890–1950* (1975). The reactions of native Americans to immigration are examined in J. Higham, *Strangers in the Land* (1955), and B. M. Solomon, *Ancestors and Immigrants* (1956).

On blacks in northern cities before the Great Migration, see A. H. Spear, *Black Chicago 1890–1920* (1967); G. Osofsky, *Harlem: The Making of a Ghetto 1890–1930* (1965); D. M. Katzman, *Before the Ghetto: Black Detroit in the Nineteenth Century* (1973); K. L. Kusmer, *A Ghetto Takes Shape: Black Cleveland, 1870–1930* (1976); and R. Lane, *Roots of Violence in Black Philadelphia, 1860–1900* (1986). On black Washington D.C., see C. M. Green, *The Secret City* (1967), and J. Borchert, *Alley Life in Washington: Family, Community, Religion, and Folklife in the City, 1850–1970* (1980).

L. Steffens, *The Shame of the Cities* (1904) remains a classic critique of city government. On the urban bosses, see Z. L. Miller, *Boss Cox's Cincinnati* (1968), and A. B. Callow, *The Tweed Ring* (1966). L. Hershkowitz, *Tweed's New York,* is sympathetic to the Tweed machine. A candid and amusing account is W. Riordan, *Plunkitt of Tammany Hall* (1963 ed.), the personal reflections of a Tammany ward boss. On urban political reform, see B. Brownell and W. Stickle (eds.), *Bosses and Reformers: Urban Politics in America 1880–1920* (1973); and B. Stave (ed.), *Urban Bosses, Machines, and Progressive Reforms* (1972).

R. H. Bremner, *From the Depths: The Discovery of Poverty in the United States* (1956), is a broad and solid study. J. Riis, *How the Other Half Lives* (1890), is a classic contemporary account, as is J. Addams, *Forty Years at Hull House* (1935). A. Mann, *Yankee Reformers in the Urban Age: Social Reform in Boston 1880–1900* (1954), and T. L. Philpott, *The Slum and the Ghetto: Neighborhood Deterioration and Middle-Class Reform, Chicago 1880–1930* (1978), are important studies of urban social reform. See also suggested readings at the end of Chapter 25.

The response of organized religion to industrialism and urban conditions is examined in A. I. Abell, *The Urban Impact upon American Protestantism 1865–1900* (1943); R. D. Cross, *The Emergence of Liberal Catholicism in America* (1958); H. F. May, *Protestant Churches and Industrial America* (1949); and C.

H. Hopkins, *The Rise of the Social Gospel in American Protestantism 1865–1915* (1940). For the impact of revivalism, see W. G. McLoughlin, *Modern Revivalism: Charles Finney to Billy Graham* (1959), and J. F. Findlay, *Dwight L. Moody: American Evangelist 1837–1899* (1969).

On urban journalism, see F. L. Mott, *A History of American Magazines 1885–1905* (1957). On urban architecture, see L. Mumford, *Sticks and Stones* (1924), and *The Brown Decades* (1931); W. Andrews, *Architecture, Ambition, and Americans* (1955); J. E. Burchard and A. Bush-Brown, *The Architecture of America* (1961); R. Twombly, *Louis Sullivan* (1986); and G. Wright, *Moralism and the Model Home: Domestic Architecture and Cultural Conflict in Chicago 1873–1913* (1980).

CULTURE
AND THOUGHT

Chapter 23

For all its impressive industrial growth, the United States, in the eyes of some American and foreign critics, remained a cultural dwarf. The Centennial Exposition at Philadelphia in 1876 celebrated the birth of the nation by demonstrating its technological maturity. What Americans came to see were not displays of painting and sculpture, but the new marvels of technology, such as the telephone, the locomotive, and the steam engine.

For the intellectual Henry Adams, however, the World's Columbian Exposition in Chicago in 1893 displayed a world on the brink of disaster:

I apprehend for the next hundred years an ultimate, colossal, cosmic collapse; but not on any of our old lines. My belief is that science is to wreck us, and that we are like monkeys monkeying with a loaded shell; we don't in the least know or care where our practically infinite energies come from or will bring us to.

Even if they had understood him, few Americans in the late nineteenth century would have appreciated Adams. For most of the visitors to the Philadelphia and Chicago expositions, what they had seen confirmed the superiority of their society and the pioneering tradition that was now conquering new frontiers in technology and science. It mattered to very few that the paintings, murals, and sculptures displayed at the expositions showed hardly a trace of originality or a hint of vitality. If that said something about how Americans chose to measure progress, it was a trait foreign visitors to this country had long recognized.

The same forces so in evidence at the Chicago and Philadelphia expositions exerted a great influence on American attitudes and culture, on educational institutions and churches, on law and philosophy, on the social sciences, and on literature. Educators and editors, economists and sociologists extolled the laws of competition; historians confirmed the superiority of Anglo-Saxon institutions; popular ministers praised making money as the highest form of public service; and writers sentimentalized literature. Defenders of society drew on every kind of belief and knowledge to support their arguments. Some even adapted the new Darwinian ideas to their purposes.

But they did not go unchallenged. Nor did the business ethics, the inequalities, the ostentation, and the vulgarity that were so characteristic of the age. A growing number of respected critics began to question and condemn business values. And in raising critical questions about the changing nature of American civilization, the work of these critics would have a lasting impact on such twentieth-century developments as the Progressive movement and the New Deal.

In literature, too, there was considerable ferment. The McGuffey reader and the Horatio Alger novels may have been widely read, but others dealt realistically with their society and offered different models of behavior. Mark Twain's Huck Finn, battling the tyranny of the village, would long outlast the boys in the Alger novels, who succeeded only by losing their identity in the urban business world. ∎

SOCIAL DARWINISM

When Charles Darwin published *The Origin of Species* in 1859, the age of the earth, the process of its formation, and the origins of its inhabitants had long been discussed by philosophers, naturalists, and other scientists. But none had reached such firm conclusions from such convincing evidence. Darwin argued that the species of life all around us, far from having been created by separate acts of God in seven days, had gradually evolved, over millions of years, through the operation of the principle of "natural selection." According to Darwin, all forms of life were engaged in an unceasing "struggle for existence" in a constantly changing natural environment. Although some species died, the "fittest" had survived and passed on to their offspring their favorable characteristics. Over long ages of time, successive adaptations had produced entirely new species, including humans.

Darwin's ideas outraged biblical fundamentalists and offended some leading scientists. More remarkable, however, was the readiness of Americans to embrace the new views, which rapidly gained popularity and acceptance in intellectual circles. Darwin's popularizers in the United States—men like the Harvard botanist Asa Gray and the historian and lecturer John Fiske—found nothing antireligious in the belief that humans were the product of a long evolutionary process; on the contrary, they viewed that process as nothing less than "God's handiwork." In this way, religion and science could be made perfectly compatible.

Darwin's Popularizers

By combining scientific Darwinism with American optimism, the English philosopher Herbert Spencer achieved an impressive following in the United States. His "synthetic philosophy," as he called it, explained the new biology in moral terms easily translated by journalists and other publicists. By ensuring the survival of the fittest, who would in turn pass on their characteristics to their offspring, the evolutionary process promised constant progress. The physical and intellectual power of the fittest would become ever greater. For God, Spencer substituted the Unknowable. This satisfied the many Americans who no longer interpreted the Bible literally, yet clung to a faith in a supernatural agency.

By 1900 about 350,000 copies of Spencer's books had been bought in America—a remarkable sale for sociological and philosophical works. Harvard in 1869 and Yale, Johns Hopkins, and other universities in the 1870s adopted his view in teaching religion as well as the biological and social sciences. William Graham Sumner (1840–1910) of Yale, the most independent thinker among American Social Darwinists, stressed inevitability more than optimism. "At the banquet of life," wrote Sumner, "there are dinners without appetites at one end of the table and appetites without dinners at the other." Sumner, like Darwin and Spencer, accepted the theory of the English economist T. R. Malthus that population increase outstrips food supply. But he rejected the idea that progress arose out of the resulting struggle for existence.

He saw reformers as meddlers engaged in an absurd attempt to make over the world. Sumner was consistent in his hands-off philosophy: he opposed government handouts in the form of high tariffs to the "fittest" industrialists. Nor had he any sympathy for racists and imperialists who cited Darwin to justify worldwide power.

Critics and Dissenters

To accept Darwin's ideas was not necessarily to accept the social implications stressed by many of his popularizers. Among the most outspoken opponents of Spencer and his American followers was the sociologist Lester Ward (1841–1913). He rejected the theory that "neither physical nor social phenomena are capable of human control" and pointed to the superiority of selectivity over natural breeding in agriculture. Ward believed in

Henry George, social reformer and activist. (*Library of Congress*)

social planning and welcomed government intervention in social matters. A democratic government operating in the interests of all, he said, would permit a truer individualism by breaking up monopolies that strangled opportunity.

Ward's first major work, *Dynamic Sociology* (1883), sold only 500 copies in ten years. Henry George (1839–1897), more of an activist than Ward, reached a far larger audience. He rejected Spencer's talk of the "survival of the fittest." Progress, he said, depended on human association and social equality that unleashed a person's creative powers. When inequality prevailed, civilization declined. George saw proof of this in California, where he went from his native Philadelphia in 1857. The frontier society of California, simple and egalitarian, had become transformed before his eyes into a wealthy and stratified society.

George felt that poverty went with progress because of the system of private land ownership. The value of land, he said, was largely a matter of accident. For example, land in metropolitan New York had grown so costly only because "the presence of the whole great population" made it worth

millions of dollars an acre. Since land grew in value because of the people who lived on it, George argued, the profit ought to return to the public in the form of a tax on the unearned increase in land values resulting from favorable location, improvements in transportation and production, and community development. He would leave the ownership of land in private hands, but socialize the rent. The single tax on land would make other taxes unnecessary and bring the government funds for many useful social purposes.

George's ideas, set down in *Progress and Poverty* (1879), attracted worldwide attention. He narrowly missed being elected mayor of New York City in 1886. He ran again in 1897, but died five days before election day.

George's contemporary Edward Bellamy (1850–1898) also rejected the fatalism of the Social Darwinists. But unlike George, he concentrated on the competitive system itself. Bellamy's radicalism had something in common with the utopian experiments of the 1840s and with the Social Gospel movement of the 1880s. In *Looking Backward*, a novel published in 1888, Bellamy offered a vision of an ideal society in the year 2000 whose beauty, tranquility, and efficiency contrasted vividly with the smoky, striving, strike-ridden America of his day. This Golden Age dawned after the nationalizing of the great trusts and the replacement of private with public capitalism.

The millions of Americans who read Bellamy's novel were delighted by the prospect of an immaculate, gadget-filled city of the future in which the people had discarded the profit motive and there were neither rich nor poor. Amazed by the impact of his book, Bellamy concluded that the American people might be ready to put his theories into practice. "Nationalism," as he called his system, was not a class movement. It rested on the idea that all people would join in an effort to build a cooperative society.

To publicize Bellamy's views, "Nationalist" clubs and periodicals advocated public ownership of railroads and utilities, civil service reform, and government aid to education. Before Bellamy's death, "Nationalism" had been absorbed by the agrarian reformers. But he had made a large audience familiar with "socialist" ideas.

Academic Rebels

The ideas of George and Bellamy found little support in the universities, where conservatism was firmly fixed. American students learned that inequality in wealth produced the incentives for progress; that labor's wages depended on the number of workers competing for jobs; and that competition was the only way for free individuals to work for "the greatest good of the greatest number." Only in an unregulated society could "natural" economic laws function properly.

These ideas began to be challenged in the mid-1880s by a group of younger scholars, many of them trained in German universities. Richard T. Ely, John R. Commons, Edward Bemis and other economists grew more and more critical of laissez faire. Under the leadership of Ely, the younger economists and some liberal clergy founded the American Economic Association in 1885. The AEA declared itself in favor of "the positive assistance of the state." While recognizing "the necessity of individual initiative in industrial life," it held that the doctrine of laissez faire was both politically and morally objectionable.

Younger sociologists had also broken out of the Spencerian straitjacket by the 1890s. E. A. Ross argued that individual personality was shaped by *social* institutions that could be controlled. In *Sin and Society* (1907) Ross tried to show that new business conditions demanded a new code of ethics, one that required the corporation to take full responsibility for its acts.

Although the younger social scientists differed in their economic and political programs, by and large they all distrusted a static view of the universe, absolute laws, and fixed conceptions. Society, they felt, was constantly changing and had to be examined as process and growth. They turned to the past in order to understand the present and looked in other disciplines for relevant facts that would help illuminate their own.

Foremost among the academic rebels was the economist Thorstein Veblen (1857–1929). Son of Norwegian immigrants, the Wisconsin-born Veblen had absorbed some frontier Populism before he completed his training at Yale, where he studied under Sumner, and at Johns Hopkins. He emerged as a biting critic of the leisure class, of "the intrusion of business ideals, aims, and methods" into the universities, and of contemporary institutions and values.

According to Veblen, millionaires were not, as Sumner had insisted, products of "natural selection." Nor were they socially useful. Captains of enterprise, he said, actually sabotaged industry through monopolistic practices. Their concern, unlike that of the engineer, was profit, not production. In displaying their wealth so conspicuously, the rich simply wished to show off. In his most widely read book, *The Theory of the Leisure Class* (1899), and in other volumes, Veblen discussed the habits and thoughts of the rich as if they were a primitive tribe.

He introduced ethical, psychological, biological, and anthropological material new to economic studies. He saw an economic community organized under a technical elite who would use their mastery of the machine for the good of society. Veblen's ideas seemed odd in the early 1900s, but his influence grew steadily as real events made it clear that neither American society nor its economic system were perfect.

NEW IDEAS: PHILOSOPHY, LAW, HISTORY

Although Darwinian ideas won acceptance in academic circles, the ways in which American scholars and intellectuals would choose to apply those ideas differed widely. Rather than use the theory of evolution to defend the economic system and laissez faire, some used it as a basis for questioning everything. Darwinism opened up new areas for exploration and speculation in philosophy, law, history, the social sciences, and education. Traditional findings and interpretations underwent much revision. Most important, the development of pragmatic philosophy, with its emphasis on ideas as tools for solving practical problems, gave social thinkers confidence in their attack on the evils of industrial and urban society.

Philosophy: Pragmatism

Before the Civil War, the standard philosophy taught in the more liberal colleges was Scottish or "commonsense" realism. It assumed that individuals possessed a natural faculty—common sense—that enabled them to arrive at the truth. In much the same way as Sir Isaac Newton had formulated the natural laws of the universe, it was possible for others to formulate the natural laws of politics, economics, and ethics. In the 1870s and after, German idealism, particularly as developed by Hegel and his followers, made inroads.

Hegel had seen the whole course of history as the working out of divine purpose according to certain general laws of change. But since Hegelians looked upon the present state of affairs as a stage in historical development, Hegelianism served as well as the Scottish philosophy to justify existing conditions. Its uniqueness lay in the fact

504

William James, psychologist and philosopher. (*Brown Brothers*)

notonous" Spencerian universe, wrote a brilliant exposition on the active role of the mind that helped to establish psychology as an academic discipline, and preached his views on pragmatism. When James argued that what is true is "whatever proves itself to be good in the way of belief, and good, too, for definite, assignable reasons," he laid himself open to the charge that pragmatism was only a high-sounding name for expediency: Anything is good that works, and the end justifies the means.

The same charge was leveled at John Dewey's "instrumentalism," a later version of pragmatism. Dewey (1859–1952) was converted to pragmatism in the 1890s after reading James, but he had less interest in proving truth than in using it. Like James, he argued the importance of practice rather than theory, and he looked on philosophy as providing an agenda for action. Like Ward, George, and other dissenters, Dewey became an early critic of laissez faire and Social Darwinism in politics and business.

John Dewey, philosopher and educator. "Education is growth. Education is not preparation for life; education is life itself." (*Library of Congress*)

that it taught reverence for the social order and preached that the individual could be truly free only by subordinating himself to the advancement of a national government and the institutions of society.

Toward the end of the century, a new school of philosophy appeared: the pragmatists. They rejected the notion of an ideal or eternally fixed system in an evolving society and chose to evaluate ideas and theories in terms of their practical results. William James and John Dewey extended pragmatic thinking into a philosophy of action that would have a profound effect on social and educational reformers.

William James (1842–1910), the brother of the novelist Henry James, asserted "the right to believe at our own risk any hypothesis that is live enough to tempt our will." In rejecting absolute truths, James argued for free will and the ability of individuals and societies to arrive at their own truths. The only way to examine those truths was to test them in the real world and see how they worked. Pragmatism, he wrote, prefers to see theories as "instruments" rather than as answers to problems.

As a philosopher and psychologist at Harvard, James developed his case against the "awfully mo-

He applied his ideas to education, which he felt must be related to the rest of life and made into a tool for social reform. Dewey saw the school as an institution through which the child would be prepared for citizenship in modern society by learning to criticize the customs and beliefs of that society. The child would acquire this knowledge not by absorbing what the teacher said or a specific body of information, but by developing a scientific approach to solving problems. Dewey wanted students to participate directly in the issues or situations that concerned them, to learn by doing. At the same time, he felt strongly that the school should help to build the child's character and teach him or her to be a good citizen.

The Law: Holmes and Brandeis

Traditionally, lawyers had acted as though the law was a body of changeless doctrine and as though judicial decisions followed inevitably from constitutions, statutes, and legal precedents. The man who perhaps did most to shake this conservatism was Oliver Wendell Holmes, Jr. (1841–1935), son of the poet and friend of William James. For twenty years he served on the Massachusetts supreme court before being appointed to the United States Supreme Court in 1902. By the time of his retirement in 1932, he had become one of the most celebrated judges in the world.

To Holmes, law, like life, was constantly evolving. In his book, *The Common Law* (1881), he demonstrated that even the decisions of judges came as much from human frailty, prejudice, and preconceptions as from logic and authority. He challenged the prevailing faith in decisions based on a mechanical application of precedents and warned that the law must reflect experience. "It is revolting," Holmes said, "to have no better reason for a rule of law than that so it was laid down in the time of Henry IV." Freed of the restraints of precedent and blind tradition, the law could develop and serve society by responding to its needs and reflecting its changes.

Louis D. Brandeis (1856–1941), appointed to the Supreme Court by Wilson in 1916, agreed with his friend and colleague Holmes that the social beliefs of judges influenced their decisions. But that was all the more reason to consider objective economic and social information in arriving at those decisions. To judge cases fairly, the law's interpreters must understand the revolutionary social and economic changes produced by the industrial transformation. Brandeis's most signifi-

cant triumph as a lawyer came in the case of *Muller v. Oregon* (1908), in which the Supreme Court, on the basis of Brandeis's overwhelming evidence from physicians, factory inspectors, social workers, and other competent observers, upheld the Oregon ten-hour law for working women.

Even the Constitution became an object of critical study. J. Allen Smith argued in *The Spirit of American Government* (1907) that the framers of the Constitution had intended not to realize democracy, but to check it. In *An Economic Interpretation of the Constitution* (1913), the brilliant Columbia University professor of politics Charles A. Beard showed how the economic holdings and investments of the framers had influenced the decisions they made at the Constitutional Convention. Later historians questioned much of Beard's scholarship as well as his conclusions. Yet few deny the lasting value of his work in depicting the framers as men who shared the prejudices and concerns of their time and in disclosing how respect for property rights shaped their ideas.

History: Frederick Jackson Turner

The parallel between Darwinian ideas of the evolution of species and the historical evolution of social institutions was too obvious to be missed. By the 1880s some historians were convinced that history could be transformed into as exact a science as biology. Academic historians under the influence of Herbert B. Adams of Johns Hopkins and John W. Burgess of Columbia, proud of their Anglo-Saxon heritage, combined the evolution of species with the evolution of race, and both with the evolution (and improvement) of social institutions. In particular, they saw American democracy as the evolutionary outcome of political practices that began with those of primitive tribes in German forests.

Inspired by popular racist theories and by expansionist sentiment at home, they argued that Anglo-Saxons had evolved the "fittest" of all political systems. For that reason, they had been entrusted with "the mission of conducting the political civilization of the modern world." At the same time, they gave academic respectability to the suppression of blacks and the exclusion of "inferior" types from American society.

To Frederick Jackson Turner (1861–1932), Wisconsin-born and Johns Hopkins-trained, the conquest of the American frontier was also part of the evolutionary process. It greatly influenced American character and institutions, and clearly distinguished the American from the European way of life. Turner argued in his essay "The Significance of the Frontier in American History" (1893) that American democracy began in the American forests and among the European settlers. In the struggle to conquer the New World wilderness, the conquerors were forced to adapt to new conditions or die.

In successive adaptations, as the frontier advanced westward, they removed themselves further from European influences and established institutions and acquired characteristics that were uniquely American. The closing of the frontier in the 1890s, Turner believed, spelled danger for America. From the frontier had sprung the toughness, resourcefulness, individualism, and versatility that made the country great. These qualities were not characteristic of the new industrialized and urbanized America, and he regarded the "new" immigrants pouring into that America as of "doubtful value."

The history taught in the schools reflected the racial, ethnic, and class biases of the historians and the teachers. If the material itself was better than the McGuffey reader, the difference lay more in the method of presentation than in the values taught. Controversial subjects were avoided, as were conflicting interpretations of the American past. The student was exposed to a glorification of America in peace and war, to safe models, and to a reverence for the law and private property. History was taught largely as a preparation for good citizenship. That, in fact, was the primary mission of American public education.

EDUCATION

Once farm families and the society of small towns had shaped the character of American youth and taught them how to survive. Now this task fell more and more to educators. Public schools, colleges, and universities experienced a phenomenal growth in the post-Civil War decades, the result of urbanization and increased support. That the average American received only about five years of schooling at the turn of the century suggests how recent has been the commitment to public education.

Illiteracy declined from 17 percent of the population in 1880 to 7.7 percent in 1910. And the educational system was undergoing significant changes not only in the number of students, but in curriculum and methods of instruction. Along with the increase in public libraries and the immense popularity of public lectures, the expanding school system reflected a growing hunger for education.

Public Education

By 1860 about 50 million acres of the public domain had been set aside for the support of common schools and colleges. With the end of the Civil War, the drive for a nationally supported system of public education became stronger. Impressive advances could be seen after 1865 in the lengthening of the school term, the higher dollar expenditure per pupil, the declining illiteracy rate, and the compulsory school attendance laws. The old prewar academy that once monopolized American secondary education gave way after 1870 to the public high school. A broadened curriculum included history and literature, as well as vocational and commercial courses designed to prepare students for work.

Between 1870 and 1910, the number of public high schools grew from 500 to more than 10,000, and a high school education had begun to be the normal expectation of great numbers of young Americans, especially white youths in towns and cities. In this forty-year period, the number of pupils attending public elementary and high schools each year rose from 6,871,000 to 17,813,000. The average number of days in the school year rose from 132 to 157, and the money spent per pupil more than doubled.

But statistics do not tell the full story. With responsibility for schooling still in the hands of local communities, the amount of support varied considerably. In the South, the level of support for black schools was considerably lower than for white schools, and the white schools themselves were inadequate.

Educating Blacks

Before the Civil War, a small minority of blacks (mostly house servants and slaves of urban owners) had learned to read and write. A much larger number had acquired mechanical skills. The vast majority were field hands to whom schooling was unknown. After the Emancipation Proclamation, education acquired almost a religious meaning for the ex-slave. Not only did northern missionary societies and the Freedmen's Bureau assist them in their quest for knowledge, but blacks themselves

Contrasting school scenes at the turn of the century; (top) a class of immigrant children in the condemned Essex Market School in New York City, and (bottom) Milton Academy, a boys school in New England. (*Top photograph by Jacob A. Riis, the Jacob A. Riis Collection, Museum of the City of New York; bottom photograph by Charles Currier, Library of Congress*)

organized educational associations, built schools, and hired teachers.

White southerners welcomed neither Yankee nor black school teachers, and many whites had resented paying taxes to support black and white schools. After the overthrow of the Radical governments, white leaders kept the educational provisions in the new state constitutions. But the schools themselves were early casualties of budget-cutting governors and legislators. Statistics of black education in the late nineteenth century confirmed W. E. B. DuBois's charge of "enforced ignorance." By 1910, despite the legal mandate for separate but equal schools, in most of the South twice as much was spent on each white student as on each black student, and the minimum salary for white teachers was nearly twice as high as the maximum salary for black teachers. Poor facilities, a shorter school term (often geared to the crops), a higher student-teacher ratio, and a restricted curriculum also set off black schools from white.

Where schools continued to be provided for blacks, vocational training suitable to their low economic position dominated the curriculum. Northern philanthropists, many of whom shared prevailing racist attitudes, funneled their contributions to vocationally oriented black colleges. Among the leaders in the campaign for industrial-vocational education for blacks was Samuel C. Armstrong, founder and headmaster of the Hampton Normal and Agricultural Institute in Virginia (1868).

The son of New England missionaries in Ha-

THE EDUCATION OF BLACKS: SEPARATE AND UNEQUAL

When Pauli Murray entered the public schools in Durham, North Carolina, in the 1920s, she inherited nearly half a century of separate and unequal education in the South—what W. E. B. DuBois called "enforced ignorance."

West End looked more like a warehouse than a school. It was a dilapidated, rickety, two-story wooden building which creaked and swayed in the wind as if it might collapse. Outside it was scarred with peeling paint from many winters of rain and snow. Inside the floors were bare and splintery, the plumbing was leaky, the drinking fountains broken and the toilets in the basement smelly and constantly out of order. . . .

It was never the hardship which hurt so much as the contrast between what we had and what the white children had. We got the greasy, torn, dog-eared books; they got the new ones. They had field day in the city park; we had it on a furrowed stubby hillside. They got wide mention in the newspaper; we got a paragraph at the bottom. The entire city officialdom from the mayor down turned out to review their pageantry; we got a solitary official.

Our seedy run-down school told us that if we had any place at all in the scheme of things it was a separate place, marked off, proscribed and unwanted by the white people. We were bottled up and labeled and set aside—sent to the Jim Crow car, the back of the bus, the side door of the theater, the side window of a restaurant. We came to know that whatever we had was always inferior. We came to understand that no matter how neat and clean, how law abiding, submissive and polite, how studious in school, how churchgoing and moral, how scrupulous in paying our bills and taxes we were, it made no essential difference in our place.

Source: Pauli Murray, *Proud Shoes* (New York: Harpers, 1956), pp. 269–70. Photograph from Valentine Museum, Richmond, Va.

waii, Armstrong had come to believe that black people, like other "backward" and "dependent" races, required special training before they could reach the level of white civilization. If the "Hampton idea" struck Henry M. Turner, a radical black clergyman, as an education in "Negro inferiority," it had no such effect on the young and impressionable Booker T. Washington, who attended the school from 1872 to 1875:

At Hampton, I found the opportunities to learn thrift, economy, and push. I was surrounded by an atmosphere of business, Christian influences, and the spirit of self-help, that seemed to have awakened every faculty in me.

When Washington opened his own normal school in 1881 at Tuskegee, Alabama, with funds supplied by an Alabama banker, he built on Armstrong's theories. Washington could see that for an indeterminate future the southern black majority would be confined to agricultural, domestic, or menial work. The best way to ensure their welfare and the tolerance of the master caste, he reasoned, was to train them in useful pursuits. When Washington made his famous speech at the Atlanta Exposition of 1895—the speech that would bring him national attention—he said little that he had not already taught at Tuskegee (see Chapter 25).

When the twentieth century began, most northern cities, finding a dual educational system too expensive, had abolished segregated schools. But the educational philosophy which had initially supported segregation remained essentially unaltered—the notion that black children had retentive memories and great quickness up to a certain point, but beyond that point they could not easily advance. Such ideas deflated black aspirations. As a result, few blacks reached high school, and still fewer got to college. (No more than 160 blacks attended white colleges in 1890).

What black children were taught in the schools, moreover, did little to enhance their self-confidence. "I am ashamed," a twelve-year-old black girl wrote in 1903, "of the names that we are called in the standard history, 'slaves and niggers,' and when we read that part of it the white children look at us real funny." Even an exceptionally educated black man like W. E. B. DuBois found his days at Harvard a mixed experience: "I was a crude brown youth, deeply opinioned, painfully aware of my color and race. I not only fiercely held to no desire to cross the color line but rather gloried in my isolation."

Higher Education

Since 1860, American colleges and universities had increased in numbers and enrollments and had grown larger and more bureaucratized in administration. At the same time, they improved steadily in quality. Public and private donations helped finance the expansion. Within a decade of the Morrill Act of 1862, Wisconsin, Minnesota, California, Texas, Massachusetts, and New York had established land grant colleges, many of them coeducational. Private money was responsible for other colleges and universities.

Ezra Cornell, who made a fortune from the electric telegraph, founded Cornell, which opened in 1868. Vanderbilt University (1873) and Stanford (1891) were the beneficiaries of two railroad millionaires, and the University of Chicago (1891) received $34 million from the oil magnate John D. Rockefeller. The Johns Hopkins University (1876) bore the name of a wealthy Baltimore banker and railroad executive; Carnegie Institute (1900) in Pittsburgh was named after the multimillionaire steel magnate.

Most of the newly endowed colleges managed to overcome or outlast any interference from their

WORDS AND NAMES IN AMERICAN HISTORY

In educational circles today, the word *deadline* normally refers to the date and or even the time of day a professor tells a student that an essay, report, or other assignment is due to be handed in. The word is also commonly used in business, in government, and even in international relations. The term conveys a certain amount of tension, even though it is quite rare for professors to gun down students who get their papers in late. What is interesting is that originally the word had much greater tension, but it concerned space rather than time. The term *deadline,* which came into our language only about a hundred years ago, originally meant something very literal: Cross this line and you're dead. This first meaning seems to have come into use in military prisons in the American Civil War. Prison camps were hastily built, often without effective walls. Most of them had lines surrounding the entire camp "drawn" by paint, by a rope, or by shovel, with the guards in towers ordered to shoot to kill any prisoner who crossed the line.

CULTURE AND THOUGHT

THE EDUCATION OF WOMEN

Two views of the benefits of colleges for women: (1) *Godey's Lady's Book* (March 1866), a highly popular magazine which celebrated the virtues of sophistication and refinement in women; and (2) Martha Carey Thomas, a leading educator at the turn of the century and president of Bryn Mawr College.

To that half education which our countrywomen now receive—the education in science and ornamental arts—add the education in useful arts and domestic knowledge necessary to fit them for the duties of their proper sphere, and they will not merely be, as at present, the "queens of society," but will be far better, the adored rulers of well-ordered and happy households.

(Godey's Lady's Book)

How vast the difference between then [1874] and now [1904] in my feelings, and in the feelings of every woman who has had to do with the education of girls! Then I was terror-struck lest I, and every other woman with me, were doomed to live as pathological invalids in a universe merciless to woman as a sex. Now we know that it is not we, but the man who believes such things about us, who is himself pathological, blinded by neurotic mists of sex, unable to see that women form one-half of the kindly race of normal, healthy, human creatures in the world; that women, like men, are quickened and inspired by the same great traditions of their race, by the same love of learning, the same love of science, the same love of abstract truth; that women, like men, are immeasurably benefited, physically, mentally, and morally, and are made vastly better mothers, as men are made vastly better fathers, by subordinating the distracting instincts of sex to the simple human fellowship of similar education, and similar intellectual and social ideals.

(Martha Carey Thomas)

Source: Martha Carey Thomas, *Publications of the Association of Collegiate Alumnae*, III (February 1908), Bryn Mawr College.

Students at Bacone College in Oklahoma (1908) marching from their dormitory. (*Culver Pictures, Inc.*)

benefactors. But college boards of trustees tended to be dominated by businessmen, some of whom demanded social and economic orthodoxy from faculty members. The same kinds of pressures were often exerted on public universities by legislators and boards of regents. Some faculty members were dismissed for teaching heretical ideas, and still others were frightened into silence. Frederick Jackson Turner could recall when the members of the Board of Regents at the University of Wisconsin "used to sit with a red lead pencil in consultation over the lists of books submitted by the professors, and strike out those that failed to please their fancy, with irreverent comments on 'fool professors.'"

Prewar colleges had confined themselves largely to traditional subjects—the classics, mathematics, and theology. The postwar institutions responded to the demand for professional, business, and technical education. The prestige of science had risen so high that such practical additions to the curriculum had to be accepted. By the end of the century, a number of American university scientists had won international reputations, and the number of professional schools in medicine, law, business, and other specialities had increased substantially.

Under the direction of Charles W. Eliot, president of Harvard, a new kind of university emerged. Undergraduates "elected" courses from an expanded curriculum, instead of being limited to required courses. Graduate schools grew, and faculties were assembled. Between 1869 and 1900, Eliot also reformed Harvard's medical and law schools, which became models for others. Premedical students, who had formerly obtained degrees with a minimum of course and clinical work, were now required to study three full years in medical school, to work in laboratories, and to take examinations. The dean of the Harvard Law School abolished the textbook and introduced a system whereby the law student gained knowledge by examining specific cases.

Not all the changes in university and college life were intellectual or administrative. The introduction of baseball, football, and other organized sports aroused an almost fanatical concern with school rivalries. By the 1890s intercollegiate football had become a mass spectacle attended by crowds of 30,000 or 40,000, and critics protested its professional emphasis.

Not all the critics, however, confined themselves to alarm over athletic programs. American universities, said Brooks Adams, graduated narrow, half-educated specialists lacking the breadth of mind needed to administer a complex, centralized economy; and Thorstein Veblen, in *The Higher Learning in America* (1918), accused the universities of producing little more than salesmen.

Although much evidence to the contrary existed, many people continued to doubt women's intellectual or physical capacity to profit from college education. The experience of higher learning, some feared, would be destructive to "the loveliness and grace and essential charm of womanhood." The founding of Vassar College at Poughkeepsie, New York, in 1861 did much to dispel such antiquated ideas. Matthew Vassar, an English-born brewer, believed that women had the same right as men to intellectual development. The course of study at Vassar became as demanding as that of any men's college of the day, and Vassar graduates quickly distinguished themselves among scholars, in the professions, and in social reform.

By 1880, most of the important midwestern universities admitted women. Smith, Bryn Mawr, and Wellesley—founded shortly after Vassar—and other women's colleges offered professional training. The number of women enrolled as undergraduates rose from about 8,000 in 1869 to more than 20,000 in 1894, and soared in the twentieth century. But for the graduates of the women's colleges, improvements in educational opportunities were not translated into improvements in economic opportunities. Rather than aspiring to careers, they were expected to find economic salvation in a well-chosen husband and cultural satisfaction in women's clubs and in the romantic novels that dominated the best seller lists.

LITERATURE IN THE GILDED AGE

Informed critics after Appomattox often remarked on the poor quality of American literature. Romance, sentimentality, and tales of success reflected the values, tastes, and stereotypes of middle-class readers. Neither the world depicted in such literature nor the characters themselves suggested that American society was being transformed.

The dividing line of the Civil War was sharpened by the death or withdrawal of the major writers of the past. By 1865 Hawthorne and Thoreau were dead. Emerson retired more and more into himself, while Melville lived virtually forgotten. Emily Dickinson, the one authentic poetic genius of the early postwar years, almost unknown to her contemporaries, wrote for herself and a few friends.

If Melville and Dickinson retreated into themselves for private reasons, other postwar writers, reflecting their rural origins and repelled by an industrializing and urbanizing America, retreated to the past. Just when country people were heading for the cities, some writers of the "local color" school, like Harriet Beecher Stowe and Edward Eggleston, retrieved the scenes and spiritual values of a pastoral America.

At the same time, Bret Harte, Joel Chandler Harris, Sarah Orne Jewett, and Mary N. Murfree sought out the "native element" of their distinctive sections—the California mining country, the southern plantation, the New England village, the Kentucky and Tennessee mountains. They did not rule out the city, as George Washington Cable's stories of New Orleans Creoles attested, but in general they stuck to what they considered to be the authentic part of America—the village, the small town, the farm—and lovingly and honestly recorded differences in dialect, manners, and customs.

Already partly visible by the 1870s was a surge of fresh talent, soon to be followed by a new generation. The new writers, many of them influenced by industrialism, Darwinian ideas, and pragmatism, explored subjects largely excluded from polite or "genteel" literature: slums, crime, class conflict, violence, divorce, racism, political corruption, drunkenness, adultery. To be sure, the dominant romantic mood had not disappeared even by the end of the century. But a new realism had given fresh life to literature, making the final break with the "genteel tradition" easier.

Mark Twain

Mark Twain (1835–1910)—the pen name of Samuel L. Clemens—belonged by temperament to the local color tradition and was regarded in his own day as a regional author. But he was a writer of far greater dimension than the others. In many respects, Mark Twain was the most revealing figure in postwar American literature, the one who best combined the virtues and defects of the society he analyzed. Born in Hannibal, Missouri, he had been reporter, river pilot, and popular lecturer before his first literary success with *The Innocents Abroad* (1869), an uproariously funny account of a junket of his countrymen through Europe and the Near East.

Mark Twain. (*UPI/Bettman Newsphotos*)

Mark Twain wrote about everything from jumping frogs to Andrew Carnegie; but his best works, *The Adventures of Tom Sawyer* (1876), *Life on the Mississippi* (1883), and *The Adventures of Huckleberry Finn* (1884), all derive from his riverboat days. It was his loyalty to the simple America of his boyhood that partly accounts for his rage over the betrayal of democratic ideals in the Gilded Age. "In my youth," wrote Twain, "there was nothing resembling a worship of money or of its possessor, in our region." It took people of the Jay Gould variety, he said, "to make a God of money and the man":

The gospel left behind by Jay Gould is doing giant work in our days. Its message is "Get money. Get it quickly. Get it in abundance. Get it dishonestly, if you can, honestly if you must."

And yet Twain enjoyed "striking it rich" as much as anyone, speculated recklessly, and wrote always with an eye on his large audience. As he put it:

I have never tried in even one single instance to help cultivate the cultivated classes. I was not equipped for it by native gifts or training. And I never had any ambition in that direction, but always hunted for bigger game—the masses.

In his own way, however, Mark Twain was a moralist who looked upon humanity with exasperation because of its cruelty, credulity, and pigheadedness, and with compassion because it was not to blame. *Huckleberry Finn* remains an assault on social hypocrisy, false respectability, and the gospel of success. In renouncing civilization, Huck remains true to his natural goodness, yet without denying human depravity or his kinship with the wicked: "I am the whole human race without a detail lacking ... the human race is a race of cowards; and I am not only marching in that procession but carrying a banner."

Realists and Naturalists

William Dean Howells (1837–1920), a friend of Mark Twain, became the leader of the postwar school of realists. Born and reared in Ohio, Howells had come to literature, like many of his contemporaries, through the printer's office and the newspaper. From 1886 to 1891 he wrote his most influential criticism in *Harper's Monthly*. By 1900, many of the younger writers considered him the dean of American letters.

"Realism," as Howells used the term, simply meant "the truthful treatment of commonplace material." The romanticism of the popular literature of his day was immoral, in Howells's opinion, because it corrupted American taste and falsified life. He wanted fiction of "fidelity, not merely to the possible, but to the probable and ordinary course of man's experience." Let the novelist, he said through one of his fictional characters, paint "life as it is, and human feelings in their true proportion and relation."

His best-known and probably his best novels are *The Rise of Silas Lapham* (1885), the story of a self-made businessman, and *A Hazard of New Fortunes* (1890), which reflected his New York experience—the mindless struggle for wealth, the paradox of Fifth Avenue luxury and East Side squalor, the degradation of the republican dream.

Although Howells's friend Henry James (1843–1916) could not find enough material for fiction in what he saw as the bleak American scene, he allied himself with the Howells camp. James was born in New York, but he spent a good part of his youth in Europe. After a halfhearted attempt to study law at Harvard, he gave himself entirely to literature, and from 1875 until his death did most of his writing abroad. Because he visited his native land so seldom, and because so many of his novels and short stories have a European setting, many critics put James outside the main current of American literature. Actually, his international plots deal almost exclusively with Americans, and from his vantage point he saw much about the American character that escaped writers who remained too close to home.

Like Hawthorne, by whom he was profoundly influenced, James liked to place his Americans in what he called "morally interesting situations." He subjected his traveling businessman (*The American*, 1877), his sensitive and intellectually curious heiresses (*The Portrait of a Lady*, 1881), his artist heroes, hungry for culture (*Roderick Hudson*, 1876), to moral tests they either passed or failed. America remained for him a land of innocence and promise; Europe was beautiful but decadent. A superb technician and psychologist, James was also a social historian who faithfully recorded the moral gaps and strains he detected in upper-class society.

As a result of the realists' efforts, the young writers who came of age in the last two decades of the century could experiment even more boldly than their predecessors with unvarnished truth. Although it no longer took courage to expose a society committed to railroads, stockyards, real estate, and Wall Street, the new literary school went much further than the realists in uncovering seamy and brutal aspects of American life. Naturalism, as the new movement was called, derived its inspiration from French novelists like Emile Zola, who believed that literature should be governed by the same scientific laws that guided the physiologist. Human fate was determined by heredity and environment, by inner drives and external circumstances over which people had no control. Theoretically, the naturalist writer put down what he or she saw, no matter how disgusting or shocking it might be.

In America, naturalists like Stephen Crane (1871–1900) and Frank Norris (1870–1902) never matched the frankness of the French school. But they dealt with themes from which even Howells flinched. In *Maggie, A Girl of the Streets* (1893), Crane wrote of the seduction and suicide of a New York slum girl; in *The Red Badge of Courage* (1895), he reproduced the animal fear of a young Civil War recruit under fire and his psychological recovery. In all his tales and sketches of derelicts and soldiers, of frightened, abandoned people, Crane suggests that human beings must confront nature without help from the supernatural.

Norris, a less able writer than Crane and more given to melodrama, disliked Howells's realism because it smelled so much of the ordinary, "the tragedy of the broken tea cup." Norris liked huge supermen clashing with titanic natural forces. In *McTeague* (1899), the story of a man's reversion to brutishness, he displayed a power new in American fiction. In his best-known novel, *The Octopus* (1901), Norris depicted an epic struggle between California wheat growers and the railroad. The apparent radicalism of this book was considerably diluted by Norris's message that wheat and the railroad represented natural forces, each governed by the law of supply and demand.

Jack London (1876–1916) repeated many of Norris's themes, especially the tendency to exalt the brutal while condemning the brutality of the social order. Born in 1876 and thrown on his own resources at an early age in the waterfront environment of Oakland, California, London became a hobo and a seaman, among other things, before settling down to write. His literary career lasted only eighteen years, but he published over fifty books.

London preached the doctrine of the awful power of the forces of nature as well as the hopeful teachings of socialism. He never reconciled these ideas, but his work expressed one or the other well enough to make him one of the most widely read writers of his time and one of the few American authors to gain recognition in Europe.

London's most interesting books are his autobiographical novel *Martin Eden* (1909) and *The Iron Heel* (1907), concerned with a fight to the death between the exploited classes and an oligarchy. His greatest success was *The Call of the Wild* (1903), a book about the Yukon.

The writings of Theodore Dreiser reflected a naturalism even more uncompromising than that of Crane, Norris, or London. But in Dreiser, the replacement of the good and the bad by the strong and the weak was accompanied by a deeper feeling for character and a profound, almost maternal tenderness. After drifting from job to job, Dreiser spent several years as a newspaperman in Chicago, St. Louis, Cleveland, and Pittsburgh, observing at first hand the hard side of big city life. His experiences inspired him with the idea of treating a great American city as realistically as Balzac wrote of Paris.

Dreiser's first novel and one of his best, *Sister Carrie*, was published in 1900 and then quickly withdrawn after the publisher's wife objected to its "indecency." *Sister Carrie* tells the story of a young girl who comes to Chicago from a small western town and succumbs to a vulgar but generous salesman and then to a restaurant manager. The best chapters of the book trace the gradual downward drift of her second seducer, Hurstwood, who moves toward ruin while Carrie becomes a successful actress.

The Romantics

Although realists and naturalists tried to deal honestly with life and gained a following among liberals who wanted to improve conditions, they failed

Jack London. (*Culver Pictures, Inc.*)

to outsell the sentimental school among the reading public. With love stories, cloak-and-dagger romances, and tales of exotic lands, the sentimentalists helped their middle-class audience, the largest in the world, avoid the raw society around them. A love story, thought Francis Marion Crawford, should "foster agreeable allusions."

During the last three decades of the nineteenth century, the romanticists and the realists engaged in a kind of journalistic warfare. The realists, said their critics, "taught pessimism in every line of their work. They taught that marriage is a failure, that home is a brothel, that courtship is lewd, that society is an aggregation of animals." The romanticists, replied the realists, supplied flimsy illusions to adults who evaded the issues of the day. In practice, however, both schools made concessions to popular taste and interests.

Since romantic fiction outsold realistic novels four to one, it is hardly surprising that both realists and naturalists injected a little exotic color, mysticism, and pseudoscientific information into their work. They also used flamboyant success stories and sensational romances in which supermen heroes triumphed over the "mongrel" races of the world. "There was a bit of lie in this attitude of mine, a bit of hypocrisy," Jack London confessed of some of his popular works; "but the lie and the hypocrisy were those of a man desiring to live." At the same time, the romantics could not ignore the social turmoil that soon involved so many of their women readers in social reform. By 1900 romantic writers and realists were appearing together in the pages of the *Saturday Evening Post* and the *La-*

LIFE AND LITERATURE

dies' Home Journal—and it was not always easy to distinguish one from another.

Whatever the inroads of the naturalists and realists, the romantics continued to dominate the best seller lists. Perhaps the major literary "craze" of the 1890s, however, revolved around the works of an English writer, Rudyard Kipling. Not only were his novels immensely popular, but his poetry was among the most frequently recited by Americans, finding its way even into the halls of Congress.

Take up the White Man's burden—
Send forth the best ye breed—

Go, bind your sons to exile
  To serve your captives' need;
To wait in heavy harness
  On fluttered folk and wild—
Your new-caught, sullen peoples,
  Half-devil and half-child.

Published in 1899 in *McClure's Magazine* and reprinted on the front pages of major newspapers, Kipling's "The White Man's Burden" expressed the feelings of a confident and self-satisfied nation in the process of becoming a world power—the America that novelist Herman Melville had once glimpsed with "law on her brow and empire in her eyes."

SUMMARY

If economic life during the Gilded Age was dominated by laissez faire and the Gospel of Success, cultural life was dominated by Social Darwinism and the Gospel of Progress.

Darwin's *Origin of Species,* published in 1859, introduced ideas of evolution and the "survival of the fittest" in biology. These ideas were soon popularized and translated into social terms. The Social Darwinism proposed by the English philosopher Herbert Spencer became another support for the Gospel of Success and brought a new creed—the Gospel of Progress. All the changes of industrialization and urbanization were not only good, they were all for the better.

Some thinkers—Lester Ward, Henry George, and Edward Bellamy—challenged these ideas and rejected the fatalism of the Social Darwinists. In the universities, younger social scientists began to break out of the conservative straitjacket and to question systems such as laissez faire. Among these academic rebels was Thorstein Veblen, whose *The Theory of the Leisure Class* (1899) became one of the most influential works of social criticism.

Darwinism also opened up new ways of thinking in

philosophy, law, education, and history. Pragmatism aimed to make philosophy useful by looking at ideas as tools for solving practical problems. Pragmatists such as William James and John Dewey had great influence on the new discipline of psychology and the older one of education. The notion that the law too should be responsive to changing needs and not rigid was held—and practiced—by such jurists as Oliver Wendell Holmes, Jr. and Louis D. Brandeis. In the field of history, Frederick Jackson Turner presented new ideas that would influence generations of American historians and students, although they were not generally accepted until the twentieth century.

All these changing ideas found wider and wider audiences as the American people became more educated and more literate. Public schools, colleges, and universities grew rapidly in number and size after the Civil War as government made a real commitment to education for all. The public school system for elementary and secondary education, though always remaining under local control, became nationwide, especially in the cities. Compulsory school attendance laws were passed, and illiteracy declined rapidly. A separate system of black

CULTURE AND THOUGHT

education began to develop in the South, but with an emphasis on technical-vocational training. It was set up by blacks themselves and financed largely by northern philanthropists.

Higher education also expanded and changed. Many new colleges were established, and under Charles W. Eliot, Harvard pioneered a new kind of university. Students chose courses from an expanded curriculum, major scholars were recruited for graduate schools, and practical training was required for certification in the professions.

Women also gained access to higher education and to professional training. By 1880, most major midwestern state universities admitted women. Vassar College for women had been founded in 1861; Smith, Bryn Mawr, and Wellesley were established soon afterward. The number of women enrolled as undergraduates rose from 8,000 in 1869 to 20,000 by 1894. But education for women still did not mean independence and equal opportunity; it would not be until well into the twentieth century that women would join the labor force on a permanent, though still unequal, basis.

American literature between 1860 and 1900 was dominated by romanticism and sentimentality, designed mainly to be read by middle- and upper-class women who had too much leisure time. But by 1870 there were the beginnings of a new literature of realism that dealt with the evils and problems of society. There was also a new generation of American writers who would become prominent not only at home, but throughout the world. Their work would establish American literature as a separate and mature cultural tradition. Among them were Mark Twain, William Dean Howells, Henry James, Stephen Crane, Frank Norris, Jack London, and Theodore Dreiser.

Suggested Readings

The best introductions to intellectual life are H. S. Commager, *The American Mind* (1950), and R. Hofstadter, *Anti-Intellectualism in American Life* (1963). More specialized treatments of ideas between 1865 and 1920 include R. Hofstadter, *Social Darwinism in American Thought* (1955); M. G. White, *Social Thought in America* (1949); Sidney Fine, *Laissez Faire and the General Welfare State* (1957); and P. A. Carter, *The Spiritual Crisis of the Gilded Age* (1971). On sexual attitudes, see R. G. Walters (ed.), *Primers for Prudery: Sexual Advice to Victorian America* (1974); D. U. Pivar, *Purity Crusade: Sexual Morality and Social Control 1868–1900* (1973), and C. Smith-Rosenberg, *Disorderly Conduct: Visions of Gender in Victorian America* (1985).

In a collective biography, *Alternative America: Henry George, Edward Bellamy, Henry Demarest Lloyd and the Adversary Tradition* (1983), J. L. Thomas advances an important reinterpretation of these important thinkers. Individual figures in American thought are examined in C. A. Barker, *Henry George* (1955); A. E. Morgan, *Edward Bellamy* (1944); Joseph Dorfman, *Thorstein Veblen and His America* (1934); R. B. Perry, *The Thought and Character of William James* (2 vols., 1954); G. W. Allen, *William James* (1967); and Ernest Samuels's multivolume biography of Henry Adams: *The Young Henry Adams* (1948), *The Middle Years* (1958), and *The Major Phase* (1964). M. D. Howe's biography of Justice Holmes, *The Shaping Years 1841–1870* (1957), and *The Proving Years 1870–1888* (1963) places the man in his times. See also R. Hofstadter, *The Progressive Historians: Turner, Beard, Parrington* (1968), and B. Kuklick, *The Rise of American Philosophy: Cambridge, Massachusetts, 1860–1930* (1977).

L. A. Cremin, *The Transformation of the School: Progressivism in American Education* (1961), is a solid work, as is M. B. Katz, *Class, Bureaucracy, and Schools* (1975). On higher education, see L. R. Veysey, *The Emergence of the American University* (1965), and B. J. Bledstein, *The Culture of Professionalism: The Middle Class and the Development of Higher Education in America* (1976). For a stimulating critique, see Thorstein Veblen, *The Higher Learning in America* (1918). The expansion of primary and secondary schools is covered in F. Butler and L. A. Cremin, *A History of Education in American Culture* (1953). Other pertinent studies include Merle Curti, *The Social Ideas of American Educators* (1935); R. Hofstadter and W. P. Metzger, *The Development of Academic Freedom in the United States* (1955); and R. Welter, *Popular Education and Democratic Thought in America* (1962). On the education of women, see B. M. Solomon, *In the Company of Educated Women: A History of Women and Higher Education in America* (1985), and the journals and letters of M. Carey Thomas, president of Bryn Mawr College, in M. H. Dobkin (ed.), *The Making of a Feminist* (1980). For Booker T. Washington's educational views, see his *Up from Slavery* (1901); L. R. Harlan, *Booker T. Washington: The Making of a Black Leader 1856–1901* (1972) and *The Wizard of Tuskegee, 1901–1915* (1983); and A. Meier, *Negro Thought in America 1880–1915* (1963).

A. Kazin, *On Native Grounds* (1942), is a perceptive literary history. See also L. Ziff, *The American 1890s: Life and Times of a Lost Generation* (1966), and the highly readable V. W. Brooks, *New England: Indian Summer* (1940) and *The Confident Years 1885–1915* (1952). On individual literary figures, see D. Wecter, *Sam Clemens of Hannibal* (1952); J. Kaplan, *Mr. Clemens and Mark Twain* (1960); E. H. Cady, *The Road to Realism* (1956) and *The Realist at War* (1958) on W. D. Howells; L. Edel, *Henry James* (5 vols., 1953–69); R. W. Stillman, *Stephen Crane* (1968); P. S. Foner, *Jack London: American Rebel* (1947); and F. O. Matthiesson, *Theodore Dreiser* (1951). Stimulating essays on Norris, Crane, and London appear in M. D. Geismar, *Rebels and Ancestors: The American Novel 1890–1915* (1953).

THE AMERICAN EMPIRE

Chapter 24

For more than five hundred years before the age of space, the history of Europeans was the history of expansion overseas. Duty moved them as much as daring, the word of God as much as the spirit of adventure, power as strongly as trade, pride as strongly as profit, the quest for personal independence as strongly as the quest for knowledge. They were impelled to spread "civilization"; but they were also impelled to escape from it.

In this long history of expansion, the European discovery of America was a single chapter—the prologue, really—for more than three centuries of rivalry among European nations for dominance in the New World, and in Africa and Asia as well. The wealth and productivity created by the Industrial Revolution stimulated the competition for world markets. France, Belgium, Holland, Russia, and Bismarck's newly unified Germany sought a share of the spoils. They were followed by Italy and a modernizing Japan. What they wanted were the same areas the United States would come to look upon with growing interest: Latin America, the islands of the Pacific, and China.

The 1890s had been a difficult decade in the United States: economic depression, labor conflict, divisive politics, "new" immigrants, racial violence, corporate abuses. Most Americans, confident of the destiny of their nation, still needed some reassurance, particularly with the closing of the frontier, that the pioneering character, the moral fiber, the power of the society remained intact. To listen to the young New York Republican leader, Theodore Roosevelt, was to believe that materialism and the pursuit of wealth had made Americans soft. The "great masterful races," he thought, "have been fighting races, and no triumph of peace is quite so great as the supreme triumphs of war." In "strict confidence," he confessed to a close friend in late 1897 that he would welcome "almost any war, for I think this country needs one."

But the new urge to spread American power and influence to other parts of the world was something more than an expression of virility. The rapid transformation of the economy had a great impact on foreign relations. With the United States now producing large quantities of manufactured goods, more than the domestic economy could absorb at profitable prices, the need to find foreign markets became urgent. With American investments abroad soaring between 1900 and 1914—from $455 million to $2.5 billion—there was also the need to protect those investments. With American manufacturers dependent on raw materials from abroad, it became imperative to try to control sources of supplies.

Concern mounted as European competitors, motivated by the same needs, became more and more active in these regions. The New Imperialism sought not so much annexation of other regions as influence. It rested on the need to make arrangements that would secure the national interest and America's position in the world community. If influence could be exerted only through outright possession, however, that would be acceptable.

Whatever the motives or the forms it would take, overseas expansion would be justified in familiar language. Having reached the limits of continental expansion, Americans were "destined" to conquer new frontiers abroad. Confident of the superiority of its institutions and values, the United States by the 1890s was ready to shoulder the "expansionist destiny" of the Anglo-Saxon race, to join "the Christian nations," as an American missionary said, who "are subduing the world, in order to make mankind free."

When applied to the competition between nations, Social Darwinism offered a convenient rationale. Progress came to nations that proved themselves superior in the world's ceaseless competition, that cultivated manly, combative instincts. Having proved themselves the ablest and strongest in that competition, the Anglo-Saxon race assumed the responsibility to rule the unfit in the interest of all mankind. Having established the "fittest" of political systems, why not bestow the blessings of Anglo-Saxon and American civilization on the less fortunate? "In the long run," said Roosevelt, "there can be no justification for one race managing or controlling another unless the management and control are exercised in the interest and for the benefit of that other race."

In the minds of policymakers and the American public, economic and humanitarian considerations reinforced each other. The idea that the United States should plant its institutions and values in the "waste places of the world" while exploiting their economic potential helped to shape American policy in the Caribbean, Mexico, Latin America, and Asia. Perhaps, Senator Albert Beveridge conceded, the "present phase" of American expansion was "personal profit." But he had no doubt about the ultimate objective. "God has marked us as His chosen people, henceforth to lead in the regeneration of the world. American law, American order, American civilization, and the American flag will plant themselves on shores hitherto bloody and benighted, but by those agencies of God henceforth to be made beautiful and bright." ∎

THE NEW EXPANSIONISM

Expansion was hardly a new idea in the United States in the 1890s. Even before the revolution, American colonists had resisted England's policy of restricting settlement to an area east of the Appalachians. Once independent, the United States rapidly spread westward across the continent. And Mexico to the south and Canada to the north were always part of expansionist plans.

Mexico and Alaska

While the United States was involved in the Civil War, Napoleon III of France attempted to establish a Catholic monarchy in Mexico. He installed his puppet, Maximilian of Austria, on a Mexican throne, backed by the French military. In 1866, Secretary of State William H. Seward told France that its presence in Mexico was unacceptable, and 50,000 American troops were sent to the Rio Grande. That was enough, along with new problems in Europe, to persuade France to withdraw. Although Maximilian tried to reign without the French, he was quickly seized, courtmartialed, and executed by Mexican nationalists. In his communications with France, Seward never mentioned the Monroe Doctrine. But it had become apparent that the United States now had the strength to enforce its will in the Western hemisphere.

While avoiding armed conflict with foreign enemies, Andrew Johnson's administration carried out successful negotiations with foreign friends. Among these was Russia, one of the few European states that had not unofficially sided with the Confederates. In March 1867 the Russian minister in Washington offered to unload distant and costly Alaska. Russia hoped to build up the United States as a counterweight to Britain. Secretary Seward, an expansionist, jumped at the chance and negotiated a purchase treaty. Despite opposition to what the press soon called Seward's Folly, the opportunity to expand America's frontier was enough to win congressional approval. The purchase price was $7.2 million.

Canada

On completing the negotiations with Russia, Seward expressed the hope that Alaska would form the northern arm of a giant pincer movement to bring Canada into the American fold. "I know that Nature," he said, "designs that this whole continent, not merely these thirty-six states, shall be sooner or later, within the magic circle of the American Union."

During the Civil War, Confederate agents and escaping Confederate prisoners of war found sanctuary in Canada, where they could mount attacks on the northern frontier. Soon after the war ended, northerners were again reminded of the potential of British control over Canada. In 1866 the Fenians, an organization of Irish-Americans in New York, began a series of assaults on Canada with the bizarre hope of capturing the country and holding it hostage until the British gave Ireland independence. The Irish vote had become an important factor in northern politics, and how to keep it while discouraging adventures of this sort presented a ticklish problem.

Rather than yield to the temptation of supporting or even approving Irish violence, the Johnson administration chose to give Great Britain a lesson in neutral conduct by taking stern measures against anyone who used American bases for foreign intrigues. British leaders chose to ignore the example. They at first refused to receive Seward's claims against Britain for wartime actions by sea raiders such as the *Alabama*, a ship built in England for the Confederacy and used to prey on Union shipping. Resentful Americans began to consider support of the Fenians as a way of forcing Britain to yield. By 1869, however, Europe was in turmoil over Bismarck's expansionist policies on the Continent. Britain, like others, wanted American friendship if these policies led to war. By the Treaty of Washington, ratified in 1871, the two nations agreed to arbitrate their differences. The next year, an arbitration tribunal awarded the United States $15.5 million for its *Alabama* claims.

But the United States continued to cast a hungry eye on Canada. In 1886, Theodore Roosevelt, bursting upon the American political stage, told a Fourth of July audience that he looked forward to the "day when not a foot of American soil will be held by any European power." In 1891, Secretary of State James G. Blaine said he expected that

Canada would "ultimately seek . . . admission to the union." Both Roosevelt and Blaine easily qualified as early American *jingoes*—the term applied to those who saw a warlike and expansionist foreign policy as in the national interest.

THE PACIFIC: TRADE AND EMPIRE

American ambitions did not end with North America or at the water's edge. In the 1850s Commodore Matthew C. Perry thought it "self-evident" that the United States would have to "extend its jurisdiction beyond the limits of the western continent." Cuba had attracted many southern expansionists, and in 1869 President Grant's cronies hungered for the annexation of Santo Domingo (now the Dominican Republic). An island rich in minerals, timber, and fruit, Santo Domingo had won its independence from Spain in 1865. Among those anxious to exploit opportunities there were two Massachusetts promoters who enjoyed influence at the White House through President Grant's secretary, Orville Babock. On visiting Santo Domingo late in 1869, Babock was able to negotiate a treaty of annexation. When Attorney General Hoar denounced the treaty as illegal, Grant removed Hoar from office. When Charles Sumner, head of the Senate Foreign Relations Committee, then denounced the entire "deal," the Senate defeated Babock's treaty in 1870. But although the United States did not annex Santo Domingo, it would exert a dominant influence in the island.

Large numbers of Americans still believed the nation should concentrate its energies on internal development and avoid foreign entanglements. But internal development would, in fact, make foreign entanglements increasingly desirable, if not absolutely essential. The construction of the transcontinental railroads after the Civil War, along with rapid industrialization, sharpened appetites for Pacific outlets and islands. If the United States was to establish its influence in the Far East and be in a position to exploit the rich economic possibilities of that region, it would need naval bases and coaling and repair stations for its ships. Both Hawaii and Samoa had already served as stopover stations for American ships in the Pacific trade, and after the Civil War attention focused on them as permanent American outposts. With the prospect of annexation of the Philippines after the Spanish-American War, this matter was quickly resolved.

Samoa

Even before the Civil War, American interest in the Pacific and the Far East had taken on economic and religious significance. Merchants wanted commercial advantages, and missionaries sought converts to Christianity. In the 1840s and 1850s the United States had acquired "most-favored nation" treaty rights in China, giving American traders terms equal to those of any other country. After Commodore Perry had forcibly opened Japan in 1854, Townsend Harris, the first American consul there, negotiated a treaty of friendship by which he became the chief advisor on international relations to the Japanese government. In 1867, the United States Navy took possession of uninhabited Midway Island in the Pacific. But the inability to dredge its harbor disappointed those who sought to use it as a stopover station for American ships.

After the opening of the first transcontinental railroad in 1869, Americans in the trade between San Francisco and Australia eyed Samoa's fine harbor of Pago Pago, with the idea of making it into a coaling station for steamships. In the mid-1880s, however, Germany, the leading economic power in Samoa, began to enlarge its activities there at the expense of British and American interests. Friction among the three powers persisted until 1899, when Samoa was formally divided between the United States and Germany. Britain received compensation elsewhere in the Pacific. The United States acquired Pago Pago and surrounding territory; Germany got the rest of the land. American Samoa would become a strategic naval station in the twentieth century. The remaining islands, after Germany's defeat in World War I, would be controlled as a mandate by New Zealand.

Hawaii

The Hawaiian Islands, closer than Samoa and strategically a natural outpost of the North American continent, had long been known to American traders. New York and New England vessels in the China trade called at the islands in the 1790s, and in the next three decades Hawaiian produce as well as ports played a part in the fur trade. As early as 1820, Yankee missionaries had settled in the islands and transformed Honolulu into a pleasant imitation of a New England town. After 1840 Hawaii became the center of South Pacific whaling. By 1860, many American citizens owned permanent homes there, and a growing local faction sought annexation.

After 1850, sugar cane replaced whaling as Hawaii's main industry, and problems of land tenure and labor supply were added to the issues between the government and outside capitalists and among the outside rivals themselves. Until 1875, American sugar producers in the Louisiana area had succeeded in keeping Hawaiian sugar out of the United States ports. That year, however, a reciprocity treaty between the United States and the islands (negotiated under threats by Hawaiian growers to look to Britain for markets and political support) admitted Hawaiian sugar into the United States and American commodities into Hawaii, both duty-free. At the same time, the islands pledged themselves not to give any territory to foreign governments or to extend to them the commercial privileges won by the United States.

Under the treaty, sugar growing boomed, and with it the rest of the business community. Native Hawaiians, however, saw more and more of their land controlled by white planters, and themselves submerged by a flood of Chinese workers.

Negotiations to renew the treaty began in 1884. But the United States Senate would not approve a new agreement until 1887 when, in recognition of the strategic importance of Hawaii, it won an amendment granting the United States exclusive use of Pearl Harbor as a coaling station and repair base for naval vessels. In the same year, Hawaiian-born white businessmen, fed up with the corrupt and authoritarian regime of King Kalakaua, brought off a bloodless revolution forcing him to accept a new government. The Bayonet Constitution, as Hawaiians called it, gave businessmen control of the government and extended the franchise to white foreigners. Property qualifications, in turn, disfranchised most native citizens.

Hawaii was moving closer to the United States. In 1890, sugar for the American mainland made up 99 percent of Hawaiian exports. In that year, Congress admitted other foreign sugars (as well as Hawaii's) duty-free, but gave United States growers a bounty of 2 cents a pound. Hawaii's economy was badly hurt by these measures. At the same time, Hawaiians grew more and more angry about the new constitution. Discontent spread after 1891, when King Kalakaua died and was succeeded by his sister, Queen Liliuokalani, a firm opponent of white rule. By 1893, "Queen Lil's" disregard of constitutional restraints, and her efforts to throw off the constitution altogether, drove white businessmen into a second rebellion. They had the support of the American minister to Hawaii, John L. Stevens, who helped protect them with American troops landed from a cruiser.

Stevens promptly recognized the provisional government set up by the rebels, who lost no time in sending a five-man commission to Washington to negotiate a treaty of annexation. The retiring President Harrison favored the treaty and sent it to the Senate, where it met Democratic opposition. Suspicious of Stevens's activities in Hawaii, the new president, Grover Cleveland, recalled the treaty and sent a special commissioner to the islands to investigate. His report charged that Stevens, by his abuse of the authority of the United States, had done a great wrong to a "feeble but independent State."

Cleveland tried to restore Queen Lil under a constitutional regime, but the provisional government would not let go. In 1894 it wrote still another constitution, proclaimed the Republic of Hawaii, and confirmed Sanford B. Dole as its first president.

Realizing he would have to use force to unseat the new government, Cleveland recognized it. But he refused its urgent requests for annexation. In 1897, under McKinley, a new annexation treaty was worked out. But the Senate, reflecting popular discontent with imperialist adventures, rejected it. Feelings changed during the Spanish-American War, when Hawaii's strategic value became more evident. In July 1898, by a joint resolution, Congress approved a new treaty making Hawaii "a part of the territory of the United States." Sixty-one years later (August 1959), about seven months after Alaska became the forty-ninth state, Hawaii became the fiftieth.

DIPLOMACY AND POWER

After the Civil War, Americans were so intent on developing domestic resources and home markets that the United States merchant marine virtually disappeared. For almost a century, it had been one of the largest in the world. The navy, once as strong as the merchant marine, had shrunk by the 1880s to a small number of wooden sailing ships worse than useless in an age of steel and steam. The United States, especially in competition with a naval power like Great Britain, hardly appeared to be in a position to establish and maintain its influence anywhere abroad. That weakness became critical as industrialization forced American manufacturers to look elsewhere for markets for surplus goods.

The need for the United States to assert itself more aggressively in its foreign relations won more support in the 1880s and 1890s. A group of spokesmen emerged to provide the necessary direction and momentum. Among these men, two were particularly important: James G. Blaine, secretary of state in 1881 under Garfield and again from 1889 to 1892 under Harrison; and Captain, later Admiral, Alfred T. Mahan, the gifted propagandist who became the model for a later generation of imperialists. Both believed in an aggressive and spirited diplomacy. Blaine focused his energies on Latin America; Mahan concerned himself with making certain the United States had the power to carry out an aggressive diplomacy.

Latin America

Latin America still had strong cultural ties with Spain and Portugal and commercial ties with Britain. In the 1870s Germany began to seek Latin American outlets for its goods and capital. To deflect Latin American trade and development toward the United States, Blaine in 1889 issued invitations to a Pan-American Conference. Delegates from eighteen nations met in Washington and formed the Pan-American Union, but accomplished little else.

Although Latin Americans bought largely from Europeans, they sold mainly to the United States, and mainly items that were duty-free. When the Latin American delegates to the 1889 conference failed to grant tariff concessions to United States exports, Blaine threatened to respond with tariffs on Latin American goods. The so-called reciprocity provision of the McKinley Tariff in 1890, which said the United States would respond to favorable treatment, was Blaine's weapon. But his tactics did not work very well. Latin Americans remained hostile and uncooperative.

Sea Power and Trade

As secretary of state, Blaine also pushed for a powerful new American navy. In 1881, Congress set up a Naval Advisory Board to work for larger appropriations. Two years later, Congress appropriated funds for the famous White Squadron of four new steel ships equipped with steam power and a full rigging of white sails. But they were only a token navy, since they had no armor. The establishment of the Naval War College at Newport in 1884 gave another push to the idea of a "big navy." At Newport in 1886, just before he was made president of the college, Captain Mahan gave the lectures that eventually became the heart of his famous series of books on sea power in history.

Britain, he said, had grown great on sea power. The United States should profit from Britain's example not simply by rebuilding its merchant marine and its navy, but by adding colonies and naval bases throughout the world. In particular, the United States must have naval bases in the Caribbean to protect a potential canal across the Isthmus of Panama and in the Pacific not only to guard American trade, but also to take part in the coming struggle between Western and Asian civilizations.

Between 1883 and 1890, Congress authorized the building of nine cruisers. Construction began on the first modern American battleship, *Maine*. After additional pressure from naval expansionists, Congress authorized construction of so many battleships, cruisers, gunboats, and torpedo boats that by 1898 only Britain and France outranked the United States.

Toward the end of the century, the position of the United States in world trade was greatly improved, as Blaine had hoped. American imports, valued at $462 million in 1870, almost doubled in the next thirty years, reaching $850 million in 1900. In the same period, American exports almost tripled, rising from $530 million to approximately $1.4 billion. The Panic of 1893, which shrank markets at home, pushed the quest for markets abroad. Senator Albert J. Beveridge, an ardent expansionist, stated the case quite clearly in April 1898: Since American factories and farms were producing more than the American people could use and consume, "the trade of the world must and shall be ours."

Hemispheric Diplomacy

While the United States was using its resources to promote the growth of foreign trade and world power, a series of diplomatic incidents in the Western Hemisphere triggered talk of war and revived the Monroe Doctrine.

One incident arose over the old problem of fishing rights in Canadian waters. Friction over these rights had increased as a result of the other issues in Canadian-American relations during and after the Civil War. The Treaty of Washington of 1871 formally resolved some of the difficulties. But American fishermen continued to be harassed and exploited by local authorities in Canada and Newfoundland. An informal arrangement with Britain, worked out through diplomatic channels by the Cleveland administration, ended the fishing

THE AMERICAN EMPIRE

controversy in the Atlantic. But another controversy over seal fisheries in the Bering Sea brought trouble once again. In 1890 rumors spread that British warships were policing the region, and some American newspapers suggested firing at British ships in those waters. Cooler heads prevailed, and an arbitration treaty was ratified in February 1892.

A third episode occurred after a revolt in 1891 against the president of Chile, in which the United States had backed the president. When the rebels won, feeling against the United States ran high. In October 1891, the captain of the *U.S.S. Baltimore*, then in Valparaiso, permitted his crew to go ashore unarmed. A riot broke out among them and some Chileans and two Americans were killed and others imprisoned. Chilean apologies were slow in coming, and President Harrison hinted that he might invite Congress to declare war. A full apology arrived just in time and Chile eventually agreed to pay $75,000 to the families of the dead sailors and to those who had been injured.

A more serious affair brought the United States closer to war in 1895. It involved disputed territory between British Guiana and neighboring Venezuela, where gold was discovered in the 1880s. When Venezuela broke off diplomatic relations with Britian in 1887, the United States offered to act as mediator. Britain rejected the idea. The last American mediation effort was made in July 1895 by Richard Olney, Cleveland's secretary of state.

In a note to Lord Salisbury, the British foreign minister, Olney charged that Great Britain had violated the Monroe Doctrine by interfering in hemispheric affairs. If Salisbury had any question as to how the Monroe Doctrine applied to a boundary dispute, Olney made himself absolutely clear: "Today, the United States is practically sovereign on this continent, and its fiat is law upon the subjects to which it confines its interposition." In what seemed more like an ultimatum than a note, Olney asked for a quick response to his demand that Britain submit the dispute to "peaceful arbitration." Salisbury took his time in replying. When he did, in November 1895, he refused arbitration and reminded the United States that the Monroe Doctrine was not recognized in international law and did not apply to boundary disputes.

Cleveland made the Olney-Salisbury correspondence public in December, when he himself delivered a message to Congress in which he asked for funds to finance a commission to determine the actual boundary between British Guiana and Venezuela. He then added the assertion that "it will . . . be the duty of the United States to resist by every means in its power, as a wilful aggression upon its rights and interests" any efforts by Great Britain to take territory that the United States, after investigation, found to be Venezuela's.

Since the Venezuelan boundary dispute coincided with mounting silverite aspirations for action against England, the alleged center of the "gold power," it was much worse than any of the earlier episodes. But the peace parties eventually won out both in the United States and in Britain. Cleveland's proposal for a boundary commission gave Americans time to simmer down, since nothing could be done until such a commission reported. Britain, meanwhile, was growing more nervous over German rivalry, and therefore more interested in American friendship. In February 1897, at America's suggestion, Britain and Venezuela negotiated a treaty turning the boundary dispute over to international arbitration. In 1899 a final settlement was made.

THE SPANISH-AMERICAN WAR

To make arrangements that would secure American markets and sources of raw materials, protect the national interest, and increase the influence of the United States in the world community had become a principal objective of American policymakers by the 1890s. Such an objective was also consistent with the American mission to spread its institutions and habits of mind. The ways in which strong diplomacy, commercial imperialism, and missionary idealism could be combined were best exemplified in the growing American concern over Spanish-held Cuba—a concern that ended in a war and in the debut of the United States as an imperial power.

The Cuban Crisis

When the Cubans rebelled against the Spanish in 1868, Americans had not cared much. The rebellion had dragged on for ten years when Spain finally agreed to undertake serious reforms. The Cubans made two major demands: emancipation of the slaves on the island and self-government for the island's inhabitants. Spain actually took another ten years to free the slaves, and postponed granting self-government indefinitely. In the meantime, it saddled a ruined Cuban economy with all the costs of the rebellion.

After the emancipation of the slaves, large amounts of European and American capital were invested in Cuba. Modern business practices were introduced, especially in the production of cane sugar. The United States gradually became Cuba's principal market and source of capital. After the removal of the American duty on Cuban sugar in 1884, production of that export reached new highs, and almost all of it went to the United States. Events then suddenly worked against Cuban prosperity.

Europe's production of beet sugar became so great that the world price of sugar fell. The worldwide depression of the 1890s further weakened prices. Finally, the Wilson-Gorman Tariff of 1894 restored a 40 percent duty on raw sugar. The acute economic distress that followed, combined with the continuing political trouble, brought another revolt against Spanish rule in 1895. And American interests were of course threatened.

Spain sent its best general, Valeriano Weyler (soon to be called Butcher Weyler), and 200,000 men to suppress the uprising. But the Spaniards could not cope with the rebel leaders and their guerrilla followers, who had taken to the hills. The rebels destroyed property in order to exhaust the government and force the withdrawal of the troops. Much American property was also deliberately destroyed in an effort to push the United States to intervene. During all this time a *junta*, or council, of Cuban exiles in New York kept pressing for American intervention and Cuban independence. Joseph Pulitzer of the *New York World* and William Randolph Hearst of the *New York Journal* engaged in a circulation battle, each trying to outdo the other in printing sensational accounts of Spanish atrocities. Mahan, Roosevelt, Senator Lodge, and other expansionists also whipped up the war spirit.

Unlike the American public, however, which focused on the Cuban struggle for liberty, the expansionists sensed there were higher stakes involved. The Spanish Philippines were a possible stronghold of American power in the Far East and a gateway to the potentially lucrative China trade. But President Cleveland refused to be stampeded: He responded to the public frenzy over Spanish atrocities in Cuba by noting that both sides had committed outrages.

William Randolph Hearst, newspaper publisher: "You furnish the pictures," he instructed his illustrator in Havana, "and I'll furnish the war." The Hearst and Pulitzer newspapers were not alone in whipping up war hysteria over Cuba. The popular magazine *Judge* showed the Spanish as vicious brutes. (*Library of Congress*)

THE AMERICAN EMPIRE

Early in 1898, two events combined to make resistance to the jingoes and public pressure difficult. On February 9, a letter stolen from the Havana post office by a rebel sympathizer fell into the hands of Hearst's *New York Journal.* In it, Dupuy de Lome, the Spanish minister to the United States, described McKinley as "weak and a bidder for the admiration of the crowd, besides being a would-be politician who tries to leave a door open behind himself while keeping on good terms with the jingoes of his party." This was a private letter, but Hearst made it as public as possible. Spain denied any evil intent on the minister's part, and de Lome himself resigned as soon as the letter was published.

The *Maine* tragedy followed in less than a week. The new battleship *Maine* had been sent to Havana in January 1898, when the American consul-general there cabled that American property and persons were in danger. On February 15, *Maine* apparently hit a mine. Two officers and 258 of the crew were lost. Although an official inquiry left the causes of the explosion uncertain, Assistant Navy Secretary Theodore Roosevelt called it "an act of dirty treachery."

Among the messages Roosevelt, in the absence of his chief, now fired off from the Navy Department was the famous one to Commodore George Dewey, who was commanding his Pacific squadron off the China shore. In case of war with Spain, he ordered Dewey to make certain the Spanish squadron did not leave the Asian coast and then to undertake "offensive operations" in the Philippine Islands.

With Americans rallying under the slogan "Remember the *Maine!*" Congress unanimously granted the president's request for $50 million for national defense. "There is no stopping place now short of the absolute independence of Cuba," declared *The New York Times.* But many Americans still wanted peace. The business community saw the economic revival after the long depression endangered by war costs and war taxes. For a time, at least, the business community thought it possible to protect its investment in Cuban sugar plantations and iron mines without armed intervention. There was considerable doubt, moreover, about the ability of the rebels to set up a stable government in case of independence.

As for McKinley, "I have been through one war," he told a friend at this time. "I have seen the dead piled up, and I do not want to see another." But the president maintained a public silence, and indecisiveness marked his policies. "I must have money to get ready for war," he told the House

leader. "I am doing everything possible to prevent war, but it must come, and we are not prepared for war. Who knows where this war will lead us."

American Intervention

Even a great leader might have found it impossible to reduce the war fever of the American people. For many of them, the struggle of the Cuban people for independence and freedom was like their own struggle in the War of Independence. On March 27, 1898, the president after consultation with his cabinet, made a series of demands on Spain. He called for an armistice on the island, during which the United States would act as mediator between the contestants. But he also made it clear that Cuban independence would be the only satisfactory outcome. Spain was willing to make many concessions, but fearing the end of his government and even of the monarchy if Cuban independence were granted, Premier Sagasta refused to accept any armistice that the rebels did not ask for first.

The singing of "Dixie" and "The Battle Hymn of the Republic" in the halls of Congress when war was declared against Spain indicated the unity of the nation. Civil War veterans here show how both North and South favored the war to make Cuba safe for democracy. (*Library of Congress*)

With their hopes for American intervention rising every day, the rebels would make no such request; their demands in fact grew harsher. Spain scrambled to find support and allies in Europe, but the German foreign minister, on April 5, expressed the attitude of most other nations when he told the Spanish ambassador: "You are isolated, because everybody wants to be pleasant to the United States, or, at any rate, nobody wants to arouse America's anger; the United States is a rich country, against which you simply cannot sustain a war." When the pope that same day agreed to suggest an armistice, saving Spain the humiliation of yielding to America, Sagasta gratefully took the offer.

The American minister in Madrid promptly cabled home Spain's consent to "immediate and unconditional suspension of hostilities." He added on his own, "I believe that this means peace." But it was too late. The public, the press, the Protestant clergy, expansionist politicians in both parties created an atmosphere in which negotiation seemed to mean giving in. On April 11, 1898, President McKinley, "in the name of humanity, in the name of civilization, in behalf of endangered American interests," sent a war message to Congress. He asked for authority to use military and naval force to end the hostilities in Cuba.

On April 20, by a joint resolution, Congress declared Cuba "free and independent," demanded that Spain withdraw from the island, and authorized the president to use military force to assure compliance. Congress added the Teller Amendment, disclaiming any intention to annex Cuba and promising "to leave the government and control of the Island to its people."

Within a week of the resolution, the United States and Spain formally declared themselves in a state of war. "I think the President could have worked the business out without a war," remarked Wisconsin's conservative Republican senator, "but the current was too strong, the demagogues too numerous, and the fall election too near."

The "Splendid Little War"

The war with Spain was almost too short for those who wanted to display American power, but the results were gratifying. In the Philippines, Commodore Dewey sailed into Manila Bay on April 30. The next day, he blasted the antiquated Spanish fleet sitting there, and by July 25 about 11,000 American troops under General Wesley Merritt had landed. Supported by Filipino insurrectionists under Emilio Aguinaldo, whom Dewey had befriended and helped arm, Merritt took Manila on August 13.

By then, the "splendid little war," as the American ambassador to Britain called it, had already ended in the West Indies. On April 29, a Spanish fleet under Admiral Cervera had sailed west from the Cape Verde Islands. American coastal cities demanded naval protection. A patrol fleet tried to find Cervera before he reached Cuba, where they decided he was headed. They did not locate him, however, until he was safely in Santiago harbor, where American ships bottled him up. A military expedition was now planned to capture Santiago, and force Cervera out under the American fleet's waiting guns.

On June 14 a poorly equipped expeditionary force of 17,000 men under General William R. Shafter finally left Tampa, Florida. Typical of this army was the First Volunteer Cavalry Regiment, the Rough Riders, who had few horses. Shafter and his men reached the Cuban coast near Santiago on June 20 and took six days to disembark. After a two-day battle, which saw Roosevelt on July 1 lead the Rough Riders up the elevation "we afterwards christened Kettle Hill" (it lay on a flank of San Juan Hill, which became famous for the Rough Riders' charge), the American attack petered out. "We are within measurable distance of a terrible military disaster," Roosevelt wrote Lodge.

Luckily for Shafter, the Spaniards were in even worse shape. On July 3 Cervera decided to escape. American firepower, however, destroyed his ships. On July 16, General Linares surrendered Santiago to the Americans, and nine days later a second American expeditionary force made a triumphant march through Puerto Rico.

The Spanish government had already begun to seek a peace treaty, and on August 12 hostilities were declared over. All told, the United States lost 5,462 men in the four-month war, but only 379 in combat. The rest died from disease and other causes. Spain's losses in the fighting were much higher, and in addition it lost the last of a once great New World empire.

The Peace and the Philippines

Few Americans doubted the nobility of their mission in assisting an oppressed native people to achieve freedom. But there was far less agreement about what the United States should do with some of the spoils of the victory. Did the "liberation" of Cuba require the annexation of the Philippines?

Theodore Roosevelt and his Rough Riders on San Juan Hill in 1898. "Did I tell you," he wrote to his friend Henry Cabot Lodge, "I killed a Spaniard with my own hand, like a jack-rabbit. . . . (*Library of Congress*)

While American negotiators worked on the treaty, hunger for the Philippines kept growing. The fear that Germany would seize the islands no doubt fed American demands, as did economic, strategic, and racial considerations. The Filipinos were not prepared for self-government, annexationists argued, and the United States had an obligation to give them proper guidance and direction. This was then, as a Presbyterian minister suggested, a special kind of imperialism—"not for domination but for civilization."

The final treaty, insuring the freedom of Cuba and granting the United States the Philippines (for a payment of $20 million), Puerto Rico, and Guam, was signed in Paris on December 10. In the debate on ratification in the Senate, the annexation of the Philippines became the principal issue. To acquire the Philippines and not admit the Filipinos to full citizenship, argued critics, violated a principle in which this nation had long believed—government by consent of the governed. But to admit Filipinos as citizens posed still other dangers. They would be entitled to vote, to send representatives to Congress, and to migrate to the United States, where they would become a source of cheap labor. (That specter helped to link Samuel Gompers of the AFL with the anti-imperialists.) Finally, both southern and northern opponents of annexation agreed that annexation would make even worse an already critical race problem. Nothing but trouble might be expected, said the editor of *Nation,* from "dependencies inhabited by ignorant and inferior races" with whom white Americans had no affinity; indeed, the biracial experiment in the South should be sufficient warning of "the danger and futility of any further attempt in the same direction." The racial argument assumed that Asians, like blacks, could never be assimilated into American life.

The Anti-Imperialist League, organized in November 1898, grew rapidly as the administration's expansionist policies developed. Its supporters included political, business, literary and intellectual leaders, among them ex-President Cleveland, William Jennings Bryan, Andrew Carnegie, Samuel Gompers, Mark Twain, William James, and Jane Addams. Some of them were horrified by the behavior of American occupation troops in the Philippines; some were fearful that imperial expansion would involve the United States in an armaments race, foreign alliances, and wars of intervention. A strange coalition of individuals holding conflicting views on domestic political issues, they were drawn together by opposition to colonial expansion.

On February 6, 1899, the Senate ratified the treaty by 57 to 27, only two votes above the required two-thirds majority. The decision might have gone the other way had it not been for the Filipinos themselves. On December 21, 1898, with the debate in the Senate at its peak, McKinley had ordered the War Department to extend the military occupation of Manila to the entire archipelago. This move promptly touched off armed Filipino resistance under Aguinaldo, who headed a group that had suffered imprisonment, exile, and death in its years of struggle for independence from Spain.

But when the Senate learned that American lives had been lost in the fighting, there were enough votes for the treaty to squeak by. The commitment to liberate the Cubans now became a war to conquer the Filipinos. "It shows how rapidly we are approaching an imperial form of government," wrote the Massachusetts anti-imperialist Moorfield Storey, "that the President should undertake operations like this without the consent of Congress or without even consulting it."

There was nothing "splendid" about this war. The Filipino rebels held off the Americans for three years in a conflict that cost more men and money than the war with Spain itself. Before the war in the Philippines ended, nearly 200,000 American soldiers had participated; over 4,000 of them were killed, and 2,800 wounded. Some 16,000 Filipinos died in combat; many more died from diseases that gained an easy foothold in undernourished bodies. The food crops which might have fed them had been destroyed in the fighting. The United States found itself using some of the same brutal methods for which it had condemned the Spanish in Cuba. One American reporter wrote home:

Hundreds of native huts were fired by the Americans to dislodge their occupants. One church, in which Filipinos had fortified themselves, was set on fire by the Americans, and the escaping Filipinos were picked off with rifles as they were smoked out.

As the war deepened, protest at home grew louder. Perhaps the bitterest comment was that of Mark Twain as he explained why an American general had shot up Filipino women and children: when he was a youth, the general's conscience had "leaked out through one of his pores."

That black American troops were among those helping to suppress the rebellion caused some dissent in the black press. Not a single black soldier, one black newspaper editorialized, should be sent overseas "to kill their own kith and kin for fighting for the cause they believed to be right." Were not black soldiers, another editor asked, "simply fighting to curse the country [the Philippines] with color-phobia; jimcrow cars, disfranchisement, lynchers, and everything that prejudice can do to blight the manhood of the darker races"? Finally, in assessing the results of American expansionism, a black newspaper observed: "When one of the great Christian countries finds a strip of land it desires to possess, it is quickly seized with a commendable desire to spread the benign influence of civilization over the natives, and what a remarkably small number of natives are left after this process has been completed."

But to Theodore Roosevelt, and to those who shared his obsession about carrying civilization into "the waste places of the earth," the critics were serving only to prolong the war. "We are fighting Filipinos," said Roosevelt, "because they are killing our soldiers. The bullets that slay our men in Luzon are inspired by the denouncers of America here. The Filipino will stop killing our soldiers very soon after he becomes convinced that he will receive no aid in the effort."

In Cuba, meanwhile, General Leonard Wood ruled as military governor until May 20, 1902, when the Cubans were compelled to accept the Platt Amendment. This amendment to an army appropriation bill sharply circumscribed Cuba's freedom of action. It limited Cuba's treaty-making powers, its right to borrow money, and other rights of sovereignty. Moreover, Cuba could not withhold lands wanted by the United States for coaling or naval stations, or give territory to any other power. Finally, the amendment permitted the United States to intervene in Cuba "for the protection of life, property, and individual liberty."

The United States required the incorporation of the Platt Amendment in any constitution drawn up by Cuba and also that Cuba make a permanent treaty with the United States, using the terms of the amendment. The Platt Amendment remained in force until 1934, when it and related treaties were canceled by agreement. At that time the United States retained Guantanamo Bay and its shore area as a naval base. Until 1959, Cuba remained a safe and tractable neighbor within the American "sphere of influence."

THE RULES OF CIVILIZED WARFARE

In testimony before a Senate committee in 1902, Brigadier General Robert P. Hughes explained why the troops under his command had destroyed the dwellings of Filipinos suspected of sympathy with the insurgents.

GEN. HUGHES: The destruction was as a punishment. They permitted these people [insurgents] to come in there and conceal themselves and they gave no sign. It is always. . . .

SEN. RAWLINS: The punishment in that case would fall, not upon the men, who could go elsewhere, but mainly upon the women and little children.

GEN. HUGHES: The women and children are part of the family, and where you wish to inflict a punishment you can punish the man probably worse in that way than in any other.

SEN. RAWLINS: But is that within the ordinary rules of civilized warfare? Of course you could exterminate the family, which would be still worse punishment.

GEN. HUGHES: These people are not civilized.

SEN. RAWLINS: But is that within the ordinary rules of civilized warfare?

GEN. HUGHES: No; I think it is not.

SEN. RAWLINS: You think it is not?

SEN. DIETRICH: In order to carry on civilized warfare both sides have to engage in such warfare.

GEN. HUGHES: Yes, sir; certainly. That is the point.

Source: Henry F. Graff (ed.), *American Imperialism and the Philippine Insurrection: Testimony Taken from Hearings on Affairs in the Philippine Islands before the Senate Committee on the Philippines—1902* (Boston: Little, Brown, 1969). Photograph from the Library of Congress.

The Imperialist Policy

In the middle of public discussion of the new imperialism, the election of 1900 took place. Not a supporter of the peace treaty, William Jennings Bryan, the Democratic candidate, had secured some Democratic votes for it in the Senate. He had done this to guard his party from charges of wanting the war renewed, and to carry the whole issue of overseas expansion into the campaign. McKinley's victory was interpreted by many as a victory for the new policy. When McKinley was assassinated a few months after his inauguration in 1901 and Theodore Roosevelt became commander-in-chief, the imperialists expected further expansionism.

In May 1901, in the so-called Insular cases, the Supreme Court added its approval to that of the president and the people. In these cases the Court held that the Constitution did not follow the flag, that the rights of United States citizens did not automatically belong to the people of the territories. Even though Hawaii had been given formal territorial status in 1900, paving the way for statehood, in 1903 the Supreme Court held that these islands had not been "incorporated" into the Union and that the native citizens had not become the equals of continental citizens of the United States.

The case in question arose out of the denial of trial by jury to the Hawaiian people. The Court decided it was lawful to follow the existing criminal procedure in the islands instead of using American procedures. In reaching this decision, the Court made a distinction between "fundamental rights," which could not be abridged, and "procedural rights," which could be. Trial by jury, it was held, was a "procedural right."

These racist distinctions, however, were soon swept aside, and even the Filipinos were quickly put on the road to self-government. The foundations were laid by the Philippine Commission appointed in 1900 under William Howard Taft. By 1907, the Filipinos had gained the right to elect the lower house of their legislature, and in 1916 the Jones Act gave them virtual control over their domestic affairs. Some of this ground was lost during the 1920s. But in 1934 the Tydings-McDuffie Act provided for independence after ten years. The Filipinos agreed to the ten-year provision in 1936. After the islands were recovered from Japan during World War II, Filipinos achieved independence, as planned, on July 4, 1946.

The United States in the Pacific

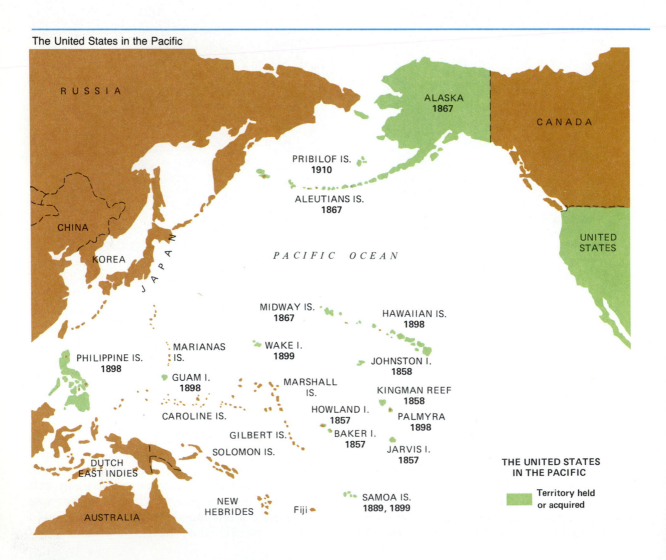

THE UNITED STATES IN THE PACIFIC

Territory held or acquired

THE AMERICAN EMPIRE

POWER POLITICS

With the acquisitions of the Spanish-American War and its industrial supremacy, the United States had become a major world power. It was a position that almost immediately demanded new commitments and entanglements. Other imperial powers were carving out spheres of influence in China. Japan was embarking on an imperial policy very much Western in inspiration. The dominant influence exercised by the United States in Cuba made its presence in the Caribbean and Central America more visible and its meddling more frequent. Expanding American interests in Latin America and the Far East also pointed up the need to construct a canal across Central America to make intercoastal shipping easier and the American navy more maneuverable.

Whether by the Open Door policy in the Far East or by the Monroe Doctrine in the Western Hemisphere, the United States reserved to itself the right to intervene to preserve stability and counteract discrimination by rival powers. These were the principles that would guide twentieth-century foreign relations—principles that bridged the political parties and the occupants of the White House.

China and the Open Door

Along with the American interest in markets, Mahan's ideas about an inevitable struggle for the world between Western and Oriental civilizations had helped push the United States into the Far East. But once there, Americans found the major struggle to be with other Western powers—France, Germany, Britain, and Russia—as well as with Japan. All were staking out *spheres of influence* in weak and still passive China. Partition of China might well ruin American hopes for further trade with that country. The problem was to find a way to gain and maintain equal trading rights without risking war and without becoming a party to further partition.

In 1898, it appeared that the British were about to use some newly leased territory on the mainland opposite Hong Kong to smuggle imports into China without paying the Chinese tariff. If the other powers followed this example, the Chinese government would soon lose all its tariff revenues. Political as well as commercial chaos would result.

In September 1899, McKinley's new Secretary of State, John Hay, sent his famous Open Door notes to Britain, Germany, and Russia—and later to Japan, Italy, and France—inviting them to agree to three points:

1. No nation was to interfere with the trading rights or privileges of other nations within its sphere of influence.
2. Chinese officials were to be permitted to collect duties under existing tariffs, which granted the United States most favored nation privileges.
3. No nation was to discriminate against nationals of other countries in levying port duties and railroad rates.

Although none of the powers would make these concessions, Hay refused to accept their vague rejections. He saved himself from disaster by calmly announcing on March 20, 1900, that all had given "final and definitive" consent to his request. Only Japan challenged his bluff.

Hardly were negotiations over the Open Door notes finished when a group of Chinese nationalists rose up against foreigners in their country. The Chinese called themselves the Order of Literary Patriotic Harmonious Fists; Westerners called them Boxers. Before they were put down by an international force to which the United States contributed 2,500 men, they had killed hundreds of persons and destroyed much property. Only swift action by Britain and the United States now prevented the other powers from retaliating by taking more Chinese territory.

Hay advised the imperial rivals that American policy was to work to "preserve Chinese territorial and administrative entity" and to "safeguard for the world the principle of equal and impartial trade with all parts of the Chinese Empire." This announcement went further than the Open Door notes and had more effect. Eventually, the nations accepted a money indemnity from China rather than new grants of territory. The United States' share of almost $25 million was larger than necessary to meet the losses it suffered. The balance was later returned to China, where it was used to help educate Chinese students in America.

Most important though, the Open Door policy had laid the basis for greater American influence in the affairs of China and Asia. At the same time, it created an impression of disinterested neutrality. Few explained the American position as clearly as did Hay himself. "The ideal policy," he wrote to Henry Adams, "is, as you justly observe, to do nothing, and yet be around when the watermelon is cut. Not that we want any watermelon, but it is always pleasant to be seen in smart colored circles on occasions of festivity."

Japan: The Russo-Japanese War

Theodore Roosevelt's preaching about the importance of what he called "the soldierly virtues" frightened many people when he became president at the age of forty-three in September 1901. Four years earlier he had said at the Naval War College: "The men who have dared greatly in war . . . are those who deserve best of their country."

But his first major international venture did not come until his second term, and then he was a peacemaker. Having beaten the Russians in Manchuria in the Russo-Japanese War of 1904–1905, the Japanese in the spring of 1905, temporarily exhausted by their efforts, secretly asked the American president to mediate. Fearful of the growing unrest at home that ended in the Revolution of October 1905, the Russians were easily persuaded to agree. But Roosevelt would take no steps until Japan consented to respect the principles of the Open Door policy. When this happened, the president invited the Japanese and the Russians to meet at Portsmouth, New Hampshire, in August. Here, among other claims, the Japanese demanded a huge money indemnity to offset their war costs. When the Russians balked, Roosevelt warned the Japanese against pressing their demand. They accepted some small territorial grants instead, along with Russia's promise to vacate Manchuria.

The Japanese people had counted on the Russian indemnity for tax relief and did not quickly forget America's role in depriving them of it. Meanwhile, Japan's emergence as a great power increased anxiety on the West coast about the "yellow peril." In October 1906 the San Francisco Board of Education ordered that the ninety-three Japanese children in the city be segregated in a separate school. Roosevelt's anger over California's action was not lessened by his realization that he had no jurisdiction over California public schools. Only after bringing a great deal of pressure on local authorities did the president succeed in getting the action reversed. At the same time, he promised Californians that Japanese immigration would be curbed. A series of notes in 1907 and 1908 made up the Gentlemen's Agreement by which Japan promised to issue no more passports to workers seeking to emigrate to the United States.

Having pacified the Japanese, Roosevelt was anxious, as he wrote to a friend, "that they should realize that I am not afraid of them." In 1907, as a demonstration of strength, he decided to send the American fleet around the world on a practice cruise. Japan welcomed the visit of the fleet as a friendly gesture, and for a time Japanese-American relations improved. The Root-Takahira Agreement of November 1908 reflected the better feeling. An executive agreement, not a treaty, the terms bound only Roosevelt's administration and its counterpart in Japan. Both powers agreed to maintain the status quo in the Pacific area, to uphold the Open Door in China, and to support that country's "independence and integrity."

Roosevelt's Far Eastern policy was upset by his successor as president, William Howard Taft, and Taft's secretary of state, the corporation lawyer Philander C. Knox. They favored a policy of promoting American investment and trade abroad, a policy that became known as Dollar Diplomacy. With the full support of the State Department, Taft encouraged investments by American bankers in China and Manchuria. These included financing China's purchase of Manchurian railroads, in which Russia and Japan were interested. His effort only aroused the suspicion of Russia and Japan, driving together the two nations Roosevelt had sought to keep apart.

The Panama Canal

Having become a world power with interests in the Pacific as well as the Caribbean, the United States began to look toward the construction of a canal to link these two great waters. Back in 1850, the United States and Britain had agreed in the Clayton-Bulwer Treaty that they would enjoy equal rights in any canal. Now, the United States pressed Britain to surrender its rights. At last, in 1901, following a new policy of keeping America as a friend, Britain gave in. The Hay-Pauncefote Treaty that year gave the United States a free hand to build, control, and fortify an isthmian canal. The United States promised to open the canal without discrimination to the commercial and fighting ships of all nations.

Two routes were possible for this canal—one through Panama in the Republic of Colombia, the other through Nicaragua. Different companies had already been at work across each route for some time. But progress had been slow and costly, and both now wanted to unload their enterprises on the United States. After much maneuvering and debate, the United States, in 1902, decided to use the Panama route. This was a triumph for the French New Panama Canal Company, which held the concession from Colombia.

By holding the alternative of a Nicaraguan canal over the heads of Colombia's negotiators, Sec-

Teddy Roosevelt, as the policeman of the hemisphere, wields the big stick—an image he cultivated. (*The Granger Collection*)

retary of State Hay was able to drive a hard bargain in a treaty approved by the United States Senate in March 1903. The treaty stated that $10 million cash and $250,000 annually were to be paid to Colombia for the rights to a canal zone 6 miles across the isthmus. In Colombia, however, a new revolutionary government resented some of the terms. Hay responded with such threats to Colombian proposals for altering these terms that, to preserve its own dignity, the Colombian Senate had to reject the treaty in August 1903. Roosevelt then lost no time in announcing that the "black-mailers of Bogota" must not be allowed "permanently to bar one of the future highways of civilization."

To break this impasse, a furious president encouraged Panamanian rebels to declare their independence from Colombia and ordered a warship to the isthmus to intimidate Colombian forces. With the "revolution" a success, Washington promptly recognized the new Republic of Panama and negotiated a treaty that gave the United States the desired strip of territory for the canal zone for $10 million and $25,000 a year. Roosevelt's be-

havior created many enemies for the United States throughout Latin America.

Within a decade of the Panamanian revolution, however, the canal was completed. On August 15, 1914, the first oceangoing steamship passed through it. In the same year, the Wilson administration tried to improve relations by apologizing for the part played by the United States in the revolution and by paying Colombia $25 million. Roosevelt's friends in the Senate would not allow this to happen, and the treaty was shelved. In 1921, after Roosevelt's death, the treaty minus the apology at last passed the Senate, and Colombia received its indemnity. If the Senate needed any incentive in this matter, the discovery of oil in Colombia was more than enough.

The Caribbean

The Panama Canal, by giving the United States a great new enterprise to protect, broadened American involvement in the Caribbean. The political

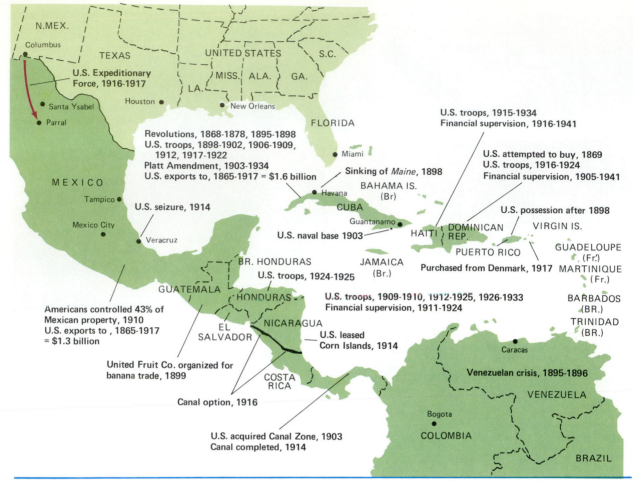

The United States and Latin America

and financial instability of its smaller republics was an especially touchy problem. Almost all their public financing had been done in Europe. If any country failed to pay interest due on its bonds, its European creditor, eager for empire, might move in with the idea of staying indefinitely—as France did in Mexico in 1863. To avert this danger, Roosevelt, in his message to Congress on December 6, 1904, set forth the Roosevelt Corollary to the Monroe Doctrine: in the event of "flagrant cases of . . . wrongdoing or impotence" in Latin America that required outside intervention to set matters right, the United States, "however reluctantly," would undertake the necessary exercise of "international police power."

The first application of the Roosevelt Corollary came in 1905, when the Dominican Republic was unable to pay its debts. After an American show of force, the Dominican government had to invite the United States to step in. The Dominican foreign debt was now scaled down and transferred from European to American bankers. A percentage of customs collections was allocated to pay future interest and to reduce the principal.

Cuba also drew the attention of the Roosevelt administration in 1906, when revolutionary disturbances led the United States to send troops to impose order. They were not withdrawn until 1909. In Taft's administration, Secretary of State Knox persuaded American bankers to increase their interest in the debt of Honduras and to put capital into the National Bank of the Republic of Haiti.

The most provocative case of Dollar Diplomacy took place in Nicaragua, where in 1909 the United States established a sympathetic government, forced it to transfer its public debt from European to American creditors, and persuaded American bankers to take charge of the nation's finances. Three years later, when a nationalist movement threatened to overthrow the American-backed ruler, President Taft rushed in 2700 marines to maintain the "legally constituted good government." Except for a brief withdrawal in 1925, the marines remained there until 1933.

These almost routine displays of force naturally deepened Latin American hostility toward the United States. When Woodrow Wilson succeeded

Taft as president in 1913, he promised to correct matters. But Caribbean diplomacy remained essentially the same. The outbreak of the European war in 1914 made the American government even more concerned about maintaining its hemispheric dominance. American marines entered Haiti in response to revolutionary disturbances in 1915 and stayed there until 1934. American forces also occupied the Dominican Republic again in 1916 and intervened once more in Cuba in 1917. By World War I, the United States had established virtual protectorates over the Dominican Republic, Haiti, Nicaragua, Panama, and Cuba, and President Wilson had become embroiled in a painful adventure in Mexico.

Wilson in Mexico

In May 1911 President Porfirio Diaz, dictator of Mexico since 1877, was overthrown by a revolutionary coalition led by the liberal idealist Francisco Madero. Unable to organize a new government rapidly enough, the revolutionaries were themselves suppressed in February 1913 by General Victoriano Huerta, who arranged Madero's assassination. Most European governments recognized the Huerta regime. American business interests, with large investments in Mexican industry, urged Wilson to do likewise. Wilson refused on the ground that Huerta's was not a free government resting on the consent of the governed. This departure from the American policy of recognizing all governments in power gave the United States the responsibility of deciding which governments were pure and which were not.

Wilson was confident of his judgment. He promised Britain to protect its oil interests in Mexico if it would abandon Huerta, which Britain did. When Huerta's government failed to collapse, as Wilson hoped it would, he offered to help the anti-Huerta Constitutionalist forces under Venustiano Carranza. But Carranza wanted no support from Yankees, and Huerta's regime stood up. Wilson now found himself unable to redeem the pledge he had made to Mexico and to the world that he would guarantee constitutional government in that country.

An incident that occurred on April 9, 1914, gave Wilson an excuse for direct intervention. One of Huerta's officers arrested the crew of an American vessel that had landed behind the government's lines at Tampico. Although the Americans were promptly released with expressions of regret, the commander of the American squadron demanded a more formal apology. This Huerta refused to make. Wilson took Huerta's action as an insult to the United States and asked Congress for authority to win an apology by force. Even before Congress could act, Wilson learned of a German steamer about to arrive at Vera Cruz with a load of ammunition for the Huerta government. To stop the delivery of armaments that might be used against American forces, Wilson ordered the navy to occupy the port. This action cost 126 Mexican lives. Even Carranza's Constitutionalists were so angered that they threatened war.

At this crucial point, the ABC powers—Argentina, Brazil, and Chile—offered to mediate. Wilson welcomed the chance to crawl away from his difficulties. Mediation failed, but Huerta's regime soon collapsed anyway. In 1914, it was unable to secure arms from European nations who were strengthening their own forces. Carranza took over the presidency, but his regime quickly became embroiled in civil war with one of his best generals, Francisco (Pancho) Villa. Disorder spread, and in March 1915 Wilson sent General John J. Pershing across the border on a "punitive expedition" against Villa, who had repeatedly raided American territory and killed American citizens. Carranza replied to this American "invasion" by mobilizing his army. Preoccupied with the war in Europe, Wilson withdrew Pershing's forces and in March 1917 recognized the Carranza regime. Peace was maintained, but only after Wilson had aroused the lasting distrust of a people he meant to help.

The Mexican policy, although pursued no doubt with the best of intentions, suggested a tendency that would persist throughout much of the century. Whether the United States chose to use its growing power for reasons of idealism or self-interest, the assumption persisted that it had an obligation to improve and shape the lives of other peoples.

The way in which Major General Arthur McArthur chose to describe his role as military governor of the Philippine Islands in 1900 and 1901 could just have easily been used by American presidents six decades later:

We are planting in those islands imperishable ideas. We are planting the best traditions, the best characteristics of Americanism in such a way that they never can be removed from that soil. . . . It encouraged me during all my efforts in those islands, even when conditions seemed most disappointing, when the people themselves, not appreciating precisely what the remote consequences of our efforts were going to be, mistrusted us; but that fact was always before me—that going down deep into that fertile soil were the imperishable ideas of Americanism.

If that remained a tenet of American foreign policy for much of the century, it was perfectly consistent with the triumph of Progressivism in the first decade. Many of those who became Progressives were expansionists who supported a strong navy and an aggressive foreign policy. To redeem "the waste places of the world" and the slums of American cities were expressions of the same missionary impulse; and both Progressivism and imperialism recognized the need to impose order and stability on societies threatened with social upheaval.

In the 1890s the United States joined the European powers in a new drive for world empire. Americans concentrated on areas of interest to them: the Caribbean and Latin America, the islands of the South Pacific, and the Philippines and China abroad; Canada and Mexico nearer home.

On the continent, American territory was expanded by the purchase of Alaska from Russia in 1867. The idea that Canada would someday be part of the United States persisted, and it kept the rivalry between the United States and Britain alive.

In the Pacific, America looked for new markets for manufactured goods, for new sources of raw materials, and for control over its own system of harbors and coaling stations for its ships. In 1854 Commodore Perry had forcibly opened Japan. In the mid-1880s the United States became involved in a three-way competition for Samoa with Britain and Germany. In 1899 Samoa was finally divided between the United States and Germany. The Hawaiian Islands had been visited by traders in the 1790s and by missionaries as early as 1820, and had a large American colony by 1860. After much political turmoil, the islands were annexed by the United States in 1898.

Part of the push for expansionism came from politicians and industrialists eager for world power and wealth. It was supported by the new idea that to be a world power, a nation needed a large and strong military establishment, and particularly a strong navy. But while the United States was using its resources to promote the growth of foreign trade and world power, a series of incidents in the Western Hemisphere brought talk of war and revived the Monroe Doctrine. One was the dispute over fishing rights with Canada, which was resolved by an arbitration treaty in February 1892. In 1891 there was an incident in Chile, where the United States had intervened in an internal revolt and backed the losing side. The boundary dispute between British Guiana and Venezuela was the most serious, because it brought the United States closest to war with Britain when the United States insisted on arbitrating the dispute.

But the ways in which strong diplomacy, commercial imperialism, and missionary idealism were combined were best shown in American actions toward Spanish-held Cuba. The result was a war with Spain, the independence of Cuba, and the debut of the United States as a world imperial power. War became unavoidable after the sinking of the battleship *Maine* in Havana harbor early in 1898. By the end of April the war was over in the Caribbean but not in the Pacific. There the American fleet under Admiral Dewey sailed into the Philippines, which was still a Spanish possession. Like Cuba, it was in revolt and seeking independence. Hostilities were declared over on August 12. The peace treaty ensured the freedom of Cuba and gave the United States the Philippines (for $20 million), Puerto Rico, and Guam.

Now a world power, the United States naturally became involved in the competition over China, where the European powers and Japan were staking out spheres of influence. To gain entry into what everyone thought would be a rich trade, the United States proposed the Open Door policy, which was in fact a proposal that each nation take its share but not poach on the shares of others. This policy, although it created an impression of disinterested neutrality, laid the foundation for greater American influence in the affairs of China and Asia.

One of the first exercises of that influence was as mediator between the Russians and the Japanese after the Russo-Japanese war of 1904–05. That conflict, which the Japanese had won, was settled by the Treaty of Portsmouth, negotiated in the United States under the sponsorship of Theodore Roosevelt, a supporter of expansionism and American power. It was during Roosevelt's presidency that the United States began to build the Panama Canal, which was opened to traffic in August 1914. But the president's heavy-handed methods of gaining the consent of the Central American nations and getting rid of British interest earned the United States many enemies in Latin America.

American meddling in the Caribbean after 1900 won no friends either. The Roosevelt Corollary of 1904 to the Monroe Doctrine set up the United States as the police officer for Latin America. In 1905 the United States took over the debt of the Dominican Republic to prevent a European creditor from moving in. Troops were sent to Cuba to keep order and protect American investments in 1906. After American bankers had taken charge of Nicaragua's finances, President Taft thought it necessary in 1912 to dispatch marines there to maintain the American-backed government. Between 1915 and 1917, the United States also intervened in Haiti, Cuba, and the Dominican Republic to maintain its interests.

Although none of this made the United States popular in the Western Hemisphere, perhaps the worst blunder was Wilson's intervention in Mexico in 1914 and 1915. The troops he sent were not withdrawn until 1917, when the United States entered the war in Europe. By that time Wilson, with the best of intentions, had succeeded in arousing the lasting distrust of the Mexicans.

The idea that the United States had a mission to improve and shape the lives of other peoples was to haunt American foreign policy throughout much of the twentieth century. The fact that the results were usually resentment rather than gratitude never seemed to make a dent in the thinking and actions of American presidents and policymakers.

Suggested Readings

On the formulation of American foreign policy in this and later periods, G. Kennan, *American Diplomacy 1900–1950* (1950); R. Osgood, *Ideals and Self-Interest in American Foreign Relations* (1953); W. A. Williams, *The Tragedy of American Diplomacy* (2nd ed., 1972); and L. C. Gardner, *Imperial America* (1976) are good introductions, with Williams and Gardner placing greater stress on economic influences. E. S. Rosenberg, *Spreading the American Dream* (1982), examines both economic and cultural expansionism from 1890 to 1945. W. LaFeber, *The New Empire: An Interpretation of American Expansion 1860–1898* (1963), is indispensable. The new expansionism is also examined in A. K. Weinberg, *Manifest Destiny* (1935); E. R. May, *Imperial Democracy: The Emergence of America as a Great Power* (1961); H. and M. Sprout, *The Rise of American Naval Power 1776–1918* (1939); and D. Healy, *U.S. Expansionism: The Imperialist Urge in the 1890s* (1970).

On John Hay, see K. J. Clymer, *John Hay: The Gentleman as Diplomat* (1975). A. T. Mahan, *The Influence of Sea Power upon History 1660–1783* (1890), exerted considerable influence on decision-makers. Leading expansionists are discussed in H. K. Beale, *Theodore Roosevelt and the Rise of America to World Power* (1956); E. Morris, *The Rise of Theodore Roosevelt* (1979); and J. A. Garraty, *Henry Cabot Lodge* (1953). On Hearst, see W. A. Swanberg, *Citizen Hearst* (1961).

On the Spanish-American War, different perspectives will be found in J. W. Pratt, *Expansionists of 1898* (1936); W. A. Williams, *The Tragedy of American Diplomacy* (1956); W. Millis, *The Martial Spirit* (1931); and R. Hofstadter, "Manifest Destiny and the Philippines," in *The Paranoid Style in American Politics and Other essays* (1958). H. F. Graff (ed.), *American Imperialism and the Philippine Insurrection* (1969), is a valuable documentary collection. The best study of the Philippine-American war is S. C. Miller, *Benevolent Assimilation: The American Conquest of the Philippines, 1899–1903* (1982). The American occupation of the Philippines is examined in W. J. Pomeroy, *American Neocolonialism: Its Emergence in the Philippines and Asia* (1970), and P. W. Stanley, *A Nation in the Making: The Philippines and the United States 1899–1921* (1975).

On the responsibilities of world power, see J. W. Pratt, *America's Colonial Experiment* (1950). The acquisition of Hawaii is examined in S. K. Stevens, *American Expansion in Hawaii 1842–1898* (1945). On American policy in Latin America, one approach is to examine case studies: D. G. Munro, *Intervention and Dollar Diplomacy in the Caribbean 1900–1921* (1964), and *The United States and the Caribbean 1921–1933* (1975); D. F. Healy, *The United States in Cuba 1898–1902* (1963); A. R. Millett, *The Politics of Intervention: The Military Occupation of Cuba 1906–1909* (1968); H. Thomas, *Cuba* (1971); H. Schmidt, *The United States Occupation of Haiti, 1915–1934* (1971). More general works focusing on United States policy in the Caribbean and Central America are W. LaFeber, *Inevitable Revolutions* (1983), and L. D. Langley, *The United States and the Caribbean, 1900–1970* (1980) and *The Banana Wars: An Inner History of American Empire, 1900–1934* (1983). On the Panama Canal, see W. LaFeber, *The Panama Canal: The Crisis in Historical Perspective* (1978). On United States policy toward Mexico, consult D. F. Smith, *The United States and Revolutionary Nationalism in Mexico 1916–1932* (1972); and P. E. Haley, *Revolution and Intervention: The Diplomacy of Taft and Wilson in Mexico 1910–1917* (1970). On American policy in the Far East, see A. Iriye, *Across the Pacific: An Inner History of American-East Asian Relations* (1969), and *Pacific Estrangement: Japanese and American Expansion 1897–1911* (1972); M. B. Young, *The Rhetoric of Empire: America's China Policy 1895–1901* (1968); P. A. Varg, *The Making of a Myth: The United States and China 1897–1912* (1968); and J. Israel, *Progressivism and the Open Door: America and China 1905–1921* (1971). On the changing relations with Britain, see B. Perkins, *The Great Rapprochement: England and the United States 1895–1914* (1968).

On the anti-imperialist movement, see E. B. Tompkins, *Anti-Imperialism in the United States: The Great Debate, 1890–1920* (1970), and R. L. Beisner, *Twelve against Empire: The Anti-Imperialists 1898–1900* (1968). For a bitter indictment of American policy overseas, see "To the Person Sitting in Darkness," in Janet Smith (ed.), *Mark Twain on the Damned Human Race* (1962). Of comparable interest is W. B. Gatewood, Jr. (ed.), *"Smoked Yankees" and the Struggle for Empire: Letters from Negro Soldiers 1898–1902* (1971) and *Black Americans and the White Man's Burden, 1898–1903* (1975).

PEOPLE AND POLITICS: THE PROGRESSIVE ERA

Chapter 25

Although what is known as the Progressive Era generally means the years between 1900 and World War I, the roots of progressivism may be found in the concern with government and business abuses in the post-Civil War decades, and its influence remained apparent as late as the New Deal of the 1930s. But its most intensive period of growth and expression was clearly the first two decades of the twentieth century. The return of prosperity seemed an ideal time for Americans to measure the damage done to their society by the rapid growth of industries and cities. Prosperity had a way of making that damage more obvious by forcing middle-class families to see and compare their comforts and advantages with those trying to survive below the subsistence level.

Progressive reformers looked for ways to make American society a more decent place in which to live. Within two decades, progressivism touched nearly every aspect of American life: the structure of city government, the conduct of corporations and trade unions, the education of children and the interpretation of laws, the conservation of natural resources and the socialization of immigrants, the status of women and the labor of children, the quality of food and the content of magazines. Where progressivism did *not* touch peoples' lives was also significant: Black Americans were relatively unaffected, as were the rural poverty of tenant farmers and migrant workers and the quality of labor of most unorganized workers. And Progressive efforts to reform humankind included some odd policies: restricting the consumption of alcoholic beverages, limiting the numbers of immigrants, and intervening in the political affairs of peoples in other parts of the world.

So varied were the makeup of the Progressive movement and its concerns that programs differed widely in the degree to which they marked new departures in thinking and in the application of ideas. But despite their differences, Progressives did share a certain optimism. National confidence, reinforced by international triumphs and an upswing in the economy, appeared to put nothing beyond the reach of goodwill. And Progressive reformers expected to tap that goodwill for the benefit of all classes. The United States, although flawed in places, remained in their estimation a model to inspire the world. To improve the society and its institutions, in fact, was to make them all the more exportable. ◼

THE PROGRESSIVE SPIRIT

The early decades of the twentieth century were marked by the vitality and breadth of the Progressive spirit. Since their purpose was not simply to make changes in society but also to free it from the past, Progressives naturally looked for support among those willing to question fixed systems of belief. They did not have far to seek. In the study of law and political science, in economics, education, philosophy, and the interpretation of history, Progressives found helpers at home and abroad. The new ideas of the social scientists and philosophers, along with the Protestant clerics who embraced the Social Gospel, provided a good atmosphere for reform. Progressives had only to test those ideas by applying them to actual situations.

The Reform Commitment

The men and women who assumed leadership roles in the Progressive movement emerged largely from the urban Protestant middle class at a time when the nation more than ever before seemed divided along class lines. The conflict between capital and labor, the changes in the sources of immigration, the squalor of the slums, the corruption of politics, the assassination of three presidents between 1865 and 1901—all had deeply impressed the Progressives in their childhood and adolescent years. Nor had they been blind to the Populist issues of the 1890s or the appeal of socialism in the early twentieth century. Not only did the Socialist party reach new sections of the country, but by 1912, 1200 Socialists held public office in 340 cities, including 79 mayors in 24 states, 160 city councilmen, and 145 aldermen.

Eugene Debs, the Socialist presidential candidate, increased his vote from 94,000 in 1900 to 900,000 (or 6 percent of the electorate) in 1912. The movement so alarmed Theodore Roosevelt that he confided to a friend in 1905 "that the growth of the Socialist party in this country [was] far more ominous than any populist or similar movement in the past."

If most Progressives could agree on the need to counter the Socialist challenge by eliminating abuses, they were less agreed on which were the worst abuses and how best to get rid of them. The Progressive movement was a coalition of many different movements, containing men and women with different degrees of commitment to reform and different priorities. Businessmen might become Progressives to prevent popular displeasure from turning to more radical channels. Crusaders for good government thought their cause was critical to progressivism, if only because reform depended on success in making government more responsive and more efficient. Women Progressives seeking to eliminate bias based on sex expanded their struggle to include those who were also oppressed by poverty and the conditions of their employment. They brought to the movement new attitudes toward poverty and a commitment, shown most vividly by the settlement house workers, to reach the people most affected by it. Protestant clerics who joined the movement did so in the spirit of the Social Gospel, convinced that to save humankind, they must save society first. Many journalists came to progressivism as a result of investigations they had conducted into abuses in almost every phase of American life. Some of the politicians who responded to the exposés with legislation also claimed to be Progressives.

Most Progressives shared a commitment to restore opportunities for the common person, broaden income distribution, rescue the poor, clean up politics, and strengthen the state. Some put strengthening the state first as the best way to deal with the question of social responsibility. The New Nationalism propounded by the Progressive theorist Herbert Croly in his influential book *The Promise of American Life* (1909) set much of the tone of the period. To free Americans from "the energetic and selfish individualism" that dominated the recent past, Croly argued, the federal government would have to assume a major responsibility. What he advocated was a positive and strong state that used professional expertise and social planning.

If progressivism often seemed elitist, it was because it reflected the conviction that the "best men" should govern—those who had the necessary courage and insight to lead the way. Supported by the work of Frederick Winslow Taylor, whose influential *Principles of Scientific Management* appeared in 1911, many Progressives looked to "social engineering" by a trained elite to administer the "means" of government, even if the people determined the "ends."

Taylor had applied his theories only to the factories. Elitist Progressives, the first generation conscious of the force of technology in amassing power as well as creating wealth, wanted to extend "scientific management" to society as a whole. In this way they hoped to bring both their primary targets, the economically wasteful wealthy and the politically warped poor, under beneficial control.

Although progressivism was a new departure in attitudes and practices, it did not result in any far-reaching redistribution of wealth or power. It aimed largely at corrective legislation, at arousing the public's conscience, not at the reorganization of society. It sought to reduce conflict and minimize abuses. It showed the ability of American society to absorb economic reforms that in no real way altered the capitalist structure or threatened corporate dominance. That feature in itself made progressivism an attractive movement to some parts of the business community.

Business and Reform

Although most businessmen defended the status quo as actively as they battled the organization of their workers, an impressive number were touched by the Progressive spirit. To some of them, progressivism was a safe and practical way to satisfy the popular demand for reform. Whether motivated by social consciousness or political need, men like E. A. Filene, the Boston department store merchant, and Joseph Fels, the soap manufacturer, supported reform movements. William Kent, a Chicago real estate operator and cattle-feed producer, became president of the Municipal Voters League and a member of the Illinois Civil Service League. Oil millionaire Samuel M. Jones and streetcar tycoon Tom Loftin Johnson emerged as model reform mayors of Toledo and Cleveland, respectively.

Some businessmen supported progressivism because they had something to gain from particular programs. As in the 1880s, many small merchants and shippers, at a disadvantage because railroads favored powerful interests, continued to seek stronger regulation. Some railroad leaders endorsed antirebating and similar federal measures to help keep favor seekers off their backs. Life insurance companies welcomed federal regulation as an alternative to more radical state controls and taxes. Wall Street and small town and midwestern bankers could agree that a conservative plan for financial reorganization would be preferable to demands by some Progressives for public control of banking. In the new public util-

Lincoln Steffens (left), muckraking journalist: "If it was privilege that caused what we called evil, it was privilege that had to be dealt with, not men. . . . To shift our votes from one to another of the two political parties, both of which are organized to serve the privileged or the privilege-seekers, was folly." (*Brown Brothers*)   Ida Tarbell (center), whose exposure of the Standard Oil Company earned her the reputation of a muckraker—much to her discomfort: "My conscience began to trouble me. Was it not as much my business as a reporter to present this [the favorable] side of the picture as to present the other? . . . The public was coming to believe . . . that the only hope was in destroying the system." (*Library of Congress*)   Upton Sinclair (right), socialist journalist whose exposure of conditions in the meatpacking plants caused a public uproar and led to demands for reform: "I realized with bitterness that I had been made a celebrity, not because the public cared anything about the workers, but simply because the public did not want to eat tubercular meat." (*Culver Pictures*)

ities that supplied services to the cities, executives sometimes asked for government regulation to avoid municipal ownership.

The effectiveness of business groups in exploiting the reform spirit to protect and consolidate their economic gains has been called "the triumph of conservatism" in the Progressive era. Federal regulation of industry, for example, came partly in response to the demands of businessmen who not only helped to write the legislation, but made certain that the regulatory commissions would be staffed with people favorable to their interests. The net effect of many of these reforms was to stabilize the industries without making competition any freer. At the same time, the public clamor for reform had been appeased.

The Muckrakers

To Progressives, disclosure of social and political evils was critical to the success of their efforts. If only the facts were known, the people would demand action. The new muckraking magazines and books supplied the facts in abundance. They exposed malpractices everywhere: in city, state, and national government; corporations; the medical profession; patent medicines; life insurance; the police; the preparation of food products; the banks. Theodore Roosevelt first pinned the label "muckrakers" on the young journalists who were exposing the worst aspects of American society. "In Bunyan's *Pilgrim's Progress*," he said, "you may recall the description of . . . the man who . . . was offered the celestial crown for his muckrake . . . but continued to rake the filth on the floor." Roosevelt agreed that many of the revelations were true, but argued that their effect was simply to make discontent worse. He felt his own Square Deal and other programs could satisfy the clamor for reform. Muckrakers argued that the American people would not fight for reform until they had been stirred up.

For many years, reporters had written stories of the kind that made the muckrakers famous. What was new after the turn of the century were the popular magazines, heavily illustrated and selling for as little as 10 cents, that provided research funds and nationwide audiences. Even such conservative magazines as the *Ladies' Home Journal* and *The Saturday Evening Post* were forced to publish muckraking articles in order to compete with *McClure's*, *Cosmopolitan*, *Everybody's*, *Arena*, and *Hampton's*, all offering outlets to writers and journalists exposing the shortcomings of American society. Between 1903 and 1906, *McClure's* circulation rose from 370,000 to more than 750,000; *Hampton's*, from 13,000 to 440,000.

Perhaps the muckrakers' most sensational accomplishment was Lincoln Steffens' series on corruption in the cities. Ida Tarbell's almost equally popular exposé of Standard Oil retold the story of the methods by which that huge combine had been built. Charles Edward Russell threw a searching light on the beef trust. Thomas Lawson, a reformed speculator, exposed Amalgamated Copper. Novel-

---

NATIONAL HOUSECLEANING

The muckraking magazines attracted the attention of Finley Peter Dunne's satirical character Mr. Dooley, the Irish saloonkeeper, and Mr. Hennessy, his steady customer. Despite the uproar created by the muckraking revelations, Mr. Dooley doubted there would be a social upheaval.

"It looks to me," said Mr. Hennessy, "as though this counthry was goin' to th' divvle."

"Put down that magazine," said Mr. Dooley. "Now d'ye feel betther? I thought so. But I can sympathize with ye. I've been readin' thim mesilf. Time was whin I sildom throubled thim. . . . But now whin I pick me fav'rite magazine off th' flure, what do I find? Ivrything has gone wrong. . . . Graft ivrywhere. 'Graft in th' Insurance Comp'nies,' 'Graft in Congress,' 'Graft in th' Supreem Coort,' 'Graft be an Old Grafter,' 'Graft in Lithrachoor,' be Hinnery James. . . . An' so it goes, Hinnissy, till I'm that blue, discouraged an' broken-hearted I cud go to th' edge iv th' wurruld an' jump off. It's a wicked, wicked, horrible place, an' this here counthry is about th' toughest spot in it. Is there an honest man among us? If there is throw him out. He's a spy. Is there an institution that isn't corrupt to its very foundations? Don't ye believe it. It on'y looks that way because our graft iditor hasn't got there on his rounds yet. . . ."

"Do I think it's all as bad as that? Well, Hinnissy, . . . I've got to tell ye that this counthry, while wan iv th' worst in th' wurruld, is about as good as th' next if it ain't a shade betther. But we're wan iv th' grreatest people in th' wurruld to clean house. . . . An' there ye ar-re Hinnissy. Th' noise ye hear is not th' first gun iv a rivolution. It's on'y th' people iv th' United States batin' a carpet. . . ."

Source: Louis Filler, ed., The World of Mr. Dooley (New York: Crowell-Collier Press, 1962), p. 148.

ist David Graham Phillips wrote for *Cosmopolitan* a lively series of articles called "The Treason of the Senate," exposing that body as a millionaire's club acting for special interests.

Muckrakers offered the public sensational disclosures rather than solutions to deal with the abuses they described. Few had any real quarrel with the basic economic institutions, only with the way some people abused them. "We muckraked," Ray Stannard Baker recalled, "not because we hated our world, but because we loved it. We were not hopeless, we were not cynical, we were not bitter." Although a Socialist rather than a muckraker, Upton Sinclair wrote the most devastating exposé of the era in his novel *The Jungle* (1906).

Having lived among meatpacking workers in Chicago during their 1904 strike, Sinclair described working conditions in the stockyards, corruption in politics and society, and the day-to-day lives of the lower-class victims. But neither his call for Socialist revolution nor his treatment of the working class affected the public nearly as much as the graphic account of how meat was handled and packaged before it reached the stores:

There would be meat that had tumbled out on the floor, in the dirt and sawdust, where the workers had tramped and spit uncounted billions of consumption germs. There would be meat stored in great piles in rooms; and the water from leaky roofs would drip over it, and thousands of rats would race about on it. It was too dark in these storage places to see well, but a man could run his hand over these piles of meat and sweep off handfuls of the dried dung of rats. These rats were nuisances, and the packers would put poisoned bread out for them, they would die, and then rats, bread, and meat would go into the hoppers together.

The book prompted several investigations of the meatpacking industry (which essentially confirmed Sinclair's findings), and led to the passage of the Meat Inspection Act and the Pure Food and Drug Act. To a bitter Upton Sinclair, who had aimed at the hearts rather than the stomachs of Americans, the people had ignored the real theme and message of his book: "I had not been nearly so interested in the condemned meat as something else, the inferno of exploitation."

PROGRESSIVISM IN POLITICS: LOCAL, STATE, NATIONAL

If the revelations of the muckrakers were to be translated into action, Progressive reformers needed to detach government at all levels from the special interests and make it more responsive to the public. Until that had been done, they could not, for example, expect to improve living conditions for slum dwellers, eliminate child labor, regulate the working hours and conditions of women workers, and enforce safety regulations in factories.

The sheer complexity of economic and political life in the early twentieth century often frustrated reform efforts. One of the effects of the Meat Inspection Act and the Pure Food and Drug Act, for example, was to make it difficult for small businesses to meet the new standards. Control of the industry was thus concentrated in the hands of fewer meat packers and drug companies. Attempts to eradicate "boss" and machine rule in the cities required Progressives to compromise between greater political participation and efficiency in government. Social reformers could expect resistance in the legislative bodies, which modified their proposals, and in the courts, which often weakened their legislative achievements. But the reformers persisted. If frustrated on a day-to-day basis, they remained confident of ultimate victory. And the new attitudes and policies they introduced eventually worked themselves into the political bloodstream and became permanent features of American government.

City Politics

By the turn of the century, municipal reform efforts had been going on for almost fifty years. The problems of corruption, inefficiency, and special privilege seemed worst on the local level, and so the cities were among the first objects of Progressive attack. The records of mayors like Samuel M. Jones of Toledo and Tom L. Johnson of Cleveland showed how much could be accomplished simply by the time-honored practice of throwing the rascals out.

While Johnson was making a fortune in street railways in Indianapolis, Detroit, and Cleveland, he saw the effects of bossism at first hand. Elected mayor of Cleveland in 1901, he won reelection three times and served until 1909. To Johnson, democracy meant public involvement. In order to interest the electorate in its own welfare, he held public meetings in a huge circus tent. And Johnson persuaded good men to work in city government. Lincoln Steffens, the best-informed and severest critic of American city life, called Johnson the "best mayor of the best-governed city in the United States."

In neighboring Toledo, Samuel M. (Golden Rule) Jones ruled from 1899 until his death in 1904. He went beyond reform to the reorganization of society on a "collective" basis, to the establishment of the "Cooperative Commonwealth, the Kingdom of Heaven on Earth." He opened free kindergartens, free playgrounds, and free golf courses; and he organized free concerts. One of his major concerns became police work, so central to the problems of the poor. He substituted light canes for the heavy clubs carried by patrolmen and stopped the system of arrests on suspicion and the jailing of people without charging them. His enemies attacked him for his "laxity" in law enforcement. When they persuaded the state legislature in 1902 to create a police commission appointed by the governor to administer the Toledo police department, Jones fought and won in the Ohio supreme court.

Many Progressives were reluctant to depend on the chance availability of good and energetic men like Johnson and Jones. They wanted institutional safeguards as well. This meant changing the structure of municpal government, removing it from state control through "home rule" charters, and creating a permanent professional staff to run the city on a nonpartisan basis.

It took a hurricane and tidal wave in Galveston, Texas, in 1900 to point a way. Politicians who made up the city council so botched the administration of relief and reconstruction that in its place, in 1901, the state appointed a five-man commission of experts. This commission did so well in rebuilding the city, restoring its credit, and rehabilitating services that Galveston kept it to run the government.

Progressives elsewhere soon adopted the Galveston system. By 1914, over 400 American cities, most of them small or middle-sized, had adopted the commission form. By then, however, the administrative experts had proved themselves less than expert in politics. And the contradiction between Progressive objectives of greater democracy and citizen participation on the one hand and nonpartisan professional experts on the other could no longer be ignored. By 1914 most city commissioners were required to run for office.

More changes in the direction of greater democracy followed another natural disaster, this one a flood in Dayton, Ohio, in 1913. Under the system adopted there, political authority was vested in a small body of elected commissioners who in turn appointed a professionally qualified city manager to run the city departments. By 1923 more than 300 cities had adopted this system.

Through the various reforms, the Progressives claimed to have democratized city government. But the evidence might also suggest the contrary. What they had introduced into municipal government was expert management based in part on corporate models. With decision-making centralized in a city manager, commission, or professional staff, city government became more efficient—but not necessarily more responsive. The urban poor, at least, seemed to have enjoyed more influence in city affairs under the "boss" than under the efficiency expert.

The State Governments

No less entrenched than the local bosses were the powerful state machines. Legally, cities are creatures of the states, operating under charters or other limited grants of power from state legislatures. In order to prevent municipal reforms from being undone by the political allies of city bosses, urban Progressives extended their attack to the state machines and the business interests they served.

Perhaps the innovation they expected to be most beneficial was the *direct primary*. Reformers hoped that this device, by leaving the choice of candidates to the people rather than to the party machines, would ensure the selection of abler and more independent officeholders. By 1916 some form of the direct primary had been adopted by every state except Rhode Island, Connecticut, and New Mexico. Several states also adopted the *initiative,* a reform that permitted the public to propose legislation, and the *referendum,* which enabled voters to approve or reject measures passed by the legislatures.

The *recall* of public officers through popular votes, another reform device, received wide support as a means of getting rid of officials before their terms expired. The proposal to recall judges and expose the judiciary to popular feelings frightened conservatives. But many judges were in low repute for having invalidated social legislation. Seven states, all west of the Mississippi, actually passed laws providing for their recall. Nowhere, however, were these laws used.

The Constitution provided for election of United States senators by the state legislatures. Since these legislatures might be controlled by party machines or by private interests, one of the reforms most in demand by Progressives was direct election of senators by the people. The Seventeenth Amendment, passed by Congress in 1912 and ratified by May 1913, provided for this change. But although the reformers succeeded in translating a great many of their political reforms into law, the results often disappointed them. The direct primary, for example, made party funds unavailable to those who wanted to run for office. That seemed to favor wealthy candidates over poor ones. Party bosses also soon discovered how to manipulate the political process despite the direct primary. The initiative and referendum became political devices that often misfired, permitting special interest groups to saddle the public with their pet projects. Recall was used only rarely.

All too often, outbursts of reform lasted only a short time, rising or falling with the enthusiasm of one outstanding leader. The professional, full-time bosses usually outlasted the amateurs; they became somewhat more careful, perhaps, but they were still powerful. The reformers held that their occasional victories might at least prevent the machines from doing greater harm.

Progressives aimed their attack not only at the corrupt state machines, but at business interests. Particular targets were the railroads and other public utilities, which relied heavily on government grants of power and political privilege. Wisconsin, where Robert M. La Follette was elected governor in 1900, provided a model for what could be done. La Follette's first step was to replace his party's strong state machine with a Progressive machine of his own. With expert advice from his "brain trust," he proceeded to please his farm constituents by establishing an effective railroad commission. Within a few years, this commission brought other utilities under its umbrella.

La Follette later agreed that his innovations had not "gone after" the corporations. The point of the reforms, he explained, had not been to destroy the corporations, but to curb their political power and subject them to the same laws as other "persons." One of his most useful measures was taxing railroad property like all other property. La Follette's career as a reformer in Wisconsin carried him to the United States Senate in 1906 and almost to the Progressive presidential candidacy in 1912.

Social Legislation

Much of the credit for achievements in social legislation belongs to Progressive women. Like Progressive groups in other fields, they based their campaigns on solid study and research, wide publicity, and the use of trained lobbyists in state capitals and Washington. Between 1902 and 1914, under the leadership of the National Child Labor Committee, new child-labor laws or amendments to old ones were adopted in nearly every state. Most of these prohibited the employment of young children (often defined as under fourteen), at least for factory work. Enforcement was made simpler in many states by laws requiring school attendance until the minimum working age. Other measures prohibited the employment of minors at night and in dangerous occupations.

In 1916 Congress passed the Keating-Owen Act, which prohibited the shipment in interstate commerce of goods made in factories, mines, or quarries that employed children under specific ages. Two years later, in *Hammer* v. *Dagenhart*, the Supreme Court declared this act unconstitutional on the grounds that it invaded the police powers of the states and attempted to use federal control of interstate commerce to attain unrelated ends. But the state laws survived.

Until 1908 the courts, while permitting state regulation of child labor as part of police power, found that control over working conditions of women infringed upon their freedom of contract. Then, in 1908, in *Muller* v. *Oregon,* the United States Supreme Court reversed its position and upheld Oregon's ten-hour law for women. This was another triumph for Progressive research, reflected in the 112-page brief submitted by Louis D. Brandeis for the state.

Brandeis offered the Court a mere two pages of the usual argument buttressed by "authorities." The rest of his brief consisted of historical, socio-

Child labor, target of progressive reformers. Shown here is a young mill worker in Fiskeville, Rhode Island, 1909. (*Library of Congress, photograph by Lewis Hine*)

logical, economic, and medical facts providing "some fair ground, reasonable in and of itself" on which the Court might find excessively long hours of work for women injurious enough to "the public health, safety, or welfare" to justify limitations. Brandeis's social "facts" swayed even the most conservative justices.

In 1917, on the basis of a 1,000-page brief modeled on Brandeis's, the Supreme Court upheld a law limiting working hours for women to ten a day. In the decision, which Progressives welcomed, the Court found labor legislation necessary for women because a woman's health "becomes an object of public interest and care in order to preserve the strength and vigor of the race." The effect, however, was less than some Progressives might have anticipated. Women found themselves excluded from occupations which required long hours and confined largely to the same menial jobs they had traditionally held.

Insurance covering industrial accidents was another Progressive objective. Under traditional common law rulings, the burden of all the hazards of industrial labor was on the worker and his or her family. To collect compensation for disabling injuries or death on the job, dependents had to go to court—a long and costly undertaking—and prove that the victim had not willingly assumed the risks of the work, that neither the victim nor any other worker had contributed to negligence that may have caused the accident, and that the employer was solely to blame. Under Progressive pressure, states began to adopt public accident insurance plans after 1909. By 1920 all but five states had taken such action.

The Progressives also succeeded in establishing a certain amount of public responsibility for the support of children and old people. States had always provided public almshouses, but only occasionally did they offer relief at home. By 1911 state legislatures began to accept the idea that it was far better, where possible, to assist dependent children in their own homes than to place them in institutions. By 1913 eight states, and by 1930 all but four, had adopted mothers' assistance acts to grant financial aid to working mothers. Such acts helped widows with dependent children, as well as families left destitute by divorce, desertion, or incapacity of the breadwinner. In 1914, states began to provide home relief for the aged poor. Urged on by the American Association for Old Age Security, thirteen states passed measures for this purpose during the 1920s. In most cases, persons sixty-five and over became eligible for pensions as high as $30 a month.

Progressive social legislation, especially legislation covering working conditions, was soon challenged, especially by those who would have to foot the bill and who were otherwise affected by bureaucratic interference. After 1900, employer associations, some of them established years earlier to combat unionization, turned their attention to politics. The National Association of Manufacturers (1895) helped to coordinate their activities.

The resistance of business interests to social legislation, and the effectiveness of the propaganda and pressure politics used by those interests, contributed to the decline of progressivism in the states. To satisfy the voters, legislators often found they had no alternative but to enact reform measures. But they did not have to provide funds and machinery for enforcement.

Progressive faith in legislation was often doomed to bitter disappointment. Perhaps that was why some Progressives, like Lincoln Steffens and Charles Edward Russell, eventually turned to socialism. "I couldn't keep it up," Russell said of his muckraking. "It was too fierce, the conditions, the facts, and what was worse, I couldn't understand them. I'd form a theory, then go out and find that the theory was all wrong. I'd set up another theory, see it blow up, and so think again and again, till I couldn't stand it. I joined the Socialist party. I had to have something to believe."

Prohibition

The reform impulse scored one of its greatest and more questionable successes in the Prohibition Amendment, the end of more than half a century of agitation to control the production and sale of alcoholic beverages. Much of the strength of the movement to abolish drinking lay in the rural, fundamentalist South and Midwest. It encountered the heaviest resistance among immigrants and Catholics in the urban centers. But it was never entirely a struggle between urban and rural America, nor did it necessarily pit liberals against conservatives. In the Progressive era it gained urban support, particularly among middle-class women reformers who saw alcohol as a social disease. They also saw its effects on the poor, and resolved their doubts about abridgments of personal freedom in favor of a reform they expected would improve the quality of human life.

Although women had played a leading role in the movement, few of them displayed the aggressiveness that brought such fame to Carry A. Nation of Kansas. Her first husband died of alcoholism just six months after their marriage in 1867. In 1890, when the "wets" of Kansas, encouraged by a favorable Supreme Court decision, opened a strong assault on the state's "dry" laws, Carry Nation organized a branch of the Women's Christian Temperance Union there. She had as little success with persuasion as the WCTU had had elsewhere. Soon she embarked on her personal vendetta against the "joints" that continued to operate more or less openly. Her weapon was her famous hatchet, used to smash saloon windows, furniture, fixtures, and supplies in many Kansas towns. In 1900 she turned her attention to cities, wielding her weapon to such effect that she was arrested some thirty-nine times, usually for "disturbing the peace."

With the formation of the Anti-Saloon League in 1893, the "drys" at last built up an agency strong enough to combat the saloon and distiller interests and the machine politicians associated with them. The Progressive assault on the machines encouraged the temperance advocates to feel their hour had also come. With the Anti-Saloon League lobby keeping the pressure on both major parties, after 1907 state after state in the West and South fell into the "dry" ranks.

The league's first national success came in March 1913, when Congress passed the Webb-Kenyon Act over President Taft's veto. This act prohibited the shipment of intoxicating liquors into any state, territory, or district where they were intended to be used in violation of local laws. The "drys" introduced a Prohibition Amendment in Congress in December 1913. Four years later, when wartime conditions brought resentment against German brewers and there was need for the materials used in distilling, Congress passed the Eighteenth Amendment. It went into effect January 1920. But to the reformers who had expected so much of this amendment, the results proved to be disappointing (see Chapter 27).

PROGRESSIVISM AND THE PARTIES

To Progressive reformers, who looked more and more to the national government to realize many of their objectives, the president had to be a person who shared their principles. That included a commitment to positive government as a tool of social and economic change. In the first two decades of the twentieth century, the three presidents—Roosevelt, Taft, and Wilson—all shared that commitment. The differences among them

pointed up some of the differences in the movement itself.

The Republicans: Roosevelt

If anyone personified progressivism, that had to be Theodore Roosevelt. He was a master politician; he knew how to respond to and manipulate public sentiment; and he had a dramatic flair that had long been missing from the presidency. His identification with the outdoors, his relentless pursuit of the "strenuous life," his exploits in the Spanish-American War, and his colorful style excited the public.

To conservatives and liberals, Roosevelt was a paradox. Although he came to symbolize Progressive reform, he was often a reluctant reformer. He made no effort to hide his dislike for the men and women who made up the radical and labor movements of his time. But like many Progressives, he saw the need to confront the abuses of the social and industrial system and to adopt reforms that would satisfy public fears and demands. As he once told a group of business leaders, he wanted to see "radicalism prosper under conservative leadership" in such a manner "that the progressive people will not part company with the bulk of the moderates."

A Republican by family tradition, an aristocrat by temperament, Roosevelt had once flirted with Mugwumpery. His love of power as well as his

Theodore Roosevelt. (*Brown Brothers*)

common touch, however, kept him "regular" enough for McKinley to appoint him assistant secretary of the navy just before the Spanish-American War. His feats as the Rough Rider added to his popularity, and in the fall of 1898 he was elected governor of New York with full party support.

He soon showed himself so independent of the Republican machine, however, that the state boss, "Tom" Platt, determined that in the election of 1900 he would bury Roosevelt in the vice-presidency. This strategy worked, and yet it worried Mark Hanna. "Don't you realize," he cried, "that there's only one life between this madman and the White House?" In September 1901, when an assassin shot McKinley, the "one life" was removed from Roosevelt's path.

Roosevelt and Big Business

Not since the days of Andrew Jackson had the White House been occupied by a president so devoted to the expansion of the role of the chief executive. But where Jackson used his position to strengthen states' rights, Roosevelt used the presidency to build federal power. In confronting private power, however, Roosevelt was always cautious. His attack on the trusts was a case in point. Despite his speeches, Roosevelt aimed not at breaking up the trusts, but at satisfying public concern about corporate power. On March 10, 1902, he ordered Attorney General Philander C. Knox to bring suit under the Sherman Antitrust Act to dissolve the Northern Securities Company. This was the company created by the country's greatest bankers to combine the holdings of the country's greatest railroad barons.

So stunning was Roosevelt's attack that J. P. Morgan himself went to Washington to find out what the president had in mind. Two years later, the Supreme Court by a 5 to 4 vote gave its verdict: The Northern Securities Company must be broken up. The company's directors gained their consolidation goals by other means, but this did not hurt the president's public or self-image. The decision, he said, was "one of the great achievements of my administration. The most powerful men in this country were held to accountability before the law."

The *Northern Securities* verdict was followed in 1905 by that in *Swift & Company* v. *United States,* breaking up the beef trust. In this case the Court reversed its decision of ten years before in the *U.S.* v. *E. C. Knight Company,* disallowing the application of the Sherman Act to manufacturing enterprises. The beef trust prosecution was one of the earliest results of Roosevelt's success in getting Congress, in 1903, to establish a Bureau of Corporations in the new Department of Commerce and Labor. In keeping with the Progressive belief in publicity as a deterrent to antisocial action, this bureau was authorized to investigate and disclose the affairs of interstate corporations.

The beef trust suit had been started on the basis of the bureau's information. Its success led to other prosecutions of such "evil" combinations as the oil trust and the tobacco trust. Despite these actions, the wave of consolidations continued, corporate power remained as strong as ever, the same men remained in control, and competition became no freer. The president had simply given notice that *unfair* combinations would be held accountable for their actions. He wanted to make clear to the American public that the government stood ready if necessary to exert its authority over big capital. Roosevelt also made it clear that big labor was no different from big business.

In October 1902, workers in the Pennsylvania anthracite pits had been on strike for months against conditions in the mines and in the company-owned mining towns. The operators, headed by George F. Baer, the Morgan-appointed head of the Reading Railroad, remained unwilling to listen to the complaints. At one stage in the strike, Baer made absolutely clear the divine right of the class he represented: "The rights and interests of the laboring man will be cared for, not by the union agitators, but by the Christian men to whom God in His infinite wisdom has given control of the property interests of the country." With winter coming and coal bins empty, coal riots broke out in northern cities.

When Roosevelt demanded that the strike be arbitrated, the operators refused until the workers went back to the pits. John Mitchell of the United Mine Workers voiced the workers' determination to stay out until their demands were met. Finally, Morgan and Roosevelt were able to agree on an arbitration commission satisfactory also to Mitchell. The settlement awarded the mine workers a nine-hour day and a 10 percent wage increase that left them only partially satisfied.

The union failed to gain recognition as labor's bargaining agent in the coal industry, and the miners were prohibited from striking for another three years. The public, however, was grateful to the president for the prospect of winter heat, and Roosevelt no doubt felt the coal operators should have been equally grateful. "I was anxious," he recalled, "to save the great coal operators and all of the class of big propertied men, of which they were members, from the dreadful punishment which their folly would have brought on them if I had not acted." After all, as he saw it, he had stood "between them and socialistic action."

In reviewing his intervention in the coal strike, Roosevelt felt he had given a "square deal" to all sides. That phrase became a hallmark of his presidency, and it seemed calculated to overwhelm any opposition to him in the election of 1904.

The Square Deal

Not long after he had ordered the prosecution of the Northern Securities Case, Roosevelt toured the nation and made a "square deal" his principal theme: "We are neither for the rich man nor the poor man as such, but for the upright man, rich or poor." Although such rhetoric was hardly new to politics, Roosevelt's actions in the coal strike and the Northern Securities case appeared to lend some substance to these words. By the 1904 presidential campaign, TR was more popular than ever. He won the Republican nomination without opposition.

Judge Alton B. Parker, the Democratic candidate, proved colorless, and Roosevelt's huge majority (7,623,000 popular votes to 5,077,000) took even him by surprise. President at last in his own right, Roosevelt now pursued a broader reform program on the national level. His major achievements were in railroad regulation, protection of consumers, and conservation of natural resources.

By 1904 the Interstate Commerce Act of 1887 regulating the railroads was practically dead, largely because of the Supreme Court's narrow interpretation of the Interstate Commerce Commission's powers. In 1903, in response to pressure from the railroads themselves, Congress had passed the Elkins Act. This made it illegal for railroads to depart from their published freight rates and made shippers as well as railroads liable for punishment for infractions. The act struck at the practice of rebating, which the railroad companies had come to regard as a major nuisance. The Elkins Act, however, failed to give the Interstate Commerce Commission any power to fix rates, which was what farmers and other shippers wanted.

Roosevelt now prodded Congress to strengthen and enlarge the commission's powers. In response, in 1906 Congress passed the Hepburn Act. The commission had been able to order alterations in railroad rates, but the roads did not have to comply until the courts ordered them to do so. Under the Hepburn Act, the commission was authorized to set maximum rates when complaints from shippers were received and to order the roads to comply within thirty days. The roads might still go to court; but in the meantime the new rates were to be in force. Within two years, shippers made more than 9000 appeals to the commission, and a great many rates were revised downward. With the Hepburn Act, Roosevelt also felt he had helped to blunt the demand for government ownership of the railroads.

In his annual message to Congress in December 1905, Roosevelt asked for an act to protect consumers from undesirable adulterants and preservatives used in food packaging. His request was made on the basis of investigations conducted by Dr. Harvey W. Wiley, a chemist in the Department of Agriculture, and by other scientists. These had shown that adulterants and preservatives were being widely used in canned foods. The packing interests naturally fought TR's proposal. But in June 1906, Congress passed the first federal meat inspection law. In the same year, it enacted a Pure Food and Drug Act, in response to Samuel Hopkins Adams's muckraking exposure of the patent medicine industry and its misleading advertising. This law did not ensure full protection for consumers, but it attacked some of the worst abuses and prepared the way for stricter regulation later on.

As an amateur naturalist and an outdoor person with a taste for natural beauty, Roosevelt took an early interest in conservation. Under the Forest Reserve Act, which had been passed in 1891, he set aside almost 150 million acres in Alaska and the Northwest in order to give the United States Geological Survey a chance to study mineral and water resources in those areas. He turned over the supervision of the national forests to the secretary of agriculture, who put a professional conservationist, Gifford Pinchot, in charge.

The "good times" that had helped to sustain the Roosevelt presidency and Progressive reform received a rude jolt in 1907 when a financial panic, brought on by speculation and mismanagement, forced a number of New York banks to the wall. Anxious to avoid a long depression, Roosevelt compromised his earlier position that the federal government could always assert its authority over large corporations. When industrialists and Wall Street representatives advised him that business would recover sooner if he permitted the United States Steel Corporation to acquire control of the Tennessee Iron and Coal Company, a firm whose shaky securities were held by many shaky brokerage houses, Roosevelt nervously approved. Whether his action saved the country from a business collapse remains doubtful.

Although Wall Street and business chose to blame the panic on Progressive reforms that were undermining the confidence of the financial community, what happened should have pointed up the need for reform of the business and financial community. Roosevelt suggested as much the next year when he called for regulation of the stock market and interstate corporations and for personal income and inheritance taxes.

But Roosevelt would not be in a position to push these ideas from the White House. The day after the election of 1904, he had announced he would not seek a third term. As the 1908 campaign neared, Roosevelt stood well enough with his party to name its next candidate, his friend William Howard Taft of Ohio, the first civil governor of the Philippines and Roosevelt's secretary of war since 1904. The president also stood well enough with the people to put Taft over. The Democrats in 1908 returned to William Jennings Bryan, but Progressive reforms under Roosevelt left Bryan issueless. Taft swept in with a vote of 7,679,000 to 6,409,000; his margin in the electoral college was 321 to 162.

Taft and Progressivism

Like Roosevelt, Taft recognized the need for social legislation and regulation of the trusts. He supported Roosevelt's Square Deal. He shared Roosevelt's ideas on most questions, and he fully expected to follow Roosevelt's policies. But he was not Roosevelt. He had no charismatic qualities. He had none of the flair of Roosevelt. His administrative skills could not make up for his lack of political skills. His loyalty to the party was not enough to hold the party together. And Taft himself helped to bring the split in party ranks when he chose to raise an issue Roosevelt had wisely evaded—the protective tariff.

By 1908, the call for a reduction of tariff duties reflected both urban and rural concern over the steadily rising cost of living. By protecting the trusts from foreign competition, the tariff, critics charged, forced the public to pay higher prices. Responding to pressures within the party, particularly from midwestern Progressives, Taft promised early action. In March 1909, he called Congress into special session to deal with the tariff question. Although Taft may have been genuinely interested in lowering tariff duties, the Old Guard in the party fought as always. Moderate reductions were adopted in the House. But when Nelson Aldrich and his conservative friends in the Senate finished with the measure, it not only failed to reduce the levies, but actually raised them.

Taft had done nothing to stop Aldrich, and this betrayal of a platform pledge so enraged certain western senators that they attacked their own party leaders. They lost the battle, but their revolt shook the Old Guard to its foundations. When Taft, after signing the Payne-Aldrich Act, declared it was the best tariff ever, he shocked the Republican rank and file as well.

With the Republican party increasingly divided between the Old Guard and Progressives, the battle shifted from the tariff issue to the sweeping powers exercised in the House by the Speaker, Joseph G. (Uncle Joe) Cannon, who had repeatedly blocked consideration of reform legislation. Taft backed the Old Guard; Roosevelt indicated his sympathy for the rebels; and the rebels won when they got enough votes to restrict the Speaker's appointive power. They followed up this victory with new railroad legislation that went beyond Taft's wishes.

In the Mann-Elkins Act of 1910, Congress empowered the Interstate Commerce Commission to suspend general rate increases (enlarging the power granted by the Hepburn Act to suspend specific increases) and to take the initiative in revising such rates. A Commerce Court was established to speed up the judicial process by hearing appeals directly from the commission. These terms were in line with Taft's desires. But the Progressives also pushed through a provision forbidding railroads from acquiring competing lines, and added another that put telephone, telegraph, cable, and wireless companies under the commission's control.

What may have remained of Republican unity was nearly wrecked by the Pinchot-Ballinger affair. The trouble began when the chief forester of the Department of Agriculture, Gifford Pinchot, heard that Secretary of the Interior Richard A. Ballinger had agreed to let private interests take over the reserved coal lands in Alaska. Pinchot attacked Ballinger, but Taft chose to believe his secretary's denials. When Pinchot continued the attack, he was removed. Progressives in Congress now investigated the Interior Department and showed that Ballinger, though not guilty of misconduct, had no sympathy with conservation policies. Somehow Taft gained the same reputation.

Taft did not disappoint the Progressives at every turn. Important measures passed during his tenure included the Sixteenth Amendment, which made the federal income tax constitutional, and the Seventeenth Amendment, providing for the direct election of United States senators, both ratified in 1913. He also initiated about twice as many prosecutions under the Sherman Act in his one administration as Roosevelt had in two.

But Taft's two leading cases, against International Harvester and United States Steel, turned out to be worse than failures. The U.S. Steel prosecution, coming after Roosevelt's virtual guarantee of immunity to the corporation, ended hope for reconciliation between Roosevelt and Taft. The Harvester action alienated the company's promoter and director, the former Morgan partner George W. Perkins, who was to become one of Roosevelt's leading backers in 1912.

The Bull Moose Party

Strife in Republican ranks broke into open warfare over Taft's using presidential patronage to build up conservative strength for the congressional elections in 1910. At first, Roosevelt made no move that would publicize his difficulties with Taft. But in August he set out in a swing through the West for a series of speeches in which he endorsed the concept of the "welfare state" under the slogan New Nationalism. In 1911, Republican insurgents helped to form the National Progressive Republican League to promote Robert La Follette.

As governor of Wisconsin, La Follette was the most successful Progressive; as United States senator, he was the most militant. Roosevelt, although pressed to head off La Follette as well as Taft, waited almost a year to make up his mind. After La Follette, worn down by campaigning, collapsed during a major speech early in 1912, Roosevelt publicly announced, "My hat is in the ring." A savage fight followed, and by the time of the Republican convention in Chicago in June, Taft's supporters were in control. Roosevelt and his followers, charging that the president had gained his delegates by fraud, stormed out.

In response to questions about his own physical energy, Roosevelt on arriving in Chicago said he felt "fit as a bull moose." His supporters now hastily organized a Progressive party convention of their own in that city, hoping to send him back to the White House. The delegates adopted a platform calling for the initiative, referendum, and recall, women's suffrage, workmen's compensation and social insurance, minimum wages for women, child-labor legislation, and federal trade and tariff commissions to regulate business.

The Democrats: Wilson

Although pleased by the Republican split in 1912, the Democrats had to mend internal divisions of their own to make the most of their opportunity. Bryan, still a power, helped matters by announcing he would not run again. At the party convention he supported Champ Clark, who had succeeded to the Speakership of the House after the 1910 elections. Though strong in the early balloting, Clark failed to get the two-thirds majority needed for the nomination. Finally, on the forty-sixth ballot, the delegates turned to a political newcomer, the Progressive Democratic governor of New Jersey, Woodrow Wilson.

Woodrow Wilson. (*Library of Congress*)

Fifty-five years old at the time of his nomination, Wilson had little political experience. While president of Princeton University from 1902 to 1910, he had been known as an educational reformer. He proved attractive to the Democratic bosses of New Jersey, who in 1910 were seeking a respectable candidate for governor, preferably one they could control. But when he won the governorship, Wilson broke with the bosses and promoted reforms that earned him Progressive support.

Born in Virginia in an intensely pious community, over which his father presided as Presbyterian minister, he learned his lessons well. The force of moral principle remained very much a part of his character and shaped his view of the world and other people; it was both his strength and his ultimate undoing.

With Roosevelt's third-party candidacy, the stage was now set for a dramatic political showdown within the ranks of Progressivism. Taft soon lagged, and the battle narrowed down to Wilson and Roosevelt and the central issue of the trusts. Louis D. Brandeis said that Wilson was for regulated competition, Roosevelt for regulated monopoly. Wilson held that the business combinations were too powerful to be regulated, "that monopoly can be broken up. If I didn't believe it, I would know that all of the roads of free development were shut in this country." A "new freedom" for the individual was more important than a "square deal" from the government.

In the election, the two overwhelmed Taft, who got only 8 electoral votes. Roosevelt won 88, Wilson 435. Eugene V. Debs, running on the Socialist ticket, won no electoral votes, yet his popular vote of over 900,000 was impressive. Although Wilson's popular vote of 6,293,000 was slightly less than 42 percent of the electorate, the Democratic party captured the House and Senate as well as the presidency. Wilson, with the additional support of a bloc of Progressive Republicans, took office with

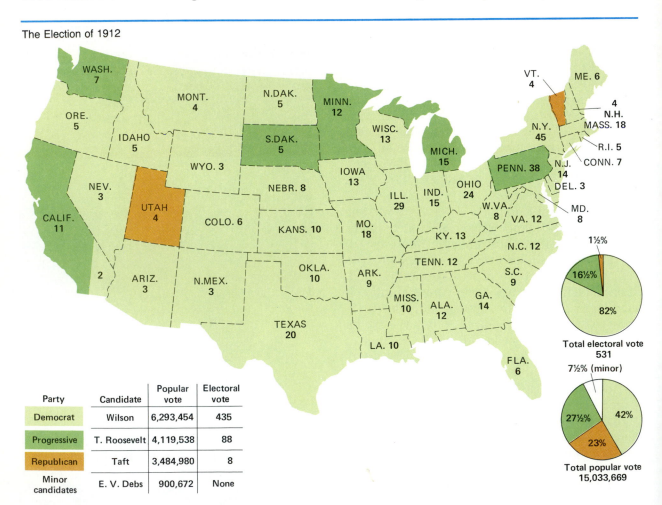

The Election of 1912

Party	Candidate	Popular vote	Electoral vote
Democrat	Wilson	6,293,454	435
Progressive	T. Roosevelt	4,119,538	88
Republican	Taft	3,484,980	8
Minor candidates	E. V. Debs	900,672	None

Total electoral vote 531

Total popular vote 15,033,669

excellent prospects for a Progressive administration.

The New Freedom

Differences on the trust issue may have dominated the election, but other subjects now demanded the president's attention. First on the list was the tariff. In 1913 Wilson called a special session of Congress on this issue. With strong support from Senator La Follette and other Republican Progressives, the Democrats that year passed the Underwood Act, the first satisfactory downward revision since the Civil War. To supply the revenue that presumably would be lost through tariff reduction, this act also placed a tax of 1 percent on personal incomes of $4000 and graduated surtaxes of from 1 to 6 percent on higher incomes.

Financial reform came next. The Panic of 1907 had revealed a poorly functioning financial system and the need for a more flexible currency. Roosevelt's efforts to resolve the crisis had also dramatized the concentration of financial power in the hands of a small group of Eastern investment bankers. A commission set up in 1908 under the chairmanship of Senator Aldrich had reported in favor of establishing a great central bank with branches dominated by the leading banking interests. Progressives led by La Follette responded with proposals for more public control, by removing financial power from the hands of private banking houses and placing it in the hands of experts who would be more responsive to the public.

As finally passed on December 23, 1913, the Federal Reserve Act set up twelve regional banking districts, each with a Federal Reserve bank. The Federal Reserve banks were owned by the member banks of the Federal Reserve system. All national banks were required to join; state banks were eligible. Member banks were required to subscribe 6 percent of their capital to the Federal Reserve bank in their region. On the security of this subscription and commercial and agricultural paper, the Federal Reserve banks would create a new currency, Federal Reserve notes, issued by the Reserve banks to member banks and circulated by them to borrowers. The Federal Reserve system was placed under the direction of the Federal Reserve Board, consisting of the secretary of the treasury and seven other persons appointed by the president.

By 1923, the Federal Reserve system covered 70 percent of the nation's banking. It created a flexible and sound currency and made it available to all sections of the country through the regional Reserve banks. It also left banking a private business under federal supervision and did not really reduce the power of the great New York financial institutions.

To improve the farmer's access to funds, Congress in May 1916 passed the Federal Farm Loan Act, creating a Federal Farm Loan Board of twelve regional Farm Loan banks patterned after the Federal Reserve system. The banks were authorized to lend money to cooperative farm-loan associations on the security of farm lands, buildings, and improvements, up to 70 percent of the value of these assets. Loans were to be on a long-range basis. Interest was not to be more than 6 percent, and profits were to be distributed to the subscribing farm-loan associations.

Like his predecessors, Wilson trusted the regulatory agencies to deal with corporate abuses and punish individual wrongdoers. The first Wilsonian antitrust measure, the Federal Trade Commission Act of September 1914, undertook to prevent rather than to punish unfair trade practices. This act created a five-person Federal Trade Commission authorized to investigate alleged violations of antitrust laws. The commission was empowered to issue "cease and desist" orders against corporations found guilty of unfair practices. If this failed, the commission could bring corporations to court.

During Wilson's administration, 379 cease-and-desist orders were issued, and a few dissolutions of trusts were initiated in cooperation with the Department of Justice. Even so, Progressives soon came to feel that the commission was not using its powers vigorously enough. Like the Interstate Commerce Commission earlier, the FTC gradually became a tool of those it was supposed to regulate.

A second antitrust law, the Clayton Act, was passed in October 1914. It prohibited a number of business practices: price discrimination that might lessen or destroy competition; *tying contracts* (that is, contracts that forced purchasers not to buy the product of competitors); the acquisition by corporations of stock in competing firms; and the creation of interlocking directorates in corporations and banks over a specified size as measured by capitalization. Officers of corporations were made personally subject to prosecution if they violated these provisions. Labor unions as such were not to be considered illegal combinations or conspiracies in restraint of trade. Labor injunctions were forbidden except when necessary to prevent "irreparable injury to property, or to a property right."

The domestic record of Wilson's first administration also included legislation to control child labor (the Keating-Owen Child Labor Act of 1916), to improve the condition of merchant seamen (the Seaman's Act of 1915), and to establish an eight-hour day for interstate railway workers (the Adamson Act of 1916). Like much of the social legislation passed during the Progressive era, however, many of these measures proved difficult to enforce—because of the way they were written, because of administrative neglect, or because of the hostility of the courts. And two groups in particular continued to struggle on their own: women and blacks.

WOMEN AND PROGRESSIVISM

In attacking glaring inequalities in American life, women played a particularly active role in the Progressive movement. By the turn of the century, the General Federation of Women's Clubs, organized in 1889, had grown into a militant organization, especially in the fight for women's suffrage and even for birth control. The discovery that some 5 million women and nearly 1 million children under the age of fifteen were now in the labor force (as reported in the census of 1900) soon pushed the General Federation and similar organizations into new fields of activity and agitation. Although the vote remained the first priority for many women activists, it was viewed not as an end in itself, but as a means for attacking a broad range of social problems.

The Suffrage

Since the 1840s, a small advance guard under the leadership of Elizabeth Cady Stanton, a graduate of Emma Willard's Female Seminary in Troy, New York, had argued that women as well as men deserved the right to vote. In 1869, angered by their failure to win the vote under the Fourteenth Amendment, suffrage groups formed the American Woman Suffrage Association, with Lucy Stone and Julia Ward Howe of Boston at its head. A more radical contingent favoring easy divorce laws and other social reforms soon split off. This group, led

by Susan B. Anthony and Elizabeth Cady Stanton, then organized the National Woman Suffrage Association. By 1898, Wyoming, Colorado, Utah, and Idaho had given women full voting rights. Other states permitted them to vote for certain offices, such as school board members. But no federal amendment was passed, despite agitation throughout the nation.

The role of women in bringing about so many Progressive reforms encouraged them to demand political rights for themselves. One of the strongest arguments for giving women the vote was their participation in business. By 1910 nearly 8 million American women were working, many of them in offices and stores as well as in factories. Some had entered the professions of law and medicine. Their number in education, even at the college level, had soared. Although Taft and Wilson evaded it, women's suffrage became an issue in the presidential campaign of 1912. The election of Wilson, with his conservative southern views on the place of women in society, was a setback. But women went right on agitating, and by 1914 they had won the franchise in eleven states.

Such limited gains dissatisfied many women, who now decided to concentrate on a federal amendment. They prepared a huge petition for Congress with 400,000 signatures and opened a lobby in Washington. Some, like Mrs. Carrie Chapman Catt and Dr. Anna Howard Shaw, preferred gradual education and propaganda. Others, who followed the lead of Alice Paul, patterned their strategy after the English suffragists and engaged in dramatic demonstrations and picketing. Eventually, even Wilson was persuaded to give the women some encouragement, and the women's role in World War I won the suffragists many new male supporters. In June 1919 Congress, by a narrow margin, passed the Nineteenth Amendment, giving women the vote. The amendment was ratified in August 1920; women throughout the country took part in the presidential election that fall.

Feminists and Suffragists

"All feminists are suffragists, but all suffragists are not feminists," Winnifred Harper Cooley correctly observed in 1913. That is, she explained, the "younger feminists" often digressed from their "elders within the fold," refusing to believe that the ballot alone, like some kind of "magician's wand," would solve the problems confronting women in American society. "They claim the vote

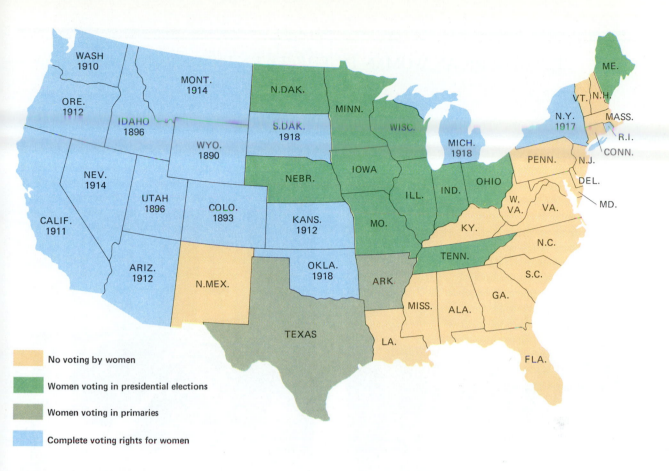

- No voting by women
- Women voting in presidential elections
- Women voting in primaries
- Complete voting rights for women

A FEMINIST MANIFESTO

Although the social revolution envisaged by feminists failed to materialize in the Progressive era, the program they set forth anticipated most of the demands that would be made by women's movements in the 1960s and the 1970s. Winnifred Harper Cooley, a writer and journalist whose mother had long been active in the struggle for the suffrage, outlined such a program in 1913.

The abolition of all arbitrary handicaps calculated to prevent woman's economic independence. . . . The woman of the future—married or single—must be absolutely free to earn her livelihood, and must receive equal pay for equal service. The younger feminists consider that the day is rapidly approaching when to be supported by a man in return for sexual privileges, or mere general housekeeping, or to be paid for motherhood, will be morally revolting to every self-respecting wife.

The opportunity for women to serve in all civic capacities—on municipal, educational, institutional and reform boards, on juries, and in every function by which they can be of service to their own sex and to children.

A demand for a single standard of morality. This is not to be interpreted arbitrarily as meaning either a strictly puritanical standard or an objectionably loose standard. It merely means that there shall be no unjust and persecuting discrimination against the woman offender, when both man and woman offend.

The abolition of white slavery and prostitution. This is only one form of the age-long insistence of man's ownership of woman. Its manifestations are quite as real in the harem, and in some phases of marriage, as in the poor creature who is sequestered, an absolute prisoner, in 'houses' in our cities.

The right to activity of expression and of creating social ideals, quite unhampered by old superstitions. . . . As a matter of fact, public opinion in the future will regard men as quite as essential to the home as are women; and women as quite as essential to the world as are men.

Source: Winnifred H. Cooley, *Harper's Weekly*, Vol. 58 (September 1913), pp. 7–8.

Anna Held. (*Library of Congress*)

An Italian mother carries home work to be finished by the family. (*Photograph by Lewis W. Hine, Library of Congress*)

Shirt waist strikers, New York, 1910. (*Bain Collection, Library of Congress*)

Ladies' luncheon at Delmonico's, 1902. (*The Byron Collection, Museum of the City of New York*)

Conforming to the traditional image of American women, the ladies of Black River Falls, Wisconsin, gather in 1905 for one of their regular tea-talk-sewing sessions. (*Photograph by Charles Van Schaick, State Historical Society of Wisconsin*)

Two black women. (*Library of Congress*)

Mother to Son

Well, son I'll tell you:
Life for me ain't been no crystal stair.
It's had tacks in it,
And splinters,
And boards torn up,
And places with no carpet on the floor—
Bare.
But all the time
I'se been a-climbin' on,
And reachin' landin's,
And turnin' corners,
And sometimes goin' in the dark
Where there ain't been no light.
So boy, don't you turn back.
Don't you set down on the steps
'Cause you finds it's kinder hard.
Don't you fall now—
For I'se still goin', honey,
I'se still climbin',
And life for me ain't been no crystal stair.

Reprinted from Selected Poems by Langston Hughes, by permission of
Alfred A. Knopf, Inc. Copyright 1926 by Alfred A. Knopf, Inc.; renewed
1954 by Langston Hughes.

May Day Parade, 1910. (*Library of Congress*)

A pro-abortion demonstration. (*UPI/Bettmann Newsphotos*)

Suffragists. (*Bain Collection, Library of Congress*)

Emma Goldman. (*Culver Pictures*)

Margaret Sanger. (*UPI*)

as 'wives and mothers,' as 'homemakers,' as 'help-meets,' " she said of the suffragists. "Just why wives should be happier, as *wives*, because they vote, is difficult to see."

Once the vote had been won, feminists argued, the ballot would amount to very little unless women waged equally vigorous battles to improve their legal position, obtain equal economic and educational opportunities, and redefine their roles in the social system. Nor should middle-class women, who dominated the suffrage movement, ignore the oppression of their working-class "sisters," to whom the ballot was far less important than the conditions of life and labor. Under the slogan "Let us be our sisters' keepers," the campaign for improvement in women's working conditions reflected the broadened interests of women's organizations.

Although never as large or influential as the General Federation, both the Women's Trade Union League and the National Consumers' League (under the leadership of Florence Kelley) publicized the exploitation of working women and successfully campaigned for legislation to restrict child labor and protect female workers.

Few working-class women belonged to any of the feminist or suffragist organizations, but they fought their own significant struggles to improve the quality of their lives. The most dramatic protest was "The Uprising of the Twenty Thousand," a general strike by shirtwaist workers in New York City. It was the largest strike of women in the nation's history, involving a rapidly expanding industry in which 80 percent of the workers were female. At the initial mass meeting, Clara Lemlich, still in her teens, offered the resolution to turn the walkouts from several shirtwaist factories into a general strike: "I am a working girl, one of those who are on strike against intolerable conditions. I am tired of listening to speakers who talk in general terms."

The young strikers, most of them between the ages of sixteen and twenty-five, proved themselves as resourceful as male workers in confronting police harassment, mass arrests, violence, and three hard months on picket lines during the winter of 1909. Although the women failed to win a clear victory, they did lay the groundwork for the successful organizing campaign of the International Ladies' Garment Workers' Union. Two years after the strike, a tragic fire at the Triangle Shirtwaist Company took the lives of 146 women and revealed the grim conditions that still prevailed in the industry (most of the fire escapes had been locked).

In the aftermath of the Triangle fire, some feminists and suffragists became more aware of how their organizations and agitation failed to address the needs of working women. Jessie Ashley, an officer in the National American Woman Suffrage Association, scolded the suffragists for their class biases. Contrasting the "handsome parading ladies" in a recent suffragist parade with the "jammed-in subway girls" on their way home from work, Ashley observed: "Only the women of the working class are really oppressed, but it is not only the working-class women to whom injustice is done. Women of the leisure class need freedom too."

Although the women's organizations lent some support to the struggles of working-class women, the question of priorities was never satisfactorily resolved. Some suffragists still insisted that their cause should not be mixed up "with outside interests." Nor did the constructive activities of social workers in the emerging urban ghettos lessen the suspicion with which black women tended to regard the largely white, middle-class women's movement. Many of the suffragists had themselves emerged from the ranks of the abolitionists. But by the turn of the century, the women's organizations had broadened their appeal and constituency to include thousands of southern white women.

To preserve national unity, these organizations were forced to make a series of crippling compromises on the explosive issue of race relations. Like so many Progressives, women reformers were not always able to overcome their own racial and class biases. To some, in fact, female suffrage promised to counter the growing influence of illiterate European immigrants and preserve white supremacy in the South.

After 1920, women would vote in substantial numbers. But men determined their role in society and still demanded conformity to stereotypes. What, then, had the suffrage accomplished? "As long as women are pictured chiefly as wife, mother, courtesan—or what not—defining merely a relationship to men, nothing new or strange or interesting is likely to happen," Florence Guy Seabury observed in 1924. "The old order is safe." Despite the suffrage amendment, the "old order" did, indeed, appear to be quite secure. Women were as reluctant as men to use the ballot as a tool for social change. It was left to a minority of feminists like Crystal Eastman to argue that the suffrage had only clarified the issues, not finished the debate.

Men are saying perhaps "Thank God, this everlasting women's fight is over!" But women, if I know them, are saying, "Now at last we can begin." . . . *Now they can say what they are really after; and what they are after, in common with all the rest of the struggling world, is freedom.*

BLACKS AND PROGRESSIVISM

Progressivism coincided with the worst period of race relations in the nation's history. During the last decade of the nineteenth century, the South moved systematically to disfranchise and segregate its black population. Although the Progressive movement also took root in the South, blacks were excluded. More often than not, Progressive and racist leaders were the same, and the two movements were barely distinguishable. With few exceptions, northern Progressives did nothing about the steady deterioration of race relations throughout the country. North and South had come together in the Spanish-American War, and northerners were beginning to face domestic and international racial problems. At home, there were "new" immigrants from eastern and southern Europe. Overseas, "inferior" colored people had to be assimilated into the American empire.

When the Supreme Court in 1898 went along with Mississippi's disfranchisement clause, *Nation* magazine thought it "an interesting coincidence that this important decision is rendered at a time when we are considering the idea of taking in a varied assortment of inferior races in different parts of the world—races, which, of course, could not be allowed to vote."

The new academic sciences such as psychology and sociology, which had become quite fashionable in intellectual and Progressive circles, tended to reinforce racist assumptions. Progressive-minded historians praised the achievements of Anglo-Saxon civilizations and documented the failure of blacks to become intelligent and useful citizens. For those who did not read learned works, there was the first great motion picture extravaganza and box-office success, *The Birth of a Nation*, which premiered in 1915.

The millions of Americans who flocked to this film would find it hard to forget the graphic portrayals of depraved, lustful, dangerous blacks seeking to impose social and political equality on a prostrate South. "It started people to thinking," one reviewer wrote. "The people of Chicago saw more in *The Birth of a Nation* than a tremendous dramatic spectacle. They saw in it the reason the South wants the Negro to 'keep in his place.' They

saw in it a new conception of southern problems." President Wilson, who saw the film at a private showing in the White House, thought it "history written in lightning." Thomas Dixon, on whose novel the film was based, assured Wilson that the movie was "transforming the entire population of the North and West into sympathetic Southern voters."

Booker T. Washington: Strategy for Survival

Against a background of white violence, disfranchisement, and segregation, Booker T. Washington followed a pragmatic policy of accommodation: "In all things that are purely social we can be as separate as the fingers, yet one as the hand in all things essential to mutual progress." Rather than agitate, black people should accumulate property: "The trouble with the Negro is that he is all the time trying to get recognition, whereas what he should do

Booker T. Washington. (*Brown Brothers*)

is to get something to recognize." Rather than intrude where they were not wanted, black people should look to their own communities: "Let us, in the future, spend *less* time talking about the part of the city that we cannot live in, and *more* time in making the part of the city that we can live in beautiful and attractive." Once black people had proved themselves, largely by measuring up to white middle-class standards, their constitutional rights would be recognized. After all, Washington observed, "There is little race prejudice in the American dollar."

Whites—North and South—supported Washington's ideas. The financial support whites funneled through Washington enabled him to monopolize black leadership and virtually control black colleges, churches, and newspapers. The success of this self-made man, who had risen from slavery, also won for him the admiration of many of his own people. "Wherever I found a prosperous Negro enterprise, a thriving business place, a good home," one reporter observed, "there I was sure to find Booker T. Washington's picture over the fireplace or a little framed motto expressing his gospel of work and service." To a small but growing black business class, most of them self-made people with a vested interest in serving a segregated black community, Washington's emphasis on pride and enterprise, rather than political agitation, simply made good sense.

W. E. B. DuBois: The Talented Tenth

Although Washington remained the dominant personality in black America for nearly two decades, his leadership did not go unchallenged. His principal critics, like W. E. B. DuBois, proved to be black intellectuals and professionals, almost all of them northerners who thought Washington had carried accommodation too far and who resented the enormous power "King Booker" wielded in the black community. Unlike Washington, DuBois had experienced neither slavery, poverty, nor personal struggle, and he readily acknowledged their diverse social backgrounds:

I was born free. Washington was born a slave. He felt the lash of an overseer across his back. I was born in Massachusetts, he on a slave plantation in the South. My great-grandfather fought with the Colonial Army in New England in the American Revolution. I had a happy childhood and acceptance in the community. Washington's childhood was hard. I had many more

W.E.B. DuBois. (*Brown Brothers*)

advantages: Fisk University, Harvard, graduate years in Europe. Washington had little formal schooling.*

Highly regarded as an authority on black social and industrial life, largely because of his research at Atlanta University, DuBois did not openly attack the Washington gospel until 1901, nor did he actively oppose the disfranchisement of the illiterate black farm worker. But he bitterly resented denial of the ballot and other elements of equality to the educated black, "the talented tenth" destined to lead their people.

Between 1901 and 1903, DuBois set down his ideas on the dual heritage of black people: Negroes were at once black and American, inheritors of a national culture, yet exhibiting unique gifts. Racial differences were beneficial; racial inequalities were insufferable. "He would not Africanize America," DuBois wrote in *The Souls of Black Folk* (1903), "for America has too much to teach the world and Africa. He would not bleach his Negro soul in a flood of white Americanism, for he knows that Negro blood has a message for the world. He simply wishes to make it possible for a man to be both a Negro and an American."†

* Quoted by permission of the Knaus-Thomson Organization, Ltd.

† Fawcett Books Group, Consumer Publishing Division, CBS, Inc.

Although DuBois acknowledged that industrial training was important, he thought blacks should also have the kind of liberating education Washington's philosophy deined them. Black advancement, he felt, depended ultimately on civil equality. Protest was essential if blacks were to maintain self-respect.

The Niagara movement, launched by DuBois and his intellectual black friends in 1905, advocated agitation rather than accommodation. But few people, black or white, listened, and the move-ment had little impact. In 1909, a group of white and black Progressives organized the National Association for the Advancement of Colored People (NAACP). As editor of its official journal, *The Crisis*, DuBois became the organization's most militant spokesman. But the NAACP's most practical work from the start was in legal action to protect civil rights and challenge disfranchisement. Although by 1914 the NAACP boasted 6000 members in fifty branches across the country, the principal officers, except for DuBois, were white

Between 1889 and 1941 an estimated 3811 blacks were lynched in this country, frequently with thousands of spectators. (*UPI/Bettmann Newsphotos*)

BLUES FALLING DOWN LIKE HAIL

To listen to Robert Johnson, the country blues singer born in 1911 in the upper Mississippi Delta, is to feel some of the tensions that pervaded his youth. In "Cross Road Blues," he finds himself in a predicament every black youth is taught to avoid. He is at a rural crossroads, trying to flag a ride. Night is approaching, he is in a place he should not be, where no one knows him, and where the common expression is: "Nigger, don't let the sun go down on you here." The crossroads are also well known in blues lore as the place where aspiring musicians make their deal with the Devil. In "Hell Hound on My Trail," Johnson conveys a similar sense of terror and paranoia, both grounded in the day-to-day experiences of southern blacks in the early twentieth century.

Cross Road Blues

I went to the crossroads, fell down on my knees.
I went to the crossroads, fell down on my knees.
I asked the Lord above, have mercy, save poor Bob if
you please.
Uumh, standing at the crossroads I tried to flag a
ride.
Ain't nobody seem to know me, everybody pass me
by.

And the sun going down, boys, dark gone catch me
here.
Uumh, oh dark gone catch me here.
I haven't got no loving sweet woman, that love will
be near.
You can run, you can run, tell my friend poor Willie
Brown.
You can run, tell my friend, poor Willie Brown
Lord, that I'm standing at the crossroads, babe,
I believe I'm sinking down.

Hell Hound on My Trail

I got to keep moving, I got to keep moving
blues falling down like hail
blues falling down like hail

Uumh, blues falling down like hail
blues falling down like hail

And the days keeps on 'minding me,
there's a hellhound on my trail,
hellhound on my trail,
hellhound on my trail.

Source: Robert Johnson: King of the Delta Blues Singers (Columbia Records, CL-1654).

---

liberal reformers. The appeal of the organization was largely to college-educated, professional blacks. Its following among the great mass of working-class blacks remained minimal.

Betrayal of Expectations

Despite their differences over strategies, priorities, and the value of agitation, DuBois and Washington both urged black people to cultivate middle-class virtues: thrift, sobriety, orderliness, cleanliness, and morality. To DuBois, "The day the Negro race courts and marries the savings-bank will be the day of its salvation." To Washington, "It is not within the province of human nature, that the man who is intelligent and virtuous, and owns and cultivates the best farm in his county, shall very long be denied the proper respect and consideration."

Contrary to their expectations, however, economic advancement failed to stop the wave of lynchings and riots that took such a dreadful toll of black lives. Even Washington had to concede in 1904 that "the custom of burning human beings has become so common as scarcely to excite interest." What Washington must have found difficult to comprehend was the fact that blacks who proved themselves economically often generated white fear and resentment rather than applause. When white mobs took to the streets, as in the Atlanta race riot of 1906, much of the violence fell on the respectable, law-abiding, middle-class blacks—those whites referred to as the "uppity, aloof, smart-ass niggers."

Politically, frustration confronted DuBois when he tried to make a choice in the 1912 election among Roosevelt, Taft, and Wilson. Neither Roosevelt nor Taft had shown any particular regard for the rights of blacks. Both had gone out of their way, in fact, to demonstrate their feeling for the white South. Although DuBois preferred Debs, the Socialist candidate, he finally cast his ballot for Wilson:

Wilson is a cultivated scholar and he has brains. We have, therefore, a conviction that Mr. Wilson will treat black men and their interests with foresighted fairness. He will not advance the cause of an oligarchy in the South, he will not seek further means of "jim crow" insult, he will not dismiss black men wholesale from

The words *lynch, lynching,* and *lynch law* all refer to a mob's seizing a suspected criminal, often from the hands of lawful authorities, sometimes giving him some sort of unauthorized trial, and then executing him, usually by hanging, sometimes after torturing him in full view of an enthusiastic crowd. This sort of lynching has taken place in the South and on the western frontier. It has been rare in Europe. Lynching reached an epidemic and most hideous form in the decades after 1889, when mobs of whites seized black men suspected of some outrage (often an attack upon a white woman). Yet the term itself originated during the American Revolution. A Virginia planter and justice of the peace, Charles Lynch, presided over an extralegal court that aimed at suppressing Tory activity in his region. At that time punishments were largely confined to seizure of the offender's property, so that the more modern meaning of the word has been considerably expanded to include mob violence as well as illegality.

office, and he will remember that the Negro has a right to be heard and considered.

On virtually every point, DuBois proved to be mistaken. When in 1914 a black delegation registered its outrage over the actions of the new administration, particularly segregation in federal departments, Wilson took offense at their language and all but ordered the black leaders out of his office. Progressivism was apparently for "white folks only."

When President Wilson called upon the American people in 1917 to help make the world "safe for democracy," Francis J. Grimke, a black clergyman, asked: "What kind of a world brotherhood can the United States, with such a man as Wilson at the head of affairs, and the Negro-hating spirit everywhere prevailing in it, represent?"

During World War I, however, some 375,000 blacks were called into military service, and none other than DuBois urged his people to "close ranks" behind the war effort: "If this is our country, then this is our war." If black people entered the war with any expectations, it was apparently the hope that through their participation both the world and the United States might be made "safe for democracy."

SUMMARY

America early in the twentieth century was the America of the Progressives, as well as the America of big business. The middle-class reformers, mostly urban and Protestant, confronted a broad range of problems: conflict between capital and labor, immigration, the terrible slums, corrupt politics. But although all could agree that there were problems to be solved, they did not agree on which to attack first and how. The movement itself was a coalition of different groups with different aims. No group tried to revolutionize society. The basic idea was to correct the evils of the system, but keep the system itself intact.

Business groups in some instances supported reform and exploited it to protect and consolidate their economic gains. Regulatory commissions, for example, were often supported by business, which helped to write the legislation establishing them. But the commissions then became tools of the groups they were intended to control.

Publicity was important for the Progressives, who saw arousing the people as the way to bring pressure for change. All during this period muckraking, the disclosure of social and political evils in the popular press, was part of the Progressive campaign.

One of its first targets was government at all levels. In municipal government Progressives fought for and introduced the idea of the commission form and the city manager. To protect these reforms, Progressives attacked state machines as well. They introduced such innovations as the direct primary, the initiative, the referendum, and the recall. They also pushed to have United States senators elected by the people rather than by the legislatures (the Seventeenth Amendment, ratified in 1913). Business interests, particularly the railroads and the public utilities that depended on government grants and political privilege, were also targets.

In the area of social legislation, Progressives worked

for child labor laws, for laws limiting the hours of work, for industrial accident insurance (compensation), and for public responsibility for the support of children and old people.

Another major Progressive campaign was to control the production and sale of alcoholic beverages and to prohibit drinking altogether. Women played a leading role in this movement. By 1913, it was strong enough to introduce an amendment to the Constitution, which Congress passed and the states ratified. The Eighteenth Amendment went into effect in January 1920 and brought a whole new era: Prohibition, the speakeasy, and large-scale organized crime.

Three presidents during this period shared the Progressive commitment, although all in different ways: Theodore Roosevelt, Taft, and Wilson. Roosevelt moved against big business by using the Sherman Antitrust Act to bring companies to court and to prosecute the beef trust, the oil trust, and tobacco trust. He considered "big labor" the same as big business, and intervened in the Pennsylvania coal strike of 1902. His theme was the Square Deal—justice for all law-abiding citizens, whether rich or poor. During his first full term as president in his own right, from 1904 to 1908, TR pursued a broad reform program at the national level. His major achievements were in railroad regulation, protection of consumers, and conservation of natural resources.

Taft, who took office in 1908, attacked the protective tariff, but had a different vision of reform from many of the Progressives in his own party. Some reforms were passed during his administration—the Sixteenth Amendment, establishing the federal income tax, and the Seventeenth. But some of his actions led to a split in the Republican party and the rise of a third party for the election of 1912. Taft was the Republican candidate; Wilson ran for the Democrats, and TR was the candidate of the Bull Moose party. Wilson won, and now the country got the Democratic version of progressivism.

Among Wilson's domestic achievements were tariff and financial reform to correct abuses in the financial system which had led to the Panic of 1907. A Federal Reserve system, created in 1913, led to a flexible and sound currency and national supervision of banking, which remained a private business. The Federal Farm Loan Act of 1916 created a financial system for farmers like the Federal Reserve for banking. Antitrust laws such as the Federal Trade Commission Act of 1914 and the Clayton Act of the same year continued the policy of relying on regulatory commissions to deal with business practices. There was more legislation to control child labor, to improve the condition of merchant seamen, and to establish an eight-hour day for interstate railway workers.

But like much of the social legislation passed during the Progressive era, these laws were seldom enforced. The Progressives' major accomplishment seems to have been to satisfy public opinion. Very few structural changes were actually made. And not all segments of society were included: women and blacks continued to struggle along on their own. Neither the women's desire for the vote nor black desires for equality of opportunity and civil rights received much attention. Both black strategies—Booker T. Washington's "survival" and W. E. B. DuBois's "talented tenth"—were doomed to betrayal by the continuation of virulent racism, and by lack of interest on the part of the nation's leaders.

Suggested Readings

The spirit and thought of the early twentieth century may best be captured by reading the contemporary literature. Of particular value are the autobiographies of Lincoln Steffens, William Allen White, Robert M. LaFollette, George Norris, Jane Addams, and Emma Goldman, as well as John Chamberlain, *Farewell to Reform* (1932); Walter Lippmann, *Drift and Mastery* (1914); Herbert Croly, *The Promise of American Life* (1909); Walter Weyl, *The New Democracy* (1912); John Spargo, *The Bitter Cry of the Children* (1906); and Ray Stannard Baker, *Following the Color Line* (1908).

The best introductions to this period are G. W. Mowry, *The Era of Theodore Roosevelt* (1958); A. S. Link, *Woodrow Wilson and the Progressive Era* (1954); O. L. Graham, *The Great Campaigns: Reform and War in America 1900–1928* (1971); and J. W. Chambers, *The Tyranny of Change 1900–1917* (1980). In *The Age of Reform* (1955), Richard Hofstadter argued that status anxiety explained the mobilization of the older middle class behind Progressive reform. S. P. Hayes, *The Response to Industrialism* (1957), and R. H. Wiebe, *The Search for Order* (1967), stress how middle-class reformers sought to impose order and efficiency on a society they thought chaotic and fragmented. G. Kolko, *The Triumph of Conservatism* (1963), and J. Weinstein, *The Corporate Ideal in the Liberal State* (1968), emphasize Progressive success in absorbing the reform impulse.

Among the principal studies of Progressive thought are D. W. Noble, *The Paradox of Progressive Thought* (1958), and *The Progressive Mind 1890–1917* (1970); C. Forcey, *The Crossroads of Liberalism* (1961); A. A. Ekirch, Jr., *Progressivism in America* (1974); C. Lasch, *The New Radicalism in America 1889–1963* (1965); S. Haber, *Efficiency and Uplift: Scientific Management in the Progressive Era 1890–1920* (1964); and R. Hofstadter, *The Progressive Historians* (1968).

The revelations of the muckrakers have been anthologized in A. and L. Weinberg (eds.), *The Muckrakers* (1961), and H. Swados (ed.), *Years of Conscience* (1962). S. S. McClure, *My Autobiography* (1914); *The Autobiography of Lincoln Steffens* (1931), and I. M.

Tarbell, *All in the Day's Work* (1939), tell much about the leading muckraker publisher and his star reporters. See also L. Filler, *Crusaders for American Liberalism* (1950 ed.); D. M. Chalmers, *The Social and Political Ideas of the Muckrakers* (1964); and H. S. Wilson, *McClure's Magazine and the Muckrakers* (1970).

The operations of progressivism on a state and local level are examined in R. B. Nye, *Midwestern Progressive Politics* (1951); D. P. Thelen, *The New Citizenship: Origins of Progressivism in Wisconsin 1885–1900* (1972); G. E. Mowry, *The California Progressives* (1951); R. M. Abrams, *Conservatism in a Progressive Era: Massachusetts Politics 1900–1912* (1964); S. Hackney, *Populism to Progressivism in Alabama* (1969); and W. E. Bean, *Boss Reuf's San Francisco* (1952). The party politics of progressivism are the subject of L. L. Gould, *Reform and Regulation: American Politics 1900–1916* (1978), and G. W. McFarland, *Mugwumps, Morals, and Politics 1884–1920* (1975). The Progressive party is examined in G. E. Mowry, *Theodore Roosevelt and the Progressive Movement* (1947).

The biographical approach to progressivism is also rewarding. The chapters on Roosevelt and Wilson in R. Hofstadter, *The American Political Tradition* (1948), are stimulating and controversial. J. M. Cooper, Jr., in *The Warrior and the Priest: Woodrow Wilson and Theodore Roosevelt* (1983), examines the ideological legacies of the two progressive reform presidents. On Roosevelt, the best works, each with its own perspective, are H. F. Pringle, *Theodore Roosevelt* (1931); J. M. Blum, *The Republican Roosevelt* (1977 ed.); and W. H. Harbaugh, *Power and Responsibility: The Life and Times of Theodore Roosevelt* (1961). A. S. Link, *Wilson* (5 vols., 1947–1965) contrasts in view with J. M. Blum, *Woodrow Wilson and the Politics of Morality* (1956). On Taft, see P. E. Coletta, *The Presidency of William Howard Taft* (1973). Principal studies of other political figures include R. Leopold, *Elihu Root and the Conservative Tradition* (1954); J. Braeman, *Albert J. Beveridge* (1971); J. A. Garraty, *Right-Hand Man: The Life of George W. Perkins* (1960); J. M. Blum, *Joe Tumulty and the Wilson Era* (1951); D. P. Thelen, *Robert M. LaFollette and the Insurgent Spirit* (1976); R. M. Lowitt, *George W. Norris* (3 vols., 1963–1978); and L. Ashby, *The Spearless Leader: Senator Borah and the Progressive Movement in the 1920s* (1972).

R. M. Crunden, *Ministers of Reform: The Progressives' Achievement in American Civilization* (1982), is a study of the culture, ideology, and politics of Progressive reform. How the Progressives confronted (or failed to confront) social and economic problems is examined in J. D. Buenker, *Urban Liberalism and Progressive Reform* (1973); S. P. Hays, *Conservation and the Gospel of Efficiency* (1959); R. Lubove, *The Progressives and the Slums 1890–1917* (1962); J. H. Timberlake, *Prohibition and the Progressive Movement 1900–1920* (1963); J. R. Gusfeld, *Symbolic Crusade: Status Politics*

and the American Temperance Movement (1963); O. E. Anderson, Jr., *The Health of a Nation* (1958); W. Graebner, *Coal-Mining Safety in the Progressive Period: The Political Economy of Reform* (1976); A. F. Davis, *Spearheads for Reform: The Social Settlements and the Progressive Movement* (1967), and *American Heroine* [Jane Addams] (1973). On judicial reform, see M. I. Urofsky, *A Mind of One Piece: Brandeis and American Reform* (1971), and J. S. Auerbach, *Unequal Justice: Lawyers and Social Change in Modern America* (1976). On radicalism in the Progressive era, see the assessments of M. Cantor, *The Divided Left: American Radicalism 1900–1975* (1978), and J. P. Diggins, *The American Left in the Twentieth Century* (1973). Studies of the Socialist party in the period of its greatest influence include H. H. Quint, *The Forging of American Socialism* (1953); I. Kipnis, *The American Socialist Movement 1897–1912* (1952); D. A. Shannon, *The Socialist Party of America* (1955); R. Ginger, *The Bending Cross: A Biography of Eugene Victor Debs* (1949); and J. Weinstein, *The Decline of Socialism in America 1912–1925* (1967).

The social history of women is examined in L. W. Banner, *Women in Modern America* (1974); S. M. Rothman, *Woman's Proper Place: A History of Changing Ideals and Practices 1870 to the Present* (1978); W. L. O'Neill, *Everyone Was Brave: The Rise and Fall of Feminism in America* (1969); and C. N. Degler, *At Odds: Women and the Family in America 1776 to the Present* (1980). N. F. Coit and E. H. Pleck (eds.), *A Heritage of Her Own* (1979), is an important collection of essays, as are Gerda Lerner, *The Majority Finds Its Past: Placing Women in History* (1979), and A. F. Scott, *Making the Invisible Woman Visible* (1984). The history of wage-earning women is examined in A. Kessler-Harris, *Out to Work* (1982). The ideology of women activists is examined in A. S. Kraditor, *The Ideas of the Woman Suffrage Movement 1890–1920* (1965). On feminist-anarchist Emma Goldman, see her autobiography, *Living My Life* (1934), and C. Falk, *Love, Anarchy, & Emma Goldman* (1984). On black woman activist Ida B. Wells, see A. M. Duster (ed.), *Crusade for Justice: The Autobiography of Ida B. Wells* (1970). Sex and race as issues in American culture are analyzed in W. H. Chafe, *Women and Equality: Changing Patterns in American Culture* (1977). On the changing status of women, as reflected in divorce and birth control, see E. T. May, *Great Expectations: Marriage and Divorce in Post-Victorian America* (1980); W. L. O'Neill, *Divorce in the Progressive Era* (1967); D. M. Kennedy, *Birth Control in America: The Career of Margaret Sanger* (1970); and L. Gordon, *Woman's Body, Woman's Right: A Social History of Birth Control in America* (1976). The "Uprising of the Twenty Thousand" is described in L. Levine, *The Women's Garment Workers* (1924). R. Rosen and S. Davidson (eds.), *The Maimie Papers* (1977) illuminates the tension between middle-class women reformers and lower-class women immigrants.

See also R. Rosen, *The Lost Sisterhood: Prostitution in America, 1900–1918* (1982). On the work and family life of black women, see J. Jones, *Labor of Love, Labor of Sorrow* (1985).

W. E. B. DuBois, *The Souls of Black Folk* (1903), explores the dilemma of racial identity. On Booker T. Washington, see his autobiography, *Up from Slavery* (1902), and L. R. Harlan, *Booker T. Washington: The Making of a Black Leader 1856–1901* (1972), and *The Wizard of Tuskegee, 1901–1915* (1983). Studies of DuBois include E. M. Rudwick, *W. E. B. DuBois: A Study in Minority Group Leadership* (1960); F. L. Broderick, *W. E. B. DuBois: Negro Leader in a Time of Crisis* (1959); and A. Rampersad, *The Art and Imagination of W. E. B. DuBois* (1976). On black ideology in this period, see A. Meier, *Negro Thought in America 1880–1915* (1963). On lynching, see W. White, *Rope and Faggot* (1929), and J. D. Hall, *Revolt Against Chivalry* (1979). The best history of the Delta blues is R. Palmer, *Deep Blues* (1981).

REMEMBER.
THE FLAG OF LIBERTY
SUPPORT IT!

BUY
U.S. Government Bond

WORLD WAR AND WORLD REVOLUTION

Chapter 26

The incident meant little to most Americans, but it would have great consequences for them and for much of the world. On June 18, 1914, Archduke Franz Ferdinand, heir to the throne of the Austro-Hungarian Empire, was shot and killed by a young Serbian nationalist at Sarajevo in the Austrian province of Bosnia. For more than a generation, the European nations had been living in fear of one another. They had been engaged in an intense competition for world markets and sources of investments and raw materials. As their suspicions and rivalries grew, so did their haste to accumulate arms and allies.

When Ferdinand died, Europe was divided roughly into two camps: the Central Powers (Germany and Austria-Hungary) and the Allied Powers (Great Britain, France, and Russia). Within six weeks, these powerful coalitions were engaged in an armed conflict that would soon engulf the rest of Europe and much of the world—the Great War, or World War I. (Italy remained neutral until May 1915. Then the Allies, in a secret treaty, promised it territory after the war, in exchange for intervention on their side.) The Central Powers and the Allies both sought American support and flooded the United States with propaganda.

Concerned with domestic problems, uncertain of what the European conflict was all about, few Americans in 1914 could have conceived that national or economic interest might force them into the war. When Wilson won reelection in 1916, with his followers shouting "He kept us out of war," he could hardly have imagined that in only five months he would be before Congress to ask for a declaration of war. When the United States entered the European conflict, which then became a world war, Wilson explained the American action in the moralistic language Americans had come to expect from him: "This is the People's War, a war for freedom and justice and self-government amongst all the nations of the world, a war to make the world safe for the peoples who live upon it." Whatever doubts Americans had had about the conflict were now resolved; few dared to question the need to work to ensure an American and Allied victory.

When it came to constructing a peace, Wilson was moved by the same moral considerations. What sustained him in his prosecution of the war and in his mission as a peacemaker was the conviction that moral principle would triumph and the world would be made safe for democracy. But the world after the Great War was far different from that of 1914. The Bolshevik Revolution in Russia, social upheavals elsewhere, colonial and nationalist stirrings complicated and frustrated his peace mission. He would be victimized not only by the legacy of Europe's long history of national jealousies, but by his own self-righteousness and sense of mission. In the end, the Allies denied him the "just" peace he had sought. The Senate denied him the means by which he had hoped to impose a kind of Progressive order on humankind. And the American people seemed to have grown weary of his rhetoric and his crusade. ■

TOWARD INTERVENTION

The preoccupation of American leaders with world power since the Spanish-American War could not hide the fact that in many ways the United States was a provincial nation in 1914. Most Americans were startled by the outbreak of fighting in Europe. When the president, in the early days of the war, appealed to them to be "impartial in thought as well as in act," they saw no reason why they should be drawn into an overseas war they barely understood.

It was not long, however, before the loyalties of the more than 30 million Americans of European birth or parentage became engaged with one side or the other. Wilson personally shared the sympathy of the majority of Americans with the Allies. Since the turn of the century, England had made an effort to keep American friendship. Language and culture joined the educated classes of both countries; trade and finance, although marked by prewar competition and wartime jealousies, also united the British and American business communities. A somewhat vaguer American enthusiasm for France dated back to the days of Lafayette and French help during the War for Independence. Belgium drew sympathy as Germany's first victim—a small, neutral nation overrun by German armies seeking to outflank the French.

In the propaganda battle for the hearts and minds of Americans, the Allies clearly had the advantage. Allied propagandists turned the conflict into a war to preserve the basic values of civilization from the German Hun. The martyrdom of Belgium confirmed in the minds of most Americans the belief that the German government was the wrongdoer. The war at sea also favored Allied public relations. The blockade of Central Europe brought hunger and malnutrition to women and children in 1916, but such slow cruelty was hard to dramatize. The German submarine, on the other hand, evoked shocking images of ships lost at sea with no chance for survivors. That warfare took on added significance when it threatened to undermine the American economy.

The Economy and Freedom of the Seas

When war broke out in Europe in 1914, the disruption of international trade and exchange threatened the United States with an economic depression. The Allied blockade so interfered with American trade with the Central Powers that it fell in value from almost $170 million in 1914 to virtually nothing in 1916. But the Allies looked to the United States for manufactured goods and food, the British Navy controlled the seas, and in 1914 and 1915 orders poured into the United States. American trade with the Allies soared from $825 million in 1914 to about $3.2 billion in 1916. The surge rescued the economy from a recession and started a boom that lasted until 1919.

Even more important was the transformation of the United States from a debtor to a creditor nation. The large amounts of American bond issues and corporate securities held by British investors were sold to pay for war materials. To finance further buying, on which Allied success in the war depended, the British and their friends had to borrow. The State Department discouraged American bankers from making loans to Allied governments, for fear the American stake in an Allied victory would become so great it would draw the country into war. To grant loans to any of the powers, Secretary of State Bryan informed J. P. Morgan, would be "inconsistent with the true spirit of neutrality." Wilson agreed.

But in June 1915, with Allied gold and dollar resources nearly gone, the administration reversed its position. Secretary of State Lansing, who had replaced Bryan, phrased the problem appropriately: "Can we afford to let a declaration as to our conception of the 'true spirit of neutrality' made in the first days of the war stand in the way of our national interests which seem to be seriously threatened?" To maintain American prosperity, Secretary of the Treasury William G. McAdoo wrote to the president, "we must finance it." By April 1917 loans to Allied governments exceeded $2 billion.

The United States, then, despite its neutrality, came to have an enormous stake in the Allies' ability to pay for the goods and loans they acquired. The United States had become in effect the principal source of supplies of the Allied Powers. This was not the work of a small group of American bankers and munitions makers, but reflected the desire of large numbers of American businessmen and farmers to profit from the war needs of the Allies and to make up for the loss of certain peacetime markets. Nor did Americans believe that this trade compromised their neutrality; on the contrary, interference with that trade was an unacceptable violation of neutrality.

To Wilson, the rights of neutrals were fully protected under international law, including the right to engage in trade with a belligerent power. He expected the nations involved in the war to respect those rights. To the European powers, in the middle of a struggle for survival, modern methods of warfare had made much of international law obsolete. Wilson soon found himself in conflict with both sides over the rights of neutral carriers. One of the earliest disputes with Britain arose over the definition of *contraband*—that is, goods that in international law may not be supplied by a neutral to one belligerent without risk of seizure by another. The British redefined contraband to include *all* articles of importance, including foodstuffs, that might give indirect aid to the enemy.

The liberties the British took with the traditional right of *visit and search* caused additional friction. Under international law, a belligerent vessel had the right to stop and search a neutral merchant ship for contraband and release it if none was found or send it to a prize court for legal action if contraband was discovered. The British insisted that the task of searching large modern vessels had grown too complicated for the usual procedure to be observed any longer. They often took neutral vessels to port for a thorough examination, thereby imposing costly delays on American ships. A third source of trouble was Britain's blockading not only enemy ports, but neutral ports near enough to Germany to serve as entry points to German markets.

In November 1914, the British declared the entire North Sea a military area and mined it so thoroughly that no neutral vessel could cross it without first receiving British directions on how to get through the mined zones. This again was a radical departure from international practice. To all complaints, Britain replied that it was fighting for its life and would not be bound by laws made under conditions now obsolete. If the United States had chosen to challenge the British action by sending its ships unescorted into the North Sea, no doubt American ships would have been sunk. But the Wilson administration decided instead to protest the British practice through a formal note. When in the summer of 1916 the London government drew up a list of eighty-five persons or firms in the United States suspected of giving aid to Germany and forbade British subjects to trade with them, Wilson was outraged.

Yet the United States never really considered going to war against the Allies. "England is fighting our fight," Wilson declared at one point. When members of his cabinet urged him to prohibit exports to Britain in 1915, Wilson replied: "Gentlemen, the Allies are standing with their backs to the wall fighting wild beasts."

But despite his sympathy for the British, Wilson did insist that both sides observe the rights of neutrals. In the first two years of the war, the United States found itself protesting British violations more frequently than German violations. The critical difference between British and German violations, however, was the fact that German violations destroyed American lives and property; British violations did not.

The War at Sea

The more deeply the United States became involved with the Allies, the more likely it was that American ships would be affected by the submarine warfare. A submarine could easily be sunk once it surfaced, even by the light deck guns of merchant ships. Submarine commanders therefore could not follow the practice of stopping a suspect vessel, discovering its identity, and providing for the safety of passengers and crew before sending it to the bottom. They had to hit and run. British practices on the high seas were less offensive; they involved legal disputes that could be adjusted at the end of the war. When the German government, on February 4, 1915, announced its intention of establishing a war area around the British Isles where all enemy ships would be destroyed without warning, it was clear that neutral vessels would not be safe.

The Germans offered to change their tactics if the Allies lifted their food blockade. But there was no hope of altering Allied policy in this respect. Early in 1915, when more and more Allied merchant vessels were being sunk, traveling on belligerent ships posed grave danger. The German government issued warnings about that danger, and Bryan, then secretary of state, urged the president to forbid Americans to take the risk. Wilson refused, insisting that American travelers were simply exercising a traditional right.

On May 7, 1915, a German submarine sank the unarmed British liner *Lusitania* with the loss of 1,198 passengers, 128 of them Americans. Although the ship was carrying rifle cartridges and other contraband, the toll of lives dramatized the submarine issue. Some Americans demanded an immediate declaration of war. Wilson chose instead to send three strong notes of protest to Germany. One was so close to a threat of war that Bryan resigned rather than sign it and acknowledge a double standard in dealing with British and German violations of neutral rights.

More sinkings occurred after the *Lusitania* tragedy, and American protests brought German promises that submarine methods would be modified. But when in March 1916 a submarine torpedoed the unarmed French ship *Sussex,* injuring Americans aboard, Wilson warned Germany that if it did not immediately abandon these tactics, "the United States can have no choice but to sever diplomatic relations." This threat drew from the Germans the *Sussex* pledge of May 4, 1916, declaring that no more merchant vessels would be sunk without warning, *provided* that the United States held Britain accountable for *its* violations of international law. By ignoring this proviso but accepting the pledge, Wilson succeeded in forcing Germany to place crippling restrictions on its principal maritime weapon.

The Decision to Fight

Wilson became convinced early in the war that the best way to keep the United States at peace was to bring an end to the fighting. In January 1915 and again a year later, he sent his personal advisor, Colonel Edward M. House, on peace missions to Europe. These visits came to nothing. Discouraged by the failure, Wilson at last gave in to the agitation for preparedness that had been organized by Roosevelt, Lodge, and others almost from the moment Belgium had been overrun. Late in January 1916 he took off on a nationwide tour to promote the preparedness idea. By June, Congress had adopted his proposals for enlargement of the army, the navy, and the merchant marine, and for opening officers' training centers at universities and elsewhere. Plans also were made for industrial mobilization.

In taking these steps, Wilson took over what might have become a useful Republican issue in the 1916 presidential campaign. Although some Progressives felt that much-needed domestic reforms were being sacrificed to military preparedness, they were few in number, even in the Progressive party. Urged to accept the Progressive presidential nomination, Roosevelt asked them instead to back the Republican nominee, Supreme Court Justice Charles Evans Hughes. Hughes, he said, stood for the "clean-cut, straight-out Americanism" Progressives themselves admired. This

WORDS AND NAMES IN AMERICAN HISTORY

Nowadays a *running mate* can be someone to jog with. Originally the term was associated with horseracing. But in 1912, the presidential nominee of the Democratic party, Woodrow Wilson, proclaimed about the Democratic candidate for vice-president: "Gov. Marshall bears the highest reputation . . . and I feel honored by having him as running mate." Ever since, the term *running mate* has usually referred to a vice-presidential candidate. The "Gov. Marshall" Wilson referred to was Thomas Marshall of Indiana, probably the most popular vice-president this nation has ever had. He was the first in a century to succeed himself when he won reelection in 1916. He was also a master of one-liners long before that phrase had been invented. As a loyal member of the Democratic party, he announced that "Democrats, like poets, are born not made." In another line, best known to fans of trivia, he said: "What this country needs is a really good 5 cent cigar." In an unanticipated development some seventy years later, the term *running mate* became an interesting bit of awkwardness for Geraldine Ferraro, the country's first woman vice-presidential candidate. During the election of 1984, the advisors of both candidates discussed at length whether they could even put an arm around each other's shoulders in public.

U.S.A.
1917

NORWAY
Oslo
Stockholm

SWEDEN

FINLAND
Indep. July, 1917
Helsinki
Petrograd

Lake Ladoga

ESTONIA
Indep.
Feb. 1918

LATVIA
Indep.
Nov. 1918
Riga

RUSSIA

Riga offensive
Sept, 1917

NORTH SEA

Edinburgh

DENMARK
Copenhagen
Kiel
Hamburg

BALTIC SEA

Memel
Konigsberg

Danzig

LITHUANIA
Indep. Feb, 1918
Vilna

Smolensk

Minsk

Masurian Lakes
Sept, 1914

Tannenberg
Aug, 1914

GREAT BRITAIN
1914

London

NETH.
Amsterdam

Berlin

GERMANY
1914

POLAND
Indep. Nov. 1918
Warsaw
Lublin

Pinsk

Brest-Litovsk

Kiev

Brussels
BELG.
1914
Cologne

Leipzig
Dresden

GERMAN INVASION
AUG-SEPT, 1914

Paris

Mainz

Prague

Cracow

GALICIA

Lemberg

Battle of Jutland
May-June, 1916

Metz

Strasbourg

Rhine R.

BAVARIA
Munich

Danube R.

Vienna

Pressburg

Budapest

AUSTRIA-HUNGARY
1914

UKRAINE

Odessa

FRANCE
1914

LUX.

Berne
SWITZ.

Piave June, 1918

Vittorio-Veneto
Oct-Nov, 1918

Milan

Trieste

Venice

Graz

Genoa

Marseilles

SPAIN

CORSICA

ITALY
1915
Withdrew from
Triple Alliance 1914

Rome

SARDINIA

Naples

BOSNIA

Sarajevo

Belgrade

SERBIA
1914

MONTENEGRO
1915

ALBANIA

Sofia

BULGARIA
1915

RUMANIA
1916

Bucharest

Danube R.

BLACK SEA

Constantinople

OTTOMAN EMPIRE
1914

Salonika

GREECE
1916

Gallipoli

Dardanelles campaign
1915-1916

Smyrna

Athens

SICILY

PORTUGAL
1916

CRETE

1916   Date of entry into the war

———   Maximum advance of the Central Powers

– – –   Maximum Russian advance

••••••   Line of the Brest-Litovsk Treaty Mar, 1918

———   Armistice lines, eastern front Dec., 1917

0   500
Miles

Central Powers   Allied Powers   Neutral Powers

World War I

the Progressives agreed to do, although some were disillusioned enough to vote for Wilson.

The Democrats renominated Wilson on the first ballot. Four years earlier Wilson had been elected only because Republican strength had been split between Roosevelt and Taft. This time, with Roosevelt campaigning for Hughes, it was hard to see how Wilson could win. Hughes, however, straddled the issue of peace and war and failed to excite the voters. Wilson, at the same time, could boast of the *Sussex* pledge, which he had wrung from the Germans while keeping the United States out of war. Wilson's domestic reforms—the child labor law, the eight-hour day for railroad workers, and low-cost loans for farmers—also helped him. But in the end, the election was close enough to hang for the first time on western ballots. Wilson carried California by a mere 4,000 votes and with it enough states in the electoral college to give him a majority of 277 to 254. In the popular vote, he received 9,129,000, to 8,538,000 for Hughes.

Wilson now renewed his attempts to bring the war to an end through mediation. He sent notes asking all the powers to state acceptable terms of peace. When nothing came of this gesture, Wilson followed with another. In a speech before the Senate on January 22, 1917, he announced to the world his own conception of a just and lasting peace and outlined ideas for a League of Nations to maintain it. "It must be a peace without victory," he said, based on the self-determination of all peoples, freedom of the seas, and disarmament. In making this plea, Wilson claimed to be speaking for "the silent mass of mankind everywhere."

Most Americans greeted this speech with enthusiasm. To the Allies, it seemed to be a withdrawal of the informal sympathy they had come to expect from the United States. Wilson's gestures also came at a time when Germany's military fortunes were high. The bloody stalemate that marked the fighting was wearing down the Allies. Within ten days of Wilson's speech, in fact, the Germans felt confident enough to revoke the *Sussex* pledge and strike for victory. On January 31, 1917, Germany announced that its submarines would again sink all vessels on sight, armed or unarmed, within a specified zone around the British Isles and in the Mediterranean. The Germans realized they now risked almost certain war with the United States, but they hoped to knock Britain out by cutting off its food supply before American forces reached the battlefields. They almost won the gamble.

As Wilson had promised, he now broke off diplomatic relations with Germany. He next called on Congress to authorize the arming of American merchant vessels. When a group in the Senate blocked this proposal with a filibuster, Wilson called them "a little group of willful men, representing no opinion but their own" and proceeded to carry out his plan by executive order. Wilson thought he still might avoid war, but several factors made this highly unlikely. Suspicion of Germany grew when in January 1917 British naval intelligence intercepted a message in code from German Foreign Secretary Alfred Zimmerman to the German minister in Mexico, instructing him to propose an alliance with Mexico in case of war with the United States. In return, Germany promised to support Mexico to recover "her lost territory in New Mexico, Texas, and Arizona."

Wilson disclosed the message on March 1 to create further support for his armed-ship bill. Two weeks later, the March revolution in Russia replaced the czarist regime with a provisional representative government, making it easier to describe the war against the Central Powers as a war for democracy and against autocracies. Finally, German submarine warfare in the Atlantic, with three American ships torpedoed in March, clarified the issue in the minds of most Americans as a question of defending national honor; neutral rights and international law obviously counted for nothing. The position of the Allies, moreover, endangered both national security and the American economy. Without American troops, as well as a continuing flow of supplies, a German victory seemed certain.

When Wilson asked Congress on April 2 for a declaration of war, he condemned German submarine warfare as "a warfare against mankind." But he placed the conflict on even higher moral grounds. The United States, by going to war, intended to fight for the liberation of all peoples, including the German people: "The world must be made safe for democracy."

By distinguishing between the "military masters of Germany" and their subjects, Wilson declared that the United States entered the war "not as a partisan" but as everybody's friend—not simply to defend neutral rights, but the rights of all people. On April 4 the Senate voted for war against Germany, 82 to 6. Two days later the House concurred, 373 to 50. Not until December 7, 1917, was war declared against Austria-Hungary.

THE WAR AT HOME AND OVERSEAS

The decision of the United States to join the fighting against Germany came when the Allies were doing badly almost everywhere. Losses in the Russian armies already exceeded a million men, and the Russian people were prepared to oppose any government that would not call a halt to the slaughter. The Bolshevik Revolution in November 1917 took Russia out of the war altogether, permitting the Germans to move men and supplies from the eastern to the western front. Worst of all, the new German submarine campaign was a great success; 880,000 tons of Allied shipping were sunk in April alone.

The United States entered the war in April 1917. Nineteen months later, with Allied and American troops advancing on all fronts, Germany agreed to an armistice. The role of the United States in achieving this victory had been considerable. The American navy almost immediately reduced the amount of tonnage lost to submarines. American ground troops ultimately helped to turn back the German armies. And the continuing flow of American supplies and money sustained the entire war effort.

To make this all possible, the United States needed to mobilize its government, people, economy, and society on a new scale. Americans had to be conditioned to make the necessary sacrifices and commitments. For a nation which had grown accustomed to Progressive ways of thinking, much of this planned effort was only a shift in goals rather than in means.

Mobilization

Even before Congress declared war, thousands of Americans had volunteered to serve with the Allies, and many of them saw the full four years of fighting. When the United States entered the war, the combined strength of the regular army and the National Guard was about 372,000 men, from whom were drawn the officers and noncoms of the new army to be created under the Selective Service Act of May 18, 1917. This act required all men between the ages of twenty-one and thirty (it was later extended to eighteen and forty-five) to register for military service. Registrants were placed in five classes, headed by able-bodied unmarried men without dependents. From this group

(*Library of Congress*)

alone the nation drew all the 2,810,000 men actually drafted, although by the end of the war as many as 4,800,000 persons had been enrolled in the army, navy, and marine corps.

Some experts recommended that the administration finance the war on a pay-as-you-go basis, by taxing wartime profits and earnings. In fact, about half of the nearly $33 billion spent on the war between April 1917 and June 1920 was raised by taxation. The rest was raised by borrowing, mainly through four Liberty Loan drives in 1917 and 1918. Backed by rallies, parades, and posters, volunteers sold the bonds directly to the public rather than to the banking community. Each issue was oversubscribed.

To mobilize the nation's other resources, Wilson created the Council of National Defense, made up of six cabinet members and an advisory commission of seven additional civilians. Under the council's supervision, huge agencies performed specific wartime tasks. The Emergency Fleet Corporation had been created as early as April 1916 to enlarge the merchant marine. The Food Administration,

(*Library of Congress*)

headed by Herbert Hoover, undertook to supply civilians and combatants. The Fuel Administration doled out coal and oil. The Railroad Administration consolidated the nation's railroads and, without removing them from private ownership, operated them as a single system.

In March 1918 the Council of National Defense placed the War Industries Board under the direction of Bernard Baruch, a Wall Street broker, and gave him dictatorial powers over American business. Great savings were effected by planning and the standardization of products.

AFL president Samuel Gompers, on becoming one of the civilian advisors of the Council of National Defense, declared that American workers backed the war, but that he hoped the government would prevent exploitation and profiteering at their expense. Early in 1918, in return for its pledge not to strike, organized labor was assured of the right of collective bargaining, maintenance of the eight-hour day where it existed, and other privileges. A National War Labor Board was created to mediate labor disputes, and a War Labor Policies Board to deal with grievances. Between 1915 and 1917, the number of strikes had tripled and the number of strikers had more than doubled.

Strikes then fell off, while the AFL pushed its membership from 1,950,000 in 1915 to 2,800,000 in 1918.

The wartime demand for labor pushed wages up as much as 20 percent in purchasing power in key military industries and approximately 4 percent overall. At the same time, salaried employees suffered from wartime inflation, losing as much as one-third of their prewar purchasing power.

Businessmen and farmers fared best of all. Baruch's War Industries Board, unwilling to delay production, gave up the traditional practice of competitive bidding and made war purchases on the basis of *cost-plus contracts*. Such contracts guaranteed sellers profits ranging from 2.5 to 15 percent of production costs. By padding costs, some contractors made enough to increase dividend payments and executive salaries and still pile up profits, despite huge taxes.

Large personal fortunes also grew. In 1914, only 5,000 persons reported annual incomes in the $50,000 to $100,000 tax brackets; in 1918, 13,000 did so. Hoover's Food Administration, meanwhile, set such a high government price on wheat and other staples that farmers stretched their resources to acquire more land. Farm operators' real income was 29 percent higher in 1918 than in 1915. Soon after the wartime demand ended, however, the farmers found themselves in deeper financial trouble than ever before (see Chapter 27).

Propaganda and Civil Liberties

Despite the success of the Liberty Loan drives, strong feeling against the war persisted. "We are going into war at the command of gold," Senator George W. Norris of Nebraska charged in a popular speech against involvement. At Canton, Ohio, Socialist leader Eugene Debs attacked the war in words that would send him to a federal prison: "The master class has always declared wars; the subject class has always fought the battles. The master class has had all to gain and nothing to lose, while the subject class has had nothing to gain and all to lose—especially their lives." Evidence of antiwar sentiment appeared in the strong showing of the Socialist party in municipal elections in 1917. In some communities, Socialists won as much as 30 or 40 percent of the vote.

To mobilize public thinking, Congress, within two weeks of the declaration of war, established the Committee on Public Information. Wilson named George Creel, once a prominent muck-

WOMEN'S WORK

Although wartime work was viewed as a patriotic duty, not as a permanent replacement of men in industrial jobs, some women managed to hold on to their positions after the war and derived considerable satisfaction from the additional income and independence. In the 1920s, Robert and Helen Lynd examined "Middletown" (Muncie, Indiana) and interviewed a forty-two-year-old woman, married to a pipefitter and the mother of two high school boys. She worked six days a week as a cleaning woman in a public building.

I began to work during the war, when every one else did; we had to meet payments on our house and everything else was getting so high. The mister objected at first, but now he don't mind. I'd rather keep on working so my boys can play football and basketball and have spending money their father can't give

them. We've built our own home, a nice brown and white bungalow, by a building and loan like every one else does. We have it almost all paid off and it's worth about $6,000. No, I don't lose out with my neighbors because I work; some of them have jobs and those who don't envy us who do. I have felt better since I worked than ever before in my life. I get up at five-thirty. My husband takes his dinner and the boys buy theirs uptown and I cook supper. We have an electric washing machine, electric iron, and vacuum sweeper. I don't even have to ask my husband any more because I buy these things with my own money. . . .

Source: Robert and Helen Lynd, *Middletown* (New York: Harcourt Brace Jovanovich, 1929), pp. 28–29. Copyright 1929 by HBJ; renewed 1957 by Robert and Helen Lynd. Photograph from the National Archives.

raker, to head it. Creel enlisted journalists, scholars, and clergy to convince the country that the Germans were depraved. Although the vast majority of German-Americans accepted the necessity of war once the United States joined the Allies, they became the most obvious targets of abuse. Libraries removed German books and sometimes publicly burned them. Schools dropped the German language from the curriculum. A peak in absurdity was reached by restaurants that renamed sauerkraut "liberty cabbage" and kennels that rechristened dachshunds "liberty pups."

But pacifists, socialists, and left-wing workers suffered the worst repression. Congress made intolerance official by adopting the Espionage Act of June 1917 and the Sedition Act of May 1918. The

Espionage Act set a fine of up to $10,000 and a prison term of twenty years for anyone who interfered with the draft or encouraged disloyalty. The Sedition Act set the same penalties for anyone who obstructed the sale of government bonds, discouraged recruiting, or did "willfully utter, print, write, or publish any disloyal, profane, scurrilous, or abusive language," about the American form of government, the Constitution, the flag, or service uniforms, or "advocate any curtailment of production . . . of anything necessary or essential to the prosecution of the war."

Although President Wilson had proclaimed in his war message "the privilege of men everywhere to choose their way of life and of obedience," he maintained a discreet silence on the widespread violation of civil liberties in the United States. Under the Espionage and Sedition laws, over 1500 persons were imprisoned, including Eugene Debs. Wilson refused to pardon Debs, even after the war had ended. "While the flower of American youth was pouring out its blood to vindicate the cause of civilization," Wilson asserted, "Debs stood behind the lines sniping, attacking, and denouncing them."

But Debs was not the only victim of this curious war for universal liberty and democracy. Several antiwar newspapers lost their mailing privileges, Department of Justice agents conducted illegal raids on antiwar organizations, judges gave harsh sentences to war critics, and patriotic mobs took out their fury in the streets. The House of Representatives voted 309 to 1 not to seat Victor Berger, a Socialist congressman from Wisconsin, because of his antiwar views and consequent indictment under the Espionage Act. "The one and only issue in this case," one congressman made clear, "is that of Americanism."

Only a few Americans protested these abridgements of their fundamental liberties, notably the newly formed Civil Liberties Bureau (the forerunner of the American Civil Liberties Union) under Roger Baldwin. But the bureau found it difficult to publicize its cause or raise funds, and some liberal

World War I: The Western Front

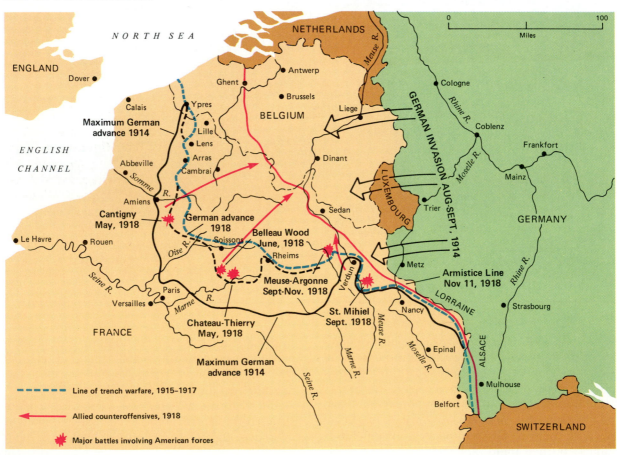

reformers who were sympathetic decided to keep silent. Jane Addams wrote to Roger Baldwin, explaining why she could not sign an appeal for funds: "I am obliged to walk very softly in all things suspect."

The Army in Action

The first American troops, under General John J. Pershing, arrived in France in June 1917 and were fed into the sagging Allied lines largely to bolster morale. When in March 1918 the Germans launched a massive spring offensive, hoping to end the war, about 300,000 American soldiers had reached France and more were arriving every day. By the war's end, of the more than 2 million men who had been carried to Europe, about 1.4 million had become actively engaged, mostly on the Western Front. In April 1918 the Germans had a numerical superiority of perhaps 320,000 on this front. By November, fresh American troops gave the Allies the advantage by 600,000.

Large numbers of Americans were thrown into battle inadequately trained, but they played a decisive role in the last eight months of the war. The Allies hoped to continue to use American troops largely as replacements and to integrate them with French or British units. Pershing, however, fought this policy. He felt the Allies had grown too defensive-minded and that the Americans would be more successful conducting independent operations. The greater part of the American army soon took its place in the lines as a separate force under Pershing's command, subject, after April 1918, to the over-all supreme command of Marshal Ferdinand Foch of France.

Pershing's men faced their first major test when assigned to help repulse a German thrust toward Paris. By May 30, 1918, the Germans had reached Château-Thierry on the Marne, only 50 miles from the French capital. The Americans drove them back, and from June 6 to 25 cleared nearby Belleau Wood of enemy forces. In July, when the German General Staff made its last great effort to break through to Paris between Rheims and Soissons, 85,000 Americans helped check the assault. In its first major offensive assignment, in September 1918, the American army launched an attack on the St. Mihiel salient, a German bulge protruding into the Allied lines across the Meuse River southeast of Verdun. Pershing sent American troops against both flanks of the salient and with some French support, reduced it in two days.

The Meuse-Argonne offensive, from late Sep-

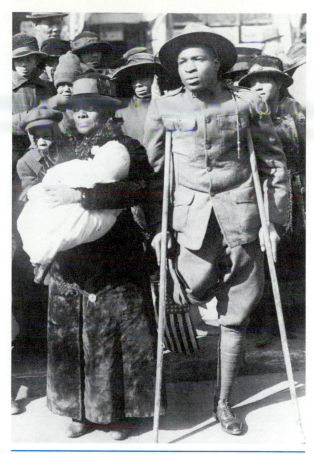

Wounded soldier viewing parade of the 369th Colored Infantry in New York City, 1919. (*UPI/Bettmann*)

tember to early November, became one of the fiercest battles in American military history. Together with the French forces on that front, Americans captured more than 25,000 prisoners and a great deal of equipment, but at a high cost in casualties. This offensive, part of a coordinated drive against the Central Powers all along the Western Front, helped defeat Germany and its allies. By early November, the German armies were everywhere in retreat, the navy was on the verge of general mutiny, and the civilian population hungry, exhausted, and dangerously discontented. On November 11, Germany gave up and signed an armistice.

The war was not over, since terms of peace had yet to be worked out. But fighting on the major fronts had ceased at last. American losses—48,000 killed in battle, 2,900 missing in action, 56,000 dead of disease—were light in comparison with those the other nations had suffered since 1914. Before pulling out of the war early in 1918, Russia counted 1,700,000 battle deaths. Germany lost

FROM THE FRONT

American Ex. [peditionary] Forces [AEF]

Dear Wife:

We pulled out about the 19th of Sept, moving towards the Argonne Forest. Finly we came to thair trenches and thair we got lots of prisiners, another fellow and myself got 13 out of one little dugout. We seen a machine gun setting in the mouth of the dugout so we stopped and decided what to do. So I asked him what he wanted to do, go get the machine gun or stay thair and keep his eye on the dugout until I could crawl up and get the gun, so he decided he would let me go.

Thair at that line of trenches one of the boys threw a hand grenade in on a Hun as he started to come out without his hands up and killed him. Well, it was along about eleven o'clock in the day now and as we hadnt had any breakfast we were getting quite tired and hungry.

In a short while we started to advance and by that time Jerry was sending shells over in a jiffy. Right thair was when I saw what war really was. The fellow on my right got hit. It was my luck that I was caught right in an open place so I dropped behind an old stump and thair I had to stay as it looked as if they were going to mow the old stump down. Well, I thought that I was a gone sucker sure. I laid thair until dark looking every minute for Fritzie to sneek up on me but he didn't come. Seven of us was sent back to gather up some ammunition and the Germans saw us and threw the shells into us. Three shells came all at once right on top of us. The man in front of me fell and the one in rear of me. The concussion from the explosion knocked me down and when I went to get up I was bured in dirt and rack and I thought I was killed as they almost knocked me senseless. Will leave out quite a bit that I witnessed now as it is too bad to write. We had 250 men when we started over the top on the 26th of Sept. and when we came out thair want but about 80 of us left. Gee, I did feel lucky, which all of us did that were still alive. Love to you.

Your Husband, Pvt. Jesse M. Maxey

Source: William Matthews and Dixon Wecter, *Our Soldiers Speak: 1885–1919* (Boston: Little, Brown and Co., 1943).

In the thick smoke and fog of the Argonne Forest, Allied and American troops suffered heavy casualties. (*National Archives*)

1,800,000 men, France 1,385,000, Britain 947,000 and Austria-Hungary 1,200,000. The war had come close to wiping out an entire generation.

PEACEMAKING AND REVOLUTION

While his administration waged a militant propaganda campaign on the home front, Wilson was seeking to clarify the objectives of the war. When the United States was still neutral, his appeal for "peace without victory" brought hope to a world already sick of war. When the United States entered the war, he kept asserting that hostilities were directed not against the German people, but against their government. Still unaware of the secret treaties among the Allies, the president held that neither punitive damages nor territorial gains were the real objectives, but rather the end of autocratic government and a settlement that would ensure permanent peace.

In the peace treaty he helped to negotiate, as in his proposal for a league of nations, Wilson hoped to translate his idea of the war's objectives into reality. What sustained him in that hope was the conviction that the peoples of the world, if not their governments, shared his views and looked to the United States for leadership and inspiration.

My dream is that as the years go by and the world knows more and more of America it will turn to America for those moral inspirations which lie at the basis of all freedom and that America will come into the full light of day when all shall know that she puts human rights above all other rights, and that her flag is the flag not only of America, but of humanity.

In an age of power politics, nationalist rivalries, and socialist revolution, to have such a vision of the world was at best a risk and at worst a dangerously foolish denial of reality.

The Fourteen Points

Soon after the United States entered the war, Wilson finally learned of the secret agreements. The Allies had already agreed to certain territorial readjustments and to taking enormous indemnities from the defeated enemy. To Wilson, such agreements violated his "peace without victory" as well as the principle of self-determination. Diplomatically and militarily, he tried to conduct the American part of the war independently. (The United States, in fact, never became one of the Allied Powers, but only an associated power among them.) The existence of the secret treaties, however, encouraged Wilson to make even clearer the American and the Allied objectives. And events in Russia added to the need for clarification.

After the Bolshevik Revolution of November 1917, the new Russian government invited all belligerents to end the entire war almost on Wilson's terms—no territory and no indemnities. No response came from the Allies. The Bolsheviks saw their silence as proof of the imperialist nature of the war. Within three weeks, Vladimir Lenin, the Bolshevik leader, began negotiations with the Central Powers to close down the Eastern Front. This step the Allies viewed as a stab in the back. The Bolsheviks next threatened to publish the secret treaties. (The deposed czar had signed them for Russia.) Wilson, after failing again to win Allied agreement to his peace plan, thought it essential to meet the Bolshevik challenge with a statement of his own.

This he did in a messge to Congress on January 8, 1918, in which he set forth in his Fourteen Points all the ideas he had been proposing during the past two years.

The first five points contained general principles aimed at removing the fundamental causes of conflict. Peace agreements should be arrived at openly, not secretly. Free use of the seas should be guaranteed to all nations, in peace as well as in war. He would remove economic barriers to free trade, and reduce armaments "to the lowest point consistent with domestic safety." The conflicting claims of the colonial powers should be settled in a way that reflected the interests of the native peoples. The next eight points dealt with territorial readjustments, based on the principle of self-determination along "historically established lines of nationality." They included "autonomous development" for the peoples of Austria-Hungary and the establishment of an independent Poland. The fourteenth point, the most important in Wilson's eyes, would establish "a general association of nations" to guarantee "political independence and territorial integrity to great and small states alike."

To Wilson, the Fourteen Points were "the moral climax of this final war for human liberty." The Allies were less certain. Some of them expressed anger over points that appeared to affect their national honor and imperial ambitions; others found Wilson's proclamation hopelessly naive. "Mr. Wilson bores me with his Fourteen Points," remarked Georges Clemenceau, the French leader. "Why, God Almighty has only ten." Whatever their feelings, however, the Allied leaders saw the propaganda value of Wilson's effort. It was for this reason that they agreed to use the Fourteen Points as at least a basis for the peace negotiations.

Intervention in Russia

When finally forced to sign a separate peace with Germany (the Treaty of Brest-Litovsk) some eight months before the armistice ended the war, the Bolsheviks yielded all of Poland, Lithuania, the Ukraine, the Baltic provinces, Finland, and neighboring territories. All told, they gave up the home of 30 percent of the czar's prewar subjects, and the source of 90 percent of Russia's coal and 80 percent of its iron. By May 1918, the British and French had also begun to send troops into Arctic Russia by way of Murmansk on the Barents Sea. Americans soon followed.

If they had intended the overthrow of the Bolshevik regime—their primary goal in the opinion of some historians—their more immediate objective was to keep the German military machine busy enough to prevent the transfer of troops to the Western Front in France. Ideological concerns probably reinforced strategic considerations. If the Bolshevik government collapsed as a result of the intervention, that would have been an added bonus.

The Allied and American presence in Russia encouraged those who opposed the Bolshevik regime. By August 1918, the Westerners had helped set up an anti-Bolshevik puppet government in northern Russia. Anti-Bolshevik groups in Siberia were aided by the arrival there of British, French, American, and Japanese forces. In this way, the Western powers became involved in the "Great Civil War" of 1918–1920, which raged across the entire Russian Empire. When the Germans collapsed in the west in November 1918, the Bolsheviks promptly renounced the Treaty of Brest-Litovsk and tried to reclaim the surrendered territories. At the same time, the armistice permitted the Allies and the United States to deal with eastern developments.

Some Americans, like Theodore Roosevelt, had urged unconditional surrender rather than an armistice. But Secretary of State Lansing recognized the need for a quick end to the war. If Germany was crushed, he argued, it would encourage social revolution there which might then spread to other European countries. The fact that Bolshevism threatened to spread was enough reason to end the war immediately and to get on with the work of containing the Bolsheviks.

Although the Soviet Union would not be invited to the Paris Peace Conference, the fear of Bolshevism played a prominent role in the deliberations. If they disagreed in other matters, the United States and the Allies shared a common alarm over the effect of the Russian Revolution. They continued to support anti-Bolshevik activity within Russia. Allied and American troops remained in northern Russia until near the end of 1919, and Japanese troops were still in Vladivostok late in 1922. To the charge that this was interference in the internal affairs of Soviet Russia, Clemenceau replied that the only objective was to "help Russia overcome anarchy and restore herself." Wilson wrote to his secretary of state: "If a stable form of government could be established through military intervention in Asiatic Russia, the moral effect upon the balance of Russia would be incalculable."

Years later, Winston Churchill recalled as one of the great mistakes of Allied statesmanship in 1919 "the failure to strangle Bolshevism at its birth and to bring Russia . . . by one means or another into the general democratic system." It remains doubtful, however, that the West could have been persuaded to make the immense effort needed to attain this goal. The White Russians, who offered the only alternative to Bolshevik rule, were in no way committed to a "democratic system." Most important, the Bolshevik regime survived. The Allies' intervention and subsequent policy of economic blockade and nonrecognition won for them the enduring suspicion of the Soviet government and of large numbers of the Russian people. Even as late as the 1930s, an Adolph Hitler could believe that the Western nations would have stood by if he had only confined himself to an anti-Soviet crusade.

The Versailles Treaty

Although Wilson's statements on peace were vague enough to be given varying interpretations, he became a hero to people everywhere who were eager for a better world and thought the president could lead them to it. Years later, his portrait could still be found hanging in peasant homes in many parts of Europe. To Wilson, his welcome in Europe confirmed him in his role as the spokesman for world humanity. That proved to be a tragic illusion. Wilson confronted mounting opposition at home. The president knew that his role as peacemaker would be weakened if the American people defeated his party at the polls.

Europe after Versailles

New independent nations

Plebiscite area

Allied occupation zone

determined promoter of French interests and French security. Vittorio Orlando, the Italian prime minister, was in Paris to see that Allied territorial promises to Italy were kept. When it became clear that they would not be, Orlando went home.

The Big Four became the Big Three—Wilson, Lloyd George, and Clemenceau. Wilson had come to Paris with three cardinal goals: (1) political self-determination for the peoples of Europe and to some extent even the peoples of colonial countries; (2) free trade; and (3) a league of nations. He left Paris with his goals only partially attained. Unfortunately, his concessions were made largely to secure the League of Nations, which the United States Senate was to forbid the United States to join. Wilson did succeed in moderating the Allied demands on Germany. But here too he was far from attaining his goal of "peace without victory." The terms of the final treaty were harsh enough almost to guarantee that the Germans would make every effort to break the agreement when they felt strong enough to do so.

The Treaty of Versailles, signed by the Germans on June 28, 1919, stripped Germany of its colonies in Africa and the Far East, and of Alsace-Lorraine and the Saar Basin north of Lorraine. France won all rights in the coal-rich Saar for fifteen years, after which a plebiscite would decide its future. On the east, German territory was given to Poland, to form the Polish Corridor to the Baltic Sea. This provision split Germany in two and was a bitter pill for Germans. The huge indemnity of $5 billion levied on the Germans and the provision for additional "reparations" later on made them look upon the Allies as vultures.

Perhaps most distressing was the "war guilt" article, which attempted to justify the indemnity and reparations by forcing Germany to acknowledge responsibility for starting the war. In an effort to prevent future aggression, the treaty deprived Germany of a navy and merchant marine and limited its army to 100,000 men. Other treaties in conjunction with the Versailles Treaty established such new states as Czechoslovakia and Yugoslavia as the Austro-Hungarian Empire was dismembered.

For all its harshness, the Versailles Treaty was no worse than the terms Germany would have imposed on the Allies had it won. (The Treaty of Brest-Litovsk made that clear.) The Versailles Treaty, however, failed to satisfy Clemenceau. He refused to sign until Britain and the United States in a separate agreement promised to come to the aid of France in the event of a future attack on

In October 1918, facing off-year elections, he issued a fatal appeal to voters to express their approval of his leadership by returning a Democratic Congress. His appeal not only failed, it also embittered the Republicans who had supported the war effort. At the polls, the voters elected Republican majorities to both houses of Congress. When Wilson went to Paris in December 1918, he seemed to have been rejected by his own country. By then, he had further angered the opposition by failing to appoint a single Republican leader or a single United States senator, even from his own party, to the peace commission that accompanied him to the peace talks.

The Paris Peace Conference, a meeting of victors to decide the fate of Germany, sat at the Versailles Palace from January to June 1919. Representing Britain was its prime minister, David Lloyd George, who had called for the punishment of Germany in a general election the preceding December and had triumphed. Representing France was Georges Clemenceau, its premier, a that country. Wilson probably suspected the Senate would reject such an "entangling alliance," which it did. His own expectation was that the League of Nations would play the role of this alliance, and he worked successfully to get the Allies to include the League Covenant in the treaty.

Under the covenant, responsibility for maintaining peace rested with an assembly (in which every member nation would be represented), a council (consisting of the United States, Britain, France, Italy, and Japan, and four others chosen by the assembly), and a Permanent Court of International Justice. Each member nation pledged itself to respect the "territorial integrity" and "political independence" of other members; to recognize the right of any nation to bring any threat to peace to the League's attention and to submit dangerous disputes to arbitration; and as a last resort, to use military and economic sanctions against aggressor nations.

Like the Versailles Treaty, however, the League Covenant failed to confront the fundamental causes of conflict—the industrial, commercial, and imperial rivalries. To some critics, in fact, it looked much more like a device to maintain the past rather than the peace.

PEACE AT HOME: WILSON, THE LEAGUE, AND THE SENATE

When Wilson returned to the United States, he faced a difficult battle. He needed to persuade a divided Senate to ratify the treaty, and he needed to keep the support of the American people, who were now concerned with unemployment and inflation. The president was confident. He had fought for the people of Europe over the heads of their rulers; he would now wage a similar struggle for the minds of Americans.

The Senate Debate

On July 10, 1919, two days after Wilson's return from Paris, he formally presented the Versailles Treaty, including the League Covenant, to the Senate. He was confronted by the Republican majority elected in 1918 and especially by his enemy, Henry Cabot Lodge, now chair of the Foreign Relations Committee. In addition, a strong group of "irreconcilables," including such western Progressives as William E. Borah, Hiram Johnson, and Robert La Follette, were determined to resist the treaty and the League. "We may become one of the four dictators of the world," Borah warned, "but we shall no longer be master of our own spirit." Nevertheless, more than the needed two-thirds of the Senate seemed ready to vote for the Versailles Treaty, with some form of League membership. There is every evidence that the majority of the people would have backed them, despite the opposition of German-Americans because of the harshness of the treaty, of Italian-Americans because of the frustration of their homeland's demands, of Irish-Americans bitter over failure to secure Irish independence, and of the American Left, which regarded the treaty and the League as nothing more than props for a decaying economic and social order.

Through the summer of 1919, as the Senate and the people debated the League, Wilson grew more and more stubborn about even minor changes in the Covenant and more tactless about his all-or-nothing stand.

When the irreconcilables opened a tremendous propaganda barrage, the president, although exhausted by work and illness, decided to take his own case to the country. In more than forty speeches delivered in some twenty-two days, he pressed home his point. For what had American youths died? he asked. "For the redemption of America? America was not directly attacked. For the salvation of America? America was not immediately in danger. No; for the salvation of mankind. It is the noblest errand that troops ever went on." If the United States rejected the treaty and League membership, it turned its back on those troops.

While the president was gone, Lodge proposed a series of reservations to the Covenant, which he knew Wilson would reject and over which the Senate might talk the whole treaty to death. Lodge's strategy worked. By the time his reservations were introduced in the Senate, Wilson had had a physical breakdown, forcing him to cancel the rest of his trip. Early in October he suffered a stroke that left him half-paralyzed. His sickbed appeal to "all true friends of the treaty" to reject the Lodge reservations helped defeat them in the Senate in November. But a resolution to ratify the treaty and the League without reservations also failed by 38 to 55, with every Republican but one voting against it.

Enough support for the League remained even in the Senate for the treaty to be brought up again in March 1920. Although a majority (49 to 35) voted for the treaty with the modified Lodge reservations, that was seven short of the necessary two-thirds. Wilson supporters remained opposed

On November 11, 1918, servicemen and women in New York City celebrated the armistice. "We hear much about ourselves as heroes," wrote a discharged soldier in May 1919. "We do not talk about the war unless the civilians ply us with questions and drive us into stories about our life on the battlefield. We have come back hating war, disgusted with the prattle about ideals, disillusioned entirely about the struggles between nations. That is why we are quiet, why we talk little, and why our friends do not understand. But the populace refuses to be disillusioned; they force us to feed their own illusions." (*The New York Times*)

to compromise. Both the Treaty and League membership were dead.

The Election of 1920

Even so, Wilson did not give up hope. The election of 1920, he announced, must be "a great and solemn referendum." The people would now vote directly on the issue. But it has rarely been possible in peacetime to make an American presidential election a clear referendum on foreign policy, and 1920 was no exception.

Deprived of their most popular leader by Roosevelt's death early in 1919, the Republicans at their national convention split so badly over the candidacy of Roosevelt's friends General Leonard Wood and Governor Frank O. Lowden of Illinois that they gave in at last to the backers of Warren G. Harding of Ohio. This small-town newspaperman, owner and editor of the *Marion Daily Star*, had been elected United States senator in 1914. When reminded that Harding still remained unknown outside Ohio, Senator Frank Brandegee of Connecticut shouted: "There ain't any first-raters this year. Harding is the best of the second-raters." Perhaps second best was the equally surprising nominee for vice-president. Calvin Coolidge, even more obscure than Harding, was governor of Massachusetts when he suddenly came to national fame by breaking the Boston police strike of September 1919.

To run against Harding, the Democrats named another Ohioan, Governor James M. Cox, who had not been closely identified with Wilson's policies. As his running mate they chose Franklin Delano Roosevelt, Wilson's assistant secretary of the navy. Meanwhile, the Socialists decided to offer an alternative by again nominating Eugene Debs. Since the president refused to pardon him, Debs would have to conduct his campaign from behind prison walls.

Although Cox strongly favored the League, he wavered on what amendments he might be willing to accept. The Republicans caught the mood of the public by evading this and all other issues. "Keep Warren at home," advised Boies Penrose, the political boss of Pennsylvania. "Don't let him make any speeches. If he goes out on a tour somebody's sure to ask him questions, and Warren's just the sort of damned fool that will try to answer them." The Republican platform condemned the League Covenant; but Harding, who had voted against the League in the Senate, promised to work for "an association of nations."

Tired of the whole debate, the American people reacted not so much to the League as to the rising cost of living, the number of people out of work, high taxes, and labor violence. Cox was crushed at the polls, 16 million to 9 million, receiving only 34 percent of the popular vote. No major party candidate had ever been defeated so badly.

In commenting on the election, the *New York World* wrote: "The American people wanted a change, and they have voted for a change. They did not know what kind of a change they wanted, and they do not know what kind of a change they have voted for." But the American electorate may have been sharper than some observers thought possible. Although Harding said little, what he did say may have been the key to his overwhelming success at the polls. He promised the American people no new crusades, no calls for self-sacrifice to save humanity, but simply a return to stability—to "normalcy." After eight years of Wilson's drives, that in itself was a welcome change.

SUMMARY

World War I officially brought the United States into the European power politics system; its entry also made the European war into a world war. At first, Americans did not understand why they should be involved. Also at first, the loyalties of Americans of European background were divided. But the Allies (Britain and France) soon won the public relations campaign. In addition, the wartime demand from the Allies for goods rescued the American economy and started a boom that lasted until 1919. Even more important, the United States was tranformed from a debtor to a creditor nation. And since the debtors were the Allied countries, America now had a huge economic stake in the outcome of the conflict.

At first, problems of neutral shipping brought the United States into conflict with both Britain and Germany, since both were battling for control of the seas and their source of supplies. Wilson's policy at the beginning was to try to bring the war quickly to an end. He was eventually forced to give in to the idea of preparing for war. The climax came in January 1917, when Germany broke its pledge on submarine warfare in a gamble to win the war before America could come to the Allies' rescue. The Allies were in deep trouble, and their defeat would have meant an economic disaster for the United States. In April 1917 the United States declared war on Germany. Nineteen months later, the Germans were forced to agree to an armistice.

The American navy reduced the amount of tonnage lost to submarines. American ground troops helped to turn back the German armies, and the flow of American supplies and money sustained the entire war effort. To do this, the United States mobilized its resources on a new and vast scale. A new army was created by the Selective Service Act of May 1917. A Council of National Defense supervised huge federal agencies that managed the merchant marine, food and fuel supplies, transportation, and industry. The war also brought some loss of civil liberties and official intolerance in the Espionage Act of June 1917 and the Sedition Act of May 1918.

When it was over, Wilson hoped to realize in the peace treaty his dream of "making the world safe for democracy." But in an age of power politics, national rivalries, and socialist revolution, such ideas were hopelessly and dangerously naive. His Fourteen Points were an effective propaganda device, but the Allies, bound by secret agreements, had no intention of negotiating anything but a punitive peace. This they did in the Treaty of Versailles, drawn up after six months of work at the Paris Peace Conference from January to June 1919. It stripped Germany of its colonies abroad and territory in Europe, saddled Germany with a $5 billion indemnity, deprived the Germans of military forces, and included a "war guilt" clause that declared the Germans responsible for the war.

Wilson did get his League of Nations, for which he sacrificed all his other objectives. But then the United States Senate, in a bitter campaign, refused to ratify the treaty and allow the United States to become a member of the League. Wilson, exhausted and ill, suffered a stroke that left him paralyzed and removed him from politics. In the election of 1920, Republican Warren Harding of Ohio became the new president. His slogan was a return to "normalcy"—to stability and to minding America's own business.

Suggested Readings

Barbara Tuchman, *The Proud Tower* (1965) is an extremely readable chronicle of Europe on the verge of war. For the diplomatic background, see A. J. P. Taylor, *The Struggle for Mastery in Europe 1848–1918* (1954), and Fritz Fischer, *Germany's Aims in the First World War* (1967).

The most comprehensive account of Wilson and World War I is the multivolume biography in progress by A. S. Link (5 vols., 1947–65). For a briefer presentation, see his *Wilson the Diplomatist* (1957), and *Woodrow Wilson and the Progressive Era* (1954). Among the numerous works examining American intervention in the war are E. R. May, *The World and American Isolation 1914–1917* (1959); R. Gregory, *The Origins of American Intervention in the First World War* (1971); P. Devlin, *Too Proud to Fight: Woodrow Wilson's Neutrality* (1975); C. P. Parrini, *Heir to Empire: United States Economic Diplomacy 1916–1923* (1969); and J. Cooper, Jr., *The Vanity of Power: American Isolationism and the First World War 1914–1917* (1969). N. G. Levin, *Woodrow Wilson and World Politics: America's Response to War and Revolution* (1969), stresses Wilson's commitment to a liberal, democratic, capitalist world order.

Walter Millis, *Road to War: America 1914–1917* (1935), and C. C. Tansill, *America Goes to War* (1938), are critiques of intervention from the isolationist view of the thirties. R. E. Osgood, *Ideals and Self-Interest in America's Foreign Relations* (1953), is a perceptive examination of the nation's motivations.

The impact of the war on American society is examined in D. M. Kennedy, *Over Here: The First World War and American Society* (1980). The mobilization of the American mind is described in G. Creel, *How We Advertised America* (1920), and S. L. Vaughn, *Holding Fast the Inner Lines: Democracy, Nationalism, and the Committee on Public Information* (1980). For wartime restraints on opinion, see D. Johnson, *Challenge to American Freedoms: World War I and the Rise of the American Civil Liberties Union* (1963); H. N. Scheiber, *The Wilson Administration and Civil Liberties 1917–1921* (1961); H. C. Peterson and G. C. Fite, *Opponents of War 1917–1918* (1957); and W. Preston, Jr.,

Aliens and Dissenters: Federal Suppression of Radicals 1903–1933 (1963). The mobilization of the universities for the war effort is described in C. S. Gruber, *Mars and Minerva: World War I and the Uses of the Higher Learning in America* (1975).

The economic conversion to war is the subject of R. D. Cuff, *The War Industries Board: Business-Government Relations during World War I* (1973). The position of the military in American life is examined in R. D. Challener, *Admirals, Generals, and American Foreign Policy 1898–1914* (1973), and J. G. Clifford, *The Citizen Soldiers: The Plattsburg Training Camp Movement 1913–1920* (1972). On the military experience, see E. M. Coffman, *The War to End All Wars* (1968); J. J. Pershing, *My Experiences in the World War* (2 vols., 1931); and F. E. Vandiver, *Black Jack: The Life and Times of John J. Pershing* (1977).

The reaction of the United States to the Russian Revolution is examined in G. F. Kennan, *Russia Leaves the War* (1956), and *The Decision to Intervene* (1958); C. Lasch, *The American Liberals and the Russian Revolution* (1962); and P. G. Filene, *Americans and the Soviet Experiment 1917–1933* (1967), and L. C. Gardner, *Safe for Democracy: The Anglo-American Response to Revolution, 1913–1923* (1984). For the impact of the Russian Revolution on the peace, see W. A. Williams, *American-Russian Relations 1781–1947* (1952); J. M. Thompson, *Russia, Bolshevism, and the Versailles Peace* (1966); and A. J. Mayer, *Political Origins of the New Diplomacy 1917–1918* (1959), and *Politics and Diplomacy of Peacemaking: Containment and Counterrevolution at Versailles 1918–1919* (1967).

T. A. Bailey, *Woodrow Wilson and the Lost Peace* (1944), and *Woodrow Wilson and the Great Betrayal* (1945), analyze Wilson's performance at Versailles and American opposition to the League. See also J. A. Garraty, *Henry Cabot Lodge* (1953). J. M. Keynes, *The Economic Consequences of the Peace* (1919), is a critical assessment of the Big Four, including Wilson. See also R. Lansing, *The Peace Negotiations: A Personal Narrative* (1921), and Harold Nicolson, *Peacemaking 1919* (1939).

THE TWENTIES: BUSINESS AND CULTURE

Chapter 27

Few decades evoke as many different and conflicting images as the twenties, and few have been subjected to more distortion and exaggeration. High-spirited college students and "flappers," emboldened by bootleg gin, danced the Charleston and the Black Bottom and went to "petting" parties. Marathon dancers competed with flagpole sitters for public attention, and both were outranked by Babe Ruth, Clara Bow, Henry Ford, and Al Capone. Sophisticated urbanites violated Prohibition in speakeasies; young and old alike satisfied their fantasies in the movie houses; the small-town elites found their outlets in Rotary, Kiwanis, or Lions clubs. Advertising became a major industry in its own right, rewarding its armies of salespeople better than most of the businesses whose products it tried to sell. The automobile became a necessity, along with the radio, the washing machine, and the refrigerator. Easy credit made these and countless other commodities available to millions of Americans.

The cultural tastes of the decade were as varied as the newly available consumer goods, and both came to be increasingly standardized. Edgar Guest, whose work appeared daily in the press, was a more widely read poet than either T. S. Eliot or Ezra Pound. Bruce Barton, the ad man who peddled an updated version of Jesus Christ, outsold Ernest Hemingway, who spent much of the decade out of the country. *The Saturday Evening Post,* whose covers and contents mirrored the middle-class vision of themselves and America, was far more popular than Henry L. Mencken's irreverent *American Mercury.* Highbrows and lowbrows alike were thrilled by the exploit of young Charles Lindbergh, whose dramatic solo flight from New York to Paris was the story of the decade; he seemed to personify the individualistic and pioneering spirit Americans still revered and the new technology they were embracing so feverishly.

But there is another side to the twenties that tends to get lost in the nostalgia Americans still feel for the Jazz Age. If the decade was a carefree fling for some, many sections of the population experienced little of the fun and none of the "good times." While ad men made a virtue out of conspicuous consumption, a lopsided distribution of income made reduced consumption necessary for millions of Americans. While the twenties tolerated bobbed hair, short skirts, cosmetics, and a relaxation of sexual rules—the trademarks of a new subculture based on age—that same decade was intolerant of radicals, union organizers, immigrants, and blacks. Even the "flaming youth" more often than not reflected and reinforced the dominant business culture. The same decade in which some Americans flaunted their liberation also witnessed a revival of the Ku Klux Klan, the Red Scare, racial violence, a court test of the right to teach evolution in the public schools, and the first restriction on the number of immigrants admitted to the United States.

The family underwent much change, as did the role of women in the household. The size of urban middle-class families continued to decline, and in the 1920s the impact of this change became more obvious. The smaller family and labor-saving devices enabled mothers to spend more time on the personality and education of their children. Knowledge of birth control, advances in the technology of contraception, and more open discussion of sex not only resulted in earlier marriages, but influenced the dominant middle-class sexual ethic. Women were encouraged to be more sexually responsive and to expect sexual gratification in marriage. While this improved the quality of sexual relationships, it may also have contributed to the rapid increase in the divorce rate. In 1890, 6 out of every 100 marriages ended in divorce; in 1930, it was 18 out of every 100 marriages.

The number of women employed increased, as did the number of women attending college. On the other hand, the percentage of women in the work force and in professional employment declined. For middle-class women, college and career were still an interval before marriage. The ideal woman of the 1920s, while encouraged to be more feminine, was asked to cultivate those qualities in order to further her husband's career, not her own. Dorothy Dix, in her widely syndicated column, advised that "a man's wife is the show window where he exhibits the measure of his achievement. . . . The woman who cultivates a circle of worth-while people, who belongs to clubs, who makes herself interesting and agreeable . . . is a help to her husband."

Women's suffrage in no way changed the quality of men elected to public office. The White House in this decade was occupied by Harding, Coolidge, and Hoover. They differed widely in talent, but were united in the conviction that "the chief business of the American people is business."

Scandals marked the Harding administration and complacency the Coolidge years, but the highest expectations greeted the Hoover presidency. "Big business in America," said a much impressed Lincoln Steffens, "is producing what the socialists held up as their goal; food, shelter and clothing for all. You will see it during the Hoover administration." Within a year of Hoover's inauguration, these expectations had been dashed. The decade closed with a mood of panic and desperation. The unemployed and the depressed of the twenties suddenly found themselves with plenty of company. ■

AFTER THE WAR: REPRESSION AND INTOLERANCE

The kind of planning that had enabled the United States to go to war was not used for demobilization afterward. With controls on the economy suddenly lifted and several million soldiers returning to civilian life, the nation found itself in a brief recession. Inflation and unemployment took their toll. Lingering wartime emotions and tensions found new outlets in hysteria over radicalism, in immigration restriction, and in racial violence. At the same time, the rapid pace of urbanization (the 1920 census revealed that for the first time most Americans lived in urban areas) fed traditional rural-urban antagonisms. And many of the 19 million Americans who moved from the farms to the cities in the twenties brought rural ways of thinking with them.

While President Harding talked of returning the nation to "normalcy," the head of the newly revived Ku Klux Klan talked of returning power to the people—"the everyday, not highly cultured, not overly intellectualized, but entirely unspoiled and not de-Americanized, average citizen of the old stock." Most Americans did not need the Klan to remind them of what they could see all too well for themselves: that traditional ways, morals, and beliefs were changing, along with the old ethnic makeup of the nation. Dangers from within had replaced the enemy abroad.

The Red Scare

During the war, Americans had grown used to the suppression of dissent. With the war's end, the intolerance that had been directed mainly against those suspected of sympathizing with Germany covered a wider range of persons—foreigners in general, Catholics, Jews, blacks, radicals, strikers. The new wave of fear found a scapegoat in the Bolshevik Revolution in Russia and the threats of worldwide revolution against capitalism. Actually, Socialists were split over the virtues of the new Soviet government. The Russian Revolution had fragmented rather than united an already demoralized American radicalism. The number of Communists in the United States did not exceed half of 1 percent of the population—and most were intellectuals, not workers. But violence in labor relations right after the war deepened concern about the safety of the social order, and a genuine bomb scare turned that concern into panic.

No longer bound by wartime no-strike pledges, trade unions made new wage demands after the armistice using their traditional weapon. They were seeking not only to maintain previous gains, but to keep up with the soaring cost of living. In 1919 alone, 3,630 strikes involved about 4 million workers. Whatever the few gains workers were able to make, industrialists quickly blamed them for the rise in prices. In February 1919 Seattle found itself paralyzed by a general strike called by the Central Labor Council to back shipyard workers seeking higher pay and shorter hours.

The tactic of a general strike revived fears of the IWW, which had been active in the Northwest, and the mayor exploited those fears in calling out troops to crush the strike. Even more spectacular, in September 1919, the Boston police struck after the city's police commissioners had refused to recognize a union organized to raise low wages. Governor Calvin Coolidge, who had done nothing to encourage a settlement, called out the state guard to maintain order in the state capital. When AFL president Samuel Gompers protested the firing of several leaders of the policemen's union for their organizing activities,

Coolidge replied: "There is no right to strike against the public safety by anybody, anywhere, anytime." This statement, despite his timid role in the entire affair, established Coolidge as a national hero and led to his nomination for the vice-presidency in 1920.

The attempts to link strike action with radicalism came to a head in September 1919, when AFL unions struck the United States Steel Corporation plants in Pittsburgh, in Gary, Indiana, and elsewhere. Since the last major steel strike at Homestead in 1892, conditions in the steel mills had only grown worse. Hours, shop conditions, and union recognition, as well as wages, were at issue. But the corporation blamed the strike on some of its Communist organizers. Using its own "security" forces along with state militia and federal troops, it broke the strike by January 1920, after eighteen workers had been killed and hundreds beaten.

The strike was thoroughly investigated by a Commission of Inquiry of the Interchurch World Movement under Bishop Francis J. McConnell of the Methodist Episcopal Church. Among the leading causes of the strike's defeat, said the commission, was the Steel Corporation's "effective mobilization of public opinion against the strikers through charges of radicalism, bolshevism, and the closed shop, none of which are justified by the facts." The working conditions that had brought on the strike, it concluded, "continue to exist."

Some union demands supported charges of radicalism. In an unsuccessful strike, the United Mine Workers had demanded nationalization of the coal pits. Railroad unions endorsed the widely discussed Plumb Plan, which called for the continuation of government operation of the railroads. The agitation sped the return of the railroads to private control in the Esch-Cummins Act of 1920, which also, for the first time, authorized the roads to plan combinations to make rail service more efficient.

Using as their excuse the influence of "foreign ideologies" in the labor movement, employer associations spent large sums of money promoting the American Plan—a set of attitudes, the most important of which was that collective bargaining and the closed or union shop were "un-American." Eventually, American Plan associations were organized in every state and nearly every industrial city in the country. Chambers of commerce, local boards of trade, "constitutional associations," and other groups all helped. The National Grange mobilized farm support.

In 1919 and 1920 a bomb scare intensified the

Seeking union recognition and an end to the 12-hour working day, steel workers went on strike in 1919, but without success. The bosses and the newspapers claimed they were led by Communist agitators. (*UPI/Bettmann*)

Red Scare. A time bomb was discovered in the mayor of Seattle's mail. Another bomb blew off the hands of a Georgia senator's house servant. No less than thirty-six bombs addressed to such prominent people as J. P. Morgan, John D. Rockefeller, and Justice Holmes of the Supreme Court were discovered in various post offices. A bomb exploded in front of the Washington home of the attorney general, and in September 1920 a bomb exploded in Wall Street, killing thirty-eight and injuring hundreds. Although the work of only a few anarchists, the bombs lent support to fears of a massive conspiracy to overthrow the government.

Wilson's attorney general, A. Mitchell Palmer, who had presidential ambitions of his own, did nothing to discourage fears of revolution. He claimed to see Reds almost everywhere he looked, and the end of the war provided him with the opportunity to hunt them down. "Like a prairie fire," he explained, "the blaze of revolution was sweeping over every American institution." On New Year's Day 1920, Palmer ordered simultaneous raids on every suspected Bolshevik cell in the country. In about a week, more than 6000 persons were arrested and their property confiscated. Friends who visited them were jailed on grounds of "solicitude for revolutionaries." Though supposedly armed to the teeth, the captives yielded the imposing total of three pistols and no explosives.

The Palmer raids were followed by the eventual deportation of 556 aliens convicted of no crime. Vigilantism spread across the nation. Students, professors, editors, writers, actors, and others suspected of subversive ideas or of engaging in un-American activities were the victims. In January 1920, five Socialist members of the New York State Assembly were expelled simply because of their party affiliation.

A few months after the Palmer raids, two Italian anarchists, Nicola Sacco and Bartolomeo Vanzetti, were arrested for a murder that had been committed in connection with a payroll robbery in South Braintree, Massachusetts. On the jury's finding them guilty, Judge Webster Thayer sentenced the two defendants to death. The actual evidence against them was not conclusive, and the suspicion grew that they had been convicted not because they had committed the crime, but because of their political beliefs. Judge Thayer's conduct of the trial, in which he made little secret of his feelings about anarchists, only deepened

suspicion of the verdict. Responding to protest in this country and abroad, Governor Alvan T. Fuller of Massachusetts appointed an advisory commission that included the president of Harvard to review the evidence. It concluded that the trial judge had been guilty of a "grave breach of official decorum," but that justice had been done.

Motions for appealing the verdict delayed the execution of the two men for years. Vanzetti's dignity and both men's quiet persistence in their anarchist beliefs, while their lives hung in the balance, won them additional sympathy. When they were electrocuted in 1927, in the middle of a new wave of worldwide protest, millions were convinced they were innocent. Millions more were convinced that, guilty or innocent, they had not been given a fair trial. "What more can the immigrants from Italy expect?" asked columnist Heywood Broun. "It is not every prisoner who has

Nicola Sacco and Bartolomeo Vanzetti, convicted anarchists who were electrocuted on August 23, 1927. "Never in our full life could we hope to do such work for tolerance, for justice, for man's understanding of man, as now we do by accident. . . . That last moment belongs to us—that agony is our triumph." (*UPI/Bettmann*)

a president of Harvard throw on the switch for him."

Although the Red Scare had quieted down after the Palmer raids, the atmosphere was hardly promising for radical activity and expression in the twenties. And the linking of radicals and immigrants added to the growing pressure for restrictions on their admission to the United States.

The "Race Suicide" Alarm: Immigration

Xenophobia, or antiforeign feeling, after the war brought to a head the anti-immigration sentiment that had been growing in the United States since the 1880s. The Immigration Restriction League had been organized by a group of New England intellectuals in 1894. It reflected fears that the "new" immigrants from southern and eastern Europe would destroy the "American character." This group had pushed for a literacy test for immigrants. During the Progressive era, xenophobes and labor and business leaders who shared hostility to newcomers were joined by liberals who feared that immigration was threatening the American way of life. The flood of "new" immigrants in the fifteen years before World War I brought some Americans to the verge of panic over "race suicide."

In the pages of the widely read *Saturday Evening Post,* Kenneth Roberts cautioned against the admission of so many Polish Jews, who were "human parasites." He argued that the mixture of Nordic with Alpine, Mediterranean, and Semitic stocks would result in "a hybrid race of people as worthless and futile as the good-for-nothing mongrels of Central America and Southeastern Europe." Such arguments, given wide national exposure, helped to pave the way for a complete reversal of the old, easygoing terms of admission to the United States.

The Immigration Restriction Act of 1921 established a quota system based on "national origins." Each European nation was assigned a quota based on 3 percent of the number of its nationals resi-

President Warren G. Harding (left) and Vice-President Calvin Coolidge (right). Their traditional Americanism and optimistic faith in business set the political tone of the decade. (*Culver Pictures*)

THE TWENTIES: BUSINESS AND CULTURE

dent in the United States in 1910. Most Asians were already barred. This law was expected to limit immigration to about 350,000 persons, largely from the United Kingdom and northwestern Europe.

The National Origins Act of 1924 cut quotas to 2 percent and made the base year 1890, when the proportion of "Nordics" in the American population had been much higher than in 1910. The National Origins Act also shut the door on Japanese immigrants. It was a national humiliation for Japan, which warned that it would have "grave consequences." The act of 1924 was to last only until 1927. Afterward, no more than 150,000 immigrants were to be admitted annually, according to quotas based on the ratio of each country's nationals to the whole American population in 1920.

In fact, the desire to restore the "Nordic" balance in the American population was frustrated because these laws did not apply to immigrants from Western Hemisphere countries. During the 1920s, almost a million Canadians, many of them French-speaking Catholics, and at least half a million Mexicans crossed their respective borders to work in the factories of New England and the fields of the South, the Southwest, and the West.

But nothing would ever again approach the earlier waves of European immigrants. With the restrictive legislation enacted in the 1920s, the idea of America as the promised land for the "huddled masses yearning to breathe free" came to an abrupt end. Only in the 1960s and 1970s—when the doors were opened to thousands of political refugees from Southeast Asia, Cuba, and Haiti—would that idea be momentarily revived.

The Great Black Migration

Although restrictions on immigrants affected the ethnic makeup of the nation, the movement of southern blacks to northern cities during and after World War I altered the racial map of the United States and introduced new tensions. Between 1910 and 1940, more than 1,750,000 black people left the South, nearly 500,000 during the war and another 800,000 in the twenties. By 1940, the black population outside the South had more than doubled. In cities such as New York, Chicago, Detroit, Cleveland, and Buffalo, the percentage of blacks in the population grew by 100 to 250 percent. Within only a few decades, a largely rural black population had become more urban than the white population. The Jim Crow restrictions, the alarming rate of lynchings and beatings, the

absence of adequate educational facilities, and the impossible tenantry and credit systems led large numbers of southern blacks to look for a better life elsewhere.

Until 1915, the North had offered the southern black migrant very little. The labor demands created by World War I and the decline in European immigration changed that situation and opened up opportunities in northern industry at wages unknown in the South. When in 1914 Henry Ford promised to pay none of his workers less than $5 a day—a sensational announcement in itself—he agreed at the same time to hire black workers for his assembly line. Before then, blacks had been barred from industrial work. Now self-interest won out over racial considerations. "These same factories, mills, and workshops that have been closed to us," said the Chicago *Defender,* "through necessity are being opened to us. We are being given a chance, not through choice but because it is expedient. Prejudice vanishes when the almighty dollar is on the wrong side of the balance sheet."

Encouraged at first by labor agents, black newspapers, and the letters of friends, the Great Migration soon had a momentum all its own. It was not uncommon for entire communites to transplant themselves. Although all classes of blacks made up the movement, many in the early waves were young, unskilled, and unmarried, the sons and daughters of sharecroppers and tenants. The chances for a rewarding life in the South had seemed increasingly dismal to these migrants, and they hoped for something beyond what their parents and grandparents had been forced to accept.

If their expectations were often disappointed, the hope still persisted that somehow they could improve the quality of their daily life. After nineteen years spent in Mississippi, Arkansas, and Tennessee, young Richard Wright headed in 1927 for Chicago, having concluded that life in a "hostile and forbidding" South made it impossible to maintain self-respect.

I had been what my surroundings had demanded, what my family—conforming to the dictates of the whites above them—had exacted of me, and what the whites had said that I must be. . . . I headed North full of a hazy notion that life could be lived with dignity, that the personalities of others should not be violated, that men should be able to confront other men without fear or shame.

The Great Migration took place in an atmosphere of growing racial intolerance. Despite the optimism with which many blacks had participated in World War I, in the first year of the ar-

A black family from the South arrives in Chicago in 1910. (*Historical Pictures Service, Chicago*)

mistice 70 blacks were lynched, 10 of them soldiers still wearing their uniforms. Between 1918 and 1927, more than 416 blacks were lynched, and 42 of them burned alive. Nor was this brutality confined to the old Confederacy. On July 2, 1917, East St. Louis, Illinois, was the scene of a savage attack on the black community in which 39 blacks and 9 whites died. Fear of black competition for white jobs and the use of black strikebreakers triggered the riot, but ignorance and bigotry accounted for its ferocity.

Two years later, on July 27, 1919, the worst race riot in the nation's history erupted in Chicago and lasted for six days and nights. Before the state militia restored some order, 38 persons (15 whites and 23 blacks) had died, 537 had been hurt, and more than a thousand were homeless. The riot

started after a seventeen-year-old black youth, swimming off a Chicago beach, accidentally crossed the unmarked line dividing the water into sectors for blacks and whites. He was stoned by white bathers until he drowned. Enraged by police indifference, black bathers attacked the whites. The bloodshed spread from there to the city streets. Quick to respond, Attorney General A. Mitchell Palmer blamed outside agitators, particularly Bolshevik sympathizers seeking black support for an insurrection. "If to fight for one's rights is to be Bolshevists," a black newspaper replied, "then we are Bolshevists and let them make the most of it."

As the black migration grew, so did white fears, resistance, and discrimination. During the Red Summer of 1919, as it came to be called, there

THE TWENTIES: BUSINESS AND CULTURE

THE PROMISED LAND

were more than twenty-five riots in various parts of the country. Several outbreaks were provoked by incidents involving urban police, bringing the charge that law enforcement officers practiced a double standard when dealing with black communities. In the black urban enclaves known as *ghettos,* the residents also faced high rents for substandard housing, high prices, poor municipal services, and white economic control. "Our money is being used by the white man," one black resident charged, "to pay us for being his cook, his valet, and his washerwoman."

Despite the expectations with which Richard Wright arrived in Chicago, he soon came to realize, as did many southern migrants, that racial oppression did not always show itself in lynchings, Jim Crow laws, or disfranchisement:

Slowly I began to forge in the depths of my mind a mechanism that repressed all the dreams and desires that the Chicago streets, the newspapers, the movies were evoking in me. I was going through a second childhood; a new sense of the limit of the possible was being born in me. What could I dream of that had the barest possibility of coming true? I could think of nothing. And slowly, it was upon exactly that nothingness that my mind began to dwell, that constant sense of wanting without having, of being hated without reason. A dim notion of what life meant to a Negro in America was coming to consciousness in me, not in terms of external events, lynchings, Jim Crowism, and the endless brutalities, but in terms of crossed up feeling, of emotional tension. I sensed that Negro life was a sprawling land of unconscious suffering, and there were but few Negroes who knew the meaning of their lives, who could tell their story.*

The Ku Klux Klan

The revival of the Ku Klux Klan in the 1920s reflected a concern not about blacks alone, but about the general erosion of the nation's moral fiber. The Klan of Reconstruction days had almost died out in the 1870s. The new Klan, founded in Georgia in 1915, grew rapidly after 1920. At its peak in 1924, no fewer than 4.5 million "white male persons, native-born Gentile citizens," as they said, had joined the hooded group. On its night rides, the Klan burned fiery crosses to advertise its presence. It flogged or kidnapped blacks and whites, acted as a moral censor, especially as the enforcement arm for Prohibition, made and unmade local politicians, and frightened union organizers.

This time around, the Klan had a much wider appeal, both geographically and ideologically. "We are a movement of plain people," explained Hiram Evans, the Grand Wizard of the Klan, "very weak in the matter of culture, intellectual support, and trained leadership. . . . It lays us open to the charge

---

*Paul R. Reynolds, Inc., for Richard Wright, "The Man Who Went to Chicago," from *Eight Men.* Copyright 1960 by World Publishing Co. Reprinted by permission.

The Ku Klux Klan marching in full regalia past the White House in 1925. "The outstanding proof of both our influence and our service . . . has been in creating, outside our ranks as well as in them, . . . a growing sentiment against radicalism, cosmopolitanism, and alienism of all kinds." (*Library of Congress*)

of being 'hicks' and 'rubes' and 'drivers of second hand Fords.' We admit it."

The Klan did well in portions of the Midwest and Far West, broadening its targets to include Jews and Catholics as well as blacks. It found support among people who felt most threatened and frustrated by the changes in American society. "One by one all our traditional moral standards went by the boards," Evans declared, "or were so disregarded that they ceased to be binding. The sacredness of our Sabbath, of our homes, of chastity, and finally even of our right to teach our own children in our own schools fundamental facts and truths were torn away from us."

By 1924 the Klan's political influence had become so great that the Democratic national convention, after days of debate, could not adopt a resolution condemning the group by name. Nor did the Democrats have a monopoly on the Klan problem. In Indiana, the group's leader, D. C. Stephenson, had built up an organization powerful enough to dominate the Republican party. Stephenson, in 1925, was convicted of second-degree murder of a young girl who took poison after he had abducted and assaulted her. He insisted he had been framed and took his revenge by giving newspapers details about state officials associated with him. Other exposés disclosed the depths of Klan corruption and soon drove people away. The Klan revival was short-lived, though it would reappear in the 1960s as one of several organizations seeking to preserve white supremacy in the South.

The Dry Decade

Although never exclusively a rural movement, Prohibition still enjoyed its greatest support in the countryside and among the fundamentalist denominations. After decades of agitation, the goal would finally be realized in the twenties. In anticipation of the Prohibition Amendment's becoming law in 1920, Congress in October 1919, over President Wilson's veto, passed the Volstead Act to implement it. This act defined intoxicating liquor as any beverage containing more than one-half of 1 percent of alcohol. It forbade any person, except for religious and medical purposes, to "manufacture, sell, barter, transport, import, export, deliver, furnish, or possess" such beverage without a license. The commissioner of internal revenue was to enforce the act.

Making liquor illegal nationwide had two immediate results. The old saloon was replaced by the "speakeasy," where drinking soon took on a new glamour. At the same time, by putting outside the law a personal habit millions of Americans would not give up, Prohibition opened up a new field for city gangs. National Prohibition made liquor a major source of gang income, raised that income to phenomenal levels, and strengthened gang domination of local police and local politics. Congress never voted enough money for more than token enforcement of the Volstead Act. The commissioner of internal revenue rarely had as many as 2000 agents to police the entire contry; the Capone gang alone had a private army in Chicago of at least a thousand. They and hundreds of other gangs gained control of the undercover liquor business—bootlegging, smuggling, and speakeasies. At its peak, the Capone gang took in $60 million a year, with gambling and liquor the principal sources of income.

Criticism of the "noble experiment," as Prohibition was called, gradually mounted. The Democratic party, although deeply divided over the issue, had to think of its urban constituents, for whom drinking in public was a social custom. It became an issue in the campaign of 1928, when Alfred E. (Al) Smith, the Democratic candidate, proposed to do away with the federal law and return the problem to the states. Herbert Hoover, his Republican opponent, did not take a stand. After his election, Hoover named a commission headed by the distinguished lawyer George W. Wickersham to study enforcement problems. Its report, published in January 1931, reviewed in frank detail all the evils of the "experiment." Yet a majority of the commission urged it be continued.

After the Democratic landslide in the election of 1932, Congress in February 1933 adopted the Twenty-first Amendment, repealing the Eighteenth. By the end of the year it had been ratified. With control of liquor returned to the states, only seven chose to continue Prohibition. Mississippi, in 1966, became the last of the seven to go "wet."

Fundamentalism and Civil Liberties

The repression of foreigners and foreign ideologies and habits soon carried over to the repression of thought and speech. Here, as among the Klansmen and the "drys," Protestant fundamentalists, demanding an absolutely literal reading of the Bible and resisting all modifications of theology in the light of modern science and biblical criticism, led the assault. The object of their attack became the public schools, where they insisted that Darwin's theory of evolution should not be taught.

In Tennessee, the fundamentalists had a success in 1925 with the passage of a state law forbidding the teaching of evolution in the state's schools and colleges. The same year, with the American Civil Liberties Union eager to test the law, John T. Scopes, a young high school teacher in the country town of Dayton, Tennessee, violated the law and was arrested. Reporters from all over the country swarmed into Dayton (population 1700) to cover the court proceedings.

To defend the Bible, William Jennings Bryan, bald and aging, joined the prosecution. Clarence Darrow, perhaps the most brilliant trial lawyer in the country, headed the defense. Bryan began his first speech by attacking the city slickers, come all the way from the Gomorrah of New York to expose the true believers. The climax came with Darrow subjecting Bryan to questioning that exposed his ignorance and inconsistencies. Bryan then allowed himself to be lured into a concession that made his followers gasp. "Do you think the earth was made in six days?" asked Darrow. "Not six days of

Clarence Darrow and William Jennings Bryan at Dayton, Tennessee. (*Brown Brothers*)

twenty-four hours," answered Bryan. In the end he conceded that the Creation might have lasted for "millions of years." The presiding judge mercifully cut the questioning short. Scopes, found guilty, was fined only $100. The national ridicule thereafter took much of the strength from fundamentalist efforts to retain a system of values by legal compulsion.

Those who cared deeply about American traditions of freedom of expression and personal liberty were most discouraged by the right-wing hysteria, ethnic intolerance, and anti-intellectualism of "normalcy." Nor could they look with much confidence to the Supreme Court, although Justice Oliver Wendell Holmes did use several cases to caution against *indiscriminate* attempts to suppress unpopular ideas. In *Schenck* v. *United States* (1919), Holmes upheld the conviction of Schenck, a Socialist, for conspiracy in distributing a circular urging draftees to refuse to report for induction into the army. In doing so, he tried to draw the line between those forms of speech that must be protected and those that were dangerous to the state. "The character of every act depends upon the cir-

cumstances in which it is done," he declared. The right of free speech would not, for example, permit anyone to shout "Fire!" in a theater and cause a panic.

The determining question, then, is whether the words are used in such a way as to create "a clear and present danger" to the national interest. Schenck, in the opinion of the Court, had clearly interfered in wartime with the power of Congress to raise armies. (The decision would be cited by the Court in 1951 in upholding the conviction of Communist Party leaders for conspiring to teach the violent overthrow of the government.)

Holmes himself applied his test in a dissenting opinion in a case superficially similar to Schenck's, *Abrams* v. *United States* (1919). Here a majority of the Court upheld the conviction of a group of Russian immigrants for distributing leaflets opposing American intervention in Russia in 1918. Holmes, with Justice Brandeis concurring, held that the specific statements made by the defendants did not constitute a threat to the government or to the conduct of its war against Germany. The Court had departed, he insisted, from the reasonable line it had drawn in the Schenck case: "Congress certainly cannot forbid all effort to change the mind of the country." Holmes closed his dissent with an appeal for "free trade in ideas."

The twenties proved less than hospitable to that "free trade in ideas." But its most fervent practitioners could be found in literary and artistic movements, which were experimenting with new ideas, undermining established beliefs, exposing absurdities in society, and promoting nonconformity.

THE CULTURE OF DISSENT

With a number of other protesters, novelist John Dos Passos stood outside the walls of Charlestown Prison on August 23, 1927, when the switch was thrown that sent Nicola Sacco and Bartolomeo Vanzetti to their deaths in the electric chair. Several years later, in his novel *The Big Money* (which completed the trilogy *U.S.A.*), Dos Passos declared that with that execution America had become two nations:

they have clubbed us off the streets they are stronger they are rich they hire and fire the politicians the newspapereditors the old judges the small men with reputations the collegepresidents the wardheelers (listen businessmen collegepresidents judges America will not forget her betrayers) they hire the men with guns the uniforms the policecars the patrolwagons

all right you have won you will kill the brave men our friends tonight . . .

America our nation has been beaten by strangers who have turned our language inside out who have taken the clean words our fathers spoke and made them slimy and foul . . .

all right we are two nations*

For a number of American intellectuals, writers, and artists, America had become two nations much earlier. The invasions of civil liberties, Prohibition, fundamentalism, Klansmen, Rotarians, the triumph of business values, the small-town and service club mentality of the White House— all had confirmed their belief that materialism, intolerance, and hypocrisy were making a shambles of American civilization. Nor did they, like some of the prewar rebels, look for a political solution. The problem with America was simply too deep to be resolved by legislation. For a nation that could boast of mass consumption on an unparalleled

scale, the American people, in their view, were suffering from emotional and esthetic poverty.

When it came to expressing their views, whether in novels, poetry, paintings, or plays, the quality of the work would vary considerably. No single writer emerged of greater stature than Melville, Emerson, Hawthorne, Whitman, Mark Twain, or Henry James. But in their willingness to question the sanity of their society and in their experiments with new ideas and forms, this generation of writers stood out from all others. Probably more good writing and more important books wer produced in these years than in any period in the nation's history.

Prelude to Rebellion: The Optimistic Years

The spirit of freedom and experimentation so eagerly taken up by writers and artists in the 1920s had found outlets for expression in the prewar years. Across the country, in large cities and in small towns, "intellectually liberated" Americans, as they liked to think of themselves, began to meet and exchange ideas. They included political radicals as well as revolutionary poets and painters. Some of them formed groups with artistic, cultural, or political programs; others preferred to work alone. Although small artist communites formed in places like Chicago, St. Louis, and even Davenport, Iowa, the mecca by 1914 had become a few blocks of downtown New York known as Greenwich Village.

The wildest young rebels from all over America came to the Village to experience "freedom," to flout convention, and to debate all the "new" ideas, from penology and poetry to birth control and sexual repression. Although the influence of Sigmund Freud, the Austrian founder of psychoanalysis, was not fully felt until the twenties, his visit to the United States in 1909 and the translation before 1925 of some of his early works had brought him to the attention of Village intellectuals. In both decades, the popularized and distorted version of Freud ignored his more complex explanations of the role of unconscious motivation in determining behavior and focused instead on the theories that seemed to advocate sexual freedom. Even to talk of Freud's ideas (few actually read them) was to feel liberated.

The cultural interlude that ushered in Wilson's presidency in 1912 has been called "The Innocent Rebellion." It continued the artistic war begun by writers like Mark Twain, Frank Norris, Stephen Crane, Jack London, and Theodore Dreiser (Chap-

---

*Copyright by Elizabeth H. Dos Passos.

ter 23). The new writers who came of age around 1912, like their predecessors, attacked the "genteel tradition" for its deliberate avoidance of reality, its polite evasions. More freely experimental, this group promised, as one of its manifestoes said, to be "skeptical of inherited values" and "ready to examine old dogmas."

In many little magazines that suddenly appeared, they published their works and criticisms. In art galleries and shows, they saw the latest experimental painting from abroad—post-Impressionists like Matisse, Braque, Picasso, and others. It was contrasted with the work of the Ashcan School of American painters, who chose to represent life around them as it really looked.

Experimental theater flourished, as did the new poetry. Both broke sharply with traditional forms and expression. In *Bound East for Cardiff,* a one-act play produced in 1916, Eugene O'Neill (1888–1953) recalled the world of tramp steamers, waterfront dives, and seamen's talk he had known. The poet Carl Sandburg (1878–1967) crowded into his verse the midwestern life he had observed in the prairie towns of Illinois and in the raw metropolis of Chicago. Robert Frost (1874–1963) evoked the black beauty of the New Hampshire hills and celebrated the taciturn and self-contained Yankees who seemed to blend into its landscape.

Both as a critic and poet, Ezra Pound had considerable influence; he promoted and associated himself with the imagists, who departed from conventional poetry by using common speech and new rhythms to evoke images of everyday life. Pound had been confident of an intellectual awakening in America, but he seemed to despair when in 1909 he chose to live abroad as an expatriate. Others would soon join him there, convinced that individual artistic fulfillment could never be realized in the machine culture of America.

The prewar writers and artists had had a certain confidence and optimism about themselves and their ability to change society. Although some were committed to socialism, the prevailing spirit was more often anarchistic or free thinking. It was rejection of all rigid ideologies. But even before America entered the war, much of the optimism had gone. And what remained failed to survive the war and the postwar repression.

Disillusion and Disenchantment

The "lost generation" was the term Gertrude Stein used to describe the postwar writers and artists, because in their youth the war had broken the continuity of their lives. But Malcolm Cowley (born in 1898) said of himself and his literary and artistic contemporaries that they had actually lost their innocence before the war. To come of age in the America of the Progressive era was to suffer from "a sense of oppression." He and his friends could feel little passion or optimism. Progressive reform threatened to create only "an intolerable utopia of dull citizens"; morality was "a lie told to our bodies"; what they learned in school was "useless or misdirected"; and "society in general was terribly secure, unexciting, middle-class, a vast reflection of the families from which we came."

But World War I, in which many of the young writers and artists participated, had a deep effect on their lives. It left them bitter, resentful, and thoroughly disillusioned. Ernest Hemingway (1899–1961) had only recently graduated high school when he enlisted in a volunteer ambulance unit in France. What he experienced of the war convinced him of its senseless brutality, stupidity, and insensitivity. "I was embarrassed," says Lieutenant Henry in Hemingway's *A Farewell to Arms* (1929), "by the words *sacred, glorious,* and *sacrifice.* . . . We had . . . read them, on proclamations, now for a long time, and I had seen nothing sacred, and the things that were glorious had no glory and the sacrifices were like the stockyards in Chicago, if nothing was done with the meat except to bury it. . . . Abstract words such as *glory, honor, courage* were obscene."[*]

Like Cowley and Hemingway, many of those who fought found it difficult to return to an America that had, in their eyes, betrayed and deceived them. The soldiers, Ezra Pound wrote:

> *walked eye-deep in hell*
> *believing in old men's lies,*
> *then unbelieving*
> *came home, home to a lie,*
> *home to deceits,*
> *home to old lies and new infamy;*
> *usury age-old and age-thick*
> *and liars in public places.*[†]

To the question of what men had died for in the war, Pound delivered the classic response of the "rebel" generation:

> *For an old bitch gone in the teeth,*
> *For a botched civilization.*[†]

Hemingway, like Pound, settled in Paris after the war. The American writers and artists who went abroad before the war had gone mostly to look, to compare, to criticize, to learn. America remained their homeland, and they believed it would yet produce a vital culture. The expatriates of the 1920s felt differently. To be sure, they considered themselves cultural representatives of their land. But few wished ever again to endure its narrow-mindedness, provincialism, and stifling conformity. In a place like Paris, artists would be free to express themselves in any way they chose. What attracted so many to France, explained e. e. cummings, the unconventional poet and writer who had also served with an American ambulance corps in the war, was that "France has happened more than she is happening, whereas America is happening more than she has happened."

Although Paris remained an intellectual and artistic center throughout the twenties, many of the expatriates eventually returned to their native America, some of them having found that even Europe afforded no real or lasting escape. After Hemingway returned to New York, he wrote *The Sun Also Rises* (1926), which told of expatriates, broken by the war, amusing themselves in a postwar wasteland—drinking, boxing, watching bullfights, making love, all to no purpose.

What made postwar America such a stifling place for the rebel writers and artists who made up the "lost generation" was its business mentality, its machine standardization, and its spiritual sterility. To these critics, the businessman was the symbol of bourgeois culture. They mocked and condemned him not as an exploiter of labor or a corrupter of politics but for his blind conformity and emotional emptiness. His motto was "Gotta hustle," he spoke in clichés, worried about trivia, and practiced bigotry and moral censorship.

George Folansbee Babbitt, the literary creation of Sinclair Lewis (1885–1951) for his novel *Babbitt,* entered the American vocabulary as a way of defining business or professional men who conform unthinkingly to middle-class standards. Babbitt was the end product of standardization and mass marketing; his very character was shaped by the goods he consumed and the material objects he worshipped:

Just as he was an Elk, a Booster, and a member of the Chamber of Commerce, just as the priests of the Presbyterian Church determined his every religious belief and the senators who controlled the Republican Party decided in little smoky rooms in Washington what he should think about disarmament, tariff, and Germany, so did the large national advertisers fix the surface of his life, fix what he believed to be his individuality.

These standard advertised wares—toothpastes, socks, tires, cameras, instantaneous hot-water-heaters—were his symbols and proofs of excellence; at first the signs, then the substitutes, for joy and passion and wisdom. *

For many of the writers of the twenties, the need to probe the sources of America's troubles required that they analyze the very places in which they had been born and nurtured—the small towns of Middle America and the Bible Belt, where "dullness is made God." Hemingway, for example, grew up in Oak Park, Illinois. "What did he fear?" he asks of one of his characters. "It was not fear or dread. It was a nothing that he knew too well."

In *Main Street*, Sinclair Lewis, whose birthplace had been Sauk Center, Minnesota, drew caricatures of small-town types obsessed with material success and standardized in their thoughts and emotions. With more compassion, Sherwood Anderson (1876–1941), born in Ohio, tried to convey how the industrial machine had destroyed the community and poetry of the village and alienated its inhabitants from each other. The loneliness of Americans—the reaching out for human contact and finding none—produced the behavior and outlook he described in *Winesburg, Ohio* (1919). The procession of grotesque characters that moved through his tales—the drunkards, keyhole peepers, bedroom murderers—had become twisted and deformed because their emotions found no outlet. As Anderson wrote of one of his characters: "The living force within could not find expression."

More concerned with a region than the small town, William Faulkner (1897–1962), a native of Mississippi, broke with conventional literary forms in novels like *The Sound and the Fury* (1929), *Light in August* (1932), and *Absalom, Absalom!* (1936). No writer, no chronicler probed more deeply into the interior life of the South, into the inner recesses of the white southern mind. Nor did any novelist write as compellingly about the tragic nature of the South's past, the terrible burden of the Civil War, and the decadence, violence, and terror that marked the transition from the old values and civilization to the New South. Human relationships fascinated Faulkner, and few American writers conveyed as many terrible truths about those relationships. "I listen to the voices," he remarked, "and when I put down what the voices say, it's right. Sometimes I don't like what they say, but I don't change it."

With little compassion of any kind, Henry L.

*From *Babbitt* by Sinclair Lewis. Reprinted by permission of Harcourt Brace Jovanovich, Inc.

MAIN STREET, USA

In the novel *Main Street* (1920), Sinclair Lewis probed his own midwestern origins. Through the character of Carol Kennicott, a recent college graduate who has married a physician of Gopher Prairie, Minnesota, Lewis sought to expose "the unsparing unapologetic ugliness" of small-town America. In a party given to welcome her to the town, Carol tries to divert the conversation from small talk to more serious topics.

"There hasn't been much labor trouble around here, has there, Mr. Stowbody [president of the Ionic Bank]?" she asked innocently..

"No, ma'am, thank God, we've been free from that, except maybe with hired girls and farmhands. Trouble enough with these foreign farmers; if you don't watch these Swedes they turn socialist or populist or some fool thing on you in a minute. Of course, if they have loans you can make 'em listen to reason. I just have 'em come into the bank for a talk, and tell 'em a few things. I don't mind their being democrats, so much, but I won't stand having socialists around. . . ."

"Do you approve of union labor?" Carol inquired of Mr. Elder.

"Me? I should say not! It's like this: I don't mind dealing with my men if they think they've got any grievances—though Lord knows what's come over workmen, nowadays—don't appreciate a good job. But still, if they come to me honestly, as man to man, I'll talk things over with them. But I'm not going to

have any outsider . . . butting in and telling me how to run my business!"

Mr. Elder was growing more excited, more belligerent and patriotic. "I stand for freedom and constitutional rights. If any man don't like my shop, he can get up and git. Same way, if I don't like him, he gits. And that's all there is to it. . . . The half-baked thinker that isn't dry behind the ears yet, and these suffragettes and God knows what all buttinskis there are that are trying to tell a business man how to run his business, and some of these college professors are just about as bad, the whole kit and bilin' of 'em are nothing in God's world but socialism in disguise! And it's my bounden duty as a producer to resist every attack on the integrity of American industry to the last ditch. Yes—SIR!"

Mr. Elder wiped his brow.

Dave Dyer added, "Sure! You bet! What they ought to do is simply to hang every one of these agitators, and that would settle the whole thing right off. Don't you think so, doc?"

"You bet," agreed Kennicott. . . .

The talk went on. It did go on! Their voices were monotonous, thick, emphatic. They were harshly pompous, like men in the smoking-compartments of Pullman cars. They did not bore Carol. They frightened her. . . .

Source: Sinclair Lewis, *Main Street* (New York: Harcourt Brace, 1920), pp. 49–52.

Mencken (1880–1956), a critic and essayist, took on Babbitts as well as social idealists in the *American Mercury*, which he helped found in 1924. In America, he insisted, the conventional middle classes, the pillars of society, even more than the masses, were boobs, yokels, or peasants. The United States was their paradise, and Harding, "the Marion stone-head," was their president. The intellectual Woodrow Wilson, on the other hand, was that "self-bamboozled Presbyterian, the right thinker, the great moral statesman, the perfect model of the Christian cad." He expressed distaste for the political reformers of his time—"the army of uplifters and world-savers," the "jitney Messiahs," and "saccharine liberals." Democracy itself was a failure, though it provided "the only really amusing form of government ever endured by mankind." Monogamy was against nature; romantic love, a lie based on "the delusion that one woman differs from another."

In one of his annual volumes of *Prejudices*, which he began publishing in 1919, he asked of

himself: "If you find so much that is unworthy of reverence in the United States, then why do you live here?" He replied with another question, "Why do men go to zoos?" Mencken's ferocious assault on every sacred conviction of "the booboisie" made the *American Mercury* an overnight sensation, delighting even those he parodied. That in itself should have forced him to consider the shallowness and sophomoric quality of many of his barbs.

Few writers came closer to symbolizing the "lost generation" than F. Scott Fitzgerald (1896–1940). He emerged as the principal spokesman for a generation "grown up to find all Gods dead, all wars fought, all faiths in man shaken." Fitzgerald, along with his wife Zelda, followed a life style of reckless and decadent abandon. *This Side of Paradise*, published in 1920 when Fitzgerald was twenty-four, made him a celebrity overnight with its vivid and daring depiction of "flaming youth." But in his best novel, *The Great Gatsby* (1925), Fitzgerald managed to suggest both the glitter of American prosperity and the treacherous foundations on which it rested. With particular skill, he exposed the success ethic for the ways in which it consumed and destroyed individuals. Jay Gatsby, the romantic bootlegger who believes every dream can come true simply by wishing for it hard enough, is betrayed by his gangster friends and by the privileged rich who "smashed up things and then retreated back into their money and their vast carelessness."

That "vast carelessness" helped to bring "the greatest, gaudiest spree in history," as Fitzgerald once called it, to a sobering end. In 1931, against the background of economic distress and widespread unemployment, Fitzgerald wrote an obituary for the decade.

Now once more the belt is tight and we summon the proper expression of horror as we look back at our wasted youth. Sometimes, though, there is a ghostly rumble among the drums, an asthmatic whisper in the trombones that swings me back into the early twenties when we drank wood alcohol and every day in every way grew better and better, and there was a first abortive shortening of the skirts, and girls all looked alike in sweater dresses, and people you didn't want to know said, "Yes, we have no bananas," and it seemed only a question of a few years before the older people would step aside and let the world be run by those who saw things as they were—and it all seems rosy and roman-tic to us who were young then, because we will never feel quite so intensely about our surroundings any more.*

Some years later, a friend visited Fitzgerald and found him reading Karl Marx. It was an odd scene—at least the visitor thought so—but Fitzgerald, like many of the other literary and artistic rebels of the twenties, was heeding the call to social responsibility. As Fitzgerald explained to his friend, "I've got to examine all my characters in the light of their class relationships."

The Harlem Renaissance

While seeking equality in white America, W. E. B. DuBois had advised his people in *The Souls of Black Folk* (1903) that blacks should not sacrifice their racial heritage or their individuality. For too long, he felt, blacks had been forced to look at themselves through white eyes, calculating every move and word in terms of white expectations. In the 1920s, the rapid urbanization of blacks in the

*From F. Scott Fitzgerald, *Taps at Reveille*. Copyright 1935 by Charles Scribner's Sons; copyright renewed. Reprinted with permission of Charles Scribner's Sons.

Claude McKay. (*Brown Brothers*)

Langston Hughes. (*New York Public Library*)

North, along with the postwar racial violence and the new cultural influences, helped to promote a movement among black writers and artists to express the "true self-consciousness" DuBois had urged.

As Greenwich Village lured white artists, so Harlem—that part of northern Manhattan formerly occupied by the Dutch, the Irish, and the Jews—became the center of black America, and an exotic attraction for the white pleasure-seeker. Black people flocked to Harlem because that was the only place to be. To young, aspiring black writers and artists, many of whom came there in the twenties, Harlem was a remarkable place that deserved to be celebrated and loved for what it was. "Where else could I have all this life but Harlem?" asks the principal character in Claude McKay's *Home to Harlem* (1928):

Good old Harlem! Chocolate Harlem! Sweet Harlem! . . . The deep-dyed color, the thickness, the closeness of it. The noises of Harlem. The sugared laughter. The honey-talk on its streets. And all night long, ragtime and "blues" playing somewhere, . . . singing somewhere, dancing somewhere! Oh, the contagious fever of Harlem. Burning everywhere in dark-eyed Harlem.*

Like the young white rebels, Harlem intellectuals and artists, in large part the children of middle-class parents, rejected many of the values and standards of their seniors. What had stood in the way of "true Negro art in America," Langston Hughes (1902—1967) insisted, was that unfortunate "urge within the race toward whiteness, the desire to pour racial individuality into the mold of American standardization, and to be as little Negro and as much American as possible." Hughes rejected such assimilationist notions:

We younger Negro artists who create now intend to express our individual dark-skinned selves without fear or shame. If white people are pleased we are glad. If they are not, it doesn't matter. We know we are beautiful. And ugly too. The tom-tom cries and the tom-tom laughs. If colored people are pleased we are glad. If they are not, their displeasure doesn't matter either. We build our temples for tomorrow, strong as we know how, and we stand on the top of the mountain, free within ourselves.†

The older generation of cultural leaders, DuBois's "talented tenth," had been so fearful of reinforcing white stereotypes about blacks that they ignored or obscured the artistic resources of

black folk forms. The more conservative among them frowned on the poets, novelists, musicians, and entertainers who celebrated black vitality and substituted anger and irony for the old strategy of humiliation or imitation. But that did not stop a new generation of black activists from preferring the black vernacular, the mournful blues of Bessie Smith, the "hot jazz" of Duke Ellington and Louis Armstrong, the soft-shoe shuffling of Bojangles Bill Robinson, the singing sermons of evangelist Elder Lightfoot Solomon Michaux.

By whatever means, the Harlem artists were intent on revealing the freshness and variety of black culture. They found inspiration and spiritual identity in their African origins. They rediscovered the spirituals, the work songs, the sermons, and the rich plantation folklore. They sought to describe, honestly and realistically, the lives and troubles of their people, both in the slave past and the urban present. Having arrived in Harlem in 1921, Langston Hughes would spend the remainder of his life there celebrating in his poetry, novels, and humor the beauty and spontaneity he found.

Of the scores of talented men and women who gave Harlem its unusual distinction in the twenties, certain names stand out. One was the Jamaican Claude McKay (1890–1948), a gifted poet and prose writer and an early leader in the Harlem movement. McKay dramatized in his life and work the New Negro's rebellion against bourgeois inhibitions. Cosmopolitan, Marxist, idealist, and realist, his serious treatment of primitivism and his militant protest against capitalism and racial bigotry linked him with both the white literary experimentalists and the radical publicists of the postwar decade.

Perhaps the most brilliant single achievement of the renaissance was Jean Toomer's (1894–1967) novel *Cane*, a series of black portraits that ranged over unexplored parts of black life in the South. But *Cane* sold less than 500 copies the year it was published, emphasizing the problem black artists faced not only in reaching their own people, but in having to cater to white expectations. If McKay's *Home to Harlem* made the best-seller charts, that was because his portrayal of Harlem life confirmed what so many whites were discovering for themselves.

The twenties, Langston Hughes recalled, was a period "when the Negro was in vogue." That is, downtown whites and tourists went to Harlem to see the action, to listen to the music, to drop their inhibitions and find emotional release. Harlem soon had a reputation among whites that few

---

*Copyright 1956 by Hope McKay Virtue; reissued 1973 by The Chatham Bookseller, Chatham, New Jersey.

†From *The Big Sea* by Langston Hughes. Copyright 1940 by Langston Hughes. Reprinted by permission of Hill and Wang, a division of Farrar, Straus and Giroux, Inc.

THE TWENTIES: BUSINESS AND CULTURE

Harlemites might have recognized. Some years later, Hughes would bitterly recall the white man's addiction:

A party of whites from Fifth Avenue
Came tippin into Dixie's to get a view,
Came tippin into Dixie's with smiles on their faces,
Knowin they can buy a dozen colored places.
Dixie grinned. Dixie bowed.
Dixie rubbed his hands and laughed out loud—
While a tall white woman
In an ermine cape
Looked at the blacks and
Thought of rape,
Looked at the blacks and
Thought of a rope,
Looked at the blacks and
Thought of flame,
And thought of something
Without a name.[*]

When Carl Van Vechten wrote *Nigger Heaven* (1926), a best-selling novel, he caught the essence of the Harlem appeal: "Jungle land. Hottentots and Bantus swaying under the amber moon. Love, sex, passion, hate." Although Van Vechten was white, he took an active interest in promoting black artists, and finding patrons and publishers for them. Their recognition, however, proved to be double-edged, and the relationship was bound to fail. "She wanted me to be primitive and know and feel the intuitions of the primitive," Hughes recalled of his white patroness. "But, unfortunately, I did not feel the rhythms of the primitive surging through me, and so I could not live and write as though I did. I was only an American Negro—who had loved the surface of Africa and the rhythms of Africa—but I was not African. I was Chicago and Kansas City and Broadway and Harlem."

Once the Great Depression struck, the patrons departed, as did the publishers. In Harlem, the exclusive clubs that had catered to white customers closed their doors. "We were no longer in vogue," Hughes recalled. Besides, he noted, the Harlem artists who thought the "Renaissance" would bring acceptance and success had only deceived themselves. "For how could a large and enthusiastic number of people be crazy about Negroes forever? . . . The ordinary Negroes hadn't heard of the Negro Renaissance. And if they had, it hadn't raised their wages any."

In 1932, Hughes and twenty-one other Harlem writers visited the Soviet Union. Claude McKay be-

came briefly interested in the Communist experiment, but came away disillusioned and entered the Catholic Church. The light-complexioned Jean Toomer found an outlet in mysticism and crossed the color line altogether. The task of expressing "our individual dark-skinned selves without fear or shame" would be largely taken on in the thirties by Hughes, DuBois, and a newcomer, Richard Wright.

THE POPULAR ARTS

Applied to the popular or "lively" arts, technology had an enormous impact in the twenties. It shaped American attitudes and tastes in ways that few if any books could. Radio reached into the homes of millions, and similar numbers flocked to the movie houses and listened to phonograph records. The effects were both liberating and conditioning. Rural isolation broke down. Americans everywhere were introduced to make-believe worlds, new styles of music, new levels of sophistication, different life styles, and new models to imitate. Movies and radio programs nationalized popular culture, revolutionzed people's expectations, and made even greater the standardization of society. With their vast potential for influencing and molding the habits and tastes of Americans, the popular arts by the end of the decade had become big businesses in their own right.

The Movies

The liveliest of the "lively arts" of the twenties, the movies, was also the most highly mechanized, the most highly capitalized, the one closest to big business in production and distribution methods. The movies began as a peep show in a penny arcade. The viewer put a nickel in a device called a kinetoscope (invented by Thomas A. Edison about 1896) and saw tiny figures moving against blurred backgrounds. Edison thought little of his invention, but others took it up and soon succeeded in projecting images on a screen for large audiences. By 1905, more than 5000 "nickelodeons," housed in converted stores and warehouses, were showing films for 5 cents admission.

Peep shows had prospered by showing short comic action. The new films introduced many inventions, most of them endless variations on the chase: cowboys after rustlers; sheriffs after badmen; city cops after bank robbers. Comedians threw pies at one another, slipped on banana peels,

[*]From *Death in Harlem*. Reprinted by permission of Harold Ober Associates Incorporated. Copyright © 1942 by Langston Hughes; copyright renewed.

A chorus line of beauties who satisfied the exacting demands of Ziegfeld. (*Culver Pictures*)

fell into manholes. The first movie with a recognizable plot was *The Great Train Robbery* (1903), and its instant success set every producer to turning out thrillers. But there were still no stars, no sex, no culture. David W. Griffith liberated the movie camera from nickelodeon themes and the limitations of the stage set. In *The Birth of a Nation* (1914), a partisan and intolerant film about the Civil War and Reconstruction, Griffith showed sweeping panoramas of massed armies, fade-outs, closeups, and other kinds of shots revealing the scope and flexibility of camera and screen. Budgeted at an unheard-of $100,000, and directed with imagination, *The Birth of a Nation* was a financial and artistic model.

The most successful of Griffith's imitators in the twenties was Cecil B. de Mille, whose religious spectacles—*The Ten Commandments* (1923) and *The King of Kings* (1927), for example—exploited the mechanical possibilities of the camera and the ways that sex could be worked into almost any subject. By 1917 the movies had become a multimillion-dollar industry, with Hollywood, California, the film capital. Luxurious movie theaters rapidly replaced the nickelodeons, and Americans were spending $175 million a year on admissions.

The first stars—Mary Pickford, Roscoe (Fatty) Arbuckle, Douglas Fairbanks, Marie Dressler—earned fabulous salaries, lived glamorous lives, and attracted incredible newspaper and magazine attention. Much of it was promoted by movie press agents to keep the stars in the public eye. The stars themselves cooperated so well, on and off stage, that Hollywood soon achieved a reputation as the Sodom of America. As if to confirm that view, films with titles like *Sinners in Silk, Ladies of Pleasure, The Joy Girl,* and *Women Who Give* exposed audiences, in the words of one press agent, to "brilliant men, beautiful jazz babies, champagne baths, midnight revels, petting parties in the purple dawn, all ending in a terrific smashing climax that makes you gasp!"

These films promised considerably more than they gave, but moralists worried about their effect on youth and agitated for official censorship. To forestall their critics by regulating their own affairs, film producers in 1922 hired Will H. Hays, former chairman of the Republican National Committee and Harding's postmaster general, to act as their conscience. Hays devised a production code setting limits on lovemaking, décolletage, crime, and profanity.

(*The Granger Collection*)

(*The Granger Collection*)

(*The Granger Collection*)

The Lyric Theatre, New York. (*Photograph by Berenice Abbott for Federal Art Project 'Changing New York,' courtesy Museum of the City of New York*)

The Rex Theatre, Lelaud, Mississippi. (*Photograph by Dorothea Lange, Library of Congress*)

Besides sex and spectacles, slapstick comedy quickly became a movie staple featuring such stars as Arbuckle, Harold Lloyd, and Buster Keaton. The greatest comic of all, Charlie Chaplin, achieved an international reputation with his brilliant characterization of the wistful little tramp with the battered derby hat, cane, and funny walk. In *Modern Times*, in which he had to escape from the clutches of enormous machines, Chaplin captured the tyranny of the assembly line.

With the opening of Al Jolson's *The Jazz Singer* in 1927, the era of sound films began. Within two years, "talkies" had replaced silents, and Hollywood, with what John Dos Passos called "its great bargain sale of five and ten cent lusts and dreams," was reaching even larger audiences.

The Phonograph: Ragtime and Jazz

What the film projector did for motion, the phonograph, another Edison invention, did for sound. By 1905 the phonograph had become a successful commercial device. Comedians, actors, singers, and musicians could be heard in the home or in places of public entertainment. By 1914 more than half a million phonographs were being manufactured each year, and soon it was nearly a million.

Before radio, the phonograph gave the greatest impetus to the spread of popular music, much of it ragtime and jazz. Ragtime had emerged in the 1890s. Scott Joplin was its best-known composer, and it borrowed heavily from black worksongs and both black and white minstrel songs—"a music," writes LeRoi Jones, "the Negro came to in imitating white imitations of Negro music." Stressing rhythm rather than melody, the instrument rather than the voice, ragtime would have a significant influence on jazz.

With the wartime and postwar migration of blacks, jazz and blues spread northward, especially to Chicago's South Side and New York's Harlem. Dixieland bands first played in these cities around 1915, the year W. C. Handy wrote his "St. Louis Blues."

In 1920, the Okeh Record company made the dramatic decision to permit a black singer to make a commercial recording. With Mamie Smith's rendition of "Crazy Blues," race records, as they were called, made a successful debut. The first jazz records were made in 1917 by a white group. Within the next several years, Paul Whiteman became known as the "King of Jazz." Blues and jazz

Bessie Smith, Empress of the Blues. (*Culver Pictures*)

Preach them blues.
Sing them blues . . .
Moan them blues.
Let me convert your soul.

recordings multiplied, and attending jazz concerts became fashionable. But as LeRoi Jones would later observe in *Blues People:* "With such displays as Whiteman's Aeolian Hall concert, complete with 'European Style' orchestra and Heifetz and Rachmaninoff in the audience, jazz had rushed into the mainstream without so much as one black face." But, he added, Americans had come to realize that there existed an American music "as

Radio

Unlike the movies, whose commercial possibilities were obvious from the first, the early development of radio was haphazard and accidental. In 1920, perhaps 20,000 amateurs listened on homemade sets to wireless messages sent mainly from ships at sea. That year, as an experiment, the Westinghouse Electric and Manufacturing Company in Pittsburgh began to broadcast musical programs. Amateurs in the area responded enthusiastically, and soon popular demand induced Westinghouse to put the programs on a regular basis and to introduce reports of baseball scores. In 1920 the first commercial broadcasting station, KDKA, was set up in Pittsburgh in time to broadcast the results of the Harding-Cox election.

Overnight, radio became big business. Within four years, 562 stations were sending out music, stock market and news reports, bedtime stories, and church services. The ringside account of the Dempsey-Carpentier fight in 1921 first realized the potential for using radio to tap the rage for mass spectator sports. By the end of the decade, broadcasts of prizefights, as well as the World Series and the Rose Bowl, ensured large audiences. The sales of radio sets boomed. Radio stations covered the country, approximately a fourth of them controlled by newspapers or newspaper chains bent on dominating news outlets. Stations were combined into networks, so programs could reach mass audiences simultaneously. In 1926, the Radio Corporation of America (RCA) established the National Broadcasting Company with nineteen stations.

Once established as a national habit, radio listening became the object of intensive study by advertisers who paid for most of the entertainment. As a selling medium, it seemed unsurpassed. The advertiser could reach into the homes of millions and repeat a message hour after hour. Most people seem to have accepted "commercials" as the price of free radio entertainment. But to Dr. Lee De Forest, whose technical breakthrough had made national radio possible, the price was too high. "What have you done with my child?" he asked. "You have sent him out on the street in rags of ragtime to collect money from all and sundry. You have made of him a laughingstock of intelligence, surely a stench in the nostrils of the gods of the ionosphere."

Now that Americans could listen to nominating conventions and campaign speeches in their homes, interest in politics increased. But that did not appear to affect the quality of politics in the twenties. Radio did enable millions to follow the Smith-Hoover campaign of 1928. Millions more would hear Franklin Delano Roosevelt seek to calm fears over the collapse of the economic order.

THE POLITICS OF COMPLACENCY

To "sell" their candidate in the 1920 election, the Republicans chose Albert Lasker of the Lord and Thomas agency, a creative genius in the newly glamorous advertising business. The selection was entirely appropriate. Having already made household words of Pepsodent and Puffed Wheat, Lasker undertook to "humanize Harding." He implanted the image of "an old-fashioned, safe, honest-to-

---

*From *Blues People* (1963) by Imamu Amiri Baraka (LeRoi Jones) by permission of William Morrow & Company.

WORDS AND NAMES IN AMERICAN HISTORY

Development of a national economy in the United States eventually brought with it "brand names" and "brand name products," ones that manufacturers hoped would be recognized by and appeal to an unprecedented number of people spread out over an enormous geographical area. Of course electronic mass media would eventually help to place these names in the living rooms of millions of American homes, but the first successful ones appeared about fifty years after newspapers became daily, cheap, and widely available in the 1830s. Toward the end of the nineteenth century, patent medicines became the first widely known name products. Lydia Pinkham's syrup (which actually contained alcohol) was downed in great quantities by teetotalling folks as a cure for almost any ailment. By the 1920s, some brand names were beginning to become the word for the new product itself: record players were "Victrolas," and paper handkerchiefs "Kleenexes."

the-core Middle Westerner who could be trusted never to rock the boat." To make that case required no distortion of Harding's character or political record.

Even without Lasker's salesmanship, the American people were bound to respond favorably to Harding. He was an easy man to like, a public favorite as long as he held office. He embodied the nation's small-town virtues. He belonged to the right clubs; he was a self-made man; he "looked like a president ought to look"; and he had a warm personality.

Unlike Wilson, Harding had no difficulty pardoning Eugene Debs for his wartime statements: "I could pick you out a half dozen members of the House and Senate," Harding explained, "who deserved quite as much to be in the penitentiary as did Debs." But he could not understand why radicals and some trade unionists persisted in their agitation rather than place their faith, as he had, in the American Dream. He had made it, and he assumed any American who had the right kind of hustle and determination would also succeed.

When Harding died in August 1923, Coolidge's oath of office as president was administered to him by his father in their Vermont farmhouse, by the light of an old-fashioned kerosene lamp. This ceremony successfully projected a taciturn Yankee rustic in the Lasker image of his unfortunate predecessor. If Harding made a virtue of humility, Coolidge made one of inactivity and dedication to the principle that "civilization and profits go hand in hand." Both men reflected the dominant business culture of the decade. And both of them, in their policies, helped to promote the maldistribution of wealth and the speculation that were speeding the nation toward economic disaster.

The Tragedy of Harding

When Harding said "we must strive for normalcy to reach stability," he had in mind his campaign promise to encourage less government in business and more business in government. To help him in that task, he said he would bring the "best minds" to Washington. He kept this promise in part by making such able men as Charles Evans Hughes secretary of state, Herbert Hoover secretary of commerce, Henry C. Wallace secretary of agriculture, and Andrew W. Mellon secretary of the treasury. But he also brought with him some lesser minds, his small-town "Ohio gang." They proceeded to make a shambles of the Harding administration.

At the head of the Ohio gang was Harry M. Daugherty, a small-time lobbyist for tobacco, meat, and utility interests, who first launched the Harding presidential boom. Rewarded with the attorney generalship, he held the position until dismissed by President Coolidge in 1924, when his activities were revealed. Daugherty had made a business, while in office, of selling liquor permits, pardons, and paroles to criminals at fancy prices. (Two divided juries in 1926 enabled him to escape prison.) Jesse Smith, who conducted a clearinghouse for the Ohio gang's graft, committed suicide, and the gang's worst secrets died with him. Even so, a number of administration insiders were soon sent to jail.

Charles R. Forbes, whom Harding had met on a vacation trip, so charmed the president that he was made director of the Veterans Bureau. In that position he swindled the country of no less than $250 million by demanding kickbacks from contractors and suppliers and by condemning supplies meant for veterans and selling them at reduced prices in return for rebates for himself. In 1925 he was sent to Leavenworth Prison. Thomas W. Miller, the alien property custodian, was convicted of conspiracy to defraud the government. For lavish gifts, Miller distributed to American firms the valuable German chemical patents confiscated during the war; the firms paid far less than the patents were worth.

The most spectacular of the Harding scandals was the notorious Teapot Dome. Since 1909, when the conservation movement was in full swing, three tracts of oil-rich public land had been set aside under the jurisdiction of the secretary of the navy for naval needs. In 1921, with Navy Secretary Edwin Denby's consent, these lands were transferred to the custody of Secretary of the Interior Albert B. Fall. A friend of private oil men, Fall secretly leased the Teapot Dome Reservation in Wyoming to Harry F. Sinclair's Mammoth Oil Company. Soon after, he leased a second reserve at Elks Hill to a company headed by Edward F. Doheny. Fall received about $300,000 in cash and negotiable securities and a herd of cattle from Sinclair, and a "loan" of $100,000 from Doheny. The wealth soon attracted the interest of watchful senators.

A committee headed by Senator Thomas J. Walsh of Montana gradually untangled the story. The Supreme Court voided the leases, and Fall, convicted of accepting a bribe, was fined $100,000 and sentenced to a year in prison. Although Doheny and Sinclair, oddly enough, were acquitted of having bribed Fall, Sinclair went to jail for

Today the word *lobby* often suggests political activity, but it still retains its ancient meaning of entrance room or hallway. Modern hotels still have lobbies. But so do state and national legislatures just outside the main halls where legislative business is carried on and where only elected members may enter. A *lobby* is a usually well-financed group of people formed with the intent of influencing legislation. Various interest groups hire *lobbyists* to *lobby* for or against certain legislation that might affect the welfare of the group, often with a great deal of money at stake. In its political sense the term originated in the Jacksonian era, when American political practices changed so drastically. In 1841 an English visitor to this country described what he saw with accuracy but obvious aristocratic distaste: "A practice exists in the State capitals, called *lobbying.* . . . A certain number of agents, selected for their skill and experience in the arts of deluding, persuading, and bribing members, are employed by public companies and private individuals, who have bills before the legislature which they are anxious to get passed. These persons attend the lobby of the House daily, talk with the members, . . . invite them to dinners and suppers, etc."

---

contempt of the Senate, and for contempt of court. He had refused to answer questions, and had hired detectives to shadow the jury at his trial.

From the start, Harding was overwhelmed by the presidency. Every decision cost him endless hesitations and torments. He expected his friends to operate as a "team" now that they were in the "big league." He found it difficult to deal with their betrayal of him. "My God, this is a hell of a job," he told a journalist. "I have no trouble with my enemies . . . But my damned friends, my God-damned friends . . . they're the ones that keep me walking the floor nights!" While on a speaking tour in the West, Harding became ill and he died on August 2, 1923, in San Francisco.

Still ignorant of the worst of this administration (as the president himself had been to the end), the public went into mourning as deep as that for any leader since Lincoln. It was as though they had lost a personal friend. Disclosures of corruption after his death only slowly eroded the popular regard in which he personally was held.

"Normalcy" in Government: Economic Policies

The transition from Harding to Coolidge was bound to be smooth. To Coolidge, as to the man he replaced, business values were sacred. "The man who builds a factory builds a temple," Coolidge observed. "The man who works there worships there." The government justified itself by its success in encouraging the business community. Beyond that objective, it needed only to cut expenses and reduce taxes.

The beginning of a business revival for which the Republicans took full credit permitted them to confront the electorate in 1924 with the slogan, "Keep Cool With Coolidge." The Democrats were badly divided. William G. McAdoo, Wilson's son-in-law and secretary of the treasury, had the support of the rural Protestant segment of the party. Alfred E. Smith, New York's Catholic governor, drew support from the city machines and the "wets." There was a deadlock until the two factions finally settled on John W. Davis, a conservative New York corporation lawyer.

Convinced that the American people needed a choice in the election, Robert M. La Follette ran as a third party candidate on a revived Progressive ticket. The platform called for nationalization of railroads, recognition of labor's right to bargain collectively, and a popular referendum for any declaration of war in cases other than invasion of the United States. Although attacked by both major party candidates as a dangerous radical, La Follette managed to poll nearly 5 million votes. Davis received over 8 million, and Coolidge well over 15 million. The vote ensured the Republican party's virtually free hand during his administration.

"No one can contemplate current conditions," said Coolidge in his inaugural address of March 1925, "without finding much that is satisfying and still more that is encouraging." The good times seemed to have justified the economic measures already taken during Harding's term. Many were the inspiration of Andrew W. Mellon, the immensely wealthy head of the aluminum trust, owner of oil companies, steel mills, utilities, and banks, a lavish contributor to the party, who became secretary of the treasury in 1921. He believed that government should promote private enterprise. He would seek to reduce the national debt by reducing government expenses and by insisting that the Allies repay the United States in full. At the same time, he wanted to lower taxes in the upper-income groups to provide incentives for the wealthy to become even wealthier.

Despite the $24 billion national debt, Congress adopted the Revenue Act of 1921. It repealed the wartime excess-profits tax and reduced the surtax on personal income from 73 to 50 percent. After Coolidge's reelection, Congress went even further in reducing the maximum income tax. During the debate on the 1925 tax cut (one of many during the next four years), a Nebraska Progressive observed that "Mr. Mellon himself gets a larger personal reduction than the aggregate of practically all the taxpayers in the state of Nebraska."

As taxes went down, tariffs went up. As early as 1916, Americans feared a postwar domestic market flooded by European manufacturers. Primed by this threat, Congress in the Fordney-McCumber Act (1922) raised duties to high levels. This prevented the Allies from reducing their war debts by exporting goods to the United States; it also caused many nations to adopt tariffs against American imports. Nevertheless, protectionism remained an essential part of Republican economic policy in the twenties. During the Hoover administration, duties would be raised even higher in the Hawley-Smoot Tariff (1930).

Under Harding and Coolidge, the principal regulatory agencies—the Interstate Commerce Commission, the Federal Trade Commission, and the Federal Reserve Board—were staffed by men who shared the belief that government serves the people best by serving the needs of business. The FTC, for example, encouraged business conferences to negotiate industrywide agreements for corporate benefit. Hoover continued this policy as secretary of commerce. Through trade associations in which companies shared product and market information, Hoover hoped to achieve his goal of industrial cooperation and standardization. In addition, the Commerce Department helped businesses to find overseas markets for materials and investments.

The Supreme Court cleared the way for cooperation and combination. By introducing the "rule of reason" into its decision dissolving the Standard Oil Company in 1911, the Court implied that from now on its antimonopoly rulings would be even less severe. This promise was tested in the antitrust suit involving the United States Steel Corporation. In 1920, the Court ruled that although the billion-dollar enterprise controlled about 40 percent of the steel industry, this did not make it powerful enough to act in "unreasonable" restraint

of trade. Encouraged by the favorable judicial atmosphere, as well as by federal agencies and cabinet-level departments, business in the 1920s went on a new merger spree. In the field of public utilities, 3,744 firms were swallowed up. Comparable consolidations occurred in manufacturing, banking, transportation, and wholesale and retail trade.

Organized labor, by contrast, lost ground. Between 1919 and 1922, strikes failed against the great steel, coal, and railroad industries. Employers pushed workers into subservient company unions, whose members numbered more than 1.5 million by 1929. AFL membership, at a peak of over 4 million in 1920, had fallen to under 3 million by 1923 and continued to fall thereafter. Most workers, particularly in the new mass-production industries, remained unorganized. Employers used various methods, including paid informers and blacklists, to keep it that way. Although workers gained modest annual improvements in real wages during the decade, the average annual income for many of them fell below the $1800 thought necessary to maintain a minimum decent standard of living.

Social legislation to help workers fared badly in the courts. Two Supreme Court decisions in 1921 exposed strikers to injunctions thought to be illegal under the Clayton Act of 1914. In 1922, the Court held that child labor could not constitutionally be regulated by a discriminatory tax levied on products manufactured by children. The next year, the Court struck down an act of Congress establishing minimum wages for women and children in the District of Columbia. Only in 1932, after the Depression had created a new political mood, did organized labor succeed in pushing through Congress the Norris-LaGuardia Act against labor injunctions.

The economic problem most troublesome to the Republicans was the distress of farmers deeply in debt from wartime overexpansion. Dairy, vegetable, and fruit farmers prospered from nearby city markets. Staple farmers had to sell in world markets, where increased competition after the war made the problem of overproduction worse. When women turned from cotton to rayon fabrics, and families changed their diets to include more fruits and vegetables at the expense of pork, beef, and flour, the pinch on staple farmers tightened. Republican leaders again urged higher tariffs as the solution. But tariffs harmed exporters by forcing up prices of farm families' purchases and by bringing foreign tariff regulation on American agricultural exports.

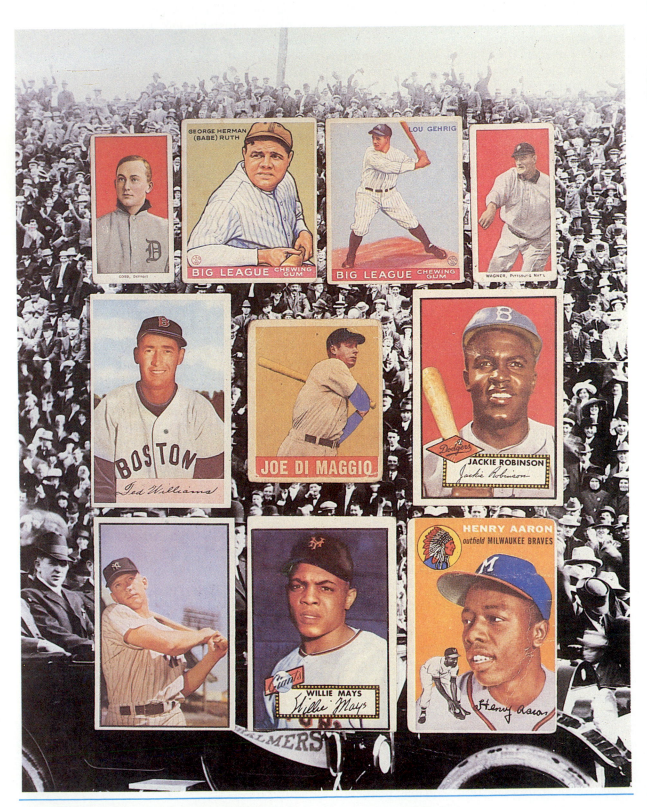

(Reproduced by permission of the players, Topps Chewing Gum Inc., and Leaf Brands, Inc.)

Babe Ruth. (*Culver Pictures*)

Joe DiMaggio. (*UPI/Bettmann Newsphotos*)

George Bellows' painting of Argentina's Luis Firpo, "Wild Bull of the Pampas," knocking Jack Dempsey out of the ring in 1923. Dempsey came back to win. (*Collection of Whitney Museum, photo by G. Clements*)

THE TWENTIES: BUSINESS AND CULTURE

Red Grange. (*Culver Pictures*)

Mud-spattered football players in a game between the Cleveland Browns and the Green Bay Packers, 1966. (*Arthur Rickerby/Life Magazine, Time, Inc.*)

Net farm income, including that of prosperous dairy and truck farmers, fell by nearly 50 percent in the 1920s—from $9.5 billion in 1919 to $5.3 billion in 1928. A strong farm bloc in Congress responded with the McNary-Haugen bill for federal government support of staple prices. Passed in 1927 and again in 1928, the president vetoed it both times. "Farmers have never made money," Coolidge said. "I don't believe we can do much about it."

"COOLIDGE PROSPERITY"

New production techniques and new consumer industries gave a golden glow to "Coolidge prosperity." Electricity was applied to the machines, and the "scientific management" theories of Frederick Winslow Taylor and his followers were applied to the people who made machines produce. The result was a substantial increase in industrial efficiency and production.

Between 1921 and 1929, industrial output almost doubled, even though the size of the labor force remained stable. At the same time, population and economic growth, as well as the wartime construction lag, pushed the demand for housing to record levels. This stimulated the private construction industry, which traditionally used more capital and labor than any other.

But the "Coolidge prosperity" rested on a slippery footing. Workers did not share adequately in the profits of increased production, resulting in an unequal distribution of purchasing power. Technological unemployment increased; and farmers failed to recover from the postwar recession. For a time, the construction and auto booms, along with speculation in real estate and securities, sustained the "good times."

New Industries

World War I itself contributed much to the prosperous side of the 1920s. Liberty Bond drives accustomed millions to investing in securities. After the war, they made it easier for corporations to finance new or expanded ventures through stock or bond issues. Many corporations made so much money during the war that they could pay for expanded or improved facilities without going to the money market at all. The excess profits tax of the war years had prompted corporations to plow back earnings into modernized plant and equipment. This paid off in productivity and profits when the war was over.

Many industries that came of age in the twenties were created by the war or matured by its demands. In 1903, Wilbur and Orville Wright made the first successful flight in a motor-driven heavier-than-air contraption at Kitty Hawk, North Carolina. But there was little interest in airplanes until they were needed in the war for scouting and combat. Transcontinental airmail service began in 1920; in 1923 came the first regularly scheduled flights between Chicago and Cheyenne, Wyoming. The Air Commerce Act of 1926 gave substantial mail subsidies to private airlines and helped make commercial flying a big business.

After Charles A. Lindbergh, Jr., in May 1927, made his solo flight from New York to Paris, flying became more popular than ever. Three years later, 122 American airlines were carrying almost half a million passengers over 50,000 miles of air routes.

The war gave the American chemical industry an even greater boost. Before 1914, American chemical companies had produced little but the simple heavy acids and alkalis used in basic industrial processes. During the war, explosives became the principal product of the industry, and many new chemical plants were built to supply Allied needs. Once the war was over, two government actions fostered the growth of a huge chemical industry. The first was the confiscation of German coal-tar patents and their assignment to American chemical corporations. The second, motivated by popular demand for chemical self-sufficiency in the event of another war, was high duties on chemical imports. By 1929, corporate beneficiaries of these measures, such as Allied Chemical, Union Carbide, and the old DuPont company, had far outstripped all foreign chemical firms or cartels.

An Electrochemical Revolution

During the twenties, the efficiency of the power industry improved significantly. By the end of the decade, 70 percent of American factory machinery was operated by electricity, compared with 30 percent fifteen years before. The most striking gains from the combination of electricity and chemical processes were made in the petroleum industry. Between 1913 and 1928, electrochemical processes tripled the quantity of gasoline that could be refined from a gallon of crude oil. Electrochemical processes in the steel industry led to higher-quality parts for internal combustion engines. Better engines made more efficient use of the gasoline, which was more efficiently produced. The combination of electricity and chemistry in metallurgy also brought gains in the manufacture of phonographs, refrigerators, radios, washing machines, vacuum cleaners, and other adjuncts of the good life.

Besides revolutionizing industrial technology in the twenties, electricity revolutionized factory organization and procedures. By permitting the transmission of power over tremendous distances, it freed the factory from the river valley and the coal field and gave management much greater opportunity to consider markets and other "location" factors in deciding on factory sites.

By permitting the even flow of power throughout huge plants, electricity added immensely to the flexibility of organization within the factory. It established the economies of the production line and put a premium on standardization of jobs and materials. "Rationalization" became the catchword of industrial planners, much as "systems" became forty years later.

The Automobile Age

No industry was more firmly rooted in the technological and managerial changes of the post-war years than automobiles. For the rubber, glass, and alloys of which body and engine parts were made, automobile manufacturers depended on the new chemical and electrical knowledge and the new electrochemical processes. Automobile manufacturers became the greatest users of each of the commodities that went into their product, and work on auto assembly lines became highly mechanized and repetitive.

American technological experience led to the growth of automobile production. From the nation's earliest days, carriage manufacturers had

Nantasket Beach, Massachusetts on a Fourth of July in the early 1920s. "Why on earth do you need to study what's changing in this country," someone asked sociologists Robert and Helen Lynd. "I can tell you what's happening in just four letters: A-U-T-O!" (*Wide World Photos*)

made bodies, springs, and wheels. Since the 1850s, the building of farm machinery had developed familiarity with small engines. In the last decades of the nineteenth century, bicycle manufacturers pushed the development of pneumatic tires. The American environment, in turn, reinforced the impact of American technological experience. The United States was a country of majestic distances and of a growing middle class prosperous enough to purchase thousand-dollar commodities that could cross the wide-open spaces with satisfying speed. Railroads had helped concentrate population in metropolises; the automobile tended to disperse it, speeding the decline of cities.

Many attempts had been made to build a "horseless carriage" run by steam, electricity, alcohol, and other fuels. After a series of experiments with a gasoline engine, in the United States and abroad, the automobile became commercially feasible about 1903. In seven years, some sixty American companies were producing cars. William C. Durant formed General Motors to control the competition, but failed to get Ford into it. Henry Ford was already a prominent automobile manufacturer in 1908. The next year he introduced the Model T, at the list price of $950 in "any color you choose so long as it's black." In five years, Model Ts were down to $550. Ford sold 168,000 cars, representing about a third of the nation's entire automobile business that year.

In 1914 Ford opened his revolutionary plant at Highland Park, Michigan. It was equipped with the first electric conveyor belt, which carried the gradually assembled car at a uniform—and rapid—speed past stationary workers. Each worker used materials and tools to perform one simple mechanical task. In 1913 it had taken 14 hours, on the average, to assemble a Model T. In the new plant it could be done in 93 minutes. In 1914, Ford built 248,000 cars—45 percent of the total automobile output—at a base price of $490. His profit that year exceeded $30 million. By 1925 Ford was turning out a complete car every 10 seconds. People, however, were beginning to tire of the Model T, and the drift toward distinctive models with more comfortable appointments had begun.

In 1920 about 9 million automobiles were registered in the United States. In ten years it was nearly 30 million. Millions of Americans came to see the automobile as part of the minimum standard of living. It broke down distances and encouraged a movement into the suburbs, created a new kind of tourist industry, and stimulated government expenditures for street and highway construction. For some, the automobile became a status symbol. In Sinclair Lewis's *Main Street*, the hero confesses four loves: his wife, his medical practice, hunting, and his automobile. He found it impossible to rate them in order of preference.

The Election of 1928

When Coolidge let slip the announcement that he did not choose to run in 1928, Republican leaders turned to his secretary of commerce. Born in modest circumstances on an Iowa farm, Herbert Hoover had had a rewarding career as an engineer and promoter. He won acclaim for his relief work in Europe during the war. After the war, he was credited with having used American wealth to stop the advance of communism. These activities gave him a reputation for practicality and humanitarianism. His attacks on the many unwise aspects of peacemaking also gave him standing as a statesman.

To oppose Hoover, the Democrats this time united behind Al Smith. As governor of New York, Smith had an outstanding record of backing liberal legislation and ideas. But that record meant nothing to the nation at large. An Irishman, a Catholic, a New Yorker, and a "wet," Smith was the incarnation of everything that aroused rural and small-town suspicions.

With Hoover's initial advantages, it seems unlikely that any Democrat could have beaten him. His popular *majority* exceeded 6 million votes, and he carried all but eight states, including, for the first time since Reconstruction, five in the Solid South. Many Catholics blamed bigotry for Smith's defeat. But "Coolidge prosperity" and Hoover's promise of more to come were more likely the decisive factors.

Despite Smith's defeat, the Democrats found some satisfaction in his showing. His vote doubled that of Davis in 1924. In the country's twelve largest cities, strongly Republican in the two preceding elections, his total exceeded Hoover's. And the future lay with the urban voter.

Calvin Coolidge left the White House confident that his administration had achieved its objective. The business community, with the active support of the government, was working economic wonders. The pockets of unemployment, the imbalance between farm and business income, the difference between wages and increases in productivity, the speculation in bonds and securities did not seem to concern him. "The country," he told Congress in 1928, "can regard the present with satisfaction, and anticipate the future with optimism."

Most Americans shared that optimism, and in 1928 they had voted accordingly. But even as the new president took the oath of office, the shaky foundations on which the "Coolidge prosperity" had rested were cracking. When the collapse came, there was little left but the dreary statistics of depression.

SUMMARY

The twenties was an extraordinary decade in America—a time when life and culture changed rapidly, when the "good times" and the prosperity of some contrasted sharply with the struggles and poverty of others.

The decade began with postwar depression and repression. Wartime tensions carried over into hysteria over radicalism, in the restriction of immigration, and in racial violence. The Ku Klux Klan was revived; a great "Red Scare" engulfed and defeated a labor movement once again pushing for better wages and working conditions. The murder trial of two Italian anarchists and their execution brought worldwide protest from millions convinced of their innocence. The "race suicide" alarm resulted in the Immigration Restriction Act of 1921 and the National Origins Act of 1924.

In the South, Jim Crow laws, lynchings and beatings, lack of educational facilities, and the misery of the sharecropper's life brought thousands of blacks to northern cities. Between 1910 and 1940, more than 1.7 million blacks left the South; by 1940, the black population outside the South had more than doubled. But the Great Migration took place in an atmosphere of growing racial intolerance in the North as well as in the South. The worst race riot in the nation's history took place in Chicago in July 1919.

Prohibition was another aspect of the twenties. Making liquor illegal nationwide had two immediate results: drinking moved from the old saloon to the speakeasy, where it took on a new glamour, and a new field was opened up for organized crime. But it was not until 1933 that Congress, with a new Democratic majority, finally passed the Twenty-first Amendment to repeal the Eighteenth.

The war between fundamentalism and "foreign" ideologies led in 1925 to the trial of a schoolteacher in Tennessee for teaching the theory of evolution. The contest set two great figures, William Jennings Bryan and Clarence Darrow, against each other as opposing legal counsel. It ended by destroying Bryan's reputation and subjecting the fundamentalists to national ridicule.

For American intellectuals, writers, and artists, the period of the twenties was enormously productive. In their willingness to question the sanity of their society and to experiment with new ideas and forms, this generation stood out; more good writing and more important books were produced in those years than in any similar period in the nation's history. Paris and New York's Greenwich Village became centers of a new American culture, of new writing, new theater, new poetry, new art. These were the writers and artists of the "lost generation," some of whom became expatriates for a while because they felt they could not work at home. Among them were Ernest Hemingway, Ezra Pound, Malcolm Cowley, e. e. cummings, Sinclair Lewis, Sherwood Anderson, William Faulkner, Henry L. Mencken, and F. Scott Fitzgerald.

This was also the time of the Harlem Renaissance, a flowering of black culture that was to spread to the white world as well. New York's Harlem became the center of culture for blacks, the "place to be." Black music—jazz and blues—became known worldwide. Among the black writers and intellectuals of this period were Langston Hughes, Claude McKay, and Jean Toomer.

The new popular arts—movies, radio, records—were all the result of technology. They shaped American attitudes and tastes in new ways. They reached mass audiences, nationalized popular culture, and speeded up the standardization of society.

Politics during the twenties were marked by a return to the American Dream—that anyone who had the right kind of ambition and determination could succeed. It was a politics of a complacency, shaken but not shattered by the scandals of the Harding administration. To Harding, as to Coolidge who succeeded him, business values were sacred. Taxes were lowered; tariffs were raised. The regulatory agencies and the Supreme Court cooperated to make life easier for business. But organized labor lost ground, social legislation had a hard time in the courts, and staple farmers were in deep trouble.

"Coolidge prosperity" was marked by new production techniques and new consumer industries. The airplane became a commercial business. Electrochemical technology made possible a revolution in the petroleum industry and the mass production of consumer goods such as phonographs, refrigerators, radios, washing machines, and vacuum cleaners. Factory organization and operation also changed because of the availability of electric power. And the automobile became part of every American's life. In 1920, about 9 million automobiles were registered in the United States; ten years later, it was nearly 30 million.

This prosperity rested on a shaky foundation. Workers did not share in the profits of increased production enough to raise their purchasing power; technological unemployment grew; the farmers did not recover; and wild speculation on the stock market blew the bubble up to the bursting point. The election of 1928 brought Herbert Hoover to the presidency, with promises of continued Republican prosperity. But the good times were not to last much beyond his inauguration in March of 1929.

Suggested Readings

The stereotypical twenties are vividly chronicled in F. L. Allen, *Only Yesterday* (1931). W. E. Leuchtenburg, *The Perils of Prosperity, 1914–1932* (1958); A. M. Schlesinger, Jr., *The Crisis of the Old Order 1919–1933* (1957); and E. W. Hawley, *The Great War and The Search for a Modern Order* (1979), are more substantial introductions to this period. The many-sided character of the twenties is underscored in two excellent anthologies, Isabel Leighton (ed.), *The Aspirin Age* (1949), and Loren Baritz (ed.), *The Culture of the Twenties* (1969). R. S. and H. M. Lynd, *Middletown* (1929), is a revealing analysis of ordinary American life in Muncie, Indiana. P. S. Fass, *The Damned and the Beautiful: American Youth in the 1920s* (1977), examines the culture of youth, focusing on the values, manners, and activities of native-born, white, middle-class college students. See also J. F. Kett, *Rites of Passage: Adolescence in America 1790 to the Present* (1977). The changing social, economic, and political role of women is examined in W. H. Chafe, *The American Woman 1920–1970* (1972).

On Harding, see S. H. Adams, *Incredible Era* (1939), and Andrew Sinclair, *The Available Man* (1965). R. K. Murray, *The Harding Era: Warren G. Harding and His Administration* (1969), and *The Politics of Normalcy: Governmental Theory and Practice in the Harding-Coolidge Era* (1973), are positive assessments.

The postwar repression is described in R. K. Murray, *Red Scare* (1955); W. Preston, Jr., *Aliens and Dissenters: Federal Suppression of Radicals 1903–1933* (1963); S. Coben, *A. Mitchell Palmer* (1963); and G. L. Joughin and E. M. Morgan, *The Legacy of Sacco and Vanzetti* (1948). On anti-immigrant feeling and legislation, see J. Higham, *Strangers in the Land: Patterns of American Nativism 1860–1925* (1955), and R. A. Divine, *American Immigration Policy 1924–1952* (1957).

D. Brody, *Steelworkers in America: The Non-Union Era* (1960), provides background for the steel strike of 1919, described in Brody, *Labor in Crisis* (1965). On the struggles of workers and farmers and their failure to share in the prosperity of the decade, see I. Bernstein, *The Lean Years: A History of the American Worker 1920–1933* (1960), and T. Saloutos and J. D. Hicks, *Twentieth Century Populism: Agricultural Discontent in the Middle West 1900–1939* (1951). The Gastonia cotton mill strike of 1929 is explored in L. Pope, *Millhands and Preachers* (1942).

The authoritative study of the South in the twentieth century is G. B. Tindall, *The Emergence of the New South 1913–1945* (1967). On the Great Migration of southern blacks to the North, see F. Henri, *Black Migration 1900–1920* (1975). Black life in the urban North is examined in G. Osofsky, *Harlem: The Making of a Ghetto 1890–1930* (1966); A. H. Spear, *Black Chicago: The Making of a Negro Ghetto 1890–1920* (1967); S. C. Drake and H. R. Cayton, *Black Metropolis* (1945); C. W. Kiser, *Sea Island to City: A Study of St. Helena Islanders in Harlem and Other Centers* (1932); K. L. Kusmer, *A Ghetto Takes Shape: Black Cleveland 1870–1930* (1976); and J. Borchert, *Alley Life in Washington, D.C.: Family, Community, Religion, Folklife in the City, 1850–1970* (1980). The personal accounts of James Weldon Johnson, *Along This Way* (1933); A. Clayton Powell, *Against the Tide* (1938); and Richard Wright, *Black Boy* (1945) illuminate the Afro-American experience, as does L. V. Levine, *Black Culture and Black Consciousness* (1977). On racial violence, see The Chicago Commission on Race Relations, *The Negro in Chicago: A Study of Race Relations and a Race Riot* (1922); W. M. Tuttle, Jr., *Race Riot: Chicago in the Red Summer of 1919* (1970); and E. M. Rudwick, *Race Riot at East St. Louis July 2, 1917* (1964). The views of the most popular black leader of this period will be found in A. Jacques-Garvey (ed.), *Philosophy and Opinions of Marcus Garvey* (1969 reprint), and J. Stein, *The World of Marcus Garvey* (1986). The best collection of black urban folklore is R. D. Abrahams, *Deep Down in the Jungle: Negro Narrative Folklore from the Streets of Philadelphia* (1964).

D. M. Chalmers, *Hooded Americanism* (1965), K. T. Jackson, *The Ku Klux Klan in the City* (1967), and C. Alexander, *The Ku Klux Klan in the Southwest* (1965) examine the impact of the KKK in the twentieth century. On Prohibition, see A. Sinclair, *Era of Excess: A Social History of the Prohibition Movement* (1962), and N. H. Clark, *Deliver Us from Evil* (1976). The battle over evolution theory is examined in N. F. Furniss, *The Fundamentalist Controversy 1918–1931* (1954), and the Scopes trial is vividly related in R. Ginger, *Six Days or Forever?* (1958). L. V. Levine, *Defender of the Faith: William Jennings Bryan: The Last Decade 1915–1925* (1965), is a study of Bryan and the period.

D. R. McCoy, *Calvin Coolidge: The Quiet President* (1967), is a revisionist biography, but W. A. White, *A Puritan in Babylon* (1938), remains rewarding reading. On Alfred E. Smith, see O. Handlin, *Al Smith and His America* (1958), and M. and H. Josephson, *Al Smith: Hero of the Cities* (1970). On the Democratic party, see D. Burner, *The Politics of Provincialism: The Democratic Party in Transition 1918–1932* (1968), and F. Freidel, *Franklin D. Roosevelt: The Ordeal* (1954).

George Soule, *Prosperity Decade: From War to De-*

pression 1917–1929 (1947), is a good introduction to the economy. See also J. W. Prothro, *The Dollar Decade: Business Ideas in the 1920s* (1954), and O. Pease, *The Responsibilities of American Advertising* (1958). The management of corporate business is examined in A. D. Chandler, Jr., *Strategy and Structure* (1962), and *Giant Enterprise: Ford, General Motors, and the Automobile Industry* (1964). On the auto industry, see also A. P. Sloan, Jr., *My Years with General Motors* (1964); C. E. Sorensen, *My Forty Years with Ford* (1956); A. Nevins and F. E. Hill, *Ford* (1954–1957); and the more critical K. Sward, *The Legend of Henry Ford* (1948). On the impact of the automobile, see J. B. Rae, *The Road and the Car in American Life* (1971), and J. Fink, *The Car Culture* (1975).

H. May, *The End of American Innocence* (1959), is a solid analysis of American culture between 1912 and 1917. The impact of radical ideas is assessed in D. Aaron, *Writers on the Left* (1961), and W. B. Rideout, *The Radical Novel in the United States 1900–1954* (1956). The avant-garde periodicals are analyzed in F. J. Hoffman and others, *The Little Magazine* (1946). Malcolm Cowley, *Exile's Return* (1951), is an indispensable personal account; see also the memoirs of Floyd Dell, Max Eastman, Mabel Dodge Luhan, Van Wyck Brooks, and Randolph Bourne. On art, consult M. Shapiro, "Rebellion in Art," in D. Aaron (ed.), *America in Crisis* (1952), and M. W. Brown, *The Story of the Armory Show* (1963).

G. Seldes, *The Seven Lively Arts* (1957 ed.), is a classic account of popular culture. The impact of the motion picture is examined in L. Jacobs, *The Rise of the American Film* (1939); E. Rosow, *Born to Lose: The Gangster Film in America* (1978); R. Sklar, *Movie-Made America: A Social History of American Movies* (1975); R. Schickel, *The Disney Version* (1968); and L. May, *Screening Out the Past: The Birth of Mass Culture and the Motion Picture Industry* (1980). J. E. O'Connor and M. A. Jackson (eds.), *American History/American Film: Interpreting the Hollywood Image* (1979), examines film as historical evidence. On radio and American life, see J. F. MacDonald, *Don't Touch That Dial! Radio Programming in American Life from 1920 to 1960* (1979), and A. F. Wertheim, *Radio Comedy* (1979).

A. Locke (ed.), *The New Negro* (1925) is indispensable as an introduction to the Harlem Renaissance. N. I. Huggins, *Harlem Renaissance* (1971), is a modern assessment. The personal accounts of Langston Hughes, *The Big Sea* (1940), and Claude McKay, *A Long Way from Home* (1937), are important, as are their literary works. See also R. E. Hemenway, *Zora Neale Hurston* (1977). On black music, see L. Jones, *Blues People* (1973), and C. Keil, *Urban Blues* (1966).

F. J. Hoffman, *The Twenties* (1955), is a thorough literary history. See also M. Geismar, *The Last of the Provincials* (1949), and *Writers in Crisis* (1947). Edmund Wilson is a perceptive social commentator in *The Shores of Light* (1952) and *The American Earthquake* (1958). On some of the principal critics and writers, see C. Bode, *Henry L. Mencken* (1969); I. Howe, *Sherwood Anderson* (1951); M. Schorer, *Sinclair Lewis* (1961); A. Mizener, *The Far Side of Paradise* (1951); A. Turnbull, *Scott Fitzgerald* (1962); C. H. Baker, *Hemingway* (1956); and C. Brooks, *William Faulkner: The Yoknapatawpha County* (1963). F. Scott Fitzgerald, *The Crack-Up* (1945), is an impressionistic account based on his letters and notes.

THE GREAT DEPRESSION AND THE NEW DEAL

Chapter 28

The presidential inaugurations of 1929 and 1933 provided a striking contrast in personalities, in issues, and in the state of the Union. In his somewhat muffled, droning voice, Herbert Hoover spoke of the "many satisfactions" he derived from surveying "the situation of our Nation at home and abroad."

Ours is a land rich in resources; stimulating in its glorious beauty; filled with millions of happy homes; blessed with comfort and opportunity. In no nation are the institutions of progress more advanced. In no nation are the fruits of accomplishment more secure.

Less than eight months later, on "Black Tuesday," October 29, 1929, stock prices at the New York Stock Exchange fell in the most disastrous trading day in the history of the market. Within a few hours, more than $10 billion of America's "fruits of accomplishment" were gone. Within the next three years, with declining consumer purchasing, manufacturers closed plants or reduced the work force. Some 100,000 workers, on the average, were fired each week. The number of unemployed stood at 2 million in 1929, at 4 million in 1930, at 8 million in 1931, at 12 million in 1932. National income was cut more than half. Over 5000 banks and 9 million savings accounts were wiped out; tens of thousands of mortgages were foreclosed.

Families found themselves evicted from their homes and barely able to exist. More than a million homeless people took to the road or settled in "Hoovervilles," shantytowns made out of old packing cartons and car bodies. They came to symbolize not only the depths of the Depression, but the president's inability to do anything about it.

By March 4, 1933, when Franklin D. Roosevelt took the oath of office as president of the United States, three and a half years had passed since October 1929, the number of unemployed had reached 13 million, and the nation was experiencing failure on a scale unprecedented in its history. But the new president, even as he described "the dark realities of the moment," conveyed a sense of confidence and determination in his voice and manner that comforted his audience:

This nation asks for action and action now. Our greatest primary task is to put people to work. . . . It can be accomplished in part by direct recruiting by the Government itself, treating the task as we would treat the emergency of a war.

The American people would respond to FDR's appeal for confidence—"the only thing we have to fear is fear itself"—with an enthusiasm matched only by the contempt they had shown for Hoover's plea for confidence—"All the evidences indicate that the worst effects of the crash . . . will have been passed during the next 60 days." But the Great Depression, as both Hoover and Roosevelt would learn from their attempts to deal with it, could not be solved with psychology. Confidence was not enough. Confidence alone could not feed hungry people or create jobs for the unemployed, and there was much more to fear than fear itself. Americans were thrilled by FDR's pledge to treat the economic crisis as he would treat a war. Few had any reason to suspect that only a war would ultimately bring them out of the crisis. ■

THE CRASH

The crash centered on the New York Stock Exchange in Wall Street, the scene in 1929 of an enormous amount of activity in stock securities. The talk was of good times and striking it rich. Overnight success stories, the assurances of business and political leaders, and easy credit terms fed the fever. Thousands of small investors, along with the wealthy, poured their savings into common stocks. The warning signs went unheeded: cutbacks in private construction, large business inventories, the decline in consumer purchasing. Industry was not making enough profit to justify the soaring stock prices. The market wavered, and on October 29, 1929, it came crashing down.

President Hoover had tried to assure the public that there was no reason to panic: "The fundamental business of this country, that is, production and distribution of commodities, is on a sound and prosperous basis." But he was wrong. And with every new assurance that the worst had passed, the depression deepened. The president would act in more decisive ways to restore confidence in the economy. But there were limits beyond which he refused to go.

A Flawed Economy

The stock market crash dramatized fundamental weaknesses in the economy. It revealed more "pockets" of economic hardship than had been acknowledged, larger ones than had been supposed, and their tendency to grow. Farm receipts had already bottomed out, as farmers throughout the twenties had to deal with large surpluses, declining prices, and higher expenses. Chronic unemployment had for many years characterized certain industries, affecting in particular textile workers and coal miners. In the twenties, the uneven distribution of income should have suggested that the nation was risking economic disaster. The slowly rising real wages of industrial workers were outdistanced by the salaries, savings, and profits of those higher on the economic ladder. In 1929, the 24,000 richest families had an aggregate income more than three times as large as that of the nearly 6 million poorest families. Forty percent of all families had incomes under $1,500.

No wonder the purchasing power of Americans did not keep up with the production potential of the industrial plant and the promotional techniques of advertising. Those who were getting

WORDS AND NAMES IN AMERICAN HISTORY

One of the most famous streets in the world is a rather short one in New York City. The name *Wall Street* has come to suggest the world of U.S. banking and trading in stocks and bonds. One of the country's foremost financial newspapers is called, simply, *The Wall Street Journal*. The New York Stock Exchange, the nation's most important Center for trading in the shares of stock and in bonds, has a Wall Street address. In Communist countries, the very term Wall Street is often a shorthand way of referring to the "evils" of capitalism. The street got its name innocently enough because it runs along the site of what was once a wall that stood at the northern edge of the little town of New Amsterdam some three hundred years ago. Today, it lies near the southern tip of Manhattan, since the original Dutch settlement occupied only a tiny part at the downriver end of that island.

rich, meanwhile, found their savings piled up out of all proportion to need. Looking for opportunities for sound investment, they turned to speculation in real estate and securities, both blown up into a bubble sure to burst.

During the twenties, the federal government had failed to deal with these matters. Tax policies favored the rich, making even more unequal the distribution of income. Labor policies were anti-union. The economic situation abroad only aggravated the domestic crisis. European nations needed goods and credit from America to restore their economies and stabilize their currencies. But American tariffs, like the Hawley-Smoot Tariff passed during the Hoover administration, presented obstacles to exports and limited Europe's buying power. American manufacturers found it ever more difficult to sell abroad. And the American and European economies were so closely linked that the Depression soon became worldwide.

Hoover himself scorned the fear of others. "Prosperity is just around the corner," he kept saying. To demonstrate his own confidence, the president made a point of attending the World Series in 1931. At the same time, he urged the American people not to give in to despair. "What the country needs," he told a newspaperman, "is a good big laugh. There seems to be a condition of hysteria. If someone could get off a good joke every ten days, I think our troubles would be over." Hoover supplied his own brand of humor with this observation: "Many persons have left their jobs for the more profitable one of selling apples." Meanwhile, Hoover's Democratic rivals made the most of the crisis. Since the Republicans had taken full credit for "Coolidge prosperity," the Democrats promptly called the new era the "Hoover Depression."

Hoover and the Depression

For all his stress on confidence, Hoover acknowledged the need for direct federal intervention. That decision in itself marked a significant break with the past. In 1930, when the slide of wheat and cotton prices became catastrophic, Hoover tried to use the extension of agricultural credit and the new Federal Farm Board to reverse the price trend by open market purchases. It was not long, however, before government warehouses bulged. Private dealers, fearful of this glut being unloaded on the market, sold their own holdings for instant cash. By 1932, cotton was 6 cents a pound, down from 16 cents in 1929; wheat, 38 cents a bushel, down from $1.

To help labor and industry, early in 1930 Congress granted the president $700 million for public works, the start of a new program that saw Hoover spend almost $3 billion on public construction. The president also tried to get companies to delay firing workers and wage cuts. But even the best-willed industrialists could not keep people at work at a living wage when there were no markets for products. By 1932, wages had plummeted, and 12 million were unemployed. Great companies faced bankruptcy.

In an effort to save insurance companies and philanthropic organizations that had invested in their securities, Congress created the Reconstruction Finance Corporation. By the end of the year, the RFC had loaned $1.5 billion to about 5000 shaky firms. But this "shot in the arm" did little to help the economy.

No previous administration had ever taken such extensive measures to revive the private economy or help the victims of its collapse. Yet they proved wholly inadequate. The crisis became even more acute when local and private welfare agencies also crashed. But Hoover's principles—his belief in the market forces, voluntarism, and self-help—did not permit him to undertake the massive federal intervention the crisis demanded. Direct federal aid to the unemployed, he feared, would make them the wards of the state and endanger the individualistic ethic. "You cannot extend the mastery of the government over the daily working life of a people without at the same time making it the master of the people's souls and thoughts." Even as the Depression deepened, he clung to the belief that the principal function of government was "to bring about a condition of affairs favorable to the beneficial development of private enterprise."

Hoover, the "great humanitarian" of the war years, soon was portrayed as the heartless villain of the Depression. Nor did the president enhance his image by minimizing the extent of the human crisis. "Nobody is actually starving," Hoover told a group of reporters. "The hoboes, for example, are better fed than they have ever been. One hobo in New York got ten meals in one day." In the summer of 1932, Hoover's image suffered another blow over the way he responded to the Bonus Army, some 12,000 jobless veterans who had marched to Washington in hopes of persuading Congress to make a veterans' bonus appropriation. On Hoover's orders and under the personal direction of Chief of Staff Douglas MacArthur, the marchers were driven from the city with tear gas and bayonets.

The Election of 1932

With unemployment increasing and local and state welfare funds nearly exhausted, Hoover faced a grim electorate in 1932 and a formidable Democratic opponent. Aware that they had to renominate Hoover or accept the charge of a Hoover Depression, the Republicans did so on the first ballot. The Democrats named Franklin D. Roosevelt, governor of New York. His victory in the state in 1928 stood out boldly against the Republicans' overwhelming national success that year. In 1930, FDR was reelected governor almost by acclamation. On receiving the presidential nomination, Roosevelt flew to Chicago to accept the honor in person, something no candidate had done before. "I pledge you, I pledge myself," he told the delegates, "to a new deal for the American people."

Despite the urgency of the Depression, neither the platforms of the two major political parties nor the candidates themselves suggested that the federal government might need to play a central role in the industrial society. Hoover stressed international economic difficulties as the main causes of the crash. Roosevelt did not deny the Depression's international character, but zeroed in on the flaws it revealed in the American economy. Hoover warned that too much government intervention would destroy individual liberty. Roosevelt called for novel methods to meet novel conditions—"bold and persistent experimentation." But his few specific commitments were conventional, and his pledge to assist the victims of the Depression while reducing government expenditures and balancing the budget must have baffled economic analysts.

Yet more voters were heartened by his promises, however vague, than were impressed by Hoover's warnings. Roosevelt received 22,821,000 votes; Hoover, 15,761,000. The victor's electoral college margin, 472 to 59, reflected his success in carrying all but six northeastern states—Maine, New Hampshire, Vermont, Connecticut, Pennsylvania, and Delaware. The Democratic party, moreover, won overwhelming majorities in both houses of Congress.

Since the campaign had turned largely on a clash of personalities rather than ideologies, few knew how to judge the new president. The people looked to Roosevelt to exert vigorous leadership, but they had only a vague notion of the direction in which he intended to lead them. The president-elect was also uncertain. He knew, however, what was expected of him. "I have looked into the faces of thousands of Americans," he told a friend during the campaign. "They have the frightened look of lost children. . . .They are saying: 'We're caught in something we don't understand; perhaps this fellow can help us out.' " That typified the kind of sensitivity FDR brought with him into the White House, and it was good enough to keep him there for twelve years.

FDR'S NEW DEAL

Charming, self-assured, energetic, and fearless, FDR was the New Deal's greatest asset. Whatever was hidden behind the famous Roosevelt smile, it was an extraordinarily effective tool in private and public relations. Unlike Hoover, the new president seemed to have both compassion and confidence, and the people responded. However erratic his actions, and despite the uncertainty with which he sometimes moved, Roosevelt knew how to communicate.

In his radio "fireside chats," he made the people feel he was discussing important national questions with them directly, that he understood

Franklin D. Roosevelt. (*AP/World Wide Photos*)

their problems and frustrations. Few expressed that reaction more clearly than the North Carolina mill worker who explained to an anti-New Deal journalist why he stood by the president: "Mr. Roosevelt is the only man we ever had in the White House who would understand that my boss is a sonofabitch."

Roosevelt was deeply moved by the plight of the poor. Unlike Cleveland and Hoover, he believed the underprivileged had a legitimate claim on the federal government. Many people during its early years spoke of the New Deal as an attempt at economic planning. Economic experimentation would be a more accurate description. No one knew of a single solution, and Roosevelt's policies proved as varied as the men around him. These included veteran politicians.

Postmaster General James A. Farley of New York had a card-index mind in which deserving and undeserving Democrats were sorted out. Secretary of State Cordell Hull, a national legislator with many years of service, reflected his Tennessee background in his support of the traditional southern quest for lower tariffs and freer world trade. William H. Woodin, a conservative industrialist who enjoyed the confidence of business, became secretary of the treasury. When Woodin resigned after the bank crisis of 1933, he was succeeded by Henry Morgenthau, Jr., an old friend of the president.

The reform element was represented in the cabinet by a veteran Progressive, Harold L. Ickes of Illinois, who became secretary of the interior. Henry A. Wallace, the son of Harding's and Coolidge's secretary of agriculture, now filled this post himself. Frances Perkins had worked with Roosevelt in Albany, and, as secretary of labor, became the first woman cabinet member. Harry Hopkins, who emerged as perhaps the most influential of all Roosevelt's advisors, although not in the cabinet until 1939, also had strong reform leanings.

Even less formally related to the administration than Hopkins were the members of the "brain trust," especially three Columbia University professors who had advised Roosevelt during the campaign: Raymond Moley, A. A. Berle, Jr., and Rexford Tugwell. Tugwell, an economist, voiced the sentiments of the social planners, those who looked for a larger degree of government control over the nation's economic life, including control of prices and profit margins.

Hoover's approach to the problem of recovery had been largely the traditional one of allowing the deflation to run its course. The New Dealers experimented with currency inflation and with heavy government spending to "prime the pump" of business. Some of them, like Tugwell, hoped also to make the crisis an occasion for reforms that went far beyond those of the Progressive movement. They began tentatively. But as the depression grew worse, public pressure for change grew stronger. Led by the president, they moved to rescue the banks, stabilize business and agriculture, reduce unemployment, and provide assistance for the victims of the Depression.

The Bank Crisis

One of the most dangerous developments of the Depression—the headlong plunge of the banks toward bankruptcy—was the first to be attacked. The first steps were taken within a day or two of Roosevelt's inauguration and gave the public a welcome taste of energetic new leadership.

So many banks had failed that even solvent institutions were menaced by frightened depositors rushing to withdraw their money. To stop the panic, the governors of almost half the states had declared "bank holidays," and most of the banks were closed when Roosevelt took office. By proclamation on March 6, Roosevelt suspended all banking operations and gold transactions. Three days later, called into special session, Congress passed the Emergency Banking Act. It ratified the president's actions and established procedures for getting sound banks back in business.

Roosevelt then went on the air with his first fireside chat, a brilliant effort to reassure people that a sound banking system was about to emerge from the reorganization. Before the end of March, most of the sound banks had reopened and the unsound ones were on the way to being permanently closed. Within another month, more than 12,000 banks, with 90 percent of the country's deposits, were functioning normally.

"In one week," wrote columnist Walter Lippmann of the bank crisis, "the nation, which had lost confidence in everything and everybody, has regained confidence in the government and in itself." Roosevelt's avoiding the more radical solution to which he could have turned—nationalizing the banks—quieted conservative suspicions. His action also made it clear that the New Deal intended to patch up the old order rather than replace it; that is, he would keep intact the basic structure of American capitalism. But to do so, he would have the federal government play a major and unprecedented role.

With his action during the banking crisis, advisor Raymond Moley recalled, Roosevelt let it be known that he would preserve and revive, not destroy the free enterprise system: "If ever there was a moment when things hung in the balance, it was on March 5, 1933—when unorthodoxy would have drained the last remaining strength of the capitalistic system."

Bank reform soon followed. One of the best reform measures was the Glass-Steagall Act of June 1933, which created the Federal Deposit Insurance Corporation (FDIC) and authorized it to guarantee bank deposits up to $5000 per depositor. Many banks had got into trouble using depositors' money to speculate in the stock market. The banks had invested through their affiliates in the securities business. The Glass-Steagall Act forbade national banks to maintain such affiliates, and it contained other reforms to divorce commercial from investment banking. The simple sanity of this law did not prevent the American Bankers Association from fighting it "to the last ditch," as its president vowed. Finally, the Banking Act of 1935 greatly increased federal authority over the banking system by empowering the Federal Reserve Board to regulate interest rates.

The administration also pressed for closer supervision of the stock market. The Securities Act of 1933 required greater publicity for the details of stock promotion and closed the mails to sellers failing to provide it. This measure was followed by the Securities Exchange Act of June 1934, creating the Securities and Exchange Commission (SEC). It was authorized to require registration of all securities traded on the stock exchanges and to cooperate with the Federal Reserve Board in regulating the purchase of securities.

Playing with Money

Business recovery proved more difficult than banking reform. The New Deal experimented with various plans aimed at stimulating industrial activity, mostly with no success. One of the earliest ideas was to cheapen the dollar. That would reduce the burden of fixed debts, which had become a drag on expansion. At the same time, it would raise domestic prices, and encourage output. Cheapening the dollar was also expected to stimulate exports, because foreign currency would buy more goods. In May 1933, Congress authorized the president to issue greenbacks, reduce the gold

content of the dollar, and provide for unlimited coinage of both gold and silver at a ratio that he could set.

The president used his new authority with great caution. To retain his flexibility with the dollar, and insisting that the United States be free to pursue its own course, Roosevelt refused in mid-1933 to join the efforts of the London Economic Conference to stabilize world currencies. In a new effort to increase the money supply and boost commodity prices by currency manipulation, Roosevelt ordered the purchase of gold on the open market. This action, he hoped, would raise the price of gold, which in turn would help to raise the general price level. Even this was given up by the end of January 1934, when the president chose to fix the price of gold at $35 an ounce, about 40 percent higher than its pre-1933 level. But despite these experiments, the price level did not rise.

Business: The NRA

The idea behind currency experiments was that under favorable monetary conditions, ordinary market mechanisms might push prices up. But the New Dealers were not alone in realizing that the market mechanisms themselves needed artificial respiration and probably a permanent iron lung. To help the economy breathe once more, Congress, in June 1933, passed the National Industrial Recovery Act (NIRA). The president hailed it as "the most important and far-reaching legislation ever enacted by the American Congress."

The point of the NIRA was not so much to expand the economy as to ration the nation's business among the surviving corporations. It had the support, and in some cases the sponsorship, of businessmen and leaders of the United States Chamber of Commerce. Under its provisions, the antitrust laws were, in effect, suspended. Trade associations and other business groups were permitted to draw up "codes of fair competition," which would include comprehensive price agreements, firm production quotas, and wage scales high enough to improve the condition of the lowest paid workers.

Each type of business was empowered to draw up its own code. The government reserved the right to accept or reject the codes, to set up its own when companies in any industry failed to agree, and to enforce them. Section 7(a) of the NIRA guaranteed labor the right of collective bargaining. A National Recovery Administration (NRA) was formed to administer the codes under the chairmanship of General Hugh Johnson, who had worked on the War Industries Board during World War I.

In order to make NRA comparable to mobilization for war, administrators organized parades and mass meetings. They adopted a placard with a blue eagle as a symbol to be awarded for display to businessmen and even to consumers who cooperated. One of their hoped-for effects was to stir up boycotts of uncooperative firms, substituting public pressure for legal enforcement. General Johnson blared forth in his characteristically grandiloquent way: "When every American housewife understands that the Blue Eagle on everything she permits to come into her home is a symbol of its restoration to security, may God have mercy on the man or group of men who attempt to trifle with this bird." Violators of the codes or objectors like Henry Ford, who met code requirements but refused to sign up, were seldom prosecuted. NRA administrators may have thought that the entire scheme would collapse if put to the judicial test.

No less than 746 NRA codes were adopted by businessmen eager to get started again. But there were problems. The paperwork required to supply needed information to the government quickly reached fantastic proportions and was resented. Big corporations resisted all further signs of bureaucratic interference. Small firms complained that the codes, drawn up by the larger firms in each industry, discriminated against small business. Workers, who at first supported NRA, soon nicknamed it the "National Run Around." Code administrators, they said, sided with anti-union employers in labor disputes. Employers detested the very existence of Section 7(a) and the expansion of organized labor it would allow. Moreover, when the codes succeeded in reviving production by raising prices, they aroused consumer discontent.

NRA had reached a low point in popularity when the Supreme Court killed it in May 1935. In the case of *Schecter Poultry Corporation* v. *United States*, the Court unanimously found that the National Recovery Act was unconstitutional on two counts. First, it improperly delegated legislative powers to the executive. Second, the provisions of the poultry code constituted a regulation of intrastate, not interstate, commerce.

NRA had not been entirely worthless. For example, when the codes were adopted, some of the most exploited workers in the textile industry had been paid as little as $5 a week. To such workers the cotton textile code, which set minimum wages

of $12 to $13 a week, was heaven-sent. NRA established the principle of maximum hours and minimum wages on a national basis. It reduced child labor. It made collective bargaining a national policy. In many instances cancellation of the codes brought a return to poor working conditions, to which the labor movement soon turned its attention.

Agriculture: The AAA

Two months before Roosevelt's inauguration, the normally conservative head of the Farm Bureau Federation, Edward A. O'Neal, warned a Senate committee: "Unless something is done for the American farmer we will have revolution in the countryside within less than 12 months." Even as he spoke, farmers were beginning to take matters into their own hands. They forced eviction sales and mortgage foreclosures to stop. They intimidated and assaulted public officials and agents of banks and insurance companies. Violence became so widespread in Iowa by April 1933 that the governor put several counties under martial law and called out the National Guard.

"Americans are slow to understand," commented the *New York World-Telegram,* "that actual revolution already exists in the farm belt. . . .When the local revolt springs from old native stock, conservatives fighting for the right to hold their homesteads, there is the warning of a larger explosion."

The New Dealers were well aware of the need for quick action to raise the prices of agricultural products to a level that would increase farmers' purchasing power. When they acted, they approached the farm problem in the same mood with which they approached the problems of industry. The farm plan was incorporated in the Agricultural Adjustment Act of May 1933, which established the Agricultural Adjustment Administration (AAA).

Abandoning all hope of regaining lost foreign markets for staples, AAA hoped to raise farm prices by cutting back production to domestic needs and rationing the domestic market among producers. In this way it planned to bring farm prices up to "parity" with those of the prosperous prewar years of 1909 to 1914. To compensate farmers for cooperating with the government plan, AAA was authorized to pay various subsidies for acreage withdrawn from production and for certain marketing practices. Funds to finance the program were to come from taxes on the processors of farm

THE FARMERS BECAME DESPERATE

Oscar Heline, an Iowa farmer, recalls the impact of the Great Depression.

The struggles people had to go through are almost unbelievable. A man lived all his life on a given farm, it was taken away from him. One after the other. . . . Not only did he lose the farm, but it was impossible for him to get out of debt. . . . First, they'd take your farm, then they took your livestock, then your farm machinery. Even your household goods. And they'd move you off. . . .

Grain was being burned. It was cheaper than coal. Corn was being burned. . . . You couldn't hardly buy groceries for corn. . . . People were determined to withhold produce from the market—livestock, cream, butter, eggs, what not. If they would dump the produce, they would force the market to a higher level. The farmers would man the highways, and cream cans were emptied in ditches and eggs dumped out. They burned the trestle bridge, so the trains wouldn't be able to haul grain. Conservatives don't like this kind of rebel attitude and aren't very sympathetic. But something had to be done.

Source: Studs Terkel, *Hard Times* (New York: Pantheon Books, 1970), pp. 252–53. Photograph by Dorothea Lange, Library of Congress.

products, such as millers, cotton ginners, and meatpackers. At first, the act provided for crop reductions only in cotton, wheat, corn, hogs, rice, tobacco, and milk. Later, other products were included.

To cut production when people were hungry was bound to bring criticism. But farm spokesmen insisted that if the profit system meant anything, the farmers had the same right as businessmen to do this. The contradiction between a program of planned scarcity and the reality of millions of Americans suffering from a lack of food and clothing was never really resolved. The United States, Secretary Wallace conceded, had "the largest wheat surplus and the longest breadlines in its history." But he saw no way out: "We must play with the cards that are dealt. Agriculture cannot survive in a capitalist society as a philanthropic enterprise."

To make matters worse, AAA did not begin to work until after the spring planting of 1933. Where acreage had not been sufficiently reduced, farmers were ordered to plow under a large part of their crops. With people reportedly starving in the cities, AAA's action seemed heartless. It also fell short of its goal. Many farmers accepted government checks for reducing acreage and then calmly cultivated their remaining acres more intensively. In 1934 Congress added production quotas to acreage restriction and imposed taxes on violators. The new and old laws helped double and triple farm staple prices. Total net income of farm operators rose dramatically from $1.8 billion in 1932 to $5 billion in 1936.

The Supreme Court ruled in January 1936 that it was unconstitutional for Congress to impose a tax on processers for the purpose of regulating farm production. Congress responded with the Soil Conservation and Domestic Allotment Act, which put crop restriction on a sounder constitutional basis. The object now was to increase soil fertilization and conserve resources. AAA was authorized to pay farmers for using soil-conservation measures and for reducing acreage used for soil-depleting crops. Congressional appropriations were to finance the new program.

When prices tumbled again in 1937, Congress passed a second Agricultural Adjustment Act. It tried to put into action Secretary Wallace's idea of the "ever-normal granary." The price fall in 1937 had come from bumper crops producd in 1936. The new act aimed to keep such bumper crops off the market by compensating farmers for storing them. Large amounts were paid to farmers, but staple growers did not really do well until wartime demand in the 1940s pushed prices up.

Millions of farm families gained nothing from legislation designed to help commercial, landowning farmers. By 1935, an estimated 46 percent of all white farmers in the country were tenants, and some 77 percent of black farmers. The problem of tenancy was worst in the South. If tenant farmers or sharecroppers owed money to the landlord or to the storekeeper, and most did, state laws required them to work the land until the debts had been paid. They lived in crudely built shacks, suffered from malnutrition, and were able to look forward to little except a lifetime of drudgery and debt.

LET US NOW PRAISE FAMOUS MEN

What is earned at the end of a given year is never to be depended on and, even late in a season, is never predictable. It can be enough to tide through the dead months of the winter, sometimes even better: it can be enough, spread very thin, to take through two months, and a sickness, or six weeks, or a month: it can be little enough to be completely meaningless: it can be nothing: it can be enough less than nothing to insure a tenant only of an equally hopeless lack of money at the end of his next year's work: and whatever one year may bring in the way of good luck, there is never any reason to hope that the luck will be repeated in the next year or the year after that.

Source: James Agee and Walker Evans, *Let us Now Praise Famous Men* (Boston: Houghton Mifflin, 1941), p. 118. Photograph by Walker Evans, Library of Congress.

Few observers described this life more vividly than James Agee in *Let Us Now Praise Famous Men* (1941).

Rarely did the benefits of the AAA seep down to the tenants and sharecroppers; 90 percent of the government payments went to the planters and landlords, and these same people usually controlled the local and county committees to which the tenants would have to appeal their case. And with acreage being removed from cultivation to qualify for AAA payments, landlords evicted many tenants rather than split the payments with them, thereby stimulating a movement of these tenants to the cities, where they could join the army of unemployed.

As the Depression wore on, concern for sharecroppers, farm tenants, and hired farm laborers grew. The New Deal's response in this area was the Resettlement Administration (RA), created in 1935. It withdrew 9 million acres of wasteland from cultivation and moved the families on them to resettlement areas. It extended loans to farmers who could not obtain credit elsewhere, and it encouraged cooperation among farmers who had always insisted on going it alone.

In response to the report of a presidential committee on rural poverty, Congress in 1937 passed the Farm Tenancy Act to provide loans to sharecroppers, tenant farmers, and farm laborers for the purchase of land, livestock, supplies, and equipment. By June 1944, 870,000 rural families had been helped. And it was the Farm Security Administration, set up under this act, that also sent out photographers like Walker Evans, Dorothea Lange, Russell Lee, and Arthur Rothstein, among others, to portray these people in all their simple dignity.

Although it recognized the problem of rural poverty, the New Deal had still done very little about it. When sharecroppers and farm laborers—white and black—began to attack their troubles through the newly formed Southern Tenant Farmers' Union, they found violent resistance from the farming interests that had benefited most from New Deal legislation. The union's newspaper finally concluded that under President Roosevelt, "too often the progressive word has been the clothing for a conservative act. Too often he has talked like a cropper and acted like a planter."

The kind of social planning necessary to deal with rural poverty and tenantry never received adequate thought or money. Instead, those who strongly supported such planning found themselves out of the Department of Agriculture. "Of course," Secretary Wallace wrote, "the liberals presented a strong case for the tenants but the reforms they wanted would have blown the department out of the water at that time."

Rural Redevelopment: The TVA

One of the poorest of all American farm areas was the Tennessee Valley, which was immensely rich in natural resources. Government projects to harness the mighty Tennessee River were begun at Muscle Shoals during World War I. Senator George W. Norris of Nebraska tried to continue them under government management. But the private power companies opposed all efforts to keep Muscle Shoals a public project, and Coolidge and Hoover vetoed the necessary legislation.

After his election, Roosevelt visited Muscle Shoals and soon had a grand plan for the whole valley. On May 18, 1933, Congress created the Tennessee Valley Authority (TVA). It was empowered to buy, build, and operate dams in the valley. It would generate and sell electric power, and plan reforestation and flood control. TVA could withdraw marginal lands from cultivation and undertake regional planning to improve the standard of living of the people who lived in the valley.

Of all the New Deal experiments in government, TVA was probably the boldest and most original. It was an independent public corporation, and its area of responsibility embraced 40,000 square miles in seven states. TVA built sixteen new dams and took over five others. By 1940, four dams were generating electric power in the TVA region. Over 40,000 users, many of them farmers with no previous access to electricity, were directly or indirectly served. TVA rates were kept low, and served as a yardstick by which to measure private rates. The result was to force private companies in the area to keep rates down. Land redeemed by TVA from flooding was made productive for the first time.

Like earlier valley plans, TVA was fought by the power companies. They gained the support of disinterested conservatives who saw in the experiment a threat to the private enterprise system. Like other New Deal measures, TVA was soon taken to court. But unlike some other measures, it survived.

Unemployment: CCC, PWA, WPA

When Roosevelt took office, at least 13 million workers were unemployed. With their families, they added up to about 50 million persons, many

BROTHER, CAN YOU SPARE A DIME?

They used to tell me I was building a dream,
And so I followed the mob;
When there was earth to plow or guns to bear
I was always there, right there on the job.

They used to tell me I was building a dream
With peace and glory ahead;
Why should I be standing in line
—just waiting for bread?

CHORUS: Once I built a railroad, made it run,
Made it race against time.
Once I built a railroad, now it's done—
Brother, can you spare a dime?

Once I built a tower, to the sun,
Brick and rivet and lime;

Once I built a tower, now it's done—
Brother, can you spare a dime?

Once in khaki suits—gee, we looked swell,
Full of that Yankee Doodle-de-dum.
Half a million boots went sloggin' thru Hell,
I was the kid with the drum.

Say, don't you remember, they called me Al,
It was Al all the time;
Say, don't you remember, I'm your pal!
Buddy, can you spare a dime?

Source: Words by E. Y. Harburg, music by Jay Gorney. Copyright 1932 by Harms, Inc. Copyright renewed. All rights reserved. Used by permission of Warner Bros. Music. Photograph by Dorothea Lange, Library of Congress.

of them on the verge of starvation. The writer Martha Gellhorn, touring the country in 1933, reported to Harry Hopkins on the unemployed: "I find them all in the same shape—fear, fear driving them into a state of semicollapse; cracking nerves; and an overpowering terror of the future . . . each family in its own miserable home going to pieces." The issue was no longer whether the federal government should act, but how. Should it give handouts to the poverty-stricken, which was the cheapest plan, or should it provide work, which seemed less wasteful and more humane.

The first New Deal assistance to the unemployed was the Civilian Conservation Corps. (CCC) for the youth of the country. At one point CCC had on its rolls 500,000 young men, eighteen to twenty-five. Recruited from cities to camps built by the War Department, they worked on reforestation, road and dam construction, control of mosquitoes and other pests, and similar tasks. Of the $30 a month wages, $22 was sent to the young men's families. By the end of 1941, some 2,750,000 youths had spent some part of their lives in CCC camps.

The first comprehensive New Deal relief measure was the act of May 1933 creating the Federal Emergency Relief Administration (FERA). Under Harry Hopkins, FERA had half a billion dollars to be used for direct emergency relief. Although the federal government provided the money, the relief itself was to be administered by the states. Cash payments were distributed at first, but Hopkins thought work relief was psychologically and economically superior. He also was concerned with quick results. When approached with a project that he was assured would "work out in the long run," Hopkins snapped, "People don't eat in the long run—they eat every day."

In time, almost half of those receiving relief were put to work on jobs that presumably did not compete with private business. Pay began at 30 cents an hour. In all, FERA spent about $4 billion before it ended in December 1935, succeeded by the Works Progress Administration (WPA).

The Civil Works Administration, set up in November 1933, was run entirely from Washington. It was wholly devoted to work relief. Widely criticized by opponents of the New Deal on the ground that it "made work," the CWA in fact performed many useful services, such as repairing roads and improving schools and parks. The Public Works Administration (PWA) under Secretary of the Interior Ickes was more a "pump-priming" than a relief agency. Its duties included planning bridges, dams, hospitals, and other public projects and contracting for their construction by private companies.

Many people complained that New Deal relief agencies, besides duplicating one another's tasks, made no effort to distinguish between employable persons who needed relief and "unemployables" who could not have found work even in good times. Early in 1935 Roosevelt proposed a reorganization of the entire relief program. The federal government would aid employables only. The care of others would be left to the states and municipalities. The Emergency Relief Act of 1935 put these proposals into effect. CCC and PWA were continued. All other federal relief was brought under a new agency, the Works Progress Administration (WPA), directed by Harry Hopkins. When its operations ended in July 1941, WPA had spent $11.3 billion. At its peak, in November 1938, nearly 3.3 million persons were on its payroll, and all told WPA provided work for 8 million people. Among its more than 250,000 projects were hospitals, bridges, municipal power plants, post offices, school buildings, slum clearance, and the rehabilitation of army posts and naval stations.

WPA also took into account the plight of the humanities and the arts, whose practitioners, like other workers, were left stranded by the Depression. Its projects in the fine arts, music, and the theater gave employment to painters, writers, actors, singers, and musicians, stimulating what *Fortune Magazine* called "a kind of cultural revolution in America." The authors of the WPA guides conducted research in local history to write the first composite survey of the American states. Still other projects recovered American folklore, conducted interviews with more than two thousand surviving ex-slaves, and recorded white and black spirituals, Indian songs, and folk tunes. On Post Office walls all over the country WPA artists painted regional scenes and memorable local episodes. Americans who had never gone to a theater or concert flocked to federal theater performances, which charged no admission from those unable to pay.

The cultural work of the WPA was supplemented by a National Youth Administration (NYA), which helped meet the needs of young persons with intellectual interests. Through NYA young people aged sixteen to twenty-five found part-time employment in high schools, colleges, and universities.

No part of the New Deal drew more criticism than its relief program. The cost was truly enormous for the times, and the tax burden had to be shouldered by the depressed private sector of the

THE GREAT DEPRESSION AND THE NEW DEAL

In 1930, when the number of unemployed went over four million, unemployment lines such as this one were a common sight. One worker described his experience to Studs Terkel in his book *Hard Times:* "I'd get up five in the morning and head for the waterfront. . . . Outside the gates there would be a thousand men. You knew dang well there's only three or four jobs. The guy would come out with two little Pinkerton cops. 'I need two guys for the bull gang. Two guys to go into the hold.' A thousand men would fight like a pack of Alaskan dogs to get through there." (*Library of Congress*)

Isaac Soyer's painting, "Employment Agency," 1937. (*Collection of Whitney Museum*)

economy. Many critics charged, usually inaccurately, that relief was inefficiently handled. Others, often justly, accused the administration of using relief for political purposes. No part of the relief program drew more criticism than its support of cultural activities. Many Americans had no sympathy with the idea that musicians, writers, and artists had as much claim on the community as workers in other fields.

Even at its peak, however, WPA had reached fewer than half of the unemployed. Despite the New Deal experiments in economic legislation, only once, in 1937, did the number of unemployed fall below 8 million. In 1940 it was back above that figure, at a level five times as high as in 1929. This failure, some critics suggested, revealed a flaw in New Deal ideas about the essential soundness of the economic system it was trying to revive.

CHALLENGE AND RESPONSE

Most of the New Deal's famous "alphabet agencies"—NRA, TVA, AAA, SEC, CCC, PWA—were begun in the first hundred days of the Roosevelt administration. The opposition was for the moment shamed, shocked, or stunned into silence. Supported by the president's optimism, relief and reform measures were adopted almost unanimously. That same enthusiasm carried over to the polls. In the congressional elections of 1934, the Democrats scored overwhelming victories, swelling their majorities in the House and Senate.

But if the election of 1934 buried the conservative critics who thought Roosevelt was going too far too fast, it might have reminded him, if he needed reminding, of several things: The spirit of protest was still rising; recovery had not yet been achieved; and those who believed the New Deal moved too little and too slowly would be heard from. The most troublesome critics in the next several years would be those who took advantage of the growing despair of the lower middle class, many of whom had been badly shaken by the collapse of a system they had never thought to question. The despair was genuine and widespread enough to move the New Deal into some new areas.

Critics and Crusaders

Most formidable among the new breed of critics was Senator Huey Long, the Kingfish of Louisiana. A skilled politician and champion of poor whites, he had as governor engineered some needed reforms, though not without corruption and invasions of constitutional liberties. He built up a national following, especially large in the Mississippi Valley and on the Pacific Coast, on the strength of his Share Our Wealth plan. This called for confiscatory taxes on the wealthy to provide every family with an income of $2500, a homestead, and an automobile. In 1935 a Democratic National Committee survey disclosed that Long might win from 3 to 4 million votes on a third-party ticket, thereby gaining the balance of power in American politics. The chance of disaster in the 1936 campaign disappeared with Long's assassination in September 1935.

A second popular challenge was mounted in California by Dr. Frances E. Townsend, an elderly physician. In January 1935 he announced the Townsend Plan, by which the government would give $200 a month to every citizen sixty years old or older. The cost would be paid by a sales tax. Each pensioner would be required to spend his or her allowance within the month. This would start such a wave of consumer buying that business would boom and make it easy for the rest of the country to bear the cost. Responsible economists dismissed the plan as a crackpot scheme; one of them estimated it would require half the national income to be turned over to 8 percent of the population.

But Townsend Clubs, organized throughout the country, attracted desperate older men and women. Their combined membership was said to be about 3 million in 1935, with perhaps as many as 7 million additional supporters. When frightened politicians began to endorse Townsend's scheme, Roosevelt had to face the possibility that a large proportion of the voters over sixty would be forged into a bloc.

More forceful and yet more vague than Dr. Townsend was the "radio priest," Father Charles E. Coughlin, who broadcast weekly from Royal Oak, Michigan. Coughlin won an enormous audience with assaults on Wall Street and the international bankers, phrased in such a way that no one could doubt the role of these groups in the Depression. His harangues seemed more satisfying to his followers than his more rational demands for a "living wage" and nationalization of banks, utilities, and natural resources. Originally one of Roosevelt's supporters, Coughlin broke with the New Deal in 1935, drifted toward fascism and anti-Semitism, and lost most of his popular appeal.

(Text continues on page 651.)

Missouri migrant farm laborer in California, 1936: "What bothers us travellin' people most is we cain't get no place to stay still." (*Photograph by Dorothea Lange, Library of Congress*)

Cotton farmer on inherited but mortgaged farm, Green County, Georgia, 1937. (*Photograph by Dorothea Lange, Library of Congress*)

Migrant workers' camp near Prague, Oklahoma, 1939. (*Photograph by Russell Lee, Library of Congress*)

Hard Times Blues

Well, I went down home 'bout a year ago,
Things so bad, Lord, my heart was sore.
Folks had nothin', it was a sin and a shame,
Ev'rybody said hard times was to blame.

> (CHORUS) Great God a-mighty, folks feelin' bad
> Lost ev'rything they ever had.
> Great God a-mighty, folks feelin' bad
> Lost ev'rything they ever had.

Now the sun was a-shinin' fourteen days and no rain,
Hoein' and plantin' was all in vain,
They had hard, hard times, Lord, all around,
Meal barrels empty, crops burnt to the ground.

They had skinny lookin' children, bellies pokin' out,
That old pellagra without a doubt.
Old folks hangin' round the cabin door
Ain't seen times so hard before.

Well, I went to the boss at the commissary store,
Folks all starvin', please don't close your door.
We want more food and a little more time to pay.
Boss man laughed and walked away.

Now your landlord comes around when your rent is due.
And if you ain't got his money, he'll take your home from you.
He'll take your mules and horse, even take your cow,
Says, "Get off my land, you're no-good, no-how!"

(This Land Is Your Land: Songs of Social Justice. *Music by Josh White; lyrics by William Waring Cuney. Copyright 1957 Charles Street Publishing Company.*)

THE GREAT DEPRESSION AND THE NEW DEAL

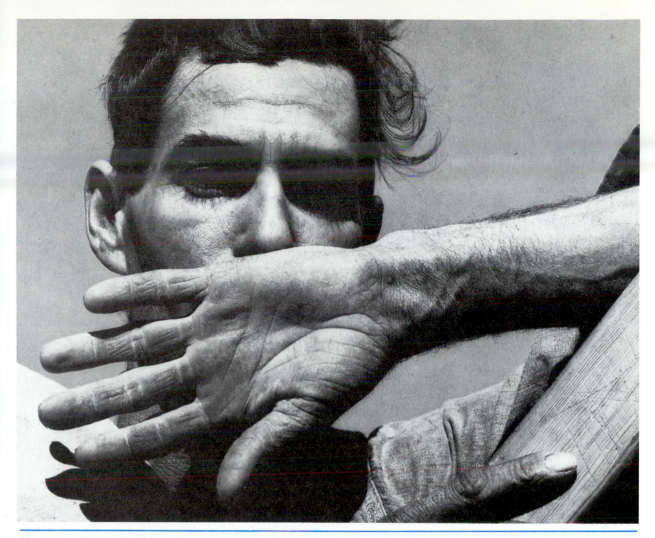

Migratory worker, 1940: "When they need us they call us migrants. When we've picked their crops we're bums and we've got to get out." (*Photograph by Dorothea Lange, Library of Congress*)

"I can count twenty-three farmers in the west half of this county that have had to leave the farms to give three men more land. Was waiting to see what would be the outcome of my hunt for a place, and the outlook right now is that I will move to town and sell my teams, tools, and cows. I have hunted from Childress, Texas, to Haskell, Texas, a distance of 200 miles, and the answer is the same. I can stay off the relief until the first of the year. After that I don't know. I've got to make a move, but I don't know where to go."

Migratory worker's wife: "If you die, you're dead—that's all." (*Photograph by Dorothea Lange, Library of Congress*)

Evicted sharecropper, 1939: "Tractors are against the black man. Every time you kill a mule you kill a black man. "You've heard about the machine picker? That's against the black man, too." (*Photograph by Arthur Rothstein, Library of Congress*)

Victim of the drought, 1937: "I want to go back to where we can live happy, live decent, and grow what we eat." (*Photograph by Dorothea Lange, Library of Congress*)

Seven Cent Cotton and Forty Cent Meat

Seven cent cotton and forty cent meat,
How in the world can a poor man eat?
Flour up high and cotton down low,
How in the world can we raise the dough?
Clothes worn out, shoes run down,
Old slouch hat with a hole in the crown.
Back nearly broken and fingers all sore,
Cotton gone down to rise no more.

Seven cent cotton and eight dollar pants,
Who in the world has got a chance?
We can't buy clothes, we can't buy meat,
Too much cotton, and not enough to eat.
Can't help each other, what'll we do?
I can't explain it, so it's up to you.
Seven cent cotton and two dollar hose,
Guess we'll have to do without any clothes.

Seven cent cotton and forty cent meat,
How in the world can a poor man eat?
Mules in the barn, no crop laid by,
Corn crib empty and the cow's gone dry;
Well water low, nearly out of sight,
Can't take a bath on a Saturday night.
No use talking, any man is beat,
With seven cent cotton and forty cent meat.

Seven cent cotton and forty cent meat,
How in the world can a poor man eat?
Poor getting poorer all around here,
Kids coming regular every year.
Fatten our hogs, take them to town,
All we get is six cents a pound.
Very next day we have to buy it back,
Forty cents a pound in a paper sack.

(*American Industrial Ballads,* Pete Seeger (*ed.*). *Words and music by Bob Miller and Emma Dermer. New York: Folkways Records, 1929.*)

Cotton chopper, White Plains, Georgia, 1941. (*Photograph by J. Delano, Library of Congress*)

Migrants moving on, 1936: "Damned if we'll work for what they pay folks hereabouts." (*Photograph by Dorothea Lange, Library of Congress*)

Harvest hand in Ohio, 1938: "We must make enough for beans, and when we have to buy gas it comes out of the beans." (*Photograph by Ben Shahn, Library of Congress*)

Goin' Down the Road

I'm goin' down the road feelin' bad,
I'm goin' down the road feelin' bad,
I'm goin' down the road feelin' bad, Lord
And I ain't gonna be treated this-a-way.

Lord I can't live on cornbread and beans, . . .
Lord I'm goin' where the water tastes like wine, . . .
Lord I'm goin' where the climate fits my clothes, . . .
Lord where I go nobody knows, . . .
I'm not goin' to be treated this-a-way.

An old Oklahoma folk song

(*Dorothea Lange and Paul S. Taylor,* An American Exodus, 57, *and John Greenway,* American Folk Songs of Protest, 206–7.)

New York City bootblack, 1937. (*Photograph by Arthur Rothstein, Library of Congress*)

The popularity of Long, Townsend, and Coughlin, coming as it did with organized labor's growing discontent, suggested in the spring of 1935 that Roosevelt's mass appeal, so strong in the early months of the New Deal, might soon dissolve. The president well understood the real grievances underlying the broad appeal of these critics and privately even spoke of doing something "to steal Long's thunder." The Revenue Tax Act, the Social Security Act, the National Labor Relations Act, and other actions were all responses to this pressure. "I am fighting Communism, Huey Longism, Coughlinism, Townsendism," Roosevelt told one of his critics. "I want to save our system, the capitalistic system; to save it is to give some heed to world thought of today. I want to equalize the distribution of wealth." The result was more reform.

New Directions: The 1935 Reforms

Three reform measures were enacted in one month, August 1935. One was inspired by the administration's desire to stop the growth of gigantic personal fortunes. This was the Revenue Tax Act of 1935, sometimes called the "wealth tax" or the "soak the rich" law. Some also suspected it was Roosevelt's way of responding to Long's Share Our Wealth scheme. Tax rates, which had already been raised by earlier New Deal measures, were now pushed much higher; they reached 75 percent on individual incomes over $5 million. Holding companies used for the management of private fortunes were also heavily taxed, and corporation taxes were raised.

Roy W. Howard, the publisher of a chain of newspapers until then sympathetic toward Roosevelt, now wrote the president in an open letter that businessmen believed the wealth tax to be a punishment. Roosevelt replied that the act was intended to "create a broader range of opportunity" and to impose taxes according to ability to pay. He did promise, however, that business would now have a "breathing spell."

The second August law was the Public Utility Holding Company Act. Holding companies were corporations permitted to hold the securities of other corporations. By holding only a tiny fraction of a great corporation's securities, but a fraction large enough to mean strong influence where other holdings were scattered, the holding company could dominate policies to its own advantage. Consumers as well as investors had suffered from public utility holding companies. In 1932, thirteen such companies controlled no less than 75 percent of the electric power market.

The new act required that those which could not, within five years, demonstrate that they had made economies in management must be dissolved. This "death sentence" clause started a bitter struggle in Congress, and holding companies spent large sums trying to defeat it. After some compromises, the "death sentence" remained in the law and the Supreme Court eventually upheld it. Every effort to impose the "death sentence," however, was stubbornly resisted, at immense legal costs. The law became a windfall for lawyers.

The third measure was the Social Security Act, to secure "the men, women and children of the nation against certain hazards and vicissitudes of life." For the first time, the federal government would make payments, directly or through the states, for pensions to the aged and the infirm, for unemployment insurance, and for benefits to dependent mothers and children. Federal pensions of up to $15 a month to the poor over sixty-five years of age were expected to be matched by the states. Federal retirement funds, ranging from $10 to $85 a month, were to be paid to workers who retired at sixty-five and who had participated in the plan before their retirement. Agricultural workers, household servants, government employees, and those working for nonprofit religious or charitable organizations were among those excluded.

The money for those included was to be raised by a payroll tax on employers and employees. Most states promptly set up old-age pension and unemployment insurance systems conforming to the provisions of the act. A worker who lost his or her job could collect from $5 to $15 a week for a period of about fifteen weeks while looking for new work.

By 1940, about 50 million workers were protected by social security. From time to time since then, new classes of workers have been covered, money payments increased, and the period for receiving unemployment insurance extended. A nonpartisan Social Security Board administers the program. The Social Security Act passed the House and Senate with far larger majorities than the other measures. Its opponents, however, made up in loudness what they lacked in numbers. Several of them asserted that it would mean the end of free government, and one critic thought social security would "take all the romance out of life."

Labor

When the Supreme Court found the NIRA unconstitutional, and invalidated its labor guarantees, Congress responded in July 1935 by enacting the National Labor Relations Act, often called the Wagner Act after the New York senator who championed it. The act guaranteed collective bargaining and prohibited employer interference with organizing activities. It provided that the representative of the majority of the employees in any plant should be the *exclusive* bargaining representative of *all* the employees. It empowered a newly established National Labor Relations Board

(NLRB) to investigate and certify the proper representatives and to hold supervised elections when there was a dispute over which union should represent employees.

The long-run effects of this measure for the political future of the New Deal, for the Democratic party, and for the country were as profound and lasting as its economic consequences. Under the new act, no less than 340 company unions were broken up. Membership in trade unions continued to grow, particularly in the unorganized mass production industries, until in 1941 it had reached 10.5 million. By then, the NLRB had handled 33,000 cases affecting more than 7 million workers.

The rise of organized labor was accompanied by conflict not only between workers and employers, but also within labor. The AFL was badly split.

Police attack strikers at the Republic Steel plant near Chicago on May 30, 1937. Republican Steel president, Tom M. Girdler was quoted as saying: "I won't have a contract, verbal or written, with an irresponsible, racketeering, violent, communistic body like the C.I.O., and until they pass a law making me do it, I am not going to do it." (*AP/World Wide Photos*)

The leaders of the old craft unions that had first come together in the federation sought to retain their power and standing as the "aristocracy of labor." Not wanting to bring in the unskilled and semi-skilled workers of mass production industries, they also refused to permit other leaders to organize such workers in new unions. The issue came to a head at the national AFL convention in October 1935, when a majority of the delegates stood fast for craft unionism.

A month later, John L. Lewis of the United Mine Workers and seven other AFL leaders met separately and organized the Committee for Industrial Organization (CIO) to advise the AFL on how to organize the mass-production industries. Lewis became chairman of the committee. In January 1936 the AFL executive council ordered the CIO to disband. The leaders refused and were suspended in August. Expelled in March 1937, they took with them unions representing 1.8 million workers. A massive organizing campaign followed, with a record 4740 strikes that year. Early in 1938, when the CIO had nearly 4 million members, the leaders formed a new, independent organization with the same initials, the Congress of Industrial Organizations.

One of the CIO's new weapons, outlawed by the Supreme Court in 1939, was the "sit-down" strike. Instead of walking off the job and picketing, workers went to their posts in the plants and stayed there, making it difficult for others to replace them. Sit-down strikes against two giant automobile companies, General Motors in January 1937 and Chrysler in April, won the CIO recognition as the bargaining agent for their workers. In March 1937 the United States Steel Corporation, once the terror of organized labor, also gave in.

"Little Steel" proved harder to crack. On Memorial Day, 1937, Chicago police killed ten pickets during a strike against the Republic Company, Little Steel's leader. Other strikes brought violence in Youngstown, Massillon, and Cleveland, Ohio. Little Steel did not fall until 1941, when the companies signed contracts conforming to the NLRB order to reinstate workers fired during the 1937 struggle.

As labor grew more aggressive and important in politics as well as business, the split in its ranks caused many difficulties. A peace movement finally brought about a merger of the AFL and CIO in 1955. By then, the complacency and conservatism of the AFL appeared to be characteristic of much of organized labor. The energy and spirit that had marked the organizing drives of the thirties were only distant memories.

The Roosevelt Coalition: White and Black

Although the New Deal failed to resolve the economic crisis, it did give the American people a sense of direction and hope. Through his personal leadership and the legislation he had helped to bring about, Roosevelt by the end of 1935 had managed to build an extraordinary political coalition. Its elements were partly old and partly new: (1) the solid Democratic South (commercial farmers in cotton and tobacco had benefited from the agricultural program); (2) Democratic machines in northern cities (FDR preferred to use, not to destroy them); (3) new immigrant groups and blacks (especially hard hit by the Depression); (4) organized labor, intellectuals, and many normally Republican farmers and businessmen.

Among ethnic elements, blacks had good reason not to support the administration. Almost all NRA codes, for example, discriminated against black workers on employment, wages, and job-improvement opportunities. AAA crop-control payments went mostly to farmers with large acreage, leaving black sharecroppers in a precarious economic position and forcing many of them off the land altogether. The CCC began as a "lily white" agency; fewer than 3 percent of the first quarter-million enrolled were blacks. Even when black participation grew, segregation remained the rule. It was also true in the model towns established by the TVA. And the New Deal housing program encouraged the development of racially segregated neighborhoods.

Most important, the New Deal had not made a significant dent in black unemployment, and blacks were not sharing in relief. When black grievances in Harlem finally exploded into a riot in 1935, the white press blamed Communist agitation. The field secretary of the Harlem YMCA saw it differently:

It is true there were Communists in the picture. But what gave them their opportunity? The fact that there were and still are thousands of Negroes standing in enforced idleness on the street corners of Harlem with no prospect of employment while their more favored Negro neighbors are compelled to spend their money with business houses directed by white absentee owners who employ white workers imported from every part of New York City.

The New Deal approached relief, reform, and recovery on a national and a general basis. Many of its leaders did not want established social patterns attacked. Party solidarity also made Democratic leaders cautious on race. They did little or nothing, for example, to fight the poll tax that disqualified most blacks of voting age in the South or to stop lynching. Between 1930 and 1934, more than sixty blacks were hanged, shot, or burned by vigilante mobs.

Black leaders, as they had in the 1920s, pressed for federal legislation against lynching. Once again, however, southern filibusters in the Senate defeated every antilynching bill. The practical-minded Roosevelt had to explain to Walter White, an NAACP official: "If I come out for the antilynching bill now, they will block every bill I ask Congress to pass to keep America from collapsing. I just can't take that risk." The best that could be said of the president on this issue, DuBois remarked, was that he had called lynching "collective murder," and that at least offered black people some hope.

And yet the president managed to convince American blacks that he cared about them. Black voters responded to the New Deal with enthusiasm and formed a strong part of the Roosevelt coalition. However little their share, they, like others, did get relief under the New Deal, where there had been little or none under Hoover. Despite almost universal second-class treatment, blacks, like others, did benefit from New Deal reforms. And they, like others, did share in economic recovery, perhaps most through the new labor movement the New Deal fostered. Roosevelt and many of his aides showed the same warmth to black leaders as they did to others, and the New Deal hired many black administrators. Finally, Eleanor Roosevelt's liberality of spirit and constant support of minorities helped to move urban black voters to the FDR bandwagon.

The success of the New Deal's agricultural program also brought many normally Republican westerners into the Democratic ranks. Iowa, for example, had gone Republican in every election from 1916 to 1928, often overwhelmingly so. In 1932, it swung to Roosevelt and in 1936 still stood solidly behind him. Labor's newly organized millions also swung heavily into the Roosevelt camp during 1935 and 1936. John L. Lewis and other CIO leaders organized Labor's Non-partisan League to mobilize the labor vote in industrial centers. The CIO gave half a million dollars to the 1936 Democratic campaign. Nor did Roosevelt suffer from the split in labor's ranks. AFL President William Green, after visiting FDR, announced that 90 percent of labor's vote would be his.

Labor's lead was followed by many intellectuals throughout the country. Suspicious at first of some of the features of NRA and AAA, and troubled by the inadequacy and inconsistency of many New Deal measures, teachers, writers, clergy, artists, and journalists rallied behind the New Deal after the 1935 reforms. Intellectuals were encouraged by the administration's receptivity to ideas and experts and by its readiness to help unemployed artists, scholars, and writers.

Nor was business altogether absent from the coalition. Roosevelt counted many loyal personal friends among businessmen. Others, especially antitariff merchants and bankers, were traditionally Democrats. Still others represented the social-minded rich. A large number also came from sectors of the economy that benefited directly from gains in mass purchasing power brought by New Deal reform and relief legislation. From them—consumer goods manufacturers, for example, and chain and department store owners and other retailers—Roosevelt won a gratifying response when the chips were down. Their contributions were feeble compared with what the Republicans got from corporate and personal holders of "the big money." But Roosevelt needed much less money than his opponents to win votes.

The Election of 1936

By the time of the 1936 elections, the New Deal had made most of the progress it was going to make. It had fostered business recovery and furthered labor organization. It had relieved distress on the farms and helped the unemployed. Economic statistics suggested that a good deal of recovery had been achieved in certain sectors of the economy. Farm income had gone up dramatically. Average weekly earnings of workers in manufacturing had risen since 1932 from $17 to almost $22. Although some 7 million remained unemployed, this figure had dropped by 4 or 5 million since Roosevelt took office, and the unemployed were receiving enough to live. The rise in national income from $40.2 billion in 1933 to $64.7 billion in 1936 reflected the general advance.

The Republicans attacked every aspect of the New Deal. "America is in peril," their 1936 platform began. "We invite all Americans, irrespective of party, to join us in defense of American institutions." For president, the convention nominated Governor Alfred M. Landon of Kansas; for vice-president, Frank Knox, a Chicago publisher. The Democrats renominated Roosevelt by acclamation. "These economic royalists," Roosevelt told the convention, "complain that we seek to overthrow the institutions of America. What they really complain of is that we seek to overthrow their power."

The critics came together in Cleveland to form a third party, the Union party. They nominated William Lemke, a Republican congressman from North Dakota. But the critics were far fewer now. The Social Security Act of 1935 had stolen much of Dr. Townsend's thunder, and Huey Long had been assassinated. Coughlin had received unmistakable evidence that the Roman Catholic Church hierarchy found his political behavior embarrassing. Lemke polled fewer than a million votes and did not carry a single state.

Some Democrats, including Al Smith, went over to Landon during the campaign. But the Republican's main support came from the Liberty League, financed by conservative millionaires. Near the end of the campaign, before a wildly enthusiastic crowd in New York's Madison Square Garden, Roosevelt declared that the New Deal had been struggling with "business and financial monopoly, speculation, reckless banking, class antagonism, sectionalism, war profiteering." He went on: "Never before in all our history have these forces been so united against one candidate as they stand today. They are unanimous in their *hate* for *me—and I welcome their hatred.*"

In the balloting, Roosevelt carried all but two states, Maine and Vermont. His 27.75 million popular votes represented 60 percent of the total cast. In the cities, his margins reached record levels. By winning even more overwhelmingly than in 1932, he made the Democratic party the normal majority party of the country.

The fate of the minor parties testified to the strength of the Roosevelt coalition. Lemke's showing disappointed the Republicans as well as his followers. Republicans had hoped he would deprive Roosevelt of enough conservative farm votes to swing some states to Landon. The record of the Socialist and Communist candidates showed that the New Deal had completely broken independent political radicalism. Four years earlier, Norman Thomas, the Socialist party nominee, won 881,000 votes; in 1936, he won only 187,000. William Z. Foster, the Communist candidate in 1932, won 102,000 votes; Earl Browder, his successor in 1936, got only 80,000.

THE CLIMAX OF THE NEW DEAL

In his second inaugural address, FDR expressed no complacency over his victory or his achievement. The problems of depression and deprivation, as he frankly confessed, persisted: "I see one-third of a nation ill-housed, ill-clad, ill-nourished." Before attacking these problems, however, Roosevelt set out to neutralize a major obstacle to the realization of his reform vision—the Supreme Court.

The Court Fight

The president's attack on the Supreme Court came as a surprise. On February 5, 1937, apparently having consulted no one but his attorney general, Roosevelt proposed to Congress what was then called his "court-packing bill." In it he asked that whenever a federal judge failed to retire within six months after reaching the age of seventy, an additional federal judge should be appointed. Although the proposal applied to the entire federal judiciary, it was obviously aimed at the Supreme Court, where six of the judges were already over seventy. Thus, as many as six judges could be added, bringing the full Court to fifteen.

Although the announcement came as a shock, the need for the bill seemed clear enough. The people had approved of the New Deal, but the Supreme Court had opposed its early legislation. In 1935 and 1936, the Court had struck down NRA and AAA. It had rejected a railroad retirement plan and the Bituminous Coat Act, which was intended to reorganize a sick industry. It had invalidated congressional legislation to protect farm mortgages, and it had thrown out a municipal bankruptcy act. To those who sympathized with the New Deal social program, the Court seemed to be creating an area where neither state nor federal power could be used to solve critical problems.

The number of Supreme Court justices had, in fact, been changed several times in the past, but the present total of nine had become fixed for so long it almost had the sanction of constitutional authority. To attempt to reduce the Court's power by a constitutional amendment would take years, and probably could not be done at all. Roosevelt's plan was a short cut. But his assertion that it was intended simply to help federal courts catch up with their business seemed not altogether true. Even for a large number of New Dealers, it gave weight to the charge that he was indeed seeking the dictatorial powers his opponents all along had said he wanted.

While debate on the bill was in progress, several events weakened its chances. Most important, within a few weeks of Roosevelt's bombshell, Justice Owen J. Roberts began to vote on the liberal side in some cases. On March 29, 1937, the Supreme Court, 5 to 4, sustained a state minimum-wage law, overruling a recent decision by the same majority. Even more important for the New Deal, the Court on April 12 upheld the National Labor Relations Act. Six weeks later, in two 5 to 4 rulings, the Court sustained the social security legislation.

In May, Justice Van Devanter, one of the most conservative justices on the bench, struck another blow at the court reform bill when he announced his intention to retire. Roosevelt would have at least one appointment of his own. On July 22, the Senate voted overwhelmingly, 70 to 20, to recommit the bill to the Judiciary Committee, where it died. And yet Roosevelt had a sort of triumph after all. In August 1937 he appointed the liberal Hugo L. Black of Alabama to Van Devanter's place.

In the next few years, six other aging justices also took the cue and began to retire. To five of the vacancies thus created, Roosevelt appointed liberals and New Dealers; to the sixth, the southern Democrat James F. Byrnes. To the Chief Justiceship vacated by Hughes, Roosevelt shifted the learned, liberal Harlan Fiske Stone, a firm supporter of federal power. New Dealers had lost the battle but won the war, even though the whole procedure opened a lasting rift in the party and cost voter support.

Housing and Labor Standards

Many reforms were gained or extended during FDR's second term. As in the Court fight, however, the political costs were high. The reform potential of the Democratic coalition was becoming exhausted.

New reforms attempted to strike harder at poor housing and low wages. As early as 1933, the administration had created the Home Owners Loan Corporation (HOLC) with huge resources to protect householders from losing their property through mortgage foreclosure. In June 1934 it had set up the Federal Housing Administration (FHA) to lend money mainly to middle-income families for repairing old homes or building new ones. But positive action on low-income housing came only with the Wagner-Steagall Housing Act of September 1937.

It created the United States Housing Authority (USHA) and authorized it to make long-term, low-interest loans to state or city public housing agencies to clear slums and build new houses that met federal standards. Occupancy of these homes was to be limited to those who could not pay rents high enough to induce private builders to construct dwellings for them. By 1941 USHA had torn down more than 78,000 substandard buildings and built new homes for 200,000 families. This accomplishment met only a tiny portion of the need, but private building interests succeeded in stopping the program at this point.

The last major New Deal reform measure was the Fair Labor Standards Act of June 1938. The outcome of liberal agitation, this measure had failed to pass Congress on its first try. Finally, after Roosevelt gave it his open endorsement, it became law over the opposition of southern Democrats. The law included most industrial workers but omitted farm labor, at the insistence of rural congressmen. It aimed to secure a minimum wage of 40 cents an hour and a maximum work week of 40 hours for those covered. Even these modest goals were to be reached gradually.

Beginning at 44 hours, the work week was to be lowered to 40 hours in three years. Beginning at 25 cents an hour, the minimum wage was to be raised to 40 cents after eight years. The law called for time-and-a-half for overtime. Many Americans were shocked to discover that over 750,000 workers were so poorly paid that they received immediate wage increases when the law first went into effect in August 1938. The hours of 1.5 million workers were shortened at the same time.

Farewell to Reform

Even before Congress unwillingly passed the Fair Labor Standards Act, a Democratic member had begged the White House not to send any more controversial legislation. Much of FDR's political difficulty came from the so-called Roosevelt recession of 1937, when no less than 4 million workers returned to the rolls of the unemployed.

The reversal appears to have happened partly because the administration, encouraged by the business advance, had called for reducing spending by WPA and other New Deal agencies. The high taxes enacted in 1935 and 1936 also seem to have cut private investment, while the accumulation of funds in the Treasury under the social security laws cut purchasing power.

The speed with which lowering government expenditures started the downward trend suggested that neither the administration nor private industry could maintain economic growth without large-scale public spending. Early in 1938, the president and Congress put the spending program back into high gear. The business revival was resumed, but at a slower pace. In the meantime, FDR attacked the "economic royalists" who, he said, were choking American opportunity.

"Big Business collectivism in industry," he told Congress, "compels ultimate collectivism in government." He now launched the broadest trust-busting campaign since Taft. At his urging, Congress created the Temporary National Economic Committee (TNEC) to restudy the whole structure of American private enterprise.

These drastic steps seemed only to strengthen the growing dissatisfaction with the New Deal. Just before the congressional elections of 1938, Roosevelt took actions similar to his efforts to pack the Supreme Court. He attempted to purge the Democratic party of conservative southerners and others who were alienated by the growing prestige of labor in the New Deal. Again, he succeeded only in adding numbers to the discontented while purging almost no one. In the elections, the Democrats—northern and southern—kept their majorities in both houses. But Republicans made large gains, raising their number in the House from 89 to 164 and in the Senate from 16 to 23.

The president acknowledged that the reform urge in the New Deal had lessened considerably. In his annual message to Congress in January 1939, he talked about the need "to invigorate the processes of recovery in order to *preserve* our reforms." Two years earlier, Harry Hopkins reached the conclusion that America had become "bored with the poor, the unemployed and the insecure." Recovery had not been achieved. It was not as though the "ill-housed," "ill-clad," and "ill-nourished" were any less visible. But the need to do something about them seemed less urgent, and

LEGACY OF THE DEPRESSION

For those who lived during the Great Depression, the memories of that event remain vivid today. In Studs Terkel's *Hard Times*, Virginia Durr and Tom Sutton offered their assessments.

Virginia Durr

Oh, no, the Depression was not a romantic time. It was a time of terrible suffering. The contradictions were so obvious that it didn't take a very bright person to realize something was terribly wrong.

Have you ever seen a child with rickets? Shaking as with palsy. No proteins, no milk. And the companies pouring milk into gutters. People with nothing to wear, and they were plowing up cotton. People with nothing to eat, and they killed the pigs. If that wasn't the craziest system in the world, could you imagine anything more idiotic? This was just insane.

And people blamed themselves, not the system. They felt they had been at fault. . . . People who were independent, who thought they were masters and mistresses of their lives, were all of a sudden dependent

on others. Relatives or relief. People of pride went into shock and sanitoriums. My mother was one.

Tom Sutton

Those who went through the Depression have a little more pride in their possessions, have a little more pride in the amount of possessions they have. They know that it was a fortunate person in the Thirties who had as much as they have today. . . .

I don't think we're basically a revolutionary country. We have too large a middle class. The middle class tends to be apathetic. An apathetic middle class gives stability to a system. They never get carried away strongly, one way or the other. Maybe we'll have riots, maybe we'll have shootings. Maybe we'll have uprisings as the farmers did in Iowa. But you won't have revolution.

Source: Studs Terkel, *Hard Times* (New York: Pantheon Books, 1970), pp. 531, 511–12.

the chances of getting more reform legislation were much less good. By 1939, moreover, the crisis in Europe and Asia occupied the president's time and energy and tended to overshadow domestic problems.

The New Deal: An Assessment

Although the New Deal commanded the loyalty of the great majority of Americans, as shown by election results, it was fought at every turn. Conservative critics pointed out invasions of individual liberty, the failure to balance the budget, the enormous increase in the national debt (from $22.5 billion in 1933 to almost $43 billion in 1940), and the growing bureaucracy in the federal government (from 600,000 civilian employees in 1932 to more than a million in 1940).

At the same time, critics noted that the New Deal had failed to restore the confidence of the business community, which held the real key to recovery. Critics on the Left raised questions about the soundness of the economic system that was being restored and the refusal of the New Deal to do the massive national and social planning that would really redistribute income. In 1939, when all the experiments were over, more than 8.7 million workers remained unemployed, and millions more were poor.

New Dealers preferred to emphasize the rise in national income from $40.2 billion in 1933 to $72.8 billion in 1939. Furthermore, if unemployment were measured in terms of real human suffering and social waste, it appeared to be less burdensome than a few years earlier. Whatever the methods by which reforms were achieved, farm prices did rise, enabling farmers to recover some lost purchasing power. Workers did gain from wage and hours legislation, and even more from protection of unionization and collective bargaining. The benefits of the New Deal may have gone mostly to the middle class, which had been given the means to preserve their savings and their homes.

The New Deal placed on the statute books a number of measures to make life more comfortable and secure, measures that would benefit millions yet to be born. To achieve such results, the federal government assumed a new and greater role in the lives of Americans—social security, minimum wages and hours, collective bargaining, improved housing for low-income families, and the insuring of bank deposits. By the end of the New Deal, only a few, even among Republicans, quarreled with this role.

When Roosevelt came into office in 1933, many Americans were flirting with thoughts of violence, doubts of democracy, political solutions of the extreme Right and the extreme Left. The New Deal restored their confidence in the ability of government to assume responsibility and to act. What the New Deal failed to restore was prosperity. Only with rearmament and World War II did the American people finally achieve economic recovery, leaving unanswered the question of whether the New Deal alone would have been able to solve the economic crisis. To win the war, the government embarked on ambitious spending programs and national mobilization, including a commitment to full employment. The eagerness with which all Americans accepted national planning for the purpose of waging war raised some troublesome questions that would persist long after the war had ended.

SUMMARY

The Great Depression, which began with the stock market crash of Black Tuesday, October 29, 1929, had a profound and lasting effect not only on the United States, but on the entire world. Americans were devastated. There were breadlines, people were homeless and starving, and there seemed to be no hope for the future.

The election of Franklin Delano Roosevelt and the Democratic landslide in 1932 brought the first attempt at a turnaround, but even the New Deal did not solve the problem.

The stock market crash pointed up the flaws in the economy. The Hoover administration did not see the flaws until much too late, and used only inadequate measures to try to fix them. The Republicans still held that federal intervention in the economy was to be avoided; FDR and his New Dealers thought the opposite. Only massive federal programs, they held, could solve some of the most urgent problems.

Beginning almost on the day of FDR's inauguration in March 1933, he moved to rescue the banks, stabilize business and agriculture, reduce unemployment and provide assistance for the victims of the crash. Most banks were closed when Roosevelt took office. Using the Emergency Banking Act, passed by a special session of Congress, the government got the sound banks back in business and the bad ones closed permanently within a month. More bank reform followed, along with laws providing for closer supervision of the stock market. The president was given authority to devalue the dollar.

Business recovery was attacked through the National Industrial Recovery Act, which set up the NRA, the first of the "alphabet" agencies of the New Deal. Agriculture was put under the AAA, the Agricultural Adjustment Administration. Laborers, sharecroppers, and farm tenants were helped by the RA, the Resettlement Administration. The federal government's first large-scale attempt at rural redevelopment was the TVA, the Tennessee Valley Authority. Unemployment was under the supervision of several agencies: the CCC (the Civilian Conservation Corps), the PWA (the Public Works Administration) and the WPA (the Works Progress Administration). Thousands of roads, hospitals, bridges, schools, post offices, and other public facilities were built under their direction.

But all these efforts still did not break the back of the Depression. A new burst of reform was attempted in 1935, after the congressional elections of 1934. By this time, the administration had to contend with a variety of dissent movements—Huey Long in Louisana, Dr. Townsend in California, and the "radio priest," Father Coughlin, in Chicago. Three reform laws were passed in August 1935: the Revenue Tax Act, to stop the growth of great personal fortunes; the Public Utility Holding Company Act, to stop manipulation and control of companies through the holding company device; and the Social Security Act, which for the first time set the federal government up as guarantor for Americans in economic trouble.

The National Labor Relations Act addressed the problems of the labor movement. It guaranteed collective bargaining and prohibited employer interference with organizing activities. It also set up the National Labor Relations Board to investigate and certify the proper bargaining representatives and to hold supervised elections if several unions wanted to organize a company. The effects were deep and lasting. Company unions were broken up, and nationwide membership in trade unions grew until it reached 10.5 million by 1941. Organized labor also split during this decade into two large organizations, the AFL and the CIO. The two remained separate until 1955, when they were joined in the AFL-CIO.

The New Deal gave Americans a sense of direction and hope. Under FDR's leadership, the Democrats built a huge new coalition that joined Americans of all classes and colors: the solid Democratic South, the Democratic machines in northern cities, the new immigrant groups and blacks, organized labor, intellectuals, and many farmers and businessmen. Despite the fact that the New Deal did nothing about black voting or lynching in the South, FDR convinced American blacks that he cared about them, and they responded.

In the election of 1936, despite fierce criticism and even the defection of Al Smith to the Republicans, FDR carried every state except two. This landslide made the Democrats the majority party of the country. But the problems were still there. This time Roosevelt set out to attack the Supreme Court by "packing" it with his own people to get the Court to be more cooperative. The attempt failed, and cost FDR political support.

Yet the coalition held, and in Roosevelt's second term many new reforms were gained and old ones extended, particularly housing for the poor and a minimum wage. But the reform drive was slowing, and by 1939, with many still unemployed, it was dead. By that time too, the crisis in Europe overshadowed all else.

Suggested Readings

On the causes of the Great Depression, J. K. Galbraith, *The Great Crash* (1955), is brief and clear. The best biography of Hoover is D. Burner, *Herbert Hoover: A Public Life* (1978). For a different view, see J. H. Wilson, *Herbert Hoover: The Forgotten Progressive* (1975). A. U. Romasco, *The Poverty of Abundance* (1965), examines Hoover's policies and the Depression. On the Bonus Army, see R. Daniels, *The Bonus March: An Episode of the Great Depression* (1971).

The impact of the Depression is clearly conveyed in the interviews collected by Studs Terkel for *Hard Times* (1970), several of which have been recorded in a two-record album, *Hard Times* (Caedmon TC2048). In addition, anyone seeking to understand how people lived during the Depression should look at its rich photographic images, which may be found in H. O'Neal (ed.), *A Vision Shared: A Classic Portrait of America and Its People 1935–1943* (1976); R. E. Stryker and N. Wood, *In This Proud Land: America 1935–1943 As Seen in the FSA Photographs* (1973); F. J. Hurley, *Portrait of a Decade: Roy Stryker and the Development of Documentary Photography in the Thirties* (1972); D. Lange and

P. S. Taylor, *An American Exodus* (1969 reprint); and W. Evans, *American Photographs* (1938), and *First and Last* (1978). Two of the finest social commentaries in American literature deal with the thirties: J. Agee and W. Evans, *Let Us Now Praise Famous Men* (1941, 1960), focusing on three tenant families, and T. Rosengarten, *All God's Dangers: The Life of Nate Shaw* (1974), the personal account of a black cotton farmer in Alabama. Illuminating in still other ways about the quality of life in the thirties are Federal Writers' Project, *These Are Our Lives* (1939); T. E. Terrill and J. Hirsch, *Such as Us: Southern Voices of the Thirties* (1978); R. S. and H. M. Lynd, *Middletown in Transition* (1937); B. Sternsher (ed.), *Hitting Home: The Great Depression in Town and Country* (1970); and W. Guthrie, *Bound for Glory* (1943). The songs of the Depression may be heard in The New Lost City Ramblers, *Songs from the Depression* (Folkways 5264); Woody Guthrie, *Talking Dust Bowl* (Folkways 2011); and in two sets of Library of Congress recordings, *Woody Guthrie* (Elektra 271/272 and *Leadbelly* (301/302).

Two popular works that assess the impact of the Depression are C. Bird, *The Invisible Scar* (1966), and E. R. Ellis, *A Nation in Torment* (1970). The best introduction to the New Deal is W. E. Leuchtenburg, *Franklin D. Roosevelt and the New Deal* (1963). See also D. Wecter, *The Age of the Great Depression 1929–1941* (1948); P. Conkin, *The New Deal* (1967); A. M. Schlesinger, Jr., *The Coming of the New Deal* (1959), and *The Politics of Upheaval* (1960); and two anthologies, H. Zinn (ed.), *New Deal Thought* (1966), and H. Swados (ed.), *The American Writer and the Great Depression* (1966). On FDR, see F. Freidel, *Franklin Delano Roosevelt* (4 vols., 1952–76); J. M. Burns, *Roosevelt: The Lion and the Fox* (1956); and R. Hofstadter, "Franklin D. Roosevelt: The Patrician as Opportunist," in *The American Political Tradition* (1948).

The best "inside" narratives include R. G. Tugwell, *The Democratic Roosevelt* (1957), *The Brain Trust* (1968), and *In Search of Roosevelt* (1972); F. Perkins, *The Roosevelt I Knew* (1946); R. Moley, *After Seven Years* (1939); R. E. Sherwood, *Roosevelt and Hopkins* (1948); D. E. Lilienthal, *Journals: The TVA Years 1939–1945* (1964); J. M. Blum, *From the Morgenthau Diaries: Years of Crisis 1928–1938* (1959), and *Years of Urgency 1938–1941* (1964); and H. L. Ickes, *The Secret Diary of Harold Ickes* (3 vols., 1953–54). Eleanor Roosevelt, *This I Remember* (1949), is a valuable personal account.

On FDR and the business community, see A. U. Romasco, *The Politics of Recovery* (1983). The spirit of the NRA is conveyed in H. S. Johnson, *The Blue Eagle: From Egg to Earth* (1935). See also S. Fine, *The Automobile under the Blue Eagle* (1963). On the AAA and farm policy, see V. L. Perkins, *Crisis in Agriculture* (1969); R. S. Kirkendall, *Social Scientists and Farm*

Politics in the Age of Roosevelt (1966); and C. M. Campbell, *The Farm Bureau and the New Deal* (1962). J. L. Shover, *Cornbelt Rebellion: The Farmers' Holiday Association* (1965), and D. E. Conrad, *The Forgotten Farmers: The Story of Sharecroppers in the New Deal* (1965), are both valuable accounts, as is S. Baldwin, *Poverty and Politics: The Rise and Decline of the Farm Security Administration* (1968). C. McWilliams has written the classic account of migratory farm labor: *Factories in the Field* (1939). P. Daniel, *Breaking the Land* (1985), is an important study of southern agriculture.

On the WPA and the arts, see W. T. MacDonald, *Federal Relief Administration and the Arts* (1969); F. V. O'Connor, *Art for the Millions* (1973); and R. D. McKinzie, *The New Deal for Artists* (1973). On the Federal Theater, H. Flannagan, *Arena* (1949), a personal memoir, may be supplemented by J. D. Matthews, *The Federal Theatre 1935–1939* (1967), a scholarly account. On the Federal Writers' Project, see J. Mangione, *The Dream and the Deal* (1972).

Labor under the New Deal is examined in I. Bernstein, *Turbulent Years* (1970), and S. Fine, *Sitdown: The General Motors Strike of 1936–1937* (1969). See also E. Levinson's vividly told *Labor on the March* (1938). On the CIO, see M. Dubofsky and W. Van Tine, *John L. Lewis: A Biography* (1977). On black workers, see H. R. Cayton and G. S. Mitchell, *Black Workers and the New Unions* (1939), and W. H. Harris, *Keeping the Faith: A. Philip Randolph, Milton P. Webster, and the Brotherhood of Sleeping Car Porters 1925–1937* (1977).

B. Mitchell, *Depression Decade* (1947), is a solid economic history. On economic planning, social programs, and the New Deal, see R. Lubove, *The Struggle for Social Security* (1968); P. Conkin, *Tomorrow a New World* (1959); E. W. Hawley, *The New Deal and the Problem of Monopoly* (1966); and O. L. Graham, Jr., *Toward a Planned Society: From Roosevelt to Nixon* (1976).

N. J. Weiss, *Farewell to the Party of Lincoln* (1983), examines black politics during the 1930s. On blacks in the New Deal, consult H. Sitkoff, *A New Deal for Blacks: The Emergence of Civil Rights as a National Issue: The Depression Decade* (1981). Bernard Sternsher (ed.), *The Negro in Depression and War: Prelude to Revolution* (1969), is a useful collection. See also R. Bunche, *The Political Status of the Negro in the Age of FDR* (1973); R. Wolters, *Negroes and the Great Depression* (1970); and H. Cruse, *The Crisis of the Negro Intellectual* (1967). On urban whites in the Roosevelt coalition, see J. J. Huthmacher, *Senator Robert Wagner and the Rise of Urban Liberalism* (1968), and C. Garrett, *The La Guardia Years* (1961). On the old Progressives and the New Deal, see O. L. Graham, Jr., *An Encore for Reform* (1967).

The challenge to the New Deal is best examined in

A. Brinkley, *Voices of Protest: Huey Long, Father Coughlin, and the Great Depression* (1982). See also T. H. Williams, *Huey Long* (1969); S. Marcus, *Father Coughlin* (1973); and A. Holtzman, *The Townsend Movement* (1963). D. R. McCoy, *Angry Voices* (1958); I. Howe and L. Coser, *The American Communist Party: A Critical History 1919–1957* (1957); and L. De Caux, *Labor Radical* (1970) discuss the radical Left. For the memoir of a black radical, see N. I. Painter, *The Nar-rative of Hosea Hudson: His Life as a Negro Commu-nist in the South* (1979). For a study of race relations and the Left, see D. T. Carter, *Scottsboro: A Tragedy of the American South* (1969). On student activism, see J. Wechsler, *Revolt on the Campus* (1935). On the chal-lenge from the Right, see J. T. Patterson, *Congressional Conservatism and the New Deal 1933–1939* (1967), and G. Wolfskill, *The Revolt of the Conservatives: A History of the American Liberty League 1934–1940* (1962).

THE AGE OF VIOLENCE: WORLD WAR II

Chapter 29

Already shaken by the experience of the Great Depression, most Americans in the 1930s refused to believe that the United States might become involved in another world war. But the news from abroad was ominous. The English writer W. H. Auden called this decade the age of anxiety. The enthusiasm with which the embittered and depressed German people rallied around Adolf Hitler's pledge to redeem their pride, race, and economy was but one example. So was Mussolini's war on the Ethiopians, Stalin's purges of Communist officials, Japan's aggression in Manchuria and China, and the civil war in Spain. All these events fed and reinforced the insecurity the deepening worldwide depression had helped set in motion.

When Americans began to understand what the events unfolding in Europe and Asia meant, the feeling was almost unanimous that the United States should avoid any involvement in another war. The poor reputation of American business leaders during the Depression fed the belief that international bankers and munitions makers had conspired to draw the United States into World War I. Public opinion polls in 1937 showed that 70 percent of the American people thought it had been a mistake for the United States to enter World War I; 95 percent thought the United States should stay out if another war developed in Europe.

But the desire to avoid involvement was not the same thing as indifference. Nazi Germany's aggressiveness and inhumanity troubled Americans. Although as late as 1939 popular polls showed 90 percent of Americans still opposed to involvement in the European war, 80 percent expressed sympathy for the Allies, Great Britain and France. Sensing this divided mood, FDR tried to balance the nation's desire to stay out of the war against the growing fear of Nazi Germany and the wish to help the Allies defeat Germany.

Hitler's invasion of Poland in September 1939 set off a new general war. The distress of America's old allies, as well as the continuing struggle for supremacy in the Pacific, encouraged Japan to strike at the United States. What confronted Americans after the attack on Pearl Harbor, December 7, 1941, was quite simply preserving a way of life. In a series of articles on "What I Am Fighting For," which appeared in the popular *Saturday Evening Post*, the theme was clear enough: "I am fighting for that big house with the bright green roof and the big front lawn." The United States fought because it had been attacked, not to make the world safe for democracy. Recognizing such feelings, Roosevelt called World War

II the War for Survival and indulged in far less speculation about the postwar world than had Wilson.

In that war some 45 million people did not survive at all: Among them were 20 million Russians, 6 million Jews, 4.2 million Germans, 2.2 million Chinese, 1.4 million Japanese, and 405,000 Americans. Methods of mass annihilation were brought to new levels of scientific perfection. Of the 344,000 people who lived in Hiroshima, Japan, nearly 100,000 died. On the night of February 13, 1945, and into the next day, at least 135,000 died in Dresden, Germany, after an Allied saturation bombing.

What happened in the Nazi extermination camps, where 6 million Jews died, had even more fearful implications. With its much revered traditions in science, medicine, and engineering, Germany demonstrated to humankind, as it had never been demonstrated before, techniques of mass extermination and bestial cruelty based on race and nationality. The Germans employed assembly-line efficiency in carrying out the executions, and the men and women—the technicians, engineers, and physicians—who acted as executioners and engaged in grisly experiments with human life looked upon themselves as perfectly normal and healthy human beings. Of all the literature that came out of World War II, few documents could approach the letter written by a child in a Nazi death camp in Poland. It said all that needed to be said about this costliest war in history: "Now I must say goodbye. Tomorrow mother goes into the gas chamber, and I will be thrown into the well."

It was a time of extraordinary violence and brutality. While the casualties soared, the technology of extermination became even more sophisticated. With the dropping of the atomic bombs on Hiroshima and Nagasaki, World War II came to a close, and the Atomic Age dawned. A world in upheaval found itself gripped by new tensions and anxieties. ■

BETWEEN THE WARS: 1920–1937

Having rejected membership in the League of Nations, the United States went its own way in international affairs. For Americans, the wisdom of this course was reinforced by the failure of the Allies to make good on their enormous war debts to the United States, and the uneasy peace in Europe. The United States made a few gestures toward international cooperation, such as joining the other world powers in naval disarmament and in vague agreements to renounce war and respect national interests. At the same time, it actively pursued its economic goals abroad, especially in Latin America and Asia, and contributed to the tariff war. And it remained alert to any international developments that posed a threat to national and economic security.

The sources of international conflict after World War I increased as the worldwide depression deepened. The economic crisis became so severe that many peoples supported totalitarian movements and justified repression that promised a solution to their insecurities. Benito Mussolini in Italy and Adolf Hitler in Germany came to power at the head of movements that replaced democratic forms with police states and adopted militant and expansionist foreign policies. In Asia, Japan emerged as the dominant power after World War I. The Japanese took formerly German islands in the Pacific, kept some troops in Siberia, cast an eye on the raw materials of Southeast Asia, and moved to shut the Open Door in China.

In the thirties, the United States often tried to interest European nations in collective action to restrain Japan's ambitions. At the same time, the United States remained outside Europe's system of collective security. Both policies failed. Weakened by American isolation, European collective security collapsed in the face of Nazi aggression. With the Europeans in trouble at home, American efforts to involve them in the Far East were doomed.

Disarmament and Stability: The Washington Conference, 1921-1922

To show that it had not abandoned its role as a great power, the United States took the lead after World War I to stop the naval race and to impose some kind of stability on the Far East. President Harding invited Britain, Japan, France, Italy, and China to meet with the United States in Washington, beginning Armistice Day, November 11, 1921.

Secretary of State Charles Evans Hughes presided over the conference. He electrified the delegates with a proposal for a ten-year suspension in the construction of capital ships—battleships and cruisers. He also proposed that the capital ship tonnage of the United States and Britain be limited to 500,000 and that of Japan to 300,000. This was in keeping with their then current power ratio of 5–5–3. But it also meant that Britain and Japan would have to get rid of no less than sixty-six ships, and the United States thirty ships. The conference ended in February 1922 with a five-power naval treaty that endorsed the 5–5–3 ratio almost at Hughes's tonnage figures. France and Italy were permitted capital ship tonnage of 175,000. Although smaller ships were not covered by the agreement, the naval race was at least partially stopped.

Two other important agreements made at the Washington meeting were the so-called Four-Power Pact and the Nine-Power Pact. The first replaced an Anglo-Japanese alliance with a new agreement including the United States and France. The four powers pledged to keep the peace in the Pacific. In the second agreement, China, Italy, Belgium, the Netherlands, and Portugal joined the other four. They reaffirmed the Open Door in China and guaranteed its sovereignty, independence, and territorial integrity. The treaties contained no real enforcement mechanism, and nothing was said about land and air forces or economic barriers to trade.

The Washington Conference was welcomed in most of the world as a triumph of diplomacy. When it was followed in 1928 by the Kellogg-Briand Pact renouncing war as an instrument of national policy (which sixty-two nations signed), a fragile international world seemed safer. Japan, however, was simply marking time.

Japan in China

Having already shattered the myth of the invincible white man by its triumph over Russia in 1904, Japan came out of World War I with renewed strength, determined to compete with the Western powers for economic advantages in Asia. If Japan came to believe that its destiny was a unified Asia under Japanese control, it was only asserting imperial ambitions that Great Britain, France, Germany, and the United States, among others, had asserted more than once in Africa, Asia, and Latin America. Japan's ambitions reflected its need for access to sources of raw materials to sustain its rapid industrialization and modernization. The Great Depression would make quite clear its economic vulnerability.

Since 1905, Japan had enjoyed special privileges in southern Manchuria, in the northeastern section of China. When in the 1920s Chinese Nationalists under Chiang Kai-shek, intent on uniting the country and ridding it of foreign powers, threatened the Japanese in Manchuria, Japan chose to strike back. In September 1931, using as an excuse an incident on the Japanese-controlled Manchurian Railway, Japanese forces moved into Manchuria. The United States and the League of Nations promptly reminded Japan of its treaty responsibilities. But by January 1932 the Japanese army had crushed all resistance in Manchuria and turned it into a puppet state.

When it was clear that reminders would have no effect, Western diplomats raised the question of economic sanctions. Secretary of State Henry L. Stimson suggested this possibility to President Hoover. But feeling that sanctions might lead the United States into war, the president opposed them. His decision, and the reluctance of the League powers to go beyond it, limited Western action to moral pressure. This Japan felt free to ignore. On January 7, 1932, Secretary Stimson stated in a note to Japan and China that the United States could not recognize any treaty or agreement in Asia that infringed its rights or violated Chinese territorial integrity. This policy of refusing to recognize territorial changes achieved by force of arms became known as the Stimson Doctrine.

The situation deteriorated after January 28, 1932. Japan invaded Shanghai, wiped out the Chinese force there, and killed civilians. For the first time, militant sentiment against Japan began to appear in the United States, but President

Hoover continued to oppose even economic pressure. Secretary Stimson decided to issue a message to the world through a letter to the chairman of the Senate Committee on Foreign Relations. In it, Stimson asserted that the United States would stand on its treaty rights in the Far East, especially those recognized in the Nine-Power Pact, and invited other nations to do the same. He warned that violation of one of the Washington treaties released the parties from the other treaties. The move was greeted with strong approval in the American press, but had little effect on Japan.

The League of Nations condemned Japanese aggression. After a League commission refused to recognize the puppet regime in Manchuria, Japan's response was to withdraw from the League in March 1933. Less than two years later, Japan also renounced the Washington Conference naval agreement. When the United States and Britain refused in 1936 to grant Japan naval equality with themselves, it began an expansion program the other two felt they had to match. And the more Japan viewed its interests as endangered by the refusal of the United States to recognize its conquests and ambitions, the closer it came to taking the chance of war.

The Soviet Union

Fear of Japan on the Asian mainland and of Hitler in Germany made the Soviet Union anxious to establish relations with the United States. All other major powers, including Japan, had long since recognized the Soviet government. The United States had equally strong reasons to extend recognition. Mutual concern over Japanese intentions in Asia might have been sufficient justification. With the Great Depression, the pressure mounted. The prospect of trade with the Soviet Union attracted American businessmen, especially those in the machine tool and agricultural implement industries. At the same time, there was growing interest among American intellectuals and writers in the Communist experiment.

Formal relations between the United States and the Soviet Union were set up by an exchange of notes in Washington on November 16, 1933. Maxim Litvinov, Stalin's emissary, gave up Soviet damage claims against the United States for its actions during the 1918–19 intervention (see Chapter 26). Litvinov in turn agreed to negotiate the claims of American and European creditors for the debts of czarist Russia. He also agreed to stop Soviet propaganda in the United States and to remove Soviet government influence from any organizations in the United States heretofore "under its direct or indirect control."

Trade relations did not really grow, but recognition gave the United States an official observation post in Moscow. Mutual suspicion persisted. It was aggravated in the Soviet Union by memories of the postwar intervention and in the United States by negotiations over debts and continued Communist activity in the Western Hemisphere.

Latin America

Despite the pretense of isolationism in American foreign affairs after World War I, the United States pursued an active policy in Latin America. Strategic, diplomatic, and economic considerations led the United States to interfere in the governments of no less than ten countries. If any justification was necessary, the Roosevelt Corollary to the Monroe Doctrine (see Chapter 24) was enough.

Often American armed forces became involved—in Panama in 1921, in the Dominican Republic from 1921 to 1924, and in Honduras in 1923. Since 1912, United States marines had been in Nicaragua. When they were withdrawn in 1925, Nicaragua again became so unstable that Coolidge almost immediately sent them back. The establishment of a "democratic" government brought some order. But rebel leader Augusto César Sandino refused to be pacified. He retired to the hills and harassed American marines until 1933, when the last of them were called home.

In Mexico, protection of private economic interests influenced United States policy. The Mexican Constitution of 1917 had reaffirmed the old Mexican principle, violated during the long Diaz regime (1877–1911), that the government retained ownership of all Mexican mineral and oil resources. American businessmen, encouraged by Diaz, had invested heavily in Mexican development. Now they feared confiscation of their properties. When President Plutarco Calles took office in 1924, he announced his desire to make just such a change. The Mexican Congress then provided that petroleum rights acquired in 1917 would be limited to fifty years.

The pressure of American oil interests and the influence of American Catholics, who resented Calles's anticlerical policy, together with the interventionist policy, soon brought talk of a new war with Mexico. But in 1927 President Coolidge sent his envoy Dwight L. Morrow to Mexico with this instruction: "Keep us out of war." Morrow worked out a compromise by which American investors could retain permanently the oil properties they had held before the Constitution of 1917. Later confiscation under the Cárdenas regime in 1938 infuriated American oil companies, brought charges of Communist influence, and revived talk of intervention. The matter was negotiated, but not until one Mexican newspaper had said: "Poor Mexico. So far from God, and so close to the United States." Under the settlement reached in 1941, the Mexican government bought out American oil properties and other claims.

In his first inaugural address in March 1933, Franklin Delano Roosevelt said he hoped "to dedicate this nation to the policy of the good neighbor." His intentions were soon tested in Cuba, where in August 1933 the regime of Gerardo Machado was overthrown, perhaps with a push from Roosevelt's ambassador, Sumner Welles. The new government of Ramón Grau San Martín, however, was far too reformist to please Cuban business interests, including the substantial American business community. On the advice of Ambassador Welles, the president withheld recognition. With the encouragement of the United States, Martín's military backers, led by Sergeant Fulgencio Batista, conducted an election in January 1934. It brought the United States-backed candidate, the first in a string of Batista puppets, to the presidency. Roosevelt quickly recognized the new government.

As a gesture of goodwill, the United States in May 1934 negotiated a treaty with Cuba giving up its right of intervention under the Platt Amendment. But it seemed clear that the United States reserved the right to impose order on the island if American economic interests or citizens were in any danger. And in keeping the naval base at Guantánamo, the United States, as *The New York Times* noted, gave "a clear indication that Cuba is embraced within the plans of the United States for national defense."

To improve the image of the United States in Latin America, Secretary Hull attended the Montevideo Conference of American States in 1933 and agreed to a proposal that "no state has the right to intervene in the internal or external affairs of another." Hull also announced a new plan to reduce tariffs through reciprocal trade agreements, further pleasing the delegates. In the spirit of the Montevideo agreement, in March 1936 United States representatives signed a treaty with Panama surrendering American rights to interfere in that nation's affairs and raising the annual pay-

ments for the canal. Not until Panama agreed in 1939 to permit the United States in emergencies to defend the canal, however, did the Senate approve the treaty.

Efforts to overcome the deep suspicion of Yankee imperialism brought only slow improvement. By the time of the attack on Pearl Harbor, relations had improved enough for the United States to be assured of cooperation in the hemisphere. But American economic domination persisted and set the stage for more conflict after World War II.

Neutrality and Aggression

The need to do something in Latin America was made more urgent by the rapid decline in sympathy and understanding between America and Europe. American immigration and protectionist policies in the twenties shut out European peoples and European goods. The arguments over Allied war debts, which the United States refused to cancel and European nations neglected to pay, reflected the breakdown in mutual respect. Nor had the United States relaxed its opposition to membership in the League of Nations. Before his nomination for the presidency, even FDR allowed himself to be pressured into attacking the League.

The desire to keep out of alliances and military confrontations became stronger in the mid-thirties. The sensational "merchants of death" investigation of 1934 conducted by a Senate committee gave weight to the view that wars were fought for the benefit of international bankers and munitions makers. The best way to stay out of war was to make it unprofitable under the law for citizens to trade with belligerents.

The first test of this policy came in mid-1935 when the fascist dictator Benito Mussolini made it clear that Italy intended to annex Ethiopia. By the time the Italians had launched a full-scale attack in October 1935, Congress had passed the first of a series of Neutrality Acts authorizing the president, after proclaiming that a state of war existed between foreign nations, to forbid Americans to sell or ship munitions to them. Basic war materials such as oil, steel, and copper were not included in the ban. Under administration pressure, Congress put a six-month limit on this embargo, and Roosevelt reluctantly signed it.

The arms embargo, he said later, by penalizing unprepared victims while leaving untouched those who had built up massive military machines, "played right into the hands of the aggressor nations [which] were actually encouraged by our laws to make war upon their neighbors." (In February 1936, Congress extended the Neutrality Act to May 1, 1937, and added loans and credits to belligerents to the ban.)

After his triumph in Ethiopia, Mussolini embarked on other adventures. In July 1936, when Spanish fascists under General Francisco Franco rebelled against their country's republican government, Mussolini promptly sent 50,000 to 75,000 "volunteers," along with planes and supplies. Not to be outdone, Hitler also sent help.

Opinion in the United States was deeply divided over the Spanish war. Many Americans sided with the government, which the United States had long recognized. Some even went to Spain to fight for it. Soviet support of the government, however, lent weight to the fascist charge that it was Communists they were opposing. It also made it easier for American fascist sympathizers and Catholic supporters of Franco's uprising to get a joint res-

olution from Congress forbidding the export of munitions to either side (January 6, 1937). Naturally this action hurt the government more than the fascists, who were receiving much foreign assistance.

In May Congress adopted a new measure authorizing the president to decide not only when wars between nations existed, but also when civil wars like that in Spain endangered world peace. In such situations, an embargo was to begin at once on the export of munitions and on credits for them. A "cash-and-carry" plan, limited to two years, empowered the president to require belligerents buying *nonmilitary* goods in this country to take them away in their own ships. The act also made it unlawful for Americans to travel on belligerent vessels.

In March 1939, after an exhausting war, Franco's forces won. General Franco was under heavy obligation to Mussolini and Hitler. He man-

Adolf Hitler: "Today there must remain no vestige of doubt—it is not a Fuehrer or a man who speaks, but the whole German people!" (*Brown Brothers*)

THE AGE OF VIOLENCE: WORLD WAR II

aged to outlive both of them, and his anticommunism would win him new friends in the post-World War II era.

THE ROAD TO WAR

After Japanese and Chinese forces met at Peking in July 1937, the Japanese overran North China. Roosevelt attacked this aggression in his famous quarantine speech of October 5, 1937. Ninety percent of the people of the world wanted peace, he said, but their security was threatened by the other 10 percent. Peace-loving nations must act together to quarantine aggressors; otherwise the disease will spread uncontrolled:

There is a solidarity, an interdependence about the modern world, both technically and morally, which makes it impossible for any nation completely to isolate itself from economic and political upheavals in the rest of the world, especially when such upheavals appear to be spreading and not declining. . . . We are determined to keep clear of war. . . . We are adopting such measures as will minimize our risk of involvement, but we cannot have complete protection in a world of disorder in which confidence and security have broken down.

The president gave no indication of what kind of collective action he had in mind. The response to the speech was so mixed in the United States that Roosevelt remarked to one of his close advisors, "It's a terrible thing to look over your shoulder when you are trying to lead—and to find no one there."

European Theater, 1939–42

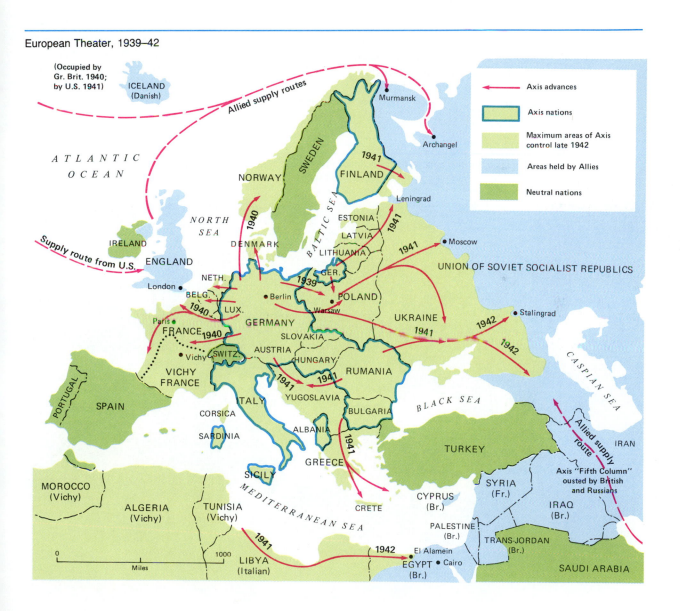

The Crisis in Europe

Although no action was taken against Japan, Roosevelt in May 1938 got a billion dollars from Congress to enlarge the navy. Within the year, aggression in Europe brought on a crisis there. Hitler had come to power in Germany in January 1933. Fifteen months later he renounced the Versailles Treaty terms on German disarmament. In March 1936, while Mussolini's invasion of Ethiopia held the attention of western Europe, German forces occupied the Rhineland. Hitler had long been campaigning for the return of German territory lost in World War I. Now, in September 1938, he was poised to grab the Sudetenland of Czechoslovakia.

France, along with Great Britain, remained unprepared to confront a rearmed Germany. At the disastrous meeting in Munich on September 29, 1938, they let Hitler have what he wanted. The world had gained "peace with honor . . . peace in our time," at Munich, British Prime Minister Neville Chamberlain told his people. But his words carried little conviction.

Having gained the Sudetenland, Hitler promised to leave the rest of Czechoslovakia alone. In March 1939 he swallowed up the remainder of the small republic. Not to be outdone, three weeks later Mussolini took Albania. Hitler's word obviously was worthless. Yet the world applauded FDR when, in April 1939, he wrote to Hitler and Mussolini, asking them to pledge, for a period of ten years, that they would not attack any one of a list of thirty-one nations.

Hitler replied for both with the suggestion that the danger existed only in Roosevelt's mind. The reality was brought closer in May 1939, when a stubborn group of Senate isolationists blocked an administration request for revisions of the neutrality laws to permit economic aid to Britain and France in case of war.

Apparently safe on his western front, Hitler shocked the world by making a nonaggression pact in August with the Soviet Union on his eastern front. This double protection left him free to attack Poland. He had demanded that Poland return territory, but Poland resisted, encouraged by France and Britain. The new pact left the Soviet Union

In August 1940 Congress enacted the first peacetime conscription in American history, and on October 29 the first draft numbers were drawn. Within two weeks, draftees, like those pictured here on their way to Fort Dix, New Jersey, were drilling in camps all over the country. (*UPI/Bettmann Newsphotos*)

free to strengthen its western frontier. On September 1, 1939, Hitler's troops invaded Poland while his air force bombed Polish cities.

Two days later, Britain and France honored their Polish commitments by declaring war on Germany. As the law still required, Roosevelt invoked the Neutrality Act. But he did not repeat Woodrow Wilson's appeal for neutrality in thought as well as in deed. "Even a neutral," said Roosevelt, "cannot be asked to close his mind or his conscience."

Before Munich, public opinion polls showed only a third of the American people in favor of selling arms to Britain and France in case of war. By mid-September 1939, when Roosevelt called a special session of Congress to revise the neutrality laws, and specifically to repeal the arms embargo so that munitions could be sold to the old Allies, he appeared to have the support of at least two-thirds of the people. In his message to Congress, Roosevelt also asked for authority to prevent American ships from sailing into danger zones, so that incidents could be avoided. Belligerents must carry their own cargoes. All these requests were noted by Congress on November 3, 1939. Lifting the arms embargo pleased the interventionists, restoration of cash-and-carry pleased the isolationists.

In September 1940, with the support of some big business opponents of the New Deal, the America First Committee was formed. General Robert E. Wood, board chairman of Sears, Roebuck, was national chairman. The committee drew many well-known people before being dissolved when Pearl Harbor was attacked. Colonel Charles A. Lindbergh, Jr., who had thrilled Americans in 1927 with his solo flight from New York to Paris, expressed the sentiments of the committee when he declared: "In the future we may have to deal with a Europe dominated by Germany. . . . An agreement between us could maintain peace and civilization throughout the world as far into the future as we can see."

Interventionists found their voice in the Committee to Defend America by Aiding the Allies. The chairman was William Allen White, a Kansas editor and Republican. White replied to Lindbergh that many countries, trying to be neutral, had been destroyed: "Hitler's whole philosophy, his idea of government, his economic setup, his insatiable ambitions, all make it impossible for a free country and a free people to live beside Hitler's world enslaved."

The mood in America remained sharply divided. One month after the Nazi invasion of Poland, polls revealed that 62 percent of the American people favored aiding the Allies short of war. Less than 30 percent wanted the United States to enter the war if it seemed the Allies would be defeated. On college campuses, students demonstrated on Armistice Day 1939 to express their desire for peace and disarmament. And the president himself insisted, "I hope the United States will keep out. . . . Every effort of your government will be directed toward that end."

Aid Short of War

When Hitler delayed moving on the Western Front, many even in Europe were lulled by the "phony war." But when Hitler did move in April 1940, he did so with terrifying speed and force. Neutral Denmark, Norway, and the Low Countries—Belgium, Holland, and Luxembourg—and France itself were defeated in seven weeks. When Belgium fell, Britain had to use every resource to rescue its own army from the Continent. Between May 28 and June 4 every available boat, including small pleasure craft piloted by their owners, evacuated the last of more than 335,000 men from Dunkirk, France, under the pounding of German planes and guns. On June 10, Mussolini attacked France from the south. On June 22, a crushed France signed an armistice.

The British now stood suddenly alone against the Berlin-Rome Axis. During the summer and fall of 1940, in a tremendous effort to bring Britain to its knees, Hitler sent clouds of planes to bomb English cities. Tens of thousands of civilians were killed and wounded. But the Royal Air Force fought back with extraordinary courage, and by autumn it was clear that Hitler's attempt would fail. If Britain was to be conquered, it must be by invasion. Winston Churchill, at the time of Dunkirk, had promised to resist "whatever the cost may be . . . until, in God's good time, the New World, with all its power and might, steps forth to the rescue and liberation of the Old."

Two months after the fall of France, Roosevelt talked with a close advisor on the situation in which he found himself. "Bill," FDR remarked, "if my neighbor's house catches fire and I know that fire will spread to my house unless it is put out, and I am watering the grass in my back yard, and I don't pass my garden hose over the fence to my neighbor, I am a fool. How do you think the country and the Congress would react if I should put aid to the British in the form of lending them my garden hose?"

Even as Roosevelt pledged to keep the nation out of war, he strengthened American defenses and took steps to assist Britain. Throughout the summer of 1940, aid was being rushed overseas. Military equipment that could not be legally transferred directly from government to government was sold to private firms which resold it to Britain.

On September 3, Roosevelt took his most daring step. By executive agreement, he made the famous deal with Britain transferring fifty old but still useful destroyers needed to keep off German submarines. In exchange, Britain gave the United States sites for naval bases in Newfoundland and Bermuda and rent-free leases on other sites in the Caribbean and South Atlantic. Although outraged by this trade, Hitler did nothing to push the United States to join the Allies. But Congress passed the first peacetime draft in American history and appropriated about $16 billion for airplanes, warships, and other defense needs.

The climax of the debate came at about the same time as the presidential election of 1940. The Democrats broke the two-term tradition and renominated FDR, naming Secretary of Agriculture Wallace as his running mate. Republicans leaned toward Senator Robert A. Taft of Ohio and the young district attorney of New York, Thomas E. Dewey. But the bright young men in the party rallied behind a newcomer to politics, Wendell L. Willkie of Indiana, and put him across on the sixth ballot.

A public utilities executive, Willkie had been a leader in the fight of private power interests against the TVA. His charm grew with his liberalism. By 1940 his stand on the war in Europe was close to Roosevelt's. This left him with a popular position, but without an issue on which to set himself off from his opponent. Willkie lost by a popular vote of 22,305,000 to 27,244,000 and an electoral vote of 82 to 449. But he restored the Republican party to a strong position without accepting the views of its isolationist wing—an outstanding personal success.

Roosevelt renewed the debate over foreign policy in a fireside chat to the people on December 29, 1940: "There will be no 'bottlenecks' in our determination to aid Great Britain," he said; "all our present efforts are not enough. . . . We must be the great arsenal of democracy." One week later, the president took steps to fulfill that role. The cash-and-carry system worked only as long as the British had the cash, and Churchill had warned Roosevelt that Britain's financial resources were nearly exhausted.

On January 6, 1941, in his annual message to Congress, Roosevelt came up with a clever solution. He proposed *lend-lease* as the most practical means by which the United States, remaining at peace itself, could help arm Britain and its allies. The lend-lease bill, to supply Britain and its allies with arms carried in their own ships and to be returned or replaced when the war ended, was fiercely opposed in Congress. Senator Burton K. Wheeler of Montana called it the "New Deal's 'triple A' foreign policy—to plow under every fourth American boy." But public opinion favored lend-lease, and Congress approved it.

Lend-lease had an effect on British finances and British morale even before the flow of material began. It also made American intervention seem definite. Admiral Harold R. Stark, United States Chief of Naval Operations, promptly wrote his fleet commanders: "The question as to our entry into the war now seems to be *when,* and not *whether.*"

To ensure that lend-lease ended up at its destination and not at the bottom of the sea, Roosevelt took steps to help Britain fight the packs of German submarines in the Atlantic. He soon extended American "defense" lines all the way to Greenland and Iceland. In a more aggressive move, on March 31, 1941, he ordered the Coast Guard to seize German or German-controlled ships in American ports. On May 15, a German torpedo sank the American merchant ship *Robin Moor* in the South Atlantic. Roosevelt responded by proclaiming an unlimited national emergency. On June 16, he requested Germany and Italy to close their consulates in the United States.

Thereafter the United States moved steadily closer to war in the Atlantic. In July the president announced that the United States, by agreement with the Icelandic government, was taking over the defense of Iceland for the duration of the war, and that the navy would keep convoy lines open as far as Iceland.

In August he met with Churchill on a British battleship at sea. The two leaders drew up the eight-point declaration named the Atlantic Charter, in which they proclaimed "certain common principles" that would ensure "a better future for the world": (1) no territorial aggrandizement; (2) self-government for all peoples; (3) free access to trade and raw materials; (4) the abandonment of war as an instrument in international relations.

The Atlantic Charter goals were very much like Wilson's Fourteen Points. Churchill accepted the "self-government" principle only with strong reservations regarding the British Empire. "We mean to hold our own," he said a year later. "I have not become the King's First Minister in order to preside over the liquidation of the British Empire."

Meanwhile, the war at sea continued. When in September 1941 a German submarine fired on the

American destroyer *Greer,* Roosevelt ordered the navy to "shoot on sight" any Axis raiders they encountered, although the *Greer* had provoked the attack. In October, the American destroyer *Kearney* was damaged near Iceland in a battle with German submarines. Roosevelt said: "America has been attacked.... The shooting has started." At the end of October the destroyer *Reuben James* was sunk off Iceland while engaged in convoy duty. Congress responded in November by authorizing American merchant ships to sail well-armed and to carry lend-lease supplies directly to Britain.

Thus, by the fall of 1941 the United States had become an open ally of Britain without formally having declared war. By then Hitler had begun his invasion of the Soviet Union, so recently his partner in the nonaggression pact. What led Hitler to take this step in June 1941 remains uncertain. Most likely he hoped to capture the wheat of the Ukraine, the oil of the Caucasus, and the greater part of the Soviet Union's industrial resources. Such conquests might make Britain and its friends across the sea more likely to negotiate rather than fight. Success might also inspire Germans with new hope of total victory.

Whatever his calculations, Hitler had obviously underestimated the Soviet potential for resistance. Others did the same. In June 1941, for example, immediately after the Nazi attack, Henry L. Stimson, now Roosevelt's secretary of war, estimated it would take Hitler from one to three months to conquer the Soviet Union. Secretary of the Navy Knox thought it would take "anywhere from six weeks to two months." Yet when winter came, the Nazi armies still were outside Moscow and Leningrad, and the Soviet Union was still mustering its strength.

Churchill welcomed the Russians as comrades in arms, just as he had welcomed the American "arsenal." "I have only one purpose, the destruction of Hitler," he told his secretary. "If Hitler invaded Hell I would make at least a favorable reference to the Devil in the House of Commons." To reverse a generation of hostility and aid the Soviet Union created a predictable controversy within the United States. Public opinion polls revealed that most Americans wanted the Soviet Union to defeat Germany. There was less enthusiasm about outright American aid. Charles Lindbergh reacted with anger to such a proposal. He preferred an alliance with Nazi Germany than with the "godlessness and barbarism that exist in the Soviet Union." The persistence of anti-Soviet feeling was perhaps best summed up by Harry S.

Truman, then a senator from Missouri: "If we see that Germany is winning we ought to help Russia and if Russia is winning we ought to help Germany and that way let them kill as many as possible, although I don't want to see Hitler victorious under any circumstances. . . ."

Fortunately, Roosevelt listened to no arguments about who should win. In November 1941, the United States extended lend-lease to the Soviet Union. "Give us anti-aircraft guns and the aluminum and we can fight for three or four years," Stalin told Harry Hopkins, Roosevelt's emissary. Despite predictions in the United States of a quick German victory, the Red Army proved Stalin correct.

Toward Pearl Harbor

Since his quarantine speech, Roosevelt had been cautious in dealing with the Japanese. As early as December 1937, when Japanese planes sank the American gunboat *Panay* in the Yangtze River in China, war had seemed possible. But Japan quickly apologized and paid reparations for the lives lost. From then on, the United States followed an unclear line. Roosevelt refused to invoke the Neutrality Act because it might stop the movement of supplies over the Burma Road to Chinese forces opposing Japan. Yet Americans continued to sell large quantities of scrap metal, steel, copper, oil, lead, and machinery to the Japanese.

It would have been possible, after January 1940, to end this traffic by embargo. But the president hesitated to take this step, because he thought it would only cause Japan to look for these commodities by further conquest in Asia. In May 1940, as a deterrent to Japan, Roosevelt ordered the transfer of the United States Pacific fleet base from San Diego, California, to Pearl Harbor.

As a further deterrent, after the fall of France in June 1940, Congress passed a law requiring Americans to obtain federal licenses for the export of oil and scrap metal. Under this law, Roosevelt, on July 26, ordered aviation gasoline withheld from Japan, a step that drew a strong Japanese protest. The next month Japan forced the helpless Vichy government in France to surrender bases in northern Indochina. This move prompted Roosevelt, on September 25, to extend the embargo to iron and steel scrap and to grant a large new loan to Chiang Kai-shek. Two days later, Japan joined the German-Italian coalition.

The formation of the Berlin-Rome-Tokyo Axis to promote Hitler's "New Order" in Europe and the prosperity of "Greater East Asia" under Japan was intended to warn the United States to keep hands off both. If America attacked any of the three, the other two agreed to come to the aid of the victim. The first major change in the Pacific followed the Nazi invasion of Russia in June 1941, which removed the last possibility that Soviet forces could be used against Japan.

That July, Tokyo compelled the Vichy government to yield bases in southern Indochina. Roosevelt responded by freezing all Japanese assets in the United States. Japan reciprocated, thereby paralyzing trade between the two countries. On August 17, 1941, Roosevelt warned the Japanese that if they made any further moves to impose military domination on neighboring countries, the United States would take "all steps which it may deem necessary toward safeguarding [its] legitimate right and interest."

The previous December, the United States Naval Intelligence cryptographers had broken Japan's secret diplomatic code, "Magic," and Washington could listen in on messages from Tokyo to its envoys in the American capital. One thing seemed certain from these messages: Japan intended to conquer China. At the same time, the United States had no intention of sacrificing Chiang Kai-shek to Japan's ambition. Negotiations between the two countries came to a halt principally on this issue.

In Japan itself in mid-October 1941 the government of Prime Minister Fumimaro Konoye was forced to resign in favor of General Hideki Tojo, who feared for the army's morale if, after years of sacrifice, it must yield China under American pressure. "If a hundred million people merge into one iron solidarity to go forward," Tojo declared, "nothing can stop us." He would have been glad to have China without war with the United States.

On October 23 his cabinet agreed to speed up military preparations. By November 3 his government had decided to attack Pearl Harbor if negotiations did not permit Japan to have its way. At the same time, the talks in Washington were to continue. After November 17 they were under the direction of Saburo Kurusu, a special envoy.

The Japanese assault on Pearl Harbor. Millions of Americans first learned of the surprise attack when they turned on their radios to hear their favorite Sunday programs. (*UPI/Bettmann Newsphotos*)

From the secret code, Washington knew that if a satisfactory agreement were not completed by November 29, "things are automatically going to happen." On November 20 Kurusu and the Japanese ambassador presented Secretary of State Hull with proposals that seemed to be a demand that the United States approve and aid Japan's conquest in Asia. Six days later, the State Department presented counterproposals. Favorable trade relations were offered in exchange for Japan's withdrawal of forces from China and Indochina and its signature to a nonaggression pact with other nations that had interests in the Far East. Japan obviously would not accept such terms. "I have washed my hands of it," said Hull to Secretary of War Stimson that day, "and it is now in the hands of you and Knox, the Army and Navy."

Hull did not realize how right he was. Unknown to the American negotiators, a Japanese carrier force had just set out. On December 1, dismissing the American demands as "fantastic," Kurusu nevertheless asked that discussions continue. Washington already knew of Japanese troop movements, which Roosevelt thought meant only an attack in the Southwest Pacific on Thailand, Malaya, and the Dutch East Indies—which were, in fact, the main Japanese objectives. On December 6 he sent the Japanese emperor a hasty peace appeal. The next day Japan made its move.

Early in the morning of Sunday, December 7, 1941, a strong carrier-borne force of Japanese planes swooped down on the American naval base at Pearl Harbor in Hawaii. Most American aircraft were destroyed on the ground, and the unprotected naval vessels suffered terrible damage. In this one assault, 2355 American servicemen and 68 civilians died; 1178 were wounded. The next day a shocked Congress voted to declare war on Japan.

Roosevelt's critics later accused him of having provoked Japan to attack in order to bring the United States into the war in Europe and of having deliberately exposed the navy at Pearl Harbor in order to create a situation that would unite Americans behind his war. That Roosevelt wanted to enter the war by November and that he knew a firm stand against Japan might bring drastic action seem beyond doubt. However, had the United States stood quietly by while Japan conquered an immensely rich empire in China and Asia, Roosevelt would have been criticized for inaction.

The notion that Roosevelt conspired to defeat and destroy a substantial part of the navy he had served and built up and that his administration and high military authorities were involved in the plot is most unlikely. No doubt there was fault

both in Washington and Pearl Harbor. But to the very end it was thought the Japanese would strike elsewhere.

On December 11, four days after Pearl Harbor, Japan's Axis partners, Germany and Italy, declared war on the United States. Congress responded immediately with declarations of war against them. The United States was now engaged in global warfare.

THE HOME FRONT

Two weeks after the attack on Pearl Harbor, Jonathan Daniels, a newspaper editor who would soon become Roosevelt's administrative assistant, wrote that the war had brought a new era in American history: "The twenties are gone with self-indulgence. The thirties have disappeared with self-pity. The forties are here in which Americans stand on a continent as men—men again fighting in the crudest man terms." Unlike World War I, there was little discussion about the need to fight. The American people—men and women—were asked to mobilize their human and physical resources for total war. It was the men who would ultimately take the war into the enemy's terrain; it was the women who built most of the bombers and fighters that pounded the enemy's cities.

To mobilize a people for war, to generate the kind of enthusiasm that will lead them to make sacrifices, it is almost always necessary to portray the enemy as an inhuman force. World War II was no exception. The Germans were the very incarnation of evil, prepared to invade the homes of American families. The Japanese were subhuman and treacherous. *Time,* the popular newsmagazine, caught the proper tone when it entitled the article on the Battle of Iwo Jima "Rodent Exterminators." "The ordinary unreasoning Jap is ignorant," *Time* observed. "Perhaps he is human. Nothing . . . indicates it." Near the close of the war, when *Time* featured on its cover Admiral William F. (Bull) Halsey, it also used his motto: "Kill Japs, kill Japs, and then kill more Japs."

Japanese-Americans

To unleash such hatred against a foreign enemy could be expected of any nation engaged in war. Less understandable was the decision in early 1942 to single out 110,000 Japanese-Americans, two-thirds of them citizens of the United States, remove them from their homes on the West Coast, and confine them in inland relocation centers. Except for President Jackson's removal of the Indians from Georgia, the action was without precedent in the nation's history.

What caused the decision was race prejudice rather than military security. It was the result of more than forty years of anti-Japanese sentiment and racial tension on the West Coast. No removal was ordered in Hawaii, where 32 percent of the population was of Japanese descent. Nor did anyone ever seriously consider doing the same to German-Americans or Italian-Americans. Earl Warren, then the California attorney general, tried to explain:

We believe that when we are dealing with the Caucasian race we have methods that will test the loyalty of them, and we believe that we can, in dealing with the Germans and the Italians, arrive at some fairly sound conclusions because of our knowledge of the way they live in the community and have lived for many years. But when we deal with the Japanese we are in an entirely different field and we cannot form any opinion that we believe to be sound.

Although there was no evidence of Japanese sabotage on the West Coast after Pearl Harbor, that only confirmed the suspicions of those who advocated removal. Lieutenant General J. L. DeWitt, head of the Western Defense Command, in recommending removal to the Secretary of War, concluded: "The very fact that no sabotage has taken place to date is a disturbing and confirming indication that such action will be taken."

Despite such hysterical racial repression, many units of Nisei (Americans of Japanese descent) performed heroically in the United States armed forces. Their work, along with the realization of how unfairly Japanese-American families had been treated, finally induced the federal government to pay more than $35 million to the evacuees for property losses. But this was very little compensation for the immense damage that had been done.

Near the end of the war, the Supreme Court, in a series of decisions, upheld the essential features of the removal program. If Justice Frank Murphy found in that program "a melancholy resemblance" to the Nazi treatment of the Jews, Justice Hugo Black expressed the more popular opinion: "Hardships are a part of war, and war is an aggregation of hardships."

Black Americans

Black America had responded with some uncertainty to the outbreak of war in Europe. "Our war," said one black newspaper, "is not against Hitler in Europe but against the Hitlers in America." After the attack on Pearl Harbor, a black sharecropper reportedly told his landlord, "By the way, Captain, I hear the Japs done declared war on you white folks." What these reactions reflected was not only skepticism about a "white man's war," but the contrast between wartime democratic slogans and the realities of black-white relations.

The vast majority of blacks no doubt reached the same conclusion as did one of their contemporary heroes, heavyweight champion Joe Louis: "America's got lots of problems, but Hitler won't fix them." Unlike World War I, when W. E. B. DuBois had urged his people to set aside their grievances and rally to the war effort, the black press and leadership vowed that World War II would be fought on two fronts: "victory over our enemies at home and victory over our enemies on the battlefields abroad."

The outlook for winning the war at home was often very bleak. While more than one million blacks entered the armed forces, over half of whom served overseas, discrimination and segregation continued in the army, navy, and marines, in USO and service clubs, even in Red Cross blood banks and entertainment centers. Nor did the war change traditional restrictions and practices. Under a "V for Victory" sign, for example, bus riders in Charleston, South Carolina, were advised. "Victory demands your cooperation. . . . Avoid friction. Be patriotic. White passengers will be seated from front to rear; colored passengers from rear to front." Between 1940 and 1943 seventeen blacks were lynched. In 1943, race riots broke out in Los Angeles, Beaumont, Mobile, New York, and worst of all, Detroit, where twenty-five blacks and nine whites died. "There ain't no North any more," a Detroit black woman observed. "Everything now is South."

Still, World War II marked a significant turning point in race relations. Even before Pearl Harbor, in early 1941, a threatened march of 100,000 blacks on Washington, D.C., forced Roosevelt to prohibit racial discrimination in defense industries and to establish a Fair Employment Practices Commission (FEPC) to protect minorities from job discrimination. During the war, blacks shared in employment opportunities. Migration of southern blacks to northern and western cities continued to change the nation's racial map. Overseas experience made black servicemen less willing to accept racial restrictions at home.

Nor was the lesson of what had happened to 6 million Jews in Europe lost on black Americans. World War II also generated revolutionary ferment

"A JAP'S A JAP"

As head of the West Coast Defense Command, General John L. DeWitt defended the removal of Japanese-Americans: "A Jap's a Jap . . . It makes no difference whether he is an American citizen or not . . . There is no way to determine their loyalty." In subsequent testimony before a Congressional committee, he advised against returning the Japanese to the West Coast.

GENERAL DE WITT: . . . I don't want any of them here. They are a dangerous element. There is no way to determine their loyalty. . . . There is a feeling developing, I think, in certain sections of the country that the Japanese should be allowed to return. I am opposing it with every proper means at my disposal.

MR. BATES: I was going to ask—would you base your determined stand on experience as a result of sabotage or racial history or what is it?

GENERAL DE WITT: I first of all base it on my responsibility. I have the mission of defending this coast and securing vital installations. The danger of the Japanese was, and is now—if they are permitted to come back—espionage and sabotage. It makes no difference whether he is an American citizen, he is still a Japanese. American citizenship does not necessarily determine loyalty.

MR. BATES: You draw a distinction then between Japanese and Italians and Germans? We have a great number of Italians and Germans and we think they are fine citizens. There may be exceptions.

GENERAL DE WITT: You needn't worry about the Italians at all except in certain cases. Also, the same for the Germans except in individual cases. But we must worry about the Japanese all the time until he is wiped off the map. Sabotage and espionage will make problems as long as he is allowed in this area— problems which I don't want to have to worry about.

Source: Hearings before Subcommittee of House Committee on Naval Affairs on H.R. 30, 78th Congress First Session (1943), pp. 739–40. Photography by National Archives, War Relocation Authority.

in Africa and Asia that would eventually force the United States to reassess its own racial policies. "The thesis of white supremacy," a State Department official remarked in 1944, "could only exist so long as the white race actually proved to be supreme."

Mobilization and Politics

At the time of Pearl Harbor, an American army of 1.6 million men already existed, most of them recruited through the first peacetime draft. Eventually, all men between eighteen and forty-five were subject to military service, and for the first time women were permitted to volunteer for the armed forces. By the war's end, 15 million men and more than 200,000 women had served in the army, navy, marines, and coast guard.

Behind these men and women stood American industry, agriculture, labor, and science. Critics of the president had dismissed as wishful thinking his call for 50,000 planes a year in 1940. In 1942, over 47,000 aircraft were built. For 1944, the figure rose above 96,000. By 1945 no less than 55 million tons of merchant shipping and 71,000 naval vessels had been launched by American yards. Because Malaysian and East Indian raw rubber supplies had been cut off early in the war, a new synthetic rubber industry had been established. In other American industries, first lend-lease and then American war production ended the Depression.

The "hate Roosevelt" attitude of big business did not die with mobilization. The steel industry, for example, was slow in responding to appeals to expand before Pearl Harbor. The automobile industry's "business as usual" policy reflected its reluctance to convert to armaments just when the boom was reviving the market for cars. Almost complete conversion was achieved; but private industry's fear of excess plant capacity forced the government, through the Defense Plant Corporation, to build about 85 percent of the new facilities needed for war production. Most of the government-built plants were run during the war by private corporations under liberal contracts with the armed services and purchased afterward on generous terms.

Depression unemployment also ended. Millions of women joined or replaced men on the assembly lines and kept war plants going day and night. A War Manpower Commission shifted workers into areas where they were most needed and made arrangements for efficient use of the labor force.

The incentive to work in war plants grew as average weekly earnings rose from $23.86 in 1939 to $46.08 in 1944. After Pearl Harbor, the AFL and CIO made no-strike pledges. Later, as prices rose and as the worst period of the war passed, strikes became frequent. Workers were widely criticized for strikes. The slogan "There are no strikes in foxholes" was easily met, however, with the reply "There are no profits either." Corporate profits after taxes rose from $5 billion in 1939 to almost $10 billion in 1944, and many new fortunes were made.

With the drafting of men into the armed forces, large numbers of women found wartime employment, particularly in the defense industries. By the fall of 1943, with war production reaching peak levels, an estimated 17 million women made up a third of the total work force. Of these, some 5 million worked in war factories. Posters of Rosie the Riveter, along with popular songs, persuaded women to leave the home for war work as a patriotic duty and reassured them they could do factory work as easily as household work: "If you've sewed on buttons, or made buttonholes, on a machine, you can learn to do spot welding on airplane parts," one billboard proclaimed. "If you've used an electric mixer in your kitchen, you can learn to run a drill press. If you've followed recipes exactly in making cakes, you can learn to load shell."

Those who had already been working, usually in service and menial jobs, eagerly applied for the better-paying positions in war industries. Many of these women, moreover, expected to keep good jobs after the war. Although war work increased the independence, income, and pride of women, men continued to dominate the supervisory positions. And the wage scales, despite government promises to the contrary, discriminated against women.

Although the farm population fell during the war (despite draft exemptions for many agricultural workers), farm production soared. In 1945 output per farm worker, responding to favorable weather and scientific aids, almost doubled that from 1910 to 1914, agriculture's golden years. Farm income also doubled. The war showed that a small farm labor force, working with improved agricultural techniques, could meet the normal needs of the domestic market. The demonstration soon influenced farm and financial policies.

A major effort was made during the war by the Office of Price Administration, under the chairmanship of Leon Henderson, to control inflation. Price ceilings were set on a wide variety of consumer goods. A few products, such as sugar, coffee, meat, and butter, were rationed. Prices had already

THE ROSIES

We were happy to be doing it. We felt terrific. Lunch hour would find us spread out on the sidewalk. Women welders with our outfits on, and usually a quart of milk in one hand and a salami sandwich in another. It was an experience that none of us had ever had before. Workers from other ships would look at us and see that we were welders and it was a terrifically wonderful thing. We had a happy attitude toward our work that they [the men] of course did not have because they were in the middle and the end of their stories and we felt we were at the beginning. (Lola Weixel in the documentary film *The Life & Times of Rosie the Riveter.*)

Women are working only to win the war and will return willingly to their home duties after the war is won. They will look on this period as an interlude, just as their men who have been called to service will consider military duties as an interlude. The women are like Cincinnatus, who left his plow to save Rome and then returned to his plow. Women will always be women. (Betty Allie, State Workmen's Compensation Official, in *Detroit News,* November 26, 1943.)

Well, the war ended. The black man went first, and I went second, and everybody else remained. We were laid off within a day of each other. In a way, I felt then that it was right. We had in us a philosophy that man is the breadwinner, and that if there's a choice between himself and you, he's entitled to more than you. . . . I finally ended up going to an office. I readjusted, but I never really liked it. (Celia Yanish)

After the war it was completely different. I went around and applied to different factories, but there were no jobs for me. So I had to fall back on the only other work I knew, and that was doing domestic work. And it was a very defeating feeling, very. (Margaret Ridell)

Rosie the Riveter

While other girls attend their fav'rite cocktail bar—
Sipping dry Martinis, munching caviar—

There's a girl who's really putting them to shame
Rosie is her name.

All the day long whether rain or shine—
She's a part of the assembly line—
She's making history working for victory,
Rosie the Riveter.

Keeps a sharp lookout for sabotage—
Sitting up there on the fuselage—
That little frail can do more than a male can do,
Rosie the Riveter.

Rosie's got a boy friend Charlie,
Charlie, he's a marine—
Rosie is protecting Charlie
Working overtime on the riveting machine.

When they gave her a production "E"
She was as proud as a girl could be,
There's something true about Red, white and blue about
Rosie the Riveter.

Ev'ry one stops to admire the scene—
Rosie at work on the B-Nineteen—
She's never twittery nervous or jittery,
Rosie the Riveter.

What if she's smeared full of oil and grease
Doing her bit for the old Lend lease
She keeps the gang around
They love to hang around,
Rosie the Riveter.

Rosie's buys a lot of war bonds
That girl really has sense
Wishes she could purchase more bonds
Putting all her cash into national defense.

Source: Interviews conducted by Connie Field, Director, *Rosie The Riveter Film Project* (Clarity Educational Productions, Inc., 5915 Hollis, Emeryville, Ca. 94608). "Rosie the Riveter" by Red Evans and John Jacob Loeb, Copyright renewed 1969 Ahlert-Burke Corp. & John J. Loeb Co. Photographs by Gordon Parks and by the Library of Congress.

risen about 25 percent when controls were first authorized in January 1942, and they continued to rise slightly. But serious inflation was avoided.

Wartime science in the United States came under the direction of the Office of Scientific Research and Development, headed by Vannevar Bush, president of the Carnegie Institution of Washington and former vice-president of the Massachusetts Institute of Technology, and James Conant, since 1933 president of Harvard. Their work profited greatly from the contributions of refugee scientists from Axis countries and the cooperation of British scientists. Among the major developments were those in radar, a British invention. The most lethal development was the atomic bomb.

Even before Munich, German scientists had become the first in the world to release energy by splitting the uranium atom. They worked feverishly to find a way to use this incredible energy in a deliverable weapon. Late in 1939 Albert Einstein, who had fled Germany when Hitler took power, and two other refugee scientists had managed to make FDR understand what atomic science could do. Roosevelt promptly established an advisory committee on uranium. But the "crash" program to produce an atomic bomb was not decided upon until the spring of 1941.

At that point the British, whose atomic research was considerably ahead of that in the United States, agreed to share their knowledge. From the very first, the scientists knew they could keep their findings from political leaders who would want to use atomic energy in warfare. Almost to a man, however, they had suffered under Axis regimes. Their hatred and fear of the Nazis had grown as strong as the new physical force itself. Either way, civilization seemed doomed. Perhaps Hitler's defeat might offer the better chance. In any case, it was they who pressed the bomb on governments, and not the other way around.

The most fruitful work on the atom was done at the University of California at Berkeley, the University of Chicago, and Columbia University in New York. This work showed that a practical bomb could be made by using plutonium. Plutonium was a new element produced by splitting the uranium atom in a cyclotron, or atom smasher. On May 1, 1943, the job of producing plutonium in large quantities was given to the secret Manhattan District Project established at Oak Ridge, Tennessee, where the immense water and electric power resources of TVA were available.

At about the same time, the responsibility for building a practical bomb was given to Dr. Robert J. Oppenheimer and the brilliant team of British, American, and European scientists he gathered at Los Alamos, New Mexico. On July 12, 1945, final assembly of the first atomic bomb began. Four days later, at Alamogordo air base in New Mexico, the weapon was detonated.

By mid-1943 American war costs, including those for atom bomb development, were running at $8 billion a month, as high as the *yearly* budgets of the peacetime New Deal. In 1945, for the first time in history, the federal government spent over $100 billion. The total cost of the war to the United States was about $350 billion—ten times the cost of World War I.

After July 1, 1943, employers began to collect income taxes for the government by withholding them from employee payrolls. This innovation continued to be used after the war. It assured the government of its revenues and kept workers up to date with taxes. Income and other taxes paid for two-fifths of the war's huge cost. Yet between 1941 and 1945, the national debt rose from about $48 to $247 billion.

Politics was not suspended in the war years. In the congressional elections of 1942, Republicans gained by capitalizing on public discontent with military defeats. But by 1944 the military situation had changed, and the Republicans had to contend once again with Roosevelt's popularity. Thomas E. Dewey, now governor of New York, became their candidate. The Democrats, with the third-term tradition shattered, nominated Roosevelt.

The convention spotlight, since FDR's health and age were in question, centered on the choice for vice-president. After a stormy session, Henry Wallace, unpopular with city bosses and southern conservatives, was dropped in favor of Senator Harry S. Truman of Missouri. He had gained attention as chairman of a Senate committee investigating malpractices under wartime production contracts.

Dewey had no real issue on which to campaign, since he and his party had accepted most of the administration's program, including the president's commitment to a new international organization. The Republicans focused on Roosevelt's health, but this tactic boomeranged. Dewey's freshness appeared to reflect his limited participation in war work, at which the president exhausted himself to save the country.

Roosevelt won by a vote of 25,602,000 to 22,006,000 and by 432 to 99 in the electoral college. The Democrats' choice of vice-president proved fateful indeed, for Roosevelt was to serve less than four months of the fourth term.

THE WAR FRONTS

In the spring of 1942, the United States and the Allied Powers did not expect to win the war quickly, if they could win at all. They outnumbered the Axis powers, but the Axis had enormous labor resources in Central Europe, the occupied part of the Soviet Union, and the Southwest Pacific. Occupied France and friendly Spain could contribute by helping to make the Atlantic and the western Mediterranean dangerous for Allied shipping. Axis forces occupied North Africa from Tunis to the Egyptian border; and Germany's formidable Afrika Korps, under General Rommel, seemed about to smash eastward to Alexandria, closing the Suez Canal and forcing Turkey to join the Axis.

When the eastern Mediterranean became impassable, Allied ships had to take the long route around the Cape of Good Hope to supply British forces in the Middle East. In southern Russia, the Germans were hammering at the Caucasus, threatening to drive through to Iraq and Iran and complete the conquest of the routes to the East. Britain would then have been cut off entirely from its empire.

The situation was no better in the Pacific. Japan followed up Pearl Harbor with successful attacks on the Philippines, Wake Island, Guam, Hong Kong, British Malaya, and Thailand. American troops in the Philippines under General Douglas MacArthur made brave stands on the Bataan Peninsula and on the fortress island of Corregidor. But after MacArthur managed to escape to Australia, Bataan surrendered in April 1942; Corregidor in May. In the Southwest Pacific, after paralyzing the British navy, the Japanese captured Singapore and crushed resistance in the Netherlands East Indies. By March 1942, they had conquered Burma and closed the Burma Road, the supply route to China.

At best, a war lasting seven to fifteen years seemed the future for the Allies. But this forecast neglected some Allied assets, notably American resources and American industrial capacity. Allied planning and administration proved vastly superior, both in individual countries and in the coordination of joint efforts. The United States and Britain in particular, through their combined chiefs of staff and the collaboration of Roosevelt and Churchill, worked together with remarkable harmony during most of the war.

At an early point in their joint effort, their military planners made an important overall decision. They would conduct a holding operation in the Pacific until the United States could mobilize enough aid for Britain and Russia to take the offensive in Europe. After the Axis had been defeated in Europe, Japan's turn would come.

To win the war in Europe, it was vital for the Western Powers to gain control of the sea and the air. For months after the United States entered the war, German submarines roamed the Caribbean and the waters off the Atlantic and Gulf coasts. Ship sinkings were extremely high. Few submarines were sunk, however, until a new system of convoys was worked out and coastal waters were patrolled. Still, the cost in tonnage and lives continued, and it was only the tremendous rate of American merchant-ship production that offset the submarine damage.

In the air, supremacy had passed to Britain's RAF during the clashes over England in 1940. By 1941, when British aircraft production surpassed Germany's, the RAF went on the offensive. It returned the terrible attacks Germany had inflicted on British cities. Sustained RAF bombing reached a peak during July 1943, when night raids over Hamburg destroyed more than a third of the port and killed over 60,000 persons. In August 1942 American airmen joined the British in raids over the Continent, supplementing RAF saturation bombings after dark with precision daylight bombing. Between them, the two air forces dropped more than 2.6 million bombs.

At one point, there was talk among the Allies of trying to bring Germany down by air attack alone. This would avoid the casualties a land invasion would almost surely mean. But the idea had to be abandoned. Air attacks never succeeded in stopping Axis production of planes, submarines, or synthetic rubber, although in the long run they crippled transportation and refineries. When the time came for the Allies to invade the Continent, Germany found its defenses gravely weakened by the damage inflicted on railways, roads, and bridges at home and in France, and by shortages of fuel for planes, tanks, and other vehicles.

North Africa and the Casablanca Conference

With an all-out assault on France still too risky, Churchill and Roosevelt decided to attack in North Africa and in Egypt, where General Rommel's Afrika Korps was pressing toward the Suez Canal. On October 23, 1942, the first great Allied land offensive of the war confronted Rommel at El Alamein, on the Mediterranean, and sent his forces streaming back toward Libya. Broadening the assault on November 8, 1942, three Allied armies, under General Dwight D. Eisenhower (who had been named Supreme Allied Commander in the Mediterranean theater),

began landing at Algiers, Oran, and Casablanca in French North Africa.

The landings had both military and political results. They affected two sets of touchy relations. One of these was between the Allies and the Vichy government, which controlled unoccupied southern France and French North Africa. The other was with General Charles de Gaulle, exiled leader of the Free French and an enemy of Vichy. Most of the French administrators and the French navy in North Africa had remained loyal to Vichy, so the Allied invaders were not necessarily greeted as liberators.

The landings at Algiers met little resistance. Those at Casablanca and Oran encountered heavy

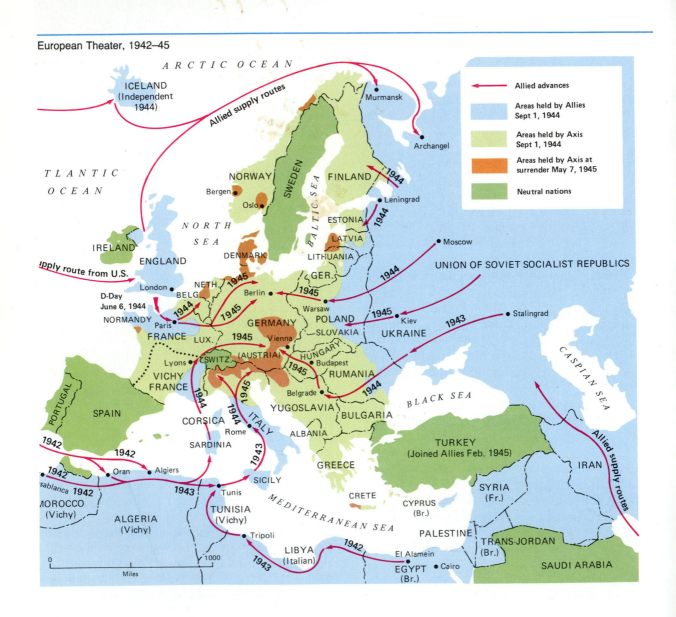

European Theater, 1942–45

THE AGE OF VIOLENCE: WORLD WAR II

fire from the French fleet, parts of which were sunk. To make matters even more difficult, French land forces would have nothing to do with General Henri Giraud, a hero of the fall of France who had escaped from prison in Germany and had been brought to North Africa by Eisenhower. The troops proved more responsive to Admiral Jean Darlan, chief of all Vichy forces, who happened to be in Algiers. Impressed with Allied strength, he agreed to an armistice.

Conveniently for the Allies, Darlan was assassinated. Giraud succeeded Darlan as head of the French government in North Africa. De Gaulle became chief of the Committee of National Liberation, which the United States recognized in July 1943 as the de facto government of all liberated parts of France. Although he became a thorn to Churchill and Roosevelt, de Gaulle's work and that of his Free French forces contributed to victory and to the French revival after the war.

The momentum of El Alamein, strengthened by the Soviet stand at Stalingrad in late 1942, gave hope to the Allies. When Churchill and Roosevelt met at Casablanca in January 1943, they made plans for victory on all fronts. The Allied leaders decided to invade Sicily and Italy after victory in North Africa. They agreed to send enough forces to the Pacific to take the offensive there, and promised to ease the pressure on the Russians by setting up another front in Europe.

They also announced that they would accept only the "unconditional surrender" of the Axis. "[We] mean that [the] will power to resist . . . of the Nazi, Fascist, and Japanese tyrannies . . . must be completely broken," Churchill explained, "and that they must yield themselves absolutely to our justice and mercy."

After the war, when searching for strong allies with whom to rebuild the balance of power on the Continent, Churchill reopened the controversy over unconditional surrender by asserting that it had made enemy resistance desperate and prolonged the slaughter. But that is not what he thought at Casablanca, where he took credit for the idea. And those who thought the threat might shorten the war by leading the enemy to sue for an early peace were soon proved wrong, at least where the Germans and Japanese were concerned.

Following the Casablanca Conference, the Allies took full possession of North Africa. General Von Arnim surrendered Rommel's army of 350,000 men (the "Fox" himself evaded capture) in Tunisia. Destruction of Nazi North African submarine and air bases followed. The southern Mediterranean again became available to the Allies at normal wartime risk, and pressure on the Middle East was eased.

The Italian Campaign

The attack on Italy began on July 10, 1943, which was as early as enough landing craft could be assembled. By August 17, when Sicily was cleared, 100,000 German prisoners had been taken. Meanwhile, King Victor Emmanuel and members of the Fascist Grand Council had deposed Mussolini and set up a new government under Marshal Pietro Badoglio, who immediately sued for peace. On September 8, 1943, the Italian government signed an unconditional surrender.

But Italy itself was still occupied by strong German forces, which Hitler strengthened. The Allied objective was to wipe out these forces, or at

WORDS AND NAMES IN AMERICAN HISTORY

Unconditional surrender is a phrase first associated with Ulysses S. Grant, during his siege of the Confederate-held Fort Donelson in Tennessee in 1862. When his opponents suggested an armistice, a stop to the fighting, Grant replied: "No terms except an unconditional and immediate surrender." The fact that he was able to enforce this demand made him a hero in the North. The same words were used during World War II, when the Allies agreed that they would not negotiate a peace, or separate peaces, with Nazi Germany or with Japan. During that war, "unconditional surrender" became a rallying cry even among civilians in the United States. These facts are well known. What is not widely recognized is that surrendering an army (let alone an entire nation) without previously agreed upon conditions, or protections for the losers, was a new phenomenon in Western warfare. Some historians argue strongly that Grant's demand marked the beginning of the "modern" age of war.

least to occupy them so they could not be used against the Russians. At the same time, the Western Powers had another objective. Control of Italy would permit them to move east into the Balkans and stop the Soviets from overrunning southern Europe when the final push against Hitler came.

The Italian campaign turned into an agonizingly slow and costly war. The Allies captured Naples on September 28, 1943. Rome, only 100 miles north, did not fall until June 4, 1944, only two days before the cross-channel invasion of France was to begin. On April 28, 1945, Italian partisans captured Mussolini, murdered him, and mutilated his body. But the Nazis in Italy fought on until May 2, five days before the Reich itself collapsed.

Conference Diplomacy: Cairo and Teheran

Although Roosevelt and Churchill met several times after the Casablanca Conference, the need to include Stalin in these meetings became more and more important. In October 1943, the foreign ministers of the Big Three—Hull for the United States, Eden for Britain, and Molotov for the USSR—met in Moscow and drew up a general understanding. The Western spokesmen promised the Russians to open the invasion of France in 1944. All three declared their intention to establish a general international organization "for the maintenance of international peace and security."

On June 6, 1944 (D-Day), Allied forces established a beachhead on the Normandy coast in the largest amphibious operation in history. "I took a walk along the historic coast of Normandy in the country of France. . . . Men were sleeping on the sand, some of them sleeping forever. Men were floating in the water, but they didn't know they were in the water, for they were dead." Ernie Pyle, noted war correspondent. (*The Bettmann Archive*)

The "Big Three," Churchill, Roosevelt, and Stalin, at Yalta, February 1945. (*Franklin D. Roosevelt Library*)

They also proposed a democratic future for Italy. Poland, where Russia's dominance was really unnegotiable, proved troublesome, but Roosevelt was still satisfied with the progress made.

And he was determined to meet with Stalin personally. This occasion, with Churchill joining the other two, was set for Teheran, the capital of Iran, late in November 1943. On the way to Teheran, FDR met with Chiang Kai-shek and Churchill at Cairo. To keep Chiang willing to fight to the finish, the three leaders promised to continue the struggle until Japan surrendered unconditionally. Occupied territories, including Manchuria and Formosa, would then be returned to China. They also foresaw a "free and independent Korea."

All of this was in the Cairo Declaration, announced December 1, after the Russians had endorsed it at Teheran. At Cairo, Roosevelt and Churchill also agreed that Eisenhower would become the supreme commander of the forces that would invade Europe.

The Big Three conference at Teheran set the Normandy invasion, under the code name Overlord, for May or June 1944. It was to be linked with a Russian offensive against Hitler from the east. Stalin also confirmed the promise made at the Moscow Conference to enter the war against Japan after Germany was defeated.

The Grand Alliance agreed to aid Marshal Tito and the Yugoslav partisans in ridding their country of German forces. Poland would again be sliced, the USSR taking some of its eastern land. But the Poles would be compensated on the west at Germany's expense. Germany was to be destroyed as a military power.

At the close of the meeting the Big Three announced: "We came here, friends in fact, in spirit, and in purpose." Roosevelt's optimism was apparent when he told Congress on his return that he "got along fine with Stalin," and predicted: "We are going to get along with him and the Russian people—very well indeed."

D Day and the German Defeat

Victory in the Battle of Britain gave the Allies command in the air. Victory in the Battle of the Atlantic and in North Africa had given them command of the seas. The amphibious landings and the establishment of beachheads at Casablanca, Oran, Sicily, and Salerno had gained them good experience. Even the stalemate in Italy, which tied down needed Allied forces, also tied down troops and equipment Hitler needed desperately in France.

For four years Hitler had concentrated on making northern France the strongest wall of his fortress. For six weeks Allied air attacks pulverized this wall and the communication lines leading to it. By June 1944, a force of nearly 2.9 million men, supported by 2.5 million tons of supplies, 11,000 airplanes, and a vast armada of ships, had been assembled in England for the invasion. On D day, June 6, the first assault troops established beachheads along the coast of Normandy.

Although caught by surprise because they had expected the attack elsewhere, the Nazis were able to mobilize quickly. But by July 24, more than a million Allied troops had taken 1500 square miles of Normandy and Brittany. The next day, General George S. Patton, Jr.'s, Third Army swept after the Germans and turned their retreat into a rout. On August 25, assisted by a Free French division, Patton liberated Paris. Two days later, De Gaulle installed himself as president of a provisional government. Patton kept going, with Omar Bradley's First Army moving more slowly on his left. Farther north, Montgomery, with Canadian and British forces, was hurtling through Belgium.

Having lost half a million men and virtually all of France, the Germans decided to take refuge behind their long-neglected west wall in the homeland across the Rhine. Patton was ready to burst

after them. Montgomery wanted permission to make "one powerful and full-bodied thrust toward Berlin." Eisenhower chose caution and consolidation.

The Allied offensives had stretched supplies of trucks, tires, and fuel. Rather than let either Patton or Montgomery go, Eisenhower decided to regroup for a final general advance into the German interior. The Germans used the time to rally their forces. On December 16, 1944, they startled the Allies with a strong counterattack in the thinly defended Ardennes forest in southern Belgium. In ten days the German armies advanced 50 miles. Finally they were stopped by the Americans at the crossroads town of Bastogne. By mid-January 1945, in the costly Battle of the Bulge (77,000 American casualties), the Germans had been pushed back to their old lines. Eisenhower now had to delay his final assault another month.

If Hitler had any thoughts about reinforcing his troops in the west, the Red Army made that impossible. The height of the Nazi invasion of the USSR, after devastating the Crimea, had been reached in the summer of 1942 at the approaches to the industrial city of Stalingrad on the Volga River. The battle for Stalingrad, which had few natural defenses and could be saved only by massed manpower, opened in July. Five months later, Marshal Zhukov ordered a sweeping counterattack that encircled the German forces. On January 31, 1943, after one of the "dourest, bloodiest, and most prolonged" battles of the war, the trapped German armies surrendered.

By D-Day in Normandy, the Red Army had completed the recapture of the Crimea and was advancing along the entire front. Elimination of Nazi forces in the Balkans started in the summer of 1944. In Greece, Churchill sent troops to turn the civil war there to the conservative side. Elsewhere in the Balkans, the Soviets were able to establish Communist regimes. By February 1945 Finland was in Soviet hands, and Poland had been organized as a Communist state. Hungary had fallen, Czechoslovakia had been penetrated. Vienna was about to collapse.

At the time of the Yalta Conference (February 4 to 11, 1945) Soviet armies were only 50 miles from Berlin. No people besides the Jews had suffered more from Nazi atrocities than the Russians. None of the Western Allies had sacrificed as much in the fighting itself. Understandably, the Soviet Union was concerned about its future security. Stalin now pressed that concern in all discussions

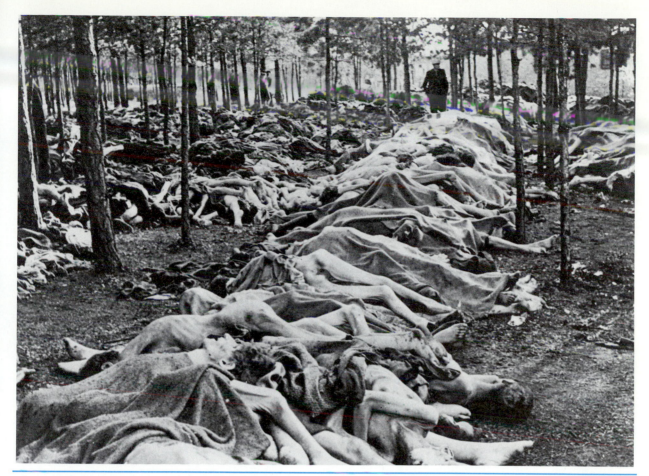

When Allied and Soviet troops finally broke through into Germany, they found the victims of the Nazi concentration camps—both the dead and the walking ghosts. One camp commander testified at Nuremberg to the cold efficiency of the Nazi plan: ". . . when I set up the extermination building at Auschwitz, I used Zyklon B, which was a crystallized prussic acid which we dropped into the death chamber from a small opening. It took from three to fifteen minutes to kill the people in the death chamber, depending on climatic conditions. Another improvement we made over Treblinka was that we built our gas chambers to accommodate 2,000 people at one time, whereas at Treblinka their ten gas chambers only accommodated 200 people each." (*AP/Wide World Photos*)

over how the postwar world would be reorganized.

Although Stalin agreed at Yalta to hold "free and unfettered elections as soon as possible" in Poland, he was determined to have no unfriendly governments on his borders. To negotiate Soviet dominance in Eastern Europe was now like asking the United States to negotiate the Monroe Doctrine. Later critics would charge that Roosevelt had given up too much at Yalta. But the fact remains that in the final phase of the war, the Red Army had overrun Eastern Europe. Stalin gave no

indication of withdrawing his troops, and the United States was not about to drive them out. Neither Roosevelt nor Churchill gave Stalin anything that was in their possession.

Anxious to get Soviet participation in the Asian war, Roosevelt made some territorial concessions to Stalin at the expense of Japan. Stalin, in turn, promised to join the war "two or three months" after the surrender of Germany. Tentative decisions at Yalta provided for the multiple administration of Berlin, the partitioning of Germany, and trials of "war criminals." (These decisions would be confirmed at the Potsdam Conference in July and August 1945.)

Finally, Stalin agreed to a United Nations Conference to be held in San Francisco in April 1945, at which a permanent international organization would be established. In Roosevelt's eyes, Stalin's agreement to participate in a United Nations was an important achievement. And with the atomic bomb still untested, American leaders welcomed

Soviet action in Manchuria to help bring about the surrender of Japan.

The European war ended after tough and costly fighting. On March 7, 1945, the Allies at last went across the Rhine over the railroad bridge at Remagen, the only bridge still standing. On April 25, American and Soviet troops made contact at the Elbe River. On or about May 1, Hitler committed suicide in Berlin, and the next day the capital surrendered. On May 7, General Jodl, chief of

The Assault on Japan

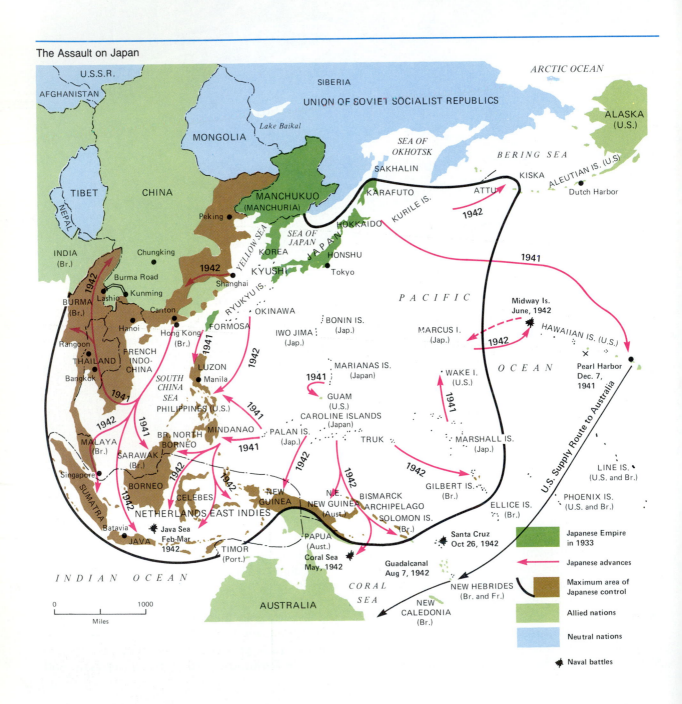

staff of the German army, signed the unconditional surrender at Eisenhower's headquarters. Within a week, half the American air force in Europe was bound for the Pacific, and the demobilization of the massive American army had begun.

On April 12, 1945, in Warm Springs, Georgia, Roosevelt died suddenly of a cerebral hemorrhage. Not since the assassination of Lincoln had the death of a president so moved the American people. Many could not even recall living under any other president. Asked if she had heard the radio bulletin, a Bronx housewife replied in tears, "For what do I need a radio? It's on everybody's face." Most appalled of all, perhaps, was FDR's successor, Harry Truman, who even as vice-president had not known the war's best-kept secret, the atomic bomb.

The War in the Pacific

In April 1942, Japan had a taste of the future. Sixteen American B-25s led by Colonel James H. Doolittle dropped a load of bombs on Tokyo. These planes had come from the aircraft carrier *Hornet*. *Hornet*'s own planes had too little range to reach Tokyo, and her deck was too short to receive Doolittle's raiders on return. All the bombers were lost in China, where their crews had to bail out. Although the raid did little damage to the target, it had great consequences and boosted American morale.

The Japanese had mounted a new offensive even before they had had time to absorb the great area conquered in their initial thrusts after Pearl Harbor. This offensive was aimed at nailing down a naval and air line of defense from Attu, the westernmost of the Arctic Aleutians, to Port Moresby, the best harbor in New Guinea. Anchor points were to be at Japanese-held Wake and American-held Midway. Inside this line Japan expected to chew up China and perhaps India.

But these plans were changed in the spring of 1942 in two important naval engagements. One was the Battle of the Coral Sea, in which a Japanese assault on Port Moresby was turned back. Coral Sea, said Admiral Ernest J. King, was "the

"Always the rain and the mud, torrid heat and teeming insect life, the stink of rotten jungle and rotting dead; malaria burning the body and fungus infection eating away the feet, and no hot chow for weeks. And fury by day and terror by night and utter weariness all the time. And death." Major Frank O. Hough, U.S. Marine Corps, as quoted in *The Island War.* (UPI/Bettmann Newsphotos)

first naval engagement in . . . history in which surface ships did not exchange a single shot." In fact, they never saw one another. The entire battle, which set a pattern for the Pacific engagements, was fought by carrier-based planes.

The second Allied victory came in the Battle of Midway Island, June 3 to 6. Japanese capture of Midway would have made Pearl Harbor unusable. To save the island, Admiral Chester Nimitz in Pearl Harbor mobilized what was left of the American fleet and sent it out to meet the much larger Japanese force. Despite heavy losses, the Americans gave the enemy its first major naval defeat.

After their failure at Midway, the Japanese had taken Attu and Kiska in the Aleutians. Alaska seemed on the verge of occupation, and Seattle was threatened. Men and materials needed elsewhere were rushed to Alaska. The Alcan Highway across Canada was begun, and plans were made for operations that would regain Attu in May and Kiska in August 1943.

The Japanese were even less successful in a second attack on Port Moresby, this one begun over land in July 1942. To protect this attack, they had begun to clear an airstrip on Guadalcanal, one of the nearby (as South Pacific distances go) Solomon Islands. The United States at the same time was looking at Guadalcanal for the starting point of its own offensive on Japan's more exposed positions.

On August 7, 1942, the first combined American and Australian landings on Guadalcanal were begun against sharp resistance. Two days later, a Japanese cruiser force swooped down on half-unloaded Allied transports in the Solomon's Savo Sea. In "the worst defeat ever suffered by the United States Navy," the cruisers sank virtually all the protective fighting ships. The transports ran, and the Japanese, mission accomplished, moved off. For six months, ill-equipped, half-starved Marines clung to Guadalcanal's airstrip while huge naval actions covering reinforcement attempts by both sides raged in the surrounding waters. Finally, on February 9, 1943, the Japanese evacuated the island.

After Guadalcanal, the Japanese became occupied with defending the Pacific and mainland positions they still held as a screen for the home islands. The defense was fierce, often fanatical. The military chiefs of staff in Washington became so impressed with the Japanese that even at the time of the Yalta Conference, when the brilliance of Allied strategy had been well demonstrated, they

advised Roosevelt that the Pacific war had at least two years to run with full Soviet assistance, and much longer without it.

Allied success in the South Pacific encouraged General Douglas MacArthur, chief of Southwest Pacific operations, in his determination to make a return to the Philippines as the last step before taking Tokyo. But the Gilbert Islands, the Marshalls, and farther north still, Wake Island stood in the way. Even barren atolls had been armed with an airstrip, artillery, and men. To the west of this arc lay the Carolines, Guam, and the Marianas. They were closer to Japan, and even more heavily armed. Farther north and west lay Iwo Jima; and in the shadow of Japan itself, Okinawa. This defense in depth, extending more than 3000 miles, shielded Tokyo. Any invasion from the Philippines would meet murderous flanking fire.

To roll back this defense, island by island, atoll by atoll, man by man, would occupy a generation and still not guarantee success. MacArthur's command devised the bold alternative of "island hopping," a strategy designed to open a path to the heart of Japan. Air power would neutralize the uncleared rear. Even so, armies as large as those that once conquered nations fought hundreds of battles on tiny unknown atolls.

The burden of this offensive was on Admiral Chester W. Nimitz and his Central Pacific Fleet. But every assault involved coordination of sea, land, and air forces. None was easy. Tarawa established the Allied hold on the Gilberts in November 1943; Kwajalein, control of the Marshalls in February 1944. In May, Wake was taken. In the immense Battle of the Philippine Sea (June 19 to 20), Admiral Raymond Spruance stopped a Japanese effort to reinforce the Marianas. By August 1, Saipan and Tinian, as well as Guam, had succumbed.

Tokyo was now within range of land-based bombers. The capital and other home island cities were systematically assaulted with fire bombs that consumed their wooden buildings and devastated the civilian population.

The island-hopping strategy had opened a path from New Guinea to the Philippines. On October 9, 1944, a grand armada carrying MacArthur and 250,000 men set out for the Philippine island of Leyte. Four days later, virtually the entire Japanese navy converged on Allied transports in Leyte Gulf, and from October 23 to 25 the greatest sea battle in history was fought. At its end the United

States emerged in complete command of the Pacific. Manila fell to MacArthur's forces on February 23, 1945. But not until July 5 were the last of the Japanese rooted out. By then, Iwo Jima and Okinawa had been taken at a cost of 70,000 men.

Kamikaze attacks by Japanese suicide fliers who plunged their bomb-laden planes into American ships accounted for many of the American casualties at Okinawa. Both campaigns—Iwo had been gained by March 16, 1945, and Okinawa by June 21—wiped out any lingering doubt that the Japanese would resist to the last knife or bullet or breath.

The island-hopping campaigns had finished all but the remnants of the Japanese navy and air force. American submarines had sunk more than half of the Japanese merchant marine, which kept them supplied with the oil, rubber, tin, and grain of their mainland conquests. These conquests had been under strong attack by British and American forces since the winter of 1943.

The Allies struggled to get Chiang Kai-shek to fight harder in China. But Chiang was preparing for a showdown with the Communists, who were gathering forces in the Chinese north. The most progress against the Japanese was made in Burma, where Rangoon, the principal port, was retaken in May 1945. But Japan did not give up the other mainland territories until its collapse at home.

The Atomic Victory

On July 16, 1945, at precisely 5:30 A.M., an atomic bomb was successfully detonated in the New Mexican desert. For those who witnessed the ex-

The mushroom cloud rises over Nagasaki, August 9, 1945. (*Official U.S. Air Force Photo*)

plosion, it was a terrifying sight. "It was as though the earth had opened and the skies had split," William L. Lawrence wrote. "One felt as though one were present at the moment of creation when God said: 'Let there be light.' "

Ten days later, Allied leaders assembled at Potsdam sent an ultimatum to the enemy: "The alternative to surrender is prompt and utter destruction." No surrender came, because Japanese military leaders overruled the government. On August 6 the first atomic bomb to be used in warfare was dropped on Hiroshima, killing instantly nearly 75,000 persons and injuring 100,000 more in a city of 344,000; many more would die from the effects of radiation. Still no word from the government. Two days later, as it had promised in Yalta, the Soviet Union entered the war and overran Japanese forces in Manchuria.

On August 9, a second bomb was dropped, this time on Nagasaki. At last, on August 10, Tokyo sued for peace, but made a condition: that Emperor Hirohito be permitted to retain his throne. This condition was accepted by the Allies. On September 2, 1945, formal surrender ceremonies were conducted in Tokyo Bay on the battleship *Missouri*, with General MacArthur accepting for the victors.

The most terrible war in history had ended in the most terrible display of force. The decision to use the bomb on a country already on the brink of collapse aroused much controversy in the world community. Those who defended the decision argued that it actually saved the lives of hundreds of thousands of Americans and Japanese by bringing the war to a quick end and making unnecessary an invasion of the Japanese mainland. If the United States had confined itself to "conventional" firebombing of Japanese cities, presumably the cost in human lives would have been much greater than the cost of the Hiroshima and Nagasaki bombs. But critics contended that Japan would have surrendered soon even if there had been no atomic bomb, invasion, or Soviet entry into the war.

Still another factor was suggested by Secretary of State James F. Byrnes, who thought the new weapon would "put us in a position to dictate our own terms at the end of the war" and "make Russia more manageable in Europe." To American soldiers in the battle areas, of course, as to their families at home, anything that contributed to a quick end to the war exceeded in importance all other considerations.

President Truman had no misgivings about his decision. "I regarded the bomb as a military weapon and never had any doubt that it should be used. The atomic bomb was no great decision, not any decision you had to worry about." No policymaker, in fact, seriously questioned the assumption that the atomic bomb would be used against Germany or Japan once it was ready. Most likely, then, the bomb was dropped to force Japanese leaders to agree to a quick surrender. That its use would also dramatize to the Soviet Union the supremacy of the United States reinforced more immediate military objectives. In any event, the United States, by becoming the only nation to have used the bomb, assumed an awesome image in the world. The atom bomb, said Truman, had become "merely another powerful weapon in the arsenal of righteousness."

The massive national mobilization of the war had significantly enlarged the role of the military in the economy, in education, and in other areas of American life. The unleashing of atomic energy at the moment of final victory, and then the international rivalry for atomic power, gave militarism new life. It also invited new worldwide responsibilities and irresponsibility—and speeded up change at home.

The war brought the end of empire: Colonial domains established by Europe in Asia and Africa over some three centuries, sources of immense manpower and natural wealth, were almost entirely dissolved in the fifteen years that followed the war. And contending for the loyalty and resources of the new nations would be the two superpowers—the United States and the Soviet Union. Both were intent on remaking the postwar world in their own image.

SUMMARY

From 1920 to about 1937, the United States went its own way in world affairs. The Washington Conference, an effort to stop the naval arms race after World War I, began late in 1921. It ended in early 1922 with a five-power naval treaty, a four-power pact, and a nine-power pact. But none of these agreements had an enforcement mechanism, and they were no more effective than the Kellogg-Briand Pact of 1928, which renounced war as an instrument of national policy and was signed by sixty-two nations.

The first signs that all these international agreements and the League of Nations were worth nothing came with Japanese expansionism. In the face of Japanese moves into Manchuria in 1931, the United States offered only the Stimson Doctrine, a policy of refusing to recognize territorial changes achieved by force of arms. Japan continued its war in China, resigned from the League in 1933, and renounced the naval agreements of 1922.

Fear of Japan and of Hitler's Germany led the United States finally to recognize the Soviet Union in November 1933. But mutual suspicion between the two continued. In Latin America, an active, interventionist policy had made the United States no friends. Roosevelt's Good Neighbor policy brought only slow improvement.

The need to do something about Latin America and the Soviets was made urgent by the deterioration of relations between America and Europe. Fascist governments had come to power in Italy and Germany. In 1936 Spanish Fascists under Franco began a civil war that lasted until 1939, when with the help of Germany and Italy, Franco won.

All these governments favored aggressive, expansionist foreign policies centered on military conquest. Mussolini took Ethiopia in Africa in 1935; German forces occupied the Rhineland in 1936; in September 1938, Hitler took the Sudetenland. At the Munich Conference, Britain and France, unprepared, let him get away with it. In March 1939, Hitler took the rest of Czechoslovakia; three weeks later, Mussolini took Albania. In August, Hitler made a nonaggression pact with the Soviet Union to protect his eastern flank. Then, on September 1, Nazi troops and planes invaded Poland. Two days later, Britain and France, honoring their Polish commitments, declared war on Germany.

The United States was officially neutral, and public opinion was sharply divided. But then in April 1940, Hitler's *blitzkrieg* (lightning war) rolled over Denmark, Norway, Belgium, Holland, Luxembourg, and even France in seven weeks. The British were left to stand alone. During the summer and fall of 1940, Hitler made a tremendous effort to bomb them into surrender. He did not succeed, and at the end the British had regained control of the air.

American policy was to strengthen its own defenses while giving aid to Britain to keep it from collapsing. Roosevelt, reelected in 1940 for a third term, began pressing the foreign policy debate in public. The lend-lease program was passed by Congress in early 1941, and the United States moved steadily closer to war in the Atlantic. At an August meeting, Churchill and Roosevelt drew up the Atlantic Charter, which set forth their goals for the postwar world. By the fall of 1941 the United States had become an open ally of Britain without having formally declared war. In November, lend-lease was extended to the Soviet Union, now under attack as Hitler opened his Eastern Front.

In the Pacific, American response to Japanese pressure had been first to embargo aviation gasoline and then iron and steel scrap shipments to Japan. Two days after the extension of the embargo in September, Japan joined the German-Italian coalition. Although negotiations with Japan continued in Washington through the autumn, the Japanese made plans to attack if the outcome was not satisfactory. These plans were carried out on Sunday, December 7, 1941, when a carrier-borne force of Japanese planes destroyed the Pacific fleet at Pearl Harbor in Hawaii. The next day Congress declared war on Japan, and four days later, Germany and Italy declared war on the United States. America was again engaged in global war.

The home front was mobilized for war; it was also mobilized in a propaganda campaign of hatred for the enemy. One result was the internment of Japanese-Americans in camps far from their West Coast homes. At the time of Pearl Harbor, an American army of 1.6 million men had been recruited in the first peacetime draft. The draft was extended to all men between certain ages, and women were allowed to volunteer. Behind the 15 million men and more than 200,000 women in active service were American industry, agriculture, labor, and science. Depression unemployment ended. Many women went to work, especially in the defense industries. Men continued to dominate in supervisory positions, and wage scales discriminated against women. Blacks continued to be segregated, even in the armed forces.

The Allied Powers did not expect to win quickly. Germany had conquered most of Europe, and Japan had taken a good bit of the Pacific islands and Southeast Asia. The Allied decision was to concentrate on Europe first. The next decision was that the Allies would have to gain control of the sea and air before land invasions could begin.

The first land operation was conducted in North Africa, where the Germans were moving toward the Suez Canal. It was followed by the invasion of Italy in July 1943, and then by the invasion of Normandy by a huge force on D day, June 6, 1944. During the whole period of the war, Allied leaders met constantly to plan strategy and conduct diplomacy. Conferences were held in 1943 at Casablanca in January, at Moscow in October, and at Cairo and Teheran in November. By the time of the Yalta Conference in February 1945, Soviet armies were only 50 miles from Berlin. The European war ended on May 7, 1945, with the unconditional surrender of Germany.

President Roosevelt died on April 12, and Harry Truman became president. By this time the campaign in the Pacific, based on an island-hopping strategy, was close to Japan itself. It was Truman's decision to use the atomic bomb, the first ever used in war, to bring the conflict to a quick end and avoid a long and costly land campaign. The most terrible war in history thus ended in the most terrible display of force. And at the end there were two superpowers, the United States and the Soviet Union, both out to reshape the postwar world according to radically opposite ideologies.

Suggested Readings

G. Wright, *The Ordeal of Total War 1939–1945* (1968), is a solid overview of the European and world situation. G. F. Kennan, *American Diplomacy 1900–1950* (1951), and *Memoirs 1925–1950* (1967), provide valuable commentary and analysis. On prewar American attitudes, see S. Adler, *The Isolationist Impulse* (1957), and *The Uncertain Giant* (1965); and M. Jonas, *Isolationism in America 1935–1941* (1966).

R. H. Ferrell, *American Diplomacy in the Great Depression: Hoover-Stimson Foreign Policy* (1957), and J. E. Wiltz, *From Isolation to War 1931–1941* (1968), provide background. But see also W. A. Williams, *The Tragedy of American Diplomacy* (2nd ed., 1972). On the development of a Far Eastern policy, see D. Borg, *The United States and the Far Eastern Crisis 1933–1938* (1964), and A. Iriye, *After Imperialism: The Search for a New Order in the Far East 1921–1931* (1965), and *Across the Pacific: An Inner History of American–East Asian Relations* (1967). On Latin American relations, see B. Wood, *The Making of the Good Neighbor Policy* (1961), and *The United States and Latin American Wars 1932–1942* (1966); and D. Green, *The Containment of Latin America* (1971). On Soviet-American relations, see W. A. Williams, *American-Russian Relations 1781–1947* (1952), and R. P. Browder, *The Origins of Soviet-American Diplomacy* (1953).

On Hitler's rise and the response, see A. Bullock, *Hitler: A Study in Tyranny* (1952); A. A. Offner, *American Appeasement: United States Foreign Policy and Germany 1933–1938* (1969); R. Dallek, *Democrat and Diplomat: The Life of William E. Dodd* (1968); and S. Friedlander, *Prelude to Downfall: Hitler and the United States 1939–1941* (1967). See also W. S. Cole, *Senator Gerald P. Nye and American Foreign Relations* (1962), and *America First: The Battle against Intervention 1940–1941* (1953). On the Spanish Civil War, see G. Jackson, *The Spanish Republic and the Civil War 1931–1939* (1965), and A. Guttman, *The Wound in the Heart: America and the Spanish Civil War* (1962).

On FDR and the war, the definitive studies are R. Dallek, *Franklin D. Roosevelt and American Foreign Policy 1932–1945* (1979), and J. M. Burns, *Roosevelt: The Soldier of Freedom 1940–1945* (1970). For the policy-makers around FDR, see E. E. Morrison, *Turmoil and Tradition: A Study of the Life and Times of Henry L. Stimson* (1960); H. L. Stimson and M. Bundy, *On Active Service in Peace and War* (1948); R. N. Current, *Secretary Stimson* (1954); Cordell Hull, *Memoirs* (2 vols., 1948); J. W. Pratt, *Cordell Hull* (1964); R. E. Sherwood, *Roosevelt and Hopkins* (1948); and J. M. Blum, *From the Morgenthau Diaries: Years of Urgency* (1965).

On the road to war, W. L. Langer and S. E. Gleason, *The Challenge to Isolation 1937–1940* (1952), and *Undeclared War 1940–1941* (1953), provide a detailed treatment. See as well R. A. Divine, *The Illusion of Neutrality* (1962), and *The Reluctant Belligerent* (1965). On the mounting crisis in the Far East, see J. C. Grew, *Turbulent Era: A Diplomatic Record of Forty Years* (1952); and H. Feis, *The Road to Pearl Harbor* (1962). Critical of American policy are C. A. Beard, *American Foreign Policy in the Making 1932–1940* (1946), and *President Roosevelt and the Coming of the War* (1948); and C. C. Tansill, *Backdoor to War* (1952). More recent revisionist studies include L. C. Gardner, *Economic Aspects of New Deal Diplomacy* (1971), and *Architects of Illusion* (1970).

J. M. Blum, *V Was for Victory* (1976), is a solid study of American politics and culture during the war. The home front is also examined in G. Perrett, *Days of Sadness, Years of Triumph* (1973); R. Polenberg, *War and Society: The United States 1941–1945* (1972); and B. Catton, *War Lords of Washington* (1948). Wartime mobilization is examined in E. Janeway, *The Struggle for Survival* (1951), and D. M. Nelson, *Arsenal for Democracy* (1944), provides an "inside" account. On the military and the economy, see R. M. Leighton and R. W. Coakley, *Global Logistics and Strategy 1940–1945* (2 vols., 1955–68); on labor, J. Seidman, *American Labor from Defense to Reconversion* (1953); on farmers, W. W. Wilcox, *The Farmer in the Second World War* (1947). On women in the war effort, see L. J. Rupp, *Mobilizing Women for War: German and American Propaganda, 1939–1945* (1978), and the engrossing documentary film, *The Life and Times of Rosie the Riveter* (Clarity Educational Productions, P. O. Box 315, Franklin Lakes, N.J. 07417).

Wartime dissent is examined in L. S. Wittner, *Rebels against War: The American Peace Movement 1941–1960* (1969). See also P. E. Jacob and M. Q. Sibley, *Conscription of Conscience* (1952), and the personal account of FDR's Attorney General Francis Biddle, *In Brief Authority* (1962). On black life and attitudes, see R. M. Dalfiume, *Desegregation of the U.S. Armed Forces 1939–1953* (1969); G. Myrdal, *An American Dilemma* (1944); H. Garfinkel, *When Negroes March* (1959); R. W. Logan (ed.), *What the Negro Wants* (1944); and W. White, *A Rising Wind* (1945). On the internment of the Japanese, see R. Daniels, *The Politics of Prejudice* (1962), and *Concentration Camps USA* (1971), and P. Irons, *Justice at War: The Story of the Japanese American Internment Cases* (1983).

On the scientific community and the development and use of the atomic bomb, see A. K. Smith, *A Peril and a Hope: The Scientists' Movement in America 1945–1947* (1965); R. G. Hewlett and O. E. Anderson, Jr., *The New World* (1962); N. P. Davis, *Lawrence and Oppenheimer* (1968); and M. J. Sherwin, *A World Destroyed: The Atomic Bomb and the Grand Alliance* (1975). The cultural "fallout" of the atomic bomb in the United States is imaginatively explored in P. Boyer, *By the Bomb's Early Light: American Thought and Culture at the Dawn of the Atomic Age* (1985).

A. R. Buchanan, *The United States and World War II* (2 vols., 1964), surveys all phases of American military involvement. See also D. D. Eisenhower, *Crusade in Europe* (1948), and D. MacArthur, *Reminiscences* (1964). The most comprehensive account of Japan's path to war and of the fighting and its aftermath is J. Toland, *The Rising Sun: The Decline and Fall of the Japanese Empire 1936–1945* (1970). See also R. H. Spector, *Eagle Against the Sun: The American War with Japan* (1985); H. Feis, *Japan Subdued: The Atomic Bomb and the End of the War in the Pacific* (1945); and J. Hersey's unforgettable *Hiroshima* (1946). The ordinary soldier is best described in E. Pyle, *The Story of G.I. Joe* (1945); B. Mauldin, *Up Front* (1945); and three novels: J. H. Burns, *The Gallery* (1947); N. Mailer, *The Naked and the Dead* (1948); and J. Heller, *Catch-22* (1961). See also an illuminating sociological study, S. A. Stouffer and others, *The American Soldier* (2 vols., 1949).

H. Feis, *Churchill, Roosevelt, Stalin* (1957), is a study of conference diplomacy. See also J. L. Snell, *Illusion and Necessity: The Diplomacy of the Global War* (1963); G. Smith, *American Diplomacy during the Second World War* (1965); W. H. McNeill, *America, Britain, and Russia* (1953); R. B. Levering, *American Opinion and the Russian Alliance 1939–1945* (1976); and the Cold War studies cited at the end of Chapter 30.

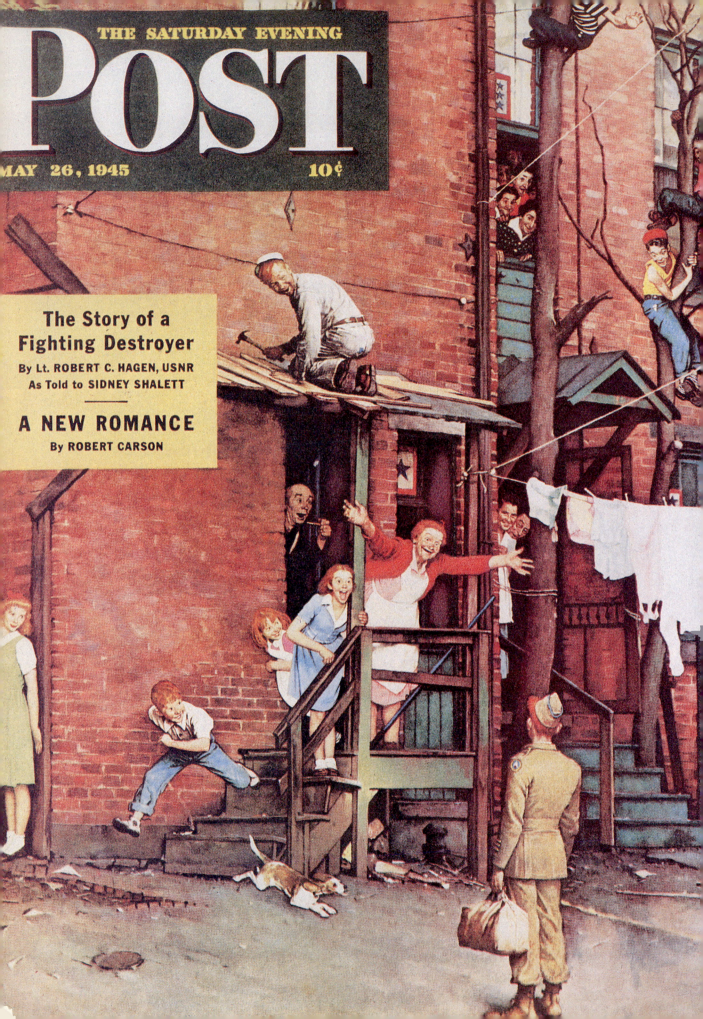

THE SEARCH FOR SECURITY

Chapter 30

The United States emerged from World War II as the most successful and dominant nation in the world, possessing, as its president said, "the greatest strength and the greatest power which man has ever reached." If greatness was measured by national income, industrial productivity, a trained work force, natural resources, scientific expertise, or by the average daily caloric intake of the population, the United States had no equal.

By contrast, the Soviet Union had seen its industrial capacity reduced by more than 40 percent. Great Britain and France faced desperate problems of economic recovery. Nationalist movements in Africa, Asia, and the Middle East threatened to topple their colonial empires. Germany and Japan were shattered and conquered territories. China was about to be engulfed by civil war. As if to underscore the position of the United States in the world community, it was also the only nation that had the atomic bomb.

But within two years after V-J Day, Americans discovered that despite all the power they commanded, their position in the world was by no means secure. Not only were nationalist movements shaking colonial empires and threatening to upset the political balance of power, but the Soviet Union refused to bend to the wishes of policymakers in Washington, D.C., or of the peoples who lived on their eastern borders.

The United States and the Soviet Union were engaged in a Cold War, a new experience for Americans. It was a war of rhetoric, the subversion and countersubversion of other governments, direct intervention in the affairs of other nations, and an armaments race with no limits. Over the next two decades, this unresolved conflict would use up a large portion of the national wealth for the perfection and accumulation of weapons designed to defend the country from nuclear destruction. It would demand from the American people the kind of loyalty usually reserved for a hot war.

The search for security was unlike anything in the American past. A nation that had always avoided "entangling alliances," the United States now entered into mutual defense pacts with forty countries. For a nation that had confined its intervention to the Caribbean and Central America, the United States found reasons to intervene, covertly or openly, in the Middle East (Iran and Lebanon) and in Asia (Korea, Vietnam, Cambodia, and Laos), as well as in its own "sphere of influence" (Cuba, the Dominican Republic, and Chile). But even with this commitment, and with American forces in bases in some thirty countries, the security Americans sought still eluded them. ■

THE NEW INTERNATIONAL ORDER

Once Japan had surrendered and the secret provisions at Yalta were revealed, Roosevelt's territorial concessions to the Soviet Union—in Eastern Europe and the northernmost islands of Japan—caused an outburst of criticism. Some of it was politically inspired and designed to pin the label of "appeasement" on the Democrats. The critics conveniently ignored the military situation at the time of Yalta, the urgent need for Soviet entry into the Asian war, and Stalin's determination to establish a defense perimeter in Eastern Europe to secure the USSR from future attack. None of the "concessions" included territory actually in control of the United States and its Western allies at the end of the war.

FDR apparently thought them necessary to reassure the Soviet Union about its security and to win Stalin's participation in the United Nations once the fighting was over. On returning from Yalta in March 1945, Roosevelt declared that the agreement there "spells the end of the system of unilateral action and exclusive alliances and balances of power" in favor of "a universal organization in which all peace-loving nations will finally have a chance to join."

The old League of Nations had failed at least as badly as traditional balance of power arrangements in keeping world peace. Whatever stability the new United Nations would be able to impose on the world rested largely on cooperation between the two dominant powers, the United States and the Soviet Union. But mutual suspicions had been aroused before the UN even had a chance to take shape. Only eleven days before his death, Roosevelt sent Stalin a sharp message about "the lack of progress" in implementing the political decisions reached at Yalta, particularly those regarding free elections in Poland.

Stalin had also grown skeptical of Western actions and intentions. No less disturbing to Stalin was the Western challenge to Soviet domination of Eastern Europe after the war. Stalin held off until the last moment before sending a delegation to San Francisco, where work on the United Nations charter began April 25, 1945. His delay only deepened Western suspicion.

The United Nations

Even before the United Nations Charter was written, certain international structures had been created to handle wartime relief and postwar reconstruction. As early as November 1943, forty-four nations had set up the United Nations Relief and Rehabilitation Administration (UNRRA) to assist areas liberated from Germany, Italy, and Japan. The first of two conferences in 1944 to plan the postwar world was held at Bretton Woods, New Hampshire. This conference created an International Monetary Fund to stabilize national currencies and an International Bank for Reconstruction and Development, called the World Bank, to extend rehabilitation loans. The second conference, at Dumbarton Oaks in Washington, D.C., drafted plans for the United Nations Charter.

The charter of the United Nations Organization provided for two major agencies, the General Assembly and the Security Council. Each member nation had a seat in the General Assembly, which was primarily an arena for discussion and debate of international questions falling within the scope of the charter. But it could recommend action to the Security Council, and if the council failed to act, the assembly was empowered by a resolution adopted in 1950 to recommend action to member nations.

The Security Council, which was to remain in continuous session in order to settle international disputes as they arose, consisted of five permanent members—the United States, the Soviet Union, Great Britain, France, and China—and six others elected for two-year terms. The council had the power to apply diplomatic, economic, or military sanctions against any nation threatening the peace. Any of the permanent members, however, could block action by exercising its veto power. This decision virtually ensured that the council would be unable to oppose aggression by the major powers. But it may have helped save the world from a collision of such powers by allowing them to check the use of force by the UN itself.

The United States Senate had debated the Covenant of the League of Nations for eight months before rejecting it. The Senate debated UN membership for six days, and approved it by a vote of 89 to 2. After the charter had been signed at San Francisco, the UN held its first meetings in London in 1946 and then moved to New York City, its permanent home. Founded with 51 charter nations, the UN by 1980 had tripled in membership to 152 nations, more than two-thirds of them in the Third World.

In the early years, the United States exercised considerable influence over the organization. In 1950, it obtained General Assembly sanction for military intervention in Korea. And until 1961 it saw to it that the question of seating the People's Republic of China was not placed on the agenda. By the early 1970s, however, that dominance had clearly passed. China had been seated, and the United States ambassador to the UN was openly expressing his concern over a new "tyranny of the majority."

If only as a discussion body, the United Nations ensured that some questions affecting world peace would be debated with words rather than with weapons. Some of its subsidiary units, like the World Health Organization (WHO) and the United Nations Educational, Scientific, and Cultural Organization (UNESCO), made important strides toward international cooperation in vital areas. But the UN failed to exert the kind of power or influence that could successfully control an armaments race, deal with the dissolution of the overseas empires of Western powers, or resolve the question of what to do with the conquered Axis powers. As the Cold War developed, those issues became more and more important.

Atomic Energy

The UN was forced to confront atomic warfare and a potential atomic arms race as its first major problem. Scientists in all industrial countries knew of the work on the atom in the 1930s, although only those in the United States could mobilize the funds, labor, and technical equipment required for A bomb development and manufacture during the war. Once the bomb was dropped, many of the scientists involved wanted to harness the monster they had created. At the same time, the evidence of its power spurred others to develop the bomb in self-defense.

In 1946, Bernard M. Baruch, as the delegate to the recently created UN Atomic Energy Commission, submitted a plan for control of atomic weapons. It called for the creation of an international agency to which the United States would turn over its atomic secrets. The agency would be able to inspect atomic installations in any country and see that weapons were not being manufactured. It could punish violators and its decisions would not be subject to veto. As soon as the inspection system was working, the United States would destroy its stock of weapons and manufacture no more.

But the USSR, suspicious of any international agency likely to be dominated by the United States and unwilling to tolerate inspection, proposed an international agreement to abandon atomic warfare and prohibit the making of weapons. The So-

viet plan had no provision for inspection. This was unacceptable to the United States. Once the USSR, in September 1949, detonated its own first atomic bomb, security by the balance of terror became part of the new world order. That balance may have done more to avert atomic warfare than the long and fruitless pursuit of control and disarmament.

While progress toward regulation dragged, the United States proceeded with development of atomic energy. In August 1946, Congress created the Atomic Energy Commission. It was placed under civilian control and a proposal to give the armed service chiefs a veto on its actions was defeated. The commission was to promote private and government research into the peaceful as well as military uses of atomic energy and to develop facilities for its production.

Cost and technical problems delayed peaceful applications for almost two decades. In the mid-sixties, nuclear generating plants began to be built by utility companies. But the danger of radioactive emissions was a source of considerable alarm. The disastrous potential of the accident at the Three Mile Island nuclear plant near Harrisburg, Pennsylvania, in April 1979 and at the Chernobyl nuclear plant near Kiev in the Soviet Union in April 1986 threw the entire future of the nuclear industry into question.

The Conquered Nations

The problem of settling the fate of the conquered nations also revealed the tension between the Soviet Union and the West. On July 17, 1945, Truman, Churchill, and Stalin met at Potsdam, Germany, to deal with the future of the old Axis members. (Following the startling defeat of his party in the British elections on July 26, Churchill gave way to the new prime minister, the Labor party leader Clement Attlee). At Potsdam the new Big Three reaffirmed the four-power occupation of Germany, worked out details of German reparations payments, and tentatively settled the Polish-German frontier.

During 1945 and 1946, the leading Nazis were tried at Nuremberg before an international military court on charges of having started the war and conducting it in ways that violated fundamental human decency. The trial revealed the full story of Nazi barbarity: the systematic torture and murder of millions of Jews and Slavs, along with other defenseless civilians. Never before had such brutality been so fully documented. Ten leading war criminals were executed. In all, over 500,000 Nazis were found guilty in the American zone and received sentences of varying severity.

Similar trials in Japan led to the execution of former Premier Tojo and six other war leaders. Lighter sentences were passed on about 4000 other war criminals. A generation later, these trials were to be recalled to the discomfort of some of the accusers, including the United States. For in the fighting against formerly colonial peoples, Europeans and Americans themelves broke many of the rules of war.

In 1948 the Soviets, irked by the friction arising from the administration of Germany, ordered a blockade of Berlin. That city, though situated deep in their zone, was jointly administered by the USSR and the Western powers. By threatening the Germans in the Western zone of Berlin with starvation, the Soviets hoped to force the Allies to leave Berlin. The challenge was met with an airlift. Food and supplies were delivered to the city by continuously shuttling cargo planes. In the end, it was the USSR that gave in and lifted the blockade in May 1949.

Frustrated by the failure to reach agreement on Germany, the Western powers met in June 1948 and consented to the creation of an unarmed German Federal Republic, embracing the three Western zones. The new state was launched in September 1949. One month later, the Soviets established the German Democratic Republic in the east.

No such divisions occurred in conquered Japan, where the United States assumed full command under General Douglas MacArthur. A new constitution went into effect in May 1947, turning the fundamental powers of government over to representatives elected by the people. The emperor renounced his claim to divinity, and the constitution renounced war as a right of the nation. Social reforms were carried out, including the dissolution of the great industrial and commercial monopolies and the restoration of large tracts of land to the poor in rural areas.

In September 1951, following Mao Tse-tung's seizure of power in 1949 and the outbreak of the Korean conflict in1950, forty-nine nations signed a general peace treaty with Japan restoring its "full sovereignty," including the right to redevelop an armaments industry and armed services. (The USSR did not sign.) The treaty was negotiated at the urging of the United States to rebuild Japan in order to offset communism in Asia—as Germany was soon to be strengthened to offset communism in Europe. At this time, mutual security agreements were also made with the Philippines, Australia, and New Zealand.

THE TRUMAN ADMINISTRATION AT HOME

The death of Roosevelt in April 1945 had brought to the presidency Harry Truman, a relatively obscure New Deal Democrat whose bland folksiness contrasted sharply with FDR's urbanity. During World War I, Truman, a farm boy from Independence, Missouri, became a captain of artillery. Soon after the demobilization in 1919, he opened a men's clothing store in Kansas City. When this business died in the postwar depression, the Pendergast political machine, which controlled

A sailor and a nurse celebrate the end of World War II on VJ Day, August 14, 1945, in New York's Times Square. (As recently as 1980, various individuals have claimed to be the man and the woman in this classic photograph by Alfred Eisenstaedt.) (*Life Magazine* © 1945, Time, Inc.)

Kansas City politics, invited Truman to run for county judge.

When the same machine needed a "clean" candidate for the United States Senate in 1934, it chose Truman. He won easily. After his reelection in 1940, he became chairman of a Senate committee to investigate defense contracts. His zeal in working over wartime big business brought him notice and won him the Democratic vice-presidential nomination four years later.

Upon becoming president, he said: "I felt like the moon, the stars, and all the planets had fallen on me. I've got the most terribly responsible job a man ever had." Neither in political wisdom nor in the ability to command confidence was he a match for FDR. But it was left to Truman to lead the nation out of one war while alerting it to the threat of still another. The problems he faced at home were enough to worry the most experienced of statesmen: a people eager to return to a peacetime footing but wanting to give up none of the economic benefits the war had brought them. The memories of the Great Depression were still much too vivid.

United States Population, 1950–60

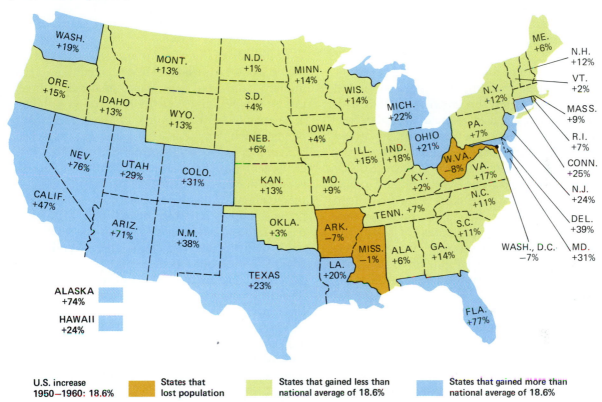

| U.S. increase 1950–1960: 18.6% | States that lost population | States that gained less than national average of 18.6% | States that gained more than national average of 18.6% |

Total Population (in millions)

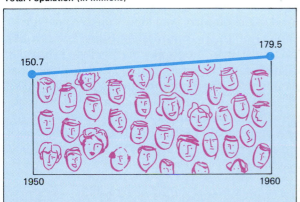

150.7
179.5
1950
1960

Suburban Growth

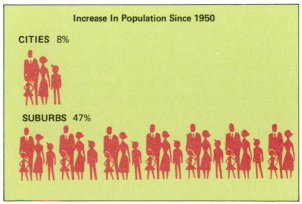

Increase In Population Since 1950

CITIES 8%

SUBURBS 47%

Demobilization

Once the war ended in August 1945, Americans' profound war weariness manifested itself in troop demonstrations and riots from Manila to Frankfurt, all of them protesting the delays in getting the troops home. The failure of military authorities to agree upon the postwar strength of the rival services explained the delays, but only added to the frustration of soldiers eager to return to civilian life.

Congress and the president bent under all this pressure. By midsummer 1946 the army and air force had been cut from over 8 million to under 2 million; the navy, from nearly 4 million to 980,000. "I termed this," Truman wrote in his *Memoirs,* "the most remarkable demobilization in the history of the world, or 'disintegration,' if you want to call it that."

Although Truman had suggested the need for universal military training, Congress hesitated until June 1948, when the growing friction with the Soviet Union led it to reenact Selective Service. In the meantime, the army and navy had offered young men of college age rewards to participate in Reserve Officer Training Corps (ROTC) units on the campuses. The expansion and extension of various veterans' benefits placed a college education within the reach of a far greater proportion of high school graduates. Under the Servicemen's Readjustment Act of June 1944, commonly known as the GI Bill of Rights, and later measures, $13.5 billion in federal funds was spent between 1945 and 1955 for veterans' education in colleges and vocational schools. Veterans of Korea were included.

This act also entitled discharged servicemen and women to medical treatment at veterans' hospitals, vocational rehabilitation for the crippled, one year's unemployment insurance, and government loans for building homes and establishing businesses.

Not long after the demobilization of military personnel, the Truman administration moved to reorganize the military establishment. The National Security Act of 1947 unified the administration of the armed services and enlarged their duties. A new National Military Establishment, soon to be renamed the Department of Defense, was established under a new secretary of defense on the cabinet level, to "be appointed from civilian life." (Navy Secretary James V. Forrestal became the first secretary of defense). Each service—army, navy, air force—was to be headed by a secretary below the cabinet level, and a uniformed chief of staff or chief of operations. The uniformed chiefs of the three services, along with the president's chief of staff, were to make up the Joint Chiefs of Staff and be the principal military advisors to the president.

The act also created the National Security Council, to be presided over by the commander in chief. Under this council the act set up a Central Intelligence Agency (CIA) to coordinate all government intelligence activities. Although its charter forbade it, the CIA would also play a role in domestic surveillance of politically suspect activity.

The Economy

With the end of the war, Americans longed for the material comforts that had been denied them when industry converted to wartime production. Backing up this longing was the massive $140 billion in savings in bank accounts and government war bonds which Americans had come out of the war anxious to spend. "The American people," Fred M. Vinson, director of war mobilization and reconversion, declared late in 1945, "are in the pleasant predicament of having to learn to live 50 percent better than they have ever lived before." The many new luxuries available to consumers, like automatic dishwashers and clothes dryers and television sets, were quickly made into necessities by a revitalized advertising industry. At the same time, Americans were able to make certain decisions the war had postponed, like marriage and having children. The average age of marriage declined, and birth rates increased rapidly. To accommodate more and larger families, the construction industry created a kind of society new to most Americans—suburbia.

The liberal heritage of the New Deal survived the war, but the sense of urgency about social and economic reform was no longer present and the mood of the country was more conservative. President Truman tried to interest Congress in a liberal legislative program that included broader social security coverage, public housing, medical insurance, a higher minimum wage (from 40 to 65 cents), a permanent Fair Employment Practices Commission, and a full employment bill. After a long debate on the relative roles of business and government, Congress in February 1946 passed the Maximum Employment Act.

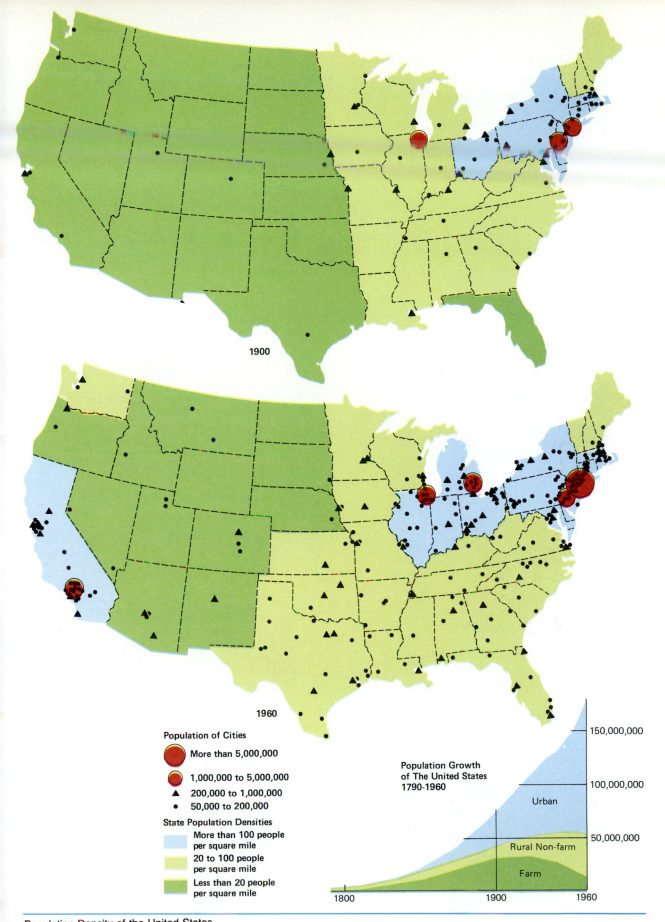

1900

1960

Population of Cities

- More than 5,000,000
- 1,000,000 to 5,000,000
- ▲ 200,000 to 1,000,000
- • 50,000 to 200,000

State Population Densities

- More than 100 people per square mile
- 20 to 100 people per square mile
- Less than 20 people per square mile

Population Growth of The United States 1790-1960

150,000,000

100,000,000

Urban

50,000,000

Rural Non-farm

Farm

1800   1900   1960

Population Density of the United States

This act for the first time committed the federal government to utilizing the nation's economic resources to ensure "maximum employment, production, and purchasing power." It created a Council of Economic Advisors to keep the president informed on economic trends and on the proper public measures to soften business downswings and sustain prosperity. Although the country did not return to prewar levels of unemployment, it did permit an unemployment rate unacceptable to many industrialized democracies. Even in a time of relative prosperity, as in the early 1960s, more than 5 percent of the work force remained unemployed, and a much higher rate prevailed for blacks.

Reconverting industry to peacetime production and the elimination of wartime controls preoccupied government and business leaders. Once the war ended, private companies that had operated Defense Plant Corporation facilities took advantage of their liberal purchase options to buy them up. The business community went on a spree of private expenditure for new plant construction. To stimulate postwar business, in November 1945 Congress cut taxes an estimated $6 billion. In November 1946, despite Truman's earlier veto of such a measure as "a sure formula for inflation," Congress swept away all wartime price controls except those on rents, sugar, and rice. With these incentives industrial production soared, as did the inflationary spiral. Between 1945 and 1947, food prices increased more than 25 percent.

So strong was the pent-up demand for consumer goods that shortages soon intensified the

Fun-seekers crowd the beach at Jones Beach, New York. In the 1950s the population increased sharply as women of child-bearing age averaged 3.35 children; by the late 1960s, that average had fallen to 2.45. (*UPI/Bettmann Newsphotos*)

already sharp inflation caused by everyone's catching up at once. Inflation broadened the wave of strikes that swept the country after the removal of wartime restraints and restrictions. Labor found that wages were simply not keeping pace with the cost of living. One of the most far-reaching strikes was that of the United Mine Workers in April 1946. Although Truman ordered government seizure of the coal pits, the mine workers eventually made important wage gains.

A nationwide railroad strike, followed by fruitless labor-management negotiations, prompted Truman to seize the railroads in May 1946. Only a last-minute settlement halted the passage of stern anti-union legislation. The president's actions no doubt reflected the lingering spirit of wartime discipline. Yet the atmosphere had changed: Militant unionism received no encouragement in the postwar decades. That was in step with the prevailing conservative mood that suddenly brought life and hope back to the Republican party.

The Eightieth Congress

Even as Truman grew more confident in the White House, the postwar inflation and labor conflicts hurt the Democratic party, especially in the cities. Despite Truman's tough anti-Soviet stand in foreign relations, the Republicans harped on the New Deal's "softness" on communism and the possibility that highly placed Americans had participated in spy rings. Using these issues, the Republicans, in the elections of 1946, won majorities in both houses of the Eightieth Congress. In March 1947 Congress passed the Twenty-second Amendment to the Constitution, limiting the president to two terms, a backhanded slap at FDR. This amendment was declared ratified in February 1951. As the incumbent, Truman was exempted from its provisions.

With his own eye on the 1948 presidential campaign, Truman pressed on the Republican-dominated Congress the liberal measures with which

After winning the election in a surprise upset, Harry Truman waved a copy of the strongly Republican *Chicago Daily Tribune,* which had gone to press confident of a Dewey landslide. (*UPI/Bettmann Newsphotos*)

he hoped to rebuild Democratic urban strength. Among his proposals were comprehensive medicare and civil rights bills. As anticipated, this program died in Congress, the victim of a Republican–southern Democrat coalition. Seeking to save something of the civil rights program, and perhaps to maximize the effectiveness of the armed forces, Truman, in July 1948, used his authority as commander-in-chief to issue an executive order for racial equality (desegregation) in the armed services.

The Eightieth Congress's most controversial domestic measure, adopted over Truman's veto in June 1947, was the Taft-Hartley Act, which (1) outlawed the closed shop (unions could not compel employers to hire only union members) but allowed the union shop (unions could negotiate contracts with employers by which newly hired workers would then have to join the union); (2) legalized "right-to work" laws by which states could prohibit the requirement of union membership as a condition of employment; (3) permitted the government to impose on unions a sixty-day "cooling off period" before striking; (4) required union leaders to file affidavits that they were not communists, or their unions could not be certified as bargaining agents under the National Labor Relations Act.

Labor leaders denounced Taft-Hartley, but it did not prevent them from making substantial gains. From 1945 to 1952, union membership rose from 14.6 to 17 million. Although the act made organizing new kinds of workers more difficult, it did weld unions together and speed the move toward unification of the AFL and the CIO. It also assured Truman of solid union support in the 1948 election.

The Election of 1948 and the Fair Deal

As the presidential election neared, Truman's prospects appeared poor. The Eightieth Congress had blocked most of his social legislation. Southern Democrats were angry over the growing concern of party liberals with civil rights. As early as 1946, moreover, Henry A. Wallace, Truman's secretary of commerce, had broken with the president over his Cold War policies and been dropped from the cabinet. In December 1947, Wallace announced he would run for president on a third party ticket. Some analysts believed he might win 5 to 8 million votes, enough to sink any Democratic candidate. The Republicans renominated

Governor Thomas E. Dewey of New York for president and named Governor Earl Warren of California for vice-president. They also adopted a platform that was internationalist on foreign policy and moderate on domestic issues.

For months before the Democrats convened, feverish efforts were made to hold the party together. Liberals led by Mayor Hubert H. Humphrey of Minneapolis formed Americans for Democratic Action (ADA) to help stop the Wallace challenge. When a broad-based movement to draft the immensely popular General Eisenhower failed, the Truman regulars closed ranks and put him over.

The ADA group, meanwhile, had carried a liberal platform defending the FDR–Truman tradition, denouncing Taft-Hartley, and promising antilynching and anti-poll-tax laws. As a sop to southerners, the convention named Acting President of the Senate Alben W. Barkley of Kentucky for vice-president.

ADA's tactics and Barkley's nomination both fell short of their goals. The so-called Dixiecrats, meeting in Birmingham, Alabama, formed the States' Rights Democratic party and nominated Governor J. Strom Thurmond of South Carolina for president. Five days later, the Wallace liberals formed the Progressive party and named their favorite as standard bearer. Wallace had hoped to offer an alternative to Truman's bipartisan Cold War foreign policy and the growing repression of civil liberties in the name of that policy.

The fact that the Communist Party endorsed Wallace and played an active role in his campaign only alienated prospective supporters and tarnished his candidacy. Although Wallace's views deserved a wider hearing, he found himself harrassed during the campaign and driven out of public life.

The failure of the efforts at unity made Truman's cause seem hopeless. But the Dixiecrat defection enhanced his appeal to the strategically important black voters of the North, and Wallace's campaign dramatized the fact that Truman was no friend of the radical Left. Dewey never caught the imagination of the voters. Truman, aware of the fight he had to make, stormed up and down the country denouncing "the do-nothing, good-for-nothing Eightieth Congress."

When the ballots were counted, Truman had pulled off the greatest upset in American political history, winning 24,105,000 popular and 303 electoral votes to Dewey's 21,969,000 and 189. Thurmond carried only four Deep South states,

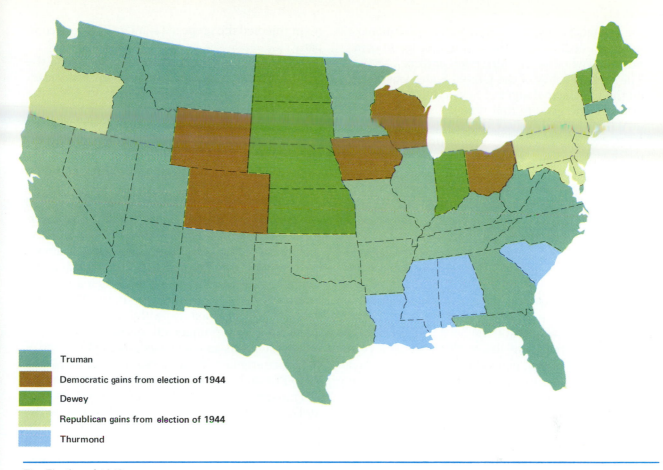

The Election of 1948

while Wallace carried not a single one. In the Eighty-first Congress, moreover, the Democrats had a Senate majority of 12 and a House majority of 93.

Convinced that he had received a popular mandate to carry on what he now called the Fair Deal, Truman drew up a program designed to go the New Deal one better. At vital points the newly influential coalition of conservative Democrats and Republicans blocked him, but he made headway. In 1949 he secured an amendment to the New Deal's Fair Labor Standards Act raising the minimum wage from 40 to 75 cents an hour. A new Social Security Act, in August 1950, added almost 10 million people to those eligible for benefits. A National Housing Act, passed in July 1949, provided large sums to cities for aid in slum clearance and the construction of over 800,000 units for low-income families.

Congress, however, defeated the Brannan Plan (an ambitious program for stabilizing farm income), turned down a strong civil rights program for blacks, and refused to repeal or significantly amend the Taft-Hartley Act.

THE TRUMAN ADMINISTRATION AND THE COLD WAR

While Americans attempted to resume politics as usual at home, the United States and the Soviet Union clashed over the reorganization of the postwar world. Even before Winston Churchill's famous pronouncement at Fulton, Missouri, that "an iron curtain has descended across the continent," Truman's new Secretary of State, James F. Byrnes, caught the mood of American decision-makers: "In many countries throughout the world our political and economic creed is in conflict with ideologies which reject both of these principles." No doubt Stalin saw things much the same way.

These conflicting ideas affected how the United States and the Soviet Union perceived each other and defined threats to their national security. To the United States, the USSR was a revolutionary monolith dedicated to the triumph of world communism, whether by subversion or force of arms. The foreign policy of the United States was based on the inevitable danger of Soviet military aggression and the need to find ways to contain it.

With equal conviction, the USSR perceived the United States as a power anxious to preserve and extend American institutions and capitalism, whether by atomic diplomacy, subversion, or force of arms. The foreign policy of the Soviet Union rested in part on the conviction that its security demanded a weak Germany and friendly governments on its borders—the kind of security the United States enjoyed in the Western Hemisphere. With the horrors of World War II and Nazi occupation still paramount in the minds of his people, Stalin felt the need to prepare for anything.

The United States and the Soviet Union viewed each other's moves in the world arena as a confirmation of these perceptions and fears. And decision-makers in each nation capitalized on those perceptions and fears to justify greater expenditures for military arms and military alliances with friendly nations. It was imperative as well for each nation to keep intact its own sphere of influence (Eastern Europe and Latin America) and to win friends among the noncommitted nations of the world. New nations only recently emerged from colonial domination became targets of competition.

Containment through Foreign Aid

With the Communists in firm control of Eastern Europe, the first skirmishes of the Cold War were fought in the Middle East, Turkey, and Greece. Seeking to establish Soviet influence in oil-rich Iran, Stalin backed a Communist movement in Azerbaijan, Iran's northernmost province on the Soviet border, and tried to secure oil concessions similar to those of Anglo-American companies. To maintain the pressure, he chose to ignore the Big Three agreement at Teheran in 1943, which called for the removal of all Allied troops from Iran by March 2, 1946.

On March 5, after Iran had complained to the UN of Soviet interference, Truman sent Stalin a stiff note. By May 1946 the troops had been withdrawn, but only after the Soviets had obtained an agreement for participation in Iranian oil production. With American aid, Iran regained control over Azerbaijan; and in early 1947, the Iranian government rejected the proposed Iranian-Soviet oil company.

For centuries Russia had sought access to the Mediterranean by way of the Turkish straits leading out from the Black Sea. When in 1945 the Soviet Union renewed its demands for joint control of the straits, the United States sent a naval task force. This action, in addition to stern American and British notes, deterred the Russians but also led them to shift the pressure westward onto Greece.

Until February 1947, British forces had assisted the Greek government against Communist guerrillas who sought the overthrow of the right-wing monarchist regime. But the British were in financial trouble. On February 24, they notified the United States that they could no longer afford the burden of resisting communism in the Mediterranean. They planned to withdraw troops from Greece and to terminate aid to Turkey.

This step was an acknowledgment of the end of British supremacy in the Mediterranean. In March 1946 Britain had acknowledged the independence of Transjordan (renamed Jordan in 1949). In April 1947, it turned over the future of Palestine to the UN. This led in May 1948 to the creation, with mixed United States reactions, of the independent state of Israel. France, meanwhile, had completed its promised withdrawal from Syria and Lebanon by August 1946. If only by default, leadership of the non-Communist world, with all the obligations it entailed, fell to the United States.

Determined to bolster the pro-Western governments in Greece and Turkey, Truman went before Congress on March 12, 1947, to enunciate what has been known since as the Truman Doctrine. He asked Congress for $400 million to assist Greece and Turkey. In addition, he wanted authority to send American civilian and military advisors to those countries, at their request, to oversee the use of American grants and to train Greek and Turkish soldiers.

To sell this program to the American people and a budget-minded Congress, Truman set down the classic justification for Cold War policies. The images and language he used would be repeated by every succeeding president, from Dwight D. Eisenhower to Ronald Reagan. The issues, as Truman protrayed them, were clear:

At the present moment in world history nearly every nation must choose between alternative ways of life. The choice is too often not a free one.

One way of life is based upon the will of the majority, and is distinguished by free institutions, representa-

tive government, free elections, guaranties of individual liberty, freedom of speech and religion, and freedom from political oppression.

The second way of life is based upon the will of a minority forcibly imposed upon the majority. It relies upon terror and oppression, a controlled press and radio, fixed elections, and the suppression of personal freedom.

I believe that it must be the policy of the United States to support free peoples who are resisting attempted subjugation by armed minorities or by outside pressures. . . . If we falter in our leadership, we may endanger the peace of the world—and we shall surely endanger the welfare of our own Nation.

If some American critics felt Truman had oversold the Communist menace, still others questioned aid to regimes whose only virtue was their opposition to communism. But Congress responded favorably. Between 1947 and 1950, the United States spent about $660 million on aid to Greece and Turkey, and their political stability was preserved. Even before success had been assured, however, Secretary of the Navy James V. Forrestal was urging Truman to wage an economic offensive to stabilize the Western world before the "Russian poison" overwhelmed Europe, South America, "and ourselves."

Through the development of the Marshall Plan in 1947, the United States again took the initiative in the Cold War. Britain's retreat from its Mediterranean lifeline brought home to the United States the economic predicament of Western Europe and underscored this region's political vulnerability as well. Britain, almost entirely dependent upon outside food supplies and on world trade to pay for them, was by far the worst off economically. The situation in France, however, appeared more ominous because a large Communist Party was able to capitalize on a century of deprivation among the working classes.

In Italy, deprivation had an even longer history than in France, and communism an even stronger hold. In defeated Germany, hunger was common and chaos ruled. To restore "the confidence of the European people in the economic future of their own countries," the United States proposed to help in the reconstruction of the entire European economy. General George C. Marshall, the first military man to become secretary of state, announced the new program in his commencement address at Harvard on June 5:

Our policy is directed not against any country or doctrine, but against hunger, poverty, desperation, and chaos. Its purpose should be the revival of a working economy in the world so as to permit the emergence of political and social conditions in which free institutions can exist.

The Soviet Union, although invited to participate in the Marshall Plan, saw it as a project to revive and preserve Western capitalism. Most likely the United States neither expected nor wanted Soviet participation, particularly with a Republican Congress controlling appropriations. Western European leaders welcomed the program and immediately drew up plans for using it. They were probably moved as well by the Communist coup in Czechoslovakia in February 1948. After considerable debate, Congress in April 1948 provided $5.3 billion for the first twelve months of Marshall Plan aid. Between 1948 and 1952, about $12 billion was distributed, more than half of the total going to Britain, France, and West Germany. By 1952, economic recovery in these countries had been completed. Western Europe began a long business boom, and the advance of communism within the West had been checked.

To solidify American influence elsewhere in the world, Truman in 1949 proposed a Point Four Program "for the improvement and growth of undeveloped areas," so resistance to communism could be strengthened. Between 1951 and 1954, Congress appropriated nearly $400 million for technical assistance to such regions, both a response and a stimulus to the growing "revolution of rising expectations" in Asia, Africa, and Latin America.

Containment through Military Alliances: NATO

The idea behind the Truman Doctrine, the Marshall Plan, and Point Four was *containment*, which after 1947 became the cornerstone of American foreign policy. The concept was set forth by George F. Kennan, a senior Foreign Service officer and Soviet expert who had spent five years in the USSR. He warned that the Soviet Union was committed to an "aggressive intransigence with respect to the outside world." But it should not be assumed that the Russians would commit themselves to some "do-or-die program" to overthrow Western society. Their own belief in the inevitable fall of capitalism had convinced them that time was on their side.

The history of Russia and the teachings of Lenin suggested to Kennan that the Soviets would move with caution, retreating when necessary "in the face of superior force." Under such circumstances, American policy must be one of "long-term, pa-

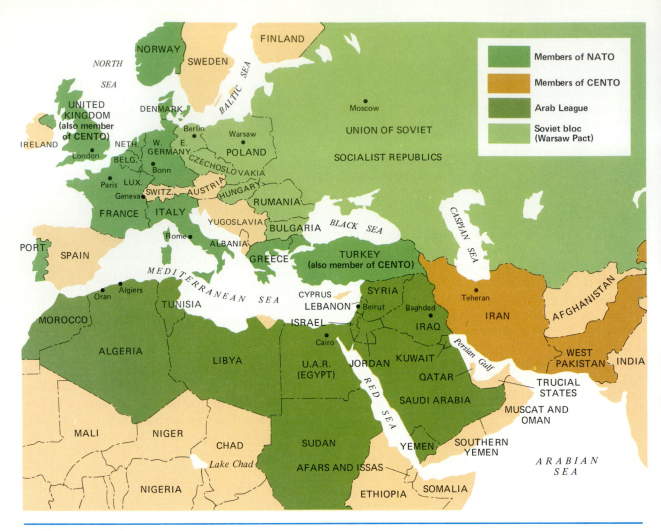

NATO and Eastern Europe

tient but firm and vigilant containment of Russian expansive tendencies" based on the "application of counter-force."

The containment policy gave little hope for an early end to the Cold War. With every new diplomatic move, the United States and the Soviet Union made assumptions about the other's motives that resulted in even more rigid and inflexible policies. As an alternative to containment, the right wing of the Republican party became infatuated with the idea of "liberation"—that is, direct action to free captive peoples behind the Iron Curtain. With far greater realism, Truman moved to consolidate recent gains. What had begun as economic and military aid to nations threatened by communism evolved into a policy of military alliances.

The UN Charter permitted "collective self-defense" arrangements until the Security Council could act "to maintain peace and security." In March 1948, under the sanction of this article and of the Marshall Plan, Britain, France, the Netherlands, Belgium, and Luxembourg signed a treaty of economic cooperation and military alliance. This step prompted the United States Senate in June 1948 to adopt the Vandenberg Resolution, by which the United States promised "to exercise the right of individual or collective self-defense" in the event of an armed attack "affecting its national security."

The ground was laid for the North Atlantic Treaty, signed April 4, 1949, by twelve Western nations and ratified overwhelmingly (82 to 13) by the United States Senate. An armed attack upon any member would be considered an attack upon all; each member promised to assist the one attacked by whatever action was thought necessary, "including the use of armed force." When asked if the treaty contemplated a rearmed Germany, Secretary of State Dean Acheson replied: "We are very clear that the disarmament and demilitarization of Germany must be complete and absolute." (In 1954 West Germany was granted full sovereignty, admitted to NATO with full equality, and permitted to raise an army of twelve divisions to become part of the NATO force.)

On September 22, 1949, President Truman made the momentous announcement that the Soviet Union had successfully exploded an atomic bomb. "This is now a different world," Senator Arthur Vandenberg remarked. Congress that same month passed the Mutual Defense Assistance Act, aimed at building up the military strength of the members of the North Atlantic Treaty Organization (NATO). During the next four years, the United States would supply almost $6 billion worth of arms and military material to European allies and another $1.7 billion to other countries.

Although the European allies strained to make their own contributions to NATO, they failed by and large to do so. NATO therefore soon came to depend on air power as the principal deterrent to the Soviet Union. It relied particularly on the American Strategic Air Command (SAC), organized in 1951. SAC, in turn, imposed on the United States the need for air bases in many parts of the world. And this need sometimes awkwardly but decisively influenced diplomatic decisions.

Latin America

During World War II, all Latin American countries except Argentina and Chile had cooperated with the Western Allies to the extent of supplying strategic materials and making bases available. Brazil and Mexico also became active belligerents against the Axis and sent troops overseas. Argentina, aspiring to leadership in competition with both Brazil and the United States, grew especially envious of Brazil because of the United States lend-lease aid Brazil received.

After the strongly pro-Axis military leader Colonel Juan D. Perón became virtual dictator of Argentina in 1944, relations between his country and the United States deteriorated. Latin American nations began to fear that the war with the Axis would be extended to their hemisphere. To consider and act upon this threat, an inter-American conference, with Argentina excluded and the United States represented, met at the Castle of Chapultepec in Mexico City in 1945. On March 6 the conference adopted the Act of Chapultepec,

an informal agreement declaring that an attack by any state against the territory, sovereignty, or political independence of an American state would be considered an act of aggression against the signers.

Argentina, aware of its growing isolation, declared war on the Axis on March 27, 1945, and a few days later accepted the Chapultepec agreement. In return the United States, over Soviet opposition, helped Argentina win a seat at the San Francisco Conference in April. It and all the Latin American countries became charter members of the UN.

The end of the war meant the end of the profitable markets for strategic raw materials that Latin American countries enjoyed during the conflict. It also saw the frustration of their hopes for industrialization, on which they had counted as a springboard for future economic growth. When neglect by the United States followed the restoration of peace, suspicion grew that the Good Neighbor policy had been merely a screen for wartime exploitation. A crushing blow came in June 1947 when Latin America found itself excluded from the Marshall Plan.

The urgency of the Cold War stirred the Truman administration to solidify hemispheric defenses. At the Inter-American Conference near Rio de Janeiro in August and September 1947, the United States helped draw up a hemispheric mutual defense pact. A second step was the creation at Bogotá, Colombia in March 1948 of the Organization of American States (OAS) to oversee the Rio Pact and other inter-American contacts. New requests were made for aid—like that of the Marshall Plan—through the OAS. When the United States rejected them, whatever small gains had been made were undone.

The Rio Pact and the OAS underscored the United States' concern for political stability. But the depth of poverty in Latin America, combined with a growing revolutionary ferment, made the status of some United States-backed regimes increasingly uncertain.

The People's Republic of China

Containment worked well enough in Europe, but in the Far East an entirely different situation developed with the triumph of the Communist forces in China in October 1949. These forces, under the leadership of Mao Tse-tung, had come into existence long before World War II. Throughout the war the United States and Britain, each for its own purposes, had tried to get them and the Nationalists under Chiang Kai-shek to work together to defeat Japan. The policy failed dismally. General Joseph W. Stilwell, in charge of coordinating Chinese wartime efforts against Japan, concluded that Chiang's government "is a structure based on fear and favor, in the hands of an ignorant, arbitrary, stubborn man."

At the war's end, the Chinese Communists, encouraged by the Russians, received the surrender of Japanese armies independently, amassed their own arms, and even engaged in skirmishes with the Nationalists. By late 1945, they controlled 225,000 square miles and more than 105 million Chinese.

In an attempt to stave off civil war in China and the extension of Communist rule there, United States Ambassador Patrick J. Hurley, in September 1945, arranged a meeting in Chungking, the Nationalist capital, between Chiang and Mao Tsetung. After a full six weeks of talks, no agreement was reached. Embittered by his failure, Hurley resigned and pointed the finger at career officers in the United States Foreign Service who, he said, undermined his efforts to "prevent the collapse of the Nationalist government."

As Chiang's regime continued to falter, Truman sent General Marshall to the divided country. But he could do nothing. At one point Marshall warned Chiang that the Communist forces were too strong for him to defeat militarily, and urged negotiations. On his return to Washington in January 1947 to become secretary of state, Marshall was most discouraged. Sincere efforts to reach a settlement, he said, had been frustrated not merely by the Communists, but also "by irreconcilable groups within the Kuomintang party interested in the preservation of their own feudal control of China."

In July 1947, Truman made still another effort to avert disaster. This time he sent General Albert C. Wedemeyer, who had served as Chiang's chief of staff from late 1945 until the middle of 1946, "to make an appraisal" of the entire situation. Wedemeyer's report of September 19, 1947, made proposals that reflected so harshly on Chiang's ability to control his own territory that Truman and Marshall kept them from the public until the summer of 1949:

Today [he wrote] China is being invaded by an idea instead of strong military forces from the outside. . . . The Central Government cannot defeat the Chinese Communists by the employment of force, but can only win the loyal, enthusiastic and realistic support of the masses of the people by improving the political and economic situation immediately.

Despite his criticism of the Nationalist government, Wedemeyer recommended that it be given aid. But the Truman administration decided that Chiang's prospects did not merit further assistance. It was right. In the great civil war that developed, the Communists swept all the way to Shanghai by May 1949.

Having rested his power on military strength, continued American assistance, and an oppressive landlord class, Chiang was unable to withstand the well-disciplined Communist forces, who had the support of millions of poverty-stricken peasants. Large numbers of Nationalist troops defected, and nearly 80 percent of the American supplies sent to Chiang fell into Communist hands. By December 1949, Nationalist forces had withdrawn to the island of Taiwan (Formosa).

In the meantime, on October 1, scarcely a week after the Soviet Union had exploded its first atomic bomb, the People's Republic of China was proclaimed. In February 1950, a treaty of alliance and mutual assistance was concluded with the USSR.

With the collapse of Chiang, the State Department in August 1949 issued a lengthy White Paper on the Chinese question. It revealed, among other items, that from 1945 to 1949 the Nationalists had received $3 billion in American aid, most of which had been squandered or permitted to fall into Communist hands. In his introduction to the White Paper, Secretary of State Acheson claimed that "the ominous result" of the civil war in China had been beyond the control of the United States. Nevertheless, Acheson still anticipated a time when the Chinese people would overthrow the "foreign yoke" of communism.

Perhaps to speed that day, the United States, unlike Britain and other major nations, until the 1970s viewed Chiang's government in Taiwan as the legitimate government of China and refused to recognize the People's Republic of China or consent to its admission to the UN. In October 1971, the United Nations admitted the People's Republic and expelled Nationalist China; in February 1972 President Nixon's trip to China opened the way for United States recognition of the People's Republic. (see Chapter 33).

The White Paper failed to silence the small but vocal China bloc in the United States, which urged continued military aid to Chiang. Ex-Ambassador Hurley denounced the White Paper as a "smooth alibi for the pro-Communists in the State Department who had engineered the overthrow of our ally." A number of congressmen joined Hurley, and bitterness rose to the point where Marshall and his advisors were charged with the deliberate betrayal of American interests. The criticism capped more than a year of controversy over how far the United States should have committed itself in defending Chiang.

The Republicans used the issue to brand the opposition as "the party of treason." Democrats too had been critical of the administration. On February 21, 1948, for example, a young congressman from Massachusetts, John F. Kennedy, charged that the State Department had betrayed China by attempting to force Chiang into a coalition with Mao and by listening to the wrong advisors. "This is the tragic story of China, whose freedom we once fought to preserve," Kennedy concluded. "What our young men saved, our diplomats and our President have frittered away."

Although China had been "lost," the United States was determined to maintain its position in the Far East. On January 12, 1950, Secretary of State Acheson announced that the "defense perimeter" of the United States ran from the Aleutians to Japan, the Ryukyus, and the Philippines. Significantly, he did not include South Korea. In case of attack west of the defense perimeter, he added, "the initial reliance . . . must be on the people attacked to resist it," and then on "the entire civilized world under the Charter of the United Nations." The day after Acheson's declaration, the UN Security Council refused to seat the People's Republic of China. The Soviet delegate promptly walked out, not to return until August 1—more than a month after the Security Council voted to support United States efforts to sustain South Korea.

The Korean Conflict

The hot war between Chiang and the Communists in China had an almost instant sequel in nearby Korea. During World War II, the Allied powers had agreed that Korea, occupied by Japan, should be made independent. In August 1945, the Soviet Union agreed to accept the surrender of the Japanese in Korea north of the 38th parallel. It left the United States, on the arrival of its forces in September, to accept the surrender below that line.

Although both the United States and the Soviet Union favored a united Korea, mutual suspicion and the unwillingness to accept unification under Communist or anti-Communist control led to the establishment of separate regimes. The United States referred the question of Korean unity to the UN in September 1947. Although opposed by the USSR, the General Assembly voted to set up a temporary commission to supervise an all-Korean election.

Elections were held in May 1948 for a national assembly in the United States zone. The new assembly then adopted a constitution, elected Syngman Rhee (a devout anti-Communist who had spent many years in the United States) as the first president, and on August 15 proclaimed the Republic of Korea. The United States and thirty

---

MY GENERATION

Let me try to define my generation . . . as those of us who approached our majority during World War II, and whose attitudes were shaped by the spirit of that time and by our common initiation into the world by that momentous event. . . . By contrast [with World War I] our war, despite a nervous overlay of the usual frivolity (do you recall Rosie the Riveter and Slap the Jap or aching erotic schmaltz that suffused those "Back Home for Keeps" ads?), was brutally businesslike and anti-romantic, a hard-boiled matter of stamping out a lot of very real and nasty totalitarianism in order to get along with the business of the American Way of Life, whatever that is. Our generation was not only not intact, it had been in many places cut to pieces. The class just ahead of me in college was virtually wiped out. Beautiful fellows who had won basketball championships and Phi Beta Kappa keys died like ants in the Normandy invasion. Others only slightly older than I—like myself young Marine Corps platoon leaders, primest cannon fodder of the Pacific war—stormed ashore at Tarawa and Iwo Jima and met ugly and horrible deaths on the hot coral and sands. . . .

We were traumatized not only by what we had been through, but by the realization that the entire mess was not finished after all: there was now the Cold War to face, and its clammy presence oozed into our nights and days. When at last the Korean War arrived, some short five years later (it was this writer's duty to serve his country in the Marines in that mean conflict, too), the cosmos seemed so unhinged as to be nearly insupportable. Surely by that time . . . we were the most mistrustful of power and the least nationalistic of any generation that America has produced.

William Styron, American novelist

Source: William Styron, "My Generation," *Esquire,* October 1973, p. 132.

U.S. soldiers move slowly down a muddy road on the central Korean battle front. "It looks like World War III is near," President Truman wrote in his private notebook. (*Official U.S. Army photo, photograph by Feldman*)

other nations promptly recognized the new nation. That very day elections above the 38th parallel led to formation of the rival Democratic People's Republic of Korea, which the Soviet Union and its allies promptly recognized.

By December, leaving the North Koreans heavily armed, the USSR had recalled its troops. At the General Assembly's suggestion, the United States recalled its troops from South Korea in June 1949, leaving behind much military material and about 500 "advisors."

North and South Korea thus faced each other across an artificial border, each backed by a rival great power and committed to unification on its own terms. Border skirmishes soon threatened to broaden into civil war. To bolster South Korea, Truman in February 1950 approved an act providing it with $110 million in economic aid. Military aid was also enlarged. On June 25, 1950, North Korea sent its forces across the 38th parallel as a reprisal for border raids. The UN commission

called it a "well-planned, concerted, and full-scale invasion."

Truman, concluding that the attack endangered American interests, both in Asia and Europe, responded decisively. At his urgent request, the UN Security Council met on the afternoon of the invasion and by a vote of 9 to 0 held North Korea accountable for a "breach of the peace." (Yugoslavia abstained; the Soviet Union was still boycotting the council over the China issue.) Within forty-eight hours, and without consulting Congress, Truman ordered American naval and air units to help push the North Koreans back over the 38th parallel. Not wishing to draw China into the war, he also ordered the fleet to keep Chiang Kai-shek from attempting to invade from Formosa.

After the Security Council urged positive action to assist South Korea, Truman broadened his earlier military instructions and with other nations sent ground troops. Although the operation was ostensibly under UN auspices, American troops

THE SEARCH FOR SECURITY

The Korean War

and "restore the border," he told the American people several months later that the Koreans "have a right to be free, independent, and united." By late September, he had accepted the recommendation of his National Security Council that MacArthur be permitted to move into North Korea.

Taking advantage of their momentary military superiority, UN forces pushed across the 38th parallel on October 9, 1950, and pressed on toward the Yalu River—the boundary between North Korea and China. Through diplomatic channels, China had already warned the Western world that it would not "sit back with folded hands and let the Americans come to the border." The United States, however, thought such intervention unlikely. MacArthur called for the surrender of North Korea, American troops advanced northward, and Chinese forces began to mass across the Yalu.

At a conference on Wake Island, MacArthur assured Truman: "We are no longer fearful of Chinese intervention. We no longer stand hat in hand." If the Chinese should move across the border, with the United States Air Force controlling the skies, "there would be the greatest slaughter." The slaughter came, but the principal victims were American and South Korean troops. On November 26, Chinese forces moved into Korea, trapped and inflicted heavy casualties on American and Korean troops at Chosin Reservoir, and pursued the fleeing armies below the 38th parallel. The United States had made a gross miscalculation. Although American troops finally regrouped and counterattacked, the war was now a military stalemate.

Restive over the restraints imposed on him by the strategy of conducting a limited war for the limited objective of restoring South Korea's frontier, General MacArthur publicly expressed his dissatisfaction with the UN and President Truman. Even at the risk of becoming involved in an open war with China, a development many observers believed might lead to war with the Soviet Union, MacArthur urged an all-out effort that included the bombing of Chinese troops and supplies in Manchuria, a naval blockade of mainland China, and the use of Nationalist Chinese troops.

General Omar N. Bradley, chairman of the joint chiefs of staff, warned that a major war against China would be "the wrong war at the wrong place, in the wrong time and with the wrong enemy." MacArthur rejected this decision and finally caused President Truman, on April 11, 1951, to relieve him of his Korean command and of his control of the occupation forces in Japan.

made up about four-fifths of the UN forces in Korea, and General Douglas MacArthur was in firm command. "The entire control of my command and everything I did came from our Chiefs of Staff," MacArthur later recalled. "I had no direct connection with the United Nations whatsoever."

The Korean fighting was as savage as many World War II campaigns, and losses ran high. By the end of August 1950, the outnumbered UN forces had been pushed almost into the sea in the area around the port of Pusan. After being heavily reinforced, however, MacArthur opened a counterattack with an amphibious landing at the port of Inchon behind the North Korean line. A full-scale offensive in November drove the North Koreans back toward the 38th parallel and destroyed a considerable part of their army. Although Truman in late June had declared that the United States aimed only to reestablish peace in Korea

MacArthur returned to the United States, where he received a hero's welcome from the public.

On June 23, 1951, the head of the Soviet delegation to the UN suggested that the Korean conflict might be settled if both parties were willing. This announcement led to armistice negotiations that began on July 10, 1951, and proceeded for two entire years, during which fighting often broke out. During the 1952 presidential campaign, General Eisenhower, the Republican candidate, dramatically announced that if elected he would fly to Korea to bring about a cease-fire. In December, a month after his victory at the polls, Eisenhower made the trip. But the cease-fire was delayed another seven months. It would have been delayed even longer, in his opinion, had he not threatened once more to extend the war beyond the Korean peninsula, unleash Chiang Kai-shek, and—despite the deep misgivings of the British and other Europeans—to employ "tactical" atomic weapons.

The touchy armistice, resolved on July 27, 1953, restored the prewar division at the 38th parallel. By then the war had cost the United States over $15 billion and more than 140,000 casualties, including 33,000 dead. The outcome was a military and political draw, with a Korea still divided but now war-ravaged as well. Although remaining separate nations, North and South Korea both seemed determined to suppress political opposition at home and rigidly control the lives and liberties of the Korean people.

McCARTHYISM: REPRESSION AT HOME

Within the United States, the strains of the Cold War manifested themselves in a desperate search for internal security. Nothing in their historical experience had equipped the American people to deal with a cold war. The same level of unity and bipartisanship asked of a people at war was now demanded in different circumstances. Never before had an individual's loyalty to country seemed more important. How to measure that loyalty was sufficiently clear—the intensity and consistency of a person's anticommunism. "I think that Owen Lattimore is not a Communist," someone observed, "but the policies he has advocated certainly cannot be described as anti-Communist." That was the essence of the new loyalty.

In conducting foreign policy, Truman reinforced traditional American fears of the Soviet Union and of communism itself. At times, the threat seemed real enough. The spectacular revelations of spy rings, like that uncovered in Canada in 1946, fed the growing suspicion that certain highly placed people were conspiring to overthrow or subvert American institutions.

For confirmation, they had only to listen to Truman's own attorney general, J. Howard McGrath: "There are today many Communists in America," he warned an audience in May 1950. "They are everywhere—in factories, offices, butcher shops, on street corners, in private business—and each carries with him the germs of death for society." At this very moment, he cautioned, they are "busy at work—undermining your government, plotting to destroy the liberties of every citizen, and feverishly trying, in whatever way they can, to aid the Soviet Union."

Sounding an almost identical warning, *Life* magazine observed as early as July 1945: "The 'fellow traveler' is everywhere, in Hollywood, on college faculties, in government bureaus, in publishing companies, in radio offices, even on the editorial staffs of eminently capitalistic journals."

Actually, the U.S. Communist Party exerted little influence in the postwar period, even on the American Left. What had robbed it of power was not so much anti-Communist vigilance as previous disillusion with the Stalin purges, the Hitler-Stalin pact, and the repressive character of Soviet communism. That helps to explain why the sensational exposures of the late forties and the fifties were so often exposures of past political sins, committed largely during the Great Depression, when the Party was respectable in intellectual circles. But if the postwar Communist hunt did little for internal security, it did serve up numerous scapegoats. By 1950, substantial numbers of Americans were ready to believe Senator Joseph R. McCarthy of Wisconsin when he branded "the whole group of twisted-thinking New Dealers" as Communists who "have led America near to ruin at home and abroad."

Loyalty Tests

Before Senator McCarthy embarked on his crusade, the groundwork for what came to be called *McCarthyism* had been laid by Republicans and Democrats, by both the Truman administration and the Republican-controlled Eightieth Congress. Responding to fear of internal subversion, President Truman in March 1947 ordered a full-scale "loyalty investigation" of all present and prospective federal employees. No source of information, however questionable, was to be ignored. Along with all "loyalty" data worked up by government bureaus since 1939, the new dossiers were to become part of a "central master index." Among the "standards for refusal of employment or removal from employment" was "sympathetic association" with any foreign or domestic organization designated by the attorney general as "subversive." A Loyalty Review Board was empowered to oversee this extensive security program.

In compliance with the president's order, Attorney General Tom C. Clark, in December 1947, issued a list of ninety organizations considered disloyal to the United States. None of these organizations had the right to defend itself. Since the list had been prepared by the federal government, with the assistance of the FBI under the direction of J. Edgar Hoover, it quickly became the principal reference for the detection of disloyalty. Not only federal agencies but private organizations, business establishments, trade unions, newspapers, entertainment agencies, and schools consulted it to discover "subversives."

During the 1948 presidential campaign, even Americans for Democratic Action published in major newspapers the names of leading Progressive party supporters along with their alleged Communist affiliations, based on the attorney general's list. Only in retrospect, in a speech nearly fifteen years later at Columbia University Law School, did former Attorney General Clark confess to the arbitrary nature of the list he had compiled: "Perhaps we should, as I look at it now, have given the parties an opportunity to be heard before we issued it."

When the federal investigation of loyalty was completed in April 1951, the records of no less than 3,225,000 civil servants had been examined. Under pressure of the inquiry, 2,900 had resigned, and only 300 had been dismissed. The broad criteria for what constituted subversion made it possible that none of these individuals was a Communist, although some might have been at one time. Little that Joseph McCarthy ever managed to do in the United States Senate could compare with the steady, although less spectacular, subversion of constitutional liberties under Truman's loyalty program. In the name of "internal security," Americans had been encouraged to spy on each other. Almost any "derogatory information" uncovered could deprive a person of job and livelihood. Rather than soften any abuses of the system, the Loyalty Review Board conducted proceedings that denied the accused the right to confront the witnesses against them.

HUAC

Even as President Truman established his own anti-Communist credentials, Republicans in the Eightieth Congress revived the House Un-American Activities Committee. HUAC was formed in 1938 as a temporary investigation unit, largely to advance the personal political fortunes of its chairman, Democrat Martin Dies of Texas. With a strong push from the freshman California Congressman Richard M. Nixon, victorious after a calculated Red-baiting campaign, the committee proceeded to hunt Communists and alleged Communists, to advance individual political careers and the fortunes of the Republican party generally.

Before long, HUAC's chief investigator reported: "We were to expand to many rooms, to agencies in leading cities, a staff of 75, and 600 filing cases containing more than one million names, records, dossiers, and data pertaining to subversion. About 20,000 accredited agents of the FBI, Treasury, Army, Navy, Civil Service, Atomic Energy Commission, and other Federal officers have used our growing files."

What HUAC did was to manipulate various channels of publicity to reveal the political associations of individuals who had unorthodox ideas. By holding over each witness a threat to his or her career, the committee exerted tremendous power. Refusal to answer the committee's questions or cooperate with its investigation was like an admission of guilt. The committee's most audacious adventure was a two-week foray in Hollywood, in October 1947, "to expose those elements that are insidiously trying to . . . poison the minds of your children, distort the history of our country, and discredit Christianity."

The attempt to prove extensive Communist influence in the film industry was a dismal failure. Even a leading Republican newspaper, the *New York Herald-Tribune*, conceded that the Hollywood investigation had "dissolved into the ludicrous." Nevertheless, it did frighten movie executives into an indiscriminate housecleaning. It soon spread to radio and television, and to the blacklisting of actors, writers, directors, and others, some of whom could not get work twenty years later.

"ARE YOU NOW OR HAVE YOU EVER BEEN?"

Typical of the quality of the investigation of the Hollywood film industry by the House Un-American Activities Committee was the testimony of film actor Adolphe Menjou on October 21, 1947. Robert E. Stripling acted as the committee's secretary, and Congressman Richard M. Nixon was a member from 1947 to 1950.

MR. STRIPLING: Do you have your very definite suspicions about some members of the Screen Actors Guild?

MR. MENJOU: I know a great many people who act an awful lot like Communists.

MR. STRIPLING: As an actor, Mr. Menjou, could you tell the Committee whether or not an actor in a picture could portray a scene which would in effect serve as propaganda for Communism or any other un-American purpose?

MR. MENJOU: Oh, yes. I believe that under certain circumstances a Communistic director, a Communistic writer, or a Communistic actor, even if he were under orders from the head of the studio not to inject Communism or un-Americanism or subversion into pictures, could easily subvert that order, under the proper circumstances, by a look, by an inflection, by a change in the voice. I have never seen it done, but I think it could be done. . . .

MR. NIXON: In answer to a question by Mr. Stripling, you indicated that, although you might not know whether a certain person was a Communist, I think you said he certainly acted like a Communist.

MR. MENJOU: If you belong to a Communist-front organization and you take no action against the Communists, if you do not resign from the organization when you know the organization is dominated by Communists, I consider that a very, very dangerous thing.

MR. NIXON: Have you any other tests which you would apply which would indicate to you that people acted like Communists?

MR. MENJOU: Well, I think attending any meeting at which Mr.Paul Robeson appeared, and applauding or listening to his Communist songs in America. I would be ashamed to be seen in an audience doing a thing of that kind.

MR. NIXON: You indicated you thought a person acted like a Communist when he stated, as one person did to you, that capitalism was through.

MR. MENJOU: That is not Communistic per se, but it is very dangerous leaning, it is very close. I see nothing wrong with the capitalistic system, the new dynamic capitalism in America today. . . .

Source: *Communist Infiltration of Hollywood Motion-Picture Industry,* Hearings before the Committee on Un-American Activities, House of Representatives, 80th Congress, October 21, 1947. Photograph from UPI/Bettmann Newsphotos.

The Hollywood probe had been preceded by HUAC's attempt, starting in February 1947, to question Communist Party officials. Many of them preferred citations for contempt to answering the summons. Eugene Dennis, general secretary of the Communist Party in the United States, was among those who defied the summons. At Congressman Nixon's suggestion, HUAC agreed to ask the House to bring contempt charges against Dennis and also to ask the Justice Department to investigate the Communist "conspiracy" to violate the Smith Act of 1940. This act made it illegal for a person to advocate "overthrowing . . . any government in the United States by force," or to "affiliate" with groups teaching this doctrine.

In July 1948, the Justice Department got the indictment of Dennis and ten other high-ranking Communist leaders under this act. Their conviction by the federal district court in New York in October 1949 and their heavy fines and prison terms were upheld by the Supreme Court, 6 to 2, in June 1951.

In upholding the conviction, the Supreme Court lent its weight to the frantic search for internal security. "Certain kinds of speech are so undesirable," Chief Justice Fred M. Vinson said for the Court in the Dennis case, "as to warrant criminal prosecution." This view diminished the value Justice Holmes in 1919 had put on "the free trade in ideas" under the guarantees of the First Amendment. The Dennis ruling also encouraged states and municipalities, under local acts and ordinances similar to the Smith Act, to pursue thousands of alleged subversives, sometimes on the basis of hearsay or even lies.

The Hiss case, HUAC's most far-reaching triumph, began on August 3, right after the Dennis indictment in July. On that day, Whittaker Chambers, an admitted former Communist who said he quit the party in 1937, was brought before the committee to support earlier testimony about the Communist "apparatus" in Washington. Chambers, an editor of *Time* magazine, told a sensational story. He named members of the Washington Communist apparatus of the 1930s, including Alger Hiss, a former State Department official and since 1947 president of the Carnegie Endowment for International Peace. On learning of Chambers's accusation, Hiss telegraphed a full denial to the committee and asked for a hearing, which was granted on August 5.

This and subsequent hearings, interspersed with reexaminations of Chambers, brought additional details of Hiss's activities in the thirties, including membership (with Chambers) in a Soviet spy ring in Washington and passing classified government documents to the Russians. Hiss persisted in his denials. Neither could be prosecuted for espionage, since the acts had taken place more than seven years before and, under the statute of

Alger Hiss. (*AP/Wide World Photos*)

Richard Nixon. (*UPI/Bettmann Newsphotos*)

limitations, were beyond legal reach. But Hiss was indicted for perjury. After two trials, the first one ending in a hung jury, Hiss was found guilty and sentenced to five years in prison and fined $10,000. After appeals to higher courts upheld the verdict, Hiss went to prison in March 1951.

A Harvard Law School graduate and secretary to Justice Holmes, Hiss had served as one of the early New Dealers in the AAA and then as a State Department official. He helped to plan the United Nations Organization and was a member of Roosevelt's Yalta delegation. Before leaving the government in 1946, he served as director of the State Department's Office of Special Political Affairs. All in all, he lent some substance to the charge that privileged individuals in high places had helped to betray the country. The controversy about Hiss's guilt or innocence continued for several decades and remains unresolved.

Despite the Hiss coup, HUAC failed to turn up any significant number of "subversives" in government, at least none that could safely be brought to trial. Meanwhile, J. Parnell Thomas, chairman of HUAC during the Eightieth Congress, was convicted of fraud on December 3, 1949, and sent to prison.

While the Hiss case was in progress, HUAC made other accusations, and the FBI bestirred itself to uncover Soviet agents. The news of the first Soviet atomic bomb explosion late in September 1949, followed in October by the Communist triumph in China and in February 1950 by the mutual-security pact between the People's Republic and the USSR, all deepened the shock of Communist gains and provoked charges that the State Department itself was filled with Communists. Senator McCarthy, having learned his lessons well from Democrats and Republicans who had successfully used the Communist issue, now pounced on this theme.

McCarthy and McCarthyism

In a speech in Wheeling, West Virginia, on February 9, 1950, Senator McCarthy declared that the United States, the strongest nation on earth on V-J Day, had been shorn of its strength "because of the traitorous actions of those who have been treated so well by this nation." None were worse than "the bright young men" in the State Department "born with silver spoons in their mouths." To add substance to his charges, McCarthy added: "I have here in my hand," the names of "two hundred and five men that were known to the Secre-

Senator Joseph R. McCarthy: "We've been losing to international Communism at the rate of 100 million people a year. Perhaps we should examine the background of the men who have done the planning, and let the American people decide whether . . . we've lost because of stumbling, fumbling idiocy, or because they planned it that way." (*UPI/Bettmann Newsphotos*)

tary of State as being members of the Communist party and who nevertheless are still working and shaping the policy of the State Department."

McCarthy could never make good on his startling revelation. He gradually backed away from the figure of 205, keeping in the limelight with new numbers until, in the end, he was unable to substantiate a single name. But nothing was done to restrain the accuser. On the contrary, the respected conservative Republican leader, Senator Robert A. Taft of Ohio, gave the full benefit of his own prestige: "McCarthy should keep talking, and if one case doesn't work he should proceed with another."

Events soon played into McCarthy's hands. While he was playing "the numbers game" with Communists in the State Department, British authorities arrested for atomic espionage Dr. Klaus Fuchs, a German-born nuclear physicist and naturalized British subject who had worked on the American bomb at Los Alamos in 1944. Fuchs admitted the charges and was sentenced to fourteen years in prison. He also implicated certain American Communists in his activities.

Acting on Fuchs's information, the FBI in the summer of 1950 arrested Ethel and Julius Rosenberg and their friend Morton Sobell. They were charged with passing atomic secrets to the Soviets and speeding up Russian success with the bomb. For a crime "worse than murder," in the words of the trial judge, the Rosenbergs, in March 1951, were sentenced to death. Sobell was sentenced to thirty years. After many appeals failed, the Rosenbergs were executed on July 19, 1953. The punishment in this case suggested the kind of fear and hysteria that had overtaken the American people and the judiciary.

Meanwhile McCarthy's charges grew in reach and recklessness as the "limited" Korean conflict eroded American morale. A low point was touched on June 14, 1951, after General MacArthur's recall. McCarthy made a bid to retrieve the headlines with a 60,000-word attack in the Senate on MacArthur's rivals, General Marshall and General Eisenhower. Marshall, perhaps the most respected military figure in the country, was accused of "serving the world policy of the Kremlin." Deeply involved with him, "in a conspiracy so immense and an infamy so black as to dwarf any previous such venture in the history of man," was Marshall's "firm supporter" and "fast-rising protege, 'Ike' Eisenhower."

"McCarthyism" by then had passed into the language as an expression for wild and unfounded charges of disloyalty. But many Americans came to believe, as the senator himself told his home following in Wisconsin, that "McCarthyism is Americanism with its sleeves rolled." Money began to pour in on McCarthy, and superpatriot societies took up the cause. His most spectacular feats still lay ahead of him. So did his downfall.

The McCarran Acts

Congress also responded to the national obsession with anticommunism. On September 23, 1950, over Truman's veto, it passed the McCarran Internal Security Act, making it unlawful to conspire "to perform any act which would substantially contribute to the establishment within the United States of a totalitarian dictatorship." All "communist-action" and "communist front" organizations were assumed to be such conspiracies and required to register with the attorney general. In case of an "internal security emergency," the act authorized the president to arrest and detain any individuals for whom there was "reasonable ground" to suspect that they would "probably" engage in acts of espionage or sabotage. Any alien, moreover, with the slightest "subversive" taint was to be excluded from admission to the United States.

Even Senator McCarran denounced the Internal Security Emergency amendment to his bill as "a concentration-camp measure pure and simple." In his veto message, Truman characterized parts of the Internal Security Act as "the greatest danger to freedom of speech, press, and assembly since the alien and sedition laws of 1798." Far from protecting the nation from dictatorship, he added, the McCarran Act took the United States "a long step toward totalitarianism."

On June 30, 1952, Congress supplemented the Internal Security Act with the McCarran-Walter Immigration Act, passed again over Truman's veto. This act updated but hardly liberalized the widely attacked quota system, which imposed exceptional hardship on displaced persons and refugees from Communist countries. More to the point, it required the attorney general to screen out "subversives" within the permitted quotas and empowered him to deport such persons even after they had become naturalized American citizens.

"Seldom," said Truman, "has a bill exhibited the distrust evidenced here for citizens and aliens alike—at a time when we need unity at home and the confidence of our friends abroad." Despite Truman's vetoes, the McCarran acts might be viewed as the logical result of earlier attacks on individual liberties, beginning with the president's

WORDS AND NAMES IN AMERICAN HISTORY

A great many American school and college students have suffered through the lines of a *cafeteria* and scarcely need to have the word defined for them. Yet the word has a somewhat curious history. It came originally from the Spanish *cafetera*, which means a coffeepot, not a place where coffee is served. The word seems to have come into U.S. usage not directly from Spain but from Mexico, since it was first used in its modern sense in the Mississippi Valley rather than along the Atlantic seaboard. Some scholars trace its earliest use to the late nineteenth century. Foreign visitors to this country are sometimes confused to learn that a *café* and a *cafeteria* are both eating and drinking establishments, but not necessarily of exactly the same kind.

federal loyalty directive. What he had already done, Truman insisted, was enough to deal with the problem.

The McCarran acts, like Truman's loyalty program and the actions of the FBI, intensified the preoccupation with internal security. McCarthy had effectively used the issue in the congressional elections of 1950 to defeat a Maryland Senator, Millard F. Tydings, who had been bold enough to oppose his reckless charges. With equal effectiveness, McCarthy capitalized on fears of communism to win reelection in 1952, and the Republican party employed such fears that same year to return to the White House.

The Election of 1952: Eisenhower

Once recovered from the shock of losing the 1948 election, Republican leaders who had opposed the nomination of Thomas E. Dewey and had favored Taft blamed the defeat on bipartisanship in foreign policy and led the attack on it. The decision in 1951 to constrain MacArthur and "contain" the Korean conflict gave weight to their charge of betrayal. At the same time, they made a calculated attempt to win the votes of millions of "ethnics"— those who had roots in countries behind the Iron Curtain—by endorsing a policy of "liberation."

The platform adopted by the Republican party in 1952 thus promised to repudiate commitments such as those made at Yalta which aid "Communist enslavement" and attacked the containment policy that "abandoned" so many millions to it.

Yet many Republicans remained committed to bipartisanship in principle and to the Truman version of it in practice. Many of them also loathed McCarthy as deeply as most Democrats, a feeling they found it easy to transfer to his misguided friend Taft. Their own choice for the nomination was the immensely popular wartime hero Dwight David Eisenhower, who had turned down the Democrats four years earlier. After tactical successes in unseating southern delegates for Taft, the Eisenhower convention team put Ike across on the first ballot. The Taft people took what solace they could from the nomination for vice-president of Richard Nixon, the former HUAC luminary who had won a seat in the United States Senate after still another demonstration of Red-baiting politics.

The Republicans' snaring of Eisenhower only deepened the pessimism with which the Democrats approached their national convention two weeks later. Many voters believed the McCarthyite

charge that their reign had been "twenty years of treason." On the home front, the inflation brought by the Korean conflict also worked against the Democrats. The inflation was dramatized by the steel strike in 1952, which Truman failed to arbitrate and which resulted in higher steel prices. Moreover, beginning in 1951, certain petty scandals came to light involving the use of influence by persons close to Truman himself.

After Truman announced in March 1952 that he would not be a candidate, the leading Democratic aspirant became Senator Estes Kefauver of Tennessee. Kefauver had gained a national reputation as head of the special Senate Committee that had in fact uncovered so much Democratic graft. When Kefauver failed to win on the first two ballots at the Chicago convention, the delegates drafted Truman's choice, Adlai E. Stevenson, governor of Illinois. Senator John J. Sparkman of Alabama became his running mate.

Stevenson conducted a vigorous and unusually eloquent campaign that won him many supporters among intellectuals. He particularly attacked the Republicans' "liberation" promises as "cynical" attempts "to play upon the anxieties of foreign nationality groups in this country."

During the campaign, Nixon's successful use of innuendo to smear opponents came back to haunt him. Even as he charged that a Stevenson triumph would ensure "more Alger Hisses, more atomic spies, more crises," newspapers revealed the existence of a "secret" contingency fund that had been raised by friends to keep Nixon in "financial comfort." With Eisenhower now on the verge of dropping him from the ticket unless he placed "all the facts before the people, fairly and squarely," Nixon took to nationwide television to explain that the fund had been used for campaign expenses, not for himself or his family.

The public responded favorably to what came to be known as the Checkers speech (referring to the family dog he refused to give up), and Eisenhower reaffirmed his confidence in Nixon's integrity. But relations between the two men would be strained for some time.

To no one's surprise, Eisenhower's vast appeal, enhanced by his campaign pledge to fly to Korea and end the stalemate there, carried him to a striking triumph. He received 33,824,000 popular votes to Stevenson's 27,314,000. In the electoral college, his margin was 422 to 89, with the Solid South for the first time since 1928 contributing to the Republican total. Yet the Republicans had

(Text continues on page 727.)

(*Bruce Davidson / Magnum Photos*)

Marilyn Monroe by Andy Warhol. (*Leo Castelli Gallery, New York*)

An outdoor movie in South Dakota. (*J. R. Eyerman/Life Magazine,* © *1958, Time, Inc.*)

THE SEARCH FOR SECURITY

3-D movie audience. (*J. R. Eyerman/Life Magazine,* © 1952, 1980, Time, Inc.)

THE SEARCH FOR SECURITY

grounds for worry. Even Eisenhower's great popularity brought the party a mere majority of eight in the House and a standoff in the Senate. With a Republican–southern Democratic coalition able to control Congress, however, the conservative mood still prevailed.

The election of Eisenhower ended twenty years of Democratic rule in the White House. But few Americans anticipated any startling changes. By this time, much of the New Deal social legislation, like social security, had become so much a part of American life that no Republican leader thought of tampering with it. The foreign policy of the United States, despite Republican charges, was still bipartisan. Democrats and Republicans alike operated from the premise that the Soviet Union represented a constant and inevitable threat to the "free world" and needed to be contained. Even the search for internal security had been largely a bipartisan effort. Finally, no political figure so exemplified the spirit of bipartisanship to the American people than Eisenhower, a candidate both parties had eagerly sought.

SUMMARY

The United States after World War II was a superpower. It was a superpower engaged in a rivalry with the other superpower, the Soviet Union, for world domination. Wartime cooperation soon returned to mutual suspicion and distrust.

The United Nations, created as the war ended in an attempt to set up an international organization that would be more effective than the old League of Nations, began with fifty-one charter members. Its charter set up two major agencies, the General Assembly, to which all members belonged, and the Security Council, made up of the Great Powers as permanent members plus a few rotating members. The council was given authority to apply sanctions to maintain peace, but each of the permanent members had a veto that could block action.

By 1980 the UN had 152 members. Over the years, it influenced some world issues. But the arms race, the dissolution of overseas empires, and the Cold War were beyond its power to solve. So was atomic energy and the development of more and more sophisticated nuclear weapons. For once the Soviet Union had detonated its own atomic bomb in September 1949, security by balance of terror became part of the new world order.

In Europe, the map was far different from what it had been before the war. Germany had been divided into two states, and the leading Nazis had been tried for war crimes by an international tribunal. In Asia, Japan was occupied by the United States until 1950, when a general peace treaty was signed. At home Truman, taking office after Roosevelt's death, had to face the problems of demobilization, reconversion of the economy to a peacetime footing, reorganization of the military establishment, and satisfaction of the pent-up demands for consumer goods.

The 1948 election is remembered as the greatest upset in American history, when Truman won the presidency in his own right against Thomas E. Dewey, whom everyone had expected to win. Truman's domestic program was called the Fair Deal, and it was designed to expand the New Deal's social programs. In foreign affairs, Truman had to deal with the Cold War and the new postwar world.

The Soviets had moved to secure their borders in Europe by creating a sphere of influence in Eastern Europe like the American control in the Western Hemisphere. The rest of the world became a battleground for an ideological war between the United States and the Soviets. And the American policy set during this period—containment of Russia and the spread of communism through foreign aid and military alliances—was to last unchanged for more than a generation.

The Truman Doctrine provided aid to bolster pro-Western governments in Greece and Turkey. The Marshall Plan, developed in 1947, helped restore the shattered European economy and stop the advance of communism in Western Europe. In 1949 Truman proposed the Point Four program to give aid to Asia, Africa, and Latin America to strengthen resistance to communism.

Collective defense in Europe was set up through NATO, the North Atlantic Treaty Organization. Its counterpart in Latin America was the Rio Pact of 1947 and the Organization of American States (OAS) set up in 1948. In the Far East, the victory of the Communists in China in 1949, despite all the aid America had given Chiang Kai-shek and the Nationalists, led the United States to extend its defense perimeter to include Japan, the Ryukyus (Okinawa), and the Philippines.

The first open conflict came in Korea, which had been divided in two after the war. When North Korea, backed by the Soviet Union, invaded the South on June 25, 1950, Truman went to the UN and then ordered American forces into the conflict. The fighting went on for two more years, and at the end no one had won; Korea remained divided, and the armistice of July 1953 was a return to the prewar boundary of the 38th parallel. The futile conflict had cost the United States more than 140,000 casualties and more than $15 billion.

At home, Cold War tensions erupted in an obsessive concern with internal security and subversion. HUAC, the House Un-American Activities Committee, looked for Communists everywhere, even in Hollywood. The Hiss case was its only "triumph." But the shadow HUAC spread ruined careers and poisoned lives. Senator Joseph McCarthy, who came to symbolize the mania for loyalty, took as his special target the State Department. "McCarthyism" became a new word in the American vocabulary, and it came to mean wild and unfounded charges of disloyalty. He never managed to prove one of the many accusations he hurled in public. The McCarran Acts of 1950 and 1952 were the congressional response to the national obsession with communism at home.

All these tensions and fears, plus the popularity of General Dwight D. Eisenhower, brought a Republican president in 1952 after twenty years of Democrats in the White House. But there were to be no startling changes; the New Deal was not dismantled, and bipartisanship and the Cold War continued.

Suggested Readings

E. F. Goldman, *The Crucial Decade—and After: America 1945–1960* (1960), H. Zinn, *Postwar America 1945–1971* (1973), G. Hodgson, *America in Our Time* (1976), and W. E. Leuchtenburg, *In the Shadow of FDR: From Harry Truman to Ronald Reagan* (rev. ed., 1985), are stimulating and often contrasting interpretations. W. Manchester, *The Glory and the Dream* (1974), is a sweeping chronicle of America between 1932 and 1972. On Truman, see M. Miller, *Plain Speaking* (1973) and R. Donovan, *Conflict and Crisis* (1977) and *Tumultuous Years* (1982). B. J. Bernstein, *Politics and Policies of the Truman Administration* (1970), is a critical assessment. A. L. Hamby, *Beyond the New Deal* (1973) is a sympathetic treatment of Truman and liberal reform. For commentary by a probing contemporary critic, see I. F. Stone, *The Truman Era* (1953).

The Yalta Conference and its aftermath are examined in H. Feis, *Churchill, Roosevelt, Stalin* (1957); W. L. Neumann, *After Victory: Churchill, Roosevelt, Stalin and the Making of the Peace* (1967); and D. S. Clemens, *Yalta* (1970). On the Potsdam Conference, see C. L. Mee, *Meeting at Potsdam* (1975), and H. Feis, *Between War and Peace: The Potsdam Conference* (1960). The conflict over control of atomic weapons is examined in R. G. Hewlett and F. Duncan, *Atomic Shield 1947–1952* (1970), M. J. Sherwin, *A World Destroyed* (1975), and in two personal accounts, B. M. Baruch, *Baruch: The Public Years* (1960), and D. E. Lilienthal, *Journals* (2 vols., 1964). Eugene Davidson examines the Nuremberg trials in *The Trial of the Germans* (1966). Telford Taylor, *Nuremberg and Vietnam: An American Tragedy* (1970), is a thoughtful review of the implications of war-crime trials by one of the American prosecutors at Nuremberg.

The best introductions to the United States and the Cold War are W. LaFeber, *America, Russia, and the Cold War* (rev. ed., 1976), and S. E. Ambrose, *Rise to Globalism: American Foreign Policy 1938–1980* (rev. ed., 1985). On the origins and development of the Cold War, see L. C. Gardner, A. Schlesinger, Jr., and H. Morgenthau, *The Origins of the Cold War* (1970); J. L. Gaddis, *The United States and the Origins of the Cold War* (1972); and D. Yergin, *Shattered Peace: The Origins of the Cold War and the National Security State* (1977). The changes in George Kennan's views are revealed in *American Diplomacy 1900–1950* (1951), *Realities of American Foreign Policy* (1954), *Russia and the West under Lenin and Stalin* (1961), *On Dealing with the Communist World* (1964), and his *Memoirs 1925–1963* (2 vols., 1967–72). The critical "revisionist" view is presented in T. G. Paterson (ed.), *Cold War Critics* (1971); W. A. Williams, *The Tragedy of American Diplomacy* (1962); G. Kolko, *The Politics of War* (1968) and *The Limits of Power* (1972); G. Alperovitz, *Atomic Diplomacy* (rev. ed., 1985); R. G. Barnet, *Intervention and Revolution: The United States in the Third World* (1968); L. C. Gardner, *Architects of Illusion* (1970); and T. J. Paterson, *Soviet-American Confrontation: Postwar Reconstruction and the Origins of the Cold War* (1973). For an additional assessment, see R. E. Osgood and others, *America and the World: From the Truman Doctrine to Vietnam* (1969). J. L. Gaddis, *Strategies of Containment* (1982) is a critical appraisal of postwar American national security policy. The military influence on decision-making is analyzed in R. K. Betts, *Soldiers, Statesmen, and Cold War Crises* (1977).

The personal accounts of decision-makers are themselves useful and revealing. Among the most important are H. S. Truman, *Memoirs* (2 vols., 1955, 1956); D. Acheson, *Present at the Creation* (1969); J. Byrnes, *Speaking Frankly* (1947); W. Millis (ed.), *The Forrestal Diaries* (1951); G. Kennan, *Memoirs 1925–1963;* and Arthur Vandenberg, *Private Papers* (1952). See also R. H. Ferrell, *George C. Marshall* (1966), and G. Smith, *Dean Acheson* (1972).

Henry Wallace's break with Truman is examined in N. D. Markowitz, *The Rise and Fall of the People's Century* (1973); A. Yarnell, *Democrats and Progressives* (1973); and J. S. Walker, *Henry A. Wallace and American Foreign Policy* (1976).

On the Truman Doctrine, J. M. Jones, *The Fifteen Weeks* (1955), conveys the crisis atmosphere in which it was formulated. The implications are discussed in R. M. Freeland, *The Truman Doctrine and the Origins of McCarthyism: Foreign Policy, Domestic Politics and Internal Security 1946–1948* (1972). On the Marshall Plan, see J. Gimbel, *The Origins of the Marshall Plan* (1976). On NATO, see R. E. Osgood, *NATO: Entangling Alliance* (1962).

The Far East and the Cold War are examined in A. Iriye, *The Cold War in Asia* (1974), and Y. Nagai and A. Iriye (eds.), *The Origins of the Cold War in Asia* (1977). The United States and China may be profitably examined in the State Department's *The China White Paper,*

August 1949 (2 vols., 1967). See also H. Feis, *The China Tangle* (1953); T. Tsou, *America's Failure in China* (1963); and M. Schaller, *The United States Crusade in China 1938–1945* (1979).

On the Korean war, the important works are D. Rees, *Korea: The Limited War* (1964); G. D. Paige, *The Korean Decision* (1968); and A. Whiting, *China Crosses the Yalu* (1960). For a vigorous contemporary dissent, see I. F. Stone, *The Hidden History of the Korean War* (1952). On Truman and MacArthur, see J. W. Spanier, *The Truman-MacArthur Controversy and the Korean War* (1959); Douglas MacArthur, *Reminiscences* (1964); and W. Manchester, *American Caesar: Douglas MacArthur 1880–1964* (1978).

The Fair Deal is examined in the general works cited in the first paragraph. See also M. S. Hartmann, *Truman and the 80th Congress* (1971). On labor, see A. F. McClure, *The Truman Administration and the Problems of Postwar Labor 1945–1948* (1969); on agriculture, see A. J. Matusow, *Farm Policies and Politics in the Truman Years* (1967), and John Shover's broader analysis of the transformation of rural life in America in *First Majority—Last Minority* (1976).

Preelection voter polling became a powerful political device after World War II. For its use in political analysis, see S. Lubell, *The Future of American Politics* (1952) and *Revolt of the Moderates* (1956). The nature of political power is examined in R. E. Neustadt's influential book, *Presidential Power* (1960). On the far Right in American politics, see R. Hofstadter, *The Paranoid Style in American Politics and Other Essays* (1965). On the radical Left, see D. A. Shannon, *The Decline of American Communism: A History of the Communist Party of the United States since 1945* (1959); J. R. Starobin, *American Communism in Crisis 1943–1957* (1972); A. Richmond, *A Long View from the Left: Memoirs of an American Revolutionary* (1972); and V. Gornick, *The Romance of American Communism* (1977). On liberalism, see Reinhold Neibuhr's influential works, such as *The Irony of American History* (1952) and *The World Crisis and American Responsibility* (1958); A. M. Schlesinger, Jr., *The Vital Center* (1949); Christopher Lasch's critical assessment in *The*

New Radicalism in America 1889–1963 (1965), and R. H. Pells, *The Liberal Mind in a Conservative Age: American Intellectuals in the 1940s and 1950s* (1985). On the Democratic party, see H. S. Parmet, *The Democrats: The Years after FDR* (1976).

David Caute, *The Great Fear: The Anti-Communist Purge under Truman and Eisenhower* (1978), surveys the deterioration of civil liberties. For the particulars, see E. Bentley (ed.), *Thirty Years of Treason: Excerpts from Hearings before the House Committee on Un-American Activities 1938–1968* (1971); W. Goodman, *The Committee* (1968); M. Lowenthal, *The Federal Bureau of Investigation* (1950); E. Bontecou, *The Federal Loyalty–Security Program* (1953); W. Gellhorn (ed.), *The States and Subversion* (1952); L. Ceplair and S. Englund, *The Inquisition in Hollywood: Politics in the Film Community 1930–1960* (1980); and V. Navasky, *Naming Names* (1980). R. Rovere, *Senator Joe McCarthy* (1959), is a critical assessment but ignores the context in which the senator launched his crusade. That context is provided in R. Griffith and A. Theoharis (eds.), *The Specter: Original Essays on the Cold War and the Origins of McCarthyism* (1974); A. D. Harper, *The Politics of Loyalty: The White House and the Communist Issue 1946–1952* (1970); R. M. Freeland, *The Truman Doctrine and the Origins of McCarthyism* (1972); R. Griffith, *The Politics of Fear* (1970); A. Theoharis, *Seeds of Repression: Harry S. Truman and the Origins of McCarthyism* (1971); and R. M. Fried, *Men against McCarthy* (1976). On the nature of McCarthy's appeal, M. P. Rogin, *The Intellectuals and McCarthy* (1967), is an important study. See also T. C. Reeves, *The Life and Times of Joe McCarthy* (1982), and D. M. Oshinsky, *A Conspiracy So Immense: The World of Joe McCarthy* (1983). The Hiss and Rosenberg cases remain controversial and unresolved. The Hiss case is examined in A. Cooke, *A Generation on Trial* (1950), without reaching a verdict. J. C. Smith, *Alger Hiss* (1976), is a strong defense; A. Weinstein finds him guilty in *Perjury* (1978). W. and M. Schneier, *Invitation to an Inquest* (1965), raises questions about the guilt of the Rosenbergs; R. Radosh and J. Milton, *The Rosenberg File* (1984), finds them guilty.

SUPERPOWERS IN THE MISSILE AGE

Chapter 31

With the presidency of Dwight D. Eisenhower, the United States embarked on a unique period of peace and relative good times. Since the end of World War II, the American people had been involved in economic reconversion, an obsessive concern with internal security, and a Cold War that defied resolution. And there was no assurance that the Eisenhower presidency would bring relief. His victory came at a moment in the Cold War when the American way of life seemed threatened by events around the world and at home. The nuclear arms race had assumed terrifying proportions. The Soviet Union had exploded its first atomic weapon in 1949. The United States three years later produced the even more destructive hydrogen bomb, and the Soviet Union in turn developed its hydrogen bomb and in 1957 reported the first successful tests of an intercontinental ballistic missile (ICBM).

Confronted with this balance of terror and with international developments they could neither control nor at times understand, the American people found in President Eisenhower the security and self-assurance they so badly needed. Although his "dynamic conservatism" envisioned a less interventionist role for the federal government, he did little to undo the Fair Deal

or the New Deal. Although his foreign policy took on a "new look" and used the language of "massive retaliation" and "brinksmanship," the substance and goals remained the same: containment by alliance and superior military power.

His conservative approach satisfied most Americans, as did his refusal to commit American youth to combat situations. Through two terms, he remained for most Americans the symbol of order, stability, and military might in the White House—precisely what the times seemed to demand.

With its avoidance of controversy, belief in organization, and celebration of "togetherness," the fifties would be called the Plastic Decade. The creative energies of the American people appeared to be absorbed in the task of combating an alien ideology. Dissent was not fashionable. What remained of the American Left had been demoralized and splintered; liberals were preoccupied with demonstrating their own anticommunism. The storm of protest that would be unleashed in the sixties was barely visible on the college campuses.

Those who made up the "silent generation," as the college students of the fifties came to be called, embraced the prevailing values of the adult society, aspired to affluence, dressed modestly, avoided controversy. They listened to Perry Como, Frank Sinatra, and the Crewcuts—a music that could easily be reconciled with the middle-class homes and suburban enclaves from which most of them came. The distinguishing characteristic of the class of 1949, *Fortune* magazine observed, was its aversion to risk and passion for security: "These men don't question the system. Their aim is to make it work better—to get in there and lubricate the machinery. They're not rebels; they'll be social technicians for a better society."*

Whatever dissent managed to surface in the fifties often took unlikely forms. Among the critics, and perhaps the most deeply probing, was a standup nightclub comic, Lenny Bruce. "People should be taught what is, not what should be," he told his audiences. "All my humor is based on destruction and despair. If the whole world were tranquil, without disease and violence, I'd be standing in the breadline—right back of J. Edgar Hoover."

Equally alienated but more popular in intellectual circles was a small group of young Bohemian writers and artists who frequented the coffeehouses of San Francisco and came to be known as Beatniks or Beats. Like Lenny Bruce, they scorned all ideologies, parodied the most cherished American myths and beliefs, celebrated absurdity, and frankly questioned the nation's sanity.

But if Bruce and the Beats anticipated the rebellion of the sixties, most Americans in the fifties found them incomprehensible and in poor taste. The literary, stage, and film success of the period was Herman Wouk's The Caine Mutiny, which celebrated the virtues of conformity and authority. "The idea is," one of the novel's characters declares, "once you get an incompetent ass as a skipper there's nothing to do but serve him as though he were the wisest and the best, cover up his mistakes, keep the ship going, and bear up."*

The same decade that would see rebellion on the campuses and a counterculture based on youth began with the election of John F. Kennedy to the presidency, the youngest person elected to that office and the first president born in the twentieth century. Perhaps it was his youth that underscored the difference between Kennedy and his predecessor in the White House, that seemed to inspire hope in the youthful population of the entire world. He conveyed the impression of new and imaginative approaches to old problems, even if his actual policies were not so different.

Two events of 1960, seemingly unrelated, heralded the decade of turbulence that lay ahead. On February 1, four black students at Greensboro, North Carolina, violated segregation laws and customs by taking seats at the lunch counter of the local F. W. Woolworth store. On May 13, the House Un-American Activities Committee tried to hold hearings in San Francisco and ran into a massive demonstration, made up in part of students from the nearby Berkeley campus of the University of California.

These rumblings were barely understood in 1960—but comprehension came soon enough. The optimism with which the sixties began and with which many young Americans responded to Kennedy's vision of a New Frontier would be shattered by assassination, racial strife, and a deepening involvement in a small Asian country previously unknown to most Americans—Vietnam. ∎

CONSERVATIVES IN POWER

In campaigning for the presidency, Eisenhower had promised to clean up the "mess in Washington," purge the disloyal, spend less money, and stem the tide of "creeping socialism." The America he venerated was best exemplified by his own boyhood home of Abilene, Kansas, which lay almost at the exact geographic center of the United States. No one stressed more than the president his dedication to the "middle way." But Eisenhower discovered, like any new president, that it was not so easy to put campaign rhetoric into action.

He had pledged himself to bring into government "men and women to whom low public morals are unthinkable," only to find his own administration by 1958 afflicted by scandals. The president's loyalty program, a continuation and elaboration of Truman's, purged some dissenters but few who were disloyal. His dislike for centralized government failed to uproot "creeping socialism." The traditional virtue of individualism was celebrated by Eisenhower, even as most Americans were embracing "togetherness" and submerging their individuality in the organizations that employed them. He also spoke frequently of "preserving" each person's "equality before the law," as though each person enjoyed this fundamental right. But even while Eisenhower was taking, as he believed, "that straight road down the middle," events were polarizing the nation and the world in profound and disconcerting ways.

The Businessman's Government

To rise in the chain of command, Eisenhower wrote in *Crusade in Europe,* the individual needed personal characteristics of a special sort: "The teams and staffs through which the modern commander absorbs information and exercises his authority must be a beautiful, interlocked, smooth-working mechanism. Ideally, the whole should be practically a single mind; consequently misfits defeat the purpose of the command organization."*

Misfits were few and short-lived on the Eisenhower team. Successful businessmen and corporation lawyers dominated the cabinet. The most controversial appointment was that of Charles E. Wilson, president of General Motors, as secretary of defense. Since GM was a major

* Reprinted by permission of Doubleday & Co., Inc.

Eisenhower prepares to make his acceptance speech at the Republican National Nominating Convention in 1952 which had nominated him on the first ballot. (*UPI/Bettmann Newsphotos*)

supplier of defense material, the appointment raised a possible conflict of interest between the public good and company profits. Wilson tried to defuse the issue with his much-quoted assertion: "I thought what was good for the country was good for General Motors, and vice versa." Eisenhower thought the conflict of interest law had been carried beyond reason. The time may come, he warned, when presidents would "be unable to get anybody to take jobs in Washington except business failures, political hacks, and New Deal lawyers."

Best known for his diplomatic experience, John Foster Dulles became secretary of state. At certain crises in foreign relations, the president overruled Dulles. Yet in this field even more than in others, his normal policy was to leave decisions to his top administrator. Operating almost independently of the State Department, Dulles established a close working relationship with the new president. His long experience in foreign affairs, dating back to a diplomatic mission under President Wilson, was enough to silence any potential critics within the administration. "After all," Eisenhower's assistant said of him, "how are you going to argue with a man who has lived with a problem—for instance

The search for national security was a bipartisan effort involving Senators of such diverse politics as (left to right) Sam Ervin, Jr., Henry Jackson, John McClellan, and Joseph McCarthy. Standing behind them is Chief Counsel Robert Kennedy. (*UPI/Bettmann Newsphotos*)

in respect to Iran—for longer than most of us knew there was such a country?"

Upon becoming president, Eisenhower had promised his business friends a more favorable political climate. His cabinet selections went far to fulfill that pledge. But the president was less successful in his efforts to cut government expenses and stabilize the agricultural sector. Although few New Deal and Fair Deal programs were enlarged, few were canceled. In September 1954, on the eve of the congressional elections, Eisenhower signed an act adding more than 7 million persons to those eligible for social security benefits. The Republicans were less generous about extending the public housing program, and their attitude toward public power development clearly favored private enterprise.

Declining farm prices proved to be the most serious domestic challenge. Faced with higher distribution costs, farmers found themselves getting less for their products but paying more for what they purchased. Under the price support policy, farm surpluses were accumulating in gov-

ernment warehouses. (The public was not willing to buy farm products at the prices being supported by the government.) To reduce the surpluses, the secretary of agriculture decreased the government's support and secured congressional authorization for a flexible system. The net result of his program was to aggravate the plight of small farmers. So many stayed poor that *Time* magazine called the new program "The $5 Billion Farm Scandal."

Significant gaps in economic performance appeared during the first Eisenhower administration. But the business boom, with a strong boost from government spending and government guarantees of home mortgages and other private credit, was sufficiently genuine for the Republicans to campaign in 1956 with the slogan of "Peace, Progress, and Prosperity."

The Decline of McCarthy

No sooner had Eisenhower come to power than Senator McCarthy used his chairmanship of the

Government Operations Committee to renew his assault on his favorite target, the State Department. In February 1953, Eisenhower nominated Charles E. Bohlen as ambassador to the Soviet Union. A veteran Foreign Service officer, Bohlen had served as Roosevelt's interpreter at Yalta. After vicious condemnations of the nominee, McCarthy and his friends permitted the Senate to approve him. But their reward was the appointment of their own man as the State Department's new "security officer." Henceforth few worked there without McCarthy's consent.

Having cleansed the stables at home, as he thought, McCarthy next turned to operations abroad. His first target was the Voice of America, the overseas broadcasting unit of the United States Information Agency. After the most demoralizing search, he failed to uncover a single Communist there. The next victim was the State Department's International Information Administration, which disseminated printed materials through libraries in many parts of the world. Many books by eminent American writers, one of them Secretary Dulles's cousin, were ordered withdrawn. To the shock of the world, some were publicly burned.

Determined to expand the dragnet for Communists, the president, on April 27, 1953, issued his own "loyalty order." The categories for "security risks" in government employment were made broader and vaguer. If charges were brought against a federal employee, he or she could now be suspended. Although the administration boasted it had fired 1,456 federal employees under this program, not one Communist could be found. Truman's program had yielded even more "risks." The net result of the Democratic-Republican loyalty purges was the demoralization of federal employees and the elimination of a generation of dissenters from public service.

The search for internal security knew few limits. In December 1953, Eisenhower dismayed the scientific community by ordering a "blank wall" to be placed between J. Robert Oppenheimer, the distinguished nuclear physicist who had directed the making of the first atomic bomb, and all secret atomic data. Oppenheimer, at this time head of the Institute for Advanced Study at Princeton, also served as chairman of the general advisory committee of the Atomic Energy Commission. The administration learned that McCarthy was on Oppenheimer's trail, and it wanted to get him first. After a humiliating hearing, a special review board cleared Oppenheimer of disloyalty. But in the eyes of AEC he remained a "misfit," unemployable because of "fundamental defects in his character."

Although Congress and the presidency had often knuckled under to McCarthy, his star began to wane in the summer of 1954. The senator's reckless attack on the "coddling" of Communists in the United States Army led to the spectacular Army–McCarthy hearings. Before a nationwide television audience, McCarthy failed to sustain his charges. He conducted himself in a manner that embarrassed many of his associates. In December 1954, by a vote of 67 to 22, the Senate censured him for "conduct unbecoming a member." Less than three years later, he died virtually unsung.

Although *McCarthyism* entered the American vocabulary as a word for "indiscriminate allegations" and "unsubstantiated charges," such fame actually distorted the senator's importance. He had exploited the art; yet the origins lay in the Cold War itself. The earliest practitioners had been Democrats and Republicans, conservatives and liberals, including many who thought McCarthy had simply carried it too far.

Columnist Murray Kempton perhaps best summed up the legacy of the Wisconsin senator by placing it in the proper context: "The enormities of the musician who abuses the piano have a way of obscuring the disharmonies of the score which was appointed as entirely appropriate for him to play. Overattendance upon the excessive can distract us from noticing how bad the normal is."

Despite vigilance, extensive loyalty programs, the continued operations of HUAC, and loyalty oaths in businesses, public schools, and universities, the internal security of the nation seemed as much in danger as ever. Two years after Kennedy assumed office, J. Edgar Hoover explained to a House subcommittee why his FBI needed additional appropriations to combat Communist influence: "They have infiltrated every conceivable sphere of activity; youth groups; radio; television; and motion picture industries; nationality minority groups and civil and political units." And Kennedy's promptness in reappointing Hoover suggested the power and influence he still commanded.

Black Rights and White Laws

Even as the United States posed abroad as a defender of oppressed peoples, it found its credentials seriously undermined and challenged at home by its own black citizens. The revolution of rising expectations in the newly liberated colonial empires in Africa and Asia also stirred the black community in the United States. Despite the persistence of traditional racial practices, a new mood emerged in black America. "We're going to take over the world," jazz artist Dizzy Gillespie told a white audience, "so you'd better get used to it. You people had better just lie down and die. You've lost Asia and Africa, and now we're cutting out from white power everywhere. You'd better give up or begin to learn how it feels being a minority."

The presidency could no longer feel immune to the international implications of racism in the United States. During the Truman administration, a Committee on Civil Rights, composed of leaders of both races, made clear the extent to which the American image abroad and the Cold War demanded a new and more realistic view of race relations:

Our position in the post-war world is so vital to the future that our smallest actions have far-reaching effects. We cannot escape the fact that our civil rights record has been an issue in world politics. The world's press and radio are full of it. Those with competing philosophies have stressed—and are shamelessly distorting—our shortcomings. They have tried to prove our democracy an empty fraud, and our nation a consistent oppressor of underprivileged people. This may seem ludicrous to Americans, but it is sufficiently important to worry our friends. The United States is not so strong, the final triumph of the democratic ideal is not so inevitable that we can ignore what the world thinks of us or our record.

In May 1954, the Supreme Court's momentous decision in *Oliver Brown et al. v. Board of Education of Topeka, Kansas*, ordered the end of public school segregation. Even earlier, the Court had begun to erode the "separate but equal" principle established by the *Plessy* v. *Ferguson* decision (1896).

In the 1930s the National Association for the Advancement of Colored People (NAACP) attacked the inequality of black educational facilities and especially of black teachers' salaries in the courts. A turning point came in the Supreme Court decision in 1938 in *Missouri ex rel. Gaines* v. *Canada*, one of a series of cases in higher education through which the idea of the inherent inequality of separate facilities was developed. The University of Missouri Law School, in the absence of a law school for blacks in the state, attempted to meet the "equal" requirement by offering to pay the tuition of Lloyd Gaines, a black, for an out-of-state school. The Court, 7 to 2, held that he must be trained in Missouri, in whose courts he would practice. In the absence of a law school for blacks

there, he must be admitted to the one at the University of Missouri.

Similar decisions covering medical as well as law schools led the NAACP to challenge not only the inequality of facilities, but segregation itself. At the time of the *Brown* ruling in May 1954, cases were pending from South Carolina, Virginia, Delaware, and the District of Columbia, as well as from Kansas. All were covered by the decision. The Department of Justice, in submitting the segregation cases to the Supreme Court, also revealed a deep concern over their implications in the Cold War struggle, claiming that racial discrimination must be viewed in the context of a world struggle between competing ideologies. "Racial discrimination furnishes grist for the Communist propaganda mills, and it raises doubt even among friendly nations as to the intensity of our devotion to the democratic faith."

In September 1953, Chief Justice Fred M. Vinson died. In his place Eisenhower named Governor Earl Warren of California. Privately, the president was to call that appointment "the biggest damn fool mistake I ever made." By that time, however, Warren had directed the Court toward a far greater protection of the civil rights of racial and political minorities. Speaking for a unanimous Court in May 1954, including three southern justices, Warren reversed the *Plessy* decision:

To separate [black children] from others of similar age and qualifications solely because of their race generates a feeling of inferiority as to their status in the community that may affect their hearts and minds in a way never to be undone. . . . We conclude that in the field of public education the doctrine of "separate but equal" has no place. Separate educational facilities are inherently unequal.

Although welcoming the decision, E. Franklin Frazier, a prominent black sociologist, recognized the mixed motives that had made it possible: "The white man is scared down to his bowels, so it's be-kind-to-Negroes-decade at last."

Much has been made of the sudden and shocking character of the Warren Court's ruling. No doubt it shocked millions who had never given a thought to the issue. It probably stunned the president. Yet the particular cases had been before the courts for years. And great care was taken in its implementation, which was placed in the hands of local courts. They were permitted to use guidelines reflecting local situations.

In the border states, considerable progress was made toward compliance within two years. In the Deep South it became clear that compliance would take time and might involve violence. In September 1957 Little Rock, Arkansas, became the focal point of southern resistance. Governor Orval E. Faubus used the National Guard to prevent nine black children from entering that city's Central High School.

President Eisenhower countered by providing the children with federal military protection, and they were subsequently enrolled. Explaining his decision to send troops to Little Rock, Eisenhower revealed on nationwide television his own awareness of Cold War pressures. After speaking of "the harm that is being done to the prestige and influence and indeed to the safety of our nation and the world," he concluded: "Our enemies are gloating

LITTLE ROCK

For a moment all I could hear was the shuffling of their feet. Then someone shouted, "Here she comes, get ready!" . . . The crowd moved in closer and then began to follow me, calling me names. I still wasn't afraid. Just a little bit nervous. Then my knees started to shake all of a sudden and I wondered whether I could make it to the center entrance a block away. It was the longest block I ever walked in my whole life. . . .

I stood looking at the school—it looked so big! Just then the guards let some white students go through. The crowd was quiet. I guess they were waiting to see what was going to happen. When I was able to steady my knees, I walked up to the guard who had let the white students in. He didn't move. When I tried to squeeze past him, he raised his bayonet and

then the other guards closed in and they raised their bayonets.

They glared at me with a mean look and I was very frightened and didn't know what to do. I turned around and the crowd came toward me. They moved closer and closer. Somebody started yelling, "Lynch her! Lynch her!" I tried to see a friendly face somewhere in the mob—someone who maybe would help. I looked into the face of an old woman and it seemed a kind face, but when I looked at her again, she spat on me.

Source: Elizabeth Eckford, as quoted in Daisy Bates, *The Long Shadow of Little Rock* (New York: David McKay, 1962). Photograph by Wide World Photos.

over this incident and using it everywhere to misrepresent our whole nation."

Faubus's overwhelming victory in winning a third term as governor in August 1958 was also an endorsement of his segregation stand and a signal to the rest of the South. When the election returns were in, Harry Ashmore, liberal editor of the *Little Rock Gazette,* asserted that the moderate position was now "clearly untenable for any man in public life anywhere in the region. A period of struggle and turmoil lies ahead." The handful of black students in Little Rock were subjected to such harassment that the local school board soon asked for a suspension of the integration program. Attorneys for the school board argued that it could not at present put integration into effect because of "the total opposition of the people and of the State Governor of Arkansas." Over a reasonable length of time, perhaps, the situation would change.

Attorneys for the NAACP, led by their chief counsel, Thurgood Marshall, replied: "There can be no equality of justice for our people if the law steps aside, even for a moment, at the command of force and violence." The Supreme Court agreed and on September 12, 1958, unanimously denied the request. Seventeen days later it delivered an unprecedented written opinion on the case in which, to underscore their unanimity, all nine Justices were listed as coauthors. This opinion declared:

The constitutional rights of respondents [Negro children] are not to be sacrificed or yielded to . . . violence and disorder. . . . The constitutional rights of children not to be discriminated against in school admissions on grounds of race or color declared by this court can neither be nullified openly and directly by state legislators or state executives or judicial officers, nor nullified by them through any evasive scheme for segregation.

The outlook, however, remained bleak. By 1959, of the 2,985 biracial southern school districts, only 792 had been integrated. None were in the Deep South or Virginia, which had taken the lead in adopting the official policy of "massive resistance." The governor could close any school ordered integrated by the courts.

While concentrating first on the school issue, blacks soon broadened their campaign to every phase of life. What was at issue was not only school integration, but the entire range of southern laws and customs that confined black people to separate and almost always inferior facilities. On December 1, 1955, Rosa Parks, a middle-aged black woman, refused an order to give up her seat to a white person on a bus in Montgomery, Alabama. After her arrest, local blacks under the leadership of a young Baptist clergyman, Martin Luther King, Jr., organized a movement to boycott the city buses.

The boycott lasted for an entire year, until the Supreme Court ruled in favor of the blacks and forced the city to desegregate its public transportation system. That proved to be only the beginning of a massive nonviolent campaign to disrupt and undermine the racial caste system in the South.

Responding to the rising militancy, Congress in 1957 and in 1960 passed the first federal civil rights acts in almost a century. Broad at the outset, these acts, as adopted, were largely confined to the right to vote. They made the procedure for federal intervention in this critical field so difficult that any gains were nullified. Nevertheless, the two measures revived dormant federal commitments. "I don't believe you can change the hearts of men with laws or decisions," Eisenhower had said, urging caution in implementing the *Brown* ruling. A few years later, Martin Luther King, Jr., observed: "The law may not change the heart—but it can restrain the heartless." That much and more, sometimes with far-reaching consequences, the law and continued black agitation were to undertake.

THE NEW LOOK IN FOREIGN POLICY

The Republicans took office promising a "new look" in foreign policy. Rather than pursue the negative Democratic policy of containment, they proposed to "liberate" the nations in communism's grip, "roll back" Soviet power in Eastern Europe, and "unleash" Chiang Kaishek in Asia. The architect of this ambitious program, John Foster Dulles, was an intractable and evangelical anti-Communist. But despite the considerable influence Dulles exerted on foreign policy, the Eisenhower years showed no significant break with the containment policies of the previous administration.

Eisenhower moved more cautiously than Dulles's rhetoric dictated. His military experience had taught him to hate war, and his search for "conciliation and compromise" appeared to be genuine. Dulles actively pursued a diplomacy of rhetoric and alliance. He sought to bolster anti-Communist regimes and to undermine Communist ones. But even if Eisenhower placed few restraints on this policy, he kept American troops out of combat.

Diplomacy by Rhetoric

Having ended the war in Korea with the armistice of July 27, 1953, the Eisenhower administration tested its "new look" in Europe. The death of Stalin in 1953 had resulted in a shared leadership in the Soviet Union, with Georgi Malenkov emerging as the new premier. He suggested "peaceful coexistence" with capitalist countries. He also relaxed controls over the peoples of Eastern Europe. That step led to an uprising in East Berlin in June 1953 that quickly spread across East Germany. This revolt, a forerunner of others in 1956, had to be suppressed by Soviet tanks and troops. "You can count on us," Dulles had told the peoples of Eastern Europe in January 1953. But in this instance, as in the others, he did nothing to implement his pledge.

For the president, "fiscal morality" meant balancing the budget, a goal attainable only by reducing military spending. Conforming to the president's guidelines, the National Security Council as early as October 1953 announced a new military strategy. Dulles soon called it "massive retaliation." Others justified it by another phrase, "more bang for a buck." Under the new "basic decision," dependence on the army's costly ground forces would be reduced or eliminated. As a bonus, the United States would no longer be lured into "police actions" like that in Korea.

Security would be attained by emphasizing air power, in which the United States still led the world. The administration would simply let the Communists in Moscow and Peking know that any new menace to American security would be met by nuclear and thermonuclear assaults on their cities and civilians. Since the United States had already used two nuclear bombs and had threatened to employ nuclear weapons in Korea, its NATO allies shuddered at the thought that any military showdown with the Soviet Union could easily obliterate all of Europe.

Despite the president's great prestige, this "basic decision" also caused trouble in the armed services. Within the Department of Defense itself, it fanned already dangerously tense interservice rivalry by its massive favoritism toward air power. The reasoning behind it was soon proved wrong by the steeply rising prices of modern air equipment and installations. By the end of 1954, "massive retaliation" had become synonymous with

massive annihilation. The USSR had detonated its own thermonuclear bombs and had developed delivery systems like SAC's. America was confronted with a "balance of terror." Dulles responded with still another empty verbal triumph: brinksmanship, the art of going "to the brink of war without being scared." But when it came to new nationalist movements that threatened American interests, the United States would not rely on rhetoric alone.

The New Nationalism: Iran, Guatemala, and Vietnam

With the collapse of colonial rule in Asia, Africa, and the Mideast, the United States faced the task of converting nationalist movements into anti-Communist allies. There were times when that objective could be realized only by helping to destroy or immobilize the movements themselves.

In Iran, Mohammed Mossadegh headed a movement that seized power in 1951 and proceeded to nationalize the Anglo-Iranian Oil Company—a combine which exploited Iran's oil reserves largely for the profit of non-Iranians. Iran was not only an oil-rich nation, but one that bordered the Soviet Union. When American officials concluded that the new government was coming under Communist influence, the United States stopped aid to Iran. It sent CIA agents to help subvert the Mossadegh regime, and provided the military equipment that enabled the Shah of Iran in August 1953 to regain control.

The payoff came in the form of a pro-Western ally, a much larger percentage of Iranian oil production, and a legacy of American intervention in the internal affairs of Iran that came back to haunt the United States twenty-six years later when the Shah's repressive regime was overthrown and replaced by an equally repressive but staunchly anti-American government.

Encouraged by its success in Iran, the United States prepared to deal with a challenge in its own hemisphere. In Guatemala, a Communist-backed reformist, Colonel Jacobo Arbenz Guzmán, headed a new government and confiscated lands belonging to the monopolistic United Fruit Company. Dulles in March 1954 successfully pushed through a resolution at the Tenth Inter-American Conference declaring "international communism. . . . incompatible with the concept of American freedom." Meanwhile, the CIA engineered a coup that toppled the constitutional Arbenz regime.

The deposed president appealed to the UN, but in vain. This was an internal matter, Dulles argued, that concerned only the OAS. When the USSR presented a similar argument to justify intervention in Czechoslovakia and Hungary, the United States reacted with outrage.

With considerably less success, the United States sought to bolster its defenses in Asia, where a nationalist movement was threatening to undermine one of the last bastions of colonialism: Indochina, a mid-nineteenth-century creation consisting of the three ancient kingdoms of Laos, Cambodia, and Vietnam. With Britain and Holland on their way out as Asian powers, the United States wished to help the French retain these valuable possessions, especially after Chinese intervention in Korea.

The situation in Indochina differed in one major way from that in other European colonies overrun by Japan. Elsewhere, the Japanese had found it advantageous to use Western-educated native leaders as occupation administrators. In Indochina, the Japanese had less need of native leaders because of the pro-Vichy French there. The nationalist Indochinese, more profoundly hostile to imperialism than most people under British rule, were driven underground. Like the partisans in Nazi-occupied countries of Europe during the war, they soon fell under the domination of highly skilled Communists led by the Russian-trained Ho Chi Minh, who had begun to work against French rule long before World War II.

The principal nationalist group in Indochina was the Vietminh in Vietnam, whose standing by the end of World War II was enhanced by its success in liberating portions of the north from the Japanese. In September 1945, its leaders had proclaimed the Democratic Republic of Vietnam, with Hanoi its capital and Ho Chi Minh its president. While colonialism crumbled elsewhere, the French sought to maintain full control over Indochina.

In September 1946, Ho Chi Minh returned from consultations in Paris disenchanted with the French attitude toward independence. By December, clashes in the north had grown into a general war. The rivalry grew more intense after June 1949. The French, having successfully set up former native rulers as puppets in Cambodia and Laos, now tried the same tactic in Vietnam. Their puppet here was Bao Dai, from an old ruling family, who had no popular following and preferred life in Paris or the French Riviera to Saigon.

This challenge led the Vietminh to intensify and extend its military activity. The emergence of the People's Republic of China in October 1949 gave a tremendous boost to Vietminh morale and soon to Vietminh strength. Early in 1950 China formally recognized the Hanoi regime. The United States and Britain, concerned at this time about French support for NATO in Europe, responded by recognizing the Saigon regime of Bao Dai. More than that, the Truman administration began to offset Chinese aid to Ho with American aid to Bao.

When the Korean conflict ended, the United States greatly enlarged its assistance to the French. By the end of 1953, American taxpayers were paying two-thirds of the cost of the French military effort, or about $1 billion per year. But it could not save the French after their main army, early in 1954, allowed itself to be trapped at Dienbienphu.

The siege of Dienbienphu intensified the debate in Washington. Eisenhower had already stated that Southeast Asia was of "transcendent importance" to American security: "You have a row of dominoes set up, and you knock over the first one, and what will happen to the last one is the certainty that it will go over very quickly."

But while taking this stance, Eisenhower resisted the advice to commit American troops. As he told a press conference on February 10, 1954: "I say that I cannot conceive of a greater tragedy for America than to get heavily involved now in an all-out war in any of those regions, particularly with large units."

Within the next several months, Eisenhower, often independent of advice from close associates, made good his promise to avoid American involvement. The French, their forces near exhaustion in Dienbienphu, urgently requested United States intervention. On April 3, 1954, Dulles, with Admiral Arthur W. Radford, chairman of the Joint Chiefs of Staff, met in private with congressional leaders to request authorization for an American air strike on Dienbienphu from navy carriers. The congressmen said no. Eisenhower refused to sanction unilateral American military action. On April 10, Dulles flew to London to seek British support, but did not get it.

On April 16, in a speech before the American Society of Newspaper Editors (intended apparently as an administration trial balloon), Vice-President Nixon declared that "if to avoid further Communist expansion in Asia and Indochina we must take the risk now of putting our boys in, I think the Executive has to take the politically unpopular decision and do it." The reaction was clearly negative. The House at this time had under consideration a rider to an appropriations bill seeking to limit the president's authority to send troops anywhere in the world without congressional consent. Eisenhower's threat to veto the bill helped kill the rider.

By the time Dienbienphu surrendered to Ho Chi Minh on May 7, 1954, the representatives of nine powers—France, the People's Republic of China, the USSR, Britain, the United States, the two Vietnams, Cambodia, and Laos—had already convened at Geneva to work out some arrangements in the light of the inevitable collapse. Dulles did not attend these discussions, which were certain to end with something less than complete victory over the Communists. The Geneva settlement, complicated and ambiguous, was meant to be temporary.

Its armistice agreement, secured on July 20, provided for a military truce between the Vietminh and the French military command, the latter openly acting for its Saigon puppet regime. The truce divided Vietnam along the 17th parallel. North of the line, Vietminh armies were to "regroup"; south of it, the armies of the French. Although Ho Chi Minh controlled two-thirds of the country, he withdrew his forces to the north, convinced that he would easily win the country-wide elections in July 1956.

Not until January 1955 did the French turn back the Saigon regime to Bao Dai and his "strongman," Prime Minister Ngo Dinh Diem. Fearful of a Communist victory, Diem found reasons for putting off the elections. Meanwhile, the United States gradually replaced the French in South Vietnam and increased its aid to Diem's regime, despite a campaign of suppression and political and religious murders that offended even his American friends. Although American aid was based upon the willingness of South Vietnam to undertake "needed reforms," Diem's government proved slow in doing anything. But the United States was reluctant to cast him adrift.

Within South Vietnam, the pro-Communist guerrillas stepped up their attacks on the regime. By 1959 the North openly aided these attacks, and in September 1960 Ho formally recognized the Vietcong as the National Front for the Liberation of South Vietnam. Within the first year of the Kennedy administration, the Vietcong had grown to nearly 10,000. The South Vietnamese Army was

unable to restrain them, and the new president felt it necessary to send his vice-president, Lyndon B. Johnson, on a fact-finding mission. Obviously, the debate over the United States role in Vietnam had by no means been settled.

Diplomacy by Alliance

Frustrated in his efforts to "liberate" Eastern Europe, Dulles envisioned encircling the Communist world with a series of military alliances by which the United States promised to defend member nations against aggression. Diplomacy by alliance would become, in fact, a hallmark of the Dulles approach in foreign affairs. The policy met with varied success. In Asia, repeated failures to check communism led Dulles to seek a collective organization that would serve as a counterpart to NATO in Europe. But he was turned down by significant new countries such as India, Burma, Indonesia, and Ceylon. They resented American intrusion and feared that efforts to isolate China might just provoke that country.

Two mainland countries, Pakistan and Thailand, along with the Philippines, Australia, and New Zealand, proved more responsive. At Manila in September 1954 they met with the United States, Britain, and France and created the Southeast Asia Treaty Organization (SEATO). The signers agreed to meet any "common danger" from "Communist aggression" in accordance with their own "constitutional processes." In case of Communist threats short of armed attack, they would simply "consult" on what should be done. In the meantime, by a provision often overlooked, and perhaps meant to be, they were obliged "to strengthen their free institutions" in order to prevent Communist provocation. No SEATO armed force similar to NATO's was contemplated or created; thermonuclear weapons were to provide security.

Between SEATO countries in the Far East and NATO countries in the West lay the oil-rich Middle East. Arab nationalism, already inflamed by the creation of Israel in 1948, was reinforced after 1952 by the overthrow of King Farouk in Egypt. A new Egyptian republic emerged, with Colonel Gamal Abdel Nasser as its strongman. He had ambitions to unite the neighboring Arab lands under Egyptian leadership. An obvious first step was eliminating the remains of colonialism, most evident in Britain's control of a powerful military base

Postwar Alliances

Members of SEATO

Nations having bilateral treaties with the U.S.

Communist bloc

at the Suez Canal. Dulles hoped to draw Nasser toward the West by pressing the British to yield the base. Reluctantly, they did.

To close the gap between SEATO and NATO, and thereby "create a solid band of resistance against the Soviet Union," Dulles had been promising a Middle East defense organization. In February 1955, Turkey and its neighbor Iraq, meeting at Baghdad, signed a mutual defense treaty. Britain, Pakistan, and Iran also subscribed. These arrangements became known as the Baghdad Pact, under which the Middle East Treaty Organization (METO) was formed. The United States agreed to "cooperate with" but not join the organization. Widespread sympathy for Israel, especially among American Jews, who contributed heavily to the urban vote, made the administration not wish to appear too close to the Arab powers, who had sworn to destroy the Jewish state. Dulles also feared that open American participation in METO, which ran across the USSR's southern frontier, might provoke the Soviets.

To Dulles's great discomfort, Egypt also stayed out. Nasser wished freedom of action in playing off the USSR and the West against each other. His policy paid dividends in September 1955, when Egypt and the Soviet Union made an arms deal. Dulles, along with Britain and the World Bank, soon offered to help Egypt build the Aswan Dam. The project was to make much more of the Nile's water available for irrigation. Nasser accepted the American offer in July 1956. But within a week, certain anti-Western gestures prompted Dulles to withdraw it. On July 26, Egypt responded by announcing the nationalization of the Suez Canal. Egypt would use the canal tolls to construct the dam itself.

Rising tensions led Israel to launch an invasion of Egypt in October 1956, with the declared objective of destroying the bases from which raids had been made on its territory. Israel's action was followed by the remarkable Anglo-French invasion of the Suez region. Even more remarkable was the collaboration of the United States and the Soviet Union in the United Nations General Assembly, where they jointly condemned this resort to arms by NATO nations. The General Assembly then voted to organize a force to supervise a cease-fire.

But the UN call for peace went unheeded until the USSR threatened to intervene unilaterally with "volunteers." American threats combined with those of the USSR brought the Israeli invasion to a stop a week later. The first detachments of the United Nations Emergency Force began to arrive on November 15 to help keep the peace. But this was only a stopgap measure that solved nothing in the Middle East. And the NATO alliance was slow to recover.

When the Soviets continued to arm Arab nations, METO members called on the United States to join the Baghdad Pact. This the administration refused to do. Instead, in a message to Congress in January 1957, the president asked for endorsement of the Eisenhower Doctrine, a unilateral warning to the USSR that the United States would defend the entire Middle East against Soviet attack.

Congress foresaw no direct Soviet attack, only increased Soviet subversion. It withheld approval until March of that year. Then, by a joint resolution, it gave the president, at his discretion, power to use American forces to help any Middle East nation, at its request, to resist "armed attack from any country controlled by international communism." In July 1958, following an anti-Western revolution in Iraq that led eventually to its withdrawal from the Baghdad Pact, the United States and Britain sent troops to Lebanon and Jordan to prevent similar uprisings in those countries.

CONCILIATION AND CONFRONTATION

Soviet-American cooperation in the UN on the issue of Egypt and Israel early in November 1956 was the last glimmer of the "thaw" that had momentarily relaxed Cold War tensions. After Stalin's death in 1953, the Soviet Union had made a series of conciliatory moves. It recognized the Federal Republic of West Germany, signed a peace treaty with Japan, and ended the four-power occupation of Austria and recognized its independence. In June 1955, Premier Nikolai Bulganin, who had succeeded Malenkov, and Nikita Khrushchev, the Communist Party head, paid a visit to Marshal Tito's Yugoslavia.

In defiance of Stalin in 1948, Tito had set up his own version of a Communist state. Now, Tito, Bulganin, and Khrushchev declared openly that "differences in the concrete forms of socialist development are exclusively the concern of the peoples of the respective countries." This acknowledgment of the first break in the Soviet structure was to have far-reaching consequences in Europe and Asia.

The high point of "peaceful coexistence" came in July 1955, when the Big Four—the United States, the USSR, Britain, and France—met in Geneva for the first summit conference since World War II. On the agenda were such troublesome old subjects as the unification of Germany, European security, and disarmament. But since they were abrasive issues, they were not pressed. The best that could be said of the conference was the "spirit of Geneva" that it fostered.

Eisenhower took a conciliatory stance: "There are no natural differences between our peoples or our nations. There are no territorial or commercial rivalries. Historically, our two countries have always been at peace." But upon returning from Geneva, Eisenhower sounded a note of warning: "We must never be deluded into believing that one week of friendly, even fruitful negotiations can wholly eliminate a problem arising out of the wide gulf that separates East and West."

Although the United States and the USSR remained militarily the world's superpowers, each capable of annihilating the other, both were to find themselves increasingly frustrated in their attempts to control other nations. Preoccupied with each other, the two superpowers seemed incapable or unwilling to grasp the implications of the revolutions that were transforming large segments of the world. All too often, they failed to understand the need of colonial and oppressed peoples to determine their own destinies. That failure would have profound consequences for the future of peaceful coexistence in a rapidly changing world.

The Second Eisenhower Administration

As the election of 1956 approached, the Republicans had every right to feel confident. "By virtually every economic measure," wrote *Time*, "1956 was the greatest year in history." Setbacks in foreign affairs had not dimmed Ike's popularity, and his heart attack in 1955 and serious surgery in 1956 brought him closer still to the people. Dependent on the general's personal appeal, Republican leaders urged him to run again, despite his health. He was renominated by acclamation, along with Vice-President Nixon.

Eisenhower's illnesses and Nixon's controversial reputation made many Democrats feel they had a chance at the White House. Despite Truman's opposition, Adlai E. Stevenson easily won renomination, with Senator Kefauver as his running mate. The Democrats made what they could of the threat of a Nixon succession, of economic discontent in the farm belt, and of the failure of the "new look" in foreign affairs. But Eisenhower's personal appeal carried him to victory even more decisively than in 1952.

With 34,751,000 votes to Stevenson's 25,427,000, he won 58 percent of the ballots. In the electoral college his margin was 457 to 73. At the same time, the Democrats maintained their 49 to 47 margin in the Senate, and enlarged by two seats their comfortable majority in the House. Not since the time of Zachary Taylor had a president been elected without carrying at least one house of Congress for his party.

In his second inaugural address, January 21, 1957, Eisenhower expressed his continuing hopes for coexistence when he said: "We honor, no less in this divided world than in a less tormented time, the people of Russia. We do not dread, rather do we welcome, their progress in education and industry." A few months later the president and the American people suffered a shock which suggested that they would not, after all, welcome Soviet progress quite so heartily.

On October 4, 1957, within six weeks after reporting the first successful tests of an intercontinental ballistic missile, the Soviet Union electrified the world by using the missile's rocket engine to launch the first unmanned space satellite, Sputnik I. During the course of the next year, the successful launching of four American satellites brought some comfort. It was dissipated by the Soviet success on January 2, 1959, with Lunik I, the first space vehicle to traverse the full distance of about 250,000 miles to the moon. Lunik did not hit the moon, but soared into space to become the first artificial planet in orbit around the sun. Two months later, on March 10, the United States successfully put a planet of its own in orbit. The next stage in space exploration involved putting a man in orbit around the earth. This feat, and more spectacular ones, were accomplished in the sixties.

During Eisenhower's second administration, the United States suddenly found itself shuffling along with a slowdown in business expansion, a disturbingly high level of unemployment, inflation, and serious racial strife. In distressed areas such as the coal regions of Pennsylvania, West Virginia, Kentucky, and the old industrial regions of New England, structural unemployment had become part of the way of life. In other sections of the country, unemployment among blacks grew especially acute. Besides encountering almost universal discrimination in the job market, blacks were prevented by lack of educational opportunities from seeking white-collar work.

The continued rapid mechanization of agriculture, meanwhile, and the operation of the price-support program for staples both so favored large farm corporations that farm family income fell off. Those who fled the land for the towns swelled the ranks of the unemployed.

The Eisenhower administration had come into office after crusading against Democratic corruption. In mid-1958, however, the administration was hit by revelations of scandals so far-reaching that Sherman Adams, the confidential assistant to the president, was forced to resign. The depth of the party's trouble on all fronts was disclosed in the 1958 congressional elections, when it suffered a defeat like those of the early New Deal years. The shadow cast by these elections was deepened during the administration's last two years when Dulles's death in May 1959 left the president largely on his own to face new crises in foreign affairs.

Coexistence and New Tensions

Using the occasion of the Twentieth Party Congress in February 1956, Nikita Khrushchev startled the world by revealing the crimes of Stalin, supporting the idea of "different paths to socialism," and suggesting the need for less rigid restrictions than those sanctioned by Stalin. This bold move, along with Khrushchev's endorsement of peaceful coexistence, his trip to the United States, and his refusal to support Mao Tse-tung's call for wars of national liberation, would soon drive a wedge between the USSR and China.

The Soviet Union found itself charged with appeasement of capitalism and with betrayal of Marxist-Leninist principles. When de-Stalinization led Poland and Hungary to seek those "different paths to socialism," the Chinese used the occasion to exploit the weaknesses in Soviet leadership and to assert their own leadership in the Communist world.

Both the Polish and Hungarian "counterrevolutions" had reached their turning points in October 1956, when the world and the UN were absorbed in the Mideast crisis. Convinced that the uprisings had been "provoked by enemy agents"

rather than Stalinist oppression, Khrushchev sent troops to crush the Hungarian revolt and tightened controls elsewhere. At the same time, he secured his position at home. In March 1958 he became premier as well as party chief.

Bolstered by space triumphs and missile gains, Khrushchev took some steps to ease the Cold War tensions. During Vice-President Nixon's visit to Moscow in July 1959, Khrushchev engaged in such a high-spirited TV debate with the vice-president that Nixon came to believe the premier should get to know more about the United States at first hand. This led to a prompt invitation from the president, and on September 14, Khrushchev arrived. After a peaceable address at the UN and a lively cross-country speaking tour, he met with Eisenhower with such success that a summit conference was informally agreed upon to continue "the spirit of Camp David," the site of their talks.

But the thaw proved to be short-lived. On May 5, 1960, less than two weeks before the scheduled summit conference in Paris, an American U-2 reconnaissance plane was shot down over Soviet territory. Before acknowledging the truth of Soviet protests that the plane was on a regular spying mission, the administration trapped itself in a web of denials and half-truths. "Up until now," *The Wall Street Journal* observed, "it has been possible to say to the world that what came out of the Kremlin was deceitful and untrustworthy but that people could depend on what they were told by the Government of the United States. Now the world may not be so sure that this country is any different from any other."

Although Eisenhower announced that further surveillance flights over the Soviet Union had been suspended and would not be resumed, the damage had been done. The spirit of Camp David instantly dissolved in Paris, with Khrushchev demanding American apologies for "aggression" and punishment of those responsible. The conference ended within three hours.

While East-West relations deteriorated, relations among the anti-Communist powers also worsened. Relations with Charles de Gaulle, who had become premier of France in June 1958, became so bad that he refused to allow the United States to build NATO missile bases in France or to store nuclear weapons there. The violence that broke out in the Congo when Belgium reluctantly agreed to the formation of the Republic of the Congo in June 1960 further weakened Western unity and raised the curtain on a new region for East-West conflict. Many Japanese resented the continuing United States occupation of Okinawa and the militarization of their homeland. When Eisenhower visited the Far East in June 1960, anti-American demonstrations in Tokyo became so militant that he was officially advised to omit Japan from his itinerary because his personal security could not be assured. Meanwhile, much closer to home, Latin America had begun to erupt.

Cuba and Castro

The deterioration of the American position in Latin America had become dramatically evident in April and May 1958, when Vice-President Nixon visited a number of countries in an effort to revive friendliness toward the United States. He was hostilely received, and in Venezuela mobs stoned and spat upon him. When Eisenhower responded by sending warships and alerting marines at nearby Caribbean bases, he succeeded only in reviving the image of Yankee imperialism. The most important challenge to United States dominance, however, came in Cuba. On January 1, 1959, Fidel Castro successfully completed a five-year struggle to overthrow the Batista regime.

Determined to make a radical social revolution, Castro moved to end the colonial relationship that had bound the Cuban government and economy to the United States. The massive confiscation of foreign holdings he ordered simply reflected the extent of outside control. More than 40 percent of sugar production, for example, and 90 percent of the cattle ranches and mineral resources belonged to American interests.

Of course, Castro's economic program and repression of civil liberties angered the United States. It led many middle-class Cubans to flee to the United States. The rapid shift of Castro to the radical Left and the Soviet trade bloc came as no surprise to the last American ambassador to Cuba: "It was not Castro's predilection for Communism," he explained, "but his pathological hatred of the American power structure as he believed it to be operative in Cuba together with his discovery of the impotence of Cuba's supposedly influential classes, that led him eventually into the Communist camp. Only from that base, he thought, could he achieve his goal of eliminating American influence."

With the threatened spread of *Fidelismo* elsewhere, the United States chose to rely on the traditional ways of dealing with hemispheric trouble. Before Eisenhower left office, he agreed to a CIA plan by which an anti-Castro army of Cubans would be trained in the United States and then landed in Cuba in early 1961. Meanwhile, the Cuban issue played a curious role in the 1960 presidential election. Kennedy talked vaguely of intervention and support of "non-Batista democratic anti-Castro forces." Nixon tried to cover his awareness, as vice-president, of the preparations already under way to overthrow the Castro regime.

Eisenhower's Farewell

Eight years in office proved a great strain on the Republican party, especially since it had failed to balance the budget, reduce the national debt, end the upward wage-price spiral, restore farm income, and significantly cut taxes. It had also failed to roll back the Communists and restore the good old days of continental security. When Republican delegates convened in the summer of 1960 to choose a candidate, the conservatives were in command of the party machinery. On the first ballot the convention named Richard M. Nixon for

WORDS AND NAMES IN AMERICAN HISTORY

There could scarcely be a more American word than *Yankee*, but few people seem to agree about its original meaning or even about how the word came into being. It is clear, though, that the word was known but not commonly used before the American Revolution. The meaning of the term depends entirely on the context in which it is used. For foreigners, outside the United States, *Yankee* applies to all Americans. To American southerners, it means anyone from the North (which in this context includes folks from California). In the northern states, it denotes people from New England. In that northeastern corner of the country it is often used to distinguish people of old English descent from newer immigrants from Ireland, Italy, Canada, and so on. Most of these later immigrants were and are members of the Roman Catholic Church, so the term *Yankee* even has religious overtones of Protestantism and Puritanism. Finally, we should bear in mind that "the Yankees" are for millions of Americans first and foremost a baseball team.

president. As a sop to the party liberals, it chose Henry Cabot Lodge, United States delegate to the UN, as his running mate.

After his extraordinary performance in a series of primaries, Senator John F. Kennedy of Massachusetts clearly overshadowed the other presidential aspirants at the Democratic convention in Los Angeles. He won on the first ballot. Fearful of the effects of the strong civil rights plank and of Kennedy's Catholicism, the Democrats, in an attempt to hold the South, nominated Senator Lyndon B. Johnson of Texas for vice-president. In Kennedy's acceptance speech, he talked about "a New Frontier—the frontier of the 1960s—a frontier of unfulfilled hopes and threats."

The campaign was highlighted by the first television debates between presidential candidates, from which Kennedy seemed to have gained more than his opponent. Nixon, moreover, had aroused considerable controversy in his political past, much of it revolving around the tactics he had used to advance his career. Nor did Eisenhower's lukewarm support help. (When asked at a press conference to name the major decisions in which his vice-president had participated, Eisenhower replied, "If you give me a week, I might think of one.")

When the results were in, Kennedy had become the first Catholic president and at forty-three, the youngest ever to be elected. But his winning margin was a mere 113,000 out of a record 68.8 million votes cast. He won by less than two-thirds of 1 percent of the popular vote, and there were reports of election irregularities in Illinois and Texas, which Kennedy narrowly carried. What probably saved him from defeat was the solid support he received from Catholics and blacks. At least 70 percent of these voters, according to reliable estimates, endorsed him. No doubt his personal intervention on behalf of Martin Luther King, Jr., who had been jailed in October for violating a Georgia Jim Crow law, helped to bring out the black vote.

Before leaving the White House, the still popular Ike wanted to give the American people the "most challenging message" possible, and he did

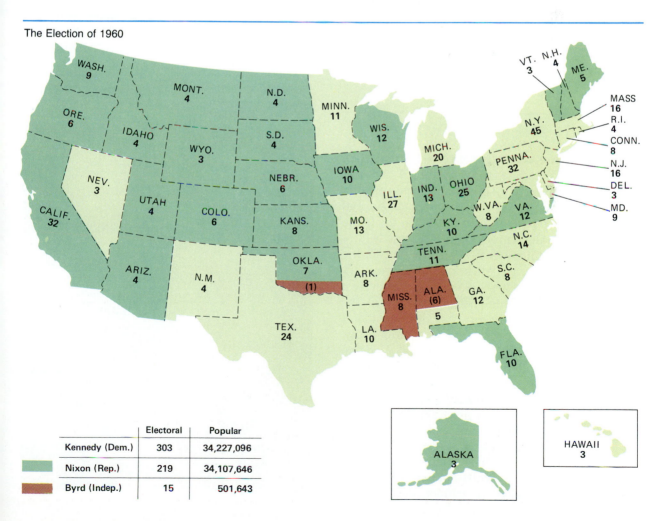

The Election of 1960

		Electoral	Popular
	Kennedy (Dem.)	303	34,227,096
	Nixon (Rep.)	219	34,107,646
	Byrd (Indep.)	15	501,643

so admirably in his famous "farewell speech" of January 17, 1961:

This conjunction of an immense military establishment and a . . . permanent armaments industry of vast proportions . . . is new in the American experience. The total influence—economic, political, even spiritual—is felt in every city, every state house, every office of the federal government. We recognize the imperative need for this development. Yet we must not fail to comprehend its grave implications. . . .

In the councils of government we must guard against the acquisition of unwarranted influence, whether sought or unsought, by the military-industrial complex. The potential for the disastrous rise of misplaced power exists and will persist. We must never let the weight of this combination endanger our liberties or democratic processes.

The warning came too late. By 1961, the "military-industrial complex" had virtually overrun the traditional instruments of American government. With confrontation in Asia and the Caribbean, the military ascendancy, like the Cold War itself, seemed destined to remain a part of the American way of life. The newly elected president must have sensed that, and he paid little heed to Eisenhower's warning. During the first year of the Kennedy administration, the military budget increased 15 percent.

JFK AND THE NEW FRONTIER

Young as he was when he delivered his first State of the Union message in January 1961, John F. Kennedy had already served fourteen years in Congress, the last eight in the Senate. He had been exposed to politics even earlier, in the home of his father, millionaire Joseph P. Kennedy, ambassador to Britain under FDR. It took time for the politically conservative environment to wear off. In Congress, he had associated with the severest critics of his party's China policy, helped carry the McCarran Internal Security Act over Truman's veto, and refrained from criticizing McCarthy. Elected to the Senate in 1952, Kennedy made an unsuccessful bid four years later for the Democratic vice-presidential nomination.

Despite his congressional experience, the young senator still lacked a national reputation; moreover, he had to overcome a political tradition in which no Catholic had ever been elected to the presidency. But he did have some important assets. His long contact with politics had not affected him personally: his candor was credible,

his humor fresh, his modesty unfeigned. And he possessed, besides, an excellent war record and an efficient campaign organization. These assets proved to be more than enough to win the Democratic nomination, but only barely so to defeat Nixon in the election.

No sooner had Kennedy taken office than he surrounded himself with youthful advisors pledged, like himself, to get the country moving again. The Kennedy team, David Halberstam would later write, "carried with them an exciting sense of American elitism, a sense that the best men had been summoned forth from the country." The dynastic heir apparent, his younger brother Robert, became attorney general with perhaps broader powers than any previous holder of that office. Robert S. McNamara, one of the statistical geniuses of the Ford Motor Company, was named secretary of defense. His assignment was, with the aid of computers, to bring Pentagon feuding under civilian control. McGeorge Bundy, a Harvard intellectual, became Kennedy's special assistant for national security affairs. In that position he may have exerted more influence than the official secretary of state, Dean Rusk. Walter C. Heller, chairman of the Council of Economic

President John F. Kennedy. (*John F. Kennedy Library*)

Advisors, offset the traditional attitudes of the secretary of treasury, the banker C. Douglas Dillon. During the campaign, Kennedy had compared himself with his also youthful rival. Nixon, said Kennedy, "has the courage of our old convictions." But "the New Frontier is here, whether we seek it or not." The New Frontier promised to pioneer in new approaches to old problems and to get the country moving again. The direction in which the country moved—toward confrontation at home and abroad—suggested how dependent Kennedy's approaches remained on the policies of his predecessors.

Civil Rights and Civil Conflict

In his first State of the Union message, Kennedy enumerated the "unfinished and neglected tasks" that faced his administration. Because of financial need, "one-third of our most promising high school graduates" prematurely ended their education. Persistent recession resulted in the "highest peak in our history" of "insured unemployment." Long-term "distressed areas" continued to decay. The drain of American gold abroad, largely for military assistance, menaced the stability of the dollar.

Growing numbers of poor old people, the ill, and others in need were neglected. Natural resources as basic as the water supply were being wasted.

But all these issues paled before that of racial equality, which Kennedy in 1961 failed to mention. By the summer of 1963, the hundredth anniversary of the Emancipation Proclamation, it dominated the headlines. Nearly a decade since the Supreme Court had ruled school segregation illegal, the pace of integration made a mockery of the court-ordered "all deliberate speed." When blacks sought admission to state universities, moreover, the resulting showdowns required the application of federal force. At the University of Mississippi, Governor Ross Barnett tried to block the admission of James Meredith. At the University of Alabama, Governor George Wallace stood in the doorway, as he had promised, to stop two black students from entering.

Meanwhile, the attack on segregation had broadened. The sit-in at the Woolworth lunch counter in Greensboro, North Carolina, on February 1, 1960, mushroomed into hundreds of similar demonstrations, all designed to desegregate public facilities and transportation. By deliberately violating Jim Crow laws, black youths defied traditions and customs that had maintained gen-

Segregated drinking fountains were symbolic of the separate worlds of the South until the 1960s. (*Elliott Erwitt, Magnum Photos*)

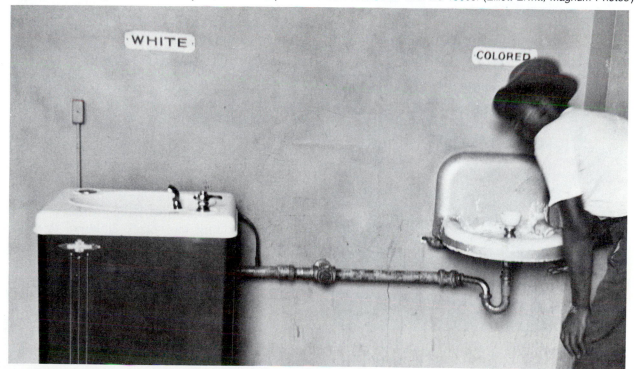

erations of white supremacy in the South. By 1963, an estimated 70,000 blacks and white sympathizers had participated in these demonstrations, and more were to come.

To the embarrassment of American foreign policy, the headlines of 1963 made known around the world the brutality with which civil rights demonstrations were suppressed. Several weeks after Kennedy proposed his first civil rights legislation to Congress, mass demonstrations began in Birmingham, Alabama. Before the summer was over, more than 800 cities and towns had had peaceful protests, often in the face of dogs and fire hoses employed by the police.

Leadership in the black nonviolent movement rested with Martin Luther King, Jr., a young minister from Atlanta barely in his thirties. If black people directed their appeal to the Christian conscience of white America, King argued, the walls of segregation and race hatred would inevitably crumble. What he asked of his followers was nonviolence, Christian love, and a belief in the essential decency of people. It would not be easy.

The climax of the nonviolent campaign came on August 3, 1963, when over 200,000 blacks and sympathetic whites marched on Washington, D.C., demanding "freedom now." Although an impressive demonstration, it was not the massive show of nonviolent civil disobedience that had been planned. Less radical organizations and leaders prevailed, and President Kennedy invited them to the White House. The March on Washington is best remembered for Martin Luther King's eloquent speech ("I Have a Dream") and the assembled multitude singing the anthem of the civil rights movement, "We Shall Overcome."

At the same time, however, the Washington rally revealed growing restlessness and divisiveness within the ranks of black leadership. It was most evident in the rapid emergence of Malcolm X, a brilliant Black Muslim leader and separatist. "They took it over," he said bitterly of the March on Washington.

It's just like when you get some coffee that's too black, which means it's too strong. What do you do? You integrate it with cream, you make it weak. But if you pour too much cream in it, you won't even know you ever had coffee. It used to be hot, it becomes cool. It used to be strong, it becomes weak. It used to wake you up, now it puts you to sleep. This is what they did with the march on Washington. Why, it even ceased to be a march. It became a picnic, a circus.

Several months before the March on Washington, on June 10, Medgar Evers, field secretary of the Mississippi NAACP, was murdered by a sniper. Less than a month after the March, a bomb exploded in the 16th Street Baptist Church in Birmingham, killing four black children. Perhaps, some argued, Martin Luther King had demanded too much of his people. His movement had yielded some positive results, but at a cost in human lives and frustration that many blacks found difficult to bear. "It's simply not possible," said Malcolm X, "to love a man whose chief purpose in life is to

Martin Luther King: "We will match your capacity to inflict suffering with our capacity to endure suffering. We will meet your physical force with our soul force. We will not hate you, but we cannot obey your unjust laws. Do to us what you will and we will still love you. Bomb our homes and threaten our children; send your hooded perpetrators of violence into our communities and drag us out on some wayside road, beating us and leaving us half dead, and we will still love you. But we will soon wear you down by our capacity to suffer. And in winning our freedom, we will so appeal to your heart and conscience that we will win you in the process." (*Declan Haun/Black Star*)

SUPERPOWERS IN THE MISSILE AGE

In Birmingham, Alabama, fire hoses and police dogs were used to disperse civil rights demonstrators. (*AP/Wide World Photos*)

humiliate you, and still be what is considered a normal human being." The black movements, increasingly independent of white liberal sympathizers, began to take on different dimensions.

Although much of the activity was confined to the South, there were no grounds for optimism or smugness in the North. If anything, the frustration and betrayal of expectations were even deeper and potentially more explosive. Even as northern whites reacted with anger to the televised brutalities inflicted on southern blacks, they paid little attention to the discrimination in housing, employment, and education in their own region. Black sharecroppers and farm laborers were flowing to northern cities in record numbers in the 1950s

and 1960s. Many whites fled to safer urban areas and to the suburbs, leaving the urban areas more and more isolated and explosive. Between 1950 and 1960, for example, the twelve largest cities lost more than 2 million white residents and gained over 2 million blacks. These cities rapidly succumbed to the poverty and frustration of their new residents.

Although northern blacks had the vote and civil rights, these were not of much value to someone facing unemployment and hunger. That was the message Malcolm X was hammering home, and he found an audience. "Well, I am one who doesn't believe in deluding myself," he said of white America. "I'm not going to sit at your table and watch you eat, with nothing on my plate, and call myself a diner. Sitting at the table doesn't make you a diner, unless you eat some of what's on that plate."

Space, Militarism, and Prosperity

"To get the country moving again" in the economic sphere, the new economists of the Kennedy administration explored every avenue for using the energies of the entire population. Early in 1962, the president proposed a broad tax cut for consumers as one way to stimulate demand for goods. But this measure, like so many of his proposals, made little headway in Congress.

The president enjoyed far more success when he asked for appropriations for defense and space. "Anybody who would spend $40 billion in a race to the moon for national prestige is nuts," Eisenhower said after he had retired from the presidency. Kennedy, although at first as doubtful as his conservative predecessor, soon held other ideas. In May 1961, under the heading: "Urgent National Needs," he told Congress: "No single space project in this period will be more impressive to mankind" than that of "landing a man on the moon and returning him safely to earth."

During Kennedy's administration, annual space appropriations soared to over $5 billion. To those who questioned such an expenditure, he responded at Rice University: "But why, some say, the moon? . . . And they may well ask, why climb the highest mountain? Why, thirty-five years ago, fly the Atlantic? Why does Rice play Texas?"

The business upswing in 1962 and 1963 followed new expenditures and appropriations not only for the space program, but for the related missile program and other "national security" items. While the strength of the country in foreign affairs depended on the strength of the domestic economy, it seemed that the strength of the domestic economy depended on the volume of military spending. Kennedy, as a senator, had become by 1959 one of the most active opponents of the growing militarization of the foreign aid program. As president, his efforts to reverse this trend were strengthened by his opposition to the military straitjacket of "massive retaliation" that so confined the Eisenhower-Dulles policy of deterrence. "We intend," he declared in July 1961, "to have a wider choice than humiliation or all-out nuclear action."

THE DIPLOMACY OF FLEXIBLE RESPONSE

Although Kennedy hoped to identify the country's power with its political ideals, its strength with its social values, he warned that "we must never be lulled into believing that either [the Soviet Union or China] has yielded its ambitions for world domination." Having accepted this basic premise of the Cold War, there were tragic ironies in Kennedy's attempts to find new approaches to foreign policy and to use the advantages of living with different cultures and governments.

While he tried to apply political solutions to "limited" international incidents, he felt obliged to build up the armed services. The "big stick" could still reduce the likelihood of extreme provocation. Admitting that, he could not stop the rapid development of the instruments of "massive retaliation." In 1962, military expenditures went over the $50 billion mark for the first time since the Korean conflict.

By then, Kennedy had taken certain steps in pursuit of a more "flexible response" in foreign policy. The Peace Corps, in which young men and women would volunteer their technical skills to help underdeveloped nations, was a different and more creative approach to diplomacy. Far less imaginative was the president's response to continuing trouble in Latin America. Determined to try to stop the spread of *Fidelismo*, Kennedy in March 1961 outlined a plan, modeled on the Marshall Plan, for an Alliance for Progress with Latin American nations. With United States assistance, these nations were expected to put into practice much needed land reforms and accelerate economic development.

But even while proposing such a program, the Kennedy administration, like its predecessors and successors, bolstered repressive regimes whose primary virtue was their commitment against communism. If that suggested inconsistency or even political bankruptcy, the response of the United States to the revolutionary upheavals in Cuba and Southeast Asia provided tragic confirmation.

Cuba: The Bay of Pigs and the Missile Crisis

In one of his last acts as president, Eisenhower had broken off diplomatic relations with Cuba in protest against "a long series of harassments, baseless accusations, and vilifications." At least one of those accusations, however, was soon proved far from baseless. For nine months, as Castro had charged, about 1500 anti-Castro Cuban exiles had been secretly training in Guatemala under United States CIA men for an invasion of their island. Mass internal uprisings were certain to follow their arrival, the exile leaders promised, and the Castro regime would be overthrown.

After repeated assurances by a unanimous Joint Chiefs of Staff, some of his own "new frontiersmen," and an enthusiastic Allan Dulles (who reminded Kennedy of how his CIA had overthrown Guatemala's Marxist government), the new president permitted the invasion to start and assured the press that "there will not be, under any conditions, any intervention in Cuba by United States forces." Five days later, on April 17, 1961, the exile forces attempted to land at the Bay of Pigs, 90 miles from Havana. At the same time, a CIA-hired firm on Madison Avenue was issuing press releases in the name of the "Cuban Revolutionary Council," which called for a "coordinated wave of sabotage and rebellion."

The anticipated popular uprising failed to happen. United States air support was inadequate; the few B-26s furnished the exiles were no match for Castro's air force, and the assault instantly collapsed. Over 1200 of the invaders were taken prisoner and held for almost two years.

The day after the abortive invasion, the president cautioned Castro that "our restraint is not inexhaustible" and that the United States would act "alone, if necessary" to protect its security. Using an odd analogy, he also warned the Soviet Union that "we do not intend to be lectured on intervention by those whose character was stamped for all time on the bloody streets of Budapest."

Castro tried to strengthen his defenses against any further United States aggression. But when the Soviet Union took this opportunity to install missile sites in Cuba, manned by Soviet technicians and capable of obliterating targets within a range of 2000 miles, it was more than the United States was willing to tolerate. On October 22, 1962, on nationwide television, Kennedy took a calculated risk that brought the world to the brink of nuclear war. He ordered Khrushchev to remove the missiles and instructed the navy to intercept and turn back Soviet ships headed for Cuba. (The Joint Chiefs of Staff and former Secretary of State Acheson had argued instead for a direct air strike on the missile sites.)

Recognizing the gravity of Kennedy's stand, the Soviet Union agreed to recall the ships and to remove the missile bases. Kennedy, on his part, assured the Soviet leader—but only in the form of a tacit understanding—that the United States would refrain from offensive action to overthrow the Castro regime. Both leaders had made their point. Kennedy emerged with enhanced prestige. The Soviet Union came out of the crisis determined never again to be placed in a position of military disadvantage.

What small chance for success the Alliance for Progress may have had was gone in the face of Castro's performance. By 1963 it had become evident that countries below the border would find it impossible to carry out the reforms that would allow the development of broad-based capitalist economies. Nor would the United States tolerate "anti-imperialists" with a popular following who might undertake even more fundamental social changes. This was made clear in Guatemala before the elections scheduled there in November 1963.

Juan José Arévalo, a former president with a Marxist following and a strong record in agricultural reforms, was the leading candidate. As one high-level Kennedy official said of Arévalo early that year: "I don't give a damn whether he is or is not a communist. He talks like a communist, he acts like a communist, and if he's elected he'll be soft on communists." In March 1963, while CIA men at least turned the other way (some suppose they helped engineer the shift), President Miguel Ydígoras Fuentes was deposed by a military faction that installed the minister of defense as president, and the November elections were not held.

Despite the Cuban confrontation and the ongoing Berlin crisis, new hopes for a detente between the Soviets and the West came out of the deepening split between the USSR and China. These hopes were strengthened in July 1963 when the three nuclear powers (the United States, Britain, and the USSR) signed a treaty pledging themselves to end nuclear testing that "causes radioactive debris" outside their own borders. This was only a first step toward "the speediest possible achievement of an agreement on general and complete disarmament."

The three powers invited others to sign the treaty. In the West, Germany had misgivings. France, eager for nuclear arms of its own, was openly hostile. In the East, China denounced the Soviets and the Western powers. In the United States, and no doubt in the USSR, armament had gained the irreversible momentum of which Eisenhower had spoken in his farewell.

Kennedy and Southeast Asia

During the early months of his administration, Kennedy found himself spending a great amount of time on the struggle to control Laos. By May 1962 the Pathet Lao, a Communist guerrilla movement, controlled almost two-thirds of the small country, apparently with little popular opposition. The conservative, pro-Western regime, which the Eisenhower administration had supported, was finally forced to flee.

The Two Vietnams

17th parallel—the temporary division between North and South Vietnam established by the Geneva Conference in 1954

Communist countries

Allied with U.S.

Neutral countries

While Kennedy hurriedly sent protective naval and military contingents to neighboring Thailand, the United States and the Soviet Union used diplomatic channels to pave the way for a coalition government in Laos under Souvanna Phouma, an avowed neutralist. The Pathet Lao maintained its pressure. More important, it kept open the path of North Vietnamese aid to the Vietcong in South Vietnam over the Ho Chi Minh trail through southeastern Laos. Meanwhile, the CIA began to supply anti-Communist guerrillas operating behind the Pathet Lao lines, and the United States soon undermined the coalition government. With the Pathet Lao now on the offensive and the United States retaliating with secret bombing raids, the situation in Laos deteriorated.

Despite Kennedy's emphasis on developing political options, the most obvious product of "flexible response" became the elaboration and application of the concept of limited war. The fatal test of this policy came in Vietnam. Although Diem had refused to hold all-Vietnam elections in 1956 (correctly fearing he would lose), and despite the fact that he had violated his pledge to Eisenhower to make needed reforms, the United States remained committed to his regime. In October 1961, General Maxwell D. Taylor went to South Vietnam as Kennedy's special representative to appraise the situation. The result of that mission was a speedup in the flow of American instructors, pilots, and other military personnel.

By the end of 1962, after Taylor had become chairman of the Joint Chiefs, the number of Americans in South Vietnam had reached 10,000. Within five years, Under Secretary of State George Ball warned the president, the United States might have as many as 300,000 troops in Vietnam. Kennedy refused to believe it. "George," he replied, "you're crazier than hell."

Although Kennedy at first resisted both the "overmilitarization" and "over-Americanization" of the war in Vietnam, he soon found himself approving the growing military intervention. Embracing Eisenhower's domino theory, he declared in July 1963 that a United States withdrawal would "mean a collapse not only of South Vietnam but Southeast Asia. So we are going to stay there." American military assistance to the Diem regime soared, and the number of American military personnel edged toward 17,000.

Earlier, the Joint Chiefs had assured the president that 40,000 troops would "clean up the Vietcong threat." McNamara had concluded: "Every quantitative measurement we have shows we're winning this war." In the meantime Diem stepped up his attacks not on the Vietcong but on the Buddhists, who made up most of the opposition to the French-oriented Catholic ruling class.

As early as 1954, military experts continued right up to the fall of Dienbienphu to forecast that "the French are going to win." (A decade later, they shamelessly forecast the always imminent but yet somehow elusive American triumph.) But Kennedy had said, "I am frankly of the belief that no amount of American military assistance in Indochina can conquer . . . 'an enemy of the people' which has the sympathy and covert support of the people." The emergence of the Vietcong some years later apparently did not alter his conviction that "counterinsurgency" must fail "if its political objectives do not coincide with the aspirations of the people, and their sympathy, cooperation and assistance cannot be gained."

In keeping with these deeper feelings, Kennedy, in September 1963, declared of the South Vietnamese: "In the final analysis, it's their war. They're the ones who have to win it or lose it. We can help them as advisers but they have to win it." To improve the prospects of winning, South Vietnamese General Duong Van Minh, with American encouragement, on November 1, 1963, overthrew the Diem regime and shortly thereafter executed Diem and his brother. The new government (the first of nine in the next five years) was given prompt American recognition. By the time of Kennedy's assassination on November 22, however, it had won few military laurels.

On October 2, 1963, Kennedy had McNamara and Taylor announce from the White House the administration's intention of withdrawing most United States forces from South Vietnam by the end of 1965. Whether Kennedy could have done this will never be known. Within three weeks of Kennedy's assassination, McNamara and CIA chief John A. McCone visited Saigon. On their return, on New Year's Day 1964, they announced they had "told the junta leaders that the United States was prepared to help . . . as long as aid was needed." This only seconded President Johnson's New Year's Eve promise to them of "the fullest measure of support . . . in achieving victory."

While these commitments were being made, the American people and Congress were not informed of the full implications of United States involvement. That "credibility gap," as historian Walter La Feber would argue, "did not begin with Lyndon Johnson's presidency. In 1963 the gap measured the growing abyss between the actual situation in Vietnam and the self-assurance of the Kennedy Administration that it could manipulate military power to control nationalist revolutions."

Death of the President

On reviewing his first two years in office, Kennedy acknowledged a large degree of frustration. "The responsibilities placed on the United States are greater than I imagined them to be and there are greater limitations upon our ability to bring about a favorable result than I had imagined them to be. . . . It is much easier to make speeches than it is finally to make the judgments."

The German problem remained unsolved. The Communists made it even more vivid by building a wall, early in August 1961, separating East from West Berlin. Periodic crises raised the threat of armed confrontation. In Africa, emerging nations were throwing off the last vestiges of colonialism and moving toward a neutral position in the East-West conflict. In Asia, the United States deepened its involvement in Vietnam.

In space, Soviet scientists continued to set the pace. The big breakthrough came on April 12, 1961, when Major Yuri Gagarin successfully orbited the earth in a Soviet space capsule. On February 20, 1962, after preliminary flights in space by Commander Alan B. Shepard, Jr. (May 5, 1961) and Captain Virgil I. Grissom (July 21, 1961), Colonel John H. Glenn, Jr., became the first American to orbit the earth.

Congress generously appropriated funds for defense and space, but proved more reluctant when it came to social legislation and the protection of civil rights. As the black movement spread, white resistance hardened. Black frustrations made Martin Luther King's hold on black leadership more precarious, and the prospect of violent confrontation grew. Meanwhile, Kennedy's civil rights program went nowhere in Congress, along with his proposals to enlarge federal aid to education and extend Medicare to the aged.

This was the state of the world and the nation in the summer of 1963. The previous November, 51 million Americans, the largest ever in a nonpresidential year, went to the polls and broke tradition by fully supporting the administration in power. The Republicans were surprised as well by Richard Nixon's defeat in the California race for governor. The leading candidate for the Republican nomination in 1964 appeared to be Senator

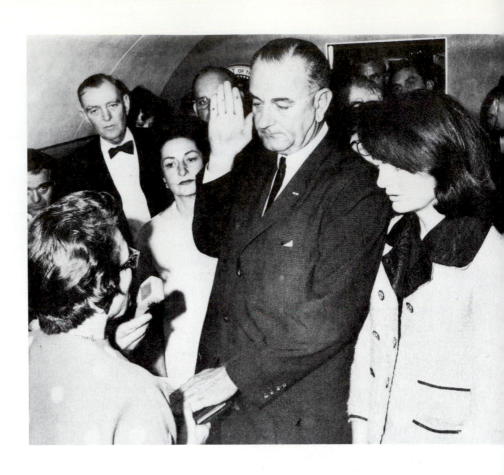

(above) Hours after the assassination of John Kennedy, Lyndon Johnson was sworn in as president, as Jacqueline Kennedy and Ladybird Johnson looked on. (*AP/Wide World Photos*)(right) Two days later, Lee Harvey Oswald, the suspected assassin, was shot to death in the Dallas city jail. (*Copyright 1963 by the Dallas Times Herald and photographer Bob Jackson*)

Barry Goldwater of Arizona, a staunch conservative who told an audience in November 1963 that the New Frontier had produced "1,026 days of wasted spending, wishful thinking, unwarranted intervention, wistful theories, and waning confidence." When asked to respond to such charges, Kennedy smiled and replied; "Not yet, not yet."

On November 22, 1963, Kennedy was in Dallas, Texas, to bolster his political position in that state. While riding in an open car, to the cheers of crowds lining the streets, the president was shot in the neck and head by an assassin. He died almost instantly. The tragic death of the young president threw the nation and the world into shock, mourning, and disbelief. The disbelief was compounded by the bizarre series of events that followed.

While a nationwide television audience looked on, Lee Harvey Oswald, the suspected assassin, was shot to death two days later by Jack Ruby, the proprietor of a small Dallas nightclub, who confronted Oswald as he was being escorted to the county jail. Although a special committee headed by Chief Justice Earl Warren could find no conspiracy in Kennedy's assassination, doubts and rumors persisted. In 1979, a congressional inquiry raised serious questions about whether Oswald had acted alone. Given all the bizarre events of the decade, the American people were prepared to believe almost anything.

SUMMARY

The eight years of the Eisenhower presidency were a time of relative peace and prosperity, although both domestic and international forces were building beneath the surface.

The Eisenhower administration, dedicated to the "middle way," was led by businessmen and lawyers. But even they were unable to cut government spending or stabilize agriculture. And the search for internal security continued, although Senator McCarthy's star began to wane in 1954, when he was censured by the Senate.

The most important domestic event of Eisenhower's first term was the Brown v. Board of Education decision by the Supreme Court, which ordered the desegregation of the public schools. Under Chief Justice Earl Warren, the Court began actively to protect the civil rights of racial and political minorities. The mood of black America now was far different; there was a new militancy and a new determination. The events at Little Rock in Arkansas in 1957, when the president sent federal troops to enforce the desegregation of the high school, symbolized both the depth of the resistance and the national commitment to change. The bus boycott in Montgomery, Alabama, in 1955–1956, marked the beginning of a massive nonviolent campaign to end the racial caste system in the South.

The "new look" in foreign policy, carried out by John Foster Dulles as secretary of state, was based on the idea of rolling back communism all over the world. It was a diplomacy of rhetoric, threat, and alliance in which the United States sought to bolster anti-Communist regimes and undermine Communist regimes. It relied on massive retaliation and brinksmanship to meet threats to world peace.

As a result of this policy, the United States intervened actively in Iran, Guatemala, and Vietnam to convert nationalist movements into anti-Communist allies. In Vietnam, the French were losing the war against the Vietminh, the Communist regime based in the North. Eisenhower had resisted the pressure to commit American troops, although the United States did extend aid to the French and did join in the truce negotiations at Geneva after the disaster of Dienbienphu in May 1954.

Gradually, the United States replaced the French in South Vietnam in support of a repressive anti-Communist regime. Pro-Communist guerrillas, supported by the North Vietnamese, continued the war—but now against the South Vietnamese Army instead of the French. These events and others in Southeast Asia led Dulles in 1954 to set up a new collective security alliance, SEATO, the counterpart of NATO in Europe. But no military force was created; thermonuclear weapons were to provide security.

In the Middle East, conflict between the oil-rich Arabs and the new state of Israel was a source of constant tension. In 1955 Dulles engineered the Baghdad Pact, under which METO, another collective security alliance, was formed. But the United States, because of Israel, did not openly join. Neither did Egypt, now under the leadership of Nasser and a new government. In July 1956, Egypt responded to American machinations in the Middle East by nationalizing the Suez Canal. In October, Israel invaded Egypt; this act was followed by an Anglo-French invasion of the Suez.

It took American-Soviet cooperation through the United Nations to force a cease-fire and avoid a new world war. But the peace was shaky, and the Middle East continued to be a powder keg. Soviet-American hostility and tension soon returned to pre-Suez levels. The Geneva Summit of 1955 had been the high point of "peaceful coexistence," and it had dealt with none of the real issues that divided the superpowers. The arms race and the rivalry continued.

Eisenhower's second administration was marked by spectacular Soviet advances in rocketry, a business slowdown, inflation, and racial strife. It was also marked by dissent within the Communist camp between China and Russia, by harshly suppressed uprisings in Poland and Hungary in 1956, and by the U-2 crisis in 1960, when an American reconnaissance plane was shot down over Soviet territory.

In addition, relations among the anti-Communist powers also worsened. Eisenhower had to omit Japan from his itinerary for a Far East tour in 1960 because of anti-American feeling there, and Vice-President Nixon was stoned on a visit to Venezuela. Nearer home, on January 1, 1959, Fidel Castro successfully completed a five-year struggle to overthrow the American-supported Batista regime. His hatred of the United States, fueled by American business's exploitation of Cuba, changed the whole situation in the Caribbean.

The election of 1960 brought John F. Kennedy to the White House—a Democrat, a Catholic, and the youngest president in American history. The Kennedy administration was staffed by youthful advisors and pledged to getting the country moving again, to the New Frontier. But many of its approaches to foreign and domestic problems were no different from those of preceding administrations.

Conflict over civil rights escalated, and the attack on segregation broadened. Before the summer of 1963 was over, peaceful protests had occurred in more than 800 towns and cities, and 200,000 blacks and whites had marched on Washington. But by this time there was division within the black leadership between the more moderate Martin Luther King, Jr., and separatist militants such as Malcolm X.

On the domestic front, the administration had far more success with defense and space programs than with measures to aid the economy. In foreign affairs, Kennedy attempted to reverse the trend toward the militarization of the foreign aid program by a diplomacy of "flexible response." It included such new ventures as the Peace Corps and the Alliance for Progress in Latin America. It also included the continuation of Cold War policies and the rapid development of new weapons.

Cuba continued to be a problem. Its leader had turned not only to the Soviet Union, but to the task of spreading *Fidelismo* throughout Latin America. American responses were conventional: an American-supported invasion, the Bay of Pigs, which ended in a fiasco in April 1961, and the threat of nuclear war in October 1962 over Soviet missile bases installed on the island, which was only 90 miles from the United States.

In Southeast Asia, Laos and Vietnam continued to be plagued by guerrilla wars, and the United States continued to be involved. The policy of flexible response became focused on the concept of "limited war," put into practice in Vietnam. By the end of 1962, there were 10,000 Americans in South Vietnam. By late 1963, the number was 17,000 and the predictions were still for an early and easy victory.

What would have happened can only remain conjecture, because on November 22, 1963, John F. Kennedy was assassinated in Dallas while riding through the city in an open car. The New Frontier was over.

Suggested Readings

Many works cited for Chapter 30 are valuable for this chapter as well. The best introduction to cultural developments in the 1950s is D. Miller and M. Nowak, *The Fifties: The Way We Really Were* (1977). Among the principal commentaries on society and culture in the fifties are D. Riesman, *The Lonely Crowd* (1950), and *Individualism Reconsidered* (1954); W. H. Whyte, Jr., *The Organization Man* (1956); C. W. Mills, *White Collar* (1951), and *The Power Elite* (1956); P. Goodman, *Growing Up Absurd* (1960); M. Mead, *And Keep Your Powder Dry* (1965); D. Bell, *The End of Ideology* (1959); D. M. Potter, *People of Plenty* (1954); and M. Kempton, *America Comes of Middle Age* (1963). A different kind of commentator but often compelling in his ability to probe society was Lenny Bruce, whose reflections are available in J. Cohen (ed.), *The Essential Lenny Bruce* (1967), and on several records. On the Beat Generation, see *Evergreen Review* (vol. 1, no. 2), devoted entirely to the "San Francisco Scene"; L. Lipton, *The Holy Barbarians* (1959); B. Cook, *The Beat Generation* (1971); A. Charters, *Kerouac* (1973); and D. McNally, *Jack Kerouac, the Beat Generation, and America* (1979). To understand the 1950s is also to visualize the decade, as in the photographs of Robert Frank in *The Americans* (reprinted 1969).

Insight into Eisenhower will be gained from his two volumes on the White House years, *Mandate for Change* (1963), and *Waging Peace* (1965). The best biographical study is S. Ambrose, *Eisenhower: Soldier, General of the Army, President-Elect, 1890–1952* (1983) and *Eisenhower: The President* (1984). See also H. S. Parmet, *Eisenhower and the American Crusades* (1972); and C. S. Alexander, *Holding the Line: The Eisenhower Era, 1952–61* (1975). The most perceptive memoir is E. J. Hughes, *The Ordeal of Power* (1963); accounts by insiders also include A. Larson, *Eisenhower: The President Nobody Knew* (1968); C. Bohlen, *Witness to History, 1929–1969* (1973); and R. M. Nixon, *Six Crises* (1962). For more critical views, see R. H. Rovere, *Affairs of State: The Eisenhower Years* (1956); I. F. Stone, *The Haunted Fifties* (1964); E. J. Dale, Jr., *Conservatives in Power: A Study in Frustration* (1960); and Herblock's contemporary cartoons and comments in *Here and Now* (1955), and *Special for Today* (1958). On farm policy, see L. Soth, *Farm Trouble in an Age of Plenty* (1957). On Robert A. Taft, see J. T. Patterson,

Mr. Republican (1972); on Adlai E. Stevenson, see J. B. Martin, *Adlai Stevenson and the World* (1977).

P. L. Murphy, *The Constitution in Crisis Times 1918–1969* (1972), is the best introduction to the Court. See also A. M. Bickel, *Politics and the Warren Court* (1965); P. B. Kurland, *Politics, the Constitution and the Warren Court* (1970); R. H. Sayler and others (eds.), *The Warren Court: A Critical Analysis* (1969); and E. Warren, *Memoirs* (1977). The desegregation decision is examined in R. Kluger, *Simple Justice: The History of Brown v. Board of Education and Black America's Struggle for Equality* (1976). On the southern response, see A. Lewis, *Portrait of a Decade* (1964); N. V. Bartley, *The Rise of Massive Resistance* (1969); R. Coles, *Children of Crisis* (1967); and a personal memoir, E. Huckaby, *Crisis at Central High: Little Rock, 1957–58* (1980). For other works on the civil rights movement, see literature cited for Chapter 32.

On McCarthyism and its origins, see the works cited for Chapter 30.

To the books on the Cold War cited in Chapter 30, add for the Eisenhower years the president's memoirs, *Mandate for Change* and *Waging Peace;* N. Graebner, *The New Isolationism* (1956); A. Wolfers (ed.), *Alliance Policy in the Cold War* (1959); E. Stillman and W. Pfaff, *The New Politics* (1961); R. A. Divine, *Eisenhower and the Cold War* (1981); H. A. Kissinger, *Nuclear Weapons and Foreign Policy* (1957), and *The Necessity for Choice* (1961); and H. Kahn, *On Thermonuclear War* (1960), an early "think-tank" product on the "unthinkable" balance of terror. On the nuclear arms race and efforts to control it, see H. York, *The Advisors* (1976); R. A. Aliano, *American Defense Policy from Eisenhower to Kennedy* (1975); R. A. Divine, *Blowing in the Wind* (1978); and M. Mandelbaum, *The Nuclear Question: The United States and Nuclear Weapons 1946–76* (1980). On Dulles, see H. J. Morgenthau, "John Foster Dulles," in N. Graebner (ed.), *An Uncertain Tradition* (1961); R. Goold-Adams, *John F. Dulles* (1962); M. A. Guhin, *John Foster Dulles* (1972); and T. Hoopes, *The Devil and John Foster Dulles* (1973). On Middle Eastern issues, see N. Safran, *The United States and Israel* (1963); H. Finer, *Dulles over Suez* (1964); H. Thomas, *Suez* (1967); and R. E. Neustadt, *Alliance Politics* (1970).

T. Draper, *Castro's Revolution* (1962); R. Ruiz, *Cuba: The Making of a Revolution;* and R. F. Smith, *The United States and Cuba* (1961) are useful introductions. H. Thomas, *Cuba* (1971), is a massive study. See also the contrasting views of two American ambassadors to Cuba, E. Smith, *The Fourth Floor* (1962), and P. W. Bonsal, *Cuba, Castro, and the United States* (1971). The literature on American policy after the Cuban revolution is cited in the Kennedy section. On the Guatemalan intervention of 1954, see S. Schlesinger and S. Kinzer, *Bitter Fruit* (1982), and R. H. Immerman, *The CIA in Guatemala: The Foreign Policy of Intervention* (1982), and the literature on the CIA cited for Chapter 33.

The place to begin any examination of Vietnam is F. Fitzgerald, *Fire in the Lake: The Vietnamese and the Americans in Vietnam* (1972). J. Buttinger, *Vietnam: A Political History* (1970), and E. Hammer, *The Struggle for Indochina 1940–1955* (1966), provide background, along with B. Fall, *The Two Viet Nams* and *Vietnam Witness 1953–1966* (1966). See also R. Shaplen, *The Lost Revolution: The U.S. in Vietnam 1946–1966* (1966), and *Time Out of Hand: Revolution and Reaction in Southeast Asia* (1969). On the deepening American military involvement, see the literature on Kennedy below and readings suggested for Chapter 32.

The 1960 campaign is covered in T. H. White, *The Making of the President* (1960). The Kennedy presidency as viewed by members of the White House staff may be found in A. M. Schlesinger, Jr., *A Thousand Days* (1965), and T. C. Sorenson, *Kennedy* (1965). For more critical assessments, see T. Wicker, *Kennedy Without Tears* (1964); H. Fairlie, *The Kennedy Promise* (1973); and H. S. Parmet, *Jack: The Struggles of John F. Kennedy* (1980), and *JFK: The Presidency of John F. Kennedy* (1983).

Economic policy in the 1960s is examined in J. Galbraith, *The New Industrial State* (1967); W. W. Heller, *New Dimensions of Political Economy* (1966); S. E. Harris, *Economics of the Kennedy Years* (1964); and The Editors of Fortune, *America in the Sixties: The Economy and the Society* (1960). The question of poverty in the affluent society was newly opened by M. Harrington, *The Other America* (1962). H. Miller, *Rich Man, Poor Man* (1964), is a commentary on Harrington's thesis. See also G. Myrdal, *Challenge to Affluence* (1963); R. L. Heilbroner, *The Limits of American Capitalism;* and O. Lewis, *La Vida: A Puerto Rican Family in the Culture of Poverty—San Juan and New York* (1966). For the literature on the civil rights movement, consult Chapter 32.

R. Hilsman, *To Move A Nation* (1967), is a firsthand report on Kennedy's foreign policy. For a critical assessment, see R. Walton, *Cold War and Counter-Revolution* (1972). On the Bay of Pigs, see T. Szulc and K. E. Meyer, *The Cuban Invasion: The Chronicle of a Disaster* (1962). On the Cuban missile crisis, see E. Abel, *The Missile Crisis* (1966); R. A. Divine (ed.), *The Cuban Missile Crisis* (1971); and R. F. Kennedy, *Thirteen Days*, a personal memoir. The ultimate failure of the Alliance for Progress is analyzed in J. Levinson and J. de Onis, *The Alliance That Lost Its Way* (1970). On Kennedy and Vietnam, see D. Halberstam, *The Best and the Brightest* (1972), and the literature cited for Chapter 32.

On Kennedy's assassination, see *A Concise Compendium of the Warren Commission Report* (1964); E. J. Epstein, *Inquest* (1966); W. Manchester, *Death of a President* (1967); and P. Scott and others, *Dallas and Beyond* (1976).

CRUMBLING CONSENSUS

Chapter 32

On Air Force One, bringing the body of John F. Kennedy back to Washington, D.C., the most dramatic presidential succession in American history took place. Jacqueline Kennedy, her clothing still stained with the blood of her husband, looked on as the oath of office was administered on November 22, 1963, to the new president, Lyndon B. Johnson. Even as Americans recovered from the shock of presidential assassination, they would learn to live in the next decade with new violence, turbulence, and uncertainty.

The deepening war abroad and civil strife at home shattered whatever remained of the consensus and complacency of the fifties. There were moments when the very survival of American society seemed threatened—not, as in the previous decade, from nuclear holocaust or Communists, but from America's own disenchanted people.

The kinds of investigatory commissions established in the sixties said a great deal about what absorbed the American people. The concerns and revelations were far different from those of the fifties, when attention had been focused on the past political "sins" of well-placed government officials. The Warren Commission examined the circumstances surrounding Kennedy's assassination. The Kerner Commission, appointed by President Johnson on July 27, 1967, investigated widespread racial violence. It concluded that the basic cause was the "white racism" that pervaded American society. The National Commission on the Causes and Prevention of Violence examined still other civil disorders, including the Democratic party's national nominating convention of 1968. It reported that "in numbers of political assassinations, riots, politically relevant armed group attacks, and demonstrations," the United States was among "the half-dozen most tumultuous nations in the world."

Major investigations of campus disorders, drugs, and pornography were also undertaken. And America's sudden awakening to the contamination of the environment would produce a huge investigatory literature that warned of cosmic disaster.

The American experience in the sixties has been compared to weird pieces of science fiction or comic book fantasy. The scenario features assassinations, cities burned out by their own people, street warfare, masked soldiers in fogs of tear gas, massed youth sprawling over the countryside at rock festivals, campus buildings under siege, cult murders, terrorist bomb factories, and courtroom shootouts. The sixties, journalist Gary Wills recalled, sometimes conveyed the feeling of being locked up with a madman whose power made no sense.

The crises of the decade were made to

order for the mass media. This was a time when government officials, politicians, professors, and priests competed with athletes, hippies, yippies, and revolutionaries for machine-made national images. Television, often feared as an instrument of centralized government information control, became a major instrument of popular education and expression. More effectively than any other medium, television brought all of life into focused image, turning all kinds of people into media performers. Combat teams and tormented villagers in Vietnam, starving children in Biafra, moonbound astronauts, striking Mexican-American grape workers, the welfare poor in New York City hotels, protest marchers, courtroom characters, celebrities from the world of sport and entertainment—all entered the living rooms of America.

Throughout the upheavals of the sixties, the war in Vietnam persisted and widened. Except for the Civil War, no previous conflict had so divided and alienated American society. With each passing month, with each new casualty list, with every promise of success, the divisiveness and disenchantment grew.

Perhaps no political rally or protest march had as much impact on the American people as one issue of *Life*, June 27, 1969, in which twelve pages were given over to the photographs of the 242 American boys who had been killed in action the week of May 28 to June 3. Not an exceptional week, said *Life*, but the "average for any seven-day period during this stage of the war." To look at these men, some of them in uniform, some wearing the caps and gowns of their high school graduation, was to be impressed not only with their youth, but with how few of them resembled the students whose protests dominated the media. The war was largely being fought by young people— white and black—from the working class, for whom draft deferments and counseling were not so easily within reach.

The war was brought home to Americans in still another way. In April 1971 a military court sentenced First Lieutenant William Calley to life imprisonment for murdering twenty-two Vietnamese civilians at My Lai village in 1968. This trial dramatized for the American people— as no previous event had done—the question of national complicity in the Vietnam holocaust. As more evidence came to light of other massacres, of saturation bombing, of forced evacuation of villages in "free-fire" zones, the line between legitimate and illegitimate warfare, if such distinctions made any sense, virtually disappeared. Who were the criminals: soldiers carrying out orders, or the men who gave them? The court-martial failed to resolve that question.

To some critics, it was Lyndon Johnson's war. But that would be a gross distortion of the historical record. The war was not the exclusive responsibility of any one president. Although Congress had not declared war, it had given the president— by overwhelming majorities—the power and the hardware required to wage war. The deepening involvement in Vietnam proved to be a tragic inheritance for LBJ, who had envisioned a Great Society that would unify the nation and inspire the world. Vietnam determined otherwise. By 1968, President Johnson himself concluded that the only way to unify the nation was to end the war and his own political career. ■

CATCH-22

The bizarre world captured by Joseph Heller in *Catch-22* (1961) did not seem at all incomprehensible to a generation that would be caught up in the tragedy of Vietnam.

"Is Orr crazy?"

"He sure is," Doc Daneeka said.

"Can you ground him?"

"I sure can. But first he has to ask me to. That's part of the rule."

"Then why doesn't he ask you to?"

"Because he's crazy," Doc Daneeka said. "He has to be crazy to keep flying combat missions after all the close calls he's had. Sure, I can ground Orr. But first he has to ask me to."

"That's all he has to do to be grounded?"

"That's all. Let him ask me."

"And then you can ground him?" Yossarian asked.

"No. Then I can't ground him."

"You mean there's a catch?"

"Sure there's a catch," Doc Daneeka replied.

"Catch-22. Anyone who wants to get out of combat duty isn't really crazy."

Source: * Joseph Heller, *Catch 22* (New York: Dell Publishing Company, 1961), pp. 46–47. Copyright 1955, 1961 by Joseph Heller. Reprinted by permission of Simon & Schuster, a Division of Gulf & Western Corporation.

THE GREAT SOCIETY

Few American presidents other than Lyndon Johnson had entered the White House with such long careers in politics. Although he retained the top Kennedy men in his cabinet, notably Rusk and McNamara, the contrast between the personalities and political styles of Johnson and Kennedy could hardly have been more striking. Johnson's wealth had been self-made, not inherited. He had none of Kennedy's charisma or urbaneness and few of his cultural pretensions. He was as skeptical of intellectuals as they were of him. ("I don't believe that I'll ever get credit for anything I do in foreign affairs, no matter how successful it is, because I didn't go to Harvard.")

But LBJ knew how to get things done. He was a shrewd manipulator, and he had already demonstrated in his long years as Senate minority and then majority leader an uncanny mastery of political techniques. (One aide called him "a Machiavelli in a Stetson.") He invited and praised "consensus," while making certain his position always prevailed.

LBJ's vision of the Great Society, although absorbing much of Kennedy's New Frontier, was more heavily influenced by his admiration for the New Deal. The ambitious domestic program he proposed was aimed at improving the quality of American life, maximizing opportunities for those who had been denied access to the "affluent society." Like FDR, he felt the need to secure Americans from the fear of hunger, unemployment, and old age. Unlike FDR, he felt the need to attack the special problems plaguing black Americans. Although Johnson's civil rights record in the Senate had been spotty, he seemed ready to extend his commitment to social justice to black people. The racial strife and agitation Johnson inherited as president also provided a stimulus for action exceeding that of any previous occupant of the White House.

Not all the Great Society measures proved workable. Some were too hastily drawn, and others suffered from lack of funding. But the commitment of the federal government to the concept of the welfare state seemed unquestioned. And it was this aspect of the Great Society that would arouse the most controversy and backlash in the seventies and eighties. For Johnson, the more immediate problem was how to wage a war on poverty while expanding the war in Vietnam. The cost of pursuing both wars at once proved too much. In the clash of priorities, the Great Society and the people of Vietnam were the principal victims.

The Transition Years

No sooner had Johnson become president than he proposed to Congress, as an appropriate memorial to Kennedy, that it act on a long-delayed prosperity tax cut and a civil rights bill. The tax reform bill helped a sagging economy. The Civil Rights Act of 1964, the most sweeping such legislation in American history, enlarged *federal* power to protect voting rights, to provide open access for all races to public facilities, to speed up school desegregation, and to ensure equal job opportunities in business and unions.

At the same time, Johnson set the stage for his Great Society program. In his first State of the Union message in January 1964, he told Congress: "Unfortunately, many Americans live on the outskirts of hope, some because of their poverty and some because of their color, and all too many because of both." To raise the hopes of such people, he proposed a "war on poverty in America." This war Congress also endorsed, in August 1964, when it appropriated almost $950 million for ten separate antipoverty programs to be supervised by a newly established Office of Economic Opportunity. Key features included (1) a Job Corps to train underprivileged youth for the labor market; (2) work-training programs to employ them; (3) a domestic peace corps (officially, Volunteers in Service to America, VISTA) to enlist the privileged on behalf of the poor; and (4) a Community Action program that would involve the poor themselves in the administration and planning of the "war."

Encouraged by his legislative triumphs, Johnson eagerly anticipated the presidential election of 1964. What he wanted was a massive triumph at the polls that would make him president in his own right. He was not disappointed. The Republicans proved accommodating in this respect by providing Johnson with an ideal target. Determined to offer the American electorate "a choice, not an echo," they nominated Senator Barry Goldwater of Arizona, star of the strong conservative wing of the party. Although segregationist Governor George C. Wallace of Alabama also entered the race by running in a number of Democratic primaries, Goldwater's nomination had deprived him of conservative support. At the Democratic convention, Johnson easily won the nomination; after a spirited contest for LBJ's nod, Senator Hubert H. Humphrey of Minnesota, identified with the liberal wing of the party, won the vice-presidential spot.

Goldwater stood for dismantling the welfare state, and many Americans suspected that the social security system would be among the victims. Nor did he help his candidacy when he suggested that NATO commanders be permitted to employ tactical nuclear weapons in a crisis. During the campaign, new uncertainties in world affairs made such statements seem particularly irresponsible. Nikita Khrushchev was out of power in the USSR, and China exploded an atomic bomb.

While Goldwater evoked visions of atomic confrontation, Johnson appeared to be a man of peace and moderation. "We don't want our American boys to do the fighting for Asian boys," he declared on September 25. "We don't want to get involved . . . and get tied down in a land war in Asia."

With 61 percent of the popular vote, Johnson surpassed even FDR's record in 1936. It was the sweeping mandate he had sought, and he intended to make the most of it. Even while preparing to escalate the Vietnam war, Johnson assured the American people: "This nation is mighty enough—its society is healthy enough—its people are strong enough—to pursue our goals in the rest of the world while still building a great society here at home."

Great Society Legislation

The Great Society was the central theme of LBJ's first message to the Eighty-ninth Congress in January 1965. When that Congress finished its business in the fall of 1966, it had made one of the most constructive records in history. It had approved nearly every one of the Great Society measures the president had proposed.

The first, adopted in April 1965, was the Elementary and Secondary Education Act, which made available for the first time massive amounts of federal aid ($1.3 billion) to school districts. If further incentive was needed for desegregation, this act provided it. The United States Office of Education, as a condition for federal aid, now demanded proof that beginning with the school term of 1966–67, desegregation both for students and for teachers had been undertaken in good faith. Despite vigorous opposition to these new "guidelines," significant increases were reported in the number of blacks going to school with whites.

A second far-reaching measure was the adoption of the Medicare amendments to the Social Security Act, which the president approved on July 30, 1965. The aged had won a significant victory over the relentless lobbying of the American Medical Association. Medicare provided hospital insurance and certain posthospital care for virtually all Americans on reaching the age of sixty-five. It also made available inexpensive medical insurance covering doctor bills, diagnostic procedures, and other medical services and supplies.

In addition, the Eighty-ninth Congress ended the discriminatory national origins quota system in immigration; provided special assistance to improve conditions in the depressed states of the Appalachian region; enacted programs to promote the purification of smog-laden air and the restoration of polluted waterways; created the National

Originally the word *grapevine* meant just what it suggests on the surface: vines that bear a fruit known as a grape. For reasons that are not clear, about the middle of the nineteenth century it began to take on a completely different meaning, often in the combined form, *grapevine telegraph* (the latter word itself being an invention of the 1840s). The *grapevine* came to mean a somewhat mysterious but very effective network of oral communication, an informal network that often conveyed scandalous, secret, or dangerous information. It came to be particularly associated with black people. Such networks did exist on and among slave plantations. After the Civil War, with so many blacks still unable to read or write, there remained a strong need for such networks. Blacks themselves embraced the term. As one popular black song of the 1960s went, "I heard it through the grapevine." Many readers of this book will be entirely familiar with the expression.

Foundation of the Arts and Humanities to encourage cultural and artistic development; and passed a Truth in Lending Act to give consumers greater protection in credit transactions.

Recognizing the critical problems of urban Americans, Congress agreed to a rent supplement program for low-income families and established the Department of Housing and Urban Development (HUD). To head it, Johnson appointed Robert C. Weaver, making him the nation's first black cabinet member. Massive new appropriations were made for older Great Society programs, including the war on poverty, regeneration of cities, and the space program. By mid-1966, the United States was looking to the moon to the tune of over $5 billion annually. This sum in the federal budget was exceeded only by expenditures for national defense and fixed commitments such as interest payments and disbursements for social security.

When the Eighty-ninth Congress adjourned in October 1966, the American economy had enjoyed six solid years of extraordinary economic expansion. But the Great Society, like the New Frontier, raised the expectations of many Americans without necessarily fulfilling them. Despite the prosperity, social dissatisfaction deepened. Life on many family farms remained dreary; city dwellers were exposed to unprecedented violence and fear. Black Americans still found it hard to get jobs or to share in the affluence that was so visible around them. They were constantly exposed to success, and yet denied it. So frustration mounted, especially among the young.

"The way these kids see it," one black remarked, "equality is like Whitey holds you by the belt at the starting line until everyone else is halfway around the track, then gives you a big slap on the rump and says, 'Go baby, you're equal.' Takes an unusual man to win a race like that. It's easier to shoot the starter."

The Black Revolution

While the "We Shall Overcome" spirit generated by the March on Washington still prevailed, the struggle to achieve racial justice in the South continued to attract national attention. During the Freedom Summer of 1964, thousands of young blacks and white students converged on Mississippi to register its nearly one million black residents. By the end of the summer, three youths—two whites and one black—had been murdered by terrorists in Neshoba County. Numerous civil rights workers had been beaten, more than a thousand had been arrested, and scores of churches and homes had been burned or bombed.

As the white youths returned to their homes and campuses in the North, the Freedom Summer revealed growing rifts within the civil rights movement. Many of these stemmed from black fears of white domination and a growing determination to plot their own strategies and make their own decisions. Beyond this urge to be independent even of their white allies, there persisted the more complex and age-old problems of white patronization.

Stokely Carmichael, a young black civil rights worker and leader in the Student Nonviolent Coordinating Committee (SNCC), tried to explain some of the dimensions of the problem. "Too many young middle-class Americans," he explained, "like some sort of Pepsi generation, wanted to come alive through the black community."

They say things without realizing what they're saying. You know—"Yeah, man, I really dig that." . . . They use words out of context. They want to be accepted right away, without being accepted for their work. They want to be accepted as a Negro, not as an individual. "Look, I'm not like the other whites you know, I dig you." The white boy putting on a show was resented. As much as it would be resented if I put on a show to show how white I was—how much I had absorbed of the culture.

THE INHERITANCE

"I wondered what it was like to live. . . . Countless nights I cried myself to sleep. Sometimes I could look at my mother and I could feel the pains her body was undergoing because of the hard work done each day to make ends meet. . . . Sometimes mother would see the tears falling from my eyes. . . . When she asked me what was wrong I told her that something stuck in my eyes or a bug was in them. I must have asked God why a thousand times but I never got an answer. Was nine of us kids in the family and we all had to work. I stayed out of school a lot of days because I couldn't let my mother go to the cotton field and try to support all of us. I picked cotton and pecans for two cents a pound. I went to the fields six in the morning and worked until seven in the afternoon. When it came time to weigh up, my heart, body and bones would be aching, burning and trembling. I stood there and looked the white men right in their eyes while they cheated me, other members of my family, and the rest of the Negroes that were working. There were times when I wanted to speak, but my fearful mother would always tell me to keep silent. The sun was awful hot and the days were long. . . . The cost of survival was high. Why I paid it I'll never know."

Charles Wingfield, a 16-year-old honor student, placed a petition on the wall of his school in Lee County, Georgia. It called for improved equipment for the all-black school. He was expelled for his action. Parents voted to boycott the school and some 1000 students (out of an enrollment of 1300) refused to attend classes. Charles Wingfield was never readmitted. He joined the Student Non-Violent Coordinating Committee (SNCC).

Source: Howard Zinn, *SNCC: The New Abolitionists* (Beacon Press, 1964), 136–37. Photograph by Danny Lyon, Magna Photos.

Before the civil rights coalition disintegrated altogether, it achieved its most dramatic hour in early 1965. The failure of certain southern states to enforce the voting provisions of the Civil Rights Act of 1964 had brought a new wave of black demonstrations, particularly in the town of Selma, Alabama. On February 1, 1965, Martin Luther King, Jr., and 770 other blacks were arrested. Early in March, Alabama state troopers and auxiliaries, using tear gas and whips, frustrated an attempted civil rights march from Selma to Montgomery, the state capital.

After President Johnson federalized the Alabama National Guard and ordered it to protect the marchers (Governor Wallace having earlier refused to do so), the procession of some 25,000 blacks and sympathetic whites from all over the country began. The night the march ended, one participant—a white woman from Detroit—was killed by Klan gunfire. Earlier, a Boston minister was slain. Their deaths enlarged the decade's toll of political activists.

With President Johnson himself now declaring that "we shall overcome," Congress responded by passing the Voting Rights Act of 1965. This measure suspended literacy tests and other devices still used to confine voting to whites. It empowered "federal examiners" to register qualified voters. The act also directed the attorney general to start suits against the surviving poll taxes in *state* elections. (The Twenty-fourth Amendment to the Constitution, ratified January 1964, had abolished the poll tax in federal elections.) On March 17, 1966, the last of the poll taxes was killed by a decision of the Supreme Court. By then a new drive to register the two million eligible blacks in eleven southern states was underway, and many black candidates appeared on the ballots within a short time.

Although the Voting Rights Act of 1965 enhanced black political power in the South, this significant triumph did little about growing racial conflict throughout the country. Public opinion polls only confirmed black suspicions that white racial attitudes had remained essentially the same. Most whites still preferred to live in exclusively white neighborhoods, feared or shunned social contact with blacks, and agreed that blacks were moving "too fast" to improve their position in American society.

The white image of black people, *Newsweek* magazine observed in late 1963, "is an implausible and contradictory caricature, half Stepin Fetchit—lazy, unwashed, shiftless, unambitious, slow-moving—half Sportin' Life—cunning, lewd, flashy, strong, fearless, immoral, and vicious."*

Other parts of the country seemed no more ready than the South for genuine integration. Although many whites had sympathized with black efforts to register voters and desegregate public facilities in the South, they had far less feeling for the grievances that were mounting in the urban North. Discrimination in employment, housing, and schooling persisted, even as more blacks poured into the cities and more whites poured into the suburbs. When Martin Luther King, Jr., prepared to attack the problems of urban blacks and staged massive demonstrations in Chicago in 1967 to mobilize support for a national open-housing bill, he met with resistance similar to that he had confronted in the South. "I have never seen such hate," he declared, "not in Mississippi, or Alabama, as I see here in Chicago." When his strategy failed and challenges to his leadership grew, King found himself addressing a hostile black audience in Chicago. He thought he knew why:

For 12 years I, and others like me, had held out radiant promises of progress. I had preached to them about my dream. I had lectured to them about the not too distant day when they would have freedom, "all, here and now." I had urged them to have faith in America and in white society. Their hopes had soared. . . . They were now hostile because they were watching the dream that they had so readily accepted turn into a nightmare.

The frustrations finally exploded. Between 1964 and 1967, more than 100 riots shattered the peace of urban America. Few were premeditated or planned. Indeed, it was the spontaneous quality of the uprisings that revealed the very depths of black disillusion and despair—the felt need to expose the deprivation and desperation of the black ghettos and ghetto dwellers and the complicity of white businessmen, shop owners, and police in maintaining those conditions. "It may be that Looting, Rioting and Burning," one observer remarked, "are really nothing more than a radical form of urban renewal, a response not only to the frustrations of the ghetto but to the collapse of all ordinary modes of change. As if a body despairing of the indifference of doctors, sought to rip a cancer out of itself."

The first of the major riots broke out in the Watts ghetto of Los Angeles—98 percent black—in mid-August 1965. Thirty-five persons died, and property damage was over $100 million. When black leaders, including Martin Luther King, Jr., came to Watts to prevent further bloodshed, they

*Copyright 1963 by Newsweek, Inc. All rights reserved Reprinted by permission.

Rioters in Washington, D.C. (*Photograph by Burt Glinn, Magnum Photos*)

were met with indifference or hostility. Later in 1965 and in 1966, similar rioting occurred in Harlem in New York City and in Chicago, San Francisco, and other cities. In the summer of 1967, racial rioting struck no fewer than 67 cities across the nation.

In Newark, New Jersey, where black unemployment rates ran spectacularly high and housing shortages were among the most acute in the country, the riots of July 12 to 17 took twenty-five lives. Rioting a week later in Detroit, Michigan, took forty-three lives. More than 4000 fires pushed property losses above even those in Watts. The violence in Detroit defeated all pacification efforts until for the first time in twenty-four years—in fact, since the 1943 Detroit riots—federal troops were called for by a governor to restore order. Army tanks on Detroit streets illustrated newspapers around the world that summer.

Meanwhile, black efforts to implement the Voting Rights Act of 1965 had brought new violent confrontations in the South. The worst of these took place in Mississippi. James Meredith, a black student whose admission to the University of Mississippi in 1962 had led to such fighting and harassment that he soon withdrew, returned to the state on June 5, 1966, for a 220-mile pilgrimage from the Tennessee border to the capital at Jackson. His object was to demonstrate to the 450,000 unregistered Mississippi adult blacks that they need no longer fear murder for attempting to sign up and cast their ballots. Only a day later, June 6, Meredith was struck three times by a shotgun blast while on the pilgrimage route. Police promptly seized his white assailant and charged him with assault with intent to kill.

Although black leaders, including King and Carmichael, promptly resumed the pilgrimage to Jackson, violence along the march route dramatized a growing fragmentation within the civil rights movement. Even as King reaffirmed his faith in nonviolence and integration, others suggested that they be abandoned as the movement's primary tactic and goal. The persistence of white hostility and disillusion with the betrayal of expectations encouraged the organization of new movements, the development of new strategies, and the enunciation of new ideologies.

The most pervasive of these was the concept of *black power,* by which black people would assume control of their own communities, lives, and destinies, establish their own economic institutions, and end the "colonialism" that had tied them to white institutions. Politically, explained Stokely Carmichael, black power envisioned black people uniting "to elect representatives and *to force those representatives to speak to their needs.*" Economically, black power demanded that the money spent by black people remain in and be shared by, the black communities themselves.

The assumptions underlying the concept of black power had been forcefully explained by Malcolm X, the Black Muslim leader. His father, the Reverend Earl Little, a Baptist minister in Omaha, Nebraska, was a devout follower of Marcus Garvey, whose campaign for racial dignity, community control, and the redemption of Africa had had the allegiance of many blacks in the twenties. The violence and humiliation Reverend Little's family suffered from "the good Christian white people" in the urban North deepened his son's alienation.

By the age of twenty-one, when Malcolm X was convicted of theft and sentenced to prison, he

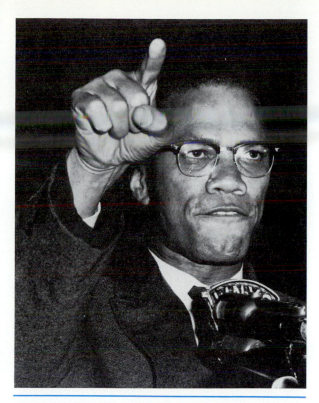

Malcom X: "The day of nonviolent resistance is over. If they have the Ku Klux Klan nonviolent, then I'll be nonviolent. . . . But as long as you've got somebody else not being nonviolent, I don't want anybody coming to me talking any nonviolent talk." (*UPI/Bettmann Newsphotos*)

found himself in a subculture of prostitutes, pimps, hustlers, numbers runners, and narcotics dealers. "I was a true hustler—uneducated, unskilled at anything honorable, and I considered myself nervy and cunning enough to live by my wits, exploiting any prey that presented itself. I would risk just about anything."

In the religion of Islam, and in Elijah Muhammad's Black Muslim movement, Malcolm X found a path from the ghetto experience he recounts so vividly in his autobiography. "Yes, I'm an extremist," he conceded. "The black race here in North America is in extremely bad condition. You show me a black man who isn't an extremist and I'll show you one who needs psychiatric attention." Strife within the black nationalist movement, after Malcolm X formed his own Organization of Afro-American Unity, appears to have brought about his assassination, February 21, 1965, while he was on stage at the Audubon Ballroom in upper Manhattan.

The violent death of Malcolm X only compounded the frustration and alienation that had overtaken so many blacks. "More than any other person," black writer Julius Lester said of him, "Malcolm X was responsible for the new militancy that entered The Movement in 1965. Malcolm X said aloud those things Negroes had been afraid to say to each other. . . . He was not concerned with stirring the moral conscience of America, because he knew—America had no moral conscience."[*]

In still another violent setback, the civil rights movement lost its apostle of nonviolence. On April 4, 1968, Martin Luther King, Jr., was assassinated in Memphis, Tennessee. King had come to Memphis to support a strike of the city's garbage men, most of them black. He was shot while standing outside his motel room, speaking to some of his co-workers. The assassin, James Earl Ray, an escapee from the Missouri state penitentiary, was later caught and convicted. Although King had been the apostle of nonviolence, his assassination set off a new wave of rioting across the country, once again requiring the intervention of federal troops. This time, the explosion centered in Washington, D.C. What Americans saw on their TV screens was the spectacle of the Capitol lit up by the nearby fires, while federal troops and troop carriers patrolled the streets.

The persistence of racial violence dramatized continued frustration in the ghettos and the limited significance of civil rights legislation in the day-to-day lives of most black people. Economic differences between black and white Americans loomed larger than ever. Yet the picture was not entirely bleak, and there were some significant breakthroughs. Middle-class blacks got substantial benefits from the "black revolution." Certain kinds of employment, formerly closed to them, were opened. Blacks were more conspicuous now in business, the professions, on the TV screen, in sports and entertainment, and on the college campuses. The new census revealed that black families whose annual incomes exceeded $10,000 had increased from 11 percent to 28 percent during the sixties.

This decade, then, was significant for black people in a number of ways, perhaps most spectacularly in enhanced racial consciousness and self-pride. Recognizing the immense problems that still persisted, Martin Luther King, Jr., sounded a note of optimism: "Lord, we ain't what we oughta be. We ain't what we wanna be. We ain't what we gonna be. But thank God, we ain't what we was."

*From *Revolutionary Notes* by Julius Lester; published by the Richard W. Baron Publishing Co.

La Raza

Since the mid-nineteenth century, Mexican-Americans had found themselves dispossessed of their lands, stereotyped, segregated, harassed, and deported at the whims of law officers. By World War II, their numbers had sharply increased, usually to meet demands for cheap labor. An unorganized labor reserve, politically powerless, they lived in *barrios* or Mex-towns of the cities.

In the 1960s and 1970s, however, the nearly 5 million "Spanish-surnamed" Americans (as the Census Bureau defined them) manifested a new sense of cultural identity. In New Mexico, Reies Lopez Tijerina headed the *Alianza,* a nationalist movement that eventually required military force to contain it. In Colorado, Rodolfo "Corky" Gonzales, an ex-prizefighter and war on poverty official, inaugurated a Crusade for Justice. Although *Chicano* (a form of *Mexicano*) had once designated Mexican refugees in the United States, it now included all Mexican-Americans, particularly those committed to the cause of *La Raza* (the Mexican "race").

Few events dramatized their quest for economic justice more than Cesar Chavez's battle in California to organize a farm laborers' union. The seasonal nature of agricultural labor, movement from crop to crop, and vigorous opposition of well-organized growers and corporate farmers had foiled previous efforts. But in 1965, in California, grape pickers struck for higher wages, improved working conditions, and union recognition. Soon the grape strike (*la huelga*) and a national consumer boycott of nonunion grapes became a rallying point of Chicano protest.

Like those he sought to organize, Chavez spent his youth in farm labor camps, left school at the seventh grade, and was a devout Roman Catholic. Like Martin Luther King, Jr., he made his religion a weapon for social justice and pledged his movement to nonviolent resistance. Through his National Farm Workers Association, Chavez hoped not only to raise living standards of Mexican-Americans, but to establish a precedent that would affect more than 4 million farm workers—brown, black, and white—who lacked job security and economic power.

Cesar Chavez speaks in support of the boycott of nonunion growers: "God knows that we are not beasts of burden, we are not agricultural implements or rented slaves, we are men." (*UPI/Bettmann Newsphotos*)

By the end of the 1970s, his efforts had aroused considerable support and controversy. Most important, the union had improved wages and working conditions for thousands of farm laborers. At the same time, and inseparable from the struggles of the farm workers, Mexican-Americans organized around a new ethnic consciousness, broadened their efforts to improve the quality of life of *barrio* dwellers, and made some significant political gains.

Native Americans

After decades of neglect and indifference, the federal government in the 1930s took a new look at Indian affairs. Under men like John Collier, a social reformer who had worked for ten years with the American Indian Defense Association, the Office of Indian Affairs under the Indian Reorganization Act of 1934 succeeded in restoring tribal landholding, self-government, and incentive. At the same time, Indians were permitted to practice their own religions, educational facilities were improved, and cultural programs were encouraged. The government had not abandoned the objective of assimilating Indians into white society, but it appeared to be willing to permit them to have a greater say in the speed and conditions of such assimilation.

Meanwhile, improvements in public health and New Deal relief policies helped to turn the "vanishing Americans" into one of the fastest-growing groups in the United States. Their number, including Eskimos, rose to over 800,000 by 1970— an increase of more than half a million in eighty years. Still another positive development was the establishment in 1946 of the Indian Claims Commission, which would seek to compensate tribes for lands earlier taken unlawfully.

Indian troubles, however, were far from over. During World War II, about 25,000 Indians served in the armed forces. The experience increased their awareness and resentment of the discrimination they suffered. Wartime employment outside the reservations led many Indians to remain in the cities, and some of these moved into the white culture. To speed that assimilation among

To call attention to their cause, American Indians briefly occupied Alcatraz Island in 1969 and took over Wounded Knee, South Dakota in 1973. "We have everything at stake, . . ." one of the Alcatraz demonstrators remarked. "Not just on Alcatraz, but everyplace else, the Indian is in his last stand for cultural survival." (*UPI/Bettmann Newsphotos*)

all Indians, westerners in Congress took the lead in trying to get "the government out of the Indian business."

At their urging, Congress in 1953 adopted two unfortunate measures that set back Indian-white relations. One, a joint resolution, set forth the intent, once and for all, to end federal responsibility for the surviving tribes. The second, a step in this direction, gave the states authority over criminal and civil issues on the reservations. The sudden ending of certain reservations threw the Indians on them into turmoil, and caused them immense losses in jointly held property and business enterprises. Individual Indians lost homes, public services, and security; many were thrown on welfare. Finally, in September 1958, Secretary of the Interior Fred A. Seaton ordered that no tribe be terminated without its consent. By this time, however, Indians had no way of knowing what to expect from the federal government.

The Great Society programs of the 1960s tried to restore purpose and incentive to Indian lives by redirecting federal policy toward such matters as health, education, housing, and vocational training. More important, the Indians themselves showed a growing ethnic consciousness. Indian groups and individual leaders in the 1970s sought to awaken their people to a new sense of dignity, self-respect, and cultural pride. Even the television and motion picture screens began to reflect a reconsideration of Indian-white relations. "The whites told only one side," Yellow Wolf of the Nez Percé Indians once complained. "Told it to please themselves. Told much that is not true. Only his own best deeds, only the worst deeds of the Indians has the white man told." But the 1970s gave clear indication that this complaint was finally being listened to.

Even so, years of repression and neglect could not be wiped away simply by correcting historical accounts. Problems persisted. In the 1970s, Indians still had one of the highest infant mortality rates in the country; their life expectancy of forty-four years was far below the national average; disease continued to take a great toll. Average family income was well below that of other groups, and the unemployment rate on some reservations was as high as 50 percent.

To draw attention to these problems and to what was seen as a paternalistic government policy, Indian militants in 1973 occupied the Bureau of Indian Affairs office in Washington, D.C., and seized Wounded Knee, South Dakota. Some years earlier, in 1969, Indians had invaded Alcatraz Island, near San Francisco, and asked that it be converted to an Indian cultural center. None of these actions proved to be anything more than symbolic reminders that native Americans, like their black and Chicano contemporaries, were no longer content to remain passive spectators; they demanded a voice in the decisions affecting their lives.

LBJ AND THE WORLD

The trouble with foreigners, Lyndon Johnson once said, "is that they're not like folks you were reared with." One trouble with Lyndon Johnson's foreign policy was his urge to make the world more congenial to Americans by making all people similar to ourselves. It was the familiar assumption, made most explicit by Woodrow Wilson, that American society could serve as a model and inspiration for all mankind. Wilson envisioned that day when the Stars and Stripes "shall be the flag not only of America but of humanity." It was in that spirit that a United States senator once declared, "With God's help we will lift Shanghai up and up, ever up, until it is just like Kansas City."

The Mekong River in Vietnam impressed Lyndon Johnson only as a larger Pedernales in his native Texas county. He saw its development with Texas knowhow and technology as the best insurance for the continued Americanization of this ancient Asian land. "I want to leave the footprints of America there," the president said of Vietnam. "I want them to say, 'This is what the Americans left—schools and hospitals and dams. . . .' We can turn the Mekong Delta into a Tennessee Valley."

Johnson told the American people, as if they needed reassurance, that "our cause has been the cause of all mankind." He repeated with approval Wilson's pronouncement that the United States was determined to make the world safe for democracy. Like his predecessors, LBJ formulated his policies from the same set of assumptions about the worldwide Communist conspiracy. "If we don't stop the Reds in South Vietnam," he instructed one senator, "tomorrow they will be in Hawaii, and next week they will be in San Francisco."

Publication of the secret Pentagon Papers by *The New York Times* in mid-1971, an "objective and encyclopedic" study of the Vietnam war ordered by Secretary of Defense McNamara, documented how successive American presidents had acted on that same premise in extending the American commitment in Vietnam. The policies of American decision-makers were based as well on the unchanging nature of world communism and on the assumption that any nationalist revolution with Communist influence posed a threat to American security. That Vietnam was no departure in American foreign policy was revealed much closer to home—in Latin America.

Intervention in the Dominican Republic

Whatever the professions of support for self-determination, neither Kennedy nor Johnson thought it inconsistent to differentiate between Communist takeovers and right-wing military coups. The United States seemed determined to crush the former, as in Cuba (1961), while tolerating if not encouraging the latter, as in Guatemala (1954) and Brazil (1964). The first major test of LBJ's Latin American policy came in the Dominican Republic in April 1965.

Four years earlier the brutal reign of Rafael Trujillo had ended after three decades when he was shot down on a lonely country road by one of his henchmen. The dispatch of American warships and 1200 marines forestalled a coup by the slain dictator's relatives. The next year, in the first free election since Trujillo's takeover, the poet Juan Bosch won the presidency. The Kennedy administration made much of this democratic development. But Bosch was soon overthrown by a military coup (supported by businessmen and landholders who resented his reforms) without United States opposition. Kennedy, however, wanted a civil regime, so one was quickly set up under Donald Reid Cabral.

The new regime soon lost whatever support it might have had. On April 24, 1965, pro-Bosch forces unseated the Reid Cabral regime. They were promptly confronted by military forces with American connections, and a civil war began. On April 28, LBJ disclosed the landing of 400 marines in Santo Domingo to protect American lives. A high-ranking navy officer said they were also "to see that no Communist government is established." By May 5, when a truce was worked out, American forces exceeded 20,000 men, a number many thought incredible. "This was a democratic revolution smashed by the leading democracy of the world," Bosch observed.

LBJ thought otherwise, and he went on nation-wide TV to share his Castroite panic with the public:

What began as a popular democratic revolution [he said] . . . moved into the hands of a band of Communist conspirators. . . . The American nation cannot, must not, will not, permit the establishment of another Communist government in the Western Hemisphere.

The administration soon backed away from these assertions and worked out a compromise settlement including Bosch men in a new government. These steps only deepened the consternation of many congressmen, other Americans, and people throughout Latin America. The whole episode enlarged the "credibility gap" already evident in White House reporting on the Vietnam war.

The Middle East: Seeds of Future Conflict

The United States position appeared to be stronger in the Middle East. But the American moral commitment to Israel and the simultaneous dependence on Arab oil suggested how difficult that position could suddenly become. In May 1967, complying with the demand of Nasser of Egypt, United Nations troops were withdrawn after keeping Egypt and Israel apart for ten years. The Egyptian leader immediately called for a "holy war" against the Jewish state. Israel, however, beat him to the punch with an overpowering assault in the Six-Day War, June 5 to 10. The extent of the defeat humiliated Egypt and the USSR as well, for it was Soviet aid that had encouraged Nasser's militancy.

But Israel's victory only intensified the already volatile tensions and fostered a bigger arms buildup. After the war, moreover, Israel cited its own security as justification for keeping some of the territory it had occupied: the Sinai Peninsula, the Golan Heights, the Gaza Strip, and the West Bank of the Jordan River. The UN Security Council in November 1967 called upon Israel to withdraw its forces from the occupied territories, while urging all states in the region to acknowledge each other's sovereignty and independence. The result was a stalemate that defied solution.

Israel continued to ignore the plight of the thousands of Palestinian refugees who had been made homeless by previous conflicts and whose mounting discontent would soon manifest itself in organized resistance movements. The Arab states cynically exploited the Palestinians as part of their overall plan to destroy Israel. With the vast oil resources at their disposal, the Arabs appeared to have time on their side. By the mid-1970s, when that oil became a potent political and economic weapon, the United States, like much of the world, would be forced to reassess its Middle East policies.

While the United States was preoccupied with Vietnam and with rebellion at home, the USSR not only regained its standing in the Middle East, but enlarged its influence in the entire Mediterranean region. Nearer home, the Soviet Union, like the United States, continued to insist on orthodoxy. This time, the victim was Czechoslovakia in August 1968.

With a show of force even greater than that used in Hungary twelve years before, the Soviets crushed the Alexander Dubcek regime and the libertarian spirit it had fostered. The manner in which Soviet leaders justified their intervention should have been all too familiar to American policymakers—to preserve Czechoslovakia from the forces of "world imperialism" and "counterrevolution." The United States was concerned with the same forces in Southeast Asia.

The Lengthening Shadow of Vietnam

Few wars in history have been marked by such an array of inconsistent, contradictory official pronouncements as to its purpose and progress as the American war in Vietnam. Nothing contributed more to public discontent over the war, except for the growing casualty lists, than the mistrust created by confusion, secrecy, and deceit. Even Congress was deliberately misled or kept ignorant by the executive department, largely for self-serving rather than security reasons.

No incidents in the war were more clouded by contradictory pronouncements and the classification of essential documents than the events in Tonkin Gulf, off North Vietnam, on August 2 and 4, 1964. Compounding the confusion was the fact that the United States at this time was in the middle of a presidential campaign. The Arizona "hawk," Senator Barry Goldwater, opposed Johnson, the Democratic seeker after "consensus." Early in July 1964, in response to saber rattling by a new Saigon regime, UN Secretary General U Thant declared that "the only sensible alternative is the political and diplomatic method of negotiations." He proposed a reconvening of the Geneva Conference for this purpose. But the new administration's response left little room for compromise or negotiation. The president himself stated: "We do not believe in conferences to ratify terror." The next day he announced a 30 percent increase in the American "military mission" to Vietnam, from 16,000 to 21,000 persons.

Neither side in the Tonkin Bay controversy three weeks later denied that on August 2, North Vietnamese PT boats attacked the U.S. destroyer *Maddox* in Tonkin Gulf, and were driven off with the help of carrier-based fighter planes. The *Maddox* suffered neither damage nor casualties. The United States asserted that the attack was "unprovoked"; *Maddox* was "on routine patrol in international waters." But Hanoi on July 30 and 31 had already filed a formal protest with the International Control Commission set up under the Geneva agreements. It declared that Siagon vessels had raided North Vietnamese fishing boats and that, under cover of protection by an American destroyer, had bombarded two North Vietnamese islands. The attack on *Maddox*, Hanoi held, was made to stop such activities.

Secretary McNamara denied American complicity: "Our Navy played absolutely no part in, was not associated with, was not aware of, any South Vietnamese actions, if there were any." Four years later, McNamara admitted before a congressional hearing what the Pentagon Papers also confirmed—that North Vietnamese islands had been bombarded and that the United States and South Vietnam had made joint raids against North Vietnam. It was also made clear that the bombardment was part of a secret and deliberate United States policy adopted in early 1964 to exert "new and significant pressures on North Vietnam." The point was to force North Vietnam to commit acts that would gain congressional authorization for whatever else "is necessary with respect to Vietnam."

This policy was stiffened after the attack on *Maddox*. The president directed the navy to assign a second destroyer to join *Maddox*'s patrol and to order both vessels, together with the necessary air power, to repel any further assaults. Two days later, on August 4, the Defense Department announced that North Vietnam had attacked both *Maddox* and its companion, 65 miles offshore in the gulf, and that the attackers had been driven off with the loss of at least two boats. North Vietnam denied that any such attack had taken place. (Congress did not learn until several years later that evidence of such an attack was, at best, inconclusive.)

That very night, allowing no time for detailed investigation and without consulting Congress, the president went on television to announce that, in response to "repeated acts of violence against the armed forces of the United States," American planes were now engaged in action "against gunboats and certain facilities in Vietnam." He called his response "limited and fitting. We Americans know, although others appear to forget, the risks of spreading conflict. We seek no wider war." Yet he must have realized that this attack on North Viet-

Infantryman in Vietnam. (*Photograph by Donald McCullin, Magnum Photos*)

nam was more than an escalation of a war officially described as one for the defense of the Saigon government against South Vietnamese guerrilla groups. Just prior to his telecast the president informed legislative leaders that he would, the next day, send Congress a retroactive joint resolution to be adopted "before dark" and without amendment.

This resolution the administration promptly and persistently interpreted as a "functional equivalent" of a formal declaration of war in Southeast Asia. Restating the United States version of the events of August 2 and 4, the Tonkin Gulf Resolution of August 7, 1964, declared:

The Congress approves and supports the determination of the President, as Commander in Chief, to take all necessary measures to repel any armed attack against the forces of the United States and to prevent further aggression.

Rushed into session in a crisis mood, the House adopted the resolution without a dissenting vote. The Senate debated the measure for two days, but only because Wayne Morse of Oregon had threatened a filibuster. Only two senators—Morse and Ernest Gruening of Alaska—stood opposed to a measure granting almost unlimited power to the president in the rapidly escalating conflict. Both, to their credit, saw through the smoke screens of at least two administrations. Gruening called the resolution "a predated declaration of war." Morse thought it a subversion of the Constitution and "a historic mistake."

But the Cold War mentality overrode reason on that day, and the president's assurances got the support of several senators who would later emerge as critics of the war. It was none other than J. William Fulbright, chairman of the Foreign Re-

lations Committee, who managed the resolution through the Senate. Among those who voted with him were Eugene McCarthy of Minnesota and George McGovern of South Dakota.

Armed with the resolution, Johnson escalated the war. The bombing of North Vietnam in August 1964 appears to have been as much a political as a military adventure. Regular missions of this sort did not begin until February 1965. During the preceding presidential election, Johnson had refused to endorse Goldwater's call for the bombing of North Vietnam. "We're not going north and drop bombs at this stage of the game," LBJ responded. "I want to think about the consequences of getting American boys into a war with 700 million Chinese."

With the election won and the new administration seated, McGeorge Bundy, now one of Johnson's hard-line advisors, returned from a visit to Saigon convinced of the need to buck up the South Vietnamese. The fear of Chinese intervention, however, still restrained the president. Even after February 1965, reporter Tom Wicker recalled, the missions went on "hesitantly and reluctantly" for six weeks.

During the spring of 1965, the administration developed a program for the systematic bombing of North Vietnam. The more intensive bombing, however, only succeeded in reinforcing North Vietnam's determination to resist. Even the CIA doubted the wisdom of the new strategy. With every new Vietcong provocation, however, Johnson stepped up the raids. And Congress, by huge majorities, voted the necessary "hardware." When pressed as to how long the war might take, LBJ was confident that the continued bombing would force Hanoi and the Vietcong to their knees within six months.

In what were described as "search and destroy" missions, American ground troops engaged the Vietcong in direct fighting for the first time in June 1965. By the end of the year, American forces in Vietnam numbered above 200,000. The South Vietnamese also promised to step up their efforts after Air Vice-Marshal Nguyen Cao Ky took over as premier of the eighth South Vietnamese government since the end of Diem. Dissent in the United States began to mount, especially on college campuses. In October 1965, the first public burning of a draft card took place. The next month, some 30,000 persons participated in a March on Washington for Peace in Vietnam. Yet the continuing escalation of military appropriations by members of Congress who were guided by their constituents' opinions suggested that most Americans still shared the president's confidence and determination. "America wins the wars that she undertakes," LBJ had made clear in 1965.

By the end of 1966, American forces in Vietnam had reached 380,000. In April, for the first time, their casualties exceeded those of the South Vietnamese: 4,800 American soldiers were killed in action that year. Meanwhile, American "hardware" commitments now probably exceeded those of any other war in history. "What kind of a war are we fighting anyway?" asked an American soldier in his Vietnam diary in 1967. "They say we've got more fire-power out here than they had in both World War I and II. Yet these damn kids in black pajamas continue to hold out. I can't understand it. Each one of them must have 40 lives."

Perhaps part of the frustration lay in the estimate that "search and destroy" missions destroyed six civilians for every one Vietcong. Widespread chemical warfare and the use of other new weaponry, largely concealed from Americans at home, also contributed heavily to the devastation of South Vietnam while contributing little to "pacification" of the Vietcong.

In a struggle that had developed into a war of "body counts," pacification had come largely to mean extermination. Vietnamese civilians, North and South, were almost routinely included in the slaughter, to help provide a better showing. "Your Secretary of Defense loves statistics," a Vietnamese general remarked. "We Vietnamese can give him all he wants. If you want them to go up, they go up. If you want them to go down, they go down." The counts grew as suspect as all other aspects of this tragedy, while the means employed added anxiety over war crimes to the other sources of revulsion.

In May 1967, Secretary McNamara himself recoiled from what was happening:

The picture of the world's greatest superpower killing or seriously injuring 1,000 noncombatants a week, while trying to pound a tiny backward nation into submission on an issue whose merits are hotly disputed, is not a pretty one.

McNamara noted that the bomb tonnage dropped every week on North Vietnam had exceeded that of all the bombings of Germany in World War II.

By the end of 1967 United States troop strength in Vietnam approached 475,000 men, about 1,500 more than at the peak of the Korean war, and casualties rose proportionately. In May, total American casualties exceeded 10,000. The futility of bombing North Vietnam and its immense political cost at home and abroad were now being acknowledged openly. McNamara admitted it publicly in August 1967, three months before his departure from the cabinet.

Despite growing dissent even within his administration, LBJ persisted. Although the president defended the right of dissent, declaring that protest was "the life breath of democracy—even when it blows heavy," he had the FBI and CIA keep him posted on the dissenters. The once gregarious president was increasingly more guarded about his movements and exposure to the public; he even declined to attend his party's national convention in August 1968.

North Vietnam's Tet (New Year's) offensive against Saigon and other South Vietnamese cities in February 1968 suggested that Ho, despite the bombing, could launch massive assaults that caught hardened United States field commanders by surprise. It also revealed that the USSR would not leave North Vietnam to confront American military technology with captured or stolen American weapons. In the Tet offensive, Hanoi used Soviet jet planes and tanks for the first time.

Although American and South Vietnamese troops recaptured several of the population centers lost in the Tet offensive, the cost was immense, and confidence in ultimate victory seriously undermined. The ancient imperial city of Hue, where pitched battles had been fought, lay in ruins. Of still another Vietnamese town, an American officer observed: "It became necessary to destroy the town to save it." The total of United States forces soared to 549,000 in April 1968, while combat deaths reached 22,951. The new campaign being planned by American field officers bore the ominous title of Operation Complete Victory.

Worldwide pressure for peace had grown very heavy by this time. Television filled America's liv-

WINNING THE VIETNAM WAR

In *Dispatches*, news correspondent Michael Herr wrote some of the most devastating personal accounts of the Vietnam War.

I knew one 4th Division Lurp [long-range reconnaissance patrollers] who took his pills by the fistful, downs from the left pocket of his tiger suit and ups from the right, one to cut the trail for him and the other to send him down it. He told me that they cooled things out just right for him, that he could see that old jungle at night like he was looking at it through a starlight scope. "They sure give you the range," he said.

This was his third tour. In 1965 he'd been the only survivor in a platoon of the Cav wiped out going into the Ia Drang Valley. In '66 he'd come back with the Special Forces and one morning after an ambush he'd hidden under the bodies of his team while the VC walked around them with knives, making sure. They stripped the bodies of their gear, the berets too, and finally went away, laughing. After that, there was nothing left for him in the war except the Lurps.

"I just can't hack it back in the World," he said. He told me that after he'd come back home the last time he would sit in his room all day, and sometimes he'd stick a hunting rifle out the window, leading people and cars as they passed his house until the only feeling he was aware of was all up in the tip of that one finger. "It used to put my folks real uptight," he said. . . .

But what a story he told me, as one-pointed and resonant as any war story I ever heard. It took me a year to understand it.

"Patrol went up the mountain. One man came back. He died before he could tell us what happened."

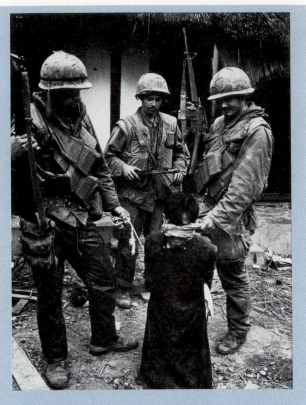

I waited for the rest, but it seemed not to be that kind of story; when I asked him what had happened he just looked like he felt sorry for me . . .

Source: Michael Herr, *Dispatches* (New York: Knopf, 1977), pp. 5–6. Copyright 1968, 1969, 1977 by Michael Herr. Reprinted by permission of Alfred A. Knopf, Inc. Photograph by Donald McCullin, Magnum Photos.

---

ing rooms with firsthand, all too realistic reports from Vietnam, in which the sight of American troops on "search and destroy" missions and setting fire to peasant huts raised doubts that were deepened by the weekly announcements of soldiers killed in action. Riots and demonstrations on college campuses attested to the antiwar sentiment there, even among usually conservative and nonpolitical students. The flow of draft resisters to Canada had reached 10,000.

The strength of the peace movement became evident in the showing of one of its leading congressional advocates, Senator Eugene J. McCarthy of Minnesota, in the Democratic presidential primary in New Hampshire on March 12, 1968. Although given little chance against LBJ, McCarthy shocked the administration by taking 42 percent of the votes to the president's 49 percent. On

March 31, Johnson said on nationwide TV: "We are prepared to move immediately toward peace through negotiations. So tonight, in the hope that this action will lead to early talks, I am taking the first step to deescalate the conflict."

This step was his order to halt all air and naval bombardment of North Vietnam, except in the area just north of the demilitarized zone where the enemy arms buildup was strongest. Even more dramatic was the president's gesture toward unifying the country; he announced that he would not seek reelection.

The North Vietnamese response came quickly. On April 3, Ho Chi Minh's government declared its readiness to talk about peace, and one month later preliminary talks began in Paris. But even as Johnson restricted the bombings, he increased the troop level in Vietnam to 535,000. On June 4 the

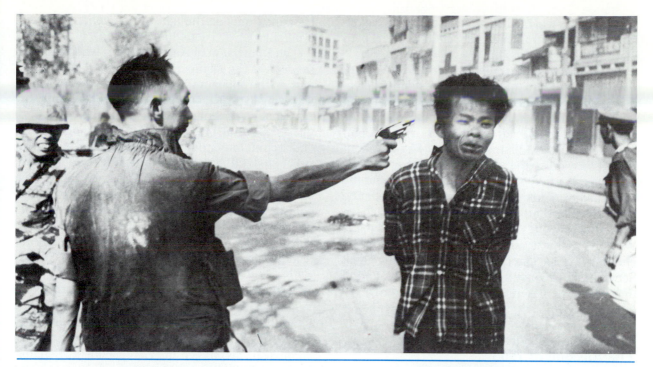

Instant justice during the Tet offensive of 1968. A Vietcong civilian carrying a pistol was captured near Quang Pagoda and taken to the police chief, General Nguyen Ngoc Loan, who shot him on the spot. (*AP/Wide World Photos*)

United States command in Vietnam announced that American battle deaths in the first six months of 1968 exceeded those of all 1967. By June 23, reckoning from December 22, 1961, the date of the first death of an American serviceman in Vietnam, the war there had become the longest in American history. The direct cost of the war also had soared to an acknowledged $25 billion a year,

Thousands of antiwar demonstrators converged on the 1968 Democratic National Convention in Chicago, which turned into one of the bloodiest and most widely publicized confrontations between America's youth and the police. (*Roger Malloch, Magnum Photos*)

with unacknowledged costs for weapons development and other programs associated with the conflict.

Little progress was reported from Paris until shortly before the United States presidential elections. Then, following favorable information from the French capital, Johnson announced: "I have now ordered that all air, naval, and artillery bombardment of North Vietnam cease." The president looked forward to the scheduled meeting at Paris on November 6, the day after the elections, for the sweet fruits of his decree. But conflicts over the Paris roles of South Vietnam and its official enemy, the Vietcong, ended his hopes. LBJ left the White House with the war still unresolved. Not only his political career but his vision of the Great Society had become a casualty of the war and of the mounting dissension and strife at home.

The "Silent Majority" on Trial: The Election of 1968

The presidential election of 1968 may be said to have begun with the decision to bomb North Vietnam in February 1965. The ranks of doves swelled not only among McCarthy's colleagues in the Senate, but among the youth of the nation as well. McCarthy's performance in the New Hampshire primary in March 1968 showed that he had grown strong enough to split the party. When, a few days later, Senator Robert F. Kennedy of New York decided to enter the campaign, it seemed that the opposition to the administration would also be split. Johnson's withdrawal two weeks later deepened the conflict between his would-be Democratic successors.

The Kennedy mantle and mystique drew millions of American young people, black and white. On June 5, however, the very night of his victory in the California primary, Robert Kennedy was shot by Sirhan Sirhan, a young Arab nationalist resentful of Kennedy's support for Israel. Coming only two months after King's murder, the Kennedy assassination shocked the nation and changed the political scene.

The Democratic nomination was now a virtual certainty for Hubert H. Humphrey, Johnson's vice-president and a firm supporter of the war. He did not enter any primaries, but his quest for delegates did not end until the very moment of the first ballot at the Democratic convention in Chicago, August 26–29. Although he easily won the nomination, the narrow victory of the plank on Vietnam revealed deep rifts in the party. What

happened outside the convention center exposed even sharper divisions in the nation.

The International Amphitheater, where official sessions of the Democratic convention were held, took on the appearance of a fortress under siege. It was ringed with barbed wire, broken only by checkpoints for entering delegates, reporters, and guests. Several blocks around the amphitheater and around major downtown hotels swarmed with police, federal agents, and finally with more than 5000 National Guardsmen called in to keep away antiwar demonstrators. In the almost inevitable confrontation between the security forces and the demonstrators, the result, an investigative report subsequently charged, "was unrestrained and indiscriminate police violence"—that is, a "police riot."

With pandemonium inside and outside the convention hall—and all visible to millions on TV—Humphrey accepted the Democratic nomination. The next day he announced, and the convention confirmed, his choice for vice-president, Senator Edmund S. Muskie of Maine.

The Republican convention, comparatively peaceful, featured the remarkable political comeback of Richard M. Nixon. Despite his defeat in the California gubernatorial election of 1962, he had remained active in Republican politics and was now given a second chance at the presidency. The platform warned that "lawlessness is crumbling the foundations of American society," and the campaign itself stressed the need for "law and order." In his acceptance speech, Nixon welcomed as the core of his constituency the "silent majority" of "forgotten Americans"—"the non-shouters, the non-demonstrators, that are not racist or sick, that are not guilty of the crime that plagues the land."

He selected as his running mate Governor Spiro T. Agnew of Maryland. The choice of Agnew, a southern candidate, could only strengthen the Republicans' "southern strategy," already manifest in Nixon's promise to southern delegations the day before the convention balloting. If elected, he said, his administration would not "ram anything down your throats." He disliked federal intervention in local school board affairs. He opposed school busing. He would appoint "strict Constitutionalists" to the Supreme Court.

Nixon's stand may have taken some of the wind out of the sails of a third candidate for president, George C. Wallace, the Alabama segregationist thought by many to be strong enough to deprive both regular party candidates of the electoral majority needed to win. Wallace delighted audiences

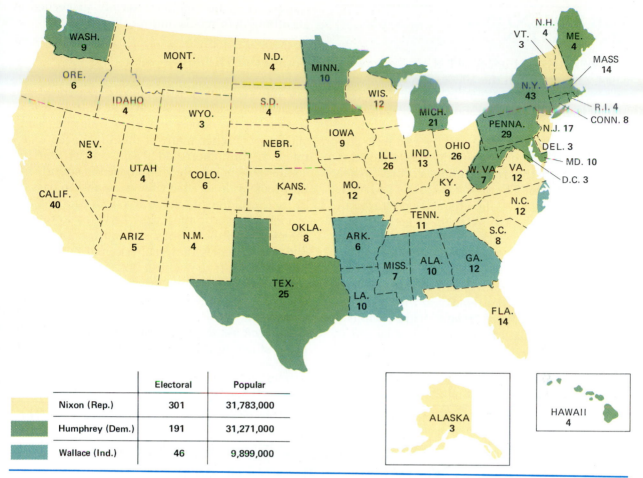

	Electoral	Popular
Nixon (Rep.)	301	31,783,000
Humphrey (Dem.)	191	31,271,000
Wallace (Ind.)	46	9,899,000

The Election of 1968

by his assaults on "scummy anarchists," "pseudo-intellectuals," federal meddlers, and those who coddled criminals. But he found it difficult to outdo the determination of Nixon and Agnew to bring "law and order" to the country.

With exceptional support from the old Democratic coalition of urban liberals, organized labor, and minority groups, Humphrey made a remarkably strong finish in the big industrial states. Nixon carried by small majorities the critical states of Ohio, Illinois, New Jersey, and California. Humphrey won in Michigan and Texas, as well as New York and Pennsylvania. Wallace's poor southern showing outside the few Deep South states he was certain to carry also helped Nixon gain a clear electoral majority.

Like Eisenhower in 1956, however, he failed to carry enough legislative candidates with him to change the Democratic majorities in House and Senate. Nixon also failed to gain a popular majority. His margin over Humphrey, a mere 510,000 out of 73.2 million votes cast, gave him only 43.4 percent of the popular vote, the lowest for a successful candidate since Wilson in 1912. Humphrey gained 42.7 percent of the popular vote; Wallace, 13.5 percent.

The new president clearly embodied the sentiments of tens of millions of Americans, angry over the threats to their personal safety, frightened by the racial violence, and frustrated by a costly and futile war. In Richard Nixon and Spiro Agnew, they found forceful spokesmen to articulate their grievances, fears, and hopes. Few could have envisioned the fate that awaited these two apostles of law and order. For the tens of thousands of young political activists who had enlisted in McCarthy's "crusade" to bring the war to an end, the disillusion was bound to be severe. The violence at the Chicago convention, the nomination of Humphrey, and the election of Nixon and Agnew reinforced for many of them the conviction that they had become strangers in their own land.

THE DISSENTING GENERATION

F. Scott Fitzgerald once said of his generation, which came of age in the 1920s, that it had found all gods dead, all wars fought in vain, and all faiths in man shaken. The generation of the 1960s, often described in similar terms, was thus not as unique as it preferred to believe. Even the relatively apathetic and silent generation of the 1950s had managed to produce the "rebel without a cause." When asked in the film *The Wild One* (1954) what he was rebelling against, the character portrayed by Marlon Brando replied "Whadda ya got?"

In the sixties, there was no end to the causes around which young people rallied. They ranged from the war in Vietnam which they wanted to stop, to the corrupt and hypocritical adult society, which they expected to remake in their own image. What most of these "rebels" had in common was the middle-class inheritance they longed to renounce. But in the end, their staying power proved brief; the dominant society succeeded in absorbing both rebels and rebellion.

Sources of Disillusionment

For the generation which had experienced the Great Depression and World War II, the relative stability of the fifties had been welcome, along with the affluence many of them managed to acquire. If they cherished their security and the comfortable homes they purchased in suburbia, if they took pride in what they were able to pass on to their children in the way of educational and economic opportunities, they had only to remind themselves of the thirties, the wartime sacrifices, and the struggles they had endured to make all this possible. If they chose not to be skeptical of their major institutions and of the Protestant ethic of hard work, it was because these had served them well.

The generation of white middle-class youth that came of age in the sixties—products of the post-

The Free Speech Movement at the University of California, Berkeley, received massive support on campus and soon spread to other universities. (*Joe Wakabayashi*)

war baby boom—had good reason, then, to feel secure and hopeful about the society they entered. Neither their families nor their teachers suggested anything else. This was the first generation to have been raised in the age of television. By the time they were fourteen, according to one estimate, they had already seen 300,000 commercials; by the time they were eighteen, they had already compiled 17,000 hours of television viewing. If they took their values and attitudes from the TV screen, they found little reason to question the dominant institutions of American society. If they responded to politics, it was to the youthful appeal of John F. Kennedy and his call for young Americans to make a commitment to the New Frontier. Some enlisted in the Peace Corps; others were drawn into the civil rights struggle and helped to register black voters in the South.

But the idealism and hope with which many young Americans entered the sixties began to come apart after the assassination of President Kennedy and the Freedom Summer of 1964. The vision of a more humane society gave way to a nightmare of violence—not the manufactured variety they had become accustomed to on TV, but real violence: the assassinations of Robert F. Kennedy, Martin Luther King, Jr., and Malcolm X; the murder and beatings of civil rights demonstrators; police violence in the ghettos; and the massive and organized violence the United States was inflicting on the people of Vietnam.

What middle-class youth began to perceive was the enormous contradiction between the ideals and virtues they had been taught by family, school, and television set and the spectacle of racism and poverty, and of the brutality of the war in Vietnam. The universities many of them were attending were so impersonal and bureaucratized as to be unable to see their own deep complicity in the war abroad and racism at home.

The "awakening" came to different people at different times. Many of them enlisted in The Movement (as it came to be called) only after observing at firsthand the attempts to repress it. When the radical Students for a Democratic Society (SDS) drew up their manifesto (The Port Huron Statement), the signers agreed that the civil rights struggle, more than any other cause, had brought most of them "from silence to activism."

The presidential election of 1964 had no sooner ended than the Free Speech Movement (FSM) on the Berkeley campus of the University of California revealed the degree to which many middle-class youths were prepared to reject the apathy and indifference of their predecessors. What be-

gan as a protest over restrictions on campus political expression evolved into a movement that seriously questioned and directly challenged the dominant values and assumptions of American society. Its purpose was to compel that society to recognize the depths of its hypocrisy.

Before 800 students staged a nonviolent sit-in at the university administration building, FSM leader Mario Savio, a veteran of the Freedom Summer earlier that year, told a massive rally outside:

There is a time when the operations of the machine become so odious, make you so sick at heart, that you can't take part, you can't even tacitly take part. And you've got to put your bodies on the gears and upon the wheels, upon the levers, upon all the apparatus, and you've got to make it stop. And you've got to indicate to the people who run it, to the people who own it, that unless you're free the machine will be prevented from working at all.

The effects would soon be felt on campuses across the country—and with ever greater intensity as American involvement in Vietnam deepened and as frustration and tension mounted at home.

The Counterculture

What emerged in the sixties was a "youth culture" (some called it a counterculture) characterized by distinct forms of expression and consciousness, including new styles of dress, social behavior, and music. Few exerted any greater influence on these styles than the Beatles, an English rock group that first visited the United States in 1963. The contagion of the Beatles and innumerable other groups and individual artists proved impossible to contain. The music suggested far different attitudes toward life and society than what the adult generation had been accustomed to hear. There was an intensity to the music, moreover, that was inseparable from the message conveyed. In form, content, and volume, the new music heralded a liberation from traditional restraints and conventions.

For many young people, the way to self-expression lay not through politics, but through the adoption of a radical life style, a redefinition of sexual mores, and the use of hallucinatory drugs. They substituted the "be-in" and the "love-in" for the protest meeting and preached an ideology of anti-ideology. Few protest marches or political rallies attracted as many young people as the countless rock festivals. The most spectacular was at Woodstock, New York, in the summer of 1969,

THE CULTURE OF ROCK

Rock music is a necessary element of contemporary society. It is functional. It is healthy and valid artistically. It is also educational (how to ask a girl for a date, what love is like). It has all the answers to what your mother and father won't tell you. It is also a big business. This is a brief history of rock and its relationship to our society. . . .

Part One: The 50s

1. Who remembers beer? White port and lemon juice? For 10 points, what was the name of the guy in your school who used to buy your juice for parties. . . .

2. Who remembers making out and getting hot? For 10 points, how old were you when it happened. . . .

3. Who remembers duck tails, peggers, leather jackets, bunny shoes, brogans, tight sweaters, teardrops, full skirts, and a million starchy petticoats, Sir Guy shirts and khakis? For 10 points, how much did you pay for your St. Christopher medallion. . . .

4. Who remembers gang fights, tire chains, boys with razor blades in the toes of their wedgies, girls with razor blades in their hair, blood and sickening crunch? For 10 points, tell why the cops were afraid of your gang.

Part Two: The 60s

5. Who remembers speed? Smoke? Acid? Transcendental meditation? For 10 points, name your connection or guru. . . .

6. Who remembers getting stoned and having an orgy? For 10 points, how old were you when you learned you were incapable of relating to others in a tender, personal way and finally discovered you had become asexual. . . .

7. Who remembers electric hair, bell bottoms, plastic jackets, sandals, high boots, bulky knit sweaters, Guccis, miniskirts, De Voss shirts and velvet pants? For 10 points, look around the house, find your beads and bells, and recite Hare Krishna without laughing. . . .

8. Who remembers demonstrations, truncheons, Mace, police dogs, the Pentagon, Century City, blood and sickening crunch? For 10 points, tell why you were afraid to cut your hair, infiltrate the establishment, and do it the easy way. . . .

Our present state of sociosexual enlightenment is, to a certain extent, attributable to the evolution of rock and vice versa. . . .

Source: Frank Zappa ("Mothers of Invention"), "The Oracle Has It All Psyched Out," *Life Magazine*, June 28, 1968. Photograph of Bob Dylan by John Launois, Black Star; photograph of Jimi Hendrix by Jim Cummins, Camera 5, Inc.

when some 400,000 came together to listen to rock bands and to share the experience and exhilaration with each other. Two years earlier, the Love Summer of 1967 had attracted thousands of "flower children" (named after their habit of handing flowers to policemen and "straights") to San Francisco, turning the city's Haight-Ashbury district into a hippy mecca.

The young political activists who made up The Movement, many of whom found the drug culture counterproductive, had been confident of their ability to turn both the Vietnam war and the nation around. Equally optimistic, Charles A. Reich, in his much discussed *The Greening of America*, forecast in 1970 that the "corporate state" would soon destroy itself, and then the emerging "youth culture" would ensure the end of established attitudes toward business, politics, leisure, and daily life. But none of these prophecies would be realized, at least not by this generation.

Youth: The Gang. (*Bruce Davidson, Magnum Photos*)

Roy Lichtenstein's "Hopeless," 1963. (*Launois Covello, Black Star*)

Drum majorette, Pittsburgh, Pennsylvania. (*I. Masser, Black Star*)

CRUMBLING CONSENSUS

The rock concert near Woodstock, New York, in the summer of 1969 attracted more than 400,000 youths. (*Dan McCoy, Black Star*)

Janis Joplin, the "rock goddess" of the Sixties. (*Dan McCoy, Black Star*)

Youth: The Gang. (*Bruce Davidson, Magnum Photos*)

Two youths at the Woodstock concert. (*Dan McCoy, Black Star*)

With relative ease, American society curbed and absorbed the radical impulses of the sixties, political and cultural. The counterculture proved short-lived. Many of its creative qualities, fads, and fashions—the hair styles, the clothes, the dancing, the music, the language, even the "pot" parties—were incorporated into the larger culture, compromising if not distorting altogether the initial spirit and ideals. In a cover story, even *Time Magazine* could recommend to its mass readership the Beatles' new album, "Sergeant Pepper's Lonely Hearts Club Band," calling it "a guaranteed package of psychic shivers," certain to turn "parents, professors, even business executives" into ardent Beatle fans.

Even as police battled and arrested thousands of antiwar demonstrators, Columbia Records in 1969 appealed to its youthful purchasers with the slogan, "The Man can't bust your music." Finally, *Rolling Stone Magazine*, founded in 1967 as an irreverent tabloid devoted to rock n' roll culture, took out a full page ad in *The New York Times* in an effort to expand its readership: "If you are a corporate executive trying to understand what is happening to youth today, you cannot afford to be without *Rolling Stone*."

Elinor Langer, who had once shared the optimism of her generation, later reflected on how short-lived it proved to be:

Youth culture was a great romance: music, energy, drugs, a cultural disguise. But it was part of our revolutionary fantasy: we were guerrillas among the people, "fish in the sea." Patton's nephew attended the premier of Patton *with long hair and we saw militarism crumbling. We forgot that America could support any life style, as long as it used money as its medium of exchange.*

The political side of The Movement succumbed to slogans, communication by invective, and sectarianism. "Our creative political potential," said one dismayed activist, "has degenerated into a short-sighted repetition of demonstrations. . . . The 'politics of apocalypse' became the 'politics of despair.'" Meanwhile, an intensive survey of the younger generation undertaken by *Fortune* in 1968, the year of the worst student riots, revealed that some 60 percent still stood on "the practical side of the line." They were preparing themselves for power and affluence, and were committed to careers in big business or big government or in adjunct professions.

The dominant society demonstrated immense staying power. The threats and warnings and the strategies for upheaval or repression produced no permanent "armies of the night" or guerrillas in the hills. Sporadic riots, street warfare, bombings, murders of and by police did not make a revolution. The Movement failed to make any inroads into the working class, those who had to send their sons into the war. Nor had liberating life styles and musical expression affected the

---

END OF AN ERA

If John Lennon of the Beatles had once epitomized the exuberance and optimism of the sixties, in 1970 he was expressing feelings far more in tune with the new decade:

I don't believe in Magic
I don't believe in I'Ching
I don't believe in the Bible
I don't believe in Hitler
I don't believe in Jesus
I don't believe in Kennedy
I don't believe in Mantra
I don't believe in Yoga
I don't believe in Kings
I don't believe in Elvis
I don't believe in Zimmerman
I don't believe in Beatles
I just believe in me,
Yoko and me
And that's reality.
The dream is over
What can I say?

The dream is over
Yesterday
I was the dreamweaver
But now I'm reborn
I was the walrus
But now I'm John
And so dear friends
You just have to carry on
The dream is over.

For Lennon, the decade ended in tragedy. On December 8, 1980, he was murdered outside his New York apartment—a victim of the senseless violence that characterized life in urban America. To the generation that had grown up with Lennon's music, his death, more than any other single event, marked the end of an era.

inequalities in the urban ghettos and barrios. With Richard Nixon's decisive victory over George McGovern in the 1972 presidential election, the familiar feeling of powerlessness, apathy, and cynicism once again gripped the college campuses. "Everything we thought was wrong is still wrong," Elinor Langer wrote, "but we are without the institutions, the influence, or the understanding to change it."

In 1963 Bob Dylan sang of far-reaching changes "blowing in the wind," far-reaching changes that would presumably radicalize and humanize the dominant society. Some years later, he sang: "Although the masters make the rules/for the wise men and the fools/I've got nothin' Ma, nothin' to live up to." The generation of the sixties ended in Watergate, economic recession, and the triumph of a new politics.

SUMMARY

The 1960s was a decade of crises and war; it was also a decade of widespread social changes.

Lyndon Johnson, who had become president in the midst of the national shock of Kennedy's assassination, set into motion new and major domestic programs: the Great Society and the war on poverty. The commitment of the federal government to the concept of the welfare state seemed unquestioned. But Johnson faced the problem of waging a war on poverty at home while waging a full-scale war on communism in Vietnam. Among his Great Society measures were the Civil Rights Act of 1964, the most sweeping such legislation in American history; a tax reform bill; and the establishment of the Office of Economic Opportunity to supervise ten separate antipoverty programs.

In the election of 1964, Johnson won a sweeping victory over the conservative Republican Barry Goldwater. Beginning in January 1965, the Eighty-ninth Congress approved nearly all the Great Society measures the president proposed: the Elementary and Secondary Education Act (April 1965); the Medicare amendments to the Social Security Act (July 1965); special assistance for Appalachia; the end of the immigration quota system; antipollution legislation; the Truth in Lending Act; the National Foundation for the Arts and Humanities; and a new cabinet department, the Department of Housing and Urban Development.

But the Great Society, like the New Frontier, raised the expectations of many Americans without necessarily fulfilling them. For blacks, frustration mounted as they found it hard to share in the affluence so visible around them. The civil rights movement reached a peak in early 1965 with the dramatic march in Alabama, for Congress responded to the violence with the Voting Rights Act of 1965, a significant triumph for southern blacks.

In the North, however, discrimination in employment, housing, and schooling persisted. Whites poured out into suburbs as blacks poured into the cities. The frustrations finally exploded in urban rioting that continued from 1964 through 1967. Watts in Los Angeles, Newark in New Jersey, and Detroit were the scenes of major violence. There were also new confrontations in the South. New black movements, more militant and separatist, developed. On April 4, 1968, the apostle of nonviolence, Martin Luther King, Jr., was assassinated.

Black activism spurred activism on the part of other minorities. Cesar Chavez battled in California to organize a farm laborers union; others organized Mexican-Americans around the cause of *La Raza,* racial and ethnic pride. Native Americans brought their cause to the public consciousness with demonstrations at Alcatraz and Wounded Knee. Minority groups gained during the decade in enhanced racial consciousness and self-pride, and in some real ways in terms of education, jobs, and political power.

In international affairs, the United States found itself in more and more difficulty. It intervened in the Dominican Republic in 1965 to prevent the establishment of a Communist government. At the end, there were 20,000 American troops in that small country, and the United States had again smashed a nationalist movement that seemed to have popular support.

In the Middle East, the situation remained explosive. As soon as UN troops were withdrawn in May 1967, Egypt and Israel went to war again. In an overpowering assault, Israel humiliated Egypt in the Six-Day War in June. It kept some of the territory it had occupied—the Sinai Peninsula, the Golan Heights, the Gaza Strip, and the West Bank. The result was an angry stalemate that defied solution, and the reassertion of Soviet influence in the Middle East and the entire Mediterranean region.

For the United States, Vietnam overshadowed everything else, as deepening involvement and confusion, secrecy, and deceit created mistrust and discontent at home. Events in the Tonkin Gulf in August 1964 led to the president's demand for, and congressional approval of, a resolution that gave him almost sole authority to act as he saw fit. Escalation of the war continued. By February 1965, bombing of North Vietnam became a systematic and regular policy. On the ground, "search and destroy" missions brought American troops in direct contact with the Vietcong. Both activities only stiffened resistance in North Vietnam.

In October 1965, the first public burning of a draft card took place in the United States. By the end of 1966, there were 380,000 troops in Vietnam; by the end of 1967, troop strength exceeded that at the peak of the Korean war. Casualties mounted accordingly. By the end of 1967, the futility of United States policies was being openly admitted. The Vietnamese success in the Tet offensive of early 1968 brought heavy pressure, both domestic and worldwide, to end the war. There were riots and demonstrations on American campuses, and more draft resisters fled to Canada.

In March 1968, LBJ announced an end to air and naval bombardment of North Vietnam; he also announced that he would not seek reelection. Talks began in Paris in April. But the number of American troops in Vietnam continued to rise, and by June, the war had become the longest in American history.

LBJ left office with the war still unresolved, and with both his career and the Great Society as additional casualties. The election of 1968 was itself a period of tragedy and violence. Robert Kennedy was assassinated in June in California, only two months after Martin Luther King, Jr., had been killed. The Democratic convention in Chicago was the scene of a "police riot" as police clashed with antiwar demonstrators. Hubert Humphrey, Johnson's vice-president and a firm supporter of the war, lost to Richard Nixon and Spiro Agnew, who campaigned for "law and order" and the rights of the "silent majority."

All these events had been accompanied by a vast youth movement of dissent and protest, and by the growth of a counterculture whose values were far different from those of the Establishment. It was characterized by distinct forms of expression and consciousness, including new styles of dress, social behavior, and music.

It was a revolt by white middle-class youth disillusioned with the world of their parents, and it focused on the confusions and contradictions of the visible tragedy of Vietnam. But "The Movement" was quickly invaded by exploiters. The drug culture itself became a tragedy for many young Americans, and political activism turned into slogans, communication by invective, sectarianism, and terrorism. In the end, its staying power proved brief; the dominant society succeeded in absorbing both rebels and rebellion.

Suggested Readings

To get close to the sixties, one might start by listening to The Beatles, *Sgt. Pepper's Lonely Hearts Club Band* (1967); The Rolling Stones, *Aftermath* (1966); Bob Dylan, *Blonde on Blonde* (1966); The Jefferson Airplane, *Surrealistic Pillow* (1967); Jimi Hendrix, *Electric Lady Land* (1968); and *Woodstock* (1970). One might also glance over M. Goodman (ed.), *The Movement Toward a New America: The Beginnings of a Long Revolution* (1970); Time-Life, *This Fabulous Century: 1960–1970* (1970); and E. Quinn and P. J. Dolan (eds.), *The Sense of the 60's* (1968). Much of the feeling of this decade is conveyed by P. Joseph (ed.), *Good Times: An Oral History of America in the Nineteen Sixties* (1974); T. Wolfe, *The Kandy-Kolored Tangerine-Flake Streamline Baby* (1965) and *The Electric Kool Aid Acid Test* (1968); and several collections of photographs: C. Harbutt and L. Jones, *America in Crisis* (1969); B. J. Fernandez, *In Opposition: Images of Dissent in the Sixties* (1968); Student Nonviolent Coordinating Committee, *The Movement* (1964); Rolling Stone, *Festival! The Book of American Music Celebrations* (1970); and B. Owens, *Suburbia* (1973). Some of the best social commentary and cultural history of the decade will be found in the issues of *Rolling Stone*. The most perceptive history is G. Hodgson, *America in Our Time* (1976). See also W. L. O'Neill, *Coming Apart* (1971); M. Viorst, *America in the 1960's* (1980); and A. J. Matusow, *The Unraveling of America: A History of Liberalism in the 1960s* (1984).

The many commission reports provide a guide to the anxieties of the sixties: Warren Commission (1964); National Advisory (Kerner) Commission on Civil Disorders (1968); (Scranton) Commission on Campus Unrest (1970); H. D. Graham and T. R. Gurr, *Violence in America: A Report to the National Commission on the Causes and Prevention of Violence* (1969); J. H. Skolnick, *The Politics of Protest* (1969); and D. Walker, *Rights in Conflict: The Violent Confrontation of Demonstrators and Police in the Parks and Streets of Chicago during the Week of the Democratic National Convention of 1968* (1968).

On the pervasive role of the media, see D. M. White and R. Averson (eds.), *Sight, Sound and Society* (1969); A. Sarris, *The American Cinema* (1968); M. McLuhan, *The Medium is the Massage* (1967); and E. Barnouw, *The Image Empire* (1970) and *Tube of Plenty* (1975). T. Gitlin, *The Whole World is Watching: The Mass Media in the Making and Unmaking of the New Left* (1980), examines the ways in which the media influenced perceptions of radical groups.

C. Lasch, *The Agony of the American Left* (1969), and I. Unger, *The Movement* (1974), are critical assessments of the New Left. On youth culture and protest, see K. Keniston, *The Uncommitted* (1965), *Young Radicals* (1968), and *Youth and Dissent* (1971); M. Mead, *Culture and Commitment* (1970); and J. Newfield, *A Prophetic Minority* (1966). The nature of the commitment will be found in P. Jacobs and S. Landau (eds.), *The New Radicals* (1966); C. Oglesby (ed.), *The Left Reader* (1969); M. V. Miller and S. Gilmore (eds.), *Revolution at Berkeley* (1965); S. M. Lipset and S. S. Wolin (eds.), *The Berkeley Student Revolt* (1965); and S. M. Lipset and P. G. Altbach (eds.), *Students in Revolt* (1969). See also K. Sale, *SDS* (1973).

R. Berman, *America in the Sixties* (1968), is an intellectual history. M. Dickstein, *Gates of Eden* (1977), is a cultural history, largely devoted to developments on the East Coast. The best studies of the music culture are C. Gillett, *The Sound of the City: The Rise of Rock and Roll* (1970), and G. Marcus, *Mystery Train: Images of America in Rock 'N' Roll Music* (1976). On the counterculture, J. Didion, *Slouching Towards Bethlehem* (1968), and *The White Album* (1979), are impressionistic works. See also T. Roszak, *The Making of a Counter Culture* (1969); H. Hopkins (ed.), *The Hippie Papers* (1968); Rolling Stone, *The Age of Paranoia: How the Sixties Ended* (1972); and H. Thompson, *Hell's Angels: A Strange and Terrible Saga* (1967).

On Lyndon B. Johnson, a place to start is the president's own memoir, *The Vantage Point* (1971). Two insiders provide a perspective in G. E. Reedy, *Lyndon Johnson: A Memoir* (1982), and E. F. Goldman, *The Tragedy of Lyndon Johnson* (1969). See also T. Wicker, *JFK and LBJ* (1968); D. Kearns, *Lyndon Johnson and the American Dream* (1976); M. Miller, *Lyndon: An Oral Biography* (1980); and R. Dugger, *The Politician: The Life and Times of Lyndon Johnson* (1982).

The brief ascendancy of Great Society thinking, its limitations and decline, are explored in M. E. Gettleman and D. Mermelstein, *The Great Society Reader* (1967). Government planning is examined in O. Graham, *Toward a Planned Society: From Roosevelt to Nixon* (1976), and M. Gelfand, *A Nation of Cities* (1976). J. C. Donovan, *The Politics of Poverty* (1967), dissects Johnson's "war on poverty." See also F. Piven and R. Cloward, *Regulating the Poor: The Function of Public Welfare* (1971). The emerging issue of ecology is studied in P. R. and A. H. Ehrlich, *Population, Resources, Environment* (1970); P. Shepherd and D. McKinley (eds.), *The Subversive Science: Essays Toward an Ecology of Man* (1969); W. Anderson, *A Place of Power: The American Episode in Human Evolution* (1976); J. Petulla, *American Environmental History* (1977); and the pioneering work of Rachel Carson, *Silent Spring* (1962).

The literature on the Black Revolution is immense. A. Meier, E. Rudwick, and F. L. Broderick (eds.), *Black Protest Thought in the Twentieth Century* (1971), is a collection of contemporary documents. Powerful black statements of the period reflect the changes in ideology and tactics: M. L. King, Jr., *Stride Toward Freedom* (1958), and *Why We Can't Wait* (1964); R. F. Williams, *Negroes with Guns* (1962); J. Baldwin, *The Fire Next Time* (1963); *The Autobiography of Malcolm X* (1964), and *Malcolm X Speaks* (1965); L. Jones, *Home: Social Essays* (1966); S. Carmichael and C. V. Hamilton, *Black Power: The Politics of Liberation in America* (1967); E. Cleaver, *Soul on Ice* (1968); J. Lester, *Look Out Whitey! Black Power's Gon' Get Your Mama!* (1968) and a moving and insightful autobiography by an activist, A. Moody, *Coming of Age in Mississippi* (1968). Two suggestive works on black ideology are H. Cruse, *The Crisis of the Negro Intellectual* (1967), and *Rebellion or Revolution* (1968). On the civil rights movement, see H. Sitkoff, *The Struggle for Black Equality 1954–1980* (1980); A. Meier and E. Rudwick, *Along the Color Line* (1976), and *CORE 1942–1968* (1973); D. L. Lewis, *King* (1970); H. Zinn, *SNCC: the New Abolitionists* (1964); W. H. Chafe, *Civilities and Civil Rights: Greensboro, North Carolina, and the Black Struggle for Freedom* (1979); D. Garrow, *Protest at Selma* (1978); and C. Carson, *In Struggle: SNCC and the Black Awakening of the 1960s* (1981). For a retrospective view, see J.

Farmer, *Lay Bare the Heart: An Autobiography of the Civil Rights Movement* (1985). On M. L. King, see S. B. Oates, *Let the Trumpet Sound: The Life of Martin Luther King, Jr.* (1982). H. Raines, *My Soul is Rested* (1977), is an excellent oral history of the movement. On black nationalism, J. H. Bracey, Jr., A. Meier, and E. Rudwick (eds.), *Black Nationalism in America* (1970), is a collection of documents. See also E. U. Essien-Udom, *Black Nationalism* (1962); C. E. Lincoln, *The Black Muslims in America* (1961); and the works of Malcolm X cited above. On racial violence, see R. Conot, *Rivers of Blood, Years of Darkness* (1967), for the Watts riot; and J. Hersey, *The Algiers Motel Incident* (1968), for the Detroit riot. On black literature, two valuable anthologies are A. Chapman (ed.), *New Black Voices* (1972), and L. Jones and L. Neal (eds.), *Black Fire* (1968). See also R. Ellison's powerful novel, *Invisible Man* (1952), and his book of essays, *Shadow and Act* (1964). On black America in the 1970s, a powerful oral history is J. L. Gwaltney, *Drylongso* (1980).

There is a growing literature on the Mexican-American. A good place to start is C. McWilliams, *North from Mexico* (1948). This may be updated with M. S. Meier and F. Rivera, *The Chicanos* (1972); S. Steiner, *La Raza* (1970); W. Moquin (ed.), *A Documentary History of the Mexican-Americans* (1971); A. Mirande and E. Enriquez, *La Chicana: The Mexican-American Woman* (1980); and R. Acuna, *Occupied America: A History of Chicanos* (2nd ed., 1980). On Cesar Chavez and the farm workers movement, see J. London and H. Anderson, *So Shall Ye Reap* (1970); P. Matthiessen, *Sal Si Puedes* (1969); R. B. Taylor, *Chavez and the Farm Workers* (1975); and J. E. Levy, *Cesar Chavez: Autobiography of La Causa* (1975).

The foreign policy of the Johnson presidency is critically examined in P. Geyelin, *Lyndon B. Johnson and the World* (1966); T. Draper, *Abuse of Power* (1967); J. W. Fulbright, *The Arrogance of Power* (1967); and I. F. Stone, *Time of Torment* (1967). For a vigorous defense, see W. W. Rostow, *The Diffusion of Power* (1972). On the intervention in the Dominican Republic, see T. Szulc, *Dominican Diary* (1965); J. B. Martin, *Overtaken by Events* (1966), the personal memoir of the American negotiator; T. Draper, *The Dominican Revolt* (1968); and A. F. Lowenthal, *The Dominican Intervention* (1972). The relationship between militarism and economic life is assessed in J. L. Clayton (ed.), *The Economic Impact of the Cold War* (1970).

The literature on Vietnam implicates not one but several administrations. *The Pentagon Papers* (1971) is an indispensable source. The best introduction to American involvement is G. C. Herring, *America's Longest War* (rev. ed., 1986). See also, in addition to the works cited in previous chapters, S. Karnow, *Vietnam* (1983); M. and S. Gettleman and L. and C. Kaplan (eds.), *Conflict in Indochina* (1970); M. G. Raskin and B. Fall (eds.), *The Vietnam Reader* (1965); and W. Brown, *The Last Chopper: The Denouement of the American Role in Vietnam 1963–1975* (1976). The deepening involvement of the United States during the Kennedy, Johnson,

CRUMBLING CONSENSUS

and Nixon administrations is also examined in F. Fitzgerald, *Fire in the Lake* (1972); D. Halberstam, *The Making of a Quagmire* (1965), and *The Best and the Brightest* (1972); R. Shaplan, *The Road from War: Vietnam 1965–1971* (1971); and J. C. Goulden, *Truth is the First Casualty: The Gulf of Tonkin Affair—Illusion and Reality* (1969).

Guenter Lewy, *America in Vietnam* (1978), is a defense of American behavior. For the view of "insiders," see C. L. Cooper, *The Lost Crusade: America in Vietnam* (1970); T. Hoopes, *The Limits of Intervention* (1969); M. Taylor, *Swords and Ploughshares* (1972); and W. W. Rostow, *The Diffusion of Power* (1972). On the tragic consequences of American involvement, see especially F. Harvey, *Air War—Vietnam* (1967); C. and S. Mydans, *The Violent Peace* (1968); R. Hammer, *One Morning in the War: The Tragedy at Son My* (1971); and S. Hersh, *My Lai 4: A Report on the Massacre and Its Aftermath* (1970), and *Cover Up* (1972). On dissent, the classic account is N. Mailer, *The Armies of the Night* (1968). See also D. Wakefield, *Supernation at Peace and War* (1968), and A. Kendrick, *The Wound Within* (1974). For personal accounts of the war, see the literature cited for Chapter 33.

Two contrasting views of the 1968 election are T. H. White, *The Making of the President 1968* (1969), and L. Chester, G. Hodgson, and B. Page, *An American Melodrama* (1969). See also N. Mailer, *Miami and the Siege of Chicago* (1968); J. McGinniss, *The Selling of the President 1968* (1969); and R. M. Scammon and B. J. Wattenberg, *The Real Majority* (1970).

THE POLITICS OF RIGHTEOUSNESS: NIXON AND CARTER

Chapter 33

Toward the end of his administration, President Jimmy Carter thought it necessary to convene a domestic summit conference on the state of the nation. For six days in July 1979, he conferred at his Camp David retreat with cabinet members, political and civic leaders, bankers, clergymen, corporation executives, university professors and presidents, trade unionists, and economists. He also ventured into several nearby communities to talk with middle-class families about what troubled them. It was an unprecedented attempt by a president to assess his own leadership and the national mood.

The concerns that prompted such an assessment were clear enough—an energy and environmental crisis, inflation and unemployment, economic stagnation and an eroding standard of living, a hostile and revolutionary world, and public opinion polls that revealed a loss of confidence in the ability of the president to meet these challenges.

These concerns had dominated most of the decade. Some ten years earlier, Richard M. Nixon, in his inaugural address, acknowledged the deepening mood of desperation in the United States. He described a nation "rich in goods, but ragged in spirit; reaching with magnificent precision for the moon, but falling into raucous discord on earth. . . . We are torn by division, wanting unity. We see around us empty lives, wanting fulfillment." He then invoked the familiar political promise to unite the nation and rally it around the proper goals: "To a crisis of the spirit, we need an answer of the spirit."

Nixon's attempt to unite the American people and regenerate them spiritually ended in abuses of public power unprecedented in the history of the nation. His successors—Jerry Ford and Jimmy Carter—restored honesty and integrity to the presidency. But Americans remained deeply troubled and frustrated about problems that seemed to defy solution. Raised on the gospel of progress, few wanted to be told that there were limits to the nation's capacities, powers, and natural resources; that they must lower their expectations and aspirations; that they would need to exercise self-discipline and be prepared to make sacrifices.

Nor did Americans accommodate easily to recession, inflation, and unemployment, polluted air and water, deteriorating neighborhood services and rising crime rates, new tax burdens, and the declining quality of public education.

Sensing a helplessness to control their lives and destinies, Americans turned to various remedies, not all of them political.

The 1970s came to be called the Me Decade, and best-seller lists were dominated by books on the pleasures of self-improvement and self-awareness, how to make oneself more powerful and wealthy, and how to refurbish one's body and psyche. Spectator sports reached new heights of popularity, as did individualized forms of recreation such as jogging. Many Americans satisfied their emotional hunger by becoming "born-again" or by embracing one of the new religious cults.

In the same decade, women experienced a self-awareness that went beyond psychological self-fulfillment. The march of 50,000 women up New York's Fifth Avenue in 1970 heralded a decade in which women organized to improve the quality of their lives and their future prospects. Inspired by the civil rights movement of the previous decade, they sought to liberate themselves from demeaning cultural stereotypes, job and wage discrimination, and sexual harassment. Although the movement embraced a number of goals, it came to focus on a proposed Equal Rights Amendment to the Constitution: "Equality of rights under law shall not be denied or abridged by any state on account of sex."

Passed by Congress early in the decade and submitted to the states for approval, it failed to obtain the number of states necessary for ratification. In the meantime, women made progress in the work force, particularly in the professions and in business, and achieved reforms in abortion laws. But they faced strong resistance as well, reflecting divisions among women as well as the hostility of many men to changes in traditional female roles.

Watergate, Vietnam, and the Iranian hostage crisis cast their shadow over much of the seventies. Without any real parallel in the past, they proved to be bitter and emotionally draining experiences, perceived by most people as part of a collective failure. Even as Americans sought for ways to improve themselves individually, they needed reassurance about the nation's moral fiber, power, virility, and destiny. Presidents Nixon, Ford, and Carter failed to provide those reassurances. That failure would be effectively exploited in 1980 by Ronald Reagan. ■

RICHARD NIXON IN POWER

The cut of Richard Nixon's clothes defined the image he wanted to convey—neat and well-tailored, with the creases in place and the tie properly knotted. The American flag he wore in his lapel exalted his patriotism. He surrounded himself with aides who shared the qualities he most admired. They were tough-minded, clean-cut, ambitious, hard-working. If at times they appeared to be cold and devoid of imagination or vision, they more than compensated for these flaws with unswerving loyalty and a grasp of what had to be done. "I'll approve of whatever will work," White House Chief of Staff H. R. Haldeman promised, "and am concerned with results—not methods." That promise set the tone for the Nixon presidency itself.

Nixon had always prided himself on his ability to know what people wanted. He claimed to understand the sources of their fears and frustrations. He felt in touch with the prevailing mood. The America that had elected him, as Nixon viewed that "silent majority," had grown weary of mounting welfare rolls crammed with chiselers, federal intervention in state and community affairs, soft and overindulgent judges, and moral permissiveness. "As long as Richard Nixon is President," Vice-President Agnew promised, "Main Street is not going to turn into Smut Alley." The quietness in Washington promised a welcome release of tensions, gratifying not only to the "silent majority" but to others as well.

Retreat from Liberalism

The reluctance of the Nixon administration to press school desegregation in the face of local resistance reflected the president's sense of the national mood. In October 1970, the U.S. Commission on Civil Rights reported that "a major breakdown" in enforcement of civil rights legislation had occurred, for which the federal government bore principal responsibility. The president

THE TRAPPED HOUSEWIFE

was undisturbed by this finding. He knew his constituents well, and he no doubt knew of the public opinion polls that showed some 78 percent of the people opposed to the idea of busing school children to effect racial integration. Most of these people, including many Democrats who had not voted for him, applauded the president's recommendation that school busing orders by federal courts be set aside until an alternative solution could be found.

This was an issue by no means confined to the South; it aroused strong emotions and resistance elsewhere in the nation. By the mid-1970s, the South had, in fact, achieved a higher degree of racial integration than had the North, and the most violent confrontations over busing were taking place in Boston. The "neighborhood school" acquired a halo that made it a convenient rallying point for those who wished to hold on to past racial patterns.

Vacancies on the Supreme Court gave the president the opportunity to redeem his campaign promise to appoint "strict constructionist" justices and to satisfy the southern constituency that had made his election possible. Nixon's selection of Warren E. Burger of Minnesota to replace Earl Warren as Chief Justice was confirmed by the Senate in June 1969. But the president's move to name a southerner to the Court led to confrontation with the Senate. The dispute had less to do with the regional background of the nominees than with Nixon's selection of mediocrities with highly questionable records.

The Senate rejected Clement F. Haynesworth, Jr., of South Carolina, largely for his past carelessness in conflict of interest cases. Shocked by this setback, Nixon next chose G. Harrold Carswell of Florida. Carswell too proved vulnerable to attack on his racial record as well as his professional competence. Nor did a Republican senator help the cause of Nixon's nominee when he observed "that even if he [Carswell] were mediocre, there are a lot of mediocre judges and people and lawyers. Aren't they entitled to a little representation and a little chance? We can't have all Brandeises and Cardozos and Frankfurters and stuff like that. I doubt we can. I doubt we want to."

When the Senate rejected Carswell as unfit, Nixon nominated Harry A. Blackmun of Minnesota, whom the Senate unanimously confirmed. When a new vacancy occurred, the president appointed a southerner, Lewis F. Powell of Virginia, a competent, conservative jurist, and the Senate had no difficulty in approving the nomination.

Economic Game Plans

The president's proposal for *revenue sharing* between federal and state governments became the avowed keystone of his domestic program. With some 10 million Americans on welfare rolls in 1969, Nixon hoped to clean up the "welfare mess" by shifting the burden of payments from the states to the federal government. At the same time, he startled some of his more conservative backers by recommending that the welfare system be replaced with a family assistance program.

This program would include a guaranteed minimum income of $1600 a year for a family of four; food stamps would add still another $820 to this sum. The amount was hardly sufficient, but the establishment of such a principle would be significant. The measure, however, died in Congress.

Depending on which economist or government expert made the assessment, recession or depression had overtaken the American economy by mid-1970. To check the inflationary spiral, President Nixon sought tighter money policies and a reduction in federal spending. But prices continued to rise. At the same time, unemployment, especially among the underprivileged and the young, added significantly to the cost of welfare. The overexpanded war industries were hard hit by the winding down of the American involvement in Vietnam. Educated, middle-income technicians and engineers suddenly found themselves out of work and competing for jobs in a glutted market.

Since 1893, the United States had enjoyed a favorable balance of trade with foreign nations. But in 1971 the money paid out for international debts exceeded the money taken in by overseas sales, and added still another dimension to domestic economic difficulties.

In his "game plan" for reversing the inflationary surge, Nixon rejected as "unworkable" Democratic proposals for wage and price controls. But as the maneuvering for the 1972 elections intensified, Nixon ordered a ninety-day wage-price freeze. Once the freeze ended, a pay board and a price commission would have the authority to rule on wage and price increases. To regain American markets abroad, the president also declared virtual economic warfare on other industrial nations. His strategy here included taking the dollar off the gold standard, with the hope that devaluation would cut the cost of American exports in terms of foreign currencies.

The business community gave the president's New Economic Policy a resounding vote of confidence. Labor leaders, however, distressed by the omission of a profit freeze, were militantly opposed to the wage freeze. For the tens of millions of unemployed, there was little relief or hope in the new policy. Joblessness among black youth, for example, soared over 40 percent in the summer of 1971. Structural unemployment, once limited to pockets of declining industries such as coal mining in Appalachia and textile manufacture in New England, had by now spread to most central cities. Its predominantly racial character had made it a social as well as an economic issue.

Even as hard times settled on the nation, the American people enjoyed the dividends of a long-term government investment in space conquest. Only six months after entering the White House, President Nixon could boast of a masterful achievement by the United States. The first successful manned space mission to the moon, Apollo 11, came on July 16, 1969. Four days later, the lunar module came down on a rock-strewn plain on the Moon's Sea of Tranquility. When Neil Armstrong set foot on the moon's surface, he declared: "That's one small step for man, one giant leap for mankind." But whatever Apollo 11 did for United States prestige in the world community, the persistent war in Vietnam continued to undermine it.

THE PRESIDENT AT WAR

The management of foreign affairs became the principal concern of Nixon's first administration. During the 1968 campaign, he ventured the opinion that the nation "could run itself domestically without a President. All you want is a competent Cabinet to run the country at home. You need a President for foreign policy; no Secretary of State is really important. The President makes foreign policy."

In foreign affairs, Henry A. Kissinger and his White House staff of 110 overshadowed not only Secretary of State William P. Rogers and the 11,000 State Department employees, but the Department of Defense and the National Security Council as well. Both as special assistant for national security affairs and later as secretary of state, Kissinger preferred secret diplomacy.

The foreign policy constructed by Nixon and Kissinger recognized that the Communist world was no longer unified. The growing tension between the Soviet Union and China underscored that recognition. Even as the United States pressed the war in Vietnam, it sought to improve relations with both major Communist powers based on mutual acceptance of the prevailing balance of power. "It will be a safer world and a better world," said Nixon, "if we have a strong, healthy United States, Europe, Soviet Union, China, Japan—each balancing the other, not playing one against the other, an even balance."

At the same time, he made clear the willingness of the United States to "participate in the defense and development of allies and friends." But he preferred, he said, to leave the "basic responsibility" to those allies and friends, particularly when it came to military action. In Southeast Asia, however, that policy proved unworkable. Success eluded the United States—with tragic consequences.

Initiatives for Peace

Although Nixon entered the White House with the reputation of a hardened cold warrior, he took the initiative to thaw the Cold War and establish a stable world order based on detente with the Soviet Union and the People's Republic of China. In August 1971 he announced that he had accepted an invitation from Premier Chou En-lai to visit China. None of his initiatives revealed the president's turnabout more dramatically and elicited such excitement and anticipation.

The "peace mission," as Nixon called it, came in February 1972 and resulted in mutual expressions of good will and agreement to settle differences peacefully and to expand trade and cultural relations. What few Democratic presidents might have been willing to risk, Nixon had successfully achieved.

Committed to a strong defense establishment, Nixon moved cautiously in the sensitive area of disarmament. With the United States and the Soviet Union spending $130 billion annually for defense, the need for some kind of mutual limitation on the balance of terror had long seemed obvious and desirable. Nixon agreed to enter strategic arms limitation (SALT) talks. To ensure the strongest possible bargaining position, however, he urged upon Congress a missile program designed to enlarge the already great strategic capacity of the United States.

Several months after his successful China mission, Nixon capped his detente diplomacy with a trip to Moscow. On May 26, 1972, the president and Leonid Brezhnev agreed to limit the number of defensive missile sites and strategic offensive missiles.

The Middle East remained a source of tension.

"One small step for man." Astronaut Buzz Aldrin as photographed on the moon by his Apollo 11 partner, Commander Neil Armstrong. (*UPI/Bettmann Newsphotos*)

Without adequate guarantees of its security, Israel defied the United Nations resolution of 1967, which called upon it to withdraw from territories occupied in the Six-Day War. The United States backed Israel with military aid and political support, while the Soviet Union helped arm Egypt and Syria. The continuing plight of Palestinian refugees and the demand for an independent Palestinian state complicated Kissinger's efforts to arrange a peace settlement between Egypt, Syria, and Israel.

In October 1973, hostilities again broke out as Egypt and Syria attacked Israel on the Jewish holy day of Yom Kippur. Both sides suffered heavy casualties, but Israel soon demonstrated its military superiority. The United Nations Security Council adopted a resolution that called for a cease-fire and peace negotiations based on its 1967 resolution. At the same time, the oil embargo imposed by the Arab nations impressed the entire world with the new reality of a unified bloc of oil-exporting nations. It raised havoc with available domestic supplies, sent gasoline prices skyrocketing, and made suddenly urgent the long-debated energy question.

But even as the Nixon administration tried to stabilize the situation in the Middle East and effect a detente with the Soviets and China, it needed to confront the continuing war in Southeast Asia.

Toward Vietnamization

Despite the Paris peace talks, the Vietnam war showed no signs of subsiding. As vice-president under Eisenhower, Nixon had initially urged military intervention to bolster the French position in Indochina. He had supported the policies of Kennedy and Johnson, differing with them only in his willingness to maximize the military thrust. Sensing widespread war weariness, however, Nixon pledged during the 1968 election campaign to end the conflict on "honorable terms" and bring home the American prisoners of war.

At the time Nixon became president, United States troop strength in Vietnam had reached a peak of 542,500. The number of Americans killed in action was about to exceed the 33,639 killed in the Korean war. More bomb tonnage had been dropped on Vietnam than had been expended by the Allies on all of Europe during World War II. Moreover, the United States was spending more than $25 billion a year on what had become the most unpopular war in the nation's history.

The president placed considerable reliance on the negotiating talents of Henry Kissinger, who had declared before joining the Nixon administration: "We fought a military war, our opponents fought a political one. We sought physical attrition; our opponents aimed for our psychological exhaustion. In the process we lost sight of one of the cardinal maxims of guerrilla war: the guerrilla wins if he does not lose. The conventional army loses if it does not win."

In June 1969, President Nixon announced his program for Vietnamization of the war. By the end of August, he would bring home 25,000 American combat troops, who would be replaced by South Vietnamese contingents. The idea was simple; the United States would maintain military pressure in the air, while the South Vietnamese would assume the bulk of the casualties and fighting on the

A South Vietnamese family struggles to escape from an aerial bombardment of their village. (*UPI, photograph by Kyoichi Sawada*)

THE POLITICS OF RIGHTEOUSNESS

ground. There was nothing particularly new about Vietnamization; both Kennedy and Johnson had talked about the Vietnamese doing their own fighting. But it had not worked. How could a hopelessly corrupt and inefficient South Vietnamese government function without large-scale American assistance?

The War at Home

Although Nixon stepped up his Vietnamization program, neither the pace of American withdrawal nor the progress of the war satisfied anyone. On October 15, 1969, in the largest public protest since the war began, hundreds of thousands across the country, most of them students and young people, observed Vietnam Moratorium Day. The most impressive of the demonstrations took place one month later in Washington, D.C., where more than 250,000 gathered. Outside the gates of the White House, some 40,000 participated in a March against Death, each holding a card with the name of an American killed in Vietnam.

The demonstrations had no apparent effect on the president. As if to underscore that fact, the White House announced that during the march, Nixon had been watching a football game on television. Convinced that the "great silent majority" stood behind him, the president lashed back at his critics: "North Vietnam cannot defeat or humiliate the United States. Only Americans can do that." He explained that the alternatives in Vietnam were to admit defeat and order an immediate and humiliating withdrawal, or to press the Vietnamization program and secure an honorable peace. When the choice was put that way, most Americans—some 77 percent, according to a Gallup poll—backed the president.

Nixon's response to war critics climaxed administration efforts to win public support. On Law Day, May 1, 1969, Attorney General John Mitchell warned that "the time has come for an end to patience" in dealing with student war dissenters. Vice-President Agnew charged that the disturbances had been instigated and manipulated by "an effete corps of impudent snobs who characterize themselves as intellectuals."

Pleased with the response to this verbal offensive, Agnew became even bolder and attacked the media, singling out the "unelected elite" of "anchormen, commentators and executive producers," who "settle upon the 20 minutes or so of film and commentary that is to reach the public."

How Many My Lais?

The administration had good reason to be concerned with the television and press coverage of the war. The barrage of pictures and words daily reminded people of the brutality and apparent futility of the conflict. Early in 1970, for example, the full details were revealed of an American attack in March 1968 on My Lai, a Vietnamese hamlet. Led by Lieutenant William L. Calley, Jr., a company of United States soldiers had massacred at least 175 and perhaps more than 500 Vietnamese, mostly old men, women, youths, and infants. The Army's official inquiry found the troops guilty of "individual and group acts of murder, rape, sodomy, maiming and assault on noncombatants and the mistreatment and killing of detainees."

The operation appeared to have been based on false intelligence reports and the difficulty of identifying Vietcong sympathizers. Women and children had been known to fire at unsuspecting American soldiers. "People were talking about killing everything that moved," one soldier remarked. "Everyone knew what we were going to do."

This was obviously not the kind of war Americans had been accustomed to fighting. Over nationwide television, a soldier described how they had entered the village: "We didn't see any VC. People began coming out of their hootches, and the guys shot them down and then burned the hootches or burned the hootches and shot the people when they came out. Sometimes they would round up a bunch and shoot them together. It went on like this all day." The lone American casualty had deliberately shot himself in the foot to avoid participating in the slaughter.

These startling revelations, given full coverage in the press and over television, confirmed what many Americans already suspected: The war had deteriorated into the kind of bloodbath the United States had initially intervened to prevent. Although wartime atrocities were hardly unique, the degree of American complicity disturbed a nation accustomed to seeing itself as civilized and decent. The conviction of Calley raised equally disturbing questions about who bore ultimate responsibility and whether My Lai had been an exceptional and isolated incident.

At his own trial, Calley's commander declared: "Every unit of brigade size had its My Lai hidden some place." Moreover, the United States had long followed a policy of destroying hamlets suspected of harboring Vietcong guerrillas. Lieutenant Calley's platoon had simply performed the task with the thoroughness characteristic of the more impersonal aerial bombardment.

From "War by Tantrum" to "Peace with Honor"

On April 20, 1970, President Nixon announced that Vietnamization and the phased withdrawal of American troops were proceeding successfully. Within ten days, however, he ordered United States troops into neighboring Cambodia to clear out "enemy sanctuaries." Unknown to Congress or the American people, United States planes had already been engaged for over a year in the bombardment of Cambodia. The administration denied that the invasion was an undeclared war on an independent nation. It was not even an invasion, said the White House, but an "incursion" (a brief raid). By June 29, all American forces had been withdrawn, their objective presumably gained.

The casualties of the expanded war reached into the very heartland of America. With massive protests that exceeded anything yet seen, college students responded to Nixon's latest move. Some schools were forced to close altogether, and disruptions hit colleges barely affected by previous protests. At Kent State University in Ohio, national guardsmen, called out during campus demonstrations, fired into a crowd of students, killing four and wounding nine. Although Nixon deplored the incident, he reminded Americans "that when dissent turns to violence, it invites tragedy."

If the demonstrations were largely confined to campuses, the war weariness was not. Among American troops in Vietnam, it had begun to show itself in declining morale, insubordination, and increased use of narcotics. To fight this kind of war, some soldiers argued, it helped to be "stoned." In Congress, meanwhile, Republican Senator Mark Hatfield of Oregon and Democratic Senator George McGovern of South Dakota proposed to amend pending legislation so that all United States troops would be removed from Vietnam by the end of 1971. Although the Senate defeated the measure 55 to 39, it revealed growing skepticism and impatience in a body that had until now supported the policies of three administrations in Vietnam.

To speed up Vietnamization, President Nixon in November 1970 resumed full-scale bombing of North Vietnam. Although the attacks were called "protective retaliation strikes," they amounted to the most massive aerial bombardment in history.

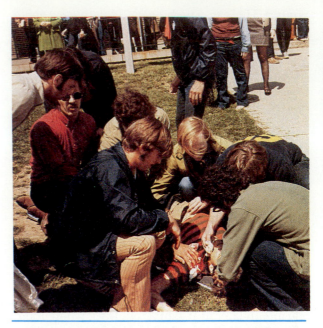

Kent State University, May 4, 1970, after campus demonstrations against Nixon's expansion of the war into Cambodia were broken up by the Ohio National Guard. (*UPI/Bettmann Newsphotos*)

In February 1971, South Vietnamese forces invaded Laos in still another "incursion" designed to ferret out enemy forces and reduce the flow of supplies from North Vietnam into the South. Despite heavy American bombing support, however, the South Vietnamese were routed by Communist counterattacks. That spectacle did little to advance the cause of Vietnamization.

In March 1972, when North Vietnamese and Vietcong forces were able to launch a major offensive in the South, Vietnamization suffered a serious setback. Nixon responded with saturation air raids on the North as well as an air and sea blockade. The action revived antiwar protest at home, but the White House reported mail favoring the president's policy by a 5 to 1 ratio; not until much later was it learned that the Committee to Re-elect the President had spent a good deal of money on bogus telegrams supporting the president.

Not long after Kissinger assured the world that agreement was near, the Paris negotiations again broke down. With the election now safely behind him, and reinforced by the large popular mandate he had received, the president in mid-December 1972 ordered B-52 bombers over Hanoi and other major northern cities. The asaults were massive, thorough, and round-the-clock. Neither hospitals, schools, nor residential areas were spared. It had

THE POLITICS OF RIGHTEOUSNESS

Reacting against student antiwar demonstrations, construction workers in New York City marched in support of the American war effort in Vietnam. (*UPI/Bettmann Newsphotos*)

come to be, as one columnist put it, "war by tantrum." Vietnamese casualties mounted, as did the number of American planes shot down and prisoners taken.

With both sides pressing for a settlement, intensive negotiations between Kissinger and Le Duc Tho of North Vietnam finally produced a cease-fire in late January 1973. United States troops would be withdrawn while North Vietnam was releasing American prisoners of war. "Peace with honor," the jubilant and relieved president announced, had finally been achieved. What remained questionable was the enormous price the United States had paid in waging the war and how long the peace could last.

Reflecting the recent Vietnam experience, Congress moved to limit the power of the president to wage war without congressional approval. The War Powers Act provided that if the president should send troops to a foreign country, he must within 48 hours fully explain the action to Congress. Moreover, he was obliged to halt the operation within 60 days unless Congress thought otherwise. President Nixon angrily vetoed the measure, but the House

and the Senate on November 7, 1973, overrode the veto.

Earlier, in August, Congress had voted to deny the president the use of federal funds in Cambodia, which the United States had continued to bomb in support of the war against Communist insurgents. In a "compromise," Nixon promised to end the bombing on August 15, thereby ending United States military action in Southeast Asia.

The Election of 1972

While the war in Vietnam still raged, the Democratic convention of 1972 had nominated Senator George McGovern of South Dakota, an avowed antiwar candidate. That convention was unique in the history of the party. Changes in delegate selection had resulted in far greater representation of minority groups, women, and young people than in any previous party convention. The party's old guard, many deprived of their traditional seats as delegates, could only look on in dismay. The expanded role of young people reflected not only their stake in the Vietnam war, but also the Twenty-Sixth Amendment to the Constitution (ratified June 30, 1971), which lowered the voting age to eighteen.

If McGovern lacked the political savvy of the professional politician, he possessed an antiwar record and a commitment to social reform that attracted the party's new constituency. But his nomination badly split the party, and the Republicans exploited domestic fears of radicalism. As *Time* magazine put it, Richard Nixon had decided to run against the sixties—"against radicalism, excess, permissiveness." McGovern was portrayed as an irresponsible leftist, committed to social reforms that would bankrupt the nation, to disarmament proposals that would endanger national security, and to an antiwar position that would result in a dishonorable peace. The contrast between the two candidates could not have been greater; the electorate had a uniquely clear-cut choice to make.

With so much at stake, the Committee to Re-elect the President took nothing for granted, sparing neither funds nor constitutional and legal scruples. John Mitchell left his post as attorney general to take over personal command of the campaign. In his mind, the reelection of the president was nothing less than a matter of national survival. With a lavish campaign treasury (enriched by illegal corporate contributions), the committee was not above falsifying documents, forging letters, burglarizing confidential files, and gathering information on the private lives of opponents.

Its tactics were not altered by the assassination attempt on Governor George Wallace of Alabama, even though he was no longer a threat as a competing spokesman for conservative principles. The attack, which left Wallace permanently paralyzed, also ended his political career as a national figure.

The incumbent president rested on his record: the China mission, detente with the Soviet Union, and a Vietnamization program that had reduced the number of American casualties. McGovern campaigned on the peace issue. However, Kissinger said, just before the election, "Peace is at hand," and the president assured the people it would be an honorable peace. McGovern called the Nixon administration "the most corrupt in history," but most Americans did not believe him. With 61 percent of the popular vote, Nixon won the victory he had coveted.

Shortly after Nixon's second inaugural, the Vietnam war ended in an uncertain truce. The president turned to persistent and mounting do-mestic problems. After his decision in early 1973 to substitute voluntary restraints for price and wage controls, the cost of living soared to new heights. In keeping with his political philosophy, Nixon tried to reduce federal spending, and the cuts came, predictably, at the expense of social programs. Even when Congress appropriated funds for such programs, the president often refused to spend the money, thereby redefining the constitutional relationship of Congress to the presidency.

Although Nixon had won a resounding mandate, he secluded himself from Congress and the public. Press conferences were infrequent. Despite his pledge to return "power to the people," the White House bureaucracy seemed more formidable and unapproachable than ever. The "palace guard" was headed by two men: John D. Ehrlichman (domestic affairs advisor) and H. R. (Bob) Haldeman (White House chief of staff). They operated as the president's shield, controlled access to him, and placed loyalty to him above the law itself. With so much power in the hands of so few, abuses were no doubt inevitable. Few people suspected their extent, and fewer still thought them possible.

ABUSE OF POWER

From the beginning of the Nixon administration, the war in Vietnam and its escalation had sharply divided the American people. On college campuses and in the streets, antiwar demonstrations had grown more militant, as had the efforts to control them. Confronted with massive protests and disruptions, the Nixon administration came to view the opposition in conspiratorial terms and as made up of the president's traditional foes: liberals, intellectuals, and reporters. In mid-1970, the president endorsed a secret plan of intelligence operations so far-reaching and so clearly above the law that FBI Director J. Edgar Hoover interceded to have it revoked. Nevertheless, a mood had been established in the White House that encouraged and justified, in the name of national security, clandestine activities infringing on the fundamental liberties of American citizens. *Time* magazine called it "a siege mentality."

The appropriate epitaph of the Nixon presidency was sounded quite inadvertently by John N. Mitchell, the president's former law partner and campaign manager and an avid champion of rigorous law enforcement. Shortly before assuming his post as attorney general, Mitchell suggested: "Watch what we do, not what we say." Less than halfway through Nixon's second term, what the American people saw and heard left them incredulous and dismayed.

Mitchell himself, among others, stood indicted on charges of conspiracy, obstruction of justice, and perjury. Through a series of events known collectively as Watergate, the public would be given an intimate glimpse of what went on in the privacy of the president's Oval Office. That was more than enough to destroy President Nixon's credibility, strip his administration of any moral authority, and pave the way for his downfall.

Break-in and Cover-up

On June 17, 1972, Frank Wills, a security guard at the elegant Watergate hotel-apartment-office-building complex in Washington, D.C., phoned the police to report suspicious activity. When they arrived, the police found five gloved men with sophisticated electronic surveillance equipment and burglary tools in the headquarters of the Democratic party. Two of the suspects turned out to be officials employed by the Committee to Re-Elect the President (CREEP, as it would be called): James W. McCord, Jr., the committee's security officer and a former CIA wiretap expert, and G. Gordon Liddy, the committee's lawyer, a former FBI agent and White House consultant. Still another suspect, E. Howard Hunt, Jr., had been a former CIA agent and White House aide.

During the presidential campaign, the Democrats tried to make the most of the Watergate incident, but most Americans preferred to believe the official denials and explanations. Attorney General Mitchell said he had been "surprised and dismayed" by the Watergate burglary. President Nixon affirmed on August 29 "that no one in the White House staff, no one in this administration presently employed, was involved in this very bizarre incident."

The president knew better. He decided, as the nation would learn only later, to tell a calculated lie. New revelations would force him to repeat that lie on numerous occasions. The Watergate break-in proved to be part of a massive, deliberate, and illegally financed operation to sabotage the opposition's campaign and ensure the reelection of Richard Nixon. Only a few persons in the White House knew all the details of the operation. The arrest of the Watergate Seven moved them into immediate action to cover their tracks by destroying relevant evidence, paying "hush money" to maintain the silence of the defendants, and lying to the grand jury of the District of Columbia.

The burglary itself infuriated the president. But a full probe of the affair, he realized, might reveal too much about White House intelligence operations and implicate several of his closest advisors, including John Mitchell. Less than a week after the break-in, President Nixon agreed to the first stage of a cover-up. Using the pretext of national security, he instructed the CIA to intercede with the FBI to stop any further investigation of Watergate. By June 23, 1972, President Nixon had become a co-conspirator in the criminal obstruction of justice.

When a grand jury indicted the Watergate Seven, Nixon was relieved that the case would proceed no further. The cover-up appeared to be working smoothly. By March 22, 1973, however, Nixon was no longer so certain. On that day, the president summoned John Mitchell, H. R. Haldeman, John Ehrlichman, and John Dean (his chief legal counsel) to the Oval Office. "I don't give a shit what happens," he told them. "I want you all to stonewall it, let them plead the Fifth Amendment, cover up or anything else if it'll save it—save the plan. That's the whole point."

What suddenly confronted the president in March 1973 was a bewildering range of options, all of them fraught with danger. He could reveal the full particulars of White House involvement, and thereby open "a can of worms." He could offer up some sacrifices, even Mitchell, without implicating himself. He could maintain the present deception. The president opted for the continued cover-up, even if that required "blackmail" money to maintain the silence of the Watergate defendants. To reveal the truth was to invite certain trouble. "There is a certain domino situation here," Dean warned Nixon. "If some things start going, a lot of other things are going to start going. . . ."

Revelations and Purges

The trial of the Watergate Seven opened in early 1973. It proved to be brief. Five of the defendants pleaded guilty to wiretapping, burglary, and attempted bugging, while two others—McCord and Liddy—were convicted by a jury. If the White House had had its way, the entire Watergate affair would have ended at that point. But before imposing sentences, John J. Sirica, the presiding judge,

IN THE OVAL OFFICE

On September 15, 1972, President Nixon congratulated his chief legal counsel, John W. Dean, for his adroitness in handling the Watergate scandal, "putting your fingers in the dikes every time that leaks have sprung here and sprung there." As if the President had learned nothing from his recent experience, he then proceeded to discuss with Dean the need to move against their political enemies. His overwhelming electoral victory in November reinforced such designs.

PRESIDENT: I think we are going to fix the son-of-a-bitch. Believe me. We are going to. We've got to, because he's a bad man.

DEAN: Absolutely . . . one of the things I've tried to do, is just keep notes on a lot of the people who are emerging as,

PRESIDENT: That's right.

DEAN: as less than our friends.

PRESIDENT: Great.

DEAN: Because this is going to be over some day and they're—We shouldn't forget the way some of them have treated us.

PRESIDENT: I want the most, I want the most com-

prehensive notes on all of those that have tried to do us in. Because they didn't have to do it.

DEAN: That's right.

PRESIDENT: They didn't have to do it. I mean, if the thing had been a clo—uh, they had a very close election, everybody on the other side would understand this game. But now they are doing this quite deliberately and they are asking for it and they are going to get it. And this, this—We, we have not used the power in this first four years, as you know.

DEAN: That's right.

PRESIDENT: We have never used it. We haven't used the Bureau [FBI] and we haven't used the Justice Department, but things are going to change now. And they're going to change, and, and they're going to get it right—

DEAN: That's an exciting prospect.

PRESIDENT: It's got to be done. It's the only thing to do.

HALDEMAN: We've got to.

Source: Transcripts of Eight Recorded Presidential Conversations, Hearings before the Committee on the Judiciary, House of Representatives, 93rd Congress, 2nd Session (Washington, D.C., 1974).

read the court a letter from McCord which charged that highly placed White House advisors had known in advance of the break-in and that perjury had been committed during the trial.

The cover-up appeared to be coming apart. McCord revealed everything he knew to a grand jury, implicating others who would soon be called to testify. With federal prosecutors closing in on his principal aides, the president, on April 17, publicly announced that he had ordered "intensive new inquiries" into the Watergate case and that no one in his administration would be given immunity from prosecution. The president indicated too that not until March 21 had he learned of any attempts to cover up the scandal. Again, the president had taken refuge in a lie.

The public statement appeared to satisfy no one. And with John Dean now talking to federal prosecutors, the "scenarios" previously worked out had to be scrapped. On April 30, the president went on nationwide television, the first of several such appearances relating to Watergate, to affirm his innocence and his determination to bring the guilty to justice and "maintain the integrity of the White House." More dramatically, he announced the resignations of his key advisors and legal counsel—Haldeman, Ehrlichman, and Dean. He would, at the same time, replace Attorney General

Richard Kleindienst with Elliot Richardson and authorize Richardson to appoint a special prosecutor to investigate Watergate.

Even as Nixon announced the departure of Haldeman and Ehrlichman, he praised them to the American people as "two of the finest public servants it has been my privilege to know." Such praise, coupled with forced resignation, obviously raised more questions than it answered.

The Ellsberg Case

The tentacles of Watergate reached out in unexpected directions. In June 1971, Daniel Ellsberg, a Defense Department analyst, had released to the press the classified Pentagon Papers, which documented the origins of United States involvement in Vietnam. Although they revealed the policies of previous presidents, the disclosures embarrassed the Nixon administration by showing there were potentially dangerous leaks within the government. The Supreme Court denied the administration's attempt to block publication of the papers. But the government did indict Ellsberg for theft, conspiracy, and espionage.

At the same time, the president authorized the formation within the White House of a special investigation unit known as the plumbers. While the Ellsberg trial was pending, the plumbers broke into the office of Ellsberg's psychiatrist to search for material that would "nail the guy cold."

Upon learning of the break-in and illegal government wiretaps, the presiding judge at the Ellsberg trial dismissed the case. By this time, several other pertinent facts had come to light: (1) Two Watergate conspirators had also been involved in the burglary of Ellsberg's psychiatrist. (2) White House aide John Ehrlichman had approved the covert operation, and had instructed the CIA deputy director to provide any necessary technical assistance. (3) While the trial was in progress, Ehrlichman had sounded out the presiding judge on becoming the new director of the FBI.

On May 22, 1973, in a public statement, President Nixon acknowledged that he had authorized wiretapping in the interest of national security, had established a White House intelligence unit under the supervision of Ehrlichman, and had instructed it to "find out all it could about Mr. Ellsberg's associates and his motives." He had not, however, condoned "any illegal means," though he understood "how highly motivated individuals could have felt justified in engaging" in such activities. Turning to Watergate, Nixon declared that he had never had any "intent" or "wish" to impede an investigation of the break-in, nor had he tried to use the CIA for that purpose.

Crisis of Credibility

The summer of 1973 proved to be a turning point. On May 17, 1973, the Senate Watergate Committee (as it came to be called), headed by Senator Sam J. Ervin, Jr., of North Carolina, began public hearings. Millions of television viewers across the country watched the mountain of testimony add up to an ugly record of deception and political sabotage carried out by the highest echelons of the White House. Several witnesses, most spectacularly John Dean, implicated themselves, top White House aides, and the president.

The hearings outdid any of the popular soap operas their television coverage had displaced. During that summer, the American people learned for the first time of "hush money" paid to the Watergate defendants, top-level discussions of executive clemency, destruction of evidence, complicity of top aides in the cover-up, and how the break-in fitted into a pattern of political subversion. Nixon aides, moreover, had tried unsuccessfully to use the Internal Revenue Service and the threat of tax audits to harass individuals thought to be hostile to the president.

With each new revelation, the credibility crisis escalated and the president's support eroded. The question was no longer whether a conspiracy had existed, but how far it extended and how many in the White House it involved. On August 15, the president reaffirmed his innocence to a nationwide television audience. Although he accepted "full responsibility" for the actions of his subordinates, he claimed to have been grossly misinformed by them. "Not only was I unaware of any cover-up, I was unaware there was anything to cover up."

The Undoing of Spiro Agnew

The Watergate scandal had in no way implicated Vice-President Agnew, who had been second only to Nixon in his moral preachments on law and order and in his attacks on "permissiveness" in the courts and the "coddling" of criminals. But even as Agnew expressed "total confidence in the Presi-

NAMES AND WORDS IN AMERICAN HISTORY

Today the words to *haze* and *hazing* can refer to the weather or to initiation procedures into some such group as a college fraternity. When referring to the weather, *haze* suggests a light and smoky or dusty-looking fog that obscures really long distance viewing. Originally the term was nautical, referring to calm seas with poor but not bad visibility. Aboard sailing ships, these conditions often led to spare time and thus the opportunity for more experienced members of the crew to initiate new hands to the proper ways and manners of on-board behavior. As a young man from Boston wrote about his first sea voyage (around Cape Horn to California): "Every shifting of the studding-sails was only to 'haze' the crew," with the note that, " 'Haze' is a word of frequent use on board ship, and never, I believe, used elsewhere. It . . . means to punish by hard work." [From Richard Henry Dana's *Two Years Before the Mast* (1840).] Sometimes hazing on college campuses has gotten drastically out of hand, but few people involved today, including students and deans, are aware of the maritime origins of the term.

dent's integrity," serious questions were raised about his own. He found himself under investigation for bribery, extortion, conspiracy, and tax evasion—charged with extorting bribes from contractors while he was a Maryland county official and governor in exchange for influencing the awarding of government contracts.

Agnew protested his innocence. But with evidence of criminal conspiracy and graft mounting, the vice-president opted on October 10, 1973, to secure immunity from further criminal prosecution and thereby escape a prison term. After "bargaining" with the Justice Department, he pleaded no contest to lesser charges of tax fraud and resigned as vice-president. The court fined him $10,000 and placed him on three years' probation. At the same time, the Justice Department released an exhaustive summary of his illegal activities. It marked the first time a vice-president had been forced from office as a convicted criminal.

To succeed Agnew, Nixon selected Gerald R. Ford, a veteran Michigan congressman and House minority leader. Almost immediately, Ford toured the country in defense of Nixon, seeking to restore confidence in the president's leadership.

The Saturday Night Massacre

Despite the Senate hearings, the extent of President Nixon's involvement in the Watergate cover-up remained debatable. Dean had implicated him, but Ehrlichman and Haldeman had backed up his contention that he knew nothing until March 21, 1973. Faced with such contradictory testimony, how would the truth ever be known? The answer came most unexpectedly. During the Senate inquiry, a former White House operations aide revealed that the president had installed secret recording devices in his office that automatically taped telephone calls and office conversations. Obviously, the Senate committee was anxious to hear those tapes, as was Archibald Cox, whom Attorney General Richardson had appointed as the special prosecutor in charge of the Watergate case. The tapes were absolutely essential to Cox's investigation, and he demanded access to them. The president, however, refused to turn them over, claiming the tapes were confidential and protected by executive privilege.

When Cox persisted, the president reached the end of his patience. Although he had no wish "to intrude upon the independence of the special prosecutor," Nixon ordered him to make no further attempts to secure records of presidential conversations. On October 20, Cox refused to accept the order and prepared to take the matter to the courts. The president, in turn, ordered Attorney General Richardson to fire Cox. Richardson refused, as did the deputy attorney general, and both men resigned their positions. Finally, on Saturday night, the solicitor general carried out the president's order.

The public reacted with outrage. Leading newspapers demanded the president's resignation, and the House Judiciary Committee for the first time in more than a century launched an inquiry to determine if there were adequate grounds for impeachment. If only to weather this "firestorm," Nixon agreed to turn over the subpoenaed tapes to Judge Sirica and to appoint a new special prosecutor and provide him with whatever materials he needed.

Toward Impeachment

Despite attempts to mobilize public support, the scandal gained momentum and reached closer to the president himself. In March 1974, a grand jury indicted three of Nixon's most intimate associates—Haldeman, Ehrlichman, and Mitchell—and four other White House aides on charges of conspiracy, obstruction of justice, and perjury. Although it was not yet publicly known, the grand jury also named an "unindicted co-conspirator"—President Nixon. (The new special prosecutor, Leon Jaworski, had told the grand jury that the indictment of a president was most likely unconstitutional.)

Meanwhile, new charges were brought against the president, including illegal income tax deductions and the expenditure of public funds to improve his Florida and California estates. Nixon appeared to be under virtual siege. At one point, the American people were presented with the sad spectacle of their president assuring them in a televised press conference, "I am not a crook."

On April 30, 1974, Nixon took his case to the people in still another television address. With pressure mounting on him to provide additional tapes, he declared his intention to make public 1254 pages of transcribed tape recordings containing "all the relevant" White House conversations about Watergate. This dramatic action, he assumed, would finally resolve the controversy. There was nothing else to disclose, Nixon insisted, and he was certain that the contents of the released tapes, although at times embarrassing, would reveal his innocence.

Appearing on nationwide TV to resign his position, Nixon declared, "In all the decisions I have made in my public life, I have always tried to do what was best for the Nation." (*UPI/Bettmann Newsphotos*)

Rather than calm the storm, the edited transcripts of White House conversations eroded still further the president's support. No matter in what context they were read, the transcripts did nothing to instill confidence in the president's leadership or truthfulness. The edited transcripts, moreover, contained sufficient ambiguities and contradictions to raise more questions than they answered. The president had not, as he had assured the public, revealed all the relevant information. In refusing to turn over additional tapes to the House Judiciary Committee and Special Prosecutor Jaworski, Nixon argued that it would only "prolong the impeachment inquiry without yielding significant additional evidence." The president knew that was not true.

While the Supreme Court readied its judgment on Nixon's refusal to provide additional materials, the House Judiciary Committee proceeded with its impeachment investigation. On July 30, 1974, after months of private and public hearings, the committee, with the support of several of its Republican members, adopted three articles of impeachment. The president was accused of obstructing justice, violating his oath of office, abusing his presidential powers, subverting the constitutional rights of citizens, and willfully disobeying lawful subpoenas for White House records and tapes. It appeared almost certain that the House would sustain the committee's recommen-

dations, impeach the president, and thereby set the stage for a trial in the Senate.

The Downfall

The climax came suddenly and spectacularly. By August 1, 1974, Nixon's credibility was nil, his state of mind, suspect. He had virtually sealed himself off from the outside world. Adding to his troubles, the Supreme Court on July 24 had unanimously ruled that executive privilege could not be invoked to withhold evidence needed for a criminal trial and had ordered Nixon to turn over the additional subpoenaed tapes to the special prosecutor. On August 5, the president agreed to release the new material, which revealed beyond any question his direct involvement in the cover-up in a criminal obstruction of justice. Nixon conceded that he had withheld relevant evidence from the House Judiciary Committee as well as from his own lawyers and that the newly released tapes were "at variance with certain of my previous statements."

With these final revelations of criminal wrongdoing, the Nixon presidency lay in shambles. Even his supporters on the House Judiciary Committee, confronted now with evidence of statutory crime, reversed their positions and made the vote recommending impeachment unanimous. Republican leaders in the House and Senate advised the president that he would be impeached and convicted. Rather than face this prospect, Richard Nixon on August 8 went on television to become the first president in American history to resign.

Less than two years after he won reelection by as huge a margin as any in the nation's history, he departed from the White House in defeat and humiliation. He left to avoid impeachment and conviction, and he still faced the prospect of criminal prosecution. In his final message to the people, Nixon admitted to no serious wrongdoing, only to exercising poor judgment, and he showed no remorse. He had acted, he insisted, "in what I believed at the time to be in the best interests of the nation."

The Legacy of Watergate

While Nixon was still en route to San Clemente, Gerald Ford took the oath of office. "Our long national nightmare is over," he declared. Nearly one month later, President Ford made a move to heal the nation's wounds and avoid the spectacle of a former president under criminal indictment. On September 8, he granted Nixon "full, free, and absolute pardon . . . for all offenses against the United States which he . . . has committed or may have committed or taken part in" during his presidency.

Rather than end the "nightmare," the pardon raised questions about a double standard of justice, with the president permitted to stand above the law while those who carried out his orders were punished. President Ford's action only confirmed, said a United States senator, "what too many Americans already believe: that there is one set of laws for the rich and powerful, another set for everyone else." The pardon raised questions about "permissiveness" and "coddling" that Nixon himself had pressed on so many occasions. And it revived controversy over the government's refusal to grant similar amnesty to deserters and draft evaders during the Vietnam war.

Nixon's aides fared badly. On New Year's Day, 1975, the jury returned its verdict in the Watergate conspiracy trial. Mitchell, Ehrlichman, and Haldeman were found guilty of conspiracy, obstruction of justice, and false testimony. Each of them was then sentenced to serve a prison term of from two and a half to eight years. Ehrlichman had previously been convicted for his part in the Ellsberg break-in.

By early 1975, nearly forty officials of the Nixon administration, including the vice-president, four cabinet officials, and top White House aides, had been named in criminal indictments. The range of the criminal charges against Nixon's men in the White House presented a sorry record: obstruction of justice, fraud, extortion, burglary, perjury, illegal campaign activities, violation of campaign funding laws, illegal wiretapping, eavesdropping, destruction of evidence, and conspiracy to commit illegal acts. Along with the ending of the Vietnam war and detente with Red China and the Soviet Union, they would constitute the mixed legacy of the Nixon presidency.

Throughout his long political career, Richard Nixon had found it difficult to tolerate criticism or to admit defeat. His hatred of the media was matched only by the contempt he felt for many of his political enemies. Eventually, these obsessions consumed him and encouraged him to stand above the law and to violate his public trust. With the pardon and the convictions, the Watergate case came to an end. The lessons of Watergate, however, would persist, if only to remind the nation of the dangers of unbridled executive power and the possibilities for political abuses in the name of national security.

In the Name of National Security

Information made public during the Ford administration focused attention on the two agencies entrusted with foreign and domestic surveillance—the Central Intelligence Agency and the Federal Bureau of Investigation. How obsession with internal security could result in gross violations of the constitutional rights of citizens was revealed in 1974 by the attorney general. Between 1956 and 1971, he reported, the FBI under J. Edgar Hoover had not only gathered data on suspect political groups, but had tried to disrupt their activities.

The CIA as well had exceeded its legal mandate. In 1975 it was revealed that this agency had participated in various questionable operations. It had spent, for example, $8 million to assist the opponents of Salvador Allende, a Marxist who had come to power in Chile in a democratic election. (A rightist military coup toppled the government in 1973.) Although the National Security Act of 1947 had confined the CIA's espionage activities to foreign operations, the agency had conducted domestic surveillance operations. It had planted undercover agents in antiwar organizations, intercepted mail, engaged in illegal wiretaps and break-ins, and compiled intelligence files on some 10,000 American citizens, including members of Congress, antiwar critics, and civil rights leaders. Most of these operations took place during the Johnson presidency and were based on his belief that hostile foreign governments might be actively supporting dissidents in the United States.

The American people were assured that such abuses of power would no longer be tolerated. The delicate balance between maintaining internal security and the constitutional rights of citizens, however, posed formidable questions for future generations of Americans.

THE FORD PRESIDENCY

The new president was personable, hard-working, and honest. To most Americans, these were attractive qualities after their recent political experience. On no issue—domestic or foreign—were there discernible differences between Ford and Nixon. Since 1949, when Ford was elected to the

House, he had reflected the views of his conservative Michigan constituency. As House minority leader, he had won the respect of Democrats and Republicans, largely because of his amiability and even temper. He also possessed a candor and openness that reflected the confidence with which he voiced the views of Middle America: "It's the quality of the ordinary, the straight, the square that accounts for the great stability and success of our nation. It's a quality to be proud of."

Middle America in Power

After the exhausting Watergate ordeal, the "good feelings" that characterized the opening weeks of the Ford administration came as a relief. Ford's selection of Governor Nelson Rockefeller of New York as vice-president pleased Republican moderates. His regular consultations with Congress provided a welcome contrast with his predecessor. His "leniency" program for Vietnam draft evaders and deserters reflected the national mood of reconciliation. But the Nixon pardon abruptly ended the political honeymoon, and the growing economic crisis provoked confrontations between Ford and a Democrat-controlled Congress.

Upon assuming office, Ford had declared war on inflation, calling it Public Enemy No. 1. The administration relied largely on fiscal restraint and tight monetary policies. By early 1975, however, the United States faced the grim prospect of the worst economic slump since the Great Depression, with the highest percentage of jobless in the work force since 1941. Although the inflation rate was reduced in the following year, unemployment and the high cost of living remained acute problems that neither the Democratic Congress nor the Republican president had done much about.

Vietnam: End of an Era

The withdrawal of United States troops in early 1973 did not bring peace to Vietnam. The fighting continued, with both sides violating the truce. South Vietnam remained dependent on United States support—$3.8 billion in 1973 alone, almost all of it for military aid. The end came quickly and unexpectedly. In March 1975, President Nguyen Van Thieu of South Vietnam ordered his forces to abandon several outlying northern provinces (nearly one-fourth of the country) that had come under Communist attack. This "strategic withdrawal" turned into a headlong retreat. Within weeks, Communist troops were in the outskirts of Saigon, Thieu had fled the country along with thousands of refugees, the South Vietnamese army had lost its will to resist, and Congress refused to invest any additional funds. In late April, Saigon and the government fell.

The chaotic exodus from Saigon—the American ambassador escaped from the embassy roof by helicopter—gave evidence of the total collapse of a government with no basis of popular support. After thirty years of war and more than a decade of American involvement, peace had finally come to Vietnam. At the same time, Cambodia fell under Communist control, and Laos came under predominantly Communist influence.

With the fall of Indochina, an era in American history ended. Four American presidents had presided over United States intervention, some 56,000 Americans had died, more than 300,000 had been wounded, and $150 billion had been spent. To Eisenhower, the future of Vietnam had assumed "a most terrible significance"; to Kennedy, Vietnam represented "the cornerstone of the Free World in Southeast Asia"; to Johnson, it was a question of confronting the Communists in Vietnam or having to face them in Hawaii or San Francisco; and to Nixon, Vietnam would be recorded in history as "one of America's finest hours." But in the end, the war's greatest significance had been in teaching the United States a difficult lesson about the limits of its power.

The Bicentennial Election: 1976

On the occasion of America's 200th birthday, the nation's voters would be given the opportunity to decide who should lead them into the third century. Memories of Vietnam, Watergate, and the Nixon pardon reinforced popular suspicions of those in power. As the incumbent, Gerald Ford should have had no difficulty in securing the Republican nomination. But he had to mobilize all his political resources to defeat challenger Ronald Reagan, a former Hollywood actor and governor of California who had emerged as the spokesman of the Republican right wing. Even as Ford nosed out Reagan for the nomination, with the support of the party's professional politicians, Reagan tightened his hold at the party's grassroots level.

Among the many Democratic contenders, James (Jimmy) E. Carter, Jr., former governor of Georgia, was the least known. In the primaries, this Annapolis graduate, nuclear engineer, successful agrarian businessman, and "born-again" Southern Baptist deacon exploited the public's discontent with professional politicians and bureaucrats and their same old programs. The American people, Carter insisted, were searching for "new voices, new ideas, new leaders," and he managed to turn into a virtue his position as an outsider. "I have been accused of being an outsider," Carter asserted. "I plead guilty. Unfortunately, the vast majority of Americans are also outsiders. We are not going to get changes by simply shifting around the same groups of insiders, the same tired old rhetoric, the same unkept promises."

The strategy worked. Bolstered by his primary victories, Carter won the nomination at the Democratic convention and named as his running mate Walter F. Mondale, an able and liberal senator from Minnesota and a protégé of Hubert Humphrey. In the campaign, Ford defended his record of restoring honesty, integrity, and stability to government (no mean achievement after the Nixon presidency), and he promised more of the same. Carter appealed to liberal Democrats with pledges of full employment and social legislation; at the same time, he appeased moderates and conservatives by promising to eliminate bureaucratic waste in government and to balance the budget. To the American people, he promised moral leadership—to be decent, truthful, fair, and compassionate.

Despite Carter's sizable lead in the early polls, the election itself was close: 40.8 million votes for Carter to 39.1 million votes for Ford (a plurality that exceeded the winning margins of Kennedy in 1960 and Nixon in 1968), and an edge in the electoral college of 297 to 241. For the first time in forty-four years, an incumbent president had been defeated. And for the first time since before the Civil War, the nation had turned to the Deep South for a president.

To win, Carter had needed to revive the New Deal coalition of urban blacks, Catholics, Jews, and blue-collar workers, along with the South. He did so, but the old coalition had been very weak; only blacks rallied in substantial numbers (about 87 percent) around Carter. Without them he would have lost the election. Only 53 percent of the people of voting age had chosen to vote. What remained uncertain was whether the results were a personal triumph and mandate for Carter "the outsider," or a rejection of Ford as the candidate of a political party still under the shadow of Watergate.

THE CRISIS OF THE AMERICAN SPIRIT: JIMMY CARTER

In his election campaign, Carter had successfully exploited the "outsider" theme. But once elected, he needed to surmount persistent doubts about his capacity to govern. The issues he confronted were as formidable as any recent president had faced, and the American people looked to Carter to make good on his promise to be a "strong, independent and aggressive President."

Four years later, with those issues still largely unresolved, many Americans had come to view him as weak, indecisive, and ineffectual. "The insiders have had their chances," Carter had declared in 1976, "and they have not delivered. Their time has run out." His Republican opponent in 1980 would campaign on essentially the same theme.

The "Outsider" in Power

President Carter inaugurated his administration with a dramatic move. Ford had hoped to end the Watergate era with his pardon of Nixon. Carter wanted to end the Vietnam era by offering full pardons to civilian Vietnam war draft resisters. By issuing pardons, he insisted, he was not justifying their actions but merely granting forgiveness. It was less than the antiwar activists had demanded, and more than some Americans thought they deserved.

In the conduct of foreign policy, an area in which Carter seemed least experienced, the president had a mixed record of impressive successes and unexpected failures. He strengthened relations with the People's Republic of China. Over strong opposition, he managed to win the Senate's ratification in 1977 of a treaty that would gradually yield to Panama control of the Panama Canal (not until the year 2000 would the United States relinquish full control of the waterway). In Africa, the United States improved its standing by supporting black majority rule in Rhodesia (Zimbabwe) and Southwest Africa (Namibia).

Even more spectacularly, Carter initiated a flexible American response to the ongoing Mideast crisis and, in a personal triumph, brought together in 1978 the leaders of Egypt and Israel at Camp David and helped them to work out the framework for a peace agreement. Any permanent settlement, however, depended on resolving the still critical issue of the Palestinian refugees and their claims to nationhood.

THE POLITICS OF RIGHTEOUSNESS

President and Mrs. Carter walk in the Inaugural Parade. (*UPI/Bettmann Newsphotos*)

Early in his presidency, Carter moved to make respect for human rights a cornerstone of American foreign policy. In this endeavor, he encountered difficulties, some of them of his own making. He singled out for condemnation Soviet treatment of dissidents and apartheid in South Africa, and he chastised several Latin American nations and South Korea for their repressive policies. But the president found it necessary to reconcile his strong convictions about human rights with pledges of support for repressive anti-Communist regimes that were thought essential to national security. He praised the shah of Iran, for example, and approved a multibillion-dollar arms sale to this "island of stability." That support soon plunged Carter into a crisis that defied any quick resolution and rapidly eroded popular support for his presidency.

Since the shah's return to power in 1953 (with the assistance of the United States), Iran had been a valuable ally against communism in the Middle East. With a steady flow of arms to back up the regime, successive American administrations tended to ignore the domestic discontent with the shah's policies. In 1979, a massive revolutionary upheaval deposed the shah and sent him into exile. Seeking to eliminate all traces of the shah's westernizing in-

fluence, Iranians embraced a religious despotism under a Muslim spiritual leader, Ayatollah Ruhollah Khomeini. At the same time, Iranians vented their anger on the United States for its support of the shah.

When Carter agreed to permit the exiled shah to enter the United States for medical treatment, mobs in Teheran attacked the American embassy and seized and held the Americans there as hostages. To secure their release, Iran demanded that the shah be returned for trial. Meanwhile, the Muslim nationalism unleashed by the revolution in Iran was being felt elsewhere in the Middle East, threatening to bring chaos to a region that supplied more than half the world's imported oil.

After the shah died in exile in Egypt, Iran continued to hold the American hostages, now demanding the return of the shah's wealth and the release of Iranian funds Carter had frozen in retaliation for that nation's actions. The president sent a military force to rescue the hostages, but the mission failed. By the time the hostages were finally released in January 1981, after more than a year in captivity, they had come to symbolize to Americans the impotence of the United States abroad—an issue the Republican candidate in 1980 successfully exploited.

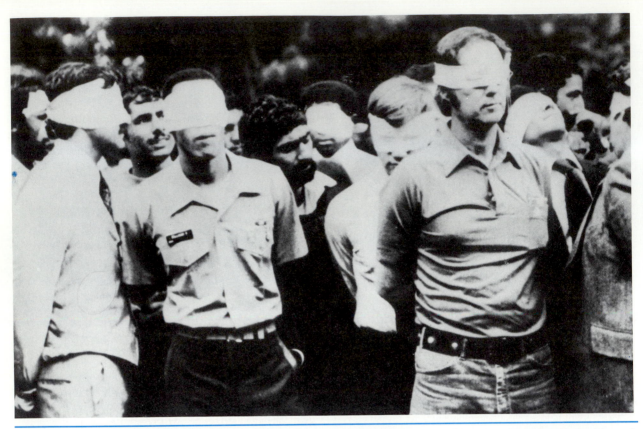

On the first day of the occupation of the U.S. Embassy in Teheran, the blindfolded American hostages were paraded before the mob by their captors. To many Americans, the prolonged captivity of the hostages was a national humiliation, dramatizing the degree to which their country had become "a helpless giant." (*UPI*)

Even as President Carter grappled with the Iranian issue, he was plunged into a new crisis in Soviet-American relations. From the outset of his presidency, his criticism of the Soviet Union for its persecution of dissidents had cooled relations between the two countries. Nevertheless, after lengthy negotiations that had begun during the Ford presidency, Carter concluded the SALT II treaty imposing restrictions on strategic nuclear weapons. But the treaty floundered in the Senate, where some critics charged that America's military defenses had been compromised.

When, in December 1979, Soviet troops moved into Afghanistan to bolster the Communist regime there, Carter reacted with outrage. He withdrew SALT II from the Senate (where its chances for passage were slim anyway), imposed a partial grain embargo on the Soviet Union, called for a boycott of the 1980 Olympic Games in Moscow, reduced cultural and technological exchanges with the Soviets, and asked Congress to authorize the registration of young Americans for a military draft.

The Soviet Union maintained that its presence in Afghanistan had been made necessary by anti-Communist rebels aided by hostile regimes, particularly China and Pakistan. The United States, along with a majority in the United Nations, condemned the move as outright aggression. With the avowed purpose of preventing "any outside force" from gaining control of the Persian Gulf region, Carter declared the region "vital" to American interests and sent in a naval force.

The crises in Iran and Afghanistan resulted in a rapid change in the foreign and military priorities of the Carter administration. Tension developed within the administration between Secretary of State Cyrus R. Vance, an experienced diplomat who favored a policy emphasizing arms control and improvement of relations with the Third World, and Zbigniew Brezezinski, national security advisor and specialist in Soviet affairs who advocated a more hard-line policy in regard to the Soviets. When Vance resigned over Carter's military mission to rescue the hostages in Iran, Brezezinski's hold on foreign policy tightened. To Carter's critics, however, the tension was reflected in the failure of the administration to articulate a clear and consistent foreign policy.

THE POLITICS OF RIGHTEOUSNESS

The Misery Index

The most conspicuous failure of the Carter presidency was its inability to stop the inflationary spiral that threatened the American people. His efforts to stimulate the economy and reduce unemployment were no more successful than his attempts to balance the budget and combat inflation. He rejected wage and price controls for voluntary guidelines, a wage and price bureaucracy to formulate and oversee the guidelines, and credit controls. In the 1976 campaign, Carter had compiled a "misery index" by adding the levels of unemployment and inflation and he had used it effectively against his opponent.

Four years later, the "misery index" stood even higher—a point his Republican opponent repeatedly stressed. To increase employment, the president proposed various programs, including job training, public service jobs, and tax incentives to private employers. But these proposals either ran aground in Congress or proved too feeble to make good on Carter's promise to reduce an unemployment level he had found "unacceptable."

Nor did Carter persuade Congress to accept his watered-down national health insurance program or his proposed reform of a tax system he had called "a disgrace to the human race." Although he had made some progress in reorganizing the civil service, he was only partly successful in reducing the "bureaucratic mess" in Washington.

Critics mocked his reform efforts by noting the addition of two new cabinet-level departments, energy and education. Carter had vowed to make the conservation of energy a top priority, calling it "the moral equivalent of war." But his energy program was less ambitious than such rhetoric suggested; special interest groups lobbied against various provisions, and Congress dismantled much of it. The United States was able to reduce its oil imports, but Americans paid higher prices for gasoline, and the decisions of the oil-producing nations remained the critical factor in determining those prices.

The achievements of the administration—in foreign policy, in energy conservation, in environmental protection, and in the unprecedented numbers of qualified minorities and women appointed to judgeships and government positions—were not enough to make up for the most conspicuous domestic and foreign failures.

What ultimately undid Carter's presidency was his failure to inspire confidence. Whether any president could have successfully dealt with the domestic and foreign crises was less important than the public's perception that Carter could not. President Carter, moreover, never developed a style that convinced Americans he could translate his high-minded rhetoric into a clearly formulated program. In the end, the very slogans he had used so successfully to win the presidency were used to ensure that he would not stay in office.

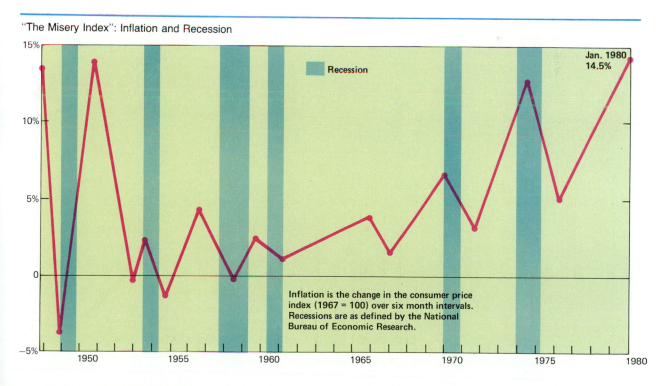

"The Misery Index": Inflation and Recession

Jan. 1980 14.5%

Recession

Inflation is the change in the consumer price index (1967 = 100) over six month intervals. Recessions are as defined by the National Bureau of Economic Research.

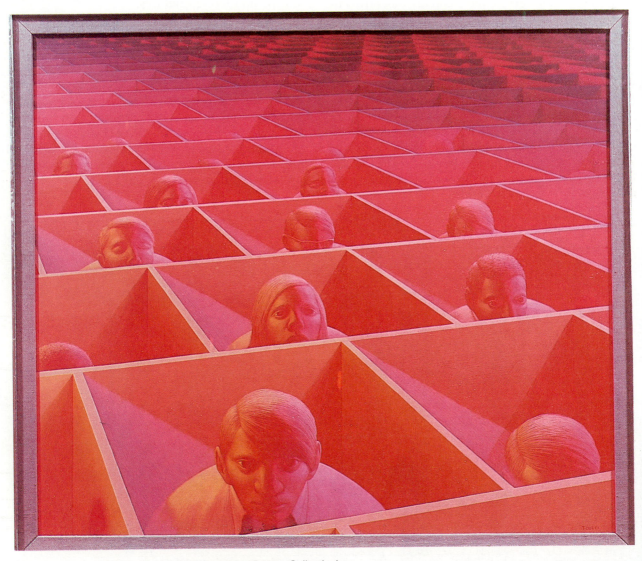

George Tooker, *Landscape with Figures*, 1963. (*Private Collection*)

George Tooker, *The Subway*, 1950. (*Whitney Museum of American Art*)

George Tooker, *Government Bureau*, 1956. (*The Metropolitan Museum of Art, George A. Hearn Fund, 1956*)

George Tooker, *The Waiting Room II*, 1982. (*Marisa Del Re Gallery*)

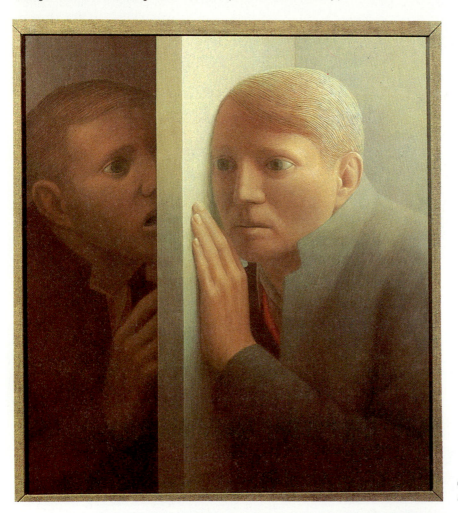

George Tooker, *Voice I*, 1963. (*Marisa Del Re Gallery*)

THE POLITICS OF RIGHTEOUSNESS

SUMMARY

Richard Nixon began his presidency in 1968 with a clear program and a clear mandate from a "silent majority" of Americans to retreat from the liberalism of the New Deal, the Fair Deal, the New Frontier, and the Great Society. For Nixon, this meant slowing down desegregation and appointing conservatives to Supreme Court vacancies. His economic game plan offered revenue sharing, tight money policies, and a reduction in federal spending. But prices and unemployment continued to rise. And although the triumph of the moon landing on July 16, 1969, raised America's prestige, Vietnam continued to undermine it.

Foreign affairs became the major concern of the first Nixon administration, and a "balance of power" a major goal, with military action left to the discretion of allies and friends. The administration did succeed in effecting détente with the Soviet Union and China, and made an effort to stabilize the Middle East. But Vietnam was different: nothing seemed to work—not more troops, nor more bombs, not Vietnamization.

At home, protest against the war mounted on and off the campuses, fueled by revelations of American atrocities in Vietnam. In 1969, Nixon secretly ordered the bombing of Cambodia, and in 1970 a resumption of full-scale bombing of North Vietnam. But neither the bombings nor "incursions" into Laos helped, and now the South Vietnamese suffered a series of major defeats. A cease-fire was negotiated in January 1973—but still the war continued, in Vietnam and in Cambodia.

The election of 1972 brought Nixon back to office on a victorious tide. The illegal activities of CREEP, the Committee to Re-Elect the President, however, soon erupted into what became known as the Watergate scandal. Before it was over, more than forty highly placed Nixon administration officials, including the president's closest aides and the attorney general, had been indicted, and the president himself had been implicated in the lies, the crimes, and the systematic deception. Faced finally in the summer of 1974 with impeachment proceedings, Nixon resigned in disgrace. His presidency was a shambles, and the American people's faith in government had been profoundly shaken. Even Nixon's vice-president, Spiro Agnew, had been forced to resign in 1973 to escape a prison term for tax fraud, bribery, extortion, and conspiracy.

Gerald Ford took office on August 9, 1974, and served out the remaining two years of Nixon's second term. He brought refreshing personal qualities to the office and tried to restore "good feelings" by such acts as leniency programs for Vietnam draft evaders and deserters. But his pardon of Nixon ended the political honeymoon, along with the growing economic crisis and confrontation with the Democrat-controlled Congress.

In Vietnam, where the fighting had continued after the American troop withdrawal of early 1973, the South Vietnamese were close to collapse by early 1975. Saigon fell in April. At the same time, Cambodia and Laos came under Communist influence and control. The policy of four American presidents had failed, and the United States had learned a difficult lesson about the limits of its power.

In the bicentennial election of 1976, Americans turned to a political "outsider," Jimmy Carter, and rejected Ford. But Carter's promises to "clean up the mess in Washington" and to balance the budget were not kept. Neither was his promise to provide moral leadership.

Economic and social problems worsened. Carter's success in the Middle East in 1978 was more than offset by what Americans saw as his failure in Iran in 1979, and the humiliation of having American citizens kept hostage there for more than a year. In 1980 Americans saw him as indecisive and ineffectual; they rejected his bid for reelection by turning to the Republicans and to Ronald Reagan, spokesman of its right wing.

Reagan ran on a conservative platform of tax cuts, a balanced budget, increased defense spending, and opposition to abortion and the ERA. His victory, along with the defeat of a number of Democratic liberal incumbents in the Senate by conservative Republicans, made the election of 1980 an impressive triumph for conservative principles and a sharp retreat from the New Deal tradition.

Suggested Readings

The best introduction to America in the seventies is P. J. Dolan and E. Quinn (eds.), *The Sense of the 70s* (1978). But no student should venture into this decade without consulting the probing and often devastating cartoons of G. B. Trudeau, many of them collected in *The Doonesbury Chronicles* (1975). C. Lasch, *The Culture of Narcissism: American Life in an Age of Diminishing Expectations* (1979), explores changing attitudes. M. Rossman, a former activist of the sixties, looks at the new religion of the counter culture—the human potential movement—in *New Age Blues: On the Politics of Consciousness* (1979).

On the modern women's movement, B. Friedan, *The Feminine Mystique* (1963), is the place to begin. Among useful anthologies are R. Morgan (ed.), *Sisterhood Is Powerful* (1970); J. Sochen (ed.), *The New Feminism in Twentieth-Century America* (1971); A. F. Scott (ed.), *The American Woman: Who Was She?* (1971); G. Lerner (ed.), *Black Women in White America* (1972), and *The Female Experience: An American Documentary* (1977);

and S. Ruth (ed.), *Issues in Feminism: A First Course in Women's Studies* (1980). See also K. Millett, *Sexual Politics* (1970). Historical assessments of women in American life, many of them applicable to the 1960s and 1970s, are cited in the literature for Chapter 25.

The expectations of a modern president and the failure to meet them are analyzed in G. Hodgson, *All Things to All Men: The False Promise of the Modern Presidency* (1980). Indispensable sources for the study of Richard Nixon are his own memoirs, *Six Crises* (1962), *RN: The Memoirs of Richard Nixon* (1978), and *The Real War* (1980). Garry Wills, *Nixon Agonistes: The Crisis of the Self-Made Man* (1970), is a critical and probing analysis that helps to make comprehensible the final debacle. Additional critical assessments are cited in the Watergate section below. The first term of the Nixon presidency is the subject of R. Evans, Jr., and R. D. Novak, *Nixon in the White House* (1971), and W. Safire, *Before the Fall: An Inside View of the Pre-Watergate White House* (1975). Nixon's economic policies are analyzed in L. Silk, *Nixonomics* (1972). On the 1972 campaign, T. H. White, *The Making of the President 1972* (1972), and H. S. Thompson, *Fear and Loathing: On the Campaign Trail '72* (1973), offer sharply contrasting views. In *Common Ground: A Turbulent Decade in the Lives of Three American Families* (1985), J. A. Lukas tells the story of Boston's public school desegregation by court order.

On Nixon and foreign policy, see H. Brandon, *The Retreat of American Power* (1972), and T. Szulc, *The Illusion of Peace* (1978). On China policy, see R. G. Sutter, *China-Watch: Toward Sino-American Reconciliation* (1978). On the Middle East, see W. C. Eveland, *Ropes of Sand: America's Failure in the Middle East* (1980); W. B. Quandt, *Decade of Decision: American Policy toward the Arab-Israel Conflict, 1967–1976* (1977); E. R. F. Sheehan, *The Arabs, Israelis and Kissinger* (1976); and B. Rubin, *Paved with Good Intentions: The American Experience and Iran* (1980). M. and B. Kalb, *Kissinger* (1974), is a sympathetic treatment. For a more critical view, see S. M. Hersh, *The Price of Power: Kissinger in the Nixon White House* (1983). Kissinger justifies his foreign policy decisions in *White House Years* (1979) and *Years of Upheaval* (1982). The most devastating indictment of those decisions is W. Shawcross, *Sideshow: Kissinger, Nixon, and the Destruction of Cambodia* (1979).

On Nixon and Vietnam, see the literature cited for Chapter 32. In the war's aftermath, a number of personal accounts underscored the tragedy of Vietnam. M. Herr, *Dispatches* (1977), is a savage, impressionistic memoir by a reporter. R. Kovic, *Born on the Fourth of July* (1976), is the autobiography of a former Marine sergeant wounded in Vietnam. P. Caputo describes in *A Rumor of War* (1977) how the reality of the war affected his thinking. C. D. B. Bryan, *Friendly Fire* (1976), focuses on the parents of a soldier killed in Vietnam. R. Stone, *Dog Soldiers* (1975), is a novel that explores parallels between the war and the home front.

The crimes of the Nixon presidency may be viewed in the context of C. Vann Woodward (ed.), *Responses of the Presidents to Charges of Misconduct* (1974), in which sixteen historians examine executive misconduct since 1789. For background, see also A. Schelsinger, Jr., *The Imperial Presidency* (1973), and the works on Nixon cited above. The Watergate scandal and the fall of Nixon produced a large number of personal and journalistic accounts. But the best place to start remains the voluminous government documents: the Senate Watergate hearings, the Nixon-edited White House tapes, and the House Judiciary Committee report and hearings. See especially *Impeachment of Richard M. Nixon* (93d Cong., 2nd Sess., House Calendar No. 426, Report of the Committee on the Judiciary, 1974), and *Transcripts of Eight Recorded Presidential Conversations* (93d Cong., 2nd Sess., Hearings before the Committee on the Judiciary, 1974). C. Bernstein and B. Woodward, two Washington *Post* reporters who helped to break the Watergate story, report their experiences in *All the President's Men* (1974), and the president's fall in *The Final Days* (1976). The undoing of the presidency is described in B. Sussman, *The Great Cover-Up: Nixon and the Scandal of Watergate* (1974); The Washington Post, *The Fall of a President* (1974); T. H. White, *Breach of Faith: The Fall of Richard Nixon* (1975); J. A. Lukas, *Nightmare: The Underside of the Nixon Years* (1976); and J. Schell, *The Time of Illusion* (1976).

Nixon defends his presidency in *RN: The Memoirs of Richard Nixon* (1978). Memoirs of the conspirators include H. R. Haldeman, *The Ends of Power* (1978); J. W. Dean, *Blind Ambition: The White House Years* (1976); J. S. Magruder, *An American Life: One Man's Road to Watergate* (1974); and E. H. Hunt, *Undercover: Memoirs of an American Secret Agent* (1974). M. H. Stans, chief fundraiser for Nixon's reelection, tells his version in *The Terrors of Justice: The Untold Side of Watergate* (1979). For the prosecution, see J. J. Sirica, *To Set the Record Straight: The Break-In, the Tapes, the Conspirators, the Pardon* (1979); S. Dash, *Chief Counsel: Inside the Ervin Committee* (1976); and L. Jaworski, *The Right and the Power: The Prosecution of Watergate* (1976).

The domestic activities of the CIA are revealed in *Report to the President by the Commission on CIA Activities within the United States* (1975). The role of the CIA at home and abroad is examined in D. Wise and T. B. Ross, *The Invisible Government* (1964); V. Marchetti and J. D. Marks, *The CIA and the Cult of Intelligence* (1974); J. J. Berman and M. H. Halperin (eds.), *The Abuses of the Intelligence Agencies* (1975); T. Powers, *The Man Who Kept the Secrets: Richard Helms and the CIA* (1979); and in three memoirs by former agents, P. Agee, *Inside the Company: CIA Diary* (1975); F. Snepp, *Decent Interval* (1977); and J. Stockwell, *In Search of Enemies* (1979).

Ford's recollections of his presidential years may be found in *A Time to Heal: The Autobiography of Gerald*

R. Ford (1979). Accounts by former aides include J. F. terHorst, *Gerald Ford and the Future of the Presidency* (1974); R. Nessen, *It Sure Looks Different from the Inside* (1978); and J. J. Casserly, *The Ford White House* (1977). On Jimmy Carter, the best work is W. L. Miller, *Yankee from Georgia: The Emergence of Jimmy Carter* (1978). See also B. Glad, *Jimmy Carter: In Search of the Great White House* (1980), and the impressionistic account by J. Wooten, *Dasher: The Roots and the Rising of Jimmy Carter* (1978).

THE POLITICS OF NOSTALGIA: THE REAGAN ERA

Chapter 34

To much of the world, the idea that a Hollywood actor would become president of the United States must have seemed characteristically American. To much of the American electorate, the candidacy of Ronald Reagan afforded them the opportunity to recover their past—a time of heroic endings and heroic lives, when the nation's military and industrial supremacy had been unquestioned. In electing Ronald Reagan to the presidency, the American people, according to pollsters, had chosen the individual they deemed most likely to "make America feel good about itself again."

No doubt Reagan's film career, although unspectacular (he made some 50 grade B movies over a 20-year period), helped make him familiar to several generations of Americans. But his considerable appeal also derived from his affability and his skill in exploiting the frustrations, fears, and hopes of the large majority. Between his film and political careers, Reagan was a successful salesman. Working for the General Electric Company between 1954 and 1962, he spoke to employees at plants across the country. He also addressed chambers of commerce, trade associations, and civic clubs. His impressive political debut, a television speech on behalf of Barry Goldwater's presidential candidacy in 1964, raised his stature in the Republican party. Two years later he

was elected governor of California, and in 1980 he was the Republican presidential candidate.

Whatever Reagan's audience, the message remained the same: the perils of government control and regulation. He was critical of much of the social legislation of the twentieth century, from the progressive income tax to social security to the Tennessee Valley Authority. But despite his strong ideas about limited government, he did not appear to most Americans as a hard-core ideologue. When he ran for president, moreover, he moderated a number of his political positions.

More effectively than any of his immediate predecessors, Reagan was able to communicate his ideas to the American people. His vision of America evoked a nostalgic view of the country, based on his own idealized midwestern boyhood in Dixon, Illinois. "There was the life," he wrote in his autobiography, "that has shaped my body and mind for all the years to come." He promised the American people an America like that of his youth, rooted in the small-town, rural values he had learned: patriotism, self-help, hard work, morality, and belief in God, family, and the flag. To Reagan, America was a land of unlimited opportunity, made up of enterprising people who had seized upon chances and made the most of them. His own life resembled in many ways the classic Horatio Alger hero, with Reagan demonstrating the necessary spunk, grit, and ability to take advantage of every break that came his way.

In the year of his election to the presidency, Reagan insisted he was "saying the same things I've been saying for twenty-five years on the mashed-potato circuit." With far greater skill than his Democratic opponent, the former actor talked to Americans about their lives and future prospects. He spoke in a language they readily understood. And he made his ideas and programs sound not only like plain common sense, but attainable. That proved to be good enough for eight years in the White House, sufficient time to inaugurate if not to realize fully the political and moral revolution he so fervently embraced. ■

REAGANISM TRIUMPHANT: NEW DEPARTURES

More fundamentally than any president since Franklin Delano Roosevelt, Ronald Reagan altered the nation's social and economic policy. For some 50 years, the nation had come to accept the idea that the welfare of Americans is a public issue. The New Deal operated under the assumption that the federal government has a responsibility to deal with the problems of poverty, unemployment, and inequality. Under subsequent presidents—Democratic and Republican—the exercise of that responsibility required considerable federal activity and spending. Truman's Fair Deal, Kennedy's New Frontier, and Johnson's Great Society inspired new and expanded programs that provided a broad range of health, education, and welfare services aimed at removing inequities in society and assisting low-income families. The Eisenhower and Nixon administrations, although professing more conservative principles, consolidated rather than curtailed federal activity in these areas.

But in the 1970s and 1980s liberal federal activism faced a more skeptical and hostile audience in Congress and the White House, climaxing in the eight years of the Reagan presidency. The role of the federal government would be redefined in accordance with a new set of priorities and some very different assumptions, the most important of which President Reagan proclaimed in his inaugural address: "Government is not the solution to our problem. Government is the problem."

The new president came to power on a wave of disillusion with the government's ability to resolve fundamental problems at home and with its apparent impotence abroad. In proclaiming that the federal government itself was the root of the problem at home and in promising to "get the government off the backs of the people," he signaled a new departure for the American people—a sharp retreat from the New Deal tradition. In proclaiming the Soviet Union to be "the focus of evil in the modern world," he signaled a more aggressive policy abroad, including the return to a Cold War rhetoric that divided the world into irreconcilable camps of good and evil.

The Election of 1980

Encouraged by the rapid decline in President Carter's popularity, the Republicans entered the 1980 election brimming with confidence. This time there was no mistaking the clear choice of the party's rank-and-file—Ronald Reagan. The Republican convention was dominated by the party's right wing, which pushed through a platform promising tax cuts, a balanced budget, increased defense spending, constitutional amendments banning nontherapeutic abortions and reinstating school prayer, the appointment of judges who opposed abortion, and opposition to the Equal Rights Amendment. As vice-president, Reagan chose George Bush of Texas, a former congressman and CIA director who had made an impressive run in the primaries.

The Democrats, rejecting a bid by Senator Edward Kennedy, renominated Carter and Mondale. But a mood of fatalism dominated the convention, and Kennedy's challenge in the primaries had already split the party. Nor was the Democratic cause aided by the independent candidacy of John Anderson, a moderate Republican and former Illinois congressman who felt the need to offer an alternative to Carter and Reagan. Although Anderson's political record was much closer to Reagan's philosophy than to Carter's, he managed to win the votes of many Democrats and self-styled liberals as well as some Republicans. But his candidacy did not affect the outcome of the election; nor did it promise a change in the nation's traditional two-party system.

In the campaign, Reagan successfully exploited domestic economic distress and international instability. He proclaimed his belief in reducing government interference in the lives of Americans while increasing the nation's military arsenal. He capitalized on the apparent disenchantment with the social ferment of the sixties, making clear his own perception of that decade: expensive and unproductive welfare systems, misguided civil rights programs, excessive environmental protection, an increasingly bloated federal bureaucracy, a morally bankrupt Supreme Court, and a post-Vietnam inertia that had reduced the nation's military defenses and jeopardized its position as a leader of the "free world."

To broaden his appeal, Reagan moderated his previous hostility to the more popular social programs, like social security. And even as he called the Vietnam war a "noble crusade," he tried to assure voters that he would not lead the country into needless foreign conflicts. In speaking to unemployed workers and to union audiences, he capitalized on dissatisfaction with inflation and promised to put people back to work. To a middle class weary of government programs and the taxes needed to pay for them, he promised a sharp reduction in federal spending (except for defense) and tax relief. To Americans concerned with the humiliations the United States had suffered in Vietnam and Iran, he promised to restore the nation's power and credibility.

When in his television debate with Carter, Reagan told the viewers "Ask yourself, are you better off than you were four years ago?", he scored a decisive point over his opponent. "The election," said Carter's political pollster, "ended up becoming exactly the referendum on unhappiness we had been trying to avoid." Not only had the Democrats underestimated Reagan's appeal, but President Carter's efforts to exploit Reagan's right-wing background had misfired badly. The confidence Carter seemed unable to inspire Reagan managed to capture with his folksy and nostalgic rhetoric about restoring the values of his youth and making Americans once again feel proud of their country.

Reagan won over the nation's increasingly white and middle-class voting population, and he effectively buried the old New Deal coalition, even in the South; only black voters remained loyal to the Democratic party. The election results, while an overwhelming triumph for Reagan, also revealed a new low in voter turnout, with only 52 percent of the eligible voters choosing to participate. The new president entered the White House having received a "landslide" of only 26 percent of the electorate.

Although Reagan's election had been expected, the success of the Republicans in securing control of the Senate for the first time in 26 years had not been. The ideological makeup of the new senators suggested that the election had been an impressive triumph for conservative principles. But with the House still Democratic, the president would face a divided Congress in his efforts to reorder federal priorities. The bipartisan coalition he managed to mobilize for that purpose confirmed Reagan's ability to make the most of his popularity with the electorate.

The Domestic Program: Reaganomics

Reagan chose a cabinet and White House staff dominated by businessmen who shared his political philosophy and priorities. Although he often professed an admiration for Franklin Delano Roosevelt ("I was an enthusiastic New Deal Democrat," he wrote in his autobiography), he took his cues as president from the example of Calvin Coolidge, whom he admired for his success in reducing taxes and government expenditures. Those same ends would constitute the cornerstone of Reagan's domestic program. "Now you hear a lot of jokes about Silent Cal Coolidge," Reagan remarked, "but I think the joke is on the people that make jokes, because if you look at his record, he cut the taxes four times. We had probably the greatest growth and prosperity that we've ever known. And I have taken heed of that because if he did nothing, maybe that's the answer [for] the federal government."

In confronting "the worst economic mess since the Great Depression," Reagan placed his confidence in orthodox conservative ideology and in supply-side economics. Previous administrations had favored the economic theories of John Maynard Keynes, the British economist, which called for measures to stimulate the economy at times of high unemployment and economic hard times, for increasing government expenditures to stimulate consumption and investment. Reagan, consistent with his conservative philosophy, called for tight money, deep federal budget cuts, and incentives for business investment, such as tax breaks.

Reagan proposed to cut income taxes across

the board. In 1981, he persuaded Congress to go along with his plan for a three-year rate reduction for both individual and corporate taxes. The principal benefits were reaped by wealthy individuals and corporations. But "Reaganomics" assumed that the tax cuts would revive a stagnant economy, that the beneficiaries would use their windfalls to improve industrial productivity. Sharp reductions in government spending along with the taxes collected after the economic revival would make up for the prospective deficits and enable the president to proceed with his military buildup. By 1984, Reagan promised, the federal budget would balance government revenues and expenditures.

The Domestic Program: Reordering Priorities

If any theme dominated Reagan's campaign, it was the promise to redefine the role of the federal government in American life. No sooner did he become president than he proceeded to implement that promise. With his commitment to an overpowering defense, the budgets he sent to Congress called mostly for cutbacks in social programs. Reagan hoped to slow the growth of those programs, and eliminate some of them altogether. The objective, he declared, was to "trim the fat" from the federal budget and to eliminate services and benefits for those who should be able to make it on their own.

Reagan promised to retain services and benefits (the "safety net") for what he called the "truly needy," defining that group more narrowly than his predecessors in the White House. The president succeeded in dismantling the antipoverty programs of previous administrations, eliminating or sharply cutting back on various services. He obtained most of the cuts he sought in the welfare and food stamp programs, both to restrict eligibility and to reduce benefits. Public pressure forced him to retreat on his plans for reductions in social security benefits, and public assistance was largely maintained for the elderly and those who, because of disability or other circumstances, were unable to work. With the social security system approaching bankruptcy, Reagan appointed a bipartisan commission to place it on a sounder financial footing. And with the cost of health care rapidly mounting, Congress agreed to substantial changes in Medicare, the health program created in 1965 for the elderly and disabled.

Reagan proved adept in persuading Congress to accede to his principal proposals. In enhancing the nation's military arsenal, for example, he got virtually everything he demanded, including appropriations for the costly MX intercontinental missile (renamed the "peacemaker"). Although questions remained about its value and feasibility, Secretary of Defense Caspar Weinberger told congress it was essential as a "bargaining chip" in arms talks with the Soviet Union. Congress went along as well with Reagan's efforts to revise the domestic agenda of previous administrations. In the Democratic-controlled House, a sufficient number of conservative southern Democrats voted with the Republicans to override liberal opposition to Reagan's deep cuts in social programs. In some cases Congress made more modest cuts than Reagan proposed, as in federal support for the arts and humanities, subsidized housing programs, child nutrition, and student loans. Although the president sought "significant reductions in funding" for almost all education programs, Congress consistently provided more money than Reagan wanted. With a presidential commission warning that "a rising tide of mediocrity" threatened American education, Reagan summoned schools "back to basics," proposed merit pay for teachers, and urged principals to crack down on disciplinary problems. But he continued to resist additional federal funding.

Although Reagan believed the nation had a God-given responsibility to preserve and protect its natural resources, he reversed the momentum of previous administrations toward more stringent environmental protection. The administration eased the impact of antipollution laws on industry and permitted more private development of resources on public lands. Environmentalists active in both parties saw to it that Congress gave the president less than he wanted, but Reagan's appointments weakened the administration of environmental and resource laws. In 1983, the director of the Environmental Protective Agency resigned along with other top agency officials amid charges that they had been lax in enforcing hazardous waste laws, had made deals with polluters, and had manipulated toxic cleanup grants for political purposes. James G. Watt, secretary of the interior, also resigned under public pressure.

Environmental groups and their allies in Congress perceived Watt as anxious to shift the emphasis from protection of public lands and resources toward their exploitation by private interests. After his appointment, Watt was almost continually embroiled in controversy, usually over policies favoring private developers and the language he used to answer his critics.

OUR NUCLEAR BUSINESS

On April 27, 1982, Major General William W. Hoover, director of the Department of Energy's Office of Military Application, appeared before the House Subcommittee on Procurement and Military Nuclear systems.

Mr. Chairman and members of the committee, it is my pleasure to appear before this committee . . . to discuss the Department of Energy's fiscal year 1983 nuclear weapons program and the funding required to execute that program.

The nuclear development and production programs are unique in Government in that they constitute an integrated Government-owned industry. . . . We are, ladies and gentlemen, talking about, in terms of assets and products, what would be a major United States industrial corporation—one that would rank in the upper quarter of the Fortune 500.

I would like you, therefore, to consider yourselves the Board of Directors of that corporation and my remarks to you the prospectus of our company's future. The record of this testimony will serve as our report to the stockholders—the American taxpayers.

Assets:

From the air, our production plants look like a cross section of American industry. Once on the inside, one begins to see the extent and diversity of their capabilities. . . .

Product Line:

Strategic weapons. . . .

Long-range theater nuclear systems. . . .

Battlefield nuclear systems. . . .

Fleet air defense. . . .

These systems constitute the near-term product line of our weapons industry. It is an impressive array, but as a product-oriented industry, we must ask: Can we keep up with the demand, and what about preparations for new products in the future?

Investment Strategy

If I may ask you again to think of the weapons complex as a business, I believe you will agree that in responding to these challenges it is important that we consider not just the program's immediate needs, but rather consider our objectives, goals, and resource requirements in the context of a long-term investment strategy. . . . Our aim is to:

Provide sufficient capacity to meet the current and planned production workload. . . .

Increase personnel levels in the weapons laboratories. . . .

Increase nuclear testing.

Revitalize the aging plant by continuing the program. . . to restore the complex to modern industrial standards . . .

Ensure that we have modern management and manufacturing techniques . . .

Mr. Chairman . . . in closing I want to say—this Government-owned industry we are managing is basically sound. There is a strong demand for our products for the foreseeable future and, if we are prudent in our care of existing facilities and equipment and future acquisitions, it will be a strong competitor in the world for the long term.

Consistent with his philosophy of government, Reagan had wanted to reduce the federal role in agriculture, particularly the costly program of price supports. But depressed export markets and bumper crops created massive surpluses, many farmers faced economic disaster, and the administration intervened with new programs to pay farmers to discourage planting excess crops. In 1983, price supports exceeded any previous year and farm foreclosures were higher than at any other time since the Great Depression.

Through much of Reagan's first term, the economic revival remained an unfulfilled promise. The policy of reviving the economy through substantial tax cuts could not be easily reconciled with the Federal Reserve board's attempt to check inflation through credit restraints. By early 1982, the United States was experiencing the highest levels of unemployment since the Great Depression. The basic industries, such as steel and automobiles, were especially hard hit, and this accelerated a decline that had begun much earlier. Many businesses went bankrupt, unemployment exceeded 10 percent of the work force (some 12 million workers were without jobs by the end of 1982), and interest rates for borrowed money remained discouragingly high.

By late 1983, however, the economy had improved sufficiently for Reagan to claim a victory for his economic theories. Inflation had been checked (with the help of declining oil prices), interest rates came down significantly, and factory production and employment increased. The renewed vigor of the economy, which persisted into Reagan's second term, surprised forecasters and did much to enhance the president's popularity.

Whether the revival and economic growth would be permanent remained debatable. The unemployment rate for blacks remained high, more than twice that of whites. Disparities between the incomes of poorer families and those of more affluent families grew markedly. The national poverty rate rose to 15.2 percent in 1983 from 13 percent in 1980, as the number of poor people grew by 6 million to a total of 35.3 million. (A family of four was classified as poor if it had a cash income of less than $10,178 in 1983.) Nearly 36 percent of all blacks lived in poverty in 1983, the highest black poverty rate since the Census Bureau began collecting data on black poverty in 1966.

The substantial increase in military spending and the consequent growth of the federal deficit to unprecedented levels also raised serious questions about the future of the economy. But for the overwhelming majority of the American electorate in 1984, Reagan's vision of a revived America—economically and militarily—seemed at hand.

Reaganism and Civil Rights

For some 20 years, the federal government had played an active role in expanding and enforcing programs designed to ensure the civil rights of black Americans. The Reagan presidency reflected growing doubts about the wisdom and effectiveness of some programs, particularly those aimed at eliminating discrimination in employment through affirmative or preferential hiring and at eliminating school segregation through busing. Despite the president's avowed support for civil rights, the Reagan administration reversed a bipartisan consensus and significantly restricted the range of remedies available to government to eliminate racial discrimination and to guarantee jobs and promotions to blacks and women.

Federal agencies charged with the enforcement of civil rights found themselves frustrated in their efforts, whether through diminished appropriations or revised guidelines. The policy embraced by the Reagan administration required people alleging discrimination in employment, for example, to prove that it was intentional. This negated broad-based affirmative action programs designed to reverse the effects of *past* discrimination. In a major victory for the administration's view, the Supreme Court ruled that judges could not alter the rules of a valid seniority system to prevent the layoff of recently hired blacks.

Once the watchdog over Democratic and Republican administrations to make certain of compliance with civil rights laws, the Civil Rights Commission came to be dominated by members who shared President Reagan's view of limited government and opposition to school busing and

affirmative action programs. On some issues, the president bowed to public or congressional pressure to moderate his civil rights positions. Despite his initial resistance, for example, he ultimately signed the bill passed overwhelmingly by Congress to extend and strengthen the Voting Rights Act of 1965. Reagan showed similar flexibility in finally yielding to bipartisan support for establishing a national holiday on the anniversary of Martin Luther King's birth.

The civil rights arena had shifted in the 1970s to the North and to the question of how to achieve genuine racial integration in the public schools. The controversy rose out of the Supreme Court's argument in the 1954 decision that segregated education was inherently unequal because it perpetuated a caste system based on race. Since in most major cities, especially in the North, integration was confined to the city limits, school systems remained in large measure segregated. Faced with this paradox, the courts held that combining urban school districts with those in the suburbs and if necessary busing pupils across municipal boundaries was a legitimate way to achieve a racially integrated system. Since nearly half of all school children in the nation already traveled to school by bus each day, desegregation by busing appeared to require no radical departure from custom.

But the prospect of busing children to achieve racial integration produced in much of urban America considerable panic and hysteria, as did various proposals to reorganize school districts for the same purpose. The controversy intensified in the 1970s, with growing political repercussions. The Reagan administration no doubt reflected strong popular feelings when it authorized the Justice Department and law enforcement officials to assist communities and individuals seeking "relief" from desegregation and busing orders.

At the same time, the Reagan administration argued—unsuccessfully—in 1982 that the Internal Revenue Service did not have the authority to deny tax-exempt status to private educational institutions that practiced racial discrimination. When the Supreme Court by 8 to 1 forced the Justice Department to back down on that decision, the administration renewed its efforts to obtain tax credits for parents to help offset tuition costs at private and parochial schools and colleges, even though this might have the effect of subsidizing "white flight" from the public schools. Congress, however, refused to approve the necessary legislation.

By the 1980s, more children in northern cities

attended racially segregated schools than at the time of the Supreme Court decision in *Brown* v. *Board of Education*. In 1954, only one city (Washington, D.C.) of the 20 largest cities in the country had a white minority in the public schools; 25 years later, whites were a minority in the schools of 18 of the 20 largest cities. By 1980, nearly three-quarters of the black children in the nation's 26 largest cities attended schools with 90 to 100 percent black enrollment. White hostility to desegregation, in both North and South, underscored the depth and complexity of racial attitudes in the nation.

FOREIGN POLICY: PEACE THROUGH STRENGTH

Like the heroes he admired in Hollywood films, Ronald Reagan wanted to make Uncle Sam respected and feared once again in the world community. He appealed to that traditional sense of the United States as a moral frontier with a special, unique destiny—a "city upon the hill" that would inspire the world to follow its example.

I've always believed that this land was placed here between the two great oceans by some divine plan. It was placed there to be found by a special kind of people. We built a new breed of human, called an American. We can meet our destiny, and that destiny is to build a land here that will be for all mankind a shining city on a hill.

The humiliations in Vietnam and Iran Reagan viewed as debilitating experiences for the American people. Respect would come, he believed, only from military strength and preparedness, and his determination to raise the level of military spending rested firmly on that belief. Once the nation had renewed its military power, it would be in a position to pursue a foreign policy that would make it once again the leader of the "free world."

Farewell to Détente

Upon becoming president Reagan chose as secretary of state Alexander Haig, a former Nixon aide and NATO commander. He seemed ideally suited for a commitment to a tougher foreign policy. "There are things worse than war," Haig told a Senate committee, and he vowed that the United States would not enter any war it was not prepared to win. That was the kind of language the president wanted to hear, and Reagan himself provided much of the inflated rhetoric for the new departure in American foreign policy.

The inauguration had hardly ended before Reagan unleashed a verbal attack on the Soviet Union that had not been heard since the 1950s. In his first press conference, he said the Russians could not be trusted because "they reserve unto themselves the right to commit any crime, to lie, to cheat" in order to achieve world domination. The Soviet Union, Reagan insisted, "underlies all the unrest" in the world. And he underscored the differences between the two great superpowers: "They don't subscribe to our sense of morality because they don't believe in any of the good things; they don't believe in an afterlife. They don't believe in a God or a religion, and . . . the only morality they recognize, therefore, is what will advance the cause of socialism." In a speech in Orlando, Florida, in 1983 to fundamentalist preachers, Reagan excoriated the Soviet Union as "an evil empire" and he called upon his audience to enlist in the new crusade: "There is sin and evil in the world and we are enjoined by Scriptures and the Lord Jesus to oppose it with all our might."

Midway through Reagan's first term, Haig's feud with White House staff members resulted in his resignation under pressure. To replace him, Reagan turned to George Shultz, a former Nixon cabinet member who was regarded as a team player. But the change brought no lessening of the growing tension in Soviet-American relations. The assumption persisted that the Soviet Union was at the head of a monstrous international conspiracy bent on world conquest and the destruction of the American way of life. To confront and contain Soviet power and international communism became once again the guiding principle of American foreign policy.

Persuaded that the Soviets understood only force, Reagan proceeded with his massive military buildup. He did agree to resume arms control talks with the Soviets, focused on mutual and balanced reductions in nuclear arsenals. But no agreement could be reached by the end of 1983, the date on which the United States had promised to deploy in Western Europe intermediate-range Pershing 2 and cruise missiles that could within a matter of minutes reach targets hundreds of miles inside the Soviet Union. The United States and NATO contended that the deployment was a necessary response to the Soviet modernization of its missiles aimed at Western Europe. The Soviet Union claimed that a balance of destructive weapons already existed and that deployment of the new missiles destabilized the nuclear power balance.

Refusing to believe the Reagan administration was interested in reaching an agreement, the Soviets broke off the arms control talks in December 1983. They resumed after Reagan's reelection, but remained unproductive.

The Reagan administration linked any reduction in Cold War tensions to a demonstrated improvement in Soviet behavior. The Soviet Union argued that its behavior in international affairs reflected a concern over threats to its own national security. Such a concern kept Soviet armed forces in Afghanistan in a frustrating, costly, and only partially successful effort to bolster the Communist government there. Of perhaps greater concern to the Soviets was the emergence in Poland of an independent trade union movement (Solidarity). That Polish authorities were forced to recognize Solidarity as a legitimate trade union was in itself an impressive triumph in a Communist nation. But when Solidarity then insisted on still more fundamental reforms—an implied challenge to Communist hegemony in Poland and Eastern Europe—officials in both Warsaw and Moscow knew that a confrontation was unavoidable.

In the winter of 1981, the Polish government imposed martial law and dissolved Solidarity. The United States denounced the action as Soviet-inspired and imposed some sanctions on both Poland and the Soviet Union. Two years later martial law was lifted, but not the ban on Solidarity.

Mounting tensions and distrust between the United States and the Soviet Union had a tragic consequence on September 1, 1983, when a Soviet fighter plane shot down a South Korean airliner that had strayed off course into militarily sensitive Soviet territory. The 269 passengers aboard, including a number of Americans, were all killed, and the world expressed profound shock. Reagan condemned it as an "act of barbarism." The Soviet Union defended the action, claiming the Korean airliner was on a spying mission or had been mistaken for one of the American spy aircraft that flew the same course. Subsequent investigation suggested that Soviet personnel had not known it was a commercial plane before ordering the attack. Ultimate responsibility, however, lay in the tensions that had provoked such an unwarranted response.

International Tensions: Old and New

In the Middle East, the Reagan administration pursued a foreign policy that differed in few respects from that of its predecessors. The United States sought a strong Israel aligned with "moderate" Arab states that would serve to discourage Soviet intrusion into the region and keep western oil supplies flowing from the Persian Gulf. But policymakers in Washington never seemed to grasp the dimensions and complexity of the various religious, ethnic, and revolutionary movements that make up this volatile area. The position of Palestinians, including the 1.2 million in Israeli-occupied Gaza and the West Bank, continued to deteriorate, and Israelis continued to construct settlements in the occupied territories, despite Reagan's criticism of the policy.

In June 1982 Israel invaded Lebanon, ostensibly to secure its northern border from raids and shellings. But the major objectives appeared to be the destruction of the military strength of the Palestine Liberation Organization (PLO) and the restructuring of Lebanon. Israeli troops reached Beirut, inflicting heavy losses on the PLO and forcing the evacuation from Lebanon of the bulk of the PLO armed forces. Public opinion in Israel was divided over the wisdom of the invasion, and many in Israel and elsewhere expressed revulsion over the consequences of an intensified civil war within Lebanon. In Muslim West Beirut, for example, Lebanese Christian militiamen supported and armed by Israel took charge of the Sabra and Shatila refugee camps, which housed the families of the evacuated Palestinian fighting men. As the Israelis stood by, Christian gunmen rampaged through the two camps, executing hundreds of Palestinians.

The United States, England, Italy, and France agreed to dispatch "peacekeeping" troops to Lebanon to replace the Israelis and to bolster the new Christian-led Lebanese government. But these troops soon became embroiled in the civil war among Muslims and Christians. Finally, the loss of American lives, including some 241 marines and sailors in a suicide truck bombing of the barracks headquarters, shocked Americans into action. In Congress, questions were raised about the wisdom of an operation designed to prop up a Christian-led government in a predominantly Muslim country. But President Reagan, using language that evoked memories of Vietnam, defended the American presence in Lebanon as "central to our credibility on a global scale" and necessary "to stop the cancerous spread of Soviet influence." In February 1984, the president reversed himself. He bowed to public concern and reluctantly withdrew the marines.

Consistent with the administration's view of the Soviet Union as an expansionist power, the United

States insisted on the need to combat Communist influence wherever it appeared and no matter what form it assumed. In a shift from the position of the Carter administration, Reagan's policymakers made it clear that the United States would in the future be more flexible in applying human rights standards to friendly (anti-Communist) governments. But congressional and public pressures and pragmatic foreign policy considerations forced some moderation of this position.

The administration followed its immediate predecessors in pursuing friendly relations with Communist China, although Reagan had once insisted on support of the Nationalist Chinese on Taiwan as a major tenet of the conservative creed. The same pragmatism in 1986 forced Reagan to abandon his friend and ally, Ferdinand Marcos, the president and strong man of the Philippines, after he was deposed in a popular and peaceful uprising. The United States also bowed to pressure and became more critical of the minority white regime in South Africa. That government, underpinned by Western capital, used the practice of segregation (Apartheid), disfranchisement, and brutal police tactics to repress the 23 million blacks who formed the overwhelming majority of the population. When Reagan came into the presidency, he pledged a policy of "constructive engagement" in South Africa, by which the United States would use quiet diplomacy and pressure to force changes in the Apartheid system. But by 1986, when those pressures failed to produce any results, sentiment increased for more forceful measures.

In Central America, the Reagan administration stood firm in its determination to contain and root out Communist influence. El Salvador had become a battleground between leftist guerrillas and a repressive military regime. The danger of a guerrilla victory took precedence over invasions of human rights and right-wing terrorism, and the Reagan administration gave its full support to the beleaguered anti-Communist regime. In May 1984 a United States-inspired election produced a new government under José Napoleon Duarte. But the problems of reform and internal rebellion remained unresolved, and Duarte was unable to halt the activities of right-wing "death squads."

Of much greater concern to the Reagan administration, a leftist government had come to power in Nicaragua in 1979. Revolutionaries won their war against Anastasio Somoza, long an ally of the United States and the head of the family that had run the country for some 45 years. The rebels, called Sandinistas, modeled themselves after Augusto Cesar Sandino, a Nicaraguan nationalist leader who had fought American marines in the early 1930s. The triumph of the Sandinistas, the revolutionary ideas they expounded, their growing ties with Castro's Cuba, and the suspicion that they actively assisted the rebels in El Salvador were deemed sufficient reason for the United States to grant covert military support to rebels (contras), many of them former Somoza supporters, seeking the overthrow of the Sandinista government.

The president went so far as to proclaim the contras "the moral equivalent of our Founding Fathers," despite their record of attacking civilians indiscriminately, torturing and mutilating prisoners, and terrorizing the countryside. The controversy over support of the contras divided the United States, with public opinion polls indicating public opposition and anxiety over the possible involvement of American troops. But Congress acceded to the president's call for continued military assistance, finding most persuasive his argument that the United States could not afford a Communist sanctuary in Central America.

To underscore its new determination, the United States also resorted to some old remedies. On October 25, 1983, Reagan ordered the invasion of the small island of Grenada in the eastern Caribbean. The administration claimed its purpose was to protect Americans on the island, to restore democratic institutions, to forestall a "Cuban occupation" and to remove "a brutal group of leftist thugs." Critics found little evidence of a major Communist threat in Grenada, but the move was popular with most Americans, and the casualties were minimal.

That the Grenada victory coincided with improved economic conditions in the United States and the patriotic frenzy that dominated the 1984 Olympic Games in Los Angeles boded well for Reagan's reelection campaign. It was less a political campaign on issues than a demonstration of Reagan's continued ability to project a favorable image for most Americans.

REAGAN'S "POLITICAL REVOLUTION": THE SECOND TERM

Even as the president often evoked the past to serve his vision of America, the Reagan administration marked a fundamental break with the past. It sought to rewrite the national agenda, to reverse previous economic and social policy. Not only did it envision dismantling all but the most basic elements of the New Deal and Great Society social programs, but it proposed to make their restoration politically and financially impractical.

After four years in the White House, Reagan could boast to the Republican nominating convention in 1984 that he had achieved many of his goals. He had reduced the growth of the federal government. He had reduced interest rates and inflation. He had reduced taxes to provide incentives for individuals and business. And, he concluded: "We said we would once again be respected throughout the world, and we are. We said we would restore our ability to protect our freedom on land, sea and in the air, and we have." He promised the delegates four more years of the same policy, striving to realize that "dream of an America that would be 'a shining city on a hill.'"

Reagan's Referendum: The Election of 1984

The election of 1984 was significant in several respects. The Democratic party became the first major party to nominate a woman, Representative Geraldine Ferraro of New York, for vice-president.

In the Democratic primaries, moreover, the Reverend Jesse Jackson, a former co-worker of Martin Luther King and a black civil rights activist, became the first black candidate to win substantial support in a bid for the presidential nomination of a major party. Second, Ronald Reagan scored a landslide victory, winning 49 states and further fragmenting the old New Deal coalition. Walter Mondale, the Democratic candidate and former senator and vice-president, managed to win only his home state of Minnesota. Third, the census of 1980 confirmed the substantial movement of Americans from the Northeast to the Sunbelt states of the South and West, where suspicion of federal power and conservative political principles had long been entrenched; those regions gave Reagan his most substantial majorities.

In the campaign, Reagan defended his administration's record, while Mondale tried unsuccessfully to exploit the huge deficit and show how the president's policies had hurt working people, farmers, and blacks. Reagan benefitted from the remarkable economic recovery, including significantly reduced inflation and lower unemployment.

More effectively than his opponent, Reagan

Ronald Reagan scored a landslide victory in the Election of 1984, winning 49 states. (*Photograph by Terry Arthur, The White House*)

conveyed to Americans a sense of the direction in which he wanted to take the country. He emphasized individual and national self-reliance, a deregulated market, and slimmed-down and decentralized government. It was a simple and consistent message that spoke in broad terms of values rather than issues, and it succeeded in spectacular fashion. Both Reagan and Mondale thought the election provided the American people with a clear ideological choice. But it appeared to be largely a contest of personalities and a referendum on Reagan's leadership, and on these grounds the incumbent held a clear advantage.

The presence of a woman on the Democratic ticket made no apparent difference in the outcome. Along with Ferraro, all the women Senate hopefuls and challengers for House seats were defeated. Reagan won 61 percent of the men's vote and 57 percent of the women's vote. The only group he lost overwhelmingly was the black electorate, with some 90 percent voting for Mondale; Hispanics voted 65 to 33 percent for Mondale. But whites voted 66 to 34 percent for Reagan. As if to remind the president that the election was not necessarily a triumph for his conservative ideology, voters returned a Democratic House of Representatives.

Farewell to the New Deal

In his State of the Union address, at the start of his second term, Ronald Reagan reiterated an essential theme of his administration. Keeping the United States militarily strong and prepared—"defense"—was the principal responsibility of the federal government. To that end, the president proposed a nearly 12 percent increase in military spending. Under the proposed military buildup, military outlays would account for 28 cents of every federal dollar spent in 1987. Consistent with the president's priorities, the new budget once again cut deeply into social programs, eliminating some of them altogether. Congress, on the other hand, preferred a more evenhanded approach, in which military and social programs would share the cuts necessary to reduce the deficit.

In agreeing to a new budget, the executive and legislative branches operated under some new constraints. To meet growing concern over the huge federal deficit, Congress in 1984 had passed a far-reaching and controversial deficit reduction act (named after the co-sponsors, Senators William Gramm of Texas, Warren Rudman of New Hampshire, and Ernest Hollings of South Carolina). The

act would force a $36 billion reduction in the deficit in each of five fiscal years ending in 1991, ostensibly achieving a balanced budget by then. If the president and Congress failed to make such cuts in the conventional manner, the president would be required to impose the necessary reductions by cutting military as well as nonmilitary spending. The act aroused considerable controversy, and the Supreme Court agreed to rule on its constitutionality. Congress also needed to consider public opinion. Although Reagan remained immensely popular, the same polls showed that sizable majorities thought the government should spend more, not less, on aid to the poor and the environment, and only 17 percent of the public favored increased military outlays.

The net result and long-range effects of Reagan's "political revolution" remained unclear. In his two terms as president, he had fundamentally altered the shape and role of government in American life, producing substantial changes in federal spending and in the substance and purposes of its domestic programs. He had succeeded, moreover, in altering the terms of the debate concerning the role of government and federal spending. The focus was no longer on which social programs to strengthen or expand, but on the size of the cuts and which programs deserved to be scrapped altogether. The focus was no longer on the expansion and enforcement of civil rights rules, but rather on limiting and in some instances abandoning their application.

In slowing the growth of federal programs, the Reagan administration reshaped the national agenda and reversed a role for government which Democratic and Republican presidents had previously embraced or accepted. Still, the federal budget accounted for more of the national wealth than it did on the day Reagan took office, mostly because of the enormous increases in military spending, interest costs on the federal debt, and the growth built into the largest automatic benefit programs, such as social security and Medicare.

When Reagan became president, he promised a moral as well as a political revolution. But his moral agenda did not fare as well as his promised military buildup and reduction of social programs. Some obvious paradoxes confronted the president. He needed to reconcile some of his strong moral convictions regarding abortion and school prayer with his pledge "to get the government off the backs of the people." To implement some of the moral reforms he desired—a constitutional amendment to outlaw abortion and to permit organized state-sponsored prayer in public schools—would increase government intervention in the day-to-day lives of people, the very trend he had promised to halt. None of the proposals came close to congressional passage.

From the outset of his presidency, Reagan had opposed the Equal Rights Amendment to the Constitution, which would have specifically banned sex discrimination. But the president claimed he had brought women into critical positions in government. The most spectacular of his nominations to public office was that of Sandra Day O'Connor to the Supreme Court—the first woman to serve in that position. Nevertheless, the number of women and members of minority groups in appointive positions was significantly lower than in the Carter administration.

Brave New World: "Terrorists" and "Star Wars"

Much of Reagan's attention in his second term focused on how to respond to the rise in terrorist attacks on Americans abroad, mostly stemming from ongoing tensions in the Middle East. In 1986 the United States retaliated by bombing alleged terrorist bases in Libya, the country Reagan considered most responsible for encouraging such activity. The problem of combatting terrorism was complicated, however, by varying perceptions of "terrorism." President Reagan, for example, referred to *contra* rebels in Nicaragua as "freedom fighters," while Sandinistas regarded them as little more than "terrorists." Moammar Khadafy, the leader of Libya, referred to the soldiers of the Palestine Liberation Organization as "freedom fighters," while many Americans and Israelis identified them as "terrorists." The cycle of retaliation, moreover, usually claimed as its victims innocent civilians rather than the actual perpetrators of the acts being avenged.

The meeting of Reagan and Mikhail Gorbachev, the new Soviet leader, in November 1985 appeared to herald a thaw in the Cold War. Nothing substantial came of the summit conference, however, except a cultural exchange agreement and the decision to meet again. Still, the very fact that the two leaders had met eased some tensions, and the prospect of additional summit conferences raised expectations. But relations between the two countries remained highly volatile, alternating between expressions of willingness to cooperate and harsh, unrelenting rhetoric.

The war of words accelerated over responsibility for the increase in terrorism and the unresolved arms race. Much of the debate over arms control revolved around alleged violations by both sides of previous agreements and President Reagan's decision to embrace the costly and still unproved Strategic Defense Initiative (popularly called Star Wars). This highly complex military system in space would, if successful, establish an impenetrable defensive shield against ballistic missiles. The Soviets denounced the proposed militarization of space and the decision by the administration in 1986 to halt its voluntary compliance with the SALT II arms control agreement limiting nuclear weaponry (never ratified by the Senate). The prospect of reducing international tensions seemed dim. The continuing war waged by Soviet troops in Afghanistan, violations of human rights within the Soviet Union and Eastern Europe, and the ongoing conflicts in Nicaragua and El Salvador remained enduring sources of tension.

THE AMERICAN DREAM IN THE 1980S

The American people celebrated in 1987 the 200th birthday of their Constitution. From the White House, President Reagan exuded optimism about the vitality and enduring qualities of the American Dream. In accepting in 1984 his party's nomination for a new term, he had talked once again of "new eras of opportunity for everyone." He had contrasted his administration of "hope, confidence, and growth" with the Democrats' stress on "pessimism, fear, and limits." He claimed to have restored to Americans a pride in their country and a confidence in their destiny. Earlier, he had evoked memories of an America that had conquered many frontiers over the past two centuries, and he remained confident that the same spirit would triumph in the future:

I'm talking about the very essence of what it is to be an American. We are different. We have always been different. If we all feel that way the world will once again look on in awe at us, astonished by the miracles of education and freedom, amazed by our rebirth of confidence and hope and progress, and when they are amazed and when it happens we'll be able to say to the world, "Well, what did you expect? After all, we're Americans."

That was the kind of confidence Reagan succeeded in conveying, and large numbers of Americans embraced his reaffirmation of the American Dream. The return of "good times" embellished the lives of many families, even as it left untouched minorities and many of the nation's farmers and industrial workers. Studies revealed that the average family was better off financially in 1984 than in 1980. But the same studies revealed persistently wide disparities in the incomes of rich and poor Americans. In 1986, one American in seven remained below the official poverty line—some 33 million people.

For black Americans, the gains of the civil rights movement were eroding, along with their standard of living. The number of black poor far exceeded those who managed to attain middle-class standing, and the economic gap between blacks and whites continued to widen. For urban whites, black and white, public schools deteriorated, as did public services and personal security. And with jobs still at a premium, the nation experienced difficulties absorbing the vast numbers of new refugees flocking to its shores, mainly Vietnamese, Laotians, Haitians, and Central Americans seeking better lives. Finally, large numbers of farmers remained in deep trouble, desperately trying to hold on to their lands.

In the American myth of success, any person could make it to the top on the basis of hard work and ambition. But for many Americans in the 1980s, the principal concern remained not so much lifting themselves up the economic ladder, as trying to keep from falling lower. If they worked, they often worked at jobs that permitted them no opportunity of self-expression and little chance for advancement. In an interview conducted in 1974 by Studs Terkel, Mike Lefevre, a steel worker, articulated feelings and frustrations about life and work that retained considerable force as Americans prepared to enter the last decade of the twentieth century.

I'm a dying breed. A laborer. Strictly muscle work . . . pick it up, put it down, pick it up, put it down. We handle between forty and fifty thousand pounds of steel a day. . . . It's hard to take pride in a bridge you're never gonna cross, in a door you're never gonna open. You're mass producing things and you never see the end result of it. . . . It isn't that the average working guy is dumb. He's tired, that's all. . . . At seven it starts. My arms get tired about the first half-hour. After that, they don't get tired any more until maybe the last half-hour at the end of the day. I work from seven to three thirty. My arms are tired at seven thirty and they're tired at three o'clock. I hope to God I never get broke in, because I always want my arms to be tired at seven thirty and three o'clock. 'Cause that's when I know that there's a beginning and there's an end. That I'm not brainwashed. In between, I don't even try to think. It's not just the work. Somebody built the pyramids. Somebody's going to build something. Pyramids, Empire State Building— these things just don't happen. There's hard work behind it. I would like to see a building, say, the Empire State, I would like to see on one side of it a foot-wide strip from top to bottom with the name of every bricklayer, the name of every electrician, with all the names. So when a guy walked by, he could take his son and say, "See, that's me over there on the forty-fifth floor. I put the steel beam in." Picasso can point to a painting. What can I point to? A writer can point to a book. Everybody should have something to point to . . .

Yes, I want my signature on 'em, too. Sometimes, out of pure meanness, when I make something, I put a little dent in it. I like to do something to make it really unique . . . just so I can say I did it. . . . I'd like to make my imprint. . . .

This is gonna sound square, but my kid is my imprint. He's my freedom. . . . You know what I mean? This is why I work. Every time I see a young guy walk by with a shirt and tie and dressed up real sharp, I'm lookin' at my kid, you know? That's it.

Two hundred years after the birth of the nation, the American Dream, though flawed and losing some of its luster, persisted. Ronald Reagan vowed

THE NEW GENERATION

Every generation has a way of categorizing and stereotyping its predecessors, sometimes drowning them in nostalgia, sometimes criticizing their excesses and exaggerating their follies. In the 1980s, commentators took note of a generation of young Americans significantly different from their predecessors, contrasting the more conservative, career-oriented academic utilitarians of the eighties with the more liberal, rebellious, and free thinking college students of the sixties. Himself a member of the sixties' generation, Garry Trudeau, the political cartoonist responsible for the popular Doonesbury series, addressed in June 1982 the graduating class at the College of William and Mary in Williamsburg, Virginia.

It is no wonder that you've given up on the culture. With no credible ego models, what's left but to flock to your bookstores and buy handbooks on living preppies, dead cats, inert cubes, living cats and dead preppies—the subjects of the five bestselling titles on American campuses last year? These are books for minds at rest. They are also the books favored by the rest of the nation, which suggests that the post-Vietnam fatigue syndrome has us all in its grip. Your values and interests are no worse or better than those that are filtering down from the larger society that nurtured you. If you have not given your elders any clear sense of who you are, perhaps it is because you are just like your elders. Your priorities do not turn out to be all that different from those of your parents.

THE 1980s: THE "LITE" DECADE

It used to take so much time—days, sometimes weeks—to read a classic. Moby Dick, alone, runs 710 pages. Today, thanks to a small publishing house called Workman, it takes a minute. Through abridging, reabridging and editing out "rambling soliloquies," Workman boasts that it has "cut down the literary canon to a lean pistol," producing an audiocassette tape that offers listeners "Ten Classics in Ten Minutes."

The result is light literature, the latest demonstration that in the 1980s light beer is not the only thing that is less filling. What started out as a way to justify drinking three beers instead of two—the creation of a light beer with a third fewer calories—has become part of a broader phenomenon in which less is valued above more. This is the Light Decade, or as some would have it, Lite.

Sociologists say that "lite," which started as a marketing term used to denote dietetic foods, has become a metaphor for what Americans are seeking in disparate parts of their lives. In their relationships, for example, they have turned away from soul-searching and stress of emotional commitment; at the movies, they would rather watch an invincible hero, like Rambo or the Karate Kid, who never lets the audience down.

"The notion of the word 'lite' tends to follow what seems to be a trend in American culture," said Ray B. Brown, chairman of the department of popular culture at Bowling Green State University in Ohio. "That is for everybody to be utterly selfish about themselves, for people to want easy cures, easy riches, easy jobs and easy wealth."

The Light Decade is a time when men and women can "fall in love without paying the price," as a Honda Civic advertisement promises. They can undergo psychoanalysis in one sitting, because today's psychotherapy skips the formative years, namely childhood. For health care, busy executives can turn to a so-called Doc in a Box, a storefront medical clinic with extended hours, higher prices and no appointment, no referral—no medical history necessary.

There is light culture (books on tape), light shopping (buying clothes by video), light politics (candidates who run on image, not issues), light responsibility (the lowest voter participation rates of any democracy) and light music (Lite FM, where the heavy bass line has been removed so that the sound does not jar or stir listeners). And of course, there is light food, with which people can cut calories without changing their diets by using products like Jell-O Light, Cornitos Light Corn Chips, Heinz Lite Ketchup and Glace Lite, which, its manufacturer, Sweet Victory, says "gives you all the rich, delicious pleasures of 300-calorie premium ice cream" at 100 calories a scoop.

Food, notably dietetic food, is where the Light Decade started. It is also the clearest example of how the philosophy has caught on. "Lite," or "light," foods are now "one of the fastest growing segments of the American food industry," according to a recent Federal Food and Drug Administration report. . . .

Bernard Phillips, a sociologist at Boston University, calls the Light decade a "smorgasbord" approach to life, where people convince themselves that they can have the best of all worlds, immediately, by having a lightened version of everything. . . .

Source: *New York Times*, August 13, 1986, "In the 'Lite' Decade, Less Has Become More," by William R. Greer.

---

to make that dream a reality in the lives of all Americans. But so had every American president in the twentieth century. Reconciling technological advances with persistent economic problems, a growing underclass, and the decline of the family farm would be a formidable challenge for any president in the remaining years of the twentieth century. If anything, the challenge took on even greater implications abroad, where the betrayed aspirations of masses of people continued to make for a turbulent and revolutionary world.

Even as Americans commemorated the bicentennial of the Constitution, the proper role of the federal government in American life remained a potent political issue. Nor did Americans agree about the results of President Reagan's massive increase in military spending. Some viewed the cost as necessary for successful bargaining with the Soviet Union and essential to national security; others feared the consequences of an escalation of the arms race, including the introduction of a whole new class of "third generation" nuclear weapons. The accident in 1986 at the nuclear power plant at Chernobyl in the Soviet Union revived questions not only about the peaceful development of nuclear energy, but about the need to reduce nuclear arsenals and halt their proliferation in the world.

For 40 years, the United States and the Soviet Union had been engaged in a Cold War. Despite enormous military expenditures by both countries, distorting their economies and eroding the quality of life, neither felt any more secure. That was a development none of the Founding Fathers had contemplated when some two hundred years ago they had met in Philadelphia to establish "a more perfect union, establish justice, insure domestic tranquility, provide for the common defense, promote the general welfare, and secure the blessings of liberty to ourselves and our posterity."

SUMMARY

Ronald Reagan in the 1980s became the first president since Franklin Delano Roosevelt to alter the nation's social and economic policy and redefine the presidency in fundamental ways. His two terms in the White House became an exercise in the politics of nostalgia—the hearkening back to "good old days" that featured a much more invisible and unobtrusive federal government. The tone of this presidency was set in his first inaugural address: "Government is not the solution to our problem. Government is the problem." And his landslide reelection in 1984 seemed to set the seal on a new direction for the federal government.

In reordering the nation's priorities, Reagan placed special emphasis on strengthening its military capability. He expected supply-side economics to cure the nation's economic ills. Through tax cuts and an easing of federal regulations, individuals and corporations would be induced to invest and stimulate economic growth. Reduced spending on social programs would help pay for the increased military budget and soften the impact of the tax cut.

The economy did revive by late 1983, but not before unemployment had reached the highest levels since the Great Depression. And there were still unprecedented federal budget deficits, which reflected the imbalance between cuts in domestic spending and massive increases in military spending.

Reagan's foreign policy was directed at containing Soviet influence and revolutionary communism. Soviet-American relations plummeted to a new low, exacerbated by Reagan's rhetoric, the deployment of new missiles in Western Europe, Soviet actions in Afghanistan and Poland, and the Soviet downing of a South Korean airliner. To check Communist influence, the United States also became involved in civil wars in the Middle East and Central America.

The election of 1984 was significant in that it ratified all these directions: Reagan's landslide (he carried 49 states) further fragmented the old New Deal coalition. And the Democrats' choice of a woman, Geraldine Ferraro of New York, as the vice-presidential candidate, seemed to make no difference in the outcome.

The net result and long-range effects of this "political revolution" remained unclear, however; Ronald Reagan had indeed fundamentally altered the shape and role of government in American life, producing substantial changes in federal spending and in the substance and purposes of its domestic programs. He had also changed the terms of the debate on the role of government and federal spending. But the federal budget still accounted for more of the national wealth than it did when Reagan took office. And some of the items on the moral agenda—abortion and school prayer—threatened to keep government active in people's lives.

Though many Americans enthusiastically applauded Ronald Reagan's reaffirmation of the American Dream and his sense of optimism and confidence, many problems, both domestic and international, remained unresolved. Nor had debate on the scope and direction of government been stilled.

Suggested Readings

The best source for Ronald Reagan is his autobiography, *Where's the Rest of Me?* (1965). Early assessments of his presidency include L. Cannon, *Reagan* (1982); L. I. Barrett, *Gambling With History* (1983); and R. Dallek, *Ronald Reagan: The Politics of Symbolism* (1984). Often more incisive and biting than any historical critique is G. B. Trudeau, *Doonesbury Dossier: The Reagan Years* (1984). On the conservative resurgence in American political and intellectual life, see A. Crawford, *Thunder on the Right: The "New Right" and the Politics of Resentment* (1980), and P. Steinfels, *The Neoconservatives: The Men Who Are Changing America's Politics* (1979).

On the American Dream in the seventies and eighties, see S. Terkel, *Working: People Talk about What They Do All Day and How They Feel about What They Do* (1974), and *American Dreams: Lost and Found* (1980), both works of oral history. On the working class, see also R. Sennett and J. Cobb, *The Hidden Injuries of Class* (1972); L. K. Howe (ed.), *The White Majority* (1970), and *Pink Collar Workers: Inside the World of Women's Work* (1977); S. Feldstein and L. Costello (eds.), *The Ordeal of Assimilation: A Documentary History of the White Working Class* (1974); and S. Aronowitz, *False Promises: The Shaping of American Working Class Consciousness* (1973). On class, race, and ethnicity in modern American society, see R. Polenberg, *One Nation Divisible* (1980).

APPENDIX

The Declaration of Independence

When in the course of human events it becomes necessary for one people to dissolve the political bands which have connected them with another and to assume, among the powers of the earth, the separate and equal station to which the laws of nature and of nature's God entitle them, a decent respect to the opinions of mankind requires that they should declare the causes which impel them to the separation.

We hold these truths to be self-evident, that all men are created equal; that they are endowed by their Creator with certain unalienable rights; that among these are life, liberty, and the pursuit of happiness. That, to secure these rights, governments are instituted among men, deriving their just powers from the consent of the governed; that, whenever any form of government becomes destructive of these ends, it is the right of the people to alter or to abolish it, and to institute a new government, laying its foundation on such principles, and organizing its powers in such form, as to them shall seem most likely to effect their safety and happiness. Prudence, indeed, will dictate that governments long established should not be changed for light and transient causes; and, accordingly, all experience hath shown that mankind are more disposed to suffer, while evils are sufferable, than to right themselves by abolishing the forms to which they are accustomed. But when a long train of abuses and usurpations, pursuing invariably the same object, evinces a design to reduce them under absolute despotism, it is their right, it is their duty, to throw off such government and to provide new guards for their future security. Such has been the patient sufferance of these colonies, and such is now the necessity which constrains them to alter their former systems of government. The history of the present King of Great Britain is a history of repeated injuries and usurpations, all having, in direct object, the establishment of an absolute tyranny over these States. To prove this, let facts be submitted to a candid world:

He has refused his assent to laws the most wholesome and necessary for the public good.

He has forbidden his governors to pass laws of immediate and pressing importance, unless suspended in their operation till his assent should be obtained; and, when so suspended, he has utterly neglected to attend to them.

He has refused to pass other laws for the accommodation of large districts of people, unless those people would relinquish the right of representation in the legislature; a right inestimable to them and formidable to tyrants only.

He has called together legislative bodies at places unusual, uncomfortable, and distant from the depository of their public records, for the sole purpose of fatiguing them into compliance with his measures.

He has dissolved representative houses, repeatedly for opposing, with manly firmness, his invasions on the rights of the people.

He has refused, for a long time after such dissolutions, to cause others to be elected; whereby the legislative powers, incapable of annihilation, have returned to the people at large for their exercise; the state remaining, in the meantime, exposed to all the danger of invasion from without and convulsions within.

He has endeavored to prevent the population of these States; for that purpose, obstructing the laws for naturalization of foreigners, refusing to pass others to encourage their migration hither, and raising the conditions of new appropriations of lands.

He has obstructed the administration of justice by refusing his assent to laws for establishing judiciary powers.

He has made judges dependent on his will alone for the tenure of their offices and the amount and payment of their salaries.

He has erected a multitude of new offices and sent hither swarms of officers to harass our people and eat out their substance.

He has kept among us, in time of peace, standing armies, without the consent of our legislatures.

He has affected to render the military independent of, and superior to, the civil power.

He has combined with others to subject us to a jurisdiction foreign to our Constitution and unacknowledged by our laws, giving his assent to their acts of pretended legislation—

For quartering large bodies of armed troops among us;

For protecting them by a mock trial from punishment for any murders which they should commit on the inhabitants of these States;

For cutting off our trade with all parts of the world;

For imposing taxes on us without our consent;

For depriving us, in many cases, of the benefit of trial by jury;

For transporting us beyond seas to be tried for pretended offences;

For abolishing the free system of English laws in a neighboring province, establishing therein an arbitrary government, and enlarging its boundaries, so as to render it at once an example and fit instrument for introducing the same absolute rule into these colonies;

For taking away our charters, abolishing our most valuable laws, and altering, fundamentally, the powers of our governments;

For suspending our own legislatures and declaring themselves invested with power to legislate for us in all cases whatsoever.

He has abdicated government here by declaring us out of his protection and waging war against us.

He has plundered our seas, ravaged our coasts, burnt our towns, and destroyed the lives of our people.

He is, at this time, transporting large armies of foreign mercenaries to complete the works of death, desolation, and tyranny already begun with circumstances of cruelty and perfidy scarcely paralleled in the most barbarous ages, and totally unworthy the head of a civilized nation.

He has constrained our fellow citizens, taken captive on the high seas, to bear arms against their country, to become the executioners of their friends and brethren, or to fall themselves by their hands.

He has excited domestic insurrections amongst us and has endeavored to bring on the inhabitants of our frontiers, the merciless Indian savages, whose known rule of warfare is an undistinguished destruction of all ages, sexes, and conditions.

In every stage of these oppressions, we have petitioned for redress in the most humble terms; our repeated petitions have been answered only by repeated injury. A prince whose character is thus marked by every act which may define a tyrant is unfit to be the ruler of a free people.

Nor have we been wanting in attention to our British brethren. We have warned them, from time to time, of attempts made by their legislature to extend an unwarrantable jurisdiction over us. We have reminded them of the circumstances of our emigration and settlement here. We have appealed to their native justice and magnanimity, and we have conjured them, by the ties of our common kindred, to disavow these usurpations, which would inevitably interrupt our connections and correspondence. They, too, have been deaf to the voice of justice and consanguinity. We must, therefore, acquiesce in the necessity which denounces our separation, and hold them, as we hold the rest of mankind, enemies in war, in peace, friends.

We, therefore, the representatives of the United States of America, in general Congress assembled, appealing to the Supreme Judge of the world for the rectitude of our intentions, do, in the name and by the authority of the good people of these colonies, solemnly publish and declare, that these united colonies are, and of right ought to be, free and independent states: that they are absolved from all allegiance to the British Crown, and that all political connection between them and the state of Great Britain is, and ought to be, totally dissolved; and that, as free and independent states, they have full power to levy war, conclude peace, contract alliances, establish commerce, and to do all other acts and things which independent states may of right do. And, for the support of this declaration, with a firm reliance on the protection of Divine Providence, we mutually pledge to each other our lives, our fortunes, and our sacred honor.

The Constitution of the United States of America

We the people of the United States, in order to form a more perfect union, establish justice, insure domestic tranquillity, provide for the common defense, promote the general welfare, and secure the blessings of liberty to ourselves and our posterity, do ordain and establish this Constitution for the United States of America.

Article I

SECTION 1.   All legislative powers herein granted shall be vested in a Congress of the United States, which shall consist of a Senate and House of Representatives.

SECTION 2.   1. The House of Representatives shall be composed of members chosen every second year by the people of the several States, and the electors in each State shall have the qualifications requisite for electors of the most numerous branch of the State legislature.

2. No person shall be a representative who shall not have attained to the age of twenty-five years, and been seven years a citizen of the United States, and who shall not, when elected, be an inhabitant of that State in which he shall be chosen.

3. Representatives and direct taxes[1] shall be apportioned among the several States which may be included within this Union, according to their respective numbers, which shall be determined by adding to the whole number of free persons, including those bound to service for a term of years, and excluding Indians not taxed, three fifths of all other persons.[2] The actual enumeration shall be made within three years after the first meeting of the Congress of the United States, and within every subsequent term of ten years, in such manner as they shall by law direct. The number of representatives shall not exceed one for every thirty thousand, but each State shall have at least one representative; and until such enumeration shall be made, the State of New Hampshire shall be entitled to choose three, Massachusetts eight, Rhode Island and Providence Plantations one, Connecticut five, New York six, New Jersey four, Pennsylvania eight, Delaware one, Maryland six, Virginia ten, North Carolina five, South Carolina five, and Georgia three.

4. When vacancies happen in the representation from any State, the executive authority thereof shall issue writs of election to fill such vacancies.

5. The House of Representatives shall choose their speaker and other officers; and shall have the sole power of impeachment.

SECTION 3.   1. The Senate of the United States shall be composed of two senators from each State, chosen by the legislature thereof,[3] for six years; and each senator shall have one vote.

2. Immediately after they shall be assembled in consequence of the first election, they shall be divided as equally as may be into three classes. The seats of the senators of the first class shall be vacated at the expiration of the second year, of the second class at the expiration of the fourth year, and of the third class at the expiration of the sixth year, so that one third may be chosen every second year; and if vacancies happen by resignation, or otherwise, during the recess of the legislature of any State, the executive thereof may make temporary appointments until the next meeting of the legislature, which shall then fill such vacancies.[4]

3. No person shall be a senator who shall not have attained to the age of thirty years, and been nine years a citizen of the United States, and who shall not, when elected, be an inhabitant of that State for which he shall be chosen.

4. The Vice President of the United States shall be President of the Senate, but shall have no vote, unless they be equally divided.

5. The Senate shall choose their other officers, and also a president pro tempore, in the absence of the Vice President, or when he shall exercise the office of the President of the United States.

---

[1] See the Sixteenth Amendment.
[2] See the Fourteenth Amendment.

[3] See the Seventeenth Amendment.
[4] See the Seventeenth Amendment.

6. The Senate shall have the sole power to try all impeachments. When sitting for that purpose, they shall be on oath or affirmation. When the President of the United States is tried, the chief justice shall preside: and no person shall be convicted without the concurrence of two thirds of the members present.

7. Judgment in cases of impeachment shall not extend further than to removal from office, and disqualification to hold and enjoy any office of honor, trust or profit under the United States: but the party convicted shall nevertheless be liable and subject to indictment, trial, judgment and punishment, according to law.

SECTION 4. 1. The times, places, and manner of holding elections for senators and representatives, shall be prescribed in each State by the legislature thereof; but the Congress may at any time by law make or alter such regulations, except as to the places of choosing senators.

2. The Congress shall assemble at least once in every year, and such meeting shall be on the first Monday in December, unless they shall by law appoint a different day.

SECTION 5. 1. Each House shall be the judge of the elections, returns and qualifications of its own members, and a majority of each shall constitute a quorum to do business; but a smaller number may adjourn from day to day, and may be authorized to compel the attendance of absent members, in such manner, and under such penalties as each House may provide.

2. Each House may determine the rules of its proceedings, punish its members for disorderly behavior, and, with the concurrence of two thirds, expel a member.

3. Each House shall keep a journal of its proceedings, and from time to time publish the same, excepting such parts as may in their judgment require secrecy; and the yeas and nays of the members of either House on any question shall, at the desire of one fifth of those present, be entered on the journal.

4. Neither House, during the session of Congress, shall, without the consent of the other, adjourn for more than three days, nor to any other place than that in which the two Houses shall be sitting.

SECTION 6. 1. The senators and representatives shall receive a compensation for their services, to be ascertained by law, and paid out of the Treasury of the United States. They shall in all cases, except treason, felony, and breach of the peace, be privileged from arrest during their attendance at the session of their respective Houses, and in going to and returning from the same; and for any speech or debate in either House, they shall not be questioned in any other place.

2. No senator or representative shall, during the time for which he was elected, be appointed to any civil office under the authority of the United States, which shall have been created, or the emoluments whereof shall have been increased, during such time; and no person holding any office under the United States shall be a member of either House during his continuance in office.

SECTION 7. 1. All bills for raising revenue shall originate in the House of Representatives; but the Senate may propose or concur with amendments as on other bills.

2. Every bill which shall have passed the House of Representatives and the Senate, shall, before it become a law, be presented to the President of the United States; If he approves he shall sign it, but if not he shall return it, with his objections, to that House in which it shall have originated, who shall enter the objections at large on their journal, and proceed to reconsider it. If after such reconsideration two thirds of that House shall agree to pass the bill, it shall be sent, together with the objections, to the other House, by which it shall likewise be reconsidered, and if approved by two thirds of that House, it shall become a law. But in all such cases the votes of both Houses shall be determined by yeas and nays, and the names of the persons voting for and against the bill shall be entered on the journal of each House respectively. If any bill shall not be returned by the President within ten days (Sundays excepted) after it shall have been presented to him, the same shall be a law, in like manner as if he had signed it, unless the Congress by their adjournment prevent its return, in which case it shall not be a law.

3. Every order, resolution, or vote to which the concurrence of the Senate and the House of Representatives may be necessary (except on a question of adjournment) shall be presented to the President of the United States; and before the same shall take effect, shall be approved by him, or being disapproved by him, shall be repassed by two thirds of the Senate and House of Representatives, according to the rules and limitations prescribed in the case of a bill.

SECTION 8. The Congress shall have the power

1. To lay and collect taxes, duties, imposts, and excises, to pay the debts and provide for the common defense and general welfare of the United States; but all duties, imposts, and excises shall be uniform throughout the United States;

2. To borrow money on the credit of the United States;

3. To regulate commerce with foreign nations, and among the several States, and with the Indian tribes;

4. To establish a uniform rule of naturalization, and uniform laws on the subject of bankruptcies throughout the United States;

5. To coin money, regulate the value thereof, and of foreign coin, and fix the standard of weights and measures;

6. To provide for the punishment of counterfeiting the securities and current coin of the United States;

7. To establish post offices and post roads;

8. To promote the progress of science and useful arts, by securing for limited times to authors and inventors the exclusive right to their respective writings and discoveries;

9. To constitute tribunals inferior to the Supreme Court;

10. To define and punish piracies and felonies committed on the high seas, and offenses against the law of nations;

11. To declare war, grant letters of marque and reprisal, and make rules concerning captures on land and water;

12. To raise and support armies, but no appropriation of money to that use shall be for a longer term than two years;

13. To provide and maintain a navy;

14. To make rules for the government and regulation of the land and naval forces;

15. To provide for calling forth the militia to execute the laws of the Union, suppress insurrections and repel invasions;

16. To provide for organizing, arming, and disciplining the militia, and for governing such part of them as may be employed in the service of the United States, reserving to the States respectively, the appointment of the officers, and the authority of training the militia according to the discipline prescribed by Congress;

17. To exercise exclusive legislation in all cases whatsoever, over such district (not exceeding ten miles square) as may, by cession of particular States, and the acceptance of Congress, become the seat of the government of the United States, and to exercise like authority over all places purchased by the consent of the legislature of the State in which the same shall be, for the erection of forts, magazines, arsenals, dockyards, and other needful buildings; and

18. To make all laws which shall be necessary and proper for carrying into execution the foregoing powers, and all other powers vested by this Constitution in the government of the United States, or any department or officer thereof.

SECTION 9. 1. The migration or importation of such persons as any of the States now existing shall think proper to admit, shall not be prohibited by the Congress prior to the year one thousand eight hundred and eight, but a tax or duty may be imposed on such importation, not exceeding ten dollars for each person.

2. The privilege of the writ of habeas corpus shall not be suspended, unless when in cases of rebellion or invasion the public safety may require it.

3. No bill of attainder or ex post facto law shall be passed.

4. No capitation, or other direct, tax shall be laid, unless in proportion to the census or enumeration hereinbefore directed to be taken.[5]

---

[5] See the Sixteenth Amendment.

5. No tax or duty shall be laid on articles exported from any State.

6. No preference shall be given by any regulation of commerce or revenue to the ports of one State over those of another: nor shall vessels bound to, or from, one State be obliged to enter, clear, or pay duties in another.

7. No money shall be drawn from the treasury, but in consequence of appropriations made by law; and a regular statement and account of the receipts and expenditures of all public money shall be published from time to time.

8. No title of nobility shall be granted by the United States: and no person holding any office of profit or trust under them, shall, without the consent of the Congress, accept of any present, emolument, office, or title, of any kind whatever, from any king, prince, or foreign State.

SECTION 10. 1. No State shall enter into any treaty, alliance, or confederation; grant letters of marque and reprisal; coin money; emit bills of credit; make any thing but gold and silver coin a tender in payment of debts; pass any bill of attainder, ex post facto law, or law impairing the obligation of contracts, or grant any title of nobility.

2. No State shall, without the consent of the Congress, lay any imposts or duties on imports or exports, except what may be absolutely necessary for executing its inspection laws: and the net produce of all duties and imposts laid by any State on imports or exports, shall be for the use of the treasury of the United States; and all such laws shall be subject to the revision and control of the Congress.

3. No State shall, without the consent of the Congress, lay any duty of tonnage, keep troops, or ships of war in time of peace, enter into any agreement or compact with another State, or with a foreign power, or engage in war, unless actually invaded, or in such imminent danger as will not admit of delay.

Article II

SECTION 1. 1. The executive power shall be vested in a President of the United States of America. He shall hold his office during the term of four years, and, together with the Vice President, chosen for the same term, be elected, as follows:

2. Each State shall appoint, in such manner as the legislature thereof may direct, a number of electors, equal to the whole number of senators and representatives to which the State may be entitled in the Congress: but no senator or representative, or person holding any office of trust or profit under the United States, shall be appointed an elector.

The electors shall meet in their respective States, and vote by ballot for two persons, of whom one at least shall not be an inhabitant of the same State with themselves. And they shall make a list of all the persons voted for, and of the number of votes for each; which list they shall sign and certify, and transmit sealed to the seat of the government of the United States, directed to the president of the Senate. The president of the Senate shall, in the presence of the Senate and House of Representatives, open all the certificates, and the votes shall then be counted. The person having the greatest number of votes shall be the President, if such number be a majority of the whole number of electors appointed; and if there be more than one who have such majority, and have an equal number of votes, then the House of Representatives shall immediately choose by ballot one of them for President; and if no person have a majority, then from the five highest on the list the said House shall in like manner choose the President. But in choosing the President, the votes shall be taken by States, the representation from each State having one vote; a quorum for this purpose shall consist of a member or members from two thirds of the States, and a majority of all the States shall be necessary to a choice. In every case after the choice of the President, the person having the greatest number of votes of the electors shall be the Vice President. But if there should remain two or more who have equal votes, the Senate shall chose from them by ballot the Vice President.[6]

3. The Congress may determine the time of choosing the electors, and the day on which they shall give their votes; which day shall be the same throughout the United States.

4. No person except a natural born citizen, or a citizen of the United States, at the time of the adoption of this Constitution, shall be eligible to the office of President; neither shall any person be eligible to the office who shall not have attained to the age of thirty-five years, and been fourteen years a resident within the United States.

5. In case of the removal of the President from office, or of his death, resignation, or inability to discharge the powers and duties of the said office, the same shall devolve on the Vice President, and the Congress may by law provide for the case of removal, death, resignation or inability, both of the President and Vice President, declaring what officer shall then act as President, and such officer shall act accordingly until the disability be removed, or a President shall be elected.

6. The President shall, at stated times, receive for his services a compensation which shall neither be increased nor diminished during the period for which he shall have been elected, and he shall not receive within that period any other emolument from the United States, or any of them.

7. Before he enter on the execution of his office, he shall take the following oath or affirmation:—"I do solemnly swear (or affirm) that I will faithfully execute the office of President of the United States, and will to the best of my ability, preserve, protect and defend the Constitution of the United States."

SECTION 2. 1. The President shall be commander in chief of the army and navy of the United States, and of the militia of the several States, when called into the actual service of the United States; he may require the opinion in writing, of the principal officer in each of the executive departments, upon any subject relating to the duties of their respective offices, and he shall have power to grant reprieves and pardons for offenses against the United States, except in cases of impeachment.

2. He shall have power, by and with the advice and consent of the Senate, to make treaties, provided two thirds of the senators present concur; and he shall nominate, and by and with the advice and consent of the Senate, shall appoint ambassadors, other public ministers and consuls, judges of the Supreme Court, and all other officers of the United States, whose appointments are not herein otherwise provided for, and which shall be established by law; but the Congress may by law vest the appointment of such inferior officers, as they think proper, in the President alone, in the courts of laws, or in the heads of departments.

3. The President shall have power to fill up all vacancies that may happen during the recess of the Senate, by granting commissions which shall expire at the end of their next session.

SECTION 3. He shall from time to time give to the Congress information of the state of the Union, and recommend to their consideration such measures as he shall judge necessary and expedient; he may, on extraordinary occasions, convene both Houses, or either of them, and in case of disagreement between them with respect to the time of adjournment, he may adjourn them to such time as he shall think proper; he shall receive ambassadors and other public ministers; he shall take care that the laws be faithfully executed, and shall commission all the officers of the United States.

SECTION 4. The President, Vice President, and all civil officers of the United States, shall be removed from office on impeachment for, and conviction of, treason, bribery, or other high crimes and misdemeanors.

Article III

SECTION 1. The judicial power of the United States shall be vested in one Supreme Court, and in such inferior courts as the Congress may from time to time ordain and establish. The judges, both of the Supreme and inferior courts, shall hold their offices during good behavior, and shall, at stated times,

---

[6] Superseded by the Twelfth Amendment.

receive for their services, a compensation, which shall not be diminished during their continuance in office.

SECTION 2.   1. The judicial power shall extend to all cases, in law and equity, arising under this Constitution, the laws of the United States, and treaties made, or which shall be made, under their authority;—to all cases affecting ambassadors, other public ministers and consuls;—to all cases of admiralty and maritime jurisdiction;—to controversies to which the United States shall be a party;[7]—to controversies between two or more States;—between a State and citizens of another State;—between citizens of different States;—between citizens of the same State claiming lands under grants of different States, and between a State, or the citizens thereof, and foreign States, citizens or subjects.

2. In all cases affecting ambassadors, other public ministers and consuls, and those in which a State shall be party, the Supreme Court shall have original jurisdiction. In all the other cases before mentioned, the Supreme Court shall have appellate jurisdiction, both as to law and fact, with such exceptions, and under such regulations as the Congress shall make.

3. The trial of all crimes, except in cases of impeachment, shall be by jury; and such trial shall be held in the State where the said crimes shall have been committed; but when not committed within any State, the trial shall be at such place or places as the Congress may by law have directed.

SECTION 3.   1. Treason against the United States shall consist only in levying war against them, or in adhering to their enemies, giving them aid and comfort. No person shall be convicted of treason unless on the testimony of two witnesses to the same overt act, or on confession in open court.

2. The Congress shall have power to declare the punishment of treason, but no attainder of treason shall work corruption of blood, or forfeiture except during the life of the person attainted.

Article IV

SECTION 1.   Full faith and credit shall be given in each State to the public acts, records, and judicial proceedings of every other State. And the Congress may by general laws prescribe the manner in which such acts, records and proceedings shall be proved, and the effect thereof.

SECTION 2.   1. The citizens of each State shall be entitled to all privileges and immunities of citizens in the several States.[8]

2. A person charged in any State with treason, felony, or other crime, who shall flee from justice, and be found in another State, shall on demand of the executive authority of the State from which he fled, be delivered up to be removed to the State having jurisdiction of the crime.

3. No person held to service or labor in one State under the laws thereof, escaping into another, shall, in consequence of any law or regulation therein, be discharged from such service or labor, but shall be delivered up on claim of the party to whom such service or labor may be due.[9]

SECTION 3.   1. New States may be admitted by the Congress into this Union; but no new State shall be formed or erected within the jurisdiction of any other State; nor any State be formed by the junction of two or more States, or parts of States, without the consent of the legislatures of the States concerned as well as of the Congress.

2. The Congress shall have power to dispose of and make all needful rules and regulations respecting the territory or other property belonging to the United States; and nothing in this Constitution shall be so construed as to prejudice any claims of the United States, or of any particular State.

SECTION 4.   The United States shall guarantee to every State in this Union a republican form of government, and shall protect each of them against invasion; and on application of the legislature, or of the executive (when the legislature cannot be convened) against domestic violence.

Article V

The Congress, whenever two thirds of both Houses shall deem it necesary, shall propose amendments to this Constitution, or, on the application of the legislatures of two thirds of the several States, shall call a convention for proposing amendments, which in either case, shall be valid to all intents and purposes, as part of this Constitution, when ratified by the legislatures of three fourths of the several States, or by conventions in three fourths thereof, as the one or the other mode of ratification may be proposed by the Congress; Provided that no amendment which may be made prior to the year one thousand eight hundred and eight shall in any manner affect the first and fourth clauses in the ninth section of the first article; and that no State, without its consent, shall be deprived of its equal suffrage in the Senate.

Article VI

1. All debts contracted and engagements entered into, before the adoption of this Constitution, shall be as valid against the United States under this Constitution, as under the Confederation.[10]

2. This Constitution, and the laws of the United States which shall be made in pursuance thereof; and all treaties made, or which shall be made, under the authority of the United States, shall be the supreme law of the land; and the judges in every State shall be bound thereby, any thing in the Constitution or laws of any State to the contrary notwithstanding.

3. The senators and representatives before mentioned, and the members of the several State legislatures, and all executive and judicial officers, both of the United States and of the several States, shall be bound by oath or affirmation to support this Constitution; but no religious test shall ever be required as a qualification to any office or public trust under the United States.

Article VII

The ratification of the conventions of nine States shall be sufficient for the establishment of this Constitution between the States so ratifying the same.

Done in Convention by the unanimous consent of the States present the seventeenth day of September in the year of our Lord one thousand seven hundred and eighty-seven, and of the independence of the United States of America the twelfth. In witness whereof we have hereunto subscribed our names.

[Names omitted]

* * *

Articles in addition to, and amendment of, the Constitution of the United States of America, proposed by Congress, and ratified by the legislatures of the several States, pursuant to the fifth article of the original Constitution.

Amendment I [First ten amendments ratified December 15, 1791]

Congress shall make no law respecting an establishment of religion, or prohibiting the free exercise thereof; or abridging the freedom of speech, or of the press; or the right of the people peaceably to assemble, and to petition the government for a redress of grievances.

Amendment II

A well regulated militia, being necessary to the security of a free State, the right of the people to keep and bear arms, shall not be infringed.

---

[7] See the Eleventh Amendment.
[8] See the Fourteenth Amendment, Sec. 1.
[9] See the Thirteenth Amendment.

[10] See the Fourteenth Amendment, Sec. 4.

Amendment III

No soldier shall, in time of peace be quartered in any house, without the consent of the owner, nor in time of war, but in a manner to be prescribed by law.

Amendment IV

The right of the people to be secure in their persons, houses, papers, and effects, against unreasonable searches and seizures, shall not be violated, and no warrants shall issue, but upon probable cause, supported by oath or affirmation, and particularly describing the place to be searched, and the persons or things to be seized.

Amendment V

No person shall be held to answer for a capital or otherwise infamous crime, unless on a presentment or indictment of a grand jury, except in cases arising in the land or naval forces, or in the militia, when in actual service in time of war or public danger; nor shall any person be subject for the same offense to be twice put in jeopardy of life or limb; nor shall be compelled in any criminal case to be a witness against himself, nor be deprived of life, liberty, or property, without due process of law; nor shall private property be taken for public use, without just compensation.

Amendment VI

In all criminal prosecutions, the accused shall enjoy the right to a speedy and public trial, by an impartial jury of the State and district wherein the crime shall have been committed, which district shall have been previously ascertained by law, and to be informed of the nature and cause of the accusation; to be confronted with the witnesses against him; to have compulsory process for obtaining witnesses in his favor, and to have the assistance of counsel for his defense.

Amendment VII

In suits at common law, where the value in controversy shall exceed twenty dollars, the right of trial by jury shall be preserved, and no fact tried by a jury shall be otherwise reexamined in any court of the United States, than according to the rules of the common law.

Amendment VIII

Excessive bail shall not be required, nor excessive fines imposed, nor cruel and unusual punishments inflicted.

Amendment IX

The enumeration in the Constitution of certain rights shall not be construed to deny or disparage others retained by the people.

Amendment X

The powers not delegated to the United States by the Constitution, nor prohibited by it to the States, are reserved to the States respectively, or to the people.

Amendment XI [January 8, 1798]

The judicial power of the United States shall not be construed to extend to any suit in law or equity, commenced or prosecuted against one of the United States by citizens of another State, or by citizens or subjects of any foreign State.

Amendment XII [September 25, 1804]

The electors shall meet in their respective States, and vote by ballot for President and Vice President, one of whom, at least, shall not be an inhabitant of the same State with themselves; they shall name in their ballots the person voted for as President, and in distinct ballots the person voted for as Vice President, and they shall make distinct lists of all persons voted for as President and of all persons voted for as Vice President, and of the number of votes for each, which lists they shall sign and certify, and transmit sealed to the seat of the government of the United States, directed to the President of the Senate;—The President of the Senate shall, in the presence of the Senate and House of Representatives, open all the certificates and the votes shall then be counted;—The person having the greatest number of votes for President, shall be the President, if such number be a majority of the whole number of electors appointed; and if no person have such majority, then from the persons having the highest numbers not exceeding three on the list of those voted for as President, the House of Representatives shall choose immediately, by ballot, the President. But in choosing the President, the votes shall be taken by States, the representation from each State having one vote; a quorum for this purpose shall consist of a member or members from two thirds of the States, and a majority of all the States shall be necessary to a choice. And if the House of Representatives shall not choose a President whenever the right of choice shall devolve upon them, before the fourth day of March next following, then the Vice President shall act as President, as in the case of the death or other constitutional disability of the President. The person having the greatest number of votes as Vice President shall be the Vice President, if such number be a majority of the whole number of electors appointed, and if no person have a majority, then from the two highest numbers on the list, the Senate shall choose the Vice President; a quorum for the purpose shall consist of two thirds of the whole number of Senators, and a majority of the whole number shall be necessary to a choice. But no person constitutionally ineligible to the office of President shall be eligible to that of Vice President of the United States.

Amendment XIII [December 18, 1865]

Section 1. Neither slavery nor involuntary servitude, except as a punishment for crime whereof the party shall have been duly convicted, shall exist within the United States, or any place subject to their jurisdiction.

Section 2. Congress shall have power to enforce this article by appropriate legislation.

Amendment XIV [July 28, 1868]

Section 1. All persons born or naturalized in the United States, and subject to the jurisdiction thereof, are citizens of the United States and of the State wherein they reside. No State shall make or enforce any law which shall abridge the privileges or immunities of citizens of the United States; nor shall any State deprive any person of life, liberty, or property, without due process of law; nor deny to any person within its jurisdiction the equal protection of the laws.

Section 2. Representatives shall be apportioned among the several States according to their respective numbers, counting the whole number of persons in each State, excluding Indians not taxed. But when the right to vote at any election for the choice of electors for President and Vice President of the United States, representatives in Congress, the executive and judicial officers of a State, or the members of the legislature thereof, is denied to any of the male inhabitants of such State, being twenty-one years of age, and citizens of the United States, or in any way abridged, except for participating in rebellion, or other crime, the basis of representation therein shall be reduced in the proportion which the number of such male citizens shall bear to the whole number of male citizens twenty-one years of age in such State.

Section 3.   No person shall be a senator or representative in Congress, or elector of President and Vice President, or hold any office, civil or military, under the United States, or under any State, who having previously taken an oath, as a member of Congress, or as an officer of the United States, or as a member of any State legislature, or as an executive or judicial officer of any State, to support the Constitution of the United States, shall have engaged in insurrection or rebellion against the same, or given aid or comfort to the enemies thereof. But Congress may by a vote of two thirds of each House, remove such disability.

Section 4.   The validity of the public debt of the United States, authorized by law, including debts incurred for payment of pensions and bounties for services in suppressing insurrection or rebellion, shall not be questioned. But neither the United States nor any State shall assume or pay any debt or obligation incurred in aid of insurrection or rebellion against the United States, or any claim for the loss or emancipation of any slave; but all such debts, obligations, and claims shall be held illegal and void.

Section 5.   The Congress shall have the power to enforce, by appropriate legislation, the provisions of this article.

Amendment XV [March 30, 1870]

Section 1.   The right of citizens of the United States to vote shall not be denied or abridged by the United States or by any State on account of race, color, or previous condition of servitude.

Section 2.   The Congress shall have power to enforce this article by appropriate legislation.

Amendment XVI [February 25, 1913]

The Congress shall have power to lay and collect taxes on incomes, from whatever source derived, without apportionment among the several States, and without regard to any census or enumeration.

Amendment XVII [May 31, 1913]

The Senate of the United States shall be composed of two senators from each State, elected by the people thereof, for six years; and each senator shall have one vote. The electors in each State shall have the qualifications requisite for electors of the most numerous branch of the State legislature.

When vacancies happen in the representation of any State in the Senate, the executive authority of such State shall issue writs of election to fill such vacancies: *Provided,* That the legislature of any State may empower the executive thereof to make temporary appointments until the people fill the vacancies by election as the legislature may direct.

This amendment shall not be so construed as to affect the election or term of any senator chosen before it becomes valid as part of the Constitution.

Amendment XVIII[11] [January 29, 1919]

After one year from the ratification of this article, the manufacture, sale, or transportation of intoxicating liquors within, the importation thereof into, or the exportation thereof from the United States and all territory subject to the jurisdiction thereof for beverage purposes is hereby prohibited.

---

[11] Repealed by the Twenty-first Amendment.

The Congress and the several States shall have concurrent power to enforce this article by appropriate legislation.

This article shall be inoperative unless it shall have been ratified as an amendment to the Constitution by the legislatures of the several States, as provided in the Constitution, within seven years from the date of the submission hereof to the States by Congress.

Amendment XIX [August 26, 1920]

The right of citizens of the United States to vote shall not be denied or abridged by the United States or by any State on account of sex.

Congress shall have the power to enforce this article by appropriate legislation.

Amendment XX [January 23, 1933]

Section 1.   The terms of the President and Vice President shall end at noon on the 20th day of January and the terms of Senators and Representatives at noon on the 3d day of January, of the years in which such terms would have ended if this article had not been ratified; and the terms of their successors shall then begin.

Section 2.   The Congress shall assemble at least once in every year, and such meeting shall begin at noon on the 3d day of January, unless they shall by law appoint a different day.

Section 3.   If, at the time fixed for the beginning of the term of President, the President-elect shall have died, the Vice President-elect shall become President. If a President shall not have been chosen before the time fixed for the beginning of his term, or if the President-elect shall have failed to qualify, then the Vice President-elect shall act as President until a President shall have qualified; and the Congress may by law provide for the case wherein neither a President-elect nor a Vice President-elect shall have qualified, declaring who shall then act as President, or the manner in which one who is to act shall be selected, and such person shall act accordingly until a President or Vice President shall have qualified.

Section 4.   The Congress may by law provide for the case of the death of any of the persons from whom the House of Representatives may choose a President whenever the right of choice shall have devolved upon them, and for the case of the death of any of the persons from whom the Senate may choose a Vice President whenever the right of choice shall have devolved upon them.

Section 5.   Sections 1 and 2 shall take effect on the 15th day of October following the ratification of this article.

Section 6.   This article shall be inoperative unless it shall have been ratified as an amendment to the Constitution by the legislatures of three-fourths of the several States within seven years from the date of its submission.

Amendment XXI [December 5, 1933]

Section 1.   The Eighteenth Article of amendment to the Constitution of the United States is hereby repealed.

Section 2.   The transportation or importation into any State, Territory, or possession of the United States for delivery or use therein of intoxicating liquors in violation of the laws thereof, is hereby prohibited.

Section 3.   This article shall be inoperative unless it shall have been ratified as an amendment to the Constitution by conventions in the several States, as provided in the Consititution, within seven years from the date of the submission thereof to the States by the Congress.

Amendment XXII [March 1, 1951]

No person shall be elected to the office of the President more than twice, and no person who has held the office of President, or acted as President, for more than two years of a term to which some other person was elected President shall be elected to the office of the President more than once.

But this article shall not apply to any person holding the office of President when this article was proposed by the Congress, and shall not prevent any person who may be holding the office of President, or acting as President, during the term within which this article becomes operative from holding the office of President or acting as President during the remainder of such term.

This article shall be inoperative unless it shall have been ratified as an amendment to the Constitution by the legislatures of three-fourths of the several States within seven years from the date of its submission to the States by the Congress.

Amendment XXIII [March 29, 1961]

SECTION 1.   The District constituting the seat of Government of the United States shall appoint in such manner as the Congress may direct.

A number of electors of President and Vice President equal to the whole number of Senators and Representatives in Congress to which the District would be entitled if it were a State, but in no event more than the least populous State; they shall be in addition to those appointed by the States, but they shall be considered, for the purposes of the election of President and Vice President, to be electors appointed by a State; and they shall meet in the District and perform such duties as provided by the twelfth article of amendment.

SECTION 2.   The Congress shall have power to enforce this article by appropriate legislation.

Amendment XXIV [January 23, 1964]

SECTION 1.   The right of citizens of the United States to vote in any primary or other election for President or Vice President, for electors for President or Vice President, or for Senator or Representative in Congress, shall not be denied or abridged by the United States or any State by reason of failure to pay any poll tax or other tax.

SECTION 2.   The Congress shall have power to enforce this article by appropriate legislation.

Amendment XXV [February 10, 1967]

SECTION 1.   In case of the removal of the President from office or of his death or resignation, the Vice President shall become President.

SECTION 2.   Whenever there is a vacancy in the office of the Vice President, the President shall nominate a Vice President who shall take office upon confirmation by a majority of both Houses of Congress.

SECTION 3.   Whenever the President transmits to the President pro tempore of the Senate and the Speaker of the House of Representatives his written declaration that he is unable to discharge the powers and duties of his office, and until he transmits to them a written declaration to the contrary, such powers and duties shall be discharged by the Vice President as Acting President.

SECTION 4.   Whenever the Vice President and a majority of either the principal officers of the executive departments or of such other body as Congress may by law provide, transmit to the President pro tempore of the Senate and the Speaker of the House of Representatives their written declaration that the President is unable to discharge the powers and duties of his office, the Vice President shall immediately assume the powers and duties of the office as Acting President.

Thereafter, when the President transmits to the President pro tempore of the Senate and the Speaker of the House of Representatives his written declaration that no inability exists, he shall resume the powers and duties of his office unless the Vice President and a majority of either the principal officers of the executive departments or of such other body as Congress may by law provide, transmit within four days to the President pro tempore of the Senate and the Speaker of the House of Representatives their written declaration that the President is unable to discharge the powers and duties of his office. Thereupon Congress shall decide the issue, assembling within forty-eight hours for that purpose if not in session. If the Congress, within twenty-one days after receipt of the latter written declaration, or, if Congress is not in session, within twenty-one days after Congress is required to assemble, determines by two-thirds vote of both Houses that the President is unable to discharge the powers and duties of his office, the Vice President shall continue to discharge the same as Acting President; otherwise, the President shall resume the powers and duties of his office.

Amendment XXVI [June 30, 1971]

SECTION 1.   The right of citizens of the United States who are eighteen years of age or older to vote shall not be denied or abridged by the United States or by any State on account of age.

SECTION 2.   The Congress shall have power to enforce this article by appropriate legislation.

YEAR	NUMBER OF STATES	CANDIDATES	PARTY	POPULAR VOTE*	ELECTORAL VOTE†	PERCENTAGE OF POPULAR VOTE
1789	11	GEORGE WASHINGTON	No party designations		69	
		John Adams			34	
		Other Candidates			35	
1792	15	GEORGE WASHINGTON	No party designations		132	
		John Adams			77	
		George Clinton			50	
		Other Candidates			5	
1796	16	JOHN ADAMS	Federalist		71	
		Thomas Jefferson	Democratic-Republican		68	
		Thomas Pinckney	Federalist		59	
		Aaron Burr	Democratic-Republican		30	
		Other Candidates			48	
1800	16	THOMAS JEFFERSON	Democratic-Republican		73	
		Aaron Burr	Democratic-Republican		73	
		John Adams	Federalist		65	
		Charles C. Pinckney	Federalist		64	
		John Jay	Federalist		1	
1804	17	THOMAS JEFFERSON	Democratic-Republican		162	
		Charles C. Pinckney	Federalist		14	
1808	17	JAMES MADISON	Democratic-Republican		122	
		Charles C. Pinckney	Federalist		47	
		George Clinton	Democratic-Republican		6	
1812	18	JAMES MADISON	Democratic-Republican		128	
		DeWitt Clinton	Federalist		89	
1816	19	JAMES MONROE	Democratic-Republican		183	
		Rufus King	Federalist		34	
1820	24	JAMES MONROE	Democratic-Republican		231	
		John Quincy Adams	Independent Republican		1	
1824	24	JOHN QUINCY ADAMS		108,740	84	30.5
		Andrew Jackson		153,544	99	43.1
		William H. Crawford		46,618	41	13.1
		Henry Clay		47,136	37	13.2
1828	24	ANDREW JACKSON	Democrat	647,286	178	56.0
		John Quincy Adams	National Republican	508,064	83	44.0
1832	24	ANDREW JACKSON	Democrat	687,502	219	55.0
		Henry Clay	National Republican	530,189	49	42.4
		William Wirt	Anti-Masonic	33,108	7	2.6
		John Floyd	National Republican		11	
1836	26	MARTIN VAN BUREN	Democrat	765,483	170	50.9
		William H. Harrison	Whig		73	
		Hugh L. White	Whig	739,795	26	49.1
		Daniel Webster	Whig		14	
		W. P. Mangum	Whig		11	
1840	26	WILLIAM H. HARRISON	Whig	1,274,624	234	53.1
		Martin Van Buren	Democrat	1,127,781	60	46.9
1844	26	JAMES K. POLK	Democrat	1,338,464	170	49.6
		Henry Clay	Whig	1,300,097	105	48.1
		James G. Birney	Liberty	62,300		2.3
1848	30	ZACHARY TAYLOR	Whig	1,360,967	163	47.4
		Lewis Cass	Democrat	1,222,342	127	42.5
		Martin Van Buren	Free Soil	291,263		10.1
1852	31	FRANKLIN PIERCE	Democrat	1,601,117	254	50.9
		Winfield Scott	Whig	1,385,453	42	44.1
		John P. Hale	Free Soil	155,825		5.0
1856	31	JAMES BUCHANAN	Democrat	1,832,955	174	45.3
		John C. Frémont	Republican	1,339,932	114	33.1
		Millard Fillmore	American	871,731	8	21.6

* Percentage of popular vote given for any election year may not total 100 percent because candidates receiving less than 1 percent of the popular vote have been omitted.
† Prior to the passage of the Twelfth Amendment in 1904, the electoral college voted for two presidential candidates; the runner-up became Vice-President. Data from *Historical Statistics of the United States, Colonial Times to 1957* (1961), pp. 682–683, and *The World Almanac.*

YEAR	NUMBER OF STATES	CANDIDATES	PARTY	POPULAR VOTE	ELECTORAL VOTE	PERCENTAGE OF POPULAR VOTE
1860	33	ABRAHAM LINCOLN	Republican	1,865,593	180	39.8
		Stephen A. Douglas	Democrat	1,382,713	12	29.5
		John C. Breckinridge	Democrat	848,356	72	18.1
		John Bell	Constitutional Union	592,906	39	12.6
1864	36	ABRAHAM LINCOLN	Republican	2,206,938	212	55.0
		George B. McClellan	Democrat	1,803,787	21	45.0
1868	37	ULYSSES S. GRANT	Republican	3,013,421	214	52.7
		Horatio Seymour	Democrat	2,706,829	80	47.3
1872	37	ULYSSES S. GRANT	Republican	3,596,745	286	55.6
		Horace Greeley	Democrat	2,843,446	*	43.9
1876	38	RUTHERFORD B. HAYES	Republican	4,036,572	185	48.0
		Samuel J. Tilden	Democrat	4,284,020	184	51.0
1880	38	JAMES A. GARFIELD	Republican	4,453,295	214	48.5
		Winfield S. Hancock	Democrat	4,414,082	155	48.1
		James B. Weaver	Greenback-Labor	308,578		3.4
1884	38	GROVER CLEVELAND	Democrat	4,879,507	219	48.5
		James G. Blaine	Republican	4,850,293	182	48.2
		Benjamin F. Butler	Greenback-Labor	175,370		1.8
		John P. St. John	Prohibition	150,369		1.5
1888	38	BENJAMIN HARRISON	Republican	5,447,129	233	47.9
		Grover Cleveland	Democrat	5,537,857	168	48.6
		Clinton B. Fisk	Prohibition	249,506		2.2
		Anson J. Streeter	Union Labor	146,935		1.3
1892	44	GROVER CLEVELAND	Democrat	5,555,426	277	46.1
		Benjamin Harrison	Republican	5,182,690	145	43.0
		James B. Weaver	People's	1,029,846	22	8.5
		John Bidwell	Prohibition	264,133		2.2
1896	45	WILLIAM MCKINLEY	Republican	7,102,246	271	51.1
		William J. Bryan	Democrat	6,492,559	176	47.7
1900	45	WILLIAM MCKINLEY	Republican	7,218,491	292	51.7
		William J. Bryan	Democrat; Populist	6,356,734	155	45.5
		John C. Woolley	Prohibition	208,914		1.5
1904	45	THEODORE ROOSEVELT	Republican	7,628,461	336	57.4
		Alton B. Parker	Democrat	5,084,223	140	37.6
		Eugene V. Debs	Socialist	402,283		3.0
		Silas C. Swallow	Prohibition	258,536		1.9
1908	46	WILLIAM H. TAFT	Republican	7,675,320	321	51.6
		William J. Bryan	Democrat	6,412,294	162	43.1
		Eugene V. Debs	Socialist	420,793		2.8
		Eugene W. Chafin	Prohibition	253,840		1.7
1912	48	WOODROW WILSON	Democrat	6,296,547	435	41.9
		Theodore Roosevelt	Progressive	4,118,571	88	27.4
		William H. Taft	Republican	3,486,720	8	23.2
		Eugene V. Debs	Socialist	900,672		6.0
		Eugene W. Chafin	Prohibition	206,275		1.4
1916	48	WOODROW WILSON	Democrat	9,127,695	277	49.4
		Charles E. Hughes	Republican	8,533,507	254	46.2
		A. L. Benson	Socialist	585,113		3.2
		J. Frank Hanly	Prohibition	220,506		1.2
1920	48	WARREN G. HARDING	Republican	16,143,407	404	60.4
		James M. Cox	Democrat	9,130,328	127	34.2
		Eugene V. Debs	Socialist	919,799		3.4
		P. P. Christensen	Farmer-Labor	265,411		1.0
1924	48	CALVIN COOLIDGE	Republican	15,718,211	382	54.0
		John W. Davis	Democrat	8,385,283	136	28.8
		Robert M. La Follette	Progressive	4,831,289	13	16.6
1928	48	HERBERT C. HOOVER	Republican	21,391,993	444	58.2
		Alfred E. Smith	Democrat	15,016,169	87	40.9

* Because of the death of Greeley, Democratic electors scattered their votes.

YEAR	NUMBER OF STATES	CANDIDATES	PARTY	POPULAR VOTE	ELECTORAL VOTE	PERCENTAGE OF POPULAR VOTE
1932	48	FRANKLIN D. ROOSEVELT	Democrat	22,809,638	472	57.4
		Herbert C. Hoover	Republican	15,758,901	59	39.7
		Norman Thomas	Socialist	881,951		2.2
1936	48	FRANKLIN D. ROOSEVELT	Democrat	27,752,869	523	60.8
		Alfred M. Landon	Republican	16,674,665	8	36.5
		William Lemke	Union	882,479		1.9
1940	48	FRANKLIN D. ROOSEVELT	Democrat	27,307,819	449	54.8
		Wendell L. Willkie	Republican	22,321,018	82	44.8
1944	48	FRANKLIN D. ROOSEVELT	Democrat	25,606,585	432	53.5
		Thomas E. Dewey	Republican	22,014,745	99	46.0
1948	48	HARRY S. TRUMAN	Democrat	24,105,812	303	49.5
		Thomas E. Dewey	Republican	21,970,065	189	45.1
		J. Strom Thurmond	States' Rights	1,169,063	39	2.4
		Henry A. Wallace	Progressive	1,157,172		2.4
1952	48	DWIGHT D. EISENHOWER	Republican	33,936,234	442	55.1
		Adlai E. Stevenson	Democrat	27,314,992	89	44.4
1956	48	DWIGHT D. EISENHOWER	Republican	35,590,472	457†	57.6
		Adlai E. Stevenson	Democrat	26,022,752	73	42.1
1960	50	JOHN F. KENNEDY	Democrat	34,227,096	303‡	49.9
		Richard M. Nixon	Republican	34,108,546	219	49.6
1964	50	LYNDON B. JOHNSON	Democrat	42,676,220	486	61.3
		Barry M. Goldwater	Republican	26,860,314	52	38.5
1968	50	RICHARD M. NIXON	Republican	31,785,480	301	43.4
		Hubert H. Humphrey	Democrat	31,275,165	191	42.7
		George C. Wallace	American Independent	9,906,473	46	13.5
1972	50	RICHARD M. NIXON*	Republican	47,165,234	520	60.6
		George S. McGovern	Democrat	29,168,110	17	37.5
1976	50	JIMMY CARTER	Democrat	40,828,929	297	50.1
		Gerald R. Ford	Republican	39,148,940	240	47.9
		Eugene McCarthy	Independent	739,256		
1980	50	RONALD REAGAN	Republican	43,201,220	489	50.9
		Jimmy Carter	Democrat	34,913,332	49	41.2
		John B. Anderson	Independent	5,581,379		
1984	50	RONALD REAGAN	Republican	53,428,357	525	59.0
		Walter F. Mondale	Democrat	36,930,923	13	41.0

† Walter B. Jones received 1 electoral vote. ‡ Harry F. Byrd received 15 electoral votes.
* Resigned August 9, 1974: Vice President Gerald R. Ford became President.

INDEX

References to pages on which an illustration or map about the topic appears are shown in *italics*.

Slave trade
  constitutional compromise over, 139
  Creole incident, 305–6
  domestic, 286
  Dutch, 30
  Puritan, 30
Slidell (Confederate diplomat), 359
Slums
  in late 19th century, 490–91
  response of churches to, 495–96
  social unrest and, 494–95
  See also Urban America
Smalls, Robert, *385*
Smede, Susan Dabney, 286
Smith, Alfred E., 603, 618, 626, 655
Smith, Bessie, 610, *615*
Smith, J. Allen, 506
Smith, Jesse, 617
Smith, John, 20–21
Smith, Joseph, 313
Smith, Mamie, 615
Smith Act (1940), 719
Smith College, 512
Snag, derivation of word, 201
Snake Indians, 404
SNCC, 765, 766
Sobell, Norton, 720–21
Social Darwinism, 424, 455, 502–4, 520
  critics and dissenters of, 502–3
  popularization of, 502
Social engineering, 542
Social Gospel movement, 495, 503, 542
Socialism, 548
Socialist Labor party, 445
Socialist party, 542, 580
Social legislation, 424
  in 1920s, 619
  in Progressive era, 547–48
Social program cutbacks under Reagan, 826
Social reform, 494–96
Social Security Act (1935), 651–52, 655
Social Security Act (1950), 707, 764
Social Security Board, 651
Social security system under Reagan, 826
Social Welfare, scientific approach to, 495
Social workers, 495
Society
  American Revolution and changes in, 121–24
  of antebellum South, 284–91
  business orientation of, 238
  colonial, 53–61
  Indian, 3–4
  in New South, 396–98
  See also Classes, social
Society for Establishing Useful Manufactures, 206
Society of the Cincinnati, 136
Sociologists in Gilded Age, 504
Sociology for the South; Or the Failure of Free Society (Fitzhugh), 297
Sod houses, 417, 418
"Soft" money, 456
Soil Conservation and Domestic Allotment Act (1936), 639
Solidarity movement, Polish, 830
Somoza, Anastasio, 831
Sons of Liberty, 94, 96, 97, 98
Souls of Black Folks, The (DuBois), 565, 609
Sound and the Fury, The (Faulkner), 607
South, the, 283–301
  advantages in Civil War, 348
  back parts of, 54–55
  black people of, 286–91
    resistance by slaves, 290–91, 306
    slaves' inner world, 289–90
    slaves' outer world, 287–89
  black revolution in 1960s and, 765, 766, 768
  Civil War in
    in defeat after, 372–78
    home front, 358–59
    secession, 339–40, 343–44
    soldiers and supplies, 348–49, *349*
  colonial, 53–55, 77
  Democratic party in, 453
  disenfranchisement of blacks in, 396–98, 564
  education for women in, 251
  Faulkner's literature on, 607
  Great Black Migration from, 599–601
  New South, after Reconstruction, 392–98
    agriculture in, 393–94
    closed society of, 396–98
    industry in, 394–96
    labor relations in, 393, 394
    legacy of, 396
    race relations in, 392–93

plantation economy, 291–94
progressivism in, 564
proprietary colonies in, 30–34, *32*, *33*
public education in, 507, 509
  integration of, 737–38
Radical rule in, 383–86
railroads in, 425, 427
response to abolition movement, 257–58
revolutionary war and, *119*, 119–20, 122
voting rights in, expansion of, 216
white people of, 284–86
  farmers, 284–85
  planter class, 285–86
  values of, 294–99
See also Reconstruction; Slavery
South Africa, 831
South Carolina
  colony, 32–34, 53
  nullification ordinance, 226
  secession of, 340
South Carolina College, 297
Southeast Asia. *See* Indochina
Southeast Asia Treaty Organization (SEATO), 741, 742
Southern Alliance, 465, 466
Southern Cultivator (journal), 248
Southern Literary Messenger, The (magazine), 248
Southern Pacific Railroad, 428
Southern Tenant Farmers' Union, 640
South Platte River, 411
Southwest Africa (Namibia), 812
Sovereign power, 139–40
Sovereignty, popular, 318, 330, 335–36, 337, 338
Soviet bloc, *710*
Soviet Union (USSR)
  atomic energy in, 699
  Cold War and, 697, 707–16
  Cuban missile crisis and, 753
  diplomacy by rhetoric and, 739
  intervention in Czechoslovakia, 774
  Korea and, 713
  Middle East in 1960s and, 773–74
  Nixon and initiatives for peace with, 799
  in period between wars (1920–1937), 666
  persecution of dissidents in, 814
  Reagan and relations with, 829–31, 834
  SALT II treaty, 814, 834
  space program, 744
  Vietnam war and, 777
  World War II and, 670, 673, 686, 692, 697, 698
Space militarization of, 834
Space program, 744, 752, 755, 798, *799*
Spain
  conflict over Florida, 177, 184–85
  Federalist administration relations with, 154
  Indian relations with settlers from, 9–11
  migration to New World from, 7–11
  Napoleon's invasion of, 185
  Pinckney's Treaty, 160, *161*
  post-revolutionary relations with, 130
  war with England in New World, 12–13
Spanish-American War, 523, 525–32
  American intervention, 527–28
  Cuban crisis, 525–27
  deaths in, 355
  imperialist policy in, 531–32
  peace and the Philippines, 528–31
Spanish Armada, 13
Spanish civil war (1936–1939), 668–69
Sparkman, John J., 722
Speakeasies, 603
Speaking, public, 247
Specialization, industrial, 277–78
Specie Circular (1836), 229
Spencer, Herbert, 424, 502
Spheres of influence, 533
Spicer, Laura, 374
Spice trade, 5–6
Spindletop fields in Texas, 412
Spinning machine, 207
Spirit of American Government, The (Smith), 506
Spiritual democracy, 70
Spoils system, 222, 455, 456, 458
Sports, 620–23
  intercollegiate, 512
Sprague, Frank Julian, 489
Springfield, Illinois, race riots in, 491
Spruance, Raymond, 690
Sputnik I, 744
Squanto, 25
Square Deal, 550–52
Squatters, 224
Squatter sovereignty, 318, 330, 335–36, 337, 338
St. Clair, Governor, 154

St. Jo Railroad, 414
St. Louis, Missouri, 486
St. Louis Post-Dispatch (newspaper), 492–93
St. Paul and Pacific Railraod, 428
Stalin, Joseph, 663, 685, 686–88, 698, 699, 708, 739, 743, 745
Stalingrad, battle for (1942–1943), 686
Stalwarts, 391, 453, 457–58
Stamp Act (1765), 92–95
Stamp Act Congress, 93, 94, 95
Standard Oil Company, 429–30, 544, 619
Standard Oil Trust, 433
"Standing army at home," 91
Standish, Miles, 24
Stanford, Leland, 428
Stanford University, 510
Stanley, William, 431
Stanton, Edwin M., 380
Stanton, Elizabeth Cady, 267, 268, 556
Stark, Harold R., 672
Starr, Helen Gates, 495
Star Wars, 834
State, Department of, 151
State/church relationship, 122
State Department, McCarthy's influence on, 735
State mental institutions, 255
States
  constitutions, 128–29, 384–85
  federal relationship with, 225–27, 233
  government, reform of, 546–47
  rights under Jackson, 222
States' Rights Democratic party, 706
Steamboats, 199–200, 248, 275
Steam power in factories, 478
Steel industry, 430–31
  during World War II, 678
Steel production, 279
Steel skyscrapers, 494
Steel strikes
  in 1952, 722
  at Republic Steel (1937), 652, 653
  United States Steel Corporation, 595
Steffens, Lincoln, 487, 544, 545, 548, 594
Stein, Gertrude, 606
Stephens, Alexander, 350, 372, 378
Stephenson, D. C., 602
Stereotyping, racial, 298. *See also* Blacks
Stevens, John L., 523
Stevens, Thaddeus, 351, 376, 377
Stevenson, Adlai E., 722, 744
Stewart, A. T., 277
Stilwell, Joseph W., 712
Stimson, Henry L., 665, 666, 673, 675
Stimson Doctrine, 666
Stockgrowers. *See* Cattle frontier
Stock market crash, 631, 632
Stockton, Robert F., 316
Stone, Harlan Fiske, 656
Stone, Lucy, 556
Storey, Moorfield, 530
Stowe, Calvin, 249
Stowe, Harriet Beecher, 241, 326, 327, *327–29*, 513
Strategic arms limitation (SALT) talks, 799
  SALT II treaty, 814, 834
Strategic Defense Initiative (Star Wars), 834
Strikes, 443–44
  of black cotton pickers, 466
  Boston police (1919), 589, 595
  general, 595
  grape, 770
  Great Strike of 1877, 439–41, 459
  Long Strike of 1875, 440
  in 1920s, 619
  no-strike pledges in World War II, 678
  of Pennsylvania anthracite workers (1902), 550
  steel
    in 1952, 722
    at Republic Steel (1937), 652, 653
    United States Steel Corporation, 595
  of textile workers, 446
  of women in garment industry, 563
  during World War I, 580
  after World War II, 705
Strikes, labor, 210–11
Stripling, Robert E., 718
Stuart, J. E. B., 338, 356
Student Nonviolent Coordinating Committee (SNCC), 765, 766
Students, anti-Vietnam war
  demonstrations of, 777, 778, 789, 801, 802, 804
Students for a Democratic Society (SDS), 783
Stump, derivation of word, 228
Sturges v. Madison, 191
Styron, William, 713

X

Y

Z